THE
BOOK
OF THE
STATES

2004 EDITION
VOLUME 36

The Council of State Governments
Lexington, Kentucky

Headquarters: (859) 244-8000
Fax: (859) 244-8001
Internet: www.csg.org

ISBN 0-87292-817-9

9 780872 928176 >

CSG The Council of State Governments

Council Offices

Headquarters:
Daniel M. Sprague, Executive Director
2760 Research Park Drive, P.O. Box 11910
Lexington, KY 40578-1910
Phone: (859) 244-8000
Internet: www.csg.org

Eastern:
Alan V. Sokolow, Director
40 Broad Street, 20th Floor
New York, NY 10004
Phone: (212) 482-2320
Internet: www.csgeast.org

Midwestern:
Michael H. McCabe, Director
641 E. Butterfield Road, Suite 401
Lombard, IL 60148
Phone: (630) 810-0210
Internet: www.csgmidwest.org

Southern:
Colleen Cousineau, Director
P.O. Box 98129
Atlanta, GA 30359
Phone: (404) 633-1866
Internet: www.slcatlanta.org

Western:
Kent Briggs, Director
1107 9th Street, Suite 650
Sacramento, CA 95814
Phone: (916) 553-4423
Internet: www.csgwest.org

Washington, D.C.:
Jim Brown, General Counsel & Director
444 N. Capitol Street, NW, Suite 401
Washington, D.C. 20001
Phone: (202) 624-5460
Internet: www.csg-dc.org

Foreword

It is with great pleasure that we offer the 2004 edition of *The Book of the States*. As mentioned in the 2003 edition, The Council of State Governments is now publishing this premier reference book annually to serve policymakers and other readers in a timely manner.

Since its establishment as the national organization of state governments more than 70 years ago, CSG has worked with state leaders and managers to put the best ideas and solutions into practice. In particular, CSG promotes the sovereignty of the states and their role in the American federal system, builds leadership skills to improve decision-making, interprets emerging trends and issues and advocates multi-state solutions to better prepare for the future. This particular edition of *The Book of the States* includes articles on most recent trends and issues with relevant tables and figures.

Although the overall picture of state budgets looks brighter in 2004 compared to 2003, policymakers and administrators are still faced with many challenges. Hopefully, this new edition will be informative and useful to them when they tackle difficult tasks, as well as for researchers when they look for emerging trends and reliable comparative data.

May 2004

Daniel M. Sprague
Executive Director
The Council of State Governments

The Book of the States 2004

Editor in Chief   Keon S. Chi
Associate Editors   Audrey S. Wall
                              Heather M. Perkins
Production Coordinators   Lisa K. Eads
                              Susie D. Bush

Acknowledgements

The editorial and production staff members wish to thank the article authors who graciously shared their expertise and insights, the hundreds of individuals in the states who responded to national surveys conducted by The Council of State Governments, and the federal agencies and think tank organizations who made their most recent data and information available for this volume.

Table of Contents

CONTENTS

Chapter Three
STATE LEGISLATIVE BRANCH 69

Chapter Four
STATE EXECUTIVE BRANCH 143

CONTENTS

Chapter Five
STATE JUDICIAL BRANCH **233**

CONTENTS

Chapter Seven
STATE FINANCE AND DEMOGRAPHICS **323**

CONTENTS

CONTENTS

Looking Ahead: Emerging Trends and Issues in State Government

By Keon S. Chi

The year 2004 may be characterized as a year of elections, tight budgets and job growth. In addition to the presidential and congressional elections, voters in many states will elect their governors and other statewide executive officials as well as legislators and judges. States will have opportunities to demonstrate how much improvement they have made in transforming their election process under the recent election reform measure. Although the picture of the nation's economy looked brighter in early 2004 compared with 2003, state policymakers are still faced with a number of challenges ahead, such as uncertainties in revenues and expenditures and unpredictable federal tax policy, mandates and financial aid to state and local government. Another major challenge for state policymakers is launching new economic development strategies to create and expand more jobs in times of changing market environments, domestic and abroad.

The 2004 edition of *The Book of the States* is designed to provide state policymakers, researchers and students of state government with the most recent information and comparative data on these and other institutional and policy issues. Like the two previous annual editions, this volume emphasizes recent and emerging trends in institutional setups, politics, management, policies and programs. This edition includes 10 chapters with 39 articles authored by top research scholars and practitioners in selected areas of state government. It also contains more than 270 up-to-date tables and figures compiled by article authors, national organizations of state officials, think tanks, the U.S. Bureau of the Census and The Council of State Governments.

State Constitutions

In Chapter 1, Janice May of the University of Texas at Austin, a long-time contributor to *The Book of the States,* summarizes constitutional developments in 2003. Although there were fewer constitutional developments in 2003 compared to other odd-numbered years, May says, there were several important developments, including the establishment of a new state constitutional commission in Alabama, the historical governor's recall and replacement election in California under the constitution of Golden State and a judicial decision regarding same-sex marriage, an interpretation of the state constitution by the Massachusetts Supreme Judicial Court. Of particular interest to observers of state constitutional developments in 2003 was the Alabama governor's proposal on tax and spending reforms. Gov. Bob Riley, who initially supported constitutional revision, but not a convention, set up the 35-member Alabama Citizens' Constitutional Commission by executive order in January, but in the end the governor's proposal met defeat by the voters in September. In 2003, according to May, none of the familiar reform proposals regarding the framework of state government were on the ballot. Regarding policy provisions, she highlights the Nevada Supreme Court case on a balanced budget, which directed the state legislature to waive the constitutional requirement of a two-thirds vote to raise tax revenues. In addition, the author touches on the developments in constitutional provisions on public education in several states. It might be interesting to watch how the constitutional conventions in Colorado and Rhode Island will turn out in 2004.

Federalism and Intergovernmental Relations

Chapter 2 contains articles on federal-state, state-local and interstate relations. The continuing trend in recent U.S. federalism is characterized as "coercive or regulatory federalism" and reduced cooperation with major intergovernmental programs. In his article on "Trends in Federalism: Continuity, Change and Polarization," John Kincaid, director of Meyner Center at Lafayette College and former director of the U.S. Advisory Commission on Intergovernmental Relations, says that the U.S. Supreme Court's 2002-2003 term did not advance the recent trend of "state-friendly federalism jurisprudence." He observes: "Although the states won many cases in the Supreme Court, the 2002-03 term was one in which, as justice Ruth Bader Ginsburg described, federalism was 'the dog that didn't bark.'" Under President George W. Bush, like other former gubernatorial presidents, the federal system has not been a more friendly environment for the states. In the area of homeland security, for example, "antiterrorism is being institutionalized with much the same patterns of cooperation, conflict, coercion and competition." In 2003, partisan polarization has strained the traditional bipartisanship of the major national organizations' state and local leaders. Kincaid also says that the federalization of state criminal law has been another trend in federal-state relations, while federal encroachment on state tax systems and powers has been a characteristic of coercive or regulatory federalism. Regarding future development, Kincaid predicts: "State activism in forging new policies and bucking federal policies continues as well and is likely to intensify in response to rising partisan polarization."

It appears no new trends are emerging in state-local relations. Based on a national survey of municipal leagues and county associations conducted in 2003, Joseph Zimmerman of the State University of New York, Albany reports that several states initiated actions to assist local governments by broadening their discretionary authority and establishing special assistance programs. At the same time, more than one-half of the 41 respondents reported the legislatures had imposed additional mandates since 1990 and one-third reported the imposition of additional restraints. He says that state mandates continue to be a problem for general-purpose local governments. In Zimmerman's words: " It is apparent mobilization of public and private resources by local governments to solve serious problems depends heavily upon the state legislature granting them broad discretionary powers and providing financial assistance in various forms: grants-in-aid, revenue sharing, municipal bond banks, municipal investment pools, municipal insurance pools, and municipal infrastructure funds." He concludes that his 2003 survey produced little evidence of new emerging trends in state-local relations.

Although states have been increasingly interconnected, the likelihood of sustained cooperative action among them remains problematic. In her article on "Trends and Issues in Interstate Cooperation," Ann O'M. Bowman of the University of South Carolina says, "The pulls and pushes of competition and cooperation lead to a constantly evolving interstate equilibrium." She presents her findings from a detailed analysis of recent cooperative efforts of the states, such as voluntary associations, multi-state legal actions, uniform laws, administrative agreements and interstate compacts. On average, a state is a party to a multi-state legal action on 25 occasions. Regarding uniform state laws, she mentions about 22 new uniform laws finalized in the 1990s. Administrative agreements can be effective interstate cooperation because they are easier to initiate, negotiate, and amend, while interstate compacts are appropriate in instances in which complex legal or fiscal issues exist. The main focus in Bowman's article is on interstate compacts. The aver-

age rate of compact membership for states is 25.4 compacts, ranging from 16 to 32. Of the interstate compacts in existence in 2003, 32 had been ratified only by one state. Although the trend is for compacts to include large numbers of states, it is interesting to note, about one third of interstate compacts are bilateral. "Because compacts require the approval of the member states' legislatures," Bowman says, "the compact negotiation and ratification process can bog down in intra-state politics."

State Legislative Branch

Chapter 3 deals with state legislatures. In 2004, three out of four state legislators are up for election, many in redrawn legislative districts. "The 2004 sessions are likely to see legislatures deal with a number of issues with budgets remaining at the top of the list," say Rich Jones of the National Conference of State Legislatures and Alan Rosenthal of Rutgers University. In their article, "Trends in State Legislatures," the two long-time observers of state legislatures identify several recent trends and offer reasons behind them. For example, they comment on the composition of state legislatures by pointing out the increasing numbers of women and minorities; greater professionalization of legislative bodies; heightened partisan competition; the use of technology to improve legislative procedures; the growing size of legislative staff and decentralized staffing patterns; and the effects of term limits. Regarding the effects of legislative term limits, Jones and Rosenthal report: "The initial effects of term limits include high turnover rates, less experience among legislative leaders and committee chairs and shifts in power between the legislature and the executive. Legislatures have responded by increasing training for new legislators, changing leadership selection processes and adjusting legislative procedures." Regarding the 2003 and 2004 sessions, the authors say: "Legislatures performed their duties admirably in the face of significant budget problems. With a couple of exceptions, they ended fiscal year 2003 in the black and passed balanced budgets for 2004. However, some legislatures acted only after considerable debate and dramatic departures from their normal processes. Most legislatures opted for spending cuts and fee increases to balance their budget... Although the national economy is recovering state tax revenues tend to lag and states must find increases in Medicaid, corrections and K-12 education costs."

State Executive Branch

Chapter 4 includes articles on key elected executive officials (constitutional officers), including governors, lieutenant governors, secretaries of state, attorneys general, auditors, comptrollers and treasurers.

Governors

The year 2003 is "a year of major changes occurring to governors" says Thad Beyle of the University of North Carolina at Chapel Hill in his article on "Governors: Elections, Campaign Costs, Profiles, Forced Exits and Powers." Such changes include the recall of former California Gov. Gray Davis and replacement election of Gov. Arnold Schwarzenegger; the elections of new Republican governors in Kentucky, Louisiana and Mississippi; the succession of governors by lieutenant governors in Indiana and Utah; and eight women serving as governors in 2004, the largest number of female governors serving at one time in the office. Beyle presents the most recent data on campaign costs of gubernatorial elections and a detailed analysis of newly-elected governors. New governors were elected in 36 of 53 elections held between 2000 and 2003, and, in 2004, 38 of the governors are serving in their first term. He also offers an overview of governors who faced impeachment, removal and resignation. He findings: between 1851 and 2003, 29 governors faced the prospect of having to leave office through impeachment, removal or resignation due to a criminal conviction. Seventeen governors have been impeached and, while eight of them were acquitted of the charges, nine were convicted by their state senates. Of these nine losers in the fight, six were removed from office and three others resigned upon their conviction. He says, "The beginning of this century has certainly proven to be a time of change in the governors' offices across the 50 states."

Lieutenant Governors

"The office of lieutenant governor is gaining recognition for its power and possibility," says Julia Hurst, executive director of the National Lieutenant Governors Association. In her article, "Lieutenant Governors: Powerful in Two Branches," she says lieutenant governors hold powers in both the executive and legislative branches, many of them are elected as a team with the governors and preside over the senate. An emerging trend is that lieutenant governors are being named to lead state agencies. Currently 42 states have lieutenant governors and 23 serve as acting governor when the governor is out of state. Every lieutenant governor becomes governor if the office is vacated. In 2003, lieutenant governors in Indiana, Utah and American Samoa succeeded their governors. Eight governors were once lieutenant governors. Although lieutenant governors in sev-

eral states have no other roles to perform other than gubernatorial succession and presiding over the senate, Hurst observes nearly all lieutenant governors actively and successfully pursue state legislation under others' sponsorship. In addition, lieutenant governors spearheaded the passage of 2003 legislation to fund costal restoration, regulated "cyberstalking," set up nursing standards and scholarships, and appropriated nearly $1 million for statewide trauma efforts. She concludes: "Lieutenant governors are also stepping up and taking greater roles through projects, initiatives and 'use of the bully pulpit'… With fiscal shortfalls, continuing globalization and homeland security among the most recent challenges to face states, it is likely that the role of lieutenant governor will continue to grow."

Secretaries of States

Major issues for secretaries of states include election reform, e-government and international relations, according an article on "Secretaries of States: Duties and Responsibilities" by Kay Stimson of the National Association of Secretaries of State. The secretary of state in each state is responsible for elections, business filings, archives, licensing, administrative rules and the publication of legislative acts. However, Stimson says, election reform is the most pressing issue in 2004 largely due to the new federal law, the Help America Vote Act of 2002 (HAVA), which makes most secretaries of state accountable for a myriad of state operations. In 2004, other election-related areas include the presidential primary schedule, the steady decline in voter turnout and methods for ensuring the continuity of Congress in the event of terrorist attacks or natural disasters. E-government related topics include voter registration, election results, historical documents, business registration as well as various statewide directories and databases. Secretaries of states in several states are actively involved in international trade. In summary, Stimson says, "While the office of secretary of state requires a core understanding of all aspects of state government, it has also evolved into a position that demands increasingly specialized skills and knowledge."

Attorneys General

Whether attorneys general are viewed as activists, advocates or interpreters of the law, they impact all areas of pubic policy and all aspects of citizen life, says Angelita Plemmer of the National Association of Attorneys General. In her article, "Attorneys General: Roles and Emerging Issues," she describes specific roles performed by attorneys general. Attorneys general serve as the chief legal officers of their states; are instrumental in efforts by the state to ensure full, free and fair competition in the marketplace through the enforcement of antitrust laws; play a pivotal role in law enforcement in the fight against crime; are looking at the increasing number of crimes occurring over the Internet, including identify theft, stalking and other crimes against children; are a leading consumer protection force in defending senior citizens from telephone and mail fraud and home repair scams; safeguarding consumers from price gouging and charities fraud in the wake of disasters; and protecting consumers from fraudulent practices. They also play a major role in the burgeoning privacy arena, and protecting and enhancing the states' natural resources. They protect against the increasing use of federal preemption in the areas where states have traditionally exercised police powers to protect their citizens, as well. Plemmer concludes: "Attorneys general occupy a position of enormous power and responsibility in state government. Whether as interpreters or advocates, state attorneys general have contributed critical momentum to the development of American law."

Treasurers

"As the chief financial officers of the states, treasurers are the guardians of taxpayer money," says the National Association of State Treasurers (NAST). In "Treasurers: Safeguarding and Growing Public Fund," NAST notes that treasurers are elected by voters in 37 states, elected by the legislatures in four states and appointed by the governor in nine states. They serve either four or two-year terms. Emerging and current issues of interest for state treasurers range from the college savings plans to general investment of taxpayer monies. State treasurers are responsible for management and investment of more than $1.5 trillion in state funds. Treasurers also deal with unclaimed (abandoned) property. Recently, they have implemented financial literacy initiatives to help people better manage their resources from birth to retirement. In some states, treasurers initiated corporate governance reforms in the wake of the Enron and Worldcom scandals. State pension plans were affected on a broad scale, making it difficult for retirees and future retirees across the county. In the past few years, numerous state treasurers have made changes in their states regarding investment and management of public funds and established investor protection principles. NAST concludes: "Sound and profitable investments made by state treasurers make it possible for budgets to be balanced, for taxpayer-supported programs to be maintained and grown, and for a posi-

tive and equitable level of investment growth for public funds to be achieved."

Auditors, Comptrollers and Treasurers

"Government accountability, advancing technological progress, and market reforms combine to influence the future direction of our state chief financial officers," says John J. Radford, president of the National Association of State Auditors, Comptrollers and Treasurers (NASACT). In his article, "Trends in State Government Accounting, Auditing and Treasury," Radford highlights major issues faced by NASACT members, such as the implementation of financial reporting standards promulgated by the Government Accounting Standards Board, e-commerce, cost recovery projects to recover losses due to erroneous payments and the efficiencies of consolidation and centralization. NASACT members also face several challenges in the areas of security issues, competent staff retention, promotion of government standards for accounting and audits, and state chief financial officers' responsibility to deal with corporate governance. According to the author, "Financial transactions are increasingly automated or outsourced, and finance officials are being challenged to apply their existing skills to strategic activities that enhance financial government performance and customer service." Regarding future developments, he says, "As public financial managers evolve beyond traditional backroom operations into a more strategic role, the demands on public finance officers will intensify. Continuing education and technical training – along with advanced college education and professional certification are the key ingredients necessary to keep and prepare public finance professionals for their future role."

State Judicial Branch

"These are challenging times for the state judicial branches. Funding has been cut, relations with the other branches of government are frayed and election campaigns for judicial office can be injudicious. Significant innovation is occurring nonetheless. Effective practices in one jurisdiction are being spread nationally." In his article, "Trends and Issues in the State Courts: Challenges and Achievements" in Chapter 5, David Rottman of the National Center for State Courts reports that emerging trends shaping state courts include adopting contemporary management principles; the declining demand for judicial intervention in some legal arenas; private judging taking major business disputes from the state courts; the public replacing lawyers as the primary constituency in the minds of the state court judges and staff;

diffusion of successful innovations reaching a national audience; and frayed relationships between executive, legislative, and judicial branches and problematic judicial elections. Rottman raises several questions about state courts: Can the growth of problem solving courts be sustained? Can non-regulatory approaches moderate judicial elections? Can courts win the public's attention? Can court budgeting be organized in a way that balances judicial accountability and independence? The author concludes: "The environment in which the state courts operate is more complicated than in the past. The state courts today are being driven by diverse trends, some playing out the logic of previous eras of reform. At the same time, courts are struggling to keep afloat in a harsh budgetary environment, to build durable processes of innovation, and to mainstream for general use approaches first created for very specific kinds of cases.

State Elections and Ethics

Chapter 6 includes articles on election reform, the recall election in California and the issue of ethics in state government.

Election Reform

Although the federal government established fundamental mandates in election reform legislation, it left to the states how to accomplish those tasks. Talking about the Help America Vote Act of 2002 (HAVA), Doug Lewis of The Election Center says, "The act itself is a watershed event in the history of American democracy because it brought, for the first time, a significant federal role to the conduct of elections in America." Under HAVA, in order to keep the U.S. Department of Justice out of an administrative role, in addition to its historic role of enforcement, states had to be willing to take on additional oversight to assure that elections met the objectives established by Congress. HAVA is also unique in that its funding comes from fiscal year budgets of the federal government, but once distributed to the states, it essentially becomes "no year money," meaning that states are not required to spend it in one specific fiscal year. The advantage of this is quite clear: states are not forced to find ways to spend. On the other hand, Congress established the new Election Assistance Commission (EAC) at the federal level but gave the EAC no authority to neither interpret nor enforce the law. It is charged with developing 'voluntary' voting machine standards (now called guidelines) to apply to any voting equipment used in federal elections. This unique law may also provide state legislatures and governors with a blueprint for

determining similar structures within state statutes. Lewis concludes: "HAVA, while not especially well written from a clarity standpoint, establishes unique concepts that bear close observation in fostering a new era of federalism where governments actually trust each other and work together to serve the public. Only time will tell whether that direction is successful."

Recall Election

"California's recall election gave voice to voter dissatisfaction with the state's direction and resulted in a return to the type of moderate Republican governor that had led the state throughout much of the 1980s and 1990s. While exciting, it does not represent a sea change in California politics." In his article on "The California Governor's Recall," Thad Kousser of University of California, San Diego presents a detailed account of a governor's recall and replacement elections, highlighting the background, politics, trends in public opinions and actual voting results with relevant statistics. With 61 percent of registered voters turning out, participation in the recall exceeded turnout in recent gubernatorial elections but fell well below California's 71 percent turnout level in the 2000 presidential election. With voters recalling Gray Davis by a 55 percent to 45 percent margin, Schwarzenegger was sworn in as his replacement on November 17, 2003. Kousser argues that the real story of the recall was that Republican and independent voters became more and more comfortable with using the recall mechanism to oust the unpopular Davis. However, he notes, the lessons of Gray Davis' defeat in the recall are less certain. That a well-funded campaign against his recall could fail in a primarily Democratic state is surprising. But so too is the level to which his approval sank, 25 percent, and the fact that he performed so poorly in the 2002 election. In summary, Kousser says, "Seen in this light, the recall does not represent a sea change in California politics. Instead, it marks the fruition of voter discontent that had grown since the energy crisis and the state's downward fiscal turn. The recall allowed Davis' critics to offer up a stronger field of alternatives, and California voters were happy to choose one."

Ethics

It is difficult to draw any meaningful comparisons of state ethics laws. The difficulty to identify trends in standards created as a remedy to ethics concerns within the states is compounded by significant differences in the manner in which jurisdictions define "ethics" and regulate oversight. Ohio Ethics Commission Director David Freel argues in his article,

"Comparing State Ethics Laws and Ethics Trends and Issues," the difficulty in drawing issues involving gifts and gratuities, and the conflicts of interest arising from family and unique non-profit and private sector relationships, continue to present trend issues for the states and the general public. As ethics comparisons or trends are summarized to generalizations, all too often they are misleading or incorrect. For many jurisdictions, however, the term ethics describes standards of official conduct. These standards are often statutory and commonly involve issues of financial or familial conflicts of interest. For entities having ethics oversight in at least 27 states, they also include some type of personal (as opposed to campaign contribution or finance) disclosure. Following his analyses of ethics oversight, jurisdiction, authority, Freel highlights recent cases and developments in several specific areas, including gifts and gratuities, misuse of public position, nepotism, conflict of interest, revolving door, funding and ethics information systems

State Finance and Census

In Chapter 7 on state finance and census, we have included articles on tax revenues, state budgets, lottery revenues, emerging immigration patterns and women in state government.

Tax Revenues

"Today, the revenue picture is a bit brighter, but not strong enough for governors to snap fiscal ships into autopilot. Many governors have now gone back to their public after a stormy year, and few are talking about federal relief." Based on her analysis of the 2004 state of the state addresses by governors, Katherine Willoughby of Georgia State University discusses what governors are proposing for increasing revenues in her article "Tax Revenues in 2004: Governors Look Inward?" State total budget balances as a percent of expenditures have stabilized, yet they remain low, according to her. The 2004 figure is estimated to be 3.2 percent, compared with 10.4 percent in 2000. Willoughby says, "It is only mildly encouraging that state budget gaps have contracted and there are fewer states currently experiencing imbalance when compared to the same period last year. Nonetheless, states have yet to realize the review growth either hoped for or forecasted." In 2004, she says, governors have proposed the same strategies to deal with fiscal problems, yet they have added new economic development strategies, public-private partnerships, tax reform, and constitutional and statutory changes regarding new funds or balanced budgets. Regarding federal aid, she says, "While the fed-

eral government came forward with $20 billion for the states just this past year, major discretionary and mandatory program funding changes from 2004 to 2005 have decreased. President Bush's 2005 budget calls for a decrease of 4 percent in mandatory and entitlement spending." The author concludes: "In the end, the governors are calling on the public again, to recognize that states are not out of the woods, that more tax, spending and debt strategies must be considered and undoubtedly that most citizens will need to contribute more for states to get the work done that is both needed and expected."

Budget

In response to budget shortfalls in 2003, states cut spending drastically, raised taxes and tapped the budget reserves. Nick Samuels of the National Association of State Budget Officers looks back and forward to identify recent and future trends in state budget situations. In his article, "Long Term Budget Stability Amidst Fiscal Crises: What Can States Do to Better Navigate the Next One?," Samuels finds that despite a decline in revenues, states were under spending pressures, especially due to Medicaid and other health care problems. States continued to enact negative growth budgets, increasing taxes and fees, drawing from reserves and reorganizing programs. While the picture of the nation's economy as of early 2004 looked brighter than in the past two years, state budget officers are still faced with a number of challenges. "These include revenue estimation uncertainty, expenditure estimation uncertainty, unpredictable federal tax policy, unpredictable federal mandates, unpredictable court decisions, unpredictable voter decisions, and even natural disasters or events such as the 2001 terrorist attacks." The author recommends states focus more on the cyclical nature of the economy and examine structural reforms that will benefit them in the long term.

Lotteries

State lottery revenues provide assistant to education, general funds and other vital state programs. In his article, "Lotteries: Where the Money Goes," Alan Yandow of the Vermont Lottery and director of the Tri-State Lotto Commission gives an overview of state-run lotteries in terms of the size of sales and profits and then shows how lottery revenues have been spent in states with lotteries. All of the net profits from lottery revenues have been used to provide financial assistant to support primary and secondary education in 13 states and a portion of lottery revenue goes to provide assistance to education in 11 states, according to Yandow. In five states, lottery revenues go directly into general funds. Other states allocated lottery revenues for a number of programs, such as environment and natural resources, parks and recreation, wildlife, open space, public building, retirements, capital projects or property tax relief. He also notes that lottery revenues have helped small retail shops by increasing "foot traffic" and paying commissions. According to the author, since the beginning of lotteries in 1964, lottery organizations have paid more than $28 billion in commissions to lottery retailers, with more than $2.5 billion paid in fiscal 2003. "This is not only a huge contribution to the financial security of many small storeowners, but also accounts for sizable sales within the larger chain stores," says Yandow. "Responsible, well run lotteries, such as the current U.S. lotteries, are the worth inheritors of a long lottery past."

Demographic Changes

An analysis of new migration data reveals distinct contributions of immigration from broad and domestic migration to population change across the nation. "Large numbers of immigrants continue to concentrate in major 'immigrant magnet' areas, at the same time that domestic migrants are gravitating to a wider range of areas, and local destinations within them," says demographer William Frey, in his article, "Where Immigrants Matter Most: Assessing New Migration Dynamics in America." Based on the 2000 census of the nation's 81 largest metropolitan areas, Frey found that between 1995 and 2000, New York, Los Angeles, San Francisco and Chicago beat all others in the number of migrants they attracted from abroad, and these metropolitan areas led all other metropolitan areas in the number of domestic migrants they lost to other parts of the country. He says these four large immigrant magnet metros possess diverse economies and populations that continue to attract immigrants to their established ethnic enclaves which provide them with social and economic support and links to established niches in their communities. At the same time, they have become highly urbanized and congested regions with rising housing costs and long commutes which have made them less attractive and affordable to longer term residents at the middle and lower end of the socioeconomic ladder. Of all US counties, 239 grew from domestic migration at rates higher than 10 percent over the 1995-2000 period. Of these, only five counties showed growth of greater than 5 percent based on migration from abroad; and 183 of these did not register as much as 2 percent growth from migration from abroad. These trends show that the broad pattern of domestic migrant dispersal tends to dominate growth on the peripheries of metropolitan areas and beyond. His conclusion: "Newly released census data

reveal a new migration dynamics that will have important impacts on demographic change in different parts of the country."

Women

Despite a recent increase in the number of women governors, women's progress, especially at the statewide elective and state legislative levels, has slowed according to Susan Carroll of the Center for American Women and Politics at Rutgers University. The future for women in state government would seem to depend, at least in part, upon the strength of efforts to actively recruit women for elective and appointive positions. She reports that in early 2004, women held 25.4 percent of the 315 statewide elective positions. In addition to the eight women governors, women served as lieutenant governors in 17 of the 43 states that elected lieutenant governors in statewide elections. Other women elected executive officials include: 10 secretaries of state, eight state treasurers, five attorneys general, nine chief education officials, eight state auditors, four public service commissioners, three state comptroller/controllers, two chief agricultural officials, two commissioners of insurance, two commissioners of labor and two corporation commissioners. By early 2004, the proportion of women serving in state legislatures across the country has increased to 22.4 percent. In state courts, 98 of the 335 justices on state courts of last resort in late 2003 were women. In her article, "Women in State Government: Historical Overview and Current Trends," she observes, "Women have significantly increased their numbers among state government officials over the past several decades." Regarding the future for women in state government, Carroll suggests: "Legislative leaders, political parties, and advocacy organizations can help by renewing their commitment and augmenting their efforts to identify and offer support to potential women candidates, especially in winnable races with open seats or vulnerable incumbents."

Management and Administration

Chapter 8 includes articles on personnel and civil service systems, workers' compensation, information technology, licensure, telecommunications and privatization in state government.

Personnel

During the next few years, state government human resource professionals will be focused on building and maintaining the workforce of the future. With budget deficits, an aging workforce and rising benefits costs, state governments are challenged and will continue to be so. "State human resources is moving from an administrative, 'paper-pushing' role to a consultative role allowing it to play a strategic part in the future success of state government," says Leslie Scott of the National Association of State Personnel Executives (NASPE). In her article, "Trends in State Personnel Administration," she discusses the effects of the aging baby boomer population, employee retirement and workforce planning. Those baby boomers are now eligible for retirement. In addition, downsizing efforts in the early 1980s and the early 1990s have left fewer younger employees in the state government ranks. Regarding workforce planning, she reports: "Most of the plans involve aggressive recruitment strategies and allowing more flexibility in hiring and implementing innovative pay practices within the confines of public-sector employment." She says that another way states are hoping to attract and retain employees is through civil service reform. Finally, she addresses the issue of healthcare benefits for employees. State governments have struggled during recent years to fund the increases in health care premiums for employees, and it is anticipated that they will continue to do so. NASPE will be working with individual states in their recruitment efforts she says.

Civil Service

In recent years, many states have restructured, renamed their personnel agencies and reduced the number of job classifications. In his article, "Trends in State Civil Service Systems: Personnel Agencies, Reform Efforts, Classifications and Workforce Planning," Keon Chi identifies recent trends in state personnel administration, civil service reform and workforce planning. He notes that the number of personnel directors appointed by and directly reporting to governors has decreased, while more personnel executives are appointed by umbrella agency directors or personnel boards. The number of states using the label "human resources" by dropping the term "personnel" has increased. Between 1998 and 2003, according to a survey of state personnel executives on state civil service reform conducted by The Council of State Governments in 2003, comprehensive civil service reform proposals have been initiated or implemented in 10 states, while partial reforms have been carried out in more than 20 states. Between 1996-2003, as many as 30 states reduced their number of position classifications, and only six states increased the number of classifications. Currently, the number of classifications ranges from a few hundred to more than 4,000. Regarding future civil service reform, he concludes: "To implement successful civil service reform, it is imperative that

governors and legislative leaders walk their talk. They must overcome political pressure to rout the status quo from all quarters, including state employee unions." The author suggests: "Without total leadership commitment, neither ongoing civil service reform efforts nor alternatives to traditional state management approaches can be successfully implemented. Without the necessary financial resources, state managers cannot give the needed higher priority to human resource management."

Workers' Compensation

The cost of workers' compensation, as measured by insurance rates or benefits paid per worker, undergoes periodic cycles. At present, insurance rates are on an upswing after years of decline. Benefits paid per worker, however, are increasing; medical costs seem to be the principal cost driver. Due to budget shortfalls, some agencies have gone through virtually no interruption in their staffing or services for workers' compensation, while others have seen substantial cutbacks, which have hurt services and system improvements. In his article, "Trends and Issues in Workers' Compensation in the States," Gregory Krohm of the International Association of Industrial Accident Boards and Commissions highlights recent changes in coverage law, benefit levels and system cost and argues that the pace and scope of change is likely to be vigorous in the foreseeable future. Workers' compensation is highly variable among the states. "The performance of systems is quite erratic, with large swings in claims, costs, and disputes over just a few years," Krohm says. "As a result of this dynamic environment, a handful of states reform their workers' compensation statues almost annually. These changes are more the result of interest group fights in the legislature than fact-based public policy analysis. Other states are more incremental and cautious in their system changes, often patterning reforms after other states with successful programs."

Information Technology

States' budget crises hit the information technology area as well. Jack Gallt, Chris Dixon and Mary Gay Whitmer of the National Association of State Chief Information Officers report: "The rapid pace of technological change and innovation that transformed government service delivery in the 1990s has been slowed in recent years by the bleak fiscal realities facing most states." Although the demand for online services and 24/7 access to information remains strong," they argue, "information technology initiatives must now demonstrate a clear return on investment with an emphasis on system integration and infrastructure consolidation. States are also recognizing the importance of centralized IT oversight, common standards and shared solutions to save money and deliver more effective services to citizens and businesses." In their article, "Trends in State Information and Technology Management," the authors say: "Despite the recent economic downturn, the public demand for more information and greater convenience in dealing with government will continue to increase... Most states have addressed these problems by adopting a more disciplined IT governance framework that focuses on improving operational efficiency and business responsiveness." They add: "Technology should be viewed as an integral part of effective program and policy solutions and the state CIO can serve as an important resource in all business process and capital planning decisions."

Licensure

There appears to be an emerging trend in the area of licensure in the states. "In what was once one of the fastest growing areas of state government, legislators now employ stringent criteria to determine when new professions should be regulated. Consequently, many emerging professions opt for credentialing in the private sector, although for some of these, a circular relationship is developing between private and public credentialing." In her article, "Trends and Issues in State Professional Licensing," Pam Brinegar of the Council on Licensure, Enforcement and Regulation says there is another trend toward a growing environmental awareness on the part of regulatory agencies and, as more readily shareable information grows, they are becoming much less insular. Other trends and issues for professional regulators include new technological tools, shifting economic terrain, increased consumer involvement and international trade agreements. According to Brinegar, three levels of state regulation exist: licensure, certification and registration, ranging from the most to least restrictive respectively. Currently, in 37 states and the District of Columbia, professions are regulated by central agencies which share varying degrees of administrative tasks with the licensing boards. In the other states, licensing boards are independent agencies. Aside from ensuring resources to carry out their missions, issues of currency for state regulators include labor shortages, practitioner quality assurance, examination fraud, identity theft, use of new technological tools, professional mobility and federal initiatives.

Telecommunications

The development and application of personal technology in a mobile environment is a key technological trend in telecommunications. In his article on "State Government Telecommunications: Personal Technology As a New Public Commons," Wayne Hall of the NASTD reports: "For legislators and other public policymakers, this trend commands attention because of what is being created: a vast social commons. In this environment, state government policymakers will be required as never before to pay attention to the information security and integrity of individuals." He says that the development of desktop computing signaled a shift toward more decentralized work arrangements. Desktop computers could be linked together and information exchanged in local networks, which created a demand for more and faster connections between computers, not only in the local area network but to the Internet as well. The rapid growth of the public Internet also signaled the end of an era of top-down information technology management in state government. He adds: "The Internet is an organizing force without peer... networking technologies increasingly amplify the voice of ordinary citizens to speak up, to communicate in a coordinated fashion their wants and needs. The volume may be a little high, but state government policymakers must listen to those voices or tempt irrelevance. Because in any thriving society this much will always be true: people have something to say."

Privatization

Privatization continues to be a controversial management issue in state governments. In their article on "Privatization in State Government: Trends and Issues" by Keon Chi, Kelley Arnold and Heather Perkins, editors of *The Book of the States* report the extent of privatization activities in the states has largely remained the same as in the previous five years or slightly increased. Only five of the 38 state budget directors who responded to a 2002 survey reported privatization has decreased in their state in the recent past. The level of privatization activities between 1997 and 2002 differs slightly in state agencies. The extent of privatization in state personnel, education, human services has remained the same. Nineteen states, or 44 percent of the state corrections agency directors who responded to the survey, reported an increase in privatization. Directors of 24 state departments of transportation, or 59 percent of the transportation survey respondents, reported an increase in privatization, while 17 directors said the level of privatization has remained the same in the past five years. The two main reasons for privatization in these agencies include a lack of personnel or expertise and cost savings. In most cases, privatized services account for less than 5 percent of agency services, while reported costs savings range from none to less than 5 percent. But many state agency directors surveyed seemed to have no clear ideas as to how much has been actually saved from privatization. Nevertheless, privatization is likely to continue in the states in the next few years as in the past decade. There are a number of key issues for state policymakers to consider when contemplating privatization either on a statewide or agency-wide basis. Such issues and questions include constitutional and legal restrictions, lessons learned from previous privatization experiments, productivity, employee displacement and the role of government and accountability due to the blurring line between the public and private sectors.

Selected State Policies and Programs

Included in Chapter 9 are articles on selected policies and programs: homeland security, education, trends in faculty salaries in institutions of higher education, agriculture, economic development, energy, environment, Medicare, mental health, corrections and welfare.

Homeland Security

The year 2003 represents a "settling in" period for the implications of homeland security on the nation's level of preparedness for all hazards, according to Amy Hughes of the National Emergency Management Association. In her article, "State Emergency Management: New Realities in a Homeland Security World," Hughes reports what states are doing in the homeland security area. In the few months since the creation of the federal Department of Homeland Security, Hughes says, the state emergency management landscape has changed significantly. "State emergency management agencies are now facing a monumental task of adapting to their new roles in homeland security, administering billions of dollars in a long stream of federal funding, serving as administrator for local jurisdictions, and facilitating regional cooperation, while maintaining a hold on the viability of the 'all-hazards preparedness' philosophy." Regarding local efforts, she says that despite the influx of new money for emergency responders, many local jurisdictions still do not have access to some of the specialized equipment and response teams needed to handle large-scale disasters and unique emergencies situations, such as hazardous materials handling and swift-water rescue. Finally, she describes how states are helping each other. Twenty-seven states have a statewide mutual aid agreement in place or have proposed legislation in the works; these states are providing added incentives, such as training, extra funding and cost share relief.

Education

"It all adds up to an unprecedented level of federal involvement in education, a shift of educational decision-making from communities and states to the federal government," says Dewayne Matthews of the Education Commission of the States. In his article, "No Child Left Behind: The Challenge of Implementation," he characterizes the No Child Left Behind (NCLB) Act as follows: "Under NCLB, states must set performance standards for every school in America and track student learning across a wide range of student subgroups. It establishes significant consequences for schools, districts and states that fail to meet performance targets. Unlike past federal education legislation, it is fair to say that NCLB affects every child in every school in America." Matthews discusses controversial issues, such as adequate yearly progress, teacher qualifications and funding. He says that the Adequate Yearly Progress (AYP) variation is primarily a result of the difference in standards and proficiency levels across states. Some in states with a large number of schools on the list questioned why they were being punished for having high standards. Aside from AYP, the provision of NCLB that poses the most difficult implementation challenge is the requirement that all teachers in the state be "highly qualified." Is NCLB an unfunded mandate? Matthews responds: "This issue is particularly sensitive because of the unprecedented financial problems of state governments. Some in states have already decided that NCLB constitutes an unfunded mandate, which will have significant short- and long-term impact on state budgets. Others believe NCLB will make the enormous national investment in education more cost-effective."

Higher Education

State policymakers need to find resources to raise salaries for faculty members in public institutions of higher learning. John Curtis of the American Association of University Professors reports several "systematic factors" to the variation in faculty salaries across the states, factors such as institutional type, rank, gender and region. In his article, "Trends in Faculty Salaries," Curtis reports that faculty members employed at private institutions of higher learning earn more than those in public institutions; the difference is between 5 to 27 percent. The average salary of women faculty members is 7 to 12 percent below that of male counterparts. The difference is greater among full professors. Regionally, professors in New England show the highest overall average. Curtis also points out the long-term decline in faculty salaries at public institutions compared with private institutions as a critical issue for state policymakers. He concludes: "States look to their higher education institutions to provide high-quality education in a range of rapidly changing fields of endeavor, as centers of innovation in science and technology, and as sources of solutions to pressing social needs. As enrollments continue to grow, and the need for expanded access to high-quality higher education becomes increasingly apparent, state policymakers must identify sufficient resources to allow their higher education sectors to meet these new demands."

Agriculture

Farmers are affected not only by agriculture programs in the federal government but also by trade policy, fiscal policy, tax laws and other programs. Otto Doering of Purdue University discusses the 2002 farm bill and looks at the future of agriculture policy in his article, "The How and Why of Agriculture Policy." He notes, "How policy affects agriculture is not just the impact of the farm bill but all affect agriculture and other enterprises to varying degrees." Regarding the 2002 farm bill, he says: "The impacts of the 2002 farm bill are likely to be regional in nature even following the location of specific crops that are addressed by the bill. Our agricultural policies are increasingly held up as too expensive, helping only large farmers, and having unintended negative side effects. Each of these criticisms contains some truth and should be of concern to us. Our dilemma is that our agricultural productivity outruns the demand for food and farm prices slowly decline over time hurting farmers and their communities." The challenge is to maintain those aspects of agricultural programs that we believe meet important goals such as protecting farmers against weather loss and extreme financial fluctuations that would drive farmers in and out of farming, meet the most critical rationale for government involvement in agriculture in the most cost effective way. According to the author, "The most important thing for economic growth will be to encourage those aspects of agriculture, value added for food products and other non-food uses that provide this growth at the local level."

Economic Development

The country's manufacturing industry is the largest contributor to economic growth and the biggest employment generator, according to Jeff Finkle of the International Economic Development Council. In his article, "Job Creation and Retention During Recession," Finkle describes recent trends in job loss and state economic development strategies to create more jobs. He observes: "The recession—officially marked as the period between March 2001 and October 2003—has left a great percentage of corporations with an overwhelming need to find more economically friendly environments, either inside or outside the United States." Finkle cites several relevant figures regarding job losses in recent years. Quoting an October 2003 *New York Times* article, he points out that 15 percent of the 2.81 million jobs that were lost over the last two years found their way to other countries. U.S. Bureau of Labor Statistics' numbers indicated that the total payroll employment since the start of the recession has decreased by an average of 1.8 percent nationally. Faced with such a situation, the domestic competition to create and retain jobs in the sour economy over the last two years has forced states to get more aggressive than ever in facilitating economic development. However, in pursuing aggressive approaches to recruiting new companies and to preserve existing jobs, state and local officials have had to contend with the ramifications of the one of the recession's largest casualties— manufacturing. The author quotes Arizona's Jim Pickens remarks, summing up the state of competition for job development and retention across the country: "Economic development is a rough and tumble sport, and it is sometimes played without pads and helmets." States will have to maintain their efforts, perhaps with the same vigor, to create and retain jobs even as the nation emerges from the recession.

What are states doing to generate jobs? "Almost universally, education and work-force training were, in fact, where most resources were allocated in 2003," says Mark Arend, editor of *Site Selection* magazine. In his article, "Trends in Job Creation Strategies in the States," Arend takes a bird's eye view of the economic development landscape and the features on it that are causing state legislators to rethink their workforce development strategies. The states are doubling their efforts to educate and train people in order to attract and grow industry domestically. But, Arend asks, are they investing in new jobs? Are the business climates in the states such that employers will hire from within the states rather than seek labor elsewhere? Is the so-called jobless recovery the end of the story or just the beginning? According to the author, state economic developers can take several steps to improve the desirability of their states as a location for business, which would in turn stimulate job growth. They include: understanding that investments in education, health, natural resources and research/ innovation are effective economic development measures, not other departments' concerns; making business-development resources available to entrepreneurs; helping existing businesses modernize and stay competitive; working to build the assets, not just incomes, of families in the state; understanding and addressing the needs of dislocated workers and businesses in disinvested communities and supporting non-traditional approaches, such as long-term educational support for retraining older workers; and being prudent in allocating the state's tax resources so they are not wasted on efforts which do not produce quality jobs.

Energy

"We must also help structure a system whereby a collaborative process is put in place to allow federal managers to begin planning for the future of public energy development in the United States in an innovative, environmentally sensitive manner." Robert Middleton of the White House Task Force on Energy Project Streamlining describes the task force's mission, plans and projects. In his article, "Energy Project Streamlining," Middleton defines the task force's mission as monitoring and assisting federal agencies in completing energy-related projects and setting up mechanisms to coordinate federal, state, tribal and local permitting. "Its intent is to provide a cost-effective and efficient means of managing valuable domestic energy resources on public lands. In doing this, it will realize a reduced cost of energy to the consumers; a savings of taxpayer dollars by the government; a more upfront collaborative, transparent decision-making process for stakeholders; sound decisions based on more complete information; and improved mitigation measures where energy development is permitted to proceed." He says, "They must look at all forms of energy to include but not limited to: renewables—such as solar, wind, biomass, geothermal, and low-impact hydropower—gas, oil, liquefied natural gas, alternate fuels, nuclear, and coal." Since its inception, task force members have held over 100 meetings to listen to the concerns of developers, environmentalists and federal and state agencies. The first year's activities and accomplishments were many mostly falling in the areas of assisting in the resolution of bottlenecks in a number of specific energy projects. In its second year the task force continues to work on individual energy related projects bottlenecked in the system.

Environment

The states have expanded their role in environmental protection over the past three decades, and now implement most of the federal environmental statutes, says Steve Brown of the Environmental Council of the States. In his article, "Trends in State Environmental Spending," Brown says that with this heightened responsibility has come an increase in state financial commitments to pay for these programs and the states have met this responsibility for years. During the past few years, however, the fiscal crisis in the states, coupled with many new federal environmental rules and a lack of new federal money, has left the states with at least a $1 billion annual gap in the amounts they need to implement current federal law. In a 2003 report, seven rules issued over the previous seven years are identified that meet the criteria, and every single one of them is an environmental rule. They include rules on waste combustion, solid waste landfills, drinking water (three of these), and storm water discharges. There are five other air rules that meet the same criteria as unfunded mandates, but which are exempted by law from the act. These shortfalls have been documented in several studies. This situation may lead to greater risks to the public from exposure to environmental hazards. The recent state budget problems indicate that states have – after 15 years of continual growth in environmental spending - reached their limit on contributions to federally imposed environmental programs. Brown argues that the federal government should provide funding to foot the costs of further state implementation of federal environmental rules.

Medicare

"The most important change for states is that the new Medicare Part D will assume responsibility for low-income Medicare beneficiary drug costs, relieving states of some of their rising prescription drug costs in Medicaid," says Trudi Matthews of The Council of State Governments. In her article, "Medicare, Prescription Drug, Improvement and Modernization Act of 2003," she describes the most recent change to Medicare and its implication for the states and territories. The Medicare drug law provides for two basic benefits, one for now and one for later. To give the U.S. Department of Health and Human Services time to set up the new prescription drug benefit, Medicare will first establish a prescription drug discount card that becomes available in May 2004. Then in January 2006, the new Medicare Part D will go into effect. In addition to establishing these two basic benefits, the law also contains a host of health care reform measures that will affect states directly and indirectly. According to Matthews, "the 30 states that have established state pharmaceutical assistance programs will need to review the future of these programs in light of Medicare changes. States are considering them as is, eliminate them or modify them to fill in the gaps in Medicare Part D. States are prohibited from using federal matching funds through

Medicaid to fill the gaps in the Medicare drug benefit." She says, "While the transfer of dual eligibles to Medicare sounds like a fiscal boon to states at first, a number of the law's provisions mean that long term savings will be more marginal than originally hoped and states may spend more in the short term."

Mental Health

In their article, "Trends in State Mental Health Agencies," Theodore C. Lutterman, Robert Shaw, Ronald Manderscheid and Noel A. Mazade of the National Association of State Mental Health Program Directors Research Institute, offer an overview of state mental health agencies in terms of structural patterns, responsibilities, specific programs, unmet needs, hospitals, patients and funding. In every state government, the state mental health agency (SMHA) has the statutory authority to organize and purchase mental health services. The SMHA is the central authority in each state responsible for developing comprehensive plans for mental health and it is organized to assure that relevant services are delivered. Within most states, the SMHA is administratively located within a larger umbrella human services agency. In 2003, 24 SMHAs were located within states' department of human services, eight SMHAs in health departments, and two SMHAs in another state department which often combines health and human services. Fifteen SMHAs were either independent state departments or mental health or departments of mental health and mental retardation. The recent state budget shortages and efforts to streamline government has led to major changes in how SMHAs are organized in recent years. In addition to the SMHA, other state agencies play significant roles in the provision of mental health services. Such roles include education, the criminal and juvenile justice systems, vocational rehabilitation, housing and employment services. According to the authors, states are continuing to downsize and close state psychiatric hospitals and hospital beds. Half the states are reorganizing their state hospitals, including downsizing, reconfiguring, closing and/or consolidation. States' estimates of population eligible for mental health services vary, but the most common (median) estimate for adults with serious mental illness was 5.2 percent of the states' adult population. The median estimate for children and adolescents with serious emotional disturbances was 8 percent. States estimated that over 10 million adults and children met the criteria for a serious mental illness or emotional disturbance. Between fiscal years 1997-2001, the 38.3 percent increase in SMHA-controlled mental health expenditures exceeded the overall growth in state government expenditures for all services (31.3 percent). In fiscal year 2001, SMHAs controlled $15.4 billion in expenditures

for a system that serves over 5 million citizens. The authors quote President George W. Bush's New Freedom Commission on Mental Health, "Yet, for too many Americans with mental illness, the mental health services and supports they need remain fragmented, disconnected and often inadequate, frustrating the opportunity for recovery."

Corrections

"As state officials struggle with budget shortfalls, it is increasingly important to understand the changing nature of state corrections, both from a demographic perspective and a programmatic one," says John Mountjoy of The Council of State Governments. His article, "Profiles of Prisoners and Prison Programming in the States," looks at the changing nature of prisoners and programming. Mountjoy says, "If state officials are to ever solve the 'revolving-door-of-corrections,' they must provide effective programming and planning whose ultimate goal is the reentry of offenders into society." As for the composition of state prisons, he says, "What was once a young-adult to middle-aged white male dominated population has evolved into one much more representative of the population in general and in some instances, over-representative of specific groups, most notably black males. In addition, more women and juveniles are being found in state prison populations. For the most part, state prisoners are male, disproportionately black and young." Currently, states provide a range of mandatory and discretionary programs covering health care, drug and alcohol treatment, education and reentry programming. The effects of recidivism are driving the costs of corrections. While the overall volume of prisoner entry has reached its plateau, sentences and the length of time served by inmates are growing. The author argues: "Corrections officials need to be respondent to these changes, providing suitable educational, health and work programs that will benefit not only the inmate, but society in general. While state budget shortfalls have forced extensive corrections program cuts, their long-term costs are immeasurable to inmates and communities."

Welfare

The weaker economy has produced weaker welfare outcomes. Caseloads generally are no longer declining; it is more difficult for welfare recipients to find paid employment and more difficult for those that left welfare to retain employment. In her article, "Trends and Issues in Welfare Reform," Sheila Zedlewski of The Urban Institute reports: "States' welfare challenges are becoming more complex. As the economy weakened, caseload decline either diminished or reversed. Employment rates declined for both welfare recipients and those who recently left welfare. More who left welfare either have returned to welfare or are disconnected, living without a job, welfare, or someone else who can support them." Zedlewski cites several relevant trends and figures. For example, Temporary Assistance for Needy Families (TANF) caseloads have hovered around 2 million families nationwide since March 2001 following the dramatic 50 percent decline that occurred between fiscal years 1996 and 2000. Caseloads have increased in 28 states since the start of the recession in March 2001 and June 2003 and have continued to decline in 22 states. More single mothers have turned to welfare for the first time as jobs became scarcer. The most vulnerable welfare recipients and leavers, those with mental and physical health issues, limited educations, and little work experience are particularly at risk. These weaker outcomes demonstrate the substantial challenges of state and local officials. While states face greater welfare program challenges in a weaker economy, they also must prepare to achieve higher work participation targets when TANF eventually is reauthorized by Congress. The author challenges state policymakers by saying: "States need to be thinking creatively about how to maximize resources by encouraging collaborations among local programs that provide employment services."

Emerging Issues

Based on a review of the articles highlighted here, we can identify three explicit trends and raise pertinent questions. First, it appears that state governments are now run by elected and appointed officials who tend to have less experiences in state government and lack institutional memories than in the past. For example, Alan Rosenthal and Rich Jones note that term limits are likely to raise the turnover rate among lawmakers even higher and that 78 percent of state legislators are up for election in November 2004, thus adding more new legislators. Thad Beyle's data indicate that in 2004 as many as 38 of the governors (or 76 percent) are serving their first term. Keon Chi's article shows that more than 40 percent of state workers in most states have served less than five years for their states. As for future trends, it is important to note that nearly half of experienced agency managers in some states are eligible for retirement. The question here is, can state leaders, managers and workers be more innovative and productive than their predecessors without as much institutional memories and experiences?

Second, there seems to be a common theme when debating on some of major policy issues: states in need of more federal funding. On homeland security, for example, Amy Hughes mentions the inaccessibility of federal funding by local jurisdictions. Many state policymakers tend to regard the No Child Left Behind Act as an unfunded federal mandate as mentioned in Dewayne Matthews' article. Steve Brown says that states have reached their limit on contributions to federally imposed environmental programs. Doug Lewis points out that although Congress authorized nearly $4 billion for the Help American Vote Act of 2002, the reform legislation left states with how to accomplish specific tasks. Trudi Matthews mentions that states may spend more in the short term for the new Medicare drug program. In the welfare area, Sheila Zedlewski says the states face greater welfare program challenges in a weak economy. Katherine Willoughby reports that the president's 2005 federal budget calls for a decrease in mandatory and entitlement spending and a decrease in selected grants-in-aid programs. States are faced with all of these and other mandates and a decrease in federal aid in an era of what John Kincaid calls "coercive or regulatory federalism." Also, the last resort of our judicial system has not been congenial to the states either in 2003. The question is, how can states meet their challenges without additional funding either from their own sources or Uncle Sam. Nick Samuels recommends states examine structural reforms that will benefit them in the long run.

Third, it seems clear that state policymakers play increasingly important roles in meeting emerging challenges with limited resources. Can state agencies be more effective and efficient in management and public service delivery through better use of technology, restructuring and public-private partnerships? Can states find more multi-state solutions through interstate agreements or compacts? Keon Chi, Kelley Arnold and Heather Perkins' article on privatization raises a series of questions regarding in-house management and contracting out selected functions or services to non-government entities. Scott and Chi's articles on state personnel systems remind state policymakers of the need for strategic plans to deal with the future workforce. Wayne Hall, Jack Gallt, Chris Dixon and Mary Gay Whitmer talk about information technology shaping future patterns of state government management. Governors in many states are proposing new reorganization and management initiatives, as highlighted in Katherine Willoughby's analysis of the 2004 gubernatorial state of the state addresses. In addition, Ann Bowman's analysis indicates, state policymakers should pay more attention to mechanisms for interstate cooperation—voluntary associations, multi-state legal actions, uniform laws, administrative agreements and interstate compacts—with which they can work together for common goals to protect the rightful place of the states within the U.S. federal system.

Finally, it should be noted, *The Book of the States* is now published annually by breaking a 70-year tradition of biennial editions. The editors of the reference book have tried to cover as many topical issues relevant to state politics, policy and administration as they could in this issue. Due to space constraints in this particular volume, however, some significant policy areas that have not been covered in this edition, such as transportation, tourism, international trade and utility regulation, will be included in the 2005 edition. Readers should find *The Book of the States* to be timely, informative, accurate and objective.

About the Author

Keon S. Chi, editor in chief of *The Book of the States*, is a senior fellow for The Council of State Governments and professor of political science at Georgetown College. He has published extensively on state politics, policy and administration.

Chapter One

STATE CONSTITUTIONS

"In recent years, a downward trend in state constitutional activity has been observed."

— **Janice C. May**

State Constitutional Developments in 2003

By Janice C. May

Reduced levels of state constitutional activity and no major new trends were recorded in 2003, a typical "off" year. Among developments were a comprehensive tax and spending proposal and an official constitutional commission, both in Alabama, and the historic use of the state constitutional recall election in California.

State constitutional developments in 2003 were typical of those in other odd-numbered years in that amendment and revision involved fewer states and fewer amendments than in the even-numbered years when general elections are held. It was also typical to the extent that major trends observed in recent years, such as the absence of state constitutional conventions and comprehensive revision or new constitutions, were also evident. Nonetheless, important constitutional developments did occur. For the first time since 1997–1998, a new official state constitutional commission was established. Also several significant constitutional amendments were on the ballot, most notably in Alabama, whose governor received accolades for his leadership in proposing substantial tax and spending reforms. In addition, state constitutions played important roles in developments other than by amendment or revision. Of national and international interest was the historic recall election in California. Added to the California Constitution by constitutional amendment in 1911, the recall removed and replaced a sitting governor who had been elected by the voters in the November 2002 general election. Several judicial decisions interpreting state constitutions were also significant. No doubt the best known was the decision by the Massachu-

setts Supreme Judicial Court that denial of marriage to same-sex couples violated the state constitution.

Use of Authorized Methods

In 2003 state constitutional amendments were proposed in 13 states, far fewer than in 2002 when 35 states were involved. Similarly, only 57 propositions were on the ballot of which 46 were adopted, compared with 175 proposed and 118 approved in 2002. One factor accounting for the lower numbers is that some state constitutions prohibit amendments elections in the odd-year. Texas is an exception. The state's constitution and election laws permit amendments to be on the ballot in either or both years, but the Texas Legislature has, at its discretion, selected the odd year for virtually all Texas amendments since the mid-1970s. In 2003, 22 amendments were on the Texas ballot, amounting to about 40 percent of all state proposals and 48 percent of all adoptions. All 22 were approved.

Table A provides information on methods of state constitutional amendments and revision and their use. (For more information on methods see the last volume of *The Book of the States* and Tables 1.2, 1.3 and 1.4 in this volume.) Figures for 2003 have been combined with those of 2002 to afford comparisons

Table A: State Constitutional Changes by Method of Initiation: 1996–97, 1998–99, 2000–01 and 2002–03

Method of initiation	Number of states involved				Total proposals				Total adopted				Percentage adopted			
	1996–1997	1998–1999	2000–2001	2002–2003	1996–1997	1998–1999	2000–2001	2002–2003	1996–1997	1998–1999	2000–2001	2002–2003	1996–1997	1998–1999	2000–2001	2002–2003
All methods	42	46	40	38	233	296	212	232	178	229 (b)	154	164	76.3 (a)	77.2 (a)(b)	72.0 (a)	70.6
Legislative proposal	42	46	38	36	193	266	180	208	159	210 (b)	141	155	82.4 (a)	78.8 (a)(b)	91.0 (a)	74.5
Constitutional initiative	12	12	10	11	40	21	32	24	19	11	13	9	47.5	52.4	40.6	37.5
Constitutional convention	. . .	. . .	. . .	. . .	. . .	. . .	. . .	. . .	. . .	. . .	. . .	. . .	. . .	. . .	. . .	. . .
Constitutional commission	. . .	1	. . .	. . .	. . .	9	. . .	. . .	. . .	8	. . .	. . .	. . .	. . .	. . .	. . .

Source: Survey conducted by Janice May, University of Texas at Austin, January 2004.

Key:
. . . — Not applicable.
(a)—In calculating these percentages, the amendments adopted in Delaware (where proposals are not submitted to the voters) are excluded.
(b)—One Alabama amendment is excluded from adoptions because the election results were in dispute.

with other bienniums in *The Book of the States*.

In recent years a downward trend in state constitutional activity has been observed. In 2002–2003 this trend was clearly evident by the fact that amendments were on the ballot in only 38 states, the lowest number since 1968–1969 when *The Book of the States* first published tables regularly incorporating this data.

Legislative Proposal and Constitutional Initiative

As Table A indicates, the only methods used to amend or revise state constitutions in 2002–2003 were legislative proposal and the constitutional initiative. In all states the legislature is empowered to propose amendments and, except in Delaware, the amendments must be referred to the voters for final action. The legislative method is clearly the dominant one historically and currently. In 2002–2003 almost 90 percent of all propositions proposed and 95 percent of those adopted were initiated by the state legislature. The constitutional initiative, which is authorized in 18 states, was a poor second with 10 percent of proposals and 5 percent adoptions. In 2003 only three amendments were constitutional initiative measures and all were rejected.

Constitutional Conventions and Constitutional Commissions

Available in all the states, the constitutional convention is the traditional method for drafting new constitutions or substantially revising existing ones. But the trend has been against constitutional conventions in recent years and in the 20th century as a whole. The Rhode Island Convention of 1986 was the most recent. In 14 states the state constitution requires a convention call to be placed periodically on the ballot. The voters have turned down these calls regularly, most recently in 2002 (in Alaska, Missouri and New Hampshire). As reported in recent volumes of *The Book of the States*, the prospects for a convention in Alabama in 2003 appeared bright. The Alabama Citizens for Constitutional Reform (ACCR) and Gov. Don Siegelman, among others, supported a convention as the best method for constitutional change. But hopes were dashed when the governor was defeated in the November 2002 election and the 2003 Alabama Legislature rejected a convention. In 2004, however, a convention will be on the agenda at least in Rhode Island and Colorado. The Rhode Island Constitution requires a convention call referendum in 2004 and a preparatory commission. As reported in recent volumes of *The Book of the States,* there has been some support for a convention to settle

a dispute over separation of powers. In Colorado, convention legislation was introduced in the General Assembly in the current session following a recommendation to do so by an interim committee. The principal reason given for a convention is that it is the best, and maybe the only way, to resolve conflicts between state constitutional provisions limiting revenues and requiring increased expenditures for public education. Research on conventions and state constitutional reform was underway in 2003.

Constitutional commissions are essentially advisory bodies established to assist the governor, the legislature or a convention on constitutional matters. The commission listed in Table A refers only to Florida commissions, which have the unique power to propose amendments directly to the voters. The Florida Constitution requires their establishment periodically. The most recent commission served from 1997–1998. The only permanent commission is the Utah Constitutional Revision Commission (see Table 1.5).

An important development in 2003 was the creation of the first new commission since the most recent Florida body. The newly elected governor of Alabama, Bob Riley, who supported constitutional revision but not a convention, set up the 35-member Alabama Citizens' Constitution Commission by executive order on January 23, 2003 (see Table 1.5). As reported in the most recent volume of *The Book of the States*, the ACCR had created its own commission whose 2003 report supported a convention and specific reforms. Gov. Riley appointed 10 members of the ACCR commission and six members of the ACCR board to his commission, which included constitutional law experts, former public officials, educators and business and civic leaders. His choice for the chair was former Secretary of State Jim Bennett who had also headed the ACCR commission. Lenora Pate, an attorney, was co-chair. Assisted by a team of technical experts, the commission was directed to study and prepare drafts for suggested constitutional changes on five subjects: county home rule, tax earmarking, line item veto, supermajority legislative vote for new or increased taxes and a recompilation of the state constitution together with elimination of racist provisions. Commission plenary sessions were open to the public and two public hearings were held, one in Montgomery and the other in Birmingham. In its report submitted to the governor on March 27, the commission proposed five constitutional amendments and a statutory recompilation of the constitution. The commission recommended optional limited home rule for counties relating to specific functions, such as zoning; reform of tax earmarking; a three-fifths rather than a simple majority of all members of each house to override a veto; a three-fifths majority of legislators to adopt new taxes or tax increases, contingent on fundamental tax reform; and a recompilation of the constitution by statute and deletion of racist language and provisions by constitutional amendment. All the proposals were introduced in the 2003 legislature. Recompilation was approved and an amendment will be on the 2004 ballot to delete racist provisions.

The recompilation of the Alabama Constitution represents a major non-substantive revision. Described as the longest in the world, the document contains over 700 amendments, which appear serially without codification. Also, an estimated 70 percent of all amendments are local. The recompilation will integrate relevant amendments into the main body of the text, delete superseded provisions and place at the end of the document all local amendments organized by county. Such an extensive revision by statute is unusual.

Alabama Constitutional Amendment of 2003

Constitutional change took an unexpected turn in Alabama after the Alabama Commission's report. Gov. Riley put together a reform plan that turned out to be the most significant and comprehensive constitutional proposal in 2003. He chose the regular amendment process as the vehicle for the constitutional changes, using an all-or-nothing approach with a single amendment.

According to his campaign pamphlet, the governor wanted to do more than resolve the current state fiscal crisis, described as the worst since the Great Depression, and move Alabama in "a new direction" to "achieve greatness." This required a "comprehensive accountability, education and tax reform plan" if fundamental problems holding Alabama back were to be resolved. Central to the governor's reforms was revision of the taxing and spending provisions of the state constitution. An indication of the plan's breadth is that the constitutional amendment as proposed by the legislature was over 30 pages long. A new income tax article and significant changes in the property tax sections were included. In addition a new fund, the Alabama Excellence Initiative Fund, was created to support programs for "excellence in public education," health care for the elderly, and job training, among others. To fully implement the constitutional provisions, 19 legislative acts had been passed contingent on the passage of the amendment.

Among the highlights of Gov. Riley's reforms were a tax increase of $1.2 billion and a redistribution of

the tax burden by taxing the poor less and the wealthy and certain businesses and corporations more. One provision raised the threshold for the income tax from $4,600 to $20,000.

The governor's proposal was met with a resounding defeat at the hands of the voters on September 9, 2003. Of the 1,284,581 votes cast, only 417,721 or about one-third were "yes" votes. The amendment was opposed by his own party, anti-tax groups and many of those who would benefit from it. But for his efforts, Gov. Riley won high praise from various quarters. *Governing* magazine placed him first on its list of public officials of 2003. Although he failed, Riley was admired for his political courage and leadership.

Substantive Changes

Substantive constitutional change in the form of a new constitution remained elusive in 2003 as it has since the 1980s when voters in Georgia and Rhode Island approved new charters. Also missing has been comprehensive revision covering multiple articles comparable to the revision package of the Florida Constitution Revision Commission of 1997–1998. In 2003 the most comprehensive amendment was the Alabama tax and spending measure, but there were some other amendments of interest particularly on civil rights. The fiscal amendments as a group show how states are responding to the current fiscal crisis.

Table B contains information on proposals and adoptions of amendments to state constitutional articles. To facilitate comparisons with other bienniums, figures for 2003 have been added to those of 2002. Because state constitutions are not only frameworks of government but also contain policy measures, it is useful to compare framework amendments with those on policy. As a rough guide to the classification, the framework articles are bills of rights, suffrage and elections, the three branches of government, local government and amending. The policy articles are finance and taxation, state and local debt, state functions and miscellaneous. Because they often amend both framework and policy, general revision and local amendments are excluded. It is clear from Table B that framework amendments in 2002–2003 are less numerous than those on policy (77 proposals and 51 adoptions compared with 114 proposals and 77 adoptions).

Framework of Government

In 2003 none of the familiar reforms altering the structure of state or local government, such as annual legislative sessions, legislative term limits or merit selection of judges, were on the ballot. But there were some substantial changes proposed. Louisiana voters turned down a system of administrative law and law judges and a plan to assure the independence of the legislative auditor by prohibiting political activities during and after service. They did allow a judge to fill out his term during the year of mandatory retirement. In Texas, an amendment to allow six-person juries to hear misdemeanor cases in district court was approved. New Mexico voters added a secretary of education to the executive cabinet and turned the elected board of education into an elected commission. In Mississippi, a restructuring of the Board of Higher Education was approved. The term of office was reduced from 12 to 9 years and the districts from which the governor makes appointments were changed from congressional to state supreme court districts.

Probably the most important amendment on governmental structure, because it affects representative democracy, was one adopted in Texas. In an attempt to help out public officers who are called up temporarily for active duty in the U.S. military forces, the amendment allows state and local public officials, elected or appointed, to keep their positions until the end of their term without creating a vacancy. To be eligible, their tour of duty must be longer than 30 days. Of particular interest is the amendment's application to the Texas Legislature. Legislators are allowed to select their own replacement who must meet the constitutional qualifications for the office, be of the legislator's political party and confirmed by a majority of the legislator's house. The replacement would enjoy the same power and "perks" such as compensation as an elected member. Had a vacancy been created, the governor would have called a special election and the voters would have elected the new legislator. There would be no un-elected legislators.

The process is somewhat different for offices other than the legislature. The officer can only recommend a replacement and the officer or body normally charged with the responsibility of filling vacancies would name the temporary officer.

A Washington amendment that also pertained to vacancies was more in keeping with the principles of representative democracy. Approved by the voters, it would provide for filling a vacancy that occurred between the election and the beginning of the term of office. The newly elected officer would fill the vacancy, and, in effect, serve before the regular term begins.

Two Texas amendments, which passed, authorized the legislature to cancel state or local elections for a given office if the candidate was unopposed. The governor vetoed enabling legislation that would have removed the name of the candidate and office from the printed ballot.

Although not an amendment in 2003, it is diffi-

Table B: Substantive Changes in State Constitutions: Proposed and Adopted: 1998–99, 2000–01 and 2002–03

Subject matter	Total proposed			Total adopted			Percentage adopted		
	1998–1999	2000–2001	2002–2003	1998–1999	2000–2001	2002–2003	1998–1999	2000–2001	2002–2003
Proposals of statewide applicability	250 (a)	162 (a)	191	188 (b)	114 (b)	128	74.8 (a)	70.3 (a)(e)	67.0
Bill of Rights	34	4	12	31	1	8	91.1	25.0	66.6
Suffrage & elections	7	6	6	7	4	3	100	66.6	50.0
Legislative branch	40	37	24	29	27	17	72.5	72.9	70.8
Executive branch	17	9	8	10	7	4	58.8	77.7	50.0
Judicial branch	19	7 (a)	19	16	8	11	84.2	100	57.8
Local government	15	9	5	10	6	5	66.6	66.6	100
Finance & taxation	61	38	65	46	25	39	75.4	65.5	60.0
State & local debt	6	5	10	4	5	5	66.6	100	50.0
State functions	24	24	16	14	17	13	58.3	70.8	81.2
Amendment & revision	3	3	3	3	0	3	100	0	100
General revision proposals	1	0	0	1	0	0	100	0	0.0
Miscellaneous proposals	23 (c)	20 (c)	23 (c)	17 (c)	14	20 (c)	77.2	70.0	86.0
Local amendments	46	50	41	41 (d)	40	36	91.1 (d)	80.0	87.8

Source: Survey conducted by Janice May, University of Texas at Austin, January 2004.

Key:
(a)—Excludes Delaware where proposals are not submitted to voters.
(b)—Includes Delaware.
(c)—Includes amendments that contain substantial editorial revision.
(d)—Excludes one Alabama amendment in a legal dispute at the time.
(e)—Excludes one Oregon amendment not canvassed by court order.

cult to ignore the historic recall election in California in 2003, an election made possible by an amendment to the California Constitution added in 1911. One of several Progressive Party measures, the amendments collectively have been described as "the most sweeping revision of the California Constitution in the twentieth century."[1] Although associated with the Progressive Era, the statewide recall has been adopted since that time, most recently in New Jersey and Rhode Island (1992) and Minnesota (1996). However, the device was omitted from the new Montana Constitution of 1972. At present, 17 state constitutions provide for the recall for statewide offices, but it has been used rarely. Gov. Gray Davis was only the second governor to be recalled; the first was in 1921. Should the recall gain favor from the California experience, it would amount to a fundamental change in the election system, the addition of a "no confidence" alternative to regular elections.

Apart from the recall, state constitutions also played a role in the contentious issue of mid-term Congressional redistricting. On December 1, the Colorado Supreme Court ruled that a Congressional redistricting law passed by the Colorado Legislature violated the state constitution.[2] According to the court, the constitution (Art. V, Sec. 14) limits redistricting to one law each decade. Because the federal courts redrew the lines when the legislature was unable to reach consensus on the issue, the legislature lost its redistricting power by default. In its current term, the U.S. Supreme Court has before it a Congressional redistricting plan enacted by the Pennsylvania Legislature, which was challenged on state constitutional grounds in a Pennsylvania Supreme Court case in which the court found no state constitutional violation.[3]

A trend that emerged from the propositions affecting state bills of rights was arguably one of diminishing state constitutional rights. In two cases legislatures gained power at the expense of the courts and judicial decisions were overturned.

A "tort reform" proposal on the Texas ballot was the amendment of greatest national interest because of the ongoing controversy over the civil justice system. The Texas measure authorizes the legislature to "cap" non-economic damages (such as pain and suffering) awarded in medical malpractice and other suits. (If not a medical malpractice suit, a three-fifths vote of the legislature is required.) The amendment overturned a Texas Supreme Court ruling that a law limiting liability claims violated the "open courts" provision of the Texas Bill of Rights. The amendment was hotly contested in what may be the most

expensive election campaign in an amendments election in Texas history. In one ad, "Remember the Alamo," much was made of the historic fight in Texas for individual rights. Supporters stressed the high cost of medical malpractice insurance premiums and the number of doctors leaving their practice. The amendment barely passed (51 percent to 49 percent) in a turnout of 12.2 percent of the registered voters which was higher than expected.

Pennsylvania voters approved an amendment to the state's Declaration of Rights changing the right of a defendant in a criminal case "to meet witnesses face to face" to the right "to confront witnesses against him," language from the Sixth Amendment of the U.S. Constitution. The amendment was occasioned by a ruling of the state's highest court that legislation allowing children to testify by such means as closed circuit television violated the state constitution. In a second amendment, the legislature was given explicit authority to allow children to testify without being physically present in court.

Two amendments concerning private property rights in the Louisiana Bill of Rights were approved. One denies protection to contraband and the other limits recovery in damages arising from coastal wetland conservation measures.

The only rights measure to fail was a successor to the California anti-affirmative action proposition approved in 1996. The California amendment prohibited state and local governments from the collection and use of information that classified individuals by race, ethnicity, color or national origin. Gender was excluded. Called the Racial Privacy Act, it contained numerous exemptions, such as medical research, law enforcement and federal government requirements, but they were not enough to save the amendment from defeat.

State constitutional provisions as they affected gay rights were also of relevance in 2003. Gay rights were an issue in court cases involving the Massachusetts and the Nebraska constitutions.

In a widely reported case, the Supreme Judicial Court of Massachusetts ruled that denial by law of marriage licenses to same-sex couples violated the Massachusetts Constitution.[4] The court ordered the legislature to rectify the situation in 180 days. The decision was similar to a Vermont case in which the highest Vermont state court held the Vermont marriage laws in violation of that state's constitution.[5] It also ordered the state legislature to resolve the problem which it did with a civil union law.

The second case concerns the constitutionality under the U.S. Constitution of the Nebraska defense of marriage amendment added in 2000. The Nebraska provision not only bans same-sex marriage but also "civil unions, domestic partnerships or similar relationships." This would cover domestic partnership benefits given by private firms. A federal district court ruled that the amendment violated the U.S. Constitution. One argument was that it was a "bill of attainder," a legislative act that punishes individuals without a court trial.[6]

Policy

State constitutions typically contain policy provisions on a wide variety of subjects. The most numerous policy amendments are fiscal, including taxes, expenditures, debt, funds and related subjects. Fiscal articles and amendments play an important role in state government.

As has been widely reported, state governments have recently been confronted with the most serious fiscal crisis in over 50 years. An infusion of federal funds and better economic conditions may provide some relief, but conditions were still serious in 2003. State constitutional provisions requiring a balanced budget and other restrictions, both procedural and substantive, have complicated efforts to keep state government afloat in a time of severe revenue shortfalls and demands for public services. The problem was well illustrated in 2003 by a Nevada Supreme Court case.[7] Following one regular and two special sessions with no budget in sight, the court ruled that the legislature, in order to provide funds for education, must waive the constitutional requirement of a two-thirds vote to raise tax revenues. The court reasoned that education was a fundamental constitutional right. Its funding trumps the two-thirds rule, which is only procedural. By a writ of mandamus, the court ordered the legislature to proceed expeditiously with a special session under a simple majority rule.

One resolution to the budget crisis is to raise taxes. However, resistance to new or increased taxes is usually described as "fierce." Apparently opponents of taxes do not agree with Supreme Court Justice Oliver Wendell Holmes who said that taxes are the price we pay for civilization. In recent years constitutional amendments to raise taxes have been rare. The overwhelming defeat of the 2003 Alabama amendment will likely discourage major tax increases in the near future. In 2003 the only other major amendment designed to increase taxes, in this case the residential property tax, was defeated in Colorado. New Jersey voters approved using an existing business tax to pay for hazardous discharge cleanups. Instead of raising

taxes, the popular constitutional trend of lowering property taxes continued. All five on the ballot (four in Texas, one in Louisiana) passed.

One alternative to taxes is to borrow money. Nine propositions concerned bonds, loans or debt limits, five of which passed. Among the successful propositions was a Texas measure providing for general obligation state bonds to assist military communities to keep military bases or cope if they are closed. Bonds for economic development failed in Louisiana and Ohio. A Louisiana infrastructure bank was also defeated.

Most fiscal amendments concerned funds, with all but two passing. Funds are frequently used to support public services, most notably public education. In an era of fiscally trying times, funds may offer an alternative to new taxes. The best example in 2003 was a Texas amendment, which passed, changing to a total-return investment strategy for the Permanent School Fund. Millions of new dollars were expected from adding a percentage of capital gains to the income from investments. Opponents were concerned about a "raid" on the corpus of the fund. A land grant-based New Mexico Education Fund was also tapped. The lottery and funds from the tobacco settlement were sources of non-tax revenues in Louisiana. Voters approved distribution of lottery funds for education and treatment for gambling addiction, and tobacco funds for environmental programs. But Colorado voters turned down a proposal for video lottery terminals to raise money for tourism. One of the two funds rejected was the Alabama Excellence Initiative Fund, already reviewed. The Alabama amendment also included other funds. The other proposition to fail was a proposed California amendment designed to pump money into infrastructure (highways, prisons, college campuses and the like), described as "crumbling." Although not relying on new taxes, the amendment called for a dedication of a percentage of General Fund revenues to the Twenty-First Century Infrastructure Investment Fund.

All 50 state constitutions contain provisions on public education, which is commonly regarded as the most important responsibility of state and local governments in the federal system. Constitutional changes by amendment are common but not as numerous as those on fiscal subjects, although many amendments concern funding of education. New taxes and spending authorized by the rejected Alabama amendment of 2003 were intended in large part to support education as a key to economic growth and modernization in general. As already reviewed, reforms concerned with the administration of education were approved in Mississippi and New Mexico. In addition, a Louisiana amendment which passed addressed the issue of failing public schools by providing for their management by the Department of Elementary and Secondary Education, or by delegation of the board to others.

Most of the other policy amendments were on the lengthy Texas ballot and were of concern mainly to Texans. Three addressed long-standing issues in the state, liquor regulation and the protection of the homestead from creditors. The legislature was authorized to regulate wineries anywhere in the state, including in "dry" areas where by local option, alcoholic beverages cannot otherwise by sold. Two allowed more flexibility in borrowing against the homestead, allowing reverse mortgages to refinance a home equity loan and home equity lines of credit.

Research Note

The Center for State Constitutional Studies at Rutgers University, Camden, continues to provide current information on state constitutions and support for research activities and conferences. Their web site is www.camlaw. rutgers.edu/statecon. A project is underway at the University of Maryland to make available online complete and accurate sources of information on all 50 state constitutions from the date of statehood to the present. Currently at least 16 state charters have been covered. They may be viewed on their web site: www.bsos.umd.edu/const.

Notes

[1] Joseph R. Grodin, Calvin R. Massey, and Richard B. Cunningham, *The California State Constitution, A Reference Guide* (Westport, CT.: Greenwood Press, 1993): 18.

[2] *People ex rel. Salazar v. Davidson*, WL 22833085, (Colorado 2003).

[3] *Vieth et. al. v. Jubelirer et. al.*, U.S. Supreme Court, Docket No. 02-1580.

[4] *Goodrich v. Department of Public Health*, WL 22701313, (Massachusetts 2003).

[5] *Baker v. State*, 704 A2d 864, (Vermont 1999).

[6] See *Citizens for Equal Protection Inc. v. Bruning*, WL 22571708, (Nebraska 2003).

[7] *Governor v. Nevada State Legislature*, 71 P.3d 1269, (Nevada 2003).

References

"Alabama Constitutional Reform." *Cumberland Law Review* 33 (2002–2003), 189: entire issue.

"Annual Issue on State Constitutional Law." *Rutgers Law Journal.* 20 (Summer 1989) to 33 (Summer 2002).

Gardner, James A. "State Constitutions as Agents of Federalism: Power and Interpretation in State Constitutional Law." *William and Mary Law Review* 44 (March 2003), 1225.

The Report of the Alabama Citizens' Constitution Commission to Governor Bob Riley. Submitted March 27, 2003.

"State Constitutional Commentary." *Albany Law Review* 66 (2003), 575. (Annual issue since 1996).

"Symposium: The 1972 Montana Constitution: Thirty Years Later." *Montana Law Review* 64 (2003), 1: entire issue.

Tarr, G. Alan. "Interpreting the Separation of Powers in State Constitutions." *New York University Annual Survey of American Law* 59 (2003).

About the Author

Janice C. May is a professor emeritus of government at the University of Texas at Austin, where she specializes in state government and politics. A regular contributor to *The Book of the States*, she is the author of numerous publications on the Texas Constitution and government, including *The Texas State Constitution: A Reference Guide*, and on state constitutional developments nationwide. She has served on two Texas constitutional commissions and on the board of directors of the Texas State Bar.

Table 1.1
GENERAL INFORMATION ON STATE CONSTITUTIONS
(As of January 1, 2004)

State or other jurisdiction	Number of constitutions*	Dates of adoption	Effective date of present constitution	Estimated length (number of words)	Number of amendments Submitted to voters	Adopted
Alabama	6	1819, 1861, 1865, 1868, 1875, 1901	Nov. 28, 1901	340,136 (a)(b)	1,028	746 (c)
Alaska	1	1956	Jan. 3, 1959	15,988 (b)	40	28
Arizona	1	1911	Feb. 14, 1912	28,876	240	133
Arkansas	5	1836, 1861, 1864, 1868, 1874	Oct. 30, 1874	59,500 (b)	186	89 (d)
California	2	1849, 1879	July 4, 1879	54,645	848	507
Colorado	1	1876	Aug. 1, 1876	74,522 (b)	299	143
Connecticut	4	1818 (f), 1965	Dec. 30, 1965	17,256 (b)	30	29
Delaware	4	1776, 1792, 1831, 1897	June 10, 1897	19,000	(e)	136
Florida	6	1839, 1861, 1865, 1868, 1886, 1968	Jan. 7, 1969	51,456 (b)	127	96
Georgia	10	1777, 1789, 1798, 1861, 1865, 1868, 1877, 1945, 1976, 1982	July 1,1983	39,526 (b)	81 (g)	61 (g)
Hawaii	1 (h)	1950	Aug. 21, 1959	20,774 (b)	119	100
Idaho	1	1889	July 3, 1890	24,232 (b)	204	117
Illinois	4	1818, 1848, 1870, 1970	July 1, 1971	16,510 (b)	17	11
Indiana	2	1816, 1851	Nov. 1, 1851	10,379 (b)	75	43
Iowa	2	1846, 1857	Sept. 3, 1857	12,616 (b)	57	52 (i)
Kansas	1	1859	Jan. 29, 1861	12,296(b)	122	92 (i)
Kentucky	4	1792, 1799, 1850, 1891	Sept. 28, 1891	23,911 (b)	74	40
Louisiana	11	1812, 1845, 1852, 1861, 1864, 1868, 1879, 1898, 1913, 1921, 1974	Jan. 1, 1975	54,112 (b)	184	124
Maine	1	1819	March 15, 1820	16,276 (b)	201	169 (j)
Maryland	4	1776, 1851, 1864, 1867	Oct. 5, 1867	46,600 (b)	254	218 (k)
Massachusetts	1	1780	Oct. 25, 1780	36,700 (l)	148	120
Michigan	4	1835, 1850, 1908, 1963	Jan. 1, 1964	34,659 (b)	61	23
Minnesota	1	1857	May 11, 1858	11,547 (b)	213	118
Mississippi	4	1817, 1832, 1869, 1890	Nov. 1, 1890	24,323 (b)	157	122
Missouri	4	1820, 1865, 1875, 1945	March 30,1945	42,600 (b)	162	103
Montana	2	1889, 1972	July 1, 1973	13,145 (b)	49	27
Nebraska	2	1866, 1875	Oct. 12, 1875	20,048	330 (m)	219 (m)
Nevada	1	1864	Oct. 31, 1864	31,377 (b)	216	131
New Hampshire	2	1776, 1784	June 2, 1784	9,200	284 (n)	143
New Jersey	3	1776, 1844, 1947	Jan. 1, 1948	22,956 (b)	69	36
New Mexico	1	1911	Jan. 6, 1912	27,200	277	148
New York	4	1777, 1822, 1846, 1894	Jan. 1, 1895	51,700	290	216
North Carolina	3	1776, 1868, 1970	July 1, 1971	16,532 (b)	39	31
North Dakota	1	1889	Nov. 2, 1889	19,130 (b)	257	144 (o)
Ohio	2	1802, 1851	Sept. 1, 1851	48,521 (b)	266	160
Oklahoma	1	1907	Nov. 16, 1907	74,075 (b)	329 (p)	165 (p)
Oregon	1	1857	Feb. 14, 1859	54,083 (b)	469 (q)	235 (q)
Pennsylvania	5	1776, 1790, 1838, 1873, 1968 (r)	1968 (r)	27,711 (b)	36(r)	30 (r)
Rhode Island	3	1842 (f) 1986 (s)	Dec. 4, 1986	10,908 (b)	7 (s)	7 (s)
South Carolina	7	1776, 1778, 1790, 1861, 1865, 1868, 1895	Jan. 1, 1896	22,300	670 (t)	484 (t)
South Dakota	1	1889	Nov. 2, 1889	27,675(b)	217	112
Tennessee	3	1796, 1835, 1870	Feb. 23, 1870	13,300	59	36
Texas	5 (u)	1845, 1861, 1866, 1869, 1876	Feb. 15, 1876	80,000	605 (v)	432
Utah	1	1895	Jan. 4, 1896	11,000	154	103
Vermont	3	1777, 1786, 1793	July 9, 1793	10,286 (b)	211	53
Virginia	6	1776, 1830, 1851, 1869, 1902, 1970	July 1, 1971	21,319 (b)	46	38
Washington	1	1889	Nov. 11, 1889	33,564 (b)	168	95
West Virginia	2	1863, 1872	April 9, 1872	26,000	119	70
Wisconsin	1	1848	May 29, 1848	14,392 (b)	181	133 (i)
Wyoming	1	1889	July 10, 1890	31,800	116	91
American Samoa	2	1960, 1967	July 1, 1967	6,000	14	7
No. Mariana Islands	1	1977	Jan. 9, 1978	11,000	55	51 (w)(x)
Puerto Rico	1	1952	July 25, 1952	9,281	6	6

See footnotes at end of table.

GENERAL INFORMATION ON STATE CONSTITUTIONS — Continued

Source: Survey conducted by Janice May, The University of Texas at Austin, January 2004.

*The constitutions referred to in this table include those Civil War documents customarily listed by the individual states.

(a) The Alabama constitution includes numerous local amendments that apply to only one county. An estimated 70 percent of all amendments are local. A 1982 amendment provides that after proposal by the legislature to which special procedures apply, only a local vote (with exceptions) is necessary to add them to the constitution.

(b) Computer word count.

(c) The total number of amendments adopted,746 includes one usually overlooked.

(d) Eight of the approved amendments have been superseded and are not printed in the current edition of the constitution. The total adopted does not include five amendments proposed and adopted since statehood.

(e) Proposed amendments are not submitted to the voters in Delaware.

(f) Colonial charters with some alterations served as the first constitutions in Connecticut (1638, 1662) and in Rhode Island (1663).

(g) The Georgia constitution requires amendments to be of "general and uniform application throughout the state," thus eliminating local amendments that accounted for most of the amendments before 1982.

(h) As a kingdom and republic, Hawaii had five constitutions.

(i) The figure includes amendments approved by the voters and later nullified by the state supreme court in Iowa (three), Kansas (one), Nevada (six) and Wisconsin (two).

(j) The figure does not include one amendment approved by the voters in 1967 that is inoperative until implemented by legislation.

(k) Two sets of identical amendments were on the ballot and adopted in the 1992 Maryland election. The four amendments are counted as two in the table.

(l) The printed constitution includes many provisions that have been annulled. The length of effective provisions is an estimated 24,122 words (12,400

annulled in Massachusetts, and in Rhode Island before the "rewrite" of the constitution in 1986, it was 11,399 words (7,627 annulled).

(m) The 1998 and 2000 Nebraska ballots allowed the voters to vote separately on "parts" of propositions. In 1998, 10 of 18 separate propositions were adopted; in 2000, 6 of 9.

(n) The constitution of 1784 was extensively revised in 1792. Figure shows proposals and adoptions since the constitution was adopted in 1784.

(o) The figures do not include submission and approval of the constitution of 1889 itself and of Article XX; these are constitutional questions included in some counts of constitutional amendments and would add two to the figure in each column.

(p) The figures include five amendments submitted to and approved by the voters which were, by decisions of the Oklahoma or U.S. Supreme Courts, rendered inoperative or ruled invalid, unconstitutional, or illegally submitted.

(q) One Oregon amendment on the 2000 ballot was not counted as approved because canvassing was enjoined by the courts.

(r) Certain sections of the constitution were revised by the limited convention of 1967-68. Amendments proposed and adopted are since 1968.

(s) Following approval of the eight amendments and a "rewrite" of the Rhode Island Constitution in 1986, the constitution has been called the 1986 Constitution.Amendments since 1986 total seven proposed and seven adopted. Otherwise, the total is 105 proposals and 59 adopted.

(t) In 1981 approximately two-thirds of 626 proposed and four-fifths of the adopted amendments were local. Since then the amendments have been statewide propositions.

(u) The Constitution of the Republic of Texas preceded five state constitutions.

(v) The number of proposed amendments to the Texas Constitution excludes three proposed by the legislature but not placed on the ballot.

(w) By 1992, 49 amendments had been proposed and 47 adopted. Since then, one was proposed but rejected in 1994, all three proposals were ratified in 1996 and in 1998, of two proposals one was adopted.

(x) The total excludes one amendment ruled void by a federal district court.

Table 1.2
CONSTITUTIONAL AMENDMENT PROCEDURE: BY THE LEGISLATURE
Constitutional Provisions

State or other jurisdiction	Legislative vote required for proposal (a)	Consideration by two sessions required	Vote required for ratification	Limitation on the number of amendments submitted at one election
Alabama	3/5	No	Majority vote on amendment	None
Alaska	2/3	No	Majority vote on amendment	None
Arizona	Majority	No	Majority vote on amendment	None
Arkansas	Majority	No	Majority vote on amendment	3
California	2/3	No	Majority vote on amendment	None
Colorado	2/3	No	Majority vote on amendment	None (b)
Connecticut	(c)	(c)	Majority vote on amendment	None
Delaware	2/3	Yes	Not required	No referendum
Florida	3/5	No	Majority vote on amendment (d)	None
Georgia	2/3	No	Majority vote on amendment	None
Hawaii	(e)	(e)	Majority vote on amendment (f)	None
Idaho	2/3	No	Majority vote on amendment	None
Illinois	3/5	No	(g)	3 articles
Indiana	Majority	Yes	Majority vote on amendment	None
Iowa	Majority	Yes	Majority vote on amendment	None
Kansas	2/3	No	Majority vote on amendment	5
Kentucky	3/5	No	Majority vote on amendment	4
Louisiana	2/3	No	Majority vote on amendment (h)	None
Maine	2/3 (i)	No	Majority vote on amendment	None
Maryland	3/5	No	Majority vote on amendment	None
Massachusetts	Majority (j)	Yes	Majority vote on amendment	None
Michigan	2/3	No	Majority vote on amendment	None
Minnesota	Majority	No	Majority vote in election	None
Mississippi	2/3 (k)	No	Majority vote on amendment	None
Missouri	Majority	No	Majority vote on amendment	None
Montana	2/3 (i)	No	Majority vote on amendment	None
Nebraska	3/5	No	Majority vote on amendment (f)	None
Nevada	Majority	Yes	Majority vote on amendment	None
New Hampshire	3/5	No	2/3 vote on amendment	None
New Jersey	(l)	(l)	Majority vote on amendment	None (m)
New Mexico	Majority (n)	No	Majority vote on amendment (n)	None
New York	Majority	Yes	Majority vote on amendment	None
North Carolina	3/5	No	Majority vote on amendment	None
North Dakota	Majority	No	Majority vote on amendment	None
Ohio	3/5	No	Majority vote on amendment	None
Oklahoma	Majority	No	Majority vote on amendment	None
Oregon	(o)	No	Majority vote on amendment (p)	None
Pennsylvania	Majority (p)	Yes (p)	Majority vote on amendment	None
Rhode Island	Majority	No	Majority vote on amendment	None
South Carolina	2/3 (q)	Yes (q)	Majority vote on amendment	None
South Dakota	Majority	No	Majority vote on amendment	None
Tennessee	(r)	Yes (r)	Majority vote in election (s)	None
Texas	2/3	No	Majority vote on amendment	None
Utah	2/3	No	Majority vote on amendment	None
Vermont	(t)	Yes	Majority vote on amendment	None
Virginia	Majority	Yes	Majority vote on amendment	None
Washington	2/3	No	Majority vote on amendment	None
West Virginia	2/3	No	Majority vote on amendment	None
Wisconsin	Majority	Yes	Majority vote on amendment	None
Wyoming	2/3	No	Majority vote in election	None
American Samoa	2/3	No	Majority vote on amendment (u)	None
No. Mariana Islands	3/4	No	Majority vote on amendment	None
Puerto Rico	2/3 (v)	No	Majority vote on amendment	3

See footnotes at end of table.

CONSTITUTIONAL AMENDMENT PROCEDURE: BY THE LEGISLATURE — Continued

Source: Survey conducted by Janice May, University of Texas at Austin, January 2004.

Key:

(a) In all states not otherwise noted, the figure shown in the column refers to the proportion of elected members in each house required for approval of proposed constitutional amendments.

(b) Legislature may not propose amendments to more than six articles of the constitution in the same legislative session.

(c) Three-fourths vote in each house at one session, or majority vote in each house in two sessions between which an election has intervened.

(d) Majority vote on amendment except amendment for new state tax or fee not in effect on Nov. 7, 1994 requires two-thirds of voters in the election.

(e) Two-thirds vote in each house at one session, or majority vote in each house in two sessions.

(f) Majority vote on amendment must be at least 50 percent of the total votes cast at the election (at least 35 percent in Nebraska); or, at a special election, a majority of the votes tallied which must be at least 30 percent of the total number of registered voters.

(g) Majority voting in election or three-fifths voting on amendment.

(h) If five or fewer political subdivisions of the state are affected, majority in state as a whole and also in affected subdivisions) is required.

(i) Two-thirds of both houses.

(j) Majority of members elected sitting in joint session.

(k) The two-thirds must include not less than a majority elected to each house.

(l) Three-fifths of all members of each house at one session, or majority of all members of each house for two successive sessions.

(m) If a proposed amendment is not approved at the election when submitted, neither the same amendment nor one which would make substantially the same change for the constitution may be again submitted to the people before the third general election thereafter.

(n) Amendments concerning certain elective franchise and education matters require three-fourths vote of members elected and approval by three-fourths of electors voting in state and two-thirds of those voting in each county.

(o) Majority vote to amend constitution, two-thirds to revise (revise includes all or a part of the constitution).

(p) Emergency amendments may be passed by two-thirds vote of each house, followed by ratification by majority vote of electors in election held at least one month after legislative approval. There is an exception for an amendment containing a supermajority voting requirement, which must be ratified by an equal supermajority.

(q) Two-thirds of members of each house, first passage; majority of members of each house after popular ratification.

(r) Majority of members elected to both houses, first passage; two-thirds of members elected to both houses, second passage.

(s) Majority of all citizens voting for governor.

(t) Two-thirds vote senate, majority vote house, first passage; majority both houses, second passage. As of 1974, amendments may be submitted only every four years.

(u) Within 30 days after voter approval, governor must submit amendment(s) to U.S. Secretary of the Interior for approval.

(v) If approved by two-thirds of members of each house, amendment(s) submitted to voters at special referendum; if approved by not less than three-fourths of total members of each house, referendum may be held at next general election.

Table 1.3
CONSTITUTIONAL AMENDMENT PROCEDURE: BY INITIATIVE
Constitutional Provisions

State or other jurisdiction	Number of signatures required on initiative petition	Distribution of signatures	Referendum vote
Arizona	15% of total votes cast for all candidates for governor at last election	None specified.	Majority vote on amendment.
Arkansas	10% of voters for governor at last election.	Must include 5% of voters for governor in each of 15 counties.	Majority vote on amendment.
California	8% of total voters for all candidates for governor at last election.	None specified.	Majority vote on amendment.
Colorado	5% of total legal votes for all candidates for secretary of state at last general election.	None specified.	Majority vote on amendment.
Florida	8% of total votes cast in the state in the last election for presidential electors.	8% of total votes cast in each of 1/2 of the congressional districts.	Majority vote on amendment except amendment for "new state tax or fee" not in effect Nov. 7, 1994 requires 2/3 of voters voting in election.
Illinois (a)	8% of total votes cast for candidates for governor at last election	None specified. 3/5 voting on amendment.	Majority voting in election or
Massachusetts (b)	3% of total votes cast for governor at preceding biennial state election (not less than 25,000 qualified voters)	No more than 1/4 from any one county.	Majority vote on amendment which must be 30% of total ballots cast at election.
Michigan	10% of total voters for all candidates at last gubernatorial election.	None specified.	Majority vote on amendment.
Mississippi	12% of total votes for all candidates for governor in last election.	No more than 20% from any one congressional district.	Majority vote on amendment and not less than 40% of total vote cast at election.
Missouri	8% of legal voters for all candidates for governor at last election.	The 8% must be in each of 2/3 of the congressional districts in the state.	Majority vote on amendment.
Montana	10% of qualified electors, the number of qualified voters to be determined by number of votes cast for governor in preceding election in each county and in the state.	The 10% to include at least 10% of qualified voters in one-half of the counties.	Majority vote on amendment.
Nebraska	10% of total votes for governor at last election.	The 10% must include 5% in each of 2/5 of the counties.	Majority vote on amendment which must be at least 35% of total vote at the election.
Nevada	10% of voters who voted in entire state in last general election.	10% of total voters who voted in each of 75% of the counties.	Majority vote on amendment in two consecutive general elections.
North Dakota	4% of population of the state.	None specified.	Majority vote on amendment.
Ohio	10% of total number of electors who voted for governor in last election.	At least 5% of qualified electors governor in last election. the state.	Majority vote on amendment. in each of 1/2 of counties in
Oklahoma	15% of legal voters for state office receiving highest number of voters at last general state election.	None specified.	Majority vote on amendment.
Oregon	8% of total votes for all candidates for governor at last election at which governor was elected for four-year term.	None specified.	Majority vote on amendment except for supermajority equal to supermajority voting requirement contained in proposed amendment.
South Dakota	10% of total votes for governor in last election.	None specified.	Majority vote on amendment.
No. Mariana Islands	50% of qualified voters of commonwealth.	In addition, 25% of qualified voters in each senatorial district.	Majority vote on amendment if legislature approved it by majority vote; if not, at least 2/3 vote in each of two senatorial districts in addition to a majority vote.

Source: Survey conducted by Janice May, University of Texas at Austin, January 2004.
Key:
(a) Only Article IV, the Legislature, may be amended by initiative petition.

(b) Before being submitted to the electorate for ratification, initiative measures must be approved at two sessions of a successively elected legislature by not less than one-fourth of all members elected, sitting in joint session.

Table 1.4
PROCEDURES FOR CALLING CONSTITUTIONAL CONVENTIONS
Constitutional Provisions

State or other jurisdiction	Provision for convention	Legislative vote for submission of convention question (a)	Popular vote to authorize convention	Periodic submission of convention question required (b)	Popular vote required for ratification of convention proposals
Alabama	Yes	Majority	ME	No	Not specified
Alaska	Yes	No provision (c)(d)	(c)	10 years (c)	Not specified (c)
Arizona	Yes	Majority	(e)	No	MP
Arkansas	No	No			
California	Yes	2/3	MP	No	MP
Colorado	Yes	2/3	MP	No	ME
Connecticut	Yes	2/3	MP	20 years (f)	MP
Delaware	Yes	2/3	MP	No	No provision
Florida	Yes	(g)	MP	No	Not specified
Georgia	Yes	(d)	No	No	MP
Hawaii	Yes	Not specified	MP	9 years	MP (h)
Idaho	Yes	2/3	MP	No	Not specified
Illinois	Yes	3/4	(i)	20 years; 1988	MP
Indiana	No	No			
Iowa	Yes	Majority	MP	10 years; 1970	MP
Kansas	Yes	2/3	MP	No	MP
Kentucky	Yes	Majority (j)	MP (k)	No	No provision
Louisiana	Yes	(d)	No	No	MP
Maine	Yes	(d)	No	No	No provision
Maryland	Yes	Majority	ME	20 years; 1970	MP
Massachusetts	No		No	Not specified	
Michigan	Yes	Majority	MP	16 years; 1978	MP
Minnesota	Yes	2/3	ME	No	3/5 voting on proposal
Mississippi	No		No		
Missouri	Yes	Majority	MP	20 years; 1962	Not specified (l)
Montana	Yes (m)	2/3	MP	20 years	MP
Nebraska	Yes	3/4	MP (o)	No	MP
Nevada	Yes	2/3	ME	No	No provision
New Hampshire	Yes	Majority	MP	10 years	2/3 voting on proposal
New Jersey	No	No			
New Mexico	Yes	2/3	MP	No	Not specified
New York	Yes	Majority	MP	20 years; 1957	MP
North Carolina	Yes	2/3	MP	No	MP
North Dakota	No	No			
Ohio	Yes	2/3	MP	20 years; 1932	MP
Oklahoma	Yes	Majority	(e)	20 years	MP
Oregon	Yes	Majority	(e)	No	No provision
Pennsylvania	No	No			
Rhode Island	Yes	Majority	MP	10 years	MP
South Carolina	Yes	(d)	ME	No	No provision
South Dakota	Yes	(d)	(d)	No	(p)
Tennessee	Yes (q)	Majority	MP	No	MP
Texas	No	No			
Utah	Yes	2/3	ME	No	MP
Vermont	No	No			
Virginia	Yes	(d)	No	No	MP
Washington	Yes	2/3	ME	No	Not specified
West Virginia	Yes	Majority	MP	No	Not specified
Wisconsin	Yes	Majority	MP	No	No provision
Wyoming	Yes	2/3	ME	No	Not specified
American Samoa	Yes	(r)	No	No	ME (s)
No. Mariana Islands	Yes	Majority (t)	2/3	No (u)	MP and at least 2/3 in each of 2 senatorial districts
Puerto Rico	Yes	2/3	MP	No	MP

See footnotes at end of table.

PROCEDURES FOR CALLING CONSTITUTIONAL CONVENTIONS — Continued

Source: Survey conducted by Janice May, University of Texas at Austin, January 2004.

Key:

MP—Majority voting on the proposal.

ME—Majority voting in the election.

(a) In all states not otherwise noted, the entries in this column refer to the proportion of members elected to each house required to submit to the electorate the question of calling a constitutional convention.

(b) The number listed is the interval between required submissions on the question of calling a constitutional convention; where given, the date is that of the first required submission of the convention question.

(c) Unless provided otherwise by law, convention calls are to conform as nearly as possible to the act calling the 1955 convention, which provided for a legislative vote of a majority of members elected to each house and ratification by a majority vote on the proposals. The legislature may call a constitutional convention at any time.

(d) In these states, the legislature may call a convention without submitting the question to the people. The legislative vote required is two-thirds of the members elected to each house in Georgia, Louisiana, South Carolina and Virginia; two-thirds concurrent vote of both branches in Maine; three-fourths of all members of each house in South Dakota; and not specified in Alaska, but bills require majority vote of membership in each house. In South Dakota, the question of calling a convention may be initiated by the people in the same manner as an amendment to the constitution (see Table 1.3) and requires a majority vote on the question for approval.

(e) The law calling a convention must be approved by the people.

(f) The legislature shall submit the question 20 years after the last convention, or 20 years after the last vote on the question of calling a convention, whichever date is last.

(g) The power to call a convention is reserved to the people by petition.

(h) The majority must be 50 percent of the total voted cast at a general election or at a special election, a majority of the votes tallied which must be at least 30 percent of the total number of registered voters.

(i) Majority voting in the election, or three-fifths voting on the question.

(j) Must be approved during two legislative sessions.

(k) Majority must equal one-fourth of qualified voters at last general election.

(l) Majority of those voting on the proposal is assumed.

(m) The question of calling a constitutional convention may be submitted either by the legislature or by initiative petition to the secretary of state in the same manner as provided for initiated amendments (see Table 1.3).

(n) Two-thirds of all members of the legislature.

(o) Majority must be 35 percent of total votes cast at the election.

(p) Convention proposals are submitted to the electorate at a special election in a manner to be determined by the convention. Ratification by a majority of votes cast.

(q) Conventions may not be held more often than once in six years.

(r) Five years after effective date of constitutions, governor shall call a constitutional convention to consider changes proposed by a constitutional committee appointed by the governor. Delegates to the convention are to be elected by their county councils. A convention was held in 1972.

(s) If proposed amendments are approved by the voters, they must be submitted to the U.S. Secretary of the Interior for approval.

(t) The initiative may also be used to place a referendum convention call on the ballot. The petition must be signed by 25 percent of the qualified voters or at least 75 percent in a senatorial district.

(u) The legislature was required to submit the referendum no later than seven years after the effective date of the constitution. The convention was held in 1985; 45 amendments were submitted to the voters.

Table 1.5
STATE CONSTITUTIONAL COMMISSIONS
(Operative during January 1, 2002 to January 1, 2004)

State	Name of commission	Method and date of creation and period of operation	Membership: number and type	Funding	Purpose of commission	Proposals and action
Alabama	Alabama Citizens' Constitution Commission	Executive Order No. 1. January 23, 2003 - March 27, 2003	35. All appointed by the governor. Including constitutional law experts, former public officers, educators, business and civic leaders. Six were board members of Alabama Citizens for Constitutional Reform (ACCR); 10 were members of ACCR's Alabama Citizens' Commission on Constitutional Reform	Unfunded.	To deliberate on and draft suggested constitutional changes on five subjects: limited county home rule; tax earmarking, stronger veto power, required super legislative majority for new or increased taxes; recompilation of constitution and elimination of racist language and provisions.	To prepare the report five committees were set up; assistance provided by team of technical advisors. Plenary meetings open to public; two public hearings, one in Montgomery and one in Birmingham. Final report presented to the governor on March 27, 2003. It contained drafts for 5 recommended amendments: optional limited county home rule, reforming tax earmarking, 305 rather than simple majority of all members of each house to override veto, 3/5 legislative vote to adopt new taxes or increase them, elimination of racist language and provisions and , by statute, recompilation of constitution. All proposals introduced in 2003 legislature. Elimination of racist language and provisions on 2004 ballot; recompilation approved.
Utah	Utah Constitutional Revision Commission	Statutory: Ch. 89, *Laws of Utah*, 1969; amended by Ch. 107, *Laws* 1977, which made the commission permanent as of July 1 1977. (Codified as Ch. 54, Title 63, *Utah Code Annotated*, 1953.)	16: 1 ex officio, 9 appointed - by the speaker of the House (3), president of the Senate (3), and governor (3) - no more than 2 of each group to be from same party; and 6 additional members appointed by the 9 previously appointed members.	Appropriations through 1995 totaled $1,023,000. In recent years,annual appropriations have been $55,000. Currently, no funding for independent office or printed annual reports.	Study constitution and recommend desirable changes including proposed drafts.	Mandated to report recommendations at least 60 days before legislature convenes. Voter action on commission recommendations through 2000 include: approval of revised articles on legislature, executive, judiciary, elections and rights of suffrage, revenue and taxation, education, and corporations. At 2000 election voters approved an amendment to revise state and local government provisions recommended by the commission and referred by the legislature. Following consideration of the method of apportionment of taxable value of commercial aircraft, the commission was expected to study the Revenue and Taxation article in 2000-2001. Following completion of the study of the Revenue and Taxation article, the voters approved the revision in 2002.

Source: Survey conducted by Janice May, University of Texas at Austin, January 2004.
Note: No constitutional conventions were held from January 1, 2000 through January 1, 2003.

Table 1.6
STATE CONSTITUTIONAL CHANGES BY CONSTITUTIONAL INITIATIVE: 2003

State	Number of proposals	Number of adoptions	Percentage adopted
Arizona	0	0	0.0%
Arkansas	1	0	0.0
California	2	0	0.0
Colorado	5	1	20.0
Florida	5	5	100.0
Illinois	0	0	0.0
Massachusetts	0	0	0.0
Michigan	2	0	0.0
Mississippi	0	0	0.0
Missouri	1	0	0.0
Montana	0	0	0.0
Nebraska	0	0	0.0
Nevada	2	1 (a)	50.0
North Dakota	1	1	100.0
Ohio	1	0	0.0
Oklahoma	0	0	0.0
Oregon	3	1	33.3
South Dakota	1	0	0.0
Total	24	9	37.5

Source: Survey conducted by Janice May, University of Texas at Austin, January 2004.

(a) Nevada approved for the second time one initiative and defeated one initiative for the first time. To be ome effective constitutional initiatives require voter approval in two elections. The defeated initiative was counted because it received its final vote.

Chapter Two

FEDERALISM AND INTERGOVERNMENTAL RELATIONS

Federal encroachment on state tax systems and powers has been a characteristic of coercive or regulatory federalism.
— **John Kincaid**

State mandates continue to be a problem for general-purpose local governments.

— **Joseph F. Zimmerman**

Although states are increasingly interconnected, the likelihood of sustained cooperative action among them remains problematic.

— **Ann O'M. Bowman**

Trends in Federalism: Continuity, Change and Polarization
By John Kincaid

Coercive regulatory trends have displayed considerable continuity since the late 1960s, including a shift of federal aid from places to persons, increased policy conditions attached to federal aid, rising preemptions, federalization of criminal law, encroachments on state tax systems, hollowed intergovernmental institutions, and reduced cooperation within major intergovernmental programs. Two other trends—unfunded federal mandates and federal court orders—have become less significant. A newer trend has been the state-friendly federalism jurisprudence of the U.S. Supreme Court since 1991, although the Court's 2002–2003 term did not advance this trend. State activism in forging new policies and bucking federal policies continues as well, and is likely to intensify in response to rising partisan polarization.

Despite having a former governor, George W. Bush, in the White House, the federal system has not been a more congenial environment for the states. Like gubernatorial presidents Bill Clinton, Ronald Reagan and Jimmy Carter, Bush has responded to national political and fiscal opportunities, not to state interests.[1]

Homeland Security

The predominance of continuity might seem surprising, because many pundits predicted that the war on terrorism would induce centralization, a seismic shift in intergovernmental relations, and even the death of federalism. Yet, despite the massive reorganization of the federal executive branch involved in establishing the Department of Homeland Security, antiterrorism is being institutionalized with much the same patterns of cooperation, conflict, coercion and competition that characterize other intergovernmental policy fields. This is because institutions are creatures of habit, and the federal system is a vast complex of interconnected semi-autonomous institutions.

Relevant federal, state and local agencies are improving cooperation, coordination and communication in ways that build on past relationships, as well as on lessons learned since the terrorist attacks of 2001. States also are reorganizing agencies and realigning practices to correspond to the new homeland security threat and to the new tasks and funding streams emanating from Washington, D.C.

At the same time, there are fears of possible federal commandeering of state and local public safety and health agencies, and federal officials have intimated that state failures to voluntarily bring practices, such as driver's license issuances, and equipment, such as computers, in line with federal guidelines will provoke coercive federal measures. Both liberal Democrats and conservative Republicans have expressed alarm about federal encroachments upon both states' rights and individual rights under the USA Patriot Act and other antiterrorism policies. However, given the political incentives for presidents to prevent terrorist attacks, and given the potential for catastrophic attacks, homeland security policy, while relying greatly on federal coordination with state and local governments, will likely lean more toward coercive than cooperative federalism.

Some state and local oppositional activism has been evident across the country. Four states and about 150 localities have passed resolutions criticizing the Patriot Act. More than 150 city councils approved resolutions opposing the war in Iraq. Many librarians oppose Patriot Act provisions that allow federal officials to examine records on library patrons. Some librarians are purging records so that information will not be available to federal investigators.[2]

The principal source of conflict, though, has been funding—the time-honored bone of intergovernmental contention. States and local governments have complained about too little federal funding, too much red tape tied to funds, delayed releases of funds, and shortfalls between funds promised and funds delivered by the federal government.[3] Large states, such as California and New York, have objected to the Patriot Act's formula for distributing funds. New York officials complained that of $600 million distributed in early 2003, for example, the Empire State received only $1.38 per resident and California received $1.33 per capita, compared to a national average of $3.29 per person and to much higher per capita payments made to small states, such as $9.78 for Wyoming.[4] New York Gov. George Pataki and

Senators Charles Schumer and Hillary Rodham Clinton argue that funding should be linked to likely threats to jurisdictions. In turn, local officials in some states, including New York, have complained that their state holds back too much homeland security money and also misallocates federal and state funds among localities.[5]

Partisan Polarization

The partisan polarization evident in the 2000 presidential election and in Washington, D.C., is a new contextual trend that is increasingly shaping federalism and intergovernmental relations. In 2003, it became evident that polarization has strained the traditional bipartisanship of the Big 7 state and local associations, especially the National Governors Association (NGA), where partisan conflict led to the firing of NGA's chief lobbyist, to reduced dues payments by some states, and to several states withdrawing from the NGA for a time. Although bipartisanship still prevails generally in these associations, continued polarization will weaken their ability to present a united front, especially on major issues that have significant impacts on both the states and the national electoral balance.

This polarization has affected public, presidential, congressional and judicial responses to virtually all public policy issues and introduced fundamental philosophical differences over some long-standing federal-state practices and intergovernmental programs. The consequences of polarization were reflected, for example, in the battles that scuttled reauthorization of three major intergovernmental programs in 2003: the 1996 welfare-reform law, the Transportation Equity Act for the 21st Century (TEA-21), and the Individuals with Disabilities Education Act (IDEA). The compromises needed to enact legislation under conditions of polarization will likely make some intergovernmental programs more complex and somewhat schizophrenic.

This polarization also makes it impossible to resurrect bipartisan and nonpartisan intergovernmental institutions, such as the U.S. Advisory Commission on Intergovernmental Relations (ACIR), which were dismantled or defunded during the 1980s and 1990s. These institutions sought to foster intergovernmental cooperation and consensus building. The ACIR, for example, an independent bipartisan commission established in 1959, was defunded in 1996.

Grants-in-Aid

Some 608 categorical grants and 17 block grants for state and local governments continue to shift federal aid from places to persons. That is, compared to 1978 when only 31.8 percent of federal aid was for payments to individuals (e.g., Medicaid and social welfare), nearly two-thirds of federal aid is now dedicated to payments to persons. Medicaid alone accounts for about 45 percent of all federal-aid money. Consequently, even though federal aid has increased annually since 1987, less and less has been available for traditional place-based functions such as economic development, transportation, criminal justice and government operations. The rise of homeland security has made this shift highly problematic because states and localities now need more placed-based aid for first responders, infrastructure protection, and the like, while more and more state and local money must be diverted to the escalating costs of key person programs, such as Medicaid.[6]

Although the recession that triggered today's state fiscal woes lasted only from March to November 2001, the effects continue to strain most states' budgets. In mid-2003, under pressure from state and local officials, Congress enacted a $20 billion aid package as part of a $330 billion tax cut deal struck with the president. The package provides $10 billion in Medicaid cost relief and $10 billion in FYs 2003 and 2004 that states can use as a "flexible grant" for other state budget relief. "The resurgence of unfunded federal mandates," commented Utah's House Speaker Martin Stephens, "has exacerbated state fiscal problems. States can use [this] money to fill holes in their budgets caused by recent federal cost shifts."[7]

A notable change in the delivery of federal aid to places, however, has been the significant increase in congressional pork-barreling. The number of earmarked projects increased from under 2,000 in 1998 to some 9,362 in FY 2003. Supporters of these projects argue that they are necessary and that members of Congress, who are elected officials, are better suited than "bureaucrats" to make these funding allocations.

Congress also continues to attach substantive conditions to grants-in-aid to accomplish policy objectives not directly achievable under Congress's constitutionally enumerated powers. For example, April 15, 2003, was the deadline for school districts to certify that they permit voluntary religious expression, such as prayer and Bible study, by students and teachers so as not to lose federal-aid money under the No Child Left Behind Act (NCLB) of 2002. May 31, 2003, was the deadline for states to submit their accountability plans under the NCLB. October 1, 2003, was the deadline for all states to enact the .08 blood alcohol level for drunk driving in order to avoid reductions in federal-aid highway funding.

Consistent with previous Republican administrations, President Bush has advocated greater administrative flexibility for states in federal-aid programs. Under Bush, the U.S. Department of Health and Human Services has issued some 3,000 Medicaid waivers, more than all earlier administrations.[8] Bush has also proposed a "superwaiver" in conjunction with welfare reform reauthorization that would allow states to alter eligibility rules and transfer funds among programs, including food stamps, public housing, homeless assistance, child care, adult education, the Social Services Block Grant, and many employment and job training programs.

Bush has proposed a voluntary block grant to provide fixed amounts of money for Medicaid and the State Children's Health Insurance Program (SCHIP) for optional beneficiaries rather than giving states matching funds as under the current program. Optional beneficiaries such as senior citizens and disabled people constitute about one-third of all Medicaid enrollees but consume about two-thirds of Medicaid spending. Under this plan, most states would receive more funds for seven years than they would under the matching program, but federal funds would decline thereafter.

Bush has proposed to replace Section 8 housing vouchers with a program run by the states with an annual lump-sum payment from the federal government. He also has proposed to block grant Head Start (in the form of a pilot program), Unemployment Insurance administration, law-enforcement grants, child-welfare foster-care grants, job training in the Workforce Investment Act, transportation aid in the Job Access program and juvenile delinquency programs.

Bush wants to shift responsibility for passenger rail service to the states. States would contract with Amtrak or other railroads for passenger service. States also would be encouraged to form regional compacts to provide interstate service. Instead of subsidizing Amtrak directly, federal aid would be given to states to support railroad infrastructure and capital investment. States would cover operating costs.

A major state and local complaint, though, is that many programs, such as the Help America Vote Act of 2002, are under funded and that Congress and the president deliver less than what was promised at the time of enactment. Most controversial has been the NCLB, which requires states, beginning in 2005, to test pupils in grades three through eight annually in reading and math, to test those in grades 10 through 12 in science every year, and to provide highly quali-

fied and subject-trained teachers in every classroom.[9] States can select their testing standards pursuant to federal guidelines, but schools that do not improve student achievement must provide tutoring and opportunities for students to transfer to higher achieving schools. After six years, failing schools can be closed and reopened under new management. The NCLB seeks to raise all students' reading and math test scores to 100 percent of state-defined proficiency by 2014.

Many state and local officials have characterized the NCLB as an unfunded mandate because the federal government provides too little money for states and school districts to meet the NCLB's requirements. U.S. Secretary of Education Rod Paige responded, however, that: "In raw terms, this president [Bush] has increased education spending by $11 billion. As a nation, we now spend $470 billion a year on K–12 education locally and federally—more than on national defense. What is 'under funded' about that?"[10] Regardless of funding, the NCLB is an unprecedented federal intrusion into a traditional state and local governmental function.

Unfunded Mandates

The robust growth of unfunded mandates on state and local governments, which began in the late 1960s, was effectively staunched by the Unfunded Mandates Reform Act (UMRA) of 1995. According to the Congressional Budget Office's (CBO) June 2003 report, only two unfunded mandates exceeding UMRA standards have been enacted since 1995: a 1996 federal minimum-wage increase and a 1998 reduction in federal reimbursement of state administrative costs for the Food Stamp program, which together imposed average annual costs of $9 million per state. A mandate violates UMRA if it imposes an annual cost on state, local and tribal governments exceeding $58 million (or about $1.2 million per state).

NGA, however, publicizes a list of unfunded mandates, which includes, among others, homeland security, Medicaid, the NCLB and special education. Although these programs are neither mandates nor unfunded obligations, state and local officials contend that they are "de facto mandates" because they are under-funded grants-in-aid that state and local governments cannot realistically reject or opt out of once in place. For instance, the Individuals with Disabilities Education Act (IDEA) of 1975 commits the federal government to funding 40 percent of each state's IDEA costs. As of FY 2003, the federal government still covered only 18 percent of those costs.

UMRA also does not take account of the costs

of federal court orders on state and local governments, some of which have imposed enormous costs for institutional change. The number, scope and costs of such orders began to increase dramatically during the 1960s. This feature of coercive federalism may be coming to an end, however, as evidenced by the closing down of the 26-year-old desegregation lawsuit against the Kansas City Missouri School District in August 2003.[11] The case, begun in 1977, cost Missouri taxpayers some $2 billion and produced a 1990 U.S. Supreme Court decision upholding the authority of a federal judge to order a state or local government to levy a tax increase to pay for his court order.[12]

A recent study suggests, however, that overall federal policies had a $467 billion positive impact on state and local finances in FY 2004 and a $153 billion negative impact, leaving a $314 billion positive-impact balance.[13]

Preemption

Federal preemption, which skyrocketed after 1969, continues to be prevalent, and even the U.S. Supreme Court justices who support the states in many 10th Amendment, 11th Amendment and commerce clause cases have upheld federal preemptions of state powers. Many preemptions do not completely occupy a field; instead, they allow states to enact their own rules or standards so long as they are equal to or higher than the federal provisions. Recently, however, there has been a tendency for more preemptions to occupy a field and deny states the authority to enact their own legislation.

For example, the Fair and Accurate Credit Transactions Act of 2003 preempts most state laws on identity theft and limits the states' authority to enact pro-consumer laws on such matters as credit reporting and financial privacy. In the past, pro-consumer laws often originated in the states. For instance, the new federal rule that merchants truncate credit-card numbers originated in California, Connecticut and Nevada. In 2001, California was the first jurisdiction to require disclosure of credit scores to consumers.

Congress enacted anti-spam legislation (Can-Spam Act) in 2003 that preempted California's and Delaware's rigorous laws as well as many provisions of anti-spam laws in about 34 other states. The federal law allows consumers to opt out of receiving junk e-mail. Only after a consumer asks to be taken off the list is the sender required to stop transmitting messages. The California and Delaware statutes contained an "opt in" provision prohibiting unrequested commercial e-mail.

Meanwhile, Attorney General John D. Ashcroft has sought to override state laws on medicinal marijuana and physician-assisted suicide. In October 2003, however, the U.S. Supreme Court let stand a ruling by the Ninth Circuit Court of Appeals that federal attempts to revoke the drug licenses of physicians who advise patients to smoke marijuana under state law violate the First Amendment as well as principles of federalism.

Federalization of State Criminal Law

Another trend has been the federalization of state criminal law, to the point where there are some 3,500 federal criminal offenses today, about half of which have been enacted since the mid-1960s. Legislation enacted in 2003 to provide grants and assistance to states to establish a national Amber Alert system (already then operating in 41 states) to notify the public of child abductions also contained many punitive sentencing provisions with respect to kidnapping and sex offenses against children, further limited federal judges' sentencing discretion, and expanded prosecutors' wiretap powers.

This trend has met criticism from some liberals and conservatives,[14] but the political incentives for presidents and members of Congress to support crime legislation are very high. Some members of the Supreme Court have evidenced concern about this trend as well. For example, in ruling in March 2003 that antiabortion protesters cannot be prosecuted as racketeers under the Racketeer Influenced and Corrupt Organizations Act (RICO), the Court expressed concern about potential uses of RICO to transform local crimes into federal crimes.

Taxation

Another characteristic of coercive or regulatory federalism has been federal encroachments on state tax systems and powers. Two issues were prominent for states in 2003: federal tax cuts and taxation of Internet and catalog sales.

The $330 billion tax cut of 2003 will likely reduce state tax collections by several billion dollars during the next two years, depending on whether states decouple affected provisions of their tax codes from the federal tax code. Decoupling, however, will make tax compliance more complex for many taxpayers and perhaps provoke more taxpayer resistance to state and local tax increases and reforms. Federal tax reductions might, over time, also reduce grant money for states and localities, and shift taxes toward more regressive levies as state and local governments enact compensating tax and fee increases.

States cannot tax out-of-state Internet and catalog sales, which may have cost them $20 billion in FY 2002, but 34 state negotiators agreed on the Streamlined Sales Tax agreement to facilitate state taxation of Internet and catalog purchases, and some major retailers (e.g., Wal-Mart, Target and Toys "R" Us) began voluntarily in early 2003 to collect online sales taxes in 37 states and Washington, D.C. The Streamlined Sales Tax Implementing States group is trying to persuade state legislatures to enact the agreement. Many states are pushing for federal enactment of the Simplified Sales and Use Tax Act that would authorize state taxation under the streamlined system.[15]

Online sales of cigarettes are another problem. The Jenkins Act of 1949 requires out-of-state retailers to provide sales records to states where cigarettes are shipped so states can collect excise taxes, but there is no enforcement of the act by the U.S. Department of Justice and the FBI. An effort is under way in Congress to strengthen the act.

U.S. Supreme Court

In contrast to the state-friendly federalism jurisprudence of the U.S. Supreme Court since 1991, the Court's 2002–2003 term was one in which, said Justice Ruth Bader Ginsburg, federalism was "the dog that didn't bark."[16] Although the states won many cases, and of cases brought by state attorneys general, the states won 13 and lost seven, they lost the bellwether federalism case, *Nevada Department of Human Resources* v. *Hibbs*.[17] In this 6–3 ruling, the Court upheld, against an 11th Amendment challenge, the right of state employees to sue their state in federal court to enforce rights under the federal Family and Medical Leave Act of 1993. This ruling was a surprising departure from the Court's recent 11th Amendment rulings, and all the more so because Chief Justice William H. Rehnquist wrote the majority opinion and Justice Sandra Day O'Connor joined the majority. Thus, two of the Court's "Federalism Five" voted against the states.

In another case limiting state involvement in foreign affairs, the Court struck down a 1999 California law that required subsidiaries of European companies to disclose the names of millions of persons who had purchased insurance policies from their parent firms in Germany and other European countries between 1920 and 1945 so as to provide payments to Holocaust survivors on unpaid insurance policies. Companies failing to make the disclosures would lose their license to practice in California. The Court also struck down a California law that retroactively eliminated statutes of limitations on sex crimes so as to allow prosecution of individuals after the expiration of a previous statute of limitation; however, the Court did uphold California's "three strikes" criminal sentencing statute.

The Court ruled that lawsuits alleging that interest rates charged by national banks are illegally excessive must be heard in federal rather than state courts because the National Bank Act preempts state usury laws. The justices also upheld the federal Children's Internet Protection Act of 2001, which requires public libraries to install anti-pornography filters on all computers that provide Internet access to library users. Important in the Court's validating this act was that it is a condition of federal aid rather than a criminal statute. Two federal programs provide about $200 million per year for libraries to establish and link to electronic networks and to offer discount access to the Internet. "Congress has wide latitude to attach conditions to the receipt of federal assistance in order to further its policy objectives," wrote Chief Justice Rehnquist.

In *Franchise Tax Board of California* v. *Hyatt*,[18] the justices ruled unanimously that Nevada courts did not have to extend full faith and credit to a California law that gives California's tax assessors and Franchise Tax Board immunity for any tort suits arising from a tax assessment. The case involved a California resident who claimed that he moved to Nevada, a state with no income tax, shortly after he earned $20 million on a patent. The former resident sued California in Nevada courts under Nevada law for intentional torts committed mostly in California. California was supported by 20 states and by many state and local associations which argued that a ruling against California would weaken legitimate tax collection efforts and encourage wealth to flee to tax havens.

The justices held 8–0 that federal courts cannot close the door to a state prisoner who is appealing a state *habeas corpus* denial because he or she seems not to have a winnable case; instead, the inmate need only present a plausible case. The decision opens the door considerably to federal appeals after many federal courts had virtually closed their doors in complying with the restrictive provisions of the 1996 Antiterrorism and Effective Death Penalty Act.

In important policy cases, the Court limited the reach of the federal Employee Retirement Income Security Act (ERISA) by upholding Kentucky's "any willing provider" law, which allows any health care provider to join an insurance network so long as the provider accepts the insurer's rules and payment levels. The insurance industry contended that ERISA preempted Kentucky's statute. This decision helps clarify the scope and conditions of ERISA's preemption of state authority to regulate health care and to facilitate greater access to private-sector health insurance. In turn, the Court lifted an injunction that had blocked implementation of the Maine Rx Program since its 2000 enactment. The program seeks to obtain discounts on prescription drugs for the state's uninsured residents. Maine was supported by an *amicus* brief filed by 29 states.

Highly publicized was the Court's validation of an affirmative action program operated by the University of Michigan law school while invalidating the university's undergraduate program that awarded 20 extra points on a 150-point scale to black, Hispanic, and Indian applicants. The Court did not, however, require states to adopt affirmative action; hence, the decisions did not overturn California's Proposition 209 on race-neutral admissions to state colleges and universities. Also highly publicized was the Court's 5–4 overturning, on broad privacy grounds, of a Texas law that criminalized same-sex sodomy, thus voiding sodomy laws still extant in 13 states in 2003.

Finally, and pertinent to partisan polarization, the Court opined that in redistricting, states can consider a minority group's general influence on the electoral process rather than only the number of minority voters in a district. The decision was a victory for Democrats who had sought to spread black voters across more districts so as to produce more victories for Democratic candidates rather than packing African-Americans into majority-minority districts where they produce fewer Democratic victories. The U.S. Department of Justice contended that any reduction in the percentage of minority voters in such a district is an unconstitutional "retrogression" or dilution of minority voting rights.

State Activism

The legal assaults on Wall Street by New York's attorney general and the influence of state treasurers on the ouster of the chairman of the New York Stock Exchange in September 2003 highlighted the policy activism that has been evident in states since the late 1970s. States have been pioneering innovative policies, some of which are adopted by the federal government, and countering federal policies with legislation and court rulings. This activism is often attributed to the reform and resurgence of state governments during the 1950s and 1960s. Although reforms strengthened state capacities, state policy activism switched into high gear in reaction to the rise of coercive federalism under which both conserva-

tives and liberals have found ever more reasons to seek refuge in state policymaking when they cannot achieve their objectives through federal policymaking.

For instance, moral conservatives appalled by U.S. Supreme Court rulings on abortion and sodomy have sought to thwart such policies through state regulation. Pro-life activists, for example, have been pressing for state laws to add requirements to abortions (e.g., a 24-hour waiting period and parental notification), to prohibit state funding, and to criminalize injury to a fetus. According to the American Life League, "You can do a lot more in the legislatures than on the federal level right now."[19]

In turn, liberal activists responding to conservative Supreme Court rulings and to deregulation since the Reagan era have also stimulated considerable state policy activism. For example, several multistate lawsuits were initiated against the U.S. Environmental Protection Agency in 2003 alleging relaxed enforcement or lack of enforcement of federal environmental standards. According to the policy director of the liberal Center for Policy Alternatives, "states are now the vanguard of the progressive movement."[20]

Conclusion

In the end, though, both conservative and liberal activists almost always prefer a preemptive or coercive federal policy over state-by-state policies when they can achieve victory in the federal arena and when state policies violate their own policy preferences. In this respect, state activism reflects more continuity than discontinuity in coercive or regulatory federalism.

Notes

[1] See also, John Kincaid, "State-Federal Relations: Continuing Regulatory Federalism," *The Book of the States*, 2002, (Lexington, KY: The Council of State Governments, 2002), 25–32; John Kincaid, "From Cooperation to Coercion in American Federalism: Housing, Fragmentation, and Preemption, 1780–1992," *Journal of Law and Politics* 9 (Winter 1993): 333–433.

[2] Dean E. Murphy, "Some Librarians Use Shredder to Show Opposition to New F.B.I. Powers," *New York Times*, April 7, 2003, A12; Marcos Mocine-McQueen, "Library thwarts Patriot Act snooping," Denver Post, July 29, 2003, 1A, 10A.

[3] See, for example, Philip Shenon, "Antiterror Money Stalls in Congress," *New York Times*, February 13, 2003, A1–A21.

[4] Raymond Hernandez, "New York Officials Complain of Unfair Share of Homeland Security Money," *New York Times*, March 30, 2003, A23. See also, John Kincaid and Richard L. Cole, "Issues of Federalism in Response to Ter-

rorism," *Public Administration Review* 62 (Special Issue 2002): 181–92.

[5] Philip Shenon, "Counterterror Aid Is Tied Up by the States, Mayors Assert," *New York Times*, September 18, 2003, A25.

[6] See also, John Kincaid, "Trends in Federalism: Is Fiscal Federalism Fizzling?" *The Book of the States*, 2003, (Lexington, KY: The Council of State Governments, 2003), 26–31.

[7] Quoted in "States Fare Well in Federal Budget," *State Legislatures* 29 (July/August 2003): 11.

[8] Marilyn Werber Serafini, "Waiving Red Flags," *National Journal* 35 (April 5, 2003): 1072–78.

[9] See, for example, Diana Jean Schemo, "Critics Say School Funding Falls Short of Promises," *New York Times*, February 5, 2003, p. A16.

[10] Rod Paige, "It's Not About the Money," *Wall Street Journal*, October 30, 2003, A16.

[11] Associated Press, "Kansas City Schools Are Held Integrated," *New York Times*, September 28, 2003, A26.

[12] *Missouri v. Jenkins*, 110 S.Ct. 1651 (1990).

[13] Iris J. Lav, "Piling on Problems: How Federal Policies affect State Fiscal Conditions," *National Tax Journal* 56 (September 2003): 535–54.

[14] Associated Press, "Fed's larger role in crime fighting met with criticism," *Express-Times* (Easton), December 28, 2003, A–2.

[15] Amol Sharma and Martin Kady II, "State Deficits Increase Pressure For Authority to Tax Internet Sales," *CQ Weekly* 62 (January 10, 2004): 101–2.

[16] CNN, "Justice Ginsburg: Supreme Court Faces Stormy Times," 12 June 2003, at www.cnn.com/2003/LAW/06/12/ginsburg.aclu.ap/.

[17] 123 S.Ct. 1972 (2003).

[18] 123 S.Ct. 1683 (2003).

[19] Quoted in Associated Press, "Activists push for limits on abortion through legislation at state level," *Express-Times* (Easton), March 12, 2003, A–5.

[20] Quoted in Dennis Cauchon, "Fed-up states defy Washington," *USA Today*, December 8, 2003, at www.usatoday.com/news/washington/2003-12-08-states-usat_x.htm.

About the Author

John Kincaid is the Robert B. and Helen S. Meyner Professor of Government and Public Service and director of the Meyner Center for the Study of State and Local Government at Lafayette College in Easton, Pennsylvania. He is also editor of *Publius: The Journal of Federalism* and former executive director of the U.S. Advisory Commission on Intergovernmental Relations.

Trends in State-Local Relations

By Joseph F. Zimmerman

A survey of municipal leagues and county associations in 41 states reveals several state legislatures initiated actions to assist general purpose local governments by broadening their discretionary authority and establishing special assistance programs. Nevertheless, more than one-half of the respondents reported the legislatures had imposed additional mandates since 1990 and one-third reported the imposition of additional restraints. Only two respondents indicated court decisions generally favored local governments, six reported narrow interpretation of local powers and the remaining respondents reported mixed decisions.

State-local relations are traceable in origin to colony-town relations in the Massachusetts Bay Colony in 1630. Town governments initially, and cities subsequently, were under the tight control of their respective colonial government. After states declared their independence of the United Kingdom, state legislatures continued to apply to their local governments the English common law *ultra vires* rule holding a local government could not exercise a power without specific legislative authorization. This rule, when applied to United States local governments, became known popularly as Dillon's Rule after Judge John F. Dillon of the Iowa Supreme Court included two of his 1868 decisions, based on the common law rule, in his *Commentaries on the Law of Municipal Corporations*.[1] Dillon's Rule does not restrict the authority of a state legislature to devolve broad powers upon local governments and several Dillon's Rule states have granted relatively broad powers to local political entities in specified functional fields.[2]

State-local relations were limited and relatively simple in nature during the late 18th century and the early decades of the 19th century when local governments were small and were assigned only a small number of functional responsibilities. Subsequently, urbanization necessitated an increase in the responsibilities of many local governments and discriminatory legislative treatment of municipalities in several states, relative to the grant of charters and/or powers, promoted a movement to amend state constitutions to prohibit legislative enactment of a special bill unless requested by the named unit. The first such amendment, forbidding the state legislature to vacate or alter a road laid out by local highway commissioners, was ratified by Michigan voters in 1850 and today a general prohibition of special legislation is found in 41 state constitutions.

Legislative interference in municipal affairs, including so-called "ripper laws," in the late 19th century and early 20th century mobilized local gov-

ernment officers to seek protection in a new type of constitutional amendment establishing an *Imperium in Imperio* or federal system within the state by granting to general purpose local governments exclusive control over their governmental structure, property and local affairs. Sixteen state constitutions contain such a home rule provision today. New York voters, for example, approved a 1923 constitutional amendment granting such powers to cities and a subsequent amendment extended these powers to counties, towns and villages. However, the grant of authority proved to be inadequate relative to local affairs when the New York Court of Appeals in *Adler v. Deegan* (1929), developed the state concern doctrine positing the state legislature may enact a special law without New York City's consent if there is a substantial "state concern" even "though intermingled with it are concerns of the locality."[3] Courts in New York and other states continue to cite *Adler v. Deegan* as a precedent in their preemption decisions.

The American Municipal Association (now National League of Cities) continued to be concerned about state legislative interference in municipal affairs and engaged Dean Jefferson B. Fordham of the University of Pennsylvania Law School to conduct a study of the legal relationship between a state government and its general purpose local governments. This study was also intended to advance recommendations for new home rule constitutional provisions designed to ensure such governments will possess increased discretionary authority. His 1953 report recommended each state constitution should be amended to require the state legislature to devolve upon each municipality adopting a new charter all powers susceptible to devolution with two exceptions—civil relations, and definition and punishment of a felony.[4]

Voters in several states approved a new constitution or a constitutional amendment devolving powers upon general purpose local governments regardless of whether they have adopted new charters. A number of these constitutional devolution provisions withhold powers from municipalities beyond the two Fordham recommended. The New York Constitution, for example, devolves upon local governments only 10 specific powers in addition "to property, affairs, or government."[5] This constitution, however, directs the state legislature to enact and as needed amend "a statute of local governments granting to local governments powers including but not limited to those of local legislation and administration in addition to the powers vested in them by this article."[6] This unusual statute was enacted in 1963, has quasi-constitutional status, and may be amended only by a bill approved by the legislature and the governor in one calendar year and its reenactment and approval by the governor the following year. The statute has not been amended to date.

One should note the devolution of powers constitutional approach to determining the respective powers of the state and its general purpose local governments is a legislative supremacy approach. This is because the devolution provision authorizes the state legislature to remove powers from all local governments or a class of such units in order to address emerging statewide problems.

State-local powers can be placed in three general classes: state controlling, local controlling and shared. The legal relationships between states and their respective political subdivisions are particularly complex in *Imperium in Imperio* and devolution of powers states as they continue to utilize Dillon's Rule relative to certain powers, particularly personnel and taxation.[7] Municipal attorneys frequently seek advisory opinions from the state attorney general, auditor or comptroller, and/or education commissioner (state superintendent of schools) relative to the authority of a local government to initiate an action. In some instances, the attorneys seek an advisory opinion from two of the state officers and receive two different opinions. Not surprisingly, suits on occasion are filed in a court against a local government alleging the unit lacks legal authority to initiate the concerned action. The decision of the trial court often is appealed to higher state courts and may be appealed to the U.S. Supreme Court if a federal question is involved.

Congressional preemption of state and local governmental powers in many regulatory fields, particularly since 1965, has produced a silent revolution in the nature of the federal system and restricted severely the discretionary authority of states and general purpose local governments.[8] Preemption statutes often include mandates requiring subnational governments to initiate a specific action and restraints forbidding the initiation of a specific action such as dumping sewage sludge in oceans. Many so-called state mandates imposed on local governments are federal mandates contained in minimum standards preemption statutes. They allow the concerned federal department or agency to delegate regulatory primacy to a state, provided it submits a plan containing regulatory standards meeting or exceeding the federal minimum ones. Evidence the state possesses the necessary equipment and qualified personnel to enforce the standards must also be provided.

It is not uncommon for state legislatures to enact two types of acceptance or permissive statutes, in lieu of mandate statutes, authorizing local governing bodies or voters to decide whether to accept the statute. The first type allows the accepting government to exercise additional discretionary authority. The second type is a market basket approach under which voters are allowed to select one of several charters contained in the statute. In Massachusetts, voters in cities, but not towns, are allowed a choice of six charters.[9]

To collect information on trends in state-local relations, a questionnaire was sent to each state municipal league, association of counties in states with county governments, and state department of community affairs or similar agency. Responses were received from 41 states, but not all respondents answered all questions.

State-Local Legal Relationships

Constitutional provisions, statutes, state administrative rules and regulations, and court decisions determine the nature of the legal relationships between a state and its political subdivisions. The latter are classified as municipal corporations possessing significant discretionary authority and quasi-municipal corporations serving as administrative arms of the state government with few functional responsibilities. Historically, all county governments were quasi-municipal corporations, but today all counties in several states, such as New York, are municipal corporations and individual counties in certain other states are municipal corporations.

Our questionnaire requested respondents to indicate whether there are more, fewer or the same number of state restraints compared to 1990. Respondents in 13 states reported additional restraints had been imposed, Montana and Vermont respondents indicated the number of restraints had declined, and respondents in the 22 remaining states checked no change in the number. Courts interpret constitutional and statutory provisions affecting local governments and a restraint may be the product of a court decision. The New Hampshire Superior Court in 2003, for example, responded to complainants in six surrounding towns alleging the city of Manchester was violating state law by ordering the city, which sells drinking water to the towns, to stop fluoridating the water (authorized by a voter referendum in 1999), because town voters had not participated in the referendum. The court in the same year also invalidated the town of Colebrook's smoking ban in restaurants on the ground it was preempted by the State Indoor Smoking Act.

Respondents in only Kentucky and Maine indicated courts tended to interpret broadly the discretionary authority of general purpose local governments since 1990. Respondents in six states reported narrow interpretation of such authority and 30 respondents checked court decisions were mixed in terms of the breadth of such authority.

State legislatures have initiated several actions to broaden the discretionary authority of municipal corporations: acceptance statutes, opt-out statutes, and authorization to enter into intergovernmental service agreements and to transfer responsibility for a function to another local government.

Acceptance Statutes. These laws become effective in a state only if the local governing body or voters accept them and stand in direct contrast to state mandates which are orders local governments are required to implement. Respondents in 27 of 41 surveyed states reported their respective state legislature enacted such statutes, while eight states checked no.

Opt-Out Provisions. These constitutional and statutory provisions automatically apply to a local government unless the governing body votes affirmatively to exclude the government from the statute. The Illinois Constitution (Art. VII, §6) contains a unique provision stipulating a home rule government by referendum may elect not to be a home rule unit. Our survey revealed 10 of 39 states employ opt-out statutes on occasion.

Intergovernmental Service Agreements. The first statute authorizing intergovernmental service agreements was an 1851 Indiana statute pertaining to the jailing of prisoners from other jurisdictions. The growth in areawide problems since 1945 induced many state legislatures to enact broad statutes permitting general purpose local governments to enter into service agreements under which one government provides services to one or more additional governments and other statutes allowing the joint provision

of services. The incorporation of the city of Lakewood, California, in 1945 led to the unusual situation in which the city initially received all of its services under contracts with Los Angles County. Subsequently, several cities incorporated in the county also initially received all services from the county.

The enabling statute in the majority of states allows agreements only if both party governments have been granted such authority. On rare occasions, the state government has ordered a local government to provide a service, such as waste water treatment, to a neighboring municipality and counties in a few states are required by statute to provide listed services when requested to do so by a city.

Agreements may be in the form of written contracts or verbal understandings, and voter approval is not required. Respondents in 39 of 41 surveyed states reported general purpose local governments could enter into service agreements. Such agreements are popular because they allow a local government to (1) obtain a service the unit can not provide, (2) lower the cost of a service through economies of scale, and (3) provide a higher quality service.

Transfer of Functions. Local governments, where authorized, voluntarily transfer responsibility for a function to another local government or the state government for a variety of reasons including the lack of equipment, facilities, and personnel; fiscal restraints; and elimination of duplication of services. Functional consolidation may provide important cost savings to participating local units and benefit residents with improved quality services. In some instances, a local government decides to contract with a private firm instead of transferring responsibility to another governmental unit.

Twenty respondents reported a constitutional and/ or statutory provision permits a local government to transfer a function or a functional component to another local government and 17 reported the lack of such authority. Transfers in Florida, New York, Ohio, Pennsylvania and Vermont require voter approval. The Ohio Constitution (Art. X, §3) requires separate voter approval in the county, the largest city and in townships as a unit before a municipal function may be transferred to the county. In addition to voluntary transfers, the state legislature in various states reassigned responsibility for a function from a class of or all local governments to the state as illustrated by the Maryland General Assembly 1973 statute (chapter 784) transferring responsibility for property tax assessment effective in 1975.

It is important to note the distinction between an intergovernmental service agreement and a transfer of functional responsibility may be blurred as a agreement may contain no sunset provision. A unit transferring a function retains no responsibility while the unit receiving services under a contract with another government remains responsible for the function.

State-Local Fiscal Relationships

Constitutional and statutory provisions limit significantly the discretionary fiscal authority of local governments including the ability to levy taxes other than the property tax in many states. Respondents in six states said state approval was required for local budgets to become effective and 31 said no. The requirement applied only to counties in Kentucky and Nevada, cities in Nebraska, cities and townships New Jersey, and cities and counties in New Mexico.

The near bankruptcy of four New York cities persuaded the state legislature to establish a state financial control board for each city: New York in 1975 (chapters 868-70), Yonkers in 1978 (chapter 871), Troy in 1995 (chapter 187), and Buffalo in 2003 (chapter 122). The New York City board continues to operate today although the term "emergency" has been dropped its title. The restoration of Yonkers and Troy to fiscal health led to the dissolution of their respective control boards. However, the 2000 state legislature created the state-controlled Nassau Interim Finance Authority for Nassau County (chapter 84).

Local government officers generally resent mandates more than restraints and often complain the state legislature in imposing a mandate failed to consider adequately the fiscal burden placed on local governments. A restraint, however, may generate considerable animosity by imposing additional costs on local governments if they must employ a more expensive alternative to achieve the same programmatic goal.

Mandates. A mandate is a legal requirement a local government must initiate a prescribed action, thereby excluding conditions attached to grants-in-aid. Our survey found the same number of mandates today, compared to 1990, in 16 states, a larger number of mandates in 18 states, and fewer mandates in four states. Constitutional amendments in 15 states and statutes in 16 states providing some form of mandate reimbursement have influenced the state mandates trend. Most relief provisions date to the 1970s although the 1959 Alaska Constitution (Art. 2, §19) stipulates a special law imposing costs upon a local government does not become effective unless approved in a voter referendum. A 1978 Tennessee constitutional amendment (Art. 2, §24) allows the General Assembly to impose mandates on cities and counties only if "the State shares in the cost." A similarly worded provision was added to the Hawaiian state constitution (Art 8, §5) in the same year by a constitutional amendment.

California initiative proposition 4 of 1979 added a new amendment to the state constitution directing the state to reimburse local governments for all mandated costs. This amendment has not stopped the imposition of mandates as California respondents reported the trend has been more mandates imposed since 1990.

A 1984 New Hampshire constitutional amendment (Part I, Art. 27a) required similar full reimbursement of mandated costs unless the local governing body, a city council or a town meeting, approves the mandates. New Hampshire's experience reveals the General Court (state legislature) constitutionally may shift a financial burden to cities and towns without providing reimbursement. In 2001, the New Hampshire Supreme Court in *Town of Nelson v. New Hampshire Department of Transportation* (145 N.H. 75) ruled the department's reclassification of sections of state highways as local roads, shifting maintenance costs to local governments, was not a mandate subject to reimbursement even though the state's *Administrative Procedures Act* (NHRSA 541-A:25) forbids state agencies to impose mandates. Similarly, the mandate reimbursement provision is not applicable to a General Court 2004-05 fiscal year budget decision to terminate payments to cities and towns for transportation of handicapped children. A Georgia respondent reported mandates are assuming a more subtle form and referred to overcrowded state prisons not accepting state prisoners from county jails and paying a county only $20 daily for each state prisoner in the jails.

A 2002 New Hampshire act requires cities and towns to comply with a new certification process developed by the State Assessing Standards Board, but in 2003 the board replaced the standards with advisory guidelines. In addition, the 2003 General Court enacted Chapter 108 exempting towns with a population of 5,000 or less from the mandate to clean up an inactive municipally owned unlined landfill provided it is monitored in accordance with state rules.

A New Mexico constitutional amendment (Art. 10, §8) ratified in 1984, gives the state legislature a choice relative to mandates imposed by "rule or regulation." The legislature may reimburse local governments or grant "a means of new funding" to the concerned political subdivisions. A 1992 Maine constitutional amendment (Art. 9, §21) stipulates the state legislature may impose a mandate only if the state funds 90 percent of the costs or the mandate is approved by a two-thirds vote of each house of the state legislature. The Maine respondent indicated the legislature has found ways to evade the requirement.

Several mandate relief statutes implement constitutional provisions and other statutes generally offer relatively little protection from imposition of new mandates. Connecticut Public Act 434 of 1993, for example, allows a city or a town to postpone execution of the mandate for one year in the event the state legislature does not cover the imposed costs. And the 1989 New York state legislature enacted chapter 377 eliminating the mandate cities annually must publish a listing of all tax-exempt property in a local newspaper.

Special State Assistance

It is well known that state legislatures appropriate funds in the form of grants-in-aid and/or revenue sharing, and authorize technical assistance to their political subdivisions. Additional assistance is provided in the form of state created and operated municipal bond banks, investment pools, insurance pools and one infrastructure pool.

Municipal Bond Banks. The current nine banks are traceable in origin to 1970 when the Vermont General Assembly established the first one (Act 216). The purpose of each bank is to assist small municipalities who may be unable to borrow funds because of their size or can borrow funds only at a high rate of interest because of their relatively low credit rating. The New Hampshire Municipal Bond Bank, for example, declares it is "The Only 'AAA' Credit" in the state.

Each bank surveys municipalities to determine their willingness to participate in a forthcoming issuance of long term bonds and to obtain data and information on their finances. Each local government desiring to participate in the borrowing is subject to all constitutional and statutory provisions relating to incurrence of debt. A local government will not be allowed to participate if such participation would affect adversely the credit rating of the issue. The bank's strong credit rating allows it to obtain a lower bond interest rate, thereby indirectly providing a financial benefit to participating units.

A municipal bond bank can be operated by a private association as illustrated by the Kentucky Municipal League's bond pool program available to its members, and the Association County Commissioners of Georgia's tax anticipation notes pool available to its members.

Municipal Investment Pools. Local governments generally have idle funds available for short-term

investment which may be deposited in one or more local banks. Twenty-nine state legislatures created municipal investment pools in recognition of the fact that smaller participating local governments would benefit from professional management of such funds, greater liquidity, lower administrative costs and a higher return.

Municipal Insurance Pools.Twenty states have followed Texas's lead in 1973 when it established the first such pool. In California, two or more local governments may utilize the state's joint exercise of powers statute to establish a pool. The Texas Municipal League also operates a Intergovernmental Risk Pool. The importance of municipal insurance pools has increased since courts in 37 states terminated general municipal governmental immunity from suit.

Pooling, by spreading the risks, reduces premium costs for member local governments. Each pool has a deductible loss requirement and stipulates a loss is covered up to a specified maximum amount. A pool can be operated by a local government association as illustrated by the Texas Municipal League's workmen's compensation joint insurance fund which provides equal coverage at a lower premium than identical commercial insurance coverage.

Infrastructure Pool. The 1991 Louisiana State Legislature (Act 813) established the Local Government Environmental Facilities Authority, reconstituted in 1997 by adding Community Development to the title, to assist local governments by authorizing them to finance infrastructure projects through the authority which can provide loans and issue revenue bonds to raise needed funds. The Association County Commissioners of Georgia arranges the leasing of equipment and buildings for its members, and currently has approximately $40 million in equipment leases.

Possible Emerging Trends

Our survey produced little evidence of possible new emerging trends. The Delaware General Assembly established a Health Care Pool for local governments and the 2003 New Hampshire General Court authorized cities and towns (NHRSA Chapter 79-D), at their discretion, to launch a barn preservation program by granting tax abatements. The 2003 Vermont General Assembly enacted Act 8 (VSA §§4(73), 1007a, 1034), permitting neighborhood electric vehicles to operate on public highways with a maximum speed of 35 miles per hour, but also allowing a municipality to prohibit their use in order to promote public safety. These vehicles are defined in law as emission free, limited to a maximum of four persons, possess four wheels in contact with the ground, an unladen maximum weight of 1,800 pounds, and conforming with safety equipment requirements.

Summary

Our survey reveals the discretionary authority of general purpose local governments has been broadened to an extent in several states, but state mandates continue to be a problem. It is apparent mobilization of public and private resources by local governments to solve serious problems depends heavily upon the state legislature granting them broad discretionary powers and providing financial assistance in various forms: grants-in-aid, revenue sharing, municipal bond banks, municipal investment pools, municipal insurance pools and municipal infrastructure funds.

Notes

[1] John F. Dillon, *Commentaries on the Law of Municipal Corporations*. (Boston: Little, Brown, and Company, 1872).

[2] Joseph F. Zimmerman, *State-Local Relations: A Partnership Approach*, 2nd ed. (Westport, CT: Praeger Publishers, 1995).

[3] *Adler v. Deegan*, 251 N.Y. 467 at 473, 167 N.E. 705 at 707 (1929).

[4] Jefferson B. Fordham, *Model Constitutional Provisions for Municipal Home Rule*. (Chicago: American Municipal Association, 1953).

[5] *Constitution of New York,* art. IX, §2(c)(1-10).

[6] *Ibid.*, 2(b).(1).

[7] Joseph F. Zimmerman, *Measuring Local Discretionary Authority* (Washington, DC: U.S. Advisory Commission on Intergovernmental Relations, 1981).

[8] Joseph F. Zimmerman, "Trends in Congressional Preemption," *The Book of the States 2003* (Lexington, KY: The Council of State Governments, 2003): 32-37. Consult also Joseph F. Zimmerman, *Federal Preemption: The Silent Revolution* (Ames: Iowa State University Press, 1991).

[9] *Massachusetts General Laws*, chap. 43, §9.

About the Author

Joseph F. Zimmerman is a professor of political science in Rockefeller College of the State University of New York in Albany. He is the author of numerous books including *Federal Preemption: The Silent Revolution* (1991), *Contemporary American Federalism: The Growth of National Power* (1992), *State-Local Relations* (1995), *Interstate Relations: The Neglected Dimension of Federalism* (1996), *Interstate Cooperation: Compacts and Agreements* (2002), and *Interstate Economic Relations* (2004).

Trends and Issues in Interstate Cooperation
By Ann O'M. Bowman

An effective system of interstate cooperation is essential to the operation of U. S. federalism. The research reported here shows that, on average, a state belongs to 25.4 interstate compacts and, during the 1990s, joined other states in 25 legal actions and enacted 7.7 uniform laws. However, the variation both across and within states as to the degree and type of cooperation reflects the tension between cooperation and competition.

In the U.S. federal system, states are in the curious position of being both rival and ally to other states. This rival-ally duality creates a fragile equilibrium among the states, one that is in continuous adjustment as states compete and cooperate with each other. In one sense, competition is the natural condition, because states depend heavily on their own sources of revenue thus creating an active rivalry for economic development.[1] However, since the colonial period, states have often found that cooperation is an appropriate or necessary course of action and have created an array of interstate connections.

Basic rules for interactions among the states are set in the U.S. Constitution. The full faith and credit clause (Article IV, Section 1) binds citizens of every state to the laws and policies of other states. The interstate rendition clause (Article IV, Section 2) requires that fugitives from justice in one state who have fled to another state, be returned upon request of the governor. In Article IV, Section 2, citizens of one state are guaranteed the "privileges and immunities," that is, the fundamental rights of citizens in other states. A formal provision for interstate compacts, established through Article I, Section 10 of the Constitution, provides a mechanism through which states can address shared problems. Because relationships between the states can be contentious and conflictual, Article III, Section 2 of the Constitution assigns "controversies between two or more states" to the federal judiciary for resolution. For instance, the two centuries-old conflict between New York and New Jersey over the ownership of Ellis Island was finally resolved by the U.S. Supreme Court in 1997.[2] To maintain a system of free trade among the states, the Constitution contains a provision authorizing Congress to regulate interstate commerce (Article I, Section 8). One other important interstate principle is implicit in the Constitution: the legal equality of each state.[3] Contemporary interstate relations have evolved from these basic provisions into a much more complex network.

Interacting States

As polities in the U.S. federal system, states can be expected to act in a self-interested manner, pursuing opportunities and resisting obstacles. Therefore, states cooperate with other states when it is perceived to be in their interest, they clash when such behavior is deemed in their interest. The assessment of self-interest is self-determined, that is, a state (or more correctly, state officials) makes the determination of self-interest, based on any number of relevant considerations.

The pursuit of self-interest puts states on a path that inevitably intersects with other states.[4] Cooperative behaviors emerge in "win-win" situations as states work together on a common problem or a shared objective. Competitive behaviors, on the other hand, develop as states vie for a prize or position in a process that typically has a zero-sum outcome. This competition can be mediated by external actors such as government institutions that determine winners and losers, as in the case of federal grant funding, or it can be unmediated, "open market" competition as when states seek tourists or firms.[5] When unmediated competition is unproductive or costly, states may reverse field and begin cooperating. For instance, in 1989 five states that had competed with each other to attract new firms pooled their efforts and created the multi-state Pacific Northwest Economic Region, a cooperative venture designed to attract investment to the region.

The pulls and pushes of competition and cooperation lead to a constantly evolving interstate equilibrium. Consider, for example, the on-going deliberations among Alabama, Florida and Georgia over a river basin they share. At issue are water levels and allocation formulas. Each state has a preferred solution that is at least partially at odds with another state's preference. Negotiating teams for each state (and a federal commissioner who represents the interests of 10 federal agencies with a stake in the resolution of the river basin conflict) have struggled to

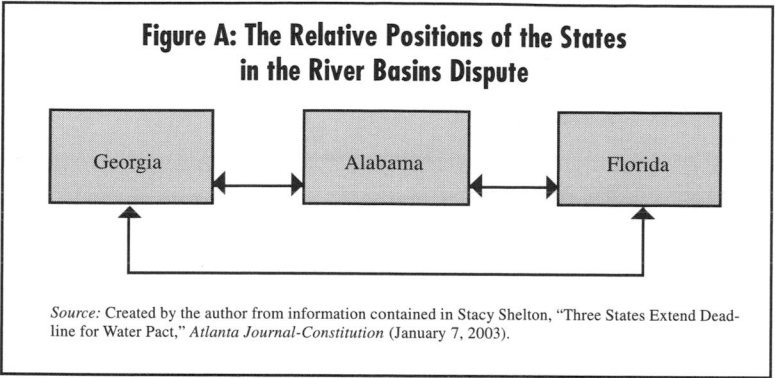

Figure A: The Relative Positions of the States in the River Basins Dispute

Georgia — Alabama — Florida

Source: Created by the author from information contained in Stacy Shelton, "Three States Extend Deadline for Water Pact," *Atlanta Journal-Constitution* (January 7, 2003).

reach agreement.[6] Complicating the resolution were partisan changes in two of the three governors' offices in 2002 and a desire by one new governor to conduct personal negotiations with his gubernatorial counterparts. The positions of the states vis-à-vis one another in 2002 are depicted in Figure A above.

Georgia and Florida were farther from the resolution of their differences than either state was with Alabama. Each wants to settle the conflict but on terms that are, if not preferential, at least acceptable to it. And each state holds a potential veto over any agreement that is reached by the other two states. In 2002, Alabama found itself in the position of broker, trying to get the other two states to compromise sufficiently to reach an accord. The presence of a federal-level official helps keep the parties at the table, because a belief shared by all three states is that a state-led solution is preferable to a federally-imposed solution. In July 2003, a memorandum of understanding was signed by the governors of the three states that set out broad guidelines for negotiators as they continue to wrestle with the details of an allocation formula. Once agreement can be achieved, a new interstate equilibrium will emerge. The larger point is quite simple: on issues that affect vital state interests, it is often difficult to reach a common accord.

Interstate Cooperation

Cooperative behaviors take many different forms including voluntary associations, optional enactment of similar laws, administrative agreements and interstate compacts.[7] In deciding whether to join other states in a collaborative venture, a state considers the anticipated costs and benefits of collective action. One can assume that a self-interested state will participate in actions in which the anticipated gains outweigh potential losses. Three specific forms of interstate cooperation are discussed in the remainder of this article:

interstate compacts, multi-state legal actions and adoption of uniform laws.

Interstate Compacts

The traditional mechanism for cooperation among states is the interstate compact, a formal agreement or contract between two or more states. A state's approval of a compact (and, when necessary, congressional approval) makes the agreements legally binding on participants. A compact establishes the policies for state compliance and the terms for state withdrawal from it. Historically, compacts were primarily used to settle boundary disputes between a pair of neighboring states but over time, the substance of compacts has broadened and the number of signatory states on a given compact has increased. Other than territorial border agreements, compacts increasingly have administrative, financial, substantive and technical dimensions.[8]

Because compacts require the approval of the member states' legislatures, the compact negotiation and ratification process can bog down in intra-state politics. Of the interstate compacts in existence in 2003, 32 had been ratified only by one state, thus they were not in effect. For instance, Indiana was the sole signatory to the Interstate Jobs Protection Compact that, when effective, would create a commission to develop strategies to prevent the "unnecessary" interstate relocation of businesses. The compact will take effect when any two of the 18 eligible states, joins Indiana. Although proportionately fewer compacts require congressional consent, for those that do, the process is lengthened.[9] A study of Michigan and its involvement in a low-level radioactive waste compact demonstrated that states do not enter into compacts casually.[10]

To determine the number and nature of interstate compacts as well as patterns of state involvement, a report from The Council of State Governments, *Interstate Compacts and Agencies 2003*, was consulted.[11] The report identifies state members of each compact currently in existence. After excluding defunct compacts (62), border compacts (26), compacts to which only one state is a party (32) and several compacts with special considerations (e.g., no states are listed as members or the compact is U.S. state-Canadian), 155 remained. In Figure B, states are as-

Figure B: State Membership in Interstate Compacts

High
> 29 compacts

9 states
N.Y., Vt., Maine, N.M., Pa., N.J., Va., Colo., Md.

High/average
28-29 compacts

7 states
Kan., Okla., Texas, W.Va., Ala., N.H., Wash.

Average
24-27 compacts

18 states
Miss., Neb., Ohio, Ore., R.I., Tenn., Ariz., Calif., Ind., Mass., Mont., Wyo., Idaho, Mo., Utah, Ark., Conn., Fla.

Average/low
22-23 compacts

8 states
Del., Ill., Ky., La., S.C., Ga., Minn., N.C.

Low
< 22 compacts

8 states
Hawaii, Wis., Alaska, S.D., Iowa, Mich., N.D., Nev.

Source: Compiled by the author from data in William Kevin Voit, Nancy J. Vickers, and Thomas L. Gavenonis, *Interstate Compacts and Agencies 2003* (Lexington, Ky: The Council of State Governments, 2003).
Note: Within each category, states range from high to low.

signed to one of five categories, based on membership in these compacts.[12]

The average rate of compact membership for states is 25.4 compacts. The lowest levels (16 compacts) are found in Hawaii and Wisconsin; the highest (32 compacts) are in Colorado and Maryland. Although the trend is for compacts to include large numbers of states, many of the extant compacts are bilateral: 57 of the 155 compacts are between two states. The New England region (Maine, New Hampshire, Vermont, Connecticut, Massachusetts and Rhode Island) has been thought of as an area especially prone to compact formation, with federalism scholar Daniel Elazar calling it "a sectional confederation within the American federal system."[13] That tendency appears to have weakened somewhat in recent years with only two of these states showing high levels of compact membership. It is true however, that the six New England states often form regional compacts but not significantly more so than other regions.

Many compacts are nationwide in scope, e.g., all states are eligible to participate, but the data show that only approximately 10 percent of the compacts have a majority of states as members. One compact that is nearly nationwide is the Interstate Compact on Adult Offender Supervision. In 1999, its first year of existence, nine states became members of the compact; by mid-2003, 47 states had joined.[14] Two of the compacts currently in force have all 50 states as members: the Interstate Compact on the Place-

ment of Children and the Uniform Interstate Compact on Juveniles. Still with so few majority-state compacts in place, the promise of the compact mechanism as an instrument of national policy is muted; it appears to be more commonly a tool for more particular use.

Multi-state Legal Action

A state's willingness to enter into lawsuits with—not against—other states is another form of cooperation. Legal action by an individual state may not represent a significant challenge to a private sector firm, but action by a group of states poses more of a threat. Furthermore, by pursuing joint legal action, states are asserting and protecting their role in the federal system. In effect, a group of proactive states can beat the national government to the punch in addressing a specific problem. Notable illustrations of this approach include state-initiated lawsuits against the tobacco industry and against Microsoft during the 1990s. In the tobacco case, although a few states acted independently and reached their own settlements with tobacco companies, most litigating states relied on joint action.[15] Eventually state attorneys general were able to broker a national agreement. In the Microsoft case, 20 states filed an antitrust lawsuit in 1998, alleging illegal anti-competitive, anti-consumer actions by the corporation.

The National Association of Attorneys General (NAAG), an organization composed of the chief le-

Figure C: State Involvement in Joint Legal Action

High
> 39 actions
11 states
Calif., Wash., Ill., Fla., N.Y., Ariz., Conn., Minn., Texas, Wis., Mass.

High/average
29-39 actions
6 states
N.M., Mich., Iowa, Vt., Mo., Pa.

Average
22-28 actions
8 states
Ore., Nev., Ohio, Idaho, Md., N.C., Tenn., W.Va.

Average/low
12-21 actions
16 states
Ala., Maine, S.D., Alaska, Mont., Neb., Hawaii, Ind., Miss., Ark., N.D., Okla., Utah, R.I., Kan., N.J.

Low
< 12 actions
9 states
Ga., S.C., Wyo., N.H., Va., Colo., Del., Ky., La.

Source: Compiled by the author from data in *AG Bulletin* (Washington, D.C.: National Association of Attorneys General, various issues 1992-1999).
Note: Within each category, states range from high to low.

gal counsels of the states (and territories), has spearheaded the push for multi-state legal action. NAAG encourages joint state efforts regarding law enforcement and legal issues, taking policy positions and issuing guidelines but avoiding official action on issues that divide its membership.[16] Collective legal action is similar to interstate compacts in that it unites states on issues of common interest. One such common interest has been protecting consumers from fraudulent practices and products of all types. As noted above, the opportunity to join other states rather than going it alone allows the strength in numbers phenomenon to emerge.

Ascertaining the degree of interstate cooperation via legal channels involved a search of the NAAG publication, *AG Bulletin*, from 1992 through 1999.

AG Bulletin is published 10 to 12 times per year to disseminate information to its members, especially updates on pending legal actions. In this regard, it reports which states have joined multi-state lawsuits.[17] To create the database, each available issue of *AG Bulletin* was reviewed and instances of joint legal actions were noted.[18] Each case was counted only once, regardless of the number of times it was mentioned in subsequent *Bulletins*. Figure C shows the level of cooperation for states, as measured by their willingness to join in multi-state legal actions.

During the period under study, on average, a state was a party to a multi-state legal action on 25 occasions. The lowest level of joint legal action (seven lawsuits) was found in three states, Georgia, South Carolina and Wyoming, while the highest level was in

Figure D: State Adoption of Uniform Laws

High
> 9 uniform laws
12 states
Alaska, Ark., Conn., Vt., Ariz., Colo., N.D., Minn., Mont., Hawaii, W.Va., N.M.

Average
6-9 uniform laws
28 states
Fla., Ind., Ky., N.J., Utah, Wash., Wyo., Calif., Ill., Iowa, Md., Mich., N.C. Ohio, Ore., R.I., Tenn., Del., Idaho, Maine, Neb., Nev., Okla., Texas, Ala., Kan., S.D., Va.

Low
< 6 uniform laws
10 states
Ga., Mass., N.Y., Wis., La., Miss., Mo., N.H., Pa., S.C.

Source: Compiled by the author from information found on the official website of the National Conference of Commissioners on Uniform State Laws, www.nccusl.org (October 2003).
Note: Within each category, states range from high to low.

Massachusetts (51 lawsuits). One trend that is discernible in the data is an increase in the rate of multi-state lawsuits during the decade. A subset of 11 states appears to have played leadership roles, given their high rate of involvement. Also, a population effect may be operative: the four states with the largest populations are in the "high" category. However, variations in state involvement may be partly attributable to an attorney general's proclivity for activism.

Uniform State Laws

A third type of interstate cooperation involves the adoption of uniform statutes. By bringing its law into conformance with other states, a state is endorsing and embracing a peer-established norm. Clearly, this form of cooperation is different from compacts and joint legal actions because it does not involve collective action per se. But the enactment of uniform laws results in a reduction of differences between states and it captures the spirit of cooperation.

The National Conference of Commissioners on Uniform State Laws (NCCUSL) was created in 1892 to draft uniform statues and model acts. The NCCUSL, a nonprofit organization funded by state appropriations, is made up of attorneys, judges and legal experts from each state. The statute-drafting process can be lengthy, involving extensive negotiations and numerous iterations. Once a law is drafted by NCCUSL, each state has the option of enacting it and thereby conforming its law on a subject to that of other enacting states.

On its website, the NCCUSL tracks state actions as model legislation wends its way (or not) through the legislative process. To explore state adoption of uniform laws, a data set was created consisting of the uniform laws finalized by NCCUSL during the 1990s. Each state was assigned a score based on the number of uniform laws it enacted during the decade. Because the range of scores was fairly narrow, the states were grouped into three categories, as shown in Figure D.[19]

There were 22 new uniform laws finalized by the NCCUSL in the 1990s and states, on average, adopted 7.7 of them. The average is as high as it is due to the nearly universal adoption of three new articles to the Uniform Commercial Code. The highest rate of enactment of uniform laws during the decade occurred in New Mexico, with 14. At the other end of the scale were Georgia, Massachusetts, New York and Wisconsin, which adopted four of the uniform laws during the time period.

Comparing the Types

The data in Figures B, C and D suggest that for an individual state, the level of cooperative behavior tends to depend on the specific form of cooperation. Wisconsin, for example, lands in the low category in terms of interstate compact membership and uniform law adoption, but has a high level of involvement in joint legal actions. Colorado is quite the opposite: high levels of compact membership and uniform law adoption, but its rate of involvement in multi-state legal actions is low. New York displays a different pattern: the top group with regard to joint lawsuits and interstate compacts, but a low level of uniform law enactment. Thus it appears that there is some differentiation in cooperative behavior, that is, an individual state tends not to pursue all three of the types of cooperation with the same degree of enthusiasm. However, one should not take the point too far, as there is some consistency in the average category, which regardless of the form of cooperation, includes Idaho, Ohio, Oregon and Tennessee. And at least two states, Georgia and South Carolina, display a general tendency toward limited willingness to cooperate with other states, scoring in the low category on two indicators and in the average/low on the third one. But the general conclusion is that states vary in their propensity toward cooperation.

Future Prospects

The analysis presented here yields several inferences about trends in interstate cooperation. Although the analysis itself was not longitudinal, the data collection process provided some evidence as to changes over time. In short, during the 1990s, both the frequency of multi-state lawsuits and the number of assenting states increased; thus this type of cooperation appears to be on the rise. State embrace of uniform laws is more problematic. Were it not for the Uniform Commercial Code, enactment rates of NCCUSL statutes during the decade would have been substantially lower. Therefore it does not appear that states are poised to adopt a set of laws that would bring their statutes in line with these model statutes. But the idea of greater uniformity across the states is popular among major corporate interests that do business nationally, thus putting pressure on states to conform.

Comparing the findings reported here to an earlier study, it appears that average state membership in compacts has risen by about 10 percent since the mid-1990s.[20] The increase appears to be due to the appeal of "nearly-national" compacts such as the Driver's License Compact that allows member states to exchange information about nonresident traffic law violators. Thus although only 15 compacts have a majority of states as members, this represents an increase from the earlier period. The next decade is likely to see more instances of cooperation that extends beyond the region. For example, many of the compacts that have evolved from the Low-Level Radioactive Waste Policy Act of 1980 (and a subsequent U.S. Supreme Court decision) link states in non-regional clusters.

While interstate compacts are appropriate in instances in which complex legal or fiscal issues exist, administrative agreements can be effective alternatives to them because they are easier to initiate, negotiate and amend.[21] Although definitive data are hard to come by, this trend seems to be on the upswing. For instance, in the "Southern Air Principles" in 2001, the governors of Georgia, North Carolina and Tennessee instructed their states' environmental agencies to develop a regional plan to address air pollution problems in the southern Appalachian Mountains. Another illustration of interstate administrative agreements is multi-state prescription drug purchasing pools. Three New England states, Maine, New Hampshire and Vermont, created the first coalition in 2001; within months, other states were exploring the benefits of collaborative action. These kinds of agreements may be less durable than compacts but in a rapidly changing environment, their flexibility may be a real advantage.

The willingness of states to cooperate with each other allows what Dale Krane, quoting Daniel Elazar, called "federalism without Washington."[22] This point is well taken. If states work together, their ability to solve major national problems is enhanced. Joint state action, especially the embrace of common policies, provides an alternative to federal legislation, and could be a means of forestalling federal preemption of the states.[23] But this recalls a point made at the beginning of this article: states are not only allies; they are rivals. Furthermore, one of the premises of a federal structure is the ability of constituent units to customize policy—the inverse of uniformity. Thus, although states are increasingly interconnected, the likelihood of sustained cooperative action is tempered by competitive pressures.

Notes

[1] Daphne A. Kenyon and John Kincaid "Introduction," In Daphne A. Kenyon and John Kincaid, eds. *Competition among States and Local Governments,* (Washington, D.C.: Urban Institute Press, 1991), 1-33.

[2] *State of New Jersey v. State of New York,* 116 S.Ct. 1726

[3] See the discussion in Joseph F. Zimmerman, *Interstate Cooperation: Compacts and Administrative Agreements,* (Westport, CT: Greenwood Press, 2002), 19-37.

[4] The possibility of noninteraction exists as well, i.e., a state may choose not to join other states in a lawsuit against the federal government or not to enter the competition for a relocating firm.

[5] John Kincaid, "The Competitive Challenge to Cooperative Federalism: A Theory of Federal Democracy," in Daphne A. Kenyon and John Kincaid, eds. *Competition among States and Local Governments.* (Washington, D.C.: Urban Institute Press, 1991), 87-114.

[6] Stacy Shelton, "Three States Extend Deadline for Water Pact," *Atlanta Journal-Constitution* (January 7, 2003).

[7] Patricia S. Florestano, "Past and Present Utilization of Interstate Compacts in the United States," *Publius: The Journal of Federalism* 24 (Fall 1994): 13-25.

[8] Zimmerman, *Interstate Cooperation.*

[9] Compacts considered to be of a political nature do not take effect without congressional consent.

[10] Jeffrey S. Hill and Carol S. Weissert, " Implementation and the Irony of Delegation: The Politics of Low-Level Radioactive Waste Disposal," *The Journal of Politics* 57 (May 1995): 344-369.

[11] William Kevin Voit, Nancy J. Vickers, and Thomas L. Gavenonis, *Interstate Compacts and Agencies 2003,* (Lexington, KY: The Council of State Governments, 2003).

[12] States are grouped around the mean, with scores within one-quarter of a standard deviation on either side of the mean deemed "average." States involved in compacts at a rate that is one full standard deviation above or below the mean were categorized as high or low, respectively. Compact use that ranged between one-quarter and a full standard deviation from the mean were labeled high/average or average/low.

[13] Daniel J. Elazar, *American Federalism: A View from the States,* 3rd ed. (New York: Harper & Row, 1984).

[14] Other compacts with more than 40 state members include the Interstate Compact for Education, the Interstate Compact on Parole and Probation, and the Interstate Compact on Mental Health.

[15] Eight states did not file a lawsuit against the tobacco industry. However, the non-filing states were included in the national agreement.

[16] Joseph F. Zimmerman, "Interstate Cooperation: The Roles of the State Attorneys General," *Publius: The Journal of Federalism* 28 (Winter 1998): 71-89.

[17] Despite concerted efforts, not all of the 1992-1999 issues of *AG Bulletin* could not be located. NAAG's headquarters did not maintain a master file, official state libraries did not archive them, and contacting the offices of the attorneys general in all fifty states yielded several hard-to-find issues, but not all of them. Therefore this analysis is based on 70 issues of *AG Bulletin* out of the 84 published during the time period. The absence of 14 issues should not be a problem because there is no pattern to the missing issues and *AG Bulletin's* updating results in multiple mentions of the cases.

[18] In a few cases, the actual cooperative act was a resolution to Congress (e.g., encouraging the passage of employment non-discrimination legislation) or the filing of comments with a federal agency (e.g., commenting on the Federal Communications Commission's proposed rules on telephone service "slamming"). These endeavors are certainly cooperative in nature, however they do not involve law-

suits, amicus briefs, or negotiated settlements. These non-legal items account for less than 15 percent of the cases.

[19] Due to the limited range of scores, three categories were created. Scores less than one full standard deviation above or below the mean were considered average while the high and low categories capture scores greater or lesser than that, respectively.

[20]Ann O'M. Bowman, "State-to-State Relationships in the U.S. Federal System," paper presented at the Annual Meeting of the American Political Science Association, San Francisco, California (2001).

[21] See Zimmerman's chapter on formal and informal administrative agreements, 163-202.

[22] Dale Krane, "The State of American Federalism, 2001-2002: Resilience in Response to Crisis," *Publius: The Journal of Federalism* 32 (Fall 2002): 1-28.

[23] See the discussion in Ann O'M. Bowman, "American Federalism on the Horizon," *Publius: The Journal of Federalism* 32 (Spring 2002): 3-22.

About the Author

Ann O'M. Bowman is the James F. and Maude B. Byrnes Professor of Government at the University of South Carolina. She has written extensively on issues in intergovernmental relations. She thanks Erica H. Carter, H. Lee Smith and Gregory K. Plagens for their assistance in collecting the data used in this research.

Table 2.1
TOTAL FEDERAL GRANTS TO STATE AND LOCAL GOVERNMENTS BY STATE AND REGION: 1993-2002
(In millions of dollars)

State or other jurisdiction	2002	2001	2000	1999	1998	1997	1996	1995	1994	1993
United States	$412,371	$338,977	$308,530	$294,469	$269,128	$229,778	$227,542	$228,936	$214,239	$195,201
Eastern Region										
Connecticut	$5,279	$4,364	$4,033	$3,846	$3,653	$2,905	$3,080	$3,195	$3,028	$2,691
Delaware	1,121	892	838	825	678	629	600	560	472	455
Maine	2,270	1,905	1,770	1,664	1,602	1,378	1,389	1,315	1,269	1,166
Massachusetts	12,339	9,718	9,070	8,838	8,019	6,365	6,813	6,829	6,261	5,520
New Hampshire	1,632	1,288	1,238	1,120	1,042	842	890	866	956	652
New Jersey	10,822	8,478	7,876	7,262	7,108	6,602	6,506	6,639	6,163	6,189
New York	42,461	32,897	31,564	28,870	28,066	24,384	24,560	24,348	22,445	21,166
Pennsylvania	18,017	14,487	13,940	13,141	12,381	10,268	10,117	10,354	9,705	8,517
Rhode Island	2,094	1,607	1,574	1,411	1,368	1,144	1,176	1,276	1,100	1,107
Vermont	1,281	1,069	929	883	803	601	641	625	546	557
Regional Total	97,316	76,705	72,832	67,860	64,720	55,118	55,772	56,007	51,945	48,020
Midwestern Region										
Illinois	14,975	$11,883	$11,228	$10,586	$10,156	$9,296	$9,229	$9,487	$8,506	$7,845
Indiana	6,969	5,850	5,108	4,706	4,152	3,539	3,657	3,546	3,553	3,732
Iowa	4,060	3,079	2,714	2,595	2,424	1,977	2,030	2,074	2,015	1,737
Kansas	3,272	2,721	2,323	2,183	1,934	1,620	1,700	1,649	1,666	1,608
Michigan	13,279	10,887	10,107	9,764	8,618	7,237	7,194	7,589	7,117	6,654
Minnesota	6,492	5,260	4,753	4,499	4,199	3,952	3,535	3,685	3,515	3,297
Nebraska	2,342	2,054	1,720	1,651	1,511	1,227	1,232	1,440	1,114	1,108
North Dakota	1,425	1,284	1,101	1,009	1,067	1,074	734	768	702	640
Ohio	14,844	11,762	10,665	10,254	9,733	8,327	8,776	9,115	8,366	7,716
South Dakota	1,506	1,254	1,088	1,056	1,007	982	867	813	724	654
Wisconsin	7,255	5,843	5,254	4,842	4,697	3,617	3,679	3,729	3,450	3,397
Regional Total	76,419	61,877	56,061	53,145	49,498	42,848	42,633	43,895	40,728	38,388
Southern Region										
Alabama	6,344	$5,298	$4,833	$4,632	$4,161	$3,483	$3,325	$3,419	$3,209	$3,081
Arkansas	4,047	3,448	2,778	2,614	2,440	2,283	2,131	2,019	1,966	1,855
Florida	16,350	13,666	12,149	11,191	10,320	8,504	8,442	9,078	8,018	7,579
Georgia	10,500	7,929	7,520	6,752	6,233	5,469	5,359	5,461	5,028	4408
Kentucky	6,346	5,100	4,687	4,395	4,236	3,702	3,355	3,437	3,096	3,041
Louisiana	7,437	6,173	5,300	5,228	4,708	4,457	4,734	5,291	5,233	4,817
Maryland	6,312	7,586	6,911	5,744	5,022	3,950	3,544	3,594	3,637	3,310
Mississippi	5,046	4,246	3,517	3,387	3,025	2,626	2,754	2,738	2,507	2,285
Missouri	8,429	6,868	5,939	5,478	5,065	4,231	4,091	4,159	3,971	3,566
North Carolina	10,939	9,122	8,158	7,608	7,133	6,284	5,227	5,487	4,862	4,498
Oklahoma	5,108	4,119	3,583	3,231	3,059	2,510	2,435	2,472	2,359	2,111
South Carolina	5,592	4,730	4,163	3,879	3,525	2,987	3,032	3,027	2,726	2,521
Tennessee	8,658	7,027	6,372	5,900	5,510	4,555	4,476	4,531	3,940	3,925
Texas	24,858	21,675	18,346	18,370	15,809	13,184	13,287	13,338	12,669	11,035
Virginia	7,714	5,908	5,163	4,749	4,423	3,518	3,403	3,504	3,180	2,945
West Virginia	3,298	2,971	2,729	2,490	2,480	2,100	2,088	2,074	2,166	1,884
Regional Total	136,978	115,866	102,148	95,648	87,149	73,843	71,683	73,629	68,567	62,861
Western Region										
Alaska	3,127	$2,314	$2,174	$1,929	$1,427	$1,303	$1,051	$1,125	$1,063	$948
Arizona	6,664	5,190	4,704	4,537	4,147	3,355	3,095	3,150	2,996	2,640
California	48,084	39,797	36,080	36,370	32,090	27,014	26,413	26,934	26,219	21,635
Colorado	4,740	3,916	3,591	3,446	3,048	2,444	2,410	2,391	2,102	2,109
Hawaii	1,835	1,514	1,348	1,335	1,190	1,184	1,126	1,162	1088	984
Idaho	1,837	1,505	1,270	1,177	1,055	936	887	849	778	712
Montana	1,912	1,665	1,474	1,399	1,139	991	964	933	906	831
Nevada	1,840	1,442	1,340	1,249	1,081	983	876	882	797	767
New Mexico	3,954	3,586	3,032	2,750	2,547	2,152	1,942	1,866	1,714	1,534
Oregon	4,814	4,308	3,684	3,518	3,275	2,853	2,797	2,763	2,355	2,099
Utah	2,697	2,244	2,065	1,994	1,727	1,355	1,446	1,318	1,209	1,173
Washington	8,296	6,794	6,345	5,720	5,422	4,496	4,152	4,351	3,924	3,722
Wyoming	1,234	1,213	1,022	933	850	762	708	748	714	645
Regional Total	91,034	75,488	68,129	66,357	58,998	49,828	47,867	48,472	45,865	39,799
Regional total without California	42,950	35,691	32,049	29,987	26,908	22,814	21,454	21,538	19,646	18,164
Dist. of Columbia	4,832	4,020	4,675	5,293	4,101	2,740	2,578	2,238	2,222	1,961
American Samoa	93	58	59	131	91	121	71	73	67	59
Federates States of Micronesia	126	94	. . .	. . .	. . .	. . .	. . .	. . .	. . .	. . .
Guam	251	176	138	188	266	125	134	162	154	161
Marshall Islands	58	48	. . .	. . .	. . .	. . .	. . .	. . .	. . .	. . .
Palau	41	35	. . .	. . .	. . .	. . .	. . .	. . .	. . .	. . .
Puerto Rico	4,828	3,899	3,842	5,284	3,895	3,719	3,387	3,535	3,388	3,132
U.S. Virgin Islands	266	111	195	216	256	371	373	217	191	181
Undistributed	65	183	10	248	116	1,032	3,009	592	1,059	592

Source: U.S. Department of Commerce, Bureau of the Census. Consolidated Federal Funds Report for Fiscal Year 2002, issued May 2003.

Key: . . .—No data available.

Table 2.2
FEDERAL AID TO STATE AND LOCAL GOVERNMENTS, SELECTED PROGRAMS BY STATE 2003
(In millions of dollars)

State or other jurisdiction	Federal aid total (a)	Department of Agriculture					Department of Education			
			Food and nutrition service						Office of Special Education and Rehabilitative Services	
		Total	Child nutrition programs (b)	supplemental Food stamp programs (c)	food program (WIC)	Other	Total	Adult education for the disadvantaged	Special education	Rehabilitation services and disability research
Total	$362,389	$21,487	$10,161	$3,859	$4,376	$3,090	$32,739	$1,356	$8,532	$2,652
United States total	355,690	19,669	9,949	2,487	4,206	3,028	32,032	1,335	8,439	2,554
Alabama	5,557	363	196	32	71	64	528	27	136	55
Alaska	2,250	117	29	8	20	61	274	9	27	11
Arizona	6,314	392	203	35	98	56	730	35	130	49
Arkansas	3,559	228	119	18	45	46	338	20	82	35
California	41,627	2,653	1,301	357	757	238	3,980	344	883	261
Colorado	3,951	209	97	27	43	41	407	24	112	27
Connecticut	4,492	158	79	25	36	18	337	9	100	20
Delaware	958	52	28	4	9	11	99	2	25	9
Florida	15,044	981	560	92	248	81	1,553	96	456	119
Georgia	9,300	650	394	62	125	69	894	27	232	74
Hawaii	1,460	100	42	11	25	22	194	3	34	11
Idaho	1,560	111	41	10	17	43	150	9	40	15
Illinois	13,296	769	408	99	169	93	1,315	60	378	100
Indiana	5,997	334	164	44	72	52	562	14	190	61
Iowa	3,391	196	84	21	34	57	294	6	93	31
Kansas	2,889	176	101	9	33	34	344	18	89	27
Kentucky	5,719	336	172	30	67	67	484	16	127	48
Louisiana	6,820	451	260	39	78	73	573	13	136	46
Maine	2,049	81	35	10	10	26	156	8	44	15
Maryland	5,660	284	146	43	53	43	497	9	150	39
Massachusetts	9,202	312	170	40	65	37	686	29	214	48
Michigan	11,185	586	257	99	119	111	1,143	60	291	92
Minnesota	5,776	329	166	44	57	62	468	9	151	44
Mississippi	4,605	351	179	33	57	83	403	9	87	40
Missouri	7,137	370	184	52	67	68	564	12	170	58
Montana	1,654	106	32	11	13	49	186	3	31	13
Nebraska	2,028	128	65	11	22	30	201	8	59	17
Nevada	1,646	90	47	10	23	10	165	3	48	13
New Hampshire	7,137	59	20	7	10	23	111	2	38	11
New Jersey	10,239	390	199	84	76	32	807	17	269	51
New Mexico	1,654	203	114	18	35	35	467	16	154	23
New York	2,028	1,353	714	236	280	124	2,468	64	576	138
North Carolina	9,510	581	325	59	111	85	803	20	238	79
North Dakota	1,189	65	25	8	10	22	131	2	20	11
Ohio	13,262	633	288	126	139	79	1,085	22	321	111
Oklahoma	4,510	332	162	38	64	68	506	9	109	42
Oregon	4,457	416	107	54	59	196	377	20	111	37
Pennsylvania	15,603	639	293	129	132	85	1,186	61	315	115
Rhode Island	1,794	62	32	7	13	10	122	2	34	10
South Carolina	4,883	312	171	32	59	50	474	9	130	45
South Dakota	1,350	86	30	11	13	32	164	3	24	11
Tennessee	7,374	427	215	39	95	78	540	10	172	60
Texas	21,955	1,690	1,036	164	361	129	2,544	111	675	185
Utah	2,208	158	81	20	32	26	267	9	83	24
Vermont	1,087	60	16	11	10	23	94	3	20	11
Virginia	6,233	342	142	72	76	52	703	11	212	61
Washington	7,103	405	166	39	93	108	644	40	164	50
West Virginia	3,034	157	76	11	29	40	235	4	58	25
Wisconsin	6,173	287	133	34	58	63	542	10	159	53
Wyoming	1,192	44	15	4	7	17	96	2	21	8
Dist. of Columbia	4,025	57	28	10	11	8	140	2	22	12
American Samoa	113	23	12	4	6	1	1	0	0	1
Fed. States of Micronesia	114	2	0	0	0	2	8	0	4	0
Guam	212	19	5	3	6	4	5	0	1	2
Marshall Islands	53	0	0	0	0	0	0	0	0	0
No. Mariana Islands	66	13	4	7	0	2	1	0	0	1
Palau	38	0	0	0	0	0	0	0	0	0
Puerto Rico	4,793	1,712	177	1,351	153	31	650	21	78	67
U.S. Virgin Islands	294	32	15	8	5	5	16	0	10	2
Undistributed	1,015	17	0	0	0	17	26	0	0	26

Source: U.S. Department of Commerce, Bureau of the Census, *Statistical Abstract of the United States, 2003*. See also <http://census.gov/prod/2003pubs/fas02.pdf>.

Note: Table in millions of dollars (204,197 represents $204,197,000,000.) For fiscal year ending September 30.

FEDERAL AID TO STATE AND LOCAL GOVERNMENTS, SELECTED PROGRAMS BY STATE 2003 — Continued

State or other jurisdiction	FEMA total (d)	Department of Housing and Urban Development							Department of Labor		
		Total	Community development block grants	Public housing programs				Other	Total	State insurance and employment service	Workforce investment
				Low-rent housing assistance	Neighborhood revitalization	Housing certificate program	Capital program				
Total	$3,406	$36,965	$5,437	$3,709	$467	$18,499	$3,767	$4,761	$8,376	$3,607	$3,431
United States total (d)	3,194	36,213	5,318	3,590	465	17,909	3,596	5,019	8,067	3,572	3,173
Alabama	27	509	68	113	2	183	86	47	130	45	59
Alaska	7	174	17	12	0	31	1	113	58	30	19
Arizona	14	489	75	30	6	157	12	205	139	48	60
Arkansas	21	236	32	27	1	121	29	25	69	31	27
California	546	4,203	685	121	25	2,690	134	534	1,207	517	564
Colorado	20	415	52	18	7	261	22	51	94	53	25
Connecticut	3	599	52	58	7	352	48	78	103	62	25
Delaware	3	104	9	10	3	54	8	19	24	11	8
Florida	178	1,324	208	96	43	412	83	470	285	118	112
Georgia	31	884	130	123	11	412	127	71	167	76	63
Hawaii	4	144	18	11	0	87	6	21	53	18	20
Idaho	3	74	12	1	0	45	2	14	50	24	17
Illinois	16	2,016	236	266	19	1,020	250	201	188	171	169
Indiana	10	538	91	40	2	298	44	60	125	61	40
Iowa	15	215	48	6	0	124	9	28	61	31	16
Kansas	44	189	43	16	0	87	15	26	54	27	15
Kentucky	21	492	68	53	10	232	76	50	104	40	27
Louisiana	22	569	108	68	13	225	80	68	120	37	76
Maine	5	179	23	9	0	115	7	25	51	19	20
Maryland	10	701	85	77	24	377	41	90	152	71	54
Massachusetts	19	1,506	154	106	9	990	82	156	173	92	59
Michigan	7	912	170	51	1	471	65	149	307	148	99
Minnesota	43	571	85	42	0	314	56	70	151	66	42
Mississippi	23	288	52	28	1	144	29	30	106	36	58
Missouri	60	589	111	45	8	274	58	89	127	62	44
Montana	20	108	14	4	0	41	3	44	35	15	16
Nebraska	6	149	31	10	0	66	19	21	39	21	11
Nevada	2	187	20	16	0	106	15	29	57	34	16
New Hampshire	5	137	19	7	0	89	8	14	32	14	13
New Jersey	82	1,381	136	155	41	768	146	120	226	125	80
New Mexico	5	180	30	9	0	79	11	49	68	19	43
New York	1,232	5,196	769	924	16	2,011	888	542	544	244	231
North Carolina	123	757	78	101	31	374	72	91	216	88	64
North Dakota	37	86	10	3	0	39	3	30	27	14	7
Ohio	11	1,473	241	161	10	739	124	183	280	114	131
Oklahoma	122	457	56	25	3	176	21	169	69	31	29
Oregon	15	359	37	15	0	227	15	62	155	62	70
Pennsylvania	16	1,808	304	240	44	775	248	177	372	179	129
Rhode Island	2	242	27	21	0	142	16	33	34	18	8
South Carolina	7	352	58	30	5	189	26	39	97	44	37
South Dakota	7	108	15	3	0	45	3	40	26	11	8
Tennessee	18	628	67	101	33	281	78	58	118	52	20
Texas	184	1,732	317	119	40	925	134	182	504	191	249
Utah	8	135	31	4	0	77	4	18	57	37	11
Vermont	4	93	19	4	0	55	3	12	18	10	7
Virginia	28	697	84	91	15	366	50	84	134	60	45
Washington	25	611	75	36	8	333	36	118	235	107	98
West Virginia	49	234	56	16	4	103	15	38	77	21	47
Wisconsin	28	462	91	19	8	244	22	75	166	85	46
Wyoming	5	36	7	1	0	18	2	8	21	11	7
Dist. of Columbia	3	686	91	51	15	165	264	92	161	69	38
American Samoa	0	0	0	0	0	0	0	0	2	0	1
Fed. States of Micronesia	0	0	0	0	0	0	0	0	2	0	2
Guam	25	25	1	2	0	18	2	2	15	2	11
Marshall Islands	0	0	0	0	0	0	0	0	1	0	1
No. Mariana Islands ..	1	0	0	0	0	0	0	0	1	0	1
Palau	0	0	0	0	0	0	0	0	0	0	0
Puerto Rico	32	674	116	98	1	260	155	37	280	28	240
U.S. Virgin Islands	12	53	2	18	1	14	14	2	8	3	2
Undistributed	141	0	0	0	0	0	0	0	0	0	0

Key:
(a) Includes programs not shown separately.
(b) Includes special milk programs.

(c) For Puerto Rico, amount shown is for nutritional assistance grant program, all other amounts are grant payments for food stamp administration.

FEDERAL AID TO STATE AND LOCAL GOVERNMENTS, SELECTED PROGRAMS BY STATE 2003 — Continued

State or other jurisdiction	Total	Department of Health and Human Services					Department of Transportation				Other federal aid
		Administration for children									
		Temporary assistance to needy families	Children and family services (Head Start)	Foster care and adoption assistance	Centers for Medicare and Medicaid Services	Other	Total	Highway trust fund	Federal transit administration	Other	
Total	$204,197	$18,538	$7,749	$5,881	$150,640	$21,388	$38,719	$29,444	$5,223	$4,052	$16,500
United States total (d)	203,343	18,471	7,494	5,881	150,351	21,146	37,618	28,539	5,024	4,055	15,554
Alabama	2,931	130	125	34	2,300	342	840	673	25	141	230
Alaska	780	75	50	16	519	120	509	328	12	168	332
Arizona	3,476	297	166	62	2,597	354	639	481	61	97	435
Arkansas	2,090	60	84	44	1,721	180	475	395	10	71	102
California	23,482	3,416	936	1,318	15,503	2,308	3,975	2,628	1,008	339	1,581
Colorado	1,976	232	125	62	1,238	318	537	342	91	103	293
Connecticut	2,576	278	64	86	1,878	270	589	493	79	17	126
Delaware	489	30	18	13	361	67	131	120	3	8	57
Florida	8,355	735	286	184	6,076	1,074	1,811	1,496	135	180	567
Georgia	5,349	449	192	111	4,078	519	1,052	873	96	82	274
Hawaii	687	70	34	29	461	94	176	122	33	21	102
Idaho	786	38	41	8	601	97	262	206	7	49	125
Illinois	7,064	600	341	389	4,783	952	1,324	889	259	177	404
Indiana	3,593	258	113	66	2,798	357	646	560	29	56	190
Iowa	2,080	118	65	40	1,667	189	404	333	22	50	128
Kansas	1,582	104	77	43	1,187	171	399	360	18	21	101
Kentucky	3,440	159	134	64	2,792	290	616	524	22	71	226
Louisiana	4,367	221	161	61	3,596	322	541	448	36	57	177
Maine	1,271	80	35	40	1,011	104	187	162	8	17	118
Maryland	3,034	306	99	158	2,023	448	727	572	105	50	255
Massachusetts	5,531	507	141	96	4,258	528	673	505	131	37	302
Michigan	6,871	926	275	242	4,649	779	1,014	823	89	102	345
Minnesota	3,375	334	109	104	2,419	409	595	384	108	104	243
Mississippi	2,803	149	179	18	2,243	214	459	385	5	69	173
Missouri	4,315	195	147	81	3,495	396	862	727	36	100	249
Montana	654	69	40	13	440	91	342	295	5	42	203
Nebraska	1,152	53	47	35	866	152	233	193	10	29	120
Nevada	736	57	31	22	485	142	234	161	16	56	176
New Hampshire	678	39	20	13	519	87	195	141	8	45	110
New Jersey	6,031	740	156	82	4,384	669	1,039	710	291	38	282
New Mexico	1,743	110	69	25	1,375	164	334	302	8	24	417
New York	24,789	2,783	515	652	19,187	1,632	2,173	1,274	773	126	901
North Carolina	5,615	361	192	84	4,395	584	1,087	959	42	86	329
North Dakota	479	29	33	15	340	61	244	216	4	24	119
Ohio	8,274	773	296	361	5,931	913	1,167	901	137	129	340
Oklahoma	2,347	150	123	44	1,751	279	432	347	20	65	246
Oregon	2,235	175	111	53	1,661	234	595	272	122	200	305
Pennsylvania	9,449	711	265	395	7,127	952	1,741	1,345	269	127	392
Rhode Island	1,027	90	32	18	796	92	221	171	26	24	85
South Carolina	2,988	131	103	51	2,415	289	482	411	14	58	170
South Dakota	539	22	44	7	391	75	241	199	5	37	178
Tennessee	4,651	248	138	39	3,813	413	617	521	39	57	375
Texas	11,949	555	589	193	9,196	1,417	2,722	2,209	271	243	631
Utah	1,063	91	52	26	749	146	321	239	55	27	198
Vermont	605	51	21	20	452	60	146	134	3	9	68
Virginia	3,002	178	181	93	2,138	412	1,036	882	66	87	290
Washington	3,988	491	155	77	2,785	480	775	548	106	121	420
West Virginia	1,686	182	57	34	1,248	165	437	318	8	111	159
Wisconsin	3,764	444	125	111	2,694	390	681	587	36	58	241
Wyoming	277	14	19	3	192	49	262	224	2	36	451
Dist. of Columbia	1,339	154	85	38	763	299	416	150	260	7	1,222
American Samoa	17	0	6	0	4	6	28	0	0	28	43
Fed. States of Micronesia	1	0	0	0	0	1	0	0	0	0	0
Guam	27	3	5	0	8	11	21	20	0	1	76
Marshall Islands	0	0	0	0	0	0	0	0	0	0	0
No. Mariana Islands	7	0	0	0	3	3	15	2	0	13	28
Palau	0	0	0	0	0	0	0	0	0	0	0
Puerto Rico	752	61	231	0	265	195	231	40	179	12	462
U.S. Virgin Islands ..	40	3	9	0	8	20	26	5	1	20	105
Undistributed	10	0	5	0	0	5	780	828	20	-68	42

(d) FEMA, Federal Emergency Management Agency.

Table 2.3
SUMMARY OF FEDERAL GOVERNMENT EXPENDITURE, BY STATE AND OUTLYING AREA:
FISCAL YEAR 2002
(In millions of dollars)

State and outlying area	Total	Retirement and disability	Other direct payments	Grants	Procurement	Salaries and wages
United States	$1,920,365	$612,996	$422,239	$415,099	$270,965	$199,066
Alabama	34,291	11,717	7,086	6,344	6,035	3,109
Alaska	7,562	981	560	3,127	1,396	1,499
Arizona	34,761	11,471	6,193	6,664	7,291	3,142
Arkansas	18,372	6,777	5,202	4,047	1,095	1,251
California	206,401	59,256	45,166	48,084	34,753	19,143
Colorado	26,229	8,073	4,753	4,740	4,526	4,138
Connecticut	25,387	7,348	5,088	5,279	6,216	1,456
Delaware	4,766	1,851	1,121	1,121	207	465
Florida	104,814	43,709	25,961	16,350	9,757	9,038
Georgia	51,336	15,945	10,160	10,500	7,364	7,366
Hawaii	10,474	2,899	1,435	1,835	1,621	2,684
Idaho	8,378	2,713	1,690	1,837	1,357	781
Illinois	70,275	24,068	20,223	14,975	4,664	6,344
Indiana	34,200	12,877	9,345	6,969	2,802	2,208
Iowa	18,839	6,570	6,169	4,060	955	1,084
Kansas	17,496	5,973	4,614	3,272	1,653	1,984
Kentucky	28,880	9,795	5,906	6,346	3,978	2,854
Louisiana	29,988	9,225	8,092	7,437	2,773	2,461
Maine	9,205	3,267	1,580	2,270	1,240	848
Maryland	52,265	12,789	7,285	9,039	13,488	9,664
Massachusetts	47,480	13,436	11,537	12,339	6,793	3,376
Michigan	55,909	21,241	14,564	13,279	3,539	3,286
Minnesota	27,056	9,225	7,089	6,492	2,228	2,022
Mississippi	21,308	6,688	5,000	5,046	2,734	1,840
Missouri	42,347	13,051	9,916	8,429	7,313	3,637
Montana	6,974	2,199	1,752	1,912	350	760
Nebraska	11,583	3,774	3,767	2,342	591	1,109
Nevada	10,737	4,425	2,126	1,840	1,250	1,096
New Hampshire	6,937	2,726	1,216	1,632	788	574
New Jersey	50,673	17,906	13,131	10,822	4,840	3,974
New Mexico	17,478	4,174	2,154	3,954	5,393	1,802
New York	128,994	39,201	31,389	42,461	7,417	8,526
North Carolina	48,180	17,971	10,369	10,939	2,923	5,978
North Dakota	6,437	1,384	2,643	1,425	329	655
Ohio	65,976	24,599	16,181	14,844	5,243	5,109
Oklahoma	24,355	8,393	5,187	5,108	2,515	3,152
Oregon	19,839	7,687	4,652	4,814	994	1,692
Pennsylvania	85,601	31,194	22,917	18,017	7,415	6,058
Rhode Island	7,503	2,479	1,650	2,094	495	786
South Carolina	26,103	9,708	5,063	5,592	3,105	2,636
South Dakota	6,315	1,702	2,099	1,506	378	631
Tennessee	39,276	13,196	8,309	8,658	5,912	3,200
Texas	123,431	37,324	27,648	24,858	20,581	13,019
Utah	12,302	3,723	1,869	2,697	2,084	1,929
Vermont	4,111	1,304	736	1,281	431	359
Virginia	74,537	18,634	8,515	7,714	26,170	13,504
Washington	40,218	13,063	7,994	8,296	5,586	5,278
West Virginia	13,361	5,460	2,780	3,298	602	1,221
Wisconsin	28,844	11,158	6,830	7,255	1,888	1,713
Wyoming	3,666	1,095	553	1,234	319	465
Dist. of Columbia	33,533	1,876	2,130	4,832	10,875	13,821
American Somoa	154	39	0	93	13	6
Fed. States of Micronesia .	140	0	0	126	1	
Guam	1,114	198	78	251	308	279
Marshall Islands	203	1	0	58	144	
No. Mariana Islands	102	21	3	66	9	3
Palau	42	0	0	41	1	0
Puerto Rico	14,062	5,282	2,658	4,828	365	930
Virgin Islands	573	138	90	266	29	50
Undistributed	18,996	17	0	65	15,844	3,071

Source: U.S. Department of Commerce, Bureau of the Census, February 2004.

Table 2.4
FEDERAL GOVERNMENT EXPENDITURE FOR DIRECT PAYMENTS FOR INDIVIDUALS FOR RETIREMENT AND DISABILITY, FOR SELECTED PROGRAMS, BY STATE AND OUTLYING AREA: FISCAL YEAR 2002
(In thousands of dollars)

State and outlying area	Total	Social Security payments				Federal retirement and disability benefits		Veteran benefits		Other
		Retirement insurance payments	Survivors insurance payments	Disability insurance payments	Supplemental security income payments	Civilian	Military	Payments for service connected disability	Other benefit payments	
United States	$612,995,927	$295,371,368	$90,311,494	$73,828,551	$31,409,951	$49,914,765	$33,803,849	$18,428,101	$6,799,971	$13,127,878
Alabama	11,717,444	4,551,821	1,760,104	1,766,334	730,450	1,211,356	874,712	387,247	209,117	226,303
Alaska	980,675	330,159	113,563	107,685	35,790	156,384	126,855	86,157	8,445	15,637
Arizona	11,471,408	5,587,186	1,435,147	1,273,898	438,478	992,489	951,674	441,014	128,829	222,694
Arkansas	6,776,748	2,879,941	993,821	1,056,809	363,545	479,617	396,353	313,042	121,677	171,943
California	59,256,019	28,696,780	8,069,092	6,570,543	4,705,930	4,629,100	3,631,119	1,485,432	549,933	918,092
Colorado	8,073,184	3,461,102	1,043,351	848,523	257,383	911,253	939,681	333,591	91,648	186,652
Connecticut	7,347,996	4,481,605	1,064,243	805,581	257,398	304,951	175,099	141,114	37,438	80,566
Delaware	1,851,031	948,098	261,903	220,321	57,560	144,024	117,311	49,731	15,102	36,981
Florida	43,708,769	22,290,331	5,548,863	4,335,954	1,899,227	3,414,287	3,574,100	1,421,017	475,483	749,507
Georgia	15,944,848	6,518,677	2,238,956	2,213,986	879,147	1,521,483	1,387,559	591,062	249,974	344,004
Hawaii	2,899,254	1,344,114	290,072	217,775	105,752	513,971	275,012	99,706	24,119	28,734
Idaho	2,712,660	1,293,095	375,927	297,174	91,390	245,939	185,683	110,122	29,248	84,080
Illinois	24,068,112	12,856,521	4,045,101	2,694,304	1,356,741	1,301,825	531,137	373,988	163,676	744,820
Indiana	12,876,771	6,915,428	2,172,924	1,609,797	459,837	692,519	319,110	281,544	94,835	330,776
Iowa	6,570,474	3,669,618	1,133,853	671,769	189,059	396,502	143,944	139,355	58,259	168,115
Kansas	5,972,825	3,020,221	914,718	588,934	175,613	472,503	336,415	163,566	62,124	238,731
Kentucky	9,795,499	3,790,491	1,550,072	1,835,211	844,847	647,194	371,433	303,178	132,469	320,603
Louisiana	9,225,492	3,619,845	1,844,925	1,387,538	784,246	521,466	439,206	294,096	169,954	164,216
Maine	3,266,654	1,467,574	431,355	460,056	135,420	286,527	180,527	192,351	48,805	64,039
Maryland	12,788,582	4,947,542	1,528,255	1,064,099	452,930	3,196,789	902,759	312,925	106,412	276,871
Massachusetts	13,435,678	7,097,728	1,894,665	1,787,885	739,757	902,136	307,628	435,004	120,390	150,486
Michigan	21,240,734	11,442,460	3,672,090	3,009,116	1,095,809	802,115	362,614	388,656	152,932	314,942
Minnesota	9,225,081	5,066,084	1,462,520	971,710	325,490	513,992	224,220	288,117	87,872	285,076
Mississippi	6,688,355	2,589,236	1,014,744	1,174,005	559,380	488,145	399,231	225,610	119,557	118,447
Missouri	13,050,932	6,313,097	2,006,354	1,753,961	547,155	1,031,703	536,770	345,605	146,972	369,315
Montana	2,198,867	992,962	315,833	239,527	66,013	233,403	118,949	97,041	25,899	109,240
Nebraska	3,773,864	1,892,406	574,483	349,698	100,592	259,008	224,245	150,341	47,065	176,025
Nevada	4,425,060	2,115,063	501,183	476,709	134,685	420,100	479,081	165,965	49,622	82,653
New Hampshire	2,726,059	1,410,457	341,406	332,506	58,429	243,099	173,033	110,719	26,762	29,649
New Jersey	17,905,840	10,396,030	2,675,257	1,976,651	684,981	1,122,191	324,852	342,885	103,780	279,212

See footnotes at end of table.

FEDERAL GOVERNMENT EXPENDITURE FOR DIRECT PAYMENTS FOR INDIVIDUALS FOR RETIREMENT AND DISABILITY, FOR SELECTED PROGRAMS, BY STATE AND OUTLYING AREA: FISCAL YEAR 2002 — Continued

State and outlying area	Total	Social Security payments				Federal retirement and disability benefits		Veteran benefits		
		Retirement insurance payments	Survivors insurance payments	Disability insurance payments	Supplemental security income payments	Civilian	Military	Payments for service connected disability	Other benefit payments	Other
New Mexico	4,173,748	1,642,988	536,797	458,776	218,051	531,284	392,144	227,979	63,043	102,686
New York	39,200,827	21,231,266	5,688,265	5,218,958	2,996,112	1,882,731	477,070	766,289	280,790	659,346
North Carolina	17,971,102	8,455,300	2,357,386	2,633,999	822,325	1,240,710	1,288,151	686,444	244,538	242,249
North Dakota	1,384,358	682,106	257,051	119,489	33,028	120,360	56,096	45,407	15,189	55,633
Ohio	24,598,782	12,429,560	4,486,906	2,781,245	1,274,988	1,496,589	650,281	557,955	231,413	689,846
Oklahoma	8,393,111	3,616,302	1,244,314	927,385	337,719	971,176	526,453	449,383	183,943	136,435
Oregon	7,686,805	3,962,868	1,069,809	831,556	271,867	637,074	348,170	301,214	98,269	165,979
Pennsylvania	31,193,997	16,257,224	5,116,559	3,396,865	1,472,830	2,104,329	721,327	670,275	275,010	1,179,579
Rhode Island	2,478,786	1,303,191	304,804	324,678	128,312	187,305	104,640	81,682	25,232	18,943
South Carolina	9,708,257	4,176,447	1,276,796	1,449,269	477,131	805,203	893,661	343,014	149,813	136,922
South Dakota	1,701,504	824,727	270,564	157,716	55,902	179,848	89,781	72,015	26,995	23,956
Tennessee	13,195,896	5,851,900	1,990,381	1,956,176	735,184	1,036,143	743,216	422,535	187,316	273,045
Texas	37,324,173	16,327,330	6,064,144	3,772,894	1,857,042	3,110,695	3,303,684	1,557,667	584,703	746,014
Utah	3,723,247	1,666,137	475,647	317,662	104,321	698,447	216,120	102,988	25,736	116,190
Vermont	1,303,516	680,419	192,145	167,639	50,449	81,398	52,291	45,241	13,510	20,424
Virginia	18,633,963	6,526,487	2,044,055	1,875,137	594,866	3,309,819	3,072,325	582,082	207,282	421,910
Washington	13,062,944	6,020,887	1,629,777	1,325,461	538,932	1,296,879	1,227,506	621,408	146,983	255,110
West Virginia	5,459,898	2,111,882	950,378	1,052,571	362,103	316,633	139,148	196,767	81,596	248,821
Wisconsin	11,157,764	6,405,434	1,787,341	1,214,910	410,682	489,407	235,391	305,027	93,808	215,765
Wyoming	1,095,230	513,404	150,831	111,352	26,532	113,608	71,539	41,230	10,066	56,670
Dist. of Columbia	1,876,039	405,102	129,564	126,515	104,673	966,893	57,806	36,245	19,951	29,290
American Samoa	39,395	9,692	10,405	10,215	0	1,556	3,290	3,309	885	44
Fed. States of Micronesia	438	137	36	5	0	197	0	0	5	0
Guam	198,143	61,279	25,533	12,798	0	59,290	29,137	7,392	1,777	938
Marshall Islands	891	543	246	51	0	21	0	8	22	0
No. Mariana Islands	20,995	4,910	4,206	1,140	3,870	4,827	1,497	462	69	13
Palau	428	136	118	10		129	0	7	26	0
Puerto Rico	5,281,765	2,140,073	951,565	1,469,432	0	201,060	88,265	232,426	172,984	25,961
Virgin Islands	138,036	77,965	21,093	16,587	0	15,019	4,548	1,412	618	796
Undistributed	16,971	0	0	0	0	65	0	0	0	16,906

Source: U.S. Department of Commerce, Bureau of the Census, February 2004.

Table 2.5
FEDERAL GOVERNMENT EXPENDITURE FOR DIRECT PAYMENTS OTHER THAN FOR RETIREMENT AND DISABILITY, FOR SELECTED PROGRAMS, BY STATE AND OUTLYING AREA: FISCAL YEAR 2002
(In thousands of dollars)

State and outlying area	Total	Medicare benefits		Excess earned income tax credits	Unemployment compensation	Food stamp payments	Housing assistance	Agricultural assistance	Federal employees life and health insurance	Other
		Hospital insurance	Supplementary medical insurance							
United States	$422,239,079	$144,095,457	$107,021,044	$28,931,014	$48,162,730	$18,243,989	$4,292,612	$33,688,183	$13,709,862	$24,094,190
Alabama	7,086,074	2,727,236	1,740,473	766,986	363,333	417,621	124,753	335,588	264,823	345,263
Alaska	560,257	121,672	74,594	36,019	137,518	59,455	12,040	10,695	1,887	106,377
Arizona	6,193,172	2,101,596	1,739,670	522,599	416,131	385,908	28,872	267,474	186,616	544,306
Arkansas	5,201,566	1,454,715	979,917	406,251	353,293	264,534	28,235	1,414,875	95,957	203,788
California	45,165,873	15,935,008	13,204,866	3,306,659	6,063,460	1,695,673	157,199	1,185,190	1,148,610	2,469,207
Colorado	4,752,721	1,453,812	1,096,056	291,486	645,106	165,442	20,977	585,564	148,080	346,199
Connecticut	5,088,004	2,111,584	1,527,094	193,084	771,795	145,798	76,292	12,626	80,284	169,447
Delaware	1,120,946	370,460	273,139	72,974	118,787	39,293	11,245	63,931	50,883	120,234
Florida	25,960,533	9,500,424	9,905,311	1,998,174	1,456,617	878,455	105,366	242,378	637,399	1,236,408
Georgia	10,159,958	3,392,738	2,343,707	1,205,149	915,764	621,291	135,580	693,990	313,533	538,206
Hawaii	1,434,696	431,084	371,941	89,144	206,908	151,769	15,207	8,645	100,062	59,936
Idaho	1,690,334	419,481	307,846	118,663	196,596	62,014	1,262	435,960	41,704	106,809
Illinois	20,223,213	6,620,287	4,453,445	1,123,898	2,820,220	923,306	308,576	2,842,847	318,046	812,587
Indiana	9,344,617	2,970,302	1,992,657	529,529	672,254	408,077	42,742	1,476,086	165,447	1,087,523
Iowa	6,169,175	1,279,669	1,072,854	189,536	405,835	128,762	6,507	2,718,225	97,080	270,706
Kansas	4,613,722	1,276,597	1,002,584	203,739	341,289	113,272	16,533	1,398,190	85,665	175,853
Kentucky	5,905,727	2,108,395	1,391,060	433,163	559,305	410,097	65,687	405,666	216,600	315,754
Louisiana	8,092,280	3,093,517	1,773,114	879,453	321,212	587,074	71,294	835,490	146,341	384,787
Maine	1,579,993	606,902	421,427	95,384	134,084	97,447	11,120	43,281	56,493	113,855
Maryland	7,285,386	2,635,119	2,021,606	435,643	550,871	215,189	93,946	171,727	857,094	304,190
Massachusetts	11,536,640	4,722,506	2,814,193	333,827	2,410,834	209,236	125,364	16,409	264,896	639,375
Michigan	14,564,196	5,210,429	4,168,116	820,009	2,208,994	644,577	60,028	636,007	207,431	608,605
Minnesota	7,089,124	1,908,643	1,354,512	270,724	960,427	200,649	66,420	1,766,454	155,522	405,773
Mississippi	5,000,373	1,609,654	983,395	626,620	223,446	297,925	31,412	837,775	112,248	277,898
Missouri	9,916,437	3,180,334	2,220,205	555,564	619,980	476,894	50,392	1,276,198	1,090,342	446,529
Montana	1,752,492	367,271	275,686	87,734	81,078	57,920	4,558	703,742	46,260	128,242
Nebraska	3,766,706	667,817	525,848	127,068	126,479	74,382	11,478	2,000,184	72,709	160,740
Nevada	2,126,161	685,682	558,200	190,513	416,641	95,508	20,764	18,721	57,716	82,416
New Hampshire	1,216,423	499,425	330,406	62,103	115,895	34,657	7,767	12,423	69,325	84,421
New Jersey	13,131,213	4,841,804	3,755,797	631,647	2,613,786	314,258	237,955	30,609	252,734	452,623
New Mexico	2,154,331	605,912	489,322	274,873	142,254	154,365	13,751	128,037	113,896	231,922
New York	31,389,154	11,610,960	8,633,195	1,943,383	4,030,266	1,478,663	1,065,087	190,931	530,084	1,906,585
North Carolina	10,369,410	3,434,028	2,319,007	1,010,709	1,403,457	536,423	110,902	846,169	194,561	514,153
North Dakota	2,642,960	292,116	222,775	45,433	43,898	31,375	2,721	1,847,901	30,655	126,085
Ohio	16,180,910	6,094,495	4,401,540	993,600	1,684,273	726,310	191,865	1,147,419	305,028	636,380

See footnotes at end of table.

FEDERAL GOVERNMENT EXPENDITURE FOR DIRECT PAYMENTS OTHER THAN FOR RETIREMENT AND DISABILITY, FOR SELECTED PROGRAMS, BY STATE AND OUTLYING AREA: FISCAL YEAR 2002 — Continued

State or other jurisdiction	Total	Medicare benefits		Excess earned income tax credits	Unemployment compensation	Food stamp payments	Housing assistance	Agricultural assistance	Federal employees life and health insurance	Other
		Hospital insurance	Supplementary medical insurance							
Oklahoma	5,187,021	1,947,458	1,168,060	411,729	274,661	288,442	29,483	537,386	192,339	337,464
Oregon	4,652,106	1,327,438	1,068,263	269,634	1,055,814	319,462	17,649	193,062	154,777	246,006
Pennsylvania	22,917,131	9,124,534	6,379,589	942,368	3,142,092	700,337	266,841	193,693	1,043,526	1,124,150
Rhode Island	1,649,862	661,077	432,183	80,428	239,977	64,256	23,479	2,130	44,423	101,908
South Carolina	5,062,678	1,678,403	1,203,238	612,782	519,149	351,662	34,926	244,109	134,274	284,135
South Dakota	2,098,567	320,973	236,088	64,496	28,869	45,324	5,630	1,177,512	19,153	200,522
Tennessee	8,309,131	3,362,251	1,882,008	726,786	726,734	551,508	110,716	351,989	176,797	420,342
Texas	27,648,089	9,160,932	5,889,165	3,077,838	2,551,571	1,522,295	137,923	2,690,529	887,425	1,730,413
Utah	1,868,695	572,804	387,844	156,184	286,624	79,709	4,463	50,603	120,938	209,526
Vermont	736,398	259,882	165,305	37,895	95,795	34,253	3,444	42,594	14,651	82,579
Virginia	8,514,779	2,677,079	1,992,550	626,908	802,473	303,674	70,056	304,979	1,067,271	669,788
Washington	7,994,305	2,141,867	1,698,435	412,666	2,112,231	317,652	41,756	447,736	316,269	505,693
West Virginia	2,779,967	1,136,843	780,055	189,608	166,949	198,011	18,928	20,275	79,820	189,476
Wisconsin	6,829,633	2,232,469	1,673,499	331,669	1,070,480	197,330	21,329	681,737	117,159	503,961
Wyoming	552,722	189,518	128,896	40,432	35,420	21,538	1,182	69,961	27,308	38,467
Dist. of Columbia	2,129,539	404,630	305,374	75,698	169,521	75,668	43,943	39,004	717,641	298,059
American Samoa	2,303	0	0	0	0	0	0	0	0	2,303
Fed. States of Micronesia	12,688	0	0	0	0	0	0	0	0	12,688
Guam	78,121	772	535	0	0	51,816	2,459	19	14,168	8,353
Marshall Islands	2	0	0	0	0	0	0	0	0	2
No. Mariana Islands	3,206	0	0	0	0	0	0	9	0	3,198
Palau	0	0	0	0	0	0	0	0	0	0
Puerto Rico	2,657,610	541,283	874,790	2,553	334,865	104,286	29,331	65,913	704,589	0
Virgin Islands	89,694	13,569	9,610	0	17,419	17,431	20,222	4,115	0	7,327
Undistributed	55	0	0	0	0	0	0	0	0	55

Source: U.S. Department of Commerce, Bureau of the Census, February 2004.

Table 2.6
FEDERAL GOVERNMENT EXPENDITURE FOR GRANTS, BY AGENCY, BY STATE, AND OUTLYING AREA: FISCAL YEAR 2002
(In thousands of dollars)

State and outlying area	Total	Department of Agriculture	Appalachian Regional Commission	Department of Commerce	Corporation for National and Community Service	Corporation for Public Broadcasting	Department of Defense	Department of Education
United States	$415,098,792	$23,882,217	$98,305	$1,593,561	$558,065	$356,694	$2,417,027	$34,286,427
Alabama	6,343,595	386,593	13,386	33,852	5,891	2,475	52,544	555,279
Alaska	3,126,749	146,661	0	116,339	4,755	5,908	37,709	285,364
Arizona	6,663,506	378,331	0	8,145	7,167	3,828	40,137	744,657
Arkansas	4,047,222	300,019	0	11,901	6,805	1,618	50,491	348,092
California	48,083,694	2,834,988	0	139,560	54,063	40,271	286,613	4,143,974
Colorado	4,739,710	213,846	0	47,698	7,176	3,532	24,551	423,604
Connecticut	5,278,748	163,678	0	10,251	6,363	2,393	35,479	352,915
Delaware	1,121,309	59,041	0	9,030	2,560	0	18,872	99,939
Florida	16,349,635	1,043,106	0	70,866	15,511	14,771	100,745	1,595,209
Georgia	10,499,924	731,442	6,312	15,873	12,739	4,924	24,616	938,587
Hawaii	1,835,296	101,120	0	27,437	2,922	2,123	5,702	221,206
Idaho	1,836,892	140,167	0	12,188	3,297	1,809	29,082	154,222
Illinois	14,975,058	768,077	0	26,119	17,325	10,268	79,747	1,360,075
Indiana	6,968,979	348,537	0	8,634	8,635	6,023	35,547	571,164
Iowa	4,060,244	226,371	0	7,838	4,584	3,164	68,782	309,271
Kansas	3,271,705	202,492	0	11,450	7,250	2,650	41,439	355,489
Kentucky	6,346,133	347,383	12,986	23,897	5,691	3,985	5,660	503,812
Louisiana	7,436,529	470,321	0	44,189	6,603	3,211	93,049	598,945
Maine	2,270,440	92,647	0	25,747	3,552	1,554	276	163,038
Maryland	9,039,490	278,943	1,260	33,412	16,145	5,533	117,239	567,740
Massachusetts	12,339,048	312,503	0	49,773	21,311	18,124	113,041	746,045
Michigan	13,279,471	631,690	0	34,167	14,777	7,426	42,241	1,159,910
Minnesota	6,491,557	361,678	0	18,163	8,991	9,077	12,714	485,373
Mississippi	5,045,908	365,243	4,711	40,687	18,275	1,935	8,692	415,351
Missouri	8,429,449	387,134	0	10,869	10,400	4,548	15,074	574,888
Montana	1,911,999	164,540	0	5,145	4,980	988	17,301	198,009
Nebraska	2,342,321	146,352	0	5,828	3,570	4,885	39,677	206,036
Nevada	1,839,768	115,309	0	7,873	3,952	2,154	1,712	168,269
New Hampshire	1,632,356	62,049	0	50,156	3,765	1,557	31,934	114,424
New Jersey	10,821,644	400,569	0	26,587	13,196	2,754	65,199	833,554
New Mexico	3,954,126	230,908	0	10,350	5,380	2,880	33,247	485,810
New York	42,460,802	2,153,760	3,027	76,573	37,019	32,222	147,666	2,567,262
North Carolina	10,939,062	629,554	11,373	39,000	9,834	55,646	47,120	839,800
North Dakota	1,425,170	181,616	0	6,393	1,225	1,130	21,213	142,778
Ohio	14,843,783	623,164	6,428	29,240	15,113	10,427	31,039	1,124,009
Oklahoma	5,107,709	511,791	0	17,111	7,182	2,175	2,559	517,497
Oregon	4,814,276	269,579	0	73,325	7,637	3,845	8,342	391,542
Pennsylvania	18,016,767	678,660	13,928	27,588	21,285	9,862	120,966	1,236,972
Rhode Island	2,093,923	61,709	0	10,500	5,092	674	27,346	127,000
South Carolina	5,591,956	327,751	4,369	61,568	6,011	3,369	44,906	499,517
South Dakota	1,505,560	96,682	0	2,588	1,555	1,114	16,853	173,841
Tennessee	8,658,179	418,995	6,724	11,656	9,211	4,526	9,173	568,067
Texas	24,858,152	2,026,826	0	71,141	24,414	12,757	131,815	2,645,316
Utah	2,697,032	193,108	0	4,853	4,989	4,467	37,283	273,760
Vermont	1,280,599	59,256	0	2,740	3,554	1,287	12,076	105,181
Virginia	7,713,799	417,476	3,638	58,027	21,684	11,077	64,550	746,642
Washington	8,296,335	393,856	0	76,062	25,288	6,747	36,754	663,516
West Virginia	3,298,202	176,450	10,129	11,198	5,782	1,237	14,399	253,534
Wisconsin	7,254,679	310,648	0	23,057	9,118	6,755	62,915	590,439
Wyoming	1,233,904	60,791	0	541	1,849	772	930	100,130
Dist. of Columbia	4,832,314	61,728	34	22,416	28,065	2,327	43,379	301,243
American Samoa	93,399	6,823	0	1,258	0	536	0	822
Fed. States of Micronesia ...	125,555	4,111	0	0	0	0	0	9,817
Guam	250,609	17,895	0	2,920	0	592	0	5,160
Marshall Islands	58,150	282	0	0	0	0	0	0
No. Mariana Islands	66,071	1,647	0	100	0	0	0	884
Palau	40,802	4	0	0	-15	0	0	0
Puerto Rico	4,828,132	1,758,866	0	17,183	4,102	3,153	1,467	678,394
Virgin Islands	266,364	17,662	0	2,498	443	568	5,166	17,480
Undistributed	65,000	9,792	0	0	0	3,061	0	25,575

Source: U.S. Department of Commerce, Bureau of the Census, January 2003.

FEDERAL GOVERNMENT EXPENDITURE FOR GRANTS, BY AGENCY, BY STATE, AND OUTLYING AREA: FISCAL YEAR 2002 — Continued

State and outlying area	Department of Energy	Environmental Protection Agency	Equal Employment Opportunity Commission	Federal Emergency Management Agency	Department of Health and Human Services	Department of Housing and Urban Development	Institute of Museum and Library Services	Department of the Interior
United States	$1,866,783	$4,259,415	$29,582	$2,584,346	$246,657,918	$28,458,983	$214,816	$2,282,312
Alabama	43,548	61,737	0	49,671	3,509,634	346,706	3,479	12,135
Alaska	26,258	92,924	184	6,591	1,554,633	45,054	1,576	43,458
Arizona	18,428	50,859	478	24,904	4,005,512	261,317	3,176	86,187
Arkansas	3,248	37,158	0	16,611	2,420,299	187,777	1,703	7,172
California	181,026	328,987	3,130	28,017	29,384,840	3,653,017	23,319	200,116
Colorado	47,013	75,518	427	26,854	2,460,396	350,476	3,024	85,816
Connecticut	44,314	47,927	650	4,985	3,188,522	480,732	3,315	5,262
Delaware	5,232	27,395	191	1,700	602,047	76,655	908	5,249
Florida	37,187	138,519	1,373	115,286	9,558,094	1,051,275	9,585	12,286
Georgia	50,915	74,553	148	12,609	6,389,999	670,141	4,464	6,356
Hawaii	5,845	30,011	131	3,039	893,291	110,314	2,073	8,397
Idaho	15,259	33,257	295	3,677	908,242	63,748	1,718	28,618
Illinois	68,224	147,957	1,520	33,643	8,470,913	1,580,123	9,086	18,767
Indiana	41,413	72,365	500	22,972	4,161,915	458,366	3,423	10,684
Iowa	24,753	41,703	832	15,018	2,544,770	194,082	2,606	4,021
Kansas	12,152	41,812	365	50,744	1,840,680	157,719	2,092	6,240
Kentucky	13,304	49,571	222	44,758	3,974,802	391,252	2,519	3,640
Louisiana	9,474	62,174	0	32,261	4,767,320	438,669	3,219	18,506
Maine	5,177	44,200	245	4,717	1,471,129	146,153	2,482	9,222
Maryland	27,800	92,832	655	16,969	5,192,278	517,459	3,863	15,001
Massachusetts	130,310	138,536	1,362	7,059	7,979,360	1,253,154	5,799	7,878
Michigan	83,582	180,217	444	19,664	8,454,558	762,236	6,328	11,129
Minnesota	41,774	77,222	564	27,676	3,955,498	465,296	3,667	9,474
Mississippi	15,285	47,596	0	14,695	3,049,929	233,019	2,962	15,975
Missouri	19,521	90,638	717	99,325	5,320,295	463,315	4,549	11,072
Montana	8,029	35,444	249	5,589	849,127	60,646	1,306	77,985
Nebraska	8,463	31,095	720	3,206	1,348,925	118,816	1,667	3,874
Nevada	55,227	38,931	505	2,184	849,188	147,649	1,310	43,104
New Hampshire	7,423	42,687	84	3,472	831,966	117,968	2,222	6,980
New Jersey	39,383	132,947	522	63,492	6,348,328	1,077,243	4,702	5,655
New Mexico	82,223	44,781	272	15,129	2,073,869	128,879	1,826	241,387
New York	135,082	292,639	2,220	1,139,922	28,308,563	3,520,303	17,478	12,901
North Carolina	39,307	91,632	135	16,792	7,041,905	546,195	5,227	6,319
North Dakota	1,155	33,432	139	19,873	581,072	54,500	1,039	25,239
Ohio	43,729	242,317	1,993	19,528	9,610,367	1,157,612	7,663	2,142
Oklahoma	10,905	67,175	391	135,361	2,847,368	264,465	2,193	9,660
Oregon	15,470	65,237	526	20,251	2,749,826	298,336	2,502	140,765
Pennsylvania	98,079	125,934	1,999	34,025	11,479,364	1,379,657	9,629	5,697
Rhode Island	4,783	36,105	193	3,039	1,274,638	187,858	1,062	3,829
South Carolina	29,083	44,652	610	7,808	3,468,131	279,257	3,010	1,470
South Dakota	2,196	28,449	163	3,825	687,669	61,500	1,123	63,454
Tennessee	22,840	50,950	346	26,213	5,809,078	437,515	4,131	6,804
Texas	67,741	194,022	941	213,015	14,067,870	1,439,287	11,447	19,870
Utah	15,995	31,446	352	10,925	1,334,174	112,966	1,681	92,918
Vermont	5,577	30,780	67	4,381	730,415	73,433	1,182	4,315
Virginia	45,029	96,242	229	39,118	3,697,948	519,747	5,527	26,223
Washington	46,306	97,937	766	59,761	5,047,878	469,715	3,620	35,482
West Virginia	21,334	32,433	172	52,669	1,903,796	170,652	1,204	4,273
Wisconsin	42,221	100,420	1,074	12,520	4,492,342	372,772	4,720	4,309
Wyoming	6,527	21,830	116	3,340	343,852	29,350	589	386,614
Dist. of Columbia	29,384	102,913	72	3,836	1,687,255	478,210	3,041	18,896
American Samoa	232	4,102	0	407	28,117	1,669	107	35,732
Fed. States of Micronesia ...	0	0	0	8,944	626	0	41	100,193
Guam	266	6,561	0	32,705	47,731	25,824	164	61,862
Marshall Islands	0	0	0	-6	5,099	0	46	51,570
No. Mariana Islands	231	816	0	507	19,302	1,636	116	21,632
Palau	0	0	0	-17	2,629	0	0	37,912
Puerto Rico	1,240	46,439	287	-57,804	971,512	535,958	2,160	724
Virgin Islands	277	3,400	10	-3,107	59,035	31,312	97	79,858
Undistributed	0	0	0	0	0	0	0	4

FEDERAL GOVERNMENT EXPENDITURE FOR GRANTS, BY AGENCY, BY STATE, AND OUTLYING AREA: FISCAL YEAR 2002 — Continued

State and outlying area	Department of Justice	Department of Labor	National Aeronautics and Space Administration	National Archives and Records Administration	National Endowment for the Arts	National Endowment for the Humanities	National Science Foundation	Small Business Administration
United States	$5,137,213	$9,356,258	$1,100,125	$6,459	$91,993	$104,512	$4,427,636	$133,749
Alabama	65,565	132,357	47,434	0	780	1,100	26,710	625
Alaska	43,907	71,110	4,649	20	808	957	28,322	688
Arizona	106,194	151,137	23,066	71	1,040	1,055	84,409	1,606
Arkansas	43,018	78,719	768	0	594	1,021	8,770	759
California	639,556	1,278,284	202,475	852	7,091	7,685	667,180	9,938
Colorado	68,294	93,652	37,448	15	2,888	1,113	238,352	919
Connecticut	96,818	111,626	14,272	230	1,276	2,240	39,700	602
Delaware	17,895	23,561	3,967	0	611	885	14,743	23
Florida	259,841	305,771	36,215	102	1,269	1,329	127,087	4,637
Georgia	164,232	168,027	19,199	63	2,310	3,497	92,259	1,240
Hawaii	25,229	55,608	26,872	0	1,016	755	28,893	844
Idaho	30,078	52,092	7,573	0	715	615	9,139	499
Illinois	163,590	394,933	13,357	199	2,895	3,732	214,979	3,112
Indiana	63,145	127,468	9,413	20	916	1,744	79,149	446
Iowa	39,417	63,682	12,002	55	834	1,098	34,246	763
Kansas	43,377	53,929	2,565	0	807	901	26,241	285
Kentucky	62,347	110,085	3,717	0	969	916	32,499	22,992
Louisiana	73,180	128,172	8,939	0	1,112	1,114	32,292	1,144
Maine	26,620	53,147	1,308	157	1,314	1,190	21,808	1,491
Maryland	142,894	229,119	88,791	153	2,538	1,338	122,073	3,405
Massachusetts	101,742	199,214	52,242	270	3,865	5,530	320,800	2,240
Michigan	104,948	310,782	15,121	0	1,347	2,579	132,970	2,129
Minnesota	65,340	155,451	5,861	154	4,514	950	57,019	1,499
Mississippi	64,494	108,801	14,291	0	719	1,021	18,507	189
Missouri	77,999	133,335	11,830	131	2,216	1,269	64,707	1,404
Montana	33,052	37,569	9,591	0	863	495	24,783	597
Nebraska	34,381	43,558	1,575	20	795	1,773	18,859	428
Nevada	47,899	57,508	1,570	0	751	472	16,670	337
New Hampshire	72,139	31,338	11,159	0	713	1,167	19,186	755
New Jersey	149,904	230,597	13,877	255	1,447	1,967	88,137	1,822
New Mexico	60,834	80,241	8,647	102	1,135	1,531	34,750	1,980
New York	493,428	628,413	53,174	938	13,848	15,808	349,379	20,797
North Carolina	89,282	241,636	15,119	180	1,744	2,790	96,193	1,902
North Dakota	19,935	28,056	5,112	0	644	623	10,982	380
Ohio	118,360	293,638	45,224	55	2,301	3,039	95,431	1,284
Oklahoma	75,395	73,492	12,908	7	663	897	24,006	2,568
Oregon	42,599	165,827	5,336	0	1,139	1,347	50,418	899
Pennsylvania	126,427	383,156	22,215	121	2,904	4,170	179,538	4,707
Rhode Island	26,997	34,456	5,010	84	920	1,858	25,845	763
South Carolina	67,911	97,396	4,530	350	1,027	638	38,734	449
South Dakota	49,231	29,492	922	0	670	691	12,020	144
Tennessee	81,856	124,646	11,009	207	865	1,338	47,600	3,166
Texas	301,952	545,546	70,140	116	2,669	4,222	163,561	4,333
Utah	47,952	58,042	5,344	0	870	912	30,740	250
Vermont	25,779	24,467	1,371	0	899	1,168	9,565	785
Virginia	229,489	286,676	47,952	491	950	3,012	164,359	6,485
Washington	93,419	247,734	10,044	143	2,024	1,470	103,097	728
West Virginia	48,184	77,528	42,274	0	680	632	13,030	8,905
Wisconsin	66,517	177,660	9,922	280	1,077	2,133	98,045	2,520
Wyoming	18,945	22,263	926	20	567	486	10,031	277
Dist. of Columbia	44,326	435,995	16,514	594	3,761	2,355	165,647	1,708
American Samoa	4,265	1,566	0	5	255	136	0	150
Fed. States of Micronesia	0	1,823	0	0	0	0	0	0
Guam	7,753	14,842	0	0	242	318	0	0
Marshall Islands	0	1,159	0	0	0	0	0	0
No. Mariana Islands	2,221	936	0	0	285	309	0	108
Palau	-3	293	0	0	0	0	0	0
Puerto Rico	49,394	281,108	5,132	0	574	861	13,224	896
Virgin Islands	17,670	7,538	151	0	270	261	952	150
Undistributed	0	0	0	0	0	0	0	0

FEDERAL GOVERNMENT EXPENDITURE FOR GRANTS, BY AGENCY, BY STATE, AND OUTLYING AREA: FISCAL YEAR 2002 — Continued

State and outlying area	Social Security Administration	Department of State	State Justice Institute	Tennessee Valley Authority	Department of Transportation	Department of the Treasury	Department of Veterans Affairs	Other
United States	$39,304	$204,780	$5,086	$328,329	$42,664,595	$1,386,236	$486,232	$79,833
Alabama	0	1,332	9	78,375	904,922	334	6,967	156
Alaska	0	389	51	0	607,461	112	105	757
Arizona	0	3,311	40	0	652,771	1,368	3,559	755
Arkansas	0	974	0	0	517,812	210	1,163	519
California	702	21,081	306	0	3,909,029	6,539	16,587	14,468
Colorado	0	3,708	215	0	507,858	352	11,096	3,869
Connecticut	0	2,590	0	0	655,396	256	5,676	1,279
Delaware	0	372	20	0	147,644	27	2,588	153
Florida	0	5,047	31	0	1,806,050	16,207	20,197	2,040
Georgia	4,458	2	5,058	1,080,926	3,665	10,507	805	
Hawaii	0	755	1	0	281,103	201	0	406
Idaho	0	736	23	0	333,450	80	5,515	800
Illinois	1,932	9,840	105	331	1,544,342	2,050	25,817	2,000
Indiana	0	3,856	62	0	925,542	587	5,053	1,397
Iowa	533	3,264	6	0	443,868	81	12,230	371
Kansas	0	1,930	2	0	401,230	167	6,856	842
Kentucky	0	1,423	41	23,912	691,308	565	11,115	762
Louisiana	0	2,824	1	0	618,455	4,634	16,125	598
Maine	0	650	48	0	181,040	70	11,398	62
Maryland	0	4,491	146	0	1,550,348	659	4,469	1,938
Massachusetts	1,677	12,046	26	0	834,945	920	14,299	4,977
Michigan	1,997	5,363	356	0	1,273,739	1,641	17,334	796
Minnesota	600	3,198	53	0	702,496	205	15,856	1,195
Mississippi	0	1,122	44	17,760	573,681	362	10,465	97
Missouri	0	2,917	1	0	1,068,585	662	50,963	1,087
Montana	0	1,010	0	0	369,981	41	3,790	890
Nebraska	0	1,164	68	0	307,131	125	9,227	101
Nevada	0	546	179	0	275,236	202	846	186
New Hampshire	499	517	34	0	204,567	172	12,549	875
New Jersey	0	2,371	2	0	1,295,312	1,273	20,017	534
New Mexico	661	1,525	278	0	400,947	440	3,214	900
New York	1,586	25,935	149	0	2,375,438	10,543	16,953	7,777
North Carolina	75	4,549	20	1,548	1,097,604	2,272	2,660	1,648
North Dakota	0	222	0	0	276,696	36	1,507	175
Ohio	655	5,852	1	0	1,327,767	692	20,990	3,723
Oklahoma	450	1,843	3	0	491,768	139	26,590	1,148
Oregon	0	3,551	24	0	491,946	1,079	2,102	827
Pennsylvania	0	9,403	37	0	2,012,200	946	25,888	1,411
Rhode Island	0	670	40	0	245,853	102	6,600	1,411
South Carolina	0	1,577	3	0	591,866	265	5,637	1,411
South Dakota	0	421	8	0	269,303	0	1,377	269
Tennessee	0	1,720	246	201,264	789,074	1,603	4,607	2,750
Texas	0	8,565	34	0	2,816,083	3,789	7,047	3,584
Utah	0	1,494	33	0	430,435	38	1,459	546
Vermont	765	757	24	0	177,030	33	2,300	1,411
Virginia	0	4,565	1,739	81	1,207,926	988	3,715	2,215
Washington	0	4,785	23	0	859,812	996	7,255	1,117
West Virginia	0	319	2	0	445,160	118	1,075	1,034
Wisconsin	950	3,041	22	0	844,711	1,457	11,782	1,252
Wyoming	0	177	7	0	221,916	228	830	0
Dist. of Columbia	358	18,984	430	0	420,082	937,226	0	1,537
American Samoa	0	0	0	0	7,217	0	0	0
Fed. States of Micronesia	0	0	0	0	0	0	0	0
Guam	0	27	0	0	25,749	0	0	0
Marshall Islands	0	0	0	0	0	0	0	0
No. Mariana Islands	0	0	0	0	15,342	0	0	0
Palau	0	0	0	0	0	0	0	0
Puerto Rico	0	1,517	91	0	131,817	379,193	276	370
Virgin Islands	0	0	0	0	24,626	0	0	48
Undistributed	25,864	0	0	0	0	286	0	418

Table 2.7
FEDERAL GOVERNMENT EXPENDITURE FOR PROCUREMENT CONTRACTS, BY AGENCY, BY STATE AND OUTLYING AREA: FISCAL YEAR 2002
(In thousands of dollars)

State and outlying area	Total	Department of Defense						Nondefense agencies		
		Total	Army	Navy	Air Force	Army Corps of Engineers	Other defense	Total	Department of Agriculture	Department of Commerce
United States	$270,965,430	$165,578,660	$38,419,875	$43,595,420	$44,009,317	$3,307,952	$36,246,096	$105,386,770	$3,644,560	$1,584,085
Alabama	6,034,798	4,637,572	1,754,159	162,775	296,713	100,646	2,323,279	1,397,226	18,351	918
Alaska	1,395,500	960,989	447,026	74,035	284,648	30,186	125,094	434,511	39,949	18,321
Arizona	7,291,158	6,460,355	2,727,721	1,401,638	1,280,085	20,504	1,030,407	830,803	24,428	4,046
Arkansas	1,095,475	831,184	500,252	33,234	139,192	101,683	56,823	264,291	21,807	216
California	34,752,544	23,991,633	3,254,802	6,065,448	10,722,009	180,206	3,769,168	10,760,911	388,393	28,807
Colorado	4,526,295	2,613,418	613,741	95,017	1,600,762	25,822	278,076	1,912,877	126,081	45,931
Connecticut	6,216,077	5,639,908	778,128	3,305,788	1,233,008	8,084	314,900	576,169	13,059	1,424
Delaware	207,209	132,721	50,321	4,470	43,666	11,299	22,965	74,488	1,213	1,427
Florida	9,757,199	6,826,049	1,694,935	1,441,312	3,022,354	214,256	453,192	2,931,150	15,879	9,407
Georgia	7,364,380	5,736,058	724,409	254,889	4,490,198	66,608	199,954	1,628,322	66,092	4,140
Hawaii	1,621,225	1,420,392	337,167	760,966	158,037	6,455	157,767	200,833	24,051	11,330
Idaho	1,356,547	157,480	60,271	11,967	58,452	10,724	16,066	1,199,067	179,142	50
Illinois	4,664,409	1,955,362	616,454	293,349	443,810	116,512	485,237	2,709,047	139,288	4,035
Indiana	2,801,574	1,843,908	758,283	295,048	217,867	30,187	542,523	957,666	17,470	163,608
Iowa	955,348	526,081	114,149	143,405	222,995	21,716	23,816	429,267	36,033	838
Kansas	1,653,500	1,107,945	411,173	31,071	580,354	26,695	58,652	545,555	83,311	745
Kentucky	3,978,175	2,135,282	365,437	79,521	108,583	72,143	1,509,598	1,842,893	19,976	541
Louisiana	2,772,520	1,655,246	181,902	646,120	45,776	262,213	519,235	1,117,274	211,847	6,484
Maine	1,239,792	1,101,138	100,391	894,167	12,868	11,032	82,680	138,654	9,320	1,467
Maryland	13,487,562	6,296,170	1,724,196	2,347,210	885,349	78,570	1,260,845	7,191,392	74,878	403,488
Massachusetts	6,793,117	4,848,119	1,390,715	1,679,982	1,264,929	82,598	429,895	1,944,998	8,157	24,600
Michigan	3,539,084	2,206,517	1,627,328	146,125	140,681	25,675	266,708	1,332,567	55,380	3,142
Minnesota	2,227,918	1,451,852	716,524	405,839	125,395	41,304	162,790	776,066	155,217	13,048
Mississippi	2,734,042	2,218,382	133,994	1,684,640	206,673	115,745	77,330	515,660	35,946	16,223
Missouri	7,312,608	5,477,168	538,046	2,883,297	1,714,893	138,723	202,209	1,835,440	200,612	8,026
Montana	350,112	127,106	21,274	1,652	76,996	11,457	15,727	223,006	48,412	392
Nebraska	590,898	298,439	46,893	70,700	150,045	18,634	12,167	292,459	82,136	1,039
Nevada	1,249,629	349,087	67,913	63,073	184,074	21,124	12,903	900,542	7,349	8,652
New Hampshire	788,132	597,346	120,709	207,783	192,284	13,445	63,125	190,786	907	1,365
New Jersey	4,840,076	3,369,738	1,107,106	1,294,994	244,437	204,005	519,196	1,470,338	9,849	6,523
New Mexico	5,393,231	781,393	338,307	27,761	310,682	32,087	72,556	4,611,838	27,167	1,379
New York	7,417,433	4,195,320	978,546	1,900,669	672,833	144,295	498,972	3,222,113	51,647	9,291
North Carolina	2,922,543	1,493,000	527,264	418,205	160,410	110,598	276,523	1,429,543	41,178	11,180
North Dakota	328,795	223,383	42,805	633	126,749	25,058	28,138	105,412	20,451	153
Ohio	5,243,370	3,365,226	563,355	327,239	1,708,075	45,841	720,716	1,878,144	15,864	4,108
Oklahoma	2,515,222	1,483,878	459,752	128,877	732,759	27,935	134,555	1,031,344	14,331	1,646
Oregon	994,352	395,161	199,658	56,073	17,375	92,755	29,300	599,191	139,651	11,722
Pennsylvania	7,414,531	4,513,490	2,107,067	968,778	313,603	100,281	1,023,761	2,901,041	78,740	73,966
Rhode Island	494,732	356,397	36,094	290,700	1,707	3,339	24,557	138,335	80	7,528
South Carolina	3,104,699	1,162,474	264,026	479,851	195,932	33,323	189,342	1,942,225	13,293	3,700
South Dakota	377,663	183,889	55,964	2,778	41,507	8,812	74,828	193,774	30,787	377
Tennessee	5,912,225	1,268,521	274,182	87,529	670,827	53,005	183,248	4,643,704	74,382	1,115
Texas	20,581,288	13,129,477	3,836,894	2,298,889	4,898,478	180,081	1,915,135	7,451,811	285,915	42,243
Utah	2,084,046	1,297,489	139,662	118,821	919,509	7,751	111,746	786,557	26,378	-140
Vermont	430,849	329,082	249,652	28,396	4,939	2,953	43,142	101,767	241	1,213
Virginia	26,170,059	17,506,203	3,559,728	7,494,984	2,056,092	86,679	4,308,540	8,663,856	65,743	423,636
Washington	5,586,182	2,377,174	573,953	614,278	786,736	80,388	321,819	3,209,008	144,245	28,930
West Virginia	601,918	143,519	14,146	31,696	7,842	63,673	26,162	458,399	26,406	13,788
Wisconsin	1,888,303	1,055,384	391,006	412,413	46,969	22,728	182,268	832,919	92,959	1,569
Wyoming	319,320	78,764	15,773	4	32,884	657	29,446	240,556	8,340	0
Dist. of Columbia	10,874,704	1,906,239	458,339	854,973	98,946	101,108	392,873	8,628,893	94,002	48,733
American Samoa	13,253	424	244	0	84	22	74	12,829	12,363	0
Fed. States of Micronesia	1,150	0	0	0	0	0	0	1,150	6	889
Guam	308,324	282,624	405	211,957	51,497	0	18,765	25,700	36	49
Marshall Islands	143,516	143,142	143,142	0	0	0	0	374	0	316
No. Mariana Islands	8,736	5,657	5,262	225	0	0	170	3,079	0	0
Palau	1,076	583	0	0	0	583	0	493	0	309
Puerto Rico	364,652	221,201	34,053	53,320	3,051	15,724	115,053	143,451	6,575	444
Virgin Islands	28,771	10,830	138	0	0	25	10,667	17,941	46	0
Undistributed	15,843,583	10,696,091	165,039	7,126	2,513	0	10,521,413	5,147,492	224,401	94,797

Source: U.S. Department of Commerce, Bureau of the Census, February 2004.

FEDERAL GOVERNMENT EXPENDITURE FOR PROCUREMENT CONTRACTS, BY AGENCY, BY STATE AND OUTLYING AREA: FISCAL YEAR 2002 — Continued

State and outlying area	Department of Education	Department of Energy	Environmental Protection Agency	Federal Emergency Management Agency	General Services Administration	Department of Health and Human Services	Department of Housing and Urban Development	Department of Interior	Department of Justice	Department of Labor
					Nondefense agencies					
United States	$941,197	$19,009,807	$1,163,719	$311,414	$13,193,202	$5,866,369	$928,215	$2,418,385	$4,585,979	$1,617,941
Alabama	379	1,079	1,539	189	150,081	41,989	5,184	5,688	27,779	17,983
Alaska	208	59	1,276	0	42,854	30,676	-21	69,854	7,788	10,477
Arizona	1,338	5,662	537	185	62,977	51,725	457	89,231	144,101	24,109
Arkansas	11	2,056	0	0	22,050	38,297	-3,463	4,610	9,866	6,196
California	46,082	2,348,812	23,740	2,766	1,006,293	498,624	66,028	407,537	221,842	107,209
Colorado	401	471,175	34,446	44	397,569	21,701	37,995	173,173	9,727	8,190
Connecticut	56,367	5,602	1,872	2	21,924	16,490	10,995	6,371	6,211	8,126
Delaware	130	39	10,566	0	9,947	2,322	1	792	1,536	455
Florida	7,042	10,597	2,066	2,063	367,246	48,836	7,665	39,342	143,931	71,998
Georgia	33,166	10,842	23,332	194	338,043	360,133	43,770	15,190	23,289	46,441
Hawaii	4,414	37	0	548	45,671	6,309	359	12,415	1,505	10,765
Idaho	94	796,054	118	189	24,623	4,103	456	44,511	4,946	10,677
Illinois	11,035	839,082	14,043	102	331,162	48,272	44,006	19,146	110,763	29,442
Indiana	718	4,489	5,629	0	46,792	63,348	16,851	8,673	120,129	15,613
Iowa	57,882	30,557	0	0	17,809	30,571	97	981	47	9,334
Kansas	93	827	22,271	0	38,257	6,905	617	4,136	7,328	6,867
Kentucky	139	89,151	11,727	1,044	86,702	8,828	2,930	11,511	24,772	18,834
Louisiana	139	157,817	215	0	62,684	10,600	-15,897	29,435	11,089	28,720
Maine	98		200	0	16,215	3,306	223	7,183	471	12,135
Maryland	215,065	146,237	69,906	62,941	741,284	2,022,023	67,059	116,091	412,403	86,023
Massachusetts	8,612	2,708	88,515	386	148,261	90,870	7,354	28,688	31,022	47,075
Michigan	109	183	28,575	800	471,395	49,956	-240	6,984	46,808	31,556
Minnesota	8,162	1,495	2,100	19	39,373	41,114	-1,225	5,045	13,197	4,852
Mississippi	89	168	-47	0	26,476	8,821	223	11,882	5,693	27,986
Missouri	3,317	488,925	12,752	23	200,375	72,737	-7,920	8,157	15,423	33,129
Montana	85	18,377	200	0	14,160	19,974	-233	34,083	10,723	5,112
Nebraska	391	2,270	0	0	21,353	26,044	1,968	4,661	586	573
Nevada	115	683,159	1,719	0	14,794	5,499	170	36,999	657	15,095
New Hampshire	153	599	402	0	21,665	6,386	0	3,144	6,078	
New Jersey	4,892	88,838	36,751	697	162,876	42,292	383	14,443	62,106	23,961
New Mexico	11	4,051,305	1,029	2,393	54,508	43,624	72	36,023	145,767	25,182
New York	121,273	721,126	41,431	1,926	331,914	125,255	96,607	26,231	85,662	52,682
North Carolina	27,804	101,363	97,946	7,527	129,895	223,690	12,492	10,564	29,619	30,444
North Dakota	15	3,739	451	0	17,083	5,092	170	4,686	4,206	4,919
Ohio	4,188	434,248	68,395	287	188,266	63,165	12,239	11,944	32,987	32,459
Oklahoma	0	4,939	2,989	1,008	447,570	10,044	3,462	8,958	105,546	23,468
Oregon	334	4,817	1,261	0	79,297	9,349	10	84,470	7,731	19,019
Pennsylvania	9,450	476,428	74,307	239	264,344	107,341	86,315	41,784	55,030	74,037
Rhode Island	225	1,240	1,708	0	10,983	8,313	2,106	2,307	817	15,047
South Carolina	1,503	1,515,181	468	0	32,219	15,514	1,584	4,445	106,951	9,630
South Dakota	8,512	3,949	100	0	8,800	26,228	26	51,820	4,887	2,073
Tennessee	110	2,189,265	-1,895	146	66,717	44,650	8,836	7,463	47,157	28,880
Texas	31,895	373,427	9,994	4,827	527,478	98,831	8,558	31,788	231,172	114,502
Utah	259	35,111	265	22	55,384	20,024	70	52,899	2,309	31,692
Vermont	110	0	1,252	0	29,069	1,900	1,722	2,568	695	8,803
Virginia	21,787	525,696	214,937	118,582	2,223,048	389,691	39,396	386,178	635,377	147,691
Washington	6,954	2,228,722	12,671	3,163	164,009	50,358	-2,171	62,787	9,953	10,384
West Virginia	565	60,114	68	15	63,352	7,155	30	10,832	24,344	25,724
Wisconsin	95	1,188	19,455	0	51,102	35,176	-674	15,389	132,662	1,920
Wyoming	129	2,477	0	0	3,127	3,597	0	33,152	-1	0
Dist. of Columbia	236,378	42,922	68,973	95,823	2,668,226	358,969	360,858	96,895	871,990	190,720
American Samoa	79	0	0	0	172	0	0	0	0	0
Fed. States of Micronesia	0	0	0	0	0	0	0	0	0	0
Guam	8	0	12	33	5,744	14	0	51	160	0
Marshall Islands	0	0	0	0	0	0	0	0	0	0
No. Mariana Islands	78	0	0	0	660	0	0	976	0	0
Palau	0	0	0	0	0	0	0	0	0	0
Puerto Rico	10	0	0	75	24,511	944	78	346	6,263	19,014
Virgin Islands	85	0	0	0	2,903	0	0	5,200	76	0
Undistributed	8,614	25,654	153,452	3,156	791,910	538,694	10,637	208,673	562,803	30,718

See footnotes at end of table.

FEDERAL GOVERNMENT EXPENDITURE FOR PROCUREMENT CONTRACTS, BY AGENCY, BY STATE AND OUTLYING AREA: FISCAL YEAR 2002 — Continued

State and outlying area	NASA	National Archives and Records Admin.	National Science Foundation	Postal Service	Small Bus. Admin.	Social Security Admin.	Dept. of State	Dept. of Transportation	Dept. of the Treasury	Dept. of Veterans Affairs	Other nondefense
United States	11,611,111	99,864	102,545	13,866,014	44,109	634,865	1,701,876	7,216,950	3,447,280	5,963,262	5,434,021
Alabama	550,363	0	0	167,571	0	4,805	10,790	14,726	3,486	60,352	313,975
Alaska	13,856	2,875	0	36,483	0	862	53,531	102,750	53	2,431	229
Arizona	53,417	0	0	218,000	0	634	2,201	94,023	873	50,789	2,070
Arkansas	-2	0	0	109,071	0	71	0	5,926	1,048	46,400	131
California	2,739,080	7,786	1,464	1,470,581	120	28,305	47,061	664,480	266,067	368,311	21,523
Colorado	143,928	0	6,000	258,163	0	1,364	10,921	55,243	12,554	39,526	58,744
Connecticut	112,390	0	150	192,525	0	447	1,123	40,454	5,520	72,238	2,879
Delaware	1,609	0	0	37,478	0	24	95	514	549	5,334	457
Florida	787,242	0	218	737,012	515	917	154,152	255,550	23,754	210,456	35,262
Georgia	9,718	2,190	0	366,334	122	2,909	1,049	76,956	108,821	60,517	35,074
Hawaii	5,802	0	0	46,623	0	165	112	23,338	151	7,100	138
Idaho	232	0	0	48,234	0	65	237	39,308	8,465	37,268	296
Illinois	4,952	110	2,938	714,664	1,594	3,321	15,634	50,383	36,612	226,936	61,527
Indiana	40,559	0	0	264,055	0	322	239	18,976	9,279	153,644	7,273
Iowa	1,114	387	0	157,589	1,000	259	56	23,162	25,868	32,995	2,688
Kansas	5,607	1,692	0	154,273	0	138	177	46,909	1,654	163,079	669
Kentucky	719	0	0	170,477	0	1,084	1,935	8,661	3,429	188,320	1,192,113
Louisiana	327,856	0	0	177,205	0	283	293	60,546	773	36,535	10,650
Maine	43	0	0	73,930	0	26	66	6,064	185	7,388	333
Maryland	1,182,337	33,984	7,370	289,546	5,150	354,185	115,756	339,285	237,947	135,095	73,339
Massachusetts	125,744	6,530	1,375	411,568	453	1,853	11,738	489,811	164,632	238,245	6,802
Michigan	6,975	6,494	0	493,758	753	7,162	1,935	21,824	51,379	44,439	3,200
Minnesota	6,506	0	29	280,591	0	779	869	64,714	972	114,450	24,759
Mississippi	145,068	0	0	94,636	0	264	31	38,937	70,372	25,946	6,946
Missouri	11,506	3,700	228	331,936	0	26,558	310	195,463	5,187	223,500	1,496
Montana	1,955	0	0	44,980	0	657	3,950	14,879	253	4,796	250
Nebraska	0	0	0	95,915	0	112	153	5,266	276	39,098	10,618
Nevada	753	0	0	83,233	0	61	0	22,135	158	19,746	248
New Hampshire	8,878	0	0	79,411	100	3,619	29,202	12,136	12,368	3,927	446
New Jersey	50,828	0	344	539,654	0	2,856	2,461	313,662	24,398	56,341	26,183
New Mexico	62,532	0	0	72,272	0	305	604	31,154	14,922	40,084	1,506
New York	23,670	15,875	0	1,082,483	609	15,740	24,081	159,632	61,298	154,759	18,920
North Carolina	19,957	0	4,833	349,704	83	963	-31,442	55,106	2,631	62,391	241,615
North Dakota	0	0	0	36,720	0	1,406	0	1,735	1,840	2,531	215
Ohio	163,720	1,042	0	557,501	425	2,638	3,028	154,033	12,606	101,922	13,079
Oklahoma	1,053	0	0	144,686	0	1,369	1,275	222,916	1,180	29,513	5,391
Oregon	6,065	0	0	147,797	0		4,220	42,832	1,597	37,988	1,031
Pennsylvania	33,690	1,332		674,469	372	17,573	1,332	87,149	49,845	406,349	286,949
Rhode Island	868	0	0	63,080	0	175	0	2,900	8,789	11,976	193
South Carolina	174	0	0	139,079	0	174	8,787	36,450	3,608	29,276	20,188
South Dakota	0	0	0	39,310	0	490	307	1,768	310	12,138	1,892
Tennessee	19,408	0	1,000	257,311	0	437	1,715	49,752	33,660	95,018	1,718,578
Texas	3,788,236	3,036	93	878,413	347	3,458	35,516	604,446	60,409	271,852	45,375
Utah	411,506	0	0	91,603	0	94	1,349	11,003	34,014	28,728	-16,013
Vermont	1,584	0	0	38,663	0	16	0	3,149	2,085	8,037	660
Virginia	494,168	6,560	22,988	357,316	742	53,414	399,389	981,806	556,592	327,940	271,079
Washington	17,014	570	0	264,718	50	1,199	4,415	137,881	4,699	52,201	6,257
West Virginia	18,913	0	0	88,713	0	138	652	4,840	80,681	21,103	10,966
Wisconsin	10,640	0	263	248,324	0	212	426	120,539	5,598	88,966	7,110
Wyoming	284	0	0	23,138	0	16	0	12,625	5,450	7,514	140,708
Dist. of Columbia	62,519	3,783	49,047	99,374	27,865	17,652	379,533	1,211,130	1,284,895	164,770	487,697
American Samoa	0	0	0	0	0	0	0	0	0	215	0
Fed. States of Micronesia	0	0	0	0	0	0	50	205	0	0	0
Guam	0	0	0	2,180	0	0	9	72	17,332	0	0
Marshall Islands	0	0	0	0	0	0	0	58	0	0	0
No. Mariana Islands	0	0	0	174	0	0	0	22	0	0	1,169
Palau	0	0	0	0	0	0	0	109	0	75	0
Puerto Rico	0	0	0	58,879	0	305	38	8,359	4,808	12,451	351
Virgin Islands	0	0	0	4,612	0	0	0	4,682	26	312	0
Undistributed	136,075	1,918	4,205	0	3,809	72,975	400,452	147,257	138,554	1,319,951	268,787

Source: U.S. Department of Commerce, Bureau of the Census, February 2004.

Table 2.8
FEDERAL GOVERNMENT EXPENDITURE FOR SALARIES AND WAGES, BY AGENCY, BY STATE AND OUTLYING AREA: FISCAL YEAR 2002
(In thousands of dollars)

State and outlying area	Total	Nondefense civilian	Department of Defense						Army	
						Military services				
			Total	Other defense civilian	Total	Active military	Inactive military	Civilian	Total	Active military
United States	199,065,805	122,965,428	76,100,377	4,633,236	71,467,141	41,216,342	7,672,851	22,577,948	24,913,663	13,438,775
Alabama	3,109,441	1,648,026	1,461,415	51,023	1,410,392	455,373	228,951	726,068	984,598	219,065
Alaska	1,498,530	648,799	849,731	8,795	840,936	636,055	45,440	159,441	320,529	232,050
Arizona	3,141,895	1,989,531	1,152,364	37,691	1,114,673	750,741	86,440	277,492	326,256	181,090
Arkansas	1,250,885	847,092	403,793	2,576	401,217	173,847	122,554	104,816	167,734	8,785
California	19,143,365	10,900,809	8,242,556	325,614	7,916,942	5,064,724	461,672	2,390,546	768,894	277,620
Colorado	4,137,514	2,471,819	1,665,695	112,884	1,552,811	1,119,988	127,966	304,857	646,592	523,285
Connecticut	1,456,289	1,066,464	389,825	33,936	355,889	222,554	66,379	66,956	56,307	770
Delaware	465,419	216,430	248,989	1,878	247,111	129,759	62,392	54,960	21,414	280
Florida	9,037,620	5,261,181	3,776,439	102,286	3,674,153	2,333,505	286,164	1,054,484	348,459	108,430
Georgia	7,366,391	3,523,815	3,842,576	76,009	3,766,567	2,376,954	285,903	1,103,710	2,220,061	1,731,590
Hawaii	2,683,526	420,994	2,262,532	31,630	2,230,902	1,507,585	91,652	631,665	734,747	559,475
Idaho	781,410	551,594	229,816	1,110	228,706	139,018	42,512	47,176	45,211	1,400
Illinois	6,344,410	4,586,375	1,758,035	58,110	1,699,925	1,031,724	217,003	451,198	395,837	24,080
Indiana	2,207,981	1,560,243	647,738	123,003	524,735	44,901	237,558	242,276	234,185	18,340
Iowa	1,084,052	909,115	174,937	2,583	172,354	22,930	101,631	47,793	106,177	9,590
Kansas	1,983,958	1,140,020	843,938	12,910	831,028	561,818	103,786	165,424	632,932	443,275
Kentucky	2,853,967	1,351,140	1,502,827	31,361	1,471,466	1,198,470	121,488	151,508	1,402,119	1,175,230
Louisiana	2,460,842	1,438,533	1,022,309	14,193	1,008,116	583,299	181,751	243,066	529,705	309,400
Maine	848,225	443,459	404,766	9,619	395,147	98,688	50,088	246,371	37,491	8,680
Maryland	9,664,051	6,760,682	2,903,369	86,464	2,816,905	1,190,006	202,838	1,424,061	850,545	249,900
Massachusetts	3,375,723	2,790,234	585,489	58,540	526,949	114,897	173,245	238,807	187,793	8,925
Michigan	3,285,526	2,762,855	522,671	75,829	446,842	54,706	134,373	257,763	305,388	17,115
Minnesota	2,022,020	1,739,479	282,541	12,720	269,821	35,858	157,278	76,685	134,866	10,780
Mississippi	1,839,820	808,613	1,031,207	8,918	1,022,289	517,261	171,836	333,192	228,294	15,715
Missouri	3,637,089	2,527,295	1,109,794	82,369	1,027,425	547,752	252,516	227,157	681,860	343,245
Montana	760,425	565,091	195,334	1,315	194,019	106,260	47,442	40,317	43,322	770
Nebraska	1,108,812	632,469	476,343	10,280	466,063	291,247	56,515	118,301	86,241	2,730
Nevada	1,096,286	682,143	414,143	4,564	409,579	296,570	37,855	75,154	33,467	3,255
New Hampshire	574,088	466,177	107,911	7,607	100,304	33,092	38,324	28,888	34,156	280
New Jersey	3,974,238	2,969,233	1,005,005	38,712	966,293	253,428	140,512	572,353	506,758	28,735
New Mexico	1,802,085	1,099,045	703,040	15,613	687,427	378,453	48,577	260,397	138,841	10,465
New York	8,526,244	7,058,510	1,467,734	65,785	1,401,949	776,377	300,580	324,992	988,054	617,050
North Carolina	5,977,658	2,259,451	3,718,207	57,323	3,660,884	2,982,152	177,611	501,121	1,718,492	1,439,200
North Dakota	655,286	329,336	325,950	2,103	323,847	216,975	51,130	55,742	39,916	665
Ohio	5,108,724	3,409,517	1,699,207	351,498	1,347,709	313,266	267,190	767,253	195,542	20,370
Oklahoma	3,151,984	1,268,343	1,883,641	47,927	1,835,714	847,911	144,421	843,382	658,983	467,775
Oregon	1,691,675	1,441,933	249,742	1,409	248,333	41,108	100,834	106,391	132,029	8,015
Pennsylvania	6,058,218	4,586,506	1,471,712	292,585	1,179,127	138,663	317,064	723,400	475,669	42,490
Rhode Island	785,941	358,432	427,509	3,311	424,198	145,543	46,722	231,933	34,310	3,780
South Carolina	2,635,610	971,953	1,663,657	40,629	1,623,028	1,187,059	133,955	302,014	531,125	363,615
South Dakota	631,461	451,204	180,257	1,308	178,949	100,135	37,978	40,836	39,868	1,435
Tennessee	3,200,111	2,669,560	530,551	26,910	503,641	109,228	189,245	205,168	247,336	12,950
Texas	13,019,462	7,317,677	5,701,785	144,551	5,557,234	3,922,698	457,001	1,177,535	2,900,831	2,137,905
Utah	1,928,950	971,909	957,041	50,748	906,293	184,357	150,105	571,831	176,326	11,200
Vermont	359,364	287,522	71,842	1,927	69,915	6,459	53,577	9,879	32,862	735
Virginia	13,503,992	4,514,780	8,989,212	974,865	8,014,347	5,245,614	193,735	2,574,998	1,782,642	872,060
Washington	5,277,826	2,419,098	2,858,728	36,078	2,822,650	1,745,807	176,810	900,033	933,027	684,425
West Virginia	1,220,745	1,043,648	177,097	871	176,226	26,090	94,184	55,952	104,566	7,070
Wisconsin	1,713,273	1,445,778	267,495	4,626	262,869	32,611	146,046	84,212	145,487	10,325
Wyoming	464,974	284,779	180,195	991	179,204	109,010	36,315	33,879	20,798	140
District Of Columbia ...	13,820,584	12,374,488	1,446,096	10,723	1,435,373	542,064	65,762	827,547	371,571	183,365
American Samoa	5,845	3,842	2,003	0	2,003	0	1,966	37	2,003	0
Micronesia	0	0	0	0	0	0	0	0	0	0
Guam	278,619	28,724	249,895	4,683	245,212	171,850	21,598	51,764	15,022	1,190
Marshall Islands	0	0	0	0	0	0	0	0	0	0
No. Mariana Islands	3,055	3,044	11	0	11	0	0	11	11	0
Palau	0	0	0	0	0	0	0	0	0	0
Puerto Rico	930,078	637,739	292,339	9,081	283,258	98,678	121,366	63,214	149,858	28,630
Virgin Islands	49,642	41,461	8,181	0	8,181	1,224	5,015	1,942	6,556	35
Undistributed	3,070,601	2,007,439	1,063,162	1,063,162	0	0	0	0	0	0

Source: U.S. Department of Commerce, Bureau of the Census, February 2004.

FEDERAL GOVERNMENT EXPENDITURE FOR SALARIES AND WAGES, BY AGENCY, BY STATE AND OUTLYING AREA: FISCAL YEAR 2002 — Continued

	Department of Defense									
	Military services									
	Army		Navy				Air Force			
State and outlying area	Inactive military	Civilian	Total	Active military	Inactive military	Civilian	Total	Active military	Inactive military	Civilian
United States	4,568,601	6,906,287	25,270,976	16,071,822	612,962	8,586,192	21,282,502	11,705,745	2,491,288	7,085,469
Alabama	159,782	605,751	34,196	24,050	8,551	1,595	391,598	212,258	60,618	118,722
Alaska	15,163	73,316	5,812	4,084	923	805	514,595	399,921	29,354	85,320
Arizona	26,350	118,816	159,174	132,320	7,986	18,868	629,243	437,331	52,104	139,808
Arkansas	83,181	75,768	3,293	911	2,086	296	230,190	164,151	37,287	28,752
California	273,170	218,104	5,798,733	4,046,277	81,571	1,670,885	1,349,315	740,827	106,931	501,557
Colorado	49,234	74,073	49,100	36,935	10,403	1,762	857,119	559,768	68,329	229,022
Connecticut	44,350	11,187	267,027	215,633	4,968	46,426	32,555	6,151	17,061	9,343
Delaware	14,530	6,604	1,560	267	1,293	224,137	129,212	46,569	48,356	
Florida	146,254	93,775	1,864,682	1,281,103	43,272	540,307	1,461,012	943,972	96,638	420,402
Georgia	167,028	321,443	445,923	263,853	24,075	157,995	1,100,583	381,511	94,800	624,272
Hawaii	46,345	128,927	1,148,389	733,153	4,202	411,034	347,766	214,957	41,105	91,704
Idaho	27,063	16,748	7,603	2,569	1,956	3,078	175,892	135,049	13,493	27,350
Illinois	144,239	227,518	833,442	743,498	22,257	67,687	470,646	264,146	50,507	155,993
Indiana	170,916	44,929	173,299	13,086	7,210	153,003	117,251	13,475	59,432	44,344
Iowa	70,516	26,071	9,356	5,440	3,793	123	56,821	7,900	27,322	21,599
Kansas	71,875	117,782	7,100	5,217	1,760	123	190,996	113,326	30,151	47,519
Kentucky	89,782	137,107	24,705	9,842	4,468	10,395	44,642	13,398	27,238	4,006
Louisiana	102,095	118,210	149,324	74,639	18,927	55,758	329,087	199,260	60,729	69,098
Maine	20,666	8,145	318,474	81,725	8,538	228,211	39,182	8,283	20,884	10,015
Maryland	137,362	463,283	1,421,467	559,100	5,265	857,102	544,893	381,006	60,211	103,676
Massachusetts	98,362	80,506	41,954	23,422	4,068	14,464	297,202	82,550	70,815	143,837
Michigan	87,572	200,701	27,954	18,504	8,555	895	113,500	19,087	38,246	56,167
Minnesota	82,415	41,671	22,202	11,560	9,743	899	112,753	13,518	65,120	34,115
Mississippi	101,127	111,452	352,597	234,325	4,712	113,560	441,398	267,221	65,997	108,180
Missouri	175,425	163,190	108,348	70,897	28,298	9,153	237,217	133,610	48,793	54,814
Montana	29,895	12,657	1,714	701	1,013	0	148,992	104,789	16,534	27,660
Nebraska	35,820	47,691	26,555	23,040	2,968	547	353,267	265,477	17,727	70,063
Nevada	21,094	9,118	49,864	35,102	2,645	12,117	326,248	258,213	14,116	53,919
New Hampshire	17,219	16,657	28,476	24,220	1,842	2,414	37,672	8,592	19,263	9,817
New Jersey	75,326	402,697	171,507	55,557	3,824	112,126	288,028	169,136	61,362	57,530
New Mexico	29,039	99,337	13,987	8,987	3,120	1,880	534,599	359,001	16,418	159,180
New York	168,501	202,503	128,296	97,499	24,340	6,457	285,599	61,828	107,739	116,032
North Carolina	117,730	161,562	1,519,316	1,215,931	13,343	290,042	423,076	327,021	46,538	49,517
North Dakota	27,562	11,689	1,133	297	789	47	282,798	216,013	22,779	44,006
Ohio	135,076	40,096	41,483	20,843	17,231	3,409	1,110,684	272,053	114,883	723,748
Oklahoma	73,873	117,335	71,598	61,702	5,941	3,955	1,105,133	318,434	64,607	722,092
Oregon	53,579	70,435	22,126	14,417	7,006	703	94,178	18,676	40,249	35,253
Pennsylvania	199,368	233,811	515,518	68,210	26,832	420,476	187,940	27,963	90,864	69,113
Rhode Island	23,922	6,608	353,618	132,440	5,617	215,561	36,270	9,323	17,183	9,764
South Carolina	98,653	68,857	704,567	529,555	8,429	166,583	387,336	293,889	26,873	66,574
South Dakota	25,377	13,056	906	197	679	30	138,175	98,503	11,922	27,750
Tennessee	109,990	124,396	126,485	71,132	11,891	43,462	129,820	25,146	67,364	37,310
Texas	277,790	485,136	440,866	340,312	40,961	59,593	2,215,537	1,444,481	138,250	632,806
Utah	102,122	63,004	11,205	6,733	3,353	1,119	718,762	166,424	44,630	507,708
Vermont	24,549	7,578	1,361	1,063	239	59	35,692	4,661	28,789	2,242
Virginia	128,893	781,689	5,175,408	3,596,146	35,866	1,543,396	1,056,297	777,408	28,976	249,913
Washington	86,229	162,373	1,481,952	802,435	22,209	657,308	407,671	258,947	68,372	80,352
West Virginia	61,874	35,622	15,568	10,990	2,152	2,426	56,092	8,030	30,158	17,904
Wisconsin	82,426	52,736	14,243	6,747	7,132	364	103,139	15,539	56,488	31,112
Wyoming	15,166	5,492	515	7	508	0	157,891	108,863	20,641	28,387
District Of Columbia	23,241	164,965	849,221	188,909	41,650	618,662	214,581	169,790	871	43,920
American Samoa	1,966	37	0	0	0	0	0	0	0	0
Micronesia	0	0	0	0	0	0	0	0	0	0
Guam	13,561	271	135,758	104,045	0	31,713	94,432	66,615	8,037	19,780
Marshall Islands	0	0	0	0	0	0	0	0	0	0
No. Mariana Islands	0	11	0	0	0	0	0	0	0	0
Palau	0	0	0	0	0	0	0	0	0	0
Puerto Rico	99,379	21,849	91,954	62,133	2,502	27,319	41,446	7,915	19,485	14,046
Virgin Islands	4,579	1,942	62	62	0	0	1,563	1,127	436	0
Undistributed	0	0	0	0	0	0	0	0	0	0

See footnotes at end of table.

FEDERAL GOVERNMENT EXPENDITURE FOR SALARIES AND WAGES, BY AGENCY, BY STATE AND OUTLYING AREA: FISCAL YEAR 2002 — Continued

					Nondefense agencies					
State and outlying area	*Total*	*Department of Agriculture*	*Department of Commerce*	*Department of Education*	*Department of Energy*	*Environmental Protection Agency*	*Federal Deposit Insurance Corporation*	*Federal Emergency Management Agency*	*General Services Administration*	*Department of Health and Human Services*
United States	122,965,428	4,942,637	2,331,403	341,304	1,299,865	1,339,697	537,273	309,109	917,579	4,295,975
Alabama	1,648,026	62,871	5,071	75	0	2,583	2,534	1,685	3,519	3,577
Alaska	648,799	48,143	28,072	0	0	2,080	0	575	3,135	36,992
Arizona	1,989,531	90,543	9,428	0	15,541	321	1,661	861	3,944	189,290
Arkansas	847,092	100,805	2,753	0	1,979	0	1,947	1,185	1,424	23,865
California	10,900,809	407,198	56,851	13,613	43,441	66,326	32,291	15,759	70,262	82,972
Colorado	2,471,819	167,881	86,323	5,052	61,014	52,868	2,877	10,619	23,936	33,630
Connecticut	1,066,464	9,320	3,488	0	0	494	2,030	693	1,018	1,787
Delaware	216,430	11,529	461	0	0	0	916	205	198	688
Florida	5,261,181	97,927	46,835	341	0	6,512	5,337	7,187	7,041	17,121
Georgia	3,523,815	140,368	13,004	14,150	6,250	79,823	17,748	15,511	46,650	446,129
Hawaii	420,994	25,829	14,177	0	302	355	108	1,439	3,575	1,654
Idaho	551,594	133,935	6,678	0	33,326	1,870	0	661	1,332	2,514
Illinois	4,586,375	88,471	13,572	13,160	28,233	91,065	25,354	7,363	48,777	53,055
Indiana	1,560,243	42,800	56,492	99	0	152	2,879	306	3,101	2,568
Iowa	909,115	100,997	4,029	63	881	292	5,085	922	1,318	1,164
Kansas	1,140,020	58,113	9,372	0	0	38,776	6,060	891	1,789	10,672
Kentucky	1,351,140	57,835	6,060	0	1,010	221	3,798	916	1,283	1,048
Louisiana	1,438,533	151,100	8,754	0	6,845	535	3,951	1,072	3,020	12,095
Maine	443,459	13,850	4,369	0	0	0	0	1,257	407	1,021
Maryland	6,760,682	206,632	730,283	0	136,011	7,127	2,295	26,161	14,925	2,258,923
Massachusetts	2,790,234	22,727	31,579	6,883	1,251	55,976	19,479	10,596	19,048	42,894
Michigan	2,762,855	64,453	16,512	0	0	24,381	2,989	966	6,805	8,641
Minnesota	1,739,479	97,628	7,221	311	62	6,035	4,550	1,147	3,225	22,432
Mississippi	808,613	99,158	12,442	0	0	2,184	2,249	817	815	1,176
Missouri	2,527,295	223,870	29,135	7,331	8,199	678	16,621	7,111	56,632	31,309
Montana	565,091	148,600	6,479	0	9,442	2,414	1,183	990	1,206	47,892
Nebraska	632,469	77,062	4,838	0	1,212	83	3,152	632	1,222	4,633
Nevada	682,143	19,590	6,530	0	31,742	11,365	0	418	1,826	4,350
New Hampshire	466,177	17,434	1,731	0	0	0	2,423	646	1,227	680
New Jersey	2,969,233	29,651	15,033	0	1,412	16,300	4,504	1,220	13,146	10,359
New Mexico	1,099,045	76,621	4,122	0	72,175	144	1,352	3,237	2,394	130,470
New York	7,058,510	63,958	25,860	6,575	17,195	53,839	19,213	10,881	46,451	65,494
North Carolina	2,259,451	98,404	27,986	0	0	88,890	3,213	2,147	3,622	67,007
North Dakota	329,336	43,043	3,521	0	3,850	0	2,580	920	849	20,886
Ohio	3,409,517	49,617	9,214	2,123	14,408	40,219	2,579	879	8,188	40,069
Oklahoma	1,268,343	51,224	18,147	0	8,917	4,004	4,024	800	2,625	66,047
Oregon	1,441,933	227,403	18,306	0	101,648	8,670	1,523	1,931	2,974	11,400
Pennsylvania	4,586,506	86,829	14,322	7,759	29,996	63,978	5,568	9,241	42,954	62,117
Rhode Island	358,432	2,113	2,766	0	0	5,458	0	333	722	1,709
South Carolina	971,953	48,749	15,943	0	39,205	75	1,766	869	1,607	1,756
South Dakota	451,204	46,005	5,118	0	11,877	54	1,963	755	875	56,577
Tennessee	2,669,560	61,911	7,516	235	51,873	390	13,546	905	2,769	7,282
Texas	7,317,677	199,562	35,121	9,123	13,308	62,969	74,408	33,541	68,272	49,990
Utah	971,909	89,551	7,456	0	1,504	77	3,070	366	1,851	2,759
Vermont	287,522	14,702	1,950	0	0	0	0	591	366	222
Virginia	4,514,780	126,540	546,969	0	5,619	102,451	933	40,566	105,397	2,369
Washington	2,419,090	115,824	76,213	4,991	165,814	39,744	3,616	13,686	30,035	46,312
West Virginia	1,043,648	39,223	2,777	0	21,970	2,056	1,046	1,343	2,143	28,195
Wisconsin	1,445,778	87,095	6,843	0	54	136	5,649	731	1,767	3,617
Wyoming	284,779	40,629	3,344	0	4,203	0	0	111	1,008	4,079
District Of Columbia	12,374,488	520,750	255,223	249,078	348,096	392,262	216,516	58,812	242,756	264,598
American Samoa	3,842	350	933	0	0	0	0	13	0	0
Micronesia	0	0	0	0	0	0	0	0	0	0
Guam	28,724	2,824	1,597	0	0	0	0	98	0	0
Marshall Islands	0	0	0	0	0	0	0	0	0	0
No. Mariana Islands	3,044	386	0	0	0	79	0	0	0	0
Palau	0	0	0	0	0	0	0	0	0	0
Puerto Rico	637,613	31,613	2,584	342	0	3,310	687	5,969	2,016	7,889
Virgin Islands	41,461	1,391	0	0	0	76	0	573	132	0
Undistributed	2,007,439	0	0	0	0	0	0	0	0	0

See footnotes at end of table.

FEDERAL GOVERNMENT EXPENDITURE FOR SALARIES AND WAGES, BY AGENCY, BY STATE AND OUTLYING AREA: FISCAL YEAR 2002 — Continued

State and outlying area	Department of Housing and Urban Development	Department of the Interior	Department of Justice	Department of Labor	National Aeronautics and Space Administration	National Archives and Records Administration	National Science Foundation	United States Postal Service	Small Business Administration
					Nondefense agencies				
United States	731,978	3,809,541	8,146,909	1,103,172	1,485,261	124,920	98,511	51,557,057	259,159
Alabama	5,854	7,599	59,871	9,264	206,359	29	0	623,068	3,172
Alaska	2,092	122,886	12,566	759	0	267	115	135,654	1,163
Arizona	7,853	220,072	228,498	3,446	259	0	0	810,575	1,749
Arkansas	3,896	15,919	34,541	3,177	0	741	0	405,552	3,089
California	44,233	359,912	856,288	57,571	184,922	5,589	0	5,467,962	31,179
Colorado	25,244	439,084	118,330	26,900	655	1,797	0	959,912	9,106
Connecticut	4,798	2,814	45,408	4,459	75	0	0	715,852	1,840
Delaware	336	2,511	8,160	620	0	0	0	139,353	384
Florida	17,518	72,037	392,129	27,573	139,991	0	0	2,740,382	4,768
Georgia	28,973	57,822	164,012	34,304	0	3,472	0	1,362,116	12,879
Hawaii	1,526	23,470	32,403	1,440	0	0	0	173,355	1,296
Idaho	902	106,420	17,017	2,121	0	0	0	179,345	859
Illinois	33,249	12,885	206,420	51,377	75	1,774	0	2,657,287	5,361
Indiana	5,551	12,969	57,286	6,297	54	0	0	981,816	1,702
Iowa	2,318	6,044	17,656	2,051	0	812	0	585,954	1,927
Kansas	11,226	19,149	54,978	3,507	0	1,434	0	573,622	1,373
Kentucky	4,456	17,188	86,732	26,043	0	0	0	633,873	2,223
Louisiana	7,228	60,185	108,642	6,231	731	0	0	658,890	1,703
Maine	464	8,917	15,807	1,778	0	0	0	274,890	1,254
Maryland	8,404	41,602	251,134	5,155	240,252	50,582	0	1,076,598	2,194
Massachusetts	15,788	62,010	90,018	30,632	243	3,945	0	1,530,304	3,285
Michigan	12,002	20,151	102,759	6,792	0	1,202	0	1,835,906	2,839
Minnesota	6,759	40,244	87,345	4,027	0	0	0	1,043,301	1,816
Mississippi	3,743	23,243	35,851	2,852	21,558	0	0	351,878	1,390
Missouri	7,330	45,805	94,632	26,631	0	24,874	0	1,234,214	5,297
Montana	685	97,931	16,072	1,502	0	0	0	167,248	979
Nebraska	2,661	22,187	35,294	2,254	0	0	0	356,634	1,275
Nevada	2,048	98,848	36,015	1,802	0	0	0	309,478	1,344
New Hampshire	2,680	4,866	10,008	2,644	91	0	0	295,267	1,017
New Jersey	9,088	18,588	211,480	11,383	147	0	0	2,006,560	2,213
New Mexico	2,194	238,853	58,231	2,163	4,319	69	0	268,724	1,328
New York	37,912	48,143	412,927	48,249	2,121	1,697	0	4,024,923	18,177
North Carolina	8,007	29,162	92,303	4,994	0	0	0	1,300,279	2,131
North Dakota	459	40,799	8,330	1,146	0	0	0	136,535	1,252
Ohio	16,933	15,449	84,742	27,595	147,780	2,413	0	2,072,918	3,664
Oklahoma	9,692	51,561	70,347	3,561	0	0	0	537,976	1,484
Oregon	3,728	171,096	48,353	3,034	84	0	0	549,544	1,769
Pennsylvania	27,868	64,100	267,411	65,390	0	2,271	0	2,507,833	5,802
Rhode Island	1,960	3,173	8,929	1,529	0	0	0	234,546	1,107
South Carolina	5,294	10,534	65,981	2,571	0	0	0	517,129	1,639
South Dakota	589	68,503	14,409	674	0	0	0	146,165	987
Tennessee	10,663	31,262	66,536	6,400	0	0	0	956,741	1,642
Texas	40,918	57,917	841,876	49,116	246,807	4,789	0	3,266,143	24,345
Utah	1,884	96,796	27,664	8,272	740	0	0	340,602	1,567
Vermont	281	2,899	59,666	426	0	0	0	143,758	1,075
Virginia	6,845	255,783	606,128	33,720	190,643	0	98,396	1,328,585	2,216
Washington	14,577	127,080	80,766	18,175	0	1,351	0	984,282	3,323
West Virginia	1,764	40,964	168,117	31,029	1,468	0	0	329,856	1,352
Wisconsin	5,134	31,607	39,886	6,739	93	0	0	923,326	1,766
Wyoming	265	84,410	6,623	1,020	0	0	0	86,031	943
District Of Columbia	249,783	277,989	1,397,008	420,223	95,794	15,812	0	369,495	66,802
American Samoa	0	1,109	0	0	0	0	0	0	0
Micronesia	0	0	0	0	0	0	0	0	0
Guam	62	2,080	7,607	34	0	0	0	8,104	804
Marshall Islands	0	0	0	0	0	0	0	0	0
No. Mariana Islands	0	425	1,036	249	0	0	0	646	0
Palau	0	0	0	0	0	0	0	0	0
Puerto Rico	6,261	8,753	60,209	2,271	0	0	0	218,925	2,654
Virgin Islands	0	5,736	8,042	0	0	0	0	17,148	654
Undistributed	0	0	156,449	0	0	0	0	0	0

See footnotes at end of table.

FEDERAL GOVERNMENT EXPENDITURE FOR SALARIES AND WAGES, BY AGENCY, BY STATE AND OUTLYING AREA: FISCAL YEAR 2002 — Continued

State and outlying area	Social Security Administration	Department of State	Department of Transportation			Department of the Treasury	Department of Veterans Affairs	All other nondefense
			Total	U.S. Coast Guard	All other Transportation			
United States	3,522,719	910,454	7,382,674	1,622,058	5,760,616	8,705,639	11,214,458	7,598,134
Alabama	124,789	338	65,668	35,526	30,142	41,064	198,733	220,304
Alaska	2,453	59	217,093	99,368	117,725	12,459	21,465	771
Arizona	28,460	983	51,049	295	50,754	89,040	221,655	14,303
Arkansas	23,670	0	21,693	1,008	20,685	17,644	180,320	2,892
California	331,948	10,725	668,098	176,262	491,836	933,118	1,056,416	104,135
Colorado	36,850	753	130,133	616	129,517	110,333	136,563	31,959
Connecticut	20,711	929	83,793	44,816	38,977	49,539	113,128	4,288
Delaware	3,568	75	3,417	702	2,715	11,169	32,279	561
Florida	122,079	23,242	488,529	199,166	289,363	328,482	691,740	24,410
Georgia	84,003	1,039	251,797	11,657	240,140	412,445	277,143	54,177
Hawaii	5,742	1,141	77,763	37,336	40,427	23,621	28,668	3,130
Idaho	6,181	0	11,428	149	11,279	9,134	37,498	373
Illinois	180,683	3,487	234,436	8,607	225,829	232,591	468,585	129,116
Indiana	41,038	0	105,041	2,073	102,968	77,297	153,182	9,612
Iowa	17,839	0	22,285	2,569	19,716	17,471	118,636	1,370
Kansas	17,949	196	104,710	6,380	98,330	95,143	125,652	5,409
Kentucky	39,601	114	43,378	5,195	38,183	222,713	142,533	60,114
Louisiana	44,196	3,661	90,839	51,385	39,454	68,442	191,334	9,079
Maine	9,761	55	39,224	20,927	18,297	18,733	51,112	561
Maryland	736,885	2,072	128,674	32,321	96,353	418,643	173,500	242,631
Massachusetts	62,969	2,863	222,925	84,163	138,762	237,754	286,381	30,685
Michigan	72,516	324	120,780	44,851	75,929	180,643	268,585	13,609
Minnesota	24,676	45	109,255	5,243	104,012	64,865	204,485	10,050
Mississippi	30,592	0	26,951	10,991	15,960	21,089	153,045	17,581
Missouri	128,253	38	115,061	6,696	108,365	196,645	256,560	11,068
Montana	6,378	114	14,009	317	13,692	12,399	28,662	907
Nebraska	9,835	0	16,168	825	15,343	18,456	73,531	1,340
Nevada	9,111	0	41,159	656	40,503	24,504	80,418	1,594
New Hampshire	7,281	3,620	68,828	4,904	63,924	13,209	31,724	800
New Jersey	57,088	898	248,980	59,645	189,335	137,163	163,952	10,068
New Mexico	38,234	401	66,280	434	65,846	26,279	98,742	2,714
New York	243,323	18,213	320,472	43,651	276,821	700,543	795,903	76,441
North Carolina	53,558	2,865	132,536	57,145	75,391	73,650	255,215	13,481
North Dakota	5,684	0	12,755	0	12,755	12,221	34,189	318
Ohio	78,586	0	165,354	19,664	145,690	191,838	412,247	22,701
Oklahoma	25,673	0	236,131	2,537	233,594	42,945	130,624	2,561
Oregon	23,749	0	66,158	38,318	27,840	39,718	158,232	2,632
Pennsylvania	210,152	3,137	104,615	14,160	90,455	428,203	495,556	81,405
Rhode Island	8,703	453	26,685	14,070	12,615	12,969	44,397	880
South Carolina	31,062	6,320	53,100	26,383	26,717	26,061	138,559	3,734
South Dakota	5,169	0	7,690	0	7,690	6,149	76,983	662
Tennessee	52,279	0	116,301	6,484	109,817	249,724	307,209	724,376
Texas	150,116	14,766	475,316	62,997	412,319	754,340	784,013	60,921
Utah	9,488	452	67,564	169	67,395	230,016	77,430	2,799
Vermont	3,271	0	9,185	947	8,238	12,577	36,246	307
Virginia	115,380	5,675	444,919	168,750	276,169	168,983	240,284	86,380
Washington	73,363	2,625	252,770	59,298	193,472	110,576	239,786	14,188
West Virginia	24,093	0	24,371	3,171	21,200	159,924	159,153	2,804
Wisconsin	35,616	0	39,517	12,350	27,167	45,199	204,319	6,683
Wyoming	2,077	0	7,855	230	7,625	5,274	36,632	275
District Of Columbia	18,773	798,776	870,103	105,425	764,678	1,252,179	391,697	3,601,963
American Samoa	250	0	1,134	177	957	0	53	0
Micronesia	0	0	0	0	0	0	0	0
Guam	549	0	3,495	125	3,370	991	460	19
Marshall Islands	0	0	0	0	0	0	0	0
No. Mariana Islands	220	0	0	0	0	0	0	3
Palau	0	0	0	0	0	0	0	0
Puerto Rico	25,505	0	51,283	28,110	23,173	54,847	128,371	24,250
Virgin Islands	741	0	1,654	547	1,107	4,625	673	17
Undistributed	0	0	2,267	2,267	0	0	0	1,848,723

Source: U.S. Department of Commerce, Bureau of the Census, February 2004.

Table 2.9
FEDERAL GOVERNMENT INSURANCE AND LOAN PROGRAMS, BY STATE AND OUTLYING AREA: FISCAL YEAR 2002
(In thousands of dollars)

State and outlying area	Direct loans by volume of assistance provided					Guaranteed loans by volume of coverage provided				
		Department of Agriculture								
	Total	Commodity loans— price supports	Other agriculture loans	Federal direct student loans	Other direct loans	Total	Mortgage insurance for homes	Federal Family Education Loan program	Veterans housing guaranteed and insured loans VA home loans	
United States	$30,873,646	$10,459,823	$4,146,409	$14,733,873	$1,533,516	$214,285,069	$138,463,669	$28,132,568	$11,664,962	
Alabama	734,982	374,940	55,315	292,601	12,126	1,883,841	1,163,414	338,397	188,309	
Alaska	120,234	0	6,997	7,024	106,213	775,532	445,064	20,033	101,382	
Arizona	359,246	7,340	30,933	307,419	13,554	6,952,936	4,676,952	1,108,555	466,411	
Arkansas	902,125	733,017	121,239	40,132	7,737	9,264,319	7,434,332	231,635	104,672	
California	2,152,143	607,581	202,413	1,289,496	52,652	27,275,702	17,839,965	2,685,029	840,802	
Colorado	477,126	142,511	44,275	262,239	28,101	1,529,664	-316	454,331	416,939	
Connecticut	66,445		11,038	45,514	9,892	2,379,775	1,488,659	342,422	51,358	
Delaware	58,569	3,741	15,075	38,266	1,486	537,375	361,599	42,841	50,817	
Florida	903,743	129,778	101,114	561,920	110,932	11,225,344	7,113,325	1,639,424	924,673	
Georgia	939,627	273,701	86,089	558,762	21,076	9,806,634	6,638,150	651,466	524,969	
Hawaii	21,142	17,412	472	3,257	691,049	175,156	79,167	34,172		
Idaho	242,163	32,268	52,367	155,895	1,634	1,017,572	728,653	35,052	78,927	
Illinois	1,420,134	453,764	97,919	832,433	36,017	9,639,125	6,678,325	1,104,335	277,699	
Indiana	1,084,755	349,544	106,684	614,988	13,538	4,744,357	3,425,788	735,852	205,970	
Iowa	1,671,484	1,076,713	143,703	445,222	5,846	1,289,992	507,977	265,606	59,777	
Kansas	431,705	107,333	87,472	227,950	8,951	1,450,587	832,591	260,995	103,859	
Kentucky	427,169	65,185	180,088	157,199	24,697	2,266,465	1,109,451	300,613	128,241	
Louisiana	395,137	221,562	115,276	52,870	5,429	2,264,561	1,157,111	625,694	121,547	
Maine	80,200	200	50,791	20,984	8,225	562,372	259,240	154,578	43,156	
Maryland	403,451	12,410	46,878	323,889	20,275	8,841,792	6,862,931	350,953	492,116	
Massachusetts	956,242	0	27,100	907,666	21,477	3,474,032	2,084,014	788,067	76,567	
Michigan	1,227,269	179,349	133,605	902,956	11,358	5,861,507	4,337,422	475,679	199,516	
Minnesota	1,328,358	811,250	150,110	319,390	47,608	4,162,646	2,313,367	532,881	152,305	
Mississippi	2,022,561	1,881,262	94,157	31,122	16,020	1,429,850	745,957	299,524	93,039	
Missouri	626,836	197,521	90,204	324,067	15,045	3,961,815	2,254,953	769,883	209,082	
Montana	122,640	36,381	37,261	44,046	4,953	658,439	270,038	101,372	33,522	
Nebraska	613,878	447,636	87,072	76,196	2,974	1,205,924	631,543	230,618	93,031	
Nevada	74,361	0	9,552	60,592	4,217	3,071,182	2,447,565	56,936	270,606	
New Hampshire	42,720	0	22,376	17,990	2,354	837,570	414,256	197,049	44,239	
New Jersey	544,578	2,594	24,761	459,091	58,133	6,471,429	4,895,267	410,995	158,384	
New Mexico	134,999	7,619	40,379	84,739	2,261	1,218,648	841,868	99,494	122,239	
New York	1,736,217	28,259	99,418	1,132,527	476,012	9,154,263	5,401,880	2,453,473	138,114	
North Carolina	667,684	240,579	197,510	217,217	12,379	5,377,638	3,466,919	626,199	546,607	
North Dakota	246,677	166,290	78,588	219	1,580	602,856	169,557	128,893	23,121	
Ohio	1,257,907	170,610	109,407	953,863	24,027	6,990,895	4,844,071	1,012,830	342,130	
Oklahoma	230,536	20,050	101,197	99,889	9,399	2,082,520	1,026,368	424,912	144,814	
Oregon	351,647	5,593	64,619	277,066	4,371	2,511,528	1,807,532	220,664	180,352	
Pennsylvania	285,036	15,430	142,792	106,879	19,935	6,439,532	2,972,504	2,506,153	252,584	
Rhode Island	102,545	0	4,493	85,419	12,633	865,155	550,459	204,948	24,271	
South Carolina	252,825	39,336	69,697	135,829	7,963	1,798,849	774,024	355,452	168,798	
South Dakota	348,800	281,256	63,944	2,685	915	609,605	169,814	142,908	29,242	
Tennessee	442,937	162,786	114,319	153,114	12,718	4,042,037	2,818,944	590,352	261,487	
Texas	1,395,750	777,923	303,014	163,744	151,070	15,588,214	10,698,589	1,914,234	1,054,129	
Utah	249,312	206,871	34,359	5,924	2,157	3,577,324	2,687,408	223,926	98,370	
Vermont	62,668	29	25,599	36,156	883	292,659	60,247	143,476	13,545	
Virginia	788,040	45,464	113,355	596,465	32,756	7,545,376	5,083,707	398,142	916,339	
Washington	444,048	40,226	71,917	317,933	13,972	5,357,183	3,593,652	397,453	555,844	
West Virginia	297,853	1,503	56,836	224,459	15,055	453,206	237,842	60,775	34,529	
Wisconsin	502,680	92,262	99,321	302,652	8,446	2,055,127	804,641	464,200	155,921	
Wyoming	26,715	10,154	14,775	100	1,686	312,838	139,596	57,824	26,581	
Dist. of Columbia	362,673	0	0	352,839	9,834	663,476	265,153	340,873	6,079	
American Samoa	26	0	0	0	0	0	0	0	0	
Fed. States of Micronesia	1,440	0	1,354	0	86	0	0	0	0	
Guam	37,735	0	1,059	4,073	32,603	37,432	645	0	1,068	
Marshall Islands	865	0	865	0	0	0	0	0	0	
No. Mariana Islands .	1,294	0	465	0	830	647	0	0	0	
Palau	552	0	26	0	526	64	0	0	0	
Puerto Rico	183,694	0	82,503	98,529	2,663	1,169,585	753,318	75,407	22,384	
Virgin Islands	9,469	0	5,323	3,163	983	5,028	2,186	0	326	
Undistributed	0	0	0	0	0	0	0	0	0	

See footnotes at end of table.

FEDERAL GOVERNMENT INSURANCE AND LOAN PROGRAMS, BY STATE AND OUTLYING AREA: FISCAL YEAR 2002 — Continued

State and outlying area	Guaranteed loans by volume of coverage provided					Insurance programs by volume of coverage provided					
	Mortgage insurance condominiums	U.S.D.A. guaranteed loans	Small business loans	Other guaranteed loans	Total	Flood insurance	Crop insurance	Foreign Investment Insurance	Life Insurance for Veterans	Other insurance
United States	$10,502,588	$11,868,186	$12,889,330	$763,766	$667,089,788	$627,522,070	$36,699,579	$606,636	$1,900,793	$360,710
Alabama	12,470	98,089	83,162	0	5,141,407	4,879,290	229,020	0	25,742	7,355
Alaska	76,667	119,358	13,029	0	355,078	349,310	619	0	2,550	2,599
Arizona	145,045	182,245	373,729	0	4,153,279	4,153,279	129,092	0	42,172	4,093
Arkansas	879,358	534,473	79,849	0	1,573,873	1,105,962	451,434	0	16,294	183
California	2,487,514	238,958	2,833,434	350,000	48,586,669	45,518,615	2,782,162	42,210	200,132	43,550
Colorado	-173	300,772	358,111	0	2,898,202	2,381,280	465,915	0	30,292	20,715
Connecticut	245,786	39,618	211,932	0	4,773,965	4,666,346	75,208	0	30,804	1,606
Delaware	4,688	53,378	24,052	0	2,673,021	2,632,562	34,627	0	5,831	0
Florida	654,312	251,113	642,497	0	267,345,522	264,475,634	2,632,304	21,273	174,773	41,538
Georgia	167,766	1,448,254	376,029	0	11,389,243	10,681,391	648,280	0	42,365	17,206
Hawaii	108,823	264,869	28,862	0	5,685,213	5,561,023	106,116	0	16,033	2,041
Idaho	3,464	92,381	79,094	0	1,249,312	844,128	396,090	0	8,114	980
Illinois	774,574	414,575	389,578	40	7,878,440	4,877,869	2,761,884	150,000	80,080	8,607
Indiana	57,448	161,228	158,071	0	3,863,954	2,415,788	1,415,336	0	28,644	4,186
Iowa	22,167	333,372	101,093	0	4,602,096	895,057	3,682,625	0	23,341	1,073
Kansas	5,198	160,262	87,682	0	2,639,664	994,549	1,619,078	0	18,854	7,184
Kentucky	43,886	576,102	108,172	0	2,170,111	1,769,747	356,822	25,000	18,542	0
Louisiana	17,007	211,028	132,174	0	45,753,979	45,338,020	374,326	0	22,604	19,029
Maine	9,744	54,193	41,461	0	966,515	899,772	56,992	0	9,751	0
Maryland	789,718	87,441	258,632	0	6,344,036	6,175,026	126,769	0	40,803	1,438
Massachusetts	195,797	23,111	306,477	0	6,100,792	6,005,084	42,450	0	52,066	1,191
Michigan	204,277	351,448	293,165	0	3,586,486	2,860,901	666,234	0	52,026	7,324
Minnesota	329,162	499,534	335,399	0	3,874,962	1,040,334	2,795,183	0	38,514	931
Mississippi	563	174,574	116,194	0	4,974,784	4,522,653	432,864	0	13,685	5,582
Missouri	52,973	456,714	218,210	0	3,219,959	2,363,901	802,654	0	36,548	16,856
Montana	7,007	180,686	65,814	0	917,995	337,051	563,908	0	7,621	9,415
Nebraska	1,759	195,064	53,910	0	3,579,788	1,240,661	2,323,117	0	13,799	2,210
Nevada	182,243	10,320	103,513	0	2,295,178	2,266,655	13,187	0	13,142	2,194
New Hampshire	74,604	27,838	79,583	0	629,568	610,512	9,014	0	9,903	139
New Jersey	519,720	13,003	474,061	0	27,642,860	27,504,001	65,870	4,250	66,653	2,086
New Mexico	9,696	74,601	70,750	0	1,279,006	1,200,694	61,661	0	13,428	3,223
New York	64,951	140,247	672,521	283,078	15,117,872	14,809,413	178,424	2,158	126,931	946
North Carolina	109,271	424,736	203,906	0	16,759,292	15,767,187	936,501	0	46,260	9,344
North Dakota	6,381	223,437	51,467	0	2,472,366	719,795	1,747,422	0	4,912	238
Ohio	200,528	279,216	312,121	0	4,166,087	3,259,810	826,493	0	71,545	8,239
Oklahoma	11,627	369,878	104,922	0	1,834,825	1,424,704	387,748	0	21,014	1,359
Oregon	58,388	101,960	142,632	0	4,421,516	3,944,450	451,871	0	23,942	1,253
Pennsylvania	102,233	216,773	389,286	0	7,284,571	6,958,382	219,464	0	99,472	7,253
Rhode Island	19,798	8,213	57,467	0	1,716,640	1,706,794	1,675	0	8,002	168
South Carolina	10,698	398,159	91,718	0	24,223,769	23,926,172	269,243	500	25,742	2,112
South Dakota	1,039	209,722	56,879	0	1,720,776	322,047	1,388,968	0	6,012	3,749
Tennessee	63,525	205,974	101,755	0	2,608,365	1,991,369	550,762	35,000	28,194	3,040
Texas	115,192	582,148	1,093,210	130,712	71,835,506	69,585,767	1,834,248	269,250	107,434	38,807
Utah	241,486	92,511	233,624	0	391,785	350,868	8,028	0	11,802	21,086
Vermont	7,139	39,135	29,118	0	332,415	317,239	10,784	0	4,374	18
Virginia	753,067	188,972	205,213	-64	11,769,662	11,406,444	299,921	0	55,786	7,511
Washington	428,421	129,783	252,029	0	4,774,022	3,910,423	785,369	30,146	41,878	6,205
West Virginia	206	87,107	32,746	0	1,474,310	1,450,815	12,715	0	10,262	518
Wisconsin	20,323	367,493	242,549	0	1,962,657	1,303,353	618,282	0	40,345	676
Wyoming	316	66,469	22,052	0	314,059	254,460	50,815	0	3,639	5,146
Dist. of Columbia	33,603	0	17,767	0	104,618	68,367	0	26,849	3,618	5,784
American Samoa	0	0	0	0	0	0	0	0	0	0
Fed. States of Micronesia	0	0	0	0	0	0	0	0	0	0
Guam	0	29,551	6,168	0	26,777	26,777	0	0	0	0
Marshall Islands	0	0	0	0	0	0	0	0	0	0
No. Mariana Islands	0	520	128	0	273	273	0	0	0	0
Palau	0	64	0	0	0	0	0	0	0	0
Puerto Rico	170,837	76,961	70,677	0	3,171,069	3,165,994	0	0	4,137	938
Virgin Islands	301	619	1,597	0	286,242	284,071	0	0	386	1,785
Undistributed	0	0	0	0	0	0	0	0	0	0

Source: U.S. Department of Commerce, Bureau of the Census, February 2004.

Table 2.10
PER CAPITA AMOUNTS OF FEDERAL GOVERNMENT EXPENDITURE, BY MAJOR OBJECT CATEGORY, BY STATE AND OUTLYING AREA: FISCAL YEAR 2002
(In dollars)

State and outlying area	United States resident population— July 1, 2002	Total	Retirement and disability	Other direct payments	Grants	Procurement	Salaries and wages
United States	288,368,698	$6,536.70	$2,105.98	$1,454.37	$1,419.38	$881.69	$675.27
Alabama	4,486,508	7,643.22	2,611.71	1,579.42	1,413.93	1,345.10	693.06
Alaska	643,786	11,745.69	1,523.29	870.25	4,856.81	2,167.65	2,327.68
Arizona	5,456,453	6,370.65	2,102.36	1,135.02	1,221.22	1,336.24	575.81
Arkansas	2,710,079	6,779.10	2,500.57	1,919.34	1,493.40	404.22	461.57
California	35,116,033	5,877.70	1,687.43	1,286.19	1,369.28	989.65	545.15
Colorado	4,506,542	5,820.30	1,791.44	1,054.63	1,051.74	1,004.38	918.11
Connecticut	3,460,503	7,336.25	2,123.39	1,470.31	1,525.43	1,796.29	420.83
Delaware	807,385	5,902.90	2,292.63	1,388.37	1,388.82	256.64	576.45
Florida	16,713,149	6,271.34	2,615.23	1,553.30	978.25	583.8	540.75
Georgia	8,560,310	5,996.92	1,862.65	1,186.87	1,226.58	860.29	860.53
Hawaii	1,244,898	8,413.54	2,328.91	1,152.46	1,474.25	1,302.30	2,155.62
Idaho	1,341,131	6,246.85	2,022.67	1,260.38	1,369.66	1,011.50	582.65
Illinois	12,600,620	5,577.12	1,910.07	1,604.94	1,188.44	370.17	503.5
Indiana	6,159,068	5,552.78	2,090.70	1,517.21	1,131.50	454.87	358.49
Iowa	2,936,760	6,414.99	2,237.32	2,100.67	1,382.56	325.31	369.13
Kansas	2,715,884	6,441.99	2,199.22	1,698.79	1,204.66	608.83	730.5
Kentucky	4,092,891	7,056.02	2,393.30	1,442.92	1,550.53	971.97	697.3
Louisiana	4,482,646	6,689.72	2,058.05	1,805.25	1,658.96	618.5	548.97
Maine	1,294,464	7,111.13	2,523.56	1,220.58	1,753.96	957.76	655.27
Maryland	5,458,137	9,575.62	2,343.03	1,334.78	1,656.15	2,471.09	1,770.58
Massachusetts	6,427,801	7,386.70	2,090.24	1,794.80	1,919.64	1,056.83	525.18
Michigan	10,050,446	5,562.84	2,113.41	1,449.11	1,321.28	352.13	326.9
Minnesota	5,019,720	5,389.88	1,837.77	1,412.25	1,293.21	443.83	402.82
Mississippi	2,871,782	7,419.96	2,328.99	1,741.21	1,757.07	952.04	640.65
Missouri	5,672,579	7,465.13	2,300.71	1,748.14	1,486.00	1,289.12	641.17
Montana	909,453	7,668.23	2,417.79	1,926.97	2,102.36	384.97	836.13
Nebraska	1,729,180	6,698.32	2,182.46	2,178.32	1,354.58	341.72	641.24
Nevada	2,173,491	4,939.93	2,035.92	978.22	846.46	574.94	504.39
New Hampshire	1,275,056	5,440.59	2,137.99	954.02	1,280.22	618.12	450.24
New Jersey	8,590,300	5,898.86	2,084.43	1,528.61	1,259.75	563.44	462.64
New Mexico	1,855,059	9,421.54	2,249.93	1,161.33	2,131.54	2,907.31	971.44
New York	19,157,532	6,733.35	2,046.24	1,638.48	2,216.40	387.18	445.06
North Carolina	8,320,146	5,790.74	2,159.95	1,246.30	1,314.77	351.26	718.46
North Dakota	634,110	10,150.56	2,183.15	4,167.98	2,247.51	518.51	1,033.40
Ohio	11,421,267	5,776.55	2,153.77	1,416.74	1,299.66	459.09	447.3
Oklahoma	3,493,714	6,971.10	2,402.35	1,484.67	1,461.97	719.93	902.19
Oregon	3,521,515	5,633.72	2,182.81	1,321.05	1,367.10	282.36	480.38
Pennsylvania	12,335,091	6,939.60	2,528.88	1,857.88	1,460.61	601.09	491.14
Rhode Island	1,069,725	7,014.18	2,317.22	1,542.32	1,957.44	462.49	734.71
South Carolina	4,107,183	6,355.50	2,363.73	1,232.64	1,361.51	755.92	641.71
South Dakota	761,063	8,297.28	2,235.69	2,757.42	1,978.23	496.23	829.71
Tennessee	5,797,289	6,774.81	2,276.22	1,433.28	1,493.49	1,019.83	552
Texas	21,779,893	5,667.21	1,713.70	1,269.43	1,141.33	944.97	597.77
Utah	2,316,256	5,311.14	1,607.44	806.77	1,164.39	899.75	832.79
Vermont	616,592	6,666.85	2,114.07	1,194.30	2,076.90	698.76	582.82
Virginia	7,293,542	10,219.53	2,554.86	1,167.44	1,057.62	3,588.11	1,851.50
Washington	6,068,996	6,626.73	2,152.41	1,317.24	1,367.00	920.45	869.64
West Virginia	1,801,873	7,414.91	3,030.12	1,542.82	1,830.43	334.05	677.49
Wisconsin	5,441,196	5,300.98	2,050.61	1,255.17	1,333.29	347.04	314.87
Wyoming	498,703	7,351.37	2,196.16	1,108.32	2,474.23	640.3	932.37
District of Columbia	570,898	58,737.60	3,286.12	3,730.16	8,464.41	19,048.42	24,208.50
American Samoa	57,291	2,691.43	687.62	40.19	1,630.26	231.33	102.02
Fed States of Micronesia	105,444	1,326.11	4.15	120.33	1,190.73	10.91	0.00
Guam	154,805	7,194.96	1,279.95	504.64	1,618.87	1,991.69	1,799.81
Marshall Islands	56,429	3,589.63	15.79	0.04	1,030.50	2,543.31	0.00
No. Mariana Islands	69,221	1,474.44	303.3	46.32	954.49	126.2	44.14
Palau	19,717	2,145.65	21.71	0.00	2,069.39	54.55	0.00
Puerto Rico	3,858,806	3,644.19	1,368.76	688.71	1,251.20	94.5	241.03
Virgin Islands	108,612	5,271.13	1,270.91	825.82	2,452.44	264.9	457.06

Source: U.S. Department of Commerce, Bureau of the Census, February 2004.

Table 2.11
PERCENT DISTRIBUTION OF FEDERAL GOVERNMENT EXPENDITURE, BY MAJOR OBJECT CATEGORY, BY STATE AND OUTLYING AREA: FISCAL YEAR 2002
(In dollars)

State and outlying area	Percent distribution of United States resident population— July 1, 2002	Total	Retirement and disability	Other direct payments	Grants	Procurement	Salaries and wages
United States	100%	100%	100%	100%	100%	100%	100%
Alabama	1.6	1.8	1.9	1.7	1.5	2.2	1.6
Alaska	0.2	0.4	0.2	0.1	0.8	0.5	0.8
Arizona	1.9	1.8	1.9	1.5	1.6	2.7	1.6
Arkansas	0.9	1.0	1.1	1.2	1.0	0.4	0.6
California	12.2	10.7	9.7	10.7	11.6	12.8	9.6
Colorado	1.6	1.4	1.3	1.1	1.1	1.7	2.1
Connecticut	1.2	1.3	1.2	1.2	1.3	2.3	0.7
Delaware	0.3	0.2	0.3	0.3	0.3	0.1	0.2
Florida	5.8	5.5	7.1	6.1	3.9	3.6	4.5
Georgia	3.0	2.7	2.6	2.4	2.5	2.7	3.7
Hawaii	0.4	0.5	0.5	0.3	0.4	0.6	1.3
Idaho	0.5	0.4	0.4	0.4	0.4	0.5	0.4
Illinois	4.4	3.7	3.9	4.8	3.6	1.7	3.2
Indiana	2.1	1.8	2.1	2.2	1.7	1.0	1.1
Iowa	1.0	1.0	1.1	1.5	1.0	0.4	0.5
Kansas	0.9	0.9	1.0	1.1	0.8	0.6	1.0
Kentucky	1.4	1.5	1.6	1.4	1.5	1.5	1.4
Louisiana	1.6	1.6	1.5	1.9	1.8	1.0	1.2
Maine	0.4	0.5	0.5	0.4	0.5	0.5	0.4
Maryland	1.9	2.7	2.1	1.7	2.2	5.0	4.9
Massachusetts	2.2	2.5	2.2	2.7	3.0	2.5	1.7
Michigan	3.5	2.9	3.5	3.4	3.2	1.3	1.7
Minnesota	1.7	1.4	1.5	1.7	1.6	0.8	1.0
Mississippi	1.0	1.1	1.1	1.2	1.2	1.0	0.9
Missouri	2.0	2.2	2.1	2.3	2.0	2.7	1.8
Montana	0.3	0.4	0.4	0.4	0.5	0.1	0.4
Nebraska	0.6	0.6	0.6	0.9	0.6	0.2	0.6
Nevada	0.8	0.6	0.7	0.5	0.4	0.5	0.6
New Hampshire	0.4	0.4	0.4	0.3	0.4	0.3	0.3
New Jersey	3.0	2.6	2.9	3.1	2.6	1.8	2.0
New Mexico	0.6	0.9	0.7	0.5	1.0	2.0	0.9
New York	6.6	6.7	6.4	7.4	10.2	2.7	4.3
North Carolina	2.9	2.5	2.9	2.5	2.6	1.1	3.0
North Dakota	0.2	0.3	0.2	0.6	0.3	0.1	0.3
Ohio	4.0	3.4	4.0	3.8	3.6	1.9	2.6
Oklahoma	1.2	1.3	1.4	1.2	1.2	0.9	1.6
Oregon	1.2	1.0	1.3	1.1	1.2	0.4	0.8
Pennsylvania	4.3	4.5	5.1	5.4	4.3	2.7	3.0
Rhode Island	0.4	0.4	0.4	0.4	0.5	0.2	0.4
South Carolina	1.4	1.4	1.6	1.2	1.3	1.1	1.3
South Dakota	0.3	0.3	0.3	0.5	0.4	0.1	0.3
Tennessee	2.0	2.0	2.2	2.0	2.1	2.2	1.6
Texas	7.6	6.4	6.1	6.5	6.0	7.6	6.5
Utah	0.8	0.6	0.6	0.4	0.6	0.8	1.0
Vermont	0.2	0.2	0.2	0.2	0.3	0.2	0.2
Virginia	2.5	3.9	3.0	2.0	1.9	9.7	6.8
Washington	2.1	2.1	2.1	1.9	2.0	2.1	2.7
West Virginia	0.6	0.7	0.9	0.7	0.8	0.2	0.6
Wisconsin	1.9	1.5	1.8	1.6	1.7	0.7	0.9
Wyoming	0.2	0.2	0.2	0.1	0.3	0.1	0.2
Dist. of Columbia	0.2	1.7	0.3	0.5	1.2	4.0	6.9
American Samoa	0.0	0.0	0.0	0.0	0.0	0.0	0.0
Fed. States of Micronesia .	0.0	0.0	0.0	0.0	0.0	0.0	0.0
Guam	0.1	0.1	0.0	0.0	0.1	0.1	0.1
Marshall Islands	0.0	0.0	0.0	0.0	0.0	0.1	0.0
No. Mariana Islands	0.0	0.0	0.0	0.0	0.0	0.0	0.0
Palau	0.0	0.0	0.0	0.0	0.0	0.0	0.0
Puerto Rico	1.3	0.7	0.9	0.6	1.2	0.1	0.5
Virgin Islands	0.0	0.0	0.0	0.0	0.1	0.0	0.0
Undistributed	0.0	1.0	0.0	0.0	0.0	5.8	1.5

Source: U.S. Department of Commerce, Bureau of the Census, February 2004.

Table 2.12
FEDERAL GOVERNMENT EXPENDITURE FOR DEFENSE DEPARTMENT AND ALL OTHER AGENCIES, BY STATE AND OUTLYING AREA: FISCAL YEAR 2002

State and outlying area	Federal expenditure (millions of dollars)		Per capita federal expenditure		Percent distribution of federal expenditure		Department of Energy, defense related activities (millions of dollars)
	Department of Defense	All other federal agencies	Department of Defense	All other federal agencies	Department of Defense	All other federal agencies	
United States	$277,900	$1,642,465	$964	$5,696	$100	$100	$13,954
Alabama	7,026	27,265	1,566.08	6,077.13	2.5	1.7	0
Alaska	1,975	5,586	3,068.23	8,677.46	0.7	0.3	2
Arizona	8,605	26,157	1,576.95	4,793.70	3.1	1.6	0
Arkansas	1,682	16,690	620.58	6,158.52	0.6	1	0
California	36,152	170,250	1,029.50	4,848.20	13	10.4	1,235
Colorado	5,243	20,986	1,163.50	4,656.80	1.9	1.3	694
Connecticut	6,240	19,147	1,803.30	5,532.95	2.2	1.2	0
Delaware	518	4,248	641.45	5,261.46	0.2	0.3	0
Florida	14,277	90,536	854.26	5,417.08	5.1	5.5	3
Georgia	10,991	40,345	1,283.93	4,712.99	4	2.5	0
Hawaii	3,964	6,510	3,183.91	5,229.63	1.4	0.4	0
Idaho	602	7,776	448.92	5,797.93	0.2	0.5	620
Illinois	4,324	65,951	343.18	5,233.94	1.6	4	157
Indiana	2,846	31,354	462.13	5,090.64	1	1.9	0
Iowa	914	17,926	311.14	6,103.85	0.3	1.1	1
Kansas	2,330	15,166	857.82	5,584.18	0.8	0.9	0
Kentucky	4,015	24,864	981.02	6,075.00	1.4	1.5	7
Louisiana	3,210	26,778	716.05	5,973.67	1.2	1.6	0
Maine	1,687	7,518	1,303.02	5,808.12	0.6	0.5	0
Maryland	10,220	42,046	1,872.35	7,703.28	3.7	2.6	113
Massachusetts	5,854	41,626	910.77	6,475.92	2.1	2.5	0
Michigan	3,134	52,775	311.83	5,251.01	1.1	3.2	0
Minnesota	1,971	25,084	392.72	4,997.17	0.7	1.5	0
Mississippi	3,658	17,651	1,273.60	6,146.35	1.3	1.1	1
Missouri	7,139	35,208	1,258.48	6,206.65	2.6	2.1	360
Montana	459	6,515	504.36	7,163.87	0.2	0.4	5
Nebraska	1,039	10,544	600.69	6,097.63	0.4	0.6	0
Nevada	1,244	9,493	572.36	4,367.57	0.4	0.6	646
New Hampshire	910	6,027	713.87	4,726.72	0.3	0.4	0
New Jersey	4,765	45,908	554.67	5,344.19	1.7	2.8	0
New Mexico	1,910	15,568	1,029.52	8,392.02	0.7	0.9	3,035
New York	6,288	122,707	328.22	6,405.14	2.3	7.5	92
North Carolina	6,546	41,633	786.82	5,003.91	2.4	2.5	0
North Dakota	627	5,810	988.22	9,162.33	0.2	0.4	0
Ohio	5,746	60,230	503.07	5,273.48	2.1	3.7	478
Oklahoma	3,897	20,459	1,115.30	5,855.81	1.4	1.2	0
Oregon	1,001	18,838	284.37	5,349.35	0.4	1.1	0
Pennsylvania	6,827	78,773	553.5	6,386.10	2.5	4.8	0
Rhode Island	916	6,587	856.19	6,157.99	0.3	0.4	0
South Carolina	3,765	22,339	916.61	5,438.89	1.4	1.4	1,320
South Dakota	471	5,844	618.58	7,678.70	0.2	0.4	0
Tennessee	2,551	36,724	440.11	6,334.70	0.9	2.2	1,085
Texas	22,267	101,164	1,022.35	4,644.85	8	6.2	387
Utah	2,508	9,794	1,082.75	4,228.39	0.9	0.6	0
Vermont	465	3,645	754.62	5,912.23	0.2	0.2	0
Virginia	29,632	44,904	4,062.81	6,156.72	10.7	2.7	0
Washington	6,500	33,717	1,071.04	5,555.69	2.3	2.1	2,037
West Virginia	474	12,887	263.15	7,151.76	0.2	0.8	65
Wisconsin	1,621	27,222	297.95	5,003.03	0.6	1.7	0
Wyoming	331	3,335	664.58	6,686.79	0.1	0.2	0
Dist. of Columbia	3,454	30,080	6,049.28	52,688.33	1.2	1.8	923
American Samoa	6	148	99.79	2,591.64	0	0	0
Fed. States of Micronesia	0	140	0	1,326.11	0	0	0
Guam	562	552	3,628.15	3,566.81	0.2	0	0
Marshall Islands	143	59	2,536.67	1,052.96	0.1	0	0
No. Mariana Islands	7	95	103.51	1,370.93	0	0	0
Palau	1	42	29.57	2,116.08	0	0	0
Puerto Rico	603	13,459	156.34	3,487.86	0.2	0.8	0
Virgin Islands	29	544	264.48	5,006.65	0	0	0
Undistributed	11,759	7,237	0	0	0	0	687

Source: U.S. Department of Commerce, Bureau of the Census, February 2004.

Table 2.13
STATE RANKINGS FOR PER CAPITA AMOUNTS
OF FEDERAL GOVERNMENT EXPENDITURE: FISCAL YEAR 2002

State	Total	Retirement and disability	Other direct payments	Grants	Procurement	Salaries and wages
Alabama	9	3	15	24	6	19
Alaska	1	50	49	1	4	1
Arizona	30	34	44	41	7	30
Arkansas	21	7	6	19	39	41
California	37	48	32	28	14	33
Colorado	38	46	46	48	13	8
Connecticut	15	31	22	17	5	45
Delaware	35	17	28	25	50	29
Florida	32	2	16	49	30	34
Georgia	34	44	40	40	21	11
Hawaii	6	14	43	21	8	2
Idaho	33	42	34	27	12	28
Illinois	43	43	14	43	42	37
Indiana	45	35	20	46	37	48
Iowa	29	20	4	26	48	47
Kansas	28	22	12	42	28	16
Kentucky	17	10	24	16	15	18
Louisiana	25	38	8	14	26	32
Maine	16	6	38	13	16	21
Maryland	4	12	29	15	3	4
Massachusetts	13	36	9	10	10	35
Michigan	44	33	23	34	43	49
Minnesota	47	45	27	37	38	46
Mississippi	11	13	11	12	17	25
Missouri	10	16	10	20	9	24
Montana	8	8	5	6	41	12
Nebraska	24	26	3	32	46	23
Nevada	50	41	47	50	31	36
New Hampshire	46	30	48	38	27	42
New Jersey	36	37	19	39	32	40
New Mexico	5	19	42	5	2	6
New York	23	40	13	4	40	44
North Carolina	39	27	36	35	44	17
North Dakota	3	24	1	3	33	5
Ohio	40	28	26	36	36	43
Oklahoma	19	9	21	22	23	9
Oregon	42	25	30	29	49	39
Pennsylvania	20	5	7	23	29	38
Rhode Island	18	15	18	9	35	15
South Carolina	31	11	37	31	22	22
South Dakota	7	21	2	8	34	14
Tennessee	22	18	25	18	11	31
Texas	41	47	33	45	18	26
Utah	48	49	50	44	20	13
Vermont	26	32	39	7	24	27
Virginia	2	4	41	47	1	3
Washington	27	29	31	30	19	10
West Virginia	12	1	17	11	47	20
Wisconsin	49	39	35	33	45	50
Wyoming	14	23	45	2	25	7

Source: U.S. Department of Commerce, Bureau of Census, February 2004.

Chapter Three

STATE LEGISLATIVE BRANCH

Because 2004 is an election year, politics will percolate just below the surface in most states and probably rise above it in a few.

— Alan Rosenthal and Rich Jones

Trends in State Legislatures
By Alan Rosenthal and Rich Jones

Legislatures are vital, strong, effective institutions. They are where the people and their representatives come together to debate conflicting values and interests, set priorities and shape public policies. They are the political institutions closest to the people and drive representative democracy. This essay describes the organization and work of state legislatures, identifies the trends shaping state legislatures and the challenges confronting them and briefly describes the critical policy issues legislatures faced in the 2003 legislative sessions.

Legislatures are vital, strong, effective institutions. They are where the people and their representatives come together to debate conflicting values and interests, set priorities and shape public policies. They are the political institutions closest to the people and they drive representative democracy. They are truly representative bodies that reflect the environment in which they exist.

This essay describes the organization and work of state legislatures by drawing on the data collected by The Council of State Governments and presented in the tables that appear in this chapter. It identifies the trends shaping state legislatures and the challenges confronting them. It offers a framework for thinking about state legislatures and briefly describes the critical policy issues legislatures faced in the 2003 legislative sessions.

Composition of State Legislatures

A major role of state legislatures is to represent their constituencies and constituents. The wants and needs of constituents are probably the most powerful influences on the behavior of individual lawmakers. One factor in describing state legislatures is the extent to which they reflect the demographic characteristics found within their states. While they do not have to match the state's make up exactly, no major groups should be excluded from serving in state legislatures. Though no groups are excluded, those that do serve in state legislatures tend to be better educated and wealthier than the general population.

Over time, the number of women lawmakers and those from racial minority groups has increased. In 2003, +1,647 women (22.3 percent) served in state legislatures up from 301 (4 percent) in 1969. The number of African-American lawmakers totaled 595 (8.1 percent) in 2003 compared to 168 (2 percent) in 1970. In 2003, 215 (2.9 percent) Latino lawmakers served in state legislatures. Although increases in the number of legislators from these groups has slowed in recent elections, given changes occurring within

the broader society, it is likely that state legislatures will have more racially diverse and more female members in the future.

Professionalization

Another factor in describing state legislatures is the extent to which they are professional institutions. Legislative scholars measure professionalism based on the number of staff professionals, compensation paid to lawmakers and the time that legislatures and legislators devote to the job. Those legislatures ranking higher on these measures are considered to be more professional. Legislatures in California, Illinois, Massachusetts, Michigan, Ohio, New Jersey, New York, Pennsylvania and Wisconsin are generally considered to be full-time, professional legislatures. Among those at the other extreme are Montana, North Dakota, South Dakota, Vermont and Wyoming, generally considered to be part-time, citizen legislatures. Roughly half of the legislatures fall somewhere in the middle.

For over three decades the trend has been toward greater professionalization. One aspect of this trend has been the turnover among lawmakers, which has declined steadily since the 1950s. Lower turnover signals more professional legislatures. However, a recent study by legislative scholars found that turnover among state legislators increased slightly during the 1990s. They concluded that this trend reversal is entirely due to the higher turnover among legislators in those states with term limits.[1]

Legislative compensation is another factor that affects professionalization. Higher salaries enable lawmakers to make the legislature a full-time career. Conversely, lower salaries and short sessions mean lawmakers must hold jobs outside of the legislature. The level of compensation also affects the type of person who can serve in state legislatures. Set it too low and only the wealthy or those just starting out can afford to serve. Set it too high and the citizens reject it as unreasonable. In 2003, 17 states paid lawmakers $30,000 or more per year and nine paid

$40,000 or more. All but six states also paid a per diem to cover living and commuting expenses associated with legislative service. (see Tables 3.9-3.12)

Political Competitiveness and Partisanship

State legislatures with the exception of Nebraska, where lawmakers are elected without party labels, are partisan bodies. They are organized and controlled by a majority of Republicans or Democrats or when tied, by some type of power sharing arrangement between the parties. Party affiliation is among the defining characteristics of a state legislature and plays a significant role in the legislative process in most states.

Partisan Composition

During the past decade state legislatures have become more competitive politically. The surge in the number of Republican legislators elected during the 1990s has resulted in more competitive bodies. While only two or three out of every five legislative districts are competitive, of the 98 partisan legislative chambers nationwide (Nebraska is nonpartisan), about 55 percent are competitive. That is, each party has had control for some time during the past two decades and/or the margin is close enough that each has a chance to win the majority in the future. For example, in 2004 a shift of two seats or less from one party to the other would change control in seven senates and a shift of four seats or less would change control in eight houses. In 2004, Republicans controlled both chambers in 21 states, Democrats controlled both chambers in 17 states and the parties split control in 11 states. When considered along with the party of the governor, Republicans control both branches in 12 states, Democrats control eight states and 29 are split between the parties.

At the start of the 2004 sessions following off year elections in Louisiana, Mississippi, New Jersey, and Virginia and special elections, there were 3,688 Republican state legislators (49.9 percent) and 3,627 Democratic state legislators (49.1 percent). A combination of independents, other parties and vacancies account for the other one percent. The election of 2002 marked the first time in fifty years that more Republican state legislators were elected than Democrats. That is a far cry from 1960 when 65 percent of all state legislators were Democrats and 35 percent were Republicans.

Because partisan control of state legislatures significantly affects the types of policies adopted by the states, legislative races have become increasingly important to the political parties and the groups that support them. The closeness of the partisan battle

over control of the U.S. House of Representatives and the important role state legislatures play in drawing congressional districts in most states has raised the stakes in legislative elections even higher. As an example of the increased partisan competition, legislatures in Colorado and Texas attempted to redraw congressional districts after courts drew them in 2002. Historically, legislatures have redrawn congressional districts once a decade following the census. These efforts raised considerable partisan rancor including a boycott by Texas Democrats and hard feelings in Colorado. The Colorado Supreme Court struck down the legislature's plan while a federal court upheld the Texas plan.

To some extent, the process of drawing legislative districts has had an effect on the partisanship within state legislatures. With the advent of sophisticated technology and more precise political data legislatures have drawn an increasing number of districts that are safe for one party or the other. Because the general election outcome is largely predetermined, most of the competition for these seats occurs during the primary elections in which strong partisans from the extremes of each party tend to be elected. As a result, the party caucuses within state legislatures tend to reflect greater political polarization than is apparent among the general public.

Tied Chambers

Parity between the political parties is manifested in tied chambers. Each even-year election since 1984 and odd-year elections in 1995, 1997 and 2001 produced at least one state where the voters elected an equal number of members from each party to a legislative chamber. The North Carolina House of Representatives and the Oregon Senate were tied at the start of the 2003 session.

Republicans picked up seats in the North Carolina House in the 2002 elections giving them a 61-59 majority. However, several weeks before the session began a Republican member switched parties throwing the chamber into a 60-60 tie. After six days and eight votes for speaker ended in a deadlock, Democrats forged a power sharing agreement with a group of dissident Republicans. (Although the member switched back to Republican the House continues to operate under the power sharing agreement.) They opted for co-speakers and co-chairs of committees except for the Rules Committee chaired by a Democrat. The leaders and committee chairs rotate between the parties daily.[2]

Oregon voters elected an equal number of Republicans and Democrats to the Senate in the 2002 election. The senators briefly considered flipping a coin to determine which party would control the Senate. They rejected that approach as well as using co-leaders. Instead they negotiated a power sharing agreement where a Democrat became the Senate president and a Republican the president pro tem. Republicans relinquished the opportunity to chair the Joint Budget Committee opting instead to chair its three subcommittees. They divided the rest of the committees and each party alternated selecting the committee they wanted to chair. The Rules Committee is the only one with co-chairs. The Republican leader acknowledged that operating under the power sharing agreement was harder than if a cross party coalition organized the Senate. However, in her view, a cross party coalition runs the risk of collapsing at any moment whereas the power sharing agreement provided more stability.[3]

Legislatures have adopted several mechanisms to organize when the parties are equally divided. A coin toss is the preferred method for breaking a tie in Wyoming; the lieutenant governor can vote to break ties in 25 state senates and did so in Idaho (1990) and Pennsylvania (1992). Indiana, Montana and South Dakota have statutes that determine which party is in control when the legislative body is deadlocked—the party of the governor or secretary of state in Indiana if the governor is not up for election. Most ties have been settled through one of three types of negotiated agreements. Some legislatures have negotiated "co" agreements where the members of each party share the leadership and committee chair duties. Others opted for a divided power agreement where the parties divide power over certain areas. Another approach used by legislatures is the negotiated resignation agreement where one party will control a specific position, such as presiding officer, for a set period, such as one year of a biennium. The other party gains control of the position for the second year.[4]

Legislative Organization and Procedures

During the past three decades legislatures have taken a more active role in policymaking and tackled increasingly complex issues. Their workloads have grown as a result and many face pressures to expand the time that they meet in session. However, most legislatures choose to remain part-time, citizen bodies comprised of lawmakers who hold other jobs outside of the legislature. To remain part time institutions yet effectively discharge their duties, legislatures have devoted considerable attention to streamlining their processes and adopting procedures to help them complete their business more efficiently.

Legislatures use technology to speed up bill processing and to increase the public's access to the legislative process. Many also limit the number of bills a lawmaker may introduce, establish session schedules with deadlines for actions and use the interim between sessions to study issues and prepare legislation for the session.

Legislative Sessions

For most of the past 40 years the trend has been to relax restrictions on legislative sessions. Legislatures went from primarily meeting biennially to holding annual sessions. Limits on the amount of time that legislatures could meet in session were removed or the time available was expanded.

Currently all but six states meet annually – Arkansas, Montana, Nevada, North Dakota, Oregon and Texas. Conversely, following World War II only four states held annual sessions and only 20 states met annually in 1966. In 2000, Kentucky voters approved a constitutional amendment allowing annual sessions. In addition, six states – Connecticut, Louisiana, Maine, New Mexico, North Carolina and Wyoming – restrict the subjects that the legislature can consider during one year of the biennium. These tend to be limited to budget, tax and fiscal bills, but the legislatures broadly interpret the types of bills that meet the criteria and the restricted sessions often resemble regular legislative sessions. In 2002, Louisiana voters adopted a constitutional amendment that switched the timing of its fiscal session from the first year of the biennium to the second year. The change, which is effective with the 2004 session, allows legislators beyond those on the fiscal committees or who sponsor fiscal legislation to more actively participate in the first session of the biennium.

The trend toward relaxed limits and longer sessions shifted somewhat in the late 1980s and early 1990s as public sentiment favored limiting legislative sessions. Voters in Alaska, Colorado, Louisiana, Nevada and Oklahoma all approved constitutional amendments that resulted in shorter legislative sessions.

Bills and Bill Processing

Among the strategies legislatures have pursued to increase efficiency is to limit the number of bills introduced and establish a schedule to process them during the session. About one out of four legislative chambers either limits the number of bills a member can introduce or request to be drafted. Many of these chambers place no limits on prefiled bills and exempt particular types of bills such as appropriations and committee bills from the limit. For example, lawmakers are limited to 40 bills in the California Assembly during a regular two-year session, five bills per year in Colorado and seven bills in the first session of the biennium and three during the second session in the Wyoming Senate.

To better deal with the end of session log jam of legislation, a number of legislatures impose deadlines for the introduction of bills, committee action, action by the house of origin, second house action and conference committee action. The deadlines spread the workflow and the essential bargaining processes throughout the session. Three quarters of the legislative chambers use some form of deadline system that requires work at critical stages in the legislative process be completed by set dates or the legislation dies.

Legislative Leaders

Legislative leaders exert considerable influence over legislative operations. They set agendas, appoint committees, formulate policy, rule on parliamentary questions, preside over legislative sessions, maintain decorum and serve as spokespersons for their chambers. More than any other members, they influence the success or failure of their legislature. They must balance support for the members while leading them to reach desired outcomes on often difficult and controversial issues.

As the demands on legislatures increase so does the difficulty of the leaders' job. Rapid turnover among legislative leaders makes the job even harder. Roughly one out of every five presiding officers, majority and minority leaders, is new to their positions at the start of each biennium. Although most are experienced legislators, they are relatively new to their leadership roles. This is a particular problem in the states with term limits where lawmakers become leaders in their second or third terms. In these states, processes have been established to try and identify potential leaders early in their careers and to increase training for new leaders once they are selected. (Tables 3.6-3.7 list the leadership positions in each legislature and how they are selected.)

Legislative Staff

A major trend that helped to transform legislatures over the past 40 years has been the introduction of legislative staff. Beginning with legislative clerks and secretaries, bill drafters, researchers and support staff for the legislative session, modern legislatures now employ a bevy of staff with professional backgrounds in fiscal analysis, media relations, auditing and information technology. Today almost 35,000 staff

work for state legislatures. According to a census of legislative staff conducted by the National Conference of State Legislatures (NCSL), the number of legislative staff grew by almost 8,000 or about 30 percent from 1979 to 2003. Most of that growth occurred from 1979 to 1988 when legislatures added over 6,000 staff. During that period legislatures increased the number of permanent staff while reducing those hired only for the session. In 2003, New York (3,428), Pennsylvania (2,947) and California (2,334) employed the most staff and South Dakota (49), Vermont (82) and Wyoming (114) employed the least. In recent years there has been a trend toward decentralized and partisan staffing patterns with more legislatures hiring staff for individual legislators, caucuses and committees.[5]

Technology

Legislatures are increasingly using technology to automate their processes such as producing bills, journals and calendars. They are also using it to provide citizens with greater access to the legislative process and information about legislative proceedings. Beginning in the mid-1990s, legislatures began equipping legislators with laptop computers and currently at least one chamber in 39 states gives all legislators laptops or personal computers. Several additional states allow lawmakers to bring their own laptop to the chambers where they can connect to the legislature's network. Legislators use the laptops to view bills and amendments, do research, write letters and access e-mail.

Legislatures also use information technology to create documents such as bills, journals, committee reports and agendas and move them throughout the legislature electronically. These document management systems cut down on the time and resources necessary to produce legislative reports and documents and enable legislatures to operate more efficiently.

Legislatures are also using technology to communicate with citizens and provide them with access to the legislative process. Every legislature has a Web site that provides information about the text of bills and their status in the legislature. Most also provide access to state statutes and biographical and contact information for legislators. Forty-five states broadcast legislative proceedings to the public via television or the Internet. In 38 states, at least one chamber (and usually both) provides live audio or video broadcast of floor proceedings on the Internet with many also broadcasting committee hearings. Several legislatures allow citizens to e-mail testimony to committees and at least 19 have teleconferencing or video-conferencing capabilities to bring committee meetings to citizens outside of the capitol.

Direct Democracy

The growing appeal of the direct democracy movement is a trend that is shaping the environment that legislatures operate within and affecting how legislatures conduct their business. The most visible method for direct democracy is the initiative, a way to bypass the legislature and legislative process. Used in 24 states the initiative process allows citizens to place constitutional amendments as well as state laws on the ballot if a required number of citizens sign a petition. The initiative language becomes law if a majority of voters approve.

Used mostly in Western states, the number of initiatives exploded in the 1990s with Arizona, California, Colorado, Oregon and Washington having the most active initiative processes. Frequently, initiatives limit the legislature's authority and prevent them from developing broad and cohesive state policies. These effects have been most pronounced in the fiscal area where initiatives have limited the legislatures' authority over tax and spending decisions.

In recent years, legislatures considered an increasing number of bills to reform the initiative process. The reforms would require fiscal notes on all initiatives, more information about the costs and methods for funding the programs contained in the initiatives, greater scrutiny of the initiative language, more flexibility to fix technical problems in initiative drafts and greater disclosure of the financing of initiative campaigns.

No states have adopted the initiative process since 1992 and legislatures in states without it are unlikely to put such a proposition on the ballot. In states that have the initiative process legislatures face the possibility that their authority will be further curtailed by the voters.[6]

Term Limits

Term limits are the most significant change in the structure and operation of state legislatures to occur in the past decade. Their adoption was made possible by the initiative process. First adopted by California, Colorado and Oklahoma voters in 1990, term limits were adopted by 18 other states. Legislatures had a direct role in adopting them in two states—Louisiana and Utah—the other 19 were adopted via citizen initiative.

Term limits laws have been changed in several states in recent years. Courts in Massachusetts, Oregon and Washington invalidated their states' term limits laws.

Legislatures in Idaho and Utah repealed their laws in 2002 and 2003 respectively. A number of legislatures considered bills to amend them generally by increasing the number of terms allowed before the limits take effect. States without the initiative process are not likely to enact term limits, although it is always possible that a concerted campaign could persuade legislators to put term limits on the ballot for voters to decide, as they did in Louisiana. It appears likely that, over time, the term limits laws will be adjusted to ameliorate the negative effects while keeping the concept of limiting the time lawmakers can serve.

The initial effects of term limits include high turnover rates, less experience among legislative leaders and committee chairs and shifts in power between the legislature and the executive. Legislatures have responded by increasing training for new legislators, changing leadership selection processes and adjusting legislative procedures. Scholars are finishing a comprehensive study of the effects of term limits and actions legislatures can take to adapt to them.

Major Issues in 2003 and 2004 Legislative Sessions

The central issue, some would say the only issue, for most legislatures in 2003 was the budget. Facing the worst fiscal condition since the Great Depression, legislatures labored mightily to balance budgets in the face of significant revenue declines. This was the third year legislatures faced an economic decline and budget problems. In fiscal year 2002, 40 states collected less revenue than they did the year before according to the Rockefeller Institute of Government. According to NCSL, a dozen states took in less revenue in fiscal year 2003 than they did in 2002. Nine states fell into both categories. The biggest factor affecting state finances was the waning national economy that was either in recession or slowly recovering during this time period. State revenues declined more than the overall economic decline mostly because revenue from capital gains dropped significantly.[7]

Legislatures performed their duties admirably in the face of significant budget problems. With a couple of exceptions, they ended fiscal year 2003 in the black and passed balanced budgets for 2004. However, some legislatures acted only after considerable debate and dramatic departures from their normal processes. Arkansas for example, adjourned for the first time in history without passing a budget. Lawmakers however returned three weeks later and adopted one during a special session. Florida set a precedent when lawmakers broke off budget talks with time left in its regular session, reconvening later in a special session to adopt the budget. Idaho's budget impasse resulted in the longest session in state history totaling 118 days, 23 days longer than the previous record. Oregon also set a record for its longest session. Pennsylvania was the last state in the nation to adopt a budget for 2004 passing it on Christmas Eve.

Most legislatures opted for spending cuts and fee increases to balance their budgets. Tax hikes totaled $8.8 billion nationally. However, this total would have been higher except that a $4 billion car tax in California that was repealed by Gov. Schwarzenegger following his victory in a recall election. The tax hikes that were approved were relatively modest and concentrated in a few states.[8]

The 2004 sessions are likely to see legislatures deal with a number of issues with budgets remaining at the top of the list. Although the national economy is recovering, state tax revenues tend to lag and states must fund increases in Medicaid, corrections and K-12 education costs.

Because 2004 is an election year, politics will percolate just below the surface in most states and probably rise above it in a few. Seventy-eight percent of all state legislative seats are up for election and given the parity between the parties all sides will be fighting for partisan advantage. Hard feelings over the 2003 battles to redraw congressional districts in Colorado and Texas are likely to seep into the 2004 session.

Notes

[1] Gary Moncrief, Richard G. Niemi and Lynda W. Powell, "Time, Term Limits and Turnover: Trends in Membership Turnover in U.S. State Legislatures," Paper presented at the 2003 State Politics and Policy Conference in Tucson, Arizona. To be published in *Legislative Studies Quarterly* in 2004.

[2] Amy Gardner, "It Takes Two in North Carolina," *State Legislatures*, 29, no. 7 (July/August 2003): 14-20.

[3] Peter Wong, "Power Parity in Oregon," *State Legislatures*, 29, no. 7, (July/August 2003): 22-6.

[4] National Conference of State Legislatures, *Legislative Deadlock: What Happens if It Happens to You?*, http://www.ncsl.org/Programs/Legman/about/tieddcmbarticle.htm.

[5] "Legislative Staff Flourish Over 30 Years," *State Legislatures*, 30, no. 2 (February 2004): 5.

[6] Jennie Drage Bowser, "Reforming the Initiative Process," *NCSL Legisbrief*, 10, no. 16 (March 2002).

[7] Corina Eckl, "Where Does the Buck Stop When the Bucks Stop?," *State Legislatures*, 29, no. 9 (October/November 2003): 18-20.

[8] Corina Eckl, "Budget Woes Push Lawmakers in Uncharted Territory," *State Legislatures*, 29, no. 9 (October/November 2003): 21-4.

About the Authors

Rich Jones is the director of Legislative Programs at the National Conference of State Legislatures (NCSL). He has written extensively about state legislatures and legislative operations and has consulted with a large number of state legislatures on issues relating to legislative procedures and staff structure.

Alan Rosenthal is a professor of public policy and political science at the Eagleton Institute of Politics at Rutgers University. He has written extensively about state legislatures, including the *Decline of Representative Democracy*. He has collaborated in activities with The Council of State Governments, National Conference of State Legislatures and the State Legislative Leaders Foundation. He has worked with legislatures in most of the states.

Table 3.1
NAMES OF STATE LEGISLATIVE BODIES AND CONVENING PLACES

State or other jurisdiction	Both bodies	Upper house	Lower house	Convening place
Alabama	Legislature	Senate	House of Representatives	State House
Alaska	Legislature	Senate	House of Representatives	State Capitol
Arizona	Legislature	Senate	House of Representatives	State Capitol
Arkansas	General Assembly	Senate	House of Representatives	State Capitol
California	Legislature	Senate	Assembly	State Capitol
Colorado	General Assembly	Senate	House of Representatives	State Capitol
Connecticut	General Assembly	Senate	House of Representatives	State Capitol
Delaware	General Assembly	Senate	House of Representatives	Legislative Hall
Florida	Legislature	Senate	House of Representatives	The Capitol
Georgia	General Assembly	Senate	House of Representatives	State Capitol
Hawaii	Legislature	Senate	House of Representatives	State Capitol
Idaho	Legislature	Senate	House of Representatives	State Capitol
Illinois	General Assembly	Senate	House of Representatives	State House
Indiana	General Assembly	Senate	House of Representatives	State House
Iowa	General Assembly	Senate	House of Representatives	State Capitol
Kansas	Legislature	Senate	House of Representatives	State Capitol
Kentucky	General Assembly	Senate	House of Representatives	State Capitol
Louisiana	Legislature	Senate	House of Representatives	State Capitol
Maine	Legislature	Senate	House of Representatives	State House
Maryland	General Assembly	Senate	House of Delegates	State House
Massachusetts	General Court	Senate	House of Representatives	State House
Michigan	Legislature	Senate	House of Representatives	State Capitol
Minnesota	Legislature	Senate	House of Representatives	State Capitol
Mississippi	Legislature	Senate	House of Representatives	State Capitol
Missouri	General Assembly	Senate	House of Representatives	State Capitol
Montana	Legislature	Senate	House of Representatives	State Capitol
Nebraska	Legislature	(a)		State Capitol
Nevada	Legislature	Senate	Assembly	Legislative Building
New Hampshire	General Court	Senate	House of Representatives	State House
New Jersey	Legislature	Senate	General Assembly	State House
New Mexico	Legislature	Senate	House of Representatives	State Capitol
New York	Legislature	Senate	Assembly	State Capitol
North Carolina	General Assembly	Senate	House of Representatives	State Legislative Building
North Dakota	Legislative Assembly	Senate	House of Representatives	State Capitol
Ohio	General Assembly	Senate	House of Representatives	State House
Oklahoma	Legislature	Senate	House of Representatives	State Capitol
Oregon	Legislative Assembly	Senate	House of Representatives	State Capitol
Pennsylvania	General Assembly	Senate	House of Representatives	Main Capitol Building
Rhode Island	General Assembly	Senate	House of Representatives	State House
South Carolina	General Assembly	Senate	House of Representatives	State House
South Dakota	Legislature	Senate	House of Representatives	State Capitol
Tennessee	General Assembly	Senate	House of Representatives	State Capitol
Texas	Legislature	Senate	House of Representatives	State Capitol
Utah	Legislature	Senate	House of Representatives	State Capitol
Vermont	General Assembly	Senate	House of Representatives	State House
Virginia	General Assembly	Senate	House of Delegates	State Capitol
Washington	Legislature	Senate	House of Representatives	State Capitol
West Virginia	Legislature	Senate	House of Delegates	State Capitol
Wisconsin	Legislature	Senate	Assembly (b)	State Capitol
Wyoming	Legislature	Senate	House of Representatives	State Capitol
Dist. of Columbia	Council of the District of Columbia	(a)		Council Chamber
American Samoa	Legislature	Senate	House of Representatives	Maota Fono
Guam	Legislature	(a)		Congress Building
No. Mariana Islands	Legislature	Senate	House of Representatives	Civic Center Building
Puerto Rico	Legislative Assembly	Senate	House of Representatives	The Capitol
U.S. Virgin Islands	Legislature	(a)		Capitol Building

Source: The Council of State Governments, *Directory I - Elective Officials 2004.*

(a) Unicameral legislature. Except in Dist. of Columbia, members go by the title Senator.

(b) Members of the lower house go by the title Representative.

Table 3.2
LEGISLATIVE SESSIONS: LEGAL PROVISIONS

State or other jurisdiction	Regular sessions				Special sessions		
	Legislature convenes			Limitation on length of session (a)	Legislature may call	Legislature may determine subject	Limitation on length of session
	Year	Month	Day				
Alabama	Annual	Jan. Mar. Feb.	2nd Tues. (b) 1st Tues. (c)(d) 1st Tues. (e)	30 L in 105 C	No	Yes (f)	12 L in 30 C
Alaska	Annual	Jan.	2nd Mon.	121 C	By petition, 2/3 members, each house	Yes	30 C
Arizona	Annual	Jan.	2nd Mon.	(i)	By petition, 2/3 members, each house	Yes	None
Arkansas	Biennial-odd year	Jan.	2nd Mon.	60 C (h)	No	No (j)	None
California	(l)	Jan.	1st Mon. (d)	None	No	No	None
Colorado	Annual	Jan.	No later than 2nd Wed.	120 C	By petition, 2/3 members, each house	Yes (g)	None
Connecticut	Annual	Jan. Feb.	Wed. after 1st Mon. (n) Wed. after 1st Mon. (o)	(p)	By petition, 2/3 members, each house (q) Joint call, presiding officers, both houses	Yes	None
Delaware	Annual	Jan.	2nd Tues.	June 30	Joint call, presiding officers, both houses	Yes	None
Florida	Annual	Mar.	1st Tues. after 1st Mon.	60 C (h)	Joint call, presiding officers, both houses or	Yes	20 C (h)
Georgia	Annual	Jan.	2nd Mon.	40 L	By petition, 3/5 members, each house	No	40 L
Hawaii	Annual	Jan.	3rd Wed.	60 L (h)	By petition, 2/3 members, each house	Yes	30 L (h)
Idaho	Annual	Jan.	Mon. on or nearest 9th day	None	No	No	20 C
Illinois	Annual	Jan.		None	Joint call, presiding officers, both houses	Yes (g)	None
Indiana	Annual	Jan.	2nd Mon. (d)(t) even-30 C or Mar. 14	odd-61 C or Apr. 29;	No	Yes	30 L or 40 C
Iowa	Annual	Jan.	2nd Mon. even-100 C	odd-110 C	By petition, 2/3 members, each house	Yes	None
Kansas	Annual	Jan.	2nd Mon.	odd-None; even-90 C (h)	Petition to governor of 2/3 members, each house	Yes	None
Kentucky	Annual	Jan.	1st Tues. after 1st Mon. even-60 L	odd-30 L	No	No	None
Louisiana	Annual	Mar. (o) Apr. (n)	last Mon. (o) last Mon. (n)	even-60 L in 85 C; odd-45 L in 60 C	By petition, majority, each house	Yes	30 C
Maine	(l)(m)	Dec. Jan.	1st Wed. (b) Wed. after 1st Tues. (o)	3rd Wed. of June 3rd Wed. of April	By petition, majority, each house	Yes	None
Maryland	Annual	Jan.	2nd Wed.	90 C	By petition, majority, each house	Yes	30 C
Massachusetts	Biennial	Jan.	1st Wed.	(w)	By petition (x)	Yes	None
Michigan	Annual	Jan.	2nd Wed.	None	No	No	None
Minnesota	(y)	Jan.	Tues. after 1st Mon. (n)	120 L or 1st Mon. after 3rd Sat. in May (y)	No	Yes	None

See footnotes at end of table.

LEGISLATIVE SESSIONS: LEGAL PROVISIONS — Continued

State or other jurisdiction	Regular sessions				Special sessions		
	Legislature convenes			Limitation on length of session (a)	Legislature may call	Legislature may determine subject	Limitation on length of session
	Year	Month	Day				
Mississippi	Annual	Jan.	Tues. after 1st Mon.	125 C (z); 90C (z)	No	No	None
Missouri	Annual	Jan.	Wed. after 1st Mon.	May 30	By petition, 3/4 members, each house	Yes (g)	30 C (aa)
Montana	Biennial-odd year	Jan.	1st Mon.	90 L	By petition, majority, each house	Yes	None
Nebraska	Annual	Jan.	Wed. after 1st Mon.	odd-90 L; even-60 L	By petition, 2/3 members	Yes	None
Nevada	Biennial-odd year	Feb.	1st Mon.	120 C	No	No	None (k)
New Hampshire	Annual	Jan.	Wed. after 1st Tues.	45 L	By petition, 2/3 members, each house	Yes	15 L (r)
New Jersey	Annual	Jan.	2nd Tues.	None	By petition, majority, each house	Yes	None
New Mexico	Annual	Jan.	3rd Tues.	odd-60 C; even-30 C	By petition, 3/5 members, each house	Yes (g)	30 C
New York	Annual	Jan.	Wed. after 1st Mon.	None	By petition, 2/3 members, each house	Yes (g)	None
North Carolina	(y)	Jan.	3rd Wed. after 2nd Mon. (n)	None	By petition, 3/5 members, each house	Yes	None
North Dakota	Biennial-odd year	Jan.	Tues. after Jan. 3, but not later than Jan. 11	80 L	Yes (ff)	Yes	None
Ohio	(s)	Jan. (n)	1st Mon. (ee)	None	Joint call, presiding officers, both houses	Yes	None
Oklahoma	Annual	Feb.	1st Mon.	last Fri. in May	By vote, 2/3 members, each house	Yes (g)	None
Oregon	Biennial-odd year	Jan.	2nd Mon.	None	By petition, majority, each house	Yes	None
Pennsylvania	(dd)	Jan.	1st Tues.	None	By petition, majority each house	No	None
Rhode Island	Annual	Jan.	1st. Tues.	None	Joint call, presiding officers, both house	Yes	None
South Carolina	Biennial	Jan.	2nd Tues.	None	By vote, 2/3 members, each house	Yes	None
South Dakota	Annual	Jan.	2nd Tues.	odd-40 L; even-35 L	By petition, 2/3 members, each house	Yes	None
Tennessee	Annual	Jan.	(bb)	90 L (u)	By petition, 2/3 members, each house	Yes	30 L (u)
Texas	Biennial-odd year	Jan.	2nd Tues.	140 C	No	No	30 C
Utah	Annual	Jan.	3rd. Mon.	45 C	(cc)	No	None
Vermont	Annual	Jan.	Wed. after 1st Mon.	None	No	Yes	None
Virginia	Annual	Jan.	2nd Wed.	odd-30 C (h); even-60 C (h)	By petition, 2/3 members, each house	Yes	None
Washington	Annual	Jan.	2nd Mon.	odd-105 C; even-60 C	By vote, 2/3 members, each house	Yes	30 C
West Virginia	Annual	Jan	2nd Wed.	60 C (h)	By petition, 3/5 members, each house	Yes (g)	None
Wisconsin	Annual (gg)	Jan.	1st Mon. (n)	None	By petition, majority members each house	No	None

See footnotes at end of table.

LEGISLATIVE SESSIONS: LEGAL PROVISIONS — Continued

State or other jurisdiction	Regular sessions Legislature convenes			Limitation on length of session (a)	Special sessions		
	Year	Month	Day		Legislature may call	Legislature may determine subject	Limitation on length of session
Wyoming	Annual	Jan. Feb.	2nd Tues. (n) 3rd Mon. (o)	odd-40 L; even-20 L;	By petition, majority members each house biennium-60 L	Yes	20 L
Dist. of Columbia	(hh)	Jan.	2nd day	None			
American Samoa	Annual	Jan. July	2nd Mon. 2nd Mon.	45 L 45 L	No	No	None
Guam	Annual	Jan.	2nd Mon. (ii)	None	No	No	None
No. Mariana Islands	Annual	(jj)	(d)(jj)	90 L (jj)	Upon request of presiding officers, both houses	Yes (g)	10 C
Puerto Rico	Annual (v)	Jan. Aug.	2nd Mon. 3rd Mon.	5 mo. 4 mo.	No	No	20 C
U.S. Virgin Islands	Annual	Jan.	2nd Mon.	None	No	No	None

Source: The Council of State Governments' survey, October 2003.

Note: Some legislatures will also reconvene after normal session to consider bills vetoed by governor. Connecticut—if governor vetoes any bill, secretary of state must reconvene General Assembly on second Monday after the last day on which governor is either authorized to transmit or has transmitted every bill with his objections, whichever occurs first: General Assembly must adjourn sine die not later than three days after its reconvening. Hawaii—legislature may reconvene on 45th day after adjournment sine die, in special session, without call. Louisiana—legislature meets in a maximum five-day veto session on the 40th day after final adjournment. Missouri—if governor returns any bill on or after the fifth day before the last day on which legislature may consider bills (in even-numbered years), legislature automatically reconvenes on first Wednesday following the second Monday in September for a maximum 10 C sessions. New Jersey—legislature meets in special session (without call or petition) to act on bills returned by governor on 45th day after sine die adjournment of the regular session; if the second year expires before the 45th day, the day preceding the end of the legislative year. Utah—if 2/3 of the members of each house favor reconvening to consider vetoed bills, a maximum five-day session is set by the presiding officers. Virginia—legislature reconvenes on sixth Wednesday after adjournment for a maximum three-day session (may be extended to seven days upon vote of majority of members elected to each house). Washington—upon petition of 2/3 of the members of each house, legislature meets 45 days after adjournment for a maximum five-day session.

Key:
C — Calendar day
L — Legislative day (in some states called a session day or workday; definition may vary slightly, however, generally refers to any day on which either house of legislature is in session).
(a) Applies to each year unless otherwise indicated.
(b) General election year (quadrennial election year).
(c) Year after quadrennial election.
(d) Legal provision for organizational session prior to stated convening date. Alabama—in the year after quadrennial election, second Tuesday in January for 10 C. California—in the even-numbered general election year, first Monday in December for an organizational session, recess until the first Monday in January of the odd-numbered year. Indiana—third Tuesday after first Monday in November. No. Mariana Islands—in year after general election, second Monday in January.
(e) Other years.
(f) By 2/3 vote each house.
(g) Only if legislature convenes itself. Special sessions called by the legislature are unlimited in scope in New Mexico.

(h) Session may be extended by vote of members in both houses. Arkansas—2/3 vote. Florida—3/5 vote, session may be extended by vote of members in each house. Hawaii—petition of 2/3 membership for maximum 15-day extension. Kansas—2/3 vote. Virginia—2/3 vote for 30 C extension. West Virginia—may be extended by the governor.
(i) No constitutional or statutory provision; however, legislative rules require that regular sessions adjourn no later than Saturday of the week during which the 100th day of the session falls.
(j) After governor's business has been disposed of, members may remain in session up to 15 C by a 2/3 vote of both houses.
(k) No limit, however legislators are only paid up to 20 calendar days during a special session.
(l) Regular sessions begin after general election, in December of even-numbered year. In California, legislature meets in December for an organizational session, recesses until the first Monday in January of the odd-numbered year and continues in session until Nov. 30 of next even-numbered year. In Maine, session which begins in December of general election year runs into the following year (odd-numbered); second session begins in next even-numbered year.
(m) Second session limited to consideration of specific types of legislation. Maine—budgetary matters; legislation in the governor's call; emergency legislation; legislation referred to committees for study.
(n) Odd-numbered years.
(o) Even-numbered years.
(p) Odd-numbered years—not later than Wednesday after first Monday in June; even-numbered years—not later than Wednesday after first Monday in May.
(q) Notice sent to secretary of state.
(r) Limitation is on payment of legislative pay and mileage.
(s) General Assembly meets during a two-year biennium that is divided into two annual regular sessions.
(t) Legislators may reconvene at any time after organizational meeting; however, second Monday in January is the final date by which regular session must be in process.
(u) Tennessee—Odd year, first half general assembly 45 legislative days; even year, second half general assembly 45 legislative days.
(v) Legislature meets twice a year. During general election years, the legislature only convenes on the January session.
(w) Legislative rules say formal business must be concluded by Nov. 15th of the 1st session in the biennium, or by July 31st of the 2nd session for the biennium.
(x) Joint rules provide for the submission of a written statement requesting special session by a specified number of members of each chamber.

LEGISLATIVE SESSIONS: LEGAL PROVISIONS — Continued

(y) Legal provision for session in odd-numbered year; however, legislature may divide, and in practice has divided, to meet in even-numbered years as well.

(z) 90 C sessions every year, except the first year of a gubernatorial administration during which the legislative session runs for 125 C.

(aa) 30 C if called by legislature; 60 C if called by governor.

(bb) Commencement of regular session depends on concluding date of organizational session. Legislature meets, in odd-numbered year, on second Tuesday in January for a maximum 15 C organizational session, then returns on the Tuesday following the conclusion of the organizational session.

(cc) Legislature may call itself into a veto override session.

(dd) Sessions are two years and begin on the 1st Tuesday of January of the odd numbered year. Session ends on November 30 of the even numbered year. Each calendar year receives its own legislative number.

(ee) Unless Monday is a legal holiday; in second year, the General Assembly convenes on the same date.

(ff) Legislative Council may reconvene the Legislature assembly. However, a reconvened session may not exceed the number of days available (80) but not used by the last regular session.

(gg) The legislature, by joint resolution, establishes the session schedule of activity for the remainder of the biennium at the beginning of the odd-numbered year.

(hh) Each Council period begins on January 2 of each odd-numbered year and ends on January 1 of the following odd-numbered year.

(ii) Legislature meets on the first Monday of each month following its initial session in January.

(jj) 60 L before April 1 and 30 L after July 31.

Table 3.3
THE LEGISLATORS: NUMBERS, TERMS, AND PARTY AFFILIATIONS: 2004

State or other jurisdiction	Senate						House/Assembly						Senate and House/ Assembly totals
	Democrats	Republicans	Other	Vacancies	Total	Term	Democrats	Republicans	Other	Vacancies	Total	Term	
State and territory totals	982	1,008	8	4	2,069*	...	2,721	2,738	19	2	5,501*	...	7,570*
State totals	941	977	2	2	1,971*	...	2,700	2,693	16	2	5,411*	...	7382*
Alabama	25	10	...	...	35	4	63	42	...	...	105	4	140
Alaska	8	12	...	...	20	4	13	27	...	...	40	2	60
Arizona	13	17	...	...	30	2	21	39	...	...	60	2	90
Arkansas	27	8	...	...	35	4	70	30	...	...	100	2	135
California	25	15	...	...	40	4	48	32	...	...	80	2	120
Colorado	17	18	...	...	35	4	28	37	...	...	65	2	100
Connecticut	21	15	...	...	36	2	95	56	...	...	151	2	187
Delaware	13	8	...	...	21	4	12	29	...	...	41	2	62
Florida	14	26	...	...	40	4	39	81	...	...	120	2	160
Georgia	26	30	...	...	56	2	107	72	1 (a)	...	180	2	236
Hawaii	20	5	...	...	25	4	36	15	...	...	51	2	76
Idaho	7	28	...	...	35	2	16	54	...	...	70	2	105
Illinois	26	32	1 (a)	...	59	(b)	66	52	...	...	118	2	177
Indiana	18	32	...	...	50	4	51	49	...	...	100	2	150
Iowa	21	29	...	...	50	4	47	53	...	...	100	2	150
Kansas	10	30	...	...	40	4	45	80	...	...	125	2	165
Kentucky	16	22	...	...	38	4	63	36	...	1	100	2	138
Louisiana	24	15	...	...	39	4	68	37	...	...	105	4	144
Maine	18	17	...	...	35	2	80	67	4 (d)	...	151	2	186
Maryland	33	14	...	...	47	4	98	43	...	...	141	4	188
Massachusetts	34	6	...	...	40	2	136	23	1 (a)	...	160	2	200
Michigan	16	22	...	...	38	4	63	47	...	...	110	2	148
Minnesota	35 (c)	31	1 (a)	...	67	4	53 (c)	81	...	...	134	2	201
Mississippi	30	22	...	...	52	4	80	42	...	...	122	4	174
Missouri	14	20	...	...	34	4	73	90	...	...	163	2	197
Montana	21	29	...	...	50	4	47	53	...	...	100	2	150
Nebraska	----------Nonpartisan election----------				49	4	-----------------------Unicameral-----------------------						49
Nevada	8	13	...	...	21	4	23	19	...	...	42	2	63
New Hampshire	6	18	...	...	24	2	119	281	...	...	400	2	424
New Jersey	22	18	...	...	40	4 (e)	47	33	...	...	80	2	120
New Mexico	24	18	...	...	42	4	43	27	...	...	70	2	112
New York	25	37	...	...	62	2	103	47	...	...	150	2	212
North Carolina	28	22	...	...	50	2	59	61	...	...	120	2	170
North Dakota	16	31	...	...	47	4	28	66	...	...	94	4	141
Ohio	11	22	...	...	33	4	37	62	...	...	99	2	132
Oklahoma	28	20	...	...	48	4	53	48	...	...	101	2	149
Oregon	14	15	...	1	30	4	25	35	...	...	60	2	90
Pennsylvania	21	29	...	...	50	4	94	108	...	1	203	2	253
Rhode Island	32	6	...	...	38	2	63	11	1 (a)	...	75	2	113
South Carolina	20	25	...	1	46	4	51	73	...	...	124	2	170
South Dakota	9	26	...	...	35	2	21	49	...	...	70	2	105
Tennessee	18	15	...	...	33	4	54	45	...	...	99	2	132
Texas	12	19	...	...	31	4	62	88	...	...	150	2	181
Utah	7	22	...	...	29	4	19	56	...	...	75	2	104
Vermont	19	11	...	...	30	2	69	74	7 (f)	...	150	2	180
Virginia	16	24	...	...	40	4	37	61	2 (a)	...	100	2	140
Washington	24	25	...	...	49	4	52	46	...	...	98	2	147
West Virginia	24	10	...	...	34	4	68	32	...	...	100	2	134
Wisconsin	15	18	...	...	33	4	40	59	...	...	99	2	132
Wyoming	10	20	...	...	30	4	15	45	...	...	60	2	90
Dist. of Columbia (g)	11	2	...	...	13	4	-----------------------Unicameral-----------------------						13
American Samoa	----------Nonpartisan election----------				18	4	-----------Nonpartisan election----------				21 (l)	2	39
Guam	9	6	...	...	15	2	-----------------------Unicameral-----------------------						15
No. Mariana Islands	2	3	2 (m)	2	9	4	0	16	2 (n)	...	18	2	27
Puerto Rico	7 (h)	20 (i)	1 (j)	...	28	4	21 (h)	29 (i)	1 (j)	...	51	4	7
U.S. Virgin Islands	12	...	3 (k)	...	15	2	-----------------------Unicameral-----------------------						15

See footnotes at end of table.

THE LEGISLATORS: NUMBERS, TERMS, AND PARTY AFFILIATIONS — Continued

Source: The Council of State Governments, December 2003.

* *Note:* Senate and combined body (Senate and House/Assembly) totals include Unicameral legislatures.

Key:

. . . - Does not apply

(a) Independent.

(b) The entire Senate is up for election every 10 years, beginning in 1972. Senate districts are divided into three groups. One group elects senators for terms of four years, four years and two years; the second group for terms of four years, two years and four years; the third group for terms of two years, four years, and four years.

(c) Democratic-Farmer-Labor.

(d) Unenrolled (3); Green Independent Party (1).

(e) The first senatorial term at the beginning of each decade is two years.

(f) Independent (3); Progressive (4).

(g) Council of the District of Columbia.

(h) New Progressive Party.

(i) Popular Democratic Party.

(j) Puerto Rico Independent Party.

(k) Independent (1); Independent Citizens Movement (2).

(l) 21 seats; 20 are elected by popular vote and one is an appointed, non-voting delegate from Swains Island.

(m) Reform (1); Covenant (1).

(n) Covenant (1); Unity (1).

Table 3.3A
THE LEGISLATORS: NUMBERS, TERMS, AND PARTY AFFILIATIONS BY REGION 2003

State	Senate Democrats	Republicans	Other	Vacancies	Total	Term	House/Assembly Democrats	Republicans	Other	Vacancies	Total	Term	Senate and House/ Assembly totals
State totals	941	977	2	2	1,971*	...	2,700	2,693	16	2	5,411*	...	7382*
Eastern Region													
Connecticut	21	15	...	...	36	2	95	56	...	...	151	2	187
Delaware	13	8	...	...	21	4	12	29	...	...	41	2	62
Maine	18	17	...	...	35	2	80	67	4 (d)	...	151	2	186
Massachusetts	34	6	...	...	40	2	136	23	1 (a)	...	160	2	200
New Hampshire ...	6	18	...	...	24	2	119	281	...	...	400	2	424
New Jersey	22	18	...	...	40	4 (e)	47	33	...	...	80	2	120
New York	25	37	...	...	62	2	103	47	...	...	150	2	212
Pennsylvania	21	29	...	...	50	4	94	108	...	1	203	2	253
Rhode Island	32	6	...	...	38	2	63	11	1 (a)	...	75	2	113
Vermont	19	11	...	...	30	2	69	74	7 (f)	...	150	2	180
Regional total	211	165	0	0	376	...	818	729	13	1	1,561	...	1,937
Midwestern Region													
Illinois	26	32	1 (a)	...	59	(b)	66	52	...	...	118	2	177
Indiana	18	32	...	...	50	4	51	49	...	...	100	2	150
Iowa	21	29	...	...	50	4	47	53	...	...	100	2	150
Kansas	10	30	...	...	40	4	45	80	...	...	125	2	165
Michigan	16	22	...	...	38	4	63	47	...	...	110	2	148
Minnesota	35 (c)	31	1 (a)	...	67	4	53 (c)	81	...	...	134	2	201
Nebraska	——————Nonpartisan election——————				49	4	——————Unicameral——————						49
North Dakota	16	31	...	...	47	4	28	66	...	...	94	4	141
Ohio	11	22	...	...	33	4	37	62	...	...	99	2	132
South Dakota	9	26	...	...	35	2	21	49	...	...	70	2	105
Wisconsin	15	18	...	...	33	4	40	59	...	...	99	2	132
Region total	177	273	2	...	501	...	451	598	0	0	1,049	...	1,550
Southern Region													
Alabama	25	10	...	...	35	4	63	42	...	...	105	4	140
Arkansas	27	8	...	...	35	4	70	30	...	...	100	2	135
Florida	14	26	...	...	40	4	39	81	...	...	120	2	160
Georgia	26	30	...	...	56	2	107	72	1 (a)	...	180	2	236
Kentucky	16	22	...	...	38	4	63	36	...	1	100	2	138
Louisiana	24	15	...	...	39	4	68	37	...	...	105	4	144
Maryland	33	14	...	...	47	4	98	43	...	...	141	4	188
Mississippi	30	22	...	...	52	4	80	42	...	...	122	4	174
Missouri	14	20	...	...	34	4	73	90	...	...	163	2	197
North Carolina	28	22	...	...	50	2	59	61	...	...	120	2	170
Oklahoma	28	20	...	...	48	4	53	48	...	...	101	2	149
South Carolina	20	25	...	1	46	4	51	73	...	...	124	2	170
Tennessee	18	15	...	...	33	4	54	45	...	...	99	2	132
Texas	12	19	...	...	31	4	62	88	...	...	150	2	181
Virginia	16	24	...	...	40	4	37	61	2 (a)	...	100	2	140
West Virginia	24	10	...	...	34	4	68	32	...	...	100	2	134
Region total	355	302	0	1	658	...	1,045	881	3	1	1,930	...	2,588
Western Region													
Alaska	8	12	...	...	20	4	13	27	...	...	40	2	60
Arizona	13	17	...	...	30	2	21	39	...	...	60	2	90
California	25	15	...	...	40	4	48	32	...	...	80	2	120
Colorado	17	18	...	...	35	4	28	37	...	...	65	2	100
Hawaii	20	5	...	...	25	4	36	15	...	...	51	2	76
Idaho	7	28	...	...	35	2	16	54	...	...	70	2	105
Montana	21	29	...	...	50	4	47	53	...	...	100	2	150
Nevada	8	13	...	...	21	4	23	19	...	...	42	2	63
New Mexico	24	18	...	...	42	4	43	27	...	...	70	2	112
Oregon	14	15	...	1	30	4	25	35	...	...	60	2	90
Utah	7	22	...	...	29	4	19	56	...	...	75	2	104
Washington	24	25	...	...	49	4	52	46	...	...	98	2	147
Wyoming	10	20	...	...	30	4	15	45	...	...	60	2	90
Regional total	198	237	0	1	436	...	386	485	0	0	871*	...	1,307

Source: The Council of State Governments, December 2003.

* *Note*: Senate and combined body (Senate and House) totals include Nebraska's unicameral legislature.

Key:

... .—Does not apply

(a) Independent.

(b) The entire Senate is up for election every 10 years, beginning in 1972. Senate districts are divided into three groups. One group elects senators for terms of four years, four years and two years; the second group for terms of four years, two years and four years; the third group for terms of two years, four years, and four years.

(c) Democratic-Farmer-Labor.

(d) Unenrolled (3); Green Independent Party (1).

(e) The first senatorial term at the beginning of each decade is two years.

(f) Independent (3); Progressive (4).

Table 3.4
MEMBERSHIP TURNOVER IN THE LEGISLATURES: 2003

State or other jurisdiction	Senate			House/Assembly		
	Total number of members	Number of membership changes	Percentage change of total	Total number of members	Number of membership changes	Percentage change of total
Alabama	35	0	0	105	0	0
Alaska	20	1	5	40	3	8
Arizona	30	2	7	60	2	3
Arkansas	35	0	0	100	0	0
California	40	0	0	80	2	3
Colorado	35	2	6	65	5	8
Connecticut	36	0	0	151	2	1
Delaware	21	0	0	41	1	2
Florida	40	1	3	120	4	3
Georgia	56	0	0	180	3	2
Hawaii	25	0	0	51	0	0
Idaho	35	0	0	70	3	4
Illinois	59	6	10	118	9	8
Indiana	50	2	4	100	1	1
Iowa	50	2	4	100	3	3
Kansas	40	3	8	125	3	2
Kentucky	38	1	3	100	1	1
Louisiana	39	8	21	105	10	10
Maine	35	0	0	151	0	0
Maryland	47	0	0	141	6	4
Massachusetts	40	1	3	160	1	1
Michigan	38	0	0	110	1	1
Minnesota	67	0	0	134	3	2
Mississippi	52	15	29	122	25	20
Missouri	34	1	3	163	3	2
Montana	50	0	0	100	0	0
Nebraska	49	0	0	------------------------Unicameral------------------------		
Nevada	21	0	0	42	0	0
New Hampshire	24	0	0	400	13	3
New Jersey	40	6	15	80	15	19
New Mexico	42	2	5	70	1	1
New York	62	0	0	150	5	3
North Carolina	50	1	2	120	2	2
North Dakota	47	1	2	94	6	6
Ohio	33	2	21	99	3	3
Oklahoma	48	2	4	101	2	2
Oregon	30	4	13	60	3	5
Pennsylvania	50	2	4	203	8	4
Rhode Island	38	0	0	75	1	1
South Carolina	46	2	4	124	3	2
South Dakota	35	3	9	70	3	4
Tennessee	33	1	3	99	1	1
Texas	31	0	0	150	3	2
Utah	29	1	3	75	2	3
Vermont	30	2	7	150	3	2
Virginia	40	5	13	100	14	14
Washington	49	3	6	98	5	5
West Virginia	34	0	0	100	0	0
Wisconsin	33	3	9	99	5	5
Wyoming	30	2	7	60	1	2
Dist. of Columbia	13	0	0	------------------------Unicameral------------------------		
American Samoa	18	0	0	21	0	0
Guam	15	0	0	------------------------Unicameral------------------------		
No. Mariana Islands	9	1	11	18	8	44
Puerto Rico	28	3	11	51	3	6
U.S. Virgin Islands	15	0	0	------------------------Unicameral------------------------		

Source: The Council of State Governments, February 2004.
Note: Turnover calculated after 2003 legislative elections.

Table 3.5
THE LEGISLATORS: QUALIFICATIONS FOR ELECTION

State or other jurisdiction	House/Assembly					Senate				
	Minimum age	U.S. citizen (years)(a)	State resident (years)(b)	District resident (years)	Qualified voter (years)	Minimum age	U.S. citizen (years)(a)	State resident (years)(b)	District resident (years)	Qualified voter (years)
Alabama	21	…	3 (c)	1	…	25	…	3 (c)	1	…
Alaska	21	★	3	1	…	25	★	3	1	★
Arizona	25	★	3	1	…	25	★	3	1	★
Arkansas	21	★	2	1	★	25	★	2	1	★
California	18	3	3 (c)	1	★	18	3	3 (c)	1	★
Colorado	25	★	1	1	★	25	★	1	1	★
Connecticut	18	★	★	★	★	18	★	★	★	★
Delaware	24	…	3	1	…	27	…	3	1	…
Florida	21	…	2	2	…	21	…	2	2	…
Georgia	21	…	2 (c)	1	★	25	…	2 (c)	1	★
Hawaii	18	★	3	(d)	★	18	★	3	(d)	★
Idaho	21	★	…	1	★	21	★	…	1	★
Illinois	21	★	★	2 (e)	★	21	★	2	2 (e)	★
Indiana	21	★	2	1	★	25	★	★	1	★
Iowa	21	★	1	60 days	…	25	★	★	60 days	…
Kansas	18	★	★ (c)	★	★	18	★	★ (c)	★	★
Kentucky	24	…	2 (c)	1	★	30	…	6 (c)	1	★
Louisiana	18	★	2	1	★	18	★	2	1	★
Maine	21	5	1	3 mo.	…	25	5	1	3 mo.	…
Maryland	21	…	1 (c)	6 mo. (f)	…	25	…	1 (c)	6 mo. (f)	…
Massachusetts	18	…	…	…	★	18	…	5	★	★
Michigan	21	★	★	(d)	…	21	★	★	(d)	…
Minnesota	18	★	1	6 mo.	★	21	★	1	6 mo.	★
Mississippi	21	…	4 (c)	2	★	25	…	4 (c)	2	4
Missouri	24	★	★	1	2	30	★	★	1	3
Montana	18	…	1	6 mo. (g)	★	18	…	1	6 mo. (g)	…
Nebraska	U	U	U	U	U	21	★	★	1	★
Nevada	21	★	1 (c)	30 days (l)	★	21	…	1 (c)	30 days (l)	★
New Hampshire	18	★	2 (c)	…	★	30	★	7 (c)	1	★
New Jersey	21	★	2 (c)	1	★	30	★	4 (c)	1	★
New Mexico	21	★	★	★	★	25	★	★	★	★
New York	18	★	5	1 (h)	★	18	★	5	1 (h)	★
North Carolina	21	…	1	1	…	25	…	2	1	…
North Dakota	18	…	1	★	★	18	…	1	★	★
Ohio	18	★	30 days	1	★	18	★	30 days	1	★
Oklahoma	21	★	★	★	★	25	★	★	★	★
Oregon	21	★	…	1	…	21	★	…	1	…
Pennsylvania	21	…	4 (c)	1	★	25	…	4 (c)	1	★
Rhode Island	18	★	30 days	30 days	★	18	★	30 days	30 days	★
South Carolina	21	…	…	★	…	25	…	…	★	…

See footnotes at end of table.

THE LEGISLATORS: QUALIFICATIONS FOR ELECTION — Continued

State or other jurisdiction	House/Assembly					Senate				
	Minimum age	U.S. citizen (years) (a)	State resident (years) (b)	District resident (years)	Qualified voter (years)	Minimum age	U.S. citizen (years) (a)	State resident (years) (b)	District resident (years)	Qualified voter (years)
South Dakota	21	★	2	★	★	21	★	★	★	★
Tennessee	21	★	3 (c)	1	★	30	★	3	1	★
Texas	21	★	2	1	★	26	★	5	1	★
Utah	25	★	3 (c)	6 mo.	★	25	★	3 (c)	6 mo.	★
Vermont	18	★	2	1	...	18	★	2	1	...
Virginia	21	★	1	★	★	21	★	1	★	★
Washington	18	★	★	(d)	★	18	★	★	(d)	★
West Virginia	18	1	1 (c)	1	★	25	5	5 (c)	1	★
Wisconsin	18	★	1	(d)	★	18	★	1	(d)	★
Wyoming	21	★	★ (c)	1	★	25	★	★ (c)	1	★
Dist. of Columbia	U	U	U	U	U	18	...	1	★	U
American Samoa	25	★ (i)	5	1	...	30 (j)	★ (i)	5	1	...
Guam	U	U	U	U	U	25	★	5	...	U
No. Mariana Islands	21	...	3	(d)	★	25	...	5	(d)	★
Puerto Rico	25	...	2	1 (k)	...	30	...	5	1 (k)	...
U.S. Virgin Islands	21	★	...	3	★	21	★	...	3	★

Source: The Council of State Governments' survey, October 2003.

Note: Many state constitutions have additional provisions disqualifying persons from holding office if they are convicted of a felony, bribery, perjury or other infamous crimes.

Key:

U—Unicameral legislature; members are called senators, except in District of Columbia.

★—Formal provision; number of years not specified.

...—No formal provision.

(a) In some states candidate must be a U.S. citizen to be an elector, and must be an elector to run.

(b) In some states candidate must be a state resident to be an elector, and must be an elector to run.

(c) State citizenship requirement.

(d) Must be a qualified voter of the district; number of years not specified.

(e) Following redistricting, a candidate may be elected from any district that contains a part of the district in which (s)he resided at the time of redistricting, and reelected if a resident of the new district he represents for 18 months prior to reelection.

(f) If the district was established for less than six months, residency is length of establishment of district.

(g) Shall be a resident of the county if it contains one or more districts or of the district if it contains all or parts of more than one county.

(h) After redistricting, must have been a resident of the county in which the district is contained for one year immediately preceding election.

(i) Or U.S. national.

(j) Must be registered matai.

(k) The district legislator must live in the municipality he/she represents.

(l) 30 days prior to close of filing for declaration of candidacy.

Table 3.6
SENATE LEADERSHIP POSITIONS: METHODS OF SELECTION

State or other jurisdiction	President	President pro tem	Majority leader	Assistant majority leader	Majority floor leader	Assistant majority floor leader	Majority whip	Majority caucus chair	Minority leader	Assistant minority leader	Minority floor leader	Assistant minority floor leader	Minority whip	Minority caucus chair
Alabama	(a)	ES	AT				EC	EC	EC				EC	
Alaska	ES	AP	EC				EC	EC	EC	EC			EC	EC
Arizona	ES	ES	EC				EC		EC	EC			EC	EC
Arkansas	(a)	ES	EC		EC		EC	EC	EC		EC		EC	EC
California	(a)	ES		EC	EC		EC	EC	EC	EC	EC		EC	EC
Colorado	ES (bb)	ES (bb)	EC	EC	AP	AP	AP	AP	EC	AL	AL	AL	AL	AL
Connecticut (b)	(a)	ES	AP	AP	AP	AP	AP	AP	EC	AL	EC	EC	EC	AL
Delaware	EC/ES	EC/ES	EC	AL	AP or AL	AP or AL	EC	AP or AL	EC	AL	AL	AL	AL	AL
Florida	(a)	AP	AP		AP or AL		AP or AL	AP or AL	EC	AL	EC	AL	AL	EC
Georgia	(a)	ES	EC				EC	EC	EC	EC			EC	EC
Hawaii	ES	ES (f)	EC		EC		EC (e)	EC (cc)	EC	EC	EC		EC	EC
Idaho	(a)	ES	EC	EC			EC	EC	EC	AL/5				AL
Illinois	ES		AP (c)	AP/6		AL	EC	AP	EC	AL	EC	AL	AL	EC
Indiana	(a)		EC	AL	AL		AL	EC	EC	EC	AL	AL	AL	EC
Iowa	ES	ES	EC	EC	EC		EC	EC	EC	EC	EC		EC	EC
Kansas	ES	ES (f)	EC	EC (d)	EC		EC (e)	(e)	EC	EC	EC	EC	EC	EC
Kentucky	ES	ES			EC	EC	EC	EC	EC	EC		EC	EC	EC
Louisiana	ES	ES					AL		EC					
Maine	ES	AP	EC	EC	EC	EC	EC	EC	EC	EC	EC	EC	EC	EC
Maryland	ES	ES	AP (n)	AP (n)	(n)	(n)	AP (bb)		EC (bb)		(bb)			
Massachusetts	EC	ES (f)	AP	AP	AP		EC (e)	(p)	EC				EC	(p)
Michigan (aa)	(a)	ES		EC	EC	EC	EC	AT (j)	EC	EC	EC	EC	EC	EC
Minnesota	ES	ES		EC		EC	AL	EC	EC	EC	EC	EC	EC	AL
Mississippi	(a)	ES	EC	EC	EC	(n)	EC				EC	EC	EC	EC
Missouri	ES	ES	AP (n)	AP (n)	(n)		EC			(bb)				
Montana	ES	ES (g)	EC	AP	ES		ES	(p)	EC	EC	ES	EC	ES	(p)
Nebraska (U)	ES (g)	ES (g)												
Nevada	(a)								EC					EC
New Hampshire	(a)	AP	AP	EC/3	EC	EC	EC	EC	EC	AL	EC	AL	EC	AL
New Jersey (h)	ES	ES	EC	EC/3	EC	(n)	AP	EC	EC	EC/3	EC	EC	EC	EC
New Mexico	(a)	ES	EC (u)	EC	EC (u)	EC	EC	EC (u)	EC (u)	AL	EC (u)	EC	EC	EC
New York (v)	(a)	ES (i)	(i)	AT/2	AP	EC	AT	AT (j)	EC	AL/3	EC	EC	AL	AL (j)
North Carolina	(a)	ES	EC	EC	EC	EC	EC	EC	EC	EC	EC	EC	EC	EC
North Dakota	(a)	ES	EC	EC			EC	EC	EC	EC	EC	EC	EC	EC
Ohio (l)	ES (p)	ES	EC		ES		ES	(p)	ES (p)	ES	ES	ES	ES	(p)
Oklahoma	(a)	ES	EC	EC	EC	EC	EC	EC	EC	EC/2	EC	EC	EC	EC
Oregon	(a)	ES	EC	AL/3	EC	EC	EC/1	(p)	EC (p)	EC	EC	EC	EC/1	(p)
Pennsylvania	(;)	ES	EC	EC	EC	EC	EC	EC	EC	EC	EC	EC	EC	EC
Rhode Island (k)	ES	ES	EC	AL/6 (o)	EC	AP	AP	EC	EC	AP/2 (o)	AP	AP	AP	
South Carolina	(a)	ES	EC						EC					

See footnotes at end of table.

SENATE LEADERSHIP POSITIONS: METHODS OF SELECTION — Continued

State or other jurisdiction	President	President pro tem	Majority leader	Assistant majority leader	Majority floor leader	Assistant majority floor leader	Majority whip	Majority caucus chair	Minority leader	Assistant minority leader	Minority floor leader	Assistant minority floor leader	Minority whip	Minority caucus chair
South Dakota	(a)	ES	EC	EC	EC	EC	EC	...	EC	EC	...	...	EC	...
Tennessee	ES	AP (m)	EC (m)	...	...	...	...	EC (m)	EC (m)	...	...	...	EC	EC (m)
Texas	(a)	ES	...	...	...	...	...	...	...	...	...	...	EC	EC (r)
Utah (q)	ES	ES	EC	...	EC (r)	...	EC	...	EC	...	EC (r)	...	EC (r)	EC (r)
Vermont	(a)	ES	EC	EC	EC (r)	EC (r)	EC (r)	EC (r)	EC (t)	EC (t)	EC (t)	EC (t)	EC (t)	EC (t)
Virginia	(a)	ES	EC	...	EC	...	...	EC	EC	EC	EC	...	EC	EC
Washington (s)	(a)	ES	EC	...	EC	...	EC	EC	EC (t)	EC (t)	EC (t)	EC (t)	AL	EC
West Virginia	ES	AP	AP	...	EC	...	AP	...	EC	EC	EC	EC	EC	EC
Wisconsin	ES	ES	EC	EC	EC	EC	EC	EC	EC	EC	EC	EC	EC	EC
Wyoming	ES	ES (f)	...	...	EC	...	EC	...	EC	EC	EC	EC	EC	EC
Dist. of Columbia (U)	(w)	(x)	...	...	...	...	...	...	...	...	...	...	...	...
American Samoa	ES	ES	...	...	...	...	...	...	...	...	...	...	...	...
Guam (U)	ES (g)	ES (f)	EC	EC	EC	EC	EC	...	EC	EC	EC	...	EC	EC
No. Mariana Islands	ES (ee)	AS	(ee)	...	ES (y)	...	...	(dd)	EC (p)	...	...	...	...	EC
Puerto Rico	ES (p)	AS	AS	...	EC (z)	...	EC (p)	...	EC (p)	EC (z)	EC (z)	...	EC (p)	(p)
U.S. Virgin Islands (U)	ES	ES (f)	ES	...	(n)	...	(n)	(n)	(n)	...	...	...	...	...

Source: The Council of State Governments' survey, October 2003.

Note: In some states, the leadership positions in the Senate are not empowered by the law or by the rules of the chamber, but rather by the party members themselves. Entry following slash indicates number of individuals holding specified position.

Key:
ES — Elected or confirmed by all members of the Senate.
EC — Elected by party caucus.
AP — Appointed by president.
AT — Appointed by president pro tempore.
AL — Appointed by party leader.
(U) — Unicameral legislative body.
... — Position does not exist or is not selected on a regular basis.

(a) Lieutenant governor is president of the Senate by virtue of the office.
(b) Position titles are as follows: chief deputy president pro tem, two deputy presidents pro tem, a chief assistant president pro tem, three assistant presidents pro tem, three deputy majority leaders (AP); a minority leader pro tem, two chief deputy minority leaders, a deputy minority leader-at-large, and three deputy minority leaders (AL).
(c) The president can, at his or her discretion, serve as majority leader and usually does.
(d) Assistant majority leader also serves as majority party caucus chairperson.
(e) Official title is assistant majority leader/whip.
(f) Official title is vice president. In Guam, vice president.
(g) Official title is speaker. In Tennessee, official also has the statutory title of "lieutenant governor."
(h) Additional positions include deputy majority leader (EC), two deputy assistant minority leaders (EC), and minority leader pro tem (EC).
(i) President pro tempore is also majority leader.
(j) Majority caucus chair: official title is majority conference chair. Minority caucus chair: official title is minority conference chair.
(k) Additional positions include deputy president pro tempore.
(l) Additional positions include assistant president pro tempore (ES) and assistant minority whip (ES).
(m) President pro tem: official title is speaker pro tem. Official titles of majority party leaders: Democratic; official titles of minority party leaders: Republican.

(n) Majority leader also serves as majority floor leader; deputy majority leader is official title and serves as assistant majority floor leader. there is also an assistant deputy majority leader; there is also a deputy majority whip and assistant deputy majority whips; minority leader also serves as minority floor leader.
(o) Assistant majority leader: official title is deputy majority leader. Assistant minority leader: official title is deputy minority leader.
(p) President and minority floor leader are also caucus chairs. In Ohio and Puerto Rico, president and minority leader. In Oregon, majority leader and minority leader.
(q) Additional positions include assistant majority whip (EC) assistant majority whip (EC), minority whip (EC), assistant minority whip (EC) and minority caucus leader (EC).
(r) Majority leader serves as majority floor leader and majority caucus chair. Assistant majority leader serves as assistant majority floor leader and majority whip. Minority leader serves as minority floor leader and minority caucus chair. Assistant minority leader serves as assistant minority floor leader and minority whip.
(s) Additional positions include vice president pro tem (ES), majority assistant whip (EC), and Republican assistant whip (EC).
(t) Customary title of minority party leaders is the party designation (Republican).
(u) Majority leader also serves as majority floor leader. Minority leader also serves as minority floor leader.
(v) Additional positions include vice president pro tem (AT), deputy majority leader (AT), majority program development chair (AT), deputy minority leader (AL), senior assistant majority leader (AT), majority conference vice chair (AT), minority conference vice chair (AL), majority conference secretary (AT), deputy majority whip (AT), majority steering committee chair (AT), minority conference secretary (AL), assistant majority whip (AT), and assistant minority whip (AL).
(w) Chair of the Council, which is an elected position.
(x) Appointed by the chair; official title is chair pro tem.
(y) Official title is floor leader.
(z) Office title is alternate floor leader.
(aa) Additional positions include assistant president, associate president pro tempore, assistant majority caucus chair, assistant minority caucus chair.
(bb) Selected informally by majority caucus shortly after November election.
(cc) Official title is majority caucus leader.
(dd) Official title is caucus chairman.
(ee) Speaker also serves as majority leader.

Table 3.7
HOUSE LEADERSHIP POSITIONS: METHODS OF SELECTION

State or other jurisdiction	Speaker	Speaker pro tem	Majority leader	Assistant majority leader	Majority floor leader	Assistant majority floor leader	Majority whip	Majority caucus chair	Minority leader	Assistant minority leader	Minority floor leader	Assistant minority floor leader	Minority whip	Minority caucus chair
Alabama	EH	EH	EC						EC					
Alaska	EH		EC				EC	EC	EC				EC	EC
Arizona	EH	AS	EC				EC		EC	EC			EC	
Arkansas	EH	AS	EC	AS			AS		EC				EC	
California	EH	AS	AS		AS	AS		EC	EC		EC			EC
Colorado	EH (x)	AS	EC	EC			EC		EC	EC			EC	EC
Connecticut	EH	AS/4 (b)	EC	EC/4 (b)		AS (b)	AS (b)	AS (b)	EC	AL (b)	AL (b)	AL (b)	AL (b)	AL (b)
Delaware	EC/EH	EH	EC			AS	AS	AS	EC	EC	AL	AL	AL	AL
Florida	EH	EH	AS	AS		AS	AS	AS	EC		AL	EC	AL	AL
Georgia	EH	EH	EC				EC	EC	EC				EC	EC
Hawaii	EH	EH (a)	EC		EC				EC	EC			EC	EC
Idaho	EH		EC	EC			EC	EC	EC	EC			EC	EC
Illinois	EH	EH	AS	AS/6	AS/2 (c)	AS	AS	AS (c)	EC	AL/6	AL/2 (c)	AL		AL (c)
Indiana	EH	AL	EC	AL	AL		AL	AL	EC	AL	EC	EC	AL	AL
Iowa	EH	EH	EC	EC		AS			EC	EC				
Kansas	EH	EH	EC	EC	EC	EC	EC	EC	EC	EC	EC	EC	EC	EC
Kentucky	EH	EH	EC	EC	EC		EC	EC	EC	EC	EC		EC	EC
Louisiana	EH	EH	EC (j)		(j)	(j)	(j)		EC (j)	EC (j)	(j)	(j)	(j)	
Maine	EH	AS (d)	EC (j)	EC (j)	(e)	AS			EC	EC (j)	(j)	(j)	EC	(g)
Maryland	EH	EH	AS (e)	AS (e)			AS	(g)	EC					
Massachusetts	EC		AS	AS				(h)	EC (h)	AL		EC	EC	(h)
Michigan	EH		EC					EC	EC	EC			EC	EC
Minnesota	EH	AS	EC	EC			EC		EC	AL				
Mississippi	EH	AS	EC						EC					
Missouri	EH	EH		EC		EC					EC	EC	EC	EC
Montana	EH	EH			EH	EH	EH	EH (g)	EH (g)		EH		EH	(g)
Nebraska	(i)													
Nevada	EH	AS (a)	AS	AS (k)	EC	EC	AS (k)	AS	AS (k)	AL (k)	EC	EC	EC	EC (m)
New Hampshire	EH	EH	EC	EC/3			EC	EC (m)	EC	EC/4			EC	EC
New Jersey (l)	EH		EC			EC	EC	EC	EC		EC		EC	
New Mexico	EH	EH	EC		EC (h)		EC	EC	EC		EC (h)	EC	EC	EC
New York (n)	EH	AS	AS	AS		AS	AS	AS (o)	EC	AL/2			AL	AL (o)
North Carolina	EH	EH	EC					EC	EC	EC	EC			EC
North Dakota	EH	EH	EC	EC			EH	EC	EC	EC	EC		EH	EC
Ohio (p)	EH (g)	EH			EH	EH	EH	(g)	EH (g)				EH	(g)
Oklahoma	EH	EH	AS		AS	AS	AS	AS	EC	EC	EC		EC	EC
Oregon	EH	EH	EC (q)	AL/7	EC		EC	(q)	EC (q)	AL/5	EC		EC/3	(q)
Pennsylvania	EH	EH	EC	EC	EC	EC	EC	EC	EC	EC	EC	EC	EC	EC
Rhode Island	EH	AS	EC	EC					EC		EC			
South Carolina	EH	EH	EC	EC/11 (f)			AL		EC	AL/3 (r)			AL	

See footnotes at end of table.

HOUSE LEADERSHIP POSITIONS — METHODS OF SELECTION — Continued

State or other jurisdiction	Speaker	Speaker pro tem	Majority leader	Assistant majority leader	Majority floor leader	Assistant majority floor leader	Majority whip	Majority caucus chair	Minority leader	Assistant minority leader	Minority floor leader	Assistant minority floor leader	Minority whip	Minority caucus chair
South Dakota	EH	EH	EC	EC	...	...	EC	...	EC	EC	...	...	EC	...
Tennessee	EH	EH	EC	EC	EC	EC	EC	EC	EC	EC	EC	...	EC	EC
Texas	EH	AS	...	...	EC	EC (s)	...	...	...	...	EC	...	...	EC
Utah	EH	AS	EC	EC	...	...	EC	EC	EC	EC (s)	...	...	EC	EC(s)
Vermont	EH	...	EC	EC	(i)	(i)	(i)	(i)	EC	EC	(i)	(i)	(i)	(i)
Virginia	EH	...	EC (h)	...	(h)	...	EC	EC	EC (h)	...	(h)	EC	...	EC
Washington (o)	EH	EH	EC	EC	...	EC/2	EC	EC (t)	EC	...	EC	EC	(EC	EC
West Virginia	EH	AS	AS	AS	EC	EC	AS	AS	EC	EC	EC	EC	...	EC
Wisconsin	EH	EH	EC	EC	EC	EC	EC	EC	EC	EC	EC	EC	EC	EC
Wyoming	EH	EH	...	...	EC	EC	EC	EC	...	...	...	...	EC	EC
Dist. of Columbia	EH	EH (a)	...	...	...	...	...	...	...	...	...	...	...	...
American Samoa	(i)	...	...	...	...	...	...	...	...	...	...	...	...	...
Guam	(i)	...	...	...	...	...	...	...	EC	...	...	...	...	...
No. Mariana Islands	EH (u)	...	(u)	...	EH (v)	...	...	...	EC	...	EC (w)	...	...	...
Puerto Rico	EH (g)	EH (a)	EC	...	EC (w)	...	...	...	EC (g)	...	EC (w)	...	...	(g)
U.S. Virgin Islands	(i)	...	...	...	...	...	...	...	...	...	...	...	...	...

Source: The Council of State Governments' survey, October 2003.

Note: In some states, the leadership positions in the house are not empowered by the law or by the rules of the chamber, but rather by the party members themselves. Entry following slash indicates number of individuals holding specified position.

Key:

EH—Elected or confirmed by all members of the house.
EC—Elected by party caucus.
AS—Appointed by speaker.
AL—Appointed by party leader.
. . .—Position does not exist or is not selected on a regular basis.
(a) Each occurance.
(e) Majority leader also serves as majority floor leader. Official title of assistant majority leader is deputy majority leader.
(f) Official title is deputy majority leader.
(g) Speaker and majority leader are also caucus chair.
(h) Majority leader also serves as majority floor leader; minority leader also serves as minority floor leader.
(i) Unicameral legislature; see entries in Table 3.6, Senate Leadership Positions—Methods of Selection.
(j) Majority floor leader is deputy majority leader, assistant majority leader also serves as assistant majority floor leader and majority whip; minority floor leader is deputy minority leader, and minority caucus chair is minority conference chair.

(k) Official titles: assistant majority leader is deputy majority leader, majority whip is deputy majority whip, minority leader is Democratic leader and assistant minority leader is deputy minority leader.
(l) Additional positions include four deputy speakers (EC), three assistant majority whips (EC), majority budget officer (EC), minority leader pro tem (EC), and three deputy minority leaders (EC).
(m) Official titles: majority caucus chair is majority conference leader and minority caucus chair is conference chair.
(n) Additional positions: deputy speaker (AS), assistant speaker (AS), assistant speaker pro tem (AS), minority leader pro tem (AL), assistant minority leader pro tem (AL), deputy majority leader (AS), deputy minority leader (AL), deputy majority whip (AS), deputy minority whip (AL), assistant minority whip (AS), assistant minority whip (AL), majority conference vice-chair (AL), majority conference secretary (AL), minority conference secretary (AL), majority conference vice-chair (AS), minority steering committee chair (AL), majority steering committee vice-chair (AS), minority steering committee vice-chair (AL), majority program committee chair (AS) and minority program committee chair (AL).
(o) Official titles: majority caucus chair is majority conference chair; minority caucus chair is minority conference chair.
(p) Additional positions include assistant majority whip (EH) and assistant minority whip (EH).
(q) Majority leader also serves as majority caucus chair; minority leader also serves as minority caucus chair.
(r) Official title is deputy minority leader.
(s) Assistant majority floor leader known as assistant majority whip, assistant minority floor leader known as assistant minority whip, minority caucus chair known as minority caucus manager.
(t) Additional position is caucus vice chair (EC).
(u) Speaker also serves as majority leader.
(v) Official title is floor leader.
(w) Official title is alternate floor leader.
(x) Selected informally by majority caucus shortly after November election.

Table 3.8
METHOD OF SETTING LEGISLATIVE COMPENSATION

State or other jurisdiction	Constitution	Statute	Compensation commission	Legislators' salaries tied or related to state employees' salaries
Alabama	★	...	...	...
Alaska	...	★	★	...
Arizona	...	...	★ (a)	...
Arkansas	★	★	...	...
California	★	...	★	...
Colorado	...	★	...	...
Connecticut	...	...	★ (b)	...
Delaware	...	★	★ (c)	...
Florida	...	★	...	Statute provides members same percentage increase as state employees.
Georgia	...	★	...	...
Hawaii	...	...	★ (d)	...
Idaho	...	...	★	...
Illinois	...	★	★	Salaries are tied to employment cost index, wages and salaries for state and local government workers.
Indiana	...	★	...	...
Iowa	...	★	★	...
Kansas	...	★	...	...
Kentucky	...	...	★ (e)	...
Louisiana	...	★	...	...
Maine	★	★ (f)	★	...
Maryland	...	...	★ (g)	...
Massachusetts	...	★ (h)	...	...
Michigan	...	...	★ (i)	...
Minnesota	...	★	★ (j)	...
Mississippi	...	★	...	...
Missouri	★	★ (k)	...	...
Montana	...	★	...	Tied to executive branch pay matrix.
Nebraska	★	★	...	...
Nevada	...	★	...	...
New Hampshire	★	...	...	...
New Jersey	★	★	★	...
New Mexico	★	★	...	...
New York	★	★	...	...
North Carolina	...	★	...	...
North Dakota	...	★	★	...
Ohio	★	★	...	...
Oklahoma	...	★	★	...
Oregon	...	★	...	...
Pennsylvania	...	★ (l)	...	...
Rhode Island	★	...	...	...
South Carolina	...	★	...	...
South Dakota	★	★	...	...
Tennessee	★	★	...	...
Texas	★ (m)	...	...	...
Utah	...	...	★	...
Vermont	...	★	...	...
Virginia	★	★ (n)	...	...
Washington	★	★	★	...
West Virginia	...	...	★ (o)	...
Wisconsin	...	★	...	The Commission plan is approved by Joint Committee on Employment Relations and the governor. It is tied to state employer compensation.
Wyoming	...	★	...	...
Dist. of Columbia	...	★	...	...

See footnotes at end of table.

METHOD OF SETTING LEGISLATIVE COMPENSATION — Continued

Source: National Conference of State Legislatures, 2003.

Key:

★— Method used to set compensation.

. . . — Method not used to set compensation.

(a) Arizona commission recommendations are put on ballot for a vote of the people.

(b) The Connecticut General Assembly takes independent action pursuant to recommendations of a Compensation Committee.

(c) Are implemented automatically if not rejected by resolution.

(d) Commission recommendations take effect unless rejected by concurrent resolution or the Governor. Any change in salary that becomes effective does not apply to the legislature to which the recommendation was submitted.

(e) The Kentucky committee has not met since 1995. The most recent pay raise was initiated and passed by the General Assembly.

(f) Presented to the Legislature in the form of legislation, the legislature must enact and the Governor must sign into law.

(g) Maryland commission meets before each four-year term of office and presents recommendations to General Assembly for its action. Recommendations may be reduced or rejected, not increased.

(h) In 1998, the voters passed a legislative referendum starting with the 2001 session, members will receive an automatic increase or decrease according to the median household income for the commonwealth for the preceding 2 year period.

(i) If resolution is offered, it is put to legislative vote; if legislature does not vote recommendations down, the new salaries take effect January 1 of the new year.

(j) By May 1 in odd numbered years the Council submits salary recommendations to the presiding officers.

(k) Recommendations are adjusted by legislature or governor if necessary.

(l) Each chamber receives a cost of living increase that is tied to the Consumer Price Index.

(m) In 1991 a constitutional amendment was approved by voters to allow the Ethics Commission to recommend the salaries of members. Any recommendations must be approved by voters to be effective. This provision has yet to be used.

(n) In 1998 the Joint Rules Committee created a Legislative Compensation Commission. It was composed of two former governors and citizens that made recommendations regarding salary, per diem and office expenses.

(o) Submits, by resolution and must be concurred by at least four members of the commission. The Legislature must enact the resolution into law and may reduce, but shall not increase, any item established in such resolution.

Table 3.9
LEGISLATIVE COMPENSATION: REGULAR SESSIONS

State or other jurisdiction	Salaries Regular sessions Per diem salary (a)	Limit on days	Annual salary	Travel allowance (2002) Cents per mile	Round trips home to capital during session	Per diem living expenses
Alabama	$10 C	...	... 32.5/int. sess.	10	One	$2,280/m plus $50/d for three days each week that the legislature actually meets during any session (U).
Alaska	...	...	$24,012	32.5	...	$161/day (U) tied to federal rate. Legislators who reside in the capitol area receive 75% of federal rate.
Arizona	...	...	$24,000	32.5	...	$35/d for the 1st 120 days of regular session and for special session and $10/d thereafter; members residing outside Maricopa County receive an additional $25/d for the 1st 120 days of regular session and for special session and an additional $10/d thereafter (V). Set by statute.
Arkansas*	...	...	$12,796	31/House 32.5/Senate 31/Sen. Int.	...	$95/d (V) plus mileage tied to federal rate.
California	...	...	$99,000	(c)	...	$121/d (V) by roll call. Maximum allowable per diem is paid regardless of actual expenses.
Colorado	...	...	$30,000 32/4wd	28	...	$45/d for members living in the Denver metro area. $99/d for members living outside Denver (V). Per diem is determined by the legislature.
Connecticut	...	...	$28,000	30	...	No per diem is paid.
Delaware	...	...	$33,400	31	...	No per diem is paid.
Florida	...	...	$27,900	29	...	$99/d (V) tied to the federal rate. Earned based on the number of days in session. Travel vouchers are filed to substantiate.
Georgia	...	...	$16,200	28	...	$128/d (U) set by the legislature.
Hawaii	...	...	$32,000	...	...	$80 for members living outside Oahu; $10/d for members living on Oahu (V) set by the legislature.
Idaho	...	...	$15,646	...	(b)	$99/d for members establishing second residence in Boise; $38/day if no second residence is established and up to $25/d travel (U) set by Compensation Commission.
Illinois	...	...	$55,788	32.5	...	$85 (U) tied to federal rate.
Indiana	...	...	$11,600	28	...	$112 (U) tied to federal rate.
Iowa	...	...	$20,758	29	...	$86/d; $65/d for Polk County legislators (U) set by the legislature. State mileage rates apply.
Kansas	$78.75 C	...	...	32.5	...	$85 (U) tied to federal rate.
Kentucky	$163.56 C	...	...	(V)	...	$93.50/d (U) tied to federal rate. (110% federal per diem rate).
Louisiana	...	...	$16,800	34.5	...	$116/d (U) tied to federal rate. Additional $6,000/yr (U) expense allowance.
Maine	...	...	$10,815 - 1st $7,725 - 2nd	28	...	$38/d housing or reimbursement for mileage in lieu of housing at the rate of .28/mile up to $38/d. $32/d meals (V) set by the legislature.
Maryland	...	...	$31,509	31 (d)	...	Lodging $96/d; meals $30/d (V) tied to federal rate and compensation commission.
Massachusetts	...	...	$50,123	(e)	...	From $10/d-$100/d, depending on distance from State House (V) set by the legislature.
Michigan	...	...	$77,400	32.5	...	$12,000 yearly expense allowance for session and interim (V) set by compensation commission.
Minnesota	...	...	$31,140	(f)	...	Senators receive $66/d and Representatives receive $56/L (U) set by the legislature.
Mississippi	...	...	$10,000	34.5	...	$85/d (U) tied to federal rate.
Missouri	...	...	$31,561	29.5	...	$72/d tied to federal rate. Verification of per diem is by roll call.
Montana	$71.832 L	...	...	(g)	...	$58/d (U) plus trip mileage reimbursement.
Nebraska	...	...	$12,000	(h)	One	$85/d outside 50-mile radius from Capitol; $30/d if member resides within 50 miles of Capitol (V) tied to federal rate.
Nevada	$130	60	...	(i)	...	Federal rate for Capitol area (V). Legislators who live more than 50 miles from the capitol, if requiring lodging, will be paid Hud single room rate for Carson City area for each month of session.

See footnotes at end of table.

LEGISLATIVE COMPENSATION: REGULAR SESSIONS — Continued

State or other jurisdiction	Salaries			Travel allowance (2002)		Per diem living expenses
	Regular sessions			Cents per mile	Round trips home to capital during session	
	Per diem salary (a)	Limit on days	Annual salary			
New Hampshire	. . .	2 yr. term	$200	38 for first 45 miles, 19 thereafter	. . .	No per diem is paid.
New Jersey	. . .	. . .	$49,000	. . .	. . .	No per diem is paid.
New Mexico	. . .	. . .	. . .	34.5 (j)	. . .	$145/d (V) tied to federal rate and the constitution.
New York	. . .	. . .	$79,500	34.5	. . .	Varies (V) tied to federal rate.
North Carolina	. . .	. . .	$13,951	29	Weekly	$104/d (U) set by statute.
North Dakota	$125 C	. . .	. . .	25	Weekly	Lodging reimbursement up to $650/m (V). $250/m additional compensation by statute.
Ohio	. . .		$51,674	30	Weekly (k)	None.
Oklahoma	. . .	. . .	$38,400	32.5 (j)	. . .	$103/d (U) tied to federal rate.
Oregon*	. . .	. . .	$15,396	34.5	. . .	$85/d (U) tied to federal rate.
Pennsylvania	. . .	. . .	$61,889	34.5 (j)	. . .	$124/d (V) tied to federal rate. Can receive actual expenses or per diem.
Rhode Island	. . .	. . .	$11,236	32.5	. . .	No per diem is paid.
South Carolina	. . .	. . .	$10,400	34.5	. . .	$95/d for meals and housing, for each statewide session day and cmte. meeting (V) tied to federal rate.
South Dakota	. . .	2 yr. term	$12,000	29 (l)	. . .	$110/L (U) set by the legislature.
Tennessee	. . .	. . .	$16,500	32	. . .	$124/L (U). Session attendance is verified by roll calls submitted by the House and Senate Chief Clerks. Committee attendance is verified by roll calls submitted by each standing committee's office.
Texas*	. . .	. . .	$7,200	28(m)	. . .	$124/d (U) set by Ethics Commission.
Utah	$120 C	. . .	. . .	32.5	. . .	$75/d (U) lodging allotment for each calendar day, tied to federal rate. $42/d (U) per diem for each calendar day.
Vermont	. . .	. . .	$536/week during session	32.5	. . .	$50/d for lodging and $37/d for meals for non-commuters; commuters receive $32/d for meals (U) set by legislature.
Virginia	. . .	. . .	Senate- $18,000 House- $17,640	32.5	. . .	$115 (U) tied to federal rate.
Washington	. . .	. . .	$32,064	Federal rate	One	$82/d (U) tied to federal rate (85% Olympia area).
West Virginia	. . .	. . .	$15,000	32.5	Weekly	$85/d ((U) set by compensation commission.
Wisconsin	. . .	. . .	$44,333	29	Weekly	$88/d maximum (U) set by compensation commission (90% of federal rate).
Wyoming	$125 L	. . .	. . .	35	. . .	$80/d (V) set by the legislature, includes travel days for those outside of Cheyenne.
Dist. of Columbia	. . .	. . .	$92,500	. . .	. . .	No per diem is paid.
Guam	. . .	. . .	N.R.	(n)	. . .	N.R.
Puerto Rico	. . .	. . .	$60,000	. . .	. . .	$93/d within 35 miles of capitol; $103 if outside 35 miles (U) tied to CPI.
U.S. Virgin Islands	. . .	. . .	$65,000	. . .	. . .	$30/d (U) set by the legislature.

See footnotes at end of table.

LEGISLATIVE COMPENSATION: REGULAR SESSIONS — Continued

Source: National Conference of State Legislatures, 2002.

Note: In many states, legislators who receive an annual salary or per diem salary also receive an additional per diem amount for living expenses. Consult appropriate columns for

a more complete picture of legislative compensation during sessions. For information on interim compensation and other direct payments and services to legislators, see table entitled

"Legislative Compensation: Interim Payments and Other Direct Payments."

* — Biennial session. In Arkansas, Oregon and Texas, legislators receive an annual salary.

Key:

C — Calendar day

L — Legislative day

U) — Unvouchered

(V) — Vouchered

d — day

w — week

m — month

y — year

. . . — Not applicable

N.R.— Not reported

(a) Legislators paid on a per diem basis receive the same rate during a special session.

(b One roundtrip per week at state rate.

(c) If legislator uses personal vehicle, mileage is reimbursed.

d) $400 allowance for in district travel as taxable income, members may decline the allowance.

(e) Between $10-100 determined by distance from State House.

(f) House: range of $75-650 for in district mileage. Senate: a reasonable allowance.

(g) Rate is based on IRS rate. Reimbursement for actual mileage traveled in connection with Legislative Business.

(h) $0.31 a mile for those who live more than 50 miles from the capitol; one round trip per calendar week; for those who live within 50 miles, a daily mileage is authorized for days in session.

(i) Equal to the federal mileage rate with upper limit of $6,800 during session.

(j) Tied to the federal rate.

(k) For legislators outside of Franklin Co. only.

(l) $0.29/mile for one round trip from Pierre to home each weekend. One trip is paid at .05/mile. During the interim, .29/mile for scheduled committee meetings.

(m) An allowance in Texas for single, twin and turbo engines from .40 - $1/mile is also given.

(n) Reimbursed for fuel purchase receipts.

Table 3.10
LEGISLATIVE COMPENSATION: INTERIM PAYMENTS AND OTHER DIRECT PAYMENTS

State or other jurisdiction	Per diem compensation and living expenses for committee or official business during interim (2002)	Other direct payments or services to legislators (2002)
Alabama	$2,280/m (U); $50/d for committee meetings and $75/d attendance other legislative business. Not restricted to meals and lodging.	None.
Alaska	$65/d (V)	Senators received $10,000/y and Representatives receive $8,000/y for postage, stationery and other legislative expenses. Staffing allowance determined by rules and presiding officers, depending on time of year.
Arizona	$35/d with prior approval of presiding officer (V) set by statute.	None.
Arkansas	$95/d with mileage (V) tied to federal rate.	Legislators are entitled to receive a maximum reimbursement of $9,600/y for legislative expenses.
California	$121/d (V) tied to federal rate.	Senators are allowed staff according to the size of their districts. Assemblymen receive $260,000/y to cover non-specified salary expenses, travel costs, publications, printing, postage, etc.
Colorado	$99/d per diem plus actual expenses (V).	$3,355/y
Connecticut	None.	Senators receive $5,500/y and Representatives receive $4,500/y (U) expense allowance.
Delaware	None.	$6,728/y for office expenses.
Florida	$50/d per diem or actual hotel plus $3 breakfast; $6 lunch; $12 dinner for authorized travel during committee weeks (V) set by Florida statutes.	$1,650/m for office expenses.
Georgia	$128/d (V) set by the Legislature. A committee roster is submitted with the members who attended the meeting. Those that did not attend do not get paid.	$7,000/y reimbursable expense account. If the member requests and provides receipts, the member is reimbursed for personal services, office equipment, rent, supplies, transportation, telecommunications, etc.
Hawaii	$10/d for official business on island of legal residence; $80/d for business on another island (V) set by the legislature.	House $4,500/m for Jan.–April staffing. Senate varies between $350–500/d for staffing allowance.
Idaho	Members are reimbursed for actual expenses (V).	$1,700/y for unvouchered constituent expense. No staffing allowance.
Illinois		Senators receive $67,000/y and Representatives $57,000/y for office expenses, including district offices and staffing.
Indiana	$112/d (V) tied to federal rate.	$25/d, 7 days a week during interim only. No staffing allowance.
Iowa	$86/d (U) set by the legislature. In addition, legislators may request reimbursement for meals, hotel/motel and air fare. State mileage rates apply.	$200/m to cover district constituency postage, travel, telephone and other expenses. No staffing allowance.
Kansas	During interim committee meetings, members receive $85/d tied to federal rate, plus round trip tolls and mileage reimbursement at 33¢. All legislators receive $270 (U) for 20 pay periods ($5,400) considered taxable income.	$5,400/y which is taxable income to the legislators. Staffing allowances vary for leadership who have their own budget. Legislators provided with secretaries during the session only.
Kentucky	$163.56 for committee meetings (U). Legislators are reimbursed for actual expenses.	$1,503.19 for district expenses.
Louisiana (b)	$116/d (U) tied to federal rate.	$500/m. Representatives receive an additional $1,500 supplemental allowance for vouchered office expenses, rent, travel mileage in district. Senators and Representatives staff allowance $2,000/m starting salary up to $3,000 with annual increases paid directly to staff person.

LEGISLATIVE COMPENSATION: INTERIM PAYMENTS AND OTHER DIRECT PAYMENTS—Continued

State or other jurisdiction	Per diem compensation and living expenses for committee or official business during interim (2002)	Other direct payments or services to legislators (2002)
Maine	Actual attendance reimbursed at: $55 per diem; actual meals and mileage/housing expense. Chair of committee or presiding officer has to review and approve.	None.
Maryland	$96/d lodging; $30/d meals related to official business (V) tied to federal rate and compensation commission.	Members, $18,265/y for normal expenses of an office with limits on postage, telephone and publications. Members must document expenses. Legislators must use $5,800 for clerical services. Senators receive one administrative assistant & session secretary. Delegates receive one benefited employee and a session secretary.
Massachusetts (b)	None.	$7,200/y for office expenses.
Michigan	None.	$30,900/y for printing, mailings, travel, furniture and district offices. Senate Majority party receives $233,918; Senate Minority party receives $136,536 for staffing.
Minnesota	Senators receive $66/d and Representatives receive $56/d per approval of committee chair or leadership (U) set by the legislature.	None.
Mississippi	$85/d for committee meetings (U) tied to federal rate. $1,500 allowance (U).	None.
Missouri	None.	$1,000/m to cover all reasonable and necessary business expenses.
Montana	In state rate for meals, receipt not required . In state rate for lodging and mileage receipt required (V). Claim form required.	None.
Nebraska	None. Actual expense reimbursed with expense vouchers provided.	No allowance; however, each member is provided with two full-time capitol staff year-round.
Nevada	Statutory amount (V) maximum allowable per diem is paid regardless of actual expenses.	None.
New Hampshire	None.	None.
New Jersey	None.	$750 for supplies, equipment and furnishings supplied through a district office program. $100,000/y for district office personnel.
New Mexico	$145/d (V) tied to federal rate.	None.
New York	Varies (V) tied to federal rate.	Staff allowance set by majority leader for majority members and by minority leader for minority members. Staff allowance covers both district and capitol; geographic location; seniority and leadership responsibilities will cause variations.
North Carolina	$104/d (V) set by statute.	Non-leaders receive $6,708/y for any legislative expenses not otherwise provided. Full-time secretarial assistance is provided during session.
North Dakota	During interim committee meetings, members receive $100/d, $20/d meals (U); $45 plus tax/d lodging (V) plus round trip mileage reimbursement at 31¢. All members receive a $250/m allowance for expenses during their term in office.	None.

See footnotes at end of table.

LEGISLATIVE COMPENSATION: INTERIM PAYMENTS AND OTHER DIRECT PAYMENTS—Continued

State or other jurisdiction	Per diem compensation and living expenses for committee or official business during interim (2002)	Other direct payments or services to legislators (2002)
Ohio	None.	None.
Oklahoma (b)	$25/d (U) set by the legislature.	$350/y for unvouchered office supplies plus seven rolls of stamps.
Oregon (h)	$85/d committee and task force meetings (U) tied to federal rate.	$2,635/session; interim allowance is $400–550/m depending on geographic size of district. Staffing allowance of $3,908/m during session; $1,846/m during interim.
Pennsylvania	$124 (V) tied to federal rate. Can receive actual expenses or per diem.	Staffing is determined by the Senate Floor Leader.
Rhode Island	None.	None.
South Carolina	Member attending official meetings is eligible for $95/d subsistence and $35/d per diem (V) tied to the federal rate.	Senate $3,400/y for postage, stationery and telephone. House $1,800/y for telephone and $1,100/y for postage. Legislators also receive $1,000/m for in district expenses that is treated as income.
South Dakota	$110 per diem for each day of a committee meeting (U). Meals and lodging expenses are paid at state rate.	None.
Tennessee	$114/d (U) tied to federal rate.	$525/m for expenses in district and staff intrastate travel (U).
Texas	Senators receive $124/d for legislative business in Travis County, not to exceed 10 d/m (V). Representatives receive $124/d in Travis County, not to exceed 12 d/m (V). Per diem amount is determined by the Ethics Commission, number of days determined by Senate Caucus and the Committee on House Administration.	Senate: $25,000/m for staff salaries. House $10,750/m for staff salaries, supplies stationery, postage, district office rental, telephone expense, etc.
Utah	$42/d meals (U); up to $75/d for lodging (V).	None.
Vermont	Actual cost plus mileage (U) set by the legislature.	None.
Virginia (b)	$200/d additional compensation for committee meeting attendance. No per diem is paid.	Legislators receive $1,250/m; leadership receives $1,750/m office expense allowance. Legislators receive a staffing allowance of $31,844/y; leadership receives $47,765/y.
Washington (b)	$82/d (V) tied to federal rate (85% Olympia area). Maximum allowable per diem is paid regardless of actual expenses.	$1,350/quarter for legislative expenses, for which the legislator has not been otherwise entitled to reimbursement. No staffing allowance.
West Virginia	$85/d (U) set by compensation commission.	None.
Wisconsin	Per diem is paid year round up to $88/d (U) set by compensation commission (90% of federal rate)	Senate receives $66,000/two-year session plus a mailing for the district each year. Covers district mileage, copying and special documents; capitol expenses include printing, postage, subscriptions, phone etc. Senators receive $186,000/two-year session for staffing. Assembly members receive $12,500 plus an allowance for district size—min. $870, max. $2,900 that covers printing and postage. Staff salary paid by state.
Wyoming	$80/d (V) set by the legislature. Includes travel for those where meetings are not in "hometown."	Up to $450 per quarter.
Dist. of Columbia	None.	None.

See footnotes at end of table.

LEGISLATIVE COMPENSATION: INTERIM PAYMENTS AND OTHER DIRECT PAYMENTS—Continued

State or other jurisdiction	Per diem compensation and living expenses for committee or official business during interim (2002)	Other direct payments or services to legislators (2002)
Guam	N.R.	None.
Puerto Rico	$93/d within 35 miles of the capitol; $103/d beyond the 35 miles limit (U) tied to CPI.	Senate receives $10,833/m for staffing. House members receive $17,000/m for staffing.
U.S. Virgin Islands	None.	Senators receive an allowance that covers day-to-day operations. Staffing allowances vary with staffing requests.

Source: National Conference of State Legislatures, March 2002.
Notes:
i) For more information on legislative compensation, see the Chapter 3 table entitled Legislative Compensation: Regular Sessions.
ii) Although the official definition of per diem is daily expense allowance, it is also used in some states to refer to an interim salary that is taxed and reported as separate income from the annual salary.

Key:
(U)—Unvouchered
(V)—Vouchered
d—day
m—month
w—week
y—year
N.R.—not reported

Table 3.11
ADDITIONAL COMPENSATION FOR SENATE LEADERS

State	Presiding officer	Majority leader	Minority leader	Other leaders
Alabama	$2/day plus $1,500/mo expense allowance	None	None	None
Alaska	$500	None	None	None
Arizona	None	None	None	None
Arkansas	None	None	None	None
California	Base plus $14,850	Base plus $7,425	Base plus $14,850	Second ranking minority leader; base plus $7,425.
Colorado	All leaders receive $99/day salary during interim when in attendance at committee or leadership meetings and committee meetings.			
Connecticut	$10,689	$8,835	$8,835	Deputy min. and maj. ldrs., $6,446/year; asst. maj. and min. ldrs. and maj. and min. whips $4,241/yr
Delaware	$16,600	$9,913	$9,913	Maj. and min. whips $6,243
Florida	$10,800	None	None	None
Georgia	$6694.68/mo	$200/mo	$200/mo	President pro tem, $400/mo; admin. flr. ldr., $100/mo; asst. admin. flr. ldr., $100/mo
Hawaii	$37,000	None	None	None
Idaho	$3,000	None	None	None
Illinois	$22,641	None	$22,641	Asst. maj. and min. ldr., $16,979; maj. and min. caucus chair, $16,979
Indiana	$6,500	$5,000	$5,500	Asst. pres. pro tem $2,500; asst. maj. flr. ldr. and maj. caucus chair, $1,000; maj. caucus chair, $5,000; min. asst. flr. ldr. and min. caucus chair, $4,500; maj. and min. whips, $1,500; asst. min. caucus chair, $500
Iowa	$11,593	$11,593	$11,593	Pres. Pro Tem $1,243
Kansas	$12,103.78/yr	$10,919.74/yr	$10,919.74/yr	Asst. maj., min. ldrs., vice pres., $6,177.86/yr
Kentucky	$38.90/day	$31.43/day	$31.43/day	Maj., min. caucus chairs and whips, $24.09/day
Louisiana	$32,000	None	None	Pres. Pro Tem $24,500
Maine	150% of base salary	125% of base salary	112.5% of base salary	Pres. Pro Tem., 100% of base salary
Maryland	$10,000/yr.	None	None	None
Massachusetts	$35,000	$22,500	$22,500	Asst. maj. and min. ldr., $15,000
Michigan	$5,513	$26,000	$22,000	Maj. flr. ldr., $12,000; min. flr. ldr., $10,000
Minnesota	None	$43,596 (a)	$43,596 (a)	Asst. maj. ldr., $35,291 (a)
Mississippi	None	None	None	Pro tem resolution, $15,000/yr
Missouri	None	None	None	None
Montana	$5/day during session	None	None	None
Nebraska	None	None	None	None
Nevada	$900	$900	$900	Pres. Pro Tem, $900
New Hampshire	$50/two-yr term	None	None	None
New Jersey	1/3 above annual salary	None	None	None
New Mexico	None	None	None	None
New York	$41,500	None	$34,500	22 other leaders with compensation ranging from $13,000 to $34,000
North Carolina	$38,151 (a) and $16,956 expense allowance	$17,048 (a) and $7,992 expense allowance	$17,048 (a) and $7,992 expense allowance	Dep. pro tem: $21,739 (a) and $10,032 expense allowance
North Dakota (b)	None	$10/day	$10/day	Asst. ldrs., $5/day

See footnotes at end of table.

ADDITIONAL COMPENSATION FOR SENATE LEADERS — Continued

State	Presiding officer	Majority leader	Minority leader	Other leaders
Ohio	$80,549 base salary	President pro tem	$73,493 salary	Asst. pres. pro tem, $69,227; maj. whip, $64,967; $73,493 maj.whip, $64,967; asst. min. ldr., $67,099; min. whip, $60,706; asst. min. whip, $54,060
Oklahoma	$17,932	$12,364	$12,364	None
Oregon	$1,283/mo.	None	None	None
Pennsylvania	$34,724.08	$27,780.58	$27,780.58	Maj. and min. whip, $21,083; maj. and min. caucus chair, $13,145; maj. and min. policy chairs, maj. and min. caucus admin., $8,681
Rhode Island	None	None	None	None
South Carolina	Lt. gov. holds	None	None	President pro tem, $11,000 this position
South Dakota	None	None	None	None
Tennessee	$49,500 (a) plus $5,700 home office allowance. Add'l $750/yr of ex officio duties	None	None	None
Texas	None	None	None	None
Utah	$2,500	$1,500	$1,500	Maj. whip, asst. maj. whip, min. whip and asst. min. whip, $1,500
Vermont	$593/week during session. No add'l salary	None	None	None
Virginia	None	None	None	None
Washington	Lt. gov. holds this position	$36,064	$36,064	None
West Virginia	$50/day during session	$25/day during session	$25/day during session	Up to 4 add'l people named by presiding officer receive $100 for a maximum of 30 days.
Wisconsin	None	None	None	None
Wyoming	$3/day	None	None	None
Dist. of Columbia	$10,000 (council chair)	Not applicable	Not applicable	Not applicable
Guam	None	None	None	None
Puerto Rico	$90,000/yr	$69,000/yr	$69,000/yr	President Pro Tem, $69,000
U.S. Virgin Islands	$10,000	None	None	None

Source: National Conference of State Legislatures, 2003.

(a) Total annual salary for this leadership position.

(b) House and Senate majority and minority leaders each receive additional compensation of $250.00 per month during their term of office, pursuant to NDCC Section 54-03-20, in addition to other compensation amounts provided by law during legislative sessions.

Table 3.12
ADDITIONAL COMPENSATION FOR HOUSE LEADERS

State or other jurisdiction	Presiding officer	Majority leader	Minority leader	Other leaders
Alabama	$2/day plus $1,500/mo. expense allowance	None	None	None
Alaska	$500	None	None	None
Arizona	None	None	None	None
Arkansas	None	None	None	$2,400 Spkr. designate
California	Base plus $14,850	Base plus $7,425	Base plus $14,850	Second ranking minority ldr., $7,425
Colorado	All leaders receive $99/day salary during interim when in attendance at committee or leadership matters.			
Connecticut	$10,689	$8,835	$8,835	Dep. spkr., dep. maj. and min. ldrs., $6,446/yr; asst. maj. and min. ldrs.; maj. and min whips, $4,241/yr
Delaware	$16,600	$9,913	$9,913	Maj. and min. whips, $6,243
Florida	$10,800	None	None	None
Georgia	$6,094.68/mo.	$200/mo.	$200/mo.	Governor's flr. ldr., $200/mo; asst. flr. ldr., $100/mo.; spkr. pro tem, $400/mo.
Hawaii	$37,000	None	None	None
Idaho	$3,000	None	None	None
Illinois	$22,641	$19,101	$22,641	Dpty. maj. and min., $16,273; asst. maj. and asst. min., $14,856; maj. and min. conference chair, $14,856
Indiana	$6,500	$5,000	$5,500	Speaker pro tem, $5,000; maj. caucus chair, $5,000; min. caucus chair, $4,500; asst. min. flr. leader, $3,500; asst. maj. flr. ldr., $1,000; maj. whip, $3,500; min. whip, $1,500
Iowa	$11,593	$11,593	$11,593	Speaker pro tem, $1,243
Kansas	$12,103.78/yr.	$10,919.74/yr.	$10,919.74/yr.	Asst. maj. and min. ldrs., spkr. pro tem, $6,177.68/yr.
Kentucky	$39.80/day	$31.43/day	$31.43/day	Maj. and min. caucus chairs & whips, $24.09/day
Louisiana	$32,000 (a)	None	None	Speaker pro tem, $24,500 (a)
Maine	150% of base salary	125% of base salary	112.5% of base salary	None
Maryland	$10,000/year	None	None	None
Massachusetts	$35,000	$22,500	$22,500	Asst. maj. and min. ldr., $15,000
Michigan	$27,000	None	$22,000	Spkr. pro tem, $5,513; min. flr. ldr., $10,000; maj. flr. ldr., $12,000
Minnesota	$43,596 (a)	$43,596 (a)	$43,596 (a)	None
Mississippi	None	None	None	None
Missouri	$208.33/mo.	$125/mo.	$125/mo.	None
Montana	$5/day during session	None	None	None
Nebraska	None	None	None	None
Nevada	$900	$900	$900	Speaker pro tem, $900
New Hampshire	$50/two-year term	None	None	None
New Jersey	1/3 above annual salary	None	None	None
New Mexico	None	None	None	None
New York	$41,500	$34,500	$34,500	31 leaders with compensation ranging from $9,000 to $25,000
North Carolina	$38,151 (a) and $16,956 expense allowance	$17,048 (a) and $7,992 expense allowance	$17,048 (a) and $7,992 expense allowance	Speaker pro tem, $21,739 and $10,032 expense allowance
North Dakota (b)	$10/day	$10/day	$10/day	Asst. ldrs., $5/day
Ohio	$80,549 base salary	$69,227 base salary	$73,493 base salary	Spkr. pro tem, $73,493; asst. maj. ldr., $64,967; asst. min. ldr., $67,099; maj. whip, $60,706; min. whip, $60,706; asst. maj. whip, $56,443; asst. min. whip, $54,060
Oklahoma	$17,932	$12,364	$12,364	Speaker pro tem, $12,364
Oregon	$1,283/month	None	None	None
Pennsylvania	$34,724.08	$27,780.58	$27,780.59	Maj. and min. whips, $21,083; maj. and min. caucus chairs, $13,145; maj. and min. policy chairs, $8,681; maj. and min. caucus admin., $8,681, maj. and min. caucus secretaries, $8,681
Rhode Island	None	None	None	None
South Carolina	$11,000/yr	None	None	Speaker pro tem, $3,600/yr

See footnotes at end of table.

ADDITIONAL COMPENSATION FOR HOUSE LEADERS — Continued

State or other jurisdiction	Presiding officer	Majority leader	Minority leader	Other leaders
South Dakota	None	None	None	None
Tennessee	$49,500 (a) plus $5,700/yr home office for allowance. Add'l $750/yr. for ex-officio duties	None	None	None
Texas	None	None	None	None
Utah	$2,500	$1,500	$1,500	Whips and asst. whips, $1,500
Vermont	$593/week during session plus an additional $9,172 in salary	None	None	None
Virginia	$18,681	None	None	None
Washington	$40,064 (a)	None	$36,064(a)	None
West Virginia	$50/day during session	$25/day during session	$25/day during session	Up to four add'l people named by presiding officer receive $100 for a maximum of 30 days
Wisconsin	None	None	None	None
Wyoming	$3/day	None	None	None
District of Columbia	$10,000 (chair of council)	Not applicable	Not applicable	Not applicable
Puerto Rico	$90,000/yr.	$69,000/yr.	$69,000/yr.	Speaker pro tem, $69,000
Guam	None	None	None	None
U.S. Virgin Islands	None	None	None	None

Source: National Conference of State Legislatures, 2003.
(a) Total annual salary for this leadership position.
(b) House and Senate majority and minority leaders each receive additional compensation of $250/mo. during their term of office, pursuant to NDCC Section 54-03-20, in addition to other compensation amounts provided by law during legislative sessions.

Table 3.13
STATE LEGISLATIVE RETIREMENT BENEFITS

State or other jurisdiction	Participation	Requirements for regular retirement	Contribution rate	Monthly benefit estimates 4 yrs.	12 yrs.	20 yrs.	Benefit formula	Same as state employee
Alabama	N.A.							
Alaska	Optional	Age 60 with 10 yrs.	Employee 6.75%; employer 8.13%	Vested at 5 yrs.	$490/mo. $540/mo. within AK	$850/mo. $935/mo. within AK	2% (first 10 yrs.); or 2.25% (second 10 yrs.); or 2.5% (third 10 yrs.) x average over highest consecutive yrs. x yrs. of service	Yes
Arizona	Optional	Age 65, 5+ yrs. service; age 62, 10+ yrs. service; or 20 yrs. service	Varies	Varies	Varies	Varies	4%/yr. of credited service x highest 3 yr. average in the past 10 yrs.	No
Arkansas	Optional	Age 65, 10 yrs. service; or age 55, 12 yrs. service; or any age, 30 yrs. service	Non-contributory	Not eligible	$420 $480 for ldrshp.	$700 $800 for ldrshp.	$35/mo. x yrs. service. If ever served as Speaker or president pro tem receive $40/mo. x yrs. of service.	No
California	N.A.							
Colorado	Mandatory	PERA: age 65, 5 yrs. service; age 50, 30yrs. service; when age + service equals 80 or more (min. age of 55). DCP: no age requirement & vested immediately	PERA: 8% of gross salary	PERA: Not yet vested	PERA: 30% of highest average salary	PERA: 50% of highest average salary	2.5% x HAS x yrs. of service (a)	No
Connecticut	Mandatory	Age 65, 5 yrs. service; age 55, 10 yrs. service	Members prior to 7/1/97-0 after 1/1/97 -2%	Not yet vested	$341	$569	(.0133 x avg. annual salary) + (.005 x avg. annual salary in excess of "breakpoint" [specified dollar amount for each yr.]) x yrs. credited service	Yes
Delaware	Mandatory	Age 62, 5 yrs. service compensation in excess of $500	3% of total monthly	N.A.	N.A.	N.A.	Years of service x highest rate of payment being paid to any retired member of the General Assembly	No
Florida	Optional	Age 62, 10 yrs. service; 30 yrs. at any age	15.19%	None	$837	$2,325.05	Yrs. creditable service x percent value x average final compensation = annual average of highest 5 yrs.	No
Georgia	Optional	Vested after 8 yrs.; age 62, with no age penalty taken;	Employee rate 3.75%+ .025%+$7	None	$336	$560	$28 x yrs. service x yrs. of service x reduction factor = monthly benefit. $28 per month for each year of service	No
Hawaii	Optional	55 yrs. if less than 10 yrs. of service, no minimum age	7.8%	0	Varies	Varies	3.5 x yrs. of service as legislator x highest average salary plus annuity based on contributions as an elected official	No
Idaho	Mandatory	5 yrs. service minimum; age 65 unreduced; age 55 reduced	6.97%	$101/mo. at age 65	$305/mo. at age 65	$508/mo. at age 65	Avg. monthly salary for highest 42 consecutive months x .02000 x months of credited service	Yes

See footnotes at end of table.

STATE LEGISLATIVE RETIREMENT BENEFITS — Continued

State or other jurisdiction	Participation	Requirements for regular retirement	Contribution rate	Monthly benefit estimates			Benefit formula	Same as state employee
				4 yrs.	12 yrs.	20 yrs.		
Illinois	Optional	Age 55, 8 yrs. service; or age 62, 4 yrs. service	8.5% for retirement; 2% for survivors; 1% for automatic increases; 11.5% total	12% of final salary	45% of final salary	85% of final salary	3% of each of 1st 4 yrs.; 3.5% for each of next 2 yrs.; 4% for each of next 2 yrs.; 4.5% for each of the next 4 yrs.; 5% for each yr. above 12	No
Indiana	Mandatory	No service requirement	Employee 5% , 20% state (of taxable income)	Varies	Varies	Varies	Yrs. of service x 1.1% x highest one-year salary	No
Iowa	Optional	Age 65, less than 30 yrs. service; age 62, 30 yrs. service; age 55, 33 yrs service	3.7% individual; 5.75% state	$133/mo.	$400/mo.	$667/mo.	60% x avg of highest 3 yrs. x yrs. of service divided by 30 (maximum no. of yrs.)	Yes
Kansas	Optional	Age 65, age 62 with 10 yrs. of service or age plus yrs. of service equals 85 pts.	4%	N.A.	N.A.	N.A.	3 highest yrs. x 1.75% x yrs. service divided by 12	No
Kentucky	Mandatory	N.A.	$114.58/mo. for both plans	N.A.	N.A.	N.A.	N.A.	Yes
Louisiana	N.A.							
Maine	Mandatory (b)	Age 60 (if 10 yrs. of service on 7/1/93) and age 62 (if less than 10 yrs. of service on 7/1/93). 5 yr. Minimum creditable service requirement for eligibility	7.65% legislators; 6.24% legislative retirement system; 21.05% ME State Retirement System	$68	$230	$383	1/50 average final compensation x number of years of creditable service	No
Maryland	Optional	Age 60, with 8 yrs.: age 50, 8+yrs creditable service (early reduced retirement)	5% of annual salary	None	$891	$1,485	3% of legislative salary for each yr of service up to a max. of 22 yrs. 3 months	No
Massachusetts	Optional	Age 55, 6 yrs. Service	9%	Varies	Varies	N.A.	N.A.	No
Michigan	Optional	Age 55, 5 yrs. or age plus service equals 70	7%-13%	Varies	Varies	Varies	Depends on when service started	No (c)
Minnesota (d)	Mandatory	LRP: Age 62, 6 yrs. service and fully vested. DCP: no age requirement and vested immediately	LRP: 9% DCP: 4%	$11,210.40 refund legislator's contribution (LRP)	$840.78/mo. (LRP)	$1401.29/mo. (LRP)	2.7% x high 5 yr. avg. salary x length of service (yrs.)	No
Mississippi	Mandatory	55 yrs. or 25 yrs. of service	Regular: 7.25% Legislator: 9.75%; State: supplemental 3%/6.33%	Varies	Varies	Varies	N.A.	Yes
Missouri	Mandatory	Age 55 + 4 yrs. or 2 sessions	11.59%	Varies	Varies	Varies	Monthly pay divided by 24 x service	No

See footnotes at end of table.

STATE LEGISLATIVE RETIREMENT BENEFITS — Continued

State or other jurisdiction	Participation	Requirements for regular retirement	Contribution rate	Monthly benefit estimates			Benefit formula	Same as state employee
				4 yrs.	12 yrs.	20 yrs.		
Montana	Optional	Age 60, at least 5 yrs. service; age 65 regardless of yrs. of service; or 30 yrs. of service regardless of age	6.9%	Varies	Varies	Varies	1/56 x yrs. service credits x final avg. salary	Yes
Nebraska	N.A.							
Nevada	Mandatory	Age 60, 10 yrs. service	15% of session salary	0	$300/mo.	$500/mo.	Minimum service = 10 years; number of yrs. x $25 = monthly allowance	No
New Hampshire	N.A.							
New Jersey	Mandatory	Age 60, 8 yrs. service; age 55 (early retirement), 25 yrs.	5% of salary	N.A.	N.A.	N.A.	Effective 1/74 all legislators received 3% per yr. pension allowance; before 1974, members received 1/60th	No
New Mexico	Optional	Age 65, 5+ yrs.; 64, 8+ yrs., 63, 11+ yrs., 60, 12+ yrs. or any age with 14+ yrs. of credited service	$100 per year for service after 1959	$83.33/mo.	$250/mo.	$416.66/mo.	$250 x yrs. of service (after 1959)	No
New York	Mandatory	Depends on tier set by date of initial membership; Minimum 10 yrs. service	Based on length of service	Varies	Varies	Varies	Depends on tier set by initial membership	Yes
North Carolina	Mandatory	Age 65, 5 yrs. service	24.58%	N.A.	N.A.	N.A.	N.A.	No
North Dakota	N.A.							
Ohio	Optional	Age 60, 5 yrs. service; or age 55, 25 yrs. service; any age, 30 yrs. service	State 13.31% Legislator 8.5% of gross salary	No benefits	Varies	Varies	2.2% of final avg. salary (FAS) x yrs. of service	Yes
Oklahoma	Optional	Age 60, 6 yrs. service	Optional contribution of 4.5%, 6%, 7.5%, 8.5%, 9%, or 10%	$426.68 at 10%	$1280.04 at 10%	$2133.40 at 10%	Avg. participating salary x length of service x computation factor depending on optional contributions ranging from .019 x .040	No
Oregon	Optional	Age 55, 30+ yrs. service	16.317% of subject wages	N.A.	N.A.	N.A.	1.67% x yrs. service and final avg. monthly salary	Yes
Pennsylvania	Optional	Age 50, 3 yrs. service	5%	N.A.	N.A.	N.A.	2% x final avg. salary x credited yrs. service x withdrawal factor if under regular retirement age (50 for legislators)	Yes
Rhode Island	No (e)							No
South Carolina	Mandatory	Age 60, 8 yrs. service; 30 yrs. of service regardless of age	10%	$359.89	$1,079.68	$1,799.47	4.82% of annual compensation x yrs. service	No
South Dakota	N.A.							No
Tennessee	Optional	Age 55, 4 yrs. service	5.43%	$280/mo.	$840/mo.	$1375/mo.	$70 per month x yrs. service with a $1,375 monthly cap	No

See footnotes at end of table.

STATE LEGISLATIVE RETIREMENT BENEFITS — Continued

State or other jurisdiction	Participation	Requirements for regular retirement	Contribution rate	Monthly benefit estimates			Benefit formula	Same as state employee
				4 yrs.	12 yrs.	20 yrs.		
Texas	Optional	Age 60, 8 yrs. service; age 50, 12 yrs. service	8%	Not eligible	$2,288.25	$3,813.75	2.25% x district judges salary (currently $8,475) x length of service	N
Utah	Mandatory	Age 62, 10 yrs. service; age 65, 4 yrs. Service	Non-contributory	Varies	Varies	Varies	$10/mo. x yrs. service; adjusted semi-annually according to consumer price index ltd. to max of 2% (current rate is $22.80)	No
Vermont	N.A.							
Virginia	Mandatory	Age 50, 30 yrs. service (unreduced); age 55, 5 yrs. service; age 50, 10 yrs. service (reduced)	10.22% of credible comp	Varies	Varies	Varies	1.7% of average final compensation x yrs. of service	Yes
Washington	Optional	Age 65, 5 yrs. service credit yrs. age 55, 20 yrs. service credit yrs.	2.43%	N.A.	N.A.	N.A.	2% x service credit yrs. X avg. final compensation	Yes
West Virginia	Optional	Age 55, if yrs. of service + age equal 80	4.5%/gross income	Not eligible	$300/mo.	$500/mo.	2% of final avg. salary x yrs. Service. Final avg. salary is based on 3 highest yrs. out of last 10 yrs.	Yes
Wisconsin	Mandatory	Age 55, 5 yrs. service	5.5% of salary	$300/mo.	$900/mo.	$1500/mo.	2% x yrs. of service x salary	Yes
Wyoming	N.A.							
Dist. of Columbia	Mandatory	Age 62, 5 yrs. service; age 55, 30 yrs. service; age 60, 20 yrs. service	Before 10/1/87, 7%; after 10/1/87, 5%	0	Varies	Varies	Multiply high 3 yrs. average pay by indicator under applicable yrs. months of service.	Yes
Puerto Rico	Optional	Age 55 with 30 yrs. service	Approximately 9%	0	18% of average 3 salaries	30% of average 3 salaries	Less than 10 yrs. 0%; 1.5% per yr.	Yes
Guam	Optional	Age 60, 30 yrs. service; age 55, 15 yrs. service	5% or 8.5%	Varies	Varies	Varies	An amount equal to 2% of avg. annual salary for each of the first 10 yrs. of credited service and 2.5% of avg. annual salary for each yr. or part thereof of credited service over 10 yrs.	Yes
U.S. Virgin Islands	Optional	Age 60, 10 yrs. service	8%	0	Varies	Varies	At age 60 with at least 10 yrs. of service, at 2.5% for each yr. of service or at any time with at least 30 yrs. service	Yes

Source: National Conference of State Legislatures, 2003.

Note: The following states do not have legislative retirement benefits: Alabama, Nebraska, New Hampshire, North Dakota, South Dakota, Vermont and Wyoming.

Key:

N.A. — Not available

(a) Colorado has two plans—a defined benefit plan (PERA) and a defined contribution plan (DCP). HAS = 1/12 x average three highest annual salaries earned during calendar year periods on which PERA contributions were paid; 15 percent limit applies to annual salary increases during three years before retirement; and partial year salaries can be combined.

(b) Members may request a waiver if they can document that participation would increase their total tax liability.

(c) Prior to 1998. Two plans are offered.

(d) Minnesota has two plans. Prior to 7/1/97 all legislators participated in the Legislators Retirement Plan (LRP). All new members must participate in the Defined Contribution Plan (DCP).

(e) Constitution has been amended effective 1/95. Any legislator elected after this date is not eligible to join the State Retirement System, but will be compensated for $10,000/yr. with cost of living increases to be adjusted annually.

Table 3.14
BILL PRE-FILING, REFERENCE, AND CARRYOVER

State or other jurisdiction	Pre-filing of bills allowed (b)	Bills referred to committee by:		Bill referral restricted by rule (a)		Bill carryover allowed (c)
		Senate	House/Assembly	Senate	House/Assembly	
Alabama	★ (d)	(e) (f)	Speaker	L	L	...
Alaska	★	President	Speaker	L, M	L, M	★
Arizona	★	President	Speaker	L	L	...
Arkansas	★	President	Speaker	L	L	...
California	★	Rules Cmte.	Rules Cmte.	L	...	★ (h)
Colorado	★	President	Speaker	L, M (i)	L (i)	...
Connecticut	★	Pres. Pro Tempore	Speaker	M	M	...
Delaware	★	Pres. Pro Tempore	Speaker	...	...	...
Florida	★	President	Speaker	L, M	M	...
Georgia	★	President (f)	Speaker	...	...	★
Hawaii	(j)	President	Speaker	...	...	★
Idaho	...	President (e)	Speaker	L	L	...
Illinois	★	Rules Cmte.	Rules Cmte.	...	...	★
Indiana	★ (o)	Pres. Pro Tempore	Speaker	...	...	...
Iowa	★	President	Speaker	M	M	★
Kansas	★	President	Speaker	L	L	★
Kentucky	★	Cmte. on Cmtes.	Cmte. on Cmtes.	L	L	...
Louisiana	★	President (l)	Speaker (l)	L	L	...
Maine	★	Secy. of Senate and Clerk of House (n)		L	L	★
Maryland	★	President	Speaker	L	L	...
Massachusetts	★	Clerk	Clerk	M	M	★
Michigan	...	Majority Ldr.	Speaker	...	...	★
Minnesota	...	President	Speaker	L, M	L, M	★
Mississippi	★	President (e)	Speaker	L	L	...
Missouri	★	Pres. Pro Tempore	Speaker	L	L	...
Montana	★	President	Speaker	...	...	...
Nebraska	★	Reference Cmte.	U	L	U	★ (p)
Nevada	★	(q)	(q)	L (t)	...	...
New Hampshire	★	President	Speaker	M	L, M	★
New Jersey	★ (m)	President	Speaker	...	...	★
New Mexico	★ (k)	(r)	Speaker	L, M	M	...
New York	★	Pres. Pro Tempore (s)	Speaker	M	M	★
North Carolina	...	Rules Chairman	Speaker	M	M	★
North Dakota	★	President (e)	Speaker	M	M	...
Ohio	★	Reference Cmte.	Rules & Reference Cmte.	L	L	★
Oklahoma	★	Majority Leader	Speaker	L	...	★
Oregon	★	President	Speaker	L	H	...
Pennsylvania	★	President Pro Tempore	Speaker	L	M	...
Rhode Island	★	President	Speaker	M	M	★
South Carolina	★	President	Speaker	M	M	★
South Dakota	★	President	Speaker	...	...	...
Tennessee	★	Speaker	Speaker	...	...	★
Texas	★	President	Speaker	L	L	...
Utah	★	President	Speaker	...	...	...
Vermont	(g)	President	Speaker	M	M	★
Virginia	★	Clerk	Clerk (u)	L	L	★
Washington	★	(v)	(v)	...	...	★
West Virginia	★	President	Speaker	L, M	L, M	★ (j)
Wisconsin	...	President	Speaker	...	...	★ (p)
Wyoming	★	President	Speaker	M	M	...
Puerto Rico	...	President	Secretary	M	M	...

See footnotes at end of table.

BILL PRE-FILING, REFERENCE, AND CARRYOVER — Continued

Source: The Council of State Governments' survey, October 2003.
Key:

★ — Yes
. . . — No
L — Rules generally require all bills be referred to the appropriate committee of jurisdiction.
M — Rules require specific types of bills be referred to specific committees (e.g., appropriations, local bills).
U — Unicameral legislature.

(a) Legislative rules specify all or certain bills go to committees of jurisdiction.

(b) Unless otherwise indicated by footnote, bills may be introduced prior to convening each session of the legislature. In this column only: ★ —pre-filing is allowed in both chambers (or in the case of Nebraska, in the unicameral legislature); . . . — pre-filing is not allowed in either chamber.

(c) Bills carry over from the first year of the legislature to the second (does not apply in Alabama, Arkansas, Montana, Nevada, North Dakota, Oregon and Texas, where legislatures meet biennially). Bills generally do not carry over after an intervening legislative election.

(d) Except between the end of the last regular session of the legislature in any quadrennium and the organizational session following the general election and special session.

(e) Lieutenant governor is the president of the Senate.

(f) Senate bills by president with concurrence of president pro tem, if no concurrence by rules committee. House bills by president pro tem with concurrence of president, if no concurrence, by rules committee.

(g) Bills are drafted prior to session but released starting first day of session.

(h) Bills introduced in the first year of the regular session and passed by the house of origin on or before the January 31st constitutional deadline are carryover bills.

(i) In either house, state law requires any bill which affects the sentencing of criminal offenders and which would result in a net increase of imprisonment in state correctional facilities must be assigned to the appropriations committee of the house in which it was introduced. In the Senate, a bill must be referred to the Appropriations Committee if it contains an appropriation from the state treasury or the increase of any salary. Each bill which provides that any state revenue be devoted to any purpose other than that to which is devoted under existing law must be referred to the Finance Committee.

(j) House only in even-numbered years.

(k) In the House only.

(l) Subject to approval or disapproval. Louisiana–majority members present.

(m) Prior to convening of first regular session only.

(n) For the joint standing committee system. Secretary of the Senate and clerk of House, after conferring, suggest an appropriate committee reference for every bill, resolve and petition offered in either house. If they are unable to agree, the question of reference is referred to a conference of the president of the Senate and speaker of the House. If the presiding officers cannot agree, the question is resolved by the Legislative Council.

(o) Only in the Senate

(p) Any bill, joint resolution on which final action has not been taken at the conclusion of the last general-business floor period in the odd-numbered year shall be carried forward to the even-numbered year.

(q) Motion for referral can be made by any member.

(r) Senator introducing the bill endorses the name of the committee to which the bill is referred. If an objection is made, the Senate determines the committee to which the bill is referred.

(s) Also serves as majority leader.

(t) Suspension of rule - Majority of elected members.

(u) Under the direction of the speaker.

(v) By the membership of the chamber.

Table 3.15
TIME LIMITS ON BILL INTRODUCTION

State or other jurisdiction	Time limit on introduction of bills	Procedures for granting exception to time limits
Alabama	House: no limit. Senate: 22nd day of regular session (a).	Unanimous vote to suspend rules
Alaska	35th C day of 2nd regular session.	Introduction by committee or by suspension of operation of limiting rule.
Arizona	House: 29th day of regular session; 10th day of special session. Senate: 22nd day of regular session; 10th day of special session.	House: Permission of rules committee. Senate: Permission of President.
Arkansas	55th day of regular session (50th day for appropriations bills).	2/3 vote of membership of each house.
California	Deadlines established by rules committee	Approval of rules committee and 2/3 vote of membership.
Colorado	House: 22nd C day of regular session. Senate: 17th C day of regular session (b).	House and Senate: Committees on delayed bills may extend deadline.
Connecticut	10 days into session in odd-numbered years, 3 days into session in even-numbered years (c).	2/3 vote of members present.
Delaware	House: no limit. Senate: no limit.	
Florida	House: noon of the first day of regular session. Senate: noon first day of regular session (b)(e).	Existence of an emergency reasonably compelling consideration notwithstanding the deadline.
Georgia	Only for specific types of bills	
Hawaii	Actual dates established during session.	Majority vote of membership.
Idaho	House: 20th day of session (d); 36th day of session (f). Senate: 12th day of session (d); 36th day of session (f).	House and Senate: Speaker/President Pro Tempore may designate any standing committee to serve as a privileged committee temporarily.
Illinois	House: determined by speaker (b)(d). Senate: determined by president.	House: rules governing limitations may not be suspended except for bills determined by a majority of members of the Rules Comm. to be an emergency bill, & appropriations bills implementing the budget. Senate: Rules may be suspended by a majority vote of members.
Indiana	House and Senate: mid-January.	House: 2/3 vote.
Iowa	House: Friday of 6th week of 1st regular session (d)(g)(i); Friday of 2nd week of 2nd regular session (d)(g)(h). Senate: Friday of 7th week of 1st regular session (d)(g); Friday of 2nd week of 2nd regular session (d)(g).	Constitutional majority.
Kansas	Actual dates established suring session	Resolution adopted by majority of members of either house may make specific exceptions to deadlines.
Kentucky	House: After 14th L day of odd-year session, during last 22 L days of even-year session Senate: After 14th L day of odd-year session, during last 20 L days of even-year session	Majority vote of membership of each house.
Louisiana	30th C day of odd-year session; 10th C day of even-year session.	2/3 vote of elected members of each house.
Maine	1st Wednesday in December of 1st regular session; deadlines for 2nd regular session established by Legislative Council.	Approval of majority of members of Legislative Council.
Maryland	No introductions during last 35 C days of regular session.	2/3 vote of elected members of each house.
Massachusetts	1st Wednesday in December even-numbered years, 1st Wednesday in November odd-numbered years.	2/3 vote of members present and voting.
Michigan	No limit.	
Minnesota	No limit	Must follow committee deadline process.
Mississippi	14th C day in 90 day session; 49th C day in 125 day session (o).	2/3 vote of members present and voting.
Missouri	House: 60th L day of regular session. Senate: March 1.	Majority vote of elected members each house; governor's request for consideration of bill by special message.
Montana	General bills & resolutions: 10th L day; revenue bills: 17th L day; committee bills and resolutions: 36th L day; committee bills implementing provisions of a general appropriation act: 75th L day; committee revenue bills: 62nd L day interim study resolutions: 75th L day (b)(i).	2/3 vote of members.
Nebraska	10th L day of any session (b).	3/5 vote of elected membership
Nevada	Actual dates established at start of session.	Waiver granted by Senate Majority Floor Leader or Assembly Speaker.
New Hampshire	Actual dates established during session.	2/3 vote of members present.

See footnotes at end of table.

TIME LIMITS ON BILL INTRODUCTION — Continued

State or other jurisdiction	Time limit on introduction of bills	Procedures for granting exception to time limits
New Jersey	Assembly: No limit. Senate: no limit.	Majority vote of members.
New Mexico	30th L day of odd-year session (j); 15th L day of even-year session (j).	None.
New York	Assembly: for unlimited introduction of bills, 1st Tuesday in March; for introduction of 10 or fewer bills, last Tuesday in March (k)(l). Senate: 1st Tuesday in March (l)(m).	Unanimous vote.
North Carolina	Actual dates established during session.	Senate: 2/3 vote of membership present and voting shall be required.
North Dakota	House: 10th L day. Senate: 15th L day	2/3 vote or approval of majority of Committee on Delayed Bills.
Ohio	No limit.	
Oklahoma	Time limit set in rules.	2/3 vote of membership.
Oregon	House: 36th C day of session (k). Senate: 36th C day of session.	2/3 vote of membership.
Pennsylvania	No limit.	
Rhode Island	2nd Tuesday in February.	Simple majority vote.
South Carolina	House: Prior to April 15 of the 2nd yr. of a two-yr. legislative session; May 1 for bills first introduced in Senate. Senate: May 1 of regular session for bills originating in House.	House: 2/3 vote of members present and voting. Senate: 2/3 vote of membership.
South Dakota	40-day session: 15th L day; committee bills and joint resolutions, 16th L day. 35-day session: 10th L day; committee bills and joint resolutions, 11th L day.	2/3 vote of membership.
Tennessee	House: general bills, 10th L day of regular session (m). Senate: general bills, 10th L day or regular session; resolutions, 40th L day (m).	Unanimous consent of Committee on Delayed Bills, or upon motion approved by 2/3 vote of members present.
Texas	60th C day of regular session.	4/5 vote of members present and voting.
Utah	12:00 p.m. on 11th day of general session.	Motion for request must be approved by 2/3 vote of members.
Vermont	House: 1st session—last day of February; 2nd session—last day of January. Senate: 1st session—53 C day; 2nd session—25 C days before start of session.	Approval by Rules Committee.
Virginia	Deadlines may be set during session.	
Washington	(Constitutional limit) No introductions during final 10 days of regular session (n).	2/3 vote of elected members of each house.
West Virginia	House: 45th C day. Senate: 41st C day.	2/3 vote of members present.
Wisconsin	No limit.	
Wyoming	House: 15th L day of session. Senate: 12th L day of session	2/3 vote of elected members.
Puerto Rico	1st session—within first 125 days; 2nd session—within first 60 days.	None.

Source: The Council of State Governments' survey, October 2003.

Key:

C—Calendar
L—Legislative

(a) Not applicable to local bills, advertised or otherwise.

(b) Not applicable to appropriations bills. In West Virginia, supplementary appropriations bills or budget bills.

(c) Not applicable to (1) bills providing for current government expenditures; (2) bills the presiding officers certify are of an emergency nature; (3) bills the governor requests because of emergency or necessity; and (4) the legislative commissioners' revisor's bills and omnibus validating act.

(d) Not applicable to standing committee bills.

(e) Not applicable to local bills and joint resolutions. Florida: Not applicable to local bills (which have no deadline) or claim bills (deadline is August 1 of the year preceding consideration or within 60 days of a senator's election).

(f) Not applicable to House State Affairs, Appropriations, Education, Revenue and Taxation, or Ways and Means committees, nor to Senate State Affairs, Finance, or Judiciary and Rules committees.

(g) Unless written request for drafting bill has been filed before deadline.

(h) Not applicable to bills co-sponsored by majority and minority floor leaders.

(i) Only certain measures may be considered in the Short Session- primarily those relating to appropriations, finance, pensions and retirement and localities; certain legislation from the 2001 Session; and legislation proposed by study commissions.

(j) Final date for consideration on floor in house of origin during first session. Bills introduced after date are not placed on calendar for consideration until second session.

(k) Not applicable to measures approved by Committee on Legislative Rules and Reorganization or by speaker; appropriation or fiscal measures sponsored by committees on Appropriations; true substitute measures sponsored by standing, special or joint committees; or measures drafted by legislative counsel.

(l) Resolutions fixing the last day for introduction of bills in the House are referred to the Rules Committee before consideration by the full House.

(m) Not applicable to certain local bills.

(n) Not applicable to substitute bills reported by standing committees for bills pending before such committees.

(o) Not applicable to Revenue & Appropriations and Local & Private bills. Time limits for those bills are: 51st calendar day (90-day session) and 86th calendar day (125-day session).

Table 3.16
ENACTING LEGISLATION: VETO, VETO OVERRIDE AND EFFECTIVE DATE

State or other jurisdiction	Governor may item veto appropriation bills: Amount	Governor may item veto appropriation bills: Other (b)	Days allowed governor to consider bill (a): During session — Bill becomes law unless vetoed	Days allowed governor to consider bill (a): After session — Bill becomes law unless vetoed	Days allowed governor to consider bill (a): After session — Bill dies unless signed	Votes required in each house to pass bills or items over veto (c)	Effective date of enacted legislation (d)
Alabama	...	...	6 (e)		10A	Majority elected	Date signed by governor
Alaska	★	...	15P	20P		2/3 elected (g)	90 days after enactment
Arizona	★	★	5	10A		2/3 elected	90 days after adjournment
Arkansas	★	...	5	20A		Majority elected	91st day after adjournment
California	(hh)	...	12	30A		2/3 elected	(j)
Colorado	★ (ff)	...	10 (h)	30A (h)		2/3 elected	90 days after adjournment (k)
Connecticut	★	...	5	15P		2/3 elected	(gg)
Delaware	★	...	10P	10P	30A	3/5 elected	Immediately
Florida	...	★	7 (h)(p)	15P (h)		2/3 present	60 days after adjournment
Georgia	★	★	6	40A		2/3 elected	July 1 for generals, date signed by governor for locals
Hawaii (l)	★ (f)	★	10 (o)(p)	45A (o)(p)	(p)	2/3 elected	Immediately
Idaho	★	★	5	10A		2/3 present	July 1
Illinois	★ (f)	...	60 (h)	60P (h)		3/5 elected (g)	(n)
Indiana	...	★	7	7P		Majority elected	(q)
Iowa	★	...	3	(r)	(r)	2/3 elected	July 1 (n)
Kansas	★ (hh)	★	10 (h)	10P		2/3 membership	Upon publication
Kentucky	★ (hh)	...	10	90A	110P	Majority elected	90 days after adjournment
Louisiana (l)	★ (hh)	★	10 (h)	20P (h)		2/3 elected	Aug. 15
Maine	★ (hh)	...	10	10P		2/3 present	90 days after adjournment
Maryland	★	★	6	30P (m)		3/5 elected	June 1 (s)
Massachusetts	★	★	10	10P	10A	2/3 present	90 days after enactment
Michigan	★	★ (hh)	14 (h)		14P (h)	2/3 elected and serving	90 days after adjournment
Minnesota	★	(hh)	3	14A, 3P	3A, 14P	2/3 elected	Aug. 1 (t)
Mississippi	★	...	5	15P (m)		2/3 elected	July 1
Missouri	★	...	15	45A		2/3 elected	August 28 (u)
Montana (l)	★	★	10 (h)	25A (h)		2/3 present	Oct. 1 (t)
Nebraska	★ (v)	...	5	5A, 5P		3/5 elected	90 days following adjournment
Nevada	...	...	5	10A		2/3 present	Oct. 1
New Hampshire	...	...	5	5P		2/3 present	60 days after enactment
New Jersey	★ (f)	...	45 (h)(w)	(w)	(w)	2/3 elected	July 4; other dates usually specified
New Mexico	★	...	3 (ee)		20A	2/3 present	90 days after adjournment
New York	★	...	10		30A	2/3 elected	20 days after enactment
North Carolina	...	...	10	30A		3/5 elected	60 days after adjournment
North Dakota	...	★	3	15A		2/3 elected	(x)
Ohio	★	★	10		10A	3/5 elected (ii)	91st day after filing with secretary of state
Oklahoma	★	★	5	15A	15A	2/3 elected (g)	90 days after adjournment
Oregon	★	★	5 (o)	30A (o)		2/3 present	90 days after adjournment
Pennsylvania	★	...	10	30A, 10P	(i)	2/3 present	60 days after signed by governor
Rhode Island	...	...	6	10A		3/5 present	Immediately
South Carolina	...	...	5	(m)		2/3 elected	Date of signature

See footnotes at end of table.

ENACTING LEGISLATION: VETO, VETO OVERRIDE AND EFFECTIVE DATE — Continued

State or other jurisdiction	Governor may veto item appropriation bills		Days allowed governor to consider bill (a)			Votes required in each house to pass bills or items over veto (c)	Effective date of enacted legislation (d)
	Amount	Other (b)	During session: Bill becomes law unless vetoed	After session: Bill becomes law unless vetoed	Bill dies unless signed		
South Dakota	★	★	5	15P		2/3 elected	July 1
Tennessee	★ (f)	...	10	10A		Majority elected	40 days after enactment
Texas	★	...	10P	20A		2/3 elected	90 days after adjournment
Utah	★	...		60A (h)		2/3 elected	60 days after adjournment
Vermont	...	...	5P		3A	2/3 present	July 1
Virginia	★	★	7 (h)		30A (h)	2/3 present (y)	July 1 (z)
Washington	★	★	5	20A		2/3 present	90 days after adjournment
West Virginia	...	(hh)	5P	15A (aa)		Majority elected	90 days after enactment
Wisconsin	★	★	6P	6P		2/3 present	Day after publication date unless otherwise specified
Wyoming	★	★	3	15A		2/3 elected	Specified in act
American Samoa	★	...	10		30A	2/3 elected	60 days after adjournment (bb)
Guam	★	★	10		30P	2/3 elected	Immediately (cc)
No. Mariana Islands	★	★	40 (h)(dd)			2/3 elected	Immediately
Puerto Rico	★	...	10		30P	2/3 elected	Specified in act
U.S. Virgin Islands	★	★	10		30P (h)	2/3 elected	Immediately

See footnotes at end of table.

ENACTING LEGISLATION: VETO, VETO OVERRIDE AND EFFECTIVE DATE — Continued

Source: The Council of State Governments' survey, October 2003.

Note: Some legislatures reconvene after normal session to consider bills vetoed by governor. Connecticut—if governor vetoes any bill, secretary of state must reconvene General Assembly on second Monday after the last day on which governor is either authorized to transmit or has transmitted every bill with his objections, which- ever occurs first; General Assembly must adjourn sine die not later than three days after its reconvening. Ha- waii—legislature may reconvene on 45th day after adjournment sine die, in special session, without call. Louisi- ana—legislature meets in a maximum five-day veto session on the 40th day after final adjournment. Missouri—if governor returns any bill on or after the fifth day before the last day on which legislature may consider bills (in even-numbered years), legislature automatically reconvenes on first Wednesday following the second Monday in September for a maximum 10-calendar day session. New Jersey—legislature meets in special session (without call or petition) to act on bills returned by governor on 45th day after sine die adjournment of the regular session; if the second year expires before the 45th day, the day preceding the end of the legislative year. Utah— if two-thirds of the members of each house favor reconvening to consider vetoed bills, a maximum five-day session is set by the presiding officers. Virginia—legislature reconvenes on sixth Wednesday after adjournment for a maximum three-day session (may be extended to seven days upon vote of majority of members elected to each house). Washington—upon petition of two-thirds of the members of each house, legislature meets 45 days after adjournment for a maximum five-day session.

Key:
★ — Yes
... — No
A — Days after adjournment of legislature.
P — Days after presentation to governor.
(a) Sundays excluded, unless otherwise indicated.
(b) Includes language in appropriations bill.
(c) Bill returned to house of origin with governor's objections.
(d) Effective date may be established by the law itself or may be otherwise changed by vote of the legislature. Special or emergency acts are usually effective immediately.
(e) Except bills presented within five days of final adjournment.
(f) Governor can also reduce amounts in appropriations bills. In Hawaii, governor can reduce items in execu- tive appropriations measures, but cannot reduce nor item veto amounts appropriated for the judicial or legisla- tive branches.
(g) Different number of votes required for revenue and appropriations bills. Alaska—three-fourths elected. Illinois—appropriations reductions, majority elected. Oklahoma—emergency bills, three-fourths vote.
(h) Sundays included.
(i) Last day of two year session.
(j) For legislation enacted in regular sessions: January of the following year. For legislation enacted in special sessions: Immediately upon chaptering by Secretary of State.
(k) An act takes effect on the date stated in the act, or if no date is stated in the act, then on its passage.
(l) Constitution withholds right to veto constitutional amendments.
(m) Bills vetoed after adjournment are returned to the legislature for reconsideration. Maryland—reconsidered at the next meeting of the same General Assembly. Mississippi—returned within three days after the beginning of the next session. South Carolina—within two days after the next meeting.
(n) Effective date for bills which become law on or after July 1. Illinois—a bill passed after May 31 cannot

take effect before June 1 of the next calendar year unless legislature by a three-fifths vote in each house, the bill provides for an earlier effective date. Iowa—if governor signs bill after July 1, bill becomes law on Aug. 15; for special sessions, 90 days after adjournment.
(o) Except Sundays and legal holidays. In Hawaii, except Saturdays, Sundays, holidays and any days in which the legislature is in recess prior to its adjournment. In Oregon, except Saturdays and Sundays.
(p) The governor must notify the legislature 10 days before the 45th day of his intent to veto a measure on that day. The legislature may convene on the 45th day after adjournment to consider the vetoed measures. If the legislature fails to reconvene, the bill does not become law. If the legislature reconvenes, it may pass the mea- sure over the governor's veto or it may amend the law to meet the governor's objections. If the law is amended, the governor must sign the bill within 10 days after it is presented to him in order for it to become law.
(q) Varies with date of the veto.
(r) Any bill presented to the governor within the last three days of a session must be acted on within 30 days after adjournment.
(s) Bills passed over governor's veto take effect 30 days after veto override or on date specified in bill, whichever is later.
(t) Different date for fiscal legislation. Minnesota, Montana—July 1.
(u) If bill has an emergency clause, it becomes effective upon governor's signature.
(v) No appropriation can be made in excess of the recommendations contained in the governor's budget except by a three-fifths vote. The excess is subject to veto by the governor.
(w) On the 45th day after the date of presentation, a bill becomes law unless the governor returns it with his objections, except that (1) if the legislature is in adjournment sine die on the 45th day, a special session is convened (without petition or call) for the sole purpose of acting upon bills returned by the governor; (2) any bill passed between the 45th day and the 10th day preceding the end of the second legislative year must be returned by the governor by the day preceding the end of the second legislative year; (3) any bill passed or reenacted within 10 days preceding the expiration of the second legislative year becomes law if signed prior to the seventh day following such expiration, or the governor returns it to the house of origin and two-thirds elected members agree to pass the bill prior to such expiration.
(x) August 1 after filing with the secretary of state. Appropriations and tax bills July 1 after filing with secretary of state, or date set in legislation by Legislative Assembly, or by date established by emergency clause.
(y) Must include majority of elected members.
(z) Special sessions—first day of fourth month after adjournment.
(aa) Five days for supplemental appropriation bills.
(bb) Laws requiring to be approved only by the governor. An act required to be approved by the U.S. Secretary of the Interior only after it is vetoed by the governor and so approved takes effect 40 days after it is returned to the governor by the secretary.
(cc) U.S. Congress may annul.
(dd) Twenty days for appropriations bills.
(ee) Except bills going up in the last three days of session, for which the governor has 20 days.
(ff) Must veto entire amount of any item; an item is an indivisible sum of money dedicated to a stated purpose.
(gg) No set date. Each section of each bill has an effective date determined by bill sponsor or sponsors.
(hh) Line item veto.
(ii) Except for bills needing 2/3 majority for original passage.

Table 3.17
LEGISLATIVE APPROPRIATIONS PROCESS: BUDGET DOCUMENTS AND BILLS

State or other jurisdiction	Budget document submission — Legal source of deadline: Constitutional	Statutory	Submission date relative to convening: Prior to session	Within one week	Within two weeks	Within one month	Over one month	Budget bill introduction — Same time as budget document	Another time	Not until committee review of budget document
Alabama	★	★	...	★	...	...	...	★	...	...
Alaska	★	★	Dec. 15	(a)	...	...	...	★	...	...
Arizona	...	★	★	...	...	...	...	...	...	★
Arkansas	...	★	★	...	...	...	...	...	...	★
California	★	...	...	...	...	...	...	★	...	...
Colorado	...	★	★ (b)	...	...	...	...	...	76th day by rule	...
Connecticut	...	★	...	...	...	(a)	...	★	...	...
Delaware	...	...	...	...	...	...	...	...	...	...
Florida	★	★	★	...	...	...	...	★	...	★
Georgia	★	...	...	(a)	...	...	...	★	...	...
Hawaii	...	★	30 days	...	...	...	...	...	★	...
Idaho	...	★	...	★	...	...	...	...	...	★
Illinois	...	★	...	...	...	...	★	...	★	...
Indiana	...	★	...	...	...	...	...	...	★	...
Iowa	...	★	...	...	...	(a)	...	...	...	★ (c)
Kansas	...	★	...	...	★ (e)	...	...	...	★	...
Kentucky	...	★	...	...	(a)	...	...	★	...	...
Louisiana	...	★	(f)	(f)	...	...	...	(g)	...	...
Maine	...	★	...	(a)	...	...	...	★	...	...
Maryland	★	...	...	★(e)	...	...	...	★ (h)	...	...
Massachusetts	...	★	...	...	...	★	...	★	...	...
Michigan	...	★	...	...	...	★ (e)	...	★	...	...
Minnesota	...	★	...	...	...	★	...	★	...	...
Mississippi	...	★	★	...	...	...	...	...	★	...
Missouri	★	...	...	...	...	★	...	...	...	★
Montana	...	★	★	...	...	...	...	...	★	...
Nebraska	...	★	★	...	...	...	...	★ (c)...	...	...
Nevada	★	...	(a)	...	...	...	...	...	...	★
New Hampshire	...	★	...	...	...	...	(a)	★	...	...
New Jersey	...	★	...	...	...	★ (e)	...	...	...	★ (k)
New Mexico	...	★	...	...	...	(l)	...	...	★	...
New York	★	...	...	...	★ (e)	...	...	★ (m)...	...	...
North Carolina	...	...	...	...	...	...	...	★	...	...
North Dakota	...	★	(n)	...	...	...	...	...	...	★
Ohio	...	★	...	...	...	★ (e)	...	★	...	...
Oklahoma	...	★	★	★	...	...	...	★	...	...
Oregon	...	★	Dec. 1 (e)	...	...	...	...	...	★ (a)	...
Pennsylvania	★	...	...	...	...	...	★	★	...	...
Rhode Island	...	★	...	...	...	...	★	★	...	...
South Carolina	...	★	...	★	...	...	...	...	...	★
South Dakota	...	★	...	...	...	...	★	...	★	...
Tennessee	...	★	...	...	★(a)(e)	★(a)(e)	...	★	...	...
Texas	...	★	...	6th day	...	...	...	...	★ (t)	...
Utah	...	★	(q)	★(r)	...	...	...	...	★ (s)	...
Vermont	...	...	...	(k)	...	...	...	...	...	★
Virginia	...	★	Dec. 20	...	...	...	...	★	(a)	...
Washington	...	★	Dec. 20 (d)	...	...	...	...	★	(i)	...
West Virginia	★	...	...	★	...	...	...	★	...	...
Wisconsin	...	★	...	...	...	★ (j)	...	★	...	...
Wyoming	...	★	Dec. 1	...	...	...	...	...	...	★
No. Mariana Islands	...	★	(a)	...	...	...	...	...	(j)	★
Puerto Rico	...	★	...	...	...	★	...	...	...	★
U.S. Virgin Islands	...	★	May 30	...	...	★ (o)	...	★	...	(u)

See footnotes at end of table.

LEGISLATIVE APPROPRIATIONS PROCESS: BUDGET DOCUMENTS AND BILLS — Continued

Source: The Council of State Governments' survey, October 2003.
Key:

★—Yes

. . . —No

(a) Specific time limitations: Alaska-4th legislative day; Connecticut- not later than the first session day following the third day in February, in each odd numbered year; Georgia-first five days of session; Iowa—no later than February 1; Kentucky—10th legislative day; Maine—by Friday following the first Monday in January; Nevada—no later than 14 days before commencement of regular session; New Hampshire—by February 15; Oregon—Dec. 15 in even-numbered years; Tennessee—on or before February 1; No. Mariana Islands—no later than 6 months before the beginning of the fiscal year.

(b) Presented by November 1 to the Joint Budget Committee.

(c) Executive budget bill is introduced and used as a working tool for committee. Nebraska—Governor must submit his/her budget by January 15th each biennium of odd numbered years.

(d) For fiscal period other than biennium, 20 days prior to first day of session.

(e) Later for first session of a new governor; Kansas—21 days; Maryland—10 days after convening; Michigan—within 60 days; New Jersey—February 15; New York—February 1; Ohio—by March 15; Oregon—February 1; Tennessee—March 1.

(f) The governor shall submit his executive budget to the Joint Legislative Committee on the budget no later than 45 days prior to each regular session; except that in the first year of each term, the executive budget shall be submitted no later than 30 days prior to the regular session. Copies shall be made available to the entire legislature on the first day of each regular session.

(g) Bills appropriating monies for the general operating budget and ancillary appropriations, bills appropriating funds for the expenses of the legislature and the judiciary must be submitted to the legislature for introduction no later than 45 days prior to each regular session, except that in the first year of each term, such appropriation bills shall be submitted no later than 30 days prior to the regular session.

(h) Appropriations bill other than the budget bill (supplementary) may be introduced at any time. They must provide their own tax source and may not be enacted until the budget bill is enacted.

(i) Even-numbered years.

(j) Last Tuesday in January. A later submission date may be requested by the governor.

(k) No official submission dates. Occurs by custom early in the session.

(l) January 1.

(m) Governor has 30 days to amend or supplement the budget; he may submit any amendments to any bills or submit supplemental bills.

(n) For whole legislature. Legislative Council's Budget Section receives budget during legislature's December organizational session.

(o) By enacting annual appropriations legislation.

(p) No later than the 16th legislative day by rule.

(q) Governor must submit budget to Legislative Fiscal Analyst 34 days before official submission to legislature.

(r) Must submit to the legislature no later than 3 days after session begins.

(s) Legislative rules require budget bills to be introduced by the 43rd day of the session, three days prior to the constitutionally mandated end of the session.

(t) Within first 30 days of session.

(u) Prior to September 30.

Table 3.18
FISCAL NOTES: CONTENT AND DISTRIBUTION

State or other jurisdiction	Intent or purpose of bill	Cost involved	Projected future cost	Proposed source of revenue	Fiscal impact on local government	Other	All	Available on request	Bill sponsor	Members	Chair only	Fiscal staff	Executive budget staff
	Content						*Distribution — Legislators*			*Appropriations committee*			*Executive*
Alabama	★	★	...	★	★	★ (a)	...	★	★	...	...	...	...
Alaska	...	★	★	★	...	...	(d)	...	...	...	...	...	...
Arizona	★	★	★	★	★	★	★	★	★	★	...	★	★
Arkansas (f)	...	★	★	...	★	★	★	...	...	...	...	...	...
California	★	★	★	★	★	...	★	★	★	...	...	★	★
Colorado	★	★	★	★	★	★	★	...	...	...	...	...	...
Connecticut	★	★	★	★	★	...	(i)	...	...	...	...	...	...
Delaware	...	★	★	...	...	...	★	...	...	...	...	★	★
Florida	★	★	★	★	★	★	★	...	...	...	...	★	...
Georgia	...	★	★	...	★	...	★	★	...	...	...	...	...
Hawaii	...	...	...	...	...	★	...	...	...	...	★	★	★
Idaho	★	★	★	...	★	★	★	...	...	...	...	...	...
Illinois	...	★	★	★	★	...	★ (l)	★ (l)	...	...	...	...	...
Indiana	★	★	★	★	★	...	★	...	...	...	...	★	★
Iowa	...	★	★	★	★	★	------------------------(b)------------------------						
Kansas	★	★	★	★	★	...	★	★	★	...	★ (m)	★	★
Kentucky	★	★	★	★	★	★	...	★	★	★	...	★	...
Louisiana	...	★	★	...	★	...	★	★	...	...	★ (o)	...	...
Maine	...	★	★	...	★	...	...	★	...	★	...	★	★
Maryland	...	★	★	★	★	★	★	★ (y)	...	...	...	...	...
Massachusetts	...	★ (q)	★	...	...	★	★	...	...	...	★	...	...
Michigan	★	★	★	★	★	★ (r)	★ (s)	★	...	...	...	★	...
Minnesota	★	★	★	★	★	★	★	★	★	★	★	★	★
Mississippi	...	★	★	★	...	...	...	...	★ (y)	...	...	...	...
Missouri	★	★	★	★	★	...	...	★	★	...	...	...	★
Montana	...	★	★	...	★	★ (k)	★	...	...	...	...	★	★
Nebraska	...	★	★	★	★	...	★	...	...	...	...	★	...
Nevada	...	★	★	★	★	★	★	...	...	...	...	...	...
New Hampshire	★	★	★	★	★	★	...	★	...	...	★	★	★
New Jersey	★	★	★	★	★	★ (r)	★	...	...	...	...	...	...
New Mexico	★	★	★	★	(t)	★	...	★	★	★	...	(v)	(v)
New York	...	★	★	...	★	★ (n)	...	★	★	★	...	★	...
North Carolina	...	★	★	...	★	★	(c)	...	...	...	...	...	...
North Dakota (w)	...	★	★ (x)	★	★	★ (n)	...	★	...	...	...	★ (z)	★
Ohio	★	★	★	★	★	...	(aa)	...	...	...	...	...	...
Oklahoma	★	★	★	★	...	...	...	★	★	...	★	★	...
Oregon	★	★	★	★	★	★ (e)	★	...	...	...	...	...	...
Pennsylvania	★	★	★	★	★	...	★	...	★	★	★	★	★
Rhode Island	...	★	★	...	★	...	...	★	...	...	★	...	...
South Carolina	★	★	★	★	★	...	...	★	...	...	★ (j)	★	...
South Dakota	...	★	...	...	★	...	...	★	...	...	...	...	...
Tennessee	★	★	★	★	★	★	★	★	★	★	...	★	★
Texas	...	★	★	★	★	★ (g)	★	★	★	★	...	...	★
Utah	...	★	★	★	★	★ (u)	★	★	★	...	...	★	★
Vermont	--------------------(h)--------------------						...	★	...	★	...	...	...
Virginia	★	★	★	★ (bb)	★	★	...	★	★	★	...	...	...
Washington	★	★	★	★	★	...	...	★	★ (m)	...	★	★ (cc)	...
West Virginia	...	★	★	★	★	...	...	...	...	...	...	★	...
Wisconsin	★	★	★	★	★	★	★	...	...	...	...	★	★
Wyoming	...	★	★	★	...	...	(dd)	...	...	...	...	...	...
No. Mariana Islands	★	★	★	★	★	★	...	...	...	...	★	★	★
Puerto Rico	--------------------(p)--------------------												
U.S. Virgin Islands	★	★	...	★	★	...	★	...	★	★	...	★	...

See footnotes at end of table.

FISCAL NOTES: CONTENT AND DISTRIBUTION — Continued

Source: The Council of State Governments' survey, October 2003.

Note: A fiscal note is a summary of the fiscal effects of a bill on government revenues, expenditures and liabilities.

Key:

★— Yes

. . .—No

(a) Fiscal notes are included in bills for final passage calendar.

(b) Fiscal notes are available to everyone.

(c) Fiscal notes are posted on the internet and available to all members.

(d) Fiscal notes are available online to anyone who wishes to review them. Formal copies go to the bill sponsor and each committee to which the bill is referred. A bill cannot be passed from committee without a fiscal note.

(e) Assumptions (methodology/explanation of fiscal figures).

(f) Only retirement, corrections and local government bills require fiscal notes.

(g) Equalized education funding impact statement and criminal justice policy impact statement.

(h) Fiscal notes are not mandatory and their content will vary.

(i) The fiscal notes are printed with the bills favorably reported by the committees.

(j) Fiscal impact statements on proposed legislation are prepared by the Office of State Budget and sent to the House or Senate standing committee that requested the impact. All fiscal impacts are posted on the OSB web page.

(k) Mechanical defects in bill.

(l) A summary of the fiscal note is attached to the summary of the relevant bill in the Legislative Synopsis and Digest. Fiscal notes are prepared for the sponsor of the bill and are attached to the bill on file in either the office of the Clerk of the House or the Secretary of the Senate.

(m) Or to the committee to which referred.

(n) Bill impacting workers compensation benefits or premiums must have actuarial impact statement. Bills proposing changes in states and local government retirement system also must have an actuarial note.

(o) Prepared by the Legislative Fiscal Office when a state agency is in-volved and prepared by Legislative Auditor's office when a local board or commission is involved; copies sent to House and Senate staff offices respectively.

(p) The Legislature of Puerto Rico does not prepare fiscal notes, but upon request the economics unit could prepare one. The Department of Treasury has the duty to analyze and prepare fiscal notes.

(q) Fiscal notes are prepared only if cost exceeds $100,000 or matter has not been acted upon by the Joint Committee on Ways and Means.

(r) Other relevant data.

(s) Analyses prepared by the Senate Fiscal Agency are distributed to Senate members only; Fiscal notes prepared by the House Fiscal Agency are prepared for bills being voted on in any standing committee and are distributed to the chairperson and all committee members.

(t) Occasionally.

(u) Fiscal notes are to include cost estimates on all proposed bills that anticipate direct expenditures by any Utah resident and the cost to the overall Utah resident population.

(v) Fiscal impact statements prepared by Legislative Finance Committee staff are available to anyone on request and on the legislature's web site.

(w) Notes required only if impact is $5,000 or more.

(x) A four-year projection.

(y) And to the committee to which referred.

(z) Only select fiscal staff.

(aa) Fiscal notes are prepared for bills before being voted on in any standing committee or floor session. Upon distribution to the legislators preparing to vote, the fiscal notes are made available to all other legislators and interested parties.

(bb) The Dept. of Planning and Budget and other relevant state agencies, including the Dept. of Taxation , prepare impact statements, The Joint Legislative Audit And Review Commission (JLARC) prepares review statements as requested by committee chairpersons.

(cc) Distributed to appropriate fiscal and policy staff.

(dd) Fiscal notes are included with the bill upon introduction.

Table 3.19
BILL AND RESOLUTION INTRODUCTIONS AND ENACTMENTS:
2003 REGULAR SESSIONS

State	Duration of session**	Introductions		Enactments		Measures vetoed by governor	Length of session
		Bills	Resolutions	Bills	Resolutions		
Alabama	Jan. 3 - June 16, 2003	1,322	532	258	54	10 (a)	27L
Alaska	Jan. 21 - May 21, 2003	567	101	154	42	0	121C
Arizona	Jan. 13 - June 19, 2003	908	90	268	24	17	158C
Arkansas	Jan. 14 - Apr. 16, 2003	2,885	214	1,816	N.A.	N.A.	94C
California (n)	Dec. 2, 2002 - Aug. 31, 2004	2,867	330	1,156	197	58	(n)
Colorado	Jan. 8 - May 7, 2003	736	178	449	132	14 (c)	120C
Connecticut	Jan. 8 - June 4, 2003	3,302	304	198 (u)	0	12	106L
Delaware	Jan. 8 - June 30, 2003	497	163	191	10	1	46L
Florida	Mar. 4 - May 2, 2003	2,553	261 (f)	412	5 (h)	22	60C
Georgia	Jan. 13 - Apr. 25, 2003	1,437	1,498	414	32	12	40L
Hawaii	Jan. 15 - May 1, 2003	3,401	803	269	282	50	60L
Idaho	Jan. 6-May 3, 2003	678	81	389	N.A.	8	118L
Illinois	Jan. 8 - May 31, 2003	5,920	1,077	600	873	105	(b)
Indiana	Nov. 19, 2002 -Apr. 26, 2003	1,587	389	277	274	6	(b)
Iowa	Jan. 13 - May 1, 2003	1,160	166	183	4	12	109C
Kansas	Jan. 13 - May 29, 2003	758	35	160	6	14 (c)	86C
Kentucky	Jan. 7 - Mar. 25, 2003	781	398	160	34	13 (a)	30L
Louisiana	Mar. 31 - June 23, 2003	3,166	740	1,307	599	15	60L
Maine	Dec. 4, 2002 - June 14, 2003	1,602	33	639	0	2	71L
Maryland	Jan. 8 - Apr. 7, 2003	1,959	33	476	0	153	90C
Massachusetts	Jan. 3, 2003 - Jan. 6, 2004 (k)	6,601	N.A.	168	N.A.	5 (a)	371C
Michigan	Jan. 3 - Dec. 30, 2003	2,313	24 (q)	322	0	14	(b)
Minnesota	Jan. 7 - May 20, 2003	1,658	0	131	0	2	120L
Mississippi	Jan. 7 - April 6, 2003	2,696	266	323	135	3	90C
Missouri	Jan. 8 - May 28, 2003	1,464	49	254	0	30 (a)	(b)
Montana	Jan. 6 - Apr. 26, 2003	1,360	92	612	70	2 (a)	89L
Nebraska	Jan. 8 - May 30, 2003	809	259	259	195	4 (a)	89L
Nevada	Feb. 3 - June 30, 2003	1,064	124	516	95	0	120C
New Hampshire	Jan. 8 - Sept. 4, 2003	988	54	318	18	10 (a)	22L
New Jersey	Jan. 8, 2002 - Jan. 13, 2004 (r)	11,176	866	457	153	19	N.A.
New Mexico	Jan. 21 - Mar. 22, 2003	1,902	66	439	7	84 (m)	60C
New York	Jan. 8 - Dec. 31, 2003	14,821	(j)	697	3,855	72 (e)	64L
North Carolina	*Jan. 29 - July 20, 2003	2,302	66	433	32	2	102L
North Dakota	Jan. 7 - Apr. 25, 2003	924	122	570	87	6 (c)	76C
Ohio	Jan. 6 - Dec. 31, 2003 (g)(l)	533	78 (d)	56	33 (d)	1 (c)	(b)
Oklahoma	Feb. 3 - May 30, 2003	1,655	42 (p)	486	5 (s)	12 (c)	(b)
Oregon	Jan. 13 - Aug. 27, 2003 (t)	2,769	153	817	45	7	227C
Pennsylvania	Jan. 7 - Dec. 23, 2003	3,284	718	67	255	1	87L
Rhode Island	Jan. 7 - July 15, 2003	2,121	678	547	345	11 (a)	(b)
South Carolina	Jan. 14 - June 5, 2003	1,330	832	114	622	39 (a)(o)	63L
South Dakota	Jan. 14 - Mar. 24, 2003	510	6	258	1	3 (a)	40L
Tennessee	Jan. 14 - May 29, 2003	2,129	1,672	483	1,599	0	(b)
Texas	Jan. 14 - June 2, 2003	5,592	3,641 (s)	1,384	3,340 (s)	48	139C
Utah	Jan. 20 - Mar. 5, 2003	628	79	343	45	1 (c)	45C
Vermont	Jan. 8 - June 19, 2003	669	273	78	253	2	(b)
Virginia	Jan. 8 - Feb.22, 2003	2,124	702	1,038	601	7	45L
Washington	Jan. 13 - Apr. 27, 2003	2,363	99	418	11	8 (i)	105C
West Virginia	Jan. 8 - Mar. 16, 2003	1,882	249	259	101	5	68C
Wisconsin	Jan. 6 - Nov. 13, 2003	1,074	168	111	46	22	(b)
Wyoming	Jan. 14 - Mar. 6, 2003	455	21	165	3	5	38L
Puerto Rico	N.A.	1412	5663	272	1308	25	N.A.

See footnotes at end of table.

INTRODUCTIONS AND ENACTMENTS: REGULAR SESSIONS — Continued

Source: The Council of State Governments legislative survey, January 2004.

**Actual adjournment dates are listed regardless of constitutional or statutory limitations. For more information on provisions, see Table 3.2, "Legislative Sessions: Legal Provisions."

*Due to an error on the part of The Council of State Governments, the information reported for North Carolina in *The Book of the States, 2003* was incorrect. The correct information for the 2002 regular session should have been as follows: Total bill introductions - 709 (includes 2 from reconvened session; also includes joint resolutions); Total joint resolution introductions - 35 (number is also included in the total bill introductions); Total bill enactments - 206 (includes 1 from the reconvened session; includes the 186 session laws and 20 resolutions); Number of joint resolution enactments - 20; Number of measures vetoed by governor - 1. Length of session - 78L (House - includes 1 day for reconvened session) and 70L (Senate - includes 1 day for reconvened session).

Key:

C - Calendar day.

L - Legislative day (in some states, called a session or workday; definition may vary slightly; however, it general refers to any day on which either chamber of the legislature is in session.)

N.A. - Not available.

(a) Number of vetoes overridden: Alabama-2; Kentucky-4; Massachusetts-There are two pending at press time (these do not include budget vetoes); Missouri-3; Montana- 1; Nebraska-4; New Hampshire-1; Rhode Island-1; South Carolina-20; South Dakota-1.

(b) Length of session: Illinois - Senate 57L and House 68L; Indiana - Senate 53L and House 54L; Michigan - Senate 107L and House 97L; Missouri - Senate 76L and House 75L; Ohio - Senate 128L and House 130L; Oklahoma-Senate 70L and House 71L; Rhode Island - Senate 70L and House 71L; Tennessee - Senate 47L and House 41L; Vermont - Senate 85L and House 83L; Wisconsin - Senate 73L and Assembly 67L.

(c) Line item or partial vetoes. Colorado - includes three partially vetoed

measures; Kansas - includes 10 line item vetoes; North Dakota - includes two line item vetoes; Ohio - One outright veto, some bills contain item vetoes; Oklahoma - Also one line tiem veto by the governor; Utah - Line item veto.

(d) Numbers include concurrent and joint resolutions only.

(e) Includes four pocket vetos.

(f) Includes one-chamber resolutions.

(g) Senate: Dec. 31, 2003 and House: Dec. 30, 2003

(h) Does not include one-chamber resolutions.

(i) 28 partial vetoes

(j) There are no official statistics for resolution introductions.

(k) Two-year session. The second year session started Jan. 7, 2004. There will be more introductions in the second year of session and there is a carryover provision.

(l) The first session of the 125th General Assembly.

(m) A total of 12 vetos and 72 pocket vetoes.

(n) California's two year session began December 2, 2002. Reconvened on January 5, 2004, final recess, August 31, 2004, sin die adjournment, November 30, 2004. Bill and resolution totals are as of February 2004. The total number of days in session for the Senate, 130 L, and 144 L, Assembly.

(o) Action on the 22 Budget Bill vetoes by the governor had not taken place at press time.

(p) Joint resolutions. Does not include simple and concurrent resolutions.

(q) Three approved by the governor and two filed with the secretary of state.

(r) New Jersey has a two-year legislative session.

(s) Resolution introductions include: 1,069 Senate resolutions, 75 Senate concurrent resolutions, 61 Senate joint resolutions, 2,030 House resolutions, 306 House concurrent resolutions and 100 House joint resolutions. Resolution enactments include: 1,056 Senate resolutions, 45 Senate concurrent resolutions, 6 Senate joint resolutions, 1,988 House resolutions, 230 House concurrent resolutions and 15 House joint resolutions.

(t) Senate: Aug. 26, 2003 and House: Aug. 27, 2003.

(u) Includes 179 public acts and 19 special acts.

Table 3.20
BILL AND RESOLUTION INTRODUCTIONS AND ENACTMENTS:
2003 SPECIAL SESSIONS

State	Duration of session**	Introductions		Enactments		Measures vetoed by governor	Length of session
		Bills	Resolutions	Bills	Resolutions		
Alabama	Jan. 14 - Jan. 21, 2003 (j)	0	38	0	21	0	3L
	May 19 - June 7, 2003	95	123	40	30	0	12L
	Sept. 15 - Sept. 26, 2003	264	94	86	45	1 (c)	8L
Alaska	No special session in 2003	20	6	5	1	0	5C
Arizona	Mar. 17, 2003	7	0	3	0	0	1C
	Oct. 20 - Dec. 20, 2003	35	1	7	1	0	61C
Arkansas	May 5 - 9, 2003	94	0	63	N.A.	N.A.	N.A.
	Dec. 8, 2003 - (f)	282	92	109 (f)	N.A.	N.A.	N.A.
California	Dec. 9, 2002 - July 29, 2003 (o)	47	2	22	0	1	(o)
	Jan. 23 - Feb. 18, 2003	2	0	2	0	0	7L
	Nov. 18, 2003 - Jan. 20, 2004 (p)	3	4	2	0	0	(b)
	Nov. 18, 2003 - (q)	20	3	N.A.	N.A.	N.A.	(r)
	Nov. 18, 2003 - (q)	16	11	N.A.	N.A.	N.A.	(r)
Colorado	No special session in 2003						
Connecticut	Jan. 6, 2003	1	5	1 (h)	5	0	1L
	June 16 - Aug. 17, 2003	0	6	0	6	0	N.A.
	June 30 - Aug. 17, 2003	7	7	7 (i)	7	2	N.A.
	Sept. 8, 2003	4	6	4 (v)	6	0	1L
Delaware	No special session in 2003						
Florida	May 12 - May 27, 2003	111	5 (k)	22	0 (l)	(a)	16C
	June 16 - June 27, 2003	63	6 (k)	4	1 (l)	0	11C
	July 9 - July 21, 2003	19	4 (k)	0	0	0	19C
	Aug. 12 - Aug. 13, 2003	17	1 (k)	2	0	0	2C
	Oct. 20 - Oct. 24, 2003	39	9 (k)	10	1 (l)	0	4C
Georgia	No special session in 2003						
Hawaii	July 8, 2003	0 (m)	4	6	4	0 (m)	1L
Idaho	No special session in 2003						
Illinois	No special session in 2003						
Indiana	No special session in 2003						
Iowa	May 29 - June 4, 2003	0	5	2	0	3 (d)	7C
Kansas	No special session in 2003						
Kentucky	No special session in 2003						
Louisiana	No special session in 2003						
Maine	Aug. 21 - Aug. 22, 2003	2	0	2	0	0	2L
Maryland	No special session in 2003						
Massachusetts	No special session in 2003						
Michigan	No special session in 2003						
Minnesota	May 20 - May 29, 2003	118	0	0	(e)	0	8L
Mississippi	No special session in 2003						
Missouri	June 2 - July 1, 2003	30	1	6	0	2	(g)
	Sept. 8 - Sept 12, 2003	14	1	1	0	0	5L
Montana	No special session in 2003						
Nebraska	No special session in 2003						
Nevada	June 3 - June 12, 2003	8	7	1	7	0	10C
	June 25 - July 22, 2003	26	10	18	10	0	28C
New Hampshire	No special session in 2003						
New Jersey	No special session in 2003						
New Mexico	Oct. 27-Nov. 5, 2003	46	2	3	0	0	10C
New York	No special session in 2003						
North Carolina	Nov. 24 - Nov. 25, 2003	8	2	1	1	0	2L
	Dec. 9 - Dec. 10, 2003	12	2	1	1	0	2L
North Dakota	May 5 - May 7, 2003	6	0	6	0	0	3C
Ohio	No special session in 2003						
Oklahoma	No special session in 2003						
Oregon	No special session in 2003						
Pennsylvania	No special session in 2003						
Rhode Island	No special session in 2003						
South Carolina	No special session in 2003						

See footnotes at end of table.

INTRODUCTIONS AND ENACTMENTS: SPECIAL SESSIONS — Continued

State	Duration of session**	Introductions		Enactments		Measures vetoed by governor	Length of session
		Bills	Resolutions	Bills	Resolutions		
South Dakota	June 26 - June 27, 2003	5	0	3	0	0	2L
Tennessee	No special session in 2003						
Texas	June 30 - July 28, 2003	181	351 (s)	4	322 (s)	0	29C
	July 28 - Aug. 26, 2003	60	245 (t)	0	196 (t)	0	30C
	Sept. 15 - Oct. 12, 2003	113	534 (u)	11	510 (u)	0	28C
Utah	May 21 - June 18, 2003	3	0	1	0	0	2L
	Nov. 19, 2003	10	0	7	0	0	1L
Vermont	No special session in 2003						
Virginia	No special session in 2003						
Washington	May 12 - June 10, 2003	29	1	28	0	3 (n)	30C
	June 11, 2003	3	0	4	0	1 (n)	1C
	Dec. 5, 2003	4	1	1	0	0	1C
West Virginia	Mar. 16, 2003	5	4	5	4	0	1L
	June 10 - July 1, 2003	41	9	27	9	0	7L
Wisconsin	Jan. 30 - Feb. 20, 2003	1	0	1	0	0	3L
Wyoming	No special session in 2003						

Source: The Council of State Governments' survey of state legislative agencies, January 2004.

** Actual adjournment dates are listed regardless of constitutional or statutory limitations. For more information on provisions, see Table 3.2, "Legislative Sessions: Legal Provisions."

Key:

N.A. — Not available

C — Calendar day.

L — Legislative day (in some states, called a session or workday; definition may vary slightly; however, it generally refers to any day on which either chamber of the legislature is in session).

(a) One of the measures was line item vetoed by the governor.

(b) Vetoes were line item vetoes.

(c) Number of vetoes overridden: Alabama-1.

(d) Includes item veto.

(e) Senate - 55 resolution enactments and House - 48 resolution enactments.

(f) At press time, the special session was still ongoing. The number of bills enacted in the special session were as of March 2004.

(g) Senate - 17L and House 12L.

(h) Public act.

(i) Includes six public acts and one special act.

(j) Organizational.

(k) Includes one-chamber resolutions.

(l) Does not include one-chamber resolutions.

(m) No bills were introduced. Instead, the Legislature convened a special session to take action on six of the 50 bills which were vetoed by the governor during the 2003 regular session. All six vetos were overridden by the Legislature.

(n) Partial.

(o) Senate ajourned on July 21, 2003. Senate - 50L and House 45L.

(p) Assembly ajourned on Jan. 15, 2004. Senate - 4L and House 5L

(q) Session still open at press time.

(r) Senate - 5L and House - 6L.

(s) Resolution introductions include: 128 Senate resolutions, 5 Senate concurrent resolutions, 5 Senate joint resolutions, 190 House resolutions, 21 House concurrent resolutions and 2 House joint resolutions. Resolution enactments include: 128 Senate resolutions, 2 Senate concurrent resolutions, 185 House resolutions and 7 House concurrent resolutions.

(t) Resolution introductions include: 22 Senate resolutions, 2 Senate concurrent resolutions, 209 House resolutions, 10 House concurrent resolutions and 2 House joint resolutions. Resolution enactments include: 196 House resolutions.

(u) Resolution introductions include: 136 Senate resolutions, 5 Senate concurrent resolutions, 1 Senate joint resolution, 355 House resolutions, 32 House concurrent resolutions and 5 House joint resolutions. Resolution enactments include: 135 Senate resolutions, 4 Senate concurrent resolutions, 348 House resolutions and 23 House concurrent resolutions.

(v) Includes two public acts and two special acts.

Table 3.21
STAFF FOR INDIVIDUAL LEGISLATORS

State or other jurisdiction	Senate Capitol Personal	Senate Capitol Shared	Senate District	House/Assembly Capitol Personal	House/Assembly Capitol Shared	House/Assembly District
Alabama	. . .	YR/2	(u)	. . .	YR/10	(u)
Alaska	SO	. . .	YR	SO	. . .	YR
Arizona	YR	. . .	. . .	. . .	YR (a)	. . .
Arkansas	. . .	YR	. . .	. . .	YR	. . .
California	YR	. . .	YR	YR	. . .	YR
Colorado (b)	YR/5, SO/35	YR/5, SO/2	. . .	YR/5, SO/65	YR/2, SO/2	. . .
Connecticut (d)	YR/36	. . .	. . .	. . .	YR/38	. . .
Delaware	--(v)--					
Florida	YR (e)	. . .	YR (e)	YR (e)	. . .	YR (e)
Georgia	. . .	YR/3, SO/68	. . .	. . .	YR/25, SO/113	. . .
Hawaii	YR	. . .	. . .	YR	. . .	. . .
Idaho	. . .	SO/1.2, YR/2	. . .	. . .	SO/.86, YR/3	. . .
Illinois	YR	YR/1 (f)	YR (g)	YR	YR/2 (f)	YR (g)
Indiana	. . .	YR	. . .	. . .	YR	. . .
Iowa	SO	. . .	. . .	SO	. . .	. . .
Kansas	SO	. . .	. . .	. . .	SO/3	. . .
Kentucky	. . .	YR (h)	. . .	. . .	YR (h)	. . .
Louisiana	(i)	YR (j)	YR (i)	(i)	YR (j)	YR (i)
Maine	YR/24, SO/8	. . .	. . .	. . .	(l)	. . .
Maryland	YR, SO (t)	. . .	YR	YR (t)	SO (t)	YR
Massachusetts	YR	. . .	. . .	YR	. . .	. . .
Michigan	. . .	YR	. . .	YR	. . .	. . .
Minnesota	YR	. . .	. . .	YR	. . .	. . .
Mississippi	. . .	YR	. . .	. . .	YR	. . .
Missouri	YR	YR	. . .	YR	YR	. . .
Montana	. . .	SO	. . .	. . .	SO	. . .
Nebraska	YR (m)	. . .	. . .	------------------Unicameral------------------		
Nevada	SO (c)	YR	. . .	SO (c)	YR	. . .
New Hampshire	. . .	SO	. . .	. . .	YR	. . .
New Jersey	YR (e)	. . .	(e)	YR (e)	. . .	. . .
New Mexico (k)	SO	. . .	. . .	. . .	SO	. . .
New York	YR	. . .	YR	YR	YR	. . .
North Carolina	YR (w)	YR	. . .	YR (w)	YR	. . .
North Dakota	. . .	SO (c)	. . .	. . .	SO (c)	. . .
Ohio	YR	YR	. . .	YR	YR	. . .
Oklahoma	YR	. . .	. . .	. . .	YR	. . .
Oregon	YR	. . .	. . .	YR	. . .	YR
Pennsylvania	YR	. . .	YR	YR	. . .	YR
Rhode Island	. . .	YR/8	. . .	. . .	YR/7	. . .
South Carolina	. . .	. . .	. . .	YR	. . .	. . .
South Dakota	. . .	SO	. . .	. . .	SO	. . .
Tennessee	YR	. . .	. . .	YR	. . .	YR
Texas	YR	. . .	YR	YR	. . .	YR
Utah	(o)	SO	. . .	(o)	SO	. . .
Vermont	YR/1 (n)	. . .	. . .	YR/1 (n)	. . .	. . .
Virginia	SO (e)	. . .	(e)	SO (e)	SO/2	(q)
Washington	YR (p)	. . .	(q)	YR	. . .	. . .
West Virginia	SO	. . .	. . .	. . .	SO/17	. . .
Wisconsin	YR (r)	YR (r)	(r)	YR	YR (r)	(r)
Wyoming	. . .	. . .	. . .	. . .	. . .	. . .
No. Mariana Islands	YR (s)	(s)	. . .	YR (s)	(s)	(r)
Puerto Rico	YR (s)	. . .	YR (s)	. . .	. . .	. . .
U.S. Virgin Islands	YR (s)	. . .	. . .	------------------Unicameral------------------		

See footnotes at end of table.

STAFF FOR INDIVIDUAL LEGISLATORS — Continued

Source: The Council of State Governments' survey, October 2003.

Note: For entries under column heading Shared, figures after slash indicated approximate number of legislators per staff person, where available.

Key:

. . .—Staff not provided for individual legislators.

YR—Year-round.

SO—Session only.

IO—Interim only.

(a) Representatives share a secretary with another legislator, however House leadership and committee chairs usually have their own secretarial staff. All legislators share professional research staff within their house.

(b) The number of year round staff is comprised of leadership staff and caucus staff. Each caucus may also hire additional shared staff during the session. During the session, each legislator can hire an aide for a limited number of hours.

(c) Secretarial staff; in North Dakota, leadership only.

(d) The numbers are for staff assigned to specific legislators. There is additional staff working in the leadership offices that also suport the rank and file members.

(e) Personal and district staff are the same. In Florida, two out of the three district employees may travel to the capitol for sessions.

(f) Partisan offices provide staff year-round.

(g) District office expenses allocated per year from which staff may be hired.

(h) Leadership offices provide staff support year-round. Individual legislators have access to clerical support year-round, augmented during a session.

(i) Each legislator may hire as many assistants as desired, but pay from public funds ranges from $2,000 to $3,000 per month per legislator. Assistant(s)

generally work in the district office but may also work at the capitol during the session.

(j) The six caucuses are assigned one full-time position each (potentially 24 legislators per one staff person).

(k) Speaker, pro tem and leadership have staff year round.

(l) The House members do not have individual staff. There are 20 people who work year round in the three partisan offices, 12 of whom are legislative aides who primarily work directly with legislators.

(m) Senators offices have 2 year round staff members. Committee chair offices have 3-4 staff members year round.

(n) No personal staff except one administrative assistant for the Speaker and one for the Sneate Pro Tempore.

(o) Legislators are provided student interns during session.

(p) Leadership, caucus chair, and Ways and Means Committee chair have two full-time staff each. All other legislators have one full-time staff year round and one additional staff session only.

(q) Full-time staff may move to the district office during interim period.

(r) Some of personal staff may work in the district office. Total of all staff salaries for each senator must be within limits established by the Senate.

(s) Individual staffing and staff pool arrangements are at the discretion of the individual legislator.

(t) Senators have one year round administrative aide and one session only secretary. Delegates have one part-time year round administrative aide and a shared session only secretary.

(u) Six counties have local delegation offices with shared staff.

(v) Staffers are a combination of full time, part time, shared, personal, etc. andtheir assignments change throughout the year.

(w) Part time during interim.

Table 3.22
STAFF FOR LEGISLATIVE STANDING COMMITTEES

| State or other jurisdiction | Committee staff assistance | | | | Source of staff services** | | | | | | | |
| | Senate | | House/Assembly | | Joint central agency (a) | | Chamber agency (b) | | Caucus or leadership | | Committee or committee chair | |
	Prof.	Cler.	Prof.	Cler.	Prof.	Cler.	Prof.	Cler.	Prof.	Cler.	Prof.	Cler.
Alabama	●	★	●	★	B	B	B	B	...	...	B	B
Alaska	★	●	★	●	B	B	...	...	B	B	...	...
Arizona	★	★	★	★	B	...	...	B	B	...	B	B
Arkansas	★	★	★	★	B	B	...	...	...	...	...	...
California	★	★	★	★	B	B	B	B	B	B	B	B
Colorado	★	...	★	...	B	...	B	B	B	B	...	...
Connecticut	...	★	...	★	B	...	...	...	...	B	...	B
Delaware	...	...	...	...	B	B	...	...	...	...	...	...
Florida	★	★	★	★	B	B	S, H	S, H	S, H	S, H	S, H	S, H
Georgia	●	★	●	★	B	B	B	B	B	B	B	...
Hawaii	●	★	★	★	B	B	B	B	B	B	B	B
Idaho	★	★	★	★	B	B	...	...	...	...	B	B
Illinois	★	★	★	★	...	...	B	B	B	B	...	...
Indiana	●	...	●	...	...	...	...	...	...	...	B	B
Iowa	★	...	★	...	B	...	B (d)	...	B	...	B	...
Kansas	★	★	★	★	B	B (e)	...	...	...	...	...	...
Kentucky	★	★	★	★	B	B	...	...	...	...	...	...
Louisiana	★ (m)	★	★ (m)	★	B	B	B	B	B	B	B (g)	B (g)
Maine	★ (c)	★ (c)	★ (c)	★ (c)	B	B	S, H	S, H	S, H	S, H	...	B
Maryland	★ (h)	★ (h)	★ (h)	★ (h)	B	B	...	...	...	...	...	...
Massachusetts	★	★	★	★	...	...	...	...	...	...	...	...
Michigan	★	★	★	★	B	...	...	H	B	B	B	S
Minnesota	★	★	★	★	...	...	B	...	H	H	B	B
Mississippi	●	★	●	★	...	...	B	B	...	...	B	B
Missouri	★	...	★	...	B		B, S, H	...	S	S	S, H	...
Montana	★	★	★	★	B	...	...	B	...	...	...	...
Nebraska	★	★	U	U	...	...	B	...	...	...	...	...
Nevada	★	★ (h)	★	★ (h)	B	...	...	B	...	...	...	...
New Hampshire	●	★	★	★	B	...	S, H	S, H	...	...	...	...
New Jersey	★	★	★	★	B	B	...	...	...	...	...	...
New Mexico	★	★	★	★	...	...	B (g)	B (g)	...	...	...	...
New York	★	★	★	★	B	B	B	B	B	B	B	B
North Carolina	★	★ (i)	★	★ (i)	B	...	...	...	...	...	...	B (i)
North Dakota	● (f)	★	● (f)	★	B	...	...	B	...	...	...	...
Ohio	★	★	★	★	B	...	...	...	...	...	B	B
Oklahoma	★	★	★	★	...	...	B	B	...	...	...	...
Oregon	★	★	★	★	B	B	...	...	...	...	B	B
Pennsylvania	★	★	★	★	B	B	B	B	B	B	B	B
Rhode Island	★	★	★	★	B	B	...	...	B	B	...	...
South Carolina	★	★	★	★	B	B	B	B	B	B	B	B
South Dakota	★	★	★	★	B (h)	...	...	...	...	...	...	...
Tennessee	★	★	★	★	B	...	...	B (j)	...	...	S	B
Texas	★	★	★	★	B	B	...	B	...	...	B	B
Utah	★	★	★	★	B	...	...	B	...	...	...	...
Vermont	★	●	★	●	B	B	...	...	...	...	...	...
Virginia	★	★	★	★	B	...	B	B	...	...	(g)	(g)
Washington	★	★	★	★	...	...	...	...	B	B	B (k)	B (k)
West Virginia	★	★	★	★	B	B	B	B	B	B	B	B
Wisconsin	★	★	★	★	B	...	B	...	...	...	B	B
Wyoming	★	★	★	★	B	...	...	B	...	B	...	B
No. Mariana Islands	★	★	★	★	B (l)	B (p)	(l)	B (l)	B (l)	B (l)	B (l)	B (l)
Puerto Rico	★	★	★	★	B (l)	B (l)	B (l)	B (l)	B (l)	B (l)	B (l)	B (l)
U.S. Virgin Islands	★	★	U	U	S (l)	S (l)	S (l)	S (l)	S (l)	S (l)	S (l)	S (l)

See footnotes at end of table.

STAFF FOR LEGISLATIVE STANDING COMMITTEES — Continued

Source: The Council of State Governments' survey, October 2003.

** — Multiple entries reflect a combination of organizations and location of services.

Key:

★ — All committees

● — Some committees

. . . — Services not provided

B — Both chambers

H — House

S — Senate

U — Unicameral

(a) Includes legislative council or service agency or central management agency.

(b) Includes chamber management agency, office of clerk or secretary and House or Senate research office.

c) Standing committees are joint House and Senate committees.

(d) The Senate secretary and House clerk maintain supervision of committee clerks. During the session each committee selects its own clerk.

(e) Senators select their secretaries and notify the central administrative services agency; all administrative employee matters handled by the agency.

(f) House and Senate Appropriations Committees have Legislative Council fiscal staff at their hearings

(g) Staff is assigned to each committee but work under the direction of the chair.

(h) Committees hire additional staff on a contractual basis during session only under direction of chair.

(i) Member's personal secretary serves as a clerk to the committee or subcommittee that the member chairs.

j) Bill clerks during session only.

(k) Each chamber has a non-partisan research staff which provides support services to committees (including chair).

(l) In general, the legislative service agency provides legal and staff assistance for legislative meetings and provides associated materials. Individual legislators hire personal or committee staff as their budgets provide and at their own discretion.

(m) House Appropriations and Senate Finance Committees have Legislative Fiscal Office staff at their hearings.

Table 3.23
STANDING COMMITTEES: APPOINTMENT AND NUMBER

State or other jurisdiction	Committee members appointed by:		Committee chairpersons appointed by:		Number of standing committees during regular 2003 session (a)	
	Senate	House	Senate	House	Senate	House
Alabama	CC	S	CC	S	25	24
Alaska	CC	CC	CC	CC	9	9
Arizona	P	S	P	S	10 (c)	16 (c)
Arkansas	(bb)	(d)	(bb)	S	10	10
California	CR	S	CR	S	25	29
Colorado	MjL, MnL	S, MnL	MjL	S	10 (a)	11 (a)
Connecticut	PT	S	PT	S	(e)	(e)
Delaware	PT	S	PT	S	26	27
Florida	P	S	P	S	20 (c)	18
Georgia	CC	S	CC	S	25	34
Hawaii	P (f)	(g)	P (f)	(g)	13	17
Idaho	PT (h)	S	PT	S	10	14
Illinois	P, MnL	S, MnL	P	S	21	37
Indiana	PT	S	PT	S	19	20
Iowa	MjL, MnL (i)	S	MjL (i)	S	16	17
Kansas	(j)	S	(j)	S	14	21
Kentucky	CC	CC	CC	CC	11	16
Louisiana	P	S (k)	P	S	17	17
Maine	P	S	P	S	4 (e)	6 (e)
Maryland	P	S	P	S	6 (c)	7 (c)
Massachusetts	P	S, MnL	P	S	9 (e)	12 (e)
Michigan	MjL	S	MjL	S	21 (c)	23 (c)
Minnesota	CR	S	MjL	S	13	24
Mississippi	P	S	P	S	30 (c)	31 (c)
Missouri	PT (l)	S	PT	S	21	31
Montana	CC	S	CC	S	13	13
Nebraska	CC	U	E	U	14	U
Nevada	MjL (m)	S (m)	MjL (m)	S (m)	9	11
New Hampshire	P (n)	S (o)	P (n)	S	16	21
New Jersey	P	S	P	S	14 (c)	20 (c)
New Mexico	CC	S	CC	S	9 (aa)	15 (aa)
New York	PT (p)	S	PT (p)	S	32	37
North Carolina	PT	S	PT	S	20 (z)	31 (z)
North Dakota	CC	CC	MjL	MjL	12	12
Ohio	P (q)	S (q)	P (q)	S (q)	14	22
Oklahoma	PT, MnL	S	PT	S	17	24
Oregon	P	S	P	S	9 (c)	13 (c)
Pennsylvania	PT	S	PT	S	22	26
Rhode Island	P	S	P	S	11	10
South Carolina	E	S	E	E	15	11
South Dakota	PT, MnL	S	PT	S	13	13
Tennessee	S	S	S	S	9	14
Texas	P	S (r)	P	S	15	40
Utah	P	S	P	S	11	14
Vermont	CC	S	CC	S	12	15
Virginia	E	S	(s)	S	11	14
Washington	P (b)(t)	S (u)	CC	S (v)	14	23
West Virginia	P	S	P	S	17	14
Wisconsin	(w)	S	(w)	S	15 (c)	42 (c)
Wyoming	P (x)	S (x)	P (x)	S (x)	12	12
Dist. of Columbia	(y)	U	(y)	U	9	U
No. Mariana Islands	P	S	P	S	8	7
Puerto Rico	P	S	P	S	22	32
U.S. Virgin Islands	P	U	P	U	9	U

See footnotes at end of table.

STANDING COMMITTEES: APPOINTMENT AND NUMBER — Continued

Source: The Council of State Governments' survey, October 2003.
Key:
CC—Committee on Committees
CR—Committee on Rules
E—Election
MjL—Majority Leader
MnL—Minority Leader
P—President
PT—President pro tempore
S—Speaker
U—Unicameral Legislature
(a) Includes appropriations committee.
(b) Lieutenant governor is president of the senate.
(c) Also, joint standing committees. Arizona, 3; Colorado, 12; Florida, 6; Maryland, 16, (joint statutory); Michigan, 5; Mississippi, 7; New Jersey, 3; Oregon, 1; Wisconsin, 9.
(d) Members of the standing committees shall be selected by House District Caucuses with each caucus selecting five members for each A standing committee and five members for each B standing committee.
(e) Substantive standing committees are joint committees. Connecticut, 18 (there are also three statutory and three select committees); Maine, 17 (also joint committee on rules and special committee on health care); Massachusetts, 21.
(f) President appoints committee members and chairs; minority members on committees are nominated by minority party caucus.
(g) By resolution, with members of majority party designating the chair, vice-chairs and majority party members of committees, and members of minority party designating minority party members.
(h) Committee members appointed by the senate leadership under the direction of the president pro tempore, by and with the senate's advice.

(i) Appointments made after consultation with the president.
(j) Committee on Organization, Calendar and Rules.
(k) Speaker appoints only 12 of the 19 members of the Committee on Appropriations.
(l) Senate minority committee members chosen by minority caucus, but appointed by president pro tempore.
(m) Committee composition and leadership usually determined by party caucus, with final decision by leader.
(n) Appointments made after consultation with the minority leader.
(o) Speaker appoints minority members with advice of the minority floor leader.
(p) President pro tempore is also majority leader.
(q) The minority leader may recommend for consideration minority party members for each committee.
(r) For each standing substantive committee of the house, except for the appropriations committee, a maximum of one-half of the membership, exclusive of chair and vice-chair, is determined by seniority; the remaining membership of the committee is determined by the speaker.
(s) Senior members of the majority part on the committee is the chair.
(t) Confirmed by the senate.
(u) By each party caucus.
(v) By majority caucus.
(w) Majority leader as chairperson, Organization Committee.
(x) With the advice and consent of the Rules and Procedures Committee.
(y) Chair of the Council.
(z) Does not include select or subcommittees.
(aa) Senate: Includes eight substantive committees and one procedural committee. House: Includes 12 substantive committees and three procedural committees.
(bb) Selection process based on seniority.

Table 3.24
RULES ADOPTION AND STANDING COMMITTEES: PROCEDURE

State or other jurisdiction	Constitution permits each legislative body to determine its own rules	Committee meetings open to public*		Specific, advance notice provisions for committee meetings or hearings	Voting/roll call provisions to report a bill to floor
		House/ Senate	Assembly		
Alabama	★	★	★	Senate: 4 hours, if possible House: 24 hours, except Rules & Local Legislations committees	Senate: final vote on a bill is recorded. House: recorded vote if requested by member of committee and sustained by one additional committee member.
Alaska	. . .	★	★	For meetings, by 4:00 p.m. on the preceding Thurs.; for first hearings on bills, 5 days	Roll call vote on any measure taken upon request by any member of either house.
Arizona	★	★	★	Senate: agenda submitted to secretary 5 days prior to meeting House: agenda distributed Wed. prior to Mon. meeting and Thurs. prior to all other meetings.	Senate: roll call vote taken upon request. House: roll call vote required for final action on any bill.
Arkansas	★	★	★	Senate: 2 days House: 24 hours	Senate: roll call votes are recorded. House: report of committee recommendation signed by committee chair.
California	★	★	★	Senate: none House: none	Senate: roll call. House: roll call.
Colorado	★	★	★	Senate: final action on a measure is prohibited unless notice is posted one calendar day prior to its consideration (f) House: none	Senate: final action by recorded roll call vote. House: final action by recorded roll call vote.
Connecticut	★	★	★	Senate: one day notice for meetings, five days notice for hearings. House: one day notice for meetings, five days notice for hearings.	Senate: roll call required. House: roll call required.
Delaware	★	★	★	Senate: agenda released the day before meetings House: agenda for meetings released on last legislative day of preceding week	Senate: results of any committee vote are recorded. House: results of any committee vote are recorded.
Florida	★	★	★	Senate: during session–3 hours notice for first 50 days, 4 hours thereafter House: two days.	Senate: vote on final passage is recorded. House: vote on final passage is recorded.
Georgia	★	★	★	Senate: a list of committee meetings shall be posted by 10:00 a.m. the preceding Friday House: none	Senate: recorded roll call taken if one-third members sustain the call for yeas and nays. House: recorded roll call taken if one-fifth members sustain the call for yeas and nays.
Hawaii	★	★ (a)	★ (a)	Senate: 72 hours before 1st referral committee meetings, 48 hours before subsequent referral committee meetings House: 48 hours	Senate: final vote is recorded. House: a record is made of a committee quorum and votes to report a bill out.
Idaho	★	★ (a)	★ (a)	Senate: none House: none	Senate: bills can be voted out by voice vote or roll call. House: bills can be voted out by voice vote or roll call.
Illinois	★	★ (a)	★ (a)	Senate: 6 days House: 6 days	Senate: votes on all legislative measures acted upon are recorded. House: votes on all legislative matters acted upon are recorded.
Indiana	★	★	★	Senate: 48 hours House: prior to adjournment or the meeting day next preceding the meeting or announced during session	Senate: majority of quorum; vote can be by roll call or consent. House: majority of quorum; vote can be by roll call or consent.
Iowa	★	★	★	Senate: none House: none	Senate: final action by roll call. House: committee reports include roll call on final disposition.
Kansas	★	★	★	Senate: none House: none	Senate: vote recorded upon request of member. House: he total for and against actions recorded.
Kentucky	★	★	★	Senate: none House: none	Senate: each member's vote recorded on each bill. House: each member's vote recorded on each bill.
Louisiana	★	★ (a)	★ (a)	Senate: no later than 1:00 p.m. the preceding day House: no later than 4:00 p.m. the preceding day	Senate: any motion to report an instrument is decided by a roll call vote. House: any motion to report an instrument is decided by a roll call vote.

See footnotes at end of table.

RULES ADOPTION AND STANDING COMMITTEES: PROCEDURE — Continued

State or other jurisdiction	Constitution permits each legislative body to determine its own rules	Committee meetings open to public* Senate	House/ Assembly	Specific, advance notice provisions for committee meetings or hearings	Voting/roll call provisions to report a bill to floor
Maine	★	★	★	Senate: must be advertised two weekends in advance. House: must be advertised two weekends in advance.	Senate: recorded vote is required to report a bill out of committee. House: recorded vote is required to report a bill out of committee.
Maryland	★	★	★	Senate: none House: none	Senate: the final vote on any bill is recorded. House: the final vote on any bill is recorded.
Massachusetts	★	★	★	Senate: 48 hours for public hearings House: 48 hours for public hearings	Senate: voice vote or recorded roll call vote at the request of 2 committee members. House: recorded vote upon request by a member.
Michigan	★	★	★	Senate: none House: none	Senate: committee reports include the vote of each member on any bill. House: the daily journal reports the roll call on all motions to report bills.
Minnesota	★	★	★	Senate: 3 days House: 3 days	Senate: recorded vote upon request of one member. Upon the request of 3 members, the record of a roll call vote and committee report are printed in the journal. House: recorded roll call vote upon request by a member.
Mississippi	★	★	★	Senate: none House: none	Senate: bills are reported out by voice vote or recorded roll call vote. House: bills are reported out by voice vote or recorded roll call vote.
Missouri	★	★	★	Senate: 24 hours House: 24 hours	Senate: yeas and nays are reported in journal. House: bills are reported out by a recorded roll call vote.
Montana	★	★	★	Senate: 3 legislative days House: none	Senate: every vote of each member is recorded and made public. House: every vote of each member is recorded and made public.
Nebraska	★	★	U	Seven calendar days notice before hearing a bill.	In executive session, majority of the committee must vote in favor of the motion made.
Nevada	★	★	★	Senate: by rule - adequate notice House: by rule - adequate notice	Senate: recorded vote is taken upon final committee action on bills. House: recorded vote is taken upon final committee action on bills.
New Hampshire	★	★	★	Senate: 5 days House: 4 days	Senate: committees may report a bill out by voice or recorded roll call vote. House: committees may report a bill out by voice or recorded roll call vote.
New Jersey	★	★	★ (a)	Senate: 5 days House: 5 days	Senate: the chair reports the vote of each member present on a motion to report a bill. House: the chair reports the vote of each member present on motions with respect to bills.
New Mexico	★	★	★	Senate: none House: none	Senate: vote on the final report of the committee taken by yeas and nays. Roll call vote upon request. House: vote on the final report of the committee taken by yeas and nays. Roll call vote upon request.
New York	(b)	★ (a)	★ (a)	Senate: 1 week House: 1 week	Senate: each report records the vote of each Senator. House: at the conclusion of a committee meeting a roll call vote is taken on each of the bills considered.
North Carolina	(c)	★	★	Senate: none (g) House: none (g)	Senate: no roll call vote may be taken in any committee. House: roll call vote taken on any question when requested by member & sustained by one-fifth of members present.
North Dakota	★	★	★	Senate: notice posted the preceding Wed. or Thurs., depending on the committee House: notice posted the preceding Wed. or Thurs., depending on the committee	Senate: minutes include recorded roll call vote on each bill referred out. House: minutes include recorded roll call vote on each bill referred out.
Ohio	★	★	★	Senate: 2 days House: 5 days	Senate: every member present shall vote unless excused by the committee. Bills are reported by recorded roll call vote. House: every member present must vote. Bills are reported by recorded roll call vote.
Oklahoma	★	★	★	Senate: none House: 3 days for hearings by author; 10 days during requested interim.	Senate: roll call vote. House: voice vote/show of hands, except that a committee member can obtain a roll call vote if requested prior to the vote.
Oregon	★	★	★	Senate: 24 hours House: 24 hours (d)	Senate: the vote on all official actions is recorded. House: motions on measures before a committee are by recorded roll call vote.

RULES ADOPTION AND STANDING COMMITTEES: PROCEDURE — Continued

State or other jurisdiction	Constitution permits each legislative body to determine its own rules	Committee meetings open to public* House/ Senate Assembly		Specific, advance notice provisions for committee meetings or hearings	Voting/roll call provisions to report a bill to floor
Pennsylvania	★	★	★	Senate: none House: none	Senate: a majority vote of committee members. House: all votes are recorded.
Rhode Island	★	★	★	Senate: 48 hours prior to meeting. House: 48 hours prior to meeting.	Senate: majority vote of the members present. House: majority vote of the members present.
South Carolina	★	★	★	Senate: 24 hours House: 24 hours	Senate: no bill may be polled out unless at least 2/3 of the members are polled. Poll results are certified and published in journal. House: favorable report out of committee (majority of committee members voting in favor).
South Dakota	★	★	★	Senate and House: at least one legislative day must intervene between the posting of the committee agenda and the committee meeting.	Senate and House: a majority vote of the members-elect taken by roll call is needed for final disposition on a bill. This applies to both houses.
Tennessee	★	★	★	Senate: 6 days House: 72 hours when House is recessed or adjourned	Senate: aye and no votes cast by name on each question are recorded. House: bills are reported out by recorded roll call vote.
Texas	★	★	★	Senate: 24 hours House: (e)	Senate: bills are reported by recorded roll call vote. House: committee reports include the record vote by which the report was adopted, including the vote of each member.
Utah	★	★	★	Senate: 24 hours House: 24 hours	Senate: each member present votes on every question and all votes are recorded. House: each member present votes on every question and all votes are recorded.
Vermont	★	★	★	Senate: none House: none	Senate: vote is recorded for each committee member for every bill considered. House: vote is recorded for each committee member for every bill considered.
Virginia	★	★ (a)	★	Senate: none House: none	Senate: generally, a recorded vote is taken for each measure. House: vote of each member is taken and recorded for each measure.
Washington	★	★	★	Senate: 5 days House: 5 days	Senate: bills reported from a committee carry a majority report which must be signed by a majority of the committee. House: every vote to report a bill out of committee is by yeas and nays; the names of the members voting are recorded in the report.
West Virginia	★	★	★	Senate: none House: none	Senate: majority of committee members voting. House: majority of committee members voting.
Wisconsin	★	★	★	Senate: a list of public hearings is filed Monday of the preceding week House: a list of public hearings is filed Monday of the preceding week	Senate: number of ayes and noes, and members absent or not voting are reported. House: number of ayes and noes are recorded.
Wyoming	★	★	★	Senate: by 3:00 p.m. of previous day House: by 3:00 p.m. of previous day	Senate: bills are reported out by recorded roll call vote. House: bills are reported out by recorded roll call vote.
Puerto Rico	★	★	★	Senate: Must be notified every Thurs., one week in advance. House: 24 hours advanced notice, no later than 4:00 p.m. previous day	Senate: bills reported from a committee carry a majority vote House: bills reported from a committee carry a majority vote by referendum or in an ordinary meeting.

Source: The Council of State Governments' survey, October 2003.
Key:
★ — Yes
* — Notice of committee meetings may also be subject to state open meetings laws; in some cases, listed times may be subject to suspension or enforceable only to the extent "feasibleÔ or "whenever possible."
U — Unicameral.
(a) Certain matters may be discussed in executive session. (Other states permit meetings to be closed for various reasons, but their rules do not specifically mention "executive session.")
(b) Not referenced specifically, but each body publishes rules and there are joint rules.

(c) Not referenced specifically, but each body publishes rules.
(d) May go to one hour notice when president and speaker proclaim sine de imminent.
(e) The House requires five calendar days notice before a public hearing at which testimony will be taken, and two hours notice or an announcement from the floor before a formal meeting (testimony cannot be taken at a formal meeting).
(f) The prohibition does not apply if the action receives a majority vote of the committee.
(g) If public hearing, five calendar days.

Table 3.25
LEGISLATIVE REVIEW OF ADMINISTRATIVE REGULATIONS: STRUCTURES AND PROCEDURES

State or other jurisdiction	Type of reviewing committee	Rules reviewed	Time limits in review process
Alabama	Joint bipartisan, standing committee	P, E (f)	35 days for action by committee.
Alaska	Joint bipartisan	P,E	. . .
Arizona	Joint bipartisan	P,E	. . .
Arkansas	Joint bipartisan	P,E	. . .
California		P,E	Regulation review conducted by independent executive branch agency.
Colorado	Joint bipartisan	E	Rules continue unless the annual legislative rule review bill discontinues a rule. The rule review bill is effective upon the Governor's signature.
Connecticut	Joint bipartisan	P	65 days for action by committee.
Delaware		P	The Attorney General shall review any rule or regulation promulgated by any state agency and inform the issuing agency in writing as to the potential of the rule or regulation to result in a taking of private property before the rule or regulation may become effective.
Florida	Joint bipartisan	P,E	. . .
Georgia	Standing committee	P	The agency notifies the Legislative Counsel 30 days prior to the effective dates of proposed rules.
Hawaii	Legislative agency (c)	P,E	. . .
Idaho	Germane joint subcommittees	P	Germane joint subcommittees vote to object or not object to a rule. They cannot reject a proposed rule directly, only advise an agency which may chose to adopt a rule subject to review by the full legislature. The legislature as a whole reviews rules during the first three weeks of session to determine if they comport with state law. The Senate and House may reject rules via resolution adopted by both. Rules imposing fees must be approved or are deemed approved unless rejected. Temporary rules expire at the end of session unless extended by concurrent resolution.
Illinois	Joint bipartisan	P,E	If the committee objects to a proposed rule, the agency can modify, adopt or withdraw within 90 days. If the agency does not act within 90 days, the rule is automatically withdrawn. If the committee determines a proposed rulemaking is objectionable and constitutes a threat to public interest, safety or welfare, it may prohibit adoption of the rule for 180 days.
Indiana	Joint bipartisan	P	. . .
Iowa	Joint bipartisan	P,E	The committee meets monthly and can delay the effective date of a proposed rule until the adjournment of the next legislative session, giving the legislature an opportunity to review the rule. The legislature can rescind any rule by joint action of the two houses.
Kansas	Joint bipartisan	P,E	Agencies must give a 60-day notice to the public and the Joint Committee of their intent to adopt or amend specific rules and regulations, a copy of which must be provided to the committee. Within the 60-day comment period, the Joint Committee must review and comment, if it feels necessary, on the proposals. Final rules and regulations are resubmitted to the committee to determine whether further expression of concern is necessary.

See footnotes at end of table.

LEGISLATIVE REVIEW OF ADMINISTRATIVE REGULATIONS: STRUCTURES AND PROCEDURES — Continued

State or other jurisdiction	Type of reviewing committee	Rules reviewed	Time limits in review process
Kentucky	Joint bipartisan statutory committee	P,E	45 days.
Louisiana (b)	Standing committee	P	All proposed rules and fees are submitted to designated standing committees of the legislature. If a rule or fee is unacceptable, the committee sends a written report to the governor. The governor has 10 days to disapprove the committee report. If both Senate and House committees fail to find the rule unacceptable, or if the governor disapproves the action of a committee within 10 days, the agency may adopt the rule change. (d)
Maine	Joint bipartisan, standing committee	P	One legislative session.
Maryland	Joint bipartisan	P,E	Proposed regulations are submitted for review at least 15 days before they are delivered for publication. The committee has 45 days from the date the regulation is published to comment or object to the regulation.
Massachusetts (b)	Public hearing by agency	P	In Massachusetts, the General Court (Legislature) may by statute authorize an administrative agency to promulgate regulations. The promulgation of such regulations are then governed by Chapter 30A of the Massachusetts General Laws. Chapter 30A requires 21 day notice to the public of a public hearing on a proposed regulation. After public hearing the proposed regulation is filed with the State Secretary who approves it if it is in conformity with Chapter 30A. The State Secretary maintains a register entitled "Massachusetts Register" and the regulation does not become effective until published in the register. The agency may promulgate amendments to the regulations following the same process.
Michigan	Joint bipartisan	P	Joint Committee on Administrative Rules (JCAR) has 21 days to approve a formal notice of objection. If no objection is made, the rules may be filed and go into effect. If JCAR does formally object, bills to block the rules are introduced in both houses of the legislature simultaneously by the committee chair, the alternate chair, or any member of the committee, and placed directly on the Senate and House calendars for action. If the bills are not enacted within 21 days, the rules may be filed and go into effect. Also, as specified in the Michigan Constitution, the committee, acting between legislative sessions, can meet and suspend rules promulgated during the interim between sessions.
Minnesota	Standing committee		
Mississippi	--(a)--		
Missouri	Joint bipartisan, standing committee	P,E	The committee must disapprove a final order of rulemaking within 30 days upon receipt or the order of rulemaking is deemed approved.
Montana	Germane joint bipartisan committees	P,E	. . .
Nebraska	Standing committee	P	If an agency proposes to repeal, adopt or amend a rule or regulation, it is required to provide the Executive Board Chairperson with the proposal at least 30 days prior to the Public Hearing, as required by law. The Executive Board Chairperson shall provide to the appropriate standing committee of the Legislature, the agency proposal for comment.

See footnotes at end of table.

LEGISLATIVE REVIEW OF ADMINISTRATIVE REGULATIONS: STRUCTURES AND PROCEDURES — Continued

State or other jurisdiction	Type of reviewing committee	Rules reviewed	Time limits in review process
Nevada	Joint bipartisan	P	If the committee objects to a rule, it is returned to the agency for revision in accordance with legislative intent and statutory authority.
New Hampshire	Joint bipartisan	P	Preliminary objections must be filed within 45 days of agency filing of final proposal. Otherwise, final proposal is automatically approved. A vote to sponsor joint resolutions must be filed within 50 days of the objection response deadline, but a final objection may be filed at any time after objection response is received.
New Jersey	The legislature	P,E	. . .
New Mexico	--(g)--		
New York	Joint bipartisan commission	P,E	Agencies must give at least 45 days notice of proposed rule making to the public and the joint commission. While there is no statutory time limit for the commission's review, any commission comments or objections are typically submitted prior to agency adoption. Agency adoption may occur until expiration of the notice of proposed rule making, which is 180 days after its publication in the "State Register," unless extended for an additional 185 days by the agency upon public notice. Whenever a proposed rule is substantially revised, the agency must give at least 30 days notice of revised rule making to the public and the joint commission.
North Carolina	Rules Review Commission; Public membership appointed by legislature	P,E	The Rules Review Commission must review a permanent rule submitted to it on or before the 20th of the month by the last day of the next month. The commission must review a permanent rule submitted to it after the 20th of the month by the last day of the second subsequent month.
North Dakota	Interim committee	E	The committee has 90 days from the time a rule is published to initially consider a rule and may carry over for one additional meeting its decision on whether to declare the rule void.
Ohio	Joint bipartisan	P,E	The committee's jurisdiction is 65 days from date of original filing plus an additional 30 days from date of re-filing. Rules filed with no changes, pursuant to the five-year review, are under a 90 day jurisdiction.
Oklahoma (b)	Standing committees	P,E	The legislature has 30 legislative days to disapprove a permanent rule. The legislature may disapprove any rule at any time by joint resolution.
Oregon (h)	Joint boint bipartisan	E	. . .
Pennsylvania	Joint bipartisan, standing committee	P,E	Time limits decided by the each house of the legislature.
Rhode Island	--(g)--		
South Carolina	Standing committee (e)	P	General Assembly has 120 days to approve or disapprove. If not disapproved by joint resolution before 120 days, regulation is automatically approved.
South Dakota	Joint bipartisan	P	Rules must be adopted within 75 days of the commencement of the public hearing; emergency rules must be adopted within 30 days of the date of the notice of intent.
Tennessee	Joint standing committee	P	All permanent rules take effect 75 days after filing with the secretary of state. Rules filed in a calendar year expire on June 30 of the following year unless extended by the General Assembly.
Texas	--(a)--		

See footnotes at end of table.

LEGISLATIVE REVIEW OF ADMINISTRATIVE REGULATIONS: STRUCTURES AND PROCEDURES — Continued

State or other jurisdiction	Type of reviewing committee	Rules reviewed	Time limits in review process
Utah	Joint bipartisan	P,E	Each rule in effect on February 28 of each year expires May 1 of that year unless reauthorized by the legislature in annual legislation.
Vermont	Joint bipartisan	P	The Joint Legislative Committee Rules must review a proposed rule within 30 days of submission to the committee.
Virginia (b)	Standing committee	P,E	Legislative review is optional. Within 21 days after the receipt of an objection, the agency shall file a response with the registrar, the objecting legislative committee and the governor. After an objection is filed, the regulation unless withdrawn by the agency shall become effective on a date specified by the agency which shall be after the 21-day extension period.
Washington (b)	Joint bipartisan	P,E	If the committee determines that a proposed rule does not comply with legislative intent, it notifies the agency, which must schedule a public hearing within 30 days of notification. The agency notifies the committee of its action within seven days after the hearing. If a hearing is not held or the agency does not amend the rule, the objection may be filed in the state register and referenced in the state code. The committee's powers, other than publication of its objections, are advisory.
West Virginia	Joint bipartisan		. . .
Wisconsin	Joint bipartisan, standing committee	P,E	The standing committee has 30 days to conduct its review for a proposed rule. The time limit can be extended in various ways. If a standing committee objects to a proposed rule, the joint committee also must object before legislation is introduced to sustain the objection. The joint committee may suspend an existing rule at any time. The suspension is followed by legislation to sustain that action.
Wyoming	Joint bipartisan	P,E	An agency shall submit copies of adopted, amended or repealed rules to the legislative services office for review within five days after the date of the agency's final action adopting, amending or repealing those rules. The legislature makes its recommendations to the governor who within 15 days after receiving any recommendation, shall either order that the rule be amended or rescinded in accordance with the recommendation or file in writing his objections to the recommendation.
Puerto Rico	--(a)--		

Source: The Council of State Governments survey, October 2003.
Key:
P—Proposed rules
E—Existing rules
. . .—No formal time limits
(a) No formal rule review is performed by both legislative and executive branches.
(b) Review of rules is performed by both legislative and executive branches.
(c) In Hawaii, the legislative reference bureau assists agencies to comply with a uniform format of style. This does not affect the status of rules.
(d) If the committees of both houses fail to find a fee unacceptable, it can be adopted. Committee action on proposed rules must be taken within 5 to 30 days after the agency reports to the committee on its public hearing (if any) and whether it is making changes on proposed rules.
(e) Submitted by General Assembly for approval.
(f) Existing rules prior to 1982.
(g) No formal review is performed by legislature. Periodic review and report to legislative finance committee is required of certain agencies.
(h) Oregon created a second kind of review. An executive department agency must submit a proposed rule to a member or committee of the legislative assembly (the recipient differs depending upon the rule) and then, if requested, a standing or interim committee must review the rule and return its comments to the adopting agency.

Table 3.26
LEGISLATIVE REVIEW OF ADMINISTRATIVE REGULATIONS: POWERS

State	Reviewing committee's powers: Advisory powers only (a)	Reviewing committee's powers: No objection constitutes approval of proposed rule	Reviewing committee's powers: Committee may suspend rule	Legislative powers: Method of legislative veto of rules
Alabama	. . .	★	★	Joint resolution (b)
Alaska	★	. . .	(c)	Statute
Arizona	★	N.A.	N.A.	Statute
Arkansas	★	. . .	. . .	. . .
California	------------------------------- (e) -------------------------------			
Colorado	. . .	★	. . .	(f)
Connecticut	. . .	★	. . .	Statute (g)
Delaware	(h)	N.A.	N.A.	N.A.
Florida	★	. . .	. . .	Statute
Georgia	. . .	★	. . .	Resolution (j)
Hawaii	★	. . .	. . .	. . .
Idaho	. . .	★	. . .	Concurrent resolution (k)
Illinois	. . .	. . .	★	Joint resolution
Indiana	★	. . .	. . .	(m)
Iowa	. . .	★	★ proposed rules	Joint resolution
Kansas	. . .	N.A.	. . .	Statute
Kentucky	. . .	★	★	(t)
Louisiana	. . .	★	(n)	Concurrent resolution to suspend, amend or repeal adopted rules or fees. For proposed rules and emergency rules, see footnote (n).
Maine	. . .	★	. . .	(o)
Maryland	(p)	. . .	(l)	Majority vote of committee. Governor can override.
Massachusetts	. . .	. . .	. . .	The legislature may pass a bill which would supersede a regulation if signed into law by the governor.
Michigan	. . .	. . .	(q)	Statute (r)
Minnesota	★	. . .	. . .	(s)
Mississippi	------------------------------- (e) -------------------------------			
Missouri	. . .	★	★	Concurrent resolution passed by both houses of the General Assembly.
Montana	. . .	. . .	★ (b)	Statute
Nebraska	. . .	★	. . .	(d)
Nevada	. . .	★	★	Vote of committee suspends regulation until the final day of next regular legislative session. Concurrent resolution of legislature required to extend suspension indefinitely.
New Hampshire	★	(u)	. . .	(v)
New Jersey	------------------------------- (w) -------------------------------			
New Mexico	------------------------------- (e) -------------------------------			
New York	★	N.A.	N.A.	The legislature may pass a bill which would supersede a regulation if signed into law by the governor.
North Carolina	★	. . .	. . .	Any member of the General Assembly may introduce a bill during first 30 days to disapprove a controversial rule that has been approved by the commission and that has not become effective or has become affective by executive order. (x)
North Dakota	. . .	★ (y)	. . .	(z)
Ohio	★	. . .	. . .	Concurrent resolution. Committee recommends to the General Assembly that a rule be invalidated. The General Assembly invalidates a rule through adoption of concurrent resolution.
Oklahoma	★	★	. . .	Joint resolution, except statutes allow for disapproval of proposed rules by concurrent resolution within review period.
Oregon	★	N.A.	N.A.	(bb)
Pennsylvania	★	★	. . .	Concurrent resolution (cc)
Rhode Island	------------------------------- (e) -------------------------------			
South Carolina	. . .	★	. . .	Joint resolution (dd)
South Dakota	. . .	★	★	(qq)
Tennessee	. . .	★	★	Statute (ee)

See footnotes at end of table.

LEGISLATIVE REVIEW OF ADMINISTRATIVE REGULATIONS: POWERS — Continued

	Reviewing committee's powers:			Legislative powers:
State	Advisory powers only (a)	No objection constitutes approval of proposed rule	Committee may suspend rule	Method of legislative veto of rules
Texas	------------------------------------- (e) -----------------------------------			Statute
Utah	★	. . .	. . .	Statute (ee)
Vermont	------------------------------------- (ff) -----------------------------------			Statute
Virginia (e)	★ (gg)	N.A.	(hh)	N.A.
Washington	★(ii)	N.A.	(jj)	N.A.
West Virginia	★	. . .	. . .	(kk)
Wisconsin	. . .	★	★	Statute (ll)
Wyoming	(mm)	. . .	. . .	Statute (aa)

Source: The Council of State Governments' survey, October 2003.

Key:

★ — Yes

. . . — No

N.A. — Not applicable

(a) This column is defined by those legislatures or legislative committees that can only recommend changes to rules but have no power to enforce a change.

(b) A rule disapproved by the reviewing committee is reinstated at the end of the next session if a joint resolution in the legislature fails to sustain committee action.

(c) Authorized, although constitutionally questionable.

(d) If an agency proposes to repeal, adopt or amend a rule or regulation, it is required to provide the Executive Board Chairperson with the proposal at least 30 days prior to the Public Hearing, as required by law. The Executive Board Chairperson shall provide to the appropriate standing committee of the Legislature, the agency proposal for comment.

(e) No formal mechanism for legislative review of administrative rules. In Virginia, legislative review is optional.

(f) A bill is introduced that includes rules the Committee on Legal Services has determined should be discontinued. The bill must be enacted for the rules to be discontinued.

(g) By February 15 of each regular session, the committee submits for study to the General Assembly a copy of all disapproved regulations. The General Assembly may by resolution sustain or reverse a vote of disapproval.

(h) During the legislative interim, July 1 and the second Tuesday in January, the chairperson of a standing committee of either house may, by majority vote, draft a committee report setting forth its suggestions and recommendations and to request the president pro tempore of the Senate or the speaker of the House to call a special session to consider the committee's recommendations. Each committee report shall be forwarded to the Sunset Committee.

(i) The interim rules review committee may, with the approval of the executive board of the legislative research council, designate any agency for a comprehensive review and evaluation of the agency's rules and rule-making authority. Proposed changes then must be submitted in the bill form to the Legislature at the next legislative session.

(j) The reviewing committee must introduce a resolution to override a rule within the first 30 days of the next regular session of the General Assembly. If the resolution passes by less than a two-thirds majority of either house, the governor has final authority to affirm or veto the resolution.

(k) All rules are terminated one year after adoption unless the legislature reauthorizes the rule.

(l) Committee approval is required for a proposed regulation to have emergency effect, and the committee may place any condition on its approval. If a member of the committee requests a public hearing on emergency adoption of the regulation, the committee must hold the hearing.

(m) None - except by passing statute.

(n) If the committee determines that a proposed rule is unacceptable, it submits a report to the governor who then has 10 days to accept or reject the report. If the governor rejects the report, the rule change may be adopted by the agency. If the governor accepts the report, the agency may not adopt the rule. Emergency rules become effective upon adoption or up to 60 days after adoption as provided in the rule, but a standing committee or governor may void the rule by finding it unacceptable within 2 to 61 days after adoption and reporting such finding to agency within four days.

(o) No veto allowed. Legislation must be enacted to prohibit agency from adopting objectionable rules.

(p) If committee cannot complete review within 45 days, it may delay the adoption of the regulation. If the promulgating agency subsequently notifies the committee of its intent to adopt the regulation, the period of delay ends on the later of the 30th day after the agency's notice to the committee or the 75th day after the initial publication of the proposed regulation. The committee may suggest changes to a regulation at any time.

(q) Committee can suspend rules during interim.

(r) JCAR has 21 days to approve a formal notice of objection. The formal notice of objection starts a 21-day time period that stays the rules and causes committee members to introduce legislation in both houses of the legislature for enactment and presentment to the Governor within 21 days. Any member of the legislature can introduce a bill at a session, which in effect amends or rescinds a rule.

(s) The Legislative Commission to Review Administrative Rules (LCRAR) ceased operating, effective July 1, 1996.

The Legislative Coordinating Commission (LCC) may perform the statutory functions of the LCRAR as it deems necessary. Contact the LCC for more information.

(t) Enacting legislation to void.

(u) Failure to object or approve within 45 days of agency filing of final proposal constitutes approval.

(v) The legislature may permanently block rules through legislation.

(w) Article V, Section IV of the Constitution, as amended in 1992, says the legislature may review any rule or regulation to determine whether the rule or regulation is consistent with legislative intent. The legislature transmits its objections to existing or proposed rules or regulations to the governor and relevant agency via concurrent resolutions. The legislature may invalidate or prohibit an existing or proposed rule from taking effect by a majority vote of the authorized membership of each house.

(x) If a rule approved by the commission is non-controversial, it is not subject to legislative disapproval.

(y) Unless formal objections are made or the rule is declared void, rules are considered approved.

(z) The Administrative Rules Committee can void a rule.

(aa) Action must be taken by legislative order adopted by both houses before the end of the next succeeding legislative session to nullify a rule.

(bb) The committee reports to the legislature during each regular session on the review of rules by the committee.

(cc) The committee has 14 days to introduce a concurrent resolution, which then must be passed by both chambers within 10 legislative days or 30 calendar days, followed by presentment to the governor.

(dd) Must be passed within 120-day review period and presented to the governor for signature.

(ee) The legislature exercises sunset control over rules. Each year a bill is filed that extends all rules promulgated the previous year, except for those rules specifically designated by the committee. In Tennessee, standing committees may suspend effectiveness of proposed rules. In Utah, each rule in effect on Feb. 28 of each year expires May 1 of that year unless reauthorized by the legislature in annual legislation.

(ff) JLCAR may recommend that an agency amend or withdraw a proposal. A vote opposing rule does not prohibit its adoption but assigns the burden of proof in any legal challenge to the agency.

(gg) The agency must respond to a legislative objection within 21 days of receipt. The regulation may become effective on a date specified by the agency, which must be after the expiration of the applicable 21-day extension period.

(hh) Standing committee of both houses in concurrence with governor may suspend effective date until the end of the next General Assembly session.

(ii) Objections are published in the Washington State Register.

(jj) By a majority vote of the committee members, the committee may request the governor to approve suspension of a rule. If the governor approves, the suspension is effective until 90 days after the end of the next regular session.

(kk) State agencies have no power to promulgate rules without first submitting proposed rules to the legislature which must enact a statute authorizing the agency to promulgate the rule. If the legislature during a regular session disapproves all or part of any legislative rule, the agency may not issue the rule nor take action to implement all or part of the rule unless authorized to do so. However, the agency may resubmit the same or a similar proposed rule to the committee.

(ll) Bills are introduced simultaneously in both houses.

(mm) Legislative Management Council can recommend action be taken by the full legislature.

Table 3.27
SUMMARY OF SUNSET LEGISLATION

State	Scope	Preliminary evaluation conducted by	Other legislative review	Other oversight mechanisms in bill	Phase-out period	Life of each agency (in years)	Other provisions
Alabama	C	Dept. of Examiners of Public Accounts	Standing Cmte.	Perf. audit	No later than Oct. 1 of the year following the regular session or a time as may be specified in the Sunset bill.	(usually 4)	Schedules of licensing boards and other enumerated agencies are repealed according to specified time tables.
Alaska	C	Budget & Audit Cmte.	...	...	1/y	...	...
Arizona	S	Off. of the Auditor General	Legis. Cmtes. of reference	Perf. audit	6/m	10	Jt. Legis. Audit Cmte. selects agencies for review and assigns responsibilities for hearings to the legis. cmtes. of reference.
Arkansas	D	...	...	...	...	...	...
California	S	St. Legis. Sunset Review Cmte. (a)	...	...	...	Varies	...
Colorado	R	Dept. of Regulatory Agencies	Legis. Cmtes. of reference	(b)	1/y	up to 15	State law provides certain criteria that are used to determine whether a public need exists for an entity or function to continue and that its regulation is the least restrictive regulation consistent with the public interest.
Connecticut	S	Legis. Program Review & Investigations Cmte.	Jt. Standing Cmte. having cognizance of govt. reorg. and admin.	...	1/y	Varies (7-11)	...
Delaware	C	Agencies under review submit reports to Del. Sunset Comm. based on criteria for review and set forth in statute. Comm. staff conducts separate review.	...	Per. audit	Dec. 31 of next succeeding calendar year	4	Yearly sunset review schedules must include at least nine agencies. If the number automatically scheduled for review or added by the General Assembly is less than a full schedule, additional agencies shall be added in order of their appearance in the Del. Code to complete the review schedule.
Florida	C	Cmte. charged with oversight of the subject area.	Jt. cmte. charged with oversight of the subject area.	...	4-6/y	10	...
Georgia	R	Dept. of Audits	Standing Cmtes.	Perf. audit	...	...	A performance audit of each regulatory agency must be conducted upon the request of the Senate or House standing committee to which an agency has been assigned for oversight and review. (e)
Hawaii	R	Legis. Auditor	Standing Cmtes.	Perf. eval.	None	Established by the legislature	Schedules various professional and vocational licensing programs for repeal.
Idaho	(f)	...	...	...	...	...	Proposed new regulatory measures must be referred to the Auditor for sunrise analysis.
Illinois	R	Bur. of the Budget	Standing Cmte.	...	...	10 (max.)	Automatic repeal if legislature fails to reenact regulatory authority before sunset.
Indiana	S	Non-partisan staff units	Interim cmte. Formed to review...	...	...	...	Smaller program review process now in place after about a dozen years of formal sunset program.
Iowa		——————————————No program——————————————					
Kansas	(g)	Administrative Regulation Review Subcommittee	Joint committee with subject matter jurisdiction.	...	...	...	...
Kentucky	R	...	...	...	...	...	...

See footnotes at end of table.

SUMMARY OF SUNSET LEGISLATION — Continued

State	Scope	Preliminary evaluation conducted by	Other legislative review	Other oversight mechanisms in bill	Phase-out period	Life of each agency (in years)	Other provisions
Louisiana	C	Standing cmtes. of the two houses with subject matter jurisdiction.	...	Perf. eval.	1/y	Up to 6	Act provides for termination of a department and all offices in a department. Also permits committees to select particular agencies or offices for more extensive evaluation. Provides for review by Jt. Legis. Cmte. on Budget of programs that were not funded during the prior fiscal year for possible repeal.
Maine	S	Joint standing cmte. of jurisdiction.	Office of Program Evaluation & Government Accountability (not yet established)	...	...	Generally 10	...
Maryland	R	Dept. of Legislative Services	Standing Cmtes.	Perf. eval.	1-2/y	Varies (usually 10)	...
Massachusetts	(f)	...	...	...	——No program——		
Michigan	(f)	...	...	...	...	...	...
Minnesota	(f)	...	...	...	...	...	...
Mississippi	(h)	...	...	...	...	...	...
Missouri	R	Oversight Division of Cmte. on Legislative Research	...	...	...	6, not to exceed total of 12	...
Montana	(f)	...	...	...	...	...	...
Nebraska	(f)	...	...	...	...	...	...
Nevada	(f)	...	...	...	...	...	...
New Hampshire	(i)	...	...	...	...	...	...
New Jersey	(f)	...	...	...	...	...	...
New Mexico	R	Legis. Finance Cmte.	...	Perf. eval., Progress	(j)	6	...
New York	(f)	...	...	...	...	...	...
North Carolina	(k)	...	...	...	...	...	...
North Dakota		...	...	...	——No program——		
Ohio	C (s)	Sunset Review Cmte.	Appropriations and Budget Cmte.	...	(l)	4	...
Oklahoma	S, D	Jt. Cmtes. With jurisdiction over sunset bills	...	...	1/y	6	...
Oregon	(m)	...	(m)	...	...	...	...
Pennsylvania	C	Leadership Cmte.	Legislative Budget & Finance Cmte.	...	...	...	...
Rhode Island	(p)	...	...	...	(o)	6	...
South Carolina	(n)	...	...	...	...	...	...
South Dakota	(q)	...	...	...	...	...	...
Tennessee	C	Jt. Govt. Operations Cmte.	...	Perf. audit	Perf. audit	1/y	Jan. 8 Sunrise review provision 2/y after creation of entity. The commission chair and vice-chair alternate between the senate and house appointees.
Texas	S	Sunset Advisory Comm.	...	Perf. eval.	1/y	12	It is the responsibility of any agency scheduled for termination or any agency which has oversight responsibilities for a statue scheduled for termination to seek its reauthorization with the Legislature.
Utah	D	Interim Study Cmte.	...	...	(d)	Up to maximum of 10/y	...
Vermont	(c)	Legis. Council staff	Senate and House Government Operations Cmtes.	...	...	...	...
Virginia	S (f)	...	Standing Cmtes.	...	...	...	General assembly places sunset on selective programs and acts. The duration varies as does the subject of the legislation.

See footnotes at end of table.

SUMMARY OF SUNSET LEGISLATION — Continued

State	Scope	Preliminary evaluation conducted by	Other legislative review	Other oversight mechanisms in bill	Phase-out period	Life of each agency (in years)	Other provisions
Washington	C	Jt. Legis. Audit and Review Cmte.	Standing Cmtes.	...	1/y	Varies	...
West Virginia	S	Jt. Cmte. on Govt. Operations	Performance Evaluation and Research Division	Perf. audit	1/y	6	Jt. Cmte. on Govt. Operations composed of five House members, five Senate members and five citizens appointed by governor. Agencies may be reviewed more frequently.
Wisconsin	(f)	...	...	...	...	...	...
Wyoming	(r)	...	...	...	...	...	...

Source: The Council of State Governments' survey, October 2003.

Key:
C - Comprehensive
R - Regulatory
S - Selective
D - Discretionary
d — day
m — month
y — year
. . . — Not applicable

(a) Review by the Jt. Legislative Sunset Review Cmte. of professional and vocational licensing boards terminates on January 1, 2004. Sunset clauses are included in other selected programs and legislation.

(b) Bills need adoption by the legislature.

(c) Sunsets are at the legislature's discretion. Their structure will vary on an individual basis.

(d) July 1 of the year next succeeding the year of termination.

(e) The automatic sunsetting of an agency every six years was eliminated in 1992. The legislature must pass a bill in order to sunset a specific agency.

(f) While they have not enacted sunset legislation in the same sense as the other states with detailed information in this table, the legislatures in Idaho, Michigan, Minnesota, Montana, Nebraska, Nevada, New Jersey, New York, Virginia and Wisconsin have included sunset clauses in selected programs or legislation.

(g) Sunset legislation terminated July 1992. Legislative oversight of designated state agencies, consisting of audit, review and evaluation, continues.

(h) Sunset Act terminated December 31, 1984.

(i) New Hampshire's Sunset Committee was repealed July 1, 1986.

(j) Agency termination is scheduled on July 1 of the year prior to the scheduled termination of statutory authority for that agency.

(k) North Carolina's sunset law terminated on July 30, 1981. Successor vehicle, the Legislative Committee on Agency Review, operated until June 30, 1983.

(l) Authority for latest review (HB 548 of the 123rd General Assembly) expires December 31, 2004. The committee is required to submit report on the need for a permanent legislative committee.

(m) Sunset legislation was repealed in 1993. Joint Legislative Audit Committee still serves as legislative review body.

(n) Law repealed by 1998 Act 419.

Chapter Four

STATE EXECUTIVE BRANCH

"The beginning of this century has certainly proven to be a time of change in the governors' offices across the 50 states."

— Thad Beyle

"The office of lieutenant governor is gaining recognition for its power and possibility."

— Julia Nienaber Hurst

"While the office of secretary of state requires a core understanding of all aspects of state government, it has also evolved into a position that demands increasingly specialized skills and knowledge."

— Kay Stimson

"Whether attorneys general are viewed as activists, advocates or interpreters of the law, they impact all areas of public policy and all aspects of citizen life."

— Angelita Plemmer

"As the chief financial officers of the states, treasurers are the guardians of taxpayer money."

— National Association of State Treasurers

"Government accountability, advancing technological progress and market reforms combine to influence the future direction of our state chief financial officers."

— John J. Radford

Governors: Elections, Campaign Costs, Profiles, Forced Exits and Powers

By Thad Beyle

The year 2003 will be etched in the future news reports and analyses as a year of major change occurring to governors. The most startling event was the recall of Gov. Gray Davis of California. The California gubernatorial recall and replacement votes highlight the fact that some elected governors faced situations in which they could lose their office without being beaten by a challenger at the ballot box, becoming ill or dying. One other unique aspect about the current governors is that there are eight women serving as governor in 2004 – the highest number of women serving at one time in the office. As we move through the first decade of the 21ˢᵗ century, we continue to find new faces in governors' offices.

The governors continue to be in the forefront of activity as we move into 21ˢᵗ century. With Republican governors across the states serving as his major supporters and guides, Texas Gov. George W. Bush sought and won the presidency in the 2000 election. He became the fourth of the last five presidents who had served as governor just prior to seeking and winning the presidency.[1] When George H. W. Bush, a non-governor, won the 1988 presidential election, he beat a governor, Michael Dukakis (D- Mass., 1975-1979 and 1983-1991). Clearly, presidential politics in the three decades following the Watergate scandal finds governors as major actors.

Additionally, the demands on the governors to propose state budgets and then to keep them in balance during the two recessions of the early 1990s and now in the early 2000s has made the governor's chair a "hot seat" in more ways than one.[2] In the current downturn, governors have moved from the half-decade of economic boom of the late 1990s, in which they could propose tax cuts and program increases, to an economic downturn period in which there is increasing demand for program support while state tax revenues fell off significantly. Proposed and adopted budgets fell victim to severe revenue shortfalls in most all of the states. Easy times had switched to hard times again.

2003 Gubernatorial Politics

The year 2003 will be etched in the future news reports and analyses as a year of major change occurring to governors. The most startling political event was the recall of incumbent Gov. Gray Davis (D-1999-2003) in California. This "grassroots" initiative effort began shortly after Davis had won his second term in the 2002 election with 3,469,025 votes

(47.4 percent). Eleven months later, he was faced with a recall election, and although he received nearly 537,000 more votes supporting his right to continue as governor than he received in his 2002 reelection bid, those wanting him recalled cast nearly 5 million votes.[3] Davis became the second governor ever removed from office through a recall initiative. The first, Gov. Lynn J. Frazier (R-N.D.), was recalled in 1921 during his third term in office.

The second question facing the California voters on October 7, 2003, was "If Davis is recalled, who should replace him?" Once the recall effort was certified on July 23, 2003, it was time for "gubernatorial wannabes" to file for the office. Over 140 filed for this contest, and 135 were certified to run on the ballot.[4] They included 49 Democrats, 42 Republicans, 33 Independents and 11 candidates from six minor parties. While initial attention focused on the wide and in some cases strange variety of individuals seeking the governorship, attention soon focused on those candidates given a chance to win. They included former Los Angeles Mayor Bill Simon (R) who lost in the 2002 gubernatorial race to Gov. Davis, Lt. Gov. Cruz Bustamante (D), state Sen. Tom McClintock (R), and actor, bodybuilder and businessman Arnold Schwarzenegger (R).

Both major parties faced a large dilemma in this short election period. For the Democrats, it was trying to win enough votes to retain Davis in office while hedging this bet by supporting Bustamante in the replacement vote should the recall succeed – a mixed message sent to the voters. For the Republicans, it was making sure that Davis was recalled and trying to focus the replacement vote on one major candidate, the well-known Schwarzenegger – and rejecting the candidacies of other solid Republicans. Also,

Table A: Gubernatorial Elections: 1970-2003

		Democratic Winner		Number of incumbent governors: Eligible to run		Actually ran		Won		Lost			
Year	Number of races	Number	Percent	Number	Percent	Number	Percent	Number	Percent	Number	Percent	In primary	In general election
1970	35	22	63	29	83	24	83	16	64	8	36	1 (a)	7 (b)
1971	3	3	100	0	...	...	...	...	...	...	...	...	...
1972	18	11	61	15	83	11	73	7	64	4	36	2 (c)	2 (d)
1973	2	1	50	1	50	1	100	...	...	1	100	1 (e)	...
1974	35	28 (f)	82	29	83	22	76	17	77	5	24	1 (g)	4 (h)
1975	3	3	100	2	66	2	100	2	100	...	...	...	...
1976	14	9	64	12	86	8	67	5	63	3	33	1 (i)	2 (j)
1977	2	1	50	1	50	1	100	1	100	...	...	...	...
1978	36	21	58	29	81	23	79	16	73	7	30	2 (k)	5 (l)
1979	3	2	67	0	...	...	...	...	...	...	...	...	...
1980	13	6	46	12	92	12	100	7	58	5	42	2 (m)	3 (n)
1981	2	1	50	0	...	...	...	...	...	...	...	...	...
1982	36	27	75	33	92	25	76	19	76	6	24	1 (o)	5 (p)
1983	3	3	100	1	33	1	100	...	...	1	100	1 (q)	...
1984	13	5	38	9	69	6	67	4	67	2	33	...	2 (r)
1985	2	1	50	1	50	1	100	1	100	...	...	...	...
1986	36	19	53	24	67	18	75	15	83	3	18	1 (s)	2 (t)
1987	3	3	100	2	67	1	50	...	...	1	100	1 (u)	...
1988	12	5	42	9	75	9	100	8	89	1	11	...	1 (v)
1989	2	2	100	0	...	...	...	...	...	...	...	...	...
1990	36	19 (w)	53	33	92	23	70	17	74	6	26	...	6 (x)
1991	3	2	67	2	67	2	100	...	...	2	100	1 (y)	1 (z)
1992	12	8	67	9	75	4	44	4	100	...	...	...	...
1993	2	0	0	1	50	1	100	...	...	1	100	...	1 (aa)
1994	36	11 (bb)	31	30	83	23	77	17	74	6	26	2 (cc)	4 (dd)
1995	3	1	33	2	67	1	50	1	100	...	...	...	...
1996	11	7	36	9	82	7	78	7	100	...	...	...	...
1997	2	0	0	1	50	1	100	1	100	...	...	...	...
1998	36	11 (ee)	31	27	75	25	93	23	92	2	8	...	2 (ff)
1999	3	2	67	2	67	2	100	2	100	...	...	...	...
2000	11	8	73	7	88	6	86	5	83	1	17	...	1 (gg)
2001	2	2	100	0	...	...	...	...	...	...	...	...	...
2002	36	14	39	22	61	16	73	12	75	4	25	...	4 (hh)
2003	4 (ii)	1	25	2	50	2	100	...	...	2	100		2 (jj)
Totals:													
Number	470	259		356		278		207		71		17	54
Percent	100	55.1		75.7		78.1		74.5		25.5		23.9	76.1

Source: The Council of State Governments, *The Book of the States, 2003*, (Lexington, KY: The Council of State Governments, 2003), 176, updated.

(a) Albert Brewer, D-Alabama.

(b) Keith Miller, R-Alaska; Winthrop Rockefeller, R-Ark.; Claude Kirk, R-Fla.; Don Samuelson, R-Idaho; Norbert Tieman, R-Neb.; Dewey Bartlett, R-Okla.; Frank Farrar, R-S.D.

(c) Walter Peterson, R-N.H.; Preston Smith, D-Texas.

(d) Russell Peterson, R-N.H.; Richard Ogilvie, R-Ill.

(e) William Cahill, R-N.J.

(f) One independent candidate won: James Longley of Maine.

(g) David Hall, D-Okla.

(h) John Vanderhoof, R-Colo.; Francis Sargent, R-Mass.; Malcolm Wilson, R-N.Y.; John Gilligan, D-Ohio.

(i) Dan Walker, D-Ill.

(j) Sherman Tribbitt, D-Del.; Christopher 'Kit' Bond, R-Mo.

(k) Michael Dukakis, D-Mass., Dolph Briscoe, D-Texas.

(l) Robert F. Bennett, R-Kan.; Rudolph G. Perpich, D-Minn.; Meldrim Thompson, R-N.H.; Robert Straub, D-Oreg.; Martin J. Schreiber, D-Wis.

(m) Thomas L. Judge, D-Mont.; Dixy Lee Ray, D-Wash.

(n) Bill Clinton, D-Ark.; Joseph P. Teasdale, D-Mo.; Arthur A. Link, D-N.D.

(o) Edward J. King, D-Mass.

(p) Frank D. White, R-Ark.; Charles Thone, R-Neb.; Robert F. List, R-Nev.; Hugh J. Gallen, D-N.H.; William P. Clements, R-Texas.

(q) David Treen, R-La.

(r) Allen I. Olson, R-N.D.; John D. Spellman, R-Wash.

(s) Bill Sheffield, D-Alaska

(t) Mark White, D-Texas; Anthony S. Earl, D-Wis.

(u) Edwin Edwards, D-La.

(v) Arch A. Moore, R- W. Va.

(w) Two Independent candidates won: Walter Hickel (Alaska) and Lowell Weiker (Conn.). Both were former statewide Republican office holders.

(x) Bob Martinez, R-Fla.; Mike Hayden, R-Kan.; James Blanchard, D-Mich.; Rudy Perpich, DFL-Minn.; Kay Orr, R-Neb.; Edward DiPrete, R-R.I.

(y) Buddy Roemer, R-La.

(z) Ray Mabus, D-Miss.

(aa) James Florio, D-N.J.

(bb) One Independent candidate won: Angus King of Maine.

(cc) Bruce Sundlun, D-R.I.; Walter Dean Miller, R-S.D.

(dd) James E. Folsom, Jr., D-Ala.; Bruce King, D-N.M.; Mario Cuomo, D-N.Y.; Ann Richards, D-Texas.

(ee) Two Independent candidates won: Angus King of Maine and Jesse Ventura of Minnesota.

(ff) Fob James, R-Ala.; David Beasley, R-S.C.

(gg) Cecil Underwood, R-W. Va.

(hh) Don Siegelman, D-Ala.; Roy Barnes, D-Ga., Jim Hodges, D-S.C.; and Scott McCallum, R-Wis.

(ii) The California recall election and replacement vote of 2003 is included in the 2003 election totals and as a general election for the last column.

(jj) Gray Davis, D-Calif., Ronnie Musgrove, D-Miss.

many observers worried that with such a large number of candidates in the race, the winner might become governor with a small percentage of the total votes cast on the second question – considerably fewer votes than Davis received in his 2002 reelection bid.

Despite some unsettling late campaign charges against Schwarzenegger, he was able to win the replacement election easily with 48.6 percent of the vote. Bustamante came in second with 31.5 percent of the vote, while McClintock at 13.5 percent of the vote was the only other of the 135 candidates to receive over 1 million votes.[5] In fact, these three candidates received nearly 94 percent of the total votes cast. And, Schwarzenegger received nearly 735,000 more votes in the replacement election than Davis had received in his 2002 reelection, so the fear of a new governor without a great political mandate from the voters was overcome. There was a 630,524 vote drop off from the number of voters on the recall question to the number of voters on the replacement question indicating that it was easier for some voters to cast their yes/no votes on the recall question than it was to figure out just which of the 135 candidates they wanted as governor.

The three Southern states that normally hold their off-year gubernatorial elections in the year before a presidential election also found change flowing from the outcome of their elections. In Kentucky, an open seat race found Republican Congressman Ernie Fletcher the winner, the first Republican gubernatorial victory there in over three and a half decades. In Louisiana, Democratic Lt. Gov. Kathleen Blanco won an open seat race, while in Mississippi former Republican Party National Chairman Haley Barbour defeated Democratic incumbent Gov. Ronnie Musgrove. As in California, each of these states saw a partisan shift in who would become the next governor.

There were also changes in two other governorships during 2003. Gov. Frank O'Bannon (D-Ind.) died after a short illness in September and was succeeded by Lt. Gov. Joe Kernan (D). This situation highlighted the problems that can occur when a governor is incapacitated but is still alive. Indiana did have a process in place that allowed the lieutenant governor to become "acting governor" until the governor resigns or dies.[6] President Bush reached into the ranks of Republican governors again in selecting Mike Leavitt (R-Utah) as the new administrator of the Environmental Protection Agency. Upon confirmation by the U.S. Senate, Leavitt resigned as governor and was succeeded by Lt. Gov. Olene Walker (R) in November.

Gubernatorial Elections

As can be seen in Table A, in the 470 gubernatorial elections held between 1970 and 2003, incumbents were eligible to seek another term in 356 (76 percent) of the contests; 278 eligible incumbents sought re-election (78 percent) and 207 of them succeeded (75 percent). Those who were defeated for re-election were more likely to lose in the general election than in their own party primary by a 3.2-to-1 ratio (see Table A).

Democratic candidates held a winning edge in these elections (55 percent). And in 191 races (41 percent) the results led to a party shift in which a candidate from a party other than the incumbent's party won. Yet these party shifts have evened out over the years so that the two major parties tie in the number of party shift races they have won.[7] But there have been some interesting patterns in these shifts over the past 34 years of gubernatorial elections.

Between 1970 and 1992, Democrats won 200 of the 324 races for governor (62 percent). Then starting in 1993, and continuing on between 1994 (when Republicans won races up and down the ballots across the states) and 1998, Republicans won 57 of 90 races (63 percent). Between 1999 and 2001, Democrats moved back into the lead by winning 12 of the 16 races (75 percent). Democratic candidates even won eight of the 11 races in 2000, when Gov. Bush won the presidency in a very close race. In the 2002-2003 races, the Republicans regained the mid-1990s momentum by winning 25 of the 40 races (63 percent). So, over the past 11 years of gubernatorial elections, the Republicans have held a 98-to-60 winning advantage (62 percent). In 2004, there is a Republican 28-to-22 seat margin in the governors' chairs.

Another factor in determining how many governors have served in the states is how many of the newly elected governors are truly new to the office and how many are returning after complying with constitutional term limits or holding other positions. Looking at the number of actual new governors taking office over a decade, the average number of new governors elected in the states dropped from 2.3 new governors per state in the 1950s to 1.9 in the 1970s and 1.1 in the 1980s. In the 1990s, the rate began to move up a bit to 1.4 new governors per state.

As we move through the first decade of the 21st century, we continue to find new faces in the governors' offices. New governors were elected in 36 of 52 elections held between 2000 and 2003 (69 percent). And as noted, two other governors succeeded to the office during 2003. So, in 2004, 38 of the governors will be serving in their first term (76 percent).

Table B: Total Costs of Gubernatorial Elections: 1977-2002
(in thousands of dollars)

Year	Number of races	Total campaign costs Actual $	Total campaign costs 2002$ (a)	Average cost per state (2002$)	Percent change in similar elections (b)
1977	2	12,312	36,535	18,268	N.A.
1978	36	102,342	282,711	7,853	N.A. (c)
1979	3	32,744	81,049	27,016	N.A.
1980	13	35,634	77,803	5,985	N.A.
1981	2	24,648	48,808	24,404	+34
1982	36	181,832	339,239	9,423	+20 (d)
1983	3	39,966	72,140	24,047	-11
1984	13	47,156	81,584	6,276	+5
1985	2	18,859	31,536	15,768	-35
1986	36	270,605	444,343	12,343	+31
1987	3	40,212	63,727	21,242	-12
1988	12 (e)	52,208	79,344	6,612	-3
1989	2	47,902	69,524	34,762	+120
1990	36	345,493	475,231	13,201	+7
1991	3	34,564	45,659	15,220	-28
1992	12	60,278	77,280	6,440	-3
1993	2	36,195	45,075	22,537	-35
1994	36	417,873	507,127	14,087	+7
1995	3	35,693	42,140	14,047	-8
1996	11 (f)	68,610	80,058	7,278	+4
1997	2	44,823	49,970	24,985	+11
1998	36	470,326	516,275	14,341	+2
1999	3	16,277	17,578	5,859	-58
2000	11	97,098	101,461	9,224	+27
2001	2	70,400	71,545	35,772	+43
2002	36	839,650	839,650	23,324	+63

Source: Thad Beyle.

(a) Developed from the Table, "Historical Consumer Price Index for All Urban Consumers (CPI-U), Bureau of Labor Statistics, U.S. Department of Labor.

Each year's actual expenditures are converted to the 2002$ value of the dollar to control for the effect of inflation over the period.

(b) This represents the percent increase or decrease in 2002$ over the last bank of similar elections, i.e., 1977 v. 1981, 1978 v. 1982, 1979 v. 1983, etc.

(c) The data for 1978 are a particular problem as the two sources compiling data on this year's elections did so in differing ways that excluded

some candidates. The result is that the numbers for 1978 under-represent the actual costs of these elections by some unknown amount. The sources are: Rhodes Cook and Stacy West, "1978 Advantage," *CQ Weekly Report,* (1979): 1757-1758, and *The Great Louisiana Spendathon* (Baton Rouge: Public Affairs Research Council, March 1980).

(d) This particular comparison with 1978 is not what it would appear to be for the reasons given in note (c).

(e) As of the 1986 election, Arkansas switched to a four-year term for the governor, hence the drop for 13 to 12 for this off-year.

(f) As of the 1996 election, Rhode Island switched to a four-year term for the governor, hence the drop from 12 to 11 for this off-year.

The beginning of this century has certainly proven to be a time of change in the governors' offices across the 50 states.

The New Governors

From 1998-2003, the 50 newly elected governors took several different routes to the governor's chair. Sixteen new governors had previously held statewide office. These included six lieutenant governors – Don Siegelman (D-Ala.), Gray Davis (D-Calif.), Ruth Ann Minner (D-Del.), Kathleen Blanco (D-La.), Ronnie Musgrove (D-Miss.) and Judy Martz (R-Mont.); five

attorneys general – Janet Napolitano (D-Ariz.), Jennifer Granholm (D-Mich.), Mike Easley (D-N.C.), Bob Taft (R-Ohio) and Jim Doyle (R-Wis.); three state treasurers – Bill Owens (R-Colo.), Bob Holden (D-Mo.) and James Douglas(R-Vt.); one secretary of state – George Ryan (R-Ill.), and one state insurance commissioner, Kathleen Sebelius (D-Kan.).

Ten of the new governors were members or former members of Congress who returned to work in the state. These included U.S. Senators Frank Murkowski (R-Alaska) and Dirk Kempthorne (R-Idaho) and U.S. Congressmen Bob Riley (R-Ala.), Rod Blagojevich

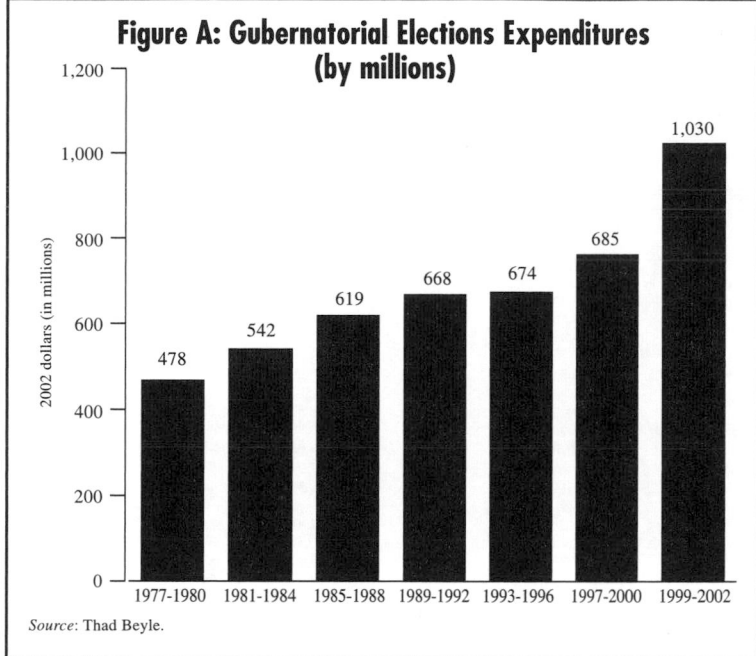

Figure A: Gubernatorial Elections Expenditures (by millions)

Source: Thad Beyle.

(D-Wyo.).

In the 360 gubernatorial races between 1977 and 2003, among the candidates were 98 lieutenant governors (27 won), 80 attorneys general (20 won), 24 secretaries of state (five won), 22 state treasurers (six won) and 13 state auditors, auditors general or comptrollers (three won). Looking at these numbers from a bettor's point of view, the odds of a lieutenant governor winning were 3.6-to-1, an attorney general 4-to-1, a secretary of state 4.8-to-1, a state treasurer 3.7-to-1 and a state auditor 4.3-to-1.

One other unique aspect about the current governors is that there will be eight women serving as

(D-Ill.), Ernie Fletcher (R-Ky.), John Baldacci (D-Maine), Robert Ehrlich (R-Md.), Mark Sanford (R-S.C.) and Bob Wise (D-W.Va.). Former Congressman Bill Richardson (D-N.M.) had also served as an administrator in the Clinton administration.

Seven legislators or former legislators moved up from a district to a statewide office. These included Roy Barnes (D-from the Ga. House) followed by Sonny Perdue (R-from the Ga. Senate), Tom Vilsack (D-from the Iowa Senate), Tim Pawlenty (R-from the Minn. House), Brad Henry (D-from the Okla. Senate), Jim Hodges (D-from the S.C. House) and Mike Rounds (R-from the S.D. Senate).

Six new governors were from the business sector: Jeb Bush (R-Fla.), Kenny Guinn (R-Nev.), Craig Benson (R-N.H.), John Hoeven (R-N.D.), Don Carcieri (R-R.I.) and Mark Warner (D-Va.).

Six new governors were mayors or former mayors. These included Linda Lingle (R-Maui, Hawaii), Jesse Ventura (Ref.-Brooklyn Park, Minn.), Mike Johanns (R-Lincoln, Neb.), Jim McGreevey (D-Woodbridge, N.J.), Ed Rendell (D-Philadelphia, Pa.) and Phil Bredesen (D-Nashville, Tenn.).

Finally, four new governors followed a unique path compared to their counterparts: actor-businessman Arnold Schwarzenegger (R-Calif.), former 2000 Winter Olympics Chairman Mitt Romney (R-Mass.), former State Supreme Court Justice Ted Kulongoski (D-Ore.) and former U.S. Attorney Dave Freudenthal

governor in 2004 - the highest number of women serving at one time in the office. This will be discussed in more detail later in this article.

Timing of Gubernatorial Elections

The election cycle for governors has settled into a regular pattern. Over the past few decades, many states have moved their elections to the off-presidential years in order to decouple the state and national level campaigns. Now, only 11 states hold their gubernatorial elections in the same year as a presidential election. Two of these states – New Hampshire and Vermont – still have two-year terms for their governor so their elections alternate between presidential and non-presidential years.

As can be seen in Table A, the year following a presidential election has only two states with gubernatorial elections.[8] Then in the even years between presidential elections, 36 states hold their gubernatorial elections, and in the year before a presidential election, three Southern states hold their gubernatorial elections.[9]

Cost of Gubernatorial Elections[10]

Table C presents data on the costs of the most recent election. There is a great range in how much these races cost, from the all-time most expensive race recorded in New York in 2002 ($146.8 million) to the

Table C: Costs of Gubernatorial Campaigns, Most Recent Elections

State	Year	Winner	Point margin	All Candidates (2002$)	Cost Per Vote (2002$)	Spent (2002$)	Percent of all expenditures	Vote percent
				Total campaign expenditures		*Winner*		
Alabama	2002	R★★★	+0.3	$31,568,741	23.09	$13,847,976	43.9	49.2
Alaska	2002	R#	+15	5,343,055	23.56	1,729,118	32.4	56.0
Arizona	2002	D#	+1	7,616,460	6.21	2,297,981	30.2	46.0
Arkansas	2002	R★	+6	4,512,521	5.60	2,730,257	60.5	53.0
California	2002	D★	+4.9	109,568,637	14.66	64,215,205	58.6	47.3
Colorado	2002	R★	+29	6,053,778	4.29	4,819,376	79.6	63.0
Connecticut	2002	R★	+12	7,869,235	7.69	6,117,067	77.7	56.0
Delaware	2000	D#	+19	3,239,556	10.01	1,393,763	43.2	59.0
Florida	2002	R#	+13	17,159,567	3.36	7,624,866	44.4	56.0
Georgia	2002	R★★★	+5	24,258,672	11.96	3,655,202	15.1	51.0
Hawaii	2002	R#	+4	9,459,227	24.76	5,408,527	57.2	51.1
Idaho	2002	R★	+14	2,236,501	5.44	1,113,300	49.8	56.0
Illinois	2002	D#	+8	48,765,754	13.78	22,409,565	46.0	53.0
Indiana	2000	D★	+14	18,867,041	8.66	10,091,908	53.5	57.0
Iowa	2002	D★	+8	13,149,081	12.82	6,051,598	46.0	52.7
Kansas	2002	D#	+8	15,261,932	18.26	4,362,442	28.6	52.9
Kentucky	1999	D★	+39	1,456,908	2.53	1,380,641	94.9	61.0
Louisiana	1999	R★	+32	7,233,356	5.58	3,845,332	53.2	62.0
Maine	2002	D	+6	4,329,123	8.57	1,584,380	36.6	47.0
Maryland	2002	R#	+4	5,136,295	3.01	2,533,835	49.3	51.6
Massachusetts	2002	R#	+5	30,601,908	13.78	9,361,003	30.6	49.8
Michigan	2002	D★★★	+4	14,451,862	4.55	8,888,296	61.5	51.4
Minnesota	2002	R#	+8	5,966,792	2.65	2,525,770	42.3	44.4
Mississippi	1999	D#	+1	8,887,524	11.63	2,972,093	33.4	49.6
Missouri	2000	D#	+1	19,571,870	8.57	10,420,305	53.2	50.5
Montana	2000	R#	+4	4,815,828	11.74	1,008,134	20.9	51.0
Nebraska	2002	R★	+41	1,598,973	3.32	1,213,155	75.9	68.7
Nevada	2002	R★	+46	2,716,694	5.39	2,644,033	97.3	68.0
New Hampshire	2002	R#	+21	18,947,338	42.77	11,164,368	58.9	59.0
New Jersey	2001	D#	+15	37,167,319	16.69	15,463,584	41.6	56.0
New Mexico	2002	D#	+15	10,022,242	20.70	7,326,497	73.1	55.0
New York	2002	R★	+16	146,751,563	31.28	44,189,099	30.1	48.2
North Carolina	2000	D#	+6	29,445,768	10.01	11,515,181	39.1	52.0
North Dakota	2000	R#	+10	2,413,485	8.31	1,174,313	48.7	55.0
Ohio	2002	R★	+20	14,471,842	4.48	12,833,724	88.7	58.0
Oklahoma	2002	D#	+0.7	11,221,349	10.84	3,231,710	28.8	43.3
Oregon	2002	D#	+2.8	15,110,672	11.99	4,167,597	27.6	49.0
Pennsylvania	2002	D	+9	65,140,806	18.19	39,163,561	60.1	53.0
Rhode Island	2002	R#	+10	6,923,727	20.87	2,441,691	35.3	55.0
South Carolina	2002	R★★★	+6	29,608,997	26.92	7,157,105	24.2	53.0
South Dakota	2002	R#	+15	9,262,918	27.69	1,624,148	17.5	56.8
Tennessee	2002	D#	+3	17,196,285	10.40	9,763,343	56.8	50.6
Texas	2002	R★	+18	105,556,032	23.18	27,899,725	26.4	57.8
Utah	2000	R★	+14	2,277,325	2.99	2,036,923	89.5	56.0
Vermont	2002	R#	+2.5	2,119,564	9.22	1,124,519	53.1	44.9
Virginia	2001	D#	+5	34,377,579	18.22	20,306,807	59.1	52.0
Washington	2000	D★	+19	6,859,375	2.78	3,953,522	57.6	58.0
West Virginia	2000	D★★★	+3	6,819,089	10.52	2,941,136	43.1	50.1
Wisconsin	2002	D★★★	+3.7	17,104,862	9.63	5,526,312	32.3	45.1
Wyoming	2002	D#	+2.1	2,576,890	13.89	748,226	29.0	50.0

Source: Thad Beyle.
Key:
D - Democrat
I - Independent
R - Republican
★ - Incumbent ran and won.
★★ - Incumbent ran and lost in party primary.
★★★ - Incumbent ran and lost in general election.
- Open seat.

Table D: Women Governors

Governor	State	Year elected or succeeded to office	How woman became governor	Tenure of service	Previous offices held	Last elected position held before governorship
Phase I - From initial statehood to adoption of the 19th Amendment to U.S. Constitution						
No women elected or served as governor						
Phase II - Wives of former governors elected governor, 1924-1926						
Nellie Tayloe Ross (D)	Wyoming	1924	E	1/1925-1/1927	F	. . .
Miriam "Ma" Ferguson (D)	Texas	1924	E	1/1925-1/1927 1/1933-1/1935	F	. . .
Lurleen Wallace (D)	Alabama	1966	E	1/1967-5/1968	F	. . .
Phase III - Women who became governor on their own merit, 1970 to date						
Ella Grasso (D)	Connecticut	1974	E	1/1975-12/1980	SH, SOS, (a)	(a)
Dixy Lee Ray (D)	Washington	1976	E	1/1977-1/1981	(b)	. . .
Vesta M. Roy (R)	New Hampshire	1982	S (c)	12/1982-1/1983	(d)	(d)
Martha Layne Collins (D)	Kentucky	1983	E	12/1983-12/1987	(e), LG	LG
Madeleine M. Kunim (D)	Vermont	1984	E	1/1985-1/1991	SH, LG	LG
Kay A. Orr (R)	Nebraska	1986	E	1/1987-1/1991	T	T
Rose Mofford (D)	Arizona	1988	S (f)	4/1988-1/1991	SOS	SOS
Joan Finney (D)	Kansas	1990	E	1/1991-1/1995	T	T
Barbara Roberts (D)	Oregon	1990	E	1/1991-1/1995	(g), C, SH, SOS	SOS
Ann Richards (D)	Texas	1990	E	1/1991-1/1995	C, T	T
Christy Whitman (R)	New Jersey	1993	E	1/1994-1/2001	(h)	(h)
Jeanne Shaheen (D)	New Hampshire	1996	E	1/1997-1/2003	(d)	(d)
Jane Dee Hull (R)	Arizona	1997	S (i)	9/1997-1/2003	(j), SOS	SOS
Nancy P. Hollister (R)	Ohio	1998	S (k)	12/1998-1/1999	LG	LG
Ruth Ann Minner (D)	Delaware	2000	E	1/2001-	SH, SS, LG	LG
Judy Martz (R)	Montana	2000	E	1/2001-	LG	LG
Sila Calderon (Pop D)	Puerto Rico	2000	E	1/2001-	M	M
Jane Swift (R)	Massachusetts	2001	S (l)	4/2001-1/2003	SS, LG	LG
Janet Napolitano (D)	Arizona	2002	E	1/2003-	(m), AG	AG
Linda Lingle (R)	Hawaii	2002	E	12/2002-	C, M (n)	M
Kathleen Sebeliu (D)	Kansas	2002	E	1/2003-	SH, (o)	(o)
Jennifer Granholm (D)	Michigan	2002	E	1/2003-	(p), AG	AG
Olene Walker (R)	Utah	2003	S (q)	11/2003-	SH, LG	LG
Kathleen Blanco (D)	Louisiana	2003	E	1/2004-	SH, LG	LG

Sources: National Governors Association Web site, www.nga.org, and individual state government Web sites.

Key:
AG – Attorney general.
C – City council or county commission.
E – Elected governor.
F – Former first lady.
LG – Lieutenant governor.
M – Mayor.
S – Succeeded to office upon death, resignation or removal of the incumbent governor.
SH – State house member.
SOS – Secretary of state.
SS – State senate.
T – State treasurer.
(a) Congresswoman.
(b) Ray served on the U.S. Atomic Energy Commission from 1972-1975 and was chair of the AEC from 1973-1975.
(c) Roy as state senate president succeeded to office upon the death of Gov. Hugh Gallen.
(d) State senate president.

(e) State supreme court clerk.
(f) Mofford as secretary of state became acting governor in February 1988 and governor in April 1988 upon the impeachment and removal of Gov. Evan Mecham.
(g) Local school board member.
(h) Whitman was a former state utilities official.
(i) Hull as secretary of state became acting governor when Gov. Fife Symington resigned. Elected to full terms in 1998.
(j) Speaker of the state house.
(k) Hollister as lieutenant governor became governor when Gov. George Voinovich stepped down to serve in the U.S. Senate.
(l) Swift as lieutenant governor succeeded Gov. Paul Celluci who resigned after being appointed ambassador to Canada. Was the first governor to give birth while serving in office.
(m) U.S. attorney.
(n) Lingle as mayor of Maui for two terms, elected in 1990 and 1996.
(o) Insurance commissioner.
(p) Federeal prosecutor.
(q) Walker as lieutenant governor succeeded to the governorship upon the resignation of Gov. Mike Leavitt in 2003.

low-cost 1998 race in Wyoming ($833,181 in 2002 dollars). Both the New York and the Wyoming races saw an incumbent successfully win re-election.

But if we look at how much was spent by all the candidates per general election vote, a slightly different picture evolves. In 2002, the New Hampshire governor's race was the most expensive at $42.77 per vote, followed by New York at $31.28 per vote, South Dakota at $27.69 per vote, South Carolina at $26.92 per vote, Hawaii at $24.76 per vote, Texas at $23.18 per vote, Alabama and Alaska both at $23.09 per vote, Rhode Island at $20.87 per vote and New Mexico at $20.70 per vote. The New Hampshire, South Dakota, Hawaii, Alaska, Rhode Island and New Mexico races were for open seats. As noted, in New York an incumbent successfully won re-election, while in Texas, an "accidental governor" won the office in his own right.[11] The Alabama and South Carolina races saw an incumbent defeated in his bid for re-election.

Table E: Impeachments and Removals of Governors

Name, party and state	Year	Process of impeachment and outcome		
Charles Robinson (R-Kan.)	1862	Impeached	Acquitted	
Harrison Reed (R-Fla.)	1868	Impeached	Acquitted	
William Holden (R-N.C.)	1870	Impeached	Convicted	Removed
Powell Clayton (R-Ark.)	1871	Impeached	Acquitted	
David Butler (R-Neb.)	1871	Impeached	Convicted	Removed
Henry Warmouth (R-La.)	1872	Impeached		Term ended
Harrison Reed (R-Fla.)	1872	Impeached	Acquitted	
Adelbert Ames (R-Miss.)	1876	Impeached		Resigned
William P. Kellogg (R-La.)	1876	Impeached	Acquitted	
Wiliam Sulzer (D-N.Y.)	1913	Impeached	Convicted	Removed
James "Pa" Ferguson (D-Texas)	1917	Impeached	Convicted	Resigned
John C. Walton (D-Okla.)	1923	Impeached	Convicted	Removed
Henry S. Johnston (D-Okla.)	1928	Impeached	Acquitted	
Henry S. Johnston (D-Okla.)	1929	Impeached	Convicted	Removed
Huey P. Long (D-La.)	1929	Impeached	Acquitted	
Henry Horton (D-Tenn.)	1931	Impeached	Acquitted	
Richard Leche (D-La.)	1939	Threatened		Resigned
Evan Mecham (R-Ariz.)	1988	Impeached	Convicted	Removed

Other removals of incumbent governors		
John A. Quitman (D-Miss.)	1851	Resigned after federal criminal indictment.
Lynn J. Frazier (R-N.D.)	1921	Recalled by voters during third term.
Warren T. McCray (R-Ind.)	1924	Resigned after federal criminal conviction.
William Langer (I-N.D.)	1934	Removed by North Dakota Supreme Court.
Thomas L. Moodie (D-N.D.)	1935	Removed by North Dakota Supreme Court.
J. Howard Pyle (R-Ariz.)	1955	Recall petition certified, but term ended before date set for recall election.
Marvin Mandel (D-Md.)	1977	Removed after federal criminal conviction.
Ray Blanton (D-Tenn.)	1979	Term shortened in bi-partisan agreement (a)
Evan Mecham (R-Ariz.)	1987	Recall petition certified, but impeached, convicted and removed from office before the date set for the recall election.
H. Guy Hunt (R-Ala.)	1993	Removed after state criminal conviction.
Jim Guy Tucker Jr. (D-Ark.)	1996	Resigned after federal criminal conviction.
J. Fife Symington (R-Ariz.)	1997	Resigned after federal criminal conviction.
Gray Davis (D-Calif.)	2003	Recalled by voters during second term.

Sources: Thad Beyle and The Council of State Governments.
Key:
(a) See Lamar Alexander, *Steps Along the War: A Governor's Scrapbook* (Nashville, TN: Thomas Nelson, 1986), 21-9 for a discussion of this unique transition between governors.

In Figure A, by converting the actual dollars spent each year into the equivalent 2002 dollars, we see how the cost of these elections has increased over time. Since 1981, we have been able to compare the costs of each 4-year cycle of elections with the previous cycle of elections.

In the 54 elections held between 1977 and 1980, the total expenditures were $478.1 million in equivalent 2002 dollars. In the 52 elections held between 1999 and 2002 - just over two decades later - the total expenditures were over $1,030 million, an increase of 115 percent. The greatest increases in ex-penditures were between the 1977-1980 and the 1987-1990 cycles, when there was a 43.9 percent increase, and between the 1992-1995 and the 1999-2002 cycles when there was a 53.4 percent increase.

These increases reflect the new style of campaigning for governor - with the candidates developing their own personal party by using outside consultants, opinion polls, media ads and buys, and extensive fundraising efforts to pay for all of this. This style has now reached into most every state. Few states will be surprised by a high-price, high-tech campaign; they are commonplace now. The "air-war" campaigns have replaced the "ground-war" campaigns across the states.

Another factor has been the increasing number of candidates who are either wealthy or who have access to wealth and are willing to spend some of this money to become governor. For some, spending a lot of money leads to winning the governor's chair. In 2002, Gov. Gray Davis spent $64.2 million in his successful bid for reelection in California, while Gov. George Pataki spent $44.2 million to win his third term. However, spending that amount of money and winning reelection did not deter those wanting to have Gov. Davis recalled from office less than a year later.

But spending a lot doesn't always lead to a win. For example, in the 2002 New York election, Thomas Golisano spent $76.3 million in his unsuccessful campaign for governor as an Independent candidate. And in Texas, Tony Sanchez also spent $76.3 million as the unsuccessful Democratic candidate. In California's 1998 gubernatorial election, three candidates spent more than $34 million each in 2002 dollars in their campaigns. Two of these candidates won their party's nomination and faced off in November, with Gray Davis (D) at $41.3 million the winner over Republican candidate Dan Lundgren at $34.6 million. The largest spender at $42.7 million, Al Checci (D), wasn't even able to win the Democratic nomination.

A Shift Toward Women Governors

One other unique aspect about the current governors is that there are eight women serving as governor in 2004 - the highest number of women serving at one time in the office. A little history helps to put this into perspective. There have been three phases in this history. In the first phase, which lasted until 1924, no woman was ever elected governor in any state. Remember, the 19th Amendment to the U.S. Constitution providing nationwide suffrage to women was only ratified in August 1920.

The second phase began in 1924, when the first two women were elected governors in the states of Texas and Wyoming - and both were the wives of former governors. Although both were elected on the same day, Wyoming's Nellie Tayloe Ross became the first woman governor to be sworn in - one week before "Ma" Ferguson in Texas took office. It wouldn't be until 1966 when outgoing Gov. George Wallace was instrumental in getting his wife Lurleen elected to succeed him that another woman was elected governor. The key to these wins was that they were wives of former and well-known governors.

The third phase began in the 1970s when women politicians began to move up the political ladder and

win the governor's chair in their own right. This began with Ella Grasso of Connecticut (1974) as she moved up from serving several terms as secretary of state and then as a U.S. congresswoman. In effect, she was the first woman governor to win the office on her own merit. There was one other woman elected governor in the 1970s on her own merit - Dixy Lee Ray of Washington, then three in the 1980s and four in the 1990s. Four other women became governor in the 1980-1999 period when as the number 2 in the line of succession they succeeded to the office upon the death, resignation or removal of the incumbent governor.

In the first decade of the 21st century we have seen 10 women become governor in the 50 states - and Puerto Rico. In the 2000 elections, three women were elected governor - Ruth Ann Minner (D-Del.), Judy Martz (R-Mont.) and Sila Caldron (Pop. D-PR). In the 2002 elections, four women were elected governor - Janet Napolitano (D-Ariz.), Linda Lingle (R-Hawaii), Kathleen Sebelius (D-Kan.) and Jennifer Granholm (D-Mich.). In the 2003 elections, Kathleen Blanco (D-La.) was elected governor and two other women moved up from lieutenant governor to governor when President Bush appointed their state's governor to a position in the Bush administration - Jane Swift (R-Mass.) in 2001 and Olene Walker (R-Utah) in 2003.

The last stepping stone to the governorship was as lieutenant governor for five of them, as attorney general for two others, mayor of a major city for two others, and as insurance commissioner for one other. And each had held other elected and appointed offices en route.

Gubernatorial Forced Exits

The California 2003 gubernatorial recall and replacement votes highlight the fact that some elected governors faced situations in which they could lose their office without being beaten by a challenger at the ballot box, becoming ill or dying. (see Table E)

Between 1851 and 2003, 29 governors have faced the prospect of having to leave office through impeachment, removal, or resignation due to a criminal conviction. Seventeen governors have been impeached by the state house and while eight of them were acquitted of the charges by the state senate, nine of them were convicted by their state senates. Of these nine losers in the fight, six were then removed from office and three others resigned upon their conviction. Henry Johnson (D-Okla.) was impeached twice and while he beat the charges in the 1928 effort, he lost the fight and was removed

Table F: Governors' Institutional Powers, 1960 v. 2004

Specific power	Scores 1960	Scores 2003	Percent change
Separately elected executive branch officials (SEP)	2.3	2.9	28
Tenure potential (TP)	3.2	4.1	28
Appointment powers (AP)	2.9	3.1	7
Budget power (BP)	3.6	3.1	-14
Veto power (VP)	2.8	4.5	61
Gubernatorial party control (PC)	3.6	3.0	-17
Totals	18.4	20.7	12.5

Notes:

SEP - Separately elected executive branch officials: 5 = only governor or governor/lieutenant governor team elected; 4.5 = governor or governor/lieutenant governor team, with one other elected official; 4 = governor/lieutenant governor team with some process officials (attorney general, secretary of state, treasurer, auditor) elected; 3 = governor/lieutenant governor team with process officials, and some major and minor policy officials elected; 2.5 = governor (no team) with six or fewer officials elected, but none are major policy officials; 2 = governor (no team) with six or fewer officials elected, including one major policy official; 1.5 = governor (no team) with six or fewer officials elected, but two are major policy officials; 1 = governor (no team) with seven or more process and several major policy officials elected. [Source: CSG, *The Book of the States, 1960-1961* (1960): 124-125 and (2003): 201-206].

TP - Tenure potential of governors: 5 = 4-year term, no restraint on reelection; 4.5 = 4-year term, only three terms permitted; 4 = 4-year term, only two terms permitted; 3 = 4-year term, no consecutive election permitted; 2 = 2-year term, no restraint on reelection; 1 = 2-year term, only two terms permitted. [Source: Joseph A. Schlesinger, "The Politics of the Executive," in Politics in the American States, edited by Herbert Jacob and Kenneth N. Vines (Boston: Little, Brown, 1965) and CSG, *The Book of the States, 2003* (2003): 183-184].

AP - Governor's appointment powers in six major functional areas: corrections, K-12 education, health, highways/transportation, public utilities regulation, and welfare. The six individual office scores are totaled and then averaged and rounded to the nearest .5 for the state score. 5 = governor appoints, no other approval needed; 4 = governor appoints, a board, council or legislature approves; 3 = someone else appoints, governor approves or shares appointment; 2 = someone else appoints, governor and others approve; 1 = someone else appoints, no approval or confirmation needed. [Source: Schlesinger (1965), and CSG, *The Book of the States, 2003* (2003): 201-206].

BP - Governor's budget power: 5 = governor has full responsibility, legislature may not increase executive budget; 4 = governor has full responsibility, legislature can increase by special majority vote or subject to item veto; 3 = governor has full responsibility, legislature has unlimited power to change executive budget; 2 = governor shares responsibility, legislature has unlimited power to change executive budget; 1 = governor shares responsibility with other elected official, legislature has unlimited power to change executive budget. [Source: Schlesinger (1965) and CSG, *The Book of the States, 2003* (2003): 188-189, 392-393 and NCSL, "Limits on Authority of Legislature to Change Budget" (1998).

VP - Governor's veto power: 5 = has item veto and a special majority vote of the legislature is needed to override a veto (3/5's of legislators elected or 2/3's of legislators present); 4 = has item veto with a majority of the legislators elected needed to override; 3 = has item veto with only a majority of the legislators present needed to override; 2 = no item veto, with a special legislative majority needed to override it; 1 = no item veto, only a simple legislative majority needed to override. (Source: Schlesinger (1965):, and CSG, *The Book of the States, 2003* (2003): 145-147, 188-189).

PC - Gubernatorial party control: 5 = has a substantial majority (75% or more) in both houses of the legislature; 4 = has a simple majority in both houses (less than 75%), or a substantial majority in one house and a simple majority in the other; 3 = split party control in the legislature or a nonpartisan legislature; 2 = has a substantial minority in both houses (25% or more), or a simple minority (25% or less) in one and a substantial minority in the other; 1 = has a simple minority in both houses. (Source: National Conference of State Legislatures web page, various dates).

Total - sum of the scores on the six individual indices. Score - total divided by six to keep 5-point scale.

Twelve governors faced other means of being forced to leave office. Eight were convicted of criminal charges, with four of them being removed from office and four others resigning upon being convicted. Four others have faced a recall initiative and while Gov. Lynn Frazier (R-N.D, 1921) and Gov. Gray Davis (D-Calif., 2003) were recalled by the voters, Gov. Evan Mecham (R-Ariz., 1988) was impeached, convicted and removed from office by the state legislature before the scheduled recall vote could be held and Gov. Howard Pyle (R-Ariz., 1955) saw his term end before a recall vote could be held. In an interesting twist on how an incumbent's tenure was shortened, Gov. Ray Blanton (D-Tenn., 1979) found his term shortened and the locks to his gubernatorial office changed to keep him out in a bi-partisan agreement tied to illegal actions he was taking at the end of his term.[14]

Much of this gubernatorial turmoil occurred to 18 governors in nine different Southern states. The leading individual states in experiencing the removal of the incumbent governor efforts were Arizona and Louisiana with four such actions each, North Dakota and Oklahoma with three such actions each, and Arkansas, Florida, Mississippi and Tennessee with two such actions each. With over a quarter of these actions occurring within the last three decades, there is heightened awareness of these options of gaining a new governor.

Gubernatorial Powers

One way to view the changes that have been occurring in gubernatorial powers is to look at the *Index of Formal Powers of the Governorship* first developed by Joseph Schlesinger in the 1960s,[15] which this author has continued to update.[16] The index used here consists of six different indices of gubernatorial power as seen in 1960 and 2004. These indices include the number and importance of separately elected executive branch officials, the tenure potential of governors, the appointment powers of governors for administrative and board positions in the executive branch, the governor's budgetary power, the governor's veto

in the 1929 effort. Another impeached governor escaped conviction as his term ended before the senate could take action.[12] And one governor resigned in the face of a threatened impeachment effort.[13]

power and the governor's party control in the legislature. Each of the individual indices is set in a five-point scale, with five being the most power and one being the least. (See Table F for details on how each of these indices and the overall index were developed).

During the four-plus decades between 1960 and 2004, the overall institutional powers of the of the nation's governors increased by 12.5 percent. The greatest increase among the individual gubernatorial powers was in their veto power (plus 61 percent) as more governors gained an item veto. And in 1996, North Carolina voters were finally able to vote on a constitutional amendment giving their governor veto power. It was approved by a 3-to-1 ratio.

The indices measuring the governors' tenure potential (length of term and ability to seek an additional term or terms) and the number of separately elected executive branch officials showed identical 28 percent increases in favor of the governor. The governors' appointment power over specific functional area executive branch officials increased by only 7 percent. In addition, the states continue to hold to the concept of the multiple executive in terms of how many statewide elected officials there are. In 2003, there were 297 separately elected executive officials covering 12 major offices in the states.[17] This compares to 306 elected officials in 1972. Ten states also have multimember boards, commissions or councils with members selected by statewide or district election.

The gubernatorial budgetary power actually declined over the period (minus 14 percent). However, we must remember that during this same period, state legislatures were also undergoing considerable reform, and gaining more power to work on the governor's proposed budget was one of those reforms. Hence, the increased legislative budgetary power more than balanced out any increases in gubernatorial budgetary power.

There has also been a drop in the gubernatorial party control in the state legislatures over the period (minus 17 percent). Much of this can be attributed to the major partisan shifts occurring in the Southern states as the region has been moving from one-party dominance to a very competitive two-party system.[18] In 1960, 13 of the 14 governors were Democrats, and all 28 state legislative chambers were under Democratic control. In 2004, Republicans control eight governorships to the Democrats six, while the Democrats hold a 17-to-10 edge in control of the legislative chambers. In the North Carolina House, a coalition of all the Democrats and a few Republicans control the chamber with dual Democratic-Republican speakers as leaders. Four Southern governors face a legisla-

ture completely controlled by the opposite party,[19] while three others - including the North Carolina governor - face a legislature with split partisan control.[20]

Notes

[1] The former governors winning the presidency over the past three decades were Jimmy Carter (D-Ga., 1971-1975) in 1976, Ronald Reagan (R-Calif., 1967-1975) in 1980 and 1984, Bill Clinton (D-Ark., 1979-1981 and 1983-1992) in 1992 and 1996, and George W. Bush (R-Texas, 1995-2001) in 2000.

[2] For an analysis of governors trying to handle the impact of the early 1990s economic downturn, see Thad Beyle, ed., *Governors in Hard Times* (Washington, D.C.: CQ Press, 1994).

[3] The actual number of recall votes was: Total – 8,978,545; Yes – 4,972,524 (55.4 percent), No – 4,006,021 (44.6 percent).

[4] The list of 135 candidates was certified on August 13, three weeks after the recall initiative was certified.

[5] The actual number of replacement votes was: Total – 8,348,021; Schwarzenegger – 4,203,596; Bustamante – 2,723,768; McClintock – 1,160,182.

[6] Brian J. Gaines, "*An Accident Waiting to Happen? Legal Provisions on Incapacity of American Governors*," Policy Forum 17:1, (Urbana, IL: University of Illinois Institute of Government and Public Affairs), 2004.

[7] For more detail on this see Beyle, "The 2002 Gubernatorial Elections," *Spectrum: The Journal of State Government* (Winter 2003), 12-14.

[8] New Jersey and Virginia.

[9] Kentucky, Louisiana and Mississippi.

[10] The data reported in this section and in Tables B and C, and Figure A reflect some changes from the data reported in recent issues of *The Book of the States*. The reason for this is that there were some errors in the data set that had been created. These errors have now been corrected. See www.unc.edu/~beyle.

[11] Lt. Gov. Rick Perry became governor upon the resignation of Gov. George W. Bush to assume the presidency after the 2000 election.

[12] Henry Warmouth (R-La.), 1872.

[13] Richard Leche (D-La.), 1939.

[14] See Lamar Alexander, *Steps Along the Way: A Governor's Scrapbook* (Nashville, TN: Thomas Nelson, 1986), 21-9 for a discussion of this unique transition between governors.

[15] Joseph A. Schlesinger, "The Politics of the Executive," *Politics in the American States*, 1st and 2nd ed, Herbert Jacob and Kenneth N. Vines, eds., (Boston: Little Brown, 1965 and 1971).

[16] Thad L. Beyle, "The Governors," *Politics in the American States* 8th ed., Virginia Gray and Russell L. Hanson, eds., (Washington, D.C.: CQ Press, 2003). Earlier versions of this index by the author appeared in the 4th edition (1983), the 5th edition (1990), the 6th edition (1996), and the 7th edition (1999).

[17] Kendra Hovey and Harold Hovey, "D-12 - Number of Statewide Elected Officials, 2003," *CQ's State Fact Finder, 2004* (Washington, D.C.: CQ Press, 2004): forthcoming.

[18] The following states are included in this definition of the South: Alabama, Arkansas, Florida, Georgia, Kentucky, Louisiana, Mississippi, North Carolina, Oklahoma, South Carolina, Tennessee, Texas, Virginia and West Virginia.

[19] Republicans Bob Riley in Ala., Mike Huckabee in Ark. and Haley Barbour in Miss., and Democrat Mark Warner in Va.

[20] Republicans Sonny Perdue in Ga., Ernie Fletcher in Ky., and Democrat Mike Easley in N.C.

About the Author

Thad Beyle is Pearsall Professor of Political Science at the University of North Carolina at Chapel Hill. A Syracuse University AB and AM, he received his Ph.D. at the University of Illinois. He spent a year in the North Carolina governor's office in the mid-1960s and has worked with the National Governors Association in several capacities on gubernatorial transitions.

Table 4.1
THE GOVERNORS, 2004

State or other jurisdiction	Name and party	Length of regular term in years	Date of first service	Present term ends	Number of previous terms	Maximum consecutive terms allowed by constitution	Joint election of governor and lieutenant governor (a)	Official who succeeds governor	Birthdate	Birthplace
Alabama	Bob Riley (R)	4	1/03	1/07	...	2	No	LG	10/3/44	AL
Alaska	Frank H. Murkowski (R)	4	12/02	12/06	...	2	Yes	LG	3/28/33	WA
Arizona	Janet Napolitano (D)	4	1/03	1/07	...	2	(k)	SS	11/29/57	NY
Arkansas	Mike Huckabee (R)	4	7/96 (b)	1/07	1	2 (b)	No	LG	8/24/55	AR
California	Arnold Swarzenegger (R)	4	11/03 (c)	1/07	...	2	No	LG	7/30/49	Aus.
Colorado	Bill Owens (R)	4	1/99	1/07	1	2	Yes	LG	10/22/50	TX
Connecticut	John G. Rowland (R)	4	1/95	1/07	2	...	Yes	LG	5/24/57	CT
Delaware	Ruth Ann Minner (D)	4	1/01	1/05	...	2 (d)	No	LG	1/17/35	DE
Florida	Jeb Bush (R)	4	1/99	1/07	1	2	Yes	LG	2/11/53	TX
Georgia	Sonny Perdue (R)	4	1/03	1/07	...	2	No	LG	12/20/46	GA
Hawaii	Linda Lingle (R)	4	12/02	12/06	...	2	Yes	LG	6/4/53	MO
Idaho	Dirk Kempthorne (R)	4	1/99	1/07	1	...	No	LG	10/29/51	CA
Illinois	Rod R. Blagojevich (D)	4	1/03	1/07	...	...	Yes	LG	12/10/56	IL
Indiana	Joseph E. Kernan (D)	4	9/03 (e)	1/05	...	2 (f)	Yes	LG	4/8/46	IL
Iowa	Tom Vilsack (D)	4	1/99	1/07	1	...	Yes	LG	12/13/50	PA
Kansas	Kathleen Sebelius (D)	4	1/03	1/07	...	2	Yes	LG	5/15/48	OH
Kentucky	Ernie Fletcher (R)	4	12/03	12/07	...	2	Yes	LG	11/12/52	KY
Louisiana	Kathleen Babineaux Blanco (D)	4	1/04	1/08	...	2	No	LG	12/15/42	LA
Maine	John Baldacci (D)	4	1/03	1/07	...	2	(k)	PS	1/30/55	ME
Maryland	Robert L. Ehrlich Jr. (R)	4	1/03	1/07	...	2	Yes	LG	11/25/57	MD
Massachusetts	Mitt Romney (R)	4	1/03	1/07	...	...	Yes	LG	3/12/47	MI
Michigan	Jennifer Granholm (D)	4	1/03	1/07	...	...	Yes	LG	2/5/59	BC
Minnesota	Tim Pawlenty (R)	4	1/03	1/07	...	...	Yes	LG	11/27/60	MN
Mississippi	Haley Barbour (R)	4	1/04	1/08	...	2	No	LG	10/22/47	MS
Missouri	Bob Holden (D)	4	1/01	1/05	...	2	No	LG	8/24/49	MO
Montana	Judy Martz (R)	4	1/01	1/05	...	2 (g)	Yes	LG	7/28/43	MT
Nebraska	Mike Johanns (R)	4	1/99	1/07	1	2	Yes	LG	6/18/50	NE
Nevada	Kenny Guinn (R)	4	1/99	1/07	1	2	No	LG	8/24/36	AR
New Hampshire	Craig Benson (R)	2	1/03	1/05	...	...	(k)	PS	10/8/54	NY
New Jersey	James E. McGreevey (D)	4	1/02	1/06	...	2	(k)	PS	8/6/57	NJ
New Mexico	Bill Richardson (D)	4	1/03	1/07	...	2	Yes	LG	11/15/47	CA
New York	George E. Pataki (R)	4	1/95	1/07	2	...	Yes	LG	6/24/45	NY
North Carolina	Michael F. Easley (D)	4	1/01	1/05	...	2 (f)	No	SS	3/23/50	NC
North Dakota	John Hoeven (R)	4	12/00	12/04	...	...	Yes	LG	3/13/57	ND
Ohio	Bob Taft (R)	4	1/99	1/07	1	2 (f)	Yes	LG	1/8/42	OH
Oklahoma	Brad Henry (D)	4	1/03	1/07	...	2	No	LG	7/10/63	OK
Oregon	Ted Kulongoski (D)	4	1/03	1/07	...	2	(k)	SS	11/5/40	MO
Pennsylvania	Edward G. Rendell (D)	4	1/03	1/07	...	2	Yes	LG	1/5/44	NY
Rhode Island	Don Carcieri (R)	4	1/03	1/07	...	2	No	LG	12/16/42	RI
South Carolina	Mark Sanford (R)	4	1/03	1/07	...	2	No	LG	5/28/60	FL

See footnotes at end of table.

THE GOVERNORS, 2004 — Continued

State or other jurisdiction	Name and party	Length of regular term in years	Date of first service	Present term ends	Number of previous terms	Maximum consecutive terms allowed by constitution	Joint election of governor and lieutenant governor (a)	Official who succeeds governor	Birthdate	Birthplace
South Dakota	Mike Rounds (R)	4	1/03	1/07	...	2	Yes	LG	10/24/54	SD
Tennessee	Phil Bredesen (D)	4	1/03	1/07	...	2	No	SpS (l)	11/21/43	NY
Texas	Rick Perry (R)	4	12/00 (h)	1/07	1	...	No	LG	3/4/50	TX
Utah	Olene S. Walker (R)	4	11/03 (i)	1/05	...	...	Yes	LG	11/15/30	UT
Vermont	Jim Douglas (R)	2	1/03	1/05	...	...	No	LG	6/21/51	MA
Virginia	Mark R. Warner (D)	4	1/02	1/06	...	(j)	No	LG	12/15/54	IN
Washington	Gary Locke (D)	4	1/97	1/05	1	...	No	LG	1/21/50	WA
West Virginia	Bob Wise (D)	4	1/01	1/05	...	2	(k)	PS	1/6/48	D.C.
Wisconsin	Jim Doyle (D)	4	1/03	1/07	...	...	Yes	LG	11/23/45	WI
Wyoming	Dave Freudenthal (D)	4	1/03	1/07	...	2 (g)	Yes	SS	10/12/50	WY
American Samoa	Togiola Tulafono (D)	4	4/03 (m)	1/05	...	2	Yes	LG	2/28/47	AS
Guam	Felix P. Camacho (R)	4	1/03	1/07	...	2	Yes	LG	10/30/57	GU
No. Mariana Islands	Juan N. Babauta (R)	4	1/02	1/06	...	2 (n)	Yes	LG	9/7/53	CNMI
Puerto Rico	Sila M. Calderon (PDP)	4	1/01	1/05	...	...	(k)	SS	9/23/42	PR
U.S. Virgin Islands	Charles W. Turnbull (D)	4	1/99	1/07	1	(f)	Yes	LG	2/5/35	VI

Sources: The Council of State Governments' survey, December 2003 and 2003 National Governors Association.

Key:

D — Democrat
PDP — Popular Democratic Party
R — Republican
LG — Lieutenant Governor
SS — Secretary of the Senate
PS — President of the Senate
SpS — Speaker of the Senate
... — Not applicable

(a) The following also choose candidates for governor and lieutenant governor through a joint nomination process: Florida, Kansas, Maryland, Minnesota, Montana, North Dakota, Ohio, Utah, American Samoa, Guam, No. Mariana Islands and U.S. Virgin Islands.

(b) Governor Huckabee, as lieutenant governor, became Governor in July 1996 after Governor Jim Guy Tucker resigned. He was elected to a full four-year term in November 1998.

(c) Governor Swarzenegger was sworn in on November 17, 2003 after defeating Governor Gray Davis in a recall election.

(d) Limited to 8 consecutive years in office.

(e) Governor Kernan, as lieutenant governor, became Governor on September 13, 2003, after Governor Frank O'Bannon's death.

(f) After two consecutive terms as Governor, the candidate must wait four years before becoming eligible to run again.

(g) Absolute limit of eight years of service out of every 16 years.

(h) Lt. Gov. Perry was sworn in on December 21, 2000 to complete President George W. Bush's term as governor of Texas.

(i) Governor Walker was sworn in on November 5, 2003 after Governor Mike Leavitt resigned to become Administrator of the U.S. Environmental Protection Agency.

(j) Governor cannot serve immediate successive terms.

(k) No lieutenant governor.

(l) Official bears the additional title of "lieutenant governor."

(m) Governor Tulafono, as lieutenant governor, became Governor in April 2003 after Governor Sunia's death.

(n) Absolute two-term limitation, but terms need not be consecutive.

Table 4.2
THE GOVERNORS: QUALIFICATIONS FOR OFFICE

State or other jurisdiction	Minimum age	State citizen (years)	U.S. citizen (years) (a)	State resident (years) (b)	Qualified voter (years)
Alabama	30	7	10	7	★
Alaska	30	7	7	7	★
Arizona	25	5	10	. . .	. . .
Arkansas	30	★	★	7	. . .
California	18	. . .	5	5	★
Colorado	30	. . .	★	2	. . .
Connecticut	30	. . .	★	★	★
Delaware	30	. . .	12	6	. . .
Florida	30	. . .	★	7	★
Georgia	30	. . .	15	6	★
Hawaii	30	. . .	. . .	5	★
Idaho	30	. . .	★	2	. . .
Illinois	25	3	★	3	★
Indiana	30	. . .	5	5	★
Iowa	30	. . .	★	2	. . .
Kansas	. . .	. . .	. . .	. . .	. . .
Kentucky	30	6	. . .	6	. . .
Louisiana	25	5	5	5	★
Maine	30	. . .	15	5	. . .
Maryland	30	. . .	(c)	5	5
Massachusetts	. . .	. . .	★	7	★
Michigan	30	. . .	★	★	4
Minnesota	25	. . .	★	1	★
Mississippi	30	. . .	20	5	★
Missouri	30	. . .	15	10	. . .
Montana	25	★	★	★	. . .
Nebraska	30	5	5	5	. . .
Nevada	25	2	2	2	★
New Hampshire	30	. . .	. . .	7	. . .
New Jersey	30	. . .	20	7	. . .
New Mexico	30	. . .	★	5	★
New York	30	. . .	★	5	. . .
North Carolina	30	. . .	5	2	★
North Dakota	30	. . .	★	5	★
Ohio	18	. . .	★	★	★
Oklahoma	31	. . .	. . .	. . .	★
Oregon	30	. . .	★	3	★
Pennsylvania	30	. . .	★	7	. . .
Rhode Island	18	30 days	★	30 days	★
South Carolina	30	5	5	5	. . .
South Dakota	21	. . .	★	2	. . .
Tennessee	30	7	★	. . .	. . .
Texas	30	. . .	★	5	. . .
Utah	30	5	★	5	★
Vermont	18	1	. . .	4	★
Virginia	30	. . .	★	5	5
Washington	18	. . .	★	★	★
West Virginia	30	5	★	1	★
Wisconsin	18	. . .	★	★	★
Wyoming	30	★	★	5	. . .
American Samoa	35	. . .	★	5	. . .
Guam	30	. . .	5	5	★
No. Mariana Islands	35	. . .	★	10	★
Puerto Rico	35	5	5	5	. . .
U.S. Virgin Islands	30	. . .	5	5	★

Sources: The Council of State Governments' survey, November 2003 and state constitutions, state statutes and secretaries of state web sites, December 2003.

Key:

★ — Formal provision; number of years not specified.

. . . — No formal provision.

(a) In some states you must be a U.S. citizen to be an elector, and must be an elector to run.

(b) In some states you must be a state resident to be an elector, and must be an elector to run.

(c) *Crosse v. Board of Supervisors of Elections* 243 Md. 555, 221A.2d431 (1966) — opinion rendered indicated that U.S. citizenship was, by necessity, a requirement for office.

Table 4.3
THE GOVERNORS: COMPENSATION

State or other jurisdiction	Salary	Governor's office staff (a)	Access to state transportation			Travel allowance	Official residence
			Automobile	Airplane	Helicopter		
Alabama	$96,361	22	★	★	★	(b)	★
Alaska	85,766	70	★	★	. . .	(k)	★
Arizona	95,000	39	★	★	. . .	(b)	. . .
Arkansas	75,296	55	★	★	★	★	★
California	175,000	86	★	. . .	. . .	(c)	(d)
Colorado	90,000	39	★	★	. . .	(e)	★
Connecticut	150,000	30	★	★	★	(e)	★
Delaware	114,000	32	★	. . .	. . .	. . .	★
Florida	120,171	310	★	★	. . .	(b)	★
Georgia	127,303	77	★	★	★	(e)	★
Hawaii	94,780	67	★	★	★	★	★
Idaho	98,500	24	★	★	. . .	(e)	. . .
Illinois	150,691	130	★	★	★	(b)	★
Indiana	95,000	34	★	★	★	$10,500 (b)	★
Iowa	107,482	19	★	★	. . .	(b)	★
Kansas	98,331	24	★	★	. . .	★	★
Kentucky	103,018	40	★	★	★	(b)	★
Louisiana	94,532	143	★	★	★	(b)	★
Maine	70,000	19	★	★	★	(b)	★
Maryland	135,000	82	★	★	★	(e)	★
Massachusetts	135,000 (j)	70	★	. . .	★	(b) (e)	. . .
Michigan	177,000	56	★	★	. . .	(e)	★
Minnesota	120,311	45	★	★	★	(e)	★
Mississippi	122,160	33	★	★	★	(e)	★
Missouri	120,087	39	★	★	. . .	(c)	★
Montana	93,089	18	★	★	★	(b)	★
Nebraska	85,000	9	★	★	. . .	(b)	★
Nevada	117,000	(g)	★	★	. . .	(c)	★
New Hampshire	96,060	23	★	. . .	. . .	(e)	★ (f)
New Jersey	157,000	156	★	. . .	★	$61,000	★
New Mexico	110,000	27	★	★	★	$79,200 (c)	★
New York	179,000	180	★	★	★	(b)	★
North Carolina	118,430	76	★	★	★	$11,500	★
North Dakota	85,506	17	★	★	. . .	(b)	★
Ohio	126,485	60	★	★	★	(f)	★
Oklahoma	110,298	34	★	★	. . .	(b)	★
Oregon	93,600	29	★	. . .	. . .	(e)	★
Pennsylvania	144,416	90	★	★	. . .	(b)	★
Rhode Island	105,194	49	★	. . .	. . .	N.A.	. . .
South Carolina	106,078	22	★	★	. . .	(b)	★
South Dakota	95,389	22.5	★	★	. . .	(b)	★
Tennessee	85,000	36	★	★	★	(e)	★
Texas	115,345	266	★	★	★	(b)	★
Utah	100,600	17.5	★	★	★	$58,900	★
Vermont	127,456	14	★	. . .	. . .	★	. . .
Virginia	124,855	34	★	★	★	(b)	★
Washington	139,087	36	★	★	. . .	(e)	★
West Virginia	90,000	56	★	★	★	(h)	★
Wisconsin	122,406	39.75	★	★	. . .	(e)	★
Wyoming	130,000	8	★	★	. . .	(b)	★
American Samoa	50,000	23	★	. . .	. . .	$105,000 (c)	★
Guam	90,000	42	★	. . .	. . .	$218/day	★
No. Mariana Islands	70,000	16	★	. . .	. . .	(e) (i)	★
Puerto Rico	70,000	352	★	. . .	. . .	. . .	★
U.S. Virgin Islands	80,000	86	★	. . .	. . .	(b)	★

See footnotes at end of table.

THE GOVERNORS: COMPENSATION — Continued

Sources: The Council of State Governments' survey, December 2003 and 2002 National Governors Association.

Key:

★ — Yes

. . . — No

N.A. — Not available.

(a) Definitions of governor's office staff vary across the states—from general office support to staffing for various operations within the executive office.

(b) Reimbursed for travel expenses. Alabama—reimbursed up to $40/day in state; actual expenses out of state. Arizona—receives up to $38/day for meals based on location; receives per diem for lodging out-of-state; default $28/day for meals and $50/day lodging in-state. Florida—reimbursed at same rate as other state officials: in state, choice between $50 per diem or actual expenses; out of state, actual expenses. Indiana—reimbursed for actual expenses for travel/lodging. Illinois—no set allowance. Iowa—limit set in annual office budget. Kentucky—mileage at same rate as other state employees. Louisiana—reimbursed for actual expenses. Massachusetts—As incurred. Montana—reimbursed for actual and necessary expenses. Nebraska—reasonable and necessary expenses. New York–reimbursed for actual and necessary expenses. North Dakota—reimbursed at state rate. Oklahoma—reimbursed for actual expenses. Pennsylvania—reimbursed for reasonable expenses. Texas—Full reimbursement. Wyoming—$85/day or actual. U.S. Virgin Islands—reimbursed 100 percent.

(c) Amount includes travel allowance for entire staff. Missouri amount not available. California–$145,000 in state; $36,000 out of state. Nevada—$30,408 in state; $21,576 out of state. New Mexico—$79,200 (in state $45,600, out of state $33,600).

(d) In California—provided by Governor's Residence Foundation, a non-profit organization which provides a residence for the governor of California. No rent is charged; maintenance and operational costs are provided by California Department of General Services.

(e) Travel allowance included in office budget.

(f) Set administratively.

(g) Eighteen active and 21 authorized staff.

(h) Included in general expense account.

(i) Governor has a contingency account that can be used for travel expenses and expenses in other departments or other projects.

(j) Governor Romney waives his salary.

(k) Alaska—$42/day per diem plus actual lodging expenses.

Table 4.4
THE GOVERNORS: POWERS

State or other jurisdiction	Budget making power		Item veto power					Authorization for reorganization through executive order (a)
	Full responsibility	Shares responsibility	Governor has item veto power on all bills	Governor has item veto power on appropriations only	Governor has no item veto power	Item veto—2/3 legislators present or 3/5 elected to override	Item veto—majority legislators elected to override	
Alabama	★		★				★	
Alaska	★							★
Arizona	★ (b)		★			★		★ ★
Arkansas		★	★			★		★ ★
California	★ (b)		★			★		
Colorado	★		★			★		
Connecticut		★	★			★		★
Delaware	★		★ ★			★		
Florida	★		★ (d)			★		★
Georgia		★		★		★		★
Hawaii	★		★			★		
Idaho	★	★	★			★		★ ★
Illinois	★	★			★	★		★ ★
Indiana	★		★			★		
Iowa	★		★			★		★
Kansas	★			★ ★ ★ ★		★ ★		
Kentucky	★ (b)					★ (k)		★ (l)
Louisiana		★				★	★	★ ★
Maine	★			★		★		★ ★
Maryland	★		★			★		
Massachusetts	★		★	★ ★		★ (k)		★ (g)
Michigan		★		★		★		★
Minnesota	★ (b)			★		★		★
Mississippi		★	★ ★			★		★
Missouri	★ (b)		★	★ ★		★		★
Montana	★		★ (j)			★		(e)
Nebraska	★	★			★ ★	★		
Nevada	★ (b)							
New Hampshire	★ (b)		★			★		
New Jersey	★		★			★		
New Mexico	★				★	★		
New York	★	★	★			★		
North Carolina	★					★		★ ★
North Dakota	★		★ (f)			★		★ ★
Ohio	★			★		★		
Oklahoma		★	★				★	
Oregon	★ (b)	★	★			★ ★		
Pennsylvania	★		★			★ ★		
Rhode Island	★ (b)			★	★			
South Carolina		★				★		

See footnotes at end of table.

THE GOVERNORS: POWERS — Continued

State or other jurisdiction	Budget making power		Item veto power					Authorization for reorganization through executive order (a)
	Full responsibility	Shares responsibility	Governor has item veto power on all bills	Governor has item veto power on appropriations only	Governor has no item veto power	Item veto—2/3 legislators present or 3/5 elected to override	Item veto—majority legislators elected to override	
South Dakota	★	...	★	...	...	★	...	★
Tennessee	...	...	...	★	...	...	★	★
Texas	...	★	...	★	...	★	...	★
Utah	★	...	...	★	...	★	...	...
Vermont	★	...	...	...	★	...	...	★
Virginia	★	...	...	★	...	★	...	★
Washington	★	...	★ (h)	...	...	★	...	...
West Virginia	★ (b)	...	...	★	...	★	...	...
Wisconsin	...	★	...	★ (i)	...	★	...	...
Wyoming	...	...	★	...	...	★	...	...
American Samoa	...	★	...	...	...	...	...	★
Guam	★	...	...	...	...	...	...	★
No. Mariana Islands	...	★	...	★	...	★	...	...
Puerto Rico	★ (b)	...	...	...	★	...	...	...
U.S. Virgin Islands	★	...	...	★	...	★	...	★

Sources: The Council of State Governments' survey, December 2003 and state constitutions and statutes.

Key:

★ — Yes; provision for.

. . . — No; not applicable.

(a) For additional information on executive orders, see Table 4.5.

(b) Full responsibility to propose; legislature adopts or revises and governor signs or vetoes.

(c) Includes only executive branch officials who are popularly elected either on a constitutional or statutory basis (elected members of state boards of education, public utilities commissions, university regents, or other state boards or commissions are also included); the number of agencies involving theses officials is also listed.

(d) Governor may only veto a specific appropriation within a general appropriation bill or an entire bill. 2/3 of both houses can override.

(e) Statutory.

(f) North Dakota has a governor's veto and a line item veto on appropriations bills.

(g) Authorization for reorganization provided for in state constitution.

(h) Governor has veto power of selections for nonappropriations and item veto in appropriations.

(i) In Wisconsin, governor has "partial" veto over appropriation bills. The partial veto is broader than item veto.

(j) Amendatory veto while legislature is in session.

(k) 2/3 of elected legislators of each house to override.

(l) Only for agencies and office within the Governor's Office

Table 4.5
GUBERNATORIAL EXECUTIVE ORDERS: AUTHORIZATION, PROVISIONS, PROCEDURES

State or other jurisdiction	Authorization for executive orders	Procedures: Civil defense disasters, public emergencies	Energy emergencies and conservation	Other emergencies	Executive branch reorganization plans and agency creation	Create advisory, coordinating, study or investigative committees/commissions	Respond to federal programs and requirements	State personnel administration	Other administration	Provisions: Filing and publication procedures	Subject to administrative procedure act	Subject to legislative review
Alabama	S, I (a)	…	…	★ (b)	★	★	…	…	…	★ (c)(d)	…	★
Alaska	C	★ (a)	…	★	★	★	…	…	…	★ (c)	…	…
Arizona	I	★	★ (a)	★ (a)	★	★	★	…	…	…	…	…
Arkansas	C	★	★	★	★	★	★	★	★	…	…	…
California	S	★	★	★ (f)	★	★	★	…	★ (gg)	…	…	…
Colorado	S, I	★	★	★	★	★	★	…	…	…	…	…
Connecticut	S	★	★	★	…	★	★	★	…	…	…	…
Delaware	C	★	★	★ (h)	★	★	★	…	…	★ (c)	…	…
Florida	C, S	★ (mm)	★	★	★	★	★	★ (mm)	★ (j)(j)(ll)	★ (c)	…	…
Georgia	S, I	★	★	★	★	★	I	…	★	★	…	…
Hawaii	S	★	I	I	…	I	I	…	…	…	…	…
Idaho	S	★	I	I	★	I	I	…	…	★ (c)	…	★
Illinois	C, S	★	★	★	★	★	★	★	★	★	…	…
Indiana	C, S, Case Law	★	★	…	★	★	★	★	…	★	★	…
Iowa	S	…	…	…	…	(s)	…	…	…	…	…	…
Kansas	C, S	★	★	★ (m)	★	★	★	★	★	★ (c)	…	…
Kentucky	C, S	★	★	★	★	★	★	★	★ (n)(o)(p)	★ (l)	…	…
Louisiana	S (g)	★	I	★	★	★	…	…	…	★	…	…
Maine	(u)	★	…	…	…	…	…	…	…	…	…	…
Maryland	C, S	★	★	★	…	★	★	★	★ (v)	★	…	★ (w)
Massachusetts	C, S	★	★	★	★	★	★	★	★	★	★	(ee)
Michigan	C	★	★ (x)	★	★	★	★	★ (y)	★ (c)(l)	★ (c)	★	★ (w)
Minnesota	S	★	★	★	★	★	★	★	★	★	★	★ (w)
Mississippi	S	★	I	…	★	★	★	S	★ (z)(aa)	★ (w)	★	…
Missouri	C, S, Common Law	★	★	★	★	★	★	★	★ (w)	★ (c)	★	★ (w)(bb)
Montana	S	★	★	★	★	★	★	★	★	★	★	★ (w)
Nebraska	C, S	★	★	★	★	★	★	★	I	★	★	…
Nevada	S, I	S	S	S	★	★	★	…	…	…	…	…
New Hampshire	S	S	…	…	…	I	★	…	★ (o)	★	…	…
New Jersey	C, S, I	★	★ (a)	★ (cc)	★ (dd)	★	★	★	★ (aa)	★	…	…
New Mexico	C	★	★	★	…	★	★	…	…	…	…	…
New York	C, S	S	S	S	★	I	S	S	I	★	★	★ (w)
North Carolina	S, I	S	S	S	S, C	I	S	…	S, C	S	★	★ (w)
North Dakota	S, I	★	S	S	…	I	S	S	…	…	…	(j)(p)(q)(r)(y)(aa)
Ohio	S, I	★	★	★	★	★	★	★	★	★	…	…

See footnotes at end of table.

GUBERNATORIAL EXECUTIVE ORDERS: AUTHORIZATION, PROVISIONS, PROCEDURES — Continued

State or other jurisdiction	Authorization for executive orders	Civil defense disasters, public emergencies	Energy emergencies and conservation	Other emergencies	Executive branch reorganization plans and agency creation	Create advisory, coordinating, study or investigative committees/commissions	Respond to federal programs and requirements	State personnel administration	Other administration	Filing and publication procedures	Subject to administrative procedure act	Subject to legislative review
Oklahoma	C	★	★	★	★	★	★	★	★ (c)			
Oregon	C, S	★	★	★	★	★	★		★★			★
Pennsylvania	C,S	★			(l)(t)(v)(ff)				★ (ff)			
Rhode Island	S (a)	★	★ (a)		(a)			★ (k)		★ (c,l)		
South Carolina	S	★	★	★		★	★	★	★	★		★
South Dakota	C	★	★	★	★	★	★	★				
Tennessee	S	★	★	★	★	★	★	★	★	★ (c)		
Texas	I	★	★	★	★	★	★	★				
Utah	S	★	★	★	★	★	★	★				
Vermont	S,I	★	★	★	★	★	★	★	★	★ (ii)		★ (ii)
Virginia	S,I	★	★	★ (g)	★	(kk)	★	★				★ (jj)
Washington	S	★										
West Virginia	C,S	★	★	★		★	★	★				
Wisconsin	C,S	★	★	★		★	★	★	(o)(aa)(dd)	★ (c)		
Wyoming	(e)		★	★	★			★	★			
American Samoa	C,S	★	★	★	★ (hh)	★	★	★	★	★ (oo)	★ (oo)	
Guam	C	★	I		(hh)	S,I	★	★	★	S	I	★
No. Mariana Islands	C	★	I	★	C	S,I	S		★			
Puerto Rico	I	★	★	★		★	★	★	★	★		★
U.S. Virgin Islands	C	★	★	★	★	★	★	★	★			

See footnotes at end of table.

GUBERNATORIAL EXECUTIVE ORDERS: AUTHORIZATION, PROVISIONS, PROCEDURES — Continued

Sources: The Council of State Governments' survey, December 2003 and January 2004, state constitutions and statutes.

Key:
C — Constitutional
S — Statutory
I — Implied
★ — Formal provision.
. . . — No formal provision.

(a) Broad interpretation of gubernatorial authority.

(b) To activate or veto environmental improvement authorities.

(c) Executive orders must be filed with secretary of state or other designated officer. In Idaho, must also be published in state general circulation newspaper.

(d) Governor required to keep record in office. In Maine, also sends copy to Legislative Counsel, State Law Library, and all county law libraries in state.

(e) No specific authorization granted, general authority only.

(f) To regulate distribution of necessities during shortages.

(g) Broad grant of authority.

(h) Local financial emergency, shore erosion, polluted discharge and energy shortage.

(i) To reassign state attorneys and public defenders.

(j) To suspend certain officials and/or other civil actions.

(k) To transfer allocated funds.

(l) Filing.

(m) To give immediate effect to state regulation in emergencies.

(n) To control administration of state contracts and procedures.

(o) To impound or freeze certain state matching funds.

(p) To reduce state expenditures in revenue shortfall.

(q) To designate game and wildlife areas or other public areas.

(r) Appointive powers.

(s) Executive Orders generally may issue with respect to both emergent and non-emergent matters falling within the Executive Branch.

(t) For fire emergencies.

(u) Authority implied statutorily and by course of practice.

(v) To control procedures for dealing with public.

(w) Reorganization plans and agency creation.

(x) If an energy emergency is declared by the state's Executive Council or legislature.

(y) To assign duties to lieutenant governor, issue writ of special election.

(z) To control prison and pardon administration.

(aa) To administer and govern the armed forces of the state.

(bb) For meeting federal program requirements.

(cc) To declare air pollution emergencies.

(dd) Relating to local governments.

(ee) Only for ERO's.

(ff) To transfer funds in an emergency.

(gg) Matters relating to the enforcement and administration of Connecticut law.

(hh) Can reorganize, but not create.

(ii) Filed with legislature.

(jj) Only if reorganization order.

(kk) To shift agencies between secretarial offices; all other reorganizations require legislative approval.

(ll) By executive order, governor may also suspend collection of fines and forfeitures, grant reprieves not exceeding 60 days and with approval of 3 cabinet members, grant full or conditional pardons, restore civil rights, commute punishment and remit fines and forfeiture for offenses.

(mm) Governor may also delineate an interjurisdictional area to prepare, plan, mitigate or respond to emergency.

(nn) Governor may also declare an office vacant.

(oo) If executive order fits definition of rule.

Table 4.6
STATE CABINET SYSTEMS

State or other jurisdiction	Authorization for cabinet system				Criteria for membership			Number of members in cabinet (including governor)	Frequency of cabinet meetings	Open cabinet meetings
	State statute	State constitution	Governor created	Tradition in state	Appointed to specific office (a)	Elected to specified office (a)	Gubernatorial appointment regardless of office			
Alabama	...	...	...	★	...	...	★	28	Gov.'s discretion (a)	...
Alaska	...	...	★	...	★	...	...	18	Gov.'s discretion	★ (b)
Arizona	...	...	★	...	★	...	★	38	Monthly	...
Arkansas	...	...	...	★	★	...	...	46	Monthly	...
California	★	...	★	...	★	...	★	13	Every two weeks	...
Colorado	...	★	...	...	★	...	...	21	Gov.'s discretion	★
Connecticut	★	...	...	...	★	...	...	27	Gov.'s discretion	...
Delaware	★	...	...	...	★	...	★	19	Gov.'s discretion	...
Florida	...	★	...	...	...	★	...	7	Every two weeks	★
Georgia						(d)				
Hawaii	★	★	...	...	★	...	★	25	Monthly	...
Idaho			(d)					22	Gov.'s discretion	...
Illinois	★	...	...	...	...	...	★	18	N.A.	...
Indiana						(d)				
Iowa						(e)				
Kansas	★	...	...	...	...	...	★	14	Biweekly	...
Kentucky	★	★	★	...	★	...	★	9	Monthly	...
Louisiana	...	...	★	★	★	...	★	14	Monthly	...
Maine	...	...	...	(i)	...	...	★	21	Weekly	...
Maryland	★	...	...	...	★ (c)	...	...	23	Weekly	...
Massachusetts	★	...	...	...	★	...	...	10	Bi-weekly	...
Michigan	...	...	★	★	...	...	★	24	Monthly	...
Minnesota	...	...	★	...	★	...	...	25	Regularly	...
Mississippi						(d)				
Missouri	...	★	...	★	★	...	...	17	Gov.'s discretion	...
Montana	★	...	★	...	★	...	...	17	Gov.'s discretion	★
Nebraska	...	...	★	★	★	...	★	29	Monthly	...
Nevada						(d)				
New Hampshire						(d)				
New Jersey	★	★	...	...	...	...	...	19	Gov.'s discretion	...
New Mexico	★	...	...	★	★	...	...	17	Weekly	...
New York	...	...	...	★	...	...	★	75	Gov.'s discretion	...
North Carolina (f)	★	★	★	...	...	...	★	10	Monthly	...
North Dakota			(g)					18	Monthly	★
Ohio	★	...	...	...	★	...	...	24	Gov.'s discretion	★
Oklahoma	★	...	...	...	...	...	★ (c)	10–15	Monthly	...
Oregon						(d)				
Pennsylvania	★	...	...	...	★ (c)	...	...	19	Weekly	★
Rhode Island			(h)						Gov.'s discretion	Gov.'s discretion
South Carolina	★	...	...	...	★ (c)	...	...	15	Monthly	★
South Dakota	★	★	...	...	★	...	...	20	Monthly	...
Tennessee	★	...	...	...	★	...	...	28	Monthly	...
Texas						(d)				
Utah	★	...	★	(h)	★	...	...	19	Monthly	...
Vermont	★	...	...	...	★	...	...	7	Gov.'s discretion	...
Virginia	★	...	...	...	★	...	...	12	Weekly	...
Washington	...	...	★	...	★	...	...	28	Bi-weekly, weekly during legislative session	...
West Virginia	...	...	★	★	★	...	...	10	Weekly	...
Wisconsin	★	...	...	...	★	...	...	16	Gov.'s discretion	★
Wyoming	★	...	...	...	...	...	★	20	Monthly	...
American Samoa	★	★	...	...	★	...	★	16	Gov.'s discretion	★
Guam	...	...	★	...	★	...	...	55	Bi-monthly	...
No. Mariana Islands	...	★	...	...	★	...	...	16	Gov.'s discretion	★
Puerto Rico	★	★	...	...	★	...	★	(j)	Monthly	...
U.S. Virgin Islands	...	★	...	...	★	...	...	21	Monthly	★

See footnotes at end of table.

STATE CABINET SYSTEMS — Continued

Sources: The Council of State Governments' survey, December 2003 and state constitutions and statutes.

Key:

★ — Yes

. . . — No

N.A. — Not available

(a) Individual is a member by virtue of election or appointment to a cabinet-level position.

(b) Except when in executive session.

(c) With the consent of the senate.

(d) No formal cabinet system. In Idaho, however, sub-cabinets have been formed, by executive order; the chairmen report to the governor when requested.

(e) Sub-cabinets meet quarterly.

(f) Constitution provides for a Council of State made up of elective state administrative officials, which makes policy decisions for the state while the cabinet acts more in an advisory capacity.

(g) Cabinet consists of agencies, created by legislation; directors of agencies appointed by the governor.

(h) In Rhode Island, department heads require advice and consent of the Senate. In Utah, department heads serve as cabinet; meets at discretion of governor, but when first appointed, department heads also require advice and consent of Senate.

(i) Authority implied statutorily and by course of practice. Some of those department heads along with other officials compose the Governor's Cabinet.

(j) 81 executive agencies, 11 government support agencies of the executive and 48 public corporations.

Table 4.7
THE GOVERNORS: PROVISIONS AND PROCEDURES FOR TRANSITION

State or other jurisdiction	Legislation pertaining to gubernatorial transition	Appropriation available to gov-elect	Gov-elect's participation in state budget for coming fiscal year	Gov-elect to hire staff to assist during transition	State personnel to be made available to assist gov-elect	Office space in buildings to be made available to gov-elect	Acquainting gov-elect staff with office procedures and routing office functions	Transfer of information (files records, etc.)
Alabama	...	...	●	(a)	●	●	●	...
Alaska	●	★ (l)	...	●	●	●	●	★
Arizona	...	...	★	...	●	●	●	●
Arkansas	●	30,000	...	●	...	●	●	●
California	★	450,000	★	★	★	★	●	●
Colorado	★	10,000	...	★	★	★	★	★
Connecticut	★	0	...	★	...	★	●	★
Delaware	★	30,000	●	★	●	●	●	●
Florida	...	300,000	★	★	●	●	●	●
Georgia	★	50,000	★	★	★	★	●	★
Hawaii	★	50,000	★	★	★	★	●	●
Idaho	★	15,000	★	★	★	★	★	★
Illinois	★	★	●	●	●	●	★	●
Indiana	★	40,000	★	...	...	★	★	★
Iowa	★ (d)	10,000	★	★	● (i)	●	●	★ (f)
Kansas	★	150,000 (g)	★	★	★	★	★	★
Kentucky	★	200,000	★	★	★	★	★	★
Louisiana	★	65,000	★	★	★	... (h)	...	... (c)
Maine	●	5,000	...	●	●	★	●	●
Maryland	★	●	...	●	★	★	★	★
Massachusetts	●	●	●	...	●	●	●	★
Michigan	...	1,200,000	...	★	...	...	★	★
Minnesota	★	★	★	★	★	★	●	●
Mississippi	★	60,000	★	★	★	★	★	★
Missouri	★	100,000	★	★	●	★	●	● (i)
Montana	★	50,000	★	★	★	★	★	★
Nebraska	★	60,879	★	★	★	★	★	★
Nevada	★	Reasonable amount	★	●	●	●	●	★ (d)
New Hampshire	★	75,000	★	★	★	★	★	...
New Jersey	★	Unspecified	★	★	★	★	●	★
New Mexico	★	(b)	★	★	●	★	●	●
New York	...	...	...	...	★	★	★	★
North Carolina	★	80,000 (j)	● (k)	★	★	★	●	●
North Dakota	●	10,000	(m)	(a)	●	...	●	★
Ohio	★	Unspecified (e)	●	★	●	...	●	★
Oklahoma	...	30,000	★	...	...	...	...	...
Oregon	★	...	★	★	★	★	★	★
Pennsylvania	★	100,000	...	★	●	●	●	...
Rhode Island	...	●	★	● (a)	●	●	●	●
South Carolina	...	●	●	●	●	●	●	●
South Dakota	●	●	●	●	●	●	●	●
Tennessee	★	★	●	★	★	★	●	●
Texas	●	●	●	●	●	●	●	●
Utah	...	● (varies)	...	...	●	●	●	●
Vermont	...	30,000	★	●	●	●	●	★
Virginia	...	●	...	●	★ (i)	★ (i)	●	...
Washington	★	★	●	★	●	★	●	●
West Virginia	...	●	...	●	...	●	●	●
Wisconsin	★	Unspecified	★	★	★	★	★	★
Wyoming	...	●	...	●	●	●	●	●
American Samoa	...	Unspecified	★ (n)	★	●	●	★	★
Guam	★	(o)	...	...	★	★	★	...
No. Mariana Islands	★	Unspecified	...	★	★	★	★	★
Puerto Rico	...	250,000 (j)	...	●	●	●	●	●
U.S. Virgin Islands	★	100,000	...	★	★	★	★	★

See footnotes at end of table.

THE GOVERNORS: PROVISIONS AND PROCEDURES FOR TRANSITION — Continued

Sources: The Council of State Governments' survey, December 2003 and state constitutions and statutes.

Key:

. . . — No provisions or procedures.

★ — Formal provisions or procedures.

● — No formal provisions, occurs informally.

N.A. — Not applicable.

(a) Governor usually hires several incoming key staff during transition.

(b) Legislature required to make appropriation; no dollar amount stated in legislation.

(c) In Louisiana—Statute directs the records and associated historical records of any governor to be transferred to the custody of the state archivist.

(d) Pertains only to funds.

(e) Determined in budget.

(f) Arrangement for transfer of criminal files.

(g) Transition funds are used by both the incoming and outgoing administrations.

(h) The $65,000 may be used to rent space.

(i) Activity is traditional and routine, although there is no specific statutory provision.

(j) Inaugural expenses are paid from this amount.

(k) New governor can submit supplemental budget.

(l) Varies.

(m) Responsible for submitting budget for coming biennium.

(n) Can submit reprogramming or supplemental appropriation measure for current fiscal year.

(o) Appropriations given upon the request of governor-elect.

Table 4.8
IMPEACHMENT PROVISIONS IN THE STATES

State or other jurisdiction	Governor and other state executive and judicial officers subject to impeachment	Legislative body which holds power of impeachment	Vote required for impeachment	Legislative body which conducts impeachment trial	Chief justice presides at impeachment trial (a)	Vote required for conviction	Official who serves as acting governor if governor impeached (b)	Legislature may call special session for impeachment
Alabama	★	H	...	S	★	...	LG	★
Alaska	★ (d)	S	2/3 mbrs.	H	(c)	2/3 mbrs.	LG	★
Arizona	★	H	maj. mbrs.	S	★ (e)	2/3 mbrs.	SS	★
Arkansas	★	H	maj. mbrs.	S	★	2/3 mbrs.	LG	...
California	★	H	...	S	...	2/3 mbrs.	LG	...
Colorado	★	H	maj. mbrs.	S	★	2/3 mbrs.	LG	...
Connecticut	★	H	...	S	★	2/3 mbrs. present	LG	...
Delaware	★	H	2/3 mbrs.	S	(f)	2/3 mbrs.	LG	...
Florida	★	H	2/3 mbrs.	S	★ (e)	2/3 mbrs.	LG	...
Georgia	★	H	...	S	(e)	2/3 mbrs.	LG	★ (g)
Hawaii	★	H	maj. mbrs.	S	★	2/3 mbrs.	LG	...
Idaho	★	H	maj. mbrs.	S	★	2/3 mbrs.	LG	★
Illinois	★	H	maj. mbrs.	S	★	2/3 mbrs.	LG	★
Indiana	★	H	2/3 mbrs.	S	...	2/3 mbrs.	LG	...
Iowa	★	H	maj. mbrs.	S	...	2/3 mbrs. present	LG	...
Kansas	★	H	...	S	...	2/3 mbrs.	LG	...
Kentucky	★	H	...	S	★	2/3 mbrs. present	LG	...
Louisiana	★	H	2/3 mbrs. elected	S	...	2/3 mbrs. elected	LG	★ (h)
Maine	★	H	...	S	★	2/3 mbrs. present	PS	...
Maryland	★	H	maj. mbrs.	S	...	2/3 mbrs.	LG	...
Massachusetts	★	H	...	S (i)	...	...	LG	★
Michigan	★	H	maj. mbrs.	S	★	2/3 mbrs.	LG	...
Minnesota	★	H	maj. mbrs.	S	...	2/3 mbrs. present	LG	...
Mississippi	★	H	2/3 mbrs. present	S	...	2/3 mbrs. present	LG	...
Missouri	★	H	maj. mbrs.	S (j)	(j)	2/3 mbrs.	LG	...
Montana	★	H	2/3 mbrs.	S	★	2/3 mbrs.	LG	★
Nebraska	★ (d)	S (k)	maj. mbrs.	S (l)	(l)	2/3 mbrs. of sup.court	LG	...
Nevada	★ (d)	H	maj. mbrs.	S	★	2/3 mbrs.	LG	★
New Hampshire	★	H	...	S	★	...	PS	...
New Jersey	★	H	maj. mbrs.	S	★	2/3 mbrs.	PS	★
New Mexico	★	H	maj. mbrs.	S (m)	★	2/3 mbrs. present	LG	★
New York	★	H	maj. mbrs.	S	★	2/3 mbrs. present	LG	★
North Carolina	★ (d)	H	...	S	★	2/3 mbrs.	LG	★
North Dakota	★ (d)	H	maj. mbrs.	S	★	2/3 mbrs.	LG	...
Ohio	★	H	maj. mbrs.	S	★	2/3 mbrs. present	LG	...
Oklahoma	★ (n)	H	...	S	★	2/3 mbrs. present	SS	★
Oregon				(o)				
Pennsylvania	★	H	maj. mbrs.	S	...	2/3 mbrs.	LG	★
Rhode Island	★	H	1/4 mbrs. (p)	S	★	2/3 mbrs.	LG	...
South Carolina	★	H	2/3 mbrs.	S	★	2/3 mbrs.	LG	...

See footnotes at end of table.

IMPEACHMENT PROVISIONS IN THE STATES —Continued

State or other jurisdiction	Governor and other state executive and judicial officers subject to impeachment	Legislative body which holds power of impeachment	Vote required for impeachment	Legislative body which conducts impeachment trial	Chief justice presides at impeachment trial (a)	Vote required for conviction	Official who serves as acting governor if governor impeached (b)	Legislature may call special session for impeachment
South Dakota	★ (d)	H	maj. mbrs.	S	★	2/3 mbrs.	LG	★
Tennessee	★	H	maj. mbrs.	S	★	2/3 mbrs. (q)	PS	★
Texas	★	H	maj. mbrs.	S	. . .	2/3 mbrs. present	LG	. . .
Utah	★ (d)	H	2/3 mbrs.	S	. . .	2/3 mbrs.	LG	. . .
Vermont	★	H	2/3 mbrs.	S	. . .	2/3 mbrs. present	LG	. . .
Virginia	★	H	. . .	S	. . .	2/3 mbrs. present	LG	★
Washington	★ (d)	H	maj. mbrs.	S	★	2/3 mbrs.	LG	★
West Virginia	★	H	maj. mbrs.	S	★	2/3 mbrs.	PS	★
Wisconsin	★	H	maj. mbrs.	S	. . .	2/3 mbrs.	LG	. . .
Wyoming	★	H	2/3 mbrs.	S	★	2/3 mbrs.	SS	. . .
Dist. of Columbia				(r)				
American Samoa	(s)	H	2/3 mbrs.	S	H	2/3 mbrs.	. . .	. . .
Guam	★	H	2/3 mbrs.	S	. . .	2/3 mbrs.	LG	★
Puerto Rico	(t)	H	2/3 mbrs.	S	★	3/4 mbrs.	SS	. . .
U.S. Virgin Islands				(r)				

Sources: The Council of State Governments' survey of governors October 2003 and state constitutions and statutes, December 2003.

Key:
★ — Yes; provision for.
. . . — Not specified, or no provision for.
H — House or Assembly (lower chamber).
S — Senate.
LG — Lieutenant Governor
PS — President or Speaker of the Senate
SS — Secretary of state.

(a) Presiding justice of state court of last resort. In many states, provision indicates that chief justice presides only on occasion of impeachment of governor.
(b) For provisions on official next in line on succession if governor is convicted and removed from office, refer to Chapter 4, "The Governors."
(c) An appointed Supreme Court justice presides.
(d) With exception of certain judicial officers. In Arizona and Washington — justices of courts not of record. In Nevada and Utah — justices of the peace. In North Dakota and South Dakota — county judges, justices of the peace, and police magistrates. In Oklahoma — all judicial officers not serving on the Supreme Court.
(e) Should the Chief Justice be on trial, or otherwise disqualified, the Senate shall elect a judge of the Supreme Court to preside.
(f) Except in a trial of the chief justice, in which case the governor shall preside.
(g) Special sessions of the General Assembly shall be limited to a period of 40 days unless extended by 3/5 vote of each house and approved by the Governor or unless at the expiration of such period an impeachment trial of some officer of state government is pending, in which event the House shall adjourn and the Senate shall remain in session until such trial is completed.

(h) In Louisiana — not specified; both the governor and the legislature appear to have authority to call a special session for impeachment.
(i) House elects three members to prosecute impeachment.
(j) All impeachments are tried before the state Supreme Court, except that the governor or a member of the Supreme Court is tried by a special commission of seven eminent jurists to be elected by the Senate. A vote of 5/7 of the court of special commission is necessary to convict.
(k) Unicameral legislature; members use the title "senator".
(l) Court of impeachment is composed of chief justice and supreme court. A vote of 2/3 of the court is necessary to convict.
(m) Court for trial of impeachment composed of president of the Senate, senators (or major part of them), and judges of Court of Appeals (or major part of them).
(n) Includes justices of Supreme Court. Other judicial officers not subject to impeachment. Seven eminent jurists to be elected by the Senate. A vote of 5/7 of the court of special commission is necessary to convict.
(o) No provision for impeachment. Public officers may be tried for incompetence, corruption, malfeasance, or delinquency in office in same manner as criminal offenses.
(p) Vote of 2/3 members required for an impeachment of the governor.
(q) Vote of 2/3 of members sworn to try the officer impeached.
(r) Removal of elected officials by recall procedure only.
(s) Governor, lieutenant governor.
(t) Governor and Supreme Court justices.

Table 4.9
CONSTITUTIONAL AND STATUTORY PROVISIONS FOR NUMBER OF CONSECUTIVE TERMS OF ELECTED STATE OFFICIALS
(All terms last four years unless otherwise noted)

State or other jurisdiction	Governor	Lt. Governor	Secretary of state	Attorney general	Treasurer	Auditor	Comptroller	Education	Agriculture	Labor	Insurance
Alabama	2	2	2	2	2	2	...	...	2	...	...
Alaska	2 (a)	2	(b)	...	(w)	...	...	...	...	...	...
Arizona	2 (a)	(e)	2 (a)	2 (a)	2 (a)	...	...	2 (a)	...	...	...
Arkansas	2	2	2	2	2	2	(e)	...	...	...	...
California	2	2	2	2	2	...	2	2	...	...	...
Colorado	2	2	2	2	2	...	...	...	...	...	...
Connecticut	N	N	N	N	N	...	N	...	...	...	...
Delaware	2 (f)	2	...	N	N	N	...	...	...	...	N
Florida	2	2	...	N	(g)	...	N	N	N	...	(g)
Georgia	2 (a)	N	N	N	...	...	...	N	N	N	N
Hawaii	2	2	(b)	...	(e)	...	...	...	...	...	...
Idaho	N	N	N	N	N	N	N	N	...	...	...
Illinois	N	N	N	N	N	...	N	...	...	...	...
Indiana	(h)	N	(h)	...	(h)	(h)	(i)	...	...	...	...
Iowa	N	N	N	N	N	N	...	...	...	...	...
Kansas	2	2	N	N	...	...	...	...	...	...	...
Kentucky	2	2	2	2	2	2	(e)	...	2	2	...
Louisiana	2 (a)	N	N	N	N	...	(j)	N	N	...	N
Maine	2 (a)	(k)	...	(o)	...	...	...	...	...	...	...
Maryland	2 (a)	2	...	N	...	...	N	...	...	...	...
Massachusetts	N	N	N	N	N	N	...	...	...	...	...
Michigan	2	2	2	2	...	...	(e)	...	...	...	...
Minnesota	N	N	N	N	(l)	N	(e)	...	...	...	(m)
Mississippi	2 (f)	2 (a)	N	N	N	N	(e)	...	...	...	...
Missouri	2 (f)	N	N	N	2 (f)	N	...	...	...	...	...
Montana	2 (n)	2 (n)	2 (n)	2 (n)	...	2 (n)	...	2 (n)	...	...	...
Nebraska	2 (a)	2 (a)	2 (a)	2 (a)	2 (a)	2 (a)	...	...	...	...	...
Nevada	2	2	2	2	2	...	2	...	...	...	...
New Hampshire	(o)	(k)	...	...	...	...	...	...	...	...	...
New Jersey	2 (a)	(k)	...	...	...	...	...	...	...	...	...
New Mexico	2 (a)	2 (a)	2 (a)	2 (a)	2 (a)	2 (a)	(p)	...	...	...	...
New York	N	N	...	N	...	(c)	N	...	...	...	...
North Carolina	2 (a)	(b)	N	N	N	N	...	N	N	N	N
North Dakota	N	N	N (q)	N (q)	N	N	...	N	N (q)(r)	N (q)	N
Ohio	2 (a)	2	2	2	2	2	(p)	...	...	...	...
Oklahoma	2 (a)	2 (a)	...	2 (a)	2 (a)	2 (a)	...	2 (a)	...	2 (a)	N
Oregon	(h)	(d)	(h)	N	(h)	...	(p)	...	...	...	...
Pennsylvania	2	2	...	2 (a)	2 (s)	2 (a)	...	...	...	...	...
Rhode Island	2	2 (a)	2 (a)	2 (a)	2 (a)	...	...	...	...	...	...
South Carolina	2 (a)	2	N	N	N	...	N	N	N	...	...
South Dakota	2 (a)	2 (a)	2 (a)	2 (a)	2 (a)	2 (a)	(i)	2 (a)	...	...	...
Tennessee	2 (a)	(k)	...	...(y)	...	(c)	...	...	...	...	...
Texas	N	N	N	...	N	(c)	...	N	...	...	...
Utah	N	N	(b)	N	N	N	...	...	...	...	...
Vermont	(o)	(o)	(o)	(o)	(o)	(o)	(e)	...	...	...	...
Virginia	(t)	(u)	...	(u)	...	...	...	...	...	...	...
Washington	N	N	N	N	N	N	(p)	N	...	...	...
West Virginia	2	(k)	N	N	N	N	(i)	...	N	...	...
Wisconsin	N	N	N	N	N	...	...	...	N	...	...
Wyoming	N (n)	(d)	N	...	N	N	(i)	...	N	...	...
Dist. of Columbia	N (v)	2	...	...	...	...	...	...	...	...	...
American Samoa	2	2	(b)	...	...	...	(p)	...	...	...	...
Guam	2 (a)	2	(b)	...	...	...	(x)	...	...	...	...
No. Mariana Islands	(h)	N	...	...	...	...	(p)	...	...	...	(m)
Puerto Rico	N	(e)	...	...	...	...	...	...	...	...	...
U.S. Virgin Islands	2 (a)	N	(c)	...	(e)	...	(e)	...	...	...	(b)

See footnotes at end of table.

CONSTITUTIONAL AND STATUTORY PROVISIONS FOR
NUMBER OF CONSECUTIVE TERMS OF ELECTED STATE OFFICIALS — Continued

---

Source: State constitutions and statutes, October 2002.

Note: All terms last four years unless otherwise noted. Footnotes specify if a position's functions are performed by an appointed official under a different title.

Key:

N—No provision specifying number of terms allowed.

. . .—Position is appointed or elected by governmental entity (not chosen by the electorate).

(a) After two consecutive terms, must wait four years and/or one full term before being eligible again.

(b) Lieutenant Governor performs this function.

(c) Comptroller performs this function.

(d) Secretary of State is next in line to the governorship.

(e) Finance Administrator performs function.

(f) Absolute two-term limitation, but not necessarily consecutive.

(g) Chief Financial Officer performs this function as of January 2003.

(h) Eligible for eight out of any period of twelve years.

(i) State auditor performs this function.

(j) Head of administration performs this function.

(k) President or Speaker of the Senate is next in line of succession to the governorship. In Tennessee, Speaker of the Senate has the statutory title Lieutenant Governor.

(l) Office of the State Treasurer was abolished on the first Monday in January 2003.

(m) Commerce administrator performs this function.

(n) Eligible for eight out of sixteen years.

(o) Serves two-year term, no provision specifying the number of terms allowed.

(p) State treasurer performs this function.

(q) The terms of the office of the elected officials are four years, except that in 2004 the agricultural commissioner, attorney general, secretary of state and the tax commissioner are elected to a term of two years.

(r) Constitution provides for a secretary of agriculture and labor. However, the legislature was given constitutional authority to provide for (and has provided for) a department of labor distinct from agriculture, and a commissioner of labor distinct from the commissioner of agriculture.

(s) Treasurer must wait four years before being eligible to the office of auditor general.

(t) Cannot serve consecutive terms, but after 4 year respite can seek re-election.

(u) Provision specifying individual may hold office for an unlimited number of terms.

(v) Mayor.

(w) Deputy Commissioner of Department of Revenue performs function.

(x) General services administrator performs function.

(y) Term is for eight years.

Table 4.10
SELECTED STATE ADMINISTRATIVE OFFICIALS: METHODS OF SELECTION

State or other jurisdiction	Governor	Lieutenant governor	Secretary of state	Attorney general	Treasurer	Adjutant general	Administration	Agriculture	Auditor	Banking
Alabama	CE	CE	CE	CE	CE	GS	G	SE	CE	GS
Alaska	CE	CE	(a-1)	GB	AG	GB	GB	AG	L	AG
Arizona	CE	(a-2)	CE	CE	CE	GS	GS	GS	L	GS
Arkansas	CE	CE	CE	CE	CE	G	G	G	CE	GS
California	CE	CE	CE	CE	CE	GS	GS	G	GB	GS
Colorado	CE	CE	CE	CE	CE	GS	GS	GS	L	CS
Connecticut	CE	CE	CE	CE	CE	GE	GE	GE	L	GE
Delaware	CE	CE	GS	CE	CE	GS	GS	GS	CE	GS
Florida	CE	CE	A	CE	CE (dd)	G	G	CE	L	CE
Georgia	CE	CE	CE	CE	G	G	G	CE	(i)	G
Hawaii	CE	CE	(a-1)	GS	GS	GS	GS (a-9)	GS	CL	AG
Idaho	CE	CE	CE	CE	CE	GS	GS	GS	LS	GS
Illinois	CE	CE	CE	CE	CE	GS	GS	GS	SL	B
Indiana	CE	CE	CE	SE	CE	G	G	LG	G	G
Iowa	CE	CE	CE	CE	CE	GS	GS	CE	CE	GS
Kansas	CE	CE	CE	CE	SE	GS	GS	GS	LS	GS
Kentucky	CE	CE	CE	CE	CE	G	CG	CE	CE	G
Louisiana	CE	CE	CE	CE	CE	GS	GS	CE	L	GLS
Maine	CE	(o)	CL	CL	CL	G	G	G	N.A	G
Maryland	CE	CE	GS	CE	CL	G	GS (a-16)	GS	LS	AG
Massachusetts	CE	CE	CE	CE	CE	G	G	CG	CE	G
Michigan	CE	CE	CE	CE	GS	GS	GS	B	CL	GS
Minnesota	CE	CE	CE	CE	(mm)	GS	GS	GS	CE	A
Mississippi	CE	CE	CE	CE	CE	GE	GS	SE	CE	GS
Missouri	CE	CE	CE	CE	CE	G	GS	GS	CE	AGS
Montana	CE	CE	CE	CE	GS	G	GS	G	CE	A
Nebraska	CE	CE	CE	CE	CE	GS	GS	GS	CE	GS
Nevada	CE	CE	CE	CE	CE	G	G	BA	LS	A
New Hampshire	CE	(o)	CL	GC	CL	GC	GC	GC	N.A.	GC
New Jersey	CE	(o)	GS	GS	GS	GS	N.A.	BG	L	GS
New Mexico	CE	CE	CE	CE	CE	G	GS (a-16)	B	CE	G
New York	CE	CE	GS	CE	A	G	. . .	GS	CE (a-9)	GS
North Carolina	CE	CE	SE	CE	CE	A	G	CE	CE	G
North Dakota	CE	CE	CE	CE	CE	G	. . .	CE	CE	GS
Ohio	SE	SE	CE	SE	SE	GS	GS	GS	CE	GS
Oklahoma	CE	CE	A	CE	CE	GS	. . .	GS	CE	GS
Oregon	CE	(a-2)	CE	SE	CE	G	GS	GS	SS	. . .
Pennsylvania	CE	CE	GS	CE	CE	GS	G	GS	CE	B
Rhode Island	SE	SE	CE	SE	SE	GB	GB	CS	LS	CS
South Carolina	CE	CE	CE	CE	CE	CE	B	CE	BA	CE
South Dakota	CE	CE	CE	CE	CE	GS	GS	GS	L	CG
Tennessee	CE	(o) (y)	CL	CT	CL	G	G (a-16)	G	SL (a-9)	G
Texas	CE	CE	G	CE	CE (a-9)	G	A	SE	L	B
Utah	CE	CE	CE (a-1)	CE	CE	G	GS	GS	CE	GS
Vermont	CE	CE	CE	CE	CE	CL	G	G	CE	G
Virginia	CE	CE	GB	CE	GB	GB	GB	GB	SL	GB
Washington	CE	CE	CE	CE	CE	GS	GS	GS	CE	GS
West Virginia	CE	(o)	CE	CE	CE	GS	GS	CE	CE	GS
Wisconsin	CE	CE	CE	CE	CE	G	GS	GS	LS	A
Wyoming	CE	CE (a-2)	CE	G	CE	G	GS	GS	CE	A
American Samoa	CE	CE	(a-1)	GB	GB	N.A.	GB	GB	N.A.	N.A.
Guam	CE	CE	. . .	CE	CS	GS	GS	GS	N.A.	GS
No. Mariana Islands	CE	CE	. . .	GS	CS	. . .	G	. . .	GB	C
U.S. Virgin Islands	SE	SE	SE (a-1)	GS	GS	GS	GS	GS	N.A.	SE (a-1)

Sources: The Council of State Governments' survey of state personnel agencies, January 2004. Information on auditor selection was provided in part by The National Association of State Auditors, Comptrollers and Treasurers, 2003.

Note: The chief administrative officials responsible for each function were determined from information given by the states for the same function as listed in *State Administrative Officials Classified by Function*, 2003, published by The Council of State Governments.

Key:
N.A.—Not available.
. . .—No specific chief administrative official or agency in charge of function.
CE—Constitutional, elected by public.
CL—Constitutional, elected by legislature.
SE—Statutory, elected by public.
SL—Statutory, elected by legislature.
L—Selected by legislature or one of its organs
CT—Constitutional, elected by state court of last resort.

Appointed by:
G—Governor
GS—Governor
GB—Governor
GE—Governor
GC—Governor
GD—Governor
GLS—Governor
GOC—Governor &
   Council or cabinet
LG—Lieutenant Governor
LGS—Lieutenant Governor
AT—Attorney General
SS—Secretary of State
C—Cabinet Secretary
CG—Cabinet Secretary

Approved by:
Senate (in Nebraska, unicameral legislature)
Both houses
Either house
Council
Departmental board
Appropriate legislative committee & Senate

Senate

Governor

SELECTED STATE ADMINISTRATIVE OFFICIALS: METHODS OF SELECTION — Continued

State or other jurisdiction	Budget	Civil rights	Commerce	Community affairs	Comptroller	Consumer affairs	Corrections	Economic development	Education	Election administration
Alabama	CS	...	G	G	CS	CS	G	G (a-8)	B	CS
Alaska	G	GB	GB	GB	AG	...	GB	AG	GD	AG
Arizona	L	AT	GS	GS (a-7)	A	AT	GS	GS (a-7)	CE	CE (a-2)
Arkansas	A	...	GS	GS	G	A	B	GS	BG	CE (a-2)
California	G	GS	N.A.	GS	CE	G	GS	N.A.	CE	CE
Colorado	G	CS	G	GS	C	CE	GS	G	AB	CS
Connecticut	CS	GE	GE	(d)	CE	N.A.	GE	GE	BG	(d)
Delaware	GS	CG	GS (a-2)	...	CG	AT	GS	GS	A	SS
Florida	G	AB	N.A.	GB	CE (dd)	A	GB	N.A.	CE	A
Georgia	G	G	BG	BG	CE	G	GD	N.A.	CE	A
Hawaii	GS	B	GS	G	GS	A	GS	GS	B	CL
Idaho	GS	GS	GS	A	CE	CE (a-3)	B	A	CE	CE
Illinois	G	GS	GS	GS (a-7)	CE	CE (a-3)	GS	GS (a-7)	B	B
Indiana	G	G	LG	G	CE	AT	G	LG	CE	(k)
Iowa	GS	GS	...	GS	...	A	GS	GS	GS	A
Kansas	G	GS	GS	A	C	AT	GS	(m)	B	(n)
Kentucky	G	B	GC	G	CG	CE (a-3)	G	GC	B	B
Louisiana	A	A	GS	A	GS	AG	GS	GS	BG	CE
Maine	C	BA	G (a-11)	...	C	C	G	G	G	SS
Maryland	GS	G	GS	A	CE	A	AGS	GS	B	B
Massachusetts	CG	G	G	G	G	G	CG	G	B	SS (e)
Michigan	GS	GS	GS	N.A.	CS	N.A.	GS	N.A.	B	(s)
Minnesota	(mm)	GS	GS	GS (a-11)	(mm)	A	GS	GS	GS	CE (a-2)
Mississippi	GS	...	SE	A	GS	A	GS	GS	BS	A (nn)
Missouri	AGS	AGS	GS (a-11)	(d)	A	CE (a-3)	GS	GS	BG	SS
Montana	G	A	GS	(d)	(d)	(d)	GS	G	CE	SS
Nebraska	A	B	GS (a-11)	A	A	CE (a-3)	GS	GS	B	A
Nevada	(a-5)	G	G	A	CE	A	G	GD	B	(z)
New Hampshire	(x)	CS	GC	G	AGC	AGC	GC	AGC	B	CL (a-2)
New Jersey	GS	A	GS	GS	(a-6)	A	GS	G	GS	A
New Mexico	G	G	GS (a-11)	G	...	G	GS	GS	B	G
New York	G	GS	GS	GS (a-2)	CE	GS	GS	GS	A	B
North Carolina	G	A	G	A	G	(d)	G	A	CE	G
North Dakota	A	G	G	CE	(qq)	AT	G	G (a-7)	CE	SS
Ohio	GS	(aa)	AG	AG	SE (a-4)	GC	GS	GS	AB	SS
Oklahoma	A	B	G	(d)	A	B	B	G (a-7)	CE	L
Oregon	A	A	GS	G	A	GS	GS	GS	SE	A
Pennsylvania	G	B	GS	AG	G	AT	GS	GS	GS	C
Rhode Island	AG	B	G (a-11)	CS	CS	SE (a-3)	GB	G	B	F
South Carolina	A	B	GS	N.A.	CE	B	GS	GS (a-7)	CE	B
South Dakota	GS (a-15)	A	GS	GS (a-11)	CE (a-23)	A	GS	GS	GS	SS
Tennessee	A	G	G (a-11)	G (a-11)	SL	A	G	G	G	SS
Texas	G	B	G	G	CE	CE (a-3)	B	G (a-7)	B	(cc)
Utah	G	A	GS	GS	A	A	GS	A	B	A
Vermont	G (a-15)	A	G	G	G (a-15)	A	G	G	G	CE (a-2)
Virginia	B	GB	GB	GB	GB	GB	GB	GB	GB	GB
Washington	GS	B	GS	G	CE (a-4)	AT	GS	GS	CE	A
West Virginia	CS	GS	GS	B	CE (a-31)	AT	GS	B (a-8)	(ee)	CE (a-2)
Wisconsin	A	A	GS	A	A	A	GS	CS	CE	B
Wyoming	A	A	G	A	CE (a-31)	A	GS	G (a-7)	CE	A
American Samoa	GB	N.A.	GB	(a-7)	(a-4)	(a-3)	A	(a-7)	GB	G
Guam	GS	...	GS	...	CS	CS	GS	B	B	GS
No. Mariana Islands	G	A	GS	GS	C	GS	C	C	B	B
U.S. Virgin Islands	GS	GS (a-3)	GS	G	GS (a-15)	GS	GS (a-3)	GS	GS	B

Appointed by:

	Approved by:
A—Agency head	
AB—Agency head	Board
AG—Agency head	Governor
AGC—Agency head	Governor & Council
AGS—Agency head	
ALS—Agency head	Appropriate legislative committee
ASH—Agency head	Senate president & House speaker
B—Board or commission	
BG—Board	Governor
BGS—Board	Governor & Senate
BS—Board or commission	Senate
BA—Board or commission	Agency head
CS—Civil Service	
LS—Legislative Committee	Senate

(a) Chief administrative official or agency in charge of function:
(a-1) Lieutenant Governor
(a-2) Secretary of state
(a-3) Attorney general
(a-4) Treasurer
(a-5) Administration
(a-6) Budget
(a-7) Commerce
(a-8) Community affairs
(a-9) Comptroller
(a-10) Consumer affairs
(a-11) Economic development
(a-12) Education (chief state school officer)
(a-13) Energy
(a-14) Environmental protection
(a-15) Finance

SELECTED STATE ADMINISTRATIVE OFFICIALS: METHODS OF SELECTION — Continued

State or other jurisdiction	Emergency management	Employment services	Energy	Environmental protection	Finance	Fish & wildlife	General services	Health	Higher education	Highways
Alabama	G	CS	CS	B	G	CS	CS	B	B	G (a-29)
Alaska	AG	AG	. . .	GB	AG	GB	. . .	AG	B	GB
Arizona	G	A	. . .	GS	A	B	A	GS	B	A
Arkansas	GS	G	A	BG/BS	G	(d)	A	BG	BG	BS (a-29)
California	GS	GS	G	GS	G	G	GS	GS	B	GS
Colorado	CS	GS	G	CS	CS	AB	GS	GS	GS	GS (a-29)
Connecticut	A	A	A	GE	GB	A	GE	GE	BG	GE (a-29)
Delaware	CG	CG	CG	GS (a-19)	GS	CG	GS (a-5)	CG	B	GS (a-29)
Florida	A	A	A	GB	CE (dd)	GB	GB	A	N.A.	GB
Georgia	G	A	G	B	G	A	A	A	B	B (a-29)
Hawaii	A	CS	CS	G	GS (a-6)	CS	GS (a-25)	GS	GS	CS
Idaho	A	GS	A	GS	GS	B	. . .	GS	B	B (a-29)
Illinois	GS	GS	GS (a-7)	GS	G (a-6)	GS (a-19)	GS (a-5)	GS	B	GS (a-29)
Indiana	G	G	LG	G	G (a-6)	A	G (a-5)	G	G	G (a-29)
Iowa	GS	GS	GS	A	A	A	A	GS	BGS	A
Kansas	CS	GS	B	C	. . .	CS	GS	C	B	GS (a-29)
Kentucky	AG	AG	AG	G	G	B	CG (a-5)	CG	B	AG
Louisiana	A	A	GS	GS	GS	GS	GS	GS	B	GS (a-29)
Maine	C	N.A.	G	G	G (a-5)	G	C	G	B	G (a-29)
Maryland	AG	A	G	GS	GS	A	GS	GS	G	AG
Massachusetts	C	CG	CG	CG	G (a-5)	CG	G (a-5)	CG	B	G
Michigan	CS	GS	. . .	GS	GS (a-6)	GS	N.A.	GS	CS	GS (a-29)
Minnesota	N.A.	A	A	A	GS	A (r)	GS (a-5)	GS	A	CE (u)
Mississippi	GS	BS	A	GS	GS	GS	N.A.	BS	BS	B (a-29)
Missouri	A	A	. . .	A	AGS	(w)	A	GS	B	B (a-29)
Montana	(d)	GS	G	GS	(d)	GS	(d)	GS	(d)	GS (a-29)
Nebraska	A	A	A	GS	(ff)	(gg)	A	GS	B	GS (a-29)
Nevada	A	A	A	A	. . .	A	A	AG	B	. . .
New Hampshire	G	GC	G	GC	GC (a-5)	BGC	GC	AGC	B	GC (a-29)
New Jersey	GS	A	A	GS	A	B	(oo)	GS	B	A
New Mexico	G	GS (a-18)	GS	GS	GS	G	GS	GS	B	GS (a-29)
New York	G	GS (a-18)	B	GS	CE (a-9)	GS	G	GS	B (a-12)	GS (a-29)
North Carolina	G	G	A	G	G (a-6)	G	G (a-5)	G	B	A
North Dakota	A	G	. . .	A	(qq)	G	G	G	B	G (a-29)
Ohio	AG	GS	AG	GS	GS(a-6)	AG	AG	GS	B	GS (a-29)
Oklahoma	GS	B	GS	B	GS	B	GS (a-5)	(d)	(d)	B (a-29)
Oregon	AG	GS	G	B	CE (a-4)	B	GS (a-5)	A	B	A
Pennsylvania	G	AG	AG	AG	G	B	GS	GS	AG	AG
Rhode Island	G	G	CS	GB	AG (a-6)	GB (bb)	GB	GB	B	GB (a-29)
South Carolina	A	B	A	B	B	B	A	GS	B	B (a-29)
South Dakota	CG	CG	A	GS	GS	CG	GS (a-5)	GS	B	GS (a-29)
Tennessee	A	G	A	G	G	B	G	G	B	G (a-29)
Texas	A	B	B	B	CE (a-9)	B	B	BG	B	B (a-29)
Utah	A	GS	A	GS	A	A	A	GS	B	GS (a-29)
Vermont	A	G	G	G	G	G	G	G	N.A.	G (a-29)
Virginia	GB	GB	GB	GB	GB	B	GB	GB	B	GB
Washington	A	A	A	GS	GS	B	GS (a-5)	GS	B	B (a-29)
West Virginia	GS	GS	GS	GS (a-13)	GS (a-5)	CS	C	GS	B	GS (a-29)
Wisconsin	A	A	A	A	A	A	GS (a-5)	A	N.A.	A
Wyoming	A	GS	A	GS	CE (a-31)	GS	GS (a-5)	GS	B	GS (a-29)
American Samoa	G	A	GB	GB	(a-4)	GB	G	GB	(a-12)	GB (a-29)
Guam	GS	GS	G	GS	GS	GS	CS	GS	B	GS
No. Mariana Islands	G	C	C	G	GS	C	GS	GS	B	C
U.S. Virgin Islands	GS	GS (a-18)	GS	GS	GS (a-4)	GS (a-14)	GS (a-5)	GS	GS	GS

(a-16) General services
(a-17) Highways
(a-18) Labor
(a-19) Natural Resources
(a-20) Parks and recreation
(a-21) Personnel
(a-22) Post-audit
(a-23) Pre-audit
(a-24) Public utility regulation
(a-25) Purchasing
(a-26) Revenue
(a-27) Social services
(a-28) Tourism
(a-29) Transportation
(a-30) Welfare
(a-31) Auditor

(b) Responsibilities shared between Commissioner of Mental Health (GE) and Commissioner of Retardation (GE).

(c) Responsibilities shared between Section Manager—Central Account Service Manager (A) and Team Leader Audit Services (CS).

(d) Method not specified.

(e) The Director of Elections (SS) post is vacant, Secretary of State William Galvin (CE) is acting director.

(f) Responsibilities shared between Director, Division of Substance Abuse and Mental Health (CG); and Director , Division of Developmental Disabilities Services (CG).

(g) Responsibilities shared between Secretary of Health and Social Services (GS) ; and Secretary, Department of Services for Children, Youth and their families (GS).

(h) Responsibilities shared between Director, Division of Licensing, Department of State (SS); and Secretary, Department of Professional Regulation (N.A.).

SELECTED STATE ADMINISTRATIVE OFFICIALS: METHODS OF SELECTION — Continued

State or other jurisdiction	Information systems	Insurance	Labor	Licensing	Mental health & retardation	Natural resources	Parks & recreation	Personnel	Planning	Post audit
Alabama	G	G	G	...	G	G	CS	B	G (a-8)	LS
Alaska	AG	AG	GB	AG	AG	GB	AG	AG	...	B
Arizona	A	GS	B	...	A	GS	B	A	L (a-6)	(d)
Arkansas	GS	GS	GS	...	A	A	GS	A	...	L
California	GS	CE	GS	G	GS	GS	GS	GS	G	(d)
Colorado	G	GS	GS	GS	GS	GS	C	GS	G	L
Connecticut	GE	GE	GE	A	GE (b)	A	A	A	A	N.A.
Delaware	GS	CE	GS	CG	CG (f)	GS	CG	GS	CG	CE (a-31)
Florida	A	CE	BGC	(h)	A	(a-14)	A	A	G	GOC
Georgia	CE	CE	CE	A	A	B	A	GS	G	(i)
Hawaii	CS	AG	GS	GS (a-7)	CS	GS	CS	GS	CS	(j)
Idaho	GS (a-5)	GS	GS	A	N.A.	GS	B	GS	GS	CE (a-9)
Illinois	GS (a-5)	GS	GS	GS	GS (a-27)	GS	GS (a-19)	GS (a-5)	...	SL
Indiana	A	G	G	(l)	A	G	A	G	...	G
Iowa	A	GS	GS	A	A	GS	A	A	...	CE
Kansas	C	SE	GS	B	C	GS	CS	C	BG	L
Kentucky	AG	G	G	AG	CG	G	G	G	G	CE
Louisiana	A	CE	GS	A	GS	GS	LGS	B	A	CL
Maine	C	G	G	C	G	G	C	C	G	CL
Maryland	A	GS	GS	A	A (p)	GS	A	A	GS	N.A.
Massachusetts	C	G	G	G	CG (q)	CG	C	CG	...	G
Michigan	CS	GS	GS (a-7)	CS	(t)	GS	CS	CS	...	CL
Minnesota	A	GS (a-7)	GS	A	GS (a-27)	GS	A	GS	N.A	CE (a-31)
Mississippi	BS	SE	...	...	B	GS (a-14)	GS	B	A	CE (a-31)
Missouri	A	GS	GS	A	A	GS	A	G	N.A	CE (a-31)
Montana	A	CE (a-31)	GS	A	A (ii)	GS	A	A	G (a-6)	L
Nebraska	A	GS	GS	A	A	GS	B	A	GS	CE (a-31)
Nevada	G	A	G	...	GD	G	G	...	...	ALS
New Hampshire	GC (a-5)	GC	GC	...	AGC	GC	AGC	AGC	G	AGC (a-9)
New Jersey	A	GS	GS	A	A (pp)	A	A	GS	A	L (a-31)
New Mexico	G	G	GS	G	G	GS	G	G	...	CE (a-31)
New York	G	GS	GS	(jj)	(kk)	GS (a-14)	GS	GS	GS (a-11)	CE (a-9)
North Carolina	G	CE	CE	...	A	G	A	G	G	CE (a-31)
North Dakota	G	CE	G	CE (a-2)	A	A	G	A	...	...
Ohio	A	G	A	AG	GS	GS	AG	AG	GS (a-6)	SE
Oklahoma	A	CE	CE	...	B	B (a-28)	B (a-28)	GS	...	...
Oregon	A	GS	SE	GS	AG	GOC	B	A	...	SS
Pennsylvania	G	GS	GS	G	AG	GS	A	G	G	CE (a-31)
Rhode Island	CS	CS	AGS	CS	GB	GB (a-14)	CS	CS	CS	CS
South Carolina	A	GS	GS	GS (a-18)	B (rr)	B	GS	A	AB	B (ss)
South Dakota	GS	GS	GS	CG	GS	GS	CG	GS	(a-15)	L
Tennessee	A	G	G	A	G	G	A	G	A	SL (a-9)
Texas	B	G	B	B	B	B	B	A	G (a-6)	L
Utah	A	GS	A	AG	AB	GS	AG	GS	G	CE (a-31)
Vermont	G	G	G	A	G	G	G	G	...	CE
Virginia	GB	SL	GB	GB	GB	GB	GB	GB	B (a-6)	SL (a-31)
Washington	GS	CE	GS	GS	A	CE	B	GS	GS (a-15)	CE
West Virginia	C	GS	GS	...	GS	GS	GS	C	GS (a-5)	LS
Wisconsin	A	GS	GS	GS	A	GS	A	GS	(a-6)	CE (a-31)
Wyoming	A	G	A	GS	A	G	A	A	G	...
American Samoa	(a-29)	G	N.A.	N.A.	(a-27)	AG	GB	A	(a-7)	G
Guam	GS	GS	GS	GS	GS (tt)	GS	GS	GS	GS	CE
No. Mariana Islands	C	CS	C	B	C	GS	C	GS	G	GS
U.S. Virgin Islands	G	SE (a-1)	GS	GS (a-10)	GS	GS (a-14)	GS	GS	G	G

(i) The State Auditor is appointed by the House and approved by the Senate.

(j) Responsibilities shared between State Auditor (CL); and Division Head, Division of Audit (CS).

(k) Responsibilities shared between Co-Directors in Election Commission (G); appointed by the Governor, subject to approval by the Chairs of the State Republican/Democratic parties.

(l) Responsibilities shared between Executive Director, Health Professions Bureau; and Executive Director, Professional Licensing Agency (G).

(m) Responsibilities shared between Lieutenant Governor (CE), Director Business Development Division (C) and President Kansas Inc.(BG).

(n) Responsibilities shared between Secretary of the State (CE); and Deputy Assistant for Elections (SS).

(o) In Maine, New Hampshire, New Jersey, Tennessee and West Virginia, the Presidents (or Speakers) of the Senate are next in line of succession to the Governorship. In Tennessee, the Speaker of the Senate bears the statutory title of Lieutenant Governor.

(p) Responsibilities shared between Director, Mental Hygiene Administration (A); and Director, Developmental Disabilities Administration, Department of Health and Mental Hygiene (A).

(q) Responsibilities shared between Commissioner, Department of Mental Retardation (CG); and Commissioner, Department of Mental Health, Executive Office of Human Services (CG).

(r) Responsibilities shared between Director of Fisheries, Department of Natural Resources (A) and Director of Wildlife, Department of Natural Resources.

(s) Responsibilities shared between Secretary of State (CE); and Director, Bureau of Elections (CS).

(t) Responsibilities shared between Director, Department of Community Health (CS); and Deputy Director, Mental Health and Substance Abuse (CS), same department.

(u) The Lieutenant Governor currently serves as the agency head of the Department of Transportation.

SELECTED STATE ADMINISTRATIVE OFFICIALS: METHODS OF SELECTION — Continued

State or other jurisdiction	Pre-audit	Public library development	Public utility regulation	Purchasing	Revenue	Social services	Solid waste management	State police	Tourism	Transportation	Welfare
Alabama	CS (a-9)	B	SE	CS	G	B	CS	G	G	G (a-17)	B (a-27)
Alaska	. . .	AG	GB	AG	GB	GB	CS	AG	AG	GB	AG
Arizona	A (a-9)	B	B	A	GS	A	A	GS	GS	GS	A
Arkansas	A	B	A	A	A	GS	A	G	GS	BS (1-17)	GS
California	CE (a-9)	GS	GS	GS	BS	GS	G	GS	G	GS	GS
Colorado	C (a-9)	A	CS	CS	GS	GS	CS	CS	CS	GS (a-17)	CS
Connecticut	CE (a-9)	A	GB	CS	GE	GE	CS	GE	A	GE (a-17)	GE
Delaware	CE (a-31)	CG	CG	CG	CG	GS (g)	B	CG	CG	GS (a-17)	CG
Florida	(a-26)	SS	L	A	GOC	N.A.	A	A	A	A	A
Georgia	(i)	AB	CE	A	G	GD	A	B	A	B (a-17)	A
Hawaii	CS	B	GS	GS	GS	GS	CS	. . .	GS (a-11)	GS	CS
Idaho	CE (a-9)	A	GS	A	GS	CE	. . .	GS	A	B (a-17)	A
Illinois	CE (a-9)	SS	GS	GS (a-5)	GS	GS	GS (a-14)	GS	GS (a-7)	GS (a-17)	GS
Indiana	CE	G	G	A	G	N.A.	A	G	LG	G (a-17)	A
Iowa	A	A	GS	A	GS	GS	A	A	A	GS	A
Kansas	(c)	GS	GS	C	GS	GS	C	GS	A	GS (a-17)	C
Kentucky	G (a-15)	G	G	CG (a-5)	G	CG	A	CG	G (a-7)	G	CG
Louisiana	A	BGS	BS	A	GS	GS	GS	GS	LGS	GS (a-17)	GS
Maine	C	B	G	CS	C	G	CS	G	C	G (a-17)	C
Maryland	A	A	GS	A	A	GS	A	GS	A	GS	GS (a-27)
Massachusetts	G (a-9)	B	G	CG	CG	CG	CG	CG	CG	G	CG
Michigan	CL	CL	GS	CS	CS	GS	CS	GS	(d)	GS (a-17)	GS (a-27)
Minnesota	CE (a-31)	N.A.	G (v)	A	GS	GS	GS	A	A	CE (u)	GS (a-27)
Mississippi	CE (a-31)	B	GS	A	GS	GS	A	GS	A	B (a-17)	GS
Missouri	A	B	GS	A	GS	GS	A	GS	A	B (a-17)	A
Montana	. . .	B	CE	A	GS	GS	GS	A	A	GS (a-17)	GS
Nebraska	A	B	B	A	GS	GS	A	GS	A	GS (a-17)	GS
Nevada	. . .	G	G	A	G	G	. . .	A	GD	BG	AG
New Hampshire	AGC (a-9)	AGC	GC	CS	GC	GC	AGC	AGC	AGC	GC (a-17)	AGC
New Jersey	. . .	. . .	GS	GS	A	GS	A	GS	A	GS	A
New Mexico	G	G	CE	G	GS	. . .	. . .	GS	GS	GS (a-17)	GS
New York	CE (a-9)	B (a-12)	GS	G (a-16)	GS	GS	GS (a-14)	G	GS (a-11)	GS (a-17)	GS (a-27)
North Carolina	CE (a-31)	A	G	A	G	A	A	A	A	G	A
North Dakota	A	A	CE	A	CE	G	A	G	G	G (a-17)	G
Ohio	SE (a-22)	B	GS	AG	GS	G	CS	GS	AG	GS (a-17)	GS
Oklahoma	A (a-9)	B	(hh)	A	GS	GS	A	GS	B	B (a-17)	GS
Oregon	A (a-6)	B	GS	A	GS	GS	B	GS	A	GS	GS
Pennsylvania	CE (a-4)	A	GS	A	GS	AG	A	GS	A	GS	GS
Rhode Island	CS (a-9)	G	(ll)	CS	CS	CS	CS	GB	A	GB (a-17)	CS
South Carolina	CE (a-9)	B	B	A	GS	GS	A	GS	A	B (a-17)	GS
South Dakota	CE	CG	CE	CG	GS	G	CG	CG	GS	GS (a-17)	GS (a-27)
Tennessee	A	A	SE	A	G	G	A	G	G	G (a-17)	G
Texas	CE (a-9)	A	B	B	CE (a-9)	G	N.A.	B	A	B (a-17)	G
Utah	A	A	A	A	BS	GS	A	A	A	GS (a-17)	GS
Vermont	G (a-15)	G	G	A	G	G	A	A	G	G (a-17)	G
Virginia	GB (a-9)	GB	SL	GB (a-16)	GB	GB	GB (a-14)	GB	CS	GB	GB (a-27)
Washington	CE (a-4)	B	GS	A	GS	GS	A	GS	A	B (a-17)	GS (a-27)
West Virginia	GS (a-5)	B	GS	CS	GS	C	B	GS	GS	GS (a-17)	GS
Wisconsin	A	A	GS	A	GS	A	A	A	GS	GS	A
Wyoming	CE (a-31)	A	G	A	GS	GS	A	A	A	GS (a-17)	GS
American Samoa	(a-4)	(a-12)	N.A.	A	(a-4)	GB	GB	GB	(a-7)	GB (a-17)	N.A.
Guam	GS	(d)	(uu)	GS	GS	GS	GS	GS	B	GS	GS
No. Mariana Islands	G	B	B	C	C	C	A	GS	GB	CS	A
U.S. Virgin Islands	GS (a-4)	GS	G	GS (a-5)	GS	G	GS	GS	GS (a-7)	GS (a-5)	GS

(v) Responsibilities shared between the five Public Utility Commissioners (G).

(w) Responsibilities shared between Administrator, Division of Fisheries, Department of Conservation; Administrator, Division of Wildlife, same department (AB).

(x) Responsibilities shared between Commissioner, Department of Administration Services (GC); and Assistant Commissioner & Budget Office, Budget Office same department (AGC).

(y) Elected to the Senate by the public and elected Lieutenant Governor by the Senate (CL).

(z) Responsibilities shared between Secretary of State (CE); Deputy Secretary of State for Elections, Office of Secretary of State (SS); and Chief Deputy Secretary of State, same office (A).

(aa) Responsibilities shares between Chair, Ohio Civil Rights Commission (GS) and Acting Executive Director, same commission.

(bb) Responsibilities shared Director Jan Reitsma (GB) and Chief John

Stolgitis(CS).

(cc) Responsibilities shared between Secretary of State (G); and Division Director of Elections, Elections Division, Secretary of State (A).

(dd) Effective Jan. 1, 2003 the positions of Commissioner & Treasurer and Comptroller will merge into one Chief Financial Officer.

(ee) Responsibilities shared between Cabinet Secretary, Department of Education and the Arts (GS); and State School Superintendent, Department of Education (B).

(ff) Responsibilities shared between State Tax Commissioner, Department of Revenue (GS); Administrator, Budget Division (A) and the Auditor of Public Accounts (CE).

(gg) Responsibilities shared between Director, Game and Parks Commission (B), Division Administrator, Wildlife Division, Game & Parks Commission (A) and Assistant Director of Fish and Wildlife (A).

(hh) Responsibilities shared between Director, Public Utility Division,

SELECTED STATE ADMINISTRATIVE OFFICIALS: METHODS OF SELECTION — Continued

Corporation Commission (A); and 3 Commissioners, Corporation Commission (CE).

(ii) Responsibilities shared two administrators (A)

(jj) Responsibilities shared between Secretary of State (GS) and Commissioner of State Education Department (B).

(kk) Responsibilities shared between Commissioner, Office of Mental Health, and Commissioner, Office of Mental Retardation and Developmental Disabilities, both (GS).

(ll) Responsibilities shared between Administrator Thomas Ahearn (G) and Chairman Elia Germani (B).

(mm) Effective January 6, 2003 the offices of State Treasurer, State Budget Director and Commerce will be abolished and the duties will be transferred to the Commissioner of Finance, (GS), in the Department of Finance.

(nn) Responsibilities shared between the Assistant Secretary of State (A) and the Senior Counsel for Elections (A).

(oo) Responsibilities shared between Director, Division of Purchasing, Dept. of Treasury (GS), and Director, Division of Property and Management, Dept. of the Treasury (A).

(pp) Responsibilities shared between Director, Division of Mental Health Services, Dept of Human Services (A) and Director, Division of Developmental Disabilities, Dept. of Human Services (A).

(qq) Responsibilities shared between Director of Fiscal Management (A) and Director of Management and Budget (G).

(rr) Responsibilities shared between Director Stan Butkus (B) and State Director George Gintoli (B).

(ss) Responsibilities shared between Director George Schroeder (B) and State Auditor Thomas Wagner (B).

(tt) Responsibilities shared between Director, Mental Health and Substance Abuse (GS) and Director, Department of Integrated Services for Individuals with Disabilities (GS).

(uu) Responsibilities shared between Public Utility Regulation (GS) and Chair, Consolidated Commission on Utilities (GS).

Table 4.11
SELECTED STATE ADMINISTRATIVE OFFICIALS: ANNUAL SALARIES BY REGION

State or other jurisdiction	Governor	Lieutenant governor	Secretary of state	Attorney general	Treasurer	Adjutant general	Administration	Agriculture	Auditor	Banking
Eastern Region										
Connecticut	$150,000	$110,000	$110,000	$110,000	$110,000	$140,272	N.A.	$110,913	(mm)	$110,914
Delaware (h)	114,000	62,400	106,000	116,700	94,000	91,800	98,800	98,800	89,900	95,700
Maine	70,000	(s)	N.A.	78,062	71,032	91,208	91,208	87,692	84,302	85,758
Massachusetts	135,000 (jj)	120,000 (jj)	120,000	122,500	120,000	N.A.	118,000	92,104	120,000	107,053
New Hampshire	100,690	(s)	65,540	85,753	76,603	81,191	85,753	64,036	89,250	81,191
New Jersey	157,000	(s)	137,165	137,165	137,165	137,165	N.A.	137,165	120,000	137,165
New York	179,000	151,500	120,800	151,500	97,000	120,800	120,800	120,800	151,500	127,000
Pennsylvania	144,416	121,309	103,980	120,154	120,154	103,980	125,000	103,980	120,154	103,980
Rhode Island	105,194	88,584	88,584	94,121	88,584	85,067	110,321	54,864	137,418	77,867
Vermont	127,456	54,080	80,808	96,752	80,808	74,901	113,901	96,574	80,808	85,010
Regional average	128,276	101,125	103,653	111,271	99,535	102,932	107,973	96,695	112,924	101,164
Midwest Region										
Illinois	150,691	115,235	132,963	132,963	115,235	98,135	120,861	113,114	112,533	115,601
Indiana	95,000	76,000	66,000	79,400	66,000	98,046	89,962	74,431	83,070	87,126
Iowa	107,482	76,698	87,990	105,430	87,990	98,411	117,458	87,990	87,990	80,000
Kansas	98,331	111,523	76,389	76,389	76,389	91,232	91,350	91,362	96,804	80,185
Michigan	177,000	123,900	124,900	124,900	167,504	123,204	124,848	124,848	135,500	114,444
Minnesota	120,311	78,196	90,222	114,297	108,388 (v)	108,388	108,388	108,388	102,249	103,627
Nebraska	85,000	60,000	65,000	75,000	60,000	79,649	85,141	87,340	60,000	83,659
North Dakota	85,506	66,380	68,108	74,668	64,236	1,203,000	. . .	69,874	68,108	64,260
Ohio	126,485	73,715 (b)	90,725	93,434	93,434	101,670	73,715 (b)	66,851 (b)	97,501	54,974 (b)
South Dakota	95,389	12,635 (ee)	64,812	80,995	64,813	92,248	89,918	89,918	76,787	84,302
Wisconsin	122,406	69,579	62,549	127,868	62,549	92,000	122,000	100,800	105,229	123,451
Regional average	114,873	78,533	84,514	98,668	87,867	198,726	102,364	92,265	93,252	90,148
Southern Region										
Alabama	96,361	45,360	71,500	163,429	71,500	76,336	76,336	71,003	71,500	132,000
Arkansas	75,296	36,392	47,060	62,746	47,060	91,097	121,491	80,090	47,060	108,363
Florida	120,171	115,112	116,056	118,957	118,957	112,594	113,877	119,415	129,240	118,957
Georgia	127,303	83,148	112,776	125,871	117,893	123,069	117,892	110,247	125,000	117,893
Kentucky	125,130	91,075	91,075	91,075	91,075	125,000	109,907	91,075	91,075	N.A.
Louisiana	94,532	85,000	85,000	85,000	85,000	129,130	171,724	85,000	114,518	85,400
Maryland	135,000	112,500	78,750	112,500	112,500	85,594 (b)	99,379 (b)	99,379 (b)	119,128	63,020 (b)
Mississippi	122,160	60,000	90,000	108,960	90,000	88,000	93,500	90,000	90,000	98,175
Missouri	120,087	77,184	96,455	104,332	96,455	80,472	111,156	95,846	96,455	N.A.
North Carolina	118,430	104,523	104,523	104,523	104,523	87,944	102,119	104,523	104,523	104,523
Oklahoma	110,298	85,500	90,000	103,109	87,875	109,162	. . .	76,000	87,876	110,000
South Carolina	106,078	46,545	92,007	92,007	92,007	92,007	148,000	92,007	101,794	(a-4)
Tennessee	85,000	49,500 (s)	131,124	121,728	131124	92268	131124	92376	131124	92376
Texas	115,345	97,200	117,546	92,217	(a-9)	94,832	115,000	92,217	96,200	118,427
Virginia	124,855	36,321	131,370	110,667	115,188	100,277	131,370	92,359	137,487	130,158
West Virginia	90,000	(s)	65,000	80,000	70,000	75,000	75,000	70,000	82,000	60,000
Regional average	110,378	75,024	95,013	104,820	92,817	98,034	116,186	91,277	99,590	102,015
Western Region										
Alaska	85,776	80,040	(a-1)	91,200	91,200	91,200	91,200	81,774	87,800	N.A.
Arizona	95,000	(a-2)	70,000	90,000	70,000	70,000	101,450	149,000	95,000	101,450
California	175,000	131,250	123,750	148,750	140,000	146,785	123,255	131,412	131,412	123,255
Colorado	90,000	68,500	68,500	80,000	68,500	121,200	121,200	121,200	120,850	95,796
Hawaii	94,780	90,041	(a-1)	85,302	(a-6)	159,600	(a-9)	85,302	85,302	74,655
Idaho	98,500	26,750	82,500	91,500	82,500	102,440	82,098	85,072	. . .	84,178
Montana	93,089	66,724	72,085	81,919	83,932	77,563	(a-4)	83,932	72,285	71,143
Nevada	117,000	50,000	80,000	110,000	80,000	91,304	107,433	82,451	94,182	80,499
New Mexico	110,000	85,000	85,000	95,000	85,000	886,000	(a-16)	115,000	85,000	75,733
Oregon	93,600	(a-2)	72,000	77,200	72,000	101,844	123,756	101,844	102,000	N.A.
Utah	100,600	78,200	(a-1)	84,600	78,200	86,736	99,702	86,736	80,700	86,736
Washington	139,087	72,705	89,004	126,443	97,446	112,594	106,130	106,130	99,708	106,130
Wyoming	130,000	(a-2)	110,000	89,067	77,000	87,719	84,067	73,568	77,000	64,800
Regional Average	109,418	77,016	84,702	96,229	85,468	166,649	103,502	96,109	95,641	87,670
Regional Average without California	103,953	72,497	81,448	91,853	80,923	168,304	101,856	93,167	92,389	84,112
Guam	90,000	85,000	. . .	90,000	58,199	68,152	74,096	60,850	82,025	74,096
No. Mariana Islands	70,000	65,000	. . .	80,000	40,800 (b)	. . .	54,000	40,800 (b)	80000	40,800 (b)
U.S. Virgin Islands	80,000	75,000	(a-1)	85,000	65,000	65,000	65,000	65,000	65,000	(a-1)

Sources: The Council of State Governments' survey of state personnel agencies, January 2004 and January 2003. The National Association of State Auditors, Comptrollers and Treasurers, 2003, provided some auditor information.

Note: The chief administrative officials responsible for each function are determined from information given by the states for the same function as listed in State Administrative Officials Classified by Function, 2002, published by The Council of State Governments.

Key:
N.A. — Not available.
. . . — No specific chief administrative official or agency in charge of function.
(a) Chief administrative official or agency in charge of function:
(a-1) Lieutenant governor.
(a-2) Secretary of state.
(a-3) Attorney general.

SELECTED OFFICIALS: ANNUAL SALARIES — Continued

State or other jurisdiction	Budget	Civil rights	Commerce	Community affairs	Comptroller	Consumer affairs	Corrections	Economic development	Education	Election administration
Eastern Region										
Connecticut	$136,624	$94,828	$83,298	$178,001	$110,000	N.A.	$140,272	$123,961	$98,872	$106,950
Delaware (h)	113,400	63,200	(a-2)	...	113,400	92,696	113,400	106,000	133,600	69,100
Maine	80,267	61,672	(a-11)	N.A.	80,267	75,171	91,208	91,208	91,208	67,330
Massachusetts	93,024	84,893	(a-11)	108,000	122,367	108,000	122,366	108,000	164,767	(a-2)
New Hampshire	85,753	54,932	85,753	69,322	67,473	67,473	83,477	64,036	85,753	(a-2)
New Jersey	120,000	107,391	137,165	137,165	(a-6)	110,000	137,165	150,000	137,165	105,365
New York	161,949	109,800	120,800	(a-2)	151,500	101,600	136,000	120,800	170,165	109,800
Pennsylvania	134,000	107,541	109,756	85,379	123,032	91,619	115,533	109,756	115,533	64,763
Rhode Island	106,679	N.A.	N.A.	N.A.	95,874	(a-3)	118,914	N.A.	135,516	N.A.
Vermont	(a-15)	76,898	90,002	70,013	(a-15)	76,898	87,006	75,005	108,000	(a-2)
Regional average	110,870	84,573	103,554	109,811	106,092	90,842	114,534	105,418	124,058	87,740
Midwest Region										
Illinois	126,240	98,135	120,861	(a-7)	115,235	(a-3)	127,576	(a-7)	225,000	115,128
Indiana	93,561	69,147	79,950	77,083	(a-23)	70,000	96,193	73,125	79,400	(m)
Iowa	126,175	73,549	N.A.	78,187	79,590	70,410	105,000	126,125	126,175	67,517
Kansas	86,528	39,354	(a-1)	64,349	79,590	70,410	93,887	(o)	137,280	(p)
Michigan	130,050	N.A.	121,500	N.A.	104,199	N.A.	130,050	...	159,885	(e)
Minnesota	108,388 (v)	108,388	108,388	(a-11)	108,388 (v)	76,943	108,388	108,388	108,388	(a-2)
Nebraska	100,697	86,558	90,000	68,707	93,009	(a-3)	98,677	90,000	127,271	60,910
North Dakota	66,912	61,812	117,312	69,874	(kk)	71,340	76,404	(a-7)	77,436	26,460
Ohio	73,715 (b)	60,611 (b)	73,715 (b)	82,326	(a-4)	124,779	73,715 (b)	(b)	190,008	45,198 (b)
South Dakota	(a-15)	N.A.	84,760	(a-11)	(a-23)	44,643	81,619	77,250	92,248	51,188
Wisconsin	91,417	83,000	101,899	N.A.	96,025	97,992	107,664	73,441	107,432	99,777
Regional average	100,012	75,617	100,991	83,003	90,569	86,211	99,925	91,322	130,048	71,797
Southern Region										
Alabama	144,979	...	130,000	76,336	118,921	110,404	95,000	(a-8)	170,754	53,775
Arkansas	99,919	...	(a-11)	(a-27)	121,491	80,767	116,897	108,798	119,768	(ll)
Florida	119,982	104,553	...	112,797	118,957	80,000	110,639	(a-28)	118,957	88,000
Georgia	120,000	N.A.	141,755	135,000	N.A.	102,648	N.A.	(a-7)	112,777	81,000
Kentucky	125,000	99,446	125,000	110,000	94,533	(a-3)	91,660	162,270	191,075	N.A.
Louisiana	113,484	65,707	(a-11)	N.A.	(a-5)	78,000	102,003	135,200	180,000	N.A.
Maryland	115,456 (b)	79,458 (b)	115,456 (b)	79,458 (b)	112,500	71,952 (b)	85,594 (b)	115,456 (b)	135,000	73,777 (b)
Mississippi	93,500	...	90,000	58,151	93,500	70,000	93,500	152,700	234,000	(q)
Missouri	90,840	67,068	95,832	75,903	85,164	(a-3)	95,844	95,832	147,924	57,888
North Carolina	(a-15)	58,501	102,119	80,916	130,078	N.A.	102,119	86,285	104,523	90,626
Oklahoma	90,000	59,220	105,660	N.A.	77,000	56,316	110,000	N.A.	95,898	73,957
South Carolina	105,168	85,000	(c)	N.A.	92,007	N.A.	124,698	(a-7)(c)	92,007	78,000
Tennessee	94728	74,028	98,316	(a-11)	131,124	62,004	92,376	98,316	98,316	N.A.
Texas	100,000	56,958	112,352	112,352	92,217	(a-3)	150,000	(a-7)	164,748	(ff)
Virginia	119,609	80,982	131,370	101,813	107,251	92,359	126,666	118,726	146,535	74,131
West Virginia	72,396	45,000	70,000	175,000	70,000	75,756	75,000	(a-8)	110,500 (gg)	65,000
Regional average	108,785	72,993	104,124	101,337	108,052	82,739	104,800	122,212	138,924	73,798
Western Region										
Alaska	105,732	98,124	91,200	91,200	97,128	...	91,200	87,852	91,200	73,752
Arizona	99,000	106,270	122,000	(a-7)	89,170	106,270	130,000	(a-7)	85,000	(a-2)
California	131,412	108,753	N.A.	108,753	140,000	123,255	131,412	N.A.	148,750	131,250
Colorado	121,200	99,036	121,200	121,200	112,968	80,000	121,200	121,200	162,000	85,908
Hawaii	(a-9)	86,041	85,302	77,966	85,302	N.A.	85,302	85,302	150,000	77,966
Idaho	(a-15)	64,438	N.A.	56,971	82,500	(a-3)	89,960	63,918	82,500	82,500
Montana	80,704	52,039	83,932	65,577	68,839	50,232	83,932	98,800	80,425	44,701
Nevada	(a-5)	70,725	107,433	70,700	80,000	73,000	107,433	94,893	107,433	(oo)
New Mexico	82,998	71,999	89,999	71,999	...	72,001	89,999	89,999	120,001	57,628
Oregon	117,840	72,576	112,272	101,844	101,844	112,272	N.A.	112,272	72,000	101,844
Utah	101,769	68,612	86,736	93,542	(a-15)	78,571	101,769	93,542	138,361	44,454
Washington	81,723	82,512	106,130	106,128	(a-4)	119,700	106,130	106,130	99,462	84,972
Wyoming	71,294	54,746	130,000	130,000	77,000	60,267	81,567	130,000	77,000	51,920
Regional average	97,737	79,682	103,291	93,683	92,053	87,915	101,659	100,492	108,779	76,030
Regional average without California	94,931	77,260	103,291	92,427	87,694	84,381	98,954	100,492	105,449	71,248
Guam	88,915	...	75,208	...	68,152	46,596	67,150	82,025	98,430	61,939
No. Mariana Islands	54,000	49,000	52,000	52,000	40,800 (b)	52,000	40,800 (b)	45,000	80,000	53,000
U.S. Virgin Islands	65,000	(a-3)	65,000	(hh)	(a-4)	65,000	(a-3)	85,000	65,000	55,000

(a-4) Treasurer.
(a-5) Administration.
(a-6) Budget.
(a-7) Commerce.
(a-8) Community affairs.
(a-9) Comptroller.
(a-10) Consumer affairs.
(a-11) Economic development.

(a-12) Education (chief state school officer).
(a-13) Energy.
(a-14) Environmental protection.
(a-15) Finance.
(a-16) General services.
(a-17) Highways.
(a-18) Labor.
(a-19) Natural resources.

SELECTED OFFICIALS: ANNUAL SALARIES — Continued

State or other jurisdiction	Emergency management	Employment services	Energy	Environmental protection	Finance	Fish & wildlife	General services	Health	Higher education	Highway
Eastern Region										
Connecticut	$89,249	$110,917	$100,000	$123,961	$178,001	$102,544	$140,272	$123,961	$140,000	$140,272
Delaware (h)	69,800	81,800	47,870	(a-19)	113,400	84,200	(a-5)	141,600	71,900	(a-29)
Maine	64,667	N.A.	80,267	91,208	(a-5)	91,208	80,267	91,208	N.A.	(a-29)
Massachusetts	82,156	96,125	92,806	110,496	(a-5)	98,334	(a-5)	116,811	180,000	102,080
New Hampshire	66,837	76,603	58,483	83,477	(a-5)	64,036	85,753	76,603	54,886	(a-29)
New Jersey	120,000	113,000	90,000	137,165	106,742	95,000	(pp)	137,165	121,900	113,000
New York	117,549	(a-18)	120,800	136,000	(a-9)	136,000	136,000	136,000	(a-12)	(a-29)
Pennsylvania	115,000	105,000	102,944	102,690	134,000	107,541	109,756	115,533	87,355	118,300
Rhode Island	68,311	108,460	77867	108,460	(a-6)	108,460	N.A.	110,321	134,639	(a-29)
Vermont	71,053	80,018	85,010	75,005	77,002	70,013	85,946	103,002	...	(a-29)
Regional average	86,462	99,880	85,605	107,446	116,229	95,734	107,088	115,220	120,106	109,995
Midwest Region										
Illinois	98,135	120,861	(a-7)	113,114	(a-6)	(a-19)	(a-5)	127,576	225,000	(a-29)
Indiana	90,480	84,766	51,831	90,090	(a-6)	74,919	(a-5)	111,286	136,000	(a-29)
Iowa	70,246	113,580	104,497	93,766	(a-9)	102,003	(a-5)	118,000	126,141	124,696
Kansas	57,948	92,086	47,789	86,525	...	46,509	(a-5)	80,000	149,025	(a-29)
Michigan	95,788	104,040	...	135,050	(a-6)	(w)	N.A.	130,050	95,789	(a-29)
Minnesota	N.A.	94,106	99,994	81,620	108,388 (v)	(l)	(a-5)	108,388	249,046	(a-1)
Nebraska	70,030	70,529	63,859	96,535	(z)	(aa)	64,482	100,501	121,550	97,995
North Dakota	65,988	72,498	...	68,676	84,000	72,600	86,000	83,820	N.A.	(a-29)
Ohio	54,974 (b)	73,715 (b)	49,941 (b)	73,715 (b)	(a-6)	54,974 (b)	54,974 (b)	73,715 (b)	190,445	(a-29)
South Dakota	59,987	68,390	38,396	(a-19)	96,445	69,390	(a-5)	89,918	157,869	97,240
Wisconsin	82,294	90,000	82,000	101,435	98,000	78,198	105,836	101,778	N.A.	87,000
Regional average	74,587	89,506	73,241	94,053	99,165	80,811	90,589	102,276	161,207	100,036
Southern Region										
Alabama	125,000	81,999	77,997	120,942	76,336	95,178	65,686	186,036	146,380	76,336
Arkansas	74,999	114,762	92,959	101,258	(a-9)	103,236	107,863	172,808	123,106	(a-29)
Florida	90,000	112,148	55,123	112,797	(a-9)	113,522	113,877	152,000	N.A.	118,589
Georgia	119,156	73,518	106,103	N.A.	120,000	76,213	90,663	162,289	272,950	(a-29)
Kentucky	51,496 (b)	N.A.	51,496 (b)	97,572	125,000	105,823	109,906	101,568 (b)	233,000	62,312 (b)
Louisiana	81,058	42,827 (b)	N.A.	N.A.	(a-5)	96,795	(a-5)	123,136	202,238	(a-29)
Maryland	55,219 (b)	58,988 (b)	67,335 (b)	107,106 (b)	107,106 (b)	58,988 (b)	(a-5)	115,456 (b)	107,106 (b)	99,379 (b)
Mississippi	71,500	90,000	85,951	98,175	93,500	104,000	...	160,600	260,000	121,755
Missouri	72,672	88,392	N.A.	85,000	81,768	(y)	80,196	111,156	110,076	125,004
North Carolina	78,603	96,260	78,603	87,472	121,435	98,292	(a-5)	138,563	299,860	129,670
Oklahoma	70,000	83,000	N.A.	82,000	90,000	87,000	74520	180,000	N.A.	(a-29)
South Carolina	80,730	112,500	90,132	132,000	148,000	111,127	126,632	116,199	N.A.	(a-29)
Tennessee	80,484	109,284	80,868	92376	131,124	92,376	92,376	136,416	155,748	92,376
Texas	75,504	120,000	81,120	132,000	(a-9)	115,000	115,000	112,352	115,000	(a-29)
Virginia	89,582	107,251	119,936	130,369	115,188	108,607	119,224	151,103	137,332	132,925
West Virginia	45,000	70,000	85,000	(a-13)	(a-5)	65,760	59,756	90,000	252,500	(a-29)
Regional average	78,813	90,729	82,509	104,576	111,803	94,635	101,928	138,105	185,792	116,152
Western Region										
Alaska	84,816	73,752	...	91,200	84,816	91,200	...	87,852	106,194	91,200
Arizona	115,000	99,700	...	124,500	102,198	122,273	110,000	126,450	172,500	80,436 (b)
California	108,753	123,255	117,818	131,412	131,412	123,255	123,255	123,255	152,060	131,412
Colorado	96,060	121,200	110,004	103,008	105,600	119,496	121,200	121,200	121,200	121,200
Hawaii	77,966	93,384	102,036	77,966	(a-6)	99,072	(a-25)	85,302	442,008	102,036
Idaho	78,333	86,278	70,054	86,528	84,178	99,091	...	99,029	104,998	(a-29)
Montana	68,787	83,932	57,200	83,932	(a-6)	77,800 (nn)	66,769	83,932	144,500	83,932
Nevada	72,792	88,456	91,703	105,016	(a-9)	107,433	N.A.	88,455	210,912	(a-29)
New Mexico	88,445	86,446	89,999	88,445	96,998	85,001	88,445	88,445	76,001	86,500
Oregon	69,156	112,272	92,436	101,844	(a-4)	101,844	(a-5)	112,272	190,008	122,376
Utah	80,743	107,908	68,612	101,769	105,903	89,993	89,993	110,873	N.A.	(a-29)
Washington	89,352	87,228	69,756	106,130	131,246	106,130	(a-5)	112,216	128,942	(a-29)
Wyoming	62,443	79,565	75,229	86,570	77,000	86,195	(a-5)	79,567	85,646	(a-29)
Regional average	84,050	95,644	85,895	99,102	94,269	100,676	98,650	101,450	161,247	108,033
Regional average without California	81,991	93,343	82,703	96,409	91,173	98,794	95,916	99,633	162,083	106,085
Guam	68,152	73,020	55,303	60,850	88,915	60,850	47,918	74,096	160,000	88,915
No. Mariana Islands	45,000	40,800 (b)	45,000	58,000	54,000	40,800 (b)	54,000	80,000	80,000	40,800 (b)
U.S. Virgin Islands	60,000	(a-18)	65,000	65,000	(a-4)	(a-14)	(a-5)	79,500	65,000	65,000

(a-20) Parks and recreation.
(a-21) Personnel.
(a-22) Post audit.
(a-23) Pre-audit.
(a-24) Public utility regulation.
(a-25) Purchasing.
(a-26) Revenue.
(a-27) Social services.

(a-28) Tourism.
(a-29) Transportation.
(a-30) Welfare.
(a-31) Auditor

(b) Salary ranges and top figure in ranges follow: Florida: Salary range for Information Systems: $48,539 - 98,912. Kentucky: Minimum figure in range: top of range follows: Election administration $84,950; Emergency management, $84,950; Energy, $84,950; Health, $162,504; Highways, $102,794; Li-

SELECTED OFFICIALS: ANNUAL SALARIES — Continued

State or other jurisdiction	Information systems	Insurance	Labor	Licensing	Mental health & retardation	Natural resources	Parks & recreation	Personnel	Planning	Post audit
Eastern Region										
Connecticut	$123,961	$110,913	$123,961	$87,896	(d)	$115,673	$102,833	$123,961	$110,913	...
Delaware (h)	133,600	89,900	95,500	75,600	(f)	106,000	85,000	106,000	81,600	(a-31)
Maine	82,451	91,208	91,208	75,171	91,208	91,208	40,134	80,267	80,267	82,659
Massachusetts	119,149	105,792	108,000	96,992	(u)	110,496	N.A.	115,307	N.A.	N.A.
New Hampshire	85,753	85,753	64,036	...	81,191	85,753	64,036	76,603	69,322	(a-9)
New Jersey	108,000	137,165	137,165	110,758	(qq)	110,000	81,995	137,165	90,000	120,000
New York	(a-16)	127,000	127,000	(bb)	(ii)	(a-14)	127,000	120,800	(a-11)	(a-9)
Pennsylvania	119,042	103,980	115,533	85,000	105,000	115,533	107,541	119,042	90,000	120,154
Rhode Island	85,067	N.A.	N.A.	N.A.	N.A.	108,460	68,311	95,874	68,311	N.A.
Vermont	85,010	85,010	70,013	75,213	81,162	90,002	70,013	75,005	...	80,808
Regional average	108,203	104,080	103,602	94,014	110,659	106,913	82,985	105,002	88,002	101,785
Midwest Region										
Illinois	(a-5)	113,114	105,366	105,366	(a-27)	113,114	(a-19)	(a-5)	...	(a-31)
Indiana	81,971	79,852	88,505	(n)	83,187	90,090	74,802	84,142	...	83,070
Iowa	126,175	103,618	89,958	76,211	107,723	105,781	75,483	94,848	...	(a-31)
Kansas	96,425	76,389	92,086	63,665	N.A.	94,311	51,272	72,100	N.A.	98,254
Michigan	146,017	112,199	(a-7)	104,900	(x)	124,848	97,223	136,578	...	135,500
Minnesota	116,114	(a-7)	108,388	94,106	108,388	108,388	96,424	108,388	N.A.	(a-31)
Nebraska	115,398	81,860	78,497	84,260	97,394	114,080	91,428	83,628	85,141	60,000
North Dakota	110,160	68,018	61,812	(a-2)	60,228	68,784	69,501	68,400	...	...
Ohio	60,611 (b)	66,851 (b)	101,442	54,974 (b)	73,715 (b)	73,715 (b)	54,974 (b)	73,715 (b)	(a-6)	93,434
South Dakota	107,682	84,760	79,602	43,493	80,000	89,918	65,124	82,451	(a-15)	76,889
Wisconsin	143,995	92,000	107,146	90,000	94,000	108,000	79,774	90,000	(a-6)	105,229
Regional average	111,401	89,732	94,027	76,644	95,424	99,184	79,011	92,283	86,680	95,515
Southern Region										
Alabama	134,565	76,336	76,336	...	134,566	76,366	70,686	137,498	(a-8)	152,305
Arkansas	109,981	101,715	100,144	...	89,347	58,469	94,829	85,831	...	123,721
Florida	48,539 (b)	(a-4)	111,718	96,411	(i)	(a-14)	(j)	85,000	119,982	123,000
Georgia	N.A.	110,234	110,260	86,415	N.A.	117,464	92,996	117,918	(a-6)	(a-31)
Kentucky	N.A.	N.A	N.A.	51,495 (b)	N.A.	95,593	N.A.	125,000	125,000	91,075
Louisiana	114,275	85,000	102,752	58,240 (b)	98,196	91,866	63,020 (b)	64,272 (b)	52,458 (b)	123,735
Maryland	92,220 (b)	99,379 (b)	99,379 (b)	79,458 (b)	(t)	107,106 (b)	85,594 (b)	99,379 (b)	119,128
Mississippi	120,481	90,000	...	...	127,726	98,175	104,000	95,750	75,000	90,000
Missouri	108,144	95,904	95,844	66,000	92,928	95,808	83,676	85,164	N.A.	(a-31)
North Carolina	130,000	104,523	104,523	...	113,000	102,119	78,603	102,119	N.A.	104,523
Oklahoma	89,000	98,875	80,749	...	125,000	74000	74000	75,000	...	N.A.
South Carolina	107,000	100,074	104,423	(a-18)	(dd)	111,127	103,000	98,476	85,214	88,496
Tennessee	231,756	92,376	109,284	88,056	98,316	92,376	90,996	92,376	N.A.	(a-9)
Texas	120,000	163,800	125,000	76,000	140,000	132,000	115,000	85,968	(a-6)	96,200
Virginia	131,370	130,158	108,127	91,423	151,103	131,370	110,057	118,613	(a-6)	137,487
West Virginia	68,556	60,000	60,000	...	90,000	70,000	70,000	55,000	(a-5)	76,000
Regional average	114,706	101,822	99,181	79,792	111,824	97,915	90,313	94,349	95,271	111,883
Western Region										
Alaska	84,816	87,852	91,200	87,852	87,852	91,200	78,756	91,156	...	87,852
Arizona	97,000	109,650	116,064	...	N.A.	108,450	111,398	94,000	(a-6)	N.A.
California	123,255	140,000	131,412	(a-10)	123,255	131,412	123,255	123,255	106,440	N.A.
Colorado	N.A.	102,269	121,200	121,200	100,284	121,200	119,500	121,200	121,200	120,850
Hawaii	93,384	74,655	85,302	(a-7)	80,664	85,302	86,448	85,302	99,072	(k)
Idaho	82098	78,250	86,278	55,994	N.A.	86,507	75,005	82,098	N.A.	82,500
Montana	105,040	72,285	83,932	71,104	81,154	83,932	65,799	66,491	80,704	108,343
Nevada	107,433	95,000	107,433	...	104,805	107,433	...	92,000	...	...
New Mexico	86,500	82,499	86,446	86,446	72,203	89,999	79,135	82,998	...	85,000
Oregon	136,416	112,272	72,000	72,576	106,992	79,908	101,844	92,436	N.A.	101,844
Utah	105,903	86,736	86,736	78,571	87,592	97,635	97,635	99,702	(a-6)	80,700
Washington	106,811	90,617	110,015	106,130	98,556	99,462	104,515	100,589	(a-15)	92,500
Wyoming	73,126	69,567	64,637	84,067	111,467	71,567	64,000	72,477	71,567	N.A.
Regional average	100,149	92,435	95,589	88,409	95,893	96,462	92,274	92,593	101,375	93,877
Regional average without California	98,048	88,471	92,604	84,924	93,157	93,550	89,458	90,037	100,651	93,877
Guam	74,096	74,096	73,020	74,096	67,150	60,850	60,850	74,096	75,208	82,025
No. Mariana Islands	45000	40,800 (b)	45,000	45,360	40,800 (b)	52,000	40,800 (b)	60,000	45,000	80,000
U.S. Virgin Islands	60,000	(a-1)	65,000	(a-10)	79,500	(a-14)	65,000	65,000	55,000	60,000

censing, $ 84,950; Solid waste management, $70,209. Louisiana: Minimum figure in range: top of range follows :Employment services,$79,622; Historic preservation, $69,555; Licensing:, $103,355; Personnel, $119,496 Planning, $97,552; Pre-audit, $97,522; Welfare, $104,374. Maryland: Minimum figure in range: top of range follows: Adjutant general, $115,014; Administration, $133,538; Agriculture, $133,538; Banking, $98,396; Budget, $155,141; Civil rights, $106,769; Commerce, $155,141; Community affairs, $106,769; Consumer affairs, $112,454; Corrections, $115,014; Economic development, $155,141; Election administration, $99,136; Emergency management, $86,118; Employment services, $92,049; Energy, $105,183; Environmental protection, $143,922; Finance, $143,922; Fish and Wildlife, $92,049; Health, $155,141; Higher education, $143,922; Highway, $133,538; Historic preservation, $99,136; Information systems, $123,919; Insurance, $133,538; Labor, $133,538; Licensing, $106,769; Natural resources, $143,922; Parks and recreation, $98,396; Personnel, $115,014; Planning, $133,538; Public library development, $106,769; Purchasing, $99,136; Revenue,

SELECTED OFFICIALS: ANNUAL SALARIES — Continued

State or other jurisdiction	Pre-audit	Public library development	Public utility regulation	Purchasing	Revenue	Social services	Solid waste management	State police	Tourism	Transportation	Welfare
Eastern Region											
Connecticut	(a-9)	$88,647	$136,635	$106,950	$140,264	$140,272	$88,060	$140,272	$106,950	$140,272	140,272
Delaware (h)	(a-31)	68,200	77,900	75,600	106,900	(g)	135,750	130,720	66,300	106,000	98,400
Maine	(a-9)	77,438	101,420	69,326	85,758	91,208	58,573	80,267	69,326	91,208	73,590
Massachusetts	(a-9)	86,592	84,441	112,142	122,366	119,149	110,496	133,976	93,443	112,500	112,018
New Hampshire	(a-9)	64,036	85,753	50,291	85,753	85,753	76,603	76,603	64,036	85,753	83,477
New Jersey	. . .	. . .	137,165	115,000	103,000	137,165	93,974	120,000	90,000	137,165	100,000
New York	(a-9)	(a-12)	127,000	(a-16)	127,000	136,000	(a-14)	127,000	(a-11)	136,000	136,000
Pennsylvania	(a-4)	90,172	112,256	80,783	109,756	100,695	102,944	109,756	56,763	115,533	115,533
Rhode Island	(a-9)	85,067	106,679	99,471	110,278	110,321	68,311	124,114	N.A.	117,337	. . .
Vermont	(a-15)	76,502	104,354	85,946	79,997	105,019	75,005	91,166	65,000	90,002	71,157
Regional average	101,615	89,647	107,360	93,151	107,107	113,528	94,572	113,387	81,402	113,177	103,383
Midwestern Region											
Illinois	(a-9)	93,636	113,836	(a-5)	120,861	127,576	(a-14)	113,114	(a-7)	127,576	120,861
Indiana	66,000	74,802	88,120	55,246	88,120	82,000	74,724	111,118	74,802	90,636	78,448
Iowa	97,510	99,559	104,497	91,790	126,175	126,175	82,410	102,794	85,218	126,173	95,826
Kansas	(r)	77,557	81,200	80,000	91,350	94,856	75,795	82,215	60,900	91,350	72,000
Michigan	N.A.	122,400	109,242	96,820	103,000	130,050	108,428	124,848	N.A.	135,000	(a-27)
Minnesota	(a-31)	N.A.	88,447	94,106	108,388	108,400	108,388	100,391	104,316	(a-1)	108,388
Nebraska	93,009	79,264	92,297	64,482	90,526	107,276	56,462	81,297	53,314	97,995	100,787
North Dakota	84,000	66,300	69,874	48,024	78,821	106,560	57,348	72,444	67,008	96,996	106,560
Ohio	(a-22)	60,611 (b)	73,715 (b)	54,974	73,715 (b)	106,683	58,968 (b)	73,715 (b)	69,805	73,715 (b)	73,715 (b)
South Dakota	64,813	53,518	75,587	49,587	79,602	89,585	58,444	75,026	84,760	97,240	95,035
Wisconsin	96,025	75,763	114,303	105,834	100,291	106,400	81,092	88,000	94,000	102,000	85,150
Regional average	87,376	80,341	91,920	78,339	96,441	107,778	79,561	93,178	81,498	101,534	96,984
Southern Region											
Alabama	(a-9)	82,750	86,801	110,404	76,336	139,310	82,000	76,336	76,336	(a-17)	(a-27)
Arkansas	59,596	84,927	77,356	85,831	91,972	125,804	51,153	91,874	94,829	130,290	(a-27)
Florida	(a-26)	98,911	119,743	88,699	114,800	N.A.	90,079	107,000	95,479	118,589	92,109
Georgia	(a-31)	119,887	106,103	91,731	117,000	N.A.	88,686	120,957	117,800	153,595	114,920
Kentucky	(a-15)	94,077	106,433	(a-5)	N.A.	N.A.	42,559 (b)	N.A.	125,000	125,000	N.A.
Louisiana	52,458 (b)	113,544	78,000	83,241	104,042	87,734	93,242	87,740	75,920	131,425	56,139 (b)
Maryland	79,458 (b)	79,458 (b)	114,400	73,777 (b)	79,458 (b)	107,106 (b)	68,518 (b)	107,106 (b)	79,458 (b)	115,456 (b)	107,106 (b)
Mississippi	90,000	80,500	107,350	65,000	111,000	93,500	64,253	88,000	87,062	121,755	85,000
Missouri	N.A.	75,000	94,029	80,196	102,024	98,004	61,104	80,040	73,000	125,004	86,988
North Carolina	(a-31)	86,285	116,405	N.A.	102,119	99,428	83,600	97,692	71,819	102,119	N.A.
Oklahoma	(a-9)	72,000	(cc)	71,200	85,000	125,000	77,697	85,000	74,000	110,000	125,000
South Carolina	(a-9)	79,403	N.A.	82,281	123,874	129,484	132,000	80,295	103,000	129,780	129,484
Tennessee	93,804	118,044	92,376	86,352	92,376	92,376	80,868	92,376	92,376	92,376	92,376
Texas	(a-9)	85,000	92,000	115,000	(a-9)	150,000	N.A.	102,000	112,352	155,000	150,000
Virginia	(a-9)	114,258	130,158	(a-16)	121,389	134,970	(a-14)	123,337	118,726	131,370	(a-27)
West Virginia	(a-5)	63,252	70,000	75,348	75,000	66,624	66,624	75,000	70,000	90,000	90,000
Regional average	93,849	90,456	98,273	89,213	99,240	111,488	80,850	94,317	91,697	119,256	109,229
Western Region											
Alaska	. . .	N.A.	84,276	84,852	91,200	91,200	N.A.	84,816	87,852	91,200	87,852
Arizona	(a-9)	112,025	97,450	82,000	130,674	130,000	86,450	126,450	108,000	121,450	99,748
California	(a-9)	108,744	117,818	123,255	123,255	123,255	117,818	131,412	106,440	123,255	123,255
Colorado	(a-9)	106,248	112,149	91,200	121,200	121,200	91,116	114,000	90,420	121,200	N.A.
Hawaii	93,384	85,000	77,966	72,886	85,302	85,302	88,824	. . .	(a-11)	85,302	90,420
Idaho	(a-9)	56,742	81,120	67,434	70,304	15,646	. . .	83,075	63,898	130,000	81,182
Montana	. . .	65,428	75,141	46,615	83,932	83,932	83,932	66,853	47,458	83,932	83,932
Nevada	98,052	90,247	99,537	81,181	107,433	107,892	. . .	102,521	94,893	107,433	101,232
New Mexico	79,135	62,400	N.A.	73,729	88,499	N.A.	. . .	88,445	86,446	(a-17)	101,982
Oregon	(a-6)	92,436	106,932	79,908	112,272	123,756	101,844	117,888	83,868	123,504	123,756
Utah	(a-15)	78,571	N.A.	89,993	93,542	110,873	92,418	89,993	73,915	110,873	107,908
Washington	(a-4)	98,553	106,130	80,892	112,216	131,246	85,296	111,000	66,060	153,472	(a-27)
Wyoming	(a-9)	68,389	75,067	62,221	79,567	79,567	78,062	68,760	81,775	83,563	(a-27)
Regional average	99,400	85,399	93,962	79,705	99,954	100,322	91,751	98,768	82,794	109,360	101,007
Regional average without California	95,340	83,276	91,577	76,076	98,012	98,238	88,493	95,800	80,824	108,202	98,984
Guam	74,096	55,303	12,000	74,096	74,096	74,096	88,915	74,096	74,096	74,096	74,096
No. Mariana Islands .	54,000	45,000	80,000	40,800 (b)	45,000	40,800 (b)	54,000	54,000	70,000	40,800 (b)	52,000
U.S. Virgin Islands ...	(a-4)	65,000	54,500	(a-5)	65,000	65,000	65,000	65,000	(a-7)	(a-5)	65,000

$106,769; Social services, $143,922; Solid waste management, $92,069; Police, $143,922; Tourism, $106,769; Transportation, $155,141; Welfare, $143,922. New Mexico: Minimum figure in range: top of range follows:134,060. Ohio: Minimum figure in range: top of range follows: Lieutenant Governor, $132,350; Administration, $132,350; Agriculture, $122,574; Banking, $102,918; Budget, $132,350; Civil Rights, $112,320; Commerce, $132,350; Corrections, $132,350; Economic development, $132,350; Elec-

tions administration, $86,258; Emergency Management, $ 102,918; Employment services, $132,350; Energy, $94,182; Environmental protection, $132,350; Fish and Wildlife, $102,918; General services, $102,918; Health, $132,350; Information systems, $112,320; Insurance, $122,574; Licensing, $102,918; Mental health and retardation, $132,350; Natural resources, $132,350; Parks and recreation, $102,918; Personnel, $102,918; Public library development, $112,320; Public utility regulation, $132,350; Purchas-

SELECTED OFFICIALS: ANNUAL SALARIES — Continued

ing, $102, 918; Revenue, $132,350; Solid waste management, $81,598; State police, $132,350; Transportation, $132,350; Welfare, $132,350 Insurance, $74,514; Licensing, $58,828; Parks & recreation, $65,369; Personnel, $91,745; Post audit, $58,828; Public library development, $105,529; Purchasing, $95,188; Revenue, $105,529; Solid waste management, $81,404; Tourism, $65,369; Welfare, $74,514 Utah: Minimum figure in range: top of range follows: Administration, $102,600; Agriculture, $87,500; Banking, $87,500; Budget, $102,600; Civil rights, $80,433; Commerce, $87,500; Community affairs, $94,300; Consumer affairs, $76,190; Corrections, $102,600; Elections administration, $41,433; Emergency management, $94,723; Employment services, $111,800; Energy, $64,750; Environmental protection, $102,600; Finance, $102,670; Fish & wildlife, $94,723; General services, $97,260; Health, $111,800; Higher education, $160,000; Highways, $111,800; Historic preservation, $80,433; Information systems, $105,500; Insurance, $87,500; Labor, $87,500; Licensing, $82,640; Mental health & retardation, $94,723; Natural resources, $102,600; Parks & recreation, $94,723; Personnel, $102,600; Planning, $102,600; Pre-audit, $102,670; Public library development, $80,433; Public utility regulation, $94,300; Purchasing, $97,260; Revenue, $94,300; Social services, $111,800; Solid waste management, $124,155; State police, $94,723; Transportation, $111,800; Welfare, $111,800 Northern Mariana Islands: $49,266 top of range applies to the following positions: Treasurer, Banking, Comptroller, Corrections, , Employment Services, Fish and Wildlife, Highways, Insurance, Mental Health and Retardation, Parks and Recreation, Purchasing, Social/Human Services, Transportation.

(c) The present Secretary of Commerce forgoes regular salary and receives $1 in compensation.

(d) Responsibilities shared between Commissioner, Mental Health: $140,272 and Commissioner, Retardation: $140,272.

(e) Responsibilities shared between Secretary of State, $124,900 and Bureau Director, $102,143.

(f) Responsibilities shared between Director, Division of Substance Abuse and Mental Health, Department of Health and Social Services, $121,800; and Director, Division of Developmental Disabilities Service, same department, $98,300.

(g) Function split between two cabinet positions: Secretary, Dept. of Health and Social Services : $113,400 (if incumbent holds a medical license, amount is increased by $12,000) and Secretary, Dept. for Children, Youth and their Families, $106,000: if a Board-certified physician , a supplement of $3,000 is added.

(h) Salaries represent those reflected for the position in section 10a of FY2004 Budget Act effective 7/21/2003.

(i) Responsibilities shared between, Director of Mental Health, Department of Children and Family Services, $83,890; and Director, Substance Abuse, same department, $77,738.

(j) Department of Fish And Wildlife, $113,522.

(k) Responsibilities shared between State Auditor, Office of the Auditor, $85,302; and Division Head, Division of Audit, Department of Accounting & General Services, vacant, salary unavailable.

(l) Responsibilities shared between Director of Fisheries, Department of Natural Resources, $96,424 and Director of Wildlife, Dept. of Natural Resources, $92,424.

(m) Responsibilities shared between Co-Directors, Election Commission, $50,500.

(n) Responsibilities shared between Executive Director, Health Professions Bureau, $54,274; and Executive Director, Professional Licensing Agency, $61,915.

(o) Responsibilities shared between Lieutenant Governor , $111,523; Director, Business Development Division, same department, $86,275; and President, Kansas Inc., salary unavailable.

(p) Responsibilities shared between Secretary of State, $76,389 and Deputy Secretary of State, $62,301.

(q) Responsibilities shared between Assistant Secretary of State, $74,600 and Senior Counsel for Elections, $68,600.

(r) Responsibilities shared between Central Account Service Manager, Division of Accounts & Reports, Department of Administration, $70,428; and

Team Leader, Audit Services, same division and department, $57,948.

(s) In Maine, New Hampshire, New Jersey, Tennessee and West Virginia, the presidents (or speakers) of the Senate are next in line of succession to the governorship. In Tennessee, the speaker of the Senate bears the statutory title of lieutenant governor.

(t) Responsibilities shared between Director, Mental Hygiene Administration, $85,594-$115,014; and Director, Developmental Disabilities Administration, Department of Health and Mental Hygiene, $85,594 - $115,014.

(u) Responsibilities shared between Commissioner, Department of Mental Retardation, $182,831; and Commissioner, Department of Mental Health, Executive Office of Human Services, $110,496; and Commissioner Gerald Morrissey, $114,258.

(v) State Treasurer Position was abolished in January 2003. Functions now served by The Department of Finance, Commissioner.

(w) Responsibilities shared between Director, Dept. of Natural Resources, $124,848 and Chief, Fish, $102,142 and Chief, Wildlife, $91,045.

(x) Responsibilities shared between Director, Dept. pf Community Health, $130,050 and Chief Deputy Director , Mental Health and Substance Abuse Services, $114,000.

(y) Responsibilities shared between Administrator, Department of Conservation, $77,508; Administration, Division of Protection, same department, $86,976.

(z) Responsibilities shared between State Tax Commissioner, Department of Revenue, $90,526; Administrator, Budget Division, Department of Administrative Services, $100,697; and Auditor of Public Accounts, $60,000.

(aa) Responsibilities shared between Director, Game & Parks Commission, $91,428; Administrator, Wildlife Division, same commission, $65,023; and Assistant Director, Fish & Wildlife, same commission, $70,874.

(bb) Responsibilities shared between Commissioner, State Education Department, $170,165; Secretary of State, Department of State, $120,800.

(cc) Responsibilities shared between Commissioners, Corporations Commission, varying salary levels for four commissioners, $72,000; $84,000; $87,875; and $87,875.

(dd) Responsibilities shared between Director for Mental Retardation , $138,396 and Director of Mental Health, $140,000.

(ee) Annual salary for duties as presiding officer of the Senate.

(ff) Responsibilities shared between Secretary of State, $117,546; and Division Director, $86,811.

(gg) Responsibilities shared between Secretary, Department of Education and the Arts, $75,000; and Superintendent, Department of Education, $146,000.

(hh) Responsibilities for St. Thomas, $60,000; St. Croix, $65,000; St. John, $60,000.

(ii) Responsibilities shared between Commissioner of Mental Health, $136,000 and Commissioner of Mental Retardation, $136,000.

(jj) Governor Romney and Lieutenant Governor Healey waive their salaries.

(kk) Responsibilities shared between Director of Fiscal Management, $84,000 and Director of Management and Budget, $86,000.

(ll) Responsibilities shared between Secretary of State, $47,060 and State Elections Director, $51,816.

(mm) Responsibilities shared between Kevin Johnston, $135,903 and Robert Jaekle, $135,903.

(nn) Responsibilities shared between Administrator, $71,683 and director, $83,932.

(oo) Responsibilities shared between Secretary of State, $80,000; Deputy Secretary of State for Elections, $78,319 and Chief Deputy Secretary of State, $86,153.

(pp) Responsibilities shared between Director, Division of Purchasing, Dept. of the Treasury, $115,000, and Director, Division of Property and Management, Dept. of the Treasury,$103,000.

(qq) Responsibilities shared between Director, Division of Mental Health Services, Dept. of Human Services, $110,365 and Director, Division of Developmental Disabilities, Dept. of Human Services, $120,000.

Lieutenant Governors: Powerful in Two Branches
By Julia Nienaber Hurst

The office of lieutenant governor is gaining recognition for its power and possibility. Lieutenant governors are unique officeholders with many having power in both the executive and legislative branches. In states in which the lieutenant governor is elected as a team with the governor and does not preside over the Senate, a trend is emerging. Lieutenant governors are being named to lead state departments and major authorities.

The Office of Lieutenant Governor

Lieutenant governors are the only state government officials with powers in both the executive and legislative branches. Most preside over their state senates, cast tie-breaking votes, and act as governor while others run state departments. Nearly all now pursue successful legislative agendas and many move on to higher office. The office of lieutenant governor is gaining recognition for its power and possibility and a trend is emerging of lieutenant governors being given or taking greater responsibilities and roles.

Twenty-four lieutenant governors are elected to office with the governor, while 18 are elected separately from the governor and may be of the opposite party. Both methods have strengths. For teams, a strong partnership with the governor is likely to continue while governing. A lieutenant governor may have a role in the budget process, a voice in vetoes, or may lead key policy. If elected separately, the lieutenant governor has the independent strength of statewide election to lead on key issues, sometimes providing an alternate view.

Executive Branch Powers

Of 42 states with a lieutenant governor, 23 serve as acting governor when the governor is out of state. Every lieutenant governor becomes governor if the office is vacated. In 2003, three lieutenant governors succeeded to governor. The country lost a long-serving public servant and former lieutenant governor in Indiana Gov. Frank O'Bannon. His unexpected incapacitation and subsequent death necessitated the succession of Joseph Kernan to governor. Utah Lt. Gov. Olene Walker became governor when Gov. Michael Leavitt was named Director of the Environmental Protection Agency. And, in the U.S. territory of American Samoa, the governor passed away unexpectedly causing the lieutenant governor to succeed to governor.

In all three cases, a new lieutenant governor was appointed. However, questions arose in each case as to succession law. In Utah, an attorney general's opinion was issued stating that the lieutenant governor would receive both the title and the authority of governor. The unfortunate events in Indiana led states like Tennessee to discover that they did not have a provision of succession addressing the incapacitation of the governor. 2003 also saw the recall of California Gov. Gray Davis which gave rise to the additional succession question of why the lieutenant governor did not become governor upon recall. The year made it clear that further research can be done in the area of succession law, particularly given homeland security issues and the need for thorough emergency planning.

Lieutenant governors often move to higher office as demonstrated in 2003 by Louisiana Lt. Gov. Kathleen Blanco who ran for governor and won. Eight governors in January of 2003 were once lieutenant governor. Statistics reveal that often 10 percent or more of the sitting governors were once lieutenant governor. For example, seven Illinois governors and four Illinois U.S. senators through history were once lieutenant governor while six South Carolina lieutenant governors became governor. Lieutenant governors have gone on to the U.S. Senate, the U.S. House, supreme courts, and to become ambassadors. Several candidates for U.S. president were once lieutenant governor. The implication for the future is that a lieutenant governor will someday be U.S. president.

Legislative Branch Powers

Thirty National Lieutenant Governors Association (NLGA) members preside over their state senates and many control the manner of debate, 14 assign bills to committee, and others determine the order bills are heard. Several also appoint committees and chairs. *Governing* magazine said presiding over the senate "arguably makes the Mississippi lieutenant governor the state's most powerful office." KVUE-TV said, "As presiding officer of the Senate, the lieutenant governor is arguably the most powerful person in Texas government."

More than half of the presiding officer lieutenant governors break tie votes in the senate. New Mexico Lt. Gov. Diane Denish and North Dakota Lt. Gov. Jack Dalrymple counsel their governors on vetoes since, as presiding officers, they hear debate on every bill.° Oklahoma Lt. Gov. Mary Fallin used the power to preside in 2000 to bring the issue of right to work to a vote of the people for the first time in 25 years.

Policy Leadership

Nearly all lieutenant governors actively and successfully pursue state legislation under others' sponsorship. Rhode Island Lt. Gov. Charles J. Fogarty, chair of the Long-Term Care Coordinating Council, won a landmark Health Quality Performance Measurement and Reporting Law which releases public reports on health care providers. He is also active in the tobacco settlement and mental health parity issues. Alaska Lt. Gov. Loren Leman will pursue faith-based social services in 2004 while lieutenant governors in Missouri and North Carolina established pioneering prescription drug programs for seniors at the state level.

Lieutenant governors also spearheaded passage of 2003 legislation to fund coastal restoration, regulate cyberstalking, set up nursing standards and scholarships, appropriate nearly $1 million for statewide trauma efforts, and more. These officeholders testify for or against bills, sometimes in Congress. North Dakota's lieutenant governor testified for teacher pay raises while Connecticut's lieutenant governor developed and promoted a plan to ensure computers and information technology for schools and libraries. Nearly one-fourth of the lieutenant governors are active on aerospace issues, an industry employing nearly 700,000 persons.

Trends for the Future

The office of lieutenant governor is gaining recognition for its possibility and a trend is emerging of lieutenant governors being given or taking greater roles. In states in which the lieutenant governor is elected as a team with the governor and does not preside over the senate, a trend is emerging of the lieutenant governor being named a member of the cabinet to lead a state department or major authority.

"Though the role of lieutenant governor changes depending on the administration, its importance does not," said Ohio Gov. Bob Taft. Taft named his previous lieutenant governor head of the Department of Public Safety based on her background. His current lieutenant governor is head of the Commerce Department based on her experience. In 2003, Minnesota's governor named the lieutenant governor head of the Department of Transportation, a groundbreaking move for the office in that state. The press noted appointing the lieutenant governor to the cabinet created fiscal savings and better government. The move eliminated one department-level salary and placed the lieutenant governor in a position to be best prepared for succession, should it happen.

"I believe the role and importance of the lieutenant governor in Nebraska is increasing and expanding," said Nebraska Gov. Mike Johanns. He named his lieutenant governor head of homeland security. "Having this issue led from the lieutenant governor's office allows a comprehensive, statewide approach to a broad and vital program," said Lt. Gov. David Heineman. Other examples include Hawaii's lieutenant governor being named to lead state efforts on drug and alcohol abuse problems and Colorado's lieutenant governor is working to achieve affordable health insurance in the state.

Lieutenant governors are also stepping up and taking greater roles through projects, initiatives and "use of the bully pulpit." As the second most powerful official in state government, lieutenant governors have the ability to draw press attention through their words and actions. In Oklahoma, the lieutenant governor worked with state officers and partnered with several private sector groups to expand the missing children "Amber Alert" system. California's lieutenant governor marched with college students at the Capitol to protest rising student fees. He then visited with thousands of high school students to promote the availability of state assistance and scholarships.

The future implication for state government is that the office of lieutenant governor will continue to gain strength, recognition and responsibility. On the succession of Indiana's lieutenant governor to governor in 2003, Senate President Bob Garton said, "If anyone has ever questioned the importance of the role of lieutenant governor, it has now been answered."

With fiscal shortfalls, continuing globalization and homeland security among the most recent challenges to face states, it is likely that the role of lieutenant governor will continue to grow. Environmental Protection Agency Administrator Michael Leavitt said, "The partnership between governor and lieutenant governor allows us to more effectively address the broad needs of the citizens."

About the Author

Julia Nienaber Hurst is executive director of the National Lieutenant Governors Association (NLGA). Hurst holds a Master's degree in Public Administration and previously was chief operating officer of The Council of State Governments. She authored government research published in *Spectrum: The Journal of State Government, State Government News* and at www.nlga.us.

Table 4.12
LIEUTENANT GOVERNORS, 2004

State or other jurisdiction	Name and party	Method of selection	Length of regular term in years	Date of first service	Present term ends	Number of previous terms	Maximum consecutive terms allowed by constitution
Alabama	Lucy Baxley (D)	CE	4	1/03	1/07	. . .	2
Alaska	Loren Leman (R)	CE	4	12/02	12/07	. . .	2
Arizona	. . . . (a)						
Arkansas	Winthrop Rockefeller (R)	CE	4	1/96 (b)	1/07	1.5 (b)	2
California	Cruz Bustamante (D)	CE	4	1/98	1/06	1	2
Colorado	Jane Norton (R)	CE	4	1/03	1/07	. . .	2
Connecticut	M. Jodi Rell (R)	CE	4	1/95	1/07	2	. . .
Delaware	John Carney (D)	CE	4	1/01	1/05	. . .	2
Florida	Toni Jennings (R)	CE	4	3/03	1/07	. . .	2
Georgia	Mark Taylor (D)	CE	4	1/99	1/07	1	. . .
Hawaii	James Aiona (R)	CE	4	12/02	12/06	. . .	2
Idaho	Jim Risch (R)	CE	4	1/03	1/07	. . .	. . .
Illinois	Pat Quinn (D)	CE	4	1/03	1/07	. . .	. . .
Indiana	Katherine Davis (D)	CE	4	10/03	1/04	1	2
Iowa	Sally Pederson (D)	CE	4	1/99	1/07	1	. . .
Kansas	John Moore (D)	CE	4	1/03	1/07	. . .	. . .
Kentucky	Steve Pence (R)	CE	4	12/03	12/07	. . .	2
Louisiana	Mitch Landrieu (D)	CE	4	1/04	1/08	. . .	. . .
Maine	. . . . (a)						
Maryland	Michael Steele (R)	CE	4	1/03	1/07	. . .	2
Massachusetts	Kerry Healey (R)	CE	4	1/03	1/07	. . .	. . .
Michigan	John D. Cherry (D)	CE	4	1/03	1/07	. . .	2
Minnesota	Carol Molnau (R)	CE	4	1/03	1/07	. . .	. . .
Mississippi	Amy Tuck (R)	CE	4	1/00	1/08	1	2
Missouri	Joe Maxwell (D)	CE	4	11/00	1/05	. . .	. . .
Montana	Karl Ohs (R)	CE	4	1/01	1/05	. . .	2 (c)
Nebraska	Dave Heineman (R)	CE	4	10/01 (e)	1/07	(e)	2
Nevada	Lorraine Hunt (R)	CE	4	1/99	1/07	1	2
New Hampshire	. . . . (a)						
New Jersey	. . . . (a)						
New Mexico	Diane Denish (D)	CE	4	1/03	1/07	. . .	2
New York	Mary Donohue (R)	CE	4	1/99	1/07	1	. . .
North Carolina	Beverly Purdue (D)	CE	4	1/01	1/05	. . .	2
North Dakota	Jack Dalrymple (R)	CE	4	12/00	12/04	. . .	. . .
Ohio	Jennette Bradley (R)	SE	4	1/03	1/07	. . .	2
Oklahoma	Mary Fallin (R)	CE	4	1/95	1/07	2	. . .
Oregon	. . . . (a)						
Pennsylvania	Catherine Baker Knoll (D)	CE	4	1/03	1/07	. . .	2
Rhode Island	Charles Fogarty (D)	SE	4	1/99	1/07	1	2
South Carolina	R. Andre Bauer (R)	CE	4	1/03	1/07	. . .	. . .
South Dakota	Dennis Daugaard (R)	CE	4	1/03	1/07	. . .	2
Tennessee	. . . . (a)						
Texas	David Dewhurst (R)	CE	4	1/03	1/07	. . .	. . .
Utah	Gayle McKeachnie (R)	CE	4	11/03	1/05	2	. . .
Vermont	Brian Dubie (R)	CE	2	1/03	1/05	. . .	. . .
Virginia	Tim Kaine (D)	CE	4	1/02	1/06	. . .	. . .
Washington	Brad Owen (D)	CE	4	1/97	1/05	1	. . .
West Virginia (d)	Earl Ray Tomblin (D)	(d)	2	1/95	1/05	5	. . .
Wisconsin	Barbara Lawton (D)	CE	4	1/03	1/07	. . .	. . .
Wyoming	. . . . (a)						
American Samoa	Aitofele T.F. Sunia (D)	CE	4	4/03 (f)	1/05	. . .	2
Guam	Kaleo Moylan (R)	CE	4	1/03	1/07	. . .	2
No. Mariana Islands	Diego T. Benavente (R)	CE	4	1/02	1/06	. . .	. . .
Puerto Rico	. . . . (a)						
U.S. Virgin Islands	Vargrave Richards (D)	SE	4	1/03	1/07	. . .	2

Source: The Council of State Governments and the National Lieutenant Governors Association, December 2003.

Key:
CE — Constitutional, elected by public.
SE — Statutory, elected by public.
. . . — Not applicable.
(a) No lieutenant governor. In Tennessee, the speaker of the Senate, elected from Senate membership, has statutory title of "lieutenant governor."
(b) Elected in November 1996 in a special election when Mike Huckabee assumed the office of governor after Governor Jim Guy Tucker's resignation on July 15, 1996.

(c) Eligible for eight out of 16 years.
(d) In West Virginia, the President of the Senate and the Lieutenant Governor are one in the same. The legislature provided the title of Lieutenant Governor upon the Senate President. The Senate President serves 2 year terms, elected by the Senate on the first day of the first session of each two year legislative term.
(e) Lt. Governor Heineman was appointed to the position of Lieutenant Governor October 1, 2001 by Governor Mike Johanns.
(f) Lt. Governor Sunia was appointed to the position of Lieutenant Governor in April 2003 by Governor Togiola Tulafono.

Table 4.13
LIEUTENANT GOVERNORS: QUALIFICATIONS AND TERMS

State or other jurisdiction	Minimum age	State citizen (years)	U.S. citizen (years) (a)	State resident (years) (b)	Qualified voter (years)	Length of term (years)	Maximum consecutive terms allowed
Alabama	30	7	10	7	★	4	2
Alaska	30	...	7	7	★	4	2
Arizona				(c)			
Arkansas	30	7	★	7	...	4	2
California	18	★	★	5	★	4	2
Colorado	30	...	★	2	★	4	2
Connecticut	...	★	★	★	★	4	...
Delaware	30	★	12	6	★	4	2
Florida	30	★	★	7	★	4	2
Georgia	30	★	15	6	★	4	...
Hawaii	30	5	...	5	★	4	2
Idaho	30	...	★	2	...	4	...
Illinois	25	...	★	3	...	4	...
Indiana	30	5	5	5	...	4	2
Iowa	30	...	2	2	...	4	...
Kansas	...	...	...	...	...	4	...
Kentucky	30	6	...	6	...	4	2
Louisiana	25	5	5	5	...	4	...
Maine				(c)			
Maryland	30	...	(d)	5	5	4	2
Massachusetts	...	★	★	★	★	4	...
Michigan	30	...	...	...	4	4	2
Minnesota	25	★	★	1	...	4	...
Mississippi	30	...	20	5	★	4	2
Missouri	30	...	15	10	...	4	...
Montana	25	2	★	2	★	4	2 (e)
Nebraska	30	5	5	5	...	4	2
Nevada	25	2	★	2	★	4	2
New Hampshire				(c)			
New Jersey				(c)			
New Mexico	30	★	★	5	★	4	2
New York	30	★	★	5	★	4	...
North Carolina	30	...	5	2	★	4	2
North Dakota	30	...	★	5	★	4	...
Ohio	18	...	★	★	★	4	2
Oklahoma	31	★	★	★	10	4	...
Oregon				(c)			
Pennsylvania	30	★	★	7	★	4	2
Rhode Island	18	★	★	★	30 days	4	2
South Carolina	30	...	★	★	★	4	...
South Dakota	21	2	★	2	...	4	2
Tennessee				(c)			
Texas	30	...	★	5	...	4	...
Utah	30	5	★	5	★	4	...
Vermont	...	...	...	4	...	2	...
Virginia	30	...	★	5	5	4	...
Washington	18	★	★	★	★	4	...
West Virginia (f)	25	1	1	1	★	2	...
Wisconsin	18	★	★	★	★	4	...
Wyoming				(c)			
American Samoa	35	(g)	★	5	★	4	2
Guam	30	...	5	5	★	4	2
No. Mariana Islands	35	...	★	10	★	4	...
Puerto Rico				(c)			
U.S. Virgin Islands	30	...	5	5	5	4	2

Sources: The Council of State Government's survey, December 2003 and state constitutions, statutes and secretaries of state web sites, December 2003.

Note: This table includes constitutional and statutory qualifications.

Key:

★— Formal provision; number of years not specified.

. . .— No formal provision.

(a) In some states you must be a U.S. citizen to be an elector, and must be an elector to run.

(b) In some states you must be a state resident to be an elector, and must be an elector to run.

(c) No lieutenant governor. In Tennessee, the speaker of the Senate, elected from Senate membership, has statutory title of "lieutenant governor."

(d) Crosse v. Board of Supervisors of Elections 243 Md. 555, 221 A.2d431 (1966)–opinion rendered indicated that U.S. citizenship was, by necessity, a requirement for office.

(e) Eligible for eight out of 16 years.

(f) In West Virginia, the President of the Senate and the Lieutenant Governor are one in the same. The legislature provided in statute the title of Lieutenant Governor upon the Senate President. The Senate President serves 2 year terms, elected by the Senate on the first day of the first session of each two year legislative term.

(g) Must be a U.S. National.

Table 4.14
LIEUTENANT GOVERNORS: POWERS AND DUTIES

State or other jurisdiction	Presides over Senate	Appoints committees	Breaks roll-call ties	Assigns bills	Authority for governor to assign duties	Member of governor's cabinet or advisory body	Serves as acting governor when governor out of state
Alabama	★	★ (p)	★	★ (p)	...	...	(q)
Alaska	...	...	...	...	★	★	...
Arizona	....(b)...						
Arkansas	★	...	★	...	...	...	★
California	...	...	★	...	...	...	★
Colorado	...	...	...	...	★	★	★
Connecticut	★	...	★	...	★	★	★
Delaware	★	...	★	...	★	...	★
Florida	...	...	...	...	★	...	★
Georgia	★	...	...	...	★	...	...
Hawaii	...	...	...	...	★	...	★
Idaho	★	...	★	★	★	...	★
Illinois	...	...	...	...	★	★	...
Indiana	★	★	★	...	...	★	...
Iowa	...	(a)	...	...	★	(g)	(f)
Kansas	...	...	...	...	...	★	...
Kentucky	...	...	...	...	★	★	...
Louisiana	...	...	...	...	★	★	★
Maine	....(c)...						
Maryland	...	...	...	...	★	★	★
Massachusetts	...	★	★	...	★	★	★
Michigan	★	...	★	...	★	★	★
Minnesota	...	...	...	...	★	★	★
Mississippi	★	★	★	★	...	...	★
Missouri	★	...	★	...	★	★	★
Montana	...	...	...	...	★	★	★
Nebraska	★ (d)	...	...	...	★	...	★
Nevada	★	...	★ (e)	...	...	...	★
New Hampshire	....(c)...						
New Jersey	....(c)...						
New Mexico	★	...	★	...	...	★	★
New York	★	...	★ (o)	...	★	★	★
North Carolina	★	...	★	...	...	...	★
North Dakota	★	...	★	...	...	★	★
Ohio	...	...	...	...	★	★	...
Oklahoma	★ (n)	...	★	...	★	★	★
Oregon	....(b)...						
Pennsylvania	★	...	★	...	...	...	...
Rhode Island	...	...	...	...	...	...	...
South Carolina	★	...	★	★	★	...	...
South Dakota	★	(h)	★	★	★	(m)	...
Tennessee	....(c)...						
Texas	★	★	★	★	...	...	★
Utah	...	...	...	...	★	★	...
Vermont	★	★ (a)	★	...	...	...	★
Virginia	★	...	★	...	...	...	...
Washington	★	★	★	...	...	...	★
West Virginia (l)	★	★	...	★	...	...	...
Wisconsin	...	...	...	...	...	...	★
Wyoming	....(b)...						
American Samoa	...	...	...	...	...	...	★
Guam	(d)	...	...	...	★	★	★
No. Mariana Islands	...	...	...	...	★	(k)	★
Puerto Rico	....(b)...						
U.S. Virgin Islands	...	...	...	...	★ (g)	★	★

See footnotes at end of table.

LIEUTENANT GOVERNORS: POWERS AND DUTIES — Continued

Sources: The Council of State Governments' survey, October 2003 and state constitutions and statutes, December 2003.

Key:

★— Provision for responsibility.

. . . — No provision for responsibility.

(a) Appoints all standing committees. Iowa—appoints some special committees; Vermont—appoints all committees as one of three members of Senate Committee on Committees.

(b) No lieutenant governor; secretary of state is next in line of succession to governorship.

(c) No lieutenant governor; senate president or speaker is next in line of succession to governorship. In Tennessee, speaker of the senate bears the additional statutory title of "lieutenant governor."

(d) Unicameral legislative body. In Guam, that body elects own presiding officer.

(e) Except on final passage of bills and joint resolutions.

(f) Only in emergency situations.

(g) Presides over cabinet meetings in absence of governor.

(h) Conference committees.

(i) Only in event of governor's continuous absence from state.

(j) Only in situations of an absence which prevents governor from discharging duties which need to be undertaken prior to his return.

(k) The Lieutenant Governor is an automatic member of the Governor's cabinet.

(l) In West Virginia, the President of the Senate and the Lieutenant Governor are one in the same. The legislature provided in statute the title of Lieutenant Governor upon the Senate President. The Senate President serves 2 year terms, elected by the Senate on the first day of the first session of each two year legislative term.

(m) If assigned.

(n) Only for joint sessions.

(o) With respect to procedural matters, not legislation.

(p) The Lieutenant Governor serves on the Assignment Committee (five members) and in such capacity has input in the appointment of committees and assigning of bills.

(q) If more than 20 days.

Secretaries of State: Duties and Responsibilities

By Kay Stimson

The office of secretary of state is evolving into a position that demands increasingly specialized skills and knowledge, particularly a thorough understanding of technology and e-government policies, and for some, experience in international trade. Recent policy trends show that election reform and e-government are demanding an increasing amount of time and effort for these state executives. For those secretaries that handle election matters, the job also comes with a new level of media and public interest in how elections are run and administered.

Overview

While today's rapid advances in technology present both opportunities and challenges for the nation's secretaries of state, the position still revolves around a basic commitment to improving the quality and scope of public administration. Each secretary of state is responsible for the functioning of diverse facets of state government, including elections, business filings, archives, licensing, administrative rules, publishing and the drafting of legislative acts.

Of all the executive positions in state government, the office of secretary of state arguably varies the most from state to state. No two offices are exactly alike. In addition to their general administrative duties, there are secretaries of state who oversee securities regulation, head the department of motor vehicles, monitor charitable giving, oversee the preparation of extraditions and warrants, direct the state libraries or museums, maintain the state capitol, commission notaries public, and participate in the state's international trade activities. "By virtue of the widespread duties that come with this office, a secretary of state acquires a very thorough understanding of state and local government," wrote one historian familiar with the post.[1]

In addition to their widespread duties and responsibilities, there are other major differences between secretary of state offices. Not counting U.S. territories, 39 members of the National Association of Secretaries of State (NASS) are elected statewide office holders, nine members (including the District of Columbia) are appointed, and three are chosen by the state legislature. Staff size can range from four people to more than 4,000.[2] Three states do not have a secretary of state position: Alaska, Hawaii and Utah. Instead, the lieutenant governors of those states have professional responsibilities that closely parallel those of the secretaries of state.

Historically speaking, the office has offered considerable career longevity. There are quite a few examples of secretaries of state spending 20 or more years in office. However, with the implementation of term limits in many states, it is becoming less common. At least seven current members of Congress held the position: Sen. Evan Bayh (D-Ind.), Rep. Roy Blunt (R-Mo.), Rep. Sherrod Brown (D-Ohio), Rep. Tom Cole (R-Okla.), Rep. Katherine Harris (R-Fla.), Rep. Jim Langevin (D-R.I.) and Rep. Candice Miller (R-Mich.). Ohio Gov. Bob Taft and Vermont Gov. Jim Douglas also served as secretary of state in their respective states, and while Utah does not have a secretary of state position (these duties are vested with the lieutenant governor), Utah Gov. Olene Walker is regarded as another distinguished alumnus of the group.

Until the turn of the century, there was also a certain level of anonymity that came with serving as secretary of state. Many secretaries take great pride in the fact that they have been able to carry out their duties in a low-key, apolitical manner; free of the usual media scrutiny that often accompanies public life.

At the same time, there can be drawbacks to playing one of the quieter roles in state government. People sometimes misinterpret what it means to be the "secretary" of state. Anne Petera, a former secretary from Virginia, used to joke about having to explain that she didn't answer the governor's phone or take notes for the governor at meetings. Others assume the title is a reference to the federal office with "secretary" in the name. Vermont Gov. Jim Douglas once wrote while serving as secretary of state, "You get used to explaining [to the public] that the U.S. secretary of state isn't your boss, that your responsibilities do not include the development and administration of U.S. foreign policy. You also learn to explain to the unenlightened just what a secretary of state does, even though your hard work touches every citizen, in some way, every day."[3]

Of course, Douglas penned his remarks more than

a decade ago. Widespread voting problems and close turnout figures during the presidential election of 2000 served as a huge catalyst for election changes, and with an unprecedented public outcry for reform came a new level of notoriety for all election officials, particularly secretaries of state. As the chief state election officials in their respective states, many secretaries are now accustomed to receiving more publicity than their predecessors. Even the most basic election matters garner attention from reporters and the public. "Depending on the situation, it can either make the job more rewarding or more frustrating," said Leslie Reynolds, executive director of NASS. "Above all, it's a different ballgame than in the past."

Duties & Responsibilities

Elections

Thirty-nine secretaries of state serve as the chief state election official, overseeing all aspects of elections and election administration. Typically, these offices supply local election officials with election materials (ballots, mailings, etc.) and training. They also collect and compile financial and campaign disclosure statements from candidates. A new federal election law, the Help America Vote Act of 2002 (HAVA), has added a whole new set of state-level administrative responsibilities, including the management of voter registration databases, provisional balloting, absentee balloting, and equipment replacement and purchasing. Voter education also figures prominently into election administration, with standard responsibilities such as public service announcements, voter information pamphlets and youth outreach programs. Some secretaries of state also investigate allegations of voter fraud and campaign reporting abuses.

Registration, Filing & Licensing

Business-related filings account for a large portion of the work of secretaries of state. Over the years, these duties have changed and expanded as government leaders have tried to make it easier for citizens to conduct their business with the state by filing documents online. Most offices oversee the registration of corporations, process and/or commission notaries public, handle professional licensing applications, and register trademarks and trade names. In addition, some offices register securities, charitable organizations and lobbyists.

It should also be noted that licensing responsibilities vary greatly from state to state. The list ranges from beauty pageants to bingo parlors to funeral directors. In Georgia and North Dakota, the secretary of state even serves as head of the state boxing commission—a rather unique responsibility.

Custodial & Publishing Duties

With few exceptions, the secretaries of state serve as the "keepers of the seal" in their respective states, an honor which establishes their position as head notary for the state. They also oversee state records archives and documents, the files on state agency rules and regulations, Uniform Commercial Code filings, and state land records and charters.

Publishing duties differ quite a bit from office to office, but about half are responsible for the state manual or directory, and most publish copies of the state constitution. In 16 states, the secretary of state handles state session laws and administrative codes and registers.

Trends for the Future

The office of secretary of state is evolving into a position that requires more focused expertise than in the past, particularly a thorough understanding of technology and e-government policies, and for some, experience in international trade. For those secretaries that handle election matters, the job also comes with a new level of media and public interest in how elections are run and administered. Major trends for secretaries of state include the following:

Election Reform

Election reform is the most pressing issue in 2004, largely due to the new federal law that makes most secretaries of state accountable for a myriad of state operations. HAVA authorizes a total of $3.9 billion over three years for states to replace outdated voting equipment and improve election administration. An additional $40 million is allocated to increase polling place access for disabled voters, improve voting technology, test voting equipment, and provide state advocacy systems for the disabled.

HAVA mandates states to abide by specific federal election requirements, including the following: provide voters with an opportunity to correct ballot errors, implement a voting system with manual audit capacity, provide at least one disability-accessible voting machine per precinct, provide alternative language accessibility for voters, allow for provisional voting, and develop a centralized, statewide voter registration base. The bill also requires states to implement statewide voter identification requirements for first-time voters.

As part of the presidential election cycle in 2004, other election-related areas that will be at the center of reform efforts are the front-loaded presidential primary schedule (NASS has a plan that advocates a regional rotating system), the steady and alarming decline in voter turnout, and methods for ensuring the continuity of Congress in the event of terrorist attacks or natural disasters.

e-Government

While serving as president of NASS, Minnesota Secretary of State Mary Kiffmeyer once noted, "The secretaries of state lead the debate on improving and increasing government services available over the Internet at the state and national levels. It is an exciting time to be holding this office."[4] One of the collective goals of the secretaries of state is to fill the digital gap in providing government information to the public. NASS released its *e-Gov Primer for Secretaries of State* in 2002, a document that details the e-government goals and progress of every state office. Topics include voter registration, election results, historical documents, business registrations and UCC filings, as well as various statewide directories and databases. Virtually every state now offers a business portal or some way to carry out transactions with the state online.

For those offices that deal with regulatory issues, fraud and other abuses within the securities market is a major concern. In early 2004, Massachusetts Secretary of State William Galvin filed suit against a Boston-based securities firm over alleged improper sales of hedge funds that resulted in investor losses totaling $3.5 million.[5] Georgia Secretary of State Cathy Cox travels the state conducting "Money Matters" forums designed to educate investors about making sound financial decisions and protecting themselves from investment fraud. This small but active group of about a dozen secretaries, under the NASS umbrella, has actively opposed congressional legislation that would seriously undermine the effectiveness of state securities regulation, including one bill aimed at preempting the states from negotiating remedial actions with firms or individuals that differ from federal or self-regulatory standards.[6] NASS Resolution on Securities Legislation and H.R. 2179 (2003), (adopted July 27, 2003).

Moreover, the secretaries of state are collectively working to combat the growing number of bogus state-level filings purporting to be legitimate financing statements under the Uniform Commercial Code. NASS formed a special Bogus Filings Task Force with the International Association of Commercial Administrators (IACA) in 2003. Their goal is to develop policies and legislation to prevent the filing of liens and other instruments intended to defraud third parties or harass individuals through the placement of holds on their assets.

International Relations

As state international engagement has rapidly increased during the past two decades, the secretaries of state have become actively involved in these activities. In Florida, the secretary of state serves as the chief cultural officer and handles all of the state's international functions. The same is true in Texas, where the secretary handles all matters with Mexico, including border relations. North Carolina Secretary of State Elaine Marshall is head of a special partnership between the state and the Republic of Moldova, overseeing work with the National Guard, trade delegations, academic partnerships and more. In addition, the secretaries of state in California, Washington, Nebraska, South Dakota, Indiana and West Virginia are currently involved in international trade at the highest levels. The most notable state office in this group may be Maryland, where an executive order issued in the 1990s created a gubernatorial sub-cabinet for international affairs headed by the secretary of state.

"It's a great move because the states need an executive-level official who can work with economic development offices and other state agencies to coordinate the work of the state and convene the meetings to discuss these matters," remarked Chris Whatley, director of international programs for The Council of State Governments.

Summary

While the office of secretary of state requires a core understanding of all aspects of state government, it has also evolved into a position that demands increasingly specialized skills and knowledge. As technology improves and diversifies, it is secretaries of state who will have to decide how to utilize the latest opportunities and make new applications available to the public. Major issue areas include elections, registration, filing, licensing, custodial duties and publishing. Recent policy trends show that election reform, e-government, and international trade are demanding an increasing amount of time and effort for these state executives. With heightened public interest in election matters, it also means that today's secretaries of state are under the media microscope more than their predecessors. Some state officials say they wouldn't be surprised if the first secretary of state to become president of the United States begins his or her political rise under these conditions.

Notes

[1] Christyn Elley Edwards, *The National Association of Secretaries of State: A Heritage*, (Jefferson City, MO: Missouri State Archives), 1996.

[2] *2002 NASS Secretary of State Office & Duties Survey*, (Washington, D.C.: National Association of Secretaries of State), 2002.

[3] Christyn Elley Edwards.

[4] Speech by Minnesota Secretary of State Mary Kiffmeyer at the 2003 NASS Summer Meeting in Portland, Maine, July 28, 2003.

[5] Reuters New Service, "Mutual Fund Probes Spread," *CNN Money*, (September 4, 2003).

About the Author

Kay Stimson is director of communications and marketing for the National Association of Secretaries of State (NASS) in Washington, D.C. Prior to her arrival at NASS, she spent more than five years in the field of television journalism as an anchor and reporter. She also has experience working as a freelance writer and media consultant. Stimson holds a master's degree in political communication from the University of Maryland and a bachelor's degree in communication from Towson University in Maryland.

Table 4.15
SECRETARIES OF STATE, 2004

State or other jurisdiction	Name and party	Method of selection	Length of regular term in years	Date of first service	Present term ends	Number of previous terms	Maximum consecutive terms allowed by constitution
Alabama	Nancy Worley (D)	E	4	1/03	1/07	...	2
Alaska	...................................(a)...................................						
Arizona	Jan Brewer (R)	E	4	1/03	1/07	...	2
Arkansas	Charlie Daniels (D)	E	4	1/03	1/07	...	2
California	Kevin Shelley (D)	E	4	1/03	1/07	...	2
Colorado	Donetta Davidson (R)	E	4	7/99 (b)	1/07	1 (b)	2 (b)
Connecticut	Susan Bysiewicz (D)	E	4	1/99	1/07	1	...
Delaware	Harriet Smith Windsor (D)	A	...	1/01	...	...	...
Florida	Glenda Hood (R)	A	...	2/03	...	...	...
Georgia	Cathy Cox (D)	E	4	1/99	1/07	1	...
Hawaii	...................................(a)...................................						
Idaho	Ben Ysursa (R)	E	4	1/03	1/07	...	...
Illinois	Jesse White (D)	E	4	1/99	1/07	1	...
Indiana	Todd Rokita (R)	E	4	1/03	1/07	...	2
Iowa	Chet Culver (D)	E	4	1/99	1/07	1	...
Kansas	Ron Thornburgh (R)	E	4	1/95	1/07	2	...
Kentucky	C.M. Grayson (R)	E	4	12/03	12/07	...	2
Louisiana	W. Fox McKeithen (R)	E	4	1/88	1/08	4	...
Maine	Dan Gwadosky (D)	L	2	1/97	12/04	3	...
Maryland	R. Karl Aumann (R)	A	...	1/03	...	...	...
Massachusetts	William Francis Galvin (D)	E	4	1/95	1/07	2	...
Michigan	Terry Lynn Land (R)	E	4	1/03	1/07	...	2
Minnesota	Mary Kiffmeyer (R)	E	4	1/99	1/07	1	...
Mississippi	Eric Clark (D)	E	4	1/96	1/08	2	...
Missouri	Matt Blunt (R)	E	4	1/01	1/05	...	...
Montana	Bob Brown (R)	E	4	1/01	1/05	...	(c)
Nebraska	John Gale (R)	E	4	12/00 (d)	1/07	(d)	2 (d)
Nevada	Dean Heller (R)	E	4	1/95	1/07	2	2 (f)
New Hampshire	William Gardner (D)	L	2	1/76	...	13	...
New Jersey	Regena Thomas (D)	A	...	1/02	...	...	...
New Mexico	Rebecca Vigil-Giron (D)	E	4	1/87 (g)	1/07	2	2
New York	Randy Daniels (R)	A	...	4/01	...	...	...
North Carolina	Elaine Marshall (D)	E	4	1/97	1/05	1	...
North Dakota	Alvin Jaeger (R)	E	4	1/93	1/05	2	...
Ohio	J. Kenneth Blackwell (R)	E	4	1/99	1/07	1	2
Oklahoma	M. Susan Savage (D)	A	...	1/03	...	...	...
Oregon	Bill Bradbury (D)	E	4	1/99 (e)	1/05	(e)	2
Pennsylvania	Pedro A. Cortes (D)	A	...	5/03	...	...	...
Rhode Island	Matthew Brown (D)	E	4	1/03	1/07	...	2
South Carolina	Mark Hammond (R)	E	4	1/03	1/07	...	...
South Dakota	Chris Nelson (R)	E	4	1/03	1/07	...	2
Tennessee	Riley Darnell (D)	L	4	1/93	1/05	2	...
Texas	Geoffrey S. Conner (R)	A	...	8/03	...	...	...
Utah	...................................(a)...................................						
Vermont	Deb Markowitz (D)	E	2	1/99	1/05	2	...
Virginia	Anita Rimler (D)	A	...	1/02	...	...	...
Washington	Sam Reed (R)	E	4	1/01	1/05	...	...
West Virginia	Joe Manchin (D)	E	4	1/01	1/05	...	...
Wisconsin	Douglas LaFollette (D)	E	4	1/99	1/07	1	...
Wyoming	Joe Meyer (R)	E	4	1/99	1/07	1	...
American Samoa	...................................(a)...................................						
Guam	...................................(a)...................................						
No. Mariana Islands	...................................(a)...................................						
Puerto Rico	Ferdinand M.Ramos (PDP)	A	...	1/01	...	...	...
U.S. Virgin Islands	...................................(a)...................................						

Source: The Council of State Governments' survey, December 2003 and The National Association of Secretaries of State, December 2003.

Key:
E — Elected by voters
A — Appointed by governor.
L — Elected by legislature.
. . . — No provision for.
(a) No secretary of state.
(b) Secretary Davidson was appointed by Gov. Bill Owens in July 1999 upon the death of Secretary Vikki Buckley. She was elected to finish out the remaining two-year term in November 2000, and then was re-elected to a full four-year term in November 2002.
(c) Eligible for eight out of 16 years.
(d) Secretary Gale was appointed by Gov. Mike Johanns in December 2000 upon the resignation of Scott Moore. He was elected to a full four-year term in November 2002.
(e) Secretary Bradbury was appointed Secretary of State in November 1999 and was elected to a four-year term in November 2000.
(f) Term limits were not effective until Secretary Heller's second term in office. His second term counts as his first.
(g) Secretary Vigil-Giron served from 1987-1991. She was elected again in 1998 and in 2002.

Table 4.16
SECRETARIES OF STATE: QUALIFICATIONS FOR OFFICE

State or other jurisdiction	Minimum age	U.S. citizen (years) (a)	State resident (years) (b)	Qualified voter (years)	Method of selection to office
Alabama	25	7	5	★	E
Alaska	...........(c)...........				E
Arizona	25	10	5	. . .	E
Arkansas	18	★	★	★	E
California	18	★	★	★	E
Colorado	25	★	2	. . .	E
Connecticut	18	★	★	★	E
Delaware	. . .	. . .	★	. . .	A
Florida	...........(f)...........				
Georgia	25	10	4	★	E
Hawaii	...........(c)...........				
Idaho	25	★	2	★	E
Illinois	25	★	3	. . .	E
Indiana	. . .	. . .	★	. . .	E
Iowa	18	. . .	. . .	. . .	E
Kansas	. . .	. . .	. . .	. . .	E
Kentucky	30	★	★	★	E
Louisiana	25	5	5	★	E
Maine	. . .	. . .	. . .	. . .	(e)
Maryland	. . .	. . .	. . .	. . .	A
Massachusetts	18	★	5	★	E
Michigan	30	★	★	4	E
Minnesota	21	★	★	★	E
Mississippi	25	★	5 (d)	★	E
Missouri	. . .	★	★	2	E
Montana	25	★	2	★	E
Nebraska	. . .	★	★	★	E
Nevada	25	2	2	. . .	E
New Hampshire	18	★	★	★	(e)
New Jersey	18	★	★	★	A
New Mexico	30	★	5	★	E
New York	18	★	★	. . .	A
North Carolina	21	. . .	. . .	★	E
North Dakota	25	★	5	★	E
Ohio	18	★	★	★	E
Oklahoma	31	★	10	★	A
Oregon	18	. . .	★	★	E
Pennsylvania	. . .	. . .	. . .	. . .	A
Rhode Island	18	★	30 days	★	E
South Carolina	18	★	★	★	E
South Dakota	. . .	. . .	. . .	. . .	E
Tennessee	. . .	. . .	. . .	. . .	(e)
Texas	18	★	1	. . .	A
Utah	...........(c)...........				
Vermont	. . .	★	★	★	E
Virginia	. . .	. . .	. . .	. . .	A
Washington	18	★	★	★	E
West Virginia	. . .	★	★	★	E
Wisconsin	18	★	★	★	E
Wyoming	25	★	1	★	E
American Samoa	...........(c)...........				
Guam	...........(c)...........				
No. Mariana Islands	...........(c)...........				
Puerto Rico	. . .	5	5	. . .	A
U.S. Virgin Islands	...........(c)...........				

Source: The Council of State Governments' survey of secretaries of state, October 2003.

Key:

★ — Formal provision; number of years not specified.

. . . — No formal provision.

A — Appointed by governor.

E — Elected by voters.

(a) In some states you must be a U.S. citizen to be an elector, and must be an elector to run.

(b) In some states you must be a state resident to be an elector, and must be an elector to run.

(c) No secretary of state.

(d) State citizenship requirement.

(e) Chosen by joint ballot of state senators and representatives. In Maine and New Hampshire, every two years. In Tennessee, every four years.

(f) As of January 1, 2003, the office of Secretary of State shall be an appointed position (appointed by the governor). It will no longer be a cabinet position, but an agency head and the Department of State shall be an agency under the governor's office.

Table 4.17
SECRETARIES OF STATE: ELECTION AND REGISTRATION DUTIES

State or other jurisdiction	Election								Registration				
	Chief election officer	Determines ballot eligibility of political parties	Receives initiative and/or referendum petition	Files certificate of nomination or election	Supplies election ballots or materials to local officials	Files candidates' expense papers	Files other campaign reports	Conducts voter education programs	Registers charitable organizations	Registers corporations (a)	Processes and/or commissions notaries public	Registers securities	Registers trade names/marks
Alabama	★	★	...	★	★	★	★	★	★	★	★	...	★
Alaska (b)	★	★	★	★	★	...	...	★	...	...	★	...	...
Arizona	★	★	★	★	...	★	★	★	★	...	★	...	★
Arkansas	★	★	★	★	...	★	★	★	★	★	★	...	★
California	★	★	★	★	...	★	★	★	...	★	★	...	★
Colorado	★	★	★	★	...	★	★	★	★	★	★	...	★
Connecticut	★	★	...	★	★	★	★	★	★	★	★	...	★
Delaware	...	...	...	(c)	...	...	(d)	...	★ (e)	★	★	...	★
Florida	★	★	★	★	...	★	★	...	★	★	...	...	★
Georgia	★	★	...	★	★	★	★	★	★	★	...	★	★
Hawaii (b)	...	...	...	...	...	...	...	...	...	...	...	...	...
Idaho	★	★	★	★	★	★	★	★	...	★	★	...	★
Illinois	...	...	★	(h)	...	...	...	...	★	★	★	★	★
Indiana	★	★	...	★	★	★	★	★	★	★	★	★	★
Iowa	★	★	...	★	...	...	...	★	...	★	★	...	★
Kansas	★	★	...	★	...	★	★	★	★	★	★	...	★
Kentucky	★	★	...	★	★	...	...	★	★	★	★	...	★
Louisiana	★	...	...	...	...	...	...	★	★	★	★	★	★
Maine	★	★	★	★	...	...	...	★	...	★	★	...	★
Maryland	...	★	★	★	...	...	...	...	★	★	...	...	★
Massachusetts	★	★	★	★	★	(d)	(d)	★	...	★	★	★	★
Michigan	★	★	★	★	...	★	★	★	...	★	★	★	...
Minnesota	★	★	★	★	...	...	...	★	★	★	★	...	★
Mississippi	★	★	★	★	★	★	★	★	★	★	★	★	★
Missouri	★	★	★	★	...	...	...	★	★	★	★	★	★
Montana	★	★	★	★	★	...	...	★	★	★	★	...	★
Nebraska	★	★	★	★	★	...	...	★	★	★	★	...	★
Nevada	★	★	★	★	★	★	★	★	...	★	★	★	★
New Hampshire	★	★	...	★	★	★	★	...	...	★	★	★	★
New Jersey	...	...	...	...	...	★	★	...	...	...	...	...	...
New Mexico	★	★	★	★	★	★	★	★	...	★	★	...	★
New York	...	...	...	...	...	...	...	...	...	★	★	...	★
North Carolina	...	...	...	...	...	...	...	...	★	★	★	★	★
North Dakota	★	★	★	★	★	★	★	★	★	★	★	...	★
Ohio	★	★	★	★	★	★	...	★	...	★	★	...	★
Oklahoma	...	...	★	★ (f)	...	...	...	...	★	★	★	...	★
Oregon	★	★	★	★	★	★	★	★	★	★	★	★	★
Pennsylvania	★	★	★	★	★	★	★	★	★	★	★	...	★
Rhode Island	★	...	...	★	★	(d)	(d)	★	...	★	★	...	★
South Carolina	...	...	...	...	...	...	...	...	★	★	★	...	★
South Dakota	★	★	★	★	...	★	★	★	...	★	★	...	★
Tennessee	...	★	...	★	★	...	...	★	★	★	★	...	★
Texas	★	★	...	★	...	...	...	★	★	★	★	...	★
Utah (b)	★	★	★	★	★	★	★	★	★	★	...	...	...
Vermont	★	★	...	★	★	★	★	★	...	★	★	...	★
Virginia	...	...	...	...	...	...	...	...	...	...	...	...	...
Washington	★	★	★	★	...	...	...	★	★	★	...	★	★
West Virginia	★	★	...	★	...	★	★	★	★	★	★	...	★
Wisconsin	...	...	...	...	...	...	...	...	...	...	★	...	★
Wyoming	★	★	★	★	(i)	★	★	★	★	★	★	★	★
American Samoa (b)	...	...	...	★	...	★	★	★	★	★	★	...	...
Guam (b)	...	...	...	...	...	...	...	...	...	...	...	...	...
Puerto Rico	...	...	...	...	...	...	...	...	★	★	★	★	★
U.S. Virgin Islands (b)	...	...	...	...	...	...	...	...	★	★ (g)	★	...	★

See footnotes at end of table.

SECRETARIES OF STATE: ELECTION AND REGISTRATION DUTIES — Continued

Source: The Council of State Governments' survey of secretaries of state, October 2003.

Key:

★ — Responsible for activity.

. . . — Not responsible for activity.

(a) Unless otherwise indicated, office registers domestic, foreign and non-profit corporations.

(b) No secretary of state. Duties indicated are performed by lieutenant governor. In Hawaii, election related responsibilities have been transferred to an independent Chief Election Officer.

(c) Files certificates of election for publication purposes only; does not file certificates of nomination.

(d) Federal candidates only.

(e) Incorporated organizations only.

(f) Files certificates of national elections only; does not file certificates of nomination.

(g) Both domestic and foreign profit; but only domestic non-profit.

(h) Office issues document, but does not receive it.

(i) Materials not ballots.

Table 4.18
SECRETARIES OF STATE: CUSTODIAL, PUBLICATION AND LEGISLATIVE DUTIES

State or other jurisdiction	Custodial			Publication					Legislative				
	Archives state records and regulations	Files state agency rules and regulations	Administers uniform commercial code provisions	Files other corporate documents	State manual or directory	Session laws	State constitution	Statutes	Administrative rules and regulations	Opens legislative sessions (a)	Enrolls or engrosses bills	Retains copies of bills	Registers lobbyists
Alabama	...	...	★	★	...	★	★	★	...	...	★	★	...
Alaska (b)	...	★	...	...	...	...	★	...	★	★	...	★	...
Arizona	★	★	★	...	...	...	★	...	★	...	...	★	★
Arkansas	★	★	★	★	...	★	★	...	★	...	...	★	★
California	★	...	★	★	...	...	...	...	...	...	...	...	★
Colorado	...	★	★	★	...	...	★	...	★	...	...	★	★
Connecticut	★(c)	★	★	★	★	...	...	...	...	S	...	★	...
Delaware	★	★	★	★	...	...	...	...	★	...	...	...	...
Florida	★	★	...	★	...	★	★	★	★	...	...	...	...
Georgia	★	★	...	...	★	...	★	...	★	...	...	...	...
Hawaii (b)	...	★	...	...	...	★	...	★	...	...	...	...	...
Idaho	...	...	...	...	★	★	★	...	...	...	...	★	★
Illinois	★	★	★	★	★	★	★	...	★	H	...	★	★
Indiana	★	★	★	★	...	...	...	...	...	...	...	★	...
Iowa	★	...	★	★	...	...	★	...	...	...	...	★	...
Kansas	...	★	★	★	...	★	...	...	★	★	...	★	★
Kentucky	★	...	★	★	...	...	...	...	...	...	★	★	...
Louisiana	★	...	★	★	★	...	...	★	...	...	...	★	...
Maine	★	★	★	★	...	...	★	★	★	...	...	...	...
Maryland	...	...	...	...	...	...	...	...	...	...	...	★	...
Massachusetts	★	★	★	★	★	★	★	★	★	...	...	★	★
Michigan	★	★	★	...	...	★	★	★	★	...	...	...	★
Minnesota	★	★	★	★	★	★	★	★	...	H	...	★	★
Mississippi	★	...	★	★	★	★	★	...	★	★	★	★	★
Missouri	★	...	★	★	★	...	★	...	★	H	★	★	...
Montana	★	★	★	★	...	...	★	...	★	H	★	★	...
Nebraska	★	★	★	★	...	...	...	...	...	...	...	★	...
Nevada	★	★	★	★	...	...	...	...	...	...	...	★	...
New Hampshire	★	...	★	★	★	...	★	...	...	...	★	★	★
New Jersey	★	...	...	...	...	...	★	...	...	...	...	...	...
New Mexico	...	...	★	...	★	★	★	★	...	H	...	★	★
New York	...	★	★	...	★	...	★	...	★	...	...	...	...
North Carolina	★	★	★	★	★	★	★	...	...	...	...	...	★
North Dakota	...	...	★	...	...	...	...	...	...	...	★	★	★
Ohio	...	★	★	★	★	★	★	...	...	...	★	★	★
Oklahoma	...	★	...	★	...	★	★	★	★	...	...	★	...
Oregon	★	★	★	★	★	...	★	...	★	...	...	★	...
Pennsylvania	...	...	★	★	...	...	...	...	...	...	★	★	...
Rhode Island	★	★	★	★	★	...	★	...	★	...	...	★	★
South Carolina	...	...	★	★	...	...	★	...	...	...	...	★	...
South Dakota	★	★	★	★	★	...	★	...	...	H	...	★	★
Tennessee	★	★	★	★	★	★	★	...	★	...	...	★	...
Texas	...	★	★	★	...	★	...	...	★	H	★	★	...
Utah (b)	...	...	...	...	...	...	...	...	...	...	...	★	★
Vermont	★	★	★	★	★	★	★	...	★	H	...	★	★
Virginia	...	...	...	...	...	...	...	...	...	...	...	...	...
Washington	★	...	...	★	★	...	...	...	...	...	...	★	...
West Virginia	★	★	★	★	...	...	★	...	★	...	...	★	...
Wisconsin	...	...	...	...	...	...	...	...	...	...	...	...	...
Wyoming	★	★	★	★	★	...	★	...	...	H	...	★	★
American Samoa (b)	...	★	...	★	...	★	★	★	★	...	...	...	...
Guam (b)	...	...	...	...	...	...	...	...	...	...	...	...	...
Puerto Rico	...	★	★	★	...	★	★	★	★	...	...	...	...
U.S. Virgin Islands (b)	...	★	★	★	...	...	...	★	...	...	★	★	...

Source: The Council of State Governments' survey of secretaries of state, October 2003.

Key:
★— Responsible for activity.
. . . — Not responsible for activity.

(a) In this column only: ★–Both houses; H–House; S–Senate.
(b) No secretary of state. Duties indicated are performed by lieutenant governor.
(c) The secretary of state is keeper of public records, but the state archives is a department of the Connecticut State Library.

Attorneys General: Roles and Emerging Issues
By Angelita Plemmer

Whether attorneys general are viewed as activists, advocates or interpreters of the law, they impact all areas of public policy and all aspects of citizen life. Emerging technologies have changed the methods used by the chief legal officers to investigate crimes, as well as enforce and prosecute all areas of the law.

The Role of Attorneys General

Keeping intrusive and unwanted telemarketers away. Protecting consumers against fraud and abuse. Ensuring a fair marketplace. Fighting crime. Defending criminal convictions on appeal. These are among the myriad of issues in which attorneys general are involved. Today, nearly every aspect of citizen life is affected in some way by the work of attorneys general.

Attorneys general serve as the chief legal officers of their states or jurisdictions. They typically provide legal advice to their governor and serve as the principal lawyer for state agencies, boards and commissions. Many have legal authority to bring independent actions in the public interest. Such actions have included lawsuits over violations of consumer and environmental protection laws, the prosecution of identity theft and cybercrime and unfair business practices by tobacco companies and others. Often, the offices of attorneys general are structured like private law firms with sections specializing in specific areas of the law.

The range of activities in which attorneys general are involved is wide and varied. The following highlights some of these activities:

Antitrust

Often characterized as "the guardians of the gates of effective antitrust enforcement," state attorneys general are instrumental in efforts to ensure full, free and fair competition in the marketplace through the enforcement of federal and state antitrust laws. Their unique ability to enforce both federal and state antitrust laws have led attorneys general to bring multistate cases that are national in scope, in addition to local bid-rigging and price-fixing cases. Even before passage of the Sherman Act in 1890, the majority of states had some form of antitrust prohibition. The Sherman Act itself was designed to supplement these state laws. State attorneys general actively enforced these laws, and important aspects of antitrust law, including the *per se* rule against price-fixing, were first developed under state law.[1]

With the enactment of the Sherman Act, attorneys general became less active in antitrust enforcement for several decades. Attorneys general resumed more vigorous antitrust enforcement in the mid-1970s. This revival stemmed in part from new state laws authorizing attorneys general to sue on behalf of their states and political subdivisions in state and federal courts. Two new federal laws, enacted in 1976, also encouraged antitrust enforcement activity by attorneys general. The State Antitrust Grant Program amendment to the Crime Control Act[2] provided seed money for states to fund antitrust enforcement programs and the Hart-Scott-Rodino Antitrust Improvements Act[3] authorized state attorneys general to maintain federal *parens patriae* treble damage antitrust actions for their respective citizens.

Today, attorneys general are using traditional enforcement tools in innovative ways, working together on multistate cases in both federal and state courts. Their goal now, as always, is to preserve competition, and accordingly, lower prices, to provide higher quality and a greater variety of innovative new products for citizens of their states.

During the past decade, the trend in state antitrust enforcement has been toward multistate litigation filed by a number of the attorneys general on cases with national impact. The Multistate Antitrust Task Force of the National Association of Attorneys General (NAAG) was created in 1983 to coordinate the exercise of the powers of individual attorneys general in antitrust matters. All states have staff representing them on the task force. The task force organizes the conduct of multistate investigations and the filing of multistate actions. A single attorney general or group of attorneys general will take the lead in an investigation, issuing administrative subpoenas or civil investigative demands. The parties are told that their responses will be shared with other interested attorneys general. The attorneys general have found that this process not only may reduce the burden on respondents, but can increase coordination among the states and allow the most efficient use of state resources. Multistate litigation typically includes cost sharing arrangements among the attorneys general and also may include deputization of staff attorneys from one state to act as assistant attorneys general in other states for investigation and litigation purposes.

Criminal Law

In most jurisdictions, the attorney general plays a pivotal role in law enforcement, as the most visible and influential state official in the fight against crime. Although the constitutional and statutory authority of attorneys general varies from state to state, in most states, the attorney general is a critical component in the successful investigation and prosecution of criminal activity and in upholding convictions challenged through direct appeal and collateral proceedings in the courts.[4] In recent years, attorneys general have emerged as leaders in the legal and policy discussions in the law enforcement community by pioneering and advocating new fields of research and expanded use of developing technologies in areas like the expanded use of DNA, the Internet and cybercrime, white collar crime detection methods, forensic analysis, surveillance and information sharing among law enforcement.

The ability of the attorney general to take an active role in criminal investigations and prosecutions is primarily dependent on statutory or constitutional authority. In many jurisdictions, the attorney general's office has its own investigative unit; in a number of jurisdictions, the statewide investigative bureau is directly under the attorney general's authority. In addition to direct investigative involvement, the attorney general, in most jurisdictions, provides important training services to peace officers and local prosecutors, ranging from manuals and newsletters, to seminars and training academies.[5]

In June 2003, California Attorney General Bill Lockyer announced that under his leadership as NAAG president, the association would focus attention on what more could be done to maximize the value and use of technology in the criminal justice system. Attorneys general could do things as practical as encouraging the wide distribution of Personal Identification Kits for use by law enforcement in helping find missing children that number nearly 800,000 each year or more than 2,000 each day across the country, including family and non-family abductions, according to a U.S. Department of Justice study released in 2002 (*The National Incidence studies of Missing, Abducted, Runaway and Thrownaway Children*). With the kits, parents would be able to gather vital identification data like DNA samples from their child's cheek using a swab and materials for simple storage on a bookshelf at home. Or, it could mean taking advantage of advances in DNA evidence analysis. Traditional investigative methods are improving due to developments in digital fingerprinting imaging and new possibilities are surfacing every day. For instance, developers say a new device inspired by NASA's Near Earth Asteroid Rendezvous mission will help detectives solve murders and shooting crimes faster using remote electron sensing to confirm quickly whether a suspect has recently fired a gun.[6] As attorneys general, it is crucial that jurisdictions have access to the best modern crime-fighting technology possible, to ensure the public trust and maintain safe communities.

Attorneys general are continuing to focus their efforts in traditional areas such as organized crime, white collar crime and Medicaid fraud, but they are also beginning to see varying responsibilities in the criminal justice arena revolving around corrections, victims' rights and drug enforcement. Other growing areas of concern, many of which have prompted the creation of a number of working groups and task forces within NAAG, are rising statistics on gang violence, prescription drug abuse — particularly Oxycontin, the civil commitment of sexually violent predators, violence against women and a number of very complex legal and ethical questions surrounding end of life issues.

Cybercrime

As the states' top law enforcers, attorneys general are looking at the increasing number of crimes occurring over the Internet – and particularly how perpetrators are becoming more adept at using the Internet to commit fraud, identity theft, stalking and other crimes against children. Traditional crimes have entered a new age. Criminal activity has become more complex and more difficult to investigate and prosecute. Today's technology-driven world provides a new arena for criminals and other unscrupulous actors. At any given moment, legions of criminals are prowling the Internet in search of unwitting targets. Children are particularly vulnerable to Internet criminals, as they are increasingly becoming victims of online luring and exposure to child pornography. Another traditional sex crime with a high-tech component, cyberstalking, is becoming one of the most terrifying computer-facilitated crimes. Scam artists are exploiting the Internet's instant access to thousands upon thousands of potential victims. Recent events in this country also have demonstrated that critical elements of our infrastructure remain vulnerable to cyber attacks.

Ubiquitous networks have facilitated the perpetration of intrusion-related crimes such as hacking, denial of service attacks, computer viruses and worms. Criminals are also harnessing the power of the Internet to commit the more traditional crimes, such as money laundering, drug smuggling and murder. In a recent Michigan homicide case, two co-conspirators plotted a murder through AOL Instant Messenger. The prosecutors handling the case were required to develop a high-level of technical expertise and then translate this digital evidence for the judge and jury. To complicate the situation further, high-tech criminals often use sophisticated encryption methods to cover their trails. Many have technical knowledge significantly beyond that of investigators and prosecutors.

The majority of state attorneys general frequently serve as the lead prosecutorial resource within their states, often sharing concurrent jurisdiction with local prosecutors. Further, many state attorneys general have taken a leadership role in high tech crime investigation and prosecution. As front-line players in the war against cybercrime, it is crucial that state prosecutors in attorneys general offices become familiar with the underlying technical concepts associated with computers, the Internet and digital evidence.

Consumer Protection

The attorneys general are a leading consumer protection force in the nation. The attorneys general can be found in the forefront of defending senior citizens from telephone and mail fraud and home repair scams, safeguarding consumers from price gouging and charities fraud in the wake of disasters, and protecting consumers from fraudulent practices as they migrate from the "brick-and-mortar" to the "online" world.

The consumer protection programs of the attorneys general are multifaceted. Most attorneys general have primary responsibility for enforcement of consumer protection statutes. Their efforts encompass civil and criminal litigation, mediation, public education, creating and commenting on state and federal legislative proposals, and cooperative enforcement ventures with state, local and federal enforcement agencies. The last part of the 20th century saw the passage of hundreds of new consumer protection laws, most of which have conveyed considerable enforcement authority to attorneys general. The growing pace of technological innovation in consumer products and the increasingly aggressive marketing and advertising strategies of manufacturers and sellers have led to an enhanced concern for and increased resource devotion to consumer protection

at the state level. The deregulation of both the telecommunications industry nationwide and the electric energy industry in selected regions, along with the explosion of Internet commerce, have expanded the attorneys general's scope of activity related to consumer protection.

The attorneys general in turn have created and added resources to consumer protection units, developed new enforcement strategies, and engaged in significant multistate projects. The continued trend toward multistate activity among the attorneys general is extremely significant. Sharing resources and acting collectively on issues that transcend state borders have produced successful results in efforts to stop consumer frauds involving sweepstakes, the Internet and tire safety.

When an attorney general brings actions on behalf of consumers, he or she does so as counsel for the state, not generally as counsel for consumers individually affected by the alleged violations. Most attorneys general do not have legal authority to litigate on behalf of individual consumers, although restitution may be obtained on their behalf. Many attorneys general offices have made use of their Internet Web sites to facilitate the submission of consumer complaints. While less than one-third of attorneys general offices accept online filing of consumer complaints, virtually every attorneys general Web site provides a "downloadable" consumer complaint that consumers can obtain through the Internet, complete, and, thereafter, submit to his or her attorney general.

Enforcement activities for attorneys general focus on a number of areas, but primarily involve: automobile-related complaints – deceptive practices by auto dealers; disaster-related scams – price gouging; home repair and improvement – shoddy contracting; Internet-based sweepstakes promotions, investment scams and pyramid schemes; and illegal Internet-based marketing schemes – auctions, online drug prescribing, and sales of candy-flavored cigarettes.

Privacy

The attorneys general have been active in the burgeoning privacy arena as well. The filing for bankruptcy by many dot–com businesses resulted in the proposed sale by those businesses of private customer information as bankruptcy assets in violation of their promises to keep such information private. Attorneys general have also tackled the emerging and burgeoning problem of identity theft. Many attorneys general have pursued criminal identity theft charges based on newly-passed identity theft and misappropriation of identity laws or more traditional credit card theft, racketeering larceny, receiving stolen property, forgery and uttering theories.

Environment

The attorney general plays a major role in protecting and enhancing the state's natural resources. Oftentimes, attorneys general work cooperatively with state agencies, local governments, private industry and public interest groups to ensure the enforcement of civil and criminal environmental protection laws.

The administration and enforcement of environmental laws involve an intricate set of relationships among the attorney general, the state regulatory agencies, and the federal government. Many federal environmental statutes authorize the federal government to transfer primary authority for the administration of those statutes to states with approved environmental programs. Once the federal government has approved a state program, the attorney general in most states is responsible for enforcing the laws that form the basis of the program.

The decade of the 1990s has seen a number of developments affecting the role and evolution of the attorney general as a key player in the enforcement of environmental law. Public awareness and attitudes toward environmental protection contributed to increases in the level of staffing in many attorneys general offices as legislatures recognized the importance to the public of environmental protection. As state environmental programs matured and federal resources devoted to environmental protection shrank or remained flat, additional responsibilities were (and continue to be) devolved to the states, and as a consequence, to state attorneys general. Many states became increasingly involved in cooperative enforcement actions with the federal government. Interest in, and involvement with, criminal enforcement of environmental laws also appeared to increase. Each of these developments has resulted in additional responsibilities for attorneys general, although, to be sure, not always coupled with an increase in resources to address them.

Preemption

Regardless of political affiliation, state attorneys general are finding themselves allied to protect against the increasing use of federal preemption in areas where states have traditionally exercised police powers to protect their citizens. A special task force was created by NAAG President Lockyer to focus attention on this important issue. The association has been involved actively in opposing the preemption efforts in litigation, amicus filings, congressional testimony and general advocacy.

Under the concept of dual sovereignty, state governments and federal governments each retain and actively exercise the functions and powers of government at the same time. Where there has been a lack of federal action, attorneys general have been able to step up state enforcement and regulatory oversight in the public interest. A disturbing reaction to this local activism has been increasing moves by federal agencies and Congress to preempt state laws and cripple the ability of states to exercise their sovereign rights.

Conclusion

Attorneys general occupy a position of enormous power and responsibility in state government. Whether as interpreters or advocates, state attorneys general have contributed critical momentum to the development of American law.[7]

Notes

[1] See *United States v. Trenton Potteries Co.*, 273 U.S. 392, 400 (1927) (holding price fixing among competitors illegal *per se*, relying on prior state case law to the same effect).

[2] Pub.L. 94-503, Title I, § 116, 90 Stat. 2415 (1976).

[3] 15 U.S.C. §18a (1994).

[4] *State Attorneys General Powers and Responsibilities.* Ed. Lynne Ross. (National Association of Attorneys General and The Bureau of National Affairs, Inc. 1990): 278.

[5] Ibid.

[6] National Association of Attorneys General. President's Message: New NAAG President Bill Lockyer Announces "Technology & Crime Fighting" Presidential Initiative. June 2003. www.naag.org.

[7] *State Attorneys General Powers and Responsibilities.*

About the Author

This article was edited and compiled by **Angelita Plemmer**, director of communications for the National Association of Attorneys General. A former print journalist, Plemmer joined the association staff in 2001. She formerly worked as the public information officer for the city of Roanoke, Va. and as the assistant city manager for public information for the city of Alexandria, Va. She holds a master's degree in journalism from Columbia University and a bachelor of arts degree from the University of Virginia.

Table 4.19
THE ATTORNEYS GENERAL, 2004

State or other jurisdiction	Name and party	Method of selection	Length of regular term in years	Date of first service	Present term ends	Number of previous terms	Maximum consecutive terms allowed
Alabama	Troy King (R)	E	4	3/04 (i)	12/06	0 (i)	2
Alaska	Gregg Renkes (R)	A	. . .	2002	2006	0	. . .
Arizona	Terry Goddard (D)	E	4	1/03	1/07	0	2 (a)
Arkansas	Mike Beebe (D)	E	4	1/03	1/07	0	2
California	Bill Lockyer (D)	E	4	1/99	1/07	1	2
Colorado	Ken Salazar (D)	E	4	1/99	1/07	1	2
Connecticut	Richard Blumenthal (D)	E	4	1/91	1/07	3	★
Delaware	M. Jane Brady (R)	E	4	1/95	1/07	2	★
Florida	Charlie Crist (R)	E	4	1/03	1/07	0	★
Georgia	Thurbert E. Baker (D)	E	4	(j)	1/07	1 (j)	★
Hawaii	Mark J. Bennett (R)	A	4	12/02	12/06	0	. . .
Idaho	Lawrence Wasden (R)	E	4	1/03	1/07	0	★
Illinois	Lisa Madigan (D)	E	4	1/03	1/07	0	★
Indiana	Steve Carter (R)	E	4	1/01	1/05	0	. . .
Iowa	Tom Miller (D)	E	4	1/79	1/07	4	★
Kansas	Phill Kline (R)	E	4	1/03	1/07	0	★
Kentucky	Greg Stumbo (D)	E	4	1/04	1/08	. . .	2
Louisiana	Charles C. Foti Jr. (D)	E	4	1/04	1/08	. . .	★
Maine	G. Steven Rowe (D)	(b)	2	1/01	1/05	0	. . .
Maryland	J. Joseph Curran Jr. (D)	E	4	1/87	1/07	4	★
Massachusetts	Tom Reilly (D)	E	4	1/99	1/07	1	2
Michigan	Mike Cox (R)	E	4	1/03	1/07	0	2
Minnesota	Mike Hatch (D)	E	4	1/97	1/07	1	★
Mississippi	Jim Hood (D)	E	4	1/04	1/08	. . .	★
Missouri	Jeremiah W. Nixon (D)	E	4	1/93	1/05	2	★
Montana	Mike McGrath (D)	E	4	1/01	1/05	0	2 (c)
Nebraska	Jon Bruning (R)	E	4	1/03	1/07	0	2 (a)
Nevada	Brian Sandoval (R)	E	4	1/03	1/07	0	2
New Hampshire	Peter W. Heed	A	4	2/03	2/05	0	. . .
New Jersey (k)	Peter C. Harvey	A	4	3/03	. . .	. . .	. . .
New Mexico	Patricia A. Madrid (D)	E	4	1/99	1/07	1	2 (a)
New York	Eliot Sptizer (D)	E	4	1/99	1/07	1	★
North Carolina	Roy Cooper (D)	E	4	1/01	1/05	0	★
North Dakota	Wayne Stenehjem (R)	E	4	12/00	12/04	0	★(d)
Ohio	Jim Petro (R)	E	4	1/03	1/07	0	2
Oklahoma	W. A. Drew Edmondson (D)	E	4	1/95	1/07	2	2 (a)
Oregon	Hardy Myers (D)	E	4	1/97	1/05	1	(e)
Pennsylvania	Gerald Pappert	E	4	1/97	2/04	0	2 (a)
Rhode Island	Patrick Lynch (D)	E	4	1/03	1/07	0	2 (a)
South Carolina	Henry McMaster (R)	E	4	1/03	1/07	0	★
South Dakota	Larry Long (R)	E	4	1/03	1/07	0	2 (a)
Tennessee	Paul G. Summers (D)	(f)	4	1/99	1/07	1	. . .
Texas	Greg Abbott (R)	E	4	1/03	1/07	0	★
Utah	Mark Shurtleff (R)	E	4	1/01	1/05	0	★
Vermont	William H. Sorrell (D)	E	2	1/99	1/07	1	★
Virginia	Jerry Kilgore (R)	E	4	1/02	1/06	0	(g)
Washington	Christine O. Gregoire (D)	E	4	1/93	1/05	2	★
West Virginia	Darrell Vivian McGraw Jr. (D)	E	4	1/93	1/07	3	★
Wisconsin	Peg Lautenschlager (D)	E	4	1/03	1/07	0	★
Wyoming	Pat Crank	A (h)	4	1/03	1/07	0	. . .
American Samoa	Fiti Sunia	A	4	N.A.	N.A.	N.A.	. . .
Guam	Douglas Moylan	E	4	1/03	1/07	0	. . .
No. Mariana Islands	(l)	A	4	N.A.	N.A.	N.A.	. . .
Puerto Rico	Anabelle Rodriguez (D)	A	4	1/01	1/05	0	. . .
U.S. Virgin Islands	Iver A. Stridiron(D)	A	4	7/99	N.A.	N.A.	. . .

Sources: National Association of Attorneys General and state web sites, March 2003.

Key:

★ — No provision specifying number of terms allowed.

. . . — No formal provision, position is appointed or elected by governmental entity (not chosen by the electorate).

A — Appointed by the governor.

E — Elected by the voters.

L — Elected by the legislature.

(a) After two consecutive terms , must wait four years and/or one full term before being eligible again.

(b) Chosen biennially by joint ballot of state senators and representatives.

(c) Eligible for eight out of 16 years.

(d) The term of the office of the elected official is four years, except that in 2004 the attorney general will be elected for a term of two years.

(e) Eligible for eight out of any period of 12 years.

(f) Appointed by judges of state Supreme Court.

(g) Provision specifying individual may hold office for an unlimited number of terms.

(h) Must be confirmed by the Senate.

(i)) Appointed to fill unexpired term in March 2004.

(j) Appointed on June 1, 1997. He was elected in 1998 to his first full term.

(k) Acting Attorney General.

(l) Appointment pending.

(m) Appointed to fill unexpired term in February 2004.

Table 4.20
ATTORNEYS GENERAL: QUALIFICATIONS FOR OFFICE

State or other jurisdiction	Minimum age	U.S. citizen (years) (a)	State resident (years) (b)	Qualified voter (years)	Licensed attorney (years)	Membership in the state bar (years)	Method of selection to office
Alabama	25	7	5	★	...	...	E
Alaska	...	★	...	...	...	...	A
Arizona	25	10	5	...	5	5	E
Arkansas	...	...	★	★	...	...	E
California	18	★	★	★	(c)	(c)	E
Colorado	25	★	2	...	★	(d)	E
Connecticut	18	★	★	★	10	10	E
Delaware	...	...	...	...	...	...	E
Florida	30	★	7	★	★	5	E
Georgia	25	10	4	★	★	7	E
Hawaii	...	1	1	...	★	(e)	A
Idaho	30	★	2	...	★	★	E
Illinois	25	★	3	★	★	...	E
Indiana	...	2	2	★	5	...	E
Iowa	18	★	★	...	...	...	E
Kansas	...	...	...	...	...	...	E
Kentucky	30	...	2 (f)	...	8	2	E
Louisiana	25	5	5 (f)	★	5	5	E
Maine	...	...	...	...	...	...	(g)
Maryland	...	★ (h)	★	★	★	10	E
Massachusetts	18	...	5	★	★	★	E
Michigan	18	★	★	...	★	★	E
Minnesota	21	★	30 days	★	...	...	E
Mississippi	26	★	★	★	5	★	E
Missouri	...	★	1	...	...	...	E
Montana	25	★	2	...	5	★	E
Nebraska	...	...	...	...	...	...	E
Nevada	25	★	2 (f)	★	...	...	E
New Hampshire	18	...	...	★	★	★	A
New Jersey	18	...	★	...	...	...	A
New Mexico	30	★	5	★	★	...	E
New York	30	★	5	...	(i)	...	E
North Carolina	21	★	★	★	★	(i)	E
North Dakota	25	★	5	★	★	★	E
Ohio	18	★	★	★	★	★	E
Oklahoma	31	★	10	10	...	...	E
Oregon	18	★	★	★	...	...	E
Pennsylvania	30	★	7	...	★	★	E
Rhode Island	18	★	30 days (f)	★	...	...	E
South Carolina	...	★	30 days	★	...	...	E
South Dakota	18	★	★	★	(i)	(i)	E
Tennessee	...	...	...	...	...	...	(j)
Texas	...	...	★	...	(i)	(i)	E
Utah	25	★	5 (f)	★	★	★	E
Vermont	18	★	★	★	...	...	E
Virginia	30	★	1 (k)	★	...	5 (k)	E
Washington	18	★	★	★	★	★	E
West Virginia	25	...	5	★	...	...	E
Wisconsin	...	★	★	...	...	...	E
Wyoming	...	★	★	★	4	4	A (l)
American Samoa	...	...	(c)	...	(i)	(i)	A
Guam	...	...	...	...	...	...	A
No. Mariana Islands	...	...	3	...	5	...	A
Puerto Rico	...	★	...	...	★	★	A
U.S. Virgin Islands	...	...	★	★	★	★	A

Sources: The Council of State Governments' survey of attorneys general, October 2003 and state constitutions and statutes, December 2003.

Key:

★ — Formal provision; number of years not specified.

. . . — No formal provision.

A — Appointed by governor.

E — Elected by voters.

(a) In some states you must be a U.S. citizen to be an elector, and must be an elector to run.

(b) In some states you must be a state resident to be an elector, and must be an elector to run.

(c) No statute specifically requires this, but the State Bar Act can be interpreted as making this a qualification.

(d) Licensed attorneys are not required to belong to the bar association.

(e) No period specified, all licensed attorneys are members of the state bar.

(f) State citizenship requirement.

(g) Chosen biennially by joint ballot of state senators and representatives.

(h) Crosse v. Board of Supervisors of Elections 243 Md. 555, 2221A.2d431 (1966)–opinion rendered indicated that U.S. citizenship was, by necessity, a requirement for office.

(i) Implied.

(j) Appointed by judges of state Supreme Court.

(k) Same as qualifications of a judge of a court of record.

(l) Must be confirmed by the Senate.

Table 4.21
ATTORNEYS GENERAL: PROSECUTORIAL AND ADVISORY DUTIES

State or other jurisdiction	Authority in local prosecutions:				Issues advisory opinions:				Reviews legislation:	
	Authority to initiate local prosection	May intervene in local prosecutions	May assist local prosecutor	May supersede local prosecutor	To state executive officials	To legislators	To local prosecutors	On the constitutionality of bills or ordinances	Prior to passage	Before signing
Alabama	A	A,D	A,D	A	★	★	★	...	★	...
Alaska	(a)	(a)	(a)	(a)	★	★	...	★	★	★
Arizona	A,B,C,D,F	B,D	B,D	B	★	★	★	...	...	...
Arkansas	D,F	...	D,F	...	★	★	★	★	...	...
California	A,B,C,D,E	A,B,C,D,E	A,B,C,D,E	A,B,C,D,E	★	★	★	...	...	...
Colorado	B,F	B	D,F (b)	B	★	★	★	★	★	★
Connecticut	...	...	...	...	★	(c)	...	★	(e)	(e)
Delaware	A (j)	(j)	(j)	(j)	★	★	...	★	...	★ (o)
Florida	F	...	D	...	★	★	★	...	...	...
Georgia	B,D,E,F,G	B,D,G	A,B,D,E,F,G	...	★	★	★	...	...	...
Hawaii	A,B,C,D,E	A,B,C,D,E	A,B,C,D,E	A,B,C,D,E	★	★	...	★ (k)	★	★
Idaho	B,D,F	...	D	...	★	★	★	★	★	★
Illinois	D,F	D,G	D	G	★	★	★	...	...	...
Indiana	F	...	D	...	★	★	★	★	...	...
Iowa	D,F	D,F	D,F	D,E,F	★	★	★	...	(p)	(p)
Kansas	A,B,C,D,F	A,D	D	A,F	★	★	★	★	...	(g)
Kentucky	D,F,G	B,D,G	D	B	★	★	★	★	...	...
Louisiana	A	A	D	G	★	★	★	★	...	...
Maine	A	A	A	A	★	★	...	★	★	★
Maryland	B,F	D	D	...	★	★	★	★	★	★
Massachusetts	A	A	A,D	A	★	★ (h)	★	★	(g)	(g)
Michigan	A	A	D	(b)	★	★	★	★	★	★
Minnesota	B,F	B,D,G	A,B,D,G	B	★	★ (h)	...	...	...	(g)
Mississippi	A,D,F	D,F	A,D,F	D,F	★	★	★	...	...	...
Missouri	F,G	...	B,F	G	★	★	★	...	(g)	(g)
Montana	D,F	A,B,D	A,B,D	A	★	★ (i)	★	...	...	...
Nebraska	A	A	A,C	A	★	★	★	★	...	...
Nevada	D,F,G	D	...	...	★	★	★	★	...	...
New Hampshire	A	A	A	A	★	★	★	...	(q)	(q)
New Jersey	A	A,B,D,G	A,D	A,B,D,G	★	★	★	★	★	★
New Mexico	B,D,E,F	D,E,F	A,B,D,E,F	D,E,F,G	★	★	★	★	★	★
New York	B,F	B,D,F	D	B	★	★ (h)	★	★	★	★
North Carolina	...	D	D	...	★	★	★	★	★	...
North Dakota	A,D,E,F,G	A,D,G	A,B,D,E,F,G	A,G	★	★	★	...	(f)	(g)
Ohio	F	D	D	F	★	(i)	★	...	...	...
Oklahoma	A,B,C,E,F	A,B,C,E,F	A,B,C,E	E	★	★	★	...	(r)	(r)
Oregon	B,D,F	B,D	B,D	...	★	★	★	...	...	★
Pennsylvania	D,F,G	...	...	G	★	...	...	★	...	...
Rhode Island	A	A	...	...	★	★	...	...	★	...
South Carolina	A,D,E,F (b)	A,B,C,D,E,F	A,D	A,E	★	(l)	A,D	B,C	★(m)	★ (g)
South Dakota	A,B,D,E,F (b)	D,G (b)	A,B,D,E	D,F	★	★	★	...	★	...
Tennessee	D,F,G (b)	D,G (b)	D	...	★	★	★	★	...	...
Texas	...	...	D	...	★ (d)	★ (d)	★ (d)	★ (d)	(n)	(n)
Utah	A,B,D,E,F,G	E,G	D,E	E	★	★ (l)	★	★	★ (g)	★(g)
Vermont	A	A	A	G	★	★	★	★	★	★
Virginia	B,F	B,D,F	B,D,F	B	★	★	★	★	★	★
Washington	B,D	D	D	...	★	★	★	...	(g)	(g)
West Virginia	...	...	...	...	★	...	...	...	...	...
Wisconsin	B,C,F	B,C,D	D	B	★	★	★	★ (k)	(e)	(e)
Wyoming	B,D,F	B,D	B,D	G	★	★	★	★ (k)	★	★
American Samoa	A (j)	(j)	(j)	(j)	★	...	(j)	(e)	(g)	(g)
Guam	A	A	A	A	★	★	★	★	(g)	B
No. Mariana Islands	A (j)	(j)	(j)	(j)	★	★	...	★	...	...
Puerto Rico	A	(j)	(j)	(j)	★	★	...	...	★	★
U.S. Virgin Islands	A (j)	(j)	(j)	(j)	★	...	...	★	★	★

See footnotes at end of table.

ATTORNEYS GENERAL: PROSECUTORIAL AND ADVISORY DUTIES — Continued

Source: The Council of State Governments' survey of attorneys general, October 2003.

Key:

A — On own initiative.
B — On request of governor.
C — On request of legislature.
D — On request of local prosecutor.
E — When in state's interest.
F — Under certain statutes for specific crimes.
G — On authorization of court or other body.
H— Has authority in area.
. . . — Does not have authority in area.
(a) Local prosecutors serve at pleasure of attorney general.
(b) Certain statutes provide for concurrent jurisdiction with local prosecutors.
(c) To legislative leadership.
(d) Only upon request by a statutorily authorized requestor.

(e) Informally reviews bills or does so upon request.
(f) Opinion may be issued to officers of either branch of General Assembly or to chairman or minority spokesman of committees or commissions thereof.
(g) Only when requested by governor or legislature.
(h) To legislature as a whole not individual legislators.
(i) To either house of legislature, not individual legislators.
(j) The attorney general functions as the local prosecutor.
(k) Bills, not ordinances.
(l) Only when requested by legislature.
(m) Has concurrent jurisdiction with states' attorneys.
(n) Official opinions, when requested, regarding proper construction or constitutionality of proposed or enacted legislation.
(o) Also at the request of agency or legislature.
(p) No requirements for review.
(q) When legislation impacts the office or upon request.
(r) If required by legislature; may assist in drafting.

Table 4.22
ATTORNEYS GENERAL: CONSUMER PROTECTION ACTIVITIES, SUBPOENA POWERS AND ANTITRUST DUTIES

State or other jurisdiction	May commence civil proceedings	May commence criminal proceedings	Represents the state before regulatory agencies (a)	Administers consumer protection programs	Handles consumer complaints	Subpoena powers (b)	Antitrust duties
Alabama	★	★	★	★	★	●	A,B
Alaska	★	★	★	★	★	★	A,B,C
Arizona	★	...	...	★	★	...	A,B,C,D
Arkansas	★	...	★	★	★	●	A,B,D
California	★	★	...	★	★	★	A,B,C
Colorado	★	★	★	★	★	★	A,B,C,D
Connecticut	★	★	★	★	★	●	A,B,D
Delaware	★	★	★	★	★	★	A,B,D
Florida	★	...	...	★	★	★	A,B,D
Georgia	★	★	...	...	...	●	...
Hawaii	★	★	★	...	...	●	A,B,C
Idaho	★	...	★	★	★	★	D
Illinois	★	...	★	★	★	●	A,B,C
Indiana	★	...	★	★	★	★	A,B
Iowa	★	★	★	★	★	★	B,C
Kansas	★	★	★	★	★	★	...
Kentucky	★	★	...	★	★	★	A,B,C,D
Louisiana	★	...	★	★	★	★	A,B
Maine	★	★	★	★	★	★	A,B,C
Maryland	★	★	...	★	★	★	B,C,D
Massachusetts	★	★	★	★	★	★	A,B,C,D
Michigan	★	★	...	★	★	●	A,B,C,D
Minnesota	★	...	★	★	★	●	A,B,C,D
Mississippi	★	★	...	★	★	★	A,B,C,D
Missouri	★	★	★	★	★	★	A,B,C
Montana (h)	...	...	...	...	...	...	A,B
Nebraska	★	★	★	★	★	...	A,B,C,D
Nevada	★	★	...	★	★	●	A,B,C,D
New Hampshire	★	★	★	★	★	★	A,B,C
New Jersey	★	★	★	★	★	★	A,B,C,D
New Mexico	★	★	★	★	★	...	A,B,C
New York	★	★	...	★	★	★	A,B,C,D
North Carolina	★	★ (e)	★	★	★	●	A,B,C,D
North Dakota	★	...	★	★	★	★	A,B,D
Ohio	★	★	...	★	★	★	A,B,D
Oklahoma	★	★	★	★	★	★	A,B,C
Oregon	★	...	★	★	★	●	A,B
Pennsylvania	★	★	...	★	★	★	A,B,C,D
Rhode Island	★	★	...	★	★	●	B, C
South Carolina	★ (a)	★ (c)	★	...	★	●	A,B,C,D
South Dakota	★	★	★	★	★	★	A,B,C
Tennessee	★	(e) (f)	(e)	...	...	★	B,C,D
Texas	★	★ (j)	★	★	★	●	A,B,D
Utah	★ (d)	★	★ (d)	...	★ (g)	●	A (i),B,C,D (i)
Vermont	★	★	★	★	★	★	A,B,C
Virginia	★	(e)	★	★ (g)	★ (g)	●	A,B,C,D
Washington	★	...	(k)	★	★	★	A,B,D
West Virginia	★	...	...	★	★	★	A,B,D
Wisconsin	★	(e)	★	...	...	●	B,C
Wyoming	★	...	★	★	★	...	...
American Samoa	★	★	★	★	★	...	...
Guam	★	★	★	★	★	●	A,B,C,D
No. Mariana Islands	★	★	★	★	★	...	A,B
Puerto Rico	★	★	...	...	...	★	A,B,C,D
U.S. Virgin Islands	★	★	★	★	★	●	A

Source: The Council of State Governments' survey, October 2003.
Key:

A — Has parens patriae authority to commence suits on behalf of consumers in state antitrust damage actions in state courts.

B — May initiate damage actions on behalf of state in state courts.

C — May commence criminal proceedings.

D — May represent cities, counties and other governmental entities in recovering civil damages under federal or state law.

★ — Has authority in area.

. . . — Does not have authority in area.

(a) May represent state on behalf of: the "people of the state; an agency of the state; or the state before a federal regulatory agency.

(b) In this column only: ★ — broad powers and ● — limited powers.

(c) When permitted to intervene.

(d) Attorney general has exclusive authority.

(e) To a limited extent.

(f) May commence criminal proceedings with local district attorney.

(g) Attorney general handles legal matters only with no administrative handling of complaints.

(h) Exercise consumer protection authority only in cooperation with the state department of administration.

(i) Opinion only, since there are no controlling precedents.

(j) Under specific statutes for specific crimes.

(k) The Public Counsel Unit appears and represents the public before the Utilities & Transportation Commission.

Table 4.23
ATTORNEYS GENERAL: DUTIES TO ADMINISTRATIVE AGENCIES AND OTHER RESPONSIBILITIES

State or other jurisdiction	Serves as counsel for state	Appears for state in criminal appeals	Issues official advice	Interprets statutes or regulations	On behalf of agency	Against agency	Prepares or reviews legal documents	Represents the public before the agency	Involved in rule-making	Reviews rules for legality
Alabama	A,B,C	★ (a)	★	★	★	★	★	(b)	(b)	★
Alaska	A,B,C	★	★	★	★	★	★	...	★	★
Arizona	A,B,C	★	★	★	★	...	★	...	★	★
Arkansas	A,B,C	★	★	★	★	★	★	★	★	★
California	A,B,C	★	★	★	★	...	★	...	...	...
Colorado	A,B,C	★ (a)	★	★	★	★	★	(e)	★	★
Connecticut	A,B,C	(b)	★	★	★	★	★	★	★	★
Delaware	A,B,C	★	★	★	★	★	★	★	★	★
Florida	A,B,C	★	★	★	★	...	★	...	...	...
Georgia	A,B,C	★	★	★	★	...	★	...	...	★
Hawaii	A,B,C	★	★	★	★	★	★	★	★	★
Idaho	A,B,C	★ (a)	★	★	★	★	★	★	★	★
Illinois	A,B,C	★	...	★	★	...	★	...	...	★
Indiana	A,B,C	★	★	★	★	...	★	...	★	★
Iowa	A,B,C	★	★	★	★	★	★	★	★	★
Kansas	A,B,C	★	★	★	★	★	★	...	★	★
Kentucky	A,B,C	★	★	★	★	...	...	★	...	★
Louisiana	A,B,C	(h)	★	★	★	...	★	...	...	★
Maine	A,B,C	★	★	★	★	...	★	...	...	★
Maryland	A,B,C	★	★	★	★	(b)	★	★	★	★
Massachusetts	A,B,C	(b)(c)(d)	★	★	★	★	★	★	★	★
Michigan	A,B,C	★	★	★	★	...	★	★	★	★
Minnesota	A,B,C	(c)(d)	★	★	(a)	★	★	★	★	★
Mississippi	A,B,C	...	★	★	★	...	★	...	...	...
Missouri	A,B,C	★	★	★	★	...	★	★	★	...
Montana	A,B,C	★	★	★	★	★	★	...	★	★
Nebraska	A,B,C	★	★	★	★	★	★	...	★	★
Nevada	A,B,C	★	★	★	★	...	★	...	★	★
New Hampshire	A,B,C	★	★	★	★	★	★	★	(f)	(f)
New Jersey	A,B,C	★	★	★	★	★	★	...	★	★
New Mexico	A,B,C	★	★	★	★	★	★	★	★	★
New York	A,B,C	(b)	...	★	★	(b)	★	(b)	...	...
North Carolina	A,B,C	★	★	★	★	★	★	(b)	★	★
North Dakota	A,B,C	(b)	★	★	★	★	★	...	★	★
Ohio	A,B,C	★	★	...	★	...	★	...	...	...
Oklahoma	A,B,C	★	★	★	★	★	★	★	★	★
Oregon	A,B	★	★	★	★	...	★	...	★	★
Pennsylvania	A,B	...	★	★	★	★	★	...	★	★
Rhode Island	A,B	★	★	★	★	★	★	...	...	...
South Carolina	A,B,C	★ (d)	(a)	★	★	(b)	★	...	★	★
South Dakota	A,B,C	★	★	★	★	★	★	...	...	★
Tennessee	A,B,C	★ (a)	★	★	★	...	★	(e)	(e)	★
Texas	A,B,C	★ (g)	★	★	★	★	★	...	★	...
Utah	A,B,C	★ (a)	★	★	★	★	★	(b)	★	★
Vermont	A,B,C	★	★	★	★	★	★	★	★	★
Virginia	A,B,C	★	★	★	★	★	★	★	★	★
Washington	A,B	★	★	★	★	★	★	★	★	★
West Virginia	A,B	★	★	★	★	★	★	...	...	...
Wisconsin	A,B,C	★	★	★	★	(b)	(b)	(b)	(b)	(b)
Wyoming	A,B,C	★	★	★	★	★	★	...	★	★
American Samoa	A,B,C	★ (a)	★	★	★	...	★	...	★	★
Guam	A,B,C	★	★	★	(d)	★	★	(b)	★	★
No. Mariana Islands	A,B,C	★	★	★	★	★	★	★	★	★
Puerto Rico	A,B,C	★	★	★	★	...	★	...	★	★
U.S. Virgin Islands	A,B	★	★	★	★	★	★	★	...	★

Source: The Council of State Governments' survey of attorneys general, October 2003.

Key:
A — Defend state law when challenged on federal constitutional grounds.
B — Conduct litigation on behalf of state in federal and other states' courts.
C — Prosecute actions against another state in U.S. Supreme Court.
★ — Has authority in area.
. . . — Does not have authority in area.
(a) Attorney general has exclusive jurisdiction.

(b) In certain cases only.
(c) When assisting local prosecutor in the appeal.
(d) Can appear on own discretion.
(e) Consumer Advocate Division represents the public in utility rate making hearings and rule making proceedings.
(f) Limited.
(g) Primarily federal habeas corpus appeals only.
(h) Upon DA recusal.

State Treasurers: Safeguarding and Growing Public Funds
By The National Association of State Treasurers

State treasurers are the chief financial officers of the states, and in this capacity, they are collectively responsible for management and investment of more than $1.5 trillion in state funds. From management of state investments in a time of profound budgetary grief to taking an active and central role in defining what is greater corporate governance, state treasurers are vital players in the healthy management of not only state budgets, but federal policy on a multitude of issues that affect citizens in each and every state of the union.

As the chief financial officers of the states, treasurers are the guardians of taxpayer money that is used to operate state governments and provide services to their residents. State treasurers have fiduciary responsibility for cash and debt management, oversight of state pension plans, sound investment of available state funds, operation of state college savings plans, return of unclaimed property to its rightful owners, and much more. As a result of these myriad responsibilities, state treasurers are collectively responsible for management and investment of more than $1.5 trillion in state funds.

State treasurers also play a unique role in policy setting at both the state and federal levels. On issues ranging from corporate governance to accounting standards, state treasurers are at the forefront of policy discussions and initiatives that attempt to safeguard investments made by and on behalf of the residents of their states.

Through this fiscal oversight and policy setting, state treasurers work daily to protect and benefit their individual states and the nation as a whole.

Selection and Term of Service

State treasurers are elected by the people in 37 states, elected by the legislature in four states and appointed by the governor in nine states. Forty state treasurers serve four-year terms in office, while the state treasurers of Maine, New Hampshire, Tennessee and Vermont serve two-year terms. The remaining state treasurers serve at the discretion and pleasure of the state official making the appointment.

Responsibilities of State Treasurers

All state treasurers are responsible for cash management, a fundamental duty of the states' chief financial officers. All but three state treasurers are responsible for banking services and in 37 states, state treasurers are responsible for some aspect of debt management – issuance, service or both. Thirty-two

state treasurers are administrators of state unclaimed property programs and 29 invest retirement or trust funds for their respective state. Several examples – though certainly not an exhaustive listing – are given below that touch on the wide array of responsibilities held by state treasurers.

Mending State Budgets with Investments

As state budgets teeter between the red and black, the role of fiscal management is now more important than ever. Managing shortfalls in state budgets, while largely viewed by the public as an issue for their state's governor and state legislature, also relies heavily on the guidance of the state's treasurer.

While the task of investing available state funds may seem fairly straightforward to the public, the process is quite complex and requires incredible knowledge and skill. Treasurers must invest using the safest, most efficient methods available to earn the highest possible return. State treasurers' performance and record of investment income critically affects the bottom line of the states' fiscal fitness, which in turn can have a measurable effect on the well being of the states' budgetary status in any given year.

College Savings Plans

One of the greatest financial worries of many American families is, "How will I be able to afford a college education for my children?" All 50 states and the District of Columbia have created innovative college savings programs designed to meet the savings needs of their citizens.

To date, nearly 6 million children across the country have been enrolled in a state college tuition or savings plan. These programs seek to make saving for college easier for the average family. These programs represent positive, productive and affordable options that can ensure the education of our most precious resources: the children of America. State sponsored savings plans promote:

- Planning for education expenses;

- Saving for education expenses instead of relying on debt;

- Reliance on family resources instead of total reliance on government aid programs; and

- State-level planning designed to meet the differing needs in each state instead of a "one size fits all" national approach.

Parents and other individuals have saved more than $40 billion to help their children and loved ones pay for future college costs. More importantly, in excess of 387,000 students have used more than $2.5 billion from these plans to fund their college education.

The mission of the state plans is to increase access to higher education by offering families a simple, safe, affordable and dedicated way to save for college tuition. Section 529 plans come in two forms, prepaid tuition programs and savings plans. The prepaid tuition program offers families a method to prepay tuition based on today's costs of college tuition and provides a guarantee to keep pace with tuition inflation. The savings plans offer dedicated qualified state college savings accounts, which provide families a variable rate of return in a tax advantaged college savings account.

In 44 states and the District of Columbia, the state treasurer has a role in the administration of the program, including program operations, serving as a board member or chairman, investment manager, or committee member.

Participants in both types of programs receive a federal tax exemption on the investment earnings of the accounts, when the funds are used to pay for qualified higher education expenses, which include tuition, room and board, books and fees, and any other expenses that students are required to pay to attend any accredited college or university in the United States.

Unclaimed Property Management

Unclaimed property (sometimes called abandoned property) refers to accounts in financial institutions and companies that have had no activity generated or contact with the owner for one year or a longer period. Common forms of unclaimed property include savings or checking accounts, stocks, uncashed dividends or payroll checks, refunds, traveler's checks, trust distributions, unredeemed money orders or gift certificates, insurance payments and life insurance policies, annuities, certificates of deposit, customer overpayments, utility security deposits, mineral royalty payments and contents of safe deposit boxes.

Fifty states and the District of Columbia operate unclaimed property programs. Treasurers in 33 states and the District of Columbia administer the states' efforts to return property to its rightful owner. Acting in the best interest of consumers, each state has enacted an unclaimed property statute that protects consumers' funds from reverting back to the company if the consumer loses contact with them. These laws instruct companies to turn forgotten funds over to a state official who will then make a diligent effort to find the rightful owner or an heir of the rightful owner. Most states hold lost funds until the rightful owner is found, returning them to the owner at no cost or for a nominal handling fee upon filing a claim form and verification of identity. Since it is impossible to store and maintain all of the contents that are turned over from safe deposit boxes, many states hold periodic auctions and hold the funds obtained from the sale of the items for the owner. Some states also sell stocks and bonds and return the proceeds to the owner in the same manner.

State unclaimed property programs work diligently on behalf of their state's citizens to return as much unclaimed property as possible through a variety of outreach programs, including: making searchable databases available via the Internet (i.e., www.missing money.com); publishing names of owners in newspapers; setting up displays at state fairs, malls and other public events; and working with other public officials such as legislators and local librarians.

Financial Literacy Initiatives

State treasurers are viewed as trusted and credible sources of sound financial advice and have long recognized the need for responsible fiscal decision-making for the management of both public funds and personal finances. Over the past few decades, more than 40 state treasurers have taken an active role in promoting financial literacy to the residents of their state. State treasurers have developed curricula and programs that help people manage their resources from birth to retirement.

Twenty-five state treasurers presently offer some type of program ranging from "Bank at School" programs designed to teach students basic monetary concepts to women's conferences that help adults gain control of their personal finances.

Corporate Governance Reform

From Enron to WorldCom, corporate misdeeds, inefficient management and unethical business practices led to the loss of billions of dollars of public funds invested in the domestic markets. The states were among the largest investors to feel the negative effects of such corporate mismanagement. State pension plans were affected on a broad scale, making it difficult for retirees and future retirees across the country to bank on investments that were made with their future economic well-being in mind.

But while the states were among the hardest hit by this corporate mismanagement, they also are among the most powerful entities that are speaking out and taking action against unfair and unjust business practices that affect the economic health of our nation's public. State elected officials have a special role in protecting their citizenry.

State treasurers, in particular, have fiduciary responsibility not only for pension plans and general state funds, but also for other investment vehicles, such as state college savings plans. State treasurers play a unique role in making sure that corporate governance reform is conducted in a manner that will protect – and in the long run, benefit – the citizens of their states.

The state treasurers, who collectively have fiduciary responsibility for more than $1 trillion dollars in public funds, contend that greater corporate responsibility is vital, since the business practices of U.S. corporations have a profound effect on public monies ranging from pension funds to state tax revenue investments.

The strength of the state treasurers on the issue of corporate governance lies in the innovative approach they have taken to enhance and improve corporate governance in their states and across the nation. Many treasurers have taken an active role in addressing the concerns raised in response to irresponsible corporate practices, calling upon corporations they do business with to verify that their accounting procedures are sound and that the money the state invests on behalf of its residents is safe.

In the past few years, numerous state treasurers have made changes in their states regarding investment and management of public funds. One way the treasurers have attempted to safeguard the investments of their state is by establishing strong "Investor Protection Principles" for investments made with public funds. The principles set out the following obligations, among others:

- Investment banks shall sever the link between compensation for analysts and investment banking.

- Investment banks shall prohibit investment banking input into analyst compensation.

- Money management firms shall disclose client relationships, including management of corporate 401(k) plans, where the money management firm could invest state or pension fund monies in the securities of a client.

- Money management firms shall, in making investment decisions, consider the quality and integrity of a company's accounting and financial data, as well as whether the company's outside auditors also provide consulting or other services to the company.

- Money management firms shall, in deciding whether to invest state or pension fund monies in a company, consider the corporate governance policies and practices of the company.

Since the time these investor protection principles were established, they have been adopted by countless states and national organizations, including the National Association of State Treasurers (NAST), as a prime way to hold businesses accountable to the shareholders and other investors who have a stake in their companies.

Conclusion

The roles and responsibilities of state treasurers are countless and critically important to the fiscal well being of their respective states. Sound and profitable investments made by state treasurers make it possible for budgets to be balanced, for taxpayer-supported programs to be maintained and grown, and for a positive and equitable level of investment growth for public funds to be achieved.

About the Author

The National Association of State Treasurers, an organization of state financial leaders, encourages the highest ethical standards, promotes education and the exchange of ideas, builds professional relationships, develops standards of excellence and influences public policy for the benefit of the citizens of the states. NAST is composed of all state treasurers, or state financial officials with comparable responsibilities from the United States, its commonwealths, territories and District of Columbia.

Table 4.24
THE TREASURERS AND CHIEF FINANCIAL OFFICERS, 2004

State or other jurisdiction	Name and party	Method of selection	Length of regular term in years	Date of first service	Present term ends	Number of previous terms	Maximum consecutive terms allowed by constitution
Alabama	Kay Ivey (R)	E	4	1/03	1/07	0	2
Alaska (a)	Tom Boutin	A	4				. . .
Arizona	David A. Petersen (R)	E	4	1/03	1/07	0	2 (b)
Arkansas	Gus Wingfield (D)	E	4	1/03	1/07	0	2
California	Philip Angelides (D)	E	4	1/99	1/07	1	2
Colorado	Mike Coffman (R)	E	4	1/99	1/07	1	2
Connecticut	Denise L. Nappier (D)	E	4	1/99	1/07	1	★
Delaware	Jack Markell (D)	E	4	1/99	1/07	1	★
Florida (c)	Tom Gallagher (R)	E	4	1/88	1/07	2	. . .
Georgia	W. Daniel Ebersole	A	Pleasure of the Board	11/97	N.A.	0	. . .
Hawaii (d)	Georgina K. Kawamura	A	4	12/02	12/06	0	. . .
Idaho	Ron G. Crane (R)	E	4	1/99	1/07	1	2
Illinois	Judy Baar Topinka (R)	E	4	1/95	1/07	2	★
Indiana	Tim Berry (R)	E	4	2/99	1/07	1	(e)
Iowa	Michael L. Fitzgerald (D)	E	4	1/83	1/07	4	★
Kansas	Lynn Jenkins (R)	E	4	1/03	1/07	0	. . .
Kentucky	Jonathan Miller (D)	E	4	1/00	12/07	1	2
Louisiana	John Kennedy (D)	E	4	1/00	1/08	1	★
Maine	Dale McCormick (D)	L	2	1/97	1/05	1	. . .
Maryland	Nancy K. Kopp (D)	L	4	2/02	1/07	1	. . .
Massachusetts	Timothy Cahill (D)	E	4	1/03	1/07	0	2
Michigan	Jay Rising	A	Governor's discretion	1/03	. . .	0	. . .
Minnesota (f)	Dan McElroy	A	. . .	1/03	. . .	0	. . .
Mississippi	Tate Reeves (R)	E	4	1/04	1/08	0	★
Missouri	Nancy Farmer (D)	E	4	1/01	1/05	0	(g)
Montana	Steve Bender	A (k)	4	1/04	N.A.	0	. . .
Nebraska	Ron Ross	E (l)	4	12/03	1/07	0	2 (b)
Nevada	Brian K. Krolicki (R)	E	4	1/99	1/07	1	2
New Hampshire	Michael A. Ablowich	L	2	3/02	12/04	1	. . .
New Jersey	John E. McCormac	A	Governor's discretion	1/02	N.A.	0	. . .
New Mexico	Robert E. Vigil (D)	E	4	1/03	1/07	0	2 (b)
New York	Aida M. Brewer	A	Governor's discretion	4/02	N.A.	0	★
North Carolina	Richard H. Moore (D)	E	4	1/01	1/05	0	★
North Dakota	Kathi Gilmore (D)	E	4	1/93	1/05	2	2
Ohio	Joseph T. Deters (R)	E	4	1/99	1/07	1	2
Oklahoma	Robert Butkin (D)	E	4	1/95	1/07	2	2 (b)
Oregon	Randall Edwards (D)	E	4	1/01	1/05	0	(e)
Pennsylvania	Barbara Hafer (R)	E	4	1/97	1/05	1	2 (h)
Rhode Island	Paul J. Tavares (D)	E	4	1/99	1/07	1	2 (b)
South Carolina	Grady L. Patterson Jr. (D)	E	4	1/66	1/07	7	★
South Dakota	Vernon L. Larson (R)	E	4	1/03	1/07	0	2 (b)
Tennessee	Dale Sims (i)	L	2	10/03	(i)	0	. . .
Texas (j)	Carole Keeton Strayhorn (R)	E	4	1/99	1/07	1	2 (b)
Utah	Edward T. Alter (R)	E	4	1/81	1/05	5	★
Vermont	Jeb Spaulding (D)	E	2	1/03	1/05	0	★
Virginia	Jody M. Wagner	A	Governor's discretion	1/02	N.A.	0	. . .
Washington	Michael J. Murphy (D)	E	4	1/97	1/05	1	★
West Virginia	John D. Perdue (D)	E	4	1/97	1/05	1	★
Wisconsin	Jack C. Voight (R)	E	4	1/95	1/07	2	★
Wyoming	Cynthia Lummis (R)	E	4	1/99	1/07	1	★
American Samoa	Francis Leasiolagi	A	4	N.A.	N.A.	N.A.	. . .
District of Columbia	N. Anthony Calhoun	A	Pleasure of CFO	1/01	N.A.	N.A.	. . .
Guam	Yasela Pereira	CS	4	N.A.	N.A.	N.A.	. . .
No. Mariana Islands	Antoinette S. Calvo	A	4	N.A.	N.A.	N.A.	. . .
Puerto Rico	Juan Flores Galarza	N.A.	4	N.A.	N.A.	N.A.	. . .
U.S. Virgin Islands	Bernice A. Turnbull	A	4	N.A.	N.A.	N.A.	. . .

Sources: National Association of State Treasurers, January 2004.

Key:

★ — No provision specifying number of terms allowed.

. . . — No formal provision, position is appointed or elected by governmental entity (not chosen by the electorate).

N.A. — Not available.

A — Appointed by the governor. (In the District of Columbia, the Treasurer is appointed by the Chief Financial Officer.)

E — Elected by the voters.

L — Elected by the legislature.

CS — Civil Service

(a) The Deputy Commissioner of Department of Revenue performs this function.

(b) After 2 consecutive terms, must wait four years and/or one full term before being eligible again.

(c) Effective January 2003, the official title of the office of state treasurer is Chief Financial Officer.

(d) The Director of Finance performs this function.

(e) Eligible for eight out of any period of twelve years.

(f) The Commissioner of Finance performs this function.

(g) Absolute two-term limitation, but not necessarily consecutive.

(h) Treasurer must wait four years before being eligible for the office of auditor general.

(i) Serving as acting treasurer until the Tennessee State Legislature selects a permanent state treasurer during the 2005 legislative session.

(j) The Comptroller of Public Accounts performs this function.

(k) Governor Martz appointed Steve Bender as Acting Director of the Department of Administration in January 2004 to fill a vacancy in the department.

(l) Governor Johanns appointed Ron Ross in December 2003 to fill a vacancy in the Treasurer's office.

Table 4.25
TREASURERS AND CHIEF FINANCIAL OFFICERS: QUALIFICATIONS FOR OFFICE

State	Minimum age	U.S. citizen (years)	State resident (years)	Qualified voter (years)	Method of selection to office
Alabama	25	7	5	★	E
Alaska	...	...	...	...	A
Arizona	25	10	5	...	E
Arkansas	21	★	★	★	E
California	18	★	★	★	E
Colorado	25	★	2	...	E
Connecticut	18	★	★	★	E
Delaware	18	★	★	★	E
Florida	30	★	7	★	E
Georgia	...	...	...	...	A
Hawaii	...	★	★	...	A
Idaho	25	★	2	★	E
Illinois	25	★	3	...	E
Indiana	18	★	★	★	E
Iowa	18	★	★	★	E
Kansas	...	...	...	...	E
Kentucky	30	★	2	...	E
Louisiana	25	5	5	★	E
Maine	...	★	★	...	L
Maryland	18	...	...	...	L
Massachusetts	...	...	5	...	E
Michigan	...	...	...	...	A
Minnesota	21	★	★	★	E
Mississippi	25	★	5	★	E
Missouri	...	★	1	...	E
Montana	...	...	...	...	A
Nebraska	19	★	★	★	E
Nevada	25	★	2	★	E
New Hampshire	...	...	...	...	L
New Jersey	...	...	★	...	A
New Mexico	30	★	5	★	E
New York	...	★	★	...	A
North Carolina	21	★	★	★	E
North Dakota	25	★	5	★	E
Ohio	18	★	★	★	E
Oklahoma	31	★	10	★	E
Oregon	18	...	★	...	E
Pennsylvania	...	...	...	...	E
Rhode Island	18	★	30 days	★	E
South Carolina	...	★	★	★	E
South Dakota	...	...	...	...	E
Tennessee	...	...	...	...	L
Texas	18	★	★	...	E
Utah	25	★	5	★	E
Vermont	18	★	2	★	E
Virginia	...	...	...	...	A
Washington	18	★	★	★	E
West Virginia	18	★	5	★	E
Wisconsin	18	★	★	★	E
Wyoming	25	★	★	★	E

Source: National Association of State Treasurers, November 2003.
Key:
★ — Formal provision; number of years not specified.
. . . — No formal provision.
A — Appointed by the governor.
E — Elected by the voters.
L — Elected by the legislature.

Table 4.26
TREASURERS AND CHIEF FINANCIAL OFFICERS: DUTIES OF OFFICE

State	Cash management	Investment of general funds	Investment of retirement and/or trust funds	Oversight of retirement funds	Oversight / management of debt issuance	Unclaimed property	Link deposit program	College Savings / Prepaid Tuition Programs
Alabama	★	★	★	★	★	★	★	★
Alaska	★	★	★	★	★	★	. . .	. . .
Arizona	★	★	★	★	N.A.	. . .	. . .	★
Arkansas	★	★	★	★	★	. . .	. . .	★
California	★	★	★	★	★	. . .	. . .	★
Colorado	★	★	★	★	★	★	★	★
Connecticut	★	★	★	★	★	★	. . .	★
Delaware	★	★	. . .	★	★	. . .	. . .	★
Florida	★	★	★	★	★	★	. . .	. . .
Georgia	★	★	★	★	★	. . .	. . .	★
Hawaii	★	★	★	★	★	★	. . .	★
Idaho	★	★	★	★	★	. . .	. . .	★
Illinois	★	★	★	★	. . .	★	★	★
Indiana	★	★	★	★	★	. . .	★	★
Iowa	★	★	★	★	★	★	★	★
Kansas	★	. . .	★	★	★	★	★	★
Kentucky	★	. . .	. . .	★	. . .	★	★	★
Louisiana	★	★	★	★	★	★	★	★
Maine	★	★	★	★	★	★	★	★
Maryland	★	★	★	★	★	. . .	★	★
Massachusetts	★	★	★	★	★	★	★	. . .
Michigan	★	★	★	★	★	★	. . .	★
Minnesota	★	★	. . .	★	★	. . .	. . .	★
Mississippi	★	★	★	★	★	★	. . .	★
Missouri	★	★	★	★	★	★	★	★
Montana	★	★	. . .	★	★	. . .	. . .	. . .
Nebraska	★	★	★	★	N.A.	★	. . .	★
Nevada	★	★	★	★	★	★	. . .	★
New Hampshire	★	★	★	★	★	★	. . .	★
New Jersey	★	★	★	★	★	★	. . .	★
New Mexico	★	★	★	★	★	. . .	. . .	. . .
New York	★	★	★	★	★	. . .	★	★
North Carolina	★	★	★	★	★	★	. . .	★
North Dakota	★	. . .	★	★	. . .	. . .	. . .	. . .
Ohio	★	★	★	★	★	. . .	★	. . .
Oklahoma	★	★	★	★	★	★	★	★
Oregon	★	★	★	★	★	. . .	. . .	★
Pennsylvania	★	★	★	★	★	★	★	★
Rhode Island	★	★	★	★	★	★	. . .	★
South Carolina	★	★	★	★	★	★	. . .	★
South Dakota	★	. . .	. . .	★	. . .	★	. . .	★
Tennessee	★	★	★	★	★	★	. . .	★
Texas (d)	★	★	★	★	★	★	★	★
Utah	★	★	★	★	★	★	. . .	★
Vermont	★	★	★	★	★	★	. . .	★
Virginia	★	★	★	. . .	★	★	. . .	★
Washington	★	★	★	★	★	. . .	★	★
West Virginia	★	★	★	★	★	★	. . .	★
Wisconsin	★	. . .	★	★	★	★	. . .	★
Wyoming	★	★	★	★	. . .	★	. . .	★

Source: National Association of State Treasurers, November 2003.

Note: For additional information on functions of the treasurers' offices, see Tables in Chapter 7 entitled Allowable Investments, Cash Management Programs and Services, and Demand Deposits.

Key:

★ — Responsible for activity.

. . . — Not responsible for activity.

N.A. — Not applicable. State does not issue debt.

Trends in State Government Accounting, Auditing and Treasury

By John J. Radford

Government accountability, advancing technological progress, and market reforms combine to influence the future direction of our state chief financial officers. Well-managed state financial organizations are not just about managing cost; they are also synonymous with the rigor of control, the delivery of accountability, the execution of technology, and the expectation of well-managed change.

Opportunities

Accounting and Financial Reporting

The Governmental Accounting Standards Board (GASB) was created in 1984 to set accounting and financial reporting standards for state and local governments. Working with the National Association of State Auditors, Comptrollers and Treasurers (NASACT) and state and local officials, GASB promulgates new financial reporting standards designed to strengthen public accountability. These standards are now embodied in the comprehensive annual financial reports of state and local governmental entities. To further enhance accountability, state officials are working to significantly decrease the amount of time to produce the annual report from an average of six months to three months or less.

In addition to improving the timeliness of annual financial reports, NASACT is working with public interest groups and state and local governments to encourage interim reporting of financial related information. Quarterly or monthly interim reports would provide timely information on changes in state revenues, expenditures and financial status. Through interim reporting, citizens, businesses and investors would have improved access to vital state information on which to base economic decisions.

Increasingly states are looking at the Internet as a way to report information about state financial operations and financial position. Nearly all states have static displays of their Comprehensive Annual Financial Reports (CAFR) available on the Web.

Governments traditionally have focused accounting and financial reporting on general ledger accounting with an emphasis on compliance with generally accepted accounting principles and financial laws. With renewed emphasis on performance measures, some states are beginning to examine the need for cost accounting. Activity Based Costing (ABC) is a methodology that links costs with specific activities and their outputs or outcomes. ABC cost information improves the credibility of efficiency based measures and enhances comparability with industry benchmarks.

Technology

E-commerce has facilitated the move of many over-the-counter or mail transactions typically found in government to the Internet. State chief financial officers (CFOs) have found themselves immersed in the design of e-commerce applications and technology infrastructures to ensure adequate controls, systems integration, and reporting of these new transaction types. State CFOs are helping to ensure business-like transaction integrity and cost efficient processing on behalf of citizens and businesses alike.

In an effort to lower transaction costs, state CFOs have implemented purchase and travel card payment programs. These programs take advantage of low transaction costs associated with credit card processors while enhancing access to low-value high-volume purchasing and payment information. State CFOs continue to provide adequate internal policy and procedural controls to ensure appropriate use and to curb instances of card fraud. Some states have projects underway to link detail bank data with state business applications. The future will look to full systems integration.

An advancement in Internet reporting capabilities has recently captured the attention of state CFOs. eXtensible Business Reporting Language (XBRL) provides a common XML-based platform for critical business reporting processes and improves the reliability and ease of communicating financial data among users that are internal and external to the reporting government. XBRL brings the publication, exchange, and analysis of the complex financial information in comprehensive annual financial reports and other business reporting documents into the dynamic and interactive realm of the Internet.

The events of terrorism and natural disasters in recent years have given all state CFOs a reason to reflect on their own capabilities to maintain services in the event of a disaster. Business continuity planning has moved up on the agenda as assessments have been undertaken and weaknesses revealed.

Cost and budget pressures continue to exact a toll on the ability of states to manage in a "do more with less" environment. Increasingly, states are looking at cross-boundary integration (XBI) with business partners, citizens and other layers of government. This level of integration may offer a way for governments to share in the cost and risk of technology infrastructure as well as a way to improve customer interaction.

Best Practice

Some states have implemented and others are looking to implement cost recovery projects to recover losses due to erroneous payments. With this practice, states engage a third party to review accounts payable and contract disbursements from the past three or four years. The state pays the contactor a portion of recovered cash. This type of project not only enhances current state revenues, it also provides states with opportunities to change business processes to eliminate payment errors.

State CFOs are examining the efficiencies of consolidation and centralization. In states with decentralized organizational structures, this will entail reaching down and across departments and agencies to identify common repetitive activities that could be concentrated and performed more efficiently as a shared service. New investments in policy, systems and procedures are usually included. This practice may offer some states an opportunity to lower cost and enhance service delivery.

Ever tightening budgets are forcing state CFOs to bring new focus, direction, and accountability to the management of state accounts receivable and cash collection activities. The current opportunity is to effectively weigh the costs and economic benefits of additional labor and technology investments. Some states have implemented outsourcing contracts to private sector collection contractors. This appears to work well in situations where central management can monitor the added value of both state and contractor collection performance. The result is usually an increase in net revenues.

The professional practice of internal auditing has languished as part of the obscure back office functions of general management. With the enactment of Sarbanes-Oxley, the establishment of the Public

Company Accounting Oversight Board (PCAOB), and renewed strength in the Securities and Exchange Commission, state CFOs are giving increasing attention to the internal audit function to add value in governance, risk mitigation and internal control management. The internal audit function is becoming a major governance tool, bringing greater accountability and control to government operations.

Challenges

Technology

Security issues seem to rise exponentially based on the number of Internet access points added to the network. The state CFO has to determine the appropriate level of security for state finance applications, build a business case that non-technical executives will understand and finance, and demonstrate a financial return. And do this so that if nothing goes wrong, nothing happens. The risks posed by cyber-terrorism are just now being understood and evaluated at the executive level by state CFOs.

The opportunities to invest information technology capital are limitless and growing. Each day brings a widening array of devices, software, innovations, and new ways to connect them all to lower long-term costs and improve customer satisfaction. At the same time, state budgets are being squeezed to respond to the more immediate needs of state programs. Borrowing is an option, but the added cost and assumed risk makes the option much less attractive then full funding from current resources. These pressures make it imperative that state CFOs construct well conceived and documented business cases for their information technology investments. Limited resources must go to those projects with the greater assumed benefit and lowest risk.

Enterprise resource planning (ERP), enterprise application integration (EAI), and Web services have given state CFOs plenty to think about in recent years. Most states continue to operate legacy applications built application upon application over a period of up to 30 years or more. ERP systems, which are currently being fully or partially implemented in a dozen or so states offer complete integration with a common design, architecture, look and feel. They offer huge operational benefits, but come with high risk and high cost. An EAI provides a middleware layer of technology that allows states to continue a "best of breed" approach in application development, but knit the system together to obtain the benefits of integration. The approach is costly, but it is less risky, and may not give the full benefits of a complete ERP system. A Web services approach uses Web technology to link data providing the ability to "Webify" current applications or build new Web based services. The tradeoff is lower change cost and more complexity, but unfortunately this approach may not achieve structural long-term benefits.

Management

The ability of state CFOs to retain competent staff and compete in the marketplace for new talent is under pressure. Changes brought about by the Sarbanes-Oxley Act and the PCAOB have spurred a hiring increase in the private sector. This increase in demand has already started raising the salaries of accountants, auditors and finance graduates. Recent policy changes in state pension plans and increased retirements have already caused labor shortages in many states. Across-the-board salary freezes and cancelled cost-of-living adjustments due to state conditions are exacerbating recruitment challenges to fill state finance professional openings. When the economy strengthens and states start to implement new systems, current salary and compensation for financial staff may not be sufficient to adequately staff state financial operations with high quality and experienced people. By not addressing these issues, states will likely incur greater risk in the conduct of their financial operations.

Accounting and Auditing Standards

As mentioned previously, the GASB was created in 1984 under the Financial Accounting Foundation. A system of voluntary contributions from state and local governments and related professional organizations was implemented to finance the operations of the GASB. Under Sarbanes-Oxley some organizations had to eliminate their contributions. Concurrently, state and local governments began to reduce GASB contributions due to economic conditions. NASACT and member states are working with other national groups to define and implement a fair, equitable and sustainable method to finance the GASB. Having a national set of accounting and financial reporting standards is critical to the municipal bond markets and government accountability.

The GASB applies limited resources to a variety of financial accounting and disclosure projects influenced by many different public interest groups. Changes in international accounting standard setting and change brought about by Sarbanes-Oxley and the PCAOB will also undoubtedly continue to have influence in the direction of U.S. financial accounting and reporting standards set for government. These changes, depending on degree and complexity, often require governments to modify existing systems and procedures. State CFOs are keenly aware of their need to stay informed, participate in the standard setting process, and to implement these changes in the most cost efficient and timely manner possible.

A long-standing issue in government financial reporting is the concept of "accountability reporting." The concept in GASB terms is noted as "service efforts and accomplishments" reporting. This type of reporting differs from the historically-based financial statement and disclosure reporting in that it attempts to link operational and financial data in support of performance measures and results. In turn, results may be tied to the budgetary process, so that the funding of various activities and programs is linked to performance. A few states have integrated performance results into their budgetary processes, and others are currently weighing the costs and benefits of accountability reporting.

Recently the U.S. Government Accounting Office updated *Government Auditing Standards* perhaps better known at the *"Yellow Book,"* which defines standards for audits and attestation engagements of government entities, programs, activities and functions, and of government assistance administered by contractors, nonprofit entities and other nongovernmental entities. These enhanced standards require a greater degree of auditor sophistication and applied procedures to conduct governmental audits. Management and users of governmental resources and programs will have higher confidence in the information used to assess government efficiency, effectiveness, economics, and compliance with laws and regulations.

Corporate Governance

In response to corporate accounting and market shenanigans, state CFOs with responsibility for auditing and managing liquidity, cash flows, financial reporting, and pension fund assets have taken leadership positions advancing new governance and market reforms. In light of Enron and other corporate scandals, state finance professionals are focusing more than ever on corporate governance. Institutional investors believe the recent reforms implemented through the Sarbanes-Oxley Act and by the major United States stock exchanges form the "first tier" of regulatory and industry response to the recent corporate scandals. Spurred by an initiative begun by state treasurers, state finance officers are seeking to promulgate the idea that all participants in the financial markets must now build on this newly laid foundation and construct a second tier of corporate responsibility reforms. This includes a continuous re-design of corporate governance systems to account for changing economic conditions and to increase accountability to shareholders. And with the notion that "actions speak louder than words," some state CFOs are taking appropriate financial actions when the affects of wrong doing have negatively impacted state assets.

Conclusions and Perspectives

For many states, current financial operations bear little resemblance to what it looked like just a few years ago. Financial transactions are increasingly automated or outsourced, and finance officials are being challenged to apply their existing skills to strategic activities that enhance financial government performance and customer service.

States continue to direct resources to traditional accounting, treasury, and auditing business functions, but increasingly state finance officials are being called upon to expand into new areas—e.g. internal consulting, organizational governance, strategic planning, performance reporting and technology management. As public financial managers evolve beyond traditional backroom operations into a more strategic role, the demands on public finance officers will intensify. Continuing education and technical training—along with advanced college education and professional certification are the key ingredients necessary to keep and prepare public finance professionals for their future role.

About the Author

John J. Radford has been the Oregon state controller since 1990 having served under five Oregon governors. He holds a Masters in Public Administration from the University of Nebraska and a Masters in Applied Information Management from the University of Oregon. He is past president of the National Association of State Comptrollers and is currently president of the National Association of State Auditors, Comptrollers and Treasurers. He is a certified internal auditor, a certified government financial manager and a certified fraud examiner.

Table 4.27
STATE AUDITORS, 2004

State or other jurisdiction	State Agency	Agency head	Title	Legal basis for office	Method of selection	Term of office	U.S. citizen	State resident	Maximum consecutive terms allowed
Alabama	Dept. of Examiners of Public Accounts	Ronald L. Jones	Chief Examiner	S	L	7 yrs.	★	★	None
Alaska	Division of Legislative Audit	Pat Davidson	Legislative Auditor	C, S	L	(a)	...	...	None
Arizona	Auditor General	Debra K. Davenport	Auditor General	S	LC	5 yrs.	...	...	None
Arkansas	Legislative Auditor	Charles L. Robinson	Legislative Auditor	N.A.	L	N.A.	...	...	None
California	Bureau of State Audits	Elaine Howle	State Auditor	S	G	4 yrs.	★	...	None
Colorado	State Auditor	Joanne Hill	State Auditor	C	L	5 yrs.	★	...	None
Connecticut	Auditors of Public Accounts	Kevin P. Johnston, Robert G. Jaekle	State Auditors	C	L	4 yrs.	...	...	None
Delaware	Auditor of Accounts	R. Thomas Wagner, Jr.	Auditor of Accounts	C, S	E	4 yrs.	★	★	None
Florida	Auditor General	William O. Monroe	Auditor General	C, S	L	(a)	...	...	None
Georgia	Dept. of Audits and Accounts	Russell W. Hinton	State Auditor	S	L	Indefinite	...	...	None
Hawaii	Office of the Auditor	Marion M. Higa	State Auditor	C, S	LC	8 yrs.	...	★	None
Idaho	Legislative Services Office–Legislative Audits	Raymond Ineck	Supervisor of Legislative Audits	S	LC	Indefinite	★	...	None
Illinois	Office of Performance Evaluations	Rakesh Mohan	Director	N.A	N.A.	N.A	N.A	N.A	None
Illinois	Auditor General	William G. Holland	Auditor General	C, S	L	10 yrs.	...	...	None
Indiana	State Board of Accounts	Charles Johnson, III	State Examiner	S	G	4 yrs.	...	...	None
Iowa	Auditor of State	David A. Vaudt	Auditor of State	C, S	E	4 yrs.	★	★	None
Kansas	Legislative Division of Post Audit	Barbara J. Hinton	Legislative Post Auditor	S	LC	(b)	...	...	None
Kentucky	Auditor of Public Accounts	Crit Luallen	Auditor of Public Accounts	C, S	E	4 yrs.	★	★	2
Louisiana	First Assistant Legislative Auditor	Grover Austin	Legislative Auditor	C, S	L	(a)	★	★	None
Maine	State Auditor	Gail M. Chase	State Auditor				★	★	None
Maryland	Office of Legislative Audits	Bruce A. Myers	Legislative Auditor	S	ED	Indefinite	...	...	None
Massachusetts	State Auditor	A. Joseph DeNucci	State Auditor	C, S	E	4 yrs.	★	★	None
Michigan	Auditor General	Thomas H. McTavish	Auditor General	C	L	8 yrs.	★	★	None
Minnesota	Legislative Auditor	James R. Nobles	Legislative Auditor	S	LC	6 yrs.	...	★	None
Mississippi	State Auditor	Phil Bryant	State Auditor	C, S	E	4 yrs.	★	★	None
Missouri	State Auditor	Claire McCaskill	State Auditor	C, S	E	4 yrs.	★	★	None
Montana	Legislative Audit Division, Legislative Branch	Scott A. Seacat	Legislative Auditor	C, S	LC	2 yrs.	...	...	None
Nebraska	Auditor of Public Accounts	Kate Witek	Auditor of Public Accounts	C, S	E	4 yrs.	★	★	None
Nevada	Legislative Auditor	Paul Townsend	Legislative Auditor	S	LC	Indefinite	...	...	None
New Hampshire	Legislative Budget Assistant	Michael L. Buckley	Legislative Budget Assistant	S	LC	2 yrs.	...	...	None
New Jersey	State Auditor	Richard L. Fair	State Auditor	C, S	L	5 yr. term and until successor is appointed	...	...	N.A.

See footnotes at end of table.

STATE AUDITORS, 2004 — Continued

State or other jurisdiction	State Agency	Agency head	Title	Legal basis for office	Method of selection	Term of office	U.S. citizen	State resident	Maximum consecutive terms allowed
New Mexico	State Auditor	Domingo Martinez	State Auditor	C	E	4 yrs.	★	★	2
New York	Office of the State Comptroller, State Audit Bureau	Lynn Canton	Deputy Comptroller– State Services	C, S	E	4 yrs.	★	★	None
North Carolina	State Auditor	Ralph Campbell, Jr.	State Auditor	C, S	E	4 yrs.	★	★	None
North Dakota	State Auditor	Robert R. Petersen	State Auditor	C, S	E	4 yrs.	...	★	None
Ohio	Auditor of State	Betty D. Montgomery	Auditor of State	C	E	4 yrs.	★	★	2
Oklahoma	State Auditor and Inspector	Jeff McMahn	State Auditor and Inspector	C, S	E	4 yrs.	★	★	None
Oregon	Secretary of State, Audits Division	Cathy Pollino	State Auditor	C	SS	(c)	...	...	N.A.
Pennsylvania	Auditor General	Robert P. Casey, Jr.	Auditor General	C	E	4 yrs.	...	...	2
Rhode Island	Legislative Finance and Budget	Philip R. Durgin	Executive Director	S	LC	(b)	...	...	None
	Auditor General	Ernest A. Almonte	Auditor General	S	LC	4 yrs.	...	...	None
South Carolina	Legislative Audit Council	George L. Schroeder	Director	S	LC	4 yrs.	...	...	None
	State Auditor	Thomas L. Wagner, Jr.	State Auditor	S	SB	Indefinite	...	...	N.A.
South Dakota	Dept. of Legislative Audit	Martin L. Guindon	Auditor General	S	L	8 yrs.	...	...	None
Tennessee	Comptroller of the Treasury, Dept. of Audit	John G. Morgan	Comptroller of the Treasury	C, S	L	2 yrs.	...	...	No
Texas	State Auditor	Lawrence F. Alwin	State Auditor	S	LC	(b)	★	★	None
Utah	Legislative Auditor	Wayne L. Welsh	Legislative Auditor General	C, S	L	6 yrs.	★	★	None
	State Auditor	Auston G. Johnson	State Auditor	C, S	E	4 yrs.	★	★	None
Vermont	State Auditor	Elizabeth M. Ready	State Auditor	C, S	E	2 yrs.	★	★	None
Virginia	Auditor of Public Accounts	Walter J. Kucharski	Auditor of Public Accounts	C	L	4 yrs.	...	...	None
Washington	Office of the State Auditor	Brian Sonntag	State Auditor	C, S	E	4 yrs.	★	...	None
West Virginia	Legislative Auditor	Aaron Allred	Legislative Auditor	C, S	L	Indefinite	...	...	None
Wisconsin	Legislative Audit Bureau	Janice Mueller	Legislative Auditor	C, S	LC	6 yrs.	...	...	None
Wyoming	Dept. of Audit	Michael Geesey	Director	S	GC	4 yrs.	...	★	None
Guam	Office of the Public Auditor	Doris Flores Brooks	Public Auditor	C, S	E	4 yrs.	★	★	2
Puerto Rico	Office of the Comptroller of Puerto Rico	Manuel Diaz Saldana	Comptroller of Puerto Rico	C, S	GL	10 yrs.	★	...	1

Source: Auditing in the States: A Summary, 2003 Edition, The National Association of Auditors, Comptrollers and Treasurers, 2003.

Key:

★ — Yes, provision for.
... — No, provision for.
E — Elected by the public.
L — Appointed by the legislature.
G — Appointed by the governor.
SS — Appointed by the secretary of state.

LC — selected by legislative committee, commission or council.
ED — appointed by the executive director of legislative services.
GC — Appointed by governor, secretary of state and treasurer.
GL — Appointed by the governor and confirmed by both changers of the legislature.
SB — Appointed by state budget and control board.
C — Constitutional
S — Statutory
N.A. — Not available.
(a) Serves at the pleasure of the legislature.
(b) Serves at the pleasure of a legislative committee.
(c) Serves at the pleasure of the secretary of state.

Table 4.28
STATE AUDITORS: SCOPE OF AGENCY AUTHORITY

State or other jurisdiction	Authority to audit all state agencies	Authority to audit local governments	Authority to obtain information	Authority to issue subpoenas	Authority to specify accounting principles for local governments	Investigations — Agency investigates fraud, waste abuse, and/or illegal acts	Agency operates a hotline
Alabama	★	★	★	★	★ (q)	★	...
Alaska	★	...	★	...	...	★	...
Arizona	★	★	★	...	★ (r)	★	...
Arkansas	N.A.	N.A.	N.A.	N.A.	N.A.	N.A.	N.A.
California	★	★	★	★	...	★	★
Colorado	★	★	★	★	★	★	...
Connecticut	★	...	★	...	...	★	★
Delaware	★	★	★	★	...	★	★
Florida	(a)	★	★	...	...	★	...
Georgia	★	(g)	★	★	★	★	...
Hawaii	(a)	★	★	★	...	★	...
Idaho	★	★	★	★	...	★	...
Illinois	★	★	★	★	...	★	...
Indiana	★	★	★	★	★	★	...
Iowa	★	★	★	★	...	★	...
Kansas	★	★	★	★	...	★	...
Kentucky	(b)	★	★	★	...	★	★
Louisiana	★	(h)	★	★	★	★	...
Maine	N.A.	N.A.	N.A.	N.A.	N.A.	N.A.	N.A.
Maryland	(a)	★	★	★	...	★	★
Massachusetts	★	★	★	...	...	★	★
Michigan	★	...	★	★	...	★	...
Minnesota							
Legislative Auditor	★	(i)	★	★	...	★	...
State Auditor	(c)	★	★	★	★	★	...
Mississippi	★	★ (j)	★	...	★	★	★
Missouri	★	★	★	★	...	★	★
Montana	★	...	★	...	...	★	★
Nebraska	★	★	★	...	★	★	★
Nevada	★	...	★	...	...	★	...
New Hampshire	★	...	★	...	...	★	...
New Jersey	★	(k)	★	...	...	★	...
New Mexico	★ (d)	★	★	...	...	★	...
New York	★	★	★	★	★	★	...
North Carolina	★	...	★	★	...	★	★
North Dakota	★	★	★	...	★	★	...
Ohio	★	★	★	★	★	★	★
Oklahoma	★ (e)	(l)	★	★	...	★	...
Oregon	★	★	★	★	★	★	★
Pennsylvania							
Auditor General	(b)	...	★	★	...	★	★
Legislative Budget and Finance Cmte.	★	...	★	★	...	...	...
Rhode Island	★	(m)	★	★	★	★	...
South Carolina							
Legislative Audit Council	★	(n)	★	...	...	★	...
State Auditor	(s)	...	★	...	...	★	...
South Dakota	★	★	★	★	★	★	...
Tennessee	★	★	★	★	★	★	★
Texas	★	...	★	★	★ (o)	★	★
Utah							
Legislative Auditor	★	★	★	★	...	★	...
State Auditor	(f)	★	★	★	★		...
Vermont	★	...	★	★	★	★	...
Virginia	★	...	★	...	★	★	...
Washington	★	★	★	★	★	★	...
West Virginia	N.A.	N.A.	N.A.	N.A.	N.A.	N.A.	N.A.
Wisconsin	★	★	★	★	...	★	...
Wyoming	★	★	★	★	(p)	★	...
Guam	...	★	★	★	★	★	★
Puerto Rico	★	★	★	★	★	★	★

See footnotes at end of table.

STATE AUDITORS: SCOPE OF AGENCY AUTHORITY — Continued

Sources: Auditing in the States, 2003 Edition, The National Association of State Auditors, Comptrollers and Treasurers 2003.

Key:

★ — Provision for responsibility.

. . . — No provision for responsibility.

N.A. — Not available.

(a) The legislature or legislative branch is excluded from audit authority.

(b) The legislative and judicial branches are excluded from audit authority.

(c) State agencies are audited by the Office of Legislative Auditor.

(d) The Gaming Commission, Mortgage Finance Authority, State Lottery Commission, Student Loan Guarantee Corporation are excluded from audit authority.

(e) Higher education and most public trusts are only audited upon request by various authorities. Commissioners of the Land Office are excluded since the State Auditor and Inspector serve on this commission.

(f) State Retirement and Worker's Compensation Fund are excluded from audit authority.

(g) All local governments are excluded from audit authority, except Public School Systems and Regional and Local libraries.

(h) Performs only investigative audits of local governments

(i) Financial audits of local governments are excluded from audit authority.

(j) All local governments excluded but municipalities.

(k) Entities not receiving state aid or state grants and school districts receiving less than 80% funding from the state are excluded from audit authority.

(l) The State Auditor and Inspector have the authority to audit counties, Generally, cities, towns, school districts, fire protection districts, rural water districts can be audited upon request by citizen petition or various authorities.

(m) No local governments are specifically excluded, but the agency goes in on orders from the Joint Cmte. and Legislative Services.

(n) County, school districts, special purpose districts are excluded from audit authority.

(o) Comptroller prescribes guidelines but SAO has responsibility to review and comment.

(p) Set by statute.

(q) Municipalities not covered.

(r) Except for cities and towns, and certain special taxing districts.

(s) Ports Authority, Public Service Authority, Research Authority and 16 technical colleges are excluded from audit authority.

Table 4.29
STATE AUDITORS: TYPES OF AUDITS

State or other jurisdiction	Financial statement	Single audit	Financial related	Compliance only	Economy and efficiency	Program	Sunset	Performance measures	IT	Accounting and review sources	Agreed upon procedures	Other audits
Alabama	★	★	★									
Alaska	★	★	★	★	★	★	★	★	★			
Arizona	★	★	★		★	★	★	★			★	(a)
Arkansas	N.A.	N.A.	N.A.	N.A.	N.A.	N.A.	N.A.	N.A.	N.A.	N.A.	N.A.	N.A.
California	★	★	★	★	★	★		★	★			(b)
Colorado	★	★	★	★	★	★	★	★	★	★	★	
Connecticut	★	★	★		★	★		★	★		★	
Delaware	★	★	★	★	★	★		★	★			(c)
Florida	★	★	★	★	★	★	★		★	★	★	
Georgia	★	★	★	★	★	★	★	★	★	★	★	
Hawaii					★	★	★	★	★			(b)
Idaho	★	★	★	★	★				★			(d)
Illinois	★	★	★	★	★	★			★		★	
Indiana	★	★	★					★	★		★	
Iowa	★	★	★					★	★		★	
Kansas	★	★	★		★	★		★	★	★	★	
Kentucky	★	★	★		★	★		★	★	★	★	
Louisiana	N.A.	N.A.	N.A.	N.A.	N.A.	N.A.	N.A.	N.A.	N.A.	N.A.	N.A.	
Maine	N.A.	N.A.	N.A.	N.A.	N.A.	N.A.	N.A.	N.A.	N.A.	N.A.	N.A.	
Maryland	★		★	★	★	★	★	★	★	★	★	(e)
Massachusetts	★	★	★	★	★	★	★	★	★	★	★	(f)
Michigan	★	★	★		★	★		★	★		★	
Minnesota												
Legislative Auditor	★	★	★			★			★			
State Auditor	★	★							★		★	(g)
Mississippi	★	★	★	★	★	★			★			
Missouri	★	★	★	★	★	★		★	★	★	★	(h)
Montana	★	★	★	★	★	★		★	★	★	★	
Nebraska	★	★	★	★	★	★			★	★	★	
Nevada	★			★	★	★		★	★			
New Hampshire	★		★		★			★	★			
New Jersey	★	★	★	★	★	★		★	★	★		
New Mexico	★	★	★		★				★		★	
New York	★	★	★		★	★			★	★	★	(i)
North Carolina	★	★	★		★	★		★	★	★		
North Dakota	★	★	★		★	★			★			
Ohio	★	★	★	★	★	★		★	★	★	★	

See footnotes at end of table.

STATE AUDITORS: TYPES OF AUDITS — Continued

State or other jurisdiction	Financial statement	Single audit	Financial related	Compliance only	Economy and efficiency	Program	Sunset	Performance measures	IT	Accounting and review sources	Agreed upon procedures	Other audits
Oklahoma	★	★	★	★	★	★	...	...	★	...	★	(j)
Oregon	★	★	★	★	★	★	...	...	★	★	★	(k)
Pennsylvania												
Auditor General	★	★	★	★	★	...	...	...	★	...	...	(l)
Legislative Budget and Finance Cmte.	...	...	...	...	★	★	...	★	★	★	...	...
Rhode Island	★	★	★	★	★	...	...	...	★	...	...	...
South Carolina												
Legislative Audit Council	...	...	...	...	★	★	...	...	...	...	...	...
State Auditor	★	★	...	...	★	...	...	...	...	...	★	...
South Dakota	★	★	★	★	...	★	...	...	...	...	★	...
Tennessee	★	★	★	★	★	★	★	...	★	★	★	(m)
Texas	★	★	★	★	★	★	...	★	★	★	★	(n)
Utah												
Legislative Auditor	...	...	...	...	★	★	★	★	...	...	...	...
State Auditor	★	★	★	★	★	...	...	★	★	...	★	(o)
Vermont	★	★	★	★	★	★	...	★	★	★	★	...
Virginia	★	★	★	...	...	...	★	★	★	...	★	...
Washington	★	★	N.A.	...	...	...	N.A.	★	★	...	★	...
West Virginia	N.A.	N.A.	N.A.	N.A.	N.A.	N.A.	N.A.	N.A.	N.A.	N.A.	N.A.	N.A.
Wisconsin	★	★	★	★	★	★	...	★	★	...	★	...
Wyoming	...	...	★	★	...	...	...	...	...	...	★	...
Guam	...	★	...	...	★	★	...	...	...	...	...	(b)
Puerto Rico	...	...	...	★	★	★	...	...	★	...	...	...

Sources: Auditing in the States: A Summary, 2003 edition. The National Association of State Auditors, Comptrollers and Treasurers.

Note: Government audits are divided into two types, financial and performance audits. Financial audits include financial statement audits and financial related audits. Performance audits include economy and efficiency audits and program audits. In addition, government auditors perform a number of other audit-related functions that do not fall into one of these categories. State audit agencies must make certain that audit coverage is broad enough to fulfill the needs of potential audit report users.

Key:
★ — Provision for responsibility.
... — No provision for responsibility.
N.A. — Not available.
(a) Fraud, special audits, studies, and program evaluations.
(b) Investigations.
(c) Attestation engagements.

(d) Sunset analyses, mandatory health insurance analyses.
(e) Federal grant audits.
(f) Special requests and follow-up reviews.
(g) Special investigation reviews.
(h) Investigations and best practices reviews.
(i) Performance reviews.
(j) Internal control reviews: studies.
(k) Quality assurance reviews.
(l) Fraud investigations.
(m) Informational reports, including referrals or investigation or fraud.
(n) Special investigations.
(o) Internal controls review, investigative, management advisory, training and other educational services.
(p) Special projects, consulting, feasibility studies.

Table 4.30
STATE COMPTROLLERS, 2004

State or other jurisdiction	Agency or office	Name and title	Title	Legal basis for office	Method of selection	Approval or confirmation, if necessary	Date of first service	Present term ends	Consecutive time in office	Length of term	Elected comptrollers maximum consecutive terms	Civil services or merit system employee
Alabama	Office of the State Comptroller	Robert L Childree	State Comptroller	S	(c)	AG	5/1987	(b)	17 yrs.	(b)	...	★
Alaska	Division of Finance	Kim J. Gamero	Director of Finance	S	(d)	AG	8/1999	(a)	4.5 yrs.	(a)	...	...
Arizona	Financial Services Division	D. Clark Partridge	State Comptroller	S	(d)	AG	4/2002	N.A.	2 yrs.	(g)	...	...
Arkansas	Dept. of Finance & Administration	Richard Weiss	Director	S	G	...	5/2002	(a)	2 yrs.	(a)	...	...
California	Office of the State Comptroller	Steve Westly (D)	State Controller	C	E	...	1/2003	1/2007	1 yr.	4 yrs.	2 terms	★
Colorado	Office of the State Controller	Arthur Barnhart	State Controller	C	CS	...	12/1998	(b)	5 yrs.	(b)	...	...
Connecticut	Office of the Controller	Nancy Wyman (D)	Comptroller	C	E	...	1/1995	1/2007	9 yrs.	4 yrs.	unlimited	...
Delaware	Dept. of Finance	David W. Singleton	Secretary of Finance	S	G	AS	1/2001	(a)	3 yrs.	(a)	...	...
Florida	Dept. of Financial Services	Tom Gallagher (R)	Chief Financial Officer	C	E	...	1/2003	12/2006	1 yr.	4 yrs.	2 terms	...
Georgia	Office of Treasury & Fiscal Services	W. Daniel Ebersole	Director	S	SDB	SDB	12/1997	(b)	6 yrs.	(b)	...	★
Hawaii	Dept. of Accounting and General Services	Russ K. Satio	State Comptroller	S	G	AS	12/2002	12/2003	1 yr.	(a)	...	...
Idaho	Office of State Controller	Keith Johnson (R)	State Controller	C,S	E	...	1/2003	1/2007	1 yr.	4 yrs.	2 terms	...
Illinois	Office of the Comptroller	Daniel W. Hynes (D)	State Comptroller	C	E	...	11/1999	1/2007	5 yrs.	4 yrs.	unlimited	...
Indiana	Office of the Auditor of State	Connie Kay Nass (R)	Auditor of State	C	E	...	1/1999	12/2006	4 yrs.	4 yrs.	2 terms	...
Iowa	Department of Administrative Services	Steve Lidner	Chief Operating Officer, State Accounting Enterprise	S	G	AS	2/2003	N.A.	1 yr.	(a)	...	...
Kansas	Division of Accounts and Reports	Dale Brunton	Director	S	(d)	...	10/2000	N.A.	2 yrs.	(b)	...	...
Kentucky	Office of the Controller	Edgar C. Ross	Controller	S	(f)	AG	6/1975	N.A.	28 yrs.	(i)	...	...
Louisiana	Division of Administration	Mark C. Drennen	Commissioner of Administration	S	G	AS	1/1996	1/2004	7 yrs.	(a)	...	...
Maine	Bureau of Accounts and Controls	Edward Karass	State Controller	S	(f)	AG	4/2003	N.A.	1 yr.	(i)	...	...
Maryland	Office of the Comptroller	William Donald Schaefer (D)	State Comptroller	C,S	E	...	1/1999	1/2007	5 yrs.	4 yrs.	unlimited	...
Massachusetts	Office of the Comptroller	Martin J. Benison	Comptroller	S	G	...	1/1999	1/2007	5 yrs.	(j)	...	...
Michigan	Office of Financial Management	Michael J. Moody	Director	S	SBD	SBD	8/2002	8/2004	2 yrs.	(k)	...	★
Minnesota	Department of Finance	Peggy Ingison	Commissioner	S	G	AS	1/2004	1/2007	0 yrs.	(a)	...	...
Mississippi	Department of Finance and Administration	J.K. Stringer Jr.	State Fiscal Officer	S	G	AS	1/2004	N.A.	0 yrs.	(a)	...	...
Missouri	Division of Accounting	James A. Carder	Director	C,S	(d)	...	9/1979	N.A.	23 yrs.	(g)	...	...
Montana	Division of Accounting	Cathy Muri	Administrator/ State Accountant	S	G	...	10/1997	Classified position	7 yrs.	4 yrs. (a)	...	...
Nebraska	Accounting Division	Paul Carlson	State Accounting Administrator	S	(d)	AG	11/2000	N.A.	3 yrs.	(g)	...	...
Nevada	Office of the State Controller	Kathy Augustine (R)	State Controller	C	E	...	1/1999	12/2006	5 yrs.	4 yrs.	2 terms	...
New Hampshire	Division of Accounting Services	Thomas E. Martin	Comptroller	S	G	...	10/1997	6/2004	5 yrs.	4 yrs.	...	...
New Jersey	Office of Management and Budget	Charlene M. Holzbaur	Director/State Controller	S	G	AS	10/1999	(b)	4 yrs.	(a)	...	...

See footnotes at end of table.

STATE COMPTROLLERS, 2004 — Continued

State or other jurisdiction	Agency or office	Name and title	Title	Legal basis for office	Method of selection	Approval or confirmation, if necessary	Date of first service	Present term ends	Consecutive time in office	Length of term	Elected comptrollers maximum consecutive terms	Civil services or merit system employee
New Mexico	Department of Finance and Administration, Financial Control Division	Anthony Armijo	State Controller and Director	N.A.	G	N.A.	1/1991	(b)	13 yrs.	N.A.	N.A.	...
New York	Office of the State Comptroller	Alan G. Hevesi (D)	State Controller	C, S	E	...	1/2003	12/2006	1 yr.	4 yrs.	unlimited	...
North Carolina	Office of the State Controller	Robert L. Powell	State Controller	S	G	GA	7/2001	7/2008	3 yrs.	7 yrs.	...	...
North Dakota	Office of Management and Budget	Pam Sharp	Director	S	G	...	6/2003	N.A	1 yr.	(a)	...	...
Ohio	Office of Management and Budget	Thomas W. Johnson	Director	S	G	AS	1/1999	N.A.	5 yrs.	(a)	...	...
Oklahoma	Office of State Finance	Brenda Bolander	State Comptroller	S	(e)	...	12/2001	(b)	2 yrs.	(h)	...	...
Oregon	State Controller's Division	John J. Radford	State Controller	S	(d)	AG	11/1989	(b)	14 yrs.	(g)	...	...
Pennsylvania	Comptroller Operations	Harvey C. Eckert	Deputy Secretary for Comptroller	S	G	...	3/1983	No exception	21 yrs.	(a)	...	...
Rhode Island	Office of Accounts and Control	Lawrence C. Franklin Jr.	State Controller	S	(d)	...	8/1986	N.A.	17 yrs.	(b)	unlimited	★
South Carolina	Office of the Comptroller General	Richard Eckstrom (R)	Comptroller General	C	E	...	1/2003	1/2007	1 yr.	4 yrs.	unlimited	...
South Dakota	Office of the State Auditor	Richard L. Sattgast (R)	State Auditor	C	E	...	1/2003	1/2007	1 yr.	4 yrs.	2 terms	...
Tennessee	Division of Accounts	Jan I. Sylvis	Chief of Accounts	S	(f)	...	12/1995	N.A.	8 yrs.	(b)	...	...
Texas	Office of the Comptroller of Public Accounts	Carole Keeton Strayhorn (R)	Comptroller of Public Accounts	C,S	E	...	1/1999	1/2007	5 yrs.	4 yrs.	unlimited	...
Utah	Division of Finance	Kim S. Thorne	Director	S	(d)	AG	4/1996	N.A.	8 yrs.	(g)	...	★
Vermont	Department of Finance	Robert D. Hofmann	Commissioner	S	G	AS	1/2003	12/2004	1 yr.	(a)	...	...
Virginia	Department of Accounts	David A. Von Moll	Comptroller	S	G	GA	1/2001	(a)	2 yrs.	(a)	...	...
Washington	Office of Financial Management	Marty Brown	Director	C,S	G	...	11/1999	N.A.	3 yrs.	(a)	...	...
West Virginia	Office of the State Auditor	Glen B. Gainer III (D)	State Auditor	C	E	...	1/1993	1/2005	11 yrs.	4 yrs.	unlimited	...
West Virginia	Division of Finance, Office of the State Comptroller	Andrew J. Fizer	State Comptroller/Director of Finance	S	(d)	AG	7/2002	N.A.	2 yrs.	(g)	...	★
Wisconsin	State Controller's Office	William J. Rafferty (R)	State Controller	S	CS	...	12/1988	N.A.	15 yrs.	(b)	...	...
Wyoming	Office of the State Auditor	Max Maxfield (R)	State Auditor	C,S	E	...	1/1999	12/2006	4 yrs.	4 yrs.	2 terms	...

Sources: Comptrollers: Technical Activities and Functions, 2003 Edition, National Association of State Auditors, Comptrollers and Treasurers, 2003.

Key:
. . . — No provision for.
C — Constitutional
S — Statutory
N.A. — Not applicable.
E — Elected by the public.
G — Appointed by the Governor.
CS — Civil Service.
AG — Approved by the governor.
AS — Approved/confirmed by the Senate.
SBD — Approved by State Budget Director.

GA — Confirmed by the General Assembly.
SDB — Confirmed by State Depository Board.
(a) Serves at the pleasure of the governor.
(b) Indefinite.
(c) Appointed by the Director of the Dept. of Finance (merit system position).
(d) Appointed by the head of the department of administration or administrative services.
(e) Appointed by the head of finance department or agency.
(f) Appointed by the head of financial and administrative services.
(g) Serves at the pleasure of the head of the department of administration or administrative services.
(h) Serves at the pleasure of the head of the finance department or agency.
(i) Serves at the pleasure of the head of the financial and administrative services.
(j) Two full terms coterminous with the governor.
(k) Two-year renewable contractual term; classified executive service.

Table 4.31
STATE COMPTROLLERS: QUALIFICATIONS FOR OFFICE

State or other jurisdiction	Minimum age	U.S. citizen (years)	State resident (years) (b)	Education years or degree	Professional experience and years	Professional certification and years	Other qualifications	No specific qualifications for office
Alabama	★	★	★	★, B.S.	★, 6 yrs.	. . .	. . .	
Alaska	. . .	. . .	. . .	. . .	. . .	. . .	. . .	★
Arizona	. . .	★, 1 yr.	★, 1 yr.	★, B.S.	★, 7–10 yrs.	★ (a)	. . .	
Arkansas	★	. . .	. . .	. . .	★	. . .	. . .	
California	★	. . .	. . .	. . .	. . .	. . .	(b)	
Colorado	. . .	. . .	★, 6 mos.	★ (i)	★	★, CPA	. . .	
Connecticut	. . .	. . .	★	. . .	. . .	. . .	. . .	
Delaware	. . .	. . .	. . .	. . .	. . .	. . .	. . .	★
Florida	★	. . .	★, 7 yrs.	. . .	. . .	. . .	. . .	
Georgia	. . .	. . .	. . .	. . .	. . .	. . .	. . .	★
Hawaii	. . .	. . .	. . .	. . .	. . .	. . .	. . .	★
Idaho	★	★ (j)	★, 2 yrs.	. . .	. . .	. . .	. . .	
Illinois	★	★	★, 3 yrs.	. . .	. . .	. . .	. . .	
Indiana	. . .	. . .	★ (j)	. . .	. . .	, , ,	. . .	
Iowa	. . .	. . .	. . .	. . .	. . .	. . .	. . .	★
Kansas	. . .	. . .	. . .	. . .	. . .	. . .	. . .	★
Kentucky	. . .	. . .	. . .	. . .	. . .	. . .	(c)	★
Louisiana	. . .	. . .	. . .	. . .	. . .	. . .	. . .	★
Maine	. . .	. . .	. . .	. . .	. . .	. . .	(d)	★
Maryland	. . .	. . .	. . .	. . .	. . .	. . .	. . .	★
Massachusetts	. . .	. . .	. . .	★ (k)	★, 7 yrs.	. . .		
Michigan	. . .	. . .	. . .	★ (l)	★, 7 yrs.	★, CPA	. . .	
Minnesota	. . .	. . .	. . .	. . .	★	. . .	. . .	. . .
Mississippi	. . .	. . .	. . .	★ (k)	★, 10 yrs.	★, CPA	(e)	. . .
Missouri	. . .	. . .	. . .	. . .	. . .	. . .	. . .	★
Montana	. . .	. . .	. . .	. . .	. . .	. . .	. . .	★
Nebraska	. . .	. . .	. . .	★ (m)	★ (n)	★, CPA	. . .	. . .
Nevada	★	★	★	. . .	. . .	. . .	. . .	. . .
New Hampshire	. . .	. . .	. . .	. . .	. . .	. . .	(f)	★
New Jersey	. . .	. . .	. . .	. . .	. . .	. . .	. . .	★
New Mexico	30	★	5	N.A.	N.A.	N.A.	N.A.	N.A.
New York	★	★	★, 5 yrs.	. . .	. . .	. . .	. . .	. . .
North Carolina	. . .	★	★	★	★	. . .	(g)	. . .
North Dakota	. . .	. . .	. . .	. . .	. . .	. . .	. . .	★
Ohio								
Oklahoma	. . .	. . .	. . .	. . .	. . .	. . .	. . .	★
Oregon	. . .	. . .	. . .	. . .	. . .	. . .	. . .	★
Pennsylvania	. . .	. . .	. . .	. . .	. . .	. . .	. . .	★
Rhode Island	. . .	. . .	★	★ (h)	★	★, CPA	. . .	. . .
South Carolina	★	★	★	. . .	. . .	. . .	. . .	. . .
South Dakota	★	★	★, 1 yr.	. . .	. . .	. . .	. . .	. . .
Tennessee	. . .	. . .	. . .	★	★, 7 yrs.	★, CPA	. . .	. . .
Texas	★	★ (j)	★, 1 yr.	. . .	. . .	. . .	. . .	. . .
Utah	. . .	. . .	. . .	★	★, 6 yrs.	★, CPA	. . .	. . .
Vermont	. . .	. . .	. . .	. . .	. . .	. . .	. . .	★
Virginia	. . .	. . .	. . .	. . .	. . .	. . .	. . .	★
Washington	★	★, Whole life	★	★ (o)	★	★, J.D.	. . .	. . .
West Virginia								
Office of State Auditor	. . .	★	★	. . .	, , ,	. . .	. . .	. . .
Division of Finance, Office of State Comptroller	. . .	★	★	★, B.S.B.A.	★, 7 yrs.	. . .	. . .	. . .
Wisconsin	. . .	. . .	. . .	★ (p)	. . .	★, CPA	. . .	. . .
Wyoming	★	★	★	. . .	. . .	. . .	. . .	. . .

Sources: Comptrollers: Technical Activities and Functions, 2003 Edition, The National Association of State Auditors, Comptrollers and Treasurers, 2003.

Key:
★ — Formal provision.
. . . — No formal provision.
(a) Any of those mentioned or CFE, CPM, etc.
(b) 18 yrs. At time of election or appointment and a citizen of the state.
(c) The Kentucky Revised Statutes state that The state controller shall be a person qualified b education and experience for the position and held in high esteem in the accounting community.
(d) There are no educational or professional mandates, yet the appointed official is generally qualified by a combination of experience and education.
(e) At least 5 yrs. experience in high level management.

(f) Education and relevant experience.
(g) Qualified by education and experience for the position.
(h) Master's degree in accounting, finance or business management or public administration.
(i) 5 yrs. or college degree.
(j) Years not specified.
(k) Master's degree.
(l) 4 yrs. and bachelor's degree.
(m) 4 yrs. with major in accounting.
(n) 3 yrs. directing the work of others.
(o) 7 yrs. and law degree.
(p) Bachelor's degree in accounting.

Table 4.32
STATE COMPTROLLERS: DUTIES AND RESPONSIBILITIES

State	Appropriation control	Budgetary reporting	Comprehensive annual financial report (CAFR)	Disbursement of state funds	Maintenance of the general ledger and chart of accounts	Payroll processing	Pre-auditing of payments	Post-audit	Operation of statewide financial management system	Management of state travel policies
Alabama	★	★	★	★ (a)	★		★		★	★
Alaska	★		★	★	★	★		★	★	★
Arizona	★	★	★	★	★	★		★	★	★
Arkansas	★		★	★	★	★	★	★	★	
California	★	★	★	★	★	★	★	★	★	
Colorado	★		★	★	★	★	★	★	★	★
Connecticut			★		★	★	★	★		★
Delaware	★		★	★ (b)	★	★	★	★	★ (c)	
Florida	★		★	★	★	★	★	★	★	★
Georgia	★				★					★
Hawaii	★ (e)		★	★	★	★	★ (d)	N.A.	★	★
Idaho	★		★	★ (f)	★	★			★	
Illinois		★	★		★	★	★ (g)	★	★	★
Indiana		★	★	★	★	★	★		★	★
Iowa	★	★	★	★	★	★	★	★	★	★
Kansas	★		★	★	★	★		★	★	★
Kentucky	★		★	★	★	★			★	★
Louisiana	★	★	★		★	★	★		★	★
Maine	★	★	★		★	★	★ (h)	★ (i)	★	★
Maryland	★	★	★	★ (a)	★	★	★	★ (j)	★	
Massachusetts		★	★	★	★	★		★	★	
Michigan	★	★	★	★	★	★			★	
Minnesota	★	★	★	★	★	★	★	★ (k)	★	★
Mississippi	★		★	★	★	★	★		★	★
Missouri	★	★	★	★	★	★	★	★	★	★
Montana	N.A.	N.A.	N.A.	N.A.	N.A.	N.A.	N.A.	N.A.	N.A.	N.A.
Nebraska		★ (l)	★	★	★	★	★		★	★
Nevada	★	★	★	★	★	★	★	★	★	
New Hampshire	★	★	★	★	★	★	★		★	★
New Jersey	★	★	★	★	★	★	★		★	
New Mexico	N.A.	N.A.	N.A.	N.A.	N.A.	N.A.	N.A.	N.A.	N.A.	N.A.
New York	★ (o)	★	★	★	★	★	★ (n)	★	★	★
North Carolina	★		★	★	★	★	★		★	
North Dakota	★	★	★	★	★	★	★	★	★	★
Ohio	★	★	★	★	★	★				★
Oklahoma	★	★	★	★	★	★	★	★	★	★
Oregon		★ (p)	★	★	★	★	★		★	★
Pennsylvania	★		★	★	★	★	★ (a)	★	★	★
Rhode Island	★		★	★	★	★	★		★	★
South Carolina	★	★	★	★ (q)	★	★	★			★

See footnotes at end of table.

STATE COMPTROLLERS: DUTIES AND RESPONSIBILITIES — Continued

State	Appropriation control	Budgetary reporting	Comprehensive annual financial report (CAFR)	Disbursement of state funds	Maintenance of the general ledger and chart of accounts	Payroll processing	Pre-auditing of payments	Post-audit	Operation of statewide financial management system	Management of state travel policies
South Dakota	...	...	...	★	NA	★	★	...	...	...
Tennessee	★	...	★	★	★	★	★ (r)	★ (s)	★	★
Texas	★	★	★	★	★	★	★ (t)	★	★	...
Utah	★	...	★	★	★	★	★ (t)	★	★	★
Vermont	★	★	★	...	★	...	★	★	★	★
Virginia	★ (u)	...	★	★	★	★	★	★ (v)	★	★
Washington	★	★ (w)	★	...	★	...	...	...	★	★
West Virginia										
Office of State Auditor	★ (x)	★ (y)	...	★	...	★	★	...	...	...
Division of Finance, Office of State Comptroller	★ (x)	...	★	...	★	...	★	...	★	★
Wisconsin	★	★	★	★	★	★	★ (z)	★	...	★
Wyoming	★	...	★	...	★	★	★	★	...	★

Sources: Comptrollers: Technical Activities and Functions, 2003 Edition, The National Association of State Auditors, Comptrollers and Treasurers 2003.

Key:
★ — Formal provision; number of years not specified.
... — No formal provision.
A — Appointed by governor.
(a) Responsibilities shared between Comptroller and Treasury.
(b) Responsibilities shared between Department of Finance and State Treasurer's Office.
(c) Responsibilities shared between Department of Finance and the Auditor of Accounts.
(d) Except for various autonomous agencies.
(e) Responsibilities shared between Office of State Controller and the Division of Financial Management.
(f) Responsibilities shared between Office of the State Controller and the State Treasurer's Office.
(g) Responsibilities shared between state agencies and the Office of the State Controller.
(h) Responsibilities shared between agencies and the Office of the State Comptroller.
(i) Responsibilities shared between Office of the State Controller and the State Auditor.
(j) Responsibilities shared between Office of the State Comptroller and the Legislative Auditor.
(k) Responsibilities shared between Dept. of Finance and the Office of the Legislative Auditor.
(l) Responsibilities shared between Accounting Division and the Dept. of Administrative Services.

(m) Responsibilities shared between Comptroller and Budget Director.
(n) Responsibilities shared between office of the State Comptroller with delegation to state agencies and universities.
(o) Responsibilities shared between shared Comptroller and Office of State Budget and Management.
(p) Responsibilities shared between State Controller and the Dept. of Administrative Services.
(q) Responsibilities shared, Comptroller General issues warrants, Treasurer issues checks, colleges maintain their own systems and write their own checks.
(r) Responsible for all departments that have not been authorized to do their own based own excellent performance.
(s) Responsibilities shared between Division of Audits and Department of Audit.
(t) Responsibilities shared between various agencies and the division of Finance.
(u) Responsibilities shared between Comptroller and Dept. of Planning and Budget.
(v) Responsibilities shared between Comptroller and Auditor.
(w) Responsibilities shared between Office of Financial Management and all state agencies.
(x) Responsibilities shared between State Budget Office within the Office of the State Comptroller and the Office of the State Auditor.
(y) Responsibilities shared between State Budget Office and the Office of the State Auditor.
(z) Responsibilities delegated to state agencies by the State Controller's Office.

Chapter Five

STATE JUDICIAL BRANCH

"The state courts today are being driven by diverse trends, some playing out the logic of previous eras of reform."

— David B. Rottman

Trends and Issues in the State Courts:
Challenges and Achievements
By David B. Rottman

These are challenging times for the state judicial branches. Funding has been cut, relations with the other branches of government are frayed, and election campaigns for judicial office can be injudicious. Significant innovation is occurring nonetheless. Effective practices in one jurisdiction are being spread nationally. Reentry courts for felons released after long incarceration is one example of the reliance federal and state officials are placing on such court innovations.

Challenges and Achievements

These are neither the best of times nor the worst of times for the state courts. On one hand, court budgets have declined, staffing levels have been reduced, court facilities have been closed, and some courts struggle to remain open to the public five days a week. Tensions with the other branches of government and problematic campaigning by judicial candidates provide additional reasons for concern. "Justice in Jeopardy" was the title chosen for the recent report of the American Bar Association's Commission on the 21st Century Judiciary.[1]

On the other hand, state courts are becoming more innovative and responsive in addressing deeply rooted, longstanding problems. Miscarriages of justice associated with inadequate translation of court proceedings are an example. With few certified translators available and steep costs of creating tests and certification procedures, observers, relatives and even defendants could be pressed into service to translate court proceedings. To rectify this situation, the courts of four states founded the Consortium for Court Interpreter Certification in 1995; 29 states now belong, accounting for three-quarters of U.S. citizens who do not speak English at home. The Kennedy School of Government at Harvard University recognized the consortium in 2003 for "creating a cost-effective yet rigorous system for education, training and certifying skilled court interpreters."[2]

One state chief justice (Jean Toal of South Carolina) chose a quote from Shakespeare—"there is a tide in the affairs of men which must be taken at the flood—to express the challenge to the state courts today."[3] This essay reviews six national trends that fed that flood and then four specific issues whose resolution will play out differently from state to state.

Six Leading Trends Shaping the State Courts

Rationalizing Justice (resumed)

From the 1960s, reformers sought to increase the ability of the judicial branch to govern itself and adapt to changing times by adopting contemporary management principles. Simplified and consolidated court structures are the most visible result. Most states now have either one or two trial court levels; this contrasts with former patchworks consisting of numerous types and levels of courts, often with overlapping jurisdiction to hear cases. Despite signs in the early 1990s that the momentum had stalled, California established a single-tier trial court in 1998, Arkansas (2000) and Oregon (1998) consolidated their general jurisdiction courts and Utah (1996) its limited jurisdiction courts (as will Arkansas in 2005).[4] This trend will continue. A recent experimental project in Michigan found continuing benefits from trial court consolidation.[5]

State court systems also centralized their budgeting, personnel management and resource allocation processes. Notably, court funding shifted to the state level. Today, the court systems of 31 states are entirely or primarily state-funded, with four others poised to make the switch (Florida, Illinois, Minnesota and Pennsylvania).[6]

In the course of these changes, the proportion of non-lawyer and part-time judges has been greatly reduced. Growth in judgeships has been at the general jurisdiction level (where judges can hear all manner of disputes). General jurisdiction court judges increased from 6,000 in 1975 to 9,000 in 1985 and to over 11,000 in 2001. The bench of limited jurisdiction courts has not grown in recent decades.

Judges' Time as a Scare Resource

The demand for judicial intervention is declining in some legal arenas: global treaties seek to supercede court jurisdiction with forums like the World Trade Organization, private judging is taking major business disputes from the state as well as federal courts, and the number of civil trials is in long-term decline in many states.

Yet the overall demand for access to state judges' time remains strong and likely to increase. Drug courts and other problem-solving courts during the 1990s demonstrated the unique ability of judges to simultaneously hold accountable and motivate people in need of treatment for substance abuse and other problems. The U.S. Department of Justice is encouraging reentry courts in which judges become in effect "reentry managers." Establishing reentry courts was a natural response to concern at the state and national level. However, it came with an unforeseen consequence of "truth in sentencing" laws that mandated all prisoners serve 85 percent of their original sentence and the abolition of the parole boards that traditionally determined release dates and provided supervision. Some 630,000 prisoners are released annually. Sentencing reform had "the perverse effect of returning the most risky offenders to the community with the least control and supervision."[7]

The impact of this change on judicial resources is substantial. Reentry court and drug court judges handle more appearances by defendants and generate more reports per defendant than traditional processes demand. The judiciary also assumes greater system-wide responsibilities for coordination and collaboration among agencies and groups.

One little discussed aspect of this use of judges' power is the degree to which it resonates with the general public, especially minority groups. Individuals most dissatisfied with traditional courts tend to be the most supportive of the new roles judges are assuming, arguably because they fill unmet expectations people hold of the courts. Nearly 90 percent of the American public agrees, for example, with the statement, "Courts should solve problems using the knowledge of psychologists and doctors."[8]

Courts and Consumers

The public is replacing lawyers as the primary constituency in the minds of the state court judges and staff. A new consumer orientation is taking hold, evident in provisions by the state courts to assist litigants without lawyers through user-friendly print material, simplified processes, and computer guided, Web-based assistance. Some courts are going further, taking steps to make legal advice available in the courthouse, previously considered unfeasible.

The Internet is being mobilized as part of the recognition that litigants, jurors and other non-lawyers in the courthouse are consumers of court services. Entire statewide court systems and individual trial and appellate courts are providing a wealth of information and services online. An annual award program identifying the top 10 court Web sites, evaluated a handful of sites in 1998 when the competition was initiated, 400 in 2002 and 900 in 2003.[9] These Web sites are becoming true points of entry to the courts. Litigants without lawyers in Orange County, California, for example, can e-file using the Superior Court's I-CAN project.

Public involvement in judicial branch decision making is another element of the enhanced public role in the state courts. Members of the public participate directly in policymaking as members of decision making and advisory committees. Less personal participation is being affected through systematic programs that build the general public's concerns and preferences into decision making, typically through scientific opinion surveys.

The Supreme Court of Virginia exemplifies both direct and indirect public participation through its Strategic Planning and Management System. Broad public involvement occurs through telephone surveys that "register the public's perceptions on how well the courts are performing and indicates where citizens perceive that improvements are needed." The survey results are combined with other information to establish future demand for court services. Emergent themes are: assigned to a focus group or "venture team" that includes a broad base of citizens, businesspersons, representatives of other government agencies, judges, clerks, magistrates, technologists and attorneys. Based on the individual and collective experience of its members, each team is asked to contribute ideas and solutions for how the courts can manage the repercussions that may flow from one of the themes.[10]

In Virginia and other states, such policies and practices represent a new mindset within the courts in which the citizen is more an actor than just a passive recipient in the life of the courts.

Diffusion

The enhanced institutional capacity of the individual state court systems is generating collective benefits because successful innovations in one state are reaching a national audience. States are working together, as in the Consortium of Language Certification, to solve problems beyond those that their individual resources can fix.

The diffusion of new approaches has been most

strongly recorded in the rapid growth of problem-solving courts. Initiated in 1989 with the opening of the Miami-Dade County Drug Court, problem-solving courts allow a judge to strictly enforce compliance with court orders, including those specifying the delivery of services to individuals with specific kinds of social and emotional problems that promote recidivism. There are now over 1,000 drug courts nationally. Drug courts exemplify court-initiated and court-based innovations that respond to longstanding concerns over ineffective policy responses to societal problems. Diffusion of a network of problem-solving courts is being undertaken in states like Ohio, which has established a Specialized Docket Section in its Supreme Court to provide "technical support to trial courts in analyzing the need for, planning, and implementing specialized docket programs."[11]

Diffusion of innovation in court practices is being facilitated by new organizations like the Center for Court Innovation, a partnership between the New York State Judicial Branch and non-profit groups, established in 1996. The center serves, in effect, as the research and development arm of the state's courts, but is administered as a project of the non-profit Fund for the City of New York. The Best Practice Institute of the National Center for State Courts identifies and promotes the adoption in other jurisdictions of practices that enhance the effective administration of justice. Emergency management for the courts was one practice identified in 2003.[12]

Mainstreaming

The state courts have drawn heavily on the organizational capacity built up during the period of unification to specialize effectively.[13] The question now is, can the benefit of that specialization be extended to the larger court systems—to civil litigants and criminal defendants generally? The stakes are high. The margins cannot be allowed to flourish at the expense of the core.

State court leaders see the promise. The two major court leadership organizations, the Conference of Chief Justices and the Conference of State Court Administrators, recently resolved to: encourage, where appropriate, the broad integration over the next decade of the principles and methods employed in the problem-solving courts into the administration of justice to improve court processes and outcomes while preserving the rule of law, enhancing judicial effectiveness, and meeting the needs and expectations of litigants, victims and the community.[14]

The immediate implications of mainstreaming are most likely to be found for the broad mix of criminal defendants whose type of offense is not currently associated with a specialized court. In mid-2003, the U.S. Department of Justice organized a focus group of criminal justice officials and experts to explore the feasibility of establishing a criminal court-wide screening, assessment and referral process that would target those "generalist" offenders. More broadly, the style of interaction used by problem-solving court judges is being extended to other categories of cases, civil and criminal, where compliance with court orders has traditionally been poor.[15] Social science research consistently demonstrates that the kind of courtroom interaction associated with problem-solving increases compliance.[16]

Inter-branch Tensions

A degree of tension inevitably characterizes the relationship between the judicial and legislative branches. After all, the judiciary is "the branch that holds the representative branches to their responsibilities."[17] And contention over budget allocations is to be expected.

In recent years, however, inter-branch relations in many states have become frayed. Contributing factors include the magnitude of state budget crises and the heightening of intrastate tensions by the involvement of national groups promoting the interests of one side or the other in litigation on such matters as the environment or tort reform. Further, lawsuits filed by citizens and organizations challenging legislative provisions on such subjects draw the courts into issues that have far-reaching policy consequences. Legislators might construe such decisions as an intrusion into policy-making. Indeed, state supreme court decisions that find a piece of legislation in violation of a state's constitution are being met with threats of retaliation by means of reducing the judiciary's budget or the threat of recall or impeachment.

Such a reaction is contrary to what we all depend on courts for: deciding fairly, even if one side has more political clout than the other. The cases that appellate courts decide are brought and shaped by others: the judges "are forced to rule."[18] Further, the policy implications of such decisions are byproducts of a finding based on facts and the applicable law. It is only the rare case, though often ones that draw attention, in which even the ablest and most neutral judges may differ on just what is the relevant law or its application to the facts. Inescapably, sometimes the law has gap and ambiguities. But in all cases, the public must be confident that the judges are doing the best humanly possible to "call 'em as they see 'em."

Problematic Judicial Elections

Judicial campaigns as of late 2003 do not look promising for those committed to keeping judicial elections different from elections for executive and legislative branch officials. In 2003, a race for an open seat on the Pennsylvania Supreme Court pitted two lower court judges each backed by different political parties in a multi-million dollar campaign received the most attention (the year's other state supreme court race involved an incumbent in Wisconsin). The successful candidate interpreted the U.S. Supreme Court's decision in *Republican Party of Minnesota v. White* (which struck down the "announce clause" of Minnesota's Code of Judicial Conduct) as freeing him to tell voters his personal beliefs in favor of abortion rights, the death penalty and unions, but opposed to capping tort judgments and gun control. The defeated candidate argued that campaigning like that would "create expectations about how she would vote if elected to the Supreme Court." Whether the race is a bellwether for campaign conduct depends on the effect of the high voter turnout, which favored the winning Democratic candidate because of events involving Philadelphia's mayoral election.[19]

Issues Facing the State Courts

Can the growth of problem solving courts be sustained? The rapid diffusion of problem-solving courts was a phenomenon. There is some evidence that the growth of the most common type of such a court is stalled, or has even reached the point of saturation.[20] There are now nearly 1,100 drug courts (adult, juvenile, family and other varieties), 20 community courts, 70 mental health courts, and perhaps as many as 300 (if loosely defined) domestic violence courts.

During 2003, 44 new drug courts were implemented, the lowest number since 1995 and one-fifth of the number recorded for 2002.[21] The potential for further expansion is clearest for mental health courts, which were backed by a federal funding initiative.[22] Otherwise, the greatest energy is evident in the creation of hybrid or more narrowly specialized courts to deal with specific, acute needs. "Dependency courts" are an example, established to provide judicial monitoring of participation in substance abuse treatment services for parents charged with child abuse and neglect.

Drug courts, however, may have a renewed spurt of growth. They have compelling advocates on the bench. They also are unique because an entire profession has grown up around them. The National Association of Drug Court Professionals (NADCP) has a membership of approximately 3,000; the degree of interest in the association's work is evident in the 15,000 individuals on its mailing list, making NADCP one of the largest national organizations of court-associated professionals.[23]

Can non-regulatory approaches moderate judicial elections?[24] In 2004, 29 states will hold supreme court elections, with at least 68 seats in contention (accounting for one out of every four seats on courts of last resort). Popular election is almost certain to remain the core element of judicial selection. No state has ever eliminated elections. Recent debates on avenues for reform have focused on methods of strengthening the credentials of those aspiring to be judges. The chief judge of New York's Commission on Public Trust and Confidence in Judicial Elections in its December 2003 preliminary report recommended that: "New York State should establish a system of state-sponsored Independent Judicial Election Qualifications Commissions to evaluate the qualifications of candidates for judicial office throughout the state."[25]

Another response to the deterioration of judicial elections was given prominence in the U.S. Supreme Court's *Republican Party of Minnesota v. White*. In concurring with the majority, Justice Anthony Kennedy wrote: "The legal profession, the legal academy, the press, voluntary groups, political and civic leaders, and all interested citizens can use their own First Amendment freedoms to protest statements inconsistent with standards of judicial neutrality and judicial excellence. Indeed, if democracy is to fulfill its promise, they must do so."[26] A National Ad Hoc Advisory Committee on Judicial Campaign Conduct has been established to provide information and assistance to states and localities that wish to respond to Justice Kennedy's call.[27]

Ultimately, public attentiveness may be the key to moderating the conduct of judicial election campaigns. Voters seek cues about a candidate but find few available beyond a person's surname, political party or public statements that may border on a commitment to decide cases before hearing the evidence.

Can courts win the public's attention? The news for the state courts about public opinion is mixed. Contrary to many claims, survey evidence over the past quarter century does not reveal a decline in the public's confidence in the state courts or show them to enjoy less public support than the executive or legislative branches. Instead, the problem may be a lack of attentiveness to the business of the courts and a corresponding stereotypical view, national in scope and resistant to local efforts that demonstrate courts are doing a better job. The important task is to build an active, critical, but supportive public constituency for the state courts that extends beyond the legal profession and understands the unique responsibilities our system of state government assigns to the judicial branch.

The extent of jury nullification, where the members of a jury vote to acquit a defendant despite what the law and the evidence indicates as an act of protest, has been taken as a symptom of public unease over the fairness of the courts. Research evidence reported in 2003 suggests that such concern is at least in part misplaced. Concerns over the persuasiveness of the evidence seem to drive hung juries.[28]

A challenge for the courts will be to develop constituencies beyond the legal profession that are constructively critical and supportive of the state courts' unique responsibilities in our system of government.

Can court budgeting be organized in a way that balances judicial accountability and independence? There are several promising developments that provide objective measurement as part of the budget process. Methodologies for translating court caseload into workload are becoming highly sophisticated. Workload assessment derives needs based on the amount of attention various types of cases require (17 states have well-established workload measures for judges). A Minnesota effort included three indices of case complexity: substantive, procedural and idiosyncratic.[29]

Conclusion

The environment in which the state courts operate is more complicated than in the past. The state courts today are being driven by diverse trends, some playing out the logic of previous eras of reform. At the same time, courts are struggling to keep afloat in a harsh budgetary environment, to build durable processes of innovation, and to mainstream for general use approaches first created for very specific kinds of cases. National interest groups are becoming involved in controversies over court decisions in individual states and global trade agreements and organizations are vying for jurisdiction over cases traditionally decided according to state law.

This flood tide challenges the institutional capacity of the state courts. Success in channeling the tide will depend on the courts' ability to build a constituency, clarify their relationship to the rest of state government, and obtain the resources commensurate with their responsibilities under our system of state government.

Notes

[1] *Justice in Jeopardy: The Report of the American Bar Association Commission on the 21st Century Judiciary*, (Chicago, IL: 2003).

[2] The Consortium was a finalist in the Kennedy School's Innovations in American Government Award, The Council for Excellence in Government, "Two Innovative Latino Service Programs Names Finalists for Prestigious American Government Award," Press release March 12, 2003.

[3] *State of the Judiciary 2002: Address of the Honorable Jean H. Toal, Chief Justice of South Carolina*, March 6, 2002 (referencing Julius Caesar IV iii 217,22).

[4] It appeared to run out of steam in the early 1990s during a previous era of severe constraints on court budgets. See David Rottman and William Hewitt, *Trial Court Structure and Performance: A Contemporary Reappraisal*, (Williamsburg, VA: National Center for State Courts, 1996).

[5] Tracy Lightcap, "Issue environments and institutionalization: structural change in U.S. State Judicial Institutions, 1975–1995," *Justice System Journal* Vol. 24, No. 2 (2003), 183-203. David C. Steelman, Michigan Trial Court Consolidation Demonstration Projects: 2001 Follow-Up Assessment Report, (Denver, CO: Court Consulting Division, National Center for State Courts, 2001).

[6] Robert W. Tobin, *Learning from Recession Experience*, (Williamsburg, VA: National Center for State Courts, 2003).

[7] U.S. Department of Justice, Office, Office of Justice Programs, "Learn about Reentry," www.ojp.usdoj.gov/reentry/learn.html. See, also, J. Travis, *But They All Come Back: Rethinking Prisoner Reenty, Research in Brief—Sentencing and Corrections: Issues for the 21st Century* (NCJ 181413), (Washington, D.C.: U.S Department of Justice, 2000).

[8] David B. Rottman, Randall Hansen, and Nicole Mott, *Perceptions of the Courts in Your Community: the Influence of Experience, Race and Ethnicity*, (Williamsburg, VA: National Center for State Courts, 2003). http://www.ncsconline.org/WC/Publications/Res_AmtPTC_PerceptionsPub.pdf.

[9] "Many courts have web sites" Criminal Justice Newsletter August 1, 2003, 1.

[10] *Judicial System of Virginia (2002) Bringing the Future to Justice: Charting the Course in the New Dominion*, http://www.courts.state.va.us/reports/2002_2004plan.pdf

[11] www.sconet.state.oh.us/spec_dockets/

[12] NCSC Best Practices Institute, Emergency Management for Courts, www.ncsconline.org/Projects_Initiatives/BPI/EmergencyMngmnt.htm.

[13] This potential was predicted by court reformers, see Robert Lipscher and Samuel Conti, "A Post- Unification Approach to Court Organizational Design and Leadership," *Justice System Journal*, Vol. 15, No. 2 (1991).

[14] Conference of Chief Justices, Resolution No. 22 (2000).

[15] Pamela Casey and David Rottman, *Problem-Solving Courts: Models and Trends*, (Williamsburg, VA: National Center for State Courts, 2003).

[16] Tom Tyler and Yuen Huo, *Trust in the Law: Encouraging Public Cooperation with the Police and Courts*, (New

York, NY: Russell Sage Foundation, 2002).

[17] Commission to Promote Public Confidence in Judicial Elections, *Interim Report to the Chief Judge of the State of New York*, (New York, NY: 2003), 1.

[18] G. Alan Tarr, "Rethinking the Selection of State Supreme Court Judges" *Willamette Law Review* Vol. 39, No. 4 (2003) 1445–70, 1456.

[19] Emily Heller, "Pennsylvania, "He speaks on issues, wins state court seat." *National Law Journal* November 10, 2003, 7. At least 13 single issue interest groups sent candidates surveys on topics from gay rights to gun control.

[20] Pamela Casey and David Rottman, *Problem-Solving Courts: Models and Trends*, (Williams-burg,VA: National Center for State Courts, 2003).

[21] Drug Court Activity Update: Composite Summary Information, Drug Court Clearinghouse, American University, December 15, 2003 (reflects only the first 11 months of 2002).

[22] Federal legislation recognized the promise of mental health courts, allocating funding for the creation of 100 additional courts (America's Law Enforcement and Mental Health Project (Public Law 106-515).

[23] Telephone conversation on January 8, 2004 with NADCP membership director Arlandis Rush.

[24] For background information, see R. A. Schotland, 2002 "Judicial elections and state court reforms," *The Book of the States* Vol. 35, (Lexington, KY: The Council of State Governments, 2003).

[25] Commission to Promote Public Confidence in Judicial Elections.

[26] 122 S. Ct. at 2545.

[27] See www.judicialcampaignconduct.org.

[28] Paula L. Hannaford-Agor and Valerie P. Hans, "Nullification at Work: A Glimpse from the National Center for State Courts Study of Hung Juries," *Chicago-Kent Law Review* 78, No. 3, 1249–1277.

[29] Brian Ostrom *et al.*, *Minnesota Judicial Workload Assessment*, 2002, (Williamsburg, VA: National Center for State Courts, 2003).

About the Author

David B. Rottman is a principal court research consultant at the National Center for State Courts, where he has worked since 1987. His current interests include the pros and cons of specialized courts, minority group perceptions of the courts, and judicial selection. He has directed the compilation of the last four editions of *State Court Organization*.

Table 5.1
STATE COURTS OF LAST RESORT

State or other jurisdiction	Name of court	Justices chosen (a) — At large	Justices chosen (a) — By district	No. of judges (b)	Term (in years) (c)	Chief justice — Method of selection	Chief justice — Term of office for chief justice
Alabama	S.C.	★		9	6	Popular election	6 years
Alaska	S.C.	★		5	10	By court	3 years (d)
Arizona	S.C.	★		5	6	By court	5 years
Arkansas	S.C.	★		7	8	Popular election	8 years
California	S.C.	★		7	12	Appointed by governor	12 years
Colorado	S.C.	★		7	10	By court	Indefinite
Connecticut	S.C.	★		7	8	Legislative appointment (e)	8 years
Delaware	S.C.	★		5	12	Appointed by governor, with consent of Senate	12 years
Florida	S.C.	(f)		7	6	By court	2 years
Georgia	S.C.	★		7	6	By court	4 years
Hawaii	S.C.	★		5	10	Appointed by governor, with consent of Senate (g)	10 years
Idaho	S.C.	★		5	6	By court	4 years
Illinois	S.C.		★	7	10	By court	3 years
Indiana	S.C.	★		5	10 (h)	Judicial nominating commission appointment	5 years
Iowa	S.C.	★		7	8	By court	8 years
Kansas	S.C.	★		7	6	Rotation by seniority	Indefinite
Kentucky	S.C.		★	7	8	By court	4 years
Louisiana	S.C.		★	7 (i)	10	By seniority of service	Duration of service
Maine	S.J.C.	★		7	7	Appointed by governor	7 years
Maryland	C.A.		★	7	10	Appointed by governor	Indefinite
Massachusetts	S.J.C.	★		7	To age 70	Appointed by governor (j)	To age 70
Michigan	S.C.	★		7	8	By court	2 years
Minnesota	S.C.	★		7	6	Popular election	6 years
Mississippi	S.C.		★	9	8	By seniority of service	Duration of service
Missouri	S.C.	★		7	12	By court (k)	2 years
Montana	S.C.	★		7	8	Popular election	8 years
Nebraska	S.C.		★ (l)	7	6 (m)	Appointed by governor from Judicial Nominating Commission	Duration of service
Nevada	S.C.	★		5	6	Rotation	2 years
New Hampshire	S.C.	★		5	To age 70	Appointed by governor with approval of elected executive council	To age 70
New Jersey	S.C.	★		7	7 (n)	Appointed by governor, with consent of Senate	Duration of service
New Mexico	S.C.	★		5	8	By court	2 years
New York	C.A.	★		7	14	Appointed by governor from Judicial Nomination Commission	14 years
North Carolina	S.C.	★		7	8	Popular election	8 years
North Dakota	S.C.	★		5 (o)	10	By Supreme and district court judges	5 years (p)
Ohio	S.C.	★		7	6	Popular election	6 years
Oklahoma	S.C.		★	9	6	By court	2 years
	C.C.A.		★	5	6	By court	2 years
Oregon	S.C.	★		7	6	By court	6 years
Pennsylvania	S.C.	★		7	10	Rotation by seniority	Duration of term
Rhode Island	S.C.	★		5	Life	Appointed by governor from Judicial Nominating Commission (t)	Life
South Carolina	S.C.	★		5	10	Legislative election	10 years

See footnotes at end of table.

STATE COURTS OF LAST RESORT — Continued

State or other jurisdiction	Name of court	Justices chosen (a) At large	Justices chosen (a) By district	No. of judges (b)	Term (in years) (c)	Chief justice Method of selection	Chief justice Term of office for chief justice
South Dakota	S.C.		★ (q)	5	8	By court	4 years
Tennessee	S.C.	★		5	8	By court	4 years
Texas	S.C.	★		9	6	Partisan election	6 years
	C.C.A.	★		9	6	Partisan election	6 years (r)
Utah	S.C.	★		5	10 (s)	By court	4 years
Vermont	S.C.	★		5	6	Appointed by governor from Judicial Nomination Commission, with consent of Senate	6 years
Virginia	S.C.	★		7	12	Seniority	Indefinite
Washington	S.C.	★		9	6	By court	4 years
West Virginia	S.C.A.		★	5	12	Rotation by seniority	1 year
Wisconsin	S.C.	★		7	10	Seniority	Until declined
Wyoming	S.C.	★		5	8	By court	4 years
Dist. of Columbia	C.A.	★		9	15	Judicial Nominating Commission appointment	4 years
Puerto Rico	S.C.	★		7	To age 70	Appointed by governor, with consent of Senate	To age 70

Sources: Number of judges from Court Statistics Project, *State Court Caseload Statistics*, 2002 (National Center for State Courts 2003). All other information from *State Court Organization* 1998 (National Center for State Courts); state constitutions, statutes and court administrative offices.

Key:
S.C. — Supreme Court
S.C.A. — Supreme Court of Appeals
S.J.C. — Supreme Judicial Court
C.A. — Court of Appeals
C.C.A. — Court of Criminal Appeals
H.C. — High Court
(a) See Chapter 5 table entitled, "Selection and Retention of Judges," for details.
(b) Number includes chief justice.
(c) The initial term may be shorter. See Chapter 5 table entitled, "Selection and Retention of Judges," for details.
(d) A justice may serve more than one term as chief justice, but may not serve consecutive terms in that position.
(e) Governor nominates from candidates submitted by Judicial Selection Commission.
(f) Regional (5), Statewide(2), Regional based on District of Appeal
(g) Judicial Selection Commission nominates.

(h) Initial two years; retention 10 years.
(i) Includes one assigned from courts of appeal.
(j) Chief Justices are appointed, until age 70, by the Governor with the advice and consent of the Executive (Governor's) Council.
(k) Selection is typically rotated among the judges.
(l) Chief justice chosen statewide; associate judges chosen by district.
(m) More than three years for first election and every six years thereafter.
(n) Followed by tenure.
(o) A temporary court of appeals was established July 1, 1987 to exercise appellate and original jurisdiction was delegated by the supreme court. This court does not sit, has no assigned judges, has heard no appeals and is currently unfunded.
(p) Or expiration of term, whichever is first.
(q) Initially chosen by district; retention determined statewide.
(r) Presiding judge of Court of Criminal Appeals.
(s) Initial three years; retention 10 years.
(t) With House and Senate confirmation.

Table 5.2
STATE INTERMEDIATE APPELLATE COURTS AND GENERAL TRIAL COURTS:
NUMBER OF JUDGES AND TERMS

State or other jurisdiction	Intermediate appellate court			General trial court		
	Name of court	No. of judges	Term (years)	Name of court	No. of judges	Term (years)
Alabama	Court of Criminal Appeals	5	6	Circuit Court	142	6
	Court of Civil Appeals	5	6			
Alaska	Court of Appeals	3	10	Superior Court	32 (a)	6
Arizona	Court of Appeals	22	6	Superior Court	160 (ii)	4
Arkansas	Court of Appeals	12	8	Chancery/Probate Court and Circuit Court	115	(b)
California	Court of Appeals	105	12	Superior Court	1,498 (c)	6
Colorado	Court of Appeals	16	10	District Court	132 (d)	6
Connecticut	Appellate Court	9	8	Superior Court	180	8
Delaware	...	...	...	Superior Court	19	12
				Court of Chancery	(e)	12
Florida	District Courts of Appeals	62	6	Circuit Court	493	6
Georgia	Court of Appeals	12	6	Superior Court	188	4
Hawaii	Intermediate Court of Appeals	4	10	Circuit Court	28 (f)	10
Idaho	Court of Appeals	3	6	District Court	39 (g)	4
Illinois	Appellate Court	52 (h)	10	Circuit Court	472 (i)	6 (j)
Indiana	Court of Appeals	15 (k)	10 (l)	Superior Court, Probate Court and Circuit Court	296	6
Iowa	Court of Appeals	9	6	District Court	179 (m)	6
Kansas	Court of Appeals	10	4	District Court	233 (n)	4
Kentucky	Court of Appeals	14	8	Circuit Court	111 (dd)	8
Louisiana	Court of Appeals	54	10	District Court	224 (o)	6
Maine	...	...	...	Superior Court	16	7
Maryland	Court of Special Appeals	13	10	Circuit Court	143	15
Massachusetts	Appeals Court	25	(p)	Superior Court	82	(p)
Michigan	Court of Appeals	28	6	Circuit Court	210	6
Minnesota	Court of Appeals	16	6	District Court	260	6
Mississippi	Court of Appeals	10	8	Circuit Court	49	4
Missouri	Court of Appeals	32	12	Circuit Court	314 (q)	6
Montana	...	...	...	District Court	48 (r)	6
Nebraska	Court of Appeals	6	6 (s)	District Court	55	6 (t)
Nevada	...	...	...	District Court	56	6
New Hampshire	...	...	...	Superior Court	29 (u)	(p)
New Jersey	Appellate Division of Superior Court	32	7 (v)	Superior Court	428 (w)	7 (x)
New Mexico	Court of Appeals	10	8	District Court	72	6
New York	Appellate Division of Supreme Court	55	5 (y)	Supreme Court and County Court	474	(z)
	Appellate Terms of Supreme Court	15	5 (y)			
North Carolina	Court of Appeals	15	8	Superior Court	105 (aa)	8
North Dakota	...	...	...	District Court	42	6
Ohio	Court of Appeals	68	6	Court of Common Pleas	375	6

See footnotes at end of table.

STATE INTERMEDIATE APPELLATE COURTS AND GENERAL TRIAL COURTS — Continued

State or other jurisdiction	Intermediate appellate court			General trial court		
	Name of court	No. of judges	Term (years)	Name of court	No. of judges	Term (years)
Oklahoma	Court of Appeals	12	6	District Court	228 (bb)	4
Oregon	Court of Appeals	10	6	Circuit Court	163	6
				Tax Court	1 (jj)	6
Pennsylvania	Superior Court	15	10	Court of Common Pleas	394	10
	Commonwealth Court	9	10			
Rhode Island	. . .	. . .	Life	Superior Court	22 (kk)	Life
South Carolina	Court of Appeals	9	6	Circuit Court	51 (cc)	6
South Dakota	. . .	. . .	. . .	Circuit Court	38	8
Tennessee	Court of Appeals	12	8	Chancery Court	33	8
	Court of Criminal Appeals	12	8	Circuit Court	85	8
				Criminal Court	31	8
				Probate Court	2	(ee)
Texas	Court of Appeals	80	6	District Court	414	4
Utah	Court of Appeals	7	10 (ff)	District Court	70 (gg)	6
Vermont	. . .	. . .	. . .	Superior Court and District Court	29 (hh)	6
Virginia	Court of Appeals	11	8	Circuit Court	150	8
Washington	Court of Appeals	22	6	Superior Court	175	4
West Virginia	. . .	. . .	. . .	Circuit Court	65	8
Wisconsin	Court of Appeals	17	6	Circuit Court	241	6
Wyoming	. . .	. . .	. . .	District Court	17	6
District of Columbia	. . .	. . .	. . .	Superior Court	58	15
Puerto Rico	Circuit Court of Appeals	33	16	Court of First Instance	328	12

Sources: National Center for State Courts, *State Court Caseload Statistics*, 2002 and *State Court Organization*, 1998.

Key:

. . . —Court does not exist in jurisdiction or not applicable.

(a) Plus nine masters.
(b) Circuit court judges serve four-year terms. Chancery probate court judges serve six-year terms. (Some judges serve both circuit and chancery courts).
(c) Plus 408 commissioners and referees.
(d) Plus 32 magistrates and 11 Water Court judges.
(e) One chancellor and four vice-chancellors.
(f) Plus 17 family judges.
(g) Plus 83 full-time magistrate/judges.
(h) Plus 10 circuit court judges assigned to the appellate court.
(i) Plus 362 associate judges.
(j) Associate judges four years.
(k) Plus one tax court judge.
(l) Two years initial; 10 years retention.
(m) Plus 135 part-time magistrates, 12 associate juvenile judges, one associate probate judge, and six part-time alternate district associate judges.
(n) Includes 74 magistrates.
(o) Plus eleven commissioners.
(p) To age 70.

(q) Plus 32 commissioners.
(r) Plus five water judges and one worker's compensation judge.
(s) More than three years for first election and every six years thereafter.
(t) The initial term is for three years but not more than five years.
(u) Plus 11 full-time martial masters.
(v) Followed by tenure.
(w) 21 surrogates are surrogates that also serve as deputy superior court clerks.
(x) On reapportionment until age 70.
(y) Or duration.
(z) Fourteen years for Supreme Court; 10 years for county court.
(aa) Plus 100 clerks who hear uncontested probate.
(bb) This includes 73 district, 77 associate district and 78 special judges.
(cc) Plus 21 masters-in-equity.
(dd) Plus 50 domestic relations commissioners.
(ee) Locally determined.
(ff) Three years initial; six years retention.
(gg) Plus seven domestic court commissioners.
(hh) Plus five child support magistrates.
(ii) Plus one part-time judge.
(jj) Plus five magistrates.
(kk) Plus four magistrates.

Table 5.3
QUALIFICATIONS OF JUDGES OF STATE APPELLATE COURTS AND GENERAL TRIAL COURTS

| State or other jurisdiction | Years of minimum residence | | | | Minimum age | | Legal credentials | |
| | In state | | In district | | | | | |
	A	T	A	T	A	T	A	T
Alabama	1	1	...	1	...	...	Licensed attorney	Licensed attorney
Alaska	5	5	...	...	...	...	8 years practice	5 years practice
Arizona	10 (a)	5	(b)	1	(ee)	30	(c)	(d)
Arkansas	2	2	(b)	...	30	28	8 years practice	6 years practice/bench
California	...	...	...	...	...	...	10 years state bar	10 years state bar
Colorado	★	★(e)	...	★	...	...	5 years state bar	5 years state bar
Connecticut	★	★	(f)	(f)	...	...	10 years state bar	Member of the bar
Delaware	★	★	(f)	(g)	...	...	Learned in law	Learned in law
Florida	★(h)	★	(i)	★(j)	...	...	10 years state bar	5 years state bar
Georgia	★	3	...	...	...	30	7 years state bar	7 years state bar
Hawaii	★	★	...	...	...	...	10 years state bar	10 years state bar
Idaho	2	1	...	...	30	...	10 years state bar	10 years state bar
Illinois	★	★	★	★	...	...	Licensed attorney	...
Indiana	...	1	(b)	★	...	...	10 years state bar (k)	...
Iowa	...	...	...	★	...	...	Licensed attorney	...
Kansas	...	...	...	★	30	...	10 years active and continuous practice (l)	5 years state bar
Kentucky	2	2	2	2	...	...	8 years state bar and licensed attorney	8 years state bar
Louisiana	2	2	2	2	...	...	5 years state bar	5 years state bar
Maine	...	...	...	...	...	...	Learned in law	Learned in law
Maryland	5	5	6 mos.	6 mos.	30	30	State bar member	State bar member
Massachusetts	...	...	...	...	...	...		No law degree required
Michigan	...	...	(b)	...	...	...	State bar member (m)	State bar member
Minnesota	...	...	(n)	...	...	...	State bar member	State bar member
Mississippi	5	5	...	...	30	26	5 years state bar	5 years practice
Missouri	(o)	(o)	(b)	★	30	30	State bar member	State bar member
Montana	2	2	...	...	...	...	5 years state bar	5 years state bar
Nebraska	3 (p)	...	★	★	30	30	5 years practice	5 years practice
Nevada	2	2	...	...	25	25	State bar member	...
New Hampshire	...	...	...	...	...	...	...	...
New Jersey	...	(q)	...	(q)	...	...	Admitted to practice in state for at least 10 years	10 years practice of law
New Mexico	3	3	...	★	35	35	10 years active practice (r)	6 years active practice
New York	★	★	(s)	(s)	...	18	10 years state bar	10 years state bar
North Carolina	...	N.A.	...	★	...	...	State bar member	State bar member
North Dakota	★(p)	★	...	★	...	...	License to practice law	State bar member
Ohio	★(p)	★	(t)	★	...	...	6 years practice	6 years practice
Oklahoma	...	(u)	1	★	30	...	5 years state bar	(v)
Oregon	3	3	...	(w)	...	...	State bar member	State bar member
Pennsylvania	1	1	(f)	★	...	...	State bar member	State bar member
Rhode Island	...	...	...	...	21	...	License to practice law	State bar member
South Carolina	5	5	...	...	32	32	8 years state bar	8 years state bar
South Dakota	★	★	★	★	...	...	State bar member	State bar member
Tennessee	5	5	★(x)	1	35	30	Qualified to practice law	Qualified to practice law
Texas	★	...	...	2	35	25	(y)	(z)
Utah	5 (aa)	3	...	★	30	25	State bar member	State bar member
Vermont	5	5	...	(bb)	...	...	5 years state bar	5 years state bar
Virginia	...	★	...	★	...	...	5 years state bar	5 years state bar
Washington	1	1	1	1	...	...	(cc)	State bar member
West Virginia	5	★	...	★	30	30	10 years state bar	5 years state bar
Wisconsin	10 days	10 days	10 days	10 days	...	...	5 years state bar	5 years state bar
Wyoming	3	2	...	...	30	28	9 years state bar	...
Dist. of Columbia	★	★	90 days	90 days	...	...	5 years state bar	5 years state bar (dd)
No. Mariana Islands	...	...	...	...	...	30	N.A.	N.A.
Puerto Rico	5	...	...	...	...	...	10 years state bar	7 years state bar

See footnotes at end of table.

QUALIFICATIONS OF JUDGES — Continued

Sources: National Center for State Courts, *State Court Organization*, 1998 and state web sites, November 2003.

Key:

A—Judges of courts of last resort and intermediate appellate courts.

T—Judges of general trial courts.

★—Provision; length of time not specified.

. . .—No specific provision.

N.A.—Not applicable

(a) For court of appeals, five years.

(b) No local residency requirement stated for Supreme Court. Local residency required for Court of Appeals.

(c) Supreme Court—ten years state bar, Court of Appeals—five years state bar.

(d) Admitted to the practice of law in Arizona for five years.

(e) State residency requirement for District Court, no residency requirement stated for Denver Probate Court, Denver Juvenile Court or Water Court.

(f) Local residency not required.

(g) Court of Chancery does not have residency requirement, Superior Court requires residency.

(h) For District Courts of Appeal must reside within the territorial jurisdiction of the court

(i) Initial appointment, must be resident of district at the time of original appointment.

(j) Circuit court judge must reside within the territorial jurisdiction of the court.

(k) In the Supreme Court and the Court of Appeals, five years service as a general jurisdiction judge may be substituted.

(l) Relevant legal experience, such as being a member of a law faculty or sitting as a judge, may qualify under the 10 year requirement.

(m) Supreme Court: state bar member and practice at least five years.

(n) No residency requirement stated for Supreme Court, Court of Appeals varies.

(o) At the appellate level must have been a state voter for nine years. At the general trial court level must have been a state voter for three years.

(p) No state residency requirement specified for Court of Appeals.

(q) For Superior court: out of a total of 427 authorized judgeships (including thirty-two in the appellate division), there are restricted superior court judgeships that require residence within the particular county of assignment at time of appointment and reappointment; there are 142 unrestricted judgeships for which assignment of county is made by the chief justice.

(r) Supreme Court and Court of Appeals: and/or judgeship in any court of the state.

(s) No local residency requirement stated for Court of Appeals, local residency requirement for presiding judge of Supreme Court, Appellate Divisions.

(t) No local residency requirement for Supreme Court, Court of Appeals requires district residency.

(u) Six months if elected.

(v) District Court: judges must be a state bar member for four years or a judge of court record. Associate judges must be a state bar member for two years or a judge of a court of record.

(w) Local residency requirement for Circuit Court, no residency requirement stated for Tax Court.

(x) Supreme Court: One justice from each of three divisions and two seats at large. Court of Appeals and Court of Criminal Appeals: Must reside in the grand division served.

(y) Ten years practicing law or a lawyer and judge of a court of record at least 10 years.

(z) District Court: judges must have been a practicing lawyer or a judge of a court in this state, or both combined, for four years.

(aa) Supreme Court is five; Court of Appeals is three.

(bb) No local residency requirement stated for Superior Court, District Court must reside in geographic unit.

(cc) Supreme Court: State bar member; Courts of Appeals: five years state bar.

(dd) Superior Court: Judge must also be an active member of the unified District of Columbia bar and have been engaged, during the five years immediately preceding the judicial nomination, in the active practice of law as an attorney by the United States, of District of Columbia government.

(ee) Court of Appeals minimum age is 30.

Table 5.4
COMPENSATION OF JUDGES OF APPELLATE COURTS AND GENERAL TRIAL COURTS

State or other jurisdiction	Appellate courts					
	Court of last resort	Salary	Intermediate appellate court	Salary	General trial courts	Salary
Alabama	Supreme Court	$152,027	Court of Criminal Appeals	$151,027	Circuit courts	$111,973
Alaska	Supreme Court	117,900	Court of Appeals	111,384	Superior courts	109,032
Arizona	Supreme Court	126,525	Court of Appeals	123,900	Superior courts	120,750
Arkansas	Supreme Court	123,475	Court of Appeals	119,569	Chancery courts	115,659
California	Supreme Court	170,319	Court of Appeals	159,657	Superior court	139,476
Colorado	Supreme Court	111,637	Court of Appeals	109,137	District courts	104,637
Connecticut	Supreme Court	138,404	Appellate Court	129,988	Superior courts	125,000
Delaware	Supreme Court	147,000	. . .	. . .	Superior courts	140,200
Florida	Supreme Court	153,750	District Court of Appeals	141,963	Circuit courts	133,250
Georgia	Supreme Court	153,086	Court of Appeals	152,139	Superior courts	121,938
Hawaii	Supreme Court	115,547	Intermediate Court	110,618	Circuit courts	196,922
Idaho	Supreme Court	102,125	Court of Appeals	101,125	District courts	95,718
Illinois	Supreme Court	158,103	Court of Appeals	148,803	Circuit courts	136,546
Indiana	Supreme Court	115,000	Court of Appeals	110,000	Circuit courts	90,000
Iowa	Supreme Court	120,100	Court of Appeals	115,540	District courts	109,810
Kansas	Supreme Court	113,073	Court of Appeals	109,157	District courts	98,744
Kentucky	Supreme Court	123,335	Court of Appeals	118,300	Circuit courts	113,266
Louisiana	Supreme Court	112,668	Court of Appeals	106,706	District courts	100,743
Maine	Supreme Judicial Court	104,929	. . .	. . .	Superior courts	98,377
Maryland	Court of Appeals	131,600	Court of Special Appeals	123,800	Circuit courts	119,600
Massachusetts	Supreme Judicial Court	126,943	Appellate Court	117,467	Superior courts	112,777
Michigan	Supreme Court	164,610	Court of Appeals	151,441	Circuit courts	139,919
Minnesota	Supreme Court	129,674	Court of Appeals	122,186	District courts	114,700
Mississippi	Supreme Court	102,000	Court of Appeals	95,500	Chancery courts	94,700
Missouri	Supreme Court	123,000	Court of Appeals	115,000	Circuit courts	108,000
Montana	Supreme Court	89,381	. . .	. . .	District courts	82,600
Nebraska	Supreme Court	119,276	Court of Appeals	113,312	District courts	110,330
Nevada	Supreme Court	140,000	. . .	. . .	District courts	130,000
New Hampshire	Supreme Court	113,266	. . .	. . .	Superior courts	106,187
New Jersey	Supreme Court	158,500	Appellate division of	150,000	Superior courts	141,000
New Mexico	Supreme Court	96,283	Court of Appeals	91,469	District courts	86,896
New York	Court of Appeals	151,200	Appellate divisions of	144,000	Supreme courts	136,700
North Carolina	Supreme Court	115,336	Court of Appeals	110,530	Superior courts	104,523
North Dakota	Supreme Court	99,122	. . .	. . .	District courts	90,671
Ohio	Supreme Court	125,500	Court of Appeals	117,000	Courts of common pleas	107,600
Oklahoma	Supreme Court	106,706	Court of Appeals	101,714	District courts	95,898
Oregon	Supreme Court	105,200	Court of Appeals	102,800	Circuit courts	95,800
Pennsylvania	Supreme Court	139,585	Superior Court	135,213	Courts of common pleas	121,225
Rhode Island	Supreme Court	132,817	. . .	. . .	Superior courts	119,579
South Carolina	Supreme Court	119,510	Court of Appeals	116,521	Circuit courts	113,535
South Dakota	Supreme Court	100,671	. . .	. . .	Circuit courts	94,029
Tennessee	Supreme Court	121,740	Court of Appeals	116,064	Chancery courts	111,060
Texas	Supreme Court	113,000	Court of Appeals	107,350	District courts	109,158
Utah	Supreme Court	114,050	Court of Appeals	108,900	District courts	103,700
Vermont	Supreme Court	102,499	. . .	. . .	. . .	
Virginia	Supreme Court	132,523	Court of Appeals	125,899	Circuit courts	123,027
Washington	Supreme Court	134,584	Court of Appeals	128,116	Superior courts	121,972
West Virginia	Supreme Court	95,000	. . .	. . .	Circuit courts	90,000
Wisconsin	Supreme Court	122,418	Court of Appeals	115,490	Circuit courts	108,950
Wyoming	Supreme Court	105,000	. . .	. . .	District courts	100,000
Dist. of Columbia	Court of Appeals	164,100	. . .	. . .	Superior courts	154,700
Guam	. . .	128,000	. . .	. . .	Superior courts	100,000
No. Mariana Islands	Commonwealth Supreme Court	126,000	. . .	. . .	Superior courts	120,000
Puerto Rico	Supreme Court	120,000	Appellate Court	90,000	Superior courts	80,000
U.S. Virgin Islands	. . .	135,000	. . .	. . .	Territorial courts	13,500

Source: National Center for State Courts, *Survey of Judicial Salaries* (April 2003).

Note: Compensation is shown according to most recent legislation, even though laws may not yet have taken effect. There are other non-salary forms of judicial compensation that can be a significant part of a judge's compensa-tion package. It should be noted that many of these can be important to judges or attorneys who might be interested in becoming judges or justices. These include retirement , disability, and death benefits, expense accounts, vaca-tion, holiday, and sick leave and various forms of insurance coverage.

Table 5.5
SELECTED DATA ON COURT ADMINISTRATIVE OFFICES

State or other jurisdiction	Title	Established	Appointed by (a)	Salary
Alabama	Administrative Director of Courts	1971	CJ (b)	$105,000
Alaska	Administrative Director	1959	CJ (b)	116,000
Arizona	Administrative Director of Courts	1960	SC	136,000
Arkansas	Director, Administrative Office of the Courts	1965	CJ (c)	91,000
California	Administrative Director of the Courts	1960	JC	176,000
Colorado	State Court Administrator	1959	SC	112,000
Connecticut	Chief Court Administrator (d)	1965	CJ	144,000
Delaware	Director, Administrative Office of the Courts	1971	CJ	108,000
Florida	State Courts Administrator	1972	SC	128,000
Georgia	Director, Administrative Office of the Courts	1973	JC	117,000
Hawaii	Administrative Director of the Courts	1959	CJ (b)	90,000
Idaho	Administrative Director of the Courts	1967	SC	97,000
Illinois	Administrative Director of the Courts	1959	SC	149,000
Indiana	Executive Director, Division of State Court Administration	1975	CJ	99,000
Iowa	Court Administrator	1971	SC	123,000
Kansas	Judicial Administrator	1965	CJ	99,000
Kentucky	Administrative Director of the Courts	1976	CJ	113,000
Louisiana	Judicial Administrator	1954	SC	107,000
Maine	Court Administrator	1975	CJ	92,000
Maryland	State Court Administrator	1955	CJ (b)	119,000
Massachusetts	Chief Justice for Administration & Management	1978	SC	122,050
Michigan	State Court Administrator	1952	SC	126,000
Minnesota	State Court Administrator	1963	SC	115,000
Mississippi	Court Administrator	1974	SC	83,000
Missouri	State Courts Administrator	1970	SC	108,000
Montana	State Court Administrator	1975	SC	91,000
Nebraska	State Court Administrator	1972	CJ	97,000
Nevada	Director, Office of Court Administration	1971	SC	100,000
New Hampshire	Director of the Administrative Office of the Court	1980	SC	96,000
New Jersey	Administrative Director of the Courts	1948	CJ	150,000
New Mexico	Director, Administrative Office of the Courts	1959	SC	94,000
New York	Chief Administrator of the Courts	1978	CJ	148,000
North Carolina	Director, Administrative Office of the Courts	1965	CJ	108,000
North Dakota	Court Administrator (h)	1971	CJ	84,000
Ohio	Administrative Director of the Courts	1955	SC	115,000
Oklahoma	Administrative Director of the Courts	1967	SC	102,000
Oregon	Court Administrator	1971	SC	108,000
Pennsylvania	Court Administrator	1968	SC	134,000
Rhode Island	State Court Administrator	1969	CJ	107,000
South Carolina	Director of Court Administration	1973	CJ	99,000
South Dakota	State Court Administrator	1974	SC	89,000
Tennessee	Director	1963	SC	116,000
Texas	Administrative Director of the Courts (i)	1977	SC	98,000
Utah	Court Administrator	1973	SC	104,000
Vermont	Court Administrator	1967	SC	103,000
Virginia	Executive Secretary to the Supreme Court	1952	SC	125,000
Washington	Administrator for the Courts	1957	SC (e)	116,000
West Virginia	Administrative Director of the Supreme Court of Appeals	1975	SC	88,000
Wisconsin	Director of State Courts	1978	SC	115,000
Wyoming	Court Coordinator	1974	SC	83,000
Dist. of Columbia	Executive Officer, Courts of D.C.	1971	(f)	154,700
Guam	Administrative Director of Superior Court	N.A.	CJ (m)	80,000
No. Mariana Islands				70,000
Puerto Rico	Administrative Director of the Courts	1952	CJ	96,000
U.S. Virgin Islands	Court/Administrative Clerk	N.A.	N.A.	85,000

Source: Salary information was taken from National Center for State Courts, *Survey of Judicial Salaries* (April 2003).

Other information from State Court Administrator web sites.

Key:
SC — State court of last resort.
CJ — Chief justice or chief judge of court of last resort.
JC — Judicial council.
N.A. — Not available.

(a) Term of office for all court administrators is at pleasure of appointing authority.
(b) With approval of Supreme Court.
(c) With approval of Judicial Council.
(d) Administrator is an associate judge of the Supreme Court.
(e) Appointed from list of five submitted by governor.
(f) Joint Committee on Judicial Administration.

Table 5.6
LENGTH OF TERMS IN OFFICE FOR STATE COURTS: STATE-BY-STATE

State or other jurisdiction	Appellate courts				Trial courts			
	Length of initial term	Length of subsequent terms			Length of initial term	Length of subsequent terms		
		6 yrs.	8 yrs.	> 8 yrs.		4 yrs.	6 yrs.	> 6 yrs.
Alabama	6	★			6		★	
Alaska	3			10 yrs. (a)	3		★ (a)	
Arizona (b)	2	★ (a)			2 or 4	★ (a)		
Arkansas (c)	8		★		4 or 6	★	★	
California	12			12 yrs. (a)	6		★	
Colorado	2			10 yrs. (a)	2		★ (a)	
Connecticut	8		★		8			8 yrs.
Delaware	12			12 yrs.	12			12 yrs.
Florida	1	★ (a)			6		★ (a)	
Georgia	6	★			4	★		
Hawaii	10			10 yrs.	10			10 yrs.
Idaho	6	★			4	★		
Illinois	10			10 yrs. (a)	6		★ (a)	
Indiana (d)	2			10 yrs. (a)	2 or 6		★(a)	
Iowa	1		★ (a)		1		★(a)	
Kansas (e)	1	★ (a)			>1 or 4	★ (a)		
Kentucky	8		★		8			8 yrs.
Louisiana	10			10 yrs.	6		★	
Maine	7		7 yrs.		7			7 yrs.
Maryland (f)	1			10 yrs. (a)	1			15 yrs.
Massachusetts	to age 70				to age 70			
Michigan	8		★		6		★	
Minnesota	6	★			6		★	
Mississippi	8		★		4	★		
Missouri (g)	1			12 yrs. (a)	1 or 6		★ (a)	
Montana	8		★		6		★	
Nebraska	3	★ (a)			3		★ (a)	
Nevada	6	★			6		★	
New Hampshire	to age 70				to age 70			
New Jersey	7			to age 70	7			to age 70
New Mexico (h)	>1		★		>1		★	
New York	14			14 yrs.	14			14 yrs.
North Carolina	8		★		8			8 yrs.
North Dakota	10			10 yrs.	6		★	
Ohio	6	★			6		★	
Oklahoma	1	★ (a)			4	★		
Oregon	6	★			6		★	
Pennsylvania	10			10 yrs. (a)	10			10 yrs. (a)
Rhode Island	Life				Life			
South Carolina	10			10 yrs.	6		★	
South Dakota	3		★		8			8 yrs.
Tennessee (i)	>2		★ (a)		>2			8 yrs.
Texas	6	★			4	★		
Utah	3			10 yrs. (a)	3		★ (a)	
Vermont	6	★			6		★	
Virginia	12			12 yrs.	8			8 yrs.
Washington	6	★			4	★		
West Virginia	12			12 yrs.	8			8 yrs.
Wisconsin	10			10 yrs.	6		★	
Wyoming	1		★ (a)		1		★ (a)	
Dist. of Columbia	15			15 yrs.	15			15 yrs.

Source: American Judicature Society's, *Judicial Selection in the States*, Updated October 2002.

Key:

(a) Judges in this state stand for retention election for subsequent terms.

(b) Trial court judges in counties with populations greater than 250,000 serve 2-year initial terms, then stand for retention for subsequent 4-year terms. All other trial court judges are elected to 4-year terms in non-partisan elections.

(c) There are two trial courts of general jurisdiction, each with its own term length. Circuit Court judges serve 4-year terms, while Chancery Court judges serve 6-year terms.

(d) Trial court judges in two counties serve 2-year initial terms, then stand for retention for subsequent 6-year terms. Judges in all other counties are elected to 6-year terms in partisan elections.

(e) District Court Judges in 7 districts are elected to 4-year terms in partisan elections. In all other districts, judges serve 1-year initial terms, then stand for retention for subsequent 4-year terms.

(f) Judges' initial terms last until the expiration of one year from the date of the occurrence of the vacancy.

(g) Circuit Court judges in four counties serve 1-year initial terms, then stand for retention for subsequent 6-year terms. Judges in all other counties are elected to 6-year terms in partisan elections.

(h) The initial term is until the next election (for appellate and trial courts). The judge then runs for a full term in a partisan election, with the winner running for retention for subsequent terms.

(i) Supreme Court justices initially serve until the next biennial general election, at which time they stand for retention.

Table 5.7
SELECTION AND RETENTION OF JUDGES

State or other jurisdiction	Court	Appointive systems Merit (a)	Appointive systems Gubernatorial or Legislative (b)	Elective systems Non-partisan	Elective systems Partisan	Initial term of office (years)	Method of retention (c)
Alabama	Supreme Court	...	...	...	★	6	Re-election (6 yr. term)
	Court of Civil App.	...	...	...	★	6	Re-election (6 yr. term)
	Court of Crim. App.	...	...	...	★	6	Re-election (6 yr. term)
	Circuit Court	...	...	...	★	6	Re-election (6 yr. term)
Alaska	Supreme Court	★	...	...	...	3	Retention election (10 yr. term)
	Court of Appeals	★	...	...	...	3	Retention election (8 yr. term)
	Superior Court	★	...	...	...	3	Retention election (6 yr. term)
Arizona	Supreme Court	★	...	...	...	2	Retention election (6 yr. term)
	Court of Appeals	★	...	...	...	2	Retention election (6 yr. term)
	Superior Court— county pop. greater than 250,000	★	...	...	...	2	Retention election (4 yr. term)
	Superior Court— county pop. less than 250,000	...	...	★	...	4	Re-election (4 yr. term)
Arkansas (d)	Supreme Court	...	...	★	...	8	Re-election for additional terms
	Court of Appeals	...	...	★	...	8	Re-election for additional terms
	Circuit Court	...	...	★	...	6	Re-election for additional terms
California	Supreme Court	...	G	...	...	12	Retention election (12 yr. term)
	Courts of Appeal	...	G	...	...	12	Retention election (12 yr. term)
	Superior Court (e)	...	...	★	...	6	Nonpartisan election (6 yr. term) (f)
Colorado	Supreme Court	★	...	...	...	2	Retention election (10 yr. term)
	Court of Appeals	★	...	...	...	2	Retention election (8 yr. term)
	District Court	★	...	...	...	2	Retention election (6 yr. term)
Connecticut	Supreme Court	★	...	...	...	8	(g)
	Appellate Court	★	...	...	...	8	(g)
	Superior Court	★	...	...	...	8	(g)
Delaware (h)	Supreme Court	★	...	...	...	12	(i)
	Court of Chancery	★	...	...	...	12	(i)
	Superior Court	★	...	...	...	12	(i)
Florida	Supreme Court	★	...	...	...	1	Retention election (6 yr. term)
	District Court of Appeal	★	...	...	...	1	Retention election (6 yr. term)
	Circuit Court	...	...	★	...	6	Re-election for additional terms
Georgia	Supreme Court	...	...	★	...	6	Re-election for additional terms
	Court of Appeals	...	...	★	...	6	Re-election for additional terms
	Superior Court	...	...	★	...	4	Re-election for additional terms
Hawaii	Supreme Court	★	...	...	...	10	Reappointed to subsequent term by Judicial Selection Comm. (10 yr. term)
	Intermediate Court of Appeals	★	...	...	...	10	Reappointed to subsequent term by Judicial Selection Comm. (10 yr. term)
	Circuit and Family Courts	★	...	...	...	10	Reappointed to subsequent term by Judicial Selection Comm. (10 yr. term)
Idaho	Supreme Court	...	...	★	...	6	Re-election for additional terms
	Court of Appeals	...	...	★	...	6	Re-election for additional terms
	District Court	...	...	★	...	4	Re-election for additional terms
Illinois	Supreme Court	...	...	...	★	10	Retention election (10 yr. term)
	Court of Appeals	...	...	...	★	10	Retention election (10 yr. term)
	District Court	...	...	...	★	6	Retention election (6 yr. term)
Indiana	Supreme Court	★	...	...	...	2	Retention election (10 yr. term)
	Court of Appeals	★	...	...	...	2	Retention election (10 yr. term)
	Circuit Court	...	...	...	★	6	Re-election for additional terms
	Circuit Court (Vanderburg Co.)	...	...	★	...	6	Re-election for additional terms
	Superior Court	...	...	...	★	6	Re-election for additional terms
	Superior Court (Allen Co.)	...	...	★	...	6	Re-election for additional terms
	Superior Court (Lake Co.)	★(j)	...	...	...	2	Retention election (6 yr. term)
	Superior Court (St. Joseph Co.)	★	...	...	...	2	Retention election (6 yr. term)
	Superior Court (Vanderburg Co.)	...	...	★	...	6	Re-election for additional terms

See footnotes at end of table.

SELECTION AND RETENTION OF JUDGES — Continued

State or other jurisdiction	Court	Methods of initial selection				Initial term of office (years)	Method of retention (c)
		Appointive systems		Elective systems			
		Merit (a)	Gubernatorial or Legislative (b)	Non-partisan	Partisan		
Iowa	Supreme Court	★	. . .	. . .	. . .	1	Retention election (8 yr. term)
	Court of Appeals	★	. . .	. . .	. . .	1	Retention election (6 yr. term)
	District Court	★	. . .	. . .	. . .	1	Retention election (6 yr. term)
Kansas	Supreme Court	★	. . .	. . .	. . .	1	Retention election (6 yr. term)
	Court of Appeals	★	. . .	. . .	. . .	1	Retention election (4 yr. term)
	District Court (17 districts)	★	. . .	. . .	. . .	1	Retention election (4 yr. term)
	District Court (14 districts)	. . .	. . .	. . .	★	4	Re-election for additional terms
Kentucky	Supreme Court	. . .	. . .	★	. . .	8	Re-election for additional terms
	Court of Appeals	. . .	. . .	★	. . .	8	Re-election for additional terms
	Circuit Court	. . .	. . .	★	. . .	8	Re-election for additional terms
Louisiana	Supreme Court	. . .	. . .	. . .	★(k)	10	Re-election for additional terms
	Court of Appeals	. . .	. . .	. . .	★(k)	10	Re-election for additional terms
	District Court	. . .	. . .	. . .	★(k)	6	Re-election for additional terms
Maine	Supreme Judicial Court	. . .	G	. . .	. . .	7	Reappointment by governor subject to legislative confirmation
	Superior Court	. . .	G	. . .	. . .	7	Reappointment by governor subject to legislative confirmation
Maryland (h)	Court of Appeals	★	. . .	. . .	. . .	(1)	Retention election (10 yr. term)
	Court of Special Appeals	★	. . .	. . .	. . .	(1)	Retention election (10 yr. term)
	Circuit Court	★	. . .	. . .	. . .	(1)	Nonpartisan election (15 yr. term) (m)
Massachusetts (h)	Supreme Judicial Court	★	. . .	. . .	. . .	to age 70	. . .
	Appeals Court	★	. . .	. . .	. . .	to age 70	. . .
	Trial Court of Massachusetts	★	. . .	. . .	. . .	to age 70	. . .
Michigan	Supreme Court	. . .	. . .	. . .	★(n)	8	Re-election for additional terms
	Court of Appeals	. . .	. . .	★	. . .	6	Re-election for additional terms
	District Court	. . .	. . .	★	. . .	6	Re-election for additional terms
Minnesota	Supreme Court	. . .	. . .	★	. . .	6	Re-election for additional terms
	Court of Appeals	. . .	. . .	★	. . .	6	Re-election for additional terms
	District Court	. . .	. . .	★	. . .	6	Re-election for additional terms
Mississippi	Supreme Court	. . .	. . .	★	. . .	8	Re-election for additional terms
	Court of Appeals	. . .	. . .	★	. . .	8	Re-election for additional terms
	Chancery Court	. . .	. . .	★	. . .	4	Re-election for additional terms
	Circuit Court	. . .	. . .	★	. . .	4	Re-election for additional terms
Missouri	Supreme Court	★	. . .	. . .	. . .	1	Retention election (12 yr. term)
	Court of Appeals	★	. . .	. . .	. . .	1	Retention election (12 yr. term)
	Circuit Court	. . .	. . .	. . .	★	6	Re-election for additional terms
	Circuit Court (Jackson, Clay, Platte & Saint Louis Counties)	★	. . .	. . .	. . .	1	Retention election (6 yr. term)
Montana	Supreme Court	. . .	. . .	★	. . .	8	Re-election; unopposed judges run for retention
	District Court	. . .	. . .	★	. . .	6	Re-election; unopposed judges run for retention
Nebraska	Supreme Court	★	. . .	. . .	. . .	3	Retention election (6 yr. term)
	Court of Appeals	★	. . .	. . .	. . .	3	Retention election (6 yr. term)
	District Court	★	. . .	. . .	. . .	3	Retention election (6 yr. term)
Nevada	Supreme Court	. . .	. . .	★	. . .	6	Re-election for additional terms
	District Court	. . .	. . .	★	. . .	6	Re-election for additional terms
New Hampshire (h)	Supreme Court	. . .	G(o)	. . .	. . .	to age 70	. . .
	Superior Court	. . .	G(o)	. . .	. . .	to age 70	. . .
New Jersey	Supreme Court	. . .	G	. . .	. . .	7	Reappointed by governor (to age 70) with advice & consent of the Senate
	Appellate Div. of Superior Court	. . .	G	. . .	. . .	7	Reappointed by governor (to age 70) with advice & consent of the Senate
	Superior Court	. . .	G	. . .	. . .	7	Reappointed by governor (to age 70) with advice & consent of the Senate

See footnotes at end of table.

SELECTION AND RETENTION OF JUDGES — Continued

State or other jurisdiction	Court	Methods of initial selection				Initial term of office (years)	Method of retention (c)
		Appointive systems		Elective systems			
		Merit (a)	Gubernatorial or Legislative (b)	Non-partisan	Partisan		
New Mexico	Supreme Court	★	. . .	. . .	. . .	(p)	(q)
	Court of Appeals	★	. . .	. . .	. . .	(p)	(q)
	District Court	★	. . .	. . .	. . .	(p)	(q)
New York	Court of Appeals	★	. . .	. . .	. . .	14	(i)
	Appellate Div. of Supreme Court	★	. . .	. . .	. . .	5	(r)
	Supreme Court	. . .	. . .	. . .	★	14	Re-election for additional terms
	County Court	. . .	. . .	. . .	★	10	Re-election for additional terms
North Carolina	Supreme Court	. . .	. . .	★(s)	. . .	8	Re-election for additional terms
	Court of Appeals	. . .	. . .	★(s)	. . .	8	Re-election for additional terms
	Superior Court	. . .	. . .	★(s)	. . .	8	Re-election for additional terms
North Dakota	Supreme Court	. . .	. . .	★	. . .	10	Re-election for additional terms
	District Court	. . .	. . .	★	. . .	6	Re-election for additional terms
Ohio	Supreme Court	. . .	. . .	. . .	★(t)	6	Re-election for additional terms
	Court of Appeals	. . .	. . .	. . .	★(t)	6	Re-election for additional terms
	Court of Common Pleas	. . .	. . .	. . .	★(t)	6	Re-election for additional terms
Oklahoma	Supreme Court	★	. . .	. . .	. . .	1	Retention election (6 yr. term)
	Court of Criminal Appeals	★	. . .	. . .	. . .	1	Retention election (6 yr. term)
	Court of Appeals	★	. . .	. . .	. . .	1	Retention election (6 yr. term)
	District Court	. . .	. . .	★	. . .	4	Re-election for additional terms
Oregon	Supreme Court	. . .	. . .	★	. . .	6	Re-election for additional terms
	Court of Appeals	. . .	. . .	★	. . .	6	Re-election for additional terms
	Circuit Court	. . .	. . .	★	. . .	6	Re-election for additional terms
	Tax Court	. . .	. . .	★	. . .	6	Re-election for additional terms
Pennsylvania	Supreme Court	. . .	. . .	. . .	★	10	Retention election (10 yr. term)
	Superior Court	. . .	. . .	. . .	★	10	Retention election (10 yr. term)
	Commonwealth Court	. . .	. . .	. . .	★	10	Retention election (10 yr. term)
	Court of Common Pleas	. . .	. . .	. . .	★	10	Retention election (10 yr. term)
Rhode Island	Supreme Court	★	. . .	. . .	. . .	Life	. . .
	Superior Court	★	. . .	. . .	. . .	Life	. . .
	Worker's Compensation Court	★	. . .	. . .	. . .	Life	. . .
South Carolina	Supreme Court	. . .	L (u)	. . .	. . .	10	Reappointment by legislature
	Court of Appeals	. . .	L (u)	. . .	. . .	6	Reappointment by legislature
	Circuit Court	. . .	L (u)	. . .	. . .	6	Reappointment by legislature
South Dakota	Supreme Court	★	. . .	. . .	. . .	3	Retention election (8 yr. term)
	Circuit Court	. . .	. . .	★	. . .	8	Re-election for additional terms
Tennessee	Supreme Court	★	. . .	. . .	. . .	(v)	Retention election (8 yr. term)
	Court of Appeals	★	. . .	. . .	. . .	(v)	Retention election (8 yr. term)
	Court of Criminal Appeals	★	. . .	. . .	. . .	(v)	Retention election (8 yr. term)
	Chancery Court	. . .	. . .	. . .	★	8	Re-election for additional terms
	Criminal Court	. . .	. . .	. . .	★	8	Re-election for additional terms
	Circuit Court	. . .	. . .	. . .	★	8	Re-election for additional terms
Texas	Supreme Court	. . .	. . .	. . .	★	6	Re-election for additional terms
	Court of Criminal Appeals	. . .	. . .	. . .	★	6	Re-election for additional terms
	Court of Appeals	. . .	. . .	. . .	★	6	Re-election for additional terms
	District Court	. . .	. . .	. . .	★	4	Re-election for additional terms
Utah	Supreme Court	★	. . .	. . .	. . .	(w)	Retention election (10 yr. term)
	Court of Appeals	★	. . .	. . .	. . .	(w)	Retention election (6 yr. term)
	District Court	★	. . .	. . .	. . .	(w)	Retention election (6 yr. term)
	Juvenile Court	★	. . .	. . .	. . .	(w)	Retention election (6 yr. term)
Vermont	Supreme Court (6 yr. term)	★	. . .	. . .	. . .	6	Retained by vote of Gen. Assembly
	Superior Court (6 yr. term)	★	. . .	. . .	. . .	6	Retained by vote of Gen. Assembly
	District Court (6 yr. term)	★	. . .	. . .	. . .	6	Retained by vote of Gen. Assembly
Virginia	Supreme Court	. . .	L	. . .	. . .	12	Reappointment by the legislature
	Court of Appeals	. . .	L	. . .	. . .	8	Reappointment by the legislature
	Circuit Court	. . .	L	. . .	. . .	8	Reappointment by the legislature
Washington	Supreme Court	. . .	. . .	★	. . .	6	Re-election for additional terms
	Court of Appeals	. . .	. . .	★	. . .	6	Re-election for additional terms
	Superior Court	. . .	. . .	★	. . .	4	Re-election for additional terms

See footnotes at end of table.

SELECTION AND RETENTION OF JUDGES — Continued

| State or other jurisdiction | Court | Methods of initial selection | | | | Initial term of office (years) | Method of retention (c) |
| | | Appointive systems | | Elective systems | | | |
		Merit (a)	Gubernatorial or Legislative (b)	Non-partisan	Partisan		
West Virginia	Supreme Court	...	...	...	★	12	Re-election for additional terms
	Circuit Court	...	...	...	★	8	Re-election for additional terms
Wisconsin	Supreme Court	...	...	★	...	10	Re-election for additional terms
	Court of Appeals	...	...	★	...	6	Re-election for additional terms
	Circuit Court	...	...	★	...	6	Re-election for additional terms
Wyoming	Supreme Court	★	...	...	...	1	Retention election (8 yr. term)
	District Court	★	...	...	...	1	Retention election (6 yr. term)
Dist. of Columbia	Court of Appeals	★	...	...	...	15	Reappointment by judicial tenure commission (x)
	Superior Court	★	...	...	...	15	Reappointment by judicial tenure commission (x)

Source: American Judicature Society's, *Judicial Selection in the States*: *Appellate and General Jurisdiction Courts*, October 2002 and state web sites, January 2004.

Key:
★—Yes
. . .—No

(a) Merit selection through nominating commission.

(b) Gubernatorial (G) or legislative (L) appointment without nominating commission.

(c) In a retention election, judges run unopposed on the basis of their record.

(d) In November 2000, Arkansas voters passed an amendment to the Arkansas constitution shifting judicial elections to a nonpartisan system.

(e) The California constitution provides that local electors may choose gubernatorial appointments instead of nonpartisan election to select superior court judges. As of July 1999, no counties have chosen gubernatorial appointments.

(f) If the election is uncontested, the incumbent's name does not appear on the ballot.

(g) Commission reviews incumbent's performance on noncompetitive basis; governor re-nominates and legislature confirms.

(h) Merit selection established by executive order in Delaware, Maryland and Massachusetts. In all other jurisdictions, merit selection established by constitutional or statutory provision.

(i) Incumbent reapplies to nominating commission and competes with other applicants for nomination to the governor. The governor may reappoint the incumbent or another nominee. The senate confirms the appointment.

(j) Three of the judges run in partisan elections for 6 years terms then have to be re-elected for additional terms.

(k) Louisiana judicial elections are partisan in as much as the candidates' party affiliations appear on the ballot. However, two factors lead a somewhat nonpartisan character to these elections: (I) primaries are open to all candidates; and (2) judicial candidates generally do not solicit party support for their campaigns.

(l) Until the first general election following the expiration of one year from the date of the occurrence of the vacancy.

(m) May be challenged by other candidates.

(n) Although party affiliations for Supreme Court candidates are not listed on the general election ballot, candidates are nominated at party conventions.

(o) The Governor's nomination is subject to the approval of a five-member executive council.

(p) Until next general election.

(q) Partisan election at next general election after appointment for eight-year term for appellate judges, six-year term for district. The winner thereafter runs in a retention election for subsequent terms.

(r) Commission reviews and recommends for or against reappointment by governor.

(s) Beginning in 2004, these elections will be nonpartisan.

(t) Although party affiliations for judicial candidates are not listed on the general election ballot, candidates are nominated in partisan party elections.

(u) South Carolina has a 10 member Judicial Merit Selection Commission that screens judicial candidates and reports the findings to the state's General Assembly. Since 1997, the Assembly is restricted to voting only on those candidates found qualified by the Judicial Merit Selection Commission. However, the nominating commission itself is not far removed from the ultimate appointing body, and cannot be considered to be nonpartisan as control over member nominations is vested in majority party leadership. Although most nominating commissions contain members appointed by the governor or legislature, no other commission actually contain the governor or current legislators who have final approval over the candidate as voting members of the commission. In contrast, the Judicial Merit Selection Commission in South Carolina contains 6 current members of the General Assembly appointed by the Speaker or the House of Representatives, the Chairman of the Senate Judiciary Committee, and the President Pro Tempore of the Senate. State legislators also choose the remaining four members of the Commission who are selected from the general public.

(v) Until next biennial general election.

(w) First general election three years after appointment.

(x) Initial appointment is made by the President of the United States and is confirmed by the Senate. Six months prior to the expiration of the term of office, the judge's performance is reviewed by the tenure commission. Those found Well Qualified are automatically reappointed. If a judge is found to be Qualified, the President may nominate the judge for an additional term (subject to Senate confirmation). If the President does not wish to re-appoint the judge, the District of Columbia Nominating Commission compiles a new list of candidates.

Table 5.8
REMOVAL OF JUDGES

State or other jurisdiction	Methods of removal			
	Judicial conduct commissions, boards, councils	Impeachment	Recall	Gubernatorial, Supreme Court and/or legislative
Alabama	Judicial conduct commissions, boards, councils The Judicial Inquiry Commission investigates complaints against judges and files complaints with the Court of the Judiciary. The Court of the Judiciary may censure, suspend, or remove a judge. Decisions of the court of the judiciary may be appealed to the Supreme Court.	Judges may be impeached.	...	...
Alaska	Judges may be suspended, removed from office, retired, or censured by the Supreme Court upon the recommendation of the Commission on Judicial Conduct.	Judges may be impeached by two-thirds of the Senate and convicted by two-thirds of the House of Representatives.	...	...
Arizona	The Supreme Court may censure, suspend, remove, or retire a judge upon recommendation of the Commission on Judicial Content.	Judges may be impeached by a majority vote of the House of Representatives and convicted by a two-thirds vote of the Senate.	Judges are subject to recall election.	...
Arkansas	The Judicial Discipline and Disability Commission, which is responsible for enforcing the Arkansas Code of Judicial Conduct, has the authority to investigate, as well as to initiate, complaints concerning misconduct of judges. After notice and hearing, the Commission may, by majority vote of the membership, recommend to the Supreme Court that a judge be suspended or removed, and the Supreme Court sitting en banc may take such action.	Judges may be impeached by the House of Representatives and convicted by two-thirds of the Senate.	...	The Governor may remove judges for good cause upon the address of two-thirds of the members of both houses of the general assembly.
California	The Commission on Judicial Performance investigates complaints of judicial misconduct and incapacity and may privately admonish, suspend, censure, retire, or remove a judge. The Commission's decisions are subject to review by the Supreme Court.	Judges may be impeached by the Assembly and convicted by two-thirds of the Senate.	Judges are subject to recall election.	...
Colorado	On the recommendation of the Judicial Discipline Commission, the Supreme Court may remove, retire, suspend, censure, reprimand, or discipline a judge.	Judges may be impeached by a majority vote of the House of Representatives and convicted by a two-thirds vote of the Senate.	Judges are subject to recall election.	...
Connecticut	The Judicial Review Council investigates complaints of Judicial misconduct. If the investigation indicated that there is probable cause that the judge is guilty of misconduct, the Council may suspend or remove the judge.	Judges may be impeached by the House of Representatives and removed by two-thirds vote of the Senate.	...	Judges may be removed by the Governor on the address of two-thirds of the general assembly.
Delaware	Judges may be removed, retired, or disciplined by a two-thirds vote of the Court on the Judiciary.	Judges may be impeached by a majority of the House of Representatives and convicted by two-thirds of the Senate.	...	...
Florida	On the recommendation of the Judicial Qualifications Commission, the Supreme Court may discipline, retire, or remove a judge.	Judges may be impeached by a two-thirds vote of the House of Representatives and convicted by a two-thirds vote of the Senate.	...	...

See footnotes at end of table.

REMOVAL OF JUDGES — Continued

State or other jurisdiction	Methods of removal			
	Judicial conduct commissions, boards, councils	Impeachment	Recall	Gubernatorial, Supreme Cout and/or legislature
Georgia	The Judicial Qualifications Commission may discipline, retire, or remove a judge. Removal and retirement decisions must be reviewed by the Supreme Court.	Judges may be impeached by the House of Representatives and convicted by a two-thirds vote of the Senate.	…	…
Hawaii	The Commission on Judicial Conduct has the authority to investigate and conduct hearings concerning allegations of judicial misconduct or disability and to recommend to the Supreme Court that a judge be reprimanded, disciplined, suspended, retired, or retired.	…	…	…
Idaho	The Idaho Judicial Council investigates complaints against Idaho judges and may recommend to the Supreme Court the discipline, removal, or retirement of judges. The Supreme Court may review the recommendation of the Judicial Council and take additional evidence. the court may then reject the recommendation of the Judicial Council, or order discipline, removal, of retirement of the judge.	Judges may be impeached by a majority vote of the House of Representatives and convicted by a two-thirds vote of the Senate.	…	…
Illinois	The Judicial Inquiry Board files complaints with the courts Commission. After notice and hearing, the Commission may reprimand, censure, retire, or remove a judge.	Judges may be impeached by a majority vote of the House of Representatives and removed by two-thirds vote of the Senate.	…	…
Indiana	On the recommendation of the Commission on Judicial Qualifications, the Supreme Court may discipline, suspend, retire, or remove a judge.	Judges may be impeached by the House of Representatives and convicted by the Senate.	…	Judges may be removed by joint resolution of the General Assembly, upon the agreement of two-thirds of each house.
Iowa	The Commission on Judicial Qualifications has the authority to investigate complaints of judicial misconduct and recommend to the Supreme Court that it retire, discipline, or remove a judge.	Judges may be impeached by a majority of the House of Representatives and convicted by two-thirds of the Senate.	…	…
Kansas	Judges of the Court of Appeals and District Court may be removed by the Supreme Court on the recommendation of the Commission on Judicial Qualifications. The Commission on Judicial Qualifications is authorized to investigate allegations of misconduct and to recommend a formal hearing. If the charges are proven by clear and convincing evidence, the Commission may admonish the judge, issue a cease-and-decease order, or recommend to the Supreme Court public censure, suspension , removal or compulsory retirement.	Judges may be removed by impeachment and conviction, as prescribed in Article 2 of the Kansas Constitution.	…	Supreme Court justices are subject to retirement upon certification to the Governor (after a hearing by the Supreme Court Nominating Commission) that the justice is so incapacitated as to be unable to perform his duties.
Kentucky	After notice and hearing the Judicial Conduct Commission may admonish, reprimand, censure, suspend, retire, or remove a judge. The commission's decisions are subject to review by the Supreme Court.	Judges may be impeached by the House of Representatives and convicted by two-thirds vote of the Senate.	…	…

See footnotes at end of table.

REMOVAL OF JUDGES — Continued

State or other jurisdiction	Methods of removal			
	Judicial conduct commissions, boards, councils	Impeachment	Recall	Gubernatorial, Supreme Court and/or legislature
Louisiana (b)	On recommendation of the Judiciary Commission, the Supreme Court may censure, suspend, remove, or retire judges.	Judges may be impeached by the House of Representatives and removed by a two-thirds vote of the Senate.	...	...
Maine	The Supreme Judicial Court may retire, remove, or discipline judges upon recommendation of the Committee on Judicial Responsibility and Disability.	Judges may be impeached by the House of Representatives and convicted by two-thirds vote of the Senate.		Judges may be removed upon the address by the Governor of both houses of the legislature.
Maryland	Judges may be removed or retired by the Court of Appeals on the recommendation of the Commission on Judicial Disabilities.	Judges may be impeached by a majority of the House of delegates and convicted by two-thirds of the Senate.	...	Judges may be removed by the Governor upon address of the General Assembly with the concurrence of two-thirds of the members of each House. Judges may also be retired by the General Assembly with a two-thirds vote of each House and the Governor's concurrence.
Massachusetts (b)	The Commission on Judicial Conduct investigates complaints of judicial misconduct. Following a formal hearing, the commission may recommend to the Supreme Judicial Court removal, retirement, or reprimand of a judge.	Judges may be impeached by the House of Representatives and convicted by the Senate.	...	The Governor, with consent of the Governor's Council, may remove judges upon the address of both Houses of the General Court. The Governor, with consent of the Governor's Council, may also retire judges because of advanced age or mental or physical disability.
Michigan	On the recommendation of the Judicial Tenure Commission, the Supreme Court may censure, suspend, retire, or remove a judge.	Judges may be impeached by a majority vote of the House of Representatives and convicted by a two-thirds vote of the Senate.	...	The Governor may remove a judge upon the concurrent resolution of two-thirds of the members of both Houses of the Legislature.
Minnesota	After a public hearing and on the recommendation of the Board on Judicial Standards, the Supreme Court may censure, retire, or remove a judge.	Judges may be impeached by a majority vote of the House of Representatives and convicted by a two-thirds vote of the Senate.	Judges are subject to recall election.	...
Mississippi	On the recommendation of the Commission on Judicial Performance, the Supreme Court may censure, remove, or retire a judge.	Judges may be impeached by two-thirds vote of the House of Representatives and removed by the Senate.	...	Judges may be removed by the Governor on the joint address of two-thirds of both Houses of the Legislature.
Missouri	On the recommendation of the Commission on Retirement, Removal, and Discipline, the Supreme Court may suspend, discipline, reprimand, retire, or remove a judge.	Judges may be impeached by the House of Representatives. Impeachments are tried by the Supreme court or by special commission in the case of impeachments of the Governor or a Supreme Court Justice. Convictions require the concurrence of five-sevenths of the court or commission.	...	...

See footnotes at end of table.

REMOVAL OF JUDGES — Continued

State or other jurisdiction	Judicial conduct commissions, boards, councils	Methods of removal		Gubernatorial, Supreme Court and/or legislature
		Impeachment	Recall	
Montana	On the recommendation of the Judicial Standards Commission, the Supreme Court may retire, censure, suspend, or remove a judge.	Judges may be impeached by a two-thirds vote of the House of Representatives and convicted by a two-thirds vote of the Senate.	. . .	. . .
Nebraska	N.A.			
Nevada	The Commission on Judicial Discipline may discipline, censure, retire, or remove a judge. Commission decisions may be appealed to the Supreme Court.	Judges may be impeached by a majority vote of the Assembly and convicted by a two-thirds vote of the Senate.	Judges are subject to recall election	Judges may be removed by legislative resolution, passed by two-thirds of the members of both Houses.
New Hampshire...............	The Governor with the consent of the Executive Council, may remove judges for reasonable cause upon the joint address of both houses of the General Court.	Judges may be impeached by the House of Representatives and convicted by the Senate.	. . .	. . .
New Jersey	When the Supreme Court certifies to the Governor that a judge is so incapacitated that she/he cannot substantially perform his/her duties, a three-person commission is appointed to look into the matter. Upon the Commission's recommendation, the Governor may retire the judge from office.	Judges may be impeached by a majority vote of all members of the General Assembly and removed by a two-thirds vote of the Senate.	. . .	Removal proceedings may be instigated by a majority of either House, by the Governor filing a complaint with the Supreme Court, or by the Supreme Court on its own motion. The Supreme Court maintains an advisory committee on judicial conduct composed of private citizens appointed by the Court. The committee reviews all allegations of misconduct and either dismisses the charges or recommends a formal hearing. Based upon the hearing, judges may be reprimanded, censured and suspended without pay, or removed from office.
New Mexico	On the recommendation of the Judicial Standards Commission, the Supreme Court may discipline, retire, or remove a judge.	Judges may be impeached by a majority vote of the House of Representatives and removed by a two-thirds vote of the Senate.	. . .	. . .
New York...........	Judges may be admonished, censured, retired, or removed from office by the Commission on Judicial Conduct. The Commission's disciplinary actions are subject to review by the Court of Appeals.	Judges may be impeached by a majority vote of the Assembly and removed by a two-thirds vote of the Court for the Trial of Impeachments. The Court consists of the President of the Senate, the Senators, and the judges of the Court of Appeals.	. . .	Judges of the Courts of Appeals and justices of the Supreme Court may be removed by two-thirds vote of both houses of the legislature. Other judges may be removed by a two-thirds vote of the senate on the recommendation of the Governor.

See footnotes at end of table.

REMOVAL OF JUDGES — Continued

State or other jurisdiction	Judicial conduct commissions, boards, councils	Methods of removal		Gubernatorial, Supreme Cout and/or legislature
		Impeachment	Recall	
North Carolina	On the recommendation of the Judicial Standards Commission, the Supreme Court may censure or remove a judge.	Judges may be impeached by the House of Representatives and convicted by a two-thirds vote of the Senate.	. . .	Judges may be removed for mental or physical incapacity by joint resolution of two-thirds of the members of the General Assembly.
North Dakota	On the recommendation of the Commission on Judicial Conduct, the Supreme Court may discipline, censure, suspend, retire, or remove a judge.	Judges may be impeached by a majority vote of the House of Representatives and convicted by a two-thirds vote of the Senate.	Judges are subject to recall election.	. . .
Ohio	Complaints alleging judicial misconduct may be filed with the Disciplinary Council or with a certified grievance committee of the Board of Commissioners on Grievances and Discipline, both of which have the authority to investigate and file formal complaints with the Board. If two-thirds of the members of the board believe there is substantial credible evidence to support the complaint, the Supreme Court appoints a commission of five judges to determine whether retirement, removal, or suspension is warranted. The Commission's decision may be appealed to the Supreme court.	. . .	. . .	Judges may be removed by a concurrent resolution of two-thirds of both Houses of the general Assembly.
Oklahoma (b)	Judges are subject to removal from office, or to compulsory retirement, by proceedings in the Court on the Judiciary.	Judges may be impeached by the House of Representatives and convicted by two-thirds of the Senate.	. . .	. . .
Oregon (h)	On the recommendation of the Commission on Judicial Fitness and Disability, the Supreme Court may censure, suspend, retire, or remove a judge.	. . .	Judges are subject to recall election.	
Pennsylvania	The Judicial Conduct Board investigates complaints regarding judicial conduct filed by individuals or initiated by the board. The board determines whether probable cause exists to file formal charges, and presents its case to the court of judicial discipline. The court has the authority to impose sanctions, ranging from a reprimand to removal from office, if the formal charges are sustained.	Judges may be impeached by the House of Representatives and convicted by a two-thirds vote of the Senate.	. . .	. . .
Rhode Island	The Commission on Judicial Tenure and Discipline reviews complaints against judges. Following a formal hearing, the Commission either dismisses the complaint or recommends to the Supreme Court that the judge be reprimanded, censured, suspended, removed, or retired. The Commission may also recommend the retirement of a judge for physical or mental disability.	Judges may be impeached by a majority of the House of Representatives and convicted by a two-thirds vote of the Senate.	. . .	. . .

See footnotes at end of table.

REMOVAL OF JUDGES — Continued

State or other jurisdiction	Judicial conduct commissions, boards, councils	Methods of removal		
		Impeachment	Recall	Gubernatorial, Supreme Cout and/or legislature
South Carolina	The Commission on Judicial Conduct is authorized to investigate complaints of judicial misconduct and incapacity. Disciplinary counsel appointed by the Supreme Court evaluates each complaint and either dismisses the complaint or conducts a preliminary investigation. If evidence supports the complaint, a full investigation is authorized. If the investigation supports the filing of formal charges, a hearing is conducted, after which recommendation is made to the Supreme Court for sanctions, dismissal, transfer to inactive status, retirement, or removal.	Judges may be impeached by a two-thirds vote of the House of Representatives and convicted by a two-thirds vote of the Senate.	. . .	Judges may be removed by the Governor upon the address of two-thirds of each house of the General Assembly.
South Dakota	On the recommendation of the Judicial Qualifications Commission , the Supreme Court, after a hearing, may censure, remove, or retire a judge,	Judges may be impeached by a majority of the House of Representatives and convicted by two-thirds vote of the Senate.	. . .	. . .
Tennessee	Upon recommendation by the Court of the Judiciary, the General Assembly may remove judges by a two-thirds vote of both Houses, with each House voting separately.	Judges may be impeached by the House of Representatives and convicted by two-thirds vote of the Senate.	. . .	. . .
Texas	The State Commission on Judicial Conduct investigates, and if warranted, prosecutes allegations of misconduct. Upon a Commission recommendation of removal or retirement, the Supreme Court selects a review tribunal from among Court of Appeals judges to verify the findings and enter a judgment. Judges may appeal decisions of the review tribunal to the Supreme Court.	Judges may be impeached by the House of Representatives and removed by two-thirds vote of the Senate.	. . .	Judges may be removed by the Governor on address of two-thirds of the House and Senate. The Supreme Court may remove District Court judges from office.
Utah	The Judicial Conduct Commission may reprimand, censure, suspend, retire, or remove a judge. The Commission's decisions are subject to review by the Supreme Court.	Judges may be impeached by a two-thirds vote of the House of Representatives and convicted by a two-thirds vote of the Senate.	. . .	. . .
Vermont	The Judicial Conduct Board investigates complaints of judicial misconduct of disability and recommends any necessary action to the Supreme Court. Possible disciplinary actions include public reprimand of the judge, suspension for a part or the remainder of the judge's term of office, or retirement of the judge if physically or mentally disabled.	Judges may be impeached by a two-thirds vote of the House of Representatives and convicted by a two-thirds vote of the Senate.	. . .	. . .
Virginia (b)	The Judicial Inquiry and Review Commission investigates complaints of judicial misconduct or serious mental or physical disability that interferes with a judges duties. The Commission may conduct hearings and gather evidence to determine whether the charges are substantial. If the Commission finds the charges to significant, a formal complaint is filed with the Supreme Court of West Virginia. The Supreme Court may dismiss the complaint or it may retire, censure, or remove the judge.	Judges may be impeached by the House of Delegates and removed by a two-thirds vote of the Senate.	. . .	. . .

See footnotes at end of table.

REMOVAL OF JUDGES — Continued

State or other jurisdiction	Methods of removal			
	Judicial conduct commissions, boards, councils	Impeachment	Recall	Gubernatorial, Supreme Cout and/or legislature
Washington (b)	The Commission on Judicial Conduct investigates complaints of judicial misconduct or disability and recommends to the Supreme Court that the judge be suspended, removed , or retired. The Supreme makes the final decision after reviewing the commission's record and hearing argument on the matter.	. . .		Judges may be removed from office by joint resolution of the legislature, in which three-fourths of the members of each house must concur.
West Virginia	The Judicial Hearing Board investigates complaints against judges and makes recommendations to the Supreme Court regarding the disposition of those complaints. The Court has the authority to censure, suspend, and retire judges.	Judges may be impeached by the House of Delegates and removed by a two-thirds vote of the Senate.		. . .
Wisconsin	On the recommendation of the Judicial Commission and after review, the Supreme Court may reprimand, censure, suspend, or remove a judge.	Judges may be impeached by a majority vote of the Assembly and convicted by a two-thirds vote of the Senate.	Judges are subject to recall election	Judges may be removed by address of both Houses of the Legislature with the concurrence of two-thirds of the members of each House.
Wyoming	The Supreme Court, on its own motion or on the recommendation of the Commission on Judicial Conduct and ethics, may censure, suspend, retire, or remove a judge.	Judges may be impeached by a majority of the House of Representatives and convicted by two-thirds of the Senate.		. . .
Dist. of Columbia	The Judicial Disabilities and Tenure Commission has the authority to suspend, involuntarily retire, or remove judges upon the filing of an order with the D.C. Court of Appeals.	. . .		. . .

Source: American Judicature Society, *Judicial Selection in the States*, January 2004 http://www.ajs.org.

Key:
. . .—No provision for method.
N.A.—Not available.

Chapter Six

STATE ELECTIONS AND ETHICS

"Although the federal government established fundamental mandates in the legislation, it left to the states how to accomplish those tasks."

— **R. Doug Lewis**

Issues involving gifts and gratuities and the conflicts of interest arising from family and unique non-profit and private sector relationships continue to present trends issues for the states and the general public.

— **David E. Freel**

"While exciting, the recall does not represent a sea change in California politics."

— **Thad Kousser**

Help America Vote Act:
A New Pattern in State Election Reform
By R. Doug Lewis

Congress enacted the Help America Vote Act (HAVA) in 2002. Supporters of HAVA would indicate that it is one of the few times that the federal government has established a national program that relies on the states to determine the best methods of implementing the mandates and goals, while opponents would point to its lack of clear direction and clear authority of the federal government to determine whether a program is meeting its objectives.

When Congress passed the Help America Vote Act (HAVA) in 2002 and the president signed it in October of that year, the act became one of the unique examples of federal mandates with Congressional funding but great state control. The specifics of the mandates, while important to elections, are not the focus of this discussion. Rather it is the way federal legislation can craft a role for each level of government and allow each level to do what it does best, that is the focus here.

State leaders at both the legislative level and the administrative level can learn useful tools by studying HAVA as an example of what to ask Congress to do in other legislation – or to avoid because of the HAVA legislation. It is somewhat unique in federalism and should become a case study for national and state programs, because it sets new precedents.

Reacting to the razor thin margins of the Florida presidential election of 2000, Congress sought to revitalize the infrastructure of American democracy by establishing "minimum standards" (called mandates in most other legislation) which had never before existed at the federal level for elections. The act itself is a watershed event in the history of American democracy because it brought for the first time, a significant federal role to the conduct of elections in America. Congress authorized $3.865 billion to be spent on updating and transforming the nation's elections process, although at this writing $3.0 billion of the money has been actually appropriated with less than $700 million actually distributed to the states.

What makes HAVA somewhat unique is that although the federal government established fundamental mandates in the legislation, it left to the states how to accomplish those tasks. The act requires some responsibilities and roles which have historically been the purview of local governments, now be the responsibility of the state, including the development and maintenance of statewide voter databases, an appeals process for complaints about elections administration

that has moved from the local level to the state level, and compliance with the provisions of the act are focused now at the state rather than local level.

While the U.S. Constitution established that states have the prime responsibility for elections, the process of administration of elections being the function of local government was the general practice throughout American history, even pre-dating the formation of a nation. (Elections in what is now the United States may have begun as early as 1610 to 1620 for local offices and a few years later for legislative offices.) This was principally because of two conditions. First, it made more sense during a period when communications were difficult and even state capitals were not easily accessible, to have elections conducted locally. Secondly, and equally as important, was the serious distrust the nation's founders had of centralized authority, especially elections authority. As rebellious colonists marshaled complaints about unpopular taxes or trade requirements, the King's British colonial governors tried to remove or limit the powers of state legislatures and to control who could serve in those bodies and how they got elected. The nation's founders got what they wanted – a system that is not terribly efficient but is exceedingly difficult to manipulate and relies on local governments to manage and make work.

Because the 2000 election revealed that there was little state control of the election administration process, Congress sought to establish more review of that process, if not at the federal level, then certainly at the state level. Many in Congress sought to give the federal government far more authority over the conduct of elections, but state and local governments fought hard to maintain state and local responsibility for the process. The result, however, established more direct authority for the process at the state level. In order to keep the U.S. Department of Justice (or any other federal agency) out of an administrative role, in addition to its historic role of enforcement, states had to be willing to take on additional oversight to assure that elections met the objectives established by Congress.

Mandating Plans without Federal Approval

One of the mandates included states accepting responsibility for creating State Plans for how HAVA funds would be spent to meet the objectives of HAVA and to have those plans developed through open public meetings and available for comment by voters and voting groups within the states. There is also a requirement that those plans be published in the *Federal Register* for 45 days prior to actual funding by the United States Election Assistance Commission (USEAC or EAC). What is unusual in this situation is that while the federal government requires written plans with accessibility and involvement of the public, those plans then become "self actuating."

No federal agency is empowered to make value judgments as to whether those plans actually accomplish the mandates of HAVA, but rather leave it to states to devise the plans, do so in an open and public manner, have them published in the *Federal Register*, and then tell the USEAC that they meet the requirements of the legislation for funding purposes. While they have to file statements that they are in compliance with a number of federal election laws (Voting Rights Act and National Voter Registration Act) and disability laws (Americans with Disabilities Act and Elderly and Handicapped Voting Accessibility Act), unless someone can show positively that they are not in compliance with one of those acts, the state gets its funding under HAVA.

The beauty of this provision is that it establishes a level of trust between governments essentially indicating that the federal government will establish overall goals to be achieved, that state government has to plan and specify how to implement those goals within their borders, and local governments must actually make the administrative functions work. This means that there is no attempt to form one national plan or program to force the states to all behave in the same manner for elections purposes. It also allows states and the District of Columbia (as well as all U.S. territories) to determine how to individually comply with the act. We have already seen that there are more solutions to some of the problems than most people envisioned.

It may be true that some of the solutions will be better than others, but some would never have been developed had there been a federal requirement to do it one way. Each state will measure its own performance against its own plan and not against another state's plan. Clearly this will frustrate some policy analysts and advocacy organizations because it becomes difficult to say with credibility that state A should have done it more like state B. The ingeniousness of HAVA is that it counts on states having very different solutions and allows the states to meet its objectives with uniqueness and originality.

For instance, a simple mandate of the legislation creates provisional ballots but leaves to the states how to determine what administrative rules and provisions go with implementing provisional ballots. Similarly, HAVA mandates that each voting site in the state have at least one voting device that makes it possible for disabled and blind persons to vote secretly and independently, without telling states exactly how to do that, or even what equipment should do that. We are likely to see a variety of answers and solutions developed over the years to comply with this mandate.

Funding and "No Year Money"

The HAVA law is also unique in that its funding comes from fiscal year budgets of the federal government. But once it is distributed to the states, it essentially becomes "no year money," meaning that states are not required to spend it in one specific fiscal year. The advantage of this is quite clear: states are not forced to either find ways to spend money in a fiscal year so they can then qualify for new funds in another fiscal year — and yet there is no advantage to holding money. The objective is to get the money in the hands of the states, and the states can utilize that money according to its own time table as long as the funds are expended for allowable projects under the law.

Clearly, the states can benefit greatly from planning their own cash flows to meet their State Plans. With proper planning and intelligent application of resources, states may find a way to earn interest on their HAVA funds and to extend the benefits of HAVA funding far beyond the actual amounts appropriated by the federal government. The law indicates even the interest earned is to be maintained for elections funding. This is not to say that states can sit on the funds for years without action or can delay action in order to "grow" their elections funds. HAVA establishes some very ambitious dates for compliance with some of the mandates and it may not be possible to delay any of those provisions to a more prudent schedule. One example of this is that statewide voter databases have to be fully functional by 2006.

History of software projects of this magnitude indicate that such databases have usually taken four to six years (or more) to develop, implement, debug and then rely on them. Congress established that it wanted these done in less time than may have been prudent, but the states have no option but to try to comply. With an accelerated deadline date, states have not had the time to develop local government "buy-in" to both the concept and the reality that it has to work. Instead states have been forced to shove the concept at the local governments and indicate that necessary deadlines mean that locals will simply have to adapt. Clearly, some states will comply and have few problems in doing so, but we can fully expect that others will have significant difficulty in making such databases function well within that time frame.

And, it is not as if the state can simply decide to take over the database input from the local governments. This is one example of the HAVA law — and elections practice — where state and local governments have to rely on each other. If one fails, both fail. Locals must rely on the state to develop a database that is useful not only in maintaining names and developing a voter registration list, but also can assist the locals in conducting their elections, tracking voter participation and voter history, tracking voter needs, determining who needs an absentee ballot, etc. States must rely on locals to correctly input data, to maintain it well for changes and updates of individual voter records, to assure that street addresses are correct and match U.S. Postal compliance needs, etc.

The point here is that each level of government, federal through local, has to rely on each other to get this done and to make it function well for the voters. If the deadline is too unrealistic, the federal government forces development of shoddy databases; if the states are too unrealistic and do not fashion a database useful for local election administration, its functionality to locals becomes void. If local governments are too unrealistic in their expectations and/or they try to drag their feet in implementing the changes, the end result is that voters suffer and/or an election disaster can happen. Clearly there are high stakes in a federalism concept that essentially requires each level to depend and support each other – when history has shown that there are traditional conflicts between and among governmental levels.

Additionally, one part of the law provides "incentive" money for the states to get rid of antiquated voting systems such as lever machines and punch card systems. And it requires the states to certify that they will be in compliance by the 2006 election in order to receive funding under that provision of the act. It relies on the state indicating that the entire state will be in compliance by the deadline. But if some of the local jurisdictions decide (for whatever reason) not to comply by the deadline, the act only requires the states to return the pro-rata share of the non-compliance, not the entire federal funding. In other words, the federal government is rewarding "substantial" compliance without forcing parts of the state to suffer because one or more local jurisdictions choose not to participate.

Federal Agency Assistance and Review

Congress established the new EAC at the federal level but gave it little authority – it can neither interpret nor enforce the law. It has no regulatory authority of any kind, but is expected to help define best practices and serve as a clearinghouse for election administration practices and procedures. It is charged with developing "voluntary" voting machine standards (now called guidelines) to apply to any voting equipment used in federal elections.

The commission can provide "advice" but state and local governments are not forced to follow or to even pay particular attention that advice. Additionally, the EAC will initiate a number of federal studies to advance the research on good elections practices. Essentially, the EAC is to be a national resource to both Congress and the states. Its standards body, in fact, is comprised of one representative from each state and territory along with one local government representative from each state (not from the same party as the state representative).

No federal program ever comes without audit capacity. What is different in this approach to a new federalism is that the traditional agencies can audit and review, but are restricted in their ability to judge levels of compliance with HAVA. The U.S. General Accounting Office (GAO) can perform its usual and customary role of determining whether federal funds were spent as Congress specified in law. But unlike most federal laws, there are no benchmark solutions for the GAO to determine how well each state performed. States must be measured against how well they performed against the plans they themselves developed.

It will be difficult (notice that we did not say impossible) for the GAO to make legitimate claims that a state spent money more wisely than another because the law does not establish a national norm, nor promote comparing a one state to another. Human nature, being what it is, will inevitably lead to some of these comparisons by not only the GAO but other groups and organizations. The point is that this law is somewhat unique in that it forces the audit groups to rely primarily on comparing the state's performance to what the state indicated in its State Plan that it will do.

Less constricted is the U.S. Department of Justice (DOJ), but it too must use a somewhat different measuring stick than in the past. The DOJ will carry its tradition of compliance review, especially when it comes to deciding whether states were truthful in stating that they already comply with the requirements of other federal laws in order to receive federal funds under HAVA. And that is a heavy stick indeed. Constitutional and federal election law provisions give the DOJ wide latitude in determining whether civil rights (voting is considered a civil right of this nation) have been restricted by a state or local government's actions.

But other sections of the law require even the DOJ to measure the state by what the actual letter of the federal law requires and then whether the state met its own plans in complying with the law. Some provisions of HAVA law do not indicate a clear answer or direction. This was done on purpose by the bill's principal backers so that states would have greater responsibility for determining their own answer and solutions as befits their own state laws and elections practices.

The HAVA law will be used for many years to come as an example of a 'good' or a 'bad' law when it comes to evaluating the appropriate actions of state and local governments. State legislators will need to look closely at the concepts established within HAVA as examples of how they want the federal government to construct future laws affecting state and local governments.

Supporters of the HAVA legislation as written will indicate that it is one of the few times that the federal government has established a national program that relies on the states to determine the best methods of implementing the mandates and goals. It takes an approach that the federal government is trusting state governments and through them, local governments, to act responsibly in serving the public and letting each level of government do determine how best to accomplish the goals.

Opponents of HAVA will point to its lack of clear direction and clear authority of the federal government to determine whether a program is meeting its objectives. Those who favor national programs, with all states doing it identically, will use HAVA as an example of how the federal government must take a stronger role in directing the activities of states to comply with Congressional intent.

Model Legislation – Is It or Isn't It?

This unique law may also provide state legislatures and governors with a blueprint for determining similar structures within state statutes. If the HAVA law works well in establishing that the federal government can set desired policies and broad goals, with state governments determining how best to accomplish those, and local governments actually implementing them. Along with the appropriate accountability at each level, the elections law passed as a result of election 2000 may have a much broader national impact for generations to come than simply its elections purposes. HAVA, while not especially well written from a clarity standpoint, establishes unique concepts that bear close observation in fostering a new era of federalism where governments actually trust each other and work together to serve the public. Only time will tell whether that direction is successful.

About the Author

R. Doug Lewis is executive director of The Election Center, a national nonpartisan, nonprofit organization serving elections and voter-registration professionals. A certified elections/registration administrator, his contributions include authoring the Professional Education Program for elections/registration officials, developing of the first Code of Ethics for voter-registration and elections administrators, establishing the Professional Practices Papers program and establishing a National Task Force on Election Reform to study the 2000 presidential election.

Table 6.1
STATE EXECUTIVE BRANCH OFFICIALS TO BE ELECTED: 2004–2008

State or other jurisdiction	2004	2005	2006	2007	2008
Alabama	...	...	G, LG, AG, AR, A, SS, T	...	...
Alaska (a)	(b)	...	G, LG	...	...
Arizona	...	...	G, AG, SS, SP, T (b)	...	...
Arkansas	...	...	G, LG, AG, A, SS, T (g)	...	...
California	...	...	G, LG, AG, SS, SP, T (c)(h)	...	...
Colorado	...	...	G, LG, AG, SS, T	...	...
Connecticut	...	...	G, LG, AG, C, SS, T	...	...
Delaware	G, LG (d)	...	AG, C, T	...	G, LG (d)
Florida	...	...	G, LG, AG, AR, CFO	...	...
Georgia	...	...	G, LG, AG, AR, SS, SP (e)(f)	...	...
Hawaii	...	...	G, LG	...	...
Idaho	...	...	G, LG, AG, SS, SP, T (h)	...	...
Illinois	...	...	G, LG, AG, C, SS, T	...	G, LG, AG, SP
Indiana	G, LG, AG, SP	...	A, SS, T	...	...
Iowa	...	...	G, LG, AG, AR, A, SS, T	...	...
Kansas	...	...	G, LG, AG, SS, T (i)	...	...
Kentucky	...	...	(j)	G, LG, AG, AR, A, SS, T	...
Louisiana	(j)	...	G	G, LG, AG, AR, SS, T (j)	(j)
Maine (k)	...	...	G, LG, AG, C	...	...
Maryland	...	...		...	...
Massachusetts	...	...	G, LG, AG, A, SS, T	...	...
Michigan	(l)	...	G, LG, AG, SS (l)	...	(l)
Minnesota	...	...	G, LG, AG, A, SS	...	...
Mississippi	...	...	A	G, LG, AG, AR, A, SS, T (m)	...
Missouri	G, LG, AG, A, SS, T	...	...	...	G, LG, AG, SS, T
Montana	G, LG, AG, A, SS, SP	...	G, LG, AG, A, SS, T	...	G, LG, AG, A, SS, SP
Nebraska	...	...	G, LG, AG, SS, T (h)	...	...
Nevada	G	...	G	...	G
New Hampshire	...	G	...	...	...
New Jersey	...	...	...	...	...
New Mexico	...	...	G, LG, AG, A, SS, T (o)	...	...
New York	G, LG, AG, AR, A, SS, SP, T (p)	...	G, LG, AG, C	...	...
North Carolina	G, LG, SS, A, T, AG, AR, SP (q)(n)(w)	...	SS, AG, AR (q)(n)	...	...
North Dakota	...	...	G, LG, A, AG, SS, T	...	G, LG, A, T (q)
Ohio	...	...	...	...	...
Oklahoma	AG, SS, T	...	G, LG, AG, A, SP, T (r)	...	AG, SS, T
Oregon	AG, A, T	...	G, SP	...	AG, A, T
Pennsylvania	...	G	G, LG	...	...
Rhode Island	...	...	G, LG, AG, SS, T	...	...
South Carolina	...	...	G, LG, AG, C, SS, SP, T (s)	...	...
South Dakota	(t)	...	G, LG, AG, A, SS, T (t)	...	(t)
Tennessee	...	G	...	...	...
Texas	(u)	...	G, LG, AG, AR, C (u)	...	(u)
Utah	G, LG, AG, A, T	...	...	...	G, LG, AG, A, T
Vermont	G, LG, AG, A, SS, T	...	G, LG, AG, A, SS, T	...	G, LG, AG, A, SS, T

See footnotes at end of table.

STATE EXECUTIVE BRANCH OFFICIALS TO BE ELECTED: 2004–2008 — Continued

State or other jurisdiction	2004	2005	2006	2007	2008
Virginia		G, LG, AG			
Washington	G, LG, AG, A, SS, SP, T (f)				G, LG, AG, A, SS, SP, T (f)
West Virginia	G, AG, AR, A, SS, T				G, AG, AR, A, SS, T
Wisconsin	. . .	SP	G, LG, AG, SS, T	. . .	. . .
Wyoming	. . .	. . .	G, A, SS, SP, T	. . .	. . .
American Samoa	G, LG				G, LG
U.S. Virgin Islands	. . .	. . .	G, LG	. . .	. . .
Totals for year					
Governor	12	2	37	3	12
Lieutenant Governor	10	1	31	3	10
Attorney General	11	1	30	3	10
Agriculture	3	0	7	3	2
Auditor	8	0	14	2	8
Chief Financial Officer ...	0	0	1	0	0
Comptroller	0	0	7	0	0
Secretary of State	8	0	26	3	7
Supt. of Public Inst. (v) ...	5	1	8	0	4
Treasurer	9	0	24	3	9

Sources: The Council of State Governments' survey, October 2003 and state election administration offices and web sites, January 2004.

Note: This table shows the executive branch officials up for election in a given year. Footnotes indicate other offices (e.g., commissioners of labor, insurance, public service, etc.) also up for election in a given year. The data contained in this table reflect information available at press time.

Key:

. . . — No regularly scheduled elections
G — Governor
LG — Lieutenant Governor
AG — Attorney General
AR — Agriculture
A — Auditor
C — Comptroller
CFO—Chief Financial Officer
SS — Secretary of State
SP — Superintendent of public instruction (v)
T — Treasurer

(a) Election of school boards established to maintain system of state dependent public school systems established in areas of the unorganized borough and military reservations not served by other public school systems.
(b) Corporation commissioners (5)–6 year terms, 2004–4 (one due to resignation), 2006–2.
(c) Insurance commissioner and Board of Equalization.
(d) Insurance Commissioner.
(e) Public service commissioners (5)–6 year terms, 2004–1, 2006–2, 2008–2. Commissioner of labor–4 year term, 2006.
(f) Insurance commissioner, commissioner of public lands.
(g) Land commissioner.
(h) Controller.
(i) Commissioner of insurance–2006; Board of education members (10)–4 year terms, 2004–5, 2006–5, 2008–5.

(j) Commissioner of elections–4 year term, 2007; commissioner of insurance–4 year term, 2007; board of elementary and secondary education (8)–4 year terms, 2007–4; public service commissioners (5)–6 year terms, 2004–2, 2006–1, 2008–2.
(k) In Maine the legislature elects constitutional officers (AG,SS,T) in even-numbered years for 2 year terms; the auditor will be elected by the legislature in 2004 and will serve a 4 year term.
(l) Michigan State University trustees (8)–8 year terms, 2004–2, 2006–2, 2008–2, 2010–2; University of Michigan regents (8)–8 year terms, 2004–2, 2006–2, 2008–2; Wayne State University governors (8)–8 year terms, 2004–2, 2006–2, 2008–2; State Board of Education (8)–8 year terms, 2004–2, 2006–2, 2008–2.
(m) Commissioner of insurance, transportation commissioners (3), public service commissioners (3).
(n) Tax Commissioner.
(o) Commissioner of public lands–4 year term, 2006; board of education (10)–6 year terms, 2004–5, 2008–5; corporation commissioners (3)–6 year terms, 2004.
(p) Commissioner of labor; commissioner of insurance.
(q) Public Service Commissioner (3)–6 year terms, 2004–1, 2006–1, 2008–1.
(r) Corporation commissioner (3)–6 year terms; commissioner of insurance–4 year term; commissioner of labor–4 year term.
(s) Adjutant general–4 year term.
(t) Commissioner of school and public lands, 2006; public utility commissioners (3)–6 year terms, 2004–1, 2006–1, 2008–1.
(u) Commissioner of general land office–4 year term, 2006; railroad commissioners (3)–6 year terms, 2004–1, 2006–1, 2008–1; board of education (15)–4 year terms, 2004–8, 2006–7, 2008–8, 2010–7.
(v) Superintendent of public instruction or commissioner of education.
(w) All of the positions will appear next on the ballot in 2004. However, the positions of secretary of state, attorney general, commissioner of agriculture and tax commissioner will only be elected to terms of two years. They will again appear on the ballot in 2006 and be elected to terms of four years and every four years thereafter. This one time ballot change is to establish a new four-year cycle as approved by the voters of North Dakota in June 2000. The remaining positions will appear on the ballot in the same four-year cycle as the governor and president of the United States.

Table 6.2
STATE LEGISLATURES: MEMBERS TO BE ELECTED, 2004-2008

State or other jurisdiction	Total legislators		2004		2005		2006		2007		2008	
	Senate	House	Senate	House	Senate	House	Senate	House	Senate	House	Senate	House
Alabama	35	105	…	…	…	…	35	105	…	…	…	…
Alaska	20	40	10	40	…	…	…	40	…	…	10	40
Arizona	30	60	30	60	…	…	30	60	…	…	30	60
Arkansas	35	100	18	100	…	…	17	100	…	…	18	100
California	40	80	20	80	…	…	20	80	…	…	20	80
Colorado	35	65	18	65	…	…	17	65	…	…	18	65
Connecticut	36	151	36	151	…	…	36	151	…	…	36	151
Delaware	21	41	10	41	…	…	11	41	…	…	10	41
Florida	40	120	20	120	…	…	20	120	…	…	20	120
Georgia	56	180	56	180	…	…	56	180	…	…	56	180
Hawaii	25	51	12	51	…	…	13	51	…	…	12	51
Idaho	35	70	35	70	…	…	35	70	…	…	35	70
Illinois	59 (a)	118	(b)	118	…	…	(b)	118	…	…	(b)	118
Indiana	50	100	25	100	…	…	25	100	…	…	25	100
Iowa	50	100	25 (c)	100	…	…	25 (d)	100	…	…	25 (c)	100
Kansas	40	125	40	125	…	…	…	125	…	…	40	125
Kentucky	38	100	19	100	…	…	19	100	…	…	19	100
Louisiana	39	105	…	…	…	…	…	…	39	105	…	…
Maine	35	151	35	151	…	…	35	151	…	…	35	151
Maryland	47	141	…	…	…	…	47	141	…	…	…	…
Massachusetts	40	160	40	160	…	…	40	160	…	…	40	160
Michigan	38	110	…	110	…	…	38	110	…	…	19	110
Minnesota	67	134	…	134	…	…	67	134	…	…	35	134
Mississippi	52	122	…	…	…	…	…	…	52	122	…	…
Missouri	34	163	17	163	…	…	17	163	…	…	17	163
Montana	50	100	25	100	…	…	25	100	…	…	25	100
Nebraska	49	U	25	U	…	…	24	U	…	…	25	U
Nevada	21	42	10	42	…	…	11	42	…	…	10	42
New Hampshire	24	400	24	400	…	…	24	400	…	…	24	400
New Jersey	40	80	…	…	…	80	…	…	40	80	…	…
New Mexico	42	70	42	70	…	…	…	70	…	…	42	70
New York	62	150	62	150	…	…	62	150	…	…	62	150
North Carolina	50	120	50	120	…	…	50	120	…	…	50	120
North Dakota	47	94	23	46	…	…	24	48	…	…	23	46
Ohio	33	99	16	99	…	…	17	99	…	…	16	99
Oklahoma	48	101	24	101	…	…	24	101	…	…	24	101
Oregon	30	60	15	60	…	…	15	60	…	…	15	60
Pennsylvania	50	203	25	203	…	…	25	203	…	…	25	203
Rhode Island	38	75	38	75	…	…	38	75	…	…	38	75
South Carolina	46	124	46	124	…	…	…	124	…	…	46	124

See footnotes at end of table.

STATE LEGISLATURES: MEMBERS TO BE ELECTED, 2004-2008 — Continued

State or other jurisdiction	Total legislators		2004		2005		2006		2007		2008	
	Senate	House	Senate	House	Senate	House	Senate	House	Senate	House	Senate	House
South Dakota	35	70	35	70	...	...	35	70	...	...	35	70
Tennessee	33	99	16	99	...	...	17	99	...	...	16	99
Texas	31	150	15	150	...	...	16	150	...	...	15	150
Utah	29	75	14	75	...	...	15	75	...	...	14	75
Vermont	30	150	30	150	...	...	30	150	...	...	30	150
Virginia	40	100	...	...	...	100	...	...	40	100	...	...
Washington	49	98	25	98	...	...	24	98	...	...	25	98
West Virginia	34	100	17	100	...	...	17	100	...	...	17	100
Wisconsin	33	99	16	99	...	...	17	99	...	...	16	99
Wyoming	30	60	15	60	...	...	15	60	...	...	15	60
American Samoa	18	20	(e)	20	...	...	(e)	20	...	...	(e)	20
U.S. Virgin Islands	15	U	15	U	...	...	15	U	...	...	15	U
Totals	2,004	5,431	1,089	4,730	0	180	1,144	4,978	171	407	1,089	4,730

Sources: The Council of State Governments' survey, October 2003 and state election web sites, January 2004.

Note: This table shows the number of legislative seats up for election in a given year. As a result of redistricting, states may adjust some elections. The data contained in this table reflect information available at press time. See the Chapter 3 table entitled, "The Legislators: Numbers, Terms, and Party Affiliations," for specific information on legislative terms.

Key:

... — No regularly scheduled elections

U — Unicameral legislature

(a) The entire Senate is up for election every 10 years, beginning in 1972. Senate districts are divided into three groups. One group of senators is elected for terms of four years, four years and two years; two years, four years and four years; four years, two years and four years.

(b) After redistricting there will be a lottery for which districts in the Senate will receive the set of terms.

(c) Even-numbered Senate districts.

(d) Odd-numbered Senate districts.

(e) In American Samoa, Senators are not elected by popular vote. They are selected by county councils of chiefs.

Table 6.3
METHODS OF NOMINATING CANDIDATES FOR STATE OFFICES

State or other jurisdiction	Method(s) of nominating candidates
Alabama	Primary election; however, the state executive committee or other governing body of any political party may choose instead to hold a state convention for the purpose of nominating candidates.
Alaska	Primary election.
Arizona	Petition.
Arkansas	Primary election.
California	Primary election or independent nomination procedure.
Colorado	Assembly/primary. Political parties hold state assemblies to nominate candidates for the primary ballot. A candidate is placed on the ballot if he/she receives 30 percent of the vote or, after two ballots, is one of the two candidates receiving the highest number of votes. Candidates (including those from major political parties) can also petition their name on the ballot. Each party's gubernatorial candidate selects a lieutenant governor candidate after the primary election.
Connecticut	Convention/primary election. Major political parties hold state conventions (convening not earlier than the 68th day and closing not later than the 50th day before the date of the primary) for the purpose of endorsing candidates. If no one challenges the endorsed candidate, no primary election is held. However, if anyone (who received at least 15 percent of the delegate vote on any roll call at the convention) challenges the endorsed candidate, a primary election is held to determine the party nominee for the general election.
Delaware	Primary election.
Florida	Primary election.
Georgia	Primary election/convention.
Hawaii	Primary election.
Idaho	Primary election. New parties nominate candidates for general election after qualifying for ballot status.
Illinois	Primary election.
Indiana	Primary election held for the nomination of candidates for governor and U.S. senator; state party conventions held for the nomination of candidates for other state offices.
Iowa	Primary election; however, if there are more than two candidates for any nomination and none receives at least 35 percent of the primary vote, the primary is deemed inconclusive and the nomination is made by the party convention. (Applicable only for recognized political parties.)
Kansas	Primary election. Minor party candidates are nominated at their respective state conventions Independent candidates are nominated by petition.
Kentucky	Primary election. A slate of candidates for governor and lieutenant governor that receives the highest number of its party's votes but which number is less than 40 percent of the votes cast for all slates of candidates of that party, shall be required to participate in a runoff primary with the slate of candidates of the same party receiving the second highest number of votes.
Louisiana	Primary election.
Maine	Primary election.
Maryland	Primary election. Petition only for unaffiliated or non-recognized parties in general elections only.
Massachusetts	Primary election.
Michigan	Primary election held for governor, state senate and state house. State convention held to nominate candidates for lieutenant governor, secretary of state and attorney general.
Minnesota	Primary election. Candidates for minor parties or independent candidates are by petition. They must have the signatures of 2,000 people who will be eligible to vote in the next general election.
Mississippi	Primary election.
Missouri	Primary election.
Montana	Primary election.
Nebraska	Primary election.
Nevada	Primary election. Independent candidates are nominated by petition for the general election. Minor parties nominated by petition or by party.
New Hampshire	Primary election.
New Jersey	Primary election. Independent candidates are nominated by petition for the general election.
New Mexico	Statewide candidates petition to go to convention and are nominated in a primary election. District and legislative candidate petition for primary ballot access.
New York	Primary election/petition.
North Carolina	Primary election. New parties by convention.
North Dakota	Convention/primary election. Political parties hold state conventions for the purpose of endorsing candidates. Endorsed candidates are automatically placed on the primary election ballot, but other candidates may also petition their name on the ballot.
Ohio	Primary election.
Oklahoma	Primary election.
Oregon	Primary election, convention and petition.
Pennsylvania	Primary election, and nomination papers for minor political parties and political bodies.
Rhode Island	Primary election.
South Carolina	Primary election for Republicans and Democrats; party conventions held for five minor parties. All must file proper forms with their political party between March 16 and March 30.

See footnotes at end of table.

METHODS OF NOMINATING CANDIDATES FOR STATE OFFICES — Continued

State or other jurisdiction	Method(s) of nominating candidates
South Dakota	Primary election. Any candidate who receives a plurality of the primary vote becomes the nominee; however, if no individual receives at least 35 percent of the vote for the candidacy for the offices of governor, U.S. senator, or U.S. congressman, a runoff election is held two weeks later. Lt. governor, attorney general, secretary of state, auditor, treasurer, school and public lands commissioner, and public utilities commissioner are nominated by party convention.
Tennessee	Primary election/petition.
Texas	Primary election/convention. Minor parties without ballot access nominate candidates for the general election after qualifying for ballot access by petition.
Utah	Convention, primary election and petition. Parties generally nominate their candidates in a convention. If one candidate does not get a certain percentage of delegate votes, the top two candidates go to a primary. Candidates not affiliated with a party can gain ballot access by petition.
Vermont	Primary election. Major parties that fail to nominate by primary election and minor parties can nominate by filing of a statement to nomination by the state party committee. Independents can be nominated by petition.
Virginia	Primary election.
Washington	Primary election; minor parties hold convention for nomination and qualify at primary election.
West Virginia	Primary election for major parties. Convention is held for official parties that received less than 10 percent of the last gubernatorial vote total. Minor parties and independent candidates nominated by petition.
Wisconsin	Primary election/petition.
Wyoming	Primary election.
Dist. of Columbia	Primary election. Independent and minor party candidates file by nominating petition.
American Samoa	Individual files petition for candidacy with the chief election officer. Petition must be signed by statutorily-mandated number of qualified voters.
U.S. Virgin Islands	Primary election.

Sources: The Council of State Governments' survey of state election administration offices, October 2003 and state election websites, January 2004.

Note: The nominating methods described here are for state offices; procedures may vary for local candidates. Also, independent candidates may have to petition for nomination.

Table 6.4
ELECTION DATES FOR NATIONAL, STATE AND LOCAL ELECTIONS
(Formulas and dates of state elections)

State or other jurisdiction	National (a)			State (b)			Local		
	Primary	Runoff	General	Primary	Runoff	General	Primary	Runoff	General
Alabama	June, 1st T June 1, 2004	…	Nov., ★ Nov. 2, 2004	June, 1st T June 1, 2004	June, Last T June 29, 2004	Nat. Nov. 2, 2004	V	V	V
Alaska	Aug., 4th T Aug. 24, 2004	…	Nov., ★ Nov. 2, 2004	Nat. Aug. 24, 2004	…	Nat. Nov. 2, 2004	…	…	V
Arizona	Feb., 4th T Feb. 3, 2004	…	Nov., ★ Nov. 2, 2004	8th T Prior Sept. 7, 2004	…	Nat. Nov. 2, 2004	Mar., 2nd T	May 3rd T	8 T prior to Nat. or Nat.
Arkansas	3 wks. Prior to Runoff May 18, 2004	June, 2nd T June 8, 2004	Nov., ★ Nov. 2, 2004	Nat. May 18, 2004	Nat. June 8, 2004	Nat. Nov. 2, 2004	Nat.	Nat.	Nat.
California	Mar., ★ Mar. 2, 2004	…	Nov., ★ Nov. 2, 2004	Mar. ★ Mar. 2, 2004	…	Nat. Nov. 2, 2004	…	…	Nat.
Colorado	(m)	…	Nov., ★ Nov. 2, 2004	Aug., 2nd T Aug. 10, 2004	…	Nat. Nov. 2, 2004	V	…	V
Connecticut	1st T in March Mar. 2, 2004	…	Nov., ★ Nov. 2, 2004	56th day Prior Sept. 7, 2004	…	Nat. Nov. 2, 2004	State	…	Nat. or May., 1st M (c)
Delaware	(l) Feb. 3, 2004	…	Nov., ★ Nov. 2, 2004	Sept., 1st S After 1st M Sept. 11, 2004	…	Nat. Nov. 2, 2004	…	…	(d)
Florida	Mar., 2nd T Mar. 9, 2004	…	Nov., ★ Nov. 2, 2004	9th T Prior Aug. 31, 2004	…	Nat. Nov. 2, 2004	State	…	Nat.
Georgia	July, 3rd T July 20, 2004	21 days AP Aug. 10, 2004	Nov., ★ Nov. 2, 2004	Nat. July 20, 2004	Nat. Aug. 10, 2004	Nat. Nov. 2, 2004	Nat.	Nat.	Nat.
Hawaii	(m)	…	Nov., ★ Nov. 2, 2004	Sept., 2nd Last S Sept. 18, 2004	…	Nat. Nov. 2, 2004	State	…	Nat.
Idaho	May, 4th T May 25, 2004	…	Nov., ★ Nov. 2, 2004	Nat. May 25, 2004	…	Nat. Nov. 2, 2004	Nat.	…	Nat.
Illinois	Mar., 3rd T Mar. 16, 2004	…	Nov., ★ Nov. 2, 2004	Nat. March 16, 2004	…	Nat. Nov. 2, 2004	…	…	…
Indiana	May, ★ May 4, 2004	…	Nov., ★ Nov. 2, 2004	Nat. May 4, 2004	…	Nat. Nov. 2, 2004	Nat.	…	Nat.
Iowa	(k) Jan. 19, 2004	…	Nov., ★ Nov. 2, 2004	June, ★ June 8, 2004	…	Nat. Nov. 2, 2004	State	…	Nat.
Kansas	(m)	…	Nov., ★ Nov. 2, 2004	Aug., 1st T (d) Aug. 3, 2004	…	Nat. (d) Nov. 2, 2004	5 wks. Prior	…	April 1st T
Kentucky	May, 1st T after 4th M May 18, 2004	…	Nov., ★ Nov. 2, 2004	Nat. May 18, 2004	35 days after P June 22, 2004	Nat. Nov. 2, 2004	Nat.	…	Nat.
Louisiana (f)	(l) Mar. 9, 2004	…	Nov., ★ Nov. 2, 2004	(p) Sept. 18, 2004	(p) Dec. 4, 2004	(p) Nov. 2, 2004	V	…	V

See footnotes at end of table.

ELECTION DATES FOR NATIONAL, STATE AND LOCAL ELECTIONS — Continued

State or other jurisdiction	National			State			Local		
	Primary	Runoff	General	Primary	Runoff	General	Primary	Runoff	General
Maine	(m)	...	Nov.,★ Nov. 2, 2004	June, 2nd T June 13, 2006	...	Nat. Nov. 7, 2006	...	...	V
Maryland	Mar., 1st T Mar. 2, 2004	...	Nov.,★ Nov. 2, 2004	Nat. Mar. 2, 2004	...	Nat. Nov. 2, 2004	Nat.	...	Nat.
Massachusetts	(l) Mar. 2, 2004	...	Nov.,★ Nov. 2, 2004	7th T Prior Sept. 19, 2006	...	Nat. Nov. 7, 2006	V	...	V
Michigan	Feb., 4th T (m)	...	Nov.,★ Nov. 2, 2004	Aug.,★ Aug. 3, 2004	...	Nat. Nov. 2, 2004	V	...	V
Minnesota	(m)	...	Nov.,★ Nov. 2, 2004	Sept., 1st T after 2nd M Sept. 12, 2006	...	Nat. Nov. 7, 2006	State (d)	...	Nat. (d)
Mississippi	June, 1st T (g) Mar. 9, 2004	...	Nov.,★ Nov. 2, 2004	Aug.,★(e) Aug. 8, 2006	3rd T AP Aug. 29, 2006	Nat. (d) Nov. 7, 2006	May, 1st T (d)	2nd T AP	June, ★ (d)
Missouri	Feb.,★ Feb. 3, 2004	...	Nov.,★ Nov. 2, 2004	Aug.,★ Aug. 3, 2004	...	Nat. Nov. 2, 2004	State	...	Nat.
Montana	June,★ June 8, 2004	...	Nov.,★ Nov. 2, 2004	Nat. June 8, 2004	...	Nat. Nov. 2, 2004	Nat.	...	Nat.
Nebraska	May, 1st T After 2nd M May 11, 2004	...	Nov.,★ Nov. 2, 2004	Nat. May 9, 2006	...	Nat. Nov. 7, 2006	Nat.	...	Nat.
Nevada	Sept., 1st T Sept. 7, 2004	...	Nov.,★ Nov. 2, 2004	Nat. Sept. 7, 2004	...	Nat. Nov. 2, 2004	Nat.	...	Nat.
New Hampshire	Sept., 2nd T Sept. 14, 2004	...	Nov.,★ Nov. 2, 2004	Nat. Sept. 14, 2004	...	Nat. Nov. 2, 2004	V	...	V
New Jersey	June,★ June 8, 2004	...	Nov.,★ Nov. 2, 2004	June,★ June 7, 2005	...	Nat. Nov. 8, 2005	June, ★	...	Nat.
New Mexico	June, 1st T June 1, 2004	...	Nov.,★ Nov. 2, 2004	Nat. June 6, 2006	...	Nat. Nov. 7, 2006	Nat.	...	Nat.
New York	Mar., 1st T Mar. 2, 2004	...	Nov.,★ Nov. 2, 2004	Sept.,★ Sept. 14, 2004	...	Nat. Nov. 2, 2004	State	Sept., 2 wks	Nat. AP (d)
North Carolina	May,★ May 4, 2004	4 wks. AP June 1, 2004	Nov.,★ Nov. 2, 2004	Nat. May 4, 2004	4 wks. AP June 1, 2004	Nat. Nov. 2, 2004	Nat.	Nat.	Nat.
North Dakota	(n) Feb. 3, 2004	...	Nov.,★ Nov. 2, 2004	June, 2nd T June 8, 2004	...	Nat. Nov. 2, 2004	...	...	June, 2nd T (e)
Ohio	Mar.,★ Mar. 2, 2004	...	Nov.,★ Nov. 2, 2004	Nat. Mar. 2, 2004	...	Nat. Nov. 2, 2004	Nat. (d)	...	Nat. (d)
Oklahoma	July, last T (h) Feb. 3, 2004	...	Nov.,★ Nov. 2, 2004	Nat. July 27, 2004	Aug., 4th T Aug. 24, 2004	Nat. Nov. 2, 2004	Nat.	Nat.	Nat.
Oregon	May, 3rd T May 18, 2004	...	Nov.,★ Nov. 2, 2004	Nat. May 18, 2004	...	Nat. Nov. 2, 2004	Nat.	...	Nat.

See footnotes at end of table.

ELECTION DATES FOR NATIONAL, STATE AND LOCAL ELECTIONS — Continued

State or other jurisdiction	National			State			Local		
	Primary	Runoff	General	Primary	Runoff	General	Primary	Runoff	General
Pennsylvania	April, 4th T Apr. 27, 2004	...	Nov., ★ Nov. 2, 2004	Nat. Apr. 27, 2004	...	Nat. Nov. 2, 2004	Nat.	...	Nat.
Rhode Island	(l) Mar. 2, 2004	...	Nov., ★ Nov. 2, 2004	Sept., 2nd T After 1st M Sept. 14, 2004	...	Nat. Nov. 2, 2004	State	...	Nat.
South Carolina	(l) Feb. 3, 2004	Nov., ★	June, 2nd T Nov. 2, 2004	2nd T AP June 8, 2004	Nat. June 22, 2004	Nat. Nov. 2, 2004	State (d)	State	Nat. (d)
South Dakota	June, 1st T June 1, 2004	2nd T AP June 15, 2004	Nov., ★ Nov. 2, 2004	Nat. June 1, 2004	Nat. June 15, 2004	Nat. Nov. 2, 2004	State	...	Nat.
Tennessee	Feb., 2nd T Feb. 10, 2004	...	Nov., ★ Nov. 2, 2004	Aug., 1st TH Aug. 5, 2004	...	Nat. Nov. 2, 2004	Feb., 2nd T May, 1st T	...	Aug 1st TH
Texas	Mar., 2nd T Mar. 9, 2004	Apr., 2nd T Apr. 13, 2004	Nov., ★ Nov. 2, 2004	Nat. Mar. 9, 2004	Nat. Apr. 13, 2004	Nat. Nov. 2, 2004	Nat.	Nat.	Nat.
Utah	(m)	...	Nov., ★	June, 4th T	...	Nat.	State	...	Nat.
Vermont (i)	(l) Mar. 2, 2004	...	Nov., ★ Nov. 2, 2004	June 22, 2004 Sept., 2nd T Sept. 14, 2004	...	Nat. Nat. Nov. 2, 2004	State	...	March., 1st T
Virginia	(l) Feb. 10, 2004	...	Nov., ★ Nov. 2, 2004	June, 2nd T June 14, 2005	...	Nat. Nov. 8, 2005	State or Feb., last T	...	Nat. or May, 1st T
Washington	(m)	...	Nov., ★ Nov. 2, 2004	Sept., 3rd T (o) Sept. 14, 2004	...	Nat. Nov. 2, 2004	State	...	Nat.
West Virginia	May, 2nd T May 11, 2004	...	Nov., ★ Nov. 2, 2004	Nat. May 11, 2004	...	Nat. Nov. 2, 2004	Nat.	...	Nat.
Wisconsin	Sept., 2nd T Sept. 14, 2004	...	Nov., ★ Nov. 2, 2004	Nat. Sept. 14, 2004	...	Nat. Nov. 2, 2004	Nat.	...	Nat.
Wyoming	(m)	...	Nov., ★ Nov. 2, 2004	Aug., 1st T After 3rd M Aug. 22, 2006	...	Nat. Nov. 7, 2006	State	...	Nat.
Dist. of Columbia	(l) Jan. 13, 2004	...	Nov., ★ Nov. 2, 2004	...	...	...	Sept., 1st T after 2nd M	...	Nov., ★
American Samoa	(j)	14 days after general Nov. 16, 2004	Nov., ★ Nov. 2, 2004	(j)	14 days after general Nov. 16, 2004	Nov., ★ Nov. 16, 2004	(j) Nov. 2, 2004	...	(o)
U.S. Virgin Islands	...	...	... Sept. 11, 2004	Sept., 2nd S Nov. 16, 2004	14 day AP Nov. 2, 2004	Nov., 1st T	Sept., 2nd S	14 days AP	Nov., 1st T

See footnotes at end of table.

ELECTION DATES FOR NATIONAL, STATE AND LOCAL ELECTIONS — Continued

Sources: The Council of State Governments' survey of state election offices, October 2003 and state web sites, February 2004.

Note: This table describes the basic formulas for determining when national, state and local elections will be held. For specific information on a particular state, the reader is advised to contact the specific state election administration office. All dates provided are based on the state election formula.

Key:

★ — First Tuesday after first Monday.

. . . — No provision.

M —Monday.

T —Tuesday.

TH —Thursday.

S — Saturday.

Nat. — Same date as national elections.

State — Same date as state elections.

Prior — Prior to general election.

AP —After primary.

V —Varies.

(a) National refers to presidential elections.

(b) State refers to election in which a state executive official or U.S. senator is to be elected. See Table 6.2, State Officials to be Elected.

(c) Unless that date conflicts with Passover, then 1st Tuesday following last day of Passover.

(d) In Delaware, elections are determined by city charter. In Iowa, partisan election only. In Kansas, state and county elections. In Minnesota, county elections only. In Mississippi, state and county elections are held separate years. In Montana, municipalities only. In Montana, municipalities and towns in odd years and counties in even years. In South Carolina, school boards vary.

(e) Cities only.

(f) Louisiana has an open primary which requires all candidates, regardless of party affiliation, to appear on a single ballot. If a candidate receives over 50 percent of the vote in the primary, that candi-

date is elected to the office. If no candidate receives a majority vote, then a single election is held between the two candidates receiving the most votes. For national elections, the first vote is held on the first Saturday in October of even-numbered years with the general election held on the first Tuesday after the first Monday in November. For state elections, the election is held on the second to last Saturday in October with the runoff being held on the fourth Saturday after first election. Local elections vary depending on the location and the year.

(g) Except in presidential election year when congressional races correspond to Super Tuesday.

(h) The primary election is held on the 4th Tuesday in August in each even-numbered year, including presidential election years. The presidential preferential primary is held on the 1st Tuesday in February during presidential election years.

(i) In Vermont, if there is a tie in a primary or general election (and a recount does not resolve the tie) the appropriate superior court could order a recessed election, among the tied candidates only, within three weeks of the recount. In state primary runoffs, the runoff election must be proclaimed within seven days after primary; after proclamation, election is held 15-22 days later. Local elections are held by annual town meetings which may vary depending on town charter.

(j) American Samoa does not conduct primary elections (In addition, elections are conducted for territory-wide offices. There are no local elections).

(k) Eight days before any other nomination process.

(l) Formula not available at press time.

(m) State did not hold a presidential primary in 2004.

(n) On one designated day, following scheduled nominating contests in the states of Iowa and New Hampshire and prior to the first Wednesday in March in every presidential election year, every political party entitled to a separate column may conduct a presidential preference caucus. Before August 15 of the odd-numbered year immediately preceding the presidential election year, the secretary of state shall designate the day after consulting with and taking recommendations from the two political parties casting the greatest vote for president of the United States at the most recent general elections when the office of president appeared on the ballot.

(o) Must be held on the third Tuesday of the preceding September or on the seventh Tuesday immediately preceding such general election, whichever occurs first.

(p) In Louisiana, a Congressional primary election is not held. The election for candidates seeking federal office is the general election scheduled for Nov. 2, 2004. If necessary, a runoff election will be held on Dec. 4, 2004.

Table 6.5
POLLING HOURS: GENERAL ELECTIONS

State or other jurisdiction	Polls open	Polls close	Notes on hours (a)
Alabama	No later than 8 a.m.	Between 6 and 8 p.m.	
Alaska	7 a.m.	8 p.m.	
Arizona	6 a.m.	7 p.m.	
Arkansas	7:30 a.m.	7:30 p.m.	
California	7 a.m.	8 p.m.	
Colorado	7 a.m.	7 p.m.	
Connecticut	6 a.m.	8 p.m.	
Delaware	7 a.m.	8 p.m.	
Florida	7 a.m.	7 p.m.	
Georgia	7 a.m.	7 p.m.	
Hawaii	7 a.m.	6 p.m.	
Idaho	8 a.m.	8 p.m.	Clerks have the option of opening polls at 7 a.m. Idaho is in two time zones—MST and PST.
Illinois	6 a.m.	7 p.m.	
Indiana	6 a.m.	6 p.m.	
Iowa	7 a.m.	9 p.m.	
Kansas	7 a.m.	7 p.m.	Counties may choose to open polls as early as 6 a.m. and close as late as 8 p.m.
Kentucky	6 a.m.	6 p.m.	
Louisiana	6 a.m.	8 p.m.	
Maine	Between 6 and 10 a.m.	8 p.m.	Applicable opening time depends on variables related to the size of the precinct.
Maryland	7 a.m.	8 p.m.	
Massachusetts	No later than 7 a.m.	8 p.m.	
Michigan	7 a.m.	8 p.m.	
Minnesota	7 a.m.	8 p.m.	Towns outside of the twin cities metro area with less than 500 inhabitants may have a later time for the polls to open as long as it is not later than 10 a.m.
Mississippi	7 a.m.	7 p.m.	
Missouri	6 a.m.	7 p.m.	
Montana	7 a.m.	8 p.m.	Polling places with fewer than 200 electors may open at noon.
Nebraska	7 a.m MST/8 a.m. CST	7 p.m. MST/8 p.m. CST	
Nevada	7 a.m.	7 p.m.	
New Hampshire	No later than 11 a.m.	No earlier than 7 p.m.	Polling hours vary from town to town. The hours of 11 a.m. to 7 p.m. are by statute.
New Jersey	6 a.m.	8 p.m.	
New Mexico	7 a.m.	7 p.m.	
New York	6 a.m.	9 p.m.	
North Carolina	6:30 a.m.	7:30 p.m.	
North Dakota	Between 7 and 9 a.m.	Between 7 and 9 p.m.	Counties must have polls open by 9 a.m., but can choose to open as early as 7 a.m. Polls must remain open until 7 p.m., but can be open as late as 9 p.m. The majority of polls in the state are open from 8 a.m. to 7 p.m. in their respective time zones (CST and MST).
Ohio	6:30 a.m.	7:30 p.m.	
Oklahoma	7 a.m.	7 p.m.	
Oregon	7 a.m.	8 p.m.	
Pennsylvania	7 a.m.	8 p.m.	
Rhode Island	7 a.m.	9 p.m.	
South Carolina	7 a.m.	7 p.m.	
South Dakota	7 a.m.	7 p.m.	
Tennessee	8 a.m.	7 p.m. CST/ 8 p.m. EST	Poll hours are set by each county election commission. Polling places shall be open a minimum of 10 hours but no more than 13 hours. All polling locations in the eastern time zone shall close at 8 p.m. and those in the central time zone shall close at 7 p.m.
Texas	7 a.m.	7 p.m.	
Utah	7 a.m.	8 p.m.	
Vermont	Between 5 and 10 a.m.	7 p.m.	The opening time for polls is set to by local boards of civil authority.
Virginia	6 a.m.	7 p.m.	
Washington	7 a.m.	8 p.m.	
West Virginia	6:30 a.m.	7:30 p.m.	
Wisconsin	7 a.m.	8 p.m.	Polls in fourth class cities, villages and towns open at 9 a.m.; extendable by the governing body to no earlier than 7 a.m.
Wyoming	7 a.m.	7 p.m.	
Dist. of Columbia	7 a.m.	8 p.m.	
Guam	8 a.m.	8 p.m.	
U.S. Virgin Islands	7 a.m.	7 p.m.	

Sources: The Council of State Governments survey, October 2003 and state election web sites, January 2004.

Note: Hours for primary, municipal and special elections may differ from those noted.

(a) In all states, voters standing in line when the polls close are allowed to vote; however, provisions for handling those voters vary across jurisdictions.

Table 6.6
VOTER REGISTRATION INFORMATION

State or other jurisdiction	Closing date for registration before general election (days)	Persons eligible for absentee registration (a)	Cut-off for receiving absentee ballots	Absentee votes signed by witness or notary	Residency requirements	Registration in other places	Criminal status	Mental competency
Alabama	10	M/O	Close of polls	N or 2W	S, C (m)	...	★	★
Alaska	30	A	10 days after election	N or 2W	...	★	★	★
Arizona	29	A	7 pm Election Day	...	S, C, 29	...	★	★
Arkansas	30	A	7:30 pm Election Day	...	(n)	★	★	...
California	15	A	8 pm Election Day	...	S	...	★	★
Colorado	29	A	7 pm Election Day	...	S, 30	...	★	...
Connecticut	14	A	8 pm Election Day	...	S, T	...	★	...
Delaware	20	A	12 pm day before election	N or W	S (o)	...	★	★
Florida	29	A	7 pm Election Day	W	S, C	...	★	★
Georgia	(b)	A	Close of polls	W (x)	S, C	...	★	★
Hawaii	30	A	Close of polls	W (x)	S	...	★	★
Idaho	25	A	8 pm Election Day	...	S, C, 30	...	★	...
Illinois	28	M/O	Close of polls	...	S, P, 30	★	★	...
Indiana	29	C, D, E, M/O O, P, T	Close of polls	...	S, P, 30	...	★	...
Iowa	10 (c)	A	Close of polls	...	S	★	★	★
Kansas	15	A	Close of polls	...	S	★	★	★
Kentucky	29	A	Close of polls	...	S, C, 28	★	★	★
Louisiana	30	A	12 am day before election	N or 2W	S	...	★	★
Maine	Election day	A	Close of polls	N or 2W	S, M	...	...	★
Maryland	21	A	Friday after election	...	S, C	...	★	★
Massachusetts	20	A	10 days after election	...	S	...	★	★
Michigan	30	A	8 pm Election Day	W (x)	S, T, 30 (p)	...	★	...
Minnesota	Election day (d)	A	Election Day	N or W	S, 20	...	★	★
Mississippi	30	A	5 pm day before election	W	S, C, 30	...	★	★
Missouri	28	A	Close of polls	N	S	...	★	★
Montana	30	A	Close of polls	...	S, C, 30	...	★	★
Nebraska	(f)	A	10 am 2 days after election	W	S	...	★	★
Nevada	(k)	M/O	Close of polls	...	S, C, 30; P, 10 (t)	...	★	★
New Hampshire	Election day (d)	B, D, E, R S, T	5 pm day before election	...	S (w)	...	★	...
New Jersey	29	A	8 pm Election Day	W or N	S, C, 30 (q)	...	★	...
New Mexico	28	T	7 pm Election Day	...	S	...	★	★
New York	25	A	Postmarked day before election	W (x)	S, C, 30 (r)	★	★	★
North Carolina	25	A	5 pm day before election	2W	S, C, 30	★	★	...
North Dakota	(e)	(e)	2 days after election	W (x)	(e)	(e)	(e)	(e)
Ohio	30	A	Close of polls	...	S, 30	...	★	★
Oklahoma	25	A	7 pm Election Day	N or W	S	...	★	★
Oregon	21	A	8 pm Election Day	...	S	...	★	...
Pennsylvania	30	B, D, M/O O, P, R, S, T	5 pm Friday before election	W (x)	S, P, 30	...	★	...
Rhode Island	30	D	9 pm Election Day	N or 2W	S, 30	...	★	★
South Carolina	30	B, C, D, S (i)	Close of polls	W	S (v)	...	★	★
South Dakota	15	A	Close of polls	...	S	...	★	★
Tennessee	30	A	Close of polls	W (x)	S	...	★	★
Texas	30	A	Before close of polls	(y)	S, C	...	★	★
Utah	20	(g)	12 pm Monday after election	W (x)	S, 30	...	★	★
Vermont	(l)	(h)	Close of polls	...	S	...	...	...
Virginia	29	(j)	Close of polls	W	S, P	...	★	★
Washington	15 (c)	M/O	10 days after election	...	S, C, P, 30	...	★	★
West Virginia	20	A	Close of polls	...	S	...	★	★
Wisconsin	Election day (c)(u)	A	Close of polls	W	S, 10	...	★	★
Wyoming	Election day (d)	A	7 pm Election Day	...	S (s)	...	★	★
Dist. of Columbia	30	A	10 days after election	...	D, 30	★	★	★
American Samoa	30	M/O	N.A.	N.A.	N.A.	N.A.	N.A.	N.A.
Guam	10	A	N.A.	N.A.	N.A.	N.A.	N.A.	N.A.
Puerto Rico	50	A	N.A.	N.A.	N.A.	N.A.	N.A.	N.A.
U.S. Virgin Islands	30	M/O	N.A.	N.A.	N.A.	N.A.	N.A.	N.A.

See footnotes at end of table.

VOTER REGISTRATION INFORMATION — Continued

Sources: Federal Election Commission, http://www.fec.gov., December 2003.

Key:

★—Column 6: State provision prohibiting registration or claiming the right to vote in another state or jurisdiction. Columns 7 and 8: State provision regarding criminal status or mental competency.

. . .—No state provision.

N.A.—Information not available.

Column 4: N—Notary, W—Witness. Numbers indicated the number of signatures required.

Column 5: S—State, C—County, D—District, M—Municipality, P—Precinct, T—Town. Numbers represent the number of days before an election for which one must be a resident.

Note: Previous editions of this chart contained a column for Automatic cancellation of registration for failure to vote for ___ years. However, the National Voter Registration Act requires a confirmation notice prior to any cancellation and thus effectively bans any automatic cancellation of voter registration. In addition, all states and territories except Puerto Rico and the U.S. Virgin Islands allow mail-in registration.

(a) In this column: A—All of these; B—Absent on business; C—Senior citizen; D—Disabled persons; E—Not absent, but prevented by employment from registering; M/O—No absentee registration except military and oversees citizens as required by federal law; O—Out of state; P—Out of precinct (or municipality in PA); R—Absent for religious reasons; S—Students; T—Temporarily out of jurisdiction.

(b) The 5th Monday before a general primary, general election, or presidential preference primary; the 5th day after the date of the call for all other special primaries and special elections.

(c) By mail: Iowa 15 days; Washington 30 days; Wisconsin, 13 days.

(d) Minnesota– delivered 21 days before an election or election-day registration at polling precincts; New Hampshire– Received by city or town clerk 10 days before or election-day registration at precincts; Wyoming– delivered 30 days before or election-day registration at polling precincts.

(e) No voter registration.

(f) Received by the 2nd Friday before election or postmarked by the 3rd Friday before the election.

(g) There are several criteria including religious reasons, disabled, etc., or if the voter otherwise expects to be absent from the precinct on election day.

(h) Anyone unable to register in person.

(i) In South Carolina, all the following are eligible for absentee registration in addition to those categories already listed: electors with a death in the family within 3 days before the election; overseas military, Red Cross, U.S.O. government employees, and their dependents and spouses residing with them; persons on vacation; persons admitted to the hospital as emergency patients 4 days prior to election; persons confined to jail or pre-trial facility pending disposition of arrest/trial; and persons attending sick/disabled persons.

(j) In Virginia, the following temporarily out of jurisdiction persons are eligible for absentee registration: (1)uniformed services voters on active duty, merchant marine, and persons temporarily residing overseas by virtue of employment (and spouse/dependents of these persons residing with them), who are not normally absent from their locality, or have been absent and returned to reside within 28 days prior to an election, may register in person up to and including the day of the election; (2) members of uniformed services discharged from active duty during 60 days preceding election (and spouse/dependents) may register, if otherwise qualified, in person up to and including the day of the election.

(k) By 9 p.m. on the 5th Saturday preceding any primary or general election.

(l) Postmarked, submitted or accepted by noon on the 2nd Saturday before an election

(m) At the time of registration.

(n) Must live in Arkansas at the address in Box 2 of your voter application.

(o) Must be a permanent state resident.

(p) Must be a resident of the town or city at least 30 days before election day.

(q) Must be a resident of the state and county at your address for 30 days before election.

(r) Must be a resident of the county or the City of New York at least 30 days before election.

(s) Must be an actual and physically bona fide resident.

(t) Must have continuously resided in the state and county at least 30 days and in precinct at least 10 days before election. Must claim no other place as legal residence.

(u) Registration may be completed in the local voter registration office 1 day before the election.

(v) Must claim the address on the application as your only legal place of residence.

(w) Must have a permanent established domicile in the state.

(x) Only if assisted by another party

(y) If unable to sign.

Table 6.7
VOTING STATISTICS FOR GUBERNATORIAL ELECTIONS BY REGION

State	Date of last election	Primary election					General election								
		Republican	Democrat	Independent	Other	Total votes	Republican	Percent	Democrat	Percent	Independent	Percent	Other	Percent	Total votes
U.S. Total		14,569,470	17,982,510	132,938	331,590	33,016,508	39,867,828	48.4	38,273,238	46.4	1,396,235	1.7	2,846,167	3.5	82,383,468
Eastern Region															
Connecticut	2002	13,893	13,847	(b)	0	27,740	573,958	56.0	448,984	44.0	0	0.0	0	0.0	1,022,942
Delaware	2000	78,783	71,735 (d)	0	1,613	152,131	191,695	59.2	128,603	39.7	0	0.0	3,271	1.1	323,569
Maine	2002						209,496	41.5	238,179	47.1	10,612	2.1	46,903	9.3	505,190
Massachusetts	2002	227,960 (d)	746,190	0	2,752	976,902	1,091,988	49.8	985,981	44.9	15,335	0.7	100,875	4.6	2,194,179
New Hampshire	2002	155,952	69,965	0	0	225,917	259,663	58.8	169,277	38.3	0	0.0	13,028	2.9	441,968
New Jersey	2001	336,948	262,086	0	0	599,034	928,174	41.7	1,256,853	56.4	0	0.0	42,138	1.9	2,227,165
New York (c)	2002	20,936	633,078	18,598	0	672,612	2,262,255	49.4	1,534,064	33.5	654,016	14.3	128,743	2.8	4,579,078
Pennsylvania	2002	538,757 (d)	1,242,236	0	0	1,780,993	1,589,408	44.4	1,913,235	53.4	0	0.0	79,346	2.2	3,581,989
Rhode Island	2002	26,824	122,535	0	399	149,758	181,827	54.8	150,229	45.2	0	0.0	0	0.0	332,056
Vermont	2002	27,462	31,143	0	2,171	60,776	103,436	45.5	97,565	42.9	22,922	10.1	3,446	1.5	227,369
Regional total		1,427,515	3,192,815	18,598	6,935	4,645,863	7,391,900	47.8	6,922,970	44.9	702,885	4.6	417,750	2.7	15,435,505
Midwest Region															
Illinois	2002	917,759	1,252,516	0	0	2,170,275	1,594,960	45.1	1,847,040	52.2	23,089	0.7	73,794	2.1	3,538,883
Indiana	2000	392,616	272,319	0	399	664,935	908,285	41.7	1,232,525	56.5	0	0.0	38,603	1.8	2,179,413
Iowa	2002	199,234	80,443 (d)	0	399	280,076	456,612	44.5	540,449	52.7	0	0.0	28,741	2.8	1,025,802
Kansas	2002	296,094	87,850 (d)	0	0	383,944	376,830	45.1	441,858	52.9	0	0.0	17,004	2.0	835,692
Michigan	2002	583,391	1,046,680	0	0	1,630,071	1,506,104	47.4	1,633,796	51.4	0	0.0	37,665	1.2	3,177,565
Minnesota	2002	195,099	224,238	0	46,269	465,606	999,473	44.4	821,268	36.5	9,698	0.4	422,034	18.7	2,252,473
Nebraska	2002	147,718	61,312	0	36	209,066	330,349	68.7	132,348	27.5	0	0.0	18,294	3.8	480,991
North Dakota	2000	40,308	34,851	0	274	75,433	159,255	55.0	130,144	45.0	0	0.0	13	0.0	289,412
Ohio	2002	658,700 (d)	585,615 (d)	0	121,438	1,365,753	1,865,007	57.7	1,236,924	38.3	0	0.0	127,061	4.0	3,228,992
South Dakota	2002	111,264	68,037	0	0	179,301	189,920	56.8	140,263	41.9	2,393	0.7	1,983	0.6	334,559
Wisconsin	2002	803,439	230,232	741	18,831	1,053,243	734,779	41.4	800,515	45.2	10,489	0.5	229,566	12.9	1,775,349
Regional total		4,345,622	3,944,093	741	187,247	8,477,703	9,121,574	47.8	8,957,130	46.8	45,669	0.2	994,758	5.2	19,119,131
Southern Region															
Alabama	2002	357,497	435,310	0	0	792,807	672,225	49.2	669,105	48.9	0	0.0	25,723	1.9	1,367,053
Arkansas	2002	92,237	279,097	0	0	371,334	427,082	53.0	378,250	46.9	0	0.0	210	0.0	805,542
Florida	2002	(d)	1,357,381	0	0	1,357,381	2,856,845	56.0	2,201,427	43.2	0	0.0	42,309	0.8	5,100,581
Georgia	2002	511,249	434,893 (d)	0	0	946,142	1,041,700	51.4	937,070	46.2	0	0.0	47,123	2.4	2,025,893
Kentucky	2003	158,528	285,149	0	0	443,677	596,284	55.0	487,159	45.0	0	0.0	0	0.0	1,083,443
Louisiana (a)	2003	(a)					676,484	48.0	731,358	52.0	0	0.0	0	0.0	1,407,842
Maryland	2002	256,486	581,885	2953	71	841,395	561,884	32.7	979,740	57.1	169,244	9.9	6,200	0.3	1,717,068
Mississippi	2003	177,122	504,319	0	0	681,441	470,404	52.6	409,787	45.8	0	0.0	14,296	1.6	894,487
Missouri	2000	350,514	362,457	741	2,009	715,721	1,131,307	48.2	1,152,752	49.1	4,916	0.2	57,855	2.5	2,346,830
North Carolina	2000	314,055	561,940	0	1,154	877,149	1,360,960	46.3	1,530,324	52.0	0	0.0	50,778	1.7	2,942,062
Oklahoma	2002	205,876	350,389	0	0	556,265	441,277	42.6	448,143	43.3	146,200	14.1	0	0.0	1,035,620
South Carolina	2002	316,255	(d)	0	0	316,255	585,422	52.8	521,140	47.1	0	0.0	1,163	0.1	1,107,725
Tennessee	2002	534,824	539,018	0	809	1,074,651	786,803	47.6	837,284	50.6	28,704	1.7	376	0.2	1,653,167
Texas	2002	1,003,388	620,463 (d)	0	0	1,623,851	2,632,591	57.8	1,819,798	40.0	0	0.0	101,538	2.2	4,553,927
Virginia	2001	108,519	(b)		0		887,234	47.0	984,177	52.2	0	0.0	15,310	0.8	1,886,721
West Virginia	2000		275,976	0	265	384,760	305,926	50.1	324,822	47.2	0	0.0	17,299	2.7	648,047
Regional total		4,386,550	6,588,277	3,694	4,308	10,982,829	15,434,428	50.5	14,412,336	47.2	349,064	1.1	380,180	1.2	30,576,008

See footnotes at end of table.

VOTING STATISTICS FOR GUBERNATORIAL ELECTIONS BY REGION — Continued

State	Date of last election	Primary election					General election								
		Republican	Democrat	Independent	Other	Total votes	Republican	Percent	Democrat	Percent	Independent	Percent	Other	Percent	Total votes
Western Region															
Alaska	2002	72,248	32,547	0	2,723	107,518	129,279	55.8	94,216	40.7	0	0.0	7,989	3.5	231,484
Arizona	2002	320,090	234,084	0	3,263	557,437	554,465	45.2	566,284	46.2	84,947	6.9	20,415	1.7	1,226,111
California	2002	2,285,452	2,169,555	0	85,749	4,540,756	3,169,801	42.4	3,533,490	47.3	0	0.0	773,020	10.3	7,476,311
Colorado	2002	189,705	98,897	0	0	288,602	884,583	62.6	475,373	33.7	0	0.0	52,646	3.7	1,412,602
Hawaii	2002	79,871	188,781	0	1,463	270,115	197,009	51.1	179,647	46.6	0	0.0	8,801	2.3	385,457
Idaho	2002	145,549	38,083	0	1,106	184,738	231,566	56.3	171,711	41.7	13	0.0	8,187	2.0	411,477
Montana	2000	113,016	96,356	0	0	209,372	209,135	51.0	193,131	47.1	0	0.0	7,926	1.9	410,192
Nevada	2002	117,474	88,974	0	0	206,448	344,001	68.2	110,935	22.0	0	0.0	49,143	9.7	504,079
New Mexico	2002	98,320	168,496	0	0	266,816	189,074	39.0	268,693	55.5	0	0.0	26,466	5.5	484,233
Oregon	2002	357,764	374,246	109,905	16,610	858,525	517,243	40.1	530,708	41.0	213,657	16.5	32,153	2.4	1,293,761
Utah	2000			(b)			424,837	55.8	321,979	42.3	0	0.0	14,990	2.0	761,806
Washington	2000	539,609	730,507	0	22,186	1,292,302	980,060	39.7	1,441,973	58.4	0	0.0	47,819	1.9	2,469,852
Wyoming	2002	90,685	36,799	0	0	127,484	88,873	47.9	92,662	50.0	0	0.0	3,924	2.1	185,459
Regional total		4,409,783	4,257,325	109,905	133,100	8,910,113	7,919,926	45.9	7,980,802	46.3	298,617	1.7	1,053,479	6.1	17,252,824
Regional total without California		2,124,331	2,087,770	109,905	47,351	4,369,357	4,750,125	48.6	4,447,312	45.5	298,617	3.0	280,459	2.9	9,776,513

Sources: The Council of State Governments' survey of election administration offices, October 2003 and state elections web sites.

Key:

(a) Louisiana has an open primary which requires all candidates, regardless of party affiliation, to appear on a single ballot. If a candidate receives over 50 percent of the vote in the primary, he is elected to the office. If no candidate receives a majority vote, then a single election is held between the two candidates receiving the most votes.

(b) Candidate nominated by convention.
(c) Total includes the Conservative Party. Governor Pataki was the candidate for both parties.
(d) Candidate ran unopposed.

Table 6.8
VOTER TURNOUT FOR PRESIDENTIAL ELECTIONS BY REGION: 1992, 1996 AND 2000
(In thousands)

State or other jurisdiction	2000 Voting age population (a)	2000 Number registered	2000 Number voting (b)	1996 Voting age population (a)	1996 Number registered	1996 Number voting (b)	1992 Voting age population (a)	1992 Number registered	1992 Number voting (b)
U.S. Total	205,815	156,420	105,587	195,193	132,796	97,050	186,995	133,321	105,344
Eastern Region									
Connecticut	2,499	1,874	1,460	2,300	1,900	750	2,535	1,962	1,616
Delaware	582	505	328	547	(c)	271	525	340	290
Maine	968	882	652	934	1,001	606	930	975	679
Massachusetts	4,749	4,009	2,734	4,623	(c)	2,556	4,607	3,346	2,774
New Hampshire	911	857	569	860	755	514	830	661	545
New Jersey	6,245	4,711	3,187	6,124	(c)	3,076	5,948	4,060	3,344
New York	13,805	11,263	6,960	13,564	9,161	6,439	13,609	9,196	7,069
Pennsylvania	9,155	7,782	4,912	9,197	6,806	4,506	9,129	5,993	4,961
Rhode Island	753	655	409	751	603	390	776	554	425
Vermont	460	427	294	430	385	261	420	383	293
Regional total	40,127	32,965	21,505	39,330	20,611	19,369	39,309	27,470	21,996
Midwest Region									
Illinois	8,983	7,129	4,742	11,431	6,663	4,418	8,568	6,600	5,164
Indiana	4,448	4,001	2,180	4,146	3,500	2,135	4,108	3,180	2,347
Iowa	2,165	1,841	1,314	2,138	1,776	1,252	2,075	1,704	1,355
Kansas	1,983	1,624	1072	1,823	1,257	1,129	1,881	1,366	1,162
Michigan	7,358	6,861	4,233	7,072	6,677	3,849	6,947	6,147	4,275
Minnesota	3,547	3,265	2,439	3,412	2,730	2,211	3,278	2,711	2,356
Nebraska	1,234	1085	697	1,208	1,015	677	1,167	951	744
North Dakota	477	(c)	288	437	(c)	272	463	(c)	315
Ohio	8,433	7,538	4,702	8,300	6,638	4,534	8,146	6,538	4,940
South Dakota	543	471	316	530	456	324	500	448	336
Wisconsin	3,930	(d)	2,599	3,786	(d)	2,196	3,677	(d)	2,531
Regional total	43,101	33,815	24,582	44,283	30,712	22,997	40,810	29,645	25,525
Southern Region									
Alabama	3,333	2,529	1,666	3,220	2,471	1,534	3,056	2,367	1,688
Arkansas	1,929	1,556	922	1,873	1,369	884	1,774	1,318	951
Florida	11,774	8,753	5,963	11,043	8,078	5,444	10,586	6,542	5,439
Georgia	5,893	3,860	2,583	5,396	3,811	2,299	4,750	3,177	2,321
Kentucky	2,993	2,557	1,544	2,928	2,391	1,388	2,779	2,076	1,493
Louisiana	3,255	2,730	1,766	3,137	(c)	1,784	2,992	2,247	1,790
Maryland	3,925	2,715	2,024	3,811	2,577	1,794	3,719	2,463	1,999
Mississippi	2,047	1,740	994	1,961	1,826	894	1,826	1,640	1,008
Missouri	4,105	3,861	2,360	3,902	3,343	2,158	3,858	3,067	2,391
North Carolina	5,797	5,122	2,915	5,800	4,300	2,515	5,217	3,817	2,612
Oklahoma	2,531	2,234	1,234	2,419	1,823	1,206	2,328	2,302	1,390
South Carolina	2,977	2,157	1,386	2,872	1,814	1,203	2,646	1,537	1,237
Tennessee	4,221	3,181	2,076	3,660	3,056	1,894	3,861	2,726	1,982
Texas	14,850	10,268	6,407	13,698	10,541	5,612	12,524	8,440	6,154
Virginia	5,263	3,770	2,790	5,089	3,323	2,417	4,842	3,055	2,559
West Virginia	1,416	1,068	648	1,414	(c)	636	1,350	956	684
Regional total	76,309	58,101	37,278	72,223	50,723	33,662	68,108	47,730	35,698
Western Region									
Alaska	430	474	286	410	415	245	404	315	261
Arizona	3,625	2,173	1,532	3,233	2,245	1,404	2,749	1,965	1,516
California	24,873	15,707	10,966	19,527	15,662	10,263	20,863	15,101	11,374
Colorado	3,067	2,274	1,741	2,843	2,285	1,551	2,501	2,003	1,597
Hawaii	909	637	368	882	545	370	856	464	383
Idaho	921	728	502	858	700	492	740	611	482
Montana	668	698	411	647	590	417	570	530	418
Nevada	1390	898	609	1,180	778	464	1,013	650	506
New Mexico	1,263	973	599	1,224	838	580	1,104	707	591
Oregon	2,530	1,944	1,534	2,344	1,962	1,399	2,210	1,775	1,499
Utah	1,465	1123	771	1,322	1,050	691	1,159	965	780
Washington	4,368	3,336	2,487	4,122	3,078	2,294	3,818	2,814	2,287
Wyoming	358	220	214	343	241	216	322	235	203
Regional total	45,867	31,185	22,020	38,935	30,389	20,836	38,309	28,135	21,897
Regional total without California	20,994	15,478	11,054	19,408	14,727	10,573	17,446	13,034	10,523
Dist. of Columbia	411	354	202	422	361	186	459	341	228

Sources: 1992 and 1996 data provided by Committee for the Study of the American Electorate, with update by the state election administration offices. 1992 base data provided by state election offices, as available; remaining data provided by Committee for the Study of the American Electorate. U.S. Congress, Clerk of the House, Statistics of the Presidential and Congressional Election. The Council of State Governments' survey of election officials, January 2002. 2000 data provided by the Federal Election Commission.

(a) Estimated population, 18 years old and over. Includes armed forces in each state, aliens, and institutional population.
(b) Number voting is number of ballots cast in presidential race.
(c) Information not available.
(d) No statewide registration required. Excluded from totals for persons registered.

Comparing State Ethics Laws and Ethics Trends and Issues
By David E. Freel

The difficulty in drawing meaningful comparisons and identifying trends in standards created as a remedy to ethics concerns within the states is compounded by significant differences in the manner in which jurisdictions define "ethics" and regulate oversight. Conflicts of interest related to gifts and gratuities, and arising from family and unique private sector relationships, represent continuing ethics trends across the nation.

Introduction—
Difficulty of Comparison Among the States

Drawing general comparisons or identifying trends among the responses of the states to any significant public policy issue is often difficult. Comparisons aimed at readily classifying or categorizing standards of conduct or noteworthy ethics developments throughout the country are no less challenging.

As ethics comparisons or trends are summarized to generalizations, all too often they are misleading or incorrect. Apart from differences in demographics, summaries commonly fail to explain legitimate regional, political, or jurisdictional factors or variations that bring about change or reconsideration. Ethics oversight presents a unique set of issues, significant examples of which are discussed below, that compound the attempt at simplifying comparison.

Attempting to do exactly this—to compare ethics statutes and identify ethical trends in this summary—it is helpful to understand why categorical assessments of ethics oversight or precedent among the states are particularly hard.[1]

Uniqueness of Ethics
Governance Approaches

Ethics oversight varies dramatically throughout the states. From the extent of conduct or persons subject to the definition of "ethics" within a state or region, to the nature of sanctions imposed upon those violating ethics standards, restrictions upon the conduct of public officials that extend beyond baseline public protections against bribery or theft vary significantly from state to state, and at times, even within political subdivisions or governmental agencies in the same state. As an example of the difficulty, one survey conducted in 2002 concluded that all states have some minimal legislative gift or gratuities restriction.[2] However, the survey noted the wide variety of standards governing gifts and the challenge of comparative analysis.

In fact, of the 50 states, there are at least 42 who actually have some structure of ethical protections to the public that limit the actions or activities of specified officials.[3] Beyond the number of jurisdictions with ethics laws or standards, a range of factors exists that the observer must contemplate in attempting to evaluate general similarities or evolving trends in ethics oversight. These issues are fundamental to any effective comparison of ethics restrictions.

Ethics—What Does it Address?

For many jurisdictions, "ethics" describes standards of official conduct. These standards are often statutory and commonly involve issues of financial or familial conflicts of interest. In addition, at least 27 states that have ethics oversight also administer some form of personal (as opposed to campaign contribution or campaign finance) financial disclosure.

Initially a post-Watergate phenomenon, jurisdictions largely began enacting ethics laws in 1973, often legislating standards of conduct together with the requirement to provide some level of personal financial disclosure. This was done in an effort to require the identification of, and then protect the larger public against, conflicts of interest likely to be inherent within ordinary personal financial interests or family or business relationships of a governing official. Some states refer to this type of disclosure as a financial disclosure statement (e.g. Delaware),[4] while other states refer to it as a statement of economic interests (e.g. Alabama);[5] both in part, to contrast the type of disclosure required in contrast to various types of campaign finance reporting. Disclosure may apply to a number of classes of public officials such as in Ohio,[6] or to a more limited class of executive branch officials, such as in Louisiana.[7] The extent and type of disclosure can also vary greatly.

At least 22 of the 27 states that combine conflict of interest and disclosure into a specific system of ethics oversight also include lobbyist regulation. (This can be significant to the observer because restrictions on gift giving or the description of a specific level or type of gratuities, for example, may be found within lobbyist restrictions, or some other area of regulation, rather than solely within ethics statutes; statutory restrictions in Minnesota and Wisconsin provide examples.)[8] Lobbyist restrictions may also overlap standards of conduct. A minimum of 15 states incorporate some responsibility for campaign finance or campaign conduct governance within the responsibility of their ethics boards, commissions or administrative structure. At least eight states provide a "one-stop shop" of public sector oversight, having subject matter responsibilities over ethics, disclosure, campaign finance, and lobbying activities placed in one entity.

One benefit of a generally inclusive model may be the convenience to the public of having a central entity examine or provide advice in response to questions involving a broad spectrum of issues viewed as having ethical implications. Other states have apparently shied away from a concentration of responsibility in one entity. They have either opted to delegate oversight by subject matter, or prioritize a more limited number of functions to their ethics entity, or within their statutory scheme.

Those Subject to Ethics Restrictions

A second concern that arises in trying to compare ethics statutes is the definition of the class of those subject to the framework of statutes or regulations. Some states, such as Alabama, Massachusetts, Ohio and Pennsylvania, subject an entire population of those in public service, at both the state and local levels, to a uniform statewide standard of ethics. States such as Indiana, New Jersey and North Carolina, subject only state employees to oversight. Others, such as Michigan and Illinois, address only executive branch officials. Some states subject judicial or legislative officials to ethical governance under professional codes of conduct or ethical policies, either in addition to state laws, or in lieu of them.

Ten states place oversight involving all of those governed by their standards in one agency. Other states may divide responsibility for legislators, judges and executive branch officials upon theoretical or interpretive views of constitutional or statutory separation of powers within the three branches. Kentucky, Ohio and Washington are examples. These states have created ethical oversight bodies for officials in the legislative, judicial, and executive branches, and therefore have a minimum of three different ethics agencies. Importantly, ethical restrictions in at least 19 states extend to persons outside the public sector, such as vendors, consultants, lobbyists or those performing some governmental function.

While some states have apparently chosen uniform standards for all those in public service, whether through one or more oversight bodies, others have limited the application of ethics statutes to one class of public officials. Some set varying standards, perhaps believing that a single standard does not address differences in authority or compensation or comparative constituent responsibility. Whatever the rationale, one area where a wide divergence of standards exists among and within the states is in gift or gratuities restrictions.[9]

Underlying Jurisdiction

A third question important to understanding similarities or trends is the source of underlying oversight jurisdiction. Many states have created boards or commissions as statutory enactments. A number of states such as Oklahoma, Rhode Island and Texas, that did not legislatively establish ethics agencies, formed them by constitutional mandate. California's Fair Political Practices Commission was created by ballot initiative through state proposition and has a mandated minimum budget.[10]

Differences in the character of underlying authority may be founded upon a specific regional response to the public interest. Despite constitutional oversight, these entities have also faced questions regarding their autonomy or separation from elected office holders, legislatures, or administrative budgeting processes.

Authority

A fourth issue that makes the comparison of states more difficult with respect to ethics laws, is the type of ethics statutes or regulations themselves—whether civil, criminal, and/or administrative in remedy, or some combination thereof—and other differences in their authority. Massachusetts and Maryland are examples of states with statutes with civil sanction, while Pennsylvania and Ohio have statutes that have potential criminal enforcement. Those states having a system of executive governance at the state level often rely on administrative application or employment sanction of their provisions. Examples of these states include Indiana and Michigan.

Among specific aspects of authority, agency power may or may not include compulsory processes to secure information such as subpoena authority. This has led to a continuing debate over a number of years regarding whether an entity may self-initiate complaints or is dependent upon sworn or formal complaint processes to initiate investigations or examinations into wrongdoing. In addition, some of these entities have advisory remedies or educational responsibilities unique to their authority.

While a state chooses a preferred mechanism for ethics oversight, each model has potential positive and negative attributes. Civil or administrative standards may be simpler to administer or test for compliance. However, civil fines or employment sanctions may not be viewed as having sufficient "teeth" to respond to public concern regarding egregious ethical misconduct. A criminal standard may be viewed as more responsive to those concerns, as a deterrent to serious unethical activity, or perhaps, more protective against indiscriminate allegations of wrongdoing. However, criminal enforcement requires a more exacting commitment to statutory drafting, factual evidence and process. Those states that have enabled education and advisory missions within their oversight structures, in addition to compliance and enforcement mechanisms, appear to have recognized that attempts to regulate unethical conduct require some interpretive and informational components to fully and effectively implement an oversight structure.

Composition of Oversight Structure

One final factor that should be taken into consideration in the comparison of ethics standards is the composition and authority of the body given ethical oversight. In states with purely executive governance, it is often a single office holder or cabinet-level subordinate who must administer the ethical standard. In many states, it is a board or commission. These bodies vary in composition and authority. Some are composed only of appointed members, with various types of qualifying criteria and appointment apparatus. Some are composed of elected office holders exclusively, and others combine both. Some boards must be bipartisan, some non-partisan; others are constituted with an even number of members, while some have an odd number of members.

Each governance makeup may have historical roots of a particular institution, office, or office holder. But cross-comparisons of caseloads, findings, or even the subject matter of ethical issues, can be dependent upon these or other unique attributes.

Municipal and Local Ethics Bodies

The concept of legislating ethical norms or restrictions argued to be in the public interest is not a unique province of the states, and exists as well in other political subdivisions. At least 11 major cities have adopted municipal ethics agencies. These include:

Buffalo, Chicago, Denver, Honolulu, Los Angeles, New York City, Oakland, San Antonio, San Diego, San Francisco and Seattle. City entities have often developed or matured in jurisdictions without statewide oversight, as in Colorado. In fact, on May 6, 2003, 80 percent of Denver voters passed a charter amendment enhancing existing ethics ordinances and requiring a code of ethics and supervising board.[11] Other municipal remedies have evolved within states having ethics statutes, such as those in major cities in California. Often the test of statewide oversight includes an examination of whether local ethical standards are as demanding as those of the state. This extent of ethical restrictions can become important to the state and municipality, as it has for Illinois and Chicago. The Chicago Board of Ethics has existed since 1987.[12] Illinois, in contrast, adopted ethics oversight on December 9, 2003, in the wake of a series of state scandals.[13]

A growing number of counties or local political subdivisions have created ethics oversight that can also be influential to any state discussion. For example, readers may quickly recognize national attention to tragic events in 2003 involving the sniper shootings in Maryland. As one of a growing number of county or regional ethics entities, the Montgomery County Ethics Commission subsequently became deeply embroiled in ethical concerns involving the lauded former chief of police that largely arose from potential compensation provided to him from private sector sources for publication or movie rights describing his public role in the successful apprehension of the snipers.[14]

National or International Influences

While the focus of this article is upon the states, and ethics enactments have been and will continue to be influenced by ethical questions resonating within a state, remedial legislation or oversight improvements can be swayed by events beyond state borders. A variety of federal institutions and cabinet departments have entities to oversee ethical issues, chief among them the Office of Governmental Ethics (OGE) in the executive branch. In 2003, OGE proposed significant legislative revisions to Congress that it described as efforts to simplify financial disclosure mandates imposed upon executive branch appointees and employees.[15]

U.S. territories and protectorates, such as Guam and the U.S. Virgin Islands, have ethics agencies. Indeed, so does the sovereign Navajo Indian Nation.

Lest the reader believe ethics oversight to be

unique to those in public sector service in the United States, the provinces of Canada and the governments in a number of Western countries, as well as developing democracies, have examined or are examining, various forms of ethics oversight that extend beyond baseline protections to the public trust. The Canadian provinces often utilize a legislatively appointed ethics officer as the responsible official. In December of 2003, the new prime minister of Canada announced proposals for the appointment of an independent federal ethics counselor by parliament, not the prime minister, and to enhance federal conflict of interest oversight in response to ethical questions involving the administration of his predecessor.[16] Some, in observance of enhanced federal sentencing guidelines in the United States courts in the mid-1990s, recent unethical activity within the private sector on Wall Street, or the implementation of Sarbannes Oxley Act of 2003 as a remedial measure, may also look to those or other events and standards to attempt to regulate unethical action.

Trends—Gifts and Gratuities

During 2003, the issue of gifts and gratuities, and their non-disclosure or insufficient disclosure, was a trend topic throughout the states. Whether fueled by pocketbook issues for consumers and voters due to conduct on Wall Street, or solely issues of local concern, the question of those doing business with government, and those in government accepting, gifts, travel, lodging or other things of value, resounded within the states in 2003.

At least four different states struggled with ethical questions involving gifts within the highest level of the executive branch, the governor. Arkansas, Connecticut, Illinois and Wisconsin all addressed allegations or findings involving prohibited gifts or travel, among other things of value, provided by businesses or persons having interests before the state or the governor. Three of the four cases entail continuing issues, including the alleged inadequacy of disclosure by the governor.

In Wisconsin, the former governor paid forfeitures totalling $13,500 for improper use of state airplanes and improper acceptance of the loan of a boat.[17] In Arkansas, litigation over gifts and disclosure filed by the governor continues into 2004, and includes his constitutional vagueness challenge to the state gift standard and its interpretation by the Arkansas Ethics Commission.[18]

In Connecticut, at the end of 2003, the *New York Times* called for the resignation of the current governor for his admission that he had not fully disclosed

the extent of gift giving by those doing business with his administration. This admission came after the governor entered into an earlier joint stipulation in June 2003 with the Connecticut State Ethics Commission in which he acknowledged the acceptance of $6,972 in vacation lodging.[19] In Illinois, the former governor was indicted by a U.S. Attorney on criminal charges stemming from gifts and vacations allegedly given to him, and alleged contract steering in his administration.[20] Gift and gratuities issues have been prominent in a number of jurisdictions at other levels of the government.

On May 12, 2003, the Massachusetts Ethics Commission issued a decision and order involving the Life Insurance Association of Massachusetts (LIAM), finding violations of the state's conflict of interest law through LIAM's provision of meals to the former insurance commissioner, and fined LIAM $4,000.[21] This case signified the commission's first reconsideration of its gratuties restrictions on direction of the Massachusetts Supreme Court as presenting similar issues and statutory language to federal statutes successfully challenged before the U.S. Supreme Court in an earlier decision on gratuities involving former Secretary of Agriculture Michael Espy.[22]

Oregon appears to have bucked the general continuing trend toward more limited and/or increased scrutiny and disclosure of gifts. In amendments in August 2003 creating new exceptions to their ethics law, the Oregon Legislative Assembly amended Oregon Revised Code Section 244.020(8)(d) to exempt from the definintion of a gift "the giving or receiving" of an unlimited amount of food and beverage for the public official and the relative of the public official, provided that the food or beverage is consumed in the presence of the provider. Iowa also enacted an exception from its gift ban in 2003 for the payment and costs of receptions where all members of the General Assembly are invited to attend.[23] However, in comparison to Oregon, the sponsors of a reception in Iowa must file a report disclosing the costs of the reception.

Misuse of Public Position

The Kentucky Executive Branch Ethics Commission brought charges against their former governor in 2003, which he ultimately admitted, for violating conflict of interest restrictions and alleged misuse of his office to benefit a businesswoman with whom he had had an alleged relationship.[24] The Ohio Ethics Commission referred criminal charges of conflict of interest and non-disclosure in 2003 involving the receipt of $1,259 in things of value, much of which were attributed to the costs of exclusive golf outings and free lodging, by the former executive director of the state's School Facilities Commission from contractors competing for $3 billion in school constructions contracts awarded for school reconstruction efforts throughout the state.[25] In 2002, the Ohio Ethics Commission had forwarded analogous questions of conflict of interest and non-disclosure involving over $1,400 worth of gift receipt by the former executive director of the Ohio Turnpike Commission to the prosecutor.[26]

Nepotism

The relationship of family or those in close proximity to the office holder is a continuing trend issue in ethics. Florida, Lousiana, Massachusetts, Ohio, Oklahoma and New York City all recorded a variety of enforcement cases in 2003 involving actions taken by public officials or employees benefiting family members close to the office holder. Oklahoma, consistent with the trend of extending ethics restrictions into issues of those related to the office holder, expanded those included within the definition of family to a child, adopted child, stepchild, or spouse of a legislator or statewide elective officer.[27] Louisiana appears to be one of the few jurisdictions to have enacted a number of statutory exceptions narrowing the impact of ethics restrictions upon family of the office holder.[28]

One challenge on the horizon for states examining the closeness of relationships to a public official as a matter of conflicting interests, is not only the extent of family included or excluded, but as already presented in personnel areas of hiring, benefits and retirement, domestic partner relationships.

Conflict of Interest

The application of ethics statutes to new and unique non-profit and private sector relationships involving public sector governance is a trend issue. Delaware wrestled in 2002 and 2003 with questions of the intersection of cabinet responsibilities with those on the cabinet simultaneously serving on the board of trustees of a charter school.[29] Ohio continues into 2004 to address issues of ethics governance involving alleged misconduct of trustees within public employees retirement systems.[30]

As Florida experienced, these issues can also involve traditional questions of conflicting interests in the misuse of public resources. The Florida Ethics Commission entered into a stipulated agreement providing for a $10,000 fine and public censure of an employee of the Correctional Privatization Commis-

sion and the misuse of state-paid long distance telephone and other public resources in the conduct of a private consulting business related to the work of the commission.[31]

Revolving Door

Revolving door statutes have existed as a part of conflict of interest restraints for some time. Of note for states looking at revising or enacting new revolving door or post-employment provisions are the 2003 efforts of the King County Board of Ethics in Washington. Having examined similar enactments from throughout the country, King County adopted substantive revisions to its revolving door restrictions in 2003.[32]

Funding

While the issue of budget may not normally be identified as a trend, reductions in operating costs in most states have taken their toll on the performance and implementation of all governmental functions. Ethics agencies have largely not been spared. In its annual survey and update of ethics agencies, conducted by the Council on Governmental Ethics Laws (COGEL) over the past two years, 11 different state ethics agencies identified significant cuts in operating budgets as resulting in delays for electronic initiatives such as online filing, the implementation of educational or informational efforts, and/or the reduction in resources to conduct ethics duties. While most states and their governmental agencies have experienced significant budget reductions in the same period, and ethics agencies have often absorbed their share, because these agencies are largely dependent upon general revenue funding, and are relatively modest in size, they commonly feel the immediate impact of even modest percentage budget reductions. Ethics oversight agencies in Connecticut, Massachusetts, North Carolina, Ohio and Oregon all experienced double-digit budget cuts over the two-year period. The New York City Conflicts of Interest Board was cut a total of 28 percent in its FY 2003 budget, and only after the city council restored some temporary budget assistance, was able to restore a portion of its entire ethics training staff.

In contrast, while California faced significant and notable budget reductions in 2003, the budget of the California Fair Political Practices Commission is fixed by proposition and contains an annual cost-of-living adjustment. At a time when states must examine the cost of baseline governmental services, jurisdictions must simultaneously weigh the import and sufficiency of ethics oversight costs.

While by no means a trend, Nevada took an interesting approach to the operating budget of its ethics agency, the Nevada Commission on Ethics. By enacting AB 551, effective on July 1, 2003, Nevada provides that county and city governments with populations over 10,000 must share the costs of operation of the commission on a percentage basis related to the number of opinion requests made, 65 percent of which were found to emanate locally. Only time will determine whether requiring those seeking advice, rather than the entire state, to directly pay for ethics consultation will undermine or generally discourage efforts to encourage ethical guidance before officials act.

Forced budget reevaluation or resolution may have other broader results in ethics policy. The New York City Conflicts of Interest Board adopted Advisory Opinion 2003–4 on the issue of fundraising in 2003.[33] The board held that city officials would not violate conflict of interest restrictions by engaging in targeted fundraising solicitations, and untargeted solicitations in certain situations, of persons having interests before the city, where the funds support the purposes and interests of the city, or a not-for-profit entity pre-certified by the board. The Connecticut State Ethics Commission issued Advisory Opinion 2003–2, in the wake of substantial layoffs, finding that a state agency could fund the continuation of a public position through contributions from entities doing business with the agency qualifying as statutory gifts to the state.[34] That opinion requires the funded public servant to refrain from taking any official action that could affect his benefactor or competing parties to his benefactor.

Information Systems

Despite funding reductions, many states and ethics agencies have been innovators in the use of technology to increase efficiency and service improvements. Indiana, Massachusetts, New York State, New York City, Pennsylvania and South Carolina all reported significant increases in the efficiency of process through online administration of disclosure and other information system enhancements. Web site software in many states now allow users to search for advisory or published enforcement precedent by names or subject matter, offering both those in the regulated community of public officials, and the greater public, the advantage of easily locating ethics guidance.

Ethics entities are increasingly utilizing online access to provide educational and training opportunities for those governed by ethical standards. Most ethics agencies offer online educational materials found on their Web sites. New York State, the Chicago Ethics Board, and the U.S. Department of Agriculture all feature online training videos, modules or testing.

Additional Resources

While comparisons or trend issues are difficult to readily identify among the states, there are resources for general assistance. COGEL conducts annual surveys in the topic areas of ethics, lobbying, campaign finance, public records and electronic filing. COGEL's membership includes many of those responsible for ethics administration in all three branches of government, at the national, state, provincial and local levels in the United States and Canada, as well as a growing number of other countries. COGEL also includes professionals, academics and individuals practicing or interested in these areas. These surveys summarize the authority and responsibility, as well as advisory, enforcement, litigative and legislative developments, of individual states and other jurisdictions. The *Ethics Update* this year is available on searchable CD, and has included in the past two years the identification of the issue or development that the ethics agency itself classifies as the year's most significant. Survey updates are available to members, and to the public for a modest cost, through COGEL's website at www.cogel.org.

Notes

[1] For those who seek to mine a definitive comparison within any state or jurisdiction, whether taken from this article or another summary, the author advises the reader to highlight the specific change or trend concern, and then conduct research specifically within the jurisdiction, including contact with more than one knowledgeable resource within that state or region. While comparisons drawn in this article come largely from summaries prepared by those agencies or individual offices charged with ethics oversight, and are often, in the author's experience, the most accurate, an agency's oversight alone may color the perception and description of the issue. For purposes of organizing this summary, the author's own identification of classifications or trends may also diverge from the category in which others identify those identical questions.

[2] *The BGA Integrity Index*, (Better Government Association, 2002), 24, relying on data from the Center For Public Integrity State Project, www.publicintegrity.org; also note the annual updates published by the Council on Governmental Ethics Laws (COGEL) described at the article's end and available through www.cogel.org.

[3] COGEL's tables, taken from the 2003 COGEL *Ethics Update*, are found at the end of this article and summarize various attributes the author has used in part to characterize ethics oversight. (Please note, while the majority of jurisdictions participate in the survey from which the gen-

eral tables are compiled, a small number of jurisdictions that have ethics laws do not, and are not listed.)

[4] Delaware Code, Title 29, Chapter 58, Section 5812.

[5] Code of Alabama, Chapter 25 of Title 36, Section 36-25-14, 1975.

[6] Ohio Ethics Law, Revised Code Sections 102.02, and Ohio Administrative Rules.

[7] Louisiana Revised Statutes, Code of Governmental Ethics, Chapter 15, Section 1114.

[8] In Minnesota, www.cfboard.state.mn.us/giftban.htm ; in Wisconsin, http://ethics.state.wi.us/Forms-Publications/Guidelines/510-3Rs.pdf.

[9] Gift limits in California are biennially adjusted based upon the Consumer Price Index by the California Fair Practices Commission, www.fppc.ca.gov/index.html?ID=52&r_id=/legal/regs/18940-2.htm.

[10] California Governmental Code, Title 9, Chapter 3, Section 83122, www.fppc.ca.gov/Act/2003Act.PDF.

[11] City of Denver Charter, Section 1.2.9.

[12] www.ci.chi.il.us/Ethics/pdf/2003AnnualReport.pdf.

[13] Illinois Public Act 093-0617; see also, www.legis.state.il.us/legislation/publicacts/fulltext.asp?Name=093-0617.

[14] www.montgomerycountymd.gov/Content/ethics/docs/moose_agreement.pdf.

[15] www.usoge.gov/pages/forms_pubs_otherdocs/fpo_files/proposed_legsltn/ega_amends_07_16_03.pdf.

[16] www.pm.gc.ca/eng/eth_conduct.asp.

[17] http://ethics.state.wi.us/NewsAndNotices/Settlement_McCallum.pdf.

[18] Declaratory Judgement and Petition for Review complaint, *Huckabee v. Kearney and Sloan*, Pulaski County Circuit Court Case No. CV-2003-1829.

[19] Stipulation and Order, Docket No. 2003–5, www.ethics.state.ct.us/Press_Releases/Rowland_Press _Release. htm.

[20] www.usdoj.gov/usao/iln/pr/2003/pr121703_01.pdf.

[21] www.state.ma.us/ethics/ENFORCEMENTACTIONS.htm#LIAM.

[22] *United States v. Sun-Diamond Growers of California*, 526 U.S.398, (1999).

[23] Section 68B.22,(4), new paragraph (r) of the Iowa Code.

[24] www.foxnews.com/story/0,2933,103280,00.html.

[25] http://ethics.ohio.gov/PressReleases/07092003.html.

[26] http://ethics.ohio.gov/PressReleases/08072002.html.

[27] Section 257:1-1-1 et seq. of the Rules of the Oklahoma Ethics Commission, 74 O.S.Supp.2002, Ch. 62, App.

[28] www.ethics.state.la.us/laws/2003legsum.htm.

[29] www.state.de.us/pic/annual03.pdf, Advisory Opinion 2–23 in Appendix B therein.

[30] www.enquirer.com/editions/2003/10/19/loc_oh-pension.html.

[31] www.ethics.state.fl.us/, Advisory Opinion 03–10

[32] www.metrokc.gov/ethics/.

[33] http://search.citylaw.org/isysquery/irldd/2/doc.

[34] www.ethics.state.ct.us/Advisory_Opinions/2003/2003_2.htm.

About the Author

David E. Freel has been the executive director of the Ohio Ethics Commission since 1994. Before joining the Ethics Commission staff, he was a faculty member of the Ohio State University College of Law. Freel has written articles on Ohio's Ethics Law and given ethics presentations at seminars and conferences in the United States and Canada. He is a past president of the Council on Governmental Ethics Laws (COGEL) and was honored with the COGEL Service Award in 2002.

Table 6.9
ETHICS AGENCIES: JURISDICTION SUBJECT AREAS

State of other jurisdiction	Agency	Campaign finance	Conflict of interest	Elections administration	Ethics	Financial disclosure	Freedom of information	Gift restriction	Lobbying	Public records
Alabama	Ethics Comm.	Y	N	Y	N	N	Y	Y	Y	Y
Alaska	Legisltv. Ethics Cmte.	N	Y	N	Y	N	N	Y	N	N
	Public Ofcs. Comm.	Y	N	N	N	N	N	Y	Y	Y
Arizona	Citizens Clean Elections Comm.	Y	N	N	N	Y	N	N	N	Y
Arkansas	Ethics Comm.	Y	Y	N	Y	Y	N	Y	Y	Y
California	Fair Political Practices Comm.;	Y	Y	N	Y	Y	N	Y	Y	Y
	L.A. Co. Metro. Transit Authority;	N	Y	N	Y	Y	N	Y	Y	Y
	L.A. Ethics Comm.;	Y	Y	N	Y	Y	N	Y	Y	Y
	Oakland Public Ethics Comm.;	Y	N	Y	Y	Y	Y	Y	N	Y
	San Diego Ethics Comm.;	Y	N	Y	Y	N	Y	Y	Y	Y
	San Francisco Ethics Comm.	Y	Y	N	Y	Y	N	Y	Y	N
Colorado	Denver Bd. of Ethics	N	Y	N	Y	N	N	Y	N	N
Connecticut	Freedom of Info. Comm.;	Y	N	N	N	Y	N	N	N	N
	State Ethics Comm.	N	Y	N	Y	Y	N	Y	Y	N
Delaware	Public Integrity Comm.	N	Y	N	Y	Y	N	Y	Y	N
Florida	City of Jacksonville;	Y	Y	N	Y	Y	N	Y	Y	Y
	Comm. on Ethics;	N	Y	N	Y	Y	N	Y	Y	N
	Elections Comm.	Y	N	N	N	N	N	N	N	N
Georgia	State Ethics Comm.	Y	N	N	N	Y	N	Y	Y	Y
Hawaii	Campaign Spending Comm.;	Y	N	N	N	N	N	N	N	N
	Honolulu Ethics Comm.	N	Y	N	Y	Y	N	N	N	N
	State Ethics Comm.;	N	Y	N	Y	Y	N	Y	Y	N
Idaho	Secretary of State	Y	N	N	N	N	N	Y	Y	Y
Illinois	Chicago Bd. of Ethics;	Y	Y	N	Y	Y	Y	Y	Y	Y
	City of Champaign	Y	N	Y	N	Y	N	Y	N	N
Indiana	Public Access Counselor's Ofc.;	Y	N	N	N	Y	N	Y	N	N
	State Ethics Comm.	N	Y	N	Y	N	N	Y	N	N
Iowa	Ethics & Campaign Discl. Bd.	Y	Y	N	Y	Y	N	Y	Y	N
Kansas	Govtl. Ethics Comm.	Y	Y	N	Y	Y	N	Y	Y	N
Kentucky	Exec. Branch Ethics Comm.;	N	Y	N	Y	Y	Y	Y	Y	N
	Legisltv. Ethics Comm.	N	Y	N	Y	Y	N	Y	Y	N
Louisiana	Ethics Admin.	Y	Y	N	Y	Y	N	Y	Y	N
Maine	Comm. on Govtl. Ethics & Election Practices	Y	N	Y	N	N	Y	Y	Y	Y
Maryland	Anne Arundel Co. Ethics Comm.;	Y	N	Y	N	N	Y	Y	Y	Y
	Montgomery Co. Ethics Comm.;	N	Y	N	Y	Y	Y	Y	Y	Y
	State Ethics Comm.	N	Y	N	Y	Y	Y	Y	Y	Y
Massachusetts	Ethics Comm.	N	Y	N	Y	Y	N	Y	N	N
Michigan	Dept. of State	Y	N	Y	N	Y	Y	Y	Y	Y
	State Bd. of Ethics	N	N	N	Y	N	N	N	N	N
Minnesota	Camp. Finance & Public Discl. Bd.	Y	Y	N	N	Y	N	Y	Y	N
Mississippi	Ethics Comm.	Y	N	N	N	N	N	Y	N	N
Missouri	Ethics Comm.	Y	Y	N	N	N	N	Y	Y	Y
Montana	Commr. of Political Practices	Y	N	N	Y	Y	N	N	Y	N
Nebraska	Accountability & Discl. Comm.	Y	Y	N	Y	Y	N	Y	Y	N
Nevada	Comm. on Ethics	N	Y	N	Y	Y	N	Y	N	N
New Hampshire	N.A.									
New Jersey	Exec. Comm. on Ethical Stds.	N	Y	N	Y	Y	N	N	N	N
New Mexico	N.A.									
New York	Buffalo Bd. of Ethics;	Y	N	Y	N	N	Y	Y	Y	N
	Dept. of State Cmte. on Open Govt.;	Y	N	N	N	Y	N	Y	Y	N
	NYC Conflicts of Interest Bd.;	N	Y	N	Y	Y	N	Y	N	N
	State Ethics Comm.;	N	Y	N	Y	Y	N	Y	N	N
	Suffolk Co. Camp. Finance Bd.;	Y	N	N	N	N	N	N	N	N
	Temp. State Comm. on Lobbying	Y	N	N	N	N	N	Y	N	Y
North Carolina	Bd. of Ethics	N	Y	N	Y	Y	N	N	N	N
North Dakota	N.A.									
Ohio	Ethics Comm.;	N	Y	N	Y	Y	N	Y	Y	N
	Legisltv. Insp. Gen. Ofc.	N	Y	N	Y	Y	N	Y	Y	N

See footnotes at end of table.

ETHICS AGENCIES: JURISDICTION SUBJECT AREAS — Continued

State of other jurisdiction	Agency	Campaign finance	Conflict of interest	Elections administration	Ethics	Financial disclosure	Freedom of information	Gift restriction	Lobbying	Public records
Oklahoma	Ethics Comm.	Y	N	Y	N	N	Y	Y	Y	Y
Oregon	Govt. Standards & Practices Comm.	N	Y	N	Y	Y	N	Y	Y	N
Pennsylvania	Ethics Comm.	N	Y	N	Y	Y	N	N	N	N
Rhode Island	Ethics Comm.	N	Y	N	Y	Y	N	Y	N	N
South Carolina	House Legisltv. Ethics Cmte.	Y	N	Y	N	N	Y	Y	Y	N
South Dakota	—————————————— N.A. ——————————————									
Tennessee	—————————————— N.A. ——————————————									
Texas	Ethics Comm.;	Y	N	Y	N	N	Y	Y	Y	Y
	San Antonio City Attorney's Ofc.	N	Y	N	Y	Y	Y	Y	Y	Y
Utah	State Elections Ofc.	Y	N	N	Y	N	N	Y	Y	Y
Vermont	—————————————— N.A. ——————————————									
Virginia	State Bd. of Elections	Y	N	N	Y	N	N	Y	Y	N
Washington	Seattle Ethics & Elections Comm.	Y	Y	Y	Y	Y	Y	Y	Y	Y
	King Co. Bd. of Ethics;	N	Y	N	Y	Y	N	Y	N	N
	King Co. Ofc. of Citizen Complaints;	Y	N	Y	N	Y	Y	Y	N	N
	State Comm. on Judcial Conduct;	Y	Y	N	N	N	Y	Y	N	N
	State Exec. Ethics Bd.;	Y	Y	Y	N	N	Y	Y	N	N
	State Legisltv. Ethics Bd.;	N	Y	N	Y	N	N	Y	N	Y
	State Public Discl. Comm.	Y	N	N	N	Y	N	N	Y	N
West Virginia	Ethics Comm.	N	Y	N	Y	Y	N	Y	Y	N
Wisconsin	Ethics Bd.	N	Y	N	Y	Y	N	Y	Y	N
Wyoming	—————————————— N.A. ——————————————									
Guam	Ethics Comm.	Y	N	N	N	N	N	Y	N	N
Puerto Rico	Ofc. of Govt. Ethics	N	Y	N	Y	Y	N	Y	N	N
U.S. Virgin Islands	Dept. of Justice	Y	N	N	N	N	N	Y	N	N

Source: The Council on Governmental Ethics Laws, *2003 Ethics Update*.
Key:
Y—Yes
N—No
N.A.—Not available.

Table 6.10
ETHICS AGENCIES: JURISDICTION

State or other jurisdiction	Agency	Executive branch employees	Judges	Judicial employees	Legislative employees	Legislators	Lobbyists	Local appointed officials	Local elected officials	Local employees	Private sector/vendors	State appointed officials	State elected officials	State employees	State colleges & universities
Alabama	Ethics Comm.	Y	Y	Y	N	Y	Y	Y	Y	Y	Y	Y	N	N	N
Alaska	Legisltv. Ethics Cmte.	N	N	N	N	Y	N	N	N	N	N	N	N	N	N
	Public Ofcs. Comm.	Y	N	N	N	Y	N	Y	N	Y	Y	Y	N	N	Y
Arizona	Citizens Clean Elections Comm.	N	N	N	N	Y	N	N	Y	N	N	Y	N	N	N
Arkansas	Ethics Comm.	Y	Y	Y	Y	Y	Y	Y	Y	Y	N	Y	Y	Y	Y
California	Fair Political Practices Comm.;	Y	Y	Y	N	Y	Y	Y	Y	Y	N	Y	Y	Y	N
	L.A. Co. Metro. Transit Authority;	N	N	N	N	N	Y	N	N	Y	Y	N	N	N	N
	L.A. Ethics Comm.;	Y	N	N	N	Y	Y	Y	Y	Y	Y	N	N	N	N
	Oakland Public Ethics Comm.;	N	N	N	N	N	N	Y	Y	Y	Y	N	N	Y	N
	San Diego Ethics Comm.;	N	N	N	N	N	Y	N	Y	N	Y	N	N	Y	N
	San Francisco Ethics Comm.	N	N	N	N	N	Y	Y	Y	Y	Y	N	N	N	N
Colorado	Denver Bd. of Ethics	N	N	N	N	N	N	Y	Y	Y	N	N	N	N	N
Connecticut	Freedom of Info. Comm.;	Y	Y	Y	Y	Y	Y	Y	Y	Y	Y	Y	Y	N	Y
	State Ethics Comm.	Y	N	Y	Y	Y	Y	N	N	N	N	Y	Y	Y	Y
Delaware	Public Integrity Comm.	Y	Y	Y	Y	Y	Y	Y	Y	Y	N	Y	Y	Y	Y
Florida	City of Jacksonville;	N	N	N	N	N	Y	Y	Y	Y	N	N	N	N	N
	Comm. on Ethics	Y	N	Y	N	Y	Y	Y	Y	Y	N	Y	Y	Y	Y
	Elections Comm.	N	N	N	N	N	N	N	N	N	N	N	N	N	N
Georgia	State Ethics Comm.	N	Y	N	N	Y	N	Y	N	Y	N	Y	N	N	N
Hawaii	Campaign Spending Comm.;	N	N	N	N	Y	N	N	Y	N	Y	N	N	N	N
	Honolulu Ethics Comm.;	Y	N	N	N	N	Y	Y	Y	Y	N	N	N	N	N
	State Ethics Comm.;	Y	Y	Y	Y	Y	Y	N	N	N	N	Y	Y	Y	Y
Idaho	Secretary of State	N	Y	N	N	Y	N	N	N	N	N	Y	N	N	N
Illinois	Chicago Bd. of Ethics;	Y	N	N	N	N	Y	Y	Y	Y	N	N	Y	N	N
	City of Champaign	N	N	N	N	N	N	Y	N	N	N	N	N	N	N
Indiana	Public Access Counselor's Ofc.;	Y	Y	Y	Y	Y	Y	Y	Y	Y	Y	Y	N	Y	Y
	State Ethics Comm.	Y	N	N	N	N	N	N	N	N	N	Y	N	N	N
Iowa	Ethics & Campaign Discl. Bd.	Y	N	N	N	Y	Y	N	N	N	N	Y	N	Y	Y
Kansas	Govtl. Ethics Comm.	Y	N	Y	Y	Y	Y	N	Y	N	Y	Y	Y	Y	Y
Kentucky	Exec. Branch Ethics Comm.;	Y	N	N	N	N	N	N	N	N	Y	Y	Y	Y	Y
	Legisltv. Ethics Comm.	N	N	N	N	Y	Y	N	N	N	N	N	N	N	N
Louisiana	Ethics Admin.	Y	N	Y	Y	Y	Y	Y	Y	Y	Y	Y	Y	Y	Y
Maine	Comm. on Govtl. Ethics & Election Practices	N	Y	Y	N	N	Y	N	N	N	Y	N	Y	N	N
Maryland	Anne Arundel Co. Ethics Comm.;	N	Y	Y	N	N	N	N	Y	N	Y	N	N	N	N
	Montgomery Co. Ethics Comm.;	Y	N	N	N	N	Y	Y	Y	Y	N	N	N	N	N
	State Ethics Comm.	Y	N	N	N	N	Y	N	N	N	N	Y	Y	Y	Y
Massachusetts	Ethics Comm.	Y	Y	Y	Y	Y	Y	Y	Y	Y	Y	Y	Y	Y	Y
Michigan	Dept. of State	N	Y	N	N	Y	Y	Y	N	N	Y	Y	Y	N	Y
	State Bd. of Ethics	N	N	N	N	N	N	N	N	N	N	Y	N	Y	N
Minnesota	Camp. Finance & Public Discl. Bd.	Y	Y	N	N	Y	Y	Y	Y	Y	N	N	N	N	N
Mississippi	Ethics Comm.	N	N	N	N	N	N	N	N	N	Y	N	N	N	N
Missouri	Ethics Comm.	Y	Y	Y	N	Y	Y	Y	Y	Y	N	Y	Y	Y	Y
Montana	Commr. of Political Practices	Y	Y	Y	Y	Y	Y	N	Y	N	N	Y	Y	Y	N
Nebraska	Accountability & Discl. Comm.	Y	N	N	Y	N	Y	Y	Y	Y	Y	Y	Y	Y	Y
Nevada	Comm. on Ethics	Y	N	N	N	Y	N	Y	Y	Y	N	Y	Y	Y	Y
New Hampshire	------------------ N.A ------------------														
New Jersey	Exec. Comm. on Ethical Stds.	Y	N	N	N	N	N	N	N	N	N	N	N	N	N
New Mexico	------------------ N.A ------------------														
New York	Buffalo Bd. of Ethics;	N	N	N	N	N	N	Y	N	Y	Y	N	N	Y	N
	Dept. of State Cmte. on Open Govt.;	Y	Y	Y	Y	Y	Y	Y	N	Y	Y	N	N	Y	Y
	NYC Conflicts of Interest Bd.;	N	N	N	N	N	Y	Y	Y	Y	N	N	N	N	N
	State Ethics Comm.;	Y	N	N	N	N	N	N	N	N	N	Y	Y	Y	Y
	Suffolk Co. Camp. Finance Bd.;	N	N	N	N	N	N	N	Y	N	N	N	N	N	N
	Temp. State Comm. on Lobbying	N	N	N	N	N	Y	N	N	N	Y	N	N	N	N
North Carolina	Bd. of Ethics	Y	N	N	N	N	N	N	N	N	N	Y	N	N	N
North Dakota	------------------ N.A ------------------														
Ohio	Ethics Comm.;	Y	N	N	N	N	N	Y	Y	Y	Y	Y	Y	Y	Y
	Legisltv. Insp. Gen. Ofc.	N	N	N	Y	Y	Y	N	N	N	N	N	N	N	N

See footnotes at end of table.

ETHICS AGENCIES: JURISDICTION — Continued

State or other jurisdiction	Agency	Executive branch employees	Judges	Judicial employees	Legislative employees	Legislators	Lobbyists	Local appointed officials	Local elected officials	Local employees	Private sector/vendors	State appointed officials	State elected officials	State employees	State colleges & universities
Oklahoma	Ethics Comm.	Y	Y	Y	N	Y	Y	Y	Y	Y	Y	N	N	Y	Y
Oregon	Govt. Standards & Practices Comm.	Y	Y	Y	Y	Y	Y	Y	Y	Y	Y	Y	Y	Y	Y
Pennsylvania	Ethics Comm.	Y	N	N	N	Y	N	Y	Y	Y	N	Y	Y	Y	Y
Rhode Island	Ethics Comm.	Y	Y	Y	Y	Y	N	Y	Y	Y	N	Y	Y	Y	Y
South Carolina	House Legisltv. Ethics Cmte.	N	N	N	N	N	N	N	N	N	Y	N	N	N	N
South Dakota	------------------------------------N.A.-----------------------------------														
Tennessee	------------------------------------N.A.-----------------------------------														
Texas	Ethics Comm.;	Y	Y	Y	N	Y	Y	N	N	N	Y	Y	N	N	Y
	San Antonio City Attorney's Ofc.	N	N	N	N	N	Y	Y	Y	Y	N	N	N	N	N
Utah	State Elections Ofc.	N	Y	Y	Y	Y	Y	N	N	N	Y	Y	N	N	N
Vermont	------------------------------------N.A.-----------------------------------														
Virginia	State Bd. of Elections	N	Y	N	N	Y	N	Y	N	N	Y	N	N	N	N
Washington	Seattle Ethics & Elections Comm.	N	N	Y	N	N	N	N	Y	Y	Y	N	N	N	N
	King Co. Bd. of Ethics;	N	N	N	N	N	N	Y	Y	Y	N	N	N	N	N
	King Co. Ofc. of Citizen Complaints;	N	N	Y	Y	N	N	N	Y	Y	N	N	N	Y	N
	State Comm. on Judcial Conduct;	N	Y	Y	N	N	N	N	Y	Y	N	Y	N	N	N
	State Exec. Ethics Bd.;	Y	N	N	N	N	N	N	N	N	Y	N	N	N	Y
	State Legisltv. Ethics Bd.;	N	N	N	Y	Y	N	N	N	N	N	N	N	N	N
	State Public Discl. Comm.	N	Y	N	N	Y	Y	N	Y	Y	N	Y	Y	N	Y
West Virginia	Ethics Comm.	Y	Y	Y	Y	Y	Y	Y	Y	Y	Y	Y	Y	Y	Y
Wisconsin	Ethics Bd.	Y	Y	Y	N	Y	Y	N	N	N	N	Y	Y	N	Y
Wyoming	------------------------------------N.A.-----------------------------------														
Guam	Ethics Comm.	N	N	N	N	N	N	N	N	N	Y	N	N	N	N
Puerto Rico	Ofc. of Govt. Ethics	Y	N	N	N	N	N	Y	Y	Y	N	Y	Y	Y	Y
U.S. Virgin Islands	Dept. of Justice	N	N	N	N	N	N	N	N	N	Y	N	N	N	N

Source: The Council on Governmental Ethics Laws, *2003 Ethics Update.*
Key:
Y - Yes
N - No
N.A. - Not available.

Table 6.11
ETHICS AGENCIES: ADVISORY OPINIONS, INVESTIGATIONS & TRAINING

State or other jurisdiction	Agency	Advisory opinions			Investigations / Authority to investigate					Training			
		Authority to issue	Binding on inquirer	Estimated number per year	On own initiative	Reimbursement	Anonymous complaints	Respond to complaint	Estimated number per year	Agency trains	Optional or required	Estimated number per year	Training methods
Alabama	State Ethics Comm.	Y	N	52	N	Y	Y	Y	329	Y	O	58	...
Alaska	Legisltv. Ethics Cmte.	Y	Y	3-5	Y	N	Y	Y	4-6	Y	Y	2	C
	Public Ofcs. Comm.	Y	Y	5-25	Y	Y	Y	Y	5-10	Y	O	20	C, T, V, VT, CD, W
Arizona	Citizens Clean Elections Comm.	N	N	...	Y	Y	N	Y	22	Y	O	5-20	C, CD, W
Arkansas	Ethics Comm.	Y	Y	12	Y	N	Y	Y	112	Y	O	13	...
California	Fair Political Practices Comm.;	Y	Y	300-400	Y	N	Y	Y	N.A.	Y	B	100	...
	L.A. Co. Metro. Trans. Authority;	Y	N	150	Y	Y	Y	Y	100	Y	R	60+	C, T
	L.A. Ethics Comm.;	Y	N	N.A.	Y	Y	Y	Y	100	N	B	35-40	...
	Oakland Public Ethics Comm.;	N	N	1-2	Y	Y	Y	Y	30-40	Y	B	4	...
	San Diego Ethics Comm.;	Y	N	4	N	Y	Y	Y	38	N	R	N.A.	C, T, V, VT, CD, W
	San Francisco Ethics Comm.	Y	N	N.A.	Y	N	N	Y	38	Y	O	20	...
Colorado	Denver Bd. of Ethics	Y	N	50	N	Y	N	Y	15 (a)	Y	R	5,000	C, T, V, VT, CD, W
Connecticut	Freedom of Info. Comm.;	Y	Y	700	Y	Y	Y	Y	N.A.	Y	O	70	...
	State Ethics Comm.	Y	Y	30	Y	Y	Y	Y	75	Y	B	35	C, VT
Delaware	Public Integrity Comm.	Y	N	60	Y	Y	N	Y	3-7	Y	O	15-20	C, T, VT, W
Florida	City of Jacksonville;	Y	N	N.A.	N	N	N	Y	N.A.	Y	R	10	C, W
	Comm. on Ethics;	Y	Y	23 (b)	N	Y	N	Y	133 (b)	N	O	25	...
	Elections Comm.	N	N	...	Y	Y	N	N	230	Y	...	...	...
Georgia	State Ethics Comm.	Y	N	1	Y	Y	Y	Y	100	Y	O	20	C, T
Hawaii	Camp. Spending Comm.;	Y	Y	12	Y	Y	Y	Y	20	Y	N.A.	5	C, VT
	Honolulu Ethics Comm.;	Y	Y	4-7	Y	N	Y	Y	20-30	Y	B	50	C, V
	State Ethics Comm.	N	N	1-5	Y	Y	Y	Y	10-20	N	O	30-60	C, T, V, VT, CD, W
Idaho	Secretary of State	N	N	...	N	Y	N	Y	5 (c)	N	...	...	...
Illinois	Chicago Bd. of Ethics	Y	N	30	Y	Y	N	Y	25	Y	B	60	C, VT, W
Indiana	Public Access Counselor's Ofc.;	Y	N	64	N	Y	Y	Y	N.A.	Y	O	29	C, T, V, VT, CD, W
	State Ethics Comm.	Y	N	225	Y	N	Y	Y	50	Y	O	22	C, VT, W
Iowa	Ethics & Camp. Discl. Bd.	Y	N	8	Y	Y	Y	N	5	Y	N.A.	5	C
Kansas	Govtl. Ethics Comm.	Y	Y	30-40	Y	Y	Y	Y	3-5	Y	O	45-55	C
Kentucky	Exec. Branch Ethics Comm.;	Y	Y	70	Y	Y	N	Y	20	Y	O	20	C
	Legisltv. Ethics Comm.	Y	Y	5	N	Y	N	N	7	Y	B	2	C, VT
Louisiana	Ethics Admin.	Y	N	390	Y	N	Y	Y	113	Y	N.A.	60	C
Maine	Comm. on Govtl. Ethics & Election Practices;	Y	Y	<6	Y	Y	Y	Y	<10	Y	1 (d)	N.A.	...
Maryland	Montgomery Co. Ethics Comm.;	Y	Y	10+	Y	Y	Y	Y	4	N	O	N.A.	W
	State Ethics Comm.	Y	Y	10	Y	Y	Y	Y	N.A.	Y	R	15	C

See footnotes at end of table.

ETHICS AGENCIES: ADVISORY OPINIONS, INVESTIGATIONS & TRAINING — Continued

State or other jurisdiction	Agency	Advisory opinions Authority to issue	Binding on inquirer	Estimated number per year	Investigations — Authority to investigate On own initiative	Reimbursement	Anonymous complaints	Respond to complaint	Estimated number per year	Agency trains	Optional or required	Training Estimated number per year	Training methods
Massachusetts	State Ethics Comm.	Y	Y	2 (e)	Y	Y	Y	Y	74 (f)	Y	O	95 (g)	⋮
Michigan	Dept. of State;	N	N	N.A.	N	N	N	N	N.A.	Y	O	6	⋮
	State Bd. of Ethics	Y	N	2	Y	N	N	N	0	N	N.A.	N.A.	N.A.
Minnesota	Camp. Finance & Public Discl. Bd.	Y	N	10	Y	Y	Y	Y	2	N	N.A.	N.A.	N.A.
Mississippi	Ethics Comm.	N	N	N.A.	N	Y	Y	N	N.A.	N	N.A.	N.A.	N.A.
Missouri	Ethics Comm.	Y	N	15	Y	N	Y	Y	180	Y	N.A.	25	⋮
Montana	Commr. of Political Practices	Y	N	50	N	Y	N	Y	15-20	N	O	2	C
Nebraska	Accountability & Discl. Comm.	Y	N	9	N	Y	N	Y	30	Y	O	8	C
Nevada	Comm. on Ethics	Y	Y	20	Y	N	N	Y	50	Y	O	20	C
New Hampshire						N.A.								
New Jersey	Exec. Comm. on Ethical Stds.	Y	N	20	Y	N	Y	Y	35	Y	B	15	C, CD
New Mexico						N.A.								
New York	Buffalo Bd. of Ethics;	Y	N	0	Y	Y	Y	Y	1-2	N	⋮	0	⋮
	Dept. of State Cmte. on Open Govt.;	Y	N	800 (h)	N	Y	Y	Y	N.A.	Y	N.A.	50	C, T, V, VT, CD, W
	NYC Conflicts of Interest Bd.;	Y	Y	505 (a)	Y	N	Y	Y	74 (a)	Y	O	377 (a)	C, VT, W
	State Ethics Comm.;	Y	Y	5-10	Y	N	Y	Y	40	N	O	65	C, VT, W
	Suffolk Co. Camp. Finance Bd.	Y	N	0	Y	Y	Y	Y	0	Y	N.A.	N.A.	N.A.
	Temp. State Comm. on Lobbying;	Y	Y	5	Y	Y	Y	Y	10	Y	N.A.	6	C, T, V, VT, CD, W
	Bd. of Ethics	Y	N	10-15	Y	N	N	Y	5-10	Y	O	100+	⋮
North Carolina						N.A.								
North Dakota						N.A.								
Ohio	Ethics Comm.;	Y	Y	151	Y	Y	Y	Y	60	Y	B	155	C
	Legisltv. Insp. Gen. Ofc.	Y	N	N.A.	Y	N	Y	Y	3	Y	N.A.	3	C
Oklahoma	Ethics Comm.	Y	N	5-7	Y	Y	Y	N	over 10	Y	O	over 10	⋮
Oregon	Govt. Standards & Practices Comm.	Y	Y	40-50	Y	N	N	Y	50-100	Y	O	50-60	C
Pennsylvania	Ethics Comm.	Y	N	125-200	Y	Y	N	Y	100	Y	O	50	C, VT
Rhode Island	Ethics Comm.	Y	N	120	Y	Y	N	Y	30	Y	O	25	C, W
South Carolina	House Legisltv. Ethics Cmte.	Y	Y	2	N	N	Y	Y	3	Y	N.A.	1	⋮
South Dakota						N.A.								
Tennessee						N.A.								
Texas	Ethics Comm.	Y	Y	10	Y	Y	Y	Y	76	Y	B	37	⋮
	San Antonio City Attorney's Ofc.	Y	N	20	Y	N	Y	Y	1-3	Y	B	30	C
Utah	State Elections Ofc.	Y	N	3	Y	Y	Y	N	3	N	N.A.	N.A.	C, T, V, VT, CD, W
Vermont	Ofc. of the Treasurer					N.A.								

See footnotes at end of table.

ETHICS AGENCIES: ADVISORY OPINIONS, INVESTIGATIONS & TRAINING — Continued

State or other jurisdiction	Agency	Advisory opinions			Investigations					Training			
		Authority to issue	Binding on inquirer	Estimated number per year	Authority to investigate					Agency trains	Optional or required	Estimated number per year	Training methods
					On own initiative	Reimbursement	Anonymous complaints	Respond to complaint	Estimated number per year				
Virginia	State Bd. of Elections	N	N	…	N	Y	Y	N	N.A.	Y	O	1–2 dozen	C, T, V, VT, CD, W
Washington	Seattle Ethics & Elections Comm.;	Y	Y	30	Y	Y	Y	Y	75	Y	O	25	C
	King Co. Bd. of Ethics;	Y	N	Varies	Y	N	Y	Y	Varies	Y	B	43 (a)	C
	King Co. Ofc. Of Citizen Complaints;	N	N	…	Y	Y	Y	Y	10–20	N	N.A.	3–5	C, T, V, VT, CD, W
	State Comm. on Judicial Conduct;	N	N	…	Y	Y	Y	Y	360	Y	O	4	C, T, V, VT, CD, W
	State Exec. Ethics Bd.;	Y	N	10	Y	Y	Y	Y	100	Y	O	40	…
	State Legisltv. Ethics Bd.;	Y	Y	8	Y	Y	N	Y	5–12	Y	B	3–10	…
	State Public Discl. Comm.	Y	Y	0–2	N	Y	N	Y	50–75	Y	O	63	C
West Virginia	Ethics Comm.	Y	N	35–40	Y	Y	Y	Y	10–15	Y	O	15–20	C
Wisconsin	State Ethics Bd.	Y	N	25	Y	Y	Y	Y	10	Y	R	25	C
Wyoming						N.A.							
Guam	Ethics Comm.	N	N	…	N	Y	Y	N	N.A.	N	…	…	…
Puerto Rico	Ofc. of Govt. Ethics	Y	Y	1,049	Y	Y	Y	Y	500	Y	R	499	…
U.S. Virgin Islands	Dept. of Justice	N	N	N.A.	N	Y	Y	N	N.A.	N	…	…	…

Source: The Council on Governmental Ethics Laws, *2003 Ethics Update.*

Key:
Y—Yes
N—No
B—Both
O—Optional
R- Required
N.A.—Not available
C—Classroom
T—Teleconference
V—Videoconference
VT—Video tape
CD—CDRom
W—Web-based
(a) In 2002.
(b) Three year average.
(c) In elections years.
(d) Biennially for new Legislature.
(e) Formal advisory opinions.
(f) In Fiscal Year 2002.
(g) In Fiscal Year 2003.
(h) Written opinions.

Table 6.12
ETHICS AGENCIES: PERSONAL FINANCIAL DISCLOSURE STATEMENTS

State or other jurisdiction	Agency	Who must file with agency								Number filed per year	File via web	File other electronic	FDS available electronically	Reviews or audits conducted	Reviews or audits available electronically
		Agency heads	Board or commission members	Judges	Legislators	Candidates for legislature	State elected officials	Candidates for statewide office	Other						
Alabama	Ethics Comm.	Y	Y	N	Y	Y	Y	Y	(a)(h)	30,000	Y	Y	N	N	N
Alaska	Public Ofcs. Comm.	Y	Y	N	Y	Y	Y	Y		2,000	Y	Y	N	Y	Y
Arizona	Citizens Clean Elections Comm.	Y	Y	Y	Y	N	N	N	(z)	6	N	Y	Y	Y	N
Arkansas	Ethics Comm.	—	—	—	— (f) —	—	—	—		240 (f)	N	N	Y	Y	N
California	Fair Political Practices Comm.;	Y	Y	Y	Y	N	Y	Y	(a)	20,000	N	N	N	Y	N
	L.A. Co. Metro. Trans. Authority	Y	Y	N	N	N	N	N	(pp)	1,200	N	N	N	Y	N
	L.A. Ethics Comm.;	Y	Y	N	N	N	N	N	(c)(aa)	6,000	N	Y	N	Y	N
	Oakland Public Ethics Comm.;	Y	Y	N	N	N	N	N	(c)(bb)	750	Y	Y	N	N	N
	San Diego Ethics Comm.;	Y	Y	N	N	N	N	N	(c)	350	Y	Y	N	N	N
	San Francisco Ethics Comm.	Y	Y	N	N	N	N	N	(gg)(kk)	650	N	N	N	Y	N
Colorado		N.A.													
Connecticut	Freedom of Info. Comm.;	Y	Y	Y	Y	N	Y	N	(i)	1,500	Y	Y	N	Y	N
	State Ethics Comm.;	Y	N	N	Y	Y	Y	N	(j)	300+	N	N	N	Y	N
Delaware	Public Integrity Comm.	Y	Y	N	Y	N	Y	Y	(gg)	100	N	N	N	N	N
Florida	City of Jacksonville;	Y	Y	N	N	N	Y	N	(k)	30,000	N	N	N	Y	N
	Comm. on Ethics	Y	Y	Y	Y	Y	Y	Y	(a)(u)	7,000	N	N	N	Y	N
Georgia	State Ethics Comm.	Y	Y	N	Y	N	Y	Y		N.A.	Y	Y	Y	Y	N
Hawaii	Campaign Spending Comm.;	N	N	N	N	N	N	N		2,000	Y	Y	N	Y	N
	State Ethics Comm.;	Y	Y	N	N	Y	Y	Y		550	N	N	Y	Y	N
	Honolulu Ethics Comm.	Y	N	N	N	N	N	Y	(a)(v)	3,000 (mm)	Y	Y	Y	Y	N
Idaho	Secretary of State	N	N	N	N	N	N	N	(ll)	12,000	N	Y	N	Y	N
Illinois	Chicago Bd. of Ethics;	N	N	N	N	N	N	N	(c)(l)	N.A.	Y	N	N	Y	N
	City of Champaign	N	N	N	N	N	N	N		N.A.	N	N	N	N	N
Indiana	Public Access Counselor's Ofc.;	N	N	N	N	N	N	N		N.A.	Y	Y	N	Y	N
	State Ethics Comm.	Y	N	N	N	N	N	Y	(mm)	400+	Y	N	N	N	N
Iowa	Ethics & Camp. Discl. Bd.	Y	Y	N	Y	N	Y	Y	(a)(cc)	600	N	Y	Y	Y	N
Kansas	Govtl. Ethics Comm.	Y	Y	N	Y	N	Y	Y		6,000	Y	N	N	Y	N
Kentucky	Exec. Branch Ethics Comm.;	Y	Y	N	N	N	Y	N	(oo)	1,300	N	N	N	Y	N
	Legisltv. Ethics Comm.	N	Y	N	Y	Y	N	N	(e)(qq)	150	N	Y	Y	Y	N
Louisiana	Ethics Admn.	N	N	N	Y	Y	N	Y		7,339	N	Y	N	Y	N
Maine	Comm. on Govtl. Ethics & Election Practices	N	N	N	Y	Y	N	N	(b)	<450	Y	Y	Y	N	N
Maryland	Anne Arundel Co. Ethics Comm.;	Y	Y	N	Y	Y	N	N	(b)(w)	200+	Y	N	N	Y	N
	Montgomery Co. Ethics Comm.;	Y	Y	N	N	N	N	N	(rr)	1,400	Y	N	N	Y	N
	State Ethics Comm.	Y	Y	Y	Y	Y	Y	Y		11,000	N	Y	N	Y	N
Massachusetts	State Ethics Comm.	Y	Y	Y	Y	Y	Y	Y	(b)(y)	4,917	N	N	N	Y	N
Michigan	Dept. of State	N	N	N	N	Y	Y	Y		10,000	Y	Y	Y	Y	Y
Minnesota	Camp. Finance & Public Discl. Bd.	Y	Y	N	Y	Y	Y	Y		1,300	N	N	N	N	N
Mississippi	Ethics Comm.	N	N	N	N	N	N	N		N.A.	N	Y	N	N	N
Missouri	Ethics Comm.	Y	Y	N	Y	Y	Y	Y	(a)(m)	9,500	N	N	N	N	N

See footnotes at end of table.

ETHICS AGENCIES: PERSONAL FINANCIAL DISCLOSURE STATEMENTS—Continued

State or other jurisdiction	Agency	Agency heads	Board or commission members	Judges	Legislators	Candidates for legislature	State elected officials	Candidates for statewide office	Other	Number filed per year	File via web	File other electronic	FDS available electronically	Reviews or audits conducted	Reviews or audits available electronically
Montana	Commr. of Political Practices	Y	N	N	Y	Y	Y	N	(a)(n)	190	N	N	N	N	N
Nebraska	Accountability & Discl. Comm.	Y	N	N	Y	Y	Y	Y	(a)(ss)	2,500	N	N	N	N	N
Nevada	Comm. on Ethics	Y	Y	N	Y	Y	Y	Y		1,800	N	N	N	N	N
New Hampshire							N.A.								N
New Jersey	Exec. Comm. on Ethical Stds.	Y	Y	N	N	N	N	N	(o)	2,000	N	N	N	Y	N
New Mexico							N.A.								
New York	Buffalo Bd. of Ethics;	Y	Y	N	N	N	N	N		550	Y	Y	N	Y	N
	Dept. of State Cmte. on Open Govt.;	N	Y	N	N	N	N	N		N.A.	N	Y	N	Y	N
	NYC Conflicts of Interest Bd.;	Y	Y	N	N	N	N	N	(c)(dd)	13,000	Y	N	N	Y	N
	State Ethics Comm.;	Y	Y	N	Y	N	Y	N	(p)	18,000	Y	Y	N	Y	N
	Temp. State Comm. on Lobbying;	Y	N	N	N	Y	N	N	(ee)	apx. 20,000	N	Y	Y	Y	N
	Suffolk Co. Camp. Finance Bd.	N	N	N	Y	Y	N	N	(b)(tt)	200	N	N	Y	Y	N
North Carolina							N.A.								N
North Dakota	Bd. of Ethics	Y	Y	N	N	Y	N	N	(q)	2500+	N	Y	N	Y	N
Ohio	Ethics Comm.;	Y	Y	N	N	N	N	Y	(a)(r)	10,500	N	N	N	Y	N
	Legisltv. Insp. Gen. Ofc.	N	N	N	Y	Y	N	N	(s)	343	N	N	N	Y	N
Oklahoma	Ethics Comm.	Y	Y	Y	Y	Y	Y	Y	(b)(ff)	6,000	Y	Y	N	Y	N
Oregon	Govt. Standards & Practices Comm.	Y	Y	Y	Y	Y	Y	Y	(b)(d)(uu)	4,200	Y	N	N	Y	N
Pennsylvania	Ethics Comm.	Y	Y	N	Y	Y	Y	Y	(a)(hh)	150,000	Y	Y	Y	Y	N
Rhode Island	Ethics Comm.	Y	Y	Y	Y	Y	Y	Y	(c)	6,500	Y	Y	Y	N	N
South Carolina	House Legisltv. Ethics Cmte.	N	N	Y	Y	Y	Y	N		800	Y	Y	N	Y	N
South Dakota							N.A.								
Tennessee							N.A.								
Texas	Ethics Comm.;	Y	Y	N	Y	Y	Y	Y	(ii)	2,500	Y	Y	N	N	N
	San Antonio City Attorney's Ofc.	N	Y	N	N	N	N	N	(c)(vv)	700	Y	Y	N	N	Y
Utah	State Elections Ofc.	N	N	N	Y	Y	Y	Y	(jj)	3,500	Y	Y	Y	Y	N
Vermont	Ofc. of the Treasurer	N	N	N	N	N	N	N		N.A.	Y	Y	N	N	N
Virginia	State Bd. of Elections	N	N	N	N	N	N	N		N.A.	Y	Y	N	N	N
Washington	Seattle Ethics & Elections Comm.;	Y	Y	N	N	N	N	N	(c)(xx)	1,964	N	Y	N	Y	N
	King Co. Bd. of Ethics;	Y	Y	N	N	N	N	N	(b)(t)	apx. 2,400	Y	Y	N	Y	N
	King Co. Ofc. of Citizen Complaints;	N	N	N	N	N	N	N		N.A.	Y	Y	N	N	N
	State Exec. Ethics Bd.;	N	N	N	N	N	N	N	(g)	N.A.	Y	Y	N	N	N
	State Legisltv. Ethics Bd.;	N	Y	N	Y	Y	N	N		N.A.	N	N	N	N	N
	State Public Discl. Bd.	Y	Y	Y	Y	Y	Y	Y	(a)	6,500-8,500	Y	Y	N	Y	N
West Virginia	Ethics Comm.	Y	Y	Y	Y	Y	Y	Y	(b)	2,600	N	N	N	N	N
Wisconsin	Ethics Bd.	N	Y	Y	Y	Y	Y	Y	(ww)	2,400	N	N	N	Y	Y
Wyoming							N.A.								
Guam	Ethics Comm.	N	N	N	N	N	N	N		N.A.	Y	Y	N	N	N
Puerto Rico	Ethics Comm.	N	Y	Y	Y	Y	Y	N	(d)(yy)	9,500	Y	Y	N	Y	N
U.S. Virgin Islands	Dept. of Justice	N	N	N	N	N	N	N		N.A.	N	N	N	N	N

See footnotes at end of table.

ETHICS AGENCIES: PERSONAL FINANCIAL DISCLOSURE STATEMENTS — Continued

Source: The Council on Governmental Ethics Laws, *2003 Ethics Update.*

Key:
Y - Yes
N - No
N.A. - Not available

(a) City and county elected officials and candidates.

(b) County elected officials and candidates.

(c) City elected officials and candidates.

(d) City elected officials.

(e) City and county office candidates.

(f) Disclosures are filed with Secretary of State. Ballot and legislative question committees make their filings with the commission.

(g) Financial statements to be filed with Public Disclosure Commission, not ethics board.

(h) Certain other employees.

(i) Senior employees; Quasi-Public Agency members and senior employees.

(j) Division directors and their equivalents.

(k) Local officers and employees file with the supervisor of elections of the county in which they reside. Candidates file with the officer before whom they qualify.

(l) Aldermen must file with the city clerk. All city employees whose annual compensation rate is at or above an amount specified by the Board each year must file with the Board.

(m) Some political subdivisions have established their own method of disclosing conflicts of interest and therefore their candidates for office are not required to file the disclosure statement.

(n) City elected officials and candidates for same file if city falls within a certain population category. Members of certain boards file if duties fall within statutory criteria.

(o) Executive branch employees from assistant division director up; casino and gaming employees.

(p) Certain political party chairs, candidates for statewide elected office.

(q) High level appointees and employees in the executive branch of state government, including gubernatorial appointees to non-advisory boards/commissions. By invitation, employees and appointees as designated by the nine elected heads of the Council of State agencies, the Board of Governors of the 16-campus University system, the president pro tempore of the Senate and the Speaker of the House of Representatives.

(r) School board treasurers, superintendents and business managers. High-ranking state employees. Public university and college presidents must file.

(s) High ranking legislative employees are also required to file. Also accept filings by other legislative employees as "voluntary filers."

(t) Local officials, candidates.

(u) State Board & Authority members, not Commission members. Do not file directly with agency; reports are filed with filing offices.

(v) City and county appointed officers and employees.

(w) County employees.

(y) Designated state and county employees in policy-making positions.

(z) Persons making independent expenditures exceeding $530.

(aa) Other employees designated in the agency Conflict of Interest Code.

(bb) Filings made with the city clerk.

(cc) Any state employee designated by an agency head who is in a major policy making position, responsible for contracting, purchasing or procurement, responsible for writing or drafting specifications for contracts, responsible for awarding grants, benefits or subsidies, or responsible for inspecting, licensing or regulating any person or entity.

(dd) Deputy and assistant agency heads, managers, annual salary over $83,500; employees involved in negotiating, authorizing or approving contracts, leases, franchises, revocable consents or land use applications; compensated board and commission members. Pursuant to legislative change, effective Jan. 1, 2004, salary threshold will be eliminated as a criterion for filing, replaced by "policymakers," and low level managers will no longer be required to file.

(ee) Lobbyists and clients.

(ff) Employees of state educational institutions who make policy or spending decisions.

(gg) City and county elected officials.

(hh) Disclosure requirements also apply to many local and state employees.

(ii) State political chairs.

(jj) Political action committees, political issues committees, political parties, corporations.

(kk) Employees who are designated in the Campaign and Governmental Conduct Code file Statements of Economic Interests with their department heads.

(ll) This is campaign disclosure, not personal financial disclosure. Reports are scanned upon receipt and available for viewing on the internet. The information is also entered into a database and available to review/search on the Internet. Desk audits are made on each report.

(mm) In an election year.

(nn) State procurement officers.

(oo) Major management personnel of Legislative Research Commission.

(pp) "Designated employees," those who are in supervisory or managerial roles or who are authorized to obligate MTA funds.

(qq) Lobbyists, in accordance with La R.S. 24:50 et seq.

(rr) All state employees who are determined by the State Ethics Commission to be "public officials," or who have procurement responsibilities for contracts in excess of $10,000 per year must file financial disclosure statements.

(ss) The 2003 Legislature passed significant changes to the financial disclosure statutes. The changes include: the secretary of state is now responsible for accepting financial disclosure statement filings of elected public officers and candidates; the annual filing date is now Jan. 15; creation of a new sections within the Ethics in Government Law regarding new filing requirements for both appointed and elected public officers.

(tt) Political committees (including PACs) which support candidates for non-judicial county elected offices.

(uu) City and county chief executive officers; designated state agency directors and superintendents and business managers of pubic school districts.

(vv) Executive level employees also file financial disclosure, e.g. the city manager and the assistant city managers; assistant department heads; members of police and fire departments involved in procurements; the city clerk; all executive secretaries. Also, "specified employees," i.e. higher-level employees who are not on executive staff file a shorter financial disclosure form reporting gifts.

(ww) Key administrators of state agencies, including the technical college and university systems.

(xx) City employees that fit criteria for filing.

(yy) High level position public servants, purchase officials and bid board members.

Table 6.13
ETHICS AGENCIES: GENERAL INFORMATION

State or other jurisdiction	Agency	Agency head	Agency telephone	Web site	Contact e-mail	Number of employees	Number on board	Current annual budget
Alabama	Ethics Comm.	James L. Sumner Jr.	(334) 242-2997	www.ethics.alalinc.net	ethics@alalinc.net	15	5	$1,024,000
Alaska	Legislative Ethics Cmte.	Joyce Anderson	(907) 269-0150	www.legis.state.ak.us	ethics_committee@legis.state.ak.us	1	9	121,700
	Public Offices Comm.	Brooke Miles	(907) 276-4176	www.state.ak.us/apoc	brooke_miles@admin.state.ak.us	11	5	752,600
Arizona	Citizens Clean Elections Comm.	Colleen Connor	(602) 364-3477	www.ccec.state.az.us	colleen.connor@ccec.state.az.us	8	5	9,000,000
Arkansas	Ethics Comm.	Graham Sloan	(501) 324-9600	www.arkansasethics.com	graham.sloan@mail.state.ar.us	9	5	582,509
California	Fair Political Practices Comm.;	Jon Matthews	(916) 322-5660	www.fppc.ca.gov	jmatthews@fppc.ca.gov	69	5	6,500,000
	L.A. Co. Metro. Trans. Authority;	Karen Gorman	(213) 922-2975	www.mta.net	gormank@mta.net		13	3,200,000,000 (a)
	L.A. Ethics Comm.;	LeeAnn Pelham	(213) 978-1960	ethics.lacity.org	lpelham@ethics.lacity.org	24	5	2,100,000
	Oakland Public Ethics Comm.;	Daniel Purnell	(510) 238-3593		dpurnell@oaklandnet.com	2	7	220,000
	San Diego Ethics Comm.;	Charles B. Walker	(619) 533-3476	www.sandiego.gov/ethics	cbwalker@sandiego.gov	3	7	398,189
	San Francisco Ethics Comm.;	Ginny Vida	(415) 581-2300	www.sfgov.org/ethics	ginny.vida@sfgov.org	10	7	909,518
	Senate Cmte. on Legisltv. Ethics	Ann Bailey	(916) 324-6929		ann.bailey@sen.ca.gov	5	5	
Colorado	Denver Bd. of Ethics	Michael Henry	(720) 865-8412	www.denvergov.org/ethics	michael.henry@ci.denver.co.us	1	7	96,000 (b)
Connecticut	Freedom of Info. Comm.;	Mitchell W. Pearlman	(860) 566-5682	www.state.ct.us/foi	foi@po.state.ct.us	16	5	1,108,379
	State Ethics Comm.	Alan S. Plofsky	(860) 566-4472	www.ethics.state.ct.us	cindy.cannata@po.state.ct.us	7	7	690,000
Delaware	New Castle Co. Ethics Comm.	Loren Grober	(302) 575-0919	www.co.new-castle.de.us	ethics@co.new-castle.de.us			164,100
	Public Integrity Comm.	Janet Wright	(302) 739-2399	www.state.de.us/pic	jwright@state.de.us	2	7	75,000
Florida	City of Jacksonville;	Carla Miller	(904) 630-1836	www.coj.net	carla@millerandskinner.com	1	9	2,087,352
	Comm. on Ethics;	Bonnie Williams	(850) 488-7864	www.ethics.state.fl.us	williams.bonnie@leg.state.fl.us	23	9	1,168,507
	Elections Comm.;	Barbara Linthicum	(850) 922-4539	www.fec.state.fl.us	barbara_linthicum@oag.state.fl.us	13	9	
	Miami-Dade Comm. On Ethics & Public Trust	Robert Meyers	(305) 579-2594		rmeyers@miamidade.gov			
Georgia	State Ethics Comm.	Theodore Lee	(770) 920-4385	www.ethics.state.ga.us	ethics@ethics.state.ga.us	10	5	779,232
Hawaii	Campaign Spending Comm.;	Bob Watada	(808) 586-0285	www.hawaii.gov/campaign	bob@csc.state.hi.us	5	5	450,000
	Honolulu Ethics Comm.;	Charles W. Totto	(808) 527-5573	www.co.honolulu.hi/us/ethics	ctotto@co.honolulu.hi.us	2.5	7	152,000
	State Ethics Comm.	Daniel J. Mollway	(808) 587-0460	www.state.hi.us/ethics	ethics@hawaiiethics.org	10	5	717,900
Idaho	Secretary of State	Pete T. Cenarrusa	(208) 334-2852	www.idsos.state.id.us	elections@idsos.state.id.us			90,000 (approx.)
Illinois	Chicago Bd. of Ethics;	Dorothy J. Eng	(312) 744-9660	www.cityofchicago.org/Ethics	deng@cityofchicago.org	10	7	620,000
	City of Champaign	Frederick Stavins	(217) 351-4471		stavins@ci.champaign.il.us			
Indiana	Public Access Counselor's Ofc.;	Anne O'Connor	(317) 234-0906	www.state.in.us/pac	aoconnor@icpr.state.in.us	5	5	152,213
	State Ethics Comm.	Timothy McClure	(317) 232-3850	www.in.gov/ethics	tmcclure@ethics.state.in.us	6	6	255,000
Iowa	Ethics & Campaign Discl. Bd.	W. Charles Smithson	(515) 281-3489	www.iowa.gov/ethics	charlie.smithson@iowa.gov	6	6	423,000
Kansas	Govtl. Ethics Comm.	Carol E. Williams	(785) 296-4219	www.accessKansas.org/ethics	ethics@cjnetworks.com	9	9	558,660
Kentucky	Exec. Branch Ethics Comm.;	Jill LeMaster	(502) 564-7954	ethics.ky.gov/	jill.lemaster@mail.state.ky.us	5	5	328,500
	Legislv. Ethics Comm.	Anthony Wilhoit	(502) 573-2863	www.lrc.state.ky.us/otherweb/ethics/ethics.htm	tony.wilhoit@lrc.state.ky.us	5	9	500,000
Louisiana	Bd. of Ethics;	R. Gray Sexton	(225) 763-8777	www.ethics.state.la.us	grays@ethics.state.la.us	20	11	1,530,782
	Ethics Admin.	Maris LeBlanc	(225) 763-8777 or (800) 842-6630	www.ethics.state.la.us	marism@ethics.state.la.us			
Maine	Comm. on Govtl. Ethics & Election Practices	William Hain	(207) 287-4179	www.state.me.us/ethics	bill.hain@state.me.us	6	5	394,000
Maryland	Anne Arundel Co. Ethics Comm.;	Betsy Dawson	(410) 222-4412	www.erols.com/wb3v/aaethics	bdawson2002@earthlink.net	2	7	143,200
	Montgomery Co. Ethics Comm.;	Barbara McNally	(240) 777-6670	www.montgomerycountymd.gov/mcnalb@co.mo.md.us		2	5	190,000
	State Ethics Comm.	Suzanne S. Fox	(410) 974-2068	ethics.gov.state.md.us	sfox@gov.state.md.us	8.5	5	660,227
Massachusetts	Ethics Comm.	Peter Sturges	(617) 727-0060	www.mass.gov/ethics	psturges@eth.state.ma.us	19		1,265,221

See footnotes at end of table.

ETHICS AGENCIES: GENERAL INFORMATION—Continued

State or other jurisdiction	Agency	Agency head	Agency telephone	Web site	Contact e-mail	Number of employees	Number on board	Current annual budget
Michigan	Dept. of State;	Glorietta Flakes	(517) 373-2540	www.michigan.gov/sos	flakesg@michigan.gov	1		5,000
	State Bd. of Ethics	Janet McClelland	(517) 373-3644	www.michigan.gov/mdcs	ethicsboard@state.mi.us	9	6	690,000
Minnesota	Camp. Finance & Public Discl. Bd.	Jeanne Olson	(651) 296-1721	www.cfboard.state.mn.us	jeanne.olson@state.mn.us	8	8	500,000
Mississippi	Ethics Comm.	Ronald E. Crowe	(601) 359-1285	www.ethics.state.ms.us	rcrowe@ethics.state.ms.us	8	6	1,385,000
Missouri	Ethics Comm.	Robert F. Connor	(800) 392-8660	www.moethics.state.mo.us	rconnor@mail.state.mo.us	21	6	
Montana	Comm. of Political Practices	Linda L. Vaughey	(406) 444-4622	www.state.mt.us/cpp	lvaughey@state.mt.us	4	1	315,000
Nebraska	Accountability & Discl. Comm.	Frank Daley	(402) 471-2522	nadc.nol.org	fdaley@mail.state.ne.us	8	9	470,245
Nevada	Comm. on Ethics	Stacy M. Jennings	(775) 687-5469	ethics.state.nv.us	sjennings@ethics.state.nv.us	3	8	362,000
New Hampshire				— N.A. —				
New Jersey	Exec. Comm. on Ethical Stds.	Rita L. Strmensky	(609) 292-1892	www.state.nj.us/lps/ethics	ethics@eces.state.nj.us	9	9	590,000
New Mexico	Sec. of State, Bureau of Elec. & Ethics Admin.	Denise Lamb	(505) 827-3600		denise.lamb@state.nm.us			
New York	Buffalo Bd. of Ethics;	Charles Michaux	(716) 851-5432		cmichaux@ch.ci.buffalo.ny.us; 7			
	Dept. of State Cmte. on Open Govt.;	Robert J. Freeman	(518) 474-2518	www.dos.state.ny.us	rfreeman@dos.state.ny.us	4	11	300,000 (approx.)
	NYC Conflicts of Interest Bd.;	Mark Davies	(212) 442-1424	nyc.gov/ethics	davies@coib.nyc.gov	19	5	1,499,752 (c)
	State Ethics Comm.;	Karl J. Sleight	(518) 432-8207	www.nysethics.com	ethics@dos.state.ny.us	20	5	1,500,000
	Suffolk Co. Camp. Finance Bd.;	Lee Lutz	(631) 853-5078	www.co.suffolk.ny.us/webtemp3.cfm?dept=38&ID=1156	Lee.Lutz@co.suffolk.ny.us	1	5	125,000
	Temp. State Comm. on Lobbying	David M. Grandeau	(518) 474-7126	www.state.ny.us/lobby	lobcom@emi.com	18	6	
North Carolina	Bd. of Ethics	Perry Y. Newson	(919) 733-2780	www.doa.state.nc.us/doa/ethics/	perry.newson@ncmail.net	2	7	207,000
North Dakota				— N.A. —				
Ohio	Ethics Comm.;	David Freel	(614) 466-7090	www.ethics.state.oh.us	david.freel@ethics.state.oh.us	19	6	1,600,000
	Legisltv. Inspctr. Gen. Ofc.	Tony Bledsoe	(614) 728-5100	www.jlec-olig.state.oh.us	tbledsoe@jlec-olig.state.oh.us	6	12	620,000
Oklahoma	Ethics Comm.	Marilyn Hughes	(405) 521-3451	www.state.ok.us/~ethics	mhughes@mhs.oklaosf.state.ok.us	7	5	524,409
Oregon	Govt. Standards & Practices Comm.	Patrick Hearn	(503) 378-5105	www.gspc.state.or.us	pat.hearn@state.or.us	3	7	291,000
Pennsylvania	Ethics Comm.	John J. Contino	(717) 783-1610	www.ethics.state.pa.us	jcontino@state.pa.us	21	7	1,761,000
Rhode Island	Ethics Comm.	Kent A. Willever	(401) 222-3790	www.ethics.state.ri.us/	ethics@ethics.state.ri.us	9	9	942,594
South Carolina	House Legisltv. Ethics Cmte.	Rep. Becky Richardson	(803) 734-3114	het@scstatehouse.net	het@scstatehouse.net; 2	6		
South Dakota				— N.A. —				
Tennessee				— N.A. —				
Texas	Ethics Comm.;	Tom Harrison	(800) 325-8506	www.ethics.state.tx.us	tom.harrison@ethics.state.tx.us	35	8	2,000,000
	San Antonio City Attorney's Ofc.	Andrew Martin	(210) 207-8940	www.sanantonio.gov/atty/	helenv@sanantonio.gov	87	11	14,000
Utah	State Elections Ofc.	Amy Naccarato	(801) 538-1041	www.elections.utah.gov	anaccarato@utah.gov	5		700,000
Vermont	Ofc. of the Treasurer	Jeb Spaulding	(802) 828-2301	www.state.vt.us/treasurer	jspaulding@tre.state.vt.us	33		
Virginia	State Bd. of Elections	Cameron Quinn	(804) 786-6551	www.sbe.state.va.us	cquinn@sbe.state.va.us	27	3	10,000,000
Washington	Seattle Ethics & Elections Comm.;	Terry Thomas	(206) 684-8500	www.ci.seattle.wa.us/ethics	ethicsandelections@seattle.gov	6	7	450,000
	King Co. Bd. of Ethics;	Catherine A. Clemens	(206) 296-1586	www.metrokc.gov/ethics/	board.ethics@metrokc.gov	1	5	113,484
	King Co. Ofc. of Citizen Complaints;	Duncan Fowler	(206) 296-3452	www.metrokc.gov/ombuds/	duncan.fowler@metrokc.gov	9		750,000
	State Exec. Ethics Bd.;	Barrie Althoff	(360) 753-4585	www.cjc.state.wa.us	balthoff@cjc.state.wa.us	7	22	912,000
	State Legisltv. Ethics Bd.;	Brian Malarky	(360) 664-0871	www.wa.gov/ethics	brianm2@atg.wa.gov	3	5	350,000
		Mike O'Connell	(360) 786-7540	www.leg.wa.gov/common/ethics/default.htm	oconnell_mi@leg.wa.gov	1	9	171,000
	State Public Discl. Comm.	Vicki Rippie	(360) 753-1111	www.pdc.wa.gov	vrippir@pdc.wa.gov	22	5	1,928,273

See footnotes at end of table.

ETHICS AGENCIES: GENERAL INFORMATION—Continued

State or other jurisdiction	Agency	Agency head	Agency telephone	Web site	Contact e-mail	Number of employees	Number on board	Current annual budget
West Virginia	Ethics Comm.	Richard M. Alker	(304) 558-0664	www.state.wv.us/ethics	ralker@gwmail.state.wv.us	3	12	319,000
Wisconsin	Ethics Bd.	Roth Judd	(608) 266-8123	ethics.state.wi.us	roth.judd@ethics.state.wi.us	5.75	6	609,800
Wyoming				—————N.A.—————				
Guam	Ethics Comm.	Madeleine Z. Bordallo	(671) 472-8931-9					
Puerto Rico	Ofc. of Govt. Ethics	Hiram R. Morales-Lugo	(787) 622-0305	www.oegpr.net	ode@oegpr.net	129	0	8,911,000
U.S. Virgin Islands	Dept. of Justice	Paul L. Gimenez	(809) 774-5666	www.usvi.org/justice/index.html	justice@usvi.org			

Source: The Council on Governmental Ethics Laws, *2003 Ethics Update.*

Key:

(a) $800,000 for the Ethics Department.

(b) Reduced in 2004 to $89,000.

(c) FY 2004.

Table 6.14
LOBBYISTS: DEFINITIONS AND PROHIBITED ACTIVITIES

State or other jurisdiction	Definition of a lobbyist includes							Prohibited activities involving lobbyists					
	Legislative lobbying	Administrative agency lobbying	Elective officials as lobbyists	Public employees as lobbyists	Compensation standard	Expenditure standard	Time standard	Making campaign contributions at any time	Making campaign contributions during legislative sessions	Making expenditures in excess of $ per official per year	Solicitation by officials or employees for contributions or gifts	Contingent compensation	Other
Alabama	★	★	…	★	…	★	★	★	★	…	…	★	…
Alaska	★	★	(ee)	(ee)	…	…	★	(x)	★	$250	…	★	★
Arizona	★	★	★	★	★	★	★	★	★	$10	★	★	(bb)
Arkansas	★	★	★	★	★	★	★	…	…	…	…	…	(z)
California	★	★	…	…	★	…	★	…	…	$10/mo.	…	★	(a)
Colorado	★	…	…	★	…	…	…	…	★	…	★	★	…
Connecticut	★	★	…	…	★	★	…	…	★	…	…	★	(d)
Delaware	★	★	…	…	…	…	…	…	…	…	…	★	★
Florida	…	★	…	…	…	…	…	…	…	$100 (dd)	★	★	…
Georgia	★	…	…	★	★	★	…	…	★	…	…	★ (b)	…
Hawaii	★	★	…	…	★	…	★	…	…	…	…	★	…
Idaho	★	…	★	…	★	…	…	…	…	…	★	★	…
Illinois	★	★	…	★	★	…	…	…	…	…	…	…	…
Indiana	★	…	…	…	★	★	…	…	★	…	…	★	(ff)
Iowa	★	★	★	★	★	★	…	★	★	★	★	★	…
Kansas	★	★	…	…	…	★	★	…	★	(c)	★	★	…
Kentucky	★	★ (j)	…	…	…	…	…	★	…	$100 (e)	★	★	…
Louisiana	★	…	…	…	★	★	★	…	★ (k)	…	…	…	…
Maine	★	(m)	…	…	★	★	…	…	★	…	★	★	…
Maryland	★	★	…	…	★	★	…	…	★	…	…	★	(n)
Massachusetts	★	★	…	★	★	★	★	…	…	…	★	★	…
Michigan (f)	★	★	…	★	★	★	★	…	…	(d)	(d)	★	(o)
Minnesota	★	★	…	★	★	★	…	…	★	…	…	★	…
Mississippi	★	★	…	★	★	★	★	…	…	…	…	★	…
Missouri	★	★	★	★	★	★	★	…	…	…	…	…	(p)
Montana	★	…	…	…	★	★	…	…	…	…	…	…	…
Nebraska	★	…	…	…	…	…	…	…	…	…	★ (q)	★	…
Nevada	★	…	…	★	…	…	…	…	★ (g)	…	★	★	…
New Hampshire	★	…	…	…	★	…	…	…	…	…	…	…	…
New Jersey	★	★	…	…	★	★	★	…	…	…	…	…	…
New Mexico	★	★	…	…	…	…	…	…	★	…	…	★	★
New York	★	★	…	…	★	★	…	…	…	$75	…	★	…
North Carolina	★	…	…	(r)	…	…	…	…	★	…	…	★	…
North Dakota	★	…	…	…	…	★	…	…	…	…	…	…	…
Ohio	★	★	…	★	★	…	…	…	…	$75	★	★	(t)
Oklahoma	★	(y)	…	…	…	…	…	…	…	$300	★ (h)	…	…
Oregon	★	…	…	★	…	★	★	…	…	$100 (u)	…	★	…
Pennsylvania	★	★	…	…	★	…	…	…	…	…	…	★	★
Rhode Island	★	…	…	★	…	★	…	…	…	…	…	★	…
South Carolina	★	★	…	★	…	★	…	★	…	$0	★	★	…
South Dakota	★	…	★	★	…	…	…	…	…	…	…	…	(cc)
Tennessee	★	★	…	…	…	…	…	…	★	…	★	…	…
Texas	★	★	…	…	★	★	★	…	★	(v)	…	★	(w)
Utah	★	★	…	…	★	★	…	…	★	…	…	★	(aa)
Vermont	★	★	…	…	…	★	…	…	★	…	…	★	…
Virginia	★	(i)	…	★	…	…	★	…	…	…	★	★	…
Washington	★	★	…	★	…	…	…	…	★	…	…	★	★
West Virginia	★	★	…	…	…	…	…	…	…	$25	★	…	(l)
Wisconsin	★	★	…	★	★	★	★	…	…	$0	★	★	…
Wyoming	★	…	★	…	★	★	…	…	…	…	…	…	(s)
Dist. of Columbia	★	★	…	…	★	★	★	…	…	$100	…	…	…

See footnotes at end of table.

LOBBYISTS: DEFINITIONS AND PROHIBITED ACTIVITIES — Continued

Sources: The Council of State Governments' survey, October 2003; The Council on Governmental Ethics Laws, *Lobbying: 2003 Update* and state statutes and rules books, February 2004.

Key:

★ — Application exists.

. . . — Not applicable.

(a) Making campaign contributions if the lobbyist's firm/employer is registered to lobby the agency of the candidate/officeholder.

(b) Not specific to lobbyists.

(c) Gift limit is $40 per calendar year, recreation limit is $100 per calendar year and honoraria is a maximum of $200 per speech.

(d) Lobbyists making gifts in excess of the following thresholds to state officials: Connecticut, $10 for gifts per year, $50 for food and drink per year; Michigan, $49 per month per official. Food and beverage for immediate consumption is reportable but not limited.

(e) Food and beverages for legislator, spouse and immediate family.

(f) The Michigan Lobby Act uses the term "lobbyist agent" to define an individual or firm compensated more than $500.00 to lobby on behalf of clients or employers. The term "lobbyist" is defined under the act as the interest group or other person that makes expenditure in excess of $500.00 to lobby a single public official or in excess of $1,975.00 to lobby any number of public officials. These thresholds are for the 2004 calendar year.

(g) Also applies to one month prior to and one month after session.

(h) By regulatory agency which sets rates, charges, fees or prices.

(i) "Administrative" does not have to register or report as long as they are lobbying in an official capacity.

(j) Lobbying definition includes governor, lt. governor, constitutional officers, secretary of the cabinets and staff.

(k) No lobbyist on behalf of himself or his principal, shall offer or provide to a legislator or his principal campaign committee any campaign contribution or loan resulting from a fundraising event held during a legislative session unless written notice of the fundraising function was given to the Board of Ethics at least 30 days prior to the function.

(l) Food and beverage expenditures, no limit, not included in the $25 prohibition.

(m) Adoptions of regulations and executive orders.

(n) Lobbyist cannot solicit or transmit political contributions on behalf of members or candidates for the General Assembly or the four statewide Executive Offices.

(o) State senators or representatives may not lobby for balance of term when they resign from office. This prohibition does not apply to other public officials.

(p) Employment of non-registered lobbyists.

(q) Gifts valued at more than $50 in a calendar month.

(r) State government agency liaisons lobbying on issues concerning their agency (no fee).

(s) Must itemize items of $50.00 or more.

(t) Campaign contributions/expenditures are specifically exempted from Ohio's lobbying laws.

(u) No limit on food and beverage consumed in presence of purchaser or provider; entertainment, such as NBA games, etc, is $100 per occasion or $250 per calendar year.

(v) Expenditures in excess of $500 for entertainment, $500 for gifts and $500 for an award momento per year.

(w) False communications, admission to floor of legislature, offering a loan, a gift of cash or negotiable instrument, an expenditure for transportation and lodging except for fact finding trips and a conference in which the member renders service.

(x) Alaska law prohibits lobbyists from giving campaign contributions to candidates for the legislature other than to the candidate(s) that are campaigning to represent the district in which the lobbyist is registered to vote.

(y) The office of the Governor and the Corporation Commission are the only two executive branch agencies/offices included in the definition of lobbying.

(z) Covered in Senate and House Rules.

(aa) Making contributions to a governor or governor's PAC during a legislative session or during the period for veto overrides.

(bb) Entertainment Ban 41-1232.08.

(cc) All costs incurred for the purpose of influencing legislation. However personal expenses of the lobbyist spent on his own meals, travel, lodging or phone while in attendance as the legislative session not be reported.

(dd) Amount is per occurrence

(ee) Specifically exempted

(ff) Having a prior felony for unlawful lobbying.

Table 6.15
LOBBYISTS: REGISTRATION AND REPORTING

State or other jurisdiction	Agency which administers registration and reports requirements for lobbyists	Frequency	Legislation/administrative action seeking to influence	Expenditures benefiting public officials or employees	Compensation received [broken down by employer(s)]	Total compensations received	Categories of expenditures	Total expenditures	Contributions received from others for lobbying purposes	Other	Number of registered lobbyists
Alabama	Ethics Comm.	Quarterly	★	...	...	...	...	...	...	...	585
Alaska	Public Offices Comm.	Monthly (b)	★	★	★	★	★	★	...	★ (pp)	211
Arizona	Secretary of State	Quarterly and Semi-annually	★	★	★	★	★	★	★	...	3,413
Arkansas	Ethics Comm.	Quarterly and Annually (jj)	★	★	...	...	★	★	★	...	302
California	Fair Political Practices Comm. Secretary of State	Quarterly Reporting Bi-annual Registration	★	★	★	★	★	★	★	(e)	1,098
Colorado	Secretary of State	Monthly	★	★	★	★	★	★	★	...	550
Connecticut	State Ethics Comm.	Biennially, Monthly (b)	★	★	★	★	★	★	★(d)	...	4,000
Delaware	Public Integrity Comm.	Quarterly	★	★	...	...	★	★	...	...	236
Florida	Executive Branch Lobbyist Registration Office	Semi-annually	...	★	...	...	★	...	...	...	1,302
Georgia	Ethics Comm.	Annually and monthly (h)	...	★	...	...	...	...	...	(qq)	1,400
Hawaii	State Ethics Comm.	Jan., March, May (o)	★(i)	★	★	★	★	★	★	...	250
Idaho	Secretary of State	Monthly (a) and annually	★	★	...	...	★	★	...	...	358
Illinois	Secretary of State	Semi-annually and annually	...	★	...	...	★	★	...	(j)	2,824
Indiana	Lobby Registration Comm.	Semi-annually	★	★	...	...	★	★	...	(k)	1,400
Iowa	Secretary of Senate, Clerk of House Ethics and Disclosure Board	Monthly (b) Quarterly	★	...	★	★	...	★	★	(p)	500
Kansas	Ethics Comm.	(m)	★	★	...	...	★	★	...	...	579
Kentucky	Legislative Ethics Comm.	(n)	★	★	★	★	★	★	★	...	650
Louisiana	Board of Ethics	Annually and semi-annually (u)	...	★	...	...	★	★	...	...	518
Maine	Comm. on Gov't'l. Ethics	Monthly (a) and after session	★	★	★	★	★	★	★	...	400
Maryland	Ethics Comm.	Semi-annually and annually	★	★	★	★	★	★	(q)	...	723
Massachusetts	Secretary of Commonwealth Public Records Division Lobbyist Section	Semi-annually	★	★	★	★	★	★	...	(w)	640
Michigan	Department of State Bureau of Elections	Semi-annually	★	★(r)	...	...	★	★	...	(s)	2,398
Minnesota	Campaign Finance & Public Disclosure Board	Semi-annually	★	★(t)	...	...	★	★	★	...	1,200
Mississippi	Secretary of State	Annually and 2 times per session	★	★	★	★	...	★	...	...	336
Missouri	Ethics Comm.	Semi-annually and annually (a)	★	★	...	...	★	★	...	(q)(v)	997
Montana	Commr. of Political Practices	Annually (non-session) Monthly (during session)	★	★	...	...	★	★	★	...	1,074
Nebraska	Clerk of Legislature	Quarterly	★	★	★	★	★	★	★	...	308
Nevada	Legislative Counsel Bureau	(x)	...	★	...	...	★	...	...	...	842
New Hampshire	Secretary of State	Three reports per year	...	★(ll)	★	★	...	★	...	(mm)	546
New Jersey	Election Law Enforcement Comm.	Annually and quarterly	★	★	★	★	★	★	...	...	564
New Mexico	Secretary of State	Before, during & after session	★	★	...	...	★	★	★	...	1,000
New York	NYTS Commission on Lobbying	Bi-monthly and semi-annually	★	★	★	★	★	★	...	...	3,412
North Carolina	Secretary of State	After session and year end	...	...	(y)	...	★	...	...	...	548
North Dakota	Secretary of State	Annually	...	...	...	...	...	★	...	...	634
Ohio	Office of the Legislative Inspector General	(kk)	★	★	...	...	★	★	...	...	1,467
Oklahoma	Ethics Comm.	Semi-annually	...	★	...	...	...	...	...	...	372
Oregon	Gov't Standards & Practices Comm.	(cc)	★(i)	★	...	...	★	★	...	(oo)	576
Pennsylvania	State Ethics Comm.	Quarterly and upon termination	★	★	★(ii)	★(ii)	★(jj)	★	...	★(ee)	747
Rhode Island	Secretary of State	(dd)	★	★	★	★	★	★	...	...	300
South Carolina	Ethics Comm.	Semi-annually	★	...	★	★	★	★	...	...	350
South Dakota	Secretary of State	Annually	★	...	...	...	...	★	...	...	532
Tennessee	Registry of Election Finance	Semi-annually	...	...	...	...	...	...	...	★(rr)	450

See footnotes at end of table.

LOBBYISTS: REGISTRATION AND REPORTING — Continued

State or other jurisdiction	Agency which administers registration and reports requirements for lobbyists	Frequency	Legislation/administrative action seeking to influence	Expenditures benefiting public officials or employees	Compensation received [broken down by employer(s)]	Total compensations received	Categories of expenditures	Total expenditures	Contributions received from others for lobbying purposes	Other	Number of registered lobbyists
Texas	Ethics Comm.	Monthly and annually (z)	★	★	★	...	★	★	...	...	1,681
Utah	State Elections Office	Annually (ff)	★	★	...	...	★	★	...	...	433
Vermont	Secretary of State	3 times per year	...	★	★	★	...	★	★	...	350
Virginia	Secretary of Commonwealth	Annually	★	★	(aa)	★	★	★	...	★	900
Washington	Public Disclosure Comm.	Monthly (nn)	...	★	★	★	★	★	★	...	832
West Virginia	Ethics Comm.	Every two years	★	★	...	...	★	★	...	(bb)	350
Wisconsin	Ethics Board	Biennially and Semi-annually	★	(gg)	★	★	...	★	★	...	775
	Secretary of State	Annually	...	...	...	...	★	★	...	...	87
Dist. of Columbia	Office of Campaign Finance	Biennially	★	★	★	★	★	★	★	...	214

Sources: The Council of State Governments' survey, October 2003; The Council on Governmental Ethics Laws, *Lobbying: 2003 Update* and state statutes and rules books, February 2004.

Key:

★—Application exists.

. . .—Not applicable.

(a) During legislative session. In Missouri, filed with the secretary of Senate and clerk of the House.

(b) During legislative session, quarterly thereafter.

(c) Must make separate disclosure report.

(d) If formed primarily for lobbying.

(e) These answers apply to reporting requirements, not registration. When registering, firm lists lobbyists, employers, agencies to be lobbied, effective date and length of contract, lobbying interest of each employer. Employer lists each employee lobbyist, firm contracted with, general lobbying interests, agencies to be lobbied and nature and interest of lobbyist employer.

(f) Also, first, second and fourth quarters.

(g) In detail, if over $10 per person.

(h) Registration annually. Monthly reporting during session, end of July and end of December.

(i) Subject areas only.

(j) Required to declare general subject matter of lobbying activity.

(k) Compensation received per employer, and total compensations received along with contributions from other for lobbying purposes is required to disclose compensation paid to others but not compensation received from others.

(l) In the Senate, reports are required only if $15 or more is provided to senators or their staff on any one day.

(m) January, February, March, April, May and September.

(n) Initial registration covers a two-year period. Reporting is monthly January, February, March, April, May, then quarterly.

(o) Register within five days of becoming a lobbyist and renew every odd-numbered year. Reporting three times a year. Reports due January 31, March 31 and May 31.

(p) Campaign contributions to state office candidates.

(q) To a limited extent.

(r) Food and beverage expenditures for public officials with itemization required over $49.99 in a 1 month period or $300 in a calendar year. Travel and lodging expenditures for public officials in excess of $650.00. Group food and beverage expenditures for public officials.

(s) Financial transactions with public officials, immediate family members or their businesses of $1,0000 or more. Name and address of employees—any person compensated or reimbursed for lobbying in excess of $20.00 during any 12 month period.

(t) Not political contributions.

(u) Register annually. Expenditure reports are filed semi-annually. First report is due on August 15th covering the period of January 1st through June 30th. The second report is due on February 15th and covers the period of July 1st through December 31st. The second report is cumulative.

(v) Business relationships with public officials, if over $50

(w) Campaign contributions are reported.

(x) Every other year in odd-number years when legislature is in session.

(y) In North Carolina, the principal shall estimate and report the compensation paid or promised directly or indirectly, to all lobbyists based on estimated time, effort and expense in connection with lobbying activities on behalf of the principal. If a lobbyist is a full-time employee of the principal, or is compensated by means of an annual fee or retainer, the principal shall estimate and report the portion of all such lobbyists' salaries or retainers that compensate the lobbyists for lobbying.

(z) Annually if expenditures are not more than $1,000 during a calendar year.

(aa) In the Commonwealth of Virginia, the lobbyist registers and reports. The employer (principal does not register and/or report).

(bb) No compensation reporting. The registered lobbyist reports expenditures made by the lobbyist or the employer for the lobbying purposes. Principal (employer or organization) represented makes no reports to us.

(cc) Registration is biennially; reporting is twice during non-session years and three times during session years.

(dd) At specified times during legislative session and at end of legislative session.

(ee) Reports required from lobbyist's principal.

(ff) Ten days after the general session, seven days before a general election, and seven days after the end of a special session or veto override session. Registrations expire at the end of even-numbered years.

(gg) Such expenditures are prohibited.

(hh) New York's Lobbying Act of 2000 requires a description of the subject lobbied or expected to be lobbied, as well as listing the legislative bill number and the rule, regulation, and ratemaking number lobbied or expected to be lobbied.

(ii) Must report all contributions to a principal in excess of 10% of principals total resources.

(jj) Reports are filed monthly if the General Assembly is in session.

(kk) Registration for executive agency lobbyists is annual. Registration for legislative lobbyists is every two years coinciding with legislative session. All lobbyists and their employers report three times per calendar year.

(ll) Expenditures benefiting public officials over $50.00.

(mm) General topic for each registration, not specific bills.

(nn) Employer's of lobbyists are required to file an annual report due by February 28th for lobbying expenses incurred during the previous period.

(oo) Expenditures for legislative officials are itemized only if they exceed $70.00 on a single occasion.

(pp) If married to or spousal equivalent of public official or legislative employee, lobbyists may only make contributions to legislative candidates in their voting district. Those contributions must be reported within 30 days.

(qq) General business of party lobbied for, employment provided, members of public officials immediate family must be disclosed.

(rr) Contributions made to candidates.

The California Governor's Recall

By Thad Kousser

California's recall election gave voice to voter dissatisfaction with the state's direction and resulted in a return to the type of moderate Republican governor that had led the state throughout much of the 1980s and 1990s. While exciting, it does not represent a sea change in California politics.

After providing the nation with a summer's worth of amusement, California's recall—which was at once a bold new use of an old Progressive institution, democracy taken to its logical extreme, and the greatest show on earth—turned into a fairly typical two-candidate race for control of the state. The major issues became the incumbent's performance and personality, set against the promises of an unproven but talented outsider to return California to greatness. Just as polls had predicted for months, Democratic Gov. Gray Davis was recalled by a fairly narrow margin in a vote that split mostly along party lines. He was replaced by Republican Arnold Schwarzenegger, who performed better than pundit predictions and nearly captured a majority of the vote in a 135-candidate field.

What sent Davis, whose fellow Democrats hold an eight percentage point edge in party registration[1] and control all seven other statewide political offices, into the record books as only the second American governor ever to be recalled? Clearly, the public's poor review of his record in five years leading California had much to do with his downfall.

A Stanford-educated lawyer and Vietnam War veteran, Davis spent most of his political career trying to find his way into the governor's office. After serving as Gov. Jerry Brown's chief of staff, Davis won a Los Angeles-area state Assembly seat in 1982. Though he did not break into Speaker Willie Brown's powerful inner circle, Davis held his seat until 1986, when he moved up the ladder to be elected the state's controller, and then, in 1994, its lieutenant governor. Davis came from behind in a primary against two self-funded candidates to become the Democratic nominee for governor in 1998. Davis swept to an impressive 58 percent to 38 percent victory over Attorney General Dan Lungren. He succeeded by balancing his pro-choice, environmentalist, and pro-gun control stances with an aggressive emphasis on his tough-on-crime credentials.[2]

Gray Davis' tenure began well enough, with a honeymoon period in which he called a special legislative session to pass a package of education reforms. Quickly, however, his relationship with his natural allies soured. When Davis felt that the Democratically-controlled Legislature was being insufficiently cooperative, he famously announced that the houses were there "to implement my vision."[3] Cruz Bustamante, the independently-elected Democratic lieutenant governor, held a press conference on the capitol steps criticizing Davis for his stance on an immigrant rights lawsuit, and promptly saw his staff lose their parking permits.

Such actions had repercussions for Davis when he ran into his own difficulties. The first obstacle was the state's energy crisis, brought by the delayed implementation of a bill proposed by Republican Gov. Pete Wilson and passed by Democrats in a Legislature that Davis had long since left. Though this was not a problem of his own making, Davis was slow to react and publicly criticized by legislators who would not simply do his bidding. The plan Davis eventually proposed avoided catastrophe, but cost the state billions in long-term energy contracts and drove his job approval ratings from 56 percent to 43 percent in the first half of 2001.[4] Shortly afterward, Davis' prodigious fundraising activities drew scrutiny from the public and from legislators. In particular, his acceptance of a $25,000 donation from the software company Oracle just after it secured a large state contract brought an investigation by the Joint Legislative Audit Committee.

As Davis' 2002 reelection neared, California's fiscal situation—like that of nearly every state—looked worse and worse. For a state that relies heavily on income taxes, the decline in revenues coming from stock options that "dot bombed" was disastrous. Because Davis and the Legislature had committed to expansions in primary education and health care spending during boom years, the bust opened up a large deficit hole. By the November general election, Davis' approval had dropped to 39 percent despite his attempts to downplay the state's fiscal problems. Yet Davis was able to survive because of a strat-

Table A: Final Campaign Contribution Totals: $80 Million for a 77-Day Contest

Candidate	Money raised in each fund	Contribution totals
Gray Davis	$2.37 million, Taxpayers Against the Governor's Recall $14.6 million, Californians Against the Costly Recall of the Governor	$16.97 million
Arnold Schwarzenegger	$18.5 million, Candidacy Fund $3.4 million, Pro-recall Fund	$21.9 million
Cruz Bustamante	$5.7 million, Candidacy Fund $5.54 million, Anti-Prop. 54 Fund $525,773, Anti-recall Fund $667,703, Old Campaign Fund	$12.4 million
Peter V. Ueberroth		$3.95 million
Tom McClintock		$1.67 million
Arianna Huffington		$812,560
Bill Simon Jr.		$588,309
Independent expenditures	$10.1 million by casino-owning tribes $10 million by organized labor $4 million combined by Democratic and Republican Parties	$24.1 million
Overal l Contributions		$82.4 million

Source: Data collected from the California secretary of state and reported in Dan Morain and Joel Rubin, "Financially, the Recall Was Business as Usual," *Los Angeles Times*, October 10, 2003.

egy that he and his canny advisors had pursued in the state's March primary: picking a weak opponent. By spending $10 million of his war chest on advertisements attacking Richard Riordan,[5] the moderate former mayor of Los Angeles, Davis was able to help conservative businessman Bill Simon defeat Riordan for the Republican nomination. Davis narrowly beat Simon in a general election marked by low turnout and much support for minor party candidates.[6] He then turned his attention to the budget deficit, which by May, 2003 grew to $38.2 billion.[7]

Putting the Recall on the Ballot

While Davis and his team congratulated each other on a close victory, Republican strategists quietly discussed the option of a recall. Mark Abernathy, who would later run DavisRecall.com, began discussing the idea with anti-tax activist Ted Costa on November 17, 2002. Convinced that Davis could be defeated if voters had a better option, Abernathy had an Arnold Schwarzenegger candidacy in mind "from day one."[8] California's recall provision places the question of whether to remove a governor on the same ballot as the election of a replacement. Added to the state's constitution in 1911,[9] the recall was part of Gov. Hiram Johnson's triumvirate of Progressive institutions—the initiative, the referendum and the recall.

Article II, Section 13 of the constitution defines the recall simply as "the power of the electors to remove an elective officer," giving no specifics about the conditions in which it should be used. An offense warranting recall in California need not be a high crime or misdemeanor. Instead, it is whatever a number equal to 12 percent of the voters in the last gubernatorial election willing to sign a petition say it is. After the November, 2002 election, this figure was 986,874,[10] which became the goal for Abernathy, Costa, and the other conservative and Republican Party activists who joined them.

Although Davis' approval rating continued to slide down to 25 percent by March 2003, collecting this many signatures was a daunting task. After all, recall petitions have been circulated for every California governor in recent memory, but none in state history had garnered sufficient support to qualify for the ballot. The key to getting an initiative or a recall on California's ballot, at least over the past two decades, is money. Recall activists drew much attention in the spring of 2003 with their public campaign, launched February 5, but it was initially unable to attract significant organizational support or resources. Although outgoing Republican Party Chair Shawn Steel backed the recall, real party powering California resides in legislative leaders. The Senate and

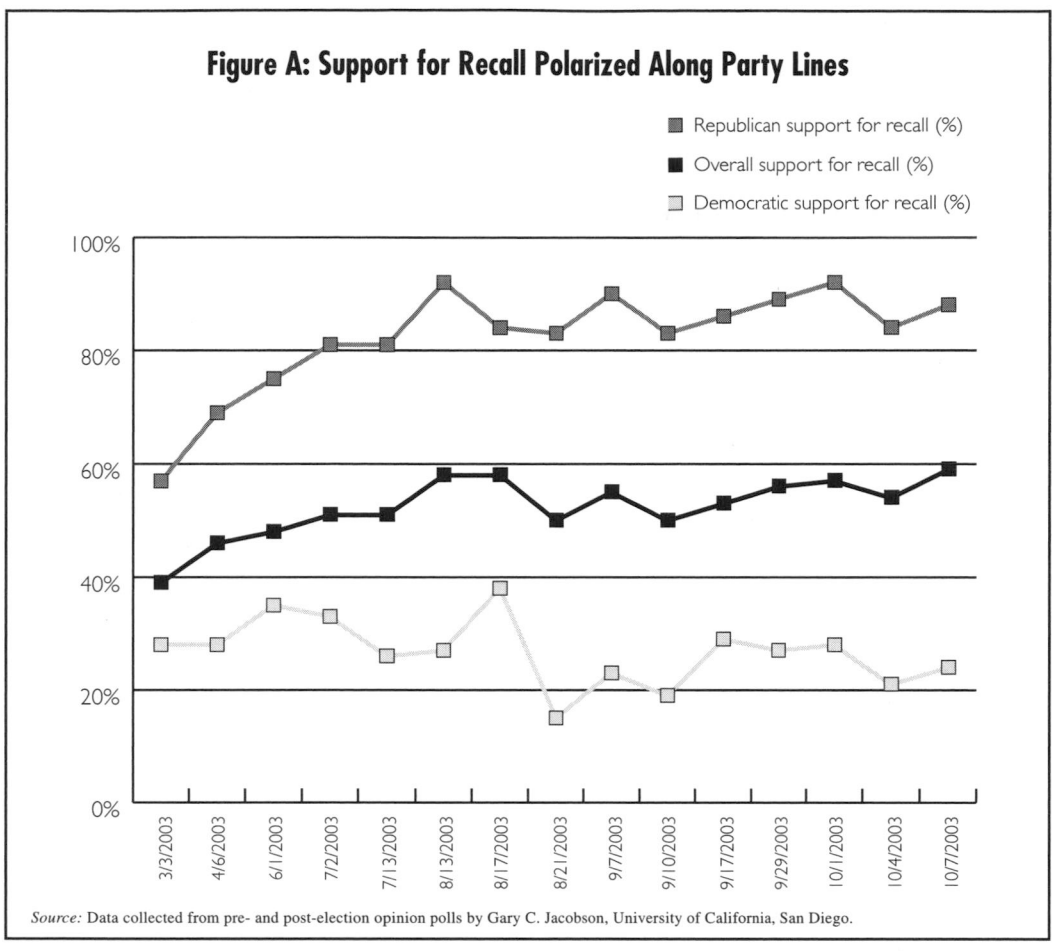

Figure A: Support for Recall Polarized Along Party Lines

■ Republican support for recall (%)

■ Overall support for recall (%)

□ Democratic support for recall (%)

Source: Data collected from pre- and post-election opinion polls by Gary C. Jacobson, University of California, San Diego.

Assembly Minority Leaders, Jim Brulte and Dave Cox, were initially cool to the idea. So were national party leaders. According to "Rescue California" leader David Gilliard, "there was no interest, zero, coming out of the White House." The recall movement had the support of activists and a vulnerable target, it had few potent backers and little money.

That changed when Darrell Issa approached recall leaders. A Republican Congressman from the San Diego area, Issa had built a personal fortune from his car alarm business and used this money in successful runs for the House and a failed bid for Barbara Boxer's Senate seat. On April 24, Issa announced that he would help fund the drive to qualify the recall for the ballot, and that he was interested in running for governor.[11] The structure of California's recall ballot likely tempted him into the race. The race to replace a recalled governor can be won with

a mere plurality of the vote, and anyone who casts a ballot can participate in this contest, regardless of whether they voted for or against the recall. A relatively new member of Congress who had not performed well in his first statewide run, Issa saw an opportunity to lead an anti-incumbent revolt and be rewarded by grateful voters with a prize that he might otherwise be unlikely to win. He began making contributions to the petition drive that would eventually total nearly $3 million.[12]

Recall proponents used this money to pay signature gatherers to supplement the efforts of volunteers who gathered an estimated 100,000 signatures by the time Issa stepped in. The presence of a patron also caused Gov. Davis' political team to take notice. "I don't think we took it at all seriously until Darrell Issa gave the money," said Davis advisor Steve Smith. Once the recall drive was flush with cash, however, it took off. The petition, accusing Davis of gross mismanagement of state money, raced around the internet and developed into the leading topic on talk radio. According to recall strategist Sal Russo, the architect of Bill Simon's 2002 gubernatorial bid, "The recall became possible because we had a tool we never had before, and that is the marriage of the internet with talk radio." Qualification for the ballot went from being a possibility before Issa's cash infusion to a probability and then, once the "Rescue California" website received 25 million hits, an inevitability. By July, organizers said they had collected 2,160,000 signatures: 1,319,000 through paid gatherers and direct mail, and 841,000 through voluntary means.[13]

On July 23, Democratic Secretary of State Kevin Shelly announced that the recall had qualified, after a month's worth of lawsuits from both sides alleged signature gathering improprieties and unlawful delays in the counting of signatures. Then it was up to Lt. Gov. Cruz Bustamante to set the timing of the election. Because the drive had progressed so quickly, constitutional provisions required that the recall be held during a special statewide election rather than put off until the March 2004 primary. Bustamante could choose any day between 60 to 80 days after Shelly certified the recall.

Since the state's election code requires that candidates file no later than 59 days before an election, some recall backers worried that Bustamante and Shelly would collaborate on a quick qualification and short filing window. Instead, the October 7 election set by Bustamante—who declared that "there's nothing Machiavellian going on"[14]—gave potential candidates plenty of time to make their choice. Both Democratic officials had dual roles, setting the rules of a game that one of them would soon enter, but took pains to be views as fair because they were constrained by public opinion.

The Field Takes Shape

In the first weeks of August, experienced officials, high profile newcomers, and local gadflies alike considered entering the race for the governorship. All that was required to join the race was $3500 and 65 signatures from members of the candidate's party. Many Republicans, outraged by Davis' handling of state finances and well aware that he was vulnerable, could not resist entering the race. Issa, whose moderate policy stances and personal fortune made his candidacy credible, had openly declared his attentions to run during the petition drive. Bill Simon quickly reassembled his 2002 campaign apparatus

and again used his own money to tout his fiscal conservatism. Still, scandals from his business practices dogged him, and his inability to defeat Davis the previous year left many wondering why he would try again.

Veteran state Sen. Tom McClintock joined the field on August 5. After many years of experience in Sacramento as an articulate leader of the state's fiscally and socially conservative forces, he had barely lost in his 2002 race to become the state's controller. McClintock was convinced that the state's budget problems made his fiscal positions more important to Californians than his less popular social prescriptions. Also in the race was Peter V. Ueberroth, a social moderate who emphasized fiscal responsibility. Another candidate with a significant personal fortune, Ueberroth hoped to parlay his success as the organizer of Los Angeles 1984 Summer Olympics and his experience as baseball's commissioner into support for his sound stewardship of the state.

The highest Republican hopes focused, of course, on bodybuilder-turned-movie star turned political activist Arnold Schwarzenegger. While he may have been new to the national political scene, Hollywood's highest-paid action hero was also one of show business' leading political voices. After considering a run for the governorship in 2002, Schwarzenegger instead led the drive for a ballot initiative that provided after school programs for California students. He won raves for his campaigning, and Proposition 49 won passage by a 57 percent to 43 percent margin, though the state's deficit has prevented it from being implemented so far. Still, Schwarzenegger remained hesitant to launch his own candidacy, and his political advisor George Gorton arrived at NBC's "Tonight Show" studios on the night of August 6 expecting to watch Schwarzenegger endorse another Republican.[15] Instead, the former Terminator announced his candidacy and immediately became the top GOP contender. Schwarzenegger fits the same mold that has led other Republicans to statewide success in California: he is a social moderate and a fiscal conservative, with the added bonus of substantial charisma and financial resources. Like Pete Wilson, the Republican governor from 1990 to 1998, Schwarzenegger favors abortion rights. He is even more centrist than Wilson on issues such as domestic partnership and gun control, which put him closely in line with California's electorate.

Another factor that gave Schwarzenegger's candidacy immediate legitimacy was his willingness to use his personal fortune. Requiring investments in five major media markets, California campaigns

Table B: Initial Results of Recall and Replacement Elections

Question/candidate	Number of votes	Percentage of the vote
Support for recall	4,851,398	55.4%
Opposition to recall	3,917,508	44.6
Arnold Schwarzenegger (R)	4,107,851	48.6
Cruz Bustamante (D)	2,668,473	31.6
Tom McClintock (R)	1,129,402	13.4
Peter Miguel Camejo (Grin)	235,286	2.8
Arianna Huffington (Ind)	46,678	0.6
Pever V. Ueberroth (R)	24,645	0.3

Source: Semifinal Official Canvas of the Vote reported by the California secretary of state, as of October 28, 2003, at http://vote2003.ss.ca.gov/.

regularly see expenditures of tens of millions of dollars. Self-financed candidates have done quite well over the last decade, with one-term Congressman Michael Huffington and political novice Bill Simon nearly pulling off upsets in statewide elections against Diane Feinstein and Gray Davis, respectively. Arnold Schwarzenegger's money gave him the resources to start a professional operation quickly and the independence to attack Gray Davis for his reliance on interest group contributions. Though Schwarzenegger would go on to raise a total of $11.9 million from real estate, farming, insurance an other interests to supplement the $10 million that he gave himself, he contended throughout his campaign that these were not the same sorts of "special interests" that had corrupted Sacramento politics.

The state's most popular Democrat, U.S. Sen. Diane Feinstein, felt strongly that recall was wrong and that the best strategy to defeat it was not to run a replacement candidate at all. This formula had allowed her to defeat a recall attempt when she was San Francisco's mayor. She reportedly put tremendous personal pressure on the state's high-profile Democrats to resist the temptation—made obvious by internal polls showing majority support for the recall—to jump into the race.[16] Attorney General Bill Lockyer and Treasurer Phil Angelides, potential candidates for the governorship in 2006, stayed out of the race.

Yet on the same day that Schwarzenegger would enter the contest, Lt. Gov. Cruz Bustamante declared his candidacy. Though Bustamante had publicly pledged on June 19 to stay off the ballot, his rocky relationship with Davis and his poor prospects in a crowded 2006 primary field tempted him into the race. According to top consultant Richie Ross, "I think [Bustamante's decision] was based on a sense that someone should do it, and he took his shot." Did this amount to a betrayal of the Democratic Party and muddle its "No on the Recall" message? Lockyer certainly thought it did, leading him after the election to criticize Bustamante's ethics and work habits when explaining why he as a lifelong Democrat voted for Schwarzenegger.[17]

Other candidates without a major party label sought the support of the 21 percent of Californians who do not register to vote as Republicans or Democrats. Arianna Huffington, the former wife of a Republican Senate nominee whose career as a political columnist had taken her from conservatism to anti-SUV activism, entered the race as an independent. Peter Miguel Camejo carried the banner of the Green Party, just as he had done when he captured 5.3 percent of the vote in the 2002 governor's race. Rounding out the field of 135 candidates were those who gave the recall its circus atmosphere. Former child actor Gary Coleman, porn star Mary Carey Cook, Los Angeles billboard queen Angelyne, and Hustler publisher Larry Flynt qualified for a ballot that was seven pages long.

Campaigns, Contributions and the Courts

Once he entered the replacement contest, Arnold Schwarzenegger began to be asked specific policy questions that the press had refrained from asking previously. In a televised interview, *The Today Show's* Matt Lauer quizzed a surprised Schwarzenegger about his positions on California's workers' compensation program. Schwarzenegger's avoidance of such concrete queries became the topic that the mainstream political media seized upon in the early days of the campaign. They challenged his assertions that he could solve the budget mess without raising taxes or cutting education.

Yet this criticism did not greatly trouble Schwarzenegger's circle of strategists, a group that combined his longtime advisors with former Gov. Pete Wilson's aides and Wilson himself.[18] The team had designed a creative media plan that bypassed traditional news outlets for appearances on shows with Jay Leno, Oprah Winfrey, Larry King and Howard Stern shows. "We ran away from the established media," explained aide Sean Walsh. "We went to the real mass media. It gave us five, seven, eight minutes of unfiltered opportunities to get out our message every day. We did it because we could."[19] Schwarzenegger's personal fortune and successful fundraising also gave him the ability to craft his own message through television ads.

Gray Davis possessed one advantage in the 77-day campaign: he was technically running against an initiative in his fight to stop the recall. A recent state campaign finance law, premised on the principle that no one can corrupt an initiative, allowed unlimited contributions to initiative campaigns but capped donations to individual candidates. Always a prolific fundraiser, Davis and the committees working on his side were able to collect nearly $17 million. The finance law, Proposition 34, imposed unexpectedly tight constraints on other candidates. Written by legislative leaders, Prop. 34 was initially thought to be a sham because it allowed mammoth contributions to parties, who could then spend money supporting local candidates. Because of the vicissitudes of the recall, though, this supposed loophole had some bite: no candidate could simply raise money through parties, because the major parties were internally divided over whom to support.

Another provision of Prop. 34 allowed candidates to accept unlimited contributions into accounts from their previous campaigns and transfer them to their recall efforts so long as $21,200-sized chunks of the transferred sums could be "attributed" to individual supporters. Cruz Bustamante attempted to take advantage of this provision. In September, his 2002 campaign account accepted nearly $4 million from Native American tribes that had casinos, and then transferred it to his recall war chest. Under pressure from popular condemnation and a lawsuit, Bustamante was forced to give this money to the fight against an initiative on the October ballot (to fund commercials in which he appeared). These TV spots likely cost Bustamante more in bad press than they were worth.[20]

Bustamante, who had been a true centrist when he served as Assembly Speaker, also moved to the left in an apparent attempt to mobilize the Democratic base. His "No on the Recall, Yes on Bustamante" campaign included a "Tough Love" budget plan raising taxes, and ads that emphasized his Latino heritage. He seemed to expect that the replacement race could be won by motivating the 30 percent of California voters who are staunch Democrats. After all, only a plurality was required to win, and an August 24 *Los Angeles Times Poll* showed Bustamante leading with 34 percent support from likely voters while the rest of the electorate was divided between Republican contend-

ers like Schwarzenegger (22 percent), McClintock (12 percent), Ueberroth (7 percent), Simon (6 percent) divided up the rest of the vote.

The Republican field did not remain crowded, though. Seeing their poll figures and knowing how unpopular they might become if their presence handed victory in the replacement race to a Democrat, the trailing Republicans eventually dropped out. Following Issa's emotional goodbye on August 7 was Bill Simon's August 23 withdrawal and Peter Ueberroth's September 9 exit. The lone major Republican remaining on Election Day was Tom McClintock. His continued presence appealed to conservatives who did not trust Schwarzenegger's qualified "no new taxes" pledge, but infuriated some Republicans who feared that it might give the election to Bustamante.

As the replacement field took shape, Gray Davis did little to help his own cause. He offered a half-hearted mea culpa in a televised appearance, though his less publicized town hall meetings across the state drew more favorable reviews. Unpopular all year because of his handling of the state's budget condition, Davis could not even count of the support of all of the state's registered Democrats. A glance at the polling figures over the course of the recall shows that a quarter of the Democratic voters consistently favored the recall. Overall support for the recall climbed over 50 percent when Republican voters, who were tepid to the idea at first, began to back it almost unanimously by October 7. Still, Davis attracted the visible support of national figures such as Bill Clinton, Jesse Jackson, and many of the 2004 presidential candidates. They campaigned alongside him, and he claimed that his campaign was just gaining momentum on September 15, when a three-judge panel of the Ninth Circuit Court of Appeals released a decision that provisionally delayed the scheduled election.

The decision ruled in favor of the Southwest Voter Registration Education Project in a suit brought on the group's behalf by the American Civil Liberties Union (ACLU). Although a slew of lawsuits were filed by both sides, this suit attracted the attention of courts because it invoked the federal constitutional rights that had been addressed in *Bush v. Gore*. The ACLU contended that holding a recall election before six counties (which had more minority voters than the rest of California) could switch from obsolete punch card balloting to secretary of state-approved devices would violate the equal protection rights of punch card voters. UC Berkeley political scientist Henry Brady, who had led efforts to study punch card voting in Florida, estimated that 40,000 fewer voters would be counted in the six counties than in areas with less error-prone voting machines. The three-judge panel accepted Brady's figures and the ACLU's reasoning, delaying the election and concluding that "This is a classic voting rights equal protection claim."[21]

The election remained in limbo until September 23, when an en banc panel of Ninth Circuit judges overruled the three initial judges. This panel was less accepting of Brady's disfranchisement estimates, and opined that the possibility that punchcard errors would be decisive was outweighed by the costs of delay. "If the recall election scheduled for October 7, 2003, is enjoined," the panel declared, "it is certain that the state of California and its citizens will suffer material hardship by virtue of the enormous resources already invested in reliance on the election's proceeding on the announced date."[22]

It is hard to say whether the court-imposed delay helped or hurt Davis' efforts, though nearly all voters told pollsters that it did not affect their decision. One event that clearly hurt Davis was the re-imposition of the state's car tax, which began to appear in collections made after August 1. In 1998, legislation signed by Pete Wilson lowered the car tax from an average of $204 per vehicle to $66. A "trigger" mechanism in the law provided that the tax would return to its initial level when the state could no longer afford to reimburse local governments for the revenue they lost when the car tax was cut. Davis invoked the trigger, effectively raising taxes and helping to plug $4 billion worth of the state's budget hole.[23]

Public outcry when the car tax returned to its 1998 levels was fierce, and Schwarzenegger made much of the issue at the only debate in which he appeared. Held in Sacramento on September 24, this "superbowl of debates" provided the candidates with questions in advance and then allowed them to challenge each other. Rather than the scripted show many had expected, the debate turned into a free-for-all that its moderator struggled to control. Post-debate polling showed that most voters thought Tom McClintock or Peter Camejo had performed best, but Schwarzenegger clearly "won" the debate by exceeding expectations in his most challenging public appearance.

Schwarzenegger's post-debate momentum carried him to a comfortable lead in the last public polls conducted before the election. Arianna Huffington, who had sparred bitterly with Schwarzenegger during the debate, dropped out on September 30 and urged her supporters to oppose the recall. Her move did not appear to put a dent in Schwarzenegger's prospects, and neither did a *Los Angeles Times* story detailing allegations that he had sexually harassed six women in graphic ways over a 25-year period. This story, which appeared only days before the recall, was an independent account that did not rely on any information leaked from opposition campaigns. Schwarzenegger immediately issued an apology, saying "Those people that I have offended, I want to say to them I am deeply sorry."[24] Many of his supporters saw the independently-researched story as another Gray Davis attack, and polls indicate that it may have paradoxically helped Schwarzenegger galvanize his supporters and pull in Tom McClintock's backers in the final days.

A Clear Schwarzenegger Victory

Schwarzenegger, who had attracted the support of 40 percent of likely voters in the last *Los Angeles Times* poll taken before the election, recovered from the harassment allegations to win the replacement election with nearly 49 percent of the vote. With voters recalling Gray Davis by a 55 percent to 45 percent margin, Schwarzenegger was sworn in as his replacement on November 17. Because the margins were so large, the ACLU announced that it would not pursue its case against punch card ballot machines any further. Comparing the number of abstentions on the recall question in punch card counties with abstentions elsewhere, Henry Brady estimated that the votes of 176,000 people were not counted.[25] But since nearly a million more people backed the recall than opposed it, voting technology did not swing the election. One of the reasons the margins were so large is that turnout was so high. With 61.2 percent of registered voters turning out, participation in the recall exceeded turnout in recent gubernatorial elections— 50.6 percent in 2002 and 57.6 percent in 1998—but fell well below California's 71.0 percent turnout level in the 2000 presidential election.

The most obvious lesson of the election was that Schwarzenegger's strategy of using nontraditional media and emphasizing his leadership skills over policy specifics was staggeringly successful. He nearly captured a majority in an election that many at the outset predicted would be won by a candidate with 20 percent of the vote. Schwarzenegger won by getting support from 76 percent of registered Republicans, 46 percent of independent voters, and 23 percent of Democrats, according to exit polling. He attracted 53 percent of white voters, 45 percent of Asians, 31 percent of Latinos and 18 percent of African-Americans. He performed relatively well in all subgroups of voters and motivated his key constituency, Republicans, to go to the polls. He did not, however, mobilize a significant group of new "Terminator Voters." Only an estimated 4 percent of those who turned out were first-time voters.

The lessons of Gray Davis' defeat in the recall are less certain. That a well-funded campaign against his recall could fail in a primarily Democratic state is surprising. So too is the level to which his approval sank, 25 percent, and the fact that he performed so poorly in the 2002 election. In that contest, 47.3 percent of voters and 81 percent of Democrats supported Davis; in 2003, 44.6 percent of voters and 75 percent of Democrats opposed the recall. Seen in this light, the recall does not represent a sea change in California politics. Instead, it marks the fruition of voter discontent that had grown since the energy crisis and the state's downward fiscal turn. The recall allowed Davis' critics to offer up a stronger field of alternatives, and California voters were happy to choose one.

And what about the circus that this contest was supposed to become, with so many candidates on a confusing ballot? There's an old saw in political science called Duverger's Law. It says that elections of the type held in the United States—races for a single office in which the top vote getter wins outright—will eventually turn into a two-way race. Voters who support candidates or parties that are running in third place or lower soon figure out that their votes will be wasted if they stick with their top choice, and strategically switch to whichever frontrunner they like better. Once the electorate sizes up the race in this way, the Peter Camejos and the Tom McClintocks of the world are doomed. So is a frontrunner who, like Cruz Bustamante, thinks that a race that starts with seven viable candidates will finish that way. Bustamante seemed to play to his Democratic base, figuring that 30 percent of the vote would make him the next governor. Schwarzenegger's centrist strategy, while risky at first, eventually paid off and made him California's newest governor.

Notes

[1] This figure and all voter registration, voter participation, and election return figures cited are taken from official reports posted on the California Secretary of State's website, www.ss.ca.gov.

[2] Biographical details and election figures taken from the 1999–2000 California Political Almanac, 6th Edition, edited by A.G. Block and Claudia Buck, Sacramento, CA: State Net, 1999.

[3] Quoted in Dan Smith, "Schwarzenegger Tells How He'd Clean Up Capitol," Sacramento Bee, September 19, 2003.

[4] All approval ratings cited come from the Los Angeles Times poll.

[5] Figure cited in "GOP Showdown in California," posted on CBSNews.com, March 4, 2002.

[6] Turnout dropped from 57.6 percent of registered voters in 1998 to 50.6 percent in 2002, according to tallies released by the Secretary of State. Davis won with 47.3 percent of the vote, while Simon garnered 42.4 percent and minor party candidates took the remaining 10.3 percent.

[7] Figure taken from the Governor's Budget May Revision, 2003–04, available online at http://www.dof.ca.gov/HTML/BUD_DOCS/May_ Revision_2003_www.pdf.

[8] Statements made by Mark Abernathy at "California's 2003 Governors Race: The Recall," a conference hosted by the University of California, Berkeley, on October 18, 2003.

[9] Current recall provisions also reflect the changes made by Proposition 9, passed in 1974.

[10] Figure reported in Daniel Borenstein and Dogen Hannah, "Recall Process Befuddles Officials," Contra Costa Times, July 23, 2003.

[11] This and other cited dates are taken from the timeline included in "An Election Like No Other," a special section of the Sacramento Bee on October 12, 2003.

[12] This figure and all other campaign finance information was collected from the California Secretary of State and reported in Dan Morain and Joel Rubin, "Financially, the Recall Was Business as Usual," Los Angeles Times, October 10, 2003.

[13] Quotes and figures in the paragraph taken from statements made by Steve Smith, Sal Russo, and Dave Gilliard at "California's 2003 Governors Race: The Recall," a conference hosted by the University of California, Berkeley, on October 18, 2003.

[14] This quote and the election rules cited in this paragraph were taken from Daniel Borenstein and Dogen Hannah, "Recall Process Befuddles Officials," Contra Costa Times, July 23, 2003.

[15] Gorton said that "I was the most surprised person in America" when Schwarzenegger made his announcement, in testimony at "California's 2003 Governors Race: The Recall," a conference hosted by the University of California, Berkeley, on October 18, 2003.

[16] Gray Davis' chief advisory, Garry South, said that, "It's fair to say that Senator Feinstein had more to do with efforts to clear the field than the Governor did," at "California's 2003 Governors Race: The Recall," a conference hosted by the University of California, Berkeley, on October 18, 2003.

[17] Lockyer and Ross made their statements at "California's 2003 Governors Race: The Recall," a conference hosted by the University of California, Berkeley, on October 18, 2003.

[18] Schwarzenegger's media consultant and his co-director on communications, Don Sipple and Sean Walsh, has served Wilson in similar positions.

[19] Quoted in James Steingold, "Celebrity Status Gave Schwarzenegger Options," San Francisco Chronicle, Monday, October 13, 2003. A study released on October 13, 2003 by the UC Berkeley/Stanford Policy Analysis for

California Education unit found that Schwarzenegger also received by far the most coverage from the traditional political media.

[20] A summary of Proposition 34 and Bustamante's actions can be found on the excellent recall website provided by the UC Berkeley Institute of Politics, at www.igs.berkeley.edu.

[21] Statement taken from page 18 of the Court's September 15 opinion, D.C. No. CV-03-05715-SVW.

[22] Statement taken from page 10 of the Court's September 23 opinion, D.C. No. CV-03-05715-SVW.

[23] Details of the "vehicle license fee: taken from a page devoted to the issue on www.igs.berkeley.edu.

[24] Quoted in Erica Werner, "Schwarzenegger Acknowl-edges 'Offensive' Behavior, Apologizes," Associated Press, October 2, 2003.

[25] Estimate and ACLU position taken from Bob Egelko, "176,000 bad punch-card ballots, ACLU Says," *San Francisco Chronicle*, October 9, 2003.

About the Author

Thad Kousser is an assistant professor of political science at the University of California, San Diego, and has worked as an aide in the California Legislature and in Congress. His book, *Term Limits and the Dismantling of Legislative Professionalism*, is forthcoming from Cambridge University Press.

Table 6.16
STATE RECALL PROVISIONS, 2004

State	Provision for recall	Officials subject to recall	Constitutional and statutory citations for recall of state officials	Constitutional or statutory language
Alabama	No			
Alaska	Yes	All (a)	Const. Art., 11 § 8; AS § 15.45.510-710, 15.60.010	All elected public officials in the State, except judicial officers, are subject to recall by the voters of the State or political subdivision from which elected. Procedures and grounds for recall shall be prescribed by the legislature.
Arizona	Yes	All	Const. Art. 8, § 1-6; ARS § 19-201-19-234	Every public officer in the state of Arizona, holding an elective office, either by election or appointment, is subject to recall from such office by the qualified electors of the electoral district from which candidates are elected to such office.
Arkansas	No			
California	Yes	All	Const. Art. 2, § 13-19; CA Election Code § 19-201-19-234	Recall is the power of the electors to remove an elective officer. Recall of a state officer is initiated by delivering to the Secretary of State a petition alleging reason for recall. Sufficiency of reason is not reviewable.
Colorado	Yes	All	Const. Art. 21, § 1; CRS § 1-12-101-1-12-122, 23-17-120.5, 31-4-501-505	Every elective public officer of the state of Colorado may be recalled from office at any time by the registered electors entitled to vote for a successor of such incumbent through the procedure and in the manner herein provided for, which procedure shall be known as the recall, and shall be in addition to and without excluding any other method of removal by law.
Connecticut	No			
Delaware	No			
Florida	No			
Georgia	Yes	All	Const. Art. 2, § 2.4; GA Code § 21-4-1 et seq.	The General Assembly is hereby authorized to provide by general law for the recall of public officials who hold elective office. The procedures, grounds, and all other matters relative to such recall shall be provided for in such law.
Hawaii	No			
Idaho	Yes	All (a)	Const. Art. 6, § 6: ID Code § 34-1701-34-1715	Every public officer in the state of Idaho, excepting the judicial officers, is subject to recall by the legal voters of the state or of the electoral district from which he is elected. The legislature shall pass the necessary laws to carry this provision into effect.
Illinois	No			
Indiana	No			
Iowa	No			
Kansas	Yes	All (a)	Const. Art. 4, § 3; KSA § 25-4301-25-4331	All elected public officials in the State, except judicial officers, shall be subject to recall by voters of the State or political subdivision from which elected. Procedures and grounds for recall shall be prescribed by law.
Kentucky	No			

See footnotes at end of table.

STATE RECALL PROVISIONS, 2004 — Continued

State	Provision for recall	Officials subject to recall	Constitutional and statutory citations for recall of state officials	Constitutional or statutory language
Louisiana	Yes	All (a)	Const. Art. 10, § 26; LRS § 18:1300.1-18:1300.17	The legislature shall provide by general law for the recall by election of any state, district, parochial, ward, or municipal officer except judges of the courts of record. The sole issue at a recall election shall be whether the official shall be recalled.
Maine	No			
Maryland	No			
Massachusetts	No			
Michigan	Yes	All (a)	Const. Art. 2, §8;MCL § 168.951-168.975	Laws shall be enacted to provide for the recall of all elective officers except judges of courts of record upon petition of electors equal in number to 25 percent of the number of persons voting in the last preceding election for the office of governor in the electoral district of the officer sought to be recalled. The sufficiency of any statement of reasons or grounds procedurally required shall be a political rather than a judicial question.
Minnesota	Yes	(b)	Const. Art. 8, § 6; MS § 211C.01 et. seq.	A member of the senate or the house of representatives, an executive officer of the state identified in section 1 of article V of the constitution, or a judge of the supreme court, the court of appeals, or a district court is subject to recall from office by the voters.
Mississippi	No			
Missouri	No			
Montana	Yes	All	Mont. Code § 2-16-601-2-16-635	Every person holding a public office of the state or any of its political subdivisions, either by election or appointment , is subject to recall from such office.
Nebraska	No			
Nevada	Yes	All	Const. Art. 2, § 9; NRS § 294A.006	Every public officer in the State of Nevada is subject, as herein provided, to recall from office by the registered voters of the state, or of the county, district, or municipality which he represents.
New Hampshire	No			
New Jersey	Yes	All	Const. Art. 1, § 2; NJRS § 19:27A-1-19:27A-18	The people reserve unto themselves the power to recall, after at least one year of service, any elected official in this State or representing this State in the Untied States Congress.
New Mexico	No			
New York	No			
North Carolina	No			
North Dakota	Yes	All (c)	Const. Art. 3, § 1 and 10; ND Century Code § 16.1-01-09.1	Any elected official of the state, of any county or of any legislative or county commissioner district shall be subject to recall by petition of electors equal in number to twenty-five percent of those who voted at the preceding general election for the office of governor in the state, county, or district in which the official is to be recalled.

See footnotes at end of table.

STATE RECALL PROVISIONS, 2004 — Continued

State	Provision for recall	Officials subject to recall	Constitutional and statutory citations for recall of state officials	Constitutional or statutory language
Ohio	No			
Oklahoma	No			
Oregon	Yes	All (c)	Const. Art. 2, § 18; ORS § 249.865-249.880	Every public official in Oregon is subject, as herein provided, to recall by the electors of the state or of the electoral district from which the public official is elected.
Pennsylvania				
Rhode Island	Yes	(d)	Const. Art. 4, § 1	Recall is authorized in the case of a general officer who has been indicted or informed against for a felony, convicted of a misdemeanor, or against whom a finding of probable cause of violation of the code of ethics has been made by the ethics commission.
South Carolina				
South Dakota	No			
Tennessee	No			
Texas	No			
Utah	No			
Vermont	No			
Virginia	No			
Washington	Yes	All (a)	Const. Art. 1, Sec. 33-34; WRC §29.82-010-29.82.220	Every elective public officer of the state of Washington except judges of courts of record is subject to recall and discharge by the legal voters of the state, or of the political subdivision of the state, from which he was elected whenever a petition demanding his recall, . . . is filed with the officer with whom a petition for nomination, or certificate for nomination, to such office must be filed under the laws of this state, and the same officer shall call a special election as provided by the general election laws of this state. and the result determined as therein provided.
West Virginia				
Wisconsin	Yes	All	Const. Art. 13, §12; Wisc. Stat. §9.10	The qualified electors of the state, of any congressional, judicial or legislative district or of any county may petition for the recall of any incumbent elective officer after the first year of the term for which the incumbent was elected, by filing a petition with the filing officer with whom the nomination petition is filed, demanding the recall of the incumbent.
Wyoming	No			

Sources: The Council of State Governments, state constitutions and statutes, December 2003.
Key:
(a) Except judicial.
(b) State executive officers, legislators, and judicial officers.
(c) Except for U.S. Congress.
(d) Governor, Lieutenant Governor, Secretary of State, and Treasurer.

Table 6.17
STATE RECALL PROVISIONS: APPLICABILITY TO STATE OFFICIALS AND PETITION CIRCULATION

State or other jurisdiction	Officers to whom recall is applicable (a)	No. of times recall can be attempted	Recall may be initiated after official has been in office	Recall may not be initiated with days remaining in term	Basis for signatures (b) (see key below)		Maximum time allowed for petition circulation (c)
					Statewide officers	*Others*	
Alabama							
Alaska	All state level officers	...	120 days	180	25% VO	25% VO	...
Arizona	All elected officials	1 (d)	6 mos./5 days legislators	...	25% VO	25% VO	120 days
Arkansas							
California	All elected officials	(e)	90 days	6 mos.	12% VO, 1% from 5 counties	20% VO	160 days
Colorado	All elected officials	(f)	6 mos./5 days legislators	6 mos.	25% VO	25% VO	60 days
Connecticut					...	...	...
Delaware					...	...	...
Florida					...	...	...
Georgia	All state level officials, county and city elected officials	...	180 days	180	15% EV (g), 1/15 from each congressional district	30% EV (g)	(t)
Hawaii					...	...	...
Idaho	All but judicial officers	(d)	90 days	...	20% EVg	50% VO	60 days
Illinois					...	...	...
Indiana					...	...	...
Iowa					...	...	...
Kansas	All but judicial officers	1	120 days	180	40% VO	40% VO	90 days
Kentucky					...	...	...
Louisiana	All officers	(h)	1 day	6 mos.	33 1/3% EV (i)	33 1/3% EV (i)	180 days
Maine					...	...	...
Maryland					...	...	...
Massachusetts	All but judicial officers	...	6 mos.	6 mos.	25% VG in district	25% VG in district	(i)
Michigan	All state level officers	...	...	6 mos.	25% VO	25% VO	90 days
Minnesota					...	...	...
Mississippi					...	...	...
Missouri					...	...	...
Montana	All state level officers & elected officials	(d)	2 mos.	...	10% EV	(k)	3 mos.
Nebraska	Elected officials from political subdivisions(u)	...	6 mos.	6 mos.	...	35-45% VO	...
Nevada	All officers	(d)	6 mos. (l)	...	25% VO in given	25% VO in given	90 days
Hampshire					...	...	...
New Jersey	All elected officials	(p)	(q)	(r)	25% VO in given jurisdiction	25% VO in given jurisdiction	(s)
New Mexico					...	...	...
New York					...	...	...
North Carolina					...	...	...
North Dakota	All elected officials	1	...	190	25% EVg	25% EV	90
Ohio					...	...	...
Oklahoma	All officers	No limit	...	...	15% (m)	15% (m)	90 days
Oregon					...	...	...
Pennsylvania					...	...	...
Rhode Island	Gov., lt. gov., atty. gen., sec. of state, treasurer	...	6 mos.	...	15% VO	...	90 days
South Carolina					...	...	...

See footnotes at end of table.

STATE RECALL PROVISIONS: APPLICABILITY TO STATE OFFICIALS AND PETITION CIRCULATION—Continued

State or other jurisdiction	Officers to whom recall is applicable (a)	No. of times recall can be attempted	Recall may be initiated after official has been in office	Recall may not be initiated with days remaining in term	Basis for signatures (b) (see key below)		Maximum time allowed for petition circulation (c)
					Statewide officers	Others	
South Dakota	...	...	...	...	...	...	...
Tennessee	...	...	...	...	...	...	...
Texas	...	...	...	...	...	...	...
Utah	...	...	...	...	...	...	...
Vermont	...	...	...	...	...	...	...
Virginia	All but judges of courts of records	...	...	...	...	...	...
Washington		...	IM	180	25% VO	35% VO	(n)
West Virginia	All elected officials	1	1 yr.	60	25% VG (o)	25% VG (o)	60 days
Wyoming		...	...	...	...	...	...
American Samoa		...	...	...	...	...	...
U.S. Virgin Islands	All elected officials	No limit	1 yr.	90	30% VO	30% VO	60 days

Sources: The Council of State Governments' survey of state election administration offices, October 2003 and state web sites.

Key:

... — Not applicable.
All — All elective officials.
VO — Number of votes cast in the last election for the office or official being recalled.
EVg — Number of eligible voters in the last general election for governor.
EV — Eligible voters.
VG — Total votes cast for the position of governor in the last election.
VP — Total votes cast for position of president in last presidential election.
IM — Immediately.

(a) An elective official may be recalled by qualified voters entitled to vote for the recalled official's successor. An appointed official may be recalled by qualified voters entitled to vote for the successor(s) of the elective officer(s) authorized to appoint an individual to the position.

(b) Signature requirements for recall of those other than state elective officials are based on votes in the jurisdiction to which the said official has been elected.

(c) The petition circulation period begins when petition forms have been approved and provided to sponsors. Sponsors are those individuals granted permission to circulate a petition, and are therefore responsible for the validity of each signature on a given petition.

(d) Additional recall attempts can be made provided that the state treasury is reimbursed the cost of the previous recall attempt(s).

(e) Open ended.

(f) One attempt unless able to gather signatures at least equal in number to 50% of those voting for the office in the last general election.

(g) Eligible voters for office at last general election to fill office.

(h) Unlimited. Once every 18 months.

(i) Basis for signatures 33 1/3 percent if over 1,000 eligible voters; 40 percent if under 1,000 eligible voters.

(j) Forty-eight hours if certified on state level and six days if certified on county level.

(k) 15-20 percent of eligible voters depending on the office.

(l) For legislators, anytime after 10 days from the beginning of the first legislative session after their election.

(m) 15 percent of the total number of votes cast in the public officer's electoral district for all candidates for governor at the last election at which a candidate for governor was elected to a full term.

(n) Statewide officials 270 days; others 180 days.

(o) At least 25 percent of the vote case for the office of governor at the last election within the same district or territory as that of the officeholder being recalled.

(p) An elected official sought to be recalled who is not recalled as the result of a recall election shall not again be subject to recall until after having served one year of a term calculated from the date of the recall election.

(q) The recall drive may not commence before the 50th day preceding the completion of the elected official's first year of the current term.

(r) No election to recall an elected official shall be held after the date occurring six months prior to the general election or regular election for that office, as appropriate, in the final year of the officials term.

(s) The maximum time allowed for petition circulation is 320 days for a governor or 160 days for other elected officials.

(t) For any statewide office, 90 days. Any officer holding an office other than statewide office and for whom no less than 5,000 signatures are required for the recall petition, 45 days. Any officer holding an office other than statewide office and for whom less than 5,000 are required, 30 days.

(u) If voted on, no recall for one year.

Table 6.18
STATE RECALL PROVISIONS: PETITION REVIEW, APPEAL AND ELECTION

State or other jurisdiction	Signatures verified (a) by:	Days to amend/appeal Days allowed for a petition that is: Incomplete (b)	Not accepted (c)	Penalty for falsifying petition (denotes fines, jail time)	Days allowed for petition to be certified (d)	Days to step down after certification (e)	Voting on the recall (f) Election held	Election type	Days to contest election results (g)
Alabama	...	...	...	...	...	...	...	...	...
Alaska	Director of elections	20	...	...	30	1	60-90 days after cert.	SP	10
Arizona	County recorder	...	...	Class 1 misdemeanor	70	5	75-120 days after cert.	(u)	5
Arkansas	...	...	...	...	...	...	...	...	...
California	County clerk/registrar of voters	10	10	...	10	(w)	60-80 days after cert.	GE	5
Colorado	SS	60 (r)	60 (r)	$1,000, 1 yr. or both	10	5	45-75 days after cert.	SP or GE	10
Connecticut	...	...	...	...	...	...	...	...	...
Delaware	...	...	...	...	...	...	...	...	...
Florida	...	...	...	...	...	...	...	...	...
Georgia	SS, registrar of voters	...	...	Misdemeanor	30-45	IM	30-45 days after cert.	SP, PR or GE	...
Hawaii	...	...	...	...	...	...	...	...	...
Idaho	County clerk	30	...	$5,000, 2 yrs.	10	5	45+ days after cert. (h)SP , PR, GE (h)	...	20 (i)
Illinois	...	...	...	...	...	...	...	...	...
Indiana	...	...	...	...	...	...	...	...	...
Iowa	...	...	...	...	...	...	...	...	...
Kansas	County clerk	...	...	Class B misdemeanor; up to $1,000, 6 mo. or both.	30	...	60-90 days after cert.	SP (v)	5 (i)
Kentucky	...	...	...	...	...	...	...	...	...
Louisiana	Registrar of voters	...	...	$100-1,000, 30-90 days	10	...	(j)	SP	30
Maine	...	...	...	...	...	...	...	...	...
Maryland	...	...	...	...	...	...	...	...	...
Massachusetts	SS, local election officials (k)	...	...	$500, 90 days	35	IM	w/i 60 days after cert.	SP	2 (i)
Minnesota	SS	...	...	Misdemeanor	10	...	Not less than 15 days after cert.	GE	7
Mississippi	...	...	...	...	...	...	...	...	...
Missouri	...	...	...	...	...	...	...	...	...
Montana	County clerk	...	...	$500, 6 mos. or both.	90	5	3 mos. after cert.	SP or GE	40
Nebraska	County clerk	...	...	Misdemeanor	15	5	30-45 days after cert.	SP	...
Nevada	County clerk, registrar of voters	5	...	Misdemeanor	(s)	5	(l)	SP	(t)
New Hampshire	...	...	...	...	...	...	...	...	...
New Jersey	Recall elections official	...	...	Crime of the 4th degree	10	5	(p)	SP or GE	(q)
New Mexico	...	...	...	...	...	...	...	...	...
New York	...	...	...	...	...	...	...	...	...
North Carolina	...	...	...	...	...	...	...	...	...
North Dakota	SS	...	...	...	30	10	...	...	14 (m)
Ohio	...	...	...	...	...	...	...	...	...
Oklahoma	...	...	...	...	...	...	...	...	...
Oregon	SS or county clerk	...	...	Class C felony	10	5	40 days after cert.	SP	35
Pennsylvania	...	...	...	...	...	...	...	...	...
Rhode Island	SBE	w/i 90 days	...	Misdemeanor and/or felony	90	...	...	SP	...
South Carolina	...	...	...	...	...	...	...	...	...

See footnotes at end of table.

STATE RECALL PROVISIONS: PETITION REVIEW, APPEAL AND ELECTION—Continued

State or other jurisdiction	Signatures verified (a) by:	Days to amend/appeal Days allowed for a petition that is:		Penalty for falsifying petition (denotes fines, jail time)	Days allowed for petition to be certified (d)	Days to step down after certification (e)	Voting on the recall (f)		Days to contest election results (g)
		Incomplete (b)	Not accepted (c)				Election held	Election type	
South Dakota	...	...	...	...	...	...	...	...	...
Tennessee	...	...	...	...	...	...	...	...	...
Texas	...	...	...	...	...	...	...	...	...
Utah	...	...	...	...	...	...	...	...	...
Vermont	...	...	...	...	...	...	...	...	...
Virginia	...	...	...	...	...	...	...	...	...
Washington	SS, county auditor	...	10 (n)	Felony	not specified	IM	45-60 days after cert.	SP	3
West Virginia	...	...	...	...	...	...	...	...	...
Wisconsin	SBE	5	...	Class 1 felony - $10,000, not more than 4 yrs. 6 mo. or both	31	10	6 weeks after cert.	GE or PR	3 (o)
Wyoming	...	...	...	...	...	...	...	...	...
American Samoa	...	...	...	...	...	...	...	...	...
U.S. Virgin Islands	Supervisor of Elections	3	...	...	60	...	60 days after cert.	SP	7

Sources: The Council of State Governments' survey of state election administration offices, October 2003 and state web sites.

Key:

...— Not applicable.

SBE - State Board of Elections.

SS — Secretary of State.

SP — Special election.

GE — General election.

PR — Primary election.

IM — Immediate and automatic removal from office.

w/i — Within

N.A. — Information not available.

(a) The validity of the signatures, as well as the correct number of required signatures must be verified before the recall is allowed on the ballot.

(b) If an insufficient number of signatures are submitted, sponsors may amend the original petition by filing additional signatures within a given number of days. If the necessary number of signatures have not been submitted by this date, the petition is declared void.

(c) In some cases, the state officer will not accept a valid petition. In such a case, sponsors may appeal this decision to the Supreme Court, where the sufficiency of the petition will be determined. When this is declared, the recall is required to be placed on the ballot.

(d) A petition is certified for the ballot when the required number of signatures has been submitted by the filing deadline, and are determined to be valid.

(e) The official to whom a recall is proposed has a certain number of days to step down from his position before a recall election is initiated, if he desires to do so.

(f) A majority of the popular vote is required to recall an official in each state.

(g) Individuals may contest the results of a vote on a recall within a certain number of days after the results are certified. In Alaska, an appeal to courts must be filed within five days of the recount.

(h) In Idaho, the dates on which elections may be conducted are the first Tuesday in February, the fourth Tuesday in May, the first Tuesday in August, or the Tuesday following the first Monday in November. In addition, an emergency election may be called upon motion of the governing board of a political subdivision. Recall elec-

tions conducted by any political subdivision shall be held on the nearest of these dates which falls more than 45 days after the clerk of the political subdivision orders that the recall election shall be held.

(i) After election is certified. In Michigan, if a petition is filed against a local officer, a recount can be requested up to 6 days after certification of recall election.

(j) The election must be held on the next available date of six dates per year allowed by the election committee.

(k) Secretary of state if filed on the state level; county or local clerks if filed on county level.

(l) In Nevada, a recall election is held 10-20 days after the Secretary of State completes notification of the petition sufficiency unless a complaint is filed, the clerk shall issue a call for the election which is to be held within 30 days after the issuance of the call.

(m) Fourteen days after the canvas board has certified the results.

(n) In Washington, a petition that is not accepted may be appealed in 10 days.

(o) Business days.

(p) New Jersey Permanent Statutes, 19:27A-13. In the case of an office which is ordinarily filed at the general election, a recall election shall be held at the next general election occurring at least 55 days following the fifth business day after service of certification, unless it was indicated in the notice of intention to recall that the recall election shall be held at a special election in which case the recall election official shall order and fix the date for holding the recall election to be the next Tuesday occurring during the period beginning with the 55th day and ending on the 61st day following the fifth business day after service of the certification of the petition.

(q) New Jersey Permanent Statutes, 19:27A-16.

(r) Petitions may be amended once during the 60 days allowed for petition circulation.

(s) Within four days, county clerks count signature totals and forward to the Secretary of State. The Secretary of State immediately notifies the clerks if they are to proceed with signature verification.

(t) Five days after recount is completed or 14 days after the election if no recount is demanded.

(u) Consolidated election dates.

(v) May be held on date of regular primary or general election if such an election is scheduled between 60 and 90 days after certification of recall petition.

(w) Prior to election being called.

Chapter Seven

STATE FINANCE AND DEMOGRAPHICS

"Today, the revenue picture is a bit brighter, but not strong enough for governors to snap fiscal ships into autopilot."

— **Katherine G. Willoughby**

States should examine structural reforms that will benefit them in the long term.

— **Nick Samuels**

All of the net profit from lottery revenues have been used to provide financial assistance to support primary and secondary education in 13 states.

— **Alan R. Yandow**

"Large numbers of immigrants continue to concentrate in major 'immigrant magnet' areas at the same time that domestic migrants are gravitating to a wider range of areas, and local destinations within them."

— **William H. Frey**

"Despite a recent increase in the number of women governors, women's progress, especially at statewide elective and state legislative levels, has slowed."

— **Susan J. Carroll**

Tax Revenues in 2004: Governors Look Inward?

By Katherine G. Willoughby

In 2003, governors brought their citizens up short, recognizing the precarious position of their governments and then calling on the federal government to provide relief. The federal government did come forward with some $20 billion in funds to states. These funds, along with numerous other tax and spending initiatives allowed the states to stay afloat, albeit just barely. Today, the revenue picture is a bit brighter, but not strong enough for governors to snap fiscal ships into autopilot. Many governors have now gone back to their public after a stormy year, and few are talking about federal relief.

In 2003, governors brought their citizens to the collective kitchen table to discuss state finances – the discussion was brutal. Governors understood the urgency with which they must address fiscal stringencies in their states and expressed this to the public, indicating the need to make painful choices in a time characterized by many as the worst fiscal crisis since WWII. Regardless of where the blame lay for the situation – 9/11, sustained economic malaise, declining federal dollars, antiquated tax structures, escalating health care, education and employee benefit costs, or historically poor management, chief executives focused their 2003 state of the state addresses on themes of pulling citizens together, returning to the primary mission of state government and then called on the federal government for fiscal relief. Many governors also made promises to tackle tax reform in their state, suppress political bickering with legislators, and enhance the performance of programs through management reforms.[1]

In actuality, states that reached balance did so only by incorporating a wide variety of rather drastic revenue, expenditure, debt and program management strategies. According to the National Association of State Budget Officers (NASBO), the most states recorded in the 23-year history of conduct of its *Fiscal Survey of the States*, "made either across-the-board or selective program cuts in fiscal 2003" totaling almost $12 billion, just about $2 billion shy of state budget cuts in 2002![2] Then for fiscal 2004, three quarters of the states imposed new taxes and fee increases, cut spending and further reduced or emptied budget reserves and used up one-time revenues. States also utilized a number of revenue enhancement and financial management strategies like tax amnesty programs or accelerating tax remittance to mute the impact on taxpayers as much as possible.[3]

What is the tone of governors' talks this year? Can we expect more of the same in terms of stated strategies and approaches to managing the states? What does the state fiscal landscape look like now and how are governors approaching the job of balancing state budgets? The following assesses the strategies that state chief executives have for addressing this task. State tax receipts are considered and conclusions drawn based on the content of governors' state of the state addresses for 2004.[4]

Governors' Considered Possibilities for Fiscal Relief

Last year, chief executives provided a cornucopia of possibilities for relief, with federal funding at the top of their wish lists. State government options for relief included political or legal strategies like reducing partisanship across branches, tax and tort reform, and advancing greater local control of education. Economic development type strategies included the enhancement of a more tax-friendly and competitive business environment, supporting partnerships, job training programs and bonding to realize a stronger in-state workforce, strengthening in-state tourism, and promoting biotechnology centers/corridors. Then, governors mentioned a number of management strategies, including support for more accurate revenue forecasting, directed expenditure cuts and grants to local governments, performance-related and privatization initiatives, reform of employee pension and benefit plans, and e-governance enhancements.[5]

In 2004, state chief executives brought up many of these same strategies, although their emphasis is different. For example, many mention economic development strategies as a primary component of their 2004 agendas. These types of efforts actually have minimal direct (short-term) effect on individual citizens, yet can realize long-term revenue gains. In Alaska, Gov. Frank H. Murkowski's address titled, "Securing Alaska's Future," lists his top priority as the construction of a pipeline to advance the production and sale of oil. In addition, this governor is calling for the development of other natural resources like timber, fisheries and minerals to advance local tax bases. In Illinois, the governor has asked for legislation to bring the coal industry back. And New Mexico's Gov. Bill Richardson is pursuing increased trade with Mexico, along with an expansion of tourism.

Other governors used their addresses to encourage partnerships and collaborations between the public, private and nonprofit sectors. Such partnerships can be used to enhance job skills of workers, advance venture capital funding, and support research leading to innovations. Results from these types of activities can be used to replace state funding for similar programs, advance local and regional economies, and eventually lead to increased state revenues by adding to the state tax base. South Dakota's governor called for an allowance to venture capitalists to be able to invest in "projects and businesses that have the potential for high return to spur long-term economic development [with the goal of increasing] gross state product by $10 billion from $24 billion to $34 billion by the year." In Michigan the governor called for working with the private sector to develop a large-scale regional distribution center for cargo. And, Arizona's governor mentioned developing "a knowledge-based economy for long term benefits."

The governors of Connecticut and Georgia mentioned the creation of partnerships specifically with faith-based organizations to share state responsibility related to human welfare programs. Delaware's Gov. Ruth Ann Minner called for matching federal and private dollars with state funds to advance investment in the manufacturing industry and biotechnology ventures in that state. Chief executives in Michigan, New Hampshire, New Jersey, North Dakota, Ohio, Rhode Island, Tennessee and West Virginia all mentioned similar types of strategies to manage through fiscal year 2005.

Tax reform remains on the minds of some governors, even in the wake of some spectacular defeats of such efforts by chief executives in the past year – Alabama Gov. Bob Riley saw his recommended changes to that state's tax structure soundly defeated this past August. This year, Iowa's Gov. Tom Vilsack has asked for expanding the sales tax base to include some services but at the same time reducing the rate. He also called for an increased cigarette tax, closing loopholes and "ending unfair preferences."[6] In Kentucky, Gov. Ernie Fletcher has a very similar plan for expansion of the sales tax and the intangibles tax, an increase to the cigarette tax, while lowering the top income and corporate income tax rates.[7] In his address, Virginia's chief executive discussed his plan to make taxes fairer by increasing the sales tax, lowering the income tax excepting approximately 8 percent of upper-income state citizens. He also pushed for a tax cut on cars and food and regarding estate taxes for farms and small businesses. According to Gov. Mark Warner, "To me, it just doesn't make any sense that someone earning only $17,000 a year in Virginia should pay the same tax rate as someone earning $500,000 a year. This plan cuts taxes for at least 65 percent of Virginians – and our methodology has been endorsed by four leading independent economists, including the president of the Federal Reserve Bank of Richmond." Finally, though not tax reform, Oklahoma's governor called for a lottery as an avenue to add revenues to the state's treasury.

Coming from the other direction, several governors (those in Georgia, New Mexico and Kansas) brought up the importance of collecting back taxes or unpaid taxes, and more vigilance in ferreting out fraudulent returns. These efforts can certainly bear fruit. For example, "in a recent report to the North Carolina General Assembly's Revenue Laws Study Committee, Secretary of Revenue Norris Tolson announced that Project Compliance, the Department of Revenue's crackdown on individual and corporate tax dodgers, is on track. The program's ultimate goal is to collect $150 million in additional revenue for the state. It has already exceeded its interim goals and recovered $47 million to date."[8] Along these same lines, New Hampshire's governor called for a "Taxpayers Bill of Rights."

Others have called for constitutional or statutory changes regarding new funds, funding strategies, or balanced budgets. Alaska's governor seeks changes regarding the use and refurbishment of two funds supported by oil revenues. Again, this governor is calling on the public to make the decision about future uses and replenishment of these funds (Permanent Fund and Constitutional Budget Reserve, respectively). According to Gov. Frank H. Murkowski, "the principal [of the Permanent Fund] has grown so large that the income created by the Fund exceeds the revenue the state receives from oil." California Gov. Arnold Schwarzenegger's 2004 state of the state address included his "California Recovery Plan" that made reference to a new balanced budget amendment as well as an incredible debt package. Schwarzenegger stated that "We took the debt we inherited from the previous administration, the debt that threatens us with bankruptcy, and we rolled it into a $15 billion recovery bond. Then we tore up the credit card. We passed a balanced budget amendment. And we created a rainy day fund for future hard times and emergencies. Never again will government be allowed to spend money it doesn't have. Never again will the state be allowed to borrow money to pay for its operating expenses." New Jersey's Gov. James McGreevey has asked for tax increases and changes coupled with $1.5 billion in borrowing to support a 9 percent increase in spending.[9]

Other constitutional changes were recommended by governors in Georgia, Hawaii, Maine and Nebraska. The governor of West Virginia asked for a constitutional amendment to provide cash bonuses to that state's military men and women who have served in Iraq, Kosovo and Afghanistan. In Wyoming, the governor discussed support for a constitutional amendment related medical malpractice tort reform. About nine other governors mentioned tort reforms and/or changes to health and other insurance to reduce premiums, avoid frivolous lawsuits and save state dollars.

Reorganizations, and/or performance and accountability measures are emphasized with regard to particular agencies especially those related to health care and education services. In Vermont, Gov. Jim Douglas remarked about a "massive reorganization" of that state's human services department. Regarding restructuring state government, South Carolina's Gov. Mark Sanford probably provided the most detailed plan. He noted dramatic changes already happening in the departments of Commerce, Corrections, and Parks and Recreation. He also suggested the creation of a sunset commission to further department restructuring in that state and called for increased accountability in South Carolina "through attitudinal change." Maryland's governor mentioned reorganization as well. Governors in Rhode Island, Virginia and Wisconsin also called for similar restructuring or accountability measures.

Kansas Gov. Kathleen Sebelius, to date, has been unsuccessful in raising taxes (property taxes for education) but she was successful with the engagement of "Kansas Budget Efficiency Savings Teams" to save "tens of millions of dollars" through management initiatives like systems that automatically turn out lights to save money.[10] Oklahoma's governor is asking the state to institute zero-based budgeting to foster improved productivity and reduced costs. Gov. Douglas also established the Vermont Institute for Government Effectiveness, "a top to bottom review of government operations to root out waste and inefficiencies that cost taxpayer dollars."

Governments are continuing the deployment of technology to advance state service delivery, many through e-governance initiatives. Several mentioned by governors in their addresses include those in Illinois where the governor talked of streamlining applications for state funding as well as "re-writing programs to cut out the bureaucracy." New Jersey's governor also talked of using "e-governance models to cut expenses." In Utah Gov. Olene S. Walker discussed the implementation of an "online service delivery system to cut costs and increase the reach amongst citizens." In West Virginia, the governor relayed that the "use of websites to garner feedback is saving taxpayers $40,000 in postage annually."

The State Fiscal Landscape

Certainly the fiscal picture has improved from 2003, but just barely. State total budget balances as a percent of expenditures have stabilized, yet remain low and reminiscent of the early 1980s' 3.8 percent. The 2004 figure is estimated to be 3.2 percent. In 2000, this ratio was 10.4 percent![11]

One recent state revenue report finds that real adjusted tax revenue has rebounded since a decade low in 2002. Specifically, "state tax revenue grew by 4.5 percent in the July-September quarter of 2003, compared to the same quarter the year before. Without the contribution of net enacted tax increases, this growth would have been only 2.6 percent. If we also take into account the effects of inflation, real adjusted state tax revenue grew by only 0.4 percent – the first real adjusted growth since the April-June quarter of 2001. This is the third straight quarter of strengthening revenue growth."[12]

It is only mildly encouraging that state budget gaps have contracted and there are fewer states currently experiencing imbalance when compared to the same period last year. Nonetheless, states have yet to realize the revenue growth either hoped for or forecasted. For example, in Georgia, a February 2004 fiscal report explained, "accounting for an expected one-time revenue influx in June of $120 million, revenues would need to grow approximately 10.8 percent over the next five months in order to meet the revised revenue estimate and avoid further FY 2004 budget cuts."[13] Unfortunately, Georgia Gov. Sonny Perdue's latest press release announces that net revenue collections for the month of February 2004 are down 1.9 percent when compared to last year at the same time – the percentage increase year-to-date for fiscal year 2004 compared to last year is 4 percent. According to Perdue, such revenue figures call for continued discipline and attest to the "seriousness of our current budget situation."[14] In fact, the National Conference of State Legislatures (NSCL) warned that states can expect a ~$35 billion total budget gap in 2005.[15] While considerably less than the cumulative budget gap last year, states are at a disadvantage in

Table A: State Tax Collections by Type of Tax, 1994 and 2003, 3rd Quarter (in percent)

	1994	2003
General sales and gross receipts	34.6%	31.4%
Individual income tax	31.5	33.1
Motor fuel sales	7.1	6.3
Corp. net income	6.6	5.0
Motor vehicles	3.3	3.0
Other sales and gross receipts	2.3	2.5
Tobacco products	2.0	2.1
Insurance	2.0	1.9
All other taxes	10.4	14.7
Including: property tax, public utilities, pari-mutuels, amusements, beverage and other licenses, death, gift and severance taxes, and taxes on document and stock transactions.		

Source: Table 3: State Tax Collections by State and Type of Tax. Data availablein Excel files qtx033t3 and qtx943t3 at http://www.census.gov/govs/www/qtax.html. Accessed on March 4, 2004.

that they have drawn down, used up or exhausted many of the funds and/or financial management strategies in an effort to keep state programs operating.

Further exacerbating state revenue problems is the fact that governors can expect little relief from the federal government in the future. While the federal government came forward with $20 billion for the states just this past year, major discretionary and mandatory program funding changes from 2004 to 2005 have decreased. President Bush's 2005 budget calls for a decrease of 4 percent in mandatory and entitlement spending (~$10 billion) and a decrease of 3 percent in selected grants-in-aid (~$11.6 billion).[16]

While states enacted net tax hikes of $2.1 billion in the July-September 2003 quarter,[17] Table A reiterates that state tax receipts, as a proportion of total receipts have barely changed in a decade. If we look at third quarter figures for 2003 and those from the same quarter almost 10 years ago, only very minor changes have occurred. Individual income tax and general sales and gross receipts still comprise the largest proportion of tax receipts at the state level. Motor fuel sales tax receipts have decreased as a proportion of total tax receipts, but just slightly. Corporate income taxes have declined as a proportion of total receipts as well. The "all other taxes" category includes a number of tax sources that contribute less than 2 percent each to total tax receipts in the states. Just a few of these taxes in this category have increased as a proportion of total receipts, most notably, documentary and stock transfer taxes, from less than 0.7 percent in 1994 to 1.5 percent in 2003.

Looking Inward

Governors undoubtedly are anxious about the fu-

ture, and with good reason. Sixty percent of governors just completed their first year as a state chief executive. And, according to one scholar, "it's asking too much for them to undertake major projects and programs with these kinds of economic conditions. If they can just manage to get the budgets to balance they're doing well."[18] Many attempted to make changes to better manage the 2003 fiscal storm, yet were unsuccessful due to intransigent legislatures or a wary public.

With tax receipts creeping up just a bit, the tone of most state of the state addresses in 2004 was less dire than in 2003, but no less worrisome. It was rare for any governors this year to plead for federal relief like they did last year. On the other hand, these chief executives remain cautious about federal involvement in their tax systems. For example, the National Governors Association (NGA) is currently monitoring possible changes to the Internet Tax Freedom Act of 1998 that could cost state governments billions of dollars in lost revenues.[19] Like last year, many governors are pushing for economic development and/or initiatives that require public input like constitutional amendments regarding balanced budgets, funding strategies, or program support (via business or nonprofit involvement). They are also continuing to call for the advancement of performance and efficiency systems and measures to keep state programs running.

Some governors have used their time in office to get to know their citizens. Michigan's governor has toured her state several times to talk with voters. Georgia's governor has held individual one-on-one visits with citizens on Saturdays to gain public insight about state operations and programs. In South Carolina the governor has held "open door after 4" sessions to talk with citizens. The governor of California took that state's fiscal troubles to citizens and they rewarded him with a balanced budget amendment and $15 billion in debt – the latter offering Californians a brief fiscal respite. In the end, the governors are calling on the public again, to recognize that states are not out of the woods, that more tax, spending and debt strategies must be considered and undoubtedly that most citizens will need to contribute more for states to get the work done that is both needed and expected.

Notes

[1] Katherine G. Willoughby, "State Revenue Choices: 2003 and Beyond," *The Book of the States*, 2003, (Lexington, KY: The Council of State Governments), 2003.

[2] NASBO and NGA, *The Fiscal Survey of the States*, (December 2003), 1.

[3] NASBO and NGA, 10.

[4] State government chief executives report annually or biennially to their legislatures regarding the fiscal condition of their state, commonwealth or territory. Governors often use their address to lay out their policy and budget agendas for their upcoming or continuing administration. The 2004 state of the state addresses were accessed from January through March 5, 2004 at the National Governors Association website: http://www.nga.org/nga/legislativeUpdate/1,1169,C_ISSUE_BRIEF^D_6252,00.html. Five states did not have state of the state addresses noted on this website during this time including, Arkansas, Montana, Nevada, North Carolina, and Texas. All quotes and data presented here are from the addresses noted on this website, unless otherwise noted.

[5] Willoughby.

[6] Jack Hunt, "Iowa: GOP Legislative Leaders Demand Tax Bill from Governor," *State Tax Notes* 31, (March 1, 2004): 698.

[7] Joe Follick, "Kentucky: Increase Cigarette Tax, Cut Income Tax," *State Tax Notes* 31, (March 1, 2004): 698.

[8] Kay Miller Hobart, "North Carolina: Revenue Secretary Says 'Project Compliance' on Track," *State Tax Notes* 31, (March 1, 2004): 707.

[9] Jeff Pillets, "New Jersey Governor Calls for $1 Billion in Tax, Fee Hikes," *State Tax Notes* 31, (March 1, 2004): 687.

[10] Alan Greenblatt, "States of Frustration," *Governing* 17, no. 4, (January 2004): 30.

[11] NASBO and NGA, 13.

[12] Nicholas W. Jenny, "State Tax Revenue Grows Slightly," *State Revenue Report* 54, (Fiscal Studies Program, The Nelson A. Rockefeller Institute of Government, December 2003): 3.

[13] Alan Essig, "Fiscal Year 2004 Revenue Estimate Update." Georgia Budget Notes no. 15, (February), http://frp.aysps.gsu.edu/frp/frpnews/budgetnotes/BudgetNote-15.pdf.

[14] Governor's Press Release, "Governor Perdue Announces February Revenue Collections," (March 3), http://www2.state.ga.us/departments/dor/pressrel/p030304.pdf.

[15] McClaughlyn, Kerrita. 2004. "NCSL: States See Decrease in Shortfalls, but Wary About Fiscal 2005," *State Tax Notes* (March 1) 31, p. 718.

[16] NASBO. *Federal Budget Update: Administration's Budget Lean for States; Cracks Down on Intergovernmental Transfers*. (February 5), Table 1. Major Discretionary and Mandatory Program Funding.

[17] Rockefeller Report, 3-4

[18] Alan Greenblatt, "States of Frustration," *Governing* 17, no.4, (January): 28.

[19] National Governors Association Homepage, http://www.nga.org/nga/lobbyIssues/1,1169,D_6383,00.html.

About the Author

Katherine G. Willoughby is professor of public administration and urban studies in the Andrew Young School of Policy Studies at Georgia State University. She is the author of numerous articles on state and local government budget and policy practices and co-author of a book on public budgeting in the United States.

Long-Term Budget Stability Amidst Fiscal Crisis:
What Can States Do to Better Navigate the Next One?

By Nick Samuels

While recent economic news suggests that the short-term cyclical fiscal hemorrhage is healing, long-term structural challenges still exist that must be examined to enable states to weather the next fiscal storm. State officials will have the opportunity and challenge to pursue durable strategies that will improve fiscal stability.

The fiscal dilemma that has dogged states for nearly three years is strikingly similar to their experiences in the early 1980s and 1990s. The economy flourished and budgets boomed, but an ebb in the cycle afflicted revenues, this time with spectacular speed and severe effects. While revenues plunged, spending pressures continued to build, particularly from Medicaid. In response, states cut spending dramatically, raised taxes, and tapped the budget reserves that, fortunately, they built up during the preceding period of prosperity. While recent economic news suggests that the short-term cyclical fiscal hemorrhage is healing, long-term structural challenges still exist that must be examined to enable states to weather the next fiscal storm. State officials will have the opportunity and challenge to pursue durable strategies that will improve fiscal stability. Budget officers will be at the forefront of the challenge to pursue such policies that reach the goal of sound financial management.

The Current State Fiscal Situation

Even as the national economy shows signs of improvement, the current state fiscal picture largely mirrors that of the last two years: states are scrambling to keep their budgets in balance. While some states are seeing positive signs in their revenue (or at least are seeing less negative ones), in others revenues remain sluggish, budget gaps are lingering, and spending pressures persist, particularly from Medicaid and other health care. States are confronting these challenges through means similar to previous years: they are enacting austere growth budgets, increasing taxes and fees, drawing from reserves and reorganizing programs.

States Have Curtailed Spending Dramatically

After relatively high rates of expenditure growth during the boom years, states have curbed spending significantly. Between fiscal 2002 and fiscal 2003, general fund spending increased by only 0.6 percent

nominally, and based on enacted budgets is expected to grow only 0.2 percent between fiscal 2003 and fiscal 2004, according to the National Association of State Budget Officers (NASBO)'s *Fiscal Survey of States* (the latter figure reflects the smallest spending increase since 1979, the first year that NASBO began tracking such data). By comparison, general fund spending increased by 8.3 percent in fiscal 2001, and between fiscal 1979 and fiscal 2004, spending has grown at an average annual nominal rate of 6.2 percent (or roughly 2 percent in real terms). To curtail spending to such an extent reflects drastic action. Incredibly, 40 states cut their budgets in fiscal 2003 (also the most since 1979) by a net $11.8 billion, resulting in 21 states ending the year with negative spending growth compared to fiscal 2002. For fiscal 2004, 13 states passed negative growth budgets compared with the previous year. Already, roughly halfway through the fiscal, 12 states have made budget cuts that total $2 billion.

As tight budgets began to set in, states tried to protect certain priority programs—such as K-12 education, Medicaid, aid to cities and towns, and public safety—from budget cuts. Many states exempted K-12 education from budget cuts altogether. However, with the fiscal crunch enduring, many of these programs also have been subjected to cuts and are in jeopardy of additional reductions the longer it takes for overall economic recovery to translate into improved state finances. Based on NASBO's most recent *State Expenditure Report*, elementary and secondary education reflect 21.6 percent of total state spending; Medicaid accounts for 20.8 percent; higher education is 11.2 percent; transportation is 8.2 percent of total state spending; corrections reflects 3.6 percent; public assistance is 2.1 percent; and "all other" spending accounts for 32.6 percent of the total. Within the general fund specifically, elementary and secondary education account for 35.4 percent of all spending; Medicaid 16 percent; higher education is 12.6 percent; corrections reflects 6.9 percent of all general fund spending; public assistance is 2.3 percent; transportation accounts for 0.7 percent; and "all other" is 26.1 percent.

States have used a variety of other tools to stop the flow of red ink, as well. In fiscal 2003, 32 states made across-the-board budget cuts, 25 tapped their rainy day funds, 16 states laid off employees, 13 states offered early retirement, and 13 reorganized programs to achieve some budget savings. They have also taken advantage of low interest rates and refinanced state debt, implemented hiring freezes, securitized their tobacco settlement funds, deferred payments, made one-time transfers from other funds and undertaken tax amnesty programs.

Revenues Suffered Severely in 2003, Hopeful for 2004

Revenue collections in most states were grim once again in fiscal 2003, echoing an economy sputtering to recover. With the economic times still tough—employment decreased during seven months of the fiscal year, for example—collections of sales, personal income and corporate income taxes were below budgeted estimates in 31 states in fiscal 2003. Overall collections of those three taxes were 6 percent lower than the amounts states budgeted for with sales taxes missing their targets by 2.9 percent, personal income taxes off by 9 percent and corporate income taxes 3.7 lower. However, halfway through fiscal 2004, states are cautiously optimistic. That hopefulness is fueled partly by an economy that finally seems to have started to recover robustly, partly by lower revenue estimates, and partly by tax increases states included in their fiscal 2004 budgets.

For fiscal 2004, 36 states enacted net tax and fee increases, totaling $9.6 billion. The largest increases were in sales taxes ($2.6 billion), personal income taxes ($2.3 billion) and fees ($1.8 billion). Additionally, states enacted $3 billion in revenue measures that do not affect taxpayer liability, such as extending a tax credit for another year or deferring a tax increase or decrease.

Balances Gave States a Much Needed Cushion

States substantially strengthened their financial reserves during the late 1990s economic boom. Those funds have played a crucial role in balancing budgets and avoiding budget cuts and tax increases even more severe than the ones states have had to apply. Total balances—states' ending balances and the amounts in their budget stabilization (or rainy day) funds—totaled a net $48.8 billion at their peak in fiscal 2000, equal to 10.4 percent of expenditures.

The situation three years after the bubble burst is much different. Reflecting a nearly 70 percent drop from their height, total balances in fiscal 2003 were $15.2 billion or 3.1 percent of expenditures (5 percent generally is considered to be a healthy level of reserves).

Looking Forward: Can States Prepare for the Next Fiscal Crunch?

States know that they will have to endure cyclical ups and downs and, as they learned during the fiscal crunch of the early 1990s and indeed, the currently subsiding downturn, healthy reserves and a willingness to make difficult decisions are necessary. However, beyond regular cyclical highs and lows, other factors play into the condition of state finances. These include revenue estimation uncertainty, expenditure estimation uncertainty, unpredictable federal tax policy, unpredictable federal mandates, unpredictable court decisions, unpredictable voter decisions, and even natural disasters or events such as the 2001 terrorist attacks.

Uncertainty is Certain

A degree of uncertainty is inherent to budgeting. For example, states must use economic forecasts in their budget process, and such projections contain uncertainty and even error. While states seek to limit the amount of uncertainty, its intrinsic nature in the budget process means that both favorable outcomes (such as the unanticipated revenue growth of the late 1990s) and unfavorable ones (such as states' more recent experiences) are magnified. This means that during periods of economic expansion, particularly such as the recent boom, states tend to adopt spending and taxing patterns that they cannot sustain during slowdowns or contractions. Conversely, during such slowdowns, states tend to react by changing their spending and taxing behavior to a mode that generates surpluses. A 3 percent budget shortfall may trigger cuts of more than 3 percent, for example. Several other factors lead to this:

- Required spending on some areas that cannot be cut, such as many non-optional parts of Medicaid, other entitlement benefits, or functions such as elementary education that are politically difficult to cut;

- The procedural and administrative difficulties of changing fiscal patterns mid-year;

- The impact of various carryovers from previous years;

- The affect of one-time measures in future years, such as the costs that result from delayed maintenance, the use of reserve funds to address structural imbalances, or issuance of debt that incurs interest costs over time.

Uncertainty and the boom-bust nature of budgeting also means that, when times are tight, some areas are burdened more heavily than others. Several budgetary "untouchables" exist, including debt service, spending that is required by formula such as much of Medicaid, and contributions to employee health and retirement plans. At least at the beginning of the recent state budget crisis, states also tried to exempt K-12 education and some other services from cuts. The result of such untouchables is that, after accounting for the protected areas, the budget must be balanced on less than 100 percent. When spending and tax changes are made, they tend to have a greater impact on future years than on the year in which they are made. Thus, budget-correcting actions that are accurate one year may be an over-correction (or an under-correction) in the next.

Budget uncertainty also has psychological impacts on decisionmakers. When their models seem too optimistic, revenue forecasters may react with ones that are overly pessimistic. Similarly, during a booming economy it can become difficult to build in an accurate degree of pessimism (as the rapid economic decline after 2000 proved).

Responding to Uncertainty

State budget officials long have understood the hazards of revenue and expenditure estimating, the perils of business cycles and their impact on the budget. Different states have different degrees of flexibility in their budget processes that determine how they can confront a budget shortfall. For example, states have different options available for how they can treat funds left over in an agency's budget; in some, they are subtracted from previously estimated spending, in others appropriated funds are compared to available resources, and other states use still other methods. Revenue volatility also varies between states, just as the strengths and weaknesses of their economies do. For example, a state that relies heavily on corporate and personal income taxes and has an economy dominated by recession-prone manufacturing may have a more unpredictable revenue stream than a state with a large percentage of retired persons and that relies on sales taxes.

Depending on demographics and how functions such as school aid or Medicaid are structured, expenditure instability between states varies, too. In some states, school aid payments are based on factors such as enrollment that are unknown until after the start of the fiscal year. A supplemental appropriation may be necessary if enrollment exceeds earlier expectorations. Such differences among states mean that no national rules about balances and budget reserves are applicable; instead, states in fiscal crisis must look at their specific circumstances and the tools available to them within their own budget process and laws.

Regardless of states' different processes and economies, budget shortfalls usually are dealt with in a crisis atmosphere. During a budget shortfall or when the ink turns from red to black as the fiscal situation begins to improve, the budgetary strategies may seem straightforward. The basic options that states choose from during budget shortfalls are tax increases, spending reductions, drawing on reserve funds and borrowing. During more thriving budget periods, when revenues exceed baseline expenditures, states may choose the opposite: cutting taxes, increasing spending, reinforcing reserve funds and paying off debt. However, the political pressures and the management atmosphere during those times are more starkly different. When revenues drop, immediate pressure exists to take action. During more robust times, that pressure does not exist, and it becomes possible to more deeply set goals, build strategies and plan around them. When fiscal times are tough, actors requesting additional funding understand being told "no" – even as they protest that the decision will hurt programs. Conversely, when treasuries are flush with revenue, budget requests multiply out of proportion to the funds available.

Conclusion: Lessons to Learn

There is no time better to plan for the next downturn than when memories of fiscal trouble and budget shortfalls are fresh. The challenge is to limit cyclical effects as much as possible and avoid spending higher than average revenues on on-going functions, especially because the dramatic drop in revenues during the past two years was worse than anyone predicted. This situation signals not only that states should focus on the cyclical nature of the economy, but that they also should examine structural reforms that will benefit them in the long term.

About the Author

Nick Samuels is a senior fiscal analyst at the National Association of State Budget Officers (NASBO).

Table 7.1
AGENCIES ADMINISTERING MAJOR STATE TAXES

State or other jurisdiction	Income	Sales	Gasoline	Motor vehicle
Alabama	Dept. of Revenue	Dept. of Revenue	Dept. of Revenue	Dept. of Revenue
Alaska	Dept. of Revenue	. . .	Dept. of Revenue	Dept. of Public Safety
Arizona	Dept. of Revenue	Dept. of Revenue	Dept. of Transportation	Dept. of Transportation
Arkansas	Dept. of Fin. & Admin.	Dept. of Fin. & Admin.	Dept. of Fin. & Admin.	Dept. of Fin. & Admin.
California	Franchise Tax Bd.	Bd. of Equalization	Bd. of Equalization	Dept. of Motor Vehicles
Colorado	Dept. of Revenue	Dept. of Revenue	Dept. of Revenue	Dept. of Revenue
Connecticut	Dept. of Revenue Serv.	Dept. of Revenue Serv.	Dept. of Revenue Serv.	Dept. of Motor Vehicles
Delaware	Div. of Revenue	. . .	Dept. of Transportation	Dept. of Public Safety
Florida	Dept. of Revenue	Dept. of Revenue	Dept. of Revenue	Dept. of Motor Vehicles
Georgia	Dept. of Revenue	Dept. of Revenue	Dept. of Revenue	Dept. of Revenue
Hawaii	Dept. of Taxation	Dept. of Taxation	Dept. of Taxation	County Treasurer
Idaho	Tax Comm.	Tax Comm.	Tax Comm.	Dept. of Transportation
Illinois	Dept. of Revenue	Dept. of Revenue	Dept. of Revenue	Secretary of State
Indiana	Dept. of Revenue	Dept. of Revenue	Dept. of Revenue	Bur. of Motor Vehicles
Iowa	Dept. of Revenue & Finance	Dept. of Revenue & Finance	Dept. of Revenue & Finance	Local
Kansas	Dept. of Revenue	Dept. of Revenue	Dept. of Revenue	Local (a)
Kentucky	Revenue Cabinet	Revenue Cabinet	Revenue Cabinet	Transportation Cabinet
Louisiana	Dept. of Revenue	Dept. of Revenue	Dept. of Revenue	Dept. of Public Safety
Maine	Revenue Services	Revenue Services	Revenue Services	Secretary of State
Maryland	Comptroller	Comptroller	Comptroller	Dept. of Transportation
Massachusetts	Dept. of Revenue	Dept. of Revenue	Dept. of Revenue	Reg. of Motor Vehicles
Michigan	Dept. of Treasury	Dept. of Treasury	Dept. of Treasury	Secretary of State
Minnesota	Dept. of Revenue	Dept. of Revenue	Dept. of Revenue	Dept. of Public Safety
Mississippi	Tax Comm.	Tax Comm.	Tax Comm.	Tax Comm.
Missouri	Dept. of Revenue	Dept. of Revenue	Dept. of Revenue	Dept. of Revenue
Montana	Dept. of Revenue	. . .	Dept. of Transportation	Local
Nebraska	Dept. of Revenue	Dept. of Revenue	Dept. of Revenue	Dept. of Motor Vehicles
Nevada	. . .	Dept. of Taxation	Dept. of Motor Vehicles	Dept. of Motor Vehicles
New Hampshire	Dept. of Revenue Admin.	. . .	Dept. of Safety	Dept. of Safety
New Jersey	Dept. of Treasury	Dept. of Treasury	Dept. of Treasury	Dept. of Law & Public Safety
New Mexico	Tax & Revenue Dept.	Tax & Revenue Dept.	Tax & Revenue Dept.	Tax & Revenue Dept.
New York	Dept. of Tax. & Finance	Dept. of Tax. & Finance	Dept. of Tax. & Finance	Dept. of Motor Vehicles
North Carolina	Dept. of Revenue	Dept. of Revenue	Dept. of Revenue	Dept. of Transportation
North Dakota	Tax. Commr.	Tax Commr.	Tax Commr.	Dept. of Transportation
Ohio	Dept. of Taxation	Dept. of Taxation	Dept. of Taxation	Bur. of Motor Vehicles
Oklahoma	Tax Comm.	Tax Comm.	Tax Comm.	Tax Comm.
Oregon	Dept. of Revenue	. . .	Dept. of Transportation	Dept. of Transportation
Pennsylvania	Dept. of Revenue	Dept. of Revenue	Dept. of Revenue	Dept. of Transportation
Rhode Island	Dept. of Administration	Dept. of Administration	Dept. of Administration	Dept. of Administration
South Carolina	Dept. of Revenue	Dept. of Revenue	Dept. of Revenue	Dept. of Public Safety
South Dakota	. . .	Dept. of Revenue	Dept. of Revenue	Dept. of Revenue
Tennessee	Dept. of Revenue	Dept. of Revenue	Dept. of Revenue	Dept. of Safety
Texas	. . .	Comptroller	Comptroller	Dept. of Transportation
Utah	Tax Comm.	Tax Comm.	Tax Comm.	Tax Comm.
Vermont	Dept. of Tax	Dept. of Tax	Commr. of Motor Vehicles	Commr. of Motor Vehicles
Virginia	Dept. of Taxation	Dept. of Taxation	Dept. of Motor Vehicles	Dept. of Motor Vehicles
Washington	. . .	Dept. of Revenue	Dept. of Licensing	Dept. of Licensing
West Virginia	Dept. of Tax & Revenue	Dept. of Tax & Revenue	Dept. of Tax & Revenue	Div. of Motor Vehicles
Wisconsin	Dept. of Revenue	Dept. of Revenue	Dept. of Revenue	Dept. of Transportation
Wyoming	. . .	Dept. of Revenue	Dept. of Revenue	Dept. of Transportation
Dist. of Columbia	Office of Tax & Rev.	Office of Tax & Rev.	Office of Tax & Rev.	Office of Tax & Rev.

See footnotes at end of table.

AGENCIES ADMINISTERING MAJOR STATE TAXES — Continued

State or other jurisdiction	Tobacco	Death	Alcoholic beverage	Number of agencies administering taxes
Alabama	Dept. of Revenue	Dept. of Revenue	Alcoh. Bev. Control Bd.	2
Alaska	Dept. of Revenue	Dept. of Revenue	Dept. of Revenue	2
Arizona	Dept. of Revenue	Dept. of Revenue	Dept. of Revenue	2
Arkansas	Dept. of Fin. & Admin.	Dept. of Fin. & Admin.	Dept. of Fin. & Admin.	1
California	Bd. of Equalization	Controller	Bd. of Equalization	4
Colorado	Dept. of Revenue	Dept. of Revenue	Dept. of Revenue	1
Connecticut	Dept. of Revenue Serv.	Dept. of Revenue Serv.	Dept. of Revenue Serv.	2
Delaware	Div. of Revenue	Div. of Revenue	Dept. of Public Safety	3
Florida	Dept. of Business Reg.	Dept. of Revenue	Dept. of Business Reg.	3
Georgia	Dept. of Revenue	Dept. of Revenue	Dept. of Revenue	1
Hawaii	Dept. of Taxation	Dept. of Taxation	Dept. of Taxation	2
Idaho	Tax Comm.	Tax Comm.	Tax Comm.	2
Illinois	Dept. of Revenue	Attorney General	Dept. of Revenue	3
Indiana	Dept. of Revenue	Dept. of Revenue	Dept. of Revenue	2
Iowa	Dept. of Revenue & Finance	Dept. of Revenue & Finance	Dept. of Revenue & Finance	2
Kansas	Dept. of Revenue	Dept. of Revenue	Dept. of Revenue	2
Kentucky	Revenue Cabinet	Revenue Cabinet	Revenue Cabinet	2
Louisiana	Dept. of Revenue	Dept. of Revenue	Dept. of Revenue	2
Maine	Revenue Services	Revenue Services	Bureau of Liquor Enf.	3
Maryland	Comptroller	Local	Comptroller	3
Massachusetts	Dept. of Revenue	Dept. of Revenue	Dept. of Revenue	2
Michigan	Dept. of Treasury	Dept. of Treasury	Liquor Control Comm.	3
Minnesota	Dept. of Revenue	Dept. of Revenue	Dept. of Revenue	2
Mississippi	Tax Comm.	Tax Comm.	Tax Comm.	1
Missouri	Dept. of Revenue	Dept. of Revenue	Dept. of Revenue	1
Montana	Dept. of Revenue	Dept. of Revenue	Dept. of Revenue	3
Nebraska	Dept. of Revenue	Dept. of Revenue	Liquor Control Comm.	3
Nevada	Dept. of Taxation	Dept. of Taxation	Dept. of Taxation	2
New Hampshire	Dept. of Revenue Admin.	Dept. of Revenue Admin.	Liquor Comm.	3
New Jersey	Dept. of Treasury	Dept. of Treasury	Dept. of Treasury	2
New Mexico	Tax & Revenue Dept.	Tax & Revenue Dept.	Tax & Revenue Dept.	1
New York	Dept. of Tax. & Finance	Dept. of Tax. & Finance	Dept. of Tax & Finance	2
North Carolina	Dept. Revenue	Dept. of Revenue	Dept. of Revenue	2
North Dakota	Tax Commr.	Tax Commr.	Treasurer	3
Ohio	Dept. of Taxation	Dept. of Taxation	State Treasurer	3
Oklahoma	Tax Comm.	Tax Comm.	Tax Comm.	1
Oregon	Dept. of Revenue	Dept. of Revenue	Liquor Control Comm.	3
Pennsylvania	Dept. of Revenue	Dept. of Revenue	Dept. of Revenue	2
Rhode Island	Dept. of Administration	Dept. of Administration	Dept. of Administration	1
South Carolina	Dept. of Revenue	Dept. of Revenue	Dept. of Revenue	2
South Dakota	Dept. of Revenue	Dept. of Revenue	Dept. of Revenue	1
Tennessee	Dept. of Revenue	Dept. of Revenue	Dept. of Revenue	2
Texas	Comptroller	Comptroller	Comptroller	2
Utah	Tax Comm.	Tax Comm.	Tax Comm.	1
Vermont	Dept. of Tax	Dept. of Tax	Dept. of Tax	2
Virginia	Dept. of Taxation	Dept. of Taxation	Alcoh. Bev. Control	3
Washington	Dept. of Revenue	Dept. of Revenue	Liquor Control Board	3
West Virginia	Dept. of Tax & Revenue	Dept. of Tax & Revenue	Dept. of Tax & Revenue	2
Wisconsin	Dept. of Revenue	Dept. of Revenue	Dept. of Revenue	2
Wyoming	Dept. of Revenue	Dept. of Revenue	Dept. of Revenue	2
Dist. of Columbia	Office of Tax & Rev.	Office of Tax & Rev.	Office of Tax & Rev.	1

Source: The Federation of Tax Administrators, December 2003.
Key:
. . . — Not applicable

(a) Joint state and local administration. State level functions are performed by the Department of Revenue in Kansas.

Table 7.2
STATE TAX AMNESTY PROGRAMS
1982 - 2004

State or other jurisdiction	Amnesty period	Legislative authorization	Major taxes covered	Accounts receivable included	Collections ($ millions) (a)	Installment arrangements permitted (b)
Alabama	1/20/84 - 4/1/84	No (c)	All	No	3.2	No
Arizona	11/22/82 - 1/20/83	No (c)	All	No	6.0	Yes
	1/1/02-2/28/02	Yes	Individual income	N.A.	N.A.	No
	9/1/03 - 10/31/03	Yes	All (t)	N.A.	73.0	Yes
Arkansas	9/1/87 - 11/30/87	Yes	All	No	1.7	Yes
California	12/10/84 - 3/15/85	Yes	Individual income	Yes	154.0	Yes
		Yes	Sales	No	43.0	Yes
Colorado	9/16/85 - 11/15/85	Yes	All	No	6.4	Yes
	6/1/03 - 6/30/03	N.A.	All	N.A.	18.4	Yes
Connecticut	9/1/90 - 11/30/90	Yes	All	Yes	54.0	Yes
	9/1/95 - 11/30/95	Yes	All	Yes	46.2	Yes
	9/1/02-12/2/02	N.A.	All	N.A.	109	N.A.
Florida	1/1/87 -6/30/87	Yes	Intangibles	No	13.0	No
	1/1/88 - 6/30/88	Yes (d)	All	No	8.4 (d)	No
	7/1/03 - 10/31/03	Yes	All	N.A.	80	N.A.
Georgia	10/1/92 - 12/5/92	Yes	All	Yes	51.3	No
Idaho	5/20/83 - 8/30/83	No (c)	Individual income	No	0.3	No
Illinois	10/1/84 - 11/30/84	Yes	All (u)	Yes	160.5	No
	10/1/03 - 11/17/03	Yes	All	N.A.	532	N.A.
Iowa	9/2/86 - 10/31/86	Yes	All	Yes	35.1	N.A.
Kansas	7/1/84 - 9/30/84	Yes	All	No	0.6	No
	10/1/03 - 11/30/03	Yes	All	Yes	53.7	N.A.
Kentucky	9/15/88 - 9/30/88	Yes (c)	All	No	100	No
	8/1/02-9/30/02	Yes (c)	All	No	100	No
Louisiana	10/1/85 - 12/31/85	Yes	All	No	1.2	Yes (f)
	10/1/87 - 12/15/87	Yes	All	No	0.3	Yes (f)
	10/1/98-12/31/98	Yes	All	No (q)	1.3	No
	9/1/01-10/30/01	Yes	All	Yes	173.1	No
Maine	11/1/90 - 12/31/90	Yes	All	Yes	29.0	Yes
	9/1/03 - 11/30/03	Yes	All	N.A.	34.7	N.A.
Maryland	9/1/87 - 11/2/87	Yes	All	Yes	34.6 (g)	No
	9/1/01-10/31/01	Yes	All	Yes	39.2	No
Massachusetts	10/17/83 - 1/17/84	Yes	All	Yes	86.5	Yes (h)
	10/1/02-11/30/02	Yes	All	Yes	91.6	Yes
	1/1/03-2/28/03	Yes	All	Yes	N.A.	N.A.
Michigan	5/12/86 - 6/30/86	Yes	All	Yes	109.8	No
	5/15/02-6/30/02	Yes	All	Yes	N.A.	N.A.
Minnesota	8/1/84 - 10/31/84	Yes	All	Yes	12.1	No
Mississippi	9/1/86 - 11/30/86	Yes	All	No	1.0	No
Missouri	9/1/83 - 10/31/83	No (c)	All	No	0.9	No
	8/1/02-10/31/02	Yes	All	Yes	76.4	N.A.
	8/1/03 - 10/31/ 03	Yes	All	Yes	20	N.A.
Nevada	2/1/02-6/30/02	N.A.	All	N.A.	7.3	N.A.
New Hampshire	12/1/97-2/17/98	Yes	All	Yes	13.5	No
	12/1/01-2/15/02	Yes	All	Yes	13.5	N.A.
New Jersey	9/10/87 - 12/8/87	Yes	All	Yes	186.5	Yes
	3/15/96 - 6/1/96	Yes	All	Yes	359.0	No
	4/15/02-6/10/02	Yes	All	Yes	276.9	N.A.
New Mexico	8/15/85 - 11/13/85	Yes	All (i)	No	13.6	Yes
	8/16/99-11/12/99	Yes	All	Yes	45	Yes
New York	11/1/85 - 1/31/86	Yes	All (j)	Yes	401.3	Yes
	11/1/96 - 1/31/97	Yes	All	Yes	253.4	Yes (o)
	11/18/02-1/31/03	Yes	All	Yes	520	Yes (s)
North Carolina	9/1/89 - 12/1/89	Yes	All (k)	Yes	37.6	No
North Dakota	9/1/83 - 11/30/83	No (c)	All	No	0.2	Yes
	10/1/03 - 1/31/04	Yes	N.A.	N.A.	N.A.	N.A.
Ohio	10/15/01-1/15/02	Yes	All	No	48.5	No

See footnotes at end of table.

STATE TAX AMNESTY PROGRAMS — Continued

State or other jurisdiction	Amnesty period	Legislative authorization	Major taxes covered	Accounts receivable included	Collections ($ millions) (a)	Installment arrangements permitted (b)
Oklahoma	7/1/84 - 12/31/84	Yes	Income, Sales	Yes	13.9	No (l)
	8/15/02-11/15/02	N.A.	All (r)	Yes	N.A.	N.A.
Pennsylvania	10/13/95 - 1/10/96	Yes	All	Yes	N.A.	No
Rhode Island	10/15/86 - 1/12/87	Yes	All	No	0.7	Yes
	4/15/96 - 6/28/96	Yes	All	Yes	7.9	Yes
South Carolina	9/1/85 - 11/30/85	Yes	All	Yes	7.1	Yes
	10/15/02-11/30/02	Yes	All	Yes	66.2	N.A.
South Dakota	4/1/99-5/15/99	Yes	All	Yes	0.5	N.A.
Texas	2/1/84 - 2/29/84	No (c)	All (m)	No	0.5	No
Vermont	5/15/90 - 6/25/90	Yes	All	Yes	1.0 (e)	No
Virginia	2/1/90 - 3/31/90	Yes	All	Yes	32.2	No
	9/2/03 - 11/3/03	Yes	All	Yes	98.3	N.A.
West Virginia	10/1/86 - 12/31/86	Yes	All	Yes	15.9	Yes
Wisconsin	9/15/85 - 11/22/85	Yes	All	Yes (n)	27.3	Yes
	6/15/98-8/14/98	Yes	All	Yes	30.9	N.A.
Dist. of Columbia	7/1/87 - 9/30/87	Yes	All	Yes	24.3	Yes
	7/10/95 - 8/31/95	Yes	All (p)	Yes	19.5	Yes (p)

Source: The Federation of Tax Administrators, January 2004.

Key:

N.A. — Not available.

(a) Where applicable, figure indicates local portions of certain taxes collected under the state tax amnesty program.

(b) "No" indicates requirement of full payment by the expiration of the amnesty period. "Yes" indicates allowance of full payment after the expiration of the amnesty period.

(c) Authority for amnesty derived from pre-existing statutory powers permitting the waiver of tax penalties.

(d) Does not include intangibles tax and drug taxes. Gross collections totaled $22.1 million, with $13.7 million in penalties withdrawn.

(e) Preliminary figure.

(f) Amnesty taxpayers were billed for the interest owed, with payment due within 30 days of notification.

(g) Figure includes $1.1 million for the separate program conducted by the Department of Natural Resources for the boat excise tax.

(h) The amnesty statute was construed to extend the amnesty to those who applied to the department before the end of the amnesty period, and permitted them to file overdue returns and pay back taxes and interest at a later date.

(i) The severance taxes, including the six oil and gas severance taxes, the resources excise tax, the corporate franchise tax, and the special fuels tax were not subject to amnesty.

(j) Availability of amnesty for the corporation tax, the oil company taxes, the transporation and transmissions companies tax, the gross receipts oil tax and the unincorporated business tax restricted to entities with 500 or fewer employees in the United States on the date of application. In addition, a taxpayer principally engaged in aviation, or a utility subject to the supervision of the State Department of Public Service was also ineligible.

(k) Local taxes and real property taxes were not included.

(l) Full payment of tax liability required before the end of the amnesty period to avoid civil penalties.

(m) Texas does not impose a corporate or individual income tax. In practical effect, the amnesty was limited to the sales tax and other excises.

(n) Waiver terms varied depending upon the date the tax liability was assessed.

(o) Installment arrangements were permitted if applicant demonstrated that payment would present a severe financial hardship.

(p) Does not include real property taxes. All interest was waived on tax payments made before July 31, 1995. After this date, only 50% of the interest was waived..

(q) Exception for individuals who owed $500 or less.

(r) Except for property and motor fuel taxes.

(s) Multiple payments can be made so long as the required balance is paid in full no later than March 15, 2003.

(t) All taxes except property, estate and unclaimed property.

(u) Does not iclude the motor fuel use tax.

Table 7.3
STATE EXCISE TAX RATES
(As of January 1, 2004)

State or other jurisdiction	General sales and gross receipts tax (percent)	Cigarettes (cents per pack of 20)	Distilled spirits ($ per gallon)	Motor fuel (cents per gallon)		
				Gasoline	Diesel	Gasohol
Alabama	4.0	16.5 (d)	(g)	18.0 (j)	19.0 (j)	18.0 (j)
Alaska	. . .	100	$12.80 (i)	8.0	8.0	. . .
Arizona	5.6	118	3.00	18.0 (l)	18.0 (l)	18.0 l)
Arkansas	5.125	59 (e)	2.50 (i)	21.5	22.5	21.5
California	7.25 (r)(w)	87	3.30 (i)	18.0 (q)	18.0 (q)	18.0 (q)
Colorado	2.9	20	2.28	22.0	20.5	22.0
Connecticut	6.0	151	4.50 (i)	25.0	26.0	24.0
Delaware	N.A.	55	3.75 (i)	23.0 (t)(n)	22.0 (t)(n)	23.0 (t)(n)
Florida	6.0	33.9	6.50 (i)	13.9 (k)(q)	26.4 (k)(q)	13.9 (k)(q)
Georgia	4.0	37	3.79 (i)	7.5 (q)	7.5 (q)	7.5 (q)
Hawaii	4.0	130 (s)	5.92	16.0 (j)(q)	16.0 (j)(q)	16.0 (j)(q)
Idaho	6.0	57	(g)	26.0 (p)(q)	26.0 (p)(q)	23.5 (p)(q)
Illinois	6.25	98 (d)	4.50 (i)	19.8 (j)(l)(q)	22.3 (l)(q)	19.8 (l)(q)
Indiana	6.0	55.5	2.68 (i)	18.0 (l)(q)	16.0 (l)(q)	18.0 (l)(q)
Iowa	5.0	36	(g)	20.1	22.5	19.0
Kansas	5.3	79	2.50 (i)	24.0	26.0	24.0
Kentucky	6.0	3 (e)	1.92 (h)(i)	16.4 (l)(m)(q)	13.4 (l)(m)(q)	16.4 (l)(m)(q)
Louisiana	4.0	36	2.50 (i)	20.0	20.0	20.0
Maine	5.0	100	(g)	24.6 (n)	25.7 (n)	24.6 (n)
Maryland	5.0	100	1.50	23.5	24.25	23.5
Massachusetts	5.0	151	4.05 (h)(i)	21.0	21.0	21.0
Michigan	6.0	125	(g)	19.0 (q)	15.0 (q)	19.0 (q)
Minnesota	6.5	48	5.03 (i)	20.0	20.0	20.0
Mississippi	7.0	18	(g)	18.4 (q)	18.4 (q)	18.4 (q)
Missouri	4.225	17 (d)	2.00	17.03 (q)	17.03 (q)	17.03 (q)
Montana	. . .	70	(g)	27.0	27.75	27.0
Nebraska	5.5	64	3.75	25.7 (i)(n)	25.7 (i)(n)	25.7 (i)(n)
Nevada	6.5	80	3.60 (i)	24.0 (j)	27.0 (j)	24.0 (j)
New Hampshire	. . .	52	(g)	19.5 (q)	19.5 (q)	19.5 (q)
New Jersey	6.0	205	4.40	14.5 (q)	17.5 (q)	14.5 (q)
New Mexico	5.0	91	6.06	18.9 (q)	19.9 (q)	18.9 (q)
New York	4.25	150 (d)	6.44 (i)	22.6 (q)	20.85 (q)	22.6 (q)
North Carolina	4.5	5	(g)(h)	24.55 (m)(q)	24.55 (m)(q)	24.55 (m)(q)
North Dakota	5.0	44	2.50 (i)	21.0	21.0	21.0
Ohio	6.0	55	(g)	22.0 (a)(q)	22.0 (a)(q)	22.0 (a)(q)
Oklahoma	4.5	23	5.56 (i)	17.0 (q)	14.0 (q)	17.0 (q)
Oregon	. . .	128	(g)	24.0 (q)	24.0 (q)	24.0 (q)
Pennsylvania	6.0	135	(g)	25.9 (q)	30.8 (q)	25.9 (q)
Rhode Island	7.0	171	3.75	31.0 (q)	31.0 (q)	31.0 (q)
South Carolina	5.0	7	2.72 (i)	16.0	16.0	16.0
South Dakota	4.0	53	3.93 (i)	22.0 (j)	22.0 (j)	20.0 (j)
Tennessee	7.0	20 (d)(e)	4.40 (i)	21.4 (j)(q)	18.4 (j)(q)	21.4 (j)(q)
Texas	6.25	41	2.40 (i)	20.0	20.0	20.0
Utah	4.75	69.5	(g)	24.5	24.5	24.5
Vermont	6.0	119	(f)(g)	20.0 (q)	26.0 (q)	20.0 (q)
Virginia	4.5 (r)	2.5 (d)	(g)	17.5 (j)(o)	16.0 (j)(o)	17.5 (j)(o)
Washington	6.5	142.5	(g)(h)	28.0 (q)	28.0 (q)	28.0 (q)
West Virginia	6.0	55	(g)	25.35 (q)	25.35 (q)	25.35 (q)
Wisconsin	5.0	77	3.25	28.5 (n)	28.5 (n)	28.5 (n)
Wyoming	4.0 (b)	60	(g)	14.0 (q)	14.0 (q)	14.0 (q)
Dist. of Columbia	5.75	100	1.50 (i)	20.0	20.0	20.0

See footnotes at end of table.

STATE EXCISE TAX RATES — Continued

Source: Compiled by The Federation of Tax Administrators from various sources, January 2004.

Key:

. . .—Tax is not applicable.

(a) Effective July 1, 2004, tax rate is scheduled to invrease to 26 cents per gallon.

(b) Tax rate may be adjusted annually according to a formaula based on balances in the unappropriated general fund and the school foundation fund.

(c) The tax rates listed are fuel excise taxes collected by distributor/retailers in each state. Additional taxes may apply to motor carriers.

(d) Counties and cities may impose an additional tax on a pack of cigarettes in Alabama, 1-6 cents; Illinois, 10-15 cents; Missouri, 4-7 cents; New York City,$1.50; Tennessee, 1 cent; and Virginia, 2-15 cents.

(e) Dealers pay an additional enforcement and administrative fee of 0.1 cents per pack in Kentucky and 0.05 cents in Tennessee. In Arkansas, a fee of $1.25/1,000 cigarette fee is imposed.

(f) 10 percent on-premise sales tax.

(g) In 18 states, the government directly controls the sales of distilled spirits. Revenue in these states is generated from various taxes, fees and net liquor profits.

(h) Sales tax is applied to on-premise sales only.

(i) Other taxes in addition to excise taxes for the following states: Alaska, under 21 percent—$2.50/gallon; Arkansas, under 5 percent—$0.50/gallon, under 21 percent—$1.00/gallon, $0.20/case and 3 percent off—14 percent on-premise retail taxes; California, over 50 percent—$6.60/gallon; Connecticut, under 7 percent—$2.05/gallon; Delaware, under 25 percent—$2.50/gallon; Florida, under 17.259 percent—$2.25/gallon, over 55.780 percent—$9.53/gallon, 6.67cents/ounce on-premise retail tax; Georgia, $0.83/gallon local tax; Illinois, under 20 percent—$0.73/gallon,$0.50/gallon in Chicago and $1.00/gallon in Cook County; Indiana, under 15 percent—$0.47/gallon; Kansas, 8 percent off—and 10 percent on-premise retail tax;Kentucky, under 6 percent—$0.25/gallon and 9 percent wholesale tax; Louisiana, under 6 percent—$0.32/gallon; Massachusetts, under 15 percent—$1.10/gallon, over 50 percent alcohol—$4.05/proof gallon, 0.57 percent on private club sales; Minnesota, $0.01/bottle (except miniatures) and 9 percent sales tax; Nebraska, petroleum fee—Nevada, under 14 percent—$0.70/gallon and under 21 percent—$1.30/gallon; New York, under 24 percent—$2.54/gallon, $1.00/gallon New York City; North Dakota, 7 percent state sales tax; Oklahoma, $1.00/bottle on-premise and 12 percent on-premise; South Carolina, $5.36/case and 9 percent surtax; South Dakota, under 14 percent—$0.93/gallon, 2 percent wholesale tax; Tennessee, $0.15/case and 15 percent on-premise, under 7 percent—$1.21/gallon; Texas, 14 percent on-premise and $0.05/drink on airline sales; and District of Columbia, 8 percent off—and 10 percent on-premise sales tax.

(j) Tax rates do not include local option taxes. In Alabama, 1-3 cents and inspection fee; Hawaii, 8–11.5 cents; Illinois, 5 cents in Chicago and 6 cents in Cook County (gasoline only); Nevada 1.75 to7.75 cents; Oregon, 1–3 cents; South Dakota, 1 cent; Tennessee, 1 cent; and Virginia, 2 percent.

(k) Local taxes for gasoline and gasohol vary from 5.5 cents to 17 cents (average is 13.4 cents). Plus a 2.07 cents/gallon pollution tax.

(l) Carriers pay an additional surcharge equal to Arizona, 8 cents; Illinois, 6.3 cents (gasoline) and 6.0 cents (diesel); Indiana, 11 cents; Kentucky, 2 percent (gasoline) and 4.7 percent (diesel).

(m) Tax rate is based on the average wholesale price and is adjusted quarterly. The actual rates are: Kentucky, 9 percent; and North Carolina, 17.5 cents plus 7 percent.

(n) A portion of the rate is adjustable based on maintenance costs, sales volume, or cost of fuel to state government.

(o) Large trucks pay an additional 3.5 cents.

(p) Tax rate is reduced by the percentage of ethanol used in blending (reported rate assumes the maximum 10 percent ethanol).

(q) Other taxes and fees; California-sales tax applicable; Florida—sales tax added to excise; Georgia—3 percent sales tax applicable; Hawaii—sales tax applicable; Idaho—clean water tax; Illinois—sales tax applicable and environmental fee; Indiana—sales tax applicable; Kentucky—environmental fee; Michigan—sales tax applicable; Mississippi—environmental fee; Missouri—inspection fee; Nebraska—petroleum fee; New Hampshire—oil discharge cleanup fee; New Jersey—petroleum fee; New Mexico—Petroleum loading fee; New York—sales tax applicable; North Carolina—Inspection tax; Ohio—plus 3 cents commercial; Oklahoma—environmental fee; Pennsylvania—oil franchise tax; Rhode Island—leaking underground storage tank tax (LUST);Tennessee—petroleum tax and environmental fee; Vermont—petroleum cleanup fee; Washington-$0.5 percent privilege tax; West Virginia—sales tax added to excise; Wyoming—license tax.

(r) Includes statewide local tax of 1.25 percent in California and 1.0 percent in Virginia.

(s) Tax rate in Hawaii is schedules to increase to $1.40 per pack on July 1, 2004.

(t) Plus 0.5 percent GRT.

Table 7.4
FOOD AND DRUG SALES TAX EXEMPTIONS
(As of January 1, 2004)

State or other jurisdiction	Tax rate (percentage)	Exemptions		
		Food (a)	Prescription drugs	Nonprescription drugs
Alabama	4	. . .	★	. . .
Alaska	none	. . .	. . .	. . .
Arizona	5.6	★	★	. . .
Arkansas	5.125	. . .	★	. . .
California (b)(c)	7.25	★	★	. . .
Colorado	2.9	★	★	
Connecticut	6	★	★	★
Delaware	none	. . .	. . .	. . .
Florida	6	★	★	★
Georgia	4	★	★	. . .
Hawaii	4	. . .	★	. . .
Idaho	6	. . .	★	. . .
Illinois	6.25	1 percent	1percent	1percent
Indiana	6	★	★	. . .
Iowa	5	★	★	. . .
Kansas	5.3	. . .	★	. . .
Kentucky	6	★	★	. . .
Louisiana	4	★ (d)	★	. . .
Maine	5	★	★	. . .
Maryland	5	★	★	★
Massachusetts	5	★	★	. . .
Michigan	6	★	★	★
Minnesota	6.5	★	★	★
Mississippi	7	. . .	★	. . .
Missouri	4.225	1.225	★	. . .
Montana	none	. . .	. . .	. . .
Nebraska	5.5	★	★	. . .
Nevada	6.5	★	★	. . .
New Hampshire	none	. . .	. . .	. . .
New Jersey	6	★	★	★
New Mexico	5	. . .	★	. . .
New York	4.25	★	★	★
North Carolina	4.5	★ (d)	★	. . .
North Dakota	5	★	★	. . .
Ohio	6	★	★	. . .
Oklahoma	4.5	. . .	★	. . .
Oregon	none	. . .	. . .	. . .
Pennsylvania	6	★	★	★
Rhode Island	7	★	★	★
South Carolina	5	. . .	★	. . .
South Dakota	4	. . .	★	. . .
Tennessee	7	6 percent	★	. . .
Texas	6.25	★	★	★
Utah	4.75	. . .	★	. . .
Vermont	6	★	★	★
Virginia (b)	4.5	4 percent (e)	★	★
Washington	6.5	★	★	. . .
West Virginia	6	. . .	★	. . .
Wisconsin	5	★	★	. . .
Wyoming (c)	4	. . .	★	. . .
Dist. of Columbia	5.75	★	★	★

Source: The Federation of Tax Administrators, January 2004.
Key:
★— Yes, exempt from tax.
. . . — Subject to general sales tax,
(a) Some states tax food, but allow an (income) tax credit to compensate poor households. They are: Idaho, Kansas, South Dakota and Wyoming.
(b) Includes statewide local tax of 1.25 percent in California and 1 percent in Virginia.

(c) The tax rate may be adjusted annually according to a formula based on balances in the unappropriated general fund and the school foundation fund.
(d) Food sales are subject to local sales tax. In Louisiana, food sales are scheduled to be exempt on 7/1/03.
(e) Tax rate on food is scheduled to decrease to 3.5 percent on 4/1/03. Statewide local tax is included.

Table 7.5
STATE INDIVIDUAL INCOME TAXES
(Tax rates for the tax year 2004—as of January 1, 2004)

State or other jurisdiction	Tax rate range (in percents) Low	High	Number of brackets	Income brackets Low	High	Personal exemptions Single	Married	Dependents	Federal income tax deductible
Alabama	2.0 –	5.0	3	500 (b) –	3,000 (b)	1,500	3,000	300	★
Alaska				----------(x)----------					...
Arizona	2.87 –	5.04	5	10,000 (b) –	150,000 (b)	2,100	4,200	2,300	...
Arkansas (a)	1.0 –	7.0 (e)	6	3,999 –	27,500	20 (c)	40 (c)	20 (c)	...
California (a)	1.0 –	9.3	6	5,962(b) –	39,133 (b)	80 (c)	160 (c)	251 (c)	...
Colorado	4.63		1	----------Flat rate----------		----------None----------			...
Connecticut	3.0 –	5	2	10,000 (b) –	10,000 (b)	12,500 (f)	24,000 (f)	0	...
Delaware	2.2 –	5.95	6	5,000 –	60,000	110 (c)	220 (c)	110 (c)	...
Florida				----------(x)----------					...
Georgia	1.0 –	6.0	6	750 (g) –	7,000 (g)	2,700	5,400	2,700	...
Hawaii	1.4 –	8.25	9	2,000 (b) –	40,000 (b)	1,040	2,080	1,040	...
Idaho (a)	1.6 –	7.8	8	1,104 (h) –	22,074 (h)	3,100 (d)	6,200 (d)	3,100 (d)	...
Illinois	3.0		1	----------Flat rate----------		2,000	4,000	2,000	...
Indiana	3.4		1	----------Flat rate----------		1,000	2,000	1,000	...
Iowa (a)	0.36 –	8.98	9	1,211 –	54,495	40 (c)	80 (c)	40 (c)	★
Kansas	3.5 –	6.45	3	15,000 (b) –	30,000 (b)	2,250	4,500	2,250	...
Kentucky	2.0 –	6.0	5	3,000 –	8,000	20 (c)	40 (c)	20 (c)	...
Louisiana	2.0 –	6.0	3	12,500 (b) –	25,000 (b)	4,500 (i)	9,000 (i)	1,000 (i)	★
Maine (a)	2.0 –	8.5	4	4,250 (b) –	16,950 (b)	4,700	7,850	1,000	...
Maryland	2.0 –	4.75	4	1,000 –	3,000	2,400	4,800	2,400	...
Massachusetts	5		1	----------Flat rate----------		3,300	6,600	1,000	...
Michigan (a)	4		1	----------Flat rate----------		3,000	6,000	3,000	...
Minnesota (a)	5.35 –	7.85	3	19,010 (j) –	62,440 (j)	3,100 (d)	6,200 (d)	3,100 (d)	...
Mississippi	3.0 –	5.0	3	5,000 –	10,000	6,000	12,000	1,500	...
Missouri	1.5 –	6.0	10	1,000 –	9,000	2,100	4,200	2,100	★ (s)
Montana (a)	2.0 –	11.0	10	2,199 –	76,199	1,740	3,480	1,740	★
Nebraska (a)	2.56 –	6.84	4	2,400 (k) –	26,500 (k)	94 (c)	188 (c)	94 (c)	...
Nevada				----------(x)----------					...
New Hampshire				----------(y)----------					...
New Jersey	1.4 –	6.37	6	20,000 (l) –	75,000 (l)	1,000	2,000	1,500	...
New Mexico	1.7 –	6.8	5	5,500 (m) –	26,000 (m)	3,100 (d)	6200 (d)	3,100 (d)	...
New York	4.0 –	7.7	7	8,000 (n) –	500,000 (n)	0	0	1,000	...
North Carolina (o)	6.0 –	8.25	4	12,750 (o) –	120,000 (o)	3,100 (d)	6,200 (d)	3,100 (d)	...
North Dakota	2.1 –	5.54 (p)	5	28,400 (p) –	311,950 (p)	3,100 (d)	6,200 (d)	3,100 (d)	...
Ohio (a)	0.743–	7.5	9	5,000 –	200,000	1,200 (q)	2,400 (q)	1,200 (q)	...
Oklahoma	0.5 –	6.65 (r)	8	1,000 (b) –	10,000 (b)	1,000	2,000	1,000	★(r)
Oregon (a)	5.0 –	9.0	3	2,500 (b) –	6,250 (b)	145 (c)	290 (c)	145 (c)	★(s)
Pennsylvania	2.8		1	----------Flat rate----------		----------None----------			...
Rhode Island				----------(t)----------					...
South Carolina (a)	2.5 –	7.0	6	2,400 –	12,000	3,000 (d)	6,000 (d)	3,000 (d)	...
South Dakota				----------(x)----------					...
Tennessee				----------(y)----------					...
Texas				----------(x)----------					...
Utah (a)	2.3 –	7.0	6	700 (b) –	3,750 (b)	2,325 (d)	4,500 (d)	2,325 (d)	★(u)
Vermont (a)	3.6 –	9.5	5	27,950 (v) –	307,050 (v)	3,100 (d)	6,200 (d)	3,100 (d)	...
Virginia	2.0 –	5.75	4	3,000 –	17,000	800	1,600	800	...
Washington				----------(x)----------					...
West Virginia	3.0 –	6.5	5	10,000 –	60,000	2,000	4,000	2,000	...
Wisconsin	4.6 –	6.75	4	8,280 (w) –	124,200 (w)	700	1,400	400	...
Wyoming				----------(x)----------					...
Dist. of Columbia	4.5 –	8.7 (z)	3	10,000 –	40,000	1,370	2,740	1,370	...

See footnotes at end of table.

STATE INDIVIDUAL INCOME TAXES — Continued

Source: The Federation of Tax Administrators from various sources, January 2004.

★—Yes

. . .—No

(a) Eight states have statutory provision for automatic adjustment of tax brackets, personal exemption or standard deductions to the rate of inflation. Michigan, Nebraska and Ohio indexes the personal exemption amounts only.

(b) For joint returns, the taxes are twice the tax imposed on half the income.

(c) Tax credits.

(d) These states allow personal exemption or standard deductions as provided in the Internal Revenue Code. Utah allows a personal exemption equal to three-fourths the federal exemptions.

(e) Plus a three percent surtax. A special tax table is available for low income taxpayers reducing their tax payments.

(f) Combined personal exemptions and standard deduction. An additional tax credit is allowed ranging from 75 percent to 0 percent based on state adjusted gross income. Exemption amounts are phased out for higher income taxpayers until they are eliminated for households earning over $54,500.

(g) The tax brackets reported are for single individuals. For married households filing separately, the same rates apply to income brackets ranging from $500 to $5,000; and the income brackets range from $1,000 to $10,000 for joint filers.

(h) For joint returns, the tax is twice the tax imposed on half of the income. A $10 filing tax is charged for each return and a $15 credit is allowed for each exemption.

(i) Combined personal exemption and standard deduction.

(j) The tax brackets reported are for single individual. For married couples filing jointly, the same rates apply for income under $27,780 to over $110,390.

(k) The tax brackets reported are for single individuals. For married couples filing jointly, the same rates apply for income under $4,000 to over $46,750.

(l) The tax brackets reported are for single individuals. For married individuals filing jointly, the same rates apply for income under $20,000 to over $150,000.

(m) The tax brackets reported are for single individuals. For married couples filing jointly, the same rates apply for income under $8,000 to over $40,000. Married households filing separately pay the tax imposed on half the income. Tax rate is scheduleed to decrease in tax year 2005.

(n) The tax brackets reported are for single individuals. For married taxpayers, the same rates apply to income brackets ranging from $16,000 to $500,000.

(o) The tax brackets reported are for single individuals. For married taxpayers, the same rates apply to income brackets ranging from $21,250 to $200,000. Lower exemption amounts allowed for high income taxpayers. Tax rates scheduled to decrease after year 2003.

(p) The tax brackets reported are for single individuals. For married taxpayers, the same rates apply to income brackets ranging from $47,450 to $311,950. An additional $300 personal exemption is allowed for joint returns or unmarried heads of households.

(q) Plus an additional $20 per exemption tax credit.

(r) The rate range reported is for single persons not deducting federal income tax. For married persons filing jointly, the same rates apply to income brackets ranging from $2,000 to $21,000. Separate schedules, with rates ranging from 0.5 percent to 10 percent, apply to taxpayers deducting federal income taxes.

(s) Deduction is limited to $10,000 for joint returns and $5,000 for individuals in Missouri and to $5,000 in Oregon.

(t) Twenty-five percent federal tax liability. Federal income tax liability prior to the Economic Growth and Tax Relief Act of 2001.

(u) One half of the federal income taxes are deductible.

(v) The tax brackets reported are for single individuals. For married couples filing jointly, the same rates apply for income under $46,700 to over $307,050.

(w) The tax brackets reported are for single individuals. For married taxpayers, the same rates apply to income brackets ranging from $11,240 to $168,560. An additional $250 exemption is provided for each taxpayer or spouse age 65 or over.

(x) No state income tax.

(y) State income tax is limited to dividends and interest income only.

(z) Tax rate decreases are scheduled for tax year 2005.

Table 7.6
STATE PERSONAL INCOME TAXES: FEDERAL STARTING POINTS
(As of January 1, 2004)

State or other jurisdiction	Relation to Internal Revenue Code	Tax base
Alabama	. . .	. . .
Alaska	(a)	(a)
Arizona	3/19/02	Federal adjusted gross income
Arkansas	. . .	. . .
California	1/1/03	Federal adjusted gross income
Colorado	Current	Federal taxable income
Connecticut	Current	Federal adjusted gross income
Delaware	Current	Federal adjusted gross income
Florida	(a)	(a)
Georgia	1/2/03	Federal adjusted gross income
Hawaii	12/31/02	Federal taxable income
Idaho	1/2/03	Federal taxable income
Illinois	Current	Federal adjusted gross income
Indiana	1/1/03	Federal adjusted gross income
Iowa	1/1/03	Federal adjusted gross income
Kansas	Current	Federal adjusted gross income
Kentucky	12/31/01	Federal adjusted gross income
Louisiana	Current	Federal adjusted gross income
Maine	5/28/03	Federal adjusted gross income
Maryland	Current	Federal adjusted gross income
Massachusetts	Current	Federal adjusted gross income
Michigan	Current (b)	Federal adjusted gross income
Minnesota	6/15/03	Federal taxable income
Mississippi	. . .	. . .
Missouri	Current	Federal adjusted gross income
Montana	Current	Federal adjusted gross income
Nebraska	2/20/03	Federal adjusted gross income
Nevada	(a)	(a)
New Hampshire	(c)	(c)
New Jersey	. . .	. . .
New Mexico	Current	Federal adjusted gross income
New York	Current	Federal adjusted gross income
North Carolina	6/1/03	Federal taxable income
North Dakota	Current	Federal taxable income
Ohio	Current	Federal adjusted gross income
Oklahoma	Current	Federal adjusted gross income
Oregon	Current	Federal taxable income
Pennsylvania	. . .	. . .
Rhode Island	6/3/01	Federal adjusted gross income
South Carolina	12/31/02	Federal taxable income
South Dakota	(a)	(a)
Tennessee	(c)	(c)
Texas	(a)	(a)
Utah	Current	Federal taxable income
Vermont	1/1/02	Federal taxable income
Virginia	12/31/02	Federal adjusted gross income
Washington	(a)	(a)
West Virginia	6/1/03	Federal adjusted gross income
Wisconsin	12/31/02	Federal adjusted gross income
Wyoming	(a)	(a)
Dist. of Columbia	Current	Federal adjusted gross income

Source: Compiled by the Federation of Tax Administrators from various sources, January 2004.

Key:

. . . — State does not employ a Federal starting point.

Current — Indicates state has adopted the Internal Revenue Code as currently in effect. Dates indicate state has adopted the IRC as amended to that date.

(a) No state income tax.

(b) Or 1/1/99, taxpayer's option.

(c) On interest and dividends only.

Table 7.7
RANGE OF STATE CORPORATE INCOME TAX RATES
(For tax year 2004—as of January 1, 2004)

State or other jurisdiction	Tax rate (percent)	Tax brackets		Number of brackets	Tax rate (a) (percent) financial institution	Federal income tax deductible
		Lowest	Highest			
Alabama	6.5	----------------Flat Rate----------------		1	6.5	★
Alaska	1.0–9.4	10,000	90,000	10	1.0–9.4	...
Arizona	6.968 (b)	----------------Flat Rate----------------		1	6.968 (b)	...
Arkansas	1.0–6.5	3,000	100,000	6	1.0–6.5	...
California	8.84 (c)	----------------Flat Rate----------------		1	10.84 (c)	...
Colorado	4.63	----------------Flat Rate----------------		1	4.63	...
Connecticut	7.5 (d)	----------------Flat Rate----------------		1	7.5 (d)	...
Delaware	8.7	----------------Flat Rate----------------		1	8.7–1.7 (e)	...
Florida	5.5 (f)	----------------Flat Rate----------------		1	5.5 (f)	...
Georgia	6.0	----------------Flat Rate----------------		1	6.0	...
Hawaii	4.4–6.4 (g)	25,000	100,000	3	7.92 (g)	...
Idaho	7.6 (h)	----------------Flat Rate----------------		1	7.6 (h)	...
Illinois	7.3 (i)	----------------Flat Rate----------------		1	7.3 (i)	...
Indiana	8.5	----------------Flat Rate----------------		1	8.5	...
Iowa	6.0–12.0	25,000	250,000	4	5.0	★(k)
Kansas	4.0 (l)	----------------Flat Rate----------------		1	2.25 (l)	...
Kentucky	4.0–8.25	25,000	250,000	5	(a)	...
Louisiana	4.0–8.0	25,000	200,000	5	(a)	★
Maine	3.5–8.93 (m)	25,000	250,000	4	1.0	...
Maryland	7.0	----------------Flat Rate----------------		1	7.0	...
Massachusetts	9.5 (n)	----------------Flat Rate----------------		1	10.5 (n)	...
Michigan	---See Note---					
Minnesota	9.8 (o)	----------------Flat Rate----------------		1	9.8 (o)	...
Mississippi	3.0–5.0	5,000	10,000	3	3.0–5.0	...
Missouri	6.25	----------------Flat Rate----------------		1	7.0	★(k)
Montana	6.75 (p)	----------------Flat Rate----------------		1	6.75 (p)	...
Nebraska	5.58–7.81	50,000		2	(a)	...
Nevada	---See Note---					
New Hampshire	8.5 (q)	----------------Flat Rate----------------		1	8.5 (q)	...
New Jersey	9.0 (r)	----------------Flat Rate----------------		1	9.0 (r)	...
New Mexico	4.8–7.6	500,000	1 million	3	4.8–7.6	...
New York	7.5 (s)	----------------Flat Rate----------------		1	7.5 (s)	...
North Carolina	6.9 (t)	----------------Flat Rate----------------		1	6.9 (t)	...
North Dakota	3.0–10.5	3,000	50,000	6	7.0 (b)	★
Ohio	5.1–8.5 (u)	50,000		2	(u)	...
Oklahoma	6.0	----------------Flat Rate----------------		1	6.0	...
Oregon	6.6 (b)	----------------Flat Rate----------------		1	6.6 (b)	...
Pennsylvania	9.99	----------------Flat Rate----------------		1	(a)	...
Rhode Island	9.0 (b)	----------------Flat Rate----------------		1	9.0 (v)	...
South Carolina	5.0	----------------Flat Rate----------------		1	4.5 (w)	...
South Dakota	...	...		...	6.0–0.25% (b)	...
Tennessee	6.5	----------------Flat Rate----------------		1	6.5	...
Texas	---See Note---					
Utah	5.0 (b)	----------------Flat Rate----------------		...	5.0 (b)	...
Vermont	7.0–9.75 (b)	10,000	250,000	4	7.0–9.75 (b)	...
Virginia	6.0	----------------Flat Rate----------------		1	6.0 (x)	...
Washington	---See Note---					
West Virginia	9.0	----------------Flat Rate----------------		1	9.0	...
Wisconsin	7.9	----------------Flat Rate----------------		1	7.9	...
Wyoming	---See Note---					
Dist. of Columbia	9.975 (y)	----------------Flat Rate----------------		...	9.975 (y)	...

See footnotes at end of table.

RANGE OF STATE CORPORATE INCOME TAX RATES — Continued

Source: Compiled by the Federation of Tax Administrators from various sources, January 2004.

Key:

★—Yes

. . .—No

Note: Michigan imposes a single business tax (sometimes described as a business activities tax or value added tax) of 1.9 percent on the sum of federal taxable income of the business, compensation paid to employees, dividends, interest, royalties paid and other items. Similarly, Texas imposes a franchise tax of 4.5 percent of earned surplus. Nevada, Washington, and Wyoming do not have state corporate income taxes.

(a) Rates listed include the corporate tax rate applied to financial institutions or excise taxes based on income. Some states have other taxes based upon the value of deposits or shares.

(b) Minimum tax is $50 in Arizona, $50 in North Dakota (banks), $10 in Oregon, $250 in Rhode Island, $500 per location in South Dakota (banks), $100 in Utah, $250 in Vermont.

(c) Minimum tax is $800. The tax rate on S-Corporations is 1.5 percent (3.5 percent for banks).

(d) Or 3.1 mills per dollar of capital stock and surplus (maximum tax $1 million) or $250.

(e) The marginal rate decreases over 4 brackets ranging from $20 to $650 million in taxable income. Building and loan associations are taxed at a flat 8.7 percent.

(f) Or 3.3 percent Alternative Minimum Tax. An exemption of $5,000 is allowed.

(g) Capital gains are taxed at 4 percent. There is also an alternative tax of 0.5 percent of gross annual sales.

(h) Minimum tax is $20. An additional tax of $10 is imposed on each return.

(i) Includes a 2.5 percent personal property replacement tax.

(j) Consists of 3.4 percent on income from sources within the state plus a 4.5 percent supplemental income tax.

(k) Fifty percent of the federal income tax is deductible.

(l) Plus a surtax of 3.35 percent (2.125 percent for banks) taxable income in excess of $50,000 ($25,000).

(m) Or a 27 percent tax on Federal Alternative Minimum Taxable Income.

(n) Rate includes a 14 percent surtax, as does the following: an additional tax of $7.00 per $1,000 on taxable tangible property (or net worth allocable to state, for intangible property corporations); minimum tax of $456.

(o) Plus a 5.8 percent tax on any Alternative Minimum Taxable Income over the base tax.

(p) A 7 percent tax on taxpayers using water's edge combination. Minimum tax is $50.

(q) Plus a 0.50 percent tax on the enterprise base (total compensation, interest and dividends paid). Business profits tax imposed on both corporations and unincorporated associations.

(r) The rate reported in the table is the business franchise tax rate. The minimum tax is $500. An Alternative Minimum Assessment based on Gross Receipts applies if greater than corporate franchise tax. Corporations not subject to the franchise tax are subject to a 7.25 percent income tax. Banking and financial corporations are subject to the franchise tax. Corporations with net income under $100,000 are taxed at 6.5 percent. The tax on S corporations is being phased out through 2007. The tax rate on a New Jersey S corporation that has entire net income not subject to federal corporate income tax in excess of $100,000 will remain at 1.33 percent for privilege periods ending on or before June 30, 2006. The rate will be 0.67 percent for privilege periods ending on or after July 1, 2006, but onor before June 30, 2007; and there will be no tax imposed for privilege periods ending on or after July 1, 2007. The tax on S corporation with entire net income not subject to federal corporate income tax of $ 100,000 or less is eliminated for privilege periods ending on or after July 1, 2007.

(s) Or 1.78 (0.1 for banks) mills per dollar of capital (up to $350,000; or 2.5 percent of the minimum taxable income); or a minimum of $100 to $1,500 depending on payroll size ($250 for banks); if any of these is greater than the tax computed on net income. An additional tax of 0.9 mills per dollar of subsidiary capital is imposed on corporations. Small corporations with income under $290,000 pay a tax of 7.5 percent on all income.

(t) Financial institutions are also subject to a tax equal to $30 per one million in assets.

(u) Or 4.0 mills times the value of the taxpayer's issued and outstanding share of stock with a maximum payment of $150,000. An additional litter tax is imposed equal to 0.11 percent on the first $50,000 of taxable income, 0.22 percent on income over $50,000; or 0.14 mills on net worth.

(v) For banks, the alternative tax is $2.50 per $10,000 of capital stock ($100 minimum).

(w) Savings and Loans are taxed at a 6 percent rate.

(x) State and national banks subject to the state's franchise tax on net capital is exempt from the income tax.

(y) Minimum tax is $100. Includes surtax.

Table 7.8
STATE SEVERANCE TAXES: 2002-2004

State	Title and application of tax (a)	Rate
Alabama	Iron Ore Mining Tax	$.03/ton
	Forest Products Severance Tax	Varies by species and ultimate use.
	Oil and Gas Conservation & Regulation of Production Tax	2% of gross value at point of production, of all oil and gas produced. 1% of the gross value (for a 5-year period from the date production begins) for well, for which the initial permit issued by the Oil and Gas Board is dated on or after July 1, 1996 and before July 1, 2002, except a replacement well for which the initial permit was dated before July 1, 1996
	Oil and Gas Privilege Tax on Production	8% of gross value at point of production; 4% of gross value at point of incremental production resulting from a qualified enhanced recovery project; 4% if wells produce 25 bbl. or less oil per day or 200,000 cu. ft. or less gas per day; 6% of gross value at point of production for certain on-shore and off-shore wells. A 50% rate reduction for wells permitted by the oil and gas board on or after July 1, 1996 and before July 1, 2002 for 5 years from initial production, except for replacement wells for which the initial permit was dated before July 1, 1996.
	Coal Severance Tax	$.135/ton
	Coal and Lignite Severance Tax	$.20/ton in addition to coal severance tax.
Alaska	Fisheries Business Tax	1% to 5% of fish value based on type of fish and processing.
	Fishery Resource Landing Tax	3% of the value of the fishery resource at the place of landing for an established commercial fish species; 1% of the value of the the of the fishery resource at the place of landing for a developing commercial fish species.
	Seafood Marketing Assessment	.03% on all commercial fish species.
	Oil and Gas Properties Production Tax	(Oil) The greater of either $0.80/bbl for old crude oil or 15% of gross value at the production point for oil fields in production more than 5 years and12.25 percent for oil fields in production less than 5 years,, multiplied by the Economic Limit Factor for oil; (Gas) The greater of either $0.64/1000 cu. ft. of gas or 10% of gross value at the production point, multiplied by the Economic Limit Factor for Gas; and conservation surcharges of $.03 cents per barrel, with an additional $.02 cents per barrel as needed to maintain a $50 million balance in the oil and hazardous substance response fund.
	Salmon Marketing Tax	1% of the value of salmon that is removed or transferred.
Arizona	Severance Tax (b)	2.5% of net severance base for mining; $1.50/1000 board ft. ($2.13 for ponderosa pine) for timbering.
Arkansas	Natural Resources Severance Tax	Separate rate for each substance.
	Oil and Gas Conservation Tax	Maximum 25 mills/bbl. of oil and 5 mills/1,000 cu. ft. of gas. (c)
California	Oil and Gas Production Tax	Rate determined annually by Department of Conservation. (d)
Colorado	Severance Tax (e)	Taxable years commencing prior to July 1, 1999, 2.25% of gross income exceeding$11 million for metallic minerals and taxable years commencing after July 1,1999, 2.25% of gross income exceeding $19 million for metallic minerals; on or after July 1,1999, $.05/ton for each ton exceeding 625,000 tons each quarter for molybdenum ore; 2% to 5% based on gross income for oil, gas, CO2, and coalbed methane; after July 1,1999, $.36/ton adjusted by the producers' prices index for each ton exceeding 300,000 tons each quarter for coal; and 4% of gross proceeds on production exceeding 15,000 tons per day for oil shale.
	Oil and Gas Conservation Levy	Maximum 1.5 mills/$1 of market value at wellhead. (f)
Florida	Oil, Gas and Sulfur Production Tax	5% of gross value for small well oil, and 8% of gross value for all other, and an additional 12.5% for escaped oil; the gas base rate times the gas base adjustment rate each fiscal year for gas; and the sulfur base rate times the sulfur base rate adjustment each fiscal year for sulfur.
	Solid Minerals Tax (g)	8% of the value of the minerals severed, except phosphate rock (rate computed annually at $1.08/ton times the changes in the producer price index) and heavy minerals (rate computed annually at a base rate of $1.34/ton times the base rate adjustment).
Idaho	Ore Severance Tax	1% of net value
	Oil and Gas Production Tax	Maximum of 5 mills/bbl. of oil and 5 mills/50,000 cu. ft. of gas. (c)
	Additional Oil and Gas Production Tax	2% of market value at site of production.

See footnotes at end of table.

STATE SEVERANCE TAXES — Continued

State	Title and application of tax (a)	Rate
Illinois	Timber Fee	4% of purchase price (h)
Indiana	Petroleum Production Tax (i)	1% of value or $.24 per barrel for oil or $.03 per 1,000 cu. Ft. of gas, whichever is greater.
Kansas	Severance Tax (j)	8% of gross value of oil and gas, less property tax credit of 3.67%; $1/ ton of coal.
	Oil and Gas Conservation Tax	27.27 mills/bbl. crude oil or petroleum marketed or used each month; 5.83 mills/1,000 cu. ft. of gas sold or marketed each month.
Kentucky	Mined-Land Conservation & Reclamation Tax	$50, plus per ton fee of between $.03 and $.10.
	Oil Production Tax	4.5% of market value
	Coal Severance Tax	4.5% of gross value, less transportation expenses
	Natural Resource Severance Tax (k)	4.5% of gross value, less transportation expenses
Louisiana	Natural Resources Severance Tax	Rate varies according to substance.
	Oil Field Site Restoration Fee	Rate varies according to type of well and production.
	Freshwater Mussel Tax	5% of revenues from the sale of whole freshwater mussels, at the point of first sale.
Maine	Mining Excise Tax	The greater of a tax on facilities and equipment or a tax on gross proceeds.
Maryland	Mine Reclamation Surcharge	$.15/ton of coal removed by open-pit, strip or deep mine methods. Of the $.15 , $.06 is remitted to the county from which the coal was removed.
Michigan	Gas and Oil Severance Tax	5% (gas), 6.6% (oil) and 4% (oil from stripper wells and marginal properties) of gross cash market value of the total production. Maximum additional fee of 1% of gross cash market value on all oil and gas produced in state in previous year.
Minnesota	Taconite and Iron Sulfides	$2.173 per ton of concentrates or pellets
	Direct Reduced Iron (l)	$2.173 per ton of concentrates plus an additional $.03 per ton for each 1% that the iron content exceeds 72%
Mississippi	Oil and Gas Severance Tax	6% of value at point of gas production; 3.5% of gross value of occluded natural gas from coal seams at point of production for well's first five years; also, maximum 35 mills/bbl. oil or 4 mills/1,000 cu. ft. gas (Oil and Gas Board maintenance tax). 6% of value at point of oil production; 3% of value at production when enhanced oil recovery method used.
	Timber Severance Tax	Varies depending on type of wood and ultimate use.
	Salt Severance Tax	3% of value of entire production in state.
Missouri	Assessment on Surface Coal Mining Permittees	$.45/ton for first 50,000 tons sold, shipped or otherwise disposed of in calendar year, and $.30/ton for next 50,000 tons. Whenever Coal Mine Land Reclamation Fund balance is less than $7 million, $.25/ ton for first 50,000 tons and $.15/ton for second 50,000 tons. Whenever Fund is less than $2 million, $.30/ton for first 50,000 tons and $.20 for the second 50,000 tons.
Montana	Coal Severance Tax	Varies by quality of coal and type of mine.
	Metalliferous Mines License Tax (m)	Progressive rate, taxed on amounts in excess of $250,000. For concentrate shipped to smelter, mill or reduction work, 1.81%. Gold, silver or any platinum group metal shipped to refinery, 1.6%.
	Oil or Gas Conservation Tax	Maximum 0.3% on the market value of each barrel of crude petroleum oil or 10,000 cu. ft. of natural gas produced, saved and marketed or stored within or exported from the state. (n)
	Oil and Natural Gas Production Tax	Varies according to the type of well and type of production.
	Micaceous Minerals License Tax	$.05/ton
	Cement License Tax (o)	$.22/ton of cement, $.05/ton of cement, plaster, gypsum or gypsum products.
	Mineral Mining Tax	$25 plus 0.5% of gross value greater than $5,000. For talc, $25 plus 4% of gross value greater than $625. For coal, $25 plus 0.40% of gross value greater than $6,250. For vermiculite, $25 plus 2% of gross value greater than $1,250. For limestone, $25 plus 10% of gross value greater than $250. For industrial garnets, $25 plus 1% of gross value greater than $2,500.00

See footnotes at end of table.

STATE SEVERANCE TAXES — Continued

State	Title and application of tax (a)	Rate
Nebraska	Oil and Gas Severance Tax	3% of value of nonstripper oil and natural gas; 2% of value of stripper oil.
	Oil and Gas Conservation Tax	Maximum 15 mills/$1 of value at wellhead, as of January 1, 2000 (c)
	Uranium Tax	2% of gross value over $5 million.
Nevada	Minerals Extraction Tax	Between 2% and 5% of net proceeds of each geographically separate extractive operation, based on ratio of net proceeds to gross proceeds of whole operation.
	Oil and Gas Conservation Tax	$50/mills/bbl. of oil and 50 mills/50,000 cu. ft. of gas.
New Hampshire	Refined Petroleum Products Tax	0.1% of fair market value
	Excavation Tax	$.02 per cubic yard of earth excavated.
	Excavation Activity Tax	Replaces real property tax on the land area that has been excavated and not reclaimed. The assessed per acre value and tax varies depending upon municipality. (x)
	Timber Tax	10% of stumpage value
New Mexico	Resources Excise Tax (p)	Varies according to substance.
	Severance Tax (p)	Varies according to substance.
	Oil and Gas Severance Tax	3.75% of value of oil, other liquid hydrocarbons, natural gas and carbon dioxide.
	Oil and Gas Emergency School Tax	3.15% of value of oil, other liquid hydrocarbons and carbon dioxide. 4% of value of natural gas.
	Natural Gas Processor's Tax	0.45% of value of products.
	Oil and Gas Ad Valorem Production Tax	Varies, based on property tax in district of production.
	Oil and Gas Conservation Tax (q)	0.19% of value.
North Carolina	Oil and Gas Conservation Tax	Maximum 5 mills/barrel of oil and 0.5 mill/1,000 cu. ft. of gas.
	Primary Forest Product Assessment Tax	Varies according to species.
North Dakota	Oil Gross Production Tax	5% of gross value at well.
	Gas Gross Production Tax	$.04/1000 cu.ft. of gas produced (the rate is subject to a a gas rate adjustment each fiscal year).
	Coal Severance Tax	$.375/ton plus $.02/ton. (r)
	Oil Extraction Tax	6.5% of gross value at well (with exceptions due to date of well completion, production volumes and production incentives).
Ohio	Resource Severance Tax	$.10/bbl. of oil; $.025/1,000 cu. ft. of natural gas; $.04/ton of salt; $.02/ ton of sand, gravel, limestone and dolomite; $.09/ton of coal; and $0.01/ton of clay, sandstone or conglomerate, shale, gypsum or quartzite.
Oklahoma	Oil, Gas and Mineral Gross Production Tax and Petroleum Excise Tax (s)	Rate; 0.75% levied on asphalt and metals. 7% casinghead gas and natural gas , as well as 0.95% being levied on crude oil, casinghead gas and natural gas. Oil Gross Production Tax is now a variable rate tax, beginning with January 1999 production, at the following rates based on the average price of Oklahoma oil: a) If the average price equals or exceeds $17/bbl, the tax shall be 7%; b) If the average price is less than $17/bbl, but is equal to or exceeds $14/bbl, the tax shall be 4%; c) If the average price is less than $14/bbl, the tax shall be 1%.
Oregon	Forest Products Harvest Tax	$2.87/1000 board ft. harvested from public and private land. (rate is for 2002 harvests)
	Oil and Gas Production Tax	6% of gross value at well.
	Privilege Tax on Eastern Oregon Timber	0.8% of immediate harvest value from privately owned land.(>=5,000 acre forestland ownership). 1.8% of immediate harvest value from privately owned land. (<5,000 acre forestland ownership)
	Privilege Tax on Western Oregon Timber	1.4% of immediate harvest value from privately owned land. (>=5,000 acre forestland ownership). 3.2% of immediate harvest value from privately owned land (<5,000 acre forestland ownership)
South Dakota	Precious Metals Severance Tax	$4 per ounce of gold severed plus additional tax depending on price of gold; 10% on net profits or royalties from sale of precious metals, and 8% of royalty value.
	Energy Minerals Severance Tax (t)	4.5% of taxable value of any energy minerals.
	Conservation Tax	2.4 mills of taxable value of any energy minerals.
Tennessee	Oil and Gas Severance Tax	3% of sales price
	Coal Severance Tax (u)	$.20/ton

See footnotes at end of table.

STATE SEVERANCE TAXES — Continued

State	Title and application of tax (a)	Rate
Texas	Gas Production Tax	7.5% of market value.
	Oil Production Tax	The greater of 4.6% of market value or $.046/bbl. 2.3% of market value for oil produced from qualified enhanced recovery projects.
	Sulphur Production Tax	$1.03/long ton or fraction thereof.
	Cement Production Tax	$.0275/100 lbs. or fraction thereof.
	Oil-Field Cleanup Regulatory Fees	5/8 of $.01/barrel; 1/15 of $.01/1000 cubic feet of gas. (v)
Utah	Metalliferous Minerals Tax	2.6% of taxable value for metals.
	Oil and Gas Tax	3% of value for the first $13 per barrel of oil, 5% from $13.01 and above; 3% of value for first $1.50/mcf, 5% from $1.51 and above; and 4% of taxable value of natural gas liquids.
	Oil and Gas Conservation Tax	.2% of market value at wellhead.
Virginia	Forest Products Tax	Varies by species and ultimate use.
	Coal Surface Mining Reclamation Tax (w)	Varies depending on balance of Coal Surface Mining Reclamation Fund.
Washington	Uranium and Thorium Milling Tax	$0.02/per kilogram.
	Enhanced Food Fish Tax	0.09% to 5.62% of value (depending on species) at point of landing.
	Timber Excise Tax	5% of stumpage value for harvests on public and private lands.
West Virginia	Natural Resource Severance Taxes	Coal, state rate is greater of 4.65% or $.75 per ton. Local rate is .35%. Special state rates for coal from new low seam mines. For seams between 37" and 45" the rate is greater of 1.65% or $.75/ton. For seams less than 37" the rate is greater of .65% or $.75/ton. Limestone or sandstone quarried or mined, 5% of gross value. Oil, 5% of gross value. Natural gas, 5% of gross value. Timber, 3.22% of gross value. Other natural resources, 5% of gross value.
Wisconsin	Mining Net Proceeds Tax	Progressive net proceeds tax ranging from 3% to 15% is imposed on the net proceeds from mining metalliferous minerals. The tax brackets are annually adjusted for inflation based on the change in the GNP deflator.
	Oil and Gas Severance Tax	7% of market value of oil or gas at the mouth of the well. There are no wells in the state
Wyoming	Severance Tax	Severance Tax is defined as an excise tax imposed on the present and continuing privilege of removing, extracting, severing or producing any mineral in this state. Except as otherwise provided by W.S. 39-14-205 (Tax Exemptions), the total severance tax on crude oil, lease condensate or natural gas shall be six percent (6%), comprising one and one-half percent (1.5%) imposed by the Wyoming constitution article 15, section 19 and four and one-half percent (4.5%) imposed by Wyoming statute. The tax shall be distributed as provided in W.S. 39-14-211 and is imposed as follows: i. One and one-half percent (1.5%);plus ii. One-half percent (.5%); plus iii. Two percent (2%); plus iv. Two percent (2%). Severance Tax is applied to the taxable value of crude oil, lease condensate or natural gas. The taxable value is the gross sales value of the product less Federal, State or Tribal Royalties paid and less allowable transportation deductions. If the product produced is natural gas, an additional deduction is allowed for processing. Rates vary from 1.50% to 6.0% on different grades of oil. Taxes on coal and other minerals varies from 2% to 4%.

See footnotes at end of table.

STATE SEVERANCE TAXES — Continued

Sources: The Council of State Governments' survey, November 2003, and state web sites, January 2004.

Key:

(a) Application of tax is same as that of title unless otherwise indicated by a footnote.

(b) Timber, metalliferous minerals.

(c) Actual rate set by administrative actions. Current conservation rate is 5 mills(.005).

(d) For 2001, $.0373354/bbl of oil or 10,000 cu. ft. of natural gas.

(e) Metallic minerals, molybdenum ore, coal, oil shale, oil, gas, CO2, and coalbed methane.

(f) As of January 31, 2000, set at 1.2 mills/$1.

(g) Clay, gravel, phosphate rock, lime, shells, stone, sand, heavy minerals and rare earths.

(h) Buyer deducts amount from payment to grower; amount forwarded to Department of Conservation.

(i) Petroleum, oil, gas and other hydrocarbons.

(j) Coal, oil and gas.

(k) Coal and oil excepted.

(l) State also has two related taxes; Mining Occupation Tax and Net Proceeds Tax. Also selected counties must impose an Aggregate Materials Tax of $.10/cubic yard or $.07/ton on materials produced in the county.

(m) Metals, precious and semi-precious stones and gems.

(n) Currently, the tax is levied at the rate of 0.3%.

(o) Cement and gypsum or allied products.

(p) Natural resources except oil, natural gas, liquid hydrocarbons or carbon dioxide.

(q) Oil, coal, gas, liquid hydrocarbons, geothermal energy, carbon dioxide and uranium.

(r) Rate reduced by 50 percent if burned in cogeneration facility using renewable resources as fuel to generate at least 10 percent of its energy output. Between June 30, 1995 and July 1, 2000, the rate is reduced by 50% for coal mined for out-of-state shipment. Between June 30, 1999 and July 1, 2003, the rate is reduced by 50% for coal burned in coal-fired boilers where the generating station has a total capacity of not more than 210 megawatts.

(s) Asphalt and ores bearing lead, zinc, jack, gold, silver, copper or petroleum or other crude oil or other mineral oil, natural gas or casinghead gas and uranium ore.

(t) Any mineral fuel used in the production of energy, including coal, lignite, petroleum, oil, natural gas, uranium and thorium.

(u) Counties and municipalities also authorized to levy severance taxes on sand, gravel, sandstone, chert and limestone and a privilege tax on nuclear materials.

(v) Fees will not be collected when Oil-Field Cleanup Fund reaches $10 million, but will again be collected when fund falls below $6 million.

(w) Until 2003, any county and city may adopt a license tax at a rate not over 1% of gross receipts on persons engaged in the business of severing coal or gases.

(x) On November 26, 2001, the New Hampshire Supreme Court issued a ruling in the case of Nash Family Investments v. Town of Hudson and Ballinger Properties, et. al. v. Town of Londonderry. The Court ruled that the method of valuing property subject to the Excavation Activity Tax as set forth in RSA 72-B: 12, III was unconstitutional.

Table 7.9
FISCAL 2003 STATE GENERAL FUND, PRELIMINARY ACTUAL, BY REGION
(In millions of dollars)

State or other jurisdiction	Beginning balance	Revenues	Adjustments	Resources	Expenditures	Adjustments	Ending balance	Budget stabilization fund
Eastern Region								
Connecticut (g)	$0	$11,531	$485	$12,016	$12,345	-$225	-$104	$0
Delaware (a) (h)	482	2,436	0	2,918	2,454	0	464	129
Maine (p)	0	2,372	192	2,564	2,540	0	24	0
Massachusetts (a)	1,388	21,975	0	23,363	22,390	0	973	726
New Hampshire (x)	-38	1,207	91	1,336	1,336	0	0	20
New Jersey (a)	292	22,931	0	23,223	22,927	46	250	0
New York (a) (z)	1,032	39,296	0	40,328	39,513	0	815	710
Pennsylvania (ff)	143	20,385	152	20,679	20,715	-245	209	70
Rhode Island (gg)	41	2,750	-56	2,735	2,699	0	36	83
Vermont (mm)	0	863	21	884	890	-6	0	24
Regional average	334	12,575	89	13,005	12,781	-43	267	176
Midwest Region								
Illinois (j)	256	21,103	3,802	25,161	21,893	2,951	317	226
Indiana (k)	0	9,945	500	10,446	10,309	0	137	279
Iowa (l)	0	4,484	0	4,484	4,529	0	-46	209
Kansas (m)	12	4,248	0	4,260	4,138	0	123	0
Michigan (r)	115	8,084	696	8,895	8,821	0	74	0
Minnesota	1,130	13,050	0	14,180	14,000	0	180	0
Nebraska (v)	56	2,456	109	2,622	2,619	0	3	59
North Dakota (bb)	-5	856	19	870	855	0	15	6
Ohio (cc)	108	22,450	0	22,558	22,653	-148	53	181
South Dakota (ii)	0	875	17	891	884	8	0	106
Wisconsin (pp)	54	10,464	255	10,772	11,033	22	-282	0
Regional average	157	8,910	491	9,558	9,249	258	52	97
Southern Region								
Alabama (b)	19	5,296	270	5,585	5,513	-41	113	68
Arkansas	0	3,251	0	3,251	3,251	0	0	0
Florida	984	20,213	0	21,197	20,707	0	491	959
Georgia (a)	2,554	13,829	0	16,383	15,271	0	1,112	562
Kentucky (n)	24	6,914	506	7,444	7,179	102	163	5
Louisiana (o)	0	6,403	259	6,662	6,617	21	23	191
Maryland (q)	309	9,377	783	10,469	10,669	-323	123	490
Mississippi (s)	4	3,443	47	3,494	3,509	-48	33	22
Missouri (t)	165	7,504	0	7,669	7,548	0	121	231
North Carolina (aa)	25	14,109	137	14,271	13,856	165	251	150
Oklahoma (dd)	75	4,581	31	4,687	4,656	0	31	0
South Carolina (a) (hh)	50	4,968	22	5,040	4,995	0	46	0
Tennessee (jj)	12	7,939	175	8,126	8,026	79	21	111
Texas (kk)	2,426	28,734	-96	31,064	30,389	592	83	561
Virginia	133	12,071	0	12,204	12,118	0	86	257
West Virginia (oo)	197	2,917	24	3,139	2,933	10	196	58
Regional average	436	9,472	135	10,043	9,827	35	181	229
Western Region								
Alaska (c)	0	1,977	494	2,471	2,471	0	0	2,142
Arizona (d)	1	5,640	391	6,031	6,014	0	18	14
California (e)	-2,133	81,527	18	79,412	78,142	-132	1,402	0
Colorado (a) (f)	138	5,665	334	6,137	5,914	0	223	0
Hawaii	134	3,789	0	3,923	3,806	0	117	53
Idaho (i)	1	1,764	176	1,941	1,926	0	16	0
Montana (u)	81	1,246	-6	1,322	1,280	0	42	0
Nevada (w)	90	1,819	229	2,139	2,036	2	100	1
New Mexico (a) (y)	320	3,944	75	4,339	4,051	43	245	N.A.
Oregon (ee)	-1,068	5,038	0	3,969	3,912	0	57	0
Utah (ll)	1	3,476	83	3,560	3,521	20	18	31
Washington (nn)	437	10,711	518	11,666	11,368	0	298	58
Wyoming (qq)	10	625	134	768	694	71	4	36
Regional average	-153	9,786	188	9,821	9,626	0	195	195
Regional average without California	12	3,808	202	4,022	3,916	11	95	212

See footnotes at end of table.

FISCAL 2003 STATE GENERAL FUND, PRELIMINARY ACTUAL, BY REGION — Continued

Source: National Association of State Budget Officers', *Fiscal Survey of States*, November 2003.

Note: For all states, unless otherwise noted, transfers into budget stabilization funds are counted as expenditures and transfers from budget stabilization funds are counted as revenues.

Key:

N.A. — Not available.

(a) In these states, the ending balance includes the balance in the budget stabilization fund.

(b) Revenue adjustments reflect a $180 million transfer from the Education Trust Fund Rainy Day Account, a $12.8 million transfer from the State General Fund Proration Prevention Fund, $75.6 million in federal assistance, and $1.9 million in land sale proceeds. Expenditure adjustments reflect $12.2 million from the repayment of 16th Section Land funds, -$47 million of reversions/adjustments, and a -$5.1 million across-the -board cut.

(c) Adjustments reflect a Constitutional Budget Reserve (CBR) draw.

(d) Revenue adjustments include a Ladewig court judgment costs set aside of ($15.0 million), $348.9 in fund transfers, a revenue generating plan $5.8 million, and asset sales of $50.9 million.

(e) Revenue adjustments include $10,675.4 million for a deficit financing bond, and also reflect a prior year revenue adjustment of $17.7 million. Expenditure adjustments of $131.8 million reflect a prior year expenditure adjustment.

(f) Revenue adjustments include a diversion to the State Education Fund and the Older Coloradoans Program, as well as $525.3 million in revenue transferred to the General Fund to mitigate revenue decline.

(g) Includes mid-year enacted legislation reducing expenditures and raising revenues. Will issue short term notes to cover estimated debt.

(h) Adjustments reflect implemented spending cuts; the Rainy Day Fund is intact.

(i) Revenue adjustments include $18.7 million in transfers to other funds and $194.7 million in transfers from other funds.

(j) Adjustments on revenues include $1,675 million received from short term borrowing proceeds and $1,827 million that were deposited into the general fund. The adjustments to expenditures include the repayment of short term borrowing of $710 million that came due in fiscal year 2003,accounts payable pay down of $210 million and transfers out of $2,031 million.

(k) Revenue adjustments represent one-time transfers from dedicated funds and the federal Jobs and Growth Tax Relief Reconciliation Act of 2003.

(l) The Rainy Day Fund balance includes $43.8 million of one-time transfers to various other funds. It is anticipated that action will occur to use the reserve funds to bring the fiscal 2003 ending balance to zero.

(m) Revenue adjustments reflect released encumbrances. Kansas does not have a separate Rainy Day Fund.

(n) Revenue includes $130.8 million in tobacco settlement funds. Adjustment for revenues includes $107.2 million that represents appropriation balances carried over from the prior fiscal year. Adjustments to revenues include $329.8 million that represents fund transfers into the General Fund and $68.7 in Federal Fiscal Relief funds. Adjustment to expenditures represents appropriation balances forwarded to the next fiscal year.

(o) Revenue adjustments include $19.9 million in carry-forward from fiscal 2001-2002, $68.4 million from the Budget Stabilization Fund and $152.2 million in one-time funds. Expenditure adjustments include $21.3 million in carry-forward expenditures.

(p) Revenue adjustments include $191.7 in legislative and statutorily authorized transfers. These include $25 million from the Federal Relief Fund Reserve, $48.7 million from transfers of unencumbered balances and lapsed balances, $38.5 million transferred from the rainy day fund,$14.6 million transferred from the Maine Learning Technology Endowment, $38.3 million transferred from the Fund for a Healthy Maine (Tobacco Settlement Payments), $10 million from operating capital, and $16.6 million from Highway Fund.

(q) Revenue adjustments reflect a transfer from Rainy day Fund ($249 million), other transfers ($501 million, and additional federal Medicaid ($33 million). Expenditure adjustments reflect cost containments of ($-218 million), targeted revisions ($-15 million), and federal funds for operating expenditures ($-90 million).

(r) Fiscal 2003 revenue adjustments include federal and state tax law changes ($-198.6 million); a Rainy Day Fund withdrawal ($124.1 million); unrestricted federal aid ($169 million): revenue sharing accounting adjustments ($181 million); legal settlement revenue ($31.9 million); and deposits from state restricted funds ($388.6 million).

(s) Fifty percent of the fiscal 2002 endi8ng balance is brought forward as the beginning balance; revenue adjustments include $8.3 million re-appropriation, $16 million transfer from working cash, and $26.7 million transfer from special funds in lieu of general fund cuts.

(t) Revenues include transfers to general revenue. Revenues include $150 million from revenue bond proceeds for capital improvement projects. Expenditures include refunds of $1,160.2 million.

(u) Adjustments primarily reflect prior year activity.

(v) Revenue adjustments are transfers between the general fund and other funds.

(w) The fiscal 2002 ending balance and fiscal 2003 beginning balance differ due to rounding.

(x) Revenue adjustments reflect $33.9 million transferred from the Health Care Fund: $35.7 million from the Rainy Day Fund: and $21.6 million from the Education Trust Fund.

(y) Adjustments reflect reserve account activity.

(z) The ending balance includes $710 million in the tax stabilization reserve fund (Rainy Day Fund), $85 million in the Community Projects Fund and $20 million in reserve funds for litigation risks.

(aa) Revenue adjustments equal $136.9 million of federal fiscal relief. Expenditure adjustments equal $150 million transfer to Rainy Day Fund and $15 million transfer to repair and renovation reserves.

(bb) Revenue adjustments reflect a transfer from the state's budget reserve at the Bank of North Dakota.

(cc) Federal reimbursements for Medicaid and other human services programs are included in t he general revenue fund. Beginning balances are undesignated, unreserved fund balances. The actual cash balances would be higher by the amount reserved for encumbrances and designated transfers from the general revenues fund. Expenditures for fiscal 2003 do not include encumbrances outstanding at the end of the year. Ohio reports expenditures based on disbursements for the general revenue fund. Expenditure adjustments reflect miscellaneous transfer- out are adjusted for an anticipated net change in encumbrances from fiscal 2002 levels of $-166.7 million.

(dd) Revenue adjustments reflect decrease in general revenue fund cash-flow reserve increasing available revenue by $31.3 million.

(ee) Oregon budgets on a biennial basis. While fiscal years may have a negative balance, the state is constitutionally requires to have a balanced budget at the end of the biennium. The Legislature held five special sessions and passed one fiscal bill during the last regular session to balance the 2001-2003 biennium.

(ff) Revenue adjustments include lapses of $151.8 million from prior-year appropriations and a $0.3 million decrease to the beginning balance. Total expenditures reflect the total amount appropriated. Expenditure adjustments include current-year lapses of $315.1 million and the year-end transfer of $69.8 million to the budget stabilization (rainy day) fund. (Note: The previously enacted transfer of $300 million to re-establish the budget stabilization (rainy day) fund was repealed).

(gg) Adjustment to revenues is contribution to budget stabilization fund.

(hh) Revenue adjustments reflect $22 million from the State's General Deposit Account used for closing fiscal 2003.

(ii) Revenue adjustments reflect $10.5 million transferred from the Property Tax Reduction Fund to cover the budget shortfall, and $6.2 million of obligated cash carried forward from fiscal 2002. Expenditure adjustments reflect $6.2 million transferred to the Budget Reserve Fund from the prior year's obligated cash, and $1.4 million of obligated cash to the Budget Reserve Fund.

(jj) Revenue adjustments reflect a $28 million transfer from debt service fund unexpected appropriations; a $30 million transfer from highway fund, a $50 million transfer from other reserves, and a $67.2 million transfer from Rainy Day Fund. Expenditure adjustments reflect a $21 million transfer to Transportation Equity Fund, a $27.9 million transfer to capital outlay projects fund, and a $29.9 million for dedicated revenue appropriations.

(kk) The revenue/balance information is from the Comptroller's September 2003 revenue update. Revenue adjustments reflect dedicated account balances. Total expenditures are preliminary 2003 budgeted, as reported by the Governor's Office, adjusted to reflect budget cuts of $1.267 billion adopted by the legislature. Total expenditures include appropriations from the Rainy Day Fund. Expenditure adjustments include a $353 million reserve for transfers to the Rainy Day Fund and other adjustments to reconcile the actual ending balance reported by the Comptroller.

(ll) (Original Budget): Revenue adjustments include: a $44.4 million transfer from tobacco settlement funds, $35 million of bonding for capital projects which originally received a general fun appropriation, a $19.4 million transfer from various restricted accounts, $10 million from designated sales taxes for water projects, $2 million reserved from the previous year, $-35.6 million reserved for following fiscal year, and $7.7 million from other miscellaneous sources. Preliminary year-end actuals subject to audit reflect: $24.1 million in additional revenue collections, including lower than budgeted sales, income, and miscellaneous tax collections ($-13.9 million) and $38 million in Federal relief aid; an expenditure reduction of $14.1 million from agency year-end lapsing balances; and expenditure adjustments of $19.9 million, including funds reserved for the next fiscal year of $8.9 million, and $11 million transferred to the Rainy Day Fund per statute.

(mm) Revenue adjustments reflect $18.1 million in direct applications and transfers in and a $2.9 million increase in property transfer tax estimate. Expenditure adjustments reflect $6.5 million from the transportation fund, $9.2 million from the tobacco settlement fund, $0.8 million from the human services caseload reserve, $.2 million from the general bond fund, and $10.8 million to the budget stabilization reserve.

(nn) Revenue adjustments reflect the transfer of fund balances from other accounts to the general fund.

(oo) Revenue adjustments reflect a $24.2 million transfer from Special Revenue and $0.2 million prior year redeposit. Expenditure adjustments reflect a $9.9 million transfer to Rainy Day Fund and a $0.2 million transfer to Special Revenue.

(pp) Revenue adjustments include the Tobacco Settlement ($153.9 million), a residual equity transfer ($67.7 million), and designated balances carried forward ($33.0 million). Expenditure adjustments included a transfer to the Tobacco Control Fund ($15.3 million) and a designation for continuing balances ($6.4 million).

(qq) The state budgets on a biennial basis. To complete the survey using annual figures, certain assumptions and estimates were required. Caution is advised when drawing conclusions or making projections.

Table 7.10
FISCAL 2004 STATE GENERAL FUND, APPROPRIATED, BY REGION
(In millions of dollars)

State or other jurisdiction	Beginning balance	Revenues	Adjustments	Resources	Expenditures	Adjustments	Ending balance	Budget stabilization fund
U.S. total	$8,348	$491,176	N.A.	$506,423	$492,160	N.A.	$9,765	$10,599
Eastern Region								
Connecticut	0	12,452	0	12,452	12,452	0	0	0
Delaware (a) (f)	464	2,514	0	2,978	2,589	0	389	137
Maine (n)	24	2,603	-59	2,568	2,556	0	12	0
Massachusetts (a)	814	22,390	0	23,205	22,344	0	861	733
New Hampshire	0	1,282	42	1,323	1,302	0	21	20
New Jersey (a)	250	23,492	0	23,742	23,493	0	249	0
New York (a) (w)	815	40,437	0	41,252	40,522	0	730	710
Pennsylvania (aa)	N.A.	N.A.	N.A.	N.A.	N.A.	N.A.	N.A.	N.A.
Rhode Island (bb)	36	2,805	-57	2,784	2,784	0	0	85
Vermont (hh)	0	881	45	925	896	30	0	41
Regional average	267	12,095	-3	12,359	12,104	3	251	192
Midwest Region								
Illinois (h)	317	22,983	3,911	27,211	22,698	4,321	192	276
Indiana (i)	137	10,855	415	11,407	11,407	0	0	273
Iowa (j)	0	4,498	0	4,498	4,561	-83	20	163
Kansas (k)	100	4,458	0	4,558	4,533	0	25	0
Michigan (p)	74	8,159	185	8,418	8,418	0	0	0
Minnesota (a) (q)	180	14,362	0	14,542	13,995	0	547	300
Nebraska (t)	3	2,732	-29	2,706	2,655	41	9	148
North Dakota	15	888	0	903	884	0	19	9
Ohio (y)	53	24,097	0	24,150	24,006	7	137	181
South Dakota (dd)	0	880	27	907	906	0	0	106
Wisconsin (kk)	-282	11,152	0	10,870	10,615	109	146	0
Regional average	54	9,551	410	10,015	9,516	400	100	132
Southern Region								
Alabama (b)	113	5,270	75	5,458	5,432	0	26	68
Arkansas	0	3,526	0	3,526	3,526	0	0	0
Florida	491	21,214	0	21,705	21,272	0	433	966
Georgia (a)	1,112	14,898	0	16,009	15,040	0	970	420
Kentucky (l)	139	7,207	198	7,543	7,420	123	0	55
Louisiana (m)	0	6,480	53	6,532	6,545	-12	0	191
Maryland (o)	123	10,083	461	10,667	10,514	-294	447	498
Mississippi (r)	17	3,582	8	3,607	3,591	0	16	72
Missouri (s)	121	7,836	0	7,957	8,058	0	-101	230
North Carolina (x)	251	14,449	246	14,945	14,775	0	170	150
Oklahoma	31	4,920	0	4,951	4,699	0	252	0
South Carolina (a) (cc)	46	4,997	0	5,043	4,944	0	99	49
Tennessee (ee)	21	8,291	0	8,312	8,239	73	0	111
Texas (ff)	83	28,750	0	28,833	28,774	111	-51	218
Virginia	86	12,208	0	12,294	12,276	0	18	129
West Virginia (jj)	196	3,041	0	3,238	3,226	10	2	68
Regional average	177	9,797	65	10,039	9,896	1	143	202
Western Region								
Alaska (c)	0	1,825	473	2,298	2,298	0	0	1,858
Arizona (d)	18	5,889	417	6,323	6,300	0	24	1
California (a)	1,402	73,353	0	74,755	71,137	0	3,618	2,216
Colorado (a) (e)	223	5,908	-254	5,877	5,647	0	230	0
Hawaii	117	3,807	0	3,924	3,825	0	99	51
Idaho (g)	16	2,022	-14	2,024	2,004	0	20	0
Montana	42	1,303	0	1,346	1,297	0	49	0
Nevada (u)	100	1,902	452	2,454	2,320	0	134	1
New Mexico (a) (v)	245	4,138	0	4,383	4,113	34	237	N.A.
Oregon (z)	57	5,067	0	5,124	5,529	0	-405	0
Utah (gg)	0	3,544	54	3,598	3,596	0	2	31
Washington (ii)	298	11,088	101	11,488	11,371	0	117	0
Wyoming (ll)	4	660	148	812	779	29	4	36
Regional average	194	9,270	106	9,570	9,247	5	318	350
Regional average without California	93	3,929	115	4,238	4,090	5	43	180

See footnotes at end of table.

FISCAL 2004 STATE GENERAL FUND, APPROPRIATED, BY REGION
(In millions of dollars)

Source: National Association of State Budget Officers, The Fiscal Survey of the States (November 2003).

Note: For all states unless otherwise noted, transfers into budget stabilization funds are counted as expenditures and transfers from budget stabilization funds are counted as revenue.

Key:

N.A.—Data are not available.

(a) In these states, the ending balance includes the balance in the budget stabilization fund.

(c) Revenue adjustments reflect a Constitutional Budget Reserve (CBR) draw.

(d) Revenue adjustments include Medicaid premium tax $69.7, DOR revenue generating plan $53.2, and DOR tax amnesty/minimum withholding $30, federal fiscal relief $174.5, fund transfers 449.5, and miscellaneous revenue adjustments $40.

(e) Revenue adjustments include a diversion to the State Education fund and the Older Coloradoans Program. Additionally , they include $14.2 million in revenue transferred to the General Fund to mitigate revenue decline.

(f) Adjustments reflect spending cuts implemented; the Rainy Day Fund is intact. Ninety-eight percent of available revenues were appropriated, and a revenue package enacted.

(g) Revenue adjustments include $13.5 million in transfers to other funds.

(h) Adjustments on revenues includes $1,600 million received from general obligation pension bond proceeds that are scheduled to be transferred into the general funds and transfers in of $2,311 million. The adjustments to expenditures includes the repayment of short term borrowing that came due in fiscal year 2004 ($1,450 million), payment of owed prior year income tax refunds ($325 million), permanent paydown of prior year carry over of accounts payable ($416 million), transfers out ($2,080 million), and a transfer to increase balance in Budget Stabilization (rainy day) Fund.

(i) Revenue adjustments represent one-time transfers from dedicated funds, the federal Jobs and Growth Tax Relief Reconciliation Act 2003 and the rainy day fund.

(j) Revenue estimates are based upon the Revenue Estimating Conference estimate for fiscal 2004 done on October 10, 2003. This estimate includes a 2.5 percent across the board reduction in allotments which will reduce spending by $82.5 million.

(k) Kansas does not have a separate rainy day fund.

(l) Revenue includes $110.2 million in tobacco settlement funds. Adjustment for revenues includes $102.2 million that represents appropriation balances carried over from the prior fiscal year. Adjustments to revenues include $95.3 million that represents fund transfers into the general fund. Adjustment to expenditures represents appropriation balances forwarded to the next fiscal year.

(m) Revenue adjustments include one-time revenue from settlements, premium generated from general obligation bond sale, and elimination of funds. Expenditure adjustments are for across the board budget cut.

(n) Revenue adjustments reflect $-59.1 million in legislative and statutorily authorized transfers. They include the following transfers: $-53 million to Affordable Health Care, $-26.7 million to the Federal Relief Fund Reserve, $6.1 million from Funds for a Healthy Maine (Tobacco Settlement Payments), $5 million from Highway Fund, $3.0 million from hospital rate adjustments and $2.4 million from Unfunded Actuarial Liability savings.

(o) Revenue adjustments reflect other transfers ($329 million) and additional federal Medicaid ($132 million); Expenditure adjustments reflect cost containments ($-204 million) and federal funds for operating expenditures ($-90 million).

(p) Fiscal 2004 revenue adjustments include federal and state tax law changes (-373.3 million); increased driver license revenue ($90.9 million); unrestricted federal aid ($169 million); and deposits from state restricted funds ($298.5 million). The Rainy Day Fund balance is equally distributed, with $73.1 million earmarked for the Budget Stabilization Fund and $73.1 million deposited to a new, School Aid Rainy Day Fund.

(q) Ending balance includes budget reserve of $300 million.

(r) Fifty percent of the fiscal 2003 preliminary ending balance is brought forward as beginning balance; revenue adjustments include an $8.2 million re-appropriation. (sate fiscal 2004 revenue estimate was revised in May 2003. Expenditures do not include Medicaid and other supplemental funding needed for fiscal 2004.the Governor withheld $240 million at the beginning of the fiscal year to balance the budget. Revenues include transfers to general revenue. Revenues also include $124.5 million from revenue bond proceeds for capital improvement projects and $387 million from federal fiscal relief. Expenditures include refunds of $2,272.1 million.

(t) Revenue adjustments are transfers between the general fund and other funds. Expenditure adjustments are carryovers from prior years and a small amount reserved for supplemental appropriations.

(u) The fiscal 2003 ending balance and fiscal 2004 beginning balance differ due to rounding.

(v) Adjustments reflect reserve account activity.

(w) The ending balance includes $710 million in the tax stabilization reserve fund (rainy day fund) and $20 million in reserve funds for litigation risks.

(x) Revenue adjustments equal $136.9 million of federal fiscal relief and $108.8 million transfer of disaster relief funds originally appropriated for Hurricane Floyd relief.

(y) Federal reimbursements for Medicaid and other human services programs are included in the general revenue fund. Beginning balances are undesignated fund balances. The actual cash balances would be higher by the amount reserved for encumbrances and designated transfers from the general revenue fund. Expenditures for fiscal 2004 do not include encumbrances outstanding at the end of the year. Ohio reports expenditures based on disbursements for the general revenue fund. Expenditure adjustments reflect miscellaneous transfers-out of $30.5 million. These transfers-out are adjusted for an anticipated net change in encumbrances from fiscal 2003 levels of $-23.8 million.

(z) Oregon budgets on a biennial basis. While fiscal years may have a negative balance, the state is constitutionally required to have a balanced budget at the end of the biennium. Current spending projection will show a $100 million ending balance at the end of the 2003-2005 biennium (fiscal year 2005).

(aa) The enactment of the fiscal 2004 budget was not yet completed at the time this report was published.

(bb) The fiscal 2004 ending balance is projected as $.5 million. Revenue adjustments reflect a contribution to budget stabilization fund.

(cc) Figures do not include funds associated with the President's Jobs and Growth Reconciliation Act of 2003.

(dd) Revenue adjustments reflect $26.8 million in one-time revenues.

(ee) Expenditure adjustments reflect a $21 million transfer to Transportation Equity Fund, a $27.5 million transfer to capital outlay projects fund, and $24.6 million for dedicated revenue appropriations.

(ff) The revenue, expenditure, and balance information is from the Comptroller's June 27, 2003 certification worksheet. Expenditure adjustments reflect the estimated reserve for transfer to the Rainy Day Fund.

(gg) Revenue adjustments include: a $35.6 million reserve from the previous year, a $9.8 million transfer from Tobacco Settlements Funds, $7.4 million in transfers from other miscellaneous sources, and $1.6 million from the sale of the Iron County Jail.

(hh) Revenue adjustments reflect $13.2 million direct applications and transfers in $4.3 million increase in property transfer revenue estimate, and $27.4 million sales tax implementation. Expenditure adjustments reflect $17.6 million to the budget stabilization reserve and$11.9 to the general fund surplus reserve.

(ii) Revenue adjustments reflect the transfer of fund balances from other accounts to the general fund.

(jj) Revenue adjustments include $0.1 million in prior year redeposits. Expenditure adjustments include a $9.8 million transfer to Rainy Day Fund.

(kk) Expenditure adjustments include Compensation Reserves ($109.2 million).

(ll) the state budgets on a biennial basis. To complete the survey using annual figures, certain assumptions and estimates were required. Caution is advised when drawing conclusions or making projections.

Table 7.11
FISCAL YEAR 2004 BUDGET GAPS

State or other jurisdiction	Gap projected in late January		Highest projected gap		Current estimated gap	
	Amount (millions)	Percent of general fund budget (%)	Amount (millions)	Percent of general fund budget (%)	Amount (millions)	Percent of general fund budget (%)
Alabama (a)	N.R.	N.R.	N.R.	N.R.	N.R.	N.R.
Alaska (b)	$ 896.0	36.0%	$ 896.0	36.0%	$ 600.0	25.0%
Arizona	1,500.0	25.0	1,500.0	25.0	1,500.0	25.0
Arkansas	0.0	0.0	0.0	0.0	0.0	0.0
California (c)	26,100.0	30.0	26,100.0	30.0	17,500.0	20.6
Colorado	398.0	6.5	398.0	6.5	869.0	15.0
Connecticut (d)	1,900.0	14.0	1,942.3	14.2	902.7	6.9
Delaware (e)	196.1	7.7	196.1	7.7	120.0	5.0
Florida (f)	N.R.	N.R.	0.0	0.0	0.0	0.0
Georgia	721.0	4.9	735.0	5.0	735.0	5.0
Hawaii	80.0	2.0	110.0	2.9	110.0	2.9
Idaho	160.0	8.8	160.0	8.8	160.0	8.8
Illinois (g)	3,500.0	13.2	3,600.0	13.6	3,600.0	13.6
Indiana	N.R.	N.R.	750.0	7.0	750.0	7.0
Iowa (h)	413.8	9.3	413.8	9.3	0.0	0.0
Kansas(i)	750.0	16.7	980.0	21.8	230.0	5.1
Kentucky (j)	N.R.	N.R.	198.2	2.7	0.0	0.0
Louisiana	600.0	8.5	600.0	8.5	600.0	8.5
Maine(k)	475.0	16.3	486.5	16.7	0.0	0.0
Maryland (l)	853.2	7.8	853.2	7.8	0.0	0.0
Massachusetts (m)	3,000.0	13.0	3,000.0	13.0	2,700.0	10.8
Michigan (n)	1,250.0	14.0	1,250.0	14.0	0.0	0.0
Minnesota (o)	2,367.0	15.0	2,375.7	15.5	2,375.7	15.5
Mississippi (p)	N.R.	N.R.	90.0	2.5	0.0	0.0
Missouri	1,000.0	15.0	1,000.0	15.0	700.0	10.5
Montana	116.0	8.3	116.0	8.3	116.0	8.3
Nebraska (q)	350.0	13.0	380.0	13.6	380.0	13.6
Nevada (r)	N.R.	N.R.	N.R.	N.R.	N.R.	N.R.
New Hampshire	148.0	6.0	148.0	6.0	39.6	3.0
New Jersey (s)	4,600.0	18.5	4,600.0	18.5	0.0	0.0
New Mexico	0.0	0.0	0.0	0.0	0.0	0.0
New York	9,300.0	24.0	9,300.0	24.0	9,300.0	24.0
North Carolina	2,000.0	14.0	2,000.0	14.0	2,000.0	14.0
North Dakota	N.R.	N.R.	0.0	0.0	0.0	0.0
Ohio (t)	N.R.	N.R.	1,700.0	7.1	1,700.0	7.1
Oklahoma	299.8	6.7	299.8	6.7	275.9	5.3
Oregon (u)	576.0	10.7	850.0	17.0	850.0	17.0
Pennsylvania (v)	N.R.	N.R.	2,402.7	10.6	0.0	0.0
Rhode Island	173.9	6.1	173.9	6.1	173.9	6.1
South Carolina (w)	400.0	7.5	400.0	7.5	400.0	7.5
South Dakota	54.2	5.9	54.2	5.9	0.0	0.0
Tennessee (x)	N.R.	N.R.	N.R.	N.R.	N.R.	N.R.
Texas	3,700.0	12.0	3,700.0	12.0	3,700.0	12.0
Utah (y)	N.R.	N.R.	79.5	2.3	0.0	0.0
Vermont (z)	30.0	3.4	30.0	3.4	0.0	0.0
Virginia (aa)	1,100.0	8.8	1,100.0	8.8	0.0	0.0
Washington (bb)	1,000.0	8.9	1,000.0	8.9	1,000.0	8.9
West Virginia (cc)	200.0	6.0	250.0	7.5	0.0	0.0
Wisconsin (dd)	1,999.0	16.0	1,999.0	16.0	N.R.	N.R.
Wyoming	0.0	0.0	0.0	0.0	0.0	0.0
Dist. of Columbia	N.R.	N.R.	143.0	4.0	143.0	4.0
Total	68,707.0 (ee)		78,360.9		53,530.8	

See footnotes at end of table.

FISCAL YEAR 2004 BUDGET GAPS — Continued

Source: Reprinted with permission from *State Budget Update 2004,* November 2003, © National Conference of State Legislatures, 2003.

Note: Puerto Rico did not respond to this survey.

Key:

N.A. - Not applicable

N.R. - No response

(a) The governor has not yet presented the revenue portion of the FY 2004 budget.

(b) Use of one-time sources may cause the gap to be smaller than $600 million.

(c) The budget gap figures provided at the end of January were based on the governor's estimate. TheLegislative Analyst's Office later provided its own figure, estimating the highest gap at $18 billion. For the purposes of this table, the governor's estimate is used to depict the highest projected gap. The figure shown for the current estimated gap in FY 2004 was provided by the Legislative Analyst's Office.

(d) PA 03-2 (HB 6495) was passed to help mitigate the FY 2003 deficit. The rollout effect of this legislation also reduces the projected FY 2004 budget gap.

(e) The governor's proposed budget includes $145 million in revenue enhancements.

(f) Projected revenues are sufficient to meet current services and Medicaid workload.

(g) The governor introduced his budget on April 9. He stated that the deficit over the two years would have been $5.186 billion. He has called for deficit reduction initiatives of $929 million in FY 2003 and $4.451 billion in FY 2004.

(h) The budget is close to enactment.

(i) The appropriation bill is awaiting the governor's signature, and the Omnibus session is scheduled to begin April 30, 2003.

(j) The budget was adopted March 23, 2003, and was balanced by a number of actions.

(k) The 2004-2005 biennial current services budget bills were enacted in late March and early April. Due to the March 2003 revenue revision, approximately $25 million per year is left "unspecified" as a statewide general fund curtailment of expenditures, absent future action of the Legislature. The "new and expanded" budget bill will be the vehicle to address those unspecified reductions. The new budget proposal should be available by late April.

(l) The budget, as enacted, estimates a $34 million closing FY 2004 fund balance, although there is a shortfall between operating revenues and expenses of $321.2 million due to the use of one-time transfers to balance the budget. Note that the gap technically rose above the prior amount because of a revenue write-down of $116.9 million in March 2003, but it was offset by withdrawn spending of $179.7 in general fund debt service through a supplemental budget and $20.8 million withdrawn by the governor in February 2003.

(m) The $2.7 billion figure was the administration's estimate in February of the preliminary gap between maintenance spending and revenue. That gap now may be closer to $2 billion to $2.5 billion as a result of cuts made to spending in FY 2003 that have annualized FY 2004 savings.

(n) Governor Granholm presented a balanced budget proposal to the Legislature on March 6, 2003. If the Legislature passes the governor's budget as presented and the revenue estimates do not change, the FY 2004 budget is balanced.

(o) The budget gap in the February forecast increased only slightly (by $9 million).

(p) The Legislature has passed the budget, but the governor had not signed the bills as of April 9.

(q) This budget gap is an artificial calculation, approximating one-half of a projected biennial gap. The gap is cumulative, including the prior year gap and the next two years of the budget biennium under consideration, which ends June 30, 2005.

(r) The FY 2004 budget will not be finalized until June 2003. However, projections of current revenue sources in FY 2004 (next fiscal year) will be insufficient to support ongoing appropriations in FY 2003 (this fiscal year).

(s) The governor's FY 2004 budget proposal would close the gap with a combination of spending and revenue measures. Many of the latter are dependent upon separate legislative enactments and the receipt of certain funds. Therefore, no gap exists on paper at this point in time. The governor's budget anticipates a $253 million (1.1%) surplus. Legislative fiscal estimates for FY 2003 and FY 2004 are $240 million lower than the executive estimate, leaving almost no surplus.

(t) The governor's FY2004 budget proposal included approximately $1,392 billion in revenue enhancements. According to testimony presented by the director of Budget and Management to the House Finance and Appropriations Committee, the $1 billion in cuts made during the past several years - which reduced many state programs and services - were carried through into the budget proposal for the 2004-2005 biennium. The budget gap estimates have ranged from $1.4 billion to $2 billion (5.8% to 8.3%). For the purposes of this table, the mid-point figure was used.

(u) The March 2003 forecast projected an additional $468 million decrease in revenue available for Oregon's 2003-2005 biennium; total general fund revenue is now projected at $10.4 billion, or approximately 3%, above levels received in 1999-2001.

(v) The new governor (Democrat) decided to introduce his budget in two phases: Part I was an austere budget with significant cuts that was introduced March 4 in accordance with state law; Part II was introduced March 25, and contained new spending initiatives. Before the governor could introduce Part II of his overall budget, however, the General Assembly (Republican) quickly passed Part I on March 10 without hearings or debate. As a result, the enacted budget does not include education funding, which currently is under consideration as a separate budget proposal.

(w) A precise number for the current FY 2004 gap is unavailable, but it is roughly in the 8% to 9% range.

(x) The governor has presented a balanced budget.

(y) The FY 2004 budget currently is balanced.

(z) The deficit ranges from zero to $10 million (1.1%). It is lower than the original estimate because the House and Senate are spending less than anticipated in their FY 2004 budget proposals.

(aa) The FY 2004 gap was addressed in 2003 legislative action.

(bb) The budget shortfall discussed here is based on the differences between projected current services spending and estimated revenues. It does not include other budget-related expenses such as salary increases, increased health benefit expenditures or other policy enhancements. If these were added in, the FY 2004 budget shortfall would increase to about $1.5 billion, or roughly 12%.

(cc) The FY 2004 budget was balanced as of the March 2003 passage of the budget bill due to increasing cigarette taxes. The budget gap that had to be closed ranged from $250 million to $280 million largely due to Medicaid expenses.

(dd) - The Joint Committee on Finance is just about to begin executive actions on the governor's 2003-2005 biennial budget. The status of FY 2003 revenue collections and current 2003-2005 estimates will be reviewed again in May 2003.

(ee) The original sum was $68.7 billion, but increased to $72.2 billion with the last-minute addition of Illinois's $3.5 billion gap.

Table 7.12
BUDGET OVERRUNS: FISCAL YEAR 2003

State	Budget Overruns		Programs
	No	*Yes*	
Alabama	★		
Alaska		★	Medicaid and fire suppression.
Arizona		★	Medicaid (already provided Title 19 Medicaid supplementals).
Arkansas	★		
California (N/R)			
Colorado (N/R)			
Connecticut		★	Medicaid is the largest account in deficiency ($82.5 million).
Delaware	★		
Florida	★		
Georgia		★	Medicaid.
Hawaii		★	Medicaid ($23 million).
Idaho	★		
Illinois		★	Medicaid and group insurance.
Indiana	★		
Iowa		★	Medicaid.
Kansas		★	Medicaid.
Kentucky		★	Medicaid benefits and corrections.
Louisiana		★	Medical costs for prisoner care ($17 million), sheriff's housing of state inmates ($8 million), state match for federal disaster aid ($34 million), minimum foundation program ($23 million) and tuition opportunity program ($8 million).
Maine		★	The second emergency budget bill for FY 2003 included $5.2 million for correctional institution health insurance contracts and correctional institution salary and benefit costs. It also provided about $10 million in additional funds for Medicaid programs.
Maryland		★	Mental health service ($30 million), human resources overestimated federal fund attainment ($25 million), various public safety and state police spending ($14.4 million), foster care ($4.9 million), non-public special education placements ($4.4 million) and other ($7.7 million).
Massachusetts		★	Medicaid, snow and ice removal.
Michigan	★		No program is over budget as yet, but the Senate Fiscal Agency is examining the need for a supplemental appropriation for Medicaid.
Minnesota	★		
Mississippi		★	Medicaid, corrections and the Department of Human Services need additional funding.
Missouri		★	Medicaid.
Montana	★		
Nebraska		★	Homestead exemption program, correctional inmate medical services costs, child welfare, Aid to Dependent Children and state ward education.
Nevada		★	A supplemental appropriation will be required to finance projected costs for Medicaid.
New Hampshire		★	Medicaid.
New Jersey		★	The state has approximately $790 million of additional spending needs in FY 2003 (compared to a more normal year where there might be $300 million to $400 million). Most of the difference is not due to program overspending, per se, but to under budgeting for Medicaid nursing home reimbursement and New Jersey's low-income senior and disabled resident prescription drug program, on the assumption the federal government would assume these costs (under a state IGT appeal and a Medicaid section 1115 waiver application). So far, neither has occurred, and it was necessary to appropriate or transfer state funds (roughly $400 million) from other areas. Other areas significantly over budget include county solid waste debt assistance, retiree medical benefits, supplemental school aid for special needs districts, Medicaid inpatient hospital costs and emergency snow removal.
New Mexico		★	Medicaid.
New York		★	Medicaid.
North Carolina	★		
North Dakota		★	Medicaid.
Ohio		★	Medicaid and disability assistance.
Oklahoma	★		
Oregon		★	Human services and public safety caseloads have not been fully funded requiring program reductions; all program areas of the budget have been reduced with resulting service elimination because of the revenue shortfall.
Pennsylvania	★		
Rhode Island		★	Mental health services, human services, corrections and K-12 education.
South Carolina		★	Department of Corrections ($27 million), State Law Enforcement Division ($2.1 million), Tax Relief Trust Fund ($9.9 million) and tuition and scholarships ($2.6 million).
South Dakota		★	Medicaid ($8.5 million) and corrections ($2.6 million).
Tennessee		★	TennCare.
Texas		★	Medicaid and Children's Health Insurance Program.
Utah	★		
Vermont		★	Corrections was taken care of in a supplemental appropriation. Social and Rehabilitative Services and child welfare may be running high. At present, these are not being addressed because overages exist only as possibilities.

See footnotes at end of table.

BUDGET OVERRUNS: FISCAL YEAR 2003 — Continued

State	Budget Overruns		Programs
	No	Yes	
Virginia		★	Medicaid and personal property tax relief.
Washington	★		The Legislature adopted a 2003 supplemental budget that added $135 million of spending authority to the general fund budget for 2001-2003.
West Virginia		★	Medicaid ($40 million).
Wisconsin		★	Shortfalls in medical assistance, Badger Care and corrections were addressed as part of the 2003 Act 1 fix-up legislation.
Wyoming	★		
Dist. of Columbia		★	Medicaid and overtime for public safety.

Source: Reprinted with permission from *State Budget Update 2004,* November 2003, © National Conference of State Legislatures, 2003.

Note: Puerto Rico did not respond to this survey.

Key:

N.R. - No response.

Table 7.13
STATE BUDGETARY CALENDARS

State or other jurisdiction	Budget guidelines to agencies	Agency requests submitted to governor	Agency hearings held	Governor's budget sent to legislature	Legislature adopts budget	Fiscal year begins	Frequency of legislative/ budget cycles
Alabama	September	November	January	February	Feb/May	October	Annual/Annual
Alaska	July	October	Sept/Nov	December	May	July	Annual/Annual
Arizona	June 1	September 1	Nov/Dec	January	Jan/April	July	Annual/Biennial
Arkansas	March	July	August	Sept/Dec	Jan/April	July	Biennial/Biennial
California	April/Nov	September	Sept–Nov	January 10	June 15	July	Biennial/Annual
Colorado	June	August 1	Aug/Sept	November 1	May	July	Annual/Annual
Connecticut	July	September	January	February	June/ May	July	Annual/Biennial
Delaware	August	Oct/Nov	Oct/Nov	January	June 30	July	Annual/Annual
Florida	June	September	September	January	April/May	July	Annual/Annual
Georgia	June	September	Nov/Dec	January	March	July	Annual/Annual
Hawaii	July/Aug	September	November	December	April/May	July	Annual/Biennial (a)
Idaho	June	September	. . .	January	March	July	Annual/Annual
Illinois	September	Oct/Nov	Nov/Dec	February	May	July	Annual/Annual
Indiana	May	August	Sept/Nov	January	April	July	Annual/Biennial
Iowa	July	October 1	Nov/Dec	January	April/May	July	Annual/Annual
Kansas	June	September	November	January	May	July	Annual/Biennial (b)
Kentucky	July	October	Nov/Dec	January	April	July	Annual/Annual
Louisiana	September	November	Jan/Feb	Feb/Mar (c)	June	July	Annual/Annual
Maine	July	September	Oct/Dec	January	June	July	Biennial/Biennial
Maryland	June	August 31	Oct/Nov	January	April	July	Annual/Annual
Massachusetts	August	October	October	January	June	July	Annual/Annual
Michigan	August	November	December	(d)	June/July	October	Annual/Annual
Minnesota	May/June	October 15	Sept/Oct	Jan (e)	May	July	Annual/Biennial
Mississippi (f)	June	August	Sept/Oct	Nov/Jan	March/April	July	Annual/Annual
Missouri	July	October	. . .	January	April/May	July	Annual/Biennial (g)
Montana (h)	Jan 31/Aug 1	May/Sept 1	May–June	January	April	July	Biennial/Biennial
Nebraska	July	September	Jan/Feb	January	April	July	Annual/Biennial
Nevada	January	August	Sept/Dec	January	May/June	July	Biennial/Biennial
New Hampshire	August	October 1	November	February 15	May	July	Annual/Biennial
New Jersey	July/August	October	Nov/Dec	January	June	July	Annual/Annual
New Mexico	July	September	Sept/Dec	January	Feb/March	July	Annual/Annual
New York	July	September	Oct/Nov	January	March	April	Annual/Annual
North Carolina	January	September	Sept/Nov	February	June	July	Biennial/Biennial (i)
North Dakota	March	June/July	July/Oct	December	Jan/April	July	Biennial/Biennial
Ohio	July	Sept/Oct	Oct/Nov	February (j)	June	July	Annual/Biennial
Oklahoma	July	October	Oct/Dec	February (k)	May (l)	July	Annual/Annual
Oregon	Jan/July	September	Sept/Nov	January	Jan/June	July	Biennial/Biennial
Pennsylvania	August	October	Dec/Jan	February (m)	May/June	July	Annual/Annual
Rhode Island	July	October	Nov/Dec	February	June	July	Annual/Annual
South Carolina	August	October	. . .	January	June	July	Annual/Annual
South Dakota	June/July	September	Sept/Oct	December	March	July	Annual/Annual
Tennessee	August	October	November	February 1 (n)	April/May	July	Annual/Annual
Texas	March	July/Sept	July/Sept	January	May	September	Biennial/Biennial
Utah	July	September	Oct/Nov	December	Feb./March	July	Annual/Annual
Vermont	October	November	Nov/Dec	January	May	July	Annual (o)/Annual
Virginia	April/August	June/Oct	Sept/Oct	December	March/April	July	Annual/Biennial
Washington	April	September	. . .	December	April/May	July	Annual/Biennial
West Virginia	July	September	Oct/Nov	Jan/Feb (p)	March/April	July	Annual/Annual
Wisconsin	June	September	. . .	January	June/July	July	Biennial/Biennial
Wyoming	May 15	September	(q)	December	March	July	Annual/Biennial
Puerto Rico	March	Sept/Dec	Aug–Sept Dec–Jan	February	June	July	Annual/Annual

See footnotes at end of table.

STATE BUDGETARY CALENDARS — Continued

Source: National Association of State Budget Officers, *Budget Processes in the States*, 2002. For additional information see http://www.nasbo.org.

Key:

. . . — Not applicable

(a) The state Constitution and statutes prescribe a biennium budget; in practice, a budget is submitted every year.

(b) Twenty agencies are on a biennial budget cycle. The rest are on an annual cycle.

(c) The governor is required to submit a copy of the executive budget to the joint legislative committee on the budget 45 days, except that during the first year of each term it shall be submitted 30 days, prior to the beginning of the regular session of the legislature. The governor shall transmit a copy to each member of the legislature on the first day of the regular session. The governor shall transmit to the legislature, no later than the eighth day of the regular session, a proposed five-year outlay program.

(d) The governor must present the budget to the legislature within 30 days after the legislature convenes in regular session, except in a year in which a newly elected governor is inaugurated into office, when 60 days are allowed.

(e) Fourth Tuesday.

(f) The executive budget is submitted in January during the first year of a governor's term. Governor does not hold separate agency hearings.

(g) There is a constitutional authority to do annual and biennial budgeting. Beginning in FY 1994, the operating budget has been on an annual basis while the capital budget has been on a biennial basis.

(h) Montana uses an Executive Planning Process (EPP) for proposals to provide new services, add FTE, change program services or alter funding sources. The earlier dates reflect this process which is linked with the regular budget in the September 1 submittal.

(i) The Constitution requires the preparation of a biennial budget, the General Assembly routinely conducts a short session for adjustments to the second year of the biennium.

(j) Budget submission delayed to mid-March for new governors.

(k) First Monday.

(l) Last Friday.

(m) Budget is submitted in March when governor has been elected for first full term.

(n) The budget may be submitted by March 1 during the first year of a governor's term.

(o) The state constitution prescribes a biennial legislature; in practice, legislature meets annually, in regular and adjourned sessions.

(p) The constitution of West Virginia requires the Governor to submit a proposed budget to the Legislature on the second Wednesday of January each year, except the year following a gubernatorial election, at which time the proposed budget is submitted on the second Wednesday in February. The Legislature has a 60 day session that starts with the budget submission.

(q) By November 20.

Table 7.14
OFFICIALS OR AGENCIES RESPONSIBLE FOR BUDGET PREPARATION, REVIEW AND CONTROLS

State or other jurisdiction	Official/agency(ies) responsible for preparing budget document	Special budget review agency in legislative branch	Official/agency(ies) responsible for budgetary and related accounting controls
Alabama	State Finance Director	Legislative Fiscal Ofc.	State Finance Director
Alaska	Director, Ofc. of Mgmt. & Budget	Div. of Legislative Audit	Director, Div. of Finance, Dept. of Administration
Arizona	Director, Ofc. of Strategic Planning & Budgeting	Jt. Legislative Budget Cmte.	Assistant Director, Financial Sacs., Dept. of Administration
Arkansas	Administrator, Ofc. of Budget, Dept. of Finance & Admn.	Fiscal & Tax Research Services, Bur. of Legislative Research	Director, Dept. of Finance & Administration
California	Director, Dept. of Finance	Ofc. of the Legislative Analyst; Senate Cmte. On Budget & Fiscal Review; Assembly Cmte. On Appropriations	Director, Dept. of Finance
Colorado	Executive Director, Ofc. of State Planning & Budgeting, Ofc. of the Governor	Jt. Budget Cmte.	State Controller, Ofc. of the State Controller, Support Services, Dept. of Personnel
Connecticut	Executive Budget Officer, Budget & Finance Div., Ofc. of Policy & Mgmt.	Ofc. of Fiscal Analysis	Secretary, Ofc. of Policy Management
Delaware	Director, Ofc. of the Budget	Legislative Info. Services; Ofc. of the Controller General	Secretary, Dept. of Finance
Florida	Director, Ofc. of Planning & Budgeting, Executive Ofc. of the Governor	Fiscal Responsibility Council; Budget Cmte.	State Comptroller
Georgia	Director, Ofc. of Planning & Budget	Legislative Budget Ofc.	Treasurer, Ofc. of Treasury & Fiscal Services
Hawaii	Director of Finance, Dept. of Budget and Finance	Ofc. of the Legislative Auditor	Director of Finance, Dept. of Budget & Finance
Idaho	Administrator, Div. of Financial Mgmt., Ofc. of the Governor	Jt. Finance Appropriations Cmte.; Budget & Policy Analysis, Legislative Services Ofc.	Administrator, Div. of Financial Mgmt., Ofc. of the Governor
Illinois	Director, Bur. of the Budget, Ofc. of the Governor	Economic & Fiscal Comm.	Director, Bur. of the Budget, Ofc. of the Governor
Indiana	Director, Budget Agcy.	Fiscal & Mgmt. Analysis Ofc., Legislative Services Agency	Director, Budget Agency
Iowa	Director, Dept. of Mgmt., Ofc. of the Governor	Legislative Fiscal Bur.	Director, Dept. of Revenue & Finance; Director, Dept. of Mgmt.
Kansas	Director, Div. of the Budget, Dept. of Admn.	Legislative Research Dept.	
Kentucky	State Budget Director, Governor's Ofc.	Ofc. of Budget Review, Legislative Research Comm.	Secretary, Finance & Administration Cabinet
Louisiana	Budget Director, Div. of Admn., Ofc. of the Governor	State Fiscal Services; Legislative Fiscal Ofc.; Fiscal Div., House Legislative Services	Commissioner, Div. of Administration
Maine	State Budget Officer, Bur. of the Budget, Dept. of Admn. & Financial Services	Ofc. of Fiscal & Program Review, Legislative Council	Commissioner, Dept. of Adm. & Financial Services
Maryland	Secretary, Ofc. of the Secretary, Dept. of Budget & Mgmt.	Ofc. of Policy Analysis, Dept. of Legislative Services	Secretary, Ofc. of the Secretary, Dept. of Budget & Mgmt.
Massachusetts	Budget Director, Executive Ofc. for Admn. & Finance	Senate, House Ways & Means Cmtes.	Secretary, Executive Ofc. for Administration & Finance
Michigan	State Budget Director, Dept. of Mgmt. & Budget	Senate, House Fiscal Agencies	State Budget Director, Dept. of Mgmt. & Budget
Minnesota	Commissioner, Dept. of Finance	Senate, House Chief Fiscal Analysts	Commissioner, Dept. of Finance
Mississippi	Director, Ofc. of Budget & Fund Mgmt., Dept. of Finance & Admn.	Jt. Legislative Budget Ofc.	Director, Dept. of Finance & Administration
Missouri	Director, Div. of Budget & Planning, Ofc. of Admn.	Senate, House Appropriations Cmtes.; Budget Cmte.; Jt. Legislative Research Cmte., Oversight Div.	Commissioner, Administration, Ofc. Of Administration
Montana	Director, Ofc. of Budget & Program Planning	Legislative Fiscal Div.	Director, Ofc. of Budget & Program Planning
Nebraska	Administrator, Budget Div., Dept. of Adm. Services	Legislative Fiscal Ofc.	State Tax Commissioner, Dept. of Revenue; Administrator, Budget Div., Dept. of Adm. Services; Auditor of Public Accounts
Nevada	Director, Dept. of Admn.	Legislative Counsel Bur., Fiscal Analysis Div.	
New Hampshire	Commissioner, Commissioner's Ofc., Dept. of Adm. Services; Asst. Commissioner Ofc., Dept. of Adm. Services & Budget Officer, Budget Ofc., Adm. Services	Ofc. of Legislative Budget Assistant	Commissioner, Commissioner's

See footnotes at end of table.

OFFICIALS OR AGENCIES RESPONSIBLE FOR BUDGET PREPARATION, REVIEW AND CONTROLS — Continued

State or other jurisdiction	Official/agency(ies) responsible for preparing budget document	Special budget review agency in legislative branch	Official/agency(ies) responsible for budgetary and related accounting controls
New Jersey	Director, Ofc. of Mgmt. & Budget; Dept. of Treasury	Assembly Majority Staff; Ofc. of Legislative Services; Budget & Fiscal Analysis, Assembly and Senate Minority Staff; Central Staff, Revenue, Finance & Appropriations	Director, Ofc. of Mgmt. & Budget, Dept. of Treasury
New Mexico	Director, Budget Div., Dept.of Finance & Admn.	Jt. Legislative Finance Cmte.	Secretary, Finance & Administration
New York	Director, Div. of Budget, Executive Dept.	Ways & Means Cmte.	Comptroller
North Carolina	State Budget Officer, Ofc. of State Budget	Fiscal Research Div.	State Budget Officer, Ofc. of the State Budget
North Dakota	Director, Budget Analyst, Ofc. of Mgmt. & Budget	Legislative Council	Director, Ofc. of Mgmt. & Budget,
Ohio	Director, Ofc. of Budget & Mgmt.	Legislative Budget Ofc.	Director, Ofc. of Budget & Mgmt.
Oklahoma	Director, Ofc. of State Finance	Fiscal Div.; Senate Fiscal Staff Div.	Director, Ofc. of State Finance
Oregon	Dpty. Director, Budget & Mgmt., Dept. of Adm. Services	Legislative Fiscal Ofc.	Deputy Director, Dept. of Adm. Services
Pennsylvania	Cabinet Secretary, Ofc. of the Budget, Budget Dept.	Appropriations Cmte.; Legislative Budget & Finance Comm.; Democratic Appropriations Cmte.	Cabinet Secretary, Ofc. of the Budget, Budget Dept.
Rhode Island	Executive Director/State Budget Officer, State Budget Ofc., Dept. of Admn.	Senate Finance Cmte.	Executive Director/State Budget Officer, State Budget Ofc., Dept. of Administration
South Carolina	Director, Ofc. of State Budget, Budget & Control Bd.	Ways & Means Cmte.; Budget & Control Board; Finance Cmte.	Executive Director, Budget & Control Board
South Dakota	Commissioner, Bur. of Finance & Mgmt.	Fiscal Research & Budget Analysis, Legislative Research Council	Commissioner, Bur. of Finance & Mgmt.
Tennessee	Assistant Commissioner, Budget Div., Dept. of Finance & Admn.	Fiscal Review Cmte.	Commissioner, Finance & Administration
Texas	Director, Budget & Planning, Ofc. of the Governor	Legislative Budget Bd.	Comptroller, Comptroller of Public Accounts
Utah	Director, Ofc. of Planning & Budget, Governor's Ofc.	Ofc. of Legislative Fiscal Analyst	Director, Div. Of Finance, Dept. of Adm. Services
Vermont	Commissioner, Agency of Admn., Dept. of Finance & Mgmt.	Jt. Fiscal Ofc.	Commissioner, Agency of Administration, Dept. of Finance & Mgmt.
Virginia	Director, Dept. of Planning & Budget	Senate Finance Cmte.; House Appropriations Cmte.	Secretary of Finance, Governor's Cabinet
Washington	Director, Ofc. of Financial Mgmt.	Legislative Transportation Cmte.; Senate Ways & Means Cmte.; House Appropriations Cmte.	Director, Ofc. of Financial Mgmt.
West Virginia	Director, Budget Div., Dept. of Finance & Admn.	Budget Div., Legislative Auditor's Ofc.; Jt. Standing Cmte. on Finance	Cabinet Secretary, Dept. of Administration
Wisconsin	Director, Div. of Executive Budget & Finance, Dept. of Admn.	Legislative Fiscal Bur.	Administrator, DOA/Div. of Technical Mgmt.
Wyoming	Administrator, Admn. & Info.	Legislative Services Ofc.	State Auditor
Dist. of Columbia	Director, Dept. of Finance & Revenue	Budget Ofc.	Chief Financial Officer, Ofc. of the Chief Financial Officer
American Samoa	Director, Program Planning & Budget	Legislative Financial Ofc.; Budget & Appropriations Cmte.	Treasurer,Dept. of the Treasury
Guam	Director, Bur. of Budget & Mgmt. Research	Legislative Accounting Div.	Director, Dept. of Administration
No. Mariana Islands	Special Assistant for Mgmt. & Budget, Ofc. of Mgmt. & Budget, Ofc. of the Governor	Finance & Accounting Div.	Secretary of Finance, Finance & Accounting, Dept. of Finance
Puerto Rico	Director, Ofc. of Budget & Mgmt.	Secretary of Administration; Speaker's Ofc.	Director, Ofc. of Budget & Mgmt.
U.S. Virgin Islands	Director, Ofc. of Mgmt. & Budget	Business & Financial Management, Legislature of U.S. Virgin Islands	Commissioner, Dept. of Finance

Sources: The Council of State Governments, *State Legislative Leadership, Committees and Staff: 2003* and *State Administrative Officials Classified by Function: 2003.*

Table 7.15
STATE BALANCED BUDGETS: CONSTITUTIONAL AND STATUTORY PROVISIONS, GUBERNATORIAL AND LEGISLATIVE AUTHORITY

State or other jurisdiction	Constitutional and Statutory Provisions			Gubernatorial Authority			Legislative Authority	
	Governor must submit a balanced budget	Legislature must pass a balanced budget	Governor must sign a balanced budget	Governor has line item veto	Can reduce budget without legislative approval	Restrictions on budget reductions	Votes required to pass revenue increase	Votes required to pass budget
Alabama	C,S	S	...	★ (a)	★	ATB	Majority	Majority
Alaska	S	S	S	★	...	...	Majority	Majority (c)
Arizona	C,S	C,S	C,S	★	...	...	2/3 elected	Majority
Arkansas	S	S	S	★	(d)	ATB	3/4 elected (b)	3/4 elected (kk)
California	C	...	S	★	...	...	2/3 elected	2/3 elected (ll)
Colorado	C	C	C	★	★	...	Majority (e)	Majority elected
Connecticut	S	C,S	C	★	★	MR	Majority	Majority (f)
Delaware	C,S	C,S	C,S	★	...	★	3/5 elected	Majority
Florida	C,S	C,S	C,S	★	★ (g)	MR	2/3 elected	Majority
Georgia	C	C	C	★	★	★ (h)	Majority	Majority
Hawaii	C,S	...	C,S	★ (ss)	partial (i)	...	Majority (j)	Majority elected (mm)
Idaho	...	C (k)	...	★	★ (l)	★ (l)	Majority	Majority
Illinois	C,S	C	S	★ (m)	★	...	Majority	Majority elected (n)
Indiana	...	...	...	...	★	...	Majority	Majority
Iowa	C,S	S	...	★	★	ATB	Majority	Majority
Kansas	S	C,S	...	★	...	ATB	Majority	Majority
Kentucky	C,S	C,S	C,S	★	...	★	2/5 elected	Majority elected
Louisiana	C,S	C,S	C,S	★	★	MR	2/3 elected	Majority
Maine	C,S	C	C,S	★	★	ATB	Majority	Majority (nn)
Maryland	C	C	C (o)	★ (tt)	★ (p)	★ (q)	Majority	Majority elected
Massachusetts	C,S	C,S	C,S	★	★	...	Majority	Majority (r)
Michigan	C,S	C	C,S	★	...	(s)	Majority (uu)	Majority
Minnesota	C,S (ww)	C,S (ww)	C,S (ww)	★	★	...	Majority	Majority elected (oo)
Mississippi	S	S	...	★	★	ATB (xx)	3/5 elected	Majority elected (oo)
Missouri	C	...	C	★	★	...	Majority (vv)	Majority elected
Montana	S	C	...	★	★	MR (t)	Majority	Majority
Nebraska	C	S	...	★	...	★	Majority	Majority elected (pp)
Nevada	S	C	C	...	★	MR	3/5 elected	Majority
New Hampshire	S	...	...	...	...	...	Majority	Majority
New Jersey	C	C	C	★	★	...	Majority	Majority
New Mexico	C	C	C	★	...	...	Majority	Majority
New York	C	...	(u)	★ (v)	★ (w)	(w)	Majority	Majority
North Carolina	C,S	S	...	...	★ (x)	(x)	Majority	Majority
North Dakota	C	C	C	★	★	ATB	Majority	Majority (qq)
Ohio	C	C	C	★ (y)	★	★	Majority	Majority
Oklahoma	S	C (z)	C (z)	★	★ (aa)	★	3/4 elected	Majority elected
Oregon	C	C	C	★	★	MR	2/3 elected	Majority
Pennsylvania	C,S	...	C,S	★	★ (bb)	★ (bb)	Majority elected	Majority elected
Rhode Island	C	C	S	...	★	★	Majority	2/3 elected
South Carolina	C	C	C	★	★ (cc)	★	Majority	Majority
South Dakota	C	C	C	★	...	★	2/3 elected	Majority elected (rr)
Tennessee	C	C	C	★	...	...	Majority	Majority
Texas	...	C,S	C	★	★	★ (yy)	Majority	Majority
Utah	C	C,S	(dd)	★	★	...	Majority	Majority elected
Vermont	...	...	...	...	★ (ee)	★ (ee)	Majority	Majority
Virginia	(ff)	...	C (ff)	★ (gg)	★ (jj)	MR	Majority (hh)	Majority elected
Washington	S	...	...	★	★	ATB	Majority	Majority
West Virginia	...	C	C	★	★ (ii)	★ (ii)	Majority	Majority elected
Wisconsin	C	C	C,S	★	★ (jj)	...	Majority	Majority
Wyoming	C	C	...	★	★	...	Majority	Majority
Puerto Rico	C	C	C	★	★	...	Majority	Majority

Source: National Association of State Budget Officers, *Budget Processes in the States,* 2002. For additional information see http://www.nasbo.org

Key:
C — Constitutional
S — Statutory
ATB — Across the board
MR — Maximum reduction dictated
★ — Yes
. . . — No

(a) The governor may return a bill without limit for recommended amend-

ments for amount and language, as long as the legislature is still in session.

(b) The constitution provides that an increase in the rate of any tax in existence in 1934 requires a 3/4 majority vote. This includes income tax, severance tax and certain excise and privilege taxes. The most significant tax not in existence in 1934 is the sales tax that requires a simple majority.

(c) A simple majority is required to pass the budget. In Alaska, a simple majority is required for most annual appropriations, but if expenditures are expected to exceed the appropriation level in the prior year's budget and a withdrawal form the budget reserve fund is needed to make up the difference, a three-fourths vote is required. Since the provision became effective in 1991,

STATE BALANCED BUDGETS: CONSTITUTIONAL AND STATUTORY PROVISIONS, GUBERNATORIAL AND LEGISLATIVE AUTHORITY — Continued

the supermajority has been necessary for few appropriation items in each budget.

(d) The governor and chief fiscal officer of the state have the authority to reduce general revenue funding to agencies should shortfalls occur in revenue collections.

(e) All tax increases must be approved by a vote of the people.

(f) Appropriations require a simple majority of members elected, unless the general fund expenditure ceiling is exceeded. In that case, the Legislature must obtain a three-fifths majority.

(g) The Legislative Budget Commission for the executive branch and the Chief Justice of the Supreme Court for the judicial branch are authorized to resolve deficits under 1.5 percent of the fiscal year appropriation. Deficits over the 1.5 percent amount shall be resolved by the legislature.

(h) The governor, during the first six months of a fiscal year in which the current revenue estimate on which appropriations are based is expected to exceed actual revenues, is authorized to require state agencies to reserve such appropriations as specified by the governor for budget reductions to be recommended to the general assembly at its next regular session.

(i) The governor's authority to reduce, expand and reorganize budgets can be done only pursuant to existing statutes.

(j) If general fund expenditure ceiling is exceeded, two-thirds vote required; otherwise majority of elected members.

(k) The governor is not required to submit a balanced budget, but it would be political suicide not to do so. The constitution requires that the legislature pass a balanced budget. The governor, as the chief budget officer of the state, has always insured that expenditures do not exceed revenues.

(l) The governor's authority to reduce budgets is temporary. The State Board of Examiners (Governor, Attorney General and Secretary of State) has permanent appropriation reduction authority.

(m) The governor can veto appropriation items entirely (Item Veto) or merely reduce an item of appropriation to a lesser amount (Reduction Veto). If the governor reduces an item of appropriation, the remaining items in the bill are not affected and can become law immediately. The governor can also veto substantive or appropriation bills entirely (Veto) or merely make changes to them (Amendatory Veto). Changes can include removing selected words or changing the meaning of words. If the governor makes amendatory language changes to an appropriation bill, the entire bill including all other appropriation items are held up until the legislature considers the governor's changes. The Legislature can add explanatory or limiting language to appropriations without violating the constitutional distinction between substantive and appropriation bills. The governor has occasionally changed language in an appropriation bill without rising to the level of an amendatory veto. For instance, the governor once changed the fund from which the appropriation was being made.

(n) A majority vote is required to pass the budget until June 1. After that date, the required vote increases to three-fifths majority.

(o) The budget bill when and as passed by both houses, shall be a law immediately without further action by the governor.

(p) With the approval of the Board of Public Works, the governor may reduce by not more than 25 percent any appropriation that the governor considers unnecessary.

(q) The governor may not, however, reduce an appropriation to the legislative or judicial branches of government; for the payment of principal and interest on state debt; the funding for public schools (K-12); or the salary of a public officer during the term of office.

(r) For capital budget, two-thirds votes required.

(s) There are both statutory and constitutional restrictions on executive branch authority to make budget reductions, involving approval by both House and Senate appropriations committees.

(t) Additional restrictions on budget reductions exclude principle and interest on state debt, legislative and judicial branches, school equalization aid and salaries of elected officials.

(u) The governor is not technically required to sign a balanced budget, but the governor, legislative leaders and the comptroller must certify the budget is in balance in order to meet borrowing requirements.

(v) Any appropriation added to the governor's budget by the legislature is subject to line item veto.

(w) May reduce budget without approval for state operations. Only restriction on reductions is that reductions in aid to localities cannot be made without legislative approval.

(x) Except for certain block grants. The governor is required to maintain a balanced budget for the fiscal period and has the authority through the Constitution and General Statutes to make reductions to insure there is no overdraft or deficit.

(y) Line item veto in appropriation act only.

(z) Legislature could pass and the governor could sign a budget where appropriations exceed cash and estimated revenues, but constitutional and statutory provisions reduce the appropriations so that the budget is balanced.

(aa) Would require agreement of agency governing boards and or CEO.

(bb) The governor may reduce budgets selectively; he must provide 10 days prior notice and the reasons for so doing before lapsing current year grant and subsidy money.

(cc) The Budget and Control Board can authorize an across-the-board agency reduction when there is a revenue shortfall. When in session, the General Assembly has five statewide session days to take action to prevent the reduction.

(dd) Governor may allow balanced budget to go into law without signature.

(ee) Reductions based on revenue shortfalls of greater than one percent require legislative approval.

(ff) Requirement applies only to budget execution. The governor is required to insure that actual expenditures do not exceed actual revenues by the end of the appropriation period.

(gg) Governor may return bill without limit for recommended amendments for amount and language. For purposes of a veto, a line item is defined as an indivisible sum of money that may or may not coincide with the way in which items are displayed in an appropriation act.

(hh) Two-thirds of members present includes a majority of the members elected.

(ii) The governor can reduce expenditures but not appropriations. Public education has priority.

(jj) Cannot reduce appropriations, but can withhold allotments.

(kk) A majority vote is required for education, highways, and paying down the state debt; a three-fourths vote of the elected members is required on all others.

(ll) A two-thirds majority is required for appropriations from the general fund, except for public school appropriations, which require a simple majority.

(mm) If the general fund expenditure ceiling is exceeded, a two-thirds vote is required, otherwise, the majority of elected members is required.

(nn) For emergency enactment, a two-thirds vote is required.

(oo) A majority is required to pass the agency appropriations bill, unless a bill is considered a donation (e.g., a donation to the Mississippi Burn Center). In this case, Joint Rule 66 requires a two-thirds vote of the elected members.

(pp) Main budget bills typically have the e (emergency) clause attached, thus requiring a two-thirds vote. The e clause is necessary for the budget to be operative by the beginning of the fiscal year.

(qq) Emergency measures and measures that amend a statute that has been referred or enacted through an initiated measure within the last seven years must pass both houses by a two-thirds majority.

(rr) A two-thirds majority is required for individual spending bills.

(ss) Governor may veto judicial and legislative appropriation bills only in their entirety.

(tt) The budget bill, when and as passed by both houses, shall be law immediately without further action by the governor. The legislature may not add to the budget bill as proposed by the governor, except in the legislative and judicial branches. The governor, however, may veto items included in supplementary appropriation bills.

(uu) The Michigan Constitution limits the amounts and types of taxes that can be imposed. In general, tax increases must be approved by a majority vote of the people.

(vv) Legislature can approve tax and fee increases during a legislative session of no more than one percent of total state revenue as proscribed by the state's constitutional revenue and spending limit—roughly $70 million in fiscal 2002. Amounts above this level must be approved by the voters.

(ww) The state constitution limits the used of public debt. The construction of this limit implicitly requires the state to have a balanced operating budget.

(xx) Above five percent or more.

(yy) May transfer, reduce and increase agency budgets through joint budget execution authority with legislative budget board.

Table 7.16
REVENUE ESTIMATING PRACTICES

State or other jurisdiction	Source of authority	Estimates bind the budget	When are official revenue estimates made (List by month)	Multi-year forecasting	Revenue Estimating Agencies or Economic Advisory Boards
Alabama	I	...	Feb.	CY + 1	Dept. of Finance
Alaska	AO	...	April, Dec. (a)	CY	Office of Management & Budget, Dept. of Revenue, Dept. of Labor
Arizona	...	...	N.A.	CY	Office of Strategic Planning & Budgeting
Arkansas	I	★	N.A.	CY	Fiscal Officer; Budget Office; Economic Analysis; Tax Research
California	I	...	Jan./May (k)	CY	Dept. of Finance
Colorado	S	...	Dec., March, June, Sept.	CY + 1	Governor's Revenue Estimating Advisory Committee
Connecticut	S	...	N.A.	CY + 3	Office of Policy & Management
Delaware	EO	★	(c)	CY + 5	Economic and Financial Advisory Council
Florida	S	★	Fall/Winter & when needed	CY	Consensus Revenue Estimating Conference
Georgia	...	★	N.A.	CY + 1	Office of Planning & Budget
Hawaii	C,S	★ (b)	June, Sept., Jan., March	CY + 4	Council on Revenues
Idaho	...	...	Jan., Aug.	CY	Division of Financial Management
Illinois	...	...	July, Oct., Feb., April	CY + 1	Budget Agency
Indiana	EO	★	N.A.	CY	Budget Agency
Iowa	...	★	N.A.	CY + 4	Dept. of Management
Kansas	I	...	N.A.	CY + 3	Budget Office; Revenue Dept.; Legislative Research Dept.
Kentucky	EO	★	N.A.	CY + 4	Finance Secretary, Legislative Research Commission
Louisiana	C,S	★	N.A.	CY + 4	Governor, Legislature, Revenue Estimating Conference
Maine	...	★	N.A.	CY + 2	State Budget Officer; Consensus Economic Forecasting Commission
Maryland	I	...	Dec.	CY + 4	Expenditures—Dept. of Budget and Management; Revenues—Board of Revenue Estimates
Massachusetts	I	★	(d)	CY + 1	Revenue Dept./Fiscal Affairs Division
Michigan	...	★	Jan., May	CY + 1	Office of Revenue and Tax Analysis—Dept. of Treasury
Minnesota	EO	★	(e)	CY + 4	Dept. of Finance
Mississippi	S	★	Oct.	CY	Office of Budget & Fund Management
Missouri	...	...	Jan.	CY + 4	Budget Office
Montana	...	...	Apr.–May/Oct./Dec. (l)	CY	Contract with forecasting firm—Wharton Economic Forecasting Assoc.
Nebraska	S	★	Feb., Apr.,Oct.	CY + 2	Revenue Dept. and Economic Forecasting Advisory Board
Nevada	S	★	Dec.—Revised in May	CY + 4-10	Economic Forum
New Hampshire	S	★	N.A.	CY	Budget Office & Dept. of Revenue Administration
New Jersey	S	★	N.A.	CY + 3	Council of Economic Advisors
New Mexico	S	...	N.A.	CY	Economic Analysis Bureau; Dept. of Finance & Administration
New York	...	★	N.A.	CY + 2	Division of the Budget
North Carolina	...	★	N.A.	CY + 4	Office of State Budget & Management
North Dakota	EO	★	(m)	CY	OMB contracts with econometrics forecasting firm
Ohio	I	...	Jan./June (f)	CY	Office of Budget & Management
Oklahoma	...	★	Dec., Feb., June (g)	CY + 5	Oklahoma Tax Commission; Office of State Finance
Oregon	EO	★	N.A.	CY + 4	Office of Economic Analysis within Dept. of Administrative Services
Pennsylvania	...	★	May/June (h)	CY + 4	Budget Office & Revenue Dept.
Rhode Island	...	★	(i)	CY + 4	Revenue Estimating Conference
South Carolina	S, Proviso	...	Nov., Feb.	CY	Board of Economic Advisors
South Dakota	EO	★	N.A.	CY + 3	Bureau of Finance & Management
Tennessee	S	...	(n)	CY	Center of Business & Economic Research—Univ. of Tennessee
Texas	...	★	Jan./May (odd years)	CY	Comptroller's Office
Utah	EO	★	N.A.	CY + 5	Office of Planning & Budget & Tax Commission
Vermont	I	...	N.A.	CY	Dept. of Finance & Management
Virginia	S	★	Dec.	CY + 4	Dept. of Taxation
Washington	EO	...	Nov.	CY + 8	Economic and Revenue Forecast Council
West Virginia	...	★	Jan. (o)	CY + 4	Dept. of Tax & Revenue
Wisconsin	...	...	Nov. 20 (even years)	CY + 2	Dept. of Revenue
Wyoming	S	...	N.A.	CY	Economic Analysis Division
Puerto Rico	EO	★	N.A.	CY	Planning Board; Government Development Bank

See footnotes at end of table.

REVENUE ESTIMATING PRACTICES — Continued

Source: National Association of State Budget Officers, *Budget Processes in the States*, 2002. For additional information see http://www.nasbo.org.

Key:

★ — Yes.

. . . — No.

N.A. — Not Available.

S — Statutory

C — Constitutional

EO — Executive Order

I — Informal

AO — Administrative Order

CY — Current Year

FY — Fiscal Year

(a) Revenue estimates must be published annually but traditionally are published semi-annually.

(b) Statutes require that estimates shall be considered; differing revenue estimates by the governor or legislature may be used if fact and reasons are made public.

(c) Quarterly estimates are done for Sept., Dec., and March; monthly estimates are done for April, May and June.

(d) Dept. of Revenue publishes estimates three times a year. Secretary for Administration and Finance and the legislature agree on revenue estimates in the spring for the fiscal year beginning in July. For fiscal 2001, the consensus was reached in May.

(e) Five-year revenue estimates are formally published twice a year in November and February.

(f) Odd numbered years. The governor must publish revenue estimates in the biennial executive budget submitted to the general assembly. A monthly financial report prepared for the governor by the Office of Budget and Management contains revenue estimates for the current fiscal year and reflects any revisions to those estimates made during the fiscal year.

(g) Revenue estimates are made by various agencies including the State Tax Commission. Economic information is provided by various private and public entities. The State Finance Office reviews, consolidates and presents the estimates to the State Equalization Board late in December and again in mid-February. The Board certifies an official estimate that is only revised if laws affecting it are passed by the state legislature. Such a revision would be made in June.

(h) Revenue estimates are updated when new legislation affects current year revenues.

(i) Per state statute, a Consensus Revenue Estimating Conference must be held within the first ten days of November and May.

(j) Advisory board planned.

(k) Revenue estimates are made public in January and May.

(l) Budget office prepares estimates in the spring and fall of even numbered years. The revenue and tax committee of the legislature adopts its estimate in December prior to convening in January.

(m) July and November of even numbered years and March of odd numbered years.

(n) February (original estimate for succeeding fiscal year); May (revised estimate); July (revised estimate for enacted budget); February (revised estimate for current fiscal year); May (revised estimate for current fiscal year).

(o) The Governor makes the official revenue estimate in January, except in the year following a gubernatorial election at which time the official revenue estimate is made in February.

Table 7.17
ALLOWABLE STATE INVESTMENTS

State	CDs within state	CDs nationally	Other time deposits	Bankers' acceptances	Commercial paper	Corporate notes/bonds	Corporate stocks (foreign)	Corporate stocks (domestic)	Derivatives	Equities	Mortgage backed securities	Mutuals	State/local government obligations	U.S. Treasury obligations	U.S. agency obligations	Eurodollars–CDs or TDs	Real Estate	Repurchase agreements	Venture capital	Other
Alabama																		★		
Alaska	(a)	★	★	★	★	★	★	★		★	★	★	★	★	★					
Arizona	★	★	★	★	★	★				★	★	★	★	★	★			★		
Arkansas	★		★	★	★	★				★	★	★	★	★	★			★		
California	★	★		★	★	★				★	★		★	★	★			★		
Colorado	★		★		★		★	★			★	★	★	★	★			★		(b)
Connecticut									★					★		★				(c)
Delaware	★	★	★	★	★	★					★		★	★	★			★		
Florida	★	★		★	★	★					★		★	★	★			★		(d)
Georgia	★	★	★	★	★	★					★		★	★	★			★		
Hawaii	★			★	★				★				★	★	★			★		(e)
Idaho	★				★	★								★	★			★		(f)
Illinois	★													★	★			★		(f)
Indiana	★													★				★		
Iowa	★													★				★		
Kansas	★		★	★	★	★	★	★		★	★	★	★	★	★			★		(g)
Kentucky	★	★		★	★			★		★	★	★	★	★	★			★		
Louisiana	★		★	★	★	★					★		★	★	★			★		
Maine	★	★	★	★	★						★		★	★	★			★		
Maryland	★	★ (h)		★	★	★							★	★	★			★		
Massachusetts	★	★		★	★	★					★		★	★	★			★		(i)
Michigan	★	★		★	★	★	★	★		★	★	★	★	★	★	★		★		(j)
Minnesota				★	★	★					★		★	★	★			★		
Mississippi	★													★				★		
Missouri	★			★	★	★								★	★			★		
Montana														★				★		
Nebraska	★	★	★	★	★	★					★		★	★	★			★		
Nevada	★	★	★	★	★	★	★	★		★	★	★	★	★	★		★	★		(k)
New Hampshire	★			★	★	★				★				★	★			★		(l)
New Jersey		★		★	★	★								★	★			★		
New Mexico	★	★		★	★	★	★	★		★	★	★	★	★	★	★		★		
New York	★	★		★	★	★					★		★	★	★			★		
North Carolina	★			★	★	★								★	★			★		
North Dakota	★	★	★	★	★	★								★	★			★		
Ohio	★		★	★	★	★					★	★	★	★	★			★		(m)

See footnotes at end of table.

ALLOWABLE STATE INVESTMENTS—Continued

State	CDs within state	CDs nationally	Other time deposits	Bankers' acceptances	Commercial paper	Corporate notes/bonds	Corporate stocks (foreign)	Corporate stocks (domestic)	Derivatives	Equities	Mortgage backed securities	Mutuals	State/local government obligations	U.S. Treasury obligations	U.S. agency obligations	Eurodollars—CDs or TDs	Real Estate	Repurchase agreements	Venture capital	Other
Oklahoma	★	★	★	★	★	. . .	. . .	. . .	(n)	. . .	. . .	(o)	★	★	★	. . .	. . .	★	. . .	. . .
Oregon	★	. . .	★	★	★	★	. . .	. . .	. . .	. . .	★	. . .	★	★	★	. . .	. . .	★	. . .	(p)
Pennsylvania	★	★	. . .	★	★	★	. . .	. . .	. . .	. . .	★	. . .	. . .	★	★	. . .	. . .	★	. . .	. . .
Rhode Island	★	★	. . .	. . .	★	★	★	★	. . .	. . .	. . .	. . .	★	★	★	. . .	★	★	★	. . .
South Carolina	★	. . .	. . .	. . .	★	★	★	★	. . .	. . .	★	★	★	★	★	. . .	★	★	. . .	. . .
South Dakota	★	★	★	★	★	★	★	★	. . .	★	★	★	★	★	★	. . .	. . .	★	. . .	. . .
Tennessee	★	. . .	★	★	★	★	. . .	. . .	. . .	. . .	. . .	★	★	★	★	. . .	. . .	★	. . .	. . .
Texas	★	★	. . .	★	★	★	. . .	(q)	. . .	(o)	★	★	★	★	★	. . .	. . .	★	. . .	. . .
Utah	. . .	. . .	. . .	★	★	★	(q)	(q)	. . .	(o)	. . .	★	★	★	★	★	. . .	★	. . .	. . .
Vermont	★	. . .	. . .	★	★	★	. . .	. . .	. . .	. . .	★	. . .	★	★	★	. . .	★	★	★	(r)
Virginia	★	★	. . .	★	★	★	. . .	. . .	. . .	. . .	★	★	★	★	★	. . .	. . .	★	. . .	. . .
Washington	★	★	★	★	★	★	★	★	. . .	★	★	★	★	★	★	. . .	★	★	. . .	. . .
West Virginia	★	★	★	★	★	. . .	★	★	. . .	★	. . .	★	★	★	★	★	★	★	★	. . .
Wisconsin	. . .	. . .	. . .	. . .	★	★	. . .	. . .	. . .	. . .	. . .	. . .	★	★	★	. . .	★	★	★	(s)
Wyoming	. . .	. . .	. . .	★	★	★	. . .	. . .	. . .	. . .	. . .	. . .	. . .	★	★	. . .	. . .	★	. . .	. . .

Source: National Association of State Treasurers, November 2003.

Key:
★—Yes
. . .—No

(a) Nothing is restricted by Statute. Commission is subject to prudent investor rule. The Commissioner evaluated each fund's time horizon and risk.
(b) Asset back securities.
(c) Convertible corporate bonds.
(d) Student loans.
(e) Money market funds, SBAs.
(f) Money market mutual funds.
(g) Collateralized mortgage obligations, other mortgages, asset backed.

(h) Authorized to do business in Massachusetts.
(i) Massachusetts Municipal Depository Trust per statute.
(j) Emergency loans to municipalities within the state.
(k) Collateralized mortgage obligations.
(l) Does not include retirement mutual funds.
(m) All fixed income.
(n) Derivatives are permitted if they otherwise meet statutory definition of permissible investment.
(o) Money market mutual funds only.
(p) Certain trust funds can invest in equities.
(q) Trust funds only.
(r) Collateralized CDs.
(s) Private equity, emerging market securities, real estate mortgages and leverage buyout funds.

Table 7.18
CASH MANAGEMENT PROGRAMS AND SERVICES

| State | Reviews of cash management programs | | | | Agency preparing cash management services | | | | | |
| | Banking relations | | Investment practices | | | | | | | |
	Reviewing agency	Frequency of review	Reviewing agency	Frequency of review	Lock boxes	Wire transfers	Zero balance accounts	Information services	Account reconciliation systems	Automated clearinghouse
Alabama	SE	...	SE	Annually	B	B	B	I	I	B
Alaska	SE	Annually	SE	N.A.	B	I	B	I	I	B
Arizona	SE	Quarterly	SE	Quarterly	B	I, B	B	I	I	I, B
Arkansas	SE	Quarterly	SE	Quarterly	NU	B	B	I, B	I, B	B
California	SE	Annually	SE	Monthly	B	I, B	I, B	I	I, B	B
Colorado	SE	Ongoing	OF	Ongoing	B	B	B	B	B	B
Connecticut	SE	Quarterly	OF	Weekly	B	I, B	B	I, B	I, B	I, B
Delaware	(a)	(b)	(a)	Annually	B	I, B	B	I, B	I	I, B
Florida	SE	(b)	SE (c)	Annually	I, B	NU	B	NU	B	B
Georgia	SE	Annually	SE	Quarterly	B	I	NU	NU	NU	NU
Hawaii	SE	(b)	SE	(d)	B	I	B	I	I	B
Idaho	SE	Quarterly	SE	Daily	B	I, B	B	I, B	I	B
Illinois	SE	(d)	SE	Quarterly	B	I, B	B	I, B	NU	I, B
Indiana	SE	Annually	SE	Annually	B	I, B	I, B	NU	I	I, B
Iowa	SE	4 years	SE	Annually	B	I	B	I	I	I
Kansas	SE	Ongoing	N.A.	N.A.	B	I	I	NU	I	I, B
Kentucky	SE	2 years	SE	Quarterly, Annually (e)	NU	B (f)	B	I	I	B
Louisiana	SE	Annually	SE	Annually	B	B	B	B	B	B
Maine	SE	3 years	SE, OF	Semi-Annually	NU	I, B	B	I, B	I, B	B
Maryland	SE	Annually	SE	Annually	B	I	B	I, B	I, B	I, B
Massachusetts	SE	Quarterly	SE	Quarterly	B	B	B	B	B	B
Michigan	SE	(d)	SE	(d)	B	I, B	B	NU	I, B	B
Minnesota	...	3 years	SE, OF	...	B	I	I	I	I	I
Mississippi	...	...	...	...	B	NU	NU	I	NU	B
Missouri	SE	Quarterly	SE	Monthly	I, B	I, B	B	I, B	I, B	I, B
Montana	SE	Monthly	SE	Monthly, Annually	NU	I, B	NU	I	NU	I, B
Nebraska	SE	Ongoing	SE	Ongoing	B	B	I, B	I	I	B
Nevada	SE	Ongoing	SE	Quarterly	B	I	B	I, B	I, B	B
New Hampshire	SE	Quarterly	SE	Quarterly	B	I	I	I	I	I
New Jersey	OF	Quarterly	OF	Annually	B	I	B	I	I, B	I
New Mexico	SE, OF	(d)	SE, OF	Monthly	B	I, B	B	I	I, B	B
New York	SE	...	SE	...	B	I	B	I	I, B	B
North Carolina	...	...	...	...	B	I	B	NU	NU	NU
North Dakota	SE	...	SE	...	NU	B	NU	NU	NU	B
Ohio	SE	Quarterly	SE	Quarterly	I, B	I, B	NU	NU	NU	NU

See footnotes at end of table.

CASH MANAGEMENT PROGRAMS AND SERVICES — Continued

State	Reviews of cash management programs				Lock boxes	Agency preparing cash management services				
	Banking relations		Investment practices			Wire transfers	Zero balance accounts	Information services	Account reconciliation systems	Automated clearinghouse
	Reviewing agency	Frequency of review	Reviewing agency	Frequency of review						
Oklahoma	SE	Ongoing	SE	Ongoing	B	NU	B	I	NU	I, B
Oregon	SE	Ongoing	SE, OF	Ongoing	I, B	I	I, B	I	I, B	I
Pennsylvania	SE	As needed	SE, OF	Daily, Monthly	B	B	B	NU	I, B	B
Rhode Island	SE	Quarterly	SE	Quarterly	B	I, B	I, B	I, B	I, B	I, B
South Carolina	SE	Annually	SE	Annually	B	I, B	I	NU	I	B
South Dakota	SE	Annually	SE	Annually	I	B	B	NU	I	B
Tennessee	SE	Annually	SE	Annually	I	I, B	B	I	I	B
Texas	SE	Annually	SE	Annually	I, B	I	B	I	I	I, B
Utah	SE	Annually	SE	Quarterly	B	I, B	B	I	NU	I
Vermont	SE	2 years	SE	Ongoing	B	B	B	I, B	I	I, B
Virginia	SE	Annually	OF	Annually	B	I	B	B	I, B	I, B
Washington	SE	Semi-Annually	SE	Annually	B	B	B	I	I, B	I, B
West Virginia	SE	Quarterly	N.A.	N.A.	I	NU	NU	I	I, B	I
Wisconsin	SE	6 years	SE	N.A.	B	B	B	I, B	I, B	B
Wyoming	SE	Daily	SE, OF	Quarterly	NU	I, B	I	NU	I	I

Source: National Association of State Treasurers, *State Treasury Activities & Functions*, 2003.
Key:
SE — State employee
N.A. — Not applicable
OF — Outside firm
B — Performed by bank
I — Within treasurer's office
NU — Not utilized

(a) Cash Management Policy Board reviews and implements.
(b) Outside firm utilized occasionally.
(c) Reviewed when contract expires.
(d) No set period for review.
(e) Quarterly review by Investment Commission, annual review by State Auditor.
(f) Initiated in-house by electronic link to bank.

Table 7.19
DEMAND DEPOSITS

State	Method for selecting depository						Treasurer's approval	Selection of depository made by	Compensation of demand depositories	Collateral above federal level	Percentage requiring collateral
	Competitive bid	Application	Negotiation	Depositor's convenience	Compensating balances	Agency's convenience					
Alabama	...	...	...	...	...	★	...	Individual agencies	CMB	Yes	100
Alaska	★	...	...	...	★	★	...	Cash manager	CMB	Yes	105
Arizona	★	...	...	★	...	...	★	Treasurer	CMB	Yes	102
Arkansas	...	...	★	★	★	...	★	Treasurer	CMB, SF	Yes	105
California	...	...	...	...	...	...	★	Treasurer	CMB	Yes	110
Colorado	★	...	...	★	...	★	★	Treasurer, Controller	CMB, SF, MB	Yes	102
Connecticut	★	...	★	★	...	★	★	Treasurer	CMB, SF, MB	Yes	(a)
Delaware	★	...	★	★	...	...	...	Treasurer, Board	CMB, SF	No (b)	102 (c)
Florida	...	...	...	...	...	...	...	Treasurer	SF	Yes	100
Georgia	...	★	...	...	...	★	★	Individual agencies	SF	Yes	...
Hawaii	★	...	...	...	...	...	★	Treasurer	SF	Yes	100
Idaho	...	★	...	★	...	...	...	Treasurer	CMB, SF	No	100
Illinois	★	...	★	★	...	...	...	Treasurer	SF	Yes	100
Indiana	★	...	★	...	...	...	★	Treasurer	CMB	No	0
Iowa	★	...	...	...	...	★	...	Treasurer	CMB, SF	No	...
Kansas	★	★	...	...	...	...	...	Treasurer, Board	SF	Yes	100
Kentucky	★	...	...	...	...	★	★	(d)	CMB, SF (e)	Yes	100
Louisiana	★	★	★	...	...	...	★	Treasurer	SF	Yes	100
Maine	...	...	...	★	...	...	★	Treasurer	CMB	Yes	10 (f)
Maryland	★	★	...	★	★	★	★	Treasurer	(g)	Yes	100 (h)
Massachusetts	★	★	...	...	...	★	★	Treasurer	CMB, SF	Yes	(i)
Michigan	...	...	...	...	...	★	★	Treasurer	CMB	Yes	25
Minnesota	★	...	...	...	...	...	...	Comm. of Finance	CMB, SF	Yes	110
Mississippi	...	...	...	★	★	...	★	Treasurer, Finance Dept.	CMB, SF	Yes	105
Missouri	★	★	...	★	★	★	★	Board (j)	CMB	Yes	100
Montana	★	...	...	...	...	...	...	Treasurer	SF	Yes	50
Nebraska	...	★	...	★	★	★	★	Treasurer	CMB	Yes	110
Nevada	★	...	...	★	...	★	★	Treasurer, Board	CMB, SF	Yes	102
New Hampshire	...	...	...	...	...	...	...	...	(k)	No	...
New Jersey	★	...	...	★	★	★	★	Treasurer	CMB, SF	Yes	100
New Mexico	...	...	...	...	...	★	★	Treasurer	SF	Yes	100
New York	★	...	...	★	...	★	★	Treasurer (l)	SF	Yes	102
North Carolina	...	...	...	...	...	...	(k)	Treasurer	(m)	Yes	100
North Dakota	(k)	(k)	(k)	(k)	(k)	(k)	(k)	State Constitution	SF	No	...
Ohio	(k)	...	★	...	...	...	★	Treasurer, Board (n)	CMB, SF	...	100

See footnotes at end of table.

DEMAND DEPOSITS—Continued

State	Method for selecting depository						Treasurer's approval	Selection of depository made by	Compensation of demand depositories	Collateral above federal level	Percentage requiring collateral
	Competitive bid	Application	Negotiation	Depositor's convenience	Compensating balances	Agency's convenience					
Oklahoma	...	...	...	★	...	...	★	Treasurer	CMB, SF	Yes	110
Oregon	...	...	...	...	...	...	★	Treasurer	CMB, SF	Yes	25
Pennsylvania	...	★	★	...	...	...	...	Board (n)	CMB	Yes	100
Rhode Island	...	★	...	★	...	★	★	Treasurer	SF	Yes	100
South Carolina	...	...	...	★	★	★	★	Treasurer	CMB	Yes	100 (o)
South Dakota	★	...	...	...	...	...	★	Treasurer	CMB, SF, MB	Yes	100
Tennessee	...	★	...	...	...	...	★	Treasurer	SF	Yes	105
Texas	★	★	...	...	...	★	★	Treasurer	CMB, SF	Yes	105
Utah	...	...	...	★	...	...	★	Treasurer	SF	No	...
Vermont	★	...	...	★	...	★	★	(p)	SF, MB	Yes	100
Virginia	...	...	...	★	...	★	★	(q)	CMB, SF	Yes	50–100 (r)
Washington	★	...	...	★	...	★	★	Treasurer	CMB, SF	Yes	10
West Virginia	...	...	...	...	...	★	...	Treasurer	CMB	Yes	65
Wisconsin	★	...	...	★	...	...	...	Treasurer, Board	CMB	No	N.A.
Wyoming	★	...	...	...	...	...	...	Treasurer	CMB, SF	Yes	102

Source: National Association of State Treasurers, *State Treasury Activities & Functions,* 2003.

Key:
★ — Method utilized.
. . . — Method not utilized.
N.A. — Not available.
CMB — Compensating balances.
SF — Service fee.
MB — Minimum balance.
(a) Varies based upon bank's risk based capitol ratios.
(b) No requirements if a bank meets credit criteria.
(c) If a bank does not meet credit criteria.
(d) Treasurer, Finance Secretary and a selection committee are responsible for the selection of institutions.
(e) CMB for Imprest and receipt accounts, SF for primary depository.
(f) Demand deposits that exceed 25 percent of a bank's retained earnings must be collateralized.

(g) Combination of fees, CMB.
(h) Any public funds in excess of FDIC must be collateralized.
(i) No deposits meet collateral requirements. A contractual $100 million collateral exists with the central depository bank but is not required by law.
(j) Must be approved by State Treasurer, State Auditor, Governor.
(k) Determined by Treasurer.
(l) RFP issued, Treasury employee committee reviews.
(m) Transaction fee.
(n) Treasurer is chair of Board.
(o) 100 percent collateralization over $300,000.
(p) State Treasurer, State Auditor, & Governor are responsible.
(q) Cash and banking services manager.
(r) Banks are required to secure all deposits in excess of FDIC insurance by 50 percent. Savings and Loans required to secure all deposits by 100 percent.

Lotteries: Where the Money Goes
By Alan R. Yandow

Lotteries exist to serve the players, and the states or jurisdictions that benefit from the proceeds. Responsible, well run lotteries, such as the current U.S. lotteries, are the worth inheritors of a long lottery past.

Lotteries—A product of our times?

Asking members of the public what they know about lotteries, one might hear references to the current large jackpot games such as Powerball or Mega Millions, or to some of the "urban myths" or stereotypes about lotteries. The truth is, lotteries, in one variation or another, have been around for centuries. And not necessarily in the formats we are used to seeing. The beneficiaries of such lotteries have varied over the years, as well. In addition to giving a bit of background on the popularity of lotteries over the years, the following will describe what sort of beneficiaries our current U.S. lotteries assist.

Overview of Lotteries Worldwide

During the Roman days, emperors would host parties where the guests could not depart until gifts had been allotted to all. At times, both valuable and valueless gifts were drawn, and many an animal was awarded.

The Bible tells of the story of how Jonas was thrown into the sea by sailors frightened by the storm. They drew lots to find out who in the ship was bringing the storm upon them, and Jonas lost the draw.

The Hindu culture relied on the ultimate lottery—trial by chance. They would place statuettes in large urns, one representing guilt and one representing innocence. The accused decided their own fate by fishing one of them out of the urn.

The ancestor of the game of Keno, invented by Chung Lung, a member of the Han dynasty, was used to raise money for his armies in the last century B.C. At that time, the game used 120 characters or Chinese proverbs, from which a certain number had to be selected. This "Chinese lottery" came with Chinese immigrants to Europe and later to America, and the modern game of Keno was born.

The emperor Nero (37 A.D.) marked his celebrations of the Eternity of the Empire by public daily draws awarding jobs, land, slaves or ships as prizes.

These few historical references show clearly that lotteries have been used in every age and in all countries as a means of solving problems, to provide recreation and integrated into customs and peoples' lives. Lotteries have always been—and always will be—a game that is fun, fascinating, entertaining and available to all.

The Modern-Day Lottery

In the United States today, there are 40 lottery organizations plus the District of Columbia. In 2003, these lottery organizations generated more than $45 billion in gross sales, resulting in net profits of more than $11 billion. Even though these numbers are huge, by comparison in 2002, more than $640 billion was wagered in all forms of gaming, including casino, riverboat, sports and Native American games. Compared to the total dollars wagered, lottery sales accounted for only about 7 percent.

Lottery Benefits

For almost 40 years, lottery organizations across the United States have provided revenue for much needed programs and/or services that otherwise would be funded by increased taxes. Even in those lottery jurisdictions where people choose not to participate in lottery games, they still benefit by the existence of their lottery through the specific programs and services provided by lottery dollars. One hundred percent of lottery revenues are used to provide financial assistance to support primary and secondary education in California, Florida, Georgia, Illinois, Michigan, Missouri, New Hampshire, New Mexico, New York, North Dakota, Ohio, Tennessee and Vermont. In Arizona, Idaho, Indiana, Kentucky, Louisiana, Montana, Nebraska, New Jersey, Oregon, Texas and West Virginia, a portion of lottery revenue goes to provide assistance to education.

In Minnesota, a share of lottery revenues are contributed to the Environment and Natural Resources fund; and to parks and recreation, wildlife, open space and public buildings in Colorado. In Indiana, lottery revenues contribute to police and fire pensions, teachers' retirements and capital projects; while lottery revenues in South Dakota, Massachusetts and Wisconsin provide property tax relief.

In Arizona, Colorado, Kansas and Oregon, lottery organizations contribute to the economic development within their states, while lottery revenues provide a variety of much needed programs and services for the senior citizens of Pennsylvania.

In Connecticut, Delaware, District of Columbia, Louisiana, Rhode Island and Washington, lottery revenues go directly into general funds, allowing for greater flexibility in the programs and/or services in which lottery revenues support.

Since New Hampshire sold its first ticket in 1964, lotteries have contributed more than $231.5 billion to support much-needed programs and/or services, on more than $506 billion in gross sales.

Where the Money Goes

Table 7.20, which can be found later in this chapter, shows a list of the programs and/or services U.S. lottery organizations have supported throughout the years, through fiscal year 2003. This is an accumulative list since the first day of ticket sales for each organization. The date listed after each organization is the year in which ticket sales began.

Since 1964, total lottery sales have generated more than $190 billion in net profits for individual states. This is a huge amount of money and would be almost impossible to replace if lotteries were not in existence today.

The Lottery Retail Network

Throughout the United States, more than 200,000 retail stores sell lottery products. Many of the lottery retailers are "mom & pop" stores that would be hard pressed to remain in business without the lottery products. It has been proven that lottery games not only generate sales of the games, but increase sales of other products as well. Foot traffic is increased with lottery products and often times, consumers frequent stores that they otherwise would not because of the lottery products. Since 1964, lottery organizations have paid more than $28 billion in commissions to lottery retailers, with more than $2.5 billion paid in FY '03. This is not only a huge contribution to the financial security of many small storeowners, but also accounts for sizable sales within the larger chain stores.

The commission paid to the lottery retail network is an important part of the overall financial strategy for most retail locations. Lottery products offer an additional convenience to customers and can increase the sales of other products at the same time. The sales generated from lottery products would be hard to replace if they were not in existence. This is just one more way state lottery revenues benefit the citizens within a particular state.

Conclusion

This article has shown that lotteries have been with us for many, many years. It has also shown how the current U.S. lotteries benefit storeowners and lottery agents, as well as those programs that would be hard pressed to exist in their current form without lotteries or major tax shifting. Lotteries exist to serve the players and the states or jurisdictions that benefit from the proceeds. Responsible, well run lotteries, such as the current U.S. lotteries, are the worth inheritors of a long lottery past.

About the Author

Alan R. Yandow has held the position of executive director of the Vermont Lottery and director of the Tri-State Lotto Commission since July 1998. He holds undergraduate and graduate degrees in Political Science and Education from the University of Vermont.

Table 7.20
CUMULATIVE LOTTERY PROCEEDS BY PROGRAM:
START-UP THROUGH FISCAL YEAR 2003

State or other jurisdiction	Organization name	Start-up date	Programs receiving funds	Cumulative total (in millions)
Alabama	---------- (a) ----------			
Alaska	---------- (a) ----------			
Arizona	Lottery	1982	Education	375.95
			Health and Welfare	148.44
			Protection and Safety	69.90
			Economic Development Fund	40.52
			General Government	41.10
			Inspection and Regulation	7.11
			Natural Resources	5.86
			Local Transportation Assistance Fund	489.00
			County Assistance Fund	129.68
			Heritage Fund	238.53
			Mass Transit	25.74
			Clean Air Fund	0.50
			Court Appointed Special Advocate Fund (Unclaimed prizes)	21.34
			State General Fund	1.50
Arkansas	---------- (a) ----------			
California	State Lottery	1985	Education	14,000.00
Colorado	Lottery	1983	Capital Construction Fund	439.80
			Division of Parks and Outdoor Recreation	128.10
			Conservation Trust Fund	512.90
			Great Outdoors Colorado Trust Fund	311.60
			General Fund	1.30
			School Fund	12.20
Connecticut	Lottery Corporation	1972	General Fund (to benefit education, roads, health and hospitals and public safety)	5,060.00
Delaware	State Lottery	1975	General Fund	1,600.00
Florida	Lottery	1987	Education Enhancement Trust Fund	13,030.00
Georgia	Lottery Corporation	1993	HOPE Scholarships	2,500.00
			Pre-Kindergarten Program	2,100.00
			Capital Outlay and Technology for Primary and Secondary Schools	1,800.00
Hawaii	---------- (a) ----------			
Idaho	Lottery	1989	Public Schools (K-12)	124.80
			Public Buildings	124.80
Illinois	Lottery	1974	Illinois Common School Fund (K-12)	11,600.00
Indiana	(Hoosier) Lottery	1989	Education	370.30
			Build Indiana Capital Projects Fund	317.10
			Teachers' Retirement Fund	402.60
			Police & Fire Pension Relief Fund	214.70
			License Plate Taxes	592.80
			Property Tax Fund	55.20
			General Fund	288.40
			Job Creation/Economic Development	30.00
Iowa	Lottery	1985	Iowa Plan (economic development)	170.31
			CLEAN Fund (environment and agriculture)	35.89
			Gambler's Treatment Program	8.68
			Special Appropriations	20.82
			Sales Tax	136.03
			General Fund	456.23
Kansas	Lottery	1987	Economic Development Initiatives Fund	519.70
			Correctional Institutions Building Fund	61.30
			County Reappraisal Project (FY 1988-1990)	17.20
			Juvenile Detention Facilities Fund	17.70
			State General Fund (FY 1995-2003)	76.50
			Problem Gambling Grant Fund (b)	240,000
Kentucky	Lottery Corporation	1989	Education	214.00
			Vietnam Veterans	32.00
			General Fund	1,300.00
			Post-Secondary & College Scholarships	316.00
			Affordable Housing Trust Fund	20.80
			Literacy Programs & Early Childhood Reading	12.00

See footnotes at end of table.

CUMULATIVE LOTTERY PROCEEDS BY PROGRAM:
START-UP THROUGH FISCAL YEAR 2003 — Continued

State or other jurisdiction	Organization name	Start-up date	Programs receiving funds	Cumulative total (in millions)
Louisiana	Lottery Corporation	1991	General Fund	1,380.00
			Problem Gambling	3.00
			Minimum Foundation Program (Public Education)- 2004 (c)	0.00
Maine	State Lottery	1974	General Fund	641.90
			Outdoor Heritage Fund	10.30
Maryland	State Lottery	1973	General Fund	7,909.00
			Subdivisions (for one year only FY 1984-1985)	20.90
			Stadium Authority	379.48
Massachusetts	State Lottery	1972	Cities and Towns	10,018.00
			Arts Council	173.65
			General Fund	2,600.00
			Compulsive Gamblers	9.80
Michigan	Bureau of State Lottery	1972	Education (K-12)	11,000.00
Minnesota	State Lottery	1989	General Fund	670.90
			Environmental and Natural Resources Trust Fund	311.80
			Game and Fish Fund	32.10
			Natural Resources Fund	32.10
			Other State Programs	36.70
			Compulsive Gambling	16.50
Mississippi	--- (a) ---			
Missouri	Lottery	1986	Public Education	1,500.00
			General Revenue Fund (1986-1993)	542.54
Montana	Lottery	1987	Education	49.40
			Juvenile Detention	2.50
			General Fund	54.60
			Study of Socioeconomic Impact on Gambling	0.10
Nebraska	Lottery	1993	Compulsive Gambling	3.90
			Education	92.50
			Environment	74.00
			Solid Waste Landfill Closure Fund	18.50
Nevada	--- (a) ---			
New Hampshire	Sweepstakes Commission	1964	Education	857.00
New Jersey	Lottery	1970	Education and Institutions	13,500.00
New Mexico	Lottery	1996	Public School Capital Outlay	66.55
			Lottery Tuition Fund	111.46
New York	Lottery	1967	Education	23,030.00
North Carolina	--- (a) ---			
North Dakota	--- (a) ---			
Ohio	Lottery Commission	1974	Education	12,400.00
Oklahoma	--- (a) ---			
Oregon	Lottery	1985	Economic Development	1,300.00
			Public Education	1,670.00
			Natural Resource Programs	186.00
Pennsylvania	State Lottery	1972	Older Pennsylvanians	13,800.00
Rhode Island	Lottery Commission	1974	General Fund	1,690.00
South Carolina	Education Lottery Commission	2002	Education Lottery	301.00
South Dakota	Lottery	1989	General Fund	358.70
			Capital Construction Fund	11.50
			Property Tax Reduction Fund	718.90
Tennessee	--- (d) ---			
Texas	Lottery Commission	1992	General Fund	4,960.00
			Foundation School Fund	5,610.00
Utah	--- (a) ---			
Vermont	Lottery	1978	General Fund	212.80
			Education Fund	88.40

See footnotes at end of table.

CUMULATIVE LOTTERY PROCEEDS BY PROGRAM:
START-UP THROUGH FISCAL YEAR 2003 — Continued

State or other jurisdiction	Organization name	Start-up date	Programs receiving funds	Cumulative total (in millions)
Virginia	Lottery	1988	General Fund (FY 1989-1998)	2,800.00
			Direct Aid to Public Education K-12 (FY 1999-present)	1,720.00
			Literary Fund (for school construction additions and renovations)	119.23
			Collection of Public Debt	10.45
Washington	State Lottery	1982	General Fund	1,800.00
			Education Funds	170.20
			Seattle Mariners Stadium	25.70
			King County Stadium and Exhibition Center	32.50
			Literacy Programs: 27,000 newchildren's books	N.A.
			Local Food Banks: 331 tons of food	N.A.
West Virginia	Lottery	1986	Education	524.80
			Senior Citizens	251.50
			Tourism	246.70
			Bonds covering profit areas	270.60
			General Fund	259.60
			Other	99.60
Wisconsin	Lottery	1988	Public Benefit such as Property Tax Relief	2,110.00
Dist. of Columbia	Lottery & Charitable Games	1982	General Fund	1,200.00
			Control Board	

Source: North American Association of State and Provincial Lotteries', *2004 Lottery Resource Handbook,* June 2003.

Key:

N.A. - Not available

(a) State does not have a lottery.

(b) The Problem Gambling Grant Fund was approved by the 2000 Kansas Legislature with $80,000 transferred each year. This fund is administered through Kansas Social and Rehabilitation Services.

(c) Constitutional Amendment passed October 2003; enabling legislation needed to enact dedication.

(d) Tennessee's lottery began in January 2004.

Table 7.21
STATE LOTTERIES' PRODUCT MIX

State or other jurisdiction	Instant	Pulltabs	3-digit	4-digit	Lotto	Powerball	Hot Lotto	Mega Millions	Cash Lotto	Spiel	Keno	Fast Keno	VLTs (c)
Alabama													
Alaska							(a)						
Arizona	★		★		★	★	(a)		★				
Arkansas			★				(a)						
California	★		★						★		(b)	★	
Colorado	★				★	★			★				
Connecticut	★		★	★	★	★			★				
Delaware	★		★	★		★			★				★
Florida	★		★	★	★				★				
Georgia	★		★	★	★			★	★			★	
Hawaii							(a)						
Idaho	★	★	★		★	★		★	★				
Illinois	★		★	★	★			★	★				
Indiana	★	★	★	★	★	★			★				
Iowa	★	★	★		★	★	★		★				
Kansas	★	★	★	★	★	★			★			★	
Kentucky	★	★	★	★	★	★			★				
Louisiana	★		★	★	★	★			★				
Maine	★		★	★	★	★			★			★	
Maryland	★		★	★	★			★	★			★	
Massachusetts	★	★	★	★	★			★	★		★	★	
Michigan	★		★	★	★			★	★		★		
Minnesota	★		★		★	★			★				
Mississippi							(a)						
Missouri	★	★	★	★	★	★			★		★		
Montana	★				★	★	★		★				
Nebraska	★					★			★				
Nevada							(a)						
New Hampshire	★		★	★		★	★	★	★				
New Jersey	★		★	★	★				★				
New Mexico	★		★		★	★			★				
New York	★		★	★	★			★	★		★	★	★
North Carolina							(a)						
North Dakota							(a)						
Ohio	★		★		★		(a)	★	★	★			
Oklahoma	★						(a)						
Oregon	★	★	★	★	★	★						★	★
Pennsylvania	★		★	★	★	★			★				
Rhode Island	★		★	★	★	★			★			★	★
South Carolina	★		★	★	★	★							

See footnotes at end of table.

STATE LOTTERIES' PRODUCT MIX — Continued

State or other jurisdiction	Instant	Pulltabs	3-digit	4-digit	Lotto	Powerball	Hot Lotto	Mega Millions	Cash Lotto	Spiel	Keno	Fast Keno	VLTs (c)
South Dakota	★	…	…	…	★	★	★	…	★	…	…	…	★
Tennessee (d)	★	…	…	…	…	★	…	…	…	…	…	…	…
Texas	★	…	★	…	★	…	…	…	★	…	…	…	…
Utah							(a)						
Vermont	★	…	★	★	★	…	…	…	★	…	…	…	…
Virginia	★	…	★	★	★	…	…	★	★	…	…	…	…
Washington	★	…	★	…	★	…	…	★	★	…	★	…	…
West Virginia	★	…	★	★	…	★	★	…	★	…	…	★	★
Wisconsin	★	★	★	★	★	★	…	…	★	…	…	…	…
Wyoming							(a)						
Dist. of Columbia	★	…	★	★	…	★	…	…	★	…	…	★	…

Sources: La Fleur's 2002 World Lottery Almanac and The Council of State Governments, February 2004.

★ — Yes
… — Not available.
(a) State does not have a lottery.
(b) Keno was ruled illegal. The lottery replaced it with Hot Spot in September 1996.
(c) Video lottery terminals.
(d) The Tennessee Education Lottery Corporation began selling instant-win tickets on January 20, 2004. Other games will be made available throughout 2004.

Table 7.22
STATE LOTTERIES' CUMULATIVE SALES, PRIZES AND PROFITS
(In millions of dollars)

State or other jurisdiction	Cumulative total, startup - FY 2002					FY 2003			
	Total sales	Total prizes	Prize payout (percent)	Government profits	Government return (percent)	Population (in millions)	Sales	Profit	Annual sales per capita
United States	$509,135.99	$268,088.99	53%	$177,134.68	35%	259.19	$45,290.57	$14,103.69	$174.74
Alabama	--(a)--								
Alaska	--(a)--								
Arizona	4,420.93	2,231.85	50	1,479.37	33	5.58	322.28	96.29	57.76
Arkansas	--(a)--								
California	37,257.82	18,857.75	51	13,880.12	37	35.48	2,781.57	1,026.48	78.40
Colorado	4,783.18	2,734.88	57	1,301.71	27	4.55	391.53	105.00	86.05
Connecticut	12,754.98	7,049.05	55	4,757.32	37	3.48	865.29	257.06	248.65
Delaware (b)	4,274.13	901.17	21	1,571.55	37	0.82	628.06	213.00	765.93
Florida	31,205.27	15,186.14	49	12,159.22	39	17.02	2,867.98	1,035.18	168.51
Georgia	16,265.55	8,572.74	53	5,291.21	33	8.68	2,604.41	751.50	300.05
Hawaii	--(a)--								
Idaho	1,008.92	578.65	57	231.65	23	1.37	97.97	20.50	71.51
Illinois	29,773.65	15,137.78	51	11,202.86	38	12.65	1,585.62	540.30	125.35
Indiana	7,227.87	4,094.87	57	2,142.45	30	6.20	664.42	175.60	107.16
Iowa	2,866.60	1,554.99	54	779.25	27	2.94	187.83	48.10	63.89
Kansas	2,096.13	1,087.97	52	633.62	30	2.72	210.83	64.30	77.51
Kentucky	6,526.43	3,889.91	60	1,717.64	26	4.12	673.49	180.76	163.47
Louisiana	3,553.47	1,782.22	50	1,273.51	36	4.50	311.46	111.05	69.21
Maine	2,142.16	1,180.61	55	612.01	29	1.31	164.60	39.25	125.65
Maryland	20,194.14	10,450.84	52	7,598.72	38	5.51	1,322.60	444.89	240.04
Massachusetts	45,811.77	27,710.32	60	11,724.54	26	6.43	4,197.75	889.49	652.84
Michigan (d)	28,466.19	14,658.14	51	11,109.57	39	10.08	1,783.38	586.04	176.92
Minnesota	3,940.74	2,334.78	59	934.93	24	5.06	351.82	79.40	69.53
Mississippi	--(a)--								
Missouri	5,670.93	3,165.09	56	1,808.68	32	5.70	708.57	193.90	124.31
Montana	425.42	211.50	50	99.15	23	0.92	34.68	7.45	37.70
Nebraska	645.08	432.42	67	161.60	25	1.74	80.92	19.97	46.51
Nevada	--(a)--								
New Hampshire..............	2,443.80	1,315.96	54	789.78	32	1.29	221.23	66.57	171.50
New Jersey	29,998.33	15,446.88	51	12,353.38	41	8.64	2,074.07	764.21	240.05
New Mexico	645.20	348.34	54	148.00	23	1.87	137.33	33.10	73.44
New York (e)	52,245.84	25,177.85	48	21,004.95	40	19.19	5,395.96	1,780.36	281.19
North Carolina	--(a)--								
North Dakota	--(a)--								
Ohio	33,733.38	18,632.15	55	11,740.69	35	11.44	2,078.20	641.40	181.66
Oklahoma	--(a)--								
Oregon (b)	10,927.21	5,345.90	49	3,018.93	28	3.56	853.16	387.70	239.65
Pennsylvania	32,897.53	16,659.87	51	12,747.66	39	12.37	2,132.98	787.70	172.43
Rhode Island (c)	6,855.94	4,429.25	65	1,460.13	21	1.08	1,290.50	241.83	1,194.91
South Carolina (h)	335.49	200.31	. . .	81.15	. . .	4.15	724.31	220.56	174.53
South Dakota (c)	6,142.27	3,932.34	64	977.88	16	0.76	646.95	112.03	851.25
Tennessee	--(i)--								
Texas (f)	29,548.85	16,467.39	56	9,755.73	33	22.12	3,130.69	955.20	141.53
Utah	--(a)--								
Vermont	977.53	574.12	59	279.80	29	0.62	79.50	16.20	128.23
Virginia	11,919.94	6,389.49	54	4,130.19	35	7.39	1,135.72	375.20	153.68
Washington	6,275.31	3,460.37	55	1,923.25	31	6.13	460.32	98.52	75.09
West Virginia (b)	3,971.90	1,156.49	29	1,282.52	32	1.81	1,081.91	411.00	597.74
Wisconsin	5,460.32	3,081.47	56	1,846.50	34	5.47	435.05	141.50	79.53
Wyoming	--(a)--								
Dist. of Columbia (d)	3,355.78	1,667.14	50	1123.45	33	0.56	237.63	72.00	424.34
Puerto Rico	. . .	. . .	. . .	. . .	. . .	3.88	338.00	113.10	87.11

Sources: Cumulative data from *LaFleur's 2003 World Lottery Almanac*; FY 2003 data from the North American Association of State and Provincial Lotteries.

Key:

. . . - Not available.

(a) State does not have a lottery.

(b) VLT net machine income is listed as sales. Total prizes do not include VLT prizes which reduce the lottery's prize payout.

(c) VLT sales are listed as "cash in." Total prizes include cash VLT prizes("cash out").

(d) Fiscal year ends December 31.

(e) Fiscal year ends March 31.

(f) Fiscal year ends August 31.

(g) U.S. Census Bureau estimated July 1, 2003 population.

(h) Sales began January 2002.

(i) Sales began in January 2004.

Where Immigrants Matter Most:
Assessing New Migration Dynamics in America
By William H. Frey

New migration data reveal the distinct contributions of immigration and domestic migration to population change across the nation. Large numbers of immigrants continue to concentrate in major "immigrant magnet" areas, at the same time that domestic migrants are gravitating to a wider range of areas, and local destinations within them.

Introduction

Newly released census data reveal a new migration dynamic that will have important impacts on demographic change in different parts of the country. Studies conducted after the 1990 census pointed out a divergence between large metropolitan areas that grew mostly from immigration, and those that grew primarily from migration within the United States. It was speculated that the continuation of these divergent migration sources of growth would lead to different demographic profiles for these "immigrant magnets" and "domestic migrant magnets" (Frey, 1996; Frey and Liaw, 1998). The former metro areas, reflecting primarily immigrant driven growth, would become more closely linked to the global economy as the nation's "world cities"—with more culturally diverse populations but also with "two tiered" economies emerging within them. The latter metro areas, reflecting domestic migrant gains, would become more "suburban" in character —with less diverse, more middle-aged, middle class populations. These distinct migration-driven differences, it has been argued, will shape each area's distinct public service needs, business patterns, political cultures and the like.

With immigration rising to even higher levels in the 1990s (Martin and Midgley, 2003), the new census migration data provide an opportunity to reassess these immigrant and domestic migration-driven growth patterns. This analysis reveals a continued divergence between these two different kinds of metropolitan "magnets." Yet the census migration data allow us to identify a new set of "domestic migrant magnet" metro areas, which are now, also attracting sizeable flows of migrants from abroad, as the new immigration waves spill out to new parts of the country.

Finally, this dichotomy in migration roles is also occurring *within* metropolitan areas. Central core and inner counties of large metropolitan areas are becoming more dependent on migration from abroad to counter declines due to domestic out-migration to their suburbs or other parts of the country. In contrast, it is domestic migration that represents a primary demographic engine for the fast growing peripheral counties in major metropolitan areas. Hence the new role of immigration toward stemming population decline in some places but not in others, finds mayors and metropolitan leaders in the latter areas examining new ways to attract more of the nation's growing immigrant populations.

This analysis focuses on the nation's 81 largest metropolitan areas with 2000 populations greater than 500,000. (Comparable data for states appears in Table D.) The migration data in this study draw from the 2000 census question "Where did you live five years ago?" which permits migration information to be obtained over the 1995–2000 period. Net domestic is defined as the difference between the numbers of in-migrants to that area from elsewhere in the United States, *minus* the number of out-migrants from that area to other parts of the country for moves taking place over the five year period. Migration from abroad (or immigration) is defined as in migration to that area for persons who resided outside of the United States at the beginning of the five-year period.

The Greatest Metropolitan Area "Magnets" for Migrants from Abroad Experience the Greatest Losses of Domestic Migrants

During the 1995–2000 period, four metropolitan areas—New York, Los Angeles, San Francisco and Chicago—exhibited a distinct profile of immigration and domestic migration patterns (see Table A). These four beat all others in the number of migrants they attracted from abroad and, at the same time, they led all others in the number of domestic migrants they lost to other parts of the United States. New York and Los Angeles had especially large gains and losses in both respects. New York's metropolitan region gained almost 1 million migrants from abroad, but at the same time, lost 874,000 domestic migrants. The Los Angeles metropolitan region gained nearly 700,000 migrants from abroad, but lost 550,000 domestic migrants.

In fact, the top six immigrant-gaining metropolitan areas each lost domestic migrants over the late 1990s, although the domestic migration losses of Washington DC and Miami metropolitan regions are much smaller than those of the other four. As a consequence, the latter two metropolitan areas showed greater overall migration gains, each exceeding 200,000 new residents over the 1995–2000 period, then is the case in the top four immigrant magnets.

This pattern of large immigrant gains and signifi-cant domestic migration losses is not a new one for some areas. It has been evident for New York and Chicago, two longstanding immigrant ports of entry, since at least the late 1960s. During this period, these large Northeast and Midwest metropolitan areas were losing both jobs and residents to newer areas in the Sunbelt. In contrast, the newest statistics show increasingly sharper net domestic out-migration from the two large California immigrant magnets (see Figure A).

Just as New York and Chicago have long experienced a demographic displacement of domestic migrants going to other parts of the country in exchange for new immigrants, the pattern has just begun to accelerate in Los Angeles and San Francisco. The

Table A: Migration Magnets: Migrants from Abroad and Domestic Migrants

| | 1995–2000 change from: | |
Metropolitan areas (a)	Migrants from abroad	Net domestic migration
I. MAGNETS FOR MIGRANTS FROM ABROAD (b)		
1. New York-Northern New Jersey-Long Island, NY-NJ-CT-PA CMSA	983,659	-874,028
2. Los Angeles-Riverside-Orange County, CA CMSA	699,573	-549,951
3. San Francisco-Oakland-San Jose, CA CMSA	373,869	-206,670
4. Chicago-Gary-Kenosha, IL-IN-WI CMSA	323,019	-318,649
5. Washington-Baltimore, DC-MD-VA-WV CMSA	300,266	-58,849
6. Miami-Fort Lauderdale, FL CMSA	299,905	-93,774
7. Dallas-Fort Worth, TX CMSA	231,494	148,644
8. Houston-Galveston-Brazoria, TX CMSA	214,268	-14,377
9. Boston-Worcester-Lawrence, MA-NH-ME-CT CMSA	196,042	-44,581
10. Atlanta, GA MSA	162,972	233,303
II. MAGNETS FOR DOMESTIC MIGRANTS (c)		
1. Phoenix-Mesa, AZ MSA	135,017	245,159
2. Atlanta, GA MSA	162,972	233,303
3. Las Vegas, NV-AZ MSA	62,255	225,266
4. Dallas-Fort Worth, TX CMSA	231,494	148,644
5. Austin-San Marcos, TX MSA	51,795	104,340
6. Tampa-St. Petersburg-Clearwater, FL MSA	67,664	103,375
7. Orlando, FL MSA	78,939	101,226
8. Denver-Boulder-Greeley, CO CMSA	93,970	93,586
9. Charlotte-Gastonia-Rock Hill, NC-SC MSA	41,485	93,505
10. Raleigh-Durham-Chapel Hill, NC MSA	47,710	91,272
III. GREATEST DOMESTIC MIGRATION LOSSES (d)		
1. New York-Northern New Jersey-Long Island, NY-NJ-CT-PA CMSA	983,659	-874,028
2. Los Angeles-Riverside-Orange County, CA CMSA	699,573	-549,951
3. Chicago-Gary-Kenosha, IL-IN-WI CMSA	323,019	-318,649
4. San Francisco-Oakland-San Jose, CA CMSA	373,869	-206,670
5. Detroit-Ann Arbor-Flint, MI CMSA	108,975	-123,009
6. Miami-Fort Lauderdale, FL CMSA	299,905	-93,774
7. Philadelphia-Wilmington-Atlantic City, PA-NJ-DE-MD CMSA	127,921	-83,539
8. Honolulu, HI MSA	38,619	-69,866
9. Cleveland-Akron, OH CMSA	36,257	-65,914
10. Washington-Baltimore, DC-MD-VA-WV CMSA	300,266	-58,849

Source: William H. Frey analysis of 2000 U.S. Census.

Key:
(a)—Metro areas are CMSAs, MSAs and (in New England) NECMAs. Names are abbreviated.
(b)—Metro areas with greatest migration from abroad, 1995–2000.
(c)—Metro with largest net domestic migration.
(d)—Large Metro area with largest negative domestic migration and not recipients of large immigration.

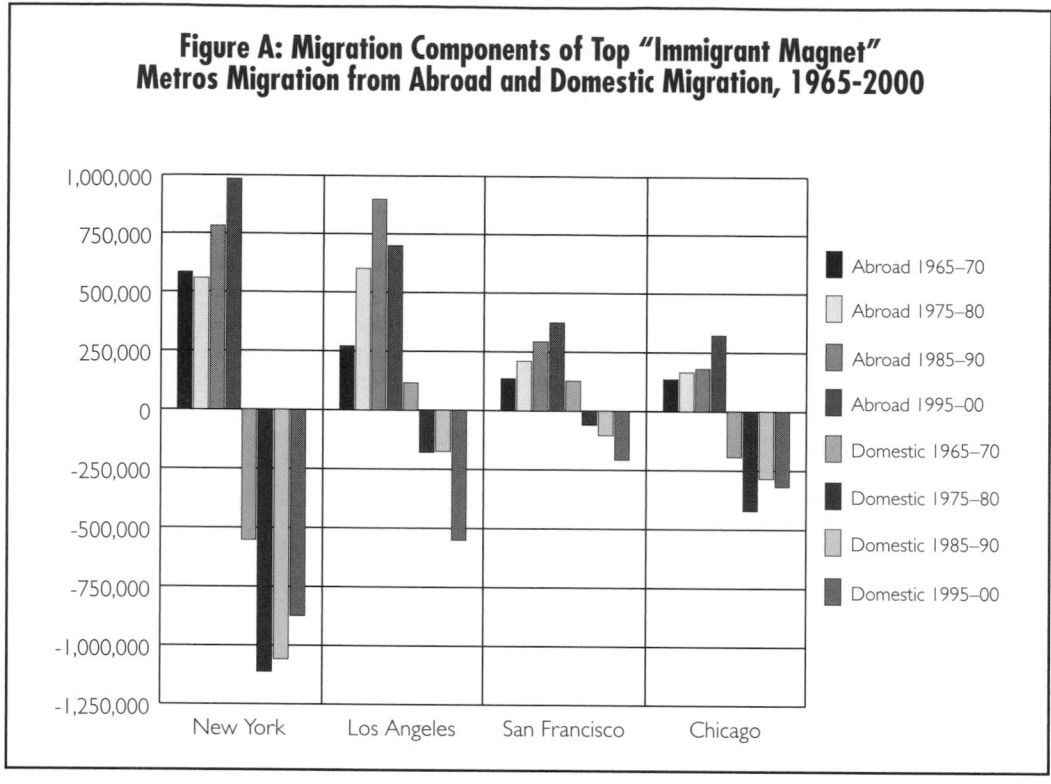

Figure A: Migration Components of Top "Immigrant Magnet" Metros Migration from Abroad and Domestic Migration, 1965-2000

net domestic out-migration in each of these two large metropolitan areas has grown significantly to that observed in the late 1990s and is reflective of a generally broad domestic out-migration observed in the state of California (*The New York Times*, 2003). While it is true that the state of California experienced sharp economic shocks during the 1990s, most of that downturn and greatest net out-migration occurred in the early part of the 1990s (Kotkin, 1997; State of California, 2003). These declines in the late 1990s, coupled with continued trends toward out-migration for these two California "immigrant magnets," suggest some linkage between immigration and domestic out-migration in these areas.

In fact, the list of metropolitan areas that sustained greatest domestic migration losses during the late 1990s is dominated by high immigration areas (see Table A, lower panel). Six of the top 10 U.S. domestic migration losing areas are also the highest "immigrant magnet" areas. The remaining four include economically stagnating metropolitan areas that are not major immigrant magnets, Detroit, Philadelphia, Honolulu and Cleveland.

The pattern of metropolitan area "donors" of do-

mestic migrants to other parts of the country has shifted over the past several decades. In the late 1960s, four of the top six domestic migration losing metros were economically declining rustbelt cities (Pittsburgh, Cleveland, Detroit and Buffalo). By the late 1990s, five of the six greatest domestic out-migrant metros were those that had become the nation's greatest immigrant magnet areas. In fact, of the net domestic migration losses experienced by all large losing metropolitan areas in the aggregate (3.1 million), the nation's six largest immigrant magnet metros contributed 70 percent to these losses.

"Domestic Migrant Magnet" Metros are also Attracting Migrants from Abroad

The list of metropolitan areas which gained the most domestic migration in the 1995–2000 period shows little overlap with those that gained the most migrants from abroad (Table A, middle panel). Led by Phoenix, Atlanta and Las Vegas, these metros are located in either the traditional Sunbelt states of Texas and Florida, or the band of "new Sunbelt" states, encompassing much of the nation's Southeast and a non-California West (Frey, 2000a). These metropolitan areas have experienced continued economic growth and new, low density urban and suburban development that have become attractive to residents and employers in the Northeast, Midwest, as well as California. Some of these metropolitan areas benefited from the 1990s growth in new economy, high tech sectors such as Atlanta, Austin, Denver and Raleigh-Durham, home of the "research triangle." Others have become attractive to particular segments of the population like retirees (e.g. Phoenix, Tampa).

The metropolitan magnets for domestic migrants are not always consistent from decade to decade, but reflect changes in the geography of employment growth and the availability of amenities in metropolitan areas. For example, in the 1975–1980 period, none of the top three 1995–2000 domestic migrant magnets were among the top six domestic migration gainers. Phoenix climbed to number three in 1975–1980; and in 1985–1990, Atlanta and Las Vegas advanced into the top six areas. Likewise, in 1965–1970, Miami ranked second in domestic migration growth, although it is now one of the nation's largest domestic migration losers. Houston is an example of an area which moved up and down over the decades as the fate of the oil industry waxed and waned. In 1975–1980, Houston ranked first of all major metros in domestic migration gains (215,000), whereas in 1975–1980 it experienced the fourth greatest domestic out migration (–142,000) of any metropolitan area of the country.

This volatility points up an important difference between areas that served as magnets for migrants from abroad, and those that attracted the most domestic migrants. The former continue to attract new immigrants to the United States since these migrants depend on their established racial and ethnic enclaves and family connections, which provide social and economic support. This is partially related to our immigration laws which give strong emphasis to family reunification in the preference system (Martin and Midgley, 2003). In contrast, domestic migrants are decidedly more "footloose" in their migration patterns and more responsive to area geographic shifts in employment location and amenities. While the list of domestic migrant magnet metros changed for each period between 1965–1970 through 1995–2000, the same six immigrant magnet metros occupied the top positions for each of these five year periods.

Of course, it is possible for a metropolitan area to attract both migrants from abroad and domestic migrants if its economy is both good and the metropolitan area serves as a port-of-entry for immigrants. This has been the case for Dallas, which during the 1995–2000 period, attracted large numbers of each. Yet, there is a new phenomenon occurring with the late 1990s that was not nearly as evident in earlier decades. This involves the increased attraction of migrants from abroad to domestic migrant magnets. It is apparent for the top domestic migrant magnets, Phoenix, Atlanta and Las Vegas, which now draw substantial numbers of migrants from abroad. Other places which previously attracted smaller numbers of immigrants, like Orlando, Charlotte and Raleigh-Durham-Chapel Hill, are now attracting many more, which are contributing to growth in their immigrant minority populations (Suro and Singer, 2002; Frey, 2002a). These immigrant newcomers are likely to be attracted by low skilled service, construction and retail jobs that are created by domestic migrants to these metropolitan areas (Frey, 2002b). The trajectories over time in gains from domestic migration and subsequently, migration from abroad, is shown in Figure B for Phoenix, Atlanta and Las Vegas, and reflects a new trend with the 1990s.

Metropolitan Core and Inner County Growth is Dependent on Migration from Abroad

Natural increase aside, the population growth in any area is dependent on the contributions of migration from abroad and domestic migration. The new census statistics indicate that the greatest domestic migration losses tend to occur in core and inner counties of major metropolitan areas. Table B lists the 30 counties with the largest domestic migration losses over 1995–2000. Nine of these lost more than 100,000 net domestic migrants over this period and include core counties of metropolitan areas such as Los Angeles Co., Calif., Cook Co., Ill., Kings and Queens counties in New York City, and Miami-Dade Co., Fla. For the most part, these counties reflect core and inner counties that lie within high immigration metropolitan areas, core counties or those that lie within stagnating Midwest or rustbelt metropolitan areas such as St. Louis, Mo., Cuyahoga Co., Ohio (in Cleveland), or Allegheny Co., Pa. (in Pittsburgh). Both the District of Columbia and inner county of Fairfax, Va. in the greater Washington, D.C. area are on this list. Overall about half of the nation's 3,141 counties, showed net out-migration over the 1990s; yet, only 95 of these counties declined by as many as 10,000 people and they are heavily represented by the kind of areas shown in Table B.

In light of these large domestic migration losses in core and inner counties of metropolitan areas, it is clear that migration from abroad is becoming an in-

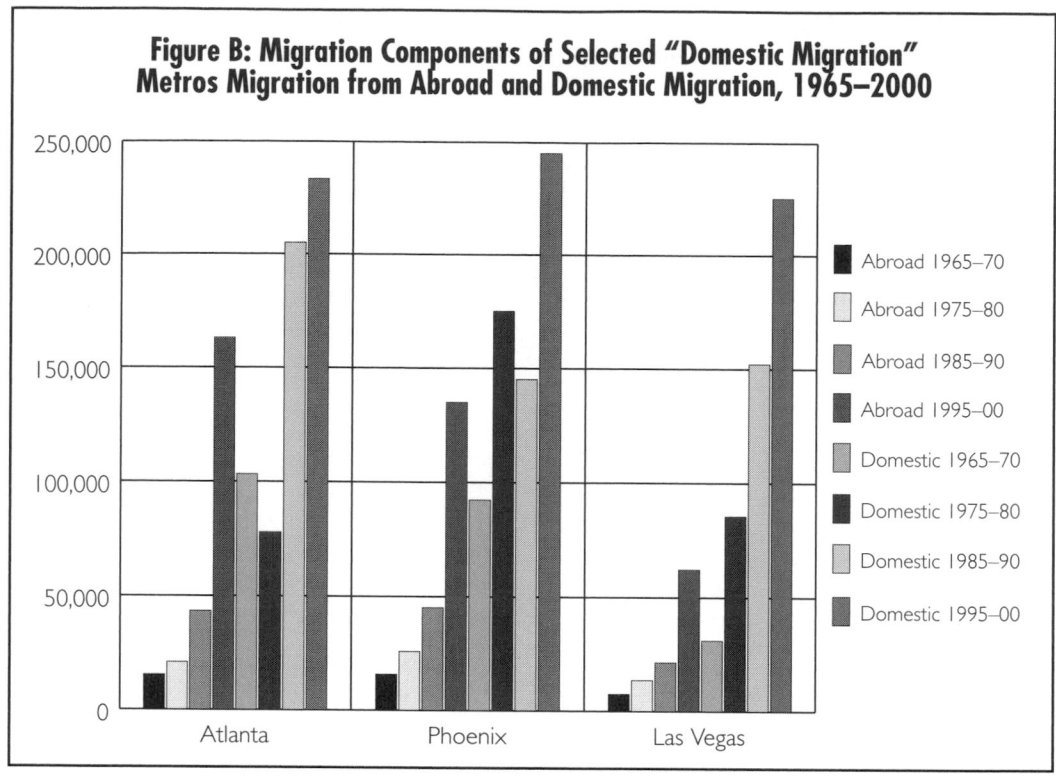

Figure B: Migration Components of Selected "Domestic Migration" Metros Migration from Abroad and Domestic Migration, 1965–2000

Legend:
- Abroad 1965–70
- Abroad 1975–80
- Abroad 1985–90
- Abroad 1995–00
- Domestic 1965–70
- Domestic 1975–80
- Domestic 1985–90
- Domestic 1995–00

creasingly important as a source of their demographic gains. For example Miami-Dade Co.'s nearly 160,000 domestic migration loss is more than compensated by a gain of 206,000 migrants from abroad. Similar loss compensations are shown in Harris Co. and Dallas Co., Texas, and in New York Co. (Manhattan), N.Y. On the other hand, many Midwest and Rustbelt cities are unable to rely on this immigration "cushion." For example, St. Louis lost 105,000 domestic migrants over the 1995–2000 period, but received less than 12,000 migrants from abroad. Similarly, small immigrant contributions can be seen in the declining core counties of Cleveland, Cincinnati, Milwaukee, Pittsburgh, Buffalo and New Orleans. It is not surprising, then, that many mayors of declining Northeast and Midwest cities are looking to immigrants as a source of potential demographic gains (Smith, 2003).

Domestic Migration Dominates Migration from Abroad in Fast-growing, Outer Metropolitan Counties

While inner counties of major metropolitan areas are increasingly dependent on migration from abroad for their growth, the opposite is occurring on the periphery of these areas. This is indicated in Table C, which shows the highest domestic migration growth rates among counties with populations greater than 30,000. This list is dominated by mostly suburban counties within the nation's largest metropolitan areas. Not surprisingly, counties within domestic migrant magnet metros like Atlanta, Phoenix, Las Vegas, Austin, Dallas and Charlotte, are heavily represented. For example, in Forsyth Co., Ga., on the periphery of the Atlanta metropolitan area, domestic migration contributed 30 percent to population growth over the 1995–2000 period. In contrast, migration abroad contributed to only 2.5 percent to Forsyth's population. This decidedly smaller contribution of migration from abroad is also apparent for other fast growing counties within Atlanta and in other large metropolitan areas.

Thus, while Atlanta began to attract larger numbers of migrants from abroad during the late 1990s, its fastest growing peripheral counties gained predominantly from domestic migration. This is not the case for some inner counties within the Atlanta's metropolitan area, however. The more centrally located Fulton Co. lost 30,013 domestic migrants during 1995–2000, but it was able to compensate for

Table B: Counties with Greatest Net Domestic Migration Losses

				1995–2000		
Rank	Country and state		Inside metro area (a)	Net domestic migration	Migration from abroad	2000 population (in thousands) (b)
1	Los Angeles County	ca06	Los Angeles-Riverside-Orange County, CA CMSA	-567,271	466,605	9,519
2	Cook County	il17	Chicago-Gary-Kenosha, IL-IN-WI CMSA	-377,902	230,922	5,377
3	Kings County	ny36	New York-Northern New Jersey-Long Island, NY-NJ-CT-PA CMSA	-233,555	160,306	2,465
4	Queens County	ny36	New York-Northern New Jersey-Long Island, NY-NJ-CT-PA CMSA	-168,505	169,784	2,229
5	Miami-Dade County	fl12	Miami-Fort Lauderdale, FL CMSA	-159,714	206,689	2,253
6	Wayne County	mi26	Detroit-Ann Arbor-Flint, MI CMSA	-115,437	42,730	2,061
7	Harris County	tx48	Houston-Galveston-Brazoria, TX CMSA	-114,892	181,509	3,401
8	St. Louis city	mo29	St. Louis, MO-IL MSA	-105,224	11,944	348
9	Santa Clara County	ca06	San Francisco-Oakland-San Jose, CA CMSA	-105,088	124,793	1,683
10	Philadelphia County	pa42	Philadelphia-Wilmington-Atlantic City, PA-NJ-DE-MD CMSA	-94,158	46,177	1,518
11	Baltimore city	md24	Washington-Baltimore, DC-MD-VA-WV CMSA	-92,223	12,656	651
12	Dallas County	tx48	Dallas-Fort Worth, TX CMSA	-89,724	137,081	2,219
13	Bronx County	ny36	New York-Northern New Jersey-Long Island, NY-NJ-CT-PA CMSA	-87,430	76,736	1,333
14	Nassau County	ny36	New York-Northern New Jersey-Long Island, NY-NJ-CT-PA CMSA	-72,284	26,840	1,335
15	Honolulu County	hi15	Honolulu, HI MSA	-69,866	38,619	876
16	Cuyahoga County	oh39	Cleveland-Akron, OH CMSA	-68,198	23,096	1,394
17	Orange County	ca06	Los Angeles-Riverside-Orange County, CA CMSA	-59,686	128,204	2,846
18	San Francisco County	ca06	San Francisco-Oakland-San Jose, CA CMSA	-58,197	49,743	777
19	New York County	ny36	New York-Northern New Jersey-Long Island, NY-NJ-CT-PA CMSA	-57,249	104,054	1,537
20	Hamilton County	oh39	Cincinnati-Hamilton, OH-KY-IN CMSA	-50,750	12,567	845
21	Essex County	nj34	New York-Northern New Jersey-Long Island, NY-NJ-CT-PA CMSA	-50,639	36,271	794
22	Milwaukee County	wi55	Milwaukee-Racine, WI CMSA	-47,965	20,561	940
23	El Paso County	tx48	El Paso, TX MSA	-47,790	31,468	680
24	Allegheny County	pa42	Pittsburgh, PA MSA	-47,757	17,230	1,282
25	Denver County	co08	Denver-Boulder-Greeley, CO CMSA	-46,872	34,194	555
26	District of Columbia	dc11	Washington-Baltimore, DC-MD-VA-WV CMSA	-45,331	30,399	572
27	Erie County	ny36	Buffalo-Niagara Falls, NY MSA	-41,115	13,901	950
28	Orleans Parish	la22	New Orleans, LA MSA	-40,825	6,372	485
29	Hudson County	nj34	New York-Northern New Jersey-Long Island, NY-NJ-CT-PA CMSA	-37,850	46,961	609
30	Fairfax County	va51	Washington-Baltimore, DC-MD-VA-WV CMSA	-36,638	72,648	970

Source: William H. Frey analysis of 2000 U.S. Census.

Key:
(a)—Names are abbreviated.
(b)—2000 Population, ages 5 and over.

this loss with a gain of 39,746 migrants from abroad.

This general pattern is pervasive nationally. Of all U.S. counties (including non-metropolitan counties), 239 grew from domestic migration at rates higher than 10 percent over the 1995–2000 period. Of these, only five counties showed growth of greater than 5 percent based on migration from abroad; and 183 of these did not register as much as 2 percent growth from migration from abroad. These trends show that the broad pattern of domestic migrant dispersal tends to dominate growth on the peripheries of metropolitan areas and beyond.

Conclusion

This analysis of census 2000 migration data reveals the distinct contributions of migration from abroad and domestic migration to population change in the nation's largest metropolitan areas. The largest "immigrant magnet" metros sustained the greatest losses of domestic migrants to other parts of the country. What was new in the late 1990s was an increased tendency for this to occur in two large California metropolitan areas, Los Angeles and San Francisco, which helped to propel the overall domestic migrant losses for the state of California during the late 1990s. It established these two West Coast immigrant ports of entry as "redistributors" of the population to fast growing interior metropolitan areas, in the same way that New York and Chicago had done in earlier decades.

These four large "immigrant magnet" metros possess diverse economies and populations that continue to attract immigrants to their established ethnic enclaves which provide them with social and economic support and links to established niches in their communities. At the same time, they have become highly urbanized and congested regions with rising housing costs and long commutes which have made them less attractive and affordable to longer term residents at the middle and lower end of the socioeconomic ladder. These areas are nonetheless dynamic "world city" regions that continue to attract highly skilled

Table C: Counties with Highest Domestic Migration Growth Rates
(among counties with greater than 30,000 population in 2000)

				1995–2000	
Rank	Country and state		Inside metro area (a)	Net domestic migration	Migration from abroad
1	Douglas County	co08	Denver-Boulder-Greeley, CO CMSA	33.3	2.4
2	Sumter County	fl12		31.2	1.5
3	Forsyth County	ga13	Atlanta, GA MSA	30.5	2.5
4	Henry County	ga13	Atlanta, GA MSA	23.3	1.2
5	Flagler County	fl12	Daytona Beach, FL MSA	22.4	1.2
6	Paulding County	ga13	Atlanta, GA MSA	22.0	0.8
7	Delaware County	oh39	Columbus, OH MSA	21.4	0.7
8	Loudoun County	va51	Washington-Baltimore, DC-MD-VA-WV CMSA	21.4	4.2
9	Williamson County	tx48	Austin-San Marcos, TX MSA	20.8	2.0
10	Lyon County	nv32		20.3	1.1
11	Nye County	nv32	Las Vegas, NV-AZ MSA	19.9	1.2
12	Tooele County	ut49		19.8	1.3
13	Collin County	tx48	Dallas-Fort Worth, TX CMSA	18.9	4.5
14	Fremont County	co08		18.1	0.5
15	Bee County	tx48		17.5	0.5
16	Christian County	mo29	Springfield, MO MSA	17.4	0.7
17	DeSoto County	ms28	Memphis, TN-AR-MS MSA	17.1	1.0
18	Hays County	tx48	Austin-San Marcos, TX MSA	17.0	1.6
19	Pinal County	az04	Phoenix-Mesa, AZ MSA	16.9	2.3
20	Cherokee County	ga13	Atlanta, GA MSA	16.3	2.4
21	Williamson County	tn47	Nashville, TN MSA	16.2	1.5
22	Effingham County	ga13	Savannah, GA MSA	16.1	0.8
23	Union County	nc37	Charlotte-Gastonia-Rock Hill, NC-SC MSA	16.1	2.5
24	Clark County	nv32	Las Vegas, NV-AZ MSA	16.0	4.7
25	Denton County	tx48	Dallas-Fort Worth, TX CMSA	15.7	3.1
26	Pike County	pa42	New York-Northern New Jersey-Long Island, NY-NJ-CT-PA CMSA	15.6	0.4
27	Isabella County	mi26		15.3	1.7
28	Barrow County	ga13	Atlanta, GA MSA	15.2	1.1
29	Fannin County	tx48		15.1	1.3
30	Shelby County	al01	Birmingham, AL MSA	15.1	1.2

Source: William H. Frey analysis of 2000 U.S. Census.

Key:
(a)—Names are abbreviated.
(b)—The rate equals the 1995–2000 migration component multiplied by 100 and divided by the 2000 population, ages 5 and over.

migrants from abroad and, among domestic migrants, show either gains or reduced losses of college graduates in comparison to their larger losses of less educated, more middle class residents.

This analysis has also identified a set of "domestic migrant magnet" metro areas that show highest gains in migrants from within the United States. They are located in much of the Southeast and *non-California* West and reflect the growth of "new economy" industries and expanding urban and suburban developments in metropolitan areas like Phoenix, Atlanta and Las Vegas. These areas attract more domestic migrants than migrants from abroad. Yet, the 1990s have shown that they are also attracting large numbers of immigrants, perhaps to lower skilled jobs in a variety of sectors, that are created by the demands of new domestic migrants (Frey, 2002b). While the new migrants from abroad will surely increase the ethnic diversity and cultural vitality to these, heretofore, largely white or (in the case of the South) white and black metropolitan areas, it remains to seen

how quickly they will be come socially integrated and incorporated into the mainstream economies of these areas.

The new census data also show that migrants from abroad and domestic migrants play different roles in contributing to growth and decline *within* metropolitan areas. Immigrants from abroad are becoming especially valuable to declining core and inner counties in large metropolitan areas that are losing domestic migrants to the suburbs and other parts of the country. Midwest and Rustbelt core counties, which are not attracting many immigrants, are sustaining some of the nation's greatest migration losses while inner counties in areas like New York, San Francisco, Washington, D.C., Boston and Houston continue to become invigorating by immigrant populations.

In contrast, the migration gains for fast growing peripheral counties in the nation's major metros accrue almost entirely from domestic migrants comprised of new suburbanites from the city, as well as migrants from other parts of the United States. The fact that these outlying counties are not attracting large numbers of migrants from abroad points out a divergence in growth dynamics within the same metropolitan area. As cities and inner suburbs become more dependent on immigration for growth, and as outer suburbs rely mostly on domestic migration, their respective demographic profiles and associated public service needs, tax bases and political orientations will also diverge. This distinct within-metropolitan migration is not just apparent in domestic migrant magnet metros like Atlanta and Denver, but they also occur in immigrant magnet metros such as New York and Washington, D.C.

The distinct roles that migration from abroad and domestic migration play in affecting demographic change in metropolitan areas make plain that new migrants from abroad and the ongoing domestic migration of U.S. residents impact metropolitan areas in sharply different ways. The large immigrant flows to the United States in the late 1990s continue to concentrate primarily in major immigrant magnet metros, at the same time that domestic migrants of all race and ethnic groups are gravitating to a wider range of metropolitan areas, and local destinations within them.

References

Frey, William H., 1994. "Immigration and Internal Migration from U.S. Metro Areas: 1990 Census Findings by Race, Poverty and Education," *Research Report No. 94-304.* Ann Arbor, MI: University of Michigan Population Studies Center.

Frey, William H., 1996. "Immigrant and Native Migrant Magnets," *American Demographics.* (November).

Frey, William H., 2002a. "Metro Magnets For Minorities and Whites: Melting Pots, The New Sunbelt and the Heartland," *Research Report No. 02-496.* Ann Arbor, Michigan: University of Michigan Population Studies Center.

Frey, William H., 2002b. "Census 2000 Reveals New Native-Born and Foreign-Born Shifts Across U.S.," *Research Report No. 02-520.* Ann Arbor, MI: University of Michigan Populations Studies Center.

Frey, William H. and Kao-Lee Liaw, 1998. "The Impact of Recent Immigration on Population Redistribution Within the United States," in James P. Smith and Barry Edmonston (Editors), *The Immigration Debate: Studies on the Economic, Demographic and Fiscal Effects of Immigration.* Washington, D.C.: National Academy of Sciences Press. 388–448.

Kotkin, Joel. 1997. California: A Twenty First Century Prospectus, Denver: Center for the New West.

Long, Larry. 1988. *Migration and Residential Mobility in the United States.* New York: Russell Sage Foundation.

Martin, Philip and Elizabeth Midgley, 2003. "Immigration to the United States: Shaping and Reshaping America," *Population Bulletin Vol 58. No. 2.* Washington, D.C.: Population and Reference Bureau. (June).

Schachter, Jason P., Rachel S. Franklin and Marc J. Perry, 2003. "Migration and Geographic Mobility in Metropolitan and Non-Metropolitan America: 1995 to 2000," *Census 2000 Special Reports,* CENSR-9. Washington, D.C.: U.S. Census Bureau.

Singer, Audrey, 2003 "At Home in the Nation's Capital: Immigrant Trends in Metropolitan Washington" *Brookings Greater Washington Research Program,* Washington, D.C.: Brookings Institution Center on Urban and Metropolitan Policy.

Smith, Robert L. 2003. "Can Immigrants Save the Region: The right kind can not only boost population, but also create jobs," *Cleveland Plain Dealer.* July 13. A1.

State of California. 2003. *Updated Revised Historical County Population Estimates and Components of Change,* 1990–1999. Sacramento, Calif.: State of California Department of Finance.

Suro, Roberto and Audrey Singer, 2002. "Latino Growth in Metropolitan America: Changing Patterns, New Locations," *Census 2000 Survey Series.* Washington, D.C.: The Brookings Institution Center on Urban and Metropolitan Policy, and Pew Hispanic Center.

The New York Times, 2003. "Census Finds More Americans Flee Than Find California Dream," August 6, p. A12

Tilove, Johnathan 2003. "Migration Patterns Point to a Nation of Three Americas," *Newhouse News Service.* Washington, D.C.: Newhouse News Service http: //www.newhousenews.com/archive/tilove073103.html.

U.S. Census Bureau, 2003. *2000 Census of Population and Housing, Public Use Microdata Sample, United States: Technical Documentation.* PUMS/01-US (Rev*).* Washington DC: U.S. Census Bureau.

About the Author

William H. Frey is a demographer known for his expertise on U.S. demographics, migration and urban and regional change. Frey is a fellow at the Brookings Institution, a research professor at the Population Studies Center, University of Michigan, a senior fellow at the Milken Institute and a contributing editor to *American Demographics* magazine.

Table D
COMPONENTS AND RATES OF MIGRATION FROM ABROAD AND NET DOMESTIC MIGRATION, 1995–2000

State or other jurisdiction	2000 population (a) age 5 and over	Components, 1995–2000		Rates, 1995–2000 (b)	
		Migration from abroad	Net domestic migration	Migration from abroad	Net domestic migration
Alabama	4,152,278	48,712	25,823	1.17	0.62
Alaska	579,740	12,564	-30,498	2.17	-5.26
Arizona	4,752,724	182,982	316,148	3.85	6.65
Arkansas	2,492,205	33,657	42,116	1.35	1.69
California	31,416,629	1,407,658	-755,536	4.48	-2.40
Colorado	4,006,285	134,715	162,633	3.36	4.06
Connecticut	3,184,514	103,805	-64,610	3.26	-2.03
Delaware	732,378	17,308	17,383	2.36	2.37
Florida	15,043,603	652,606	607,023	4.34	4.04
Georgia	7,594,476	243,421	340,705	3.21	4.49
Hawaii	1,134,351	46,751	-76,133	4.12	-6.71
Idaho	1,196,793	20,966	33,847	1.75	2.83
Illinois	11,547,505	353,831	-342,616	3.06	-2.97
Indiana	5,657,818	75,149	21,625	1.33	0.38
Iowa	2,738,499	38,160	-33,012	1.39	-1.21
Kansas	2,500,360	51,463	-7,792	2.06	-0.31
Kentucky	3,776,230	45,981	34,127	1.22	0.90
Louisiana	4,153,367	42,026	-75,759	1.01	-1.82
Maine	1,204,164	10,513	3,640	0.87	0.30
Maryland	4,945,043	147,307	-19,723	2.98	-0.40
Massachusetts	5,954,249	205,722	-54,708	3.46	-0.92
Michigan	9,268,782	159,662	-91,930	1.72	-0.99
Minnesota	4,591,491	84,505	29,169	1.84	0.64
Mississippi	2,641,453	25,269	26,930	0.96	1.02
Missouri	5,226,022	67,363	46,053	1.29	0.88
Montana	847,362	6,884	-5,166	0.81	-0.61
Nebraska	1,594,700	28,282	-15,353	1.77	-0.96
Nevada	1,853,720	75,212	233,934	4.06	12.62
New Hampshire	1,160,340	16,608	27,903	1.43	2.40
New Jersey	7,856,268	311,765	-182,829	3.97	-2.33
New Mexico	1,689,911	38,706	-29,945	2.29	-1.77
New York	17,749,110	720,748	-874,248	4.06	-4.93
North Carolina	7,513,165	196,337	337,883	2.61	4.50
North Dakota	603,106	7,216	-25,207	1.20	-4.18
Ohio	10,599,968	120,585	-116,940	1.14	-1.10
Oklahoma	3,215,719	55,161	16,887	1.72	0.53
Oregon	3,199,323	83,361	74,665	2.61	2.33
Pennsylvania	11,555,538	165,231	-131,296	1.43	-1.14
Rhode Island	985,184	25,546	3,236	2.59	0.33
South Carolina	3,748,669	59,378	132,205	1.58	3.53
South Dakota	703,820	7,125	-12,468	1.01	-1.77
Tennessee	5,315,920	77,972	146,314	1.47	2.75
Texas	19,241,518	725,960	148,240	3.77	0.77
Utah	2,023,875	64,663	25,296	3.20	1.25
Vermont	574,842	7,393	2,254	1.29	0.39
Virginia	6,619,266	205,451	75,730	3.10	1.14
Washington	5,501,398	175,667	75,330	3.19	1.37
West Virginia	1,706,931	8,334	-10,754	0.49	-0.63
Wisconsin	5,022,073	64,529	7,282	1.28	0.14
Wyoming	462,809	5,237	-12,527	1.13	-2.71
Dist. of Columbia	539,658	30,399	-45,331	5.63	-8.40

Source: William H. Frey analysis of 2000 U.S. Census.
Key:
(a) Population ages 5 and over in 2000.
(b) The rate equals the 1995-2000 migration component muliplied by 100 and divided by the 2000 population, ages 5 and over.

Women in State Government: Historical Overview and Current Trends

By Susan J. Carroll

Women have significantly increased their numbers among state government officials over the past several decades. However, despite a recent increase in the number of women governors, women's progress, especially at the statewide elective and state legislative levels, has slowed. The future for women in state government would seem to depend, at least in part, upon the strength of efforts to actively recruit women for elective and appointive positions.

In the history of our nation, women are relative newcomers among state elected and appointed officials. Women first entered state-level offices in the 1920s following passage and ratification of the 19th Amendment to the U.S. Constitution which granted women suffrage. However, significant growth in the number of women in office occurred only after the emergence of the contemporary women's movement during the late-1960s and early-1970s. Since the mid-1970s, as data collected by the Center for American Women and Politics show,[1] women have greatly increased their number among elected and appointed officials in state government. In recent years, however, progress seems to have slowed, and nationwide statistics show a leveling off in the number of women serving in certain state-level offices.

Governors

Since the founding of our country, only 26 women (17 Democrats, 9 Republicans) have served as state governors (Table A), and only one woman has served as governor of a U.S. territory (Puerto Rico). A majority of the states, 29, have never had a woman chief executive. Arizona is the only state to have had three women governors as well as the only state where a woman succeeded another as governor. Texas, Kansas and New Hampshire have each had two women governors although one of the governors of New Hampshire, Vesta Roy, served for only seven days following the death of an incumbent.

The first woman governor, Nellie Tayloe Ross of Wyoming, was selected in a special election to succeed her deceased husband in 1925. Fifteen days later a second woman, Miriam "Ma" Ferguson, was inaugurated as governor of Texas, having been elected as a surrogate for her husband, a former governor who had been impeached and consequently was barred constitutionally from running again. Ferguson's campaign slogan was "Two governors for

the price of one."[2] The third woman to serve as a governor, Lurleen Wallace of Alabama, who campaigned on the slogan, "Let George do it," was similarly elected to replace a husband who was constitutionally prohibited from seeking another term.[3]

The first woman elected in her own right (i.e., without following her husband) into the governorship was Ella Grasso, who presided over the state of Connecticut from 1975 to 1980. Seventeen of the women governors (including Grasso) who have served since the mid-1970s were elected in their own right. The other six became governor through constitutional succession; only one of these six was subsequently elected to a full term.

More women currently hold governorships simultaneously than ever before. In early 2004 a record eight women (5D, 3R) serve as chief executives of their states–Judy Martz (R-Montana), Ruth Ann Minner (D-Delaware), Jennifer M. Granholm (D-Michigan), Linda Lingle (R-Hawaii), Janet Napolitano (D-Arizona), Kathleen Sebelius (D-Kansas), Olene Walker (R-Utah) and Kathleen Blanco (D-Louisiana). In addition, Sila Calderon (Popular Democratic Party), the only woman of color to ever serve as a chief executive, is governor of Puerto Rico.

Other Statewide Elected and Appointed Officials in the Executive Branch

The states vary greatly in their numbers of statewide elected and appointed officials. For example, Maine, New Hampshire, New Jersey and Tennessee have only one statewide elected official, the governor, while North Dakota, at the other extreme, has 12.

The first woman to ever hold a major statewide office was Soledad C. Chacon (D-New Mexico) who was secretary of state in New Mexico from 1923–26;[4] Delaware, Kentucky, New York, South Dakota and Texas also had women secretaries of state in the 1920s. The first woman treasurer, Grace B. Urbahns

Table A: Women Governors Throughout History

Name (party-state)	Dates served	Special circumstances
Nellie Tayloe Ross (D-WY)	1925–1927	Won special election to replace deceased husband.
Miriam "Ma" Ferguson (D-TX)	1925–1927, 1933–1935	Inaugurated 15 days after Ross; elected as surrogate for husband who could not succeed himself.
Lurleen Wallace (D-AL)	1967–1968	Elected as surrogate for husband who could not succeed himself.
Ella Grasso (D-CT)	1975–1980	First woman elected governor in her own right; resigned for health reasons.
Dixy Lee Ray (D-WA)	1977–1981	
Vesta Roy (R-NH)	1982–1983	Elected to state senate and chosen as senate president; served as governor for seven days when incumbent died.
Martha Layne Collins (D-KY)	1984–1987	
Madeleine Kunin (D-VT)	1985–1991	First woman to serve three terms as governor.
Kay Orr (R-NE)	1987–1991	First Republican woman governor and first woman to defeat another woman in a gubernatorial race.
Rose Mofford (D-AZ)	1988–1991	Elected as secretary of state, succeeded governor who was impeached and convicted.
Joan Finney (D-KS)	1991–1995	First woman to defeat an incumbent governor.
Ann Richards (D-TX)	1991–1995	
Barbara Roberts (D-OR)	1991–1995	
Christine Todd Whitman (R-NJ)	1994–2001	Resigned to take presidential appointment as commissioner of the Environmental Protection Agency.
Jeanne Shaheen (D-NH)	1997–2003	
Jane Dee Hull (R-AZ)	1997–2003	Elected as secretary of state, succeeded governor who resigned; later elected to a full term.
Nancy Hollister (R-OH)	1998–1999	Elected lieutenant governor; served as governor for 11 days when predecessor took U.S. Senate seat and successor had not yet been sworn in.
Jane Swift (R-MA)	2001–2003	Elected as lieutenant governor, succeeded governor who resigned for an ambassadorial appointment.
Judy Martz (R-MT)	2001–present	
Ruth Ann Minner (D-DE)	2001–present	
Jennifer M. Granholm (D-MI)	2003–present	
Linda Lingle (R-HI)	2003–present	
Janet Napolitano (D-AZ)	2003–present	First woman to succeed another woman as governor.
Kathleen Sebelius (D-KS)	2003–present	Father was governor of Ohio.
Olene Walker (R-UT)	2003–present	Elected as lieutenant governor, succeeded governor who resigned to take a federal appointment.
Sila Calderon	2001–present	Former mayor of San Juan, first woman governor of Puerto Rico.
Kathleen Blanco	2004–present	

Source: Center for American Women and Politics, Eagleton Institute of Politics, Rutgers University.

(R-Indiana), served during this same time period, from 1926–32.

Several more years passed before a woman became lieutenant governor. Matilda R. Wilson (R-Michigan) served briefly as lieutenant governor of Michigan in 1940 when she was appointed to fill an expiring term. However, the first woman elected as a lieutenant governor was Consuelo N. Bailey (R-Vermont) who served from 1955–56. An additional three decades passed before a woman became attorney general of a state; the first was Arlene Violet (R-Rhode Island) who served from 1985–87.

As evident from Figure A, the proportion of women among statewide elective officials has grown substantially over the past three decades. From 1971 to 1985 the increases were small and incremental. Then, between 1983 and 1995, a period of signifi-

cant growth, the numbers and proportions of women serving in statewide office more than doubled. Since 1995, the numbers and proportions have leveled off. In fact, fewer women, 80, currently hold statewide offices than in 1995 when there were 84 women.

In early 2004, women hold 25.4 percent of the 315 statewide elective positions. In addition to the eight women governors, women serve as lieutenant governors in 17, or 39.5 percent, of the 43 states that elect lieutenant governors in statewide elections. Other women statewide elected officials include: 10 secretaries of state, eight state treasurers, five attorney generals, nine chief education officials, eight state auditors, four public service commissioners, three state comptroller/controllers, two chief agricultural officials, two commissioners of insurance, two commissioners of labor and two corporation com-

Table B: Women Statewide Elected and Appointed Officials, 2004

	Elected officials					Appointed officials		
State	Governor	Lieutenant governor	Attorney general	Secretary of state	Treasurer	% Women among top advisors (a)	% Women among department heads (b)	State rank (dept. heads & top advisors combined) (c)
Alabama	★	W	★	W	W	25.0%	13.6%	49
Alaska	★	★	. . .	. . .	. . .	45.5	7.1	41
Arizona	W	. . .	★	W	★	42.9	25.9	27
Arkansas	★	★	★	★	★	42.9	21.1	37
California	★	★	★	★	★	37.5	31.0	24
Colorado	★	W	★	W	★	33.3	23.5	36
Connecticut	★	W	★	W	W	40.0	35.5	15
Delaware	W	★	W	. . .	★	45.5	29.4	17
Florida	★	W	★	. . .	. . .	66.7	29.4	3
Georgia	★	★	★	W	. . .	16.7	25.0	44
Hawaii	W	★	. . .	. . .	. . .	14.3	31.3	38
Idaho	★	★	★	★	★	33.3	18.8	42
Illinois	★	★	W	★	W	53.8	19.4	35
Indiana	★	W	★	★	★	25.0	35.0	26
Iowa	★	W	★	★	★	66.7	40.4	4
Kansas	W	★	★	★	W	62.5	30.0	6
Kentucky	★	★	★	★	★	23.1	47.1	12
Louisiana	W	★	★	★	★	27.3	25.0	40
Maine	★	. . .	. . .	. . .	. . .	50.0	23.8	29
Maryland	★	★	★	. . .	. . .	30.8	16.0	47
Massachusetts	★	W	★	★	★	44.4	54.5	1
Michigan	W	★	★	W	. . .	33.3	38.9	11
Minnesota	★	W	★	W	. . .	0.0	26.9	43
Mississippi	★	W	★	★	★	60.0	20.0	16
Missouri	★	★	★	★	W	57.1	35.7	5
Montana	W	★	★	★	. . .	30.8	29.4	31
Nebraska	★	★	★	★	★	63.6	25.9	8
Nevada	★	W	★	★	★	33.3	35.7	13
New Hampshire	★	. . .	. . .	. . .	. . .	0.0	20.0	50
New Jersey	★	. . .	. . .	. . .	. . .	36.4	35.3	19
New Mexico	★	W	W	W	★	27.3	39.1	18
New York	★	W	★	. . .	. . .	38.9	27.7	32
North Carolina	★	W	★	W	★	45.5	23.1	23
North Dakota	★	★	★	★	W	33.3	31.8	25
Ohio	★	W	★	★	★	35.7	15.4	45
Oklahoma	★	W	★	. . .	★	28.6	25.0	39
Oregon	★	. . .	★	★	★	37.5	53.3	2
Pennsylvania	★	W	★	. . .	W	50.0	20.6	33
Rhode Island	★	★	★	★	★	37.5	33.3	22
South Carolina	★	★	★	★	★	25.0	17.6	48
South Dakota	★	★	★	★	★	0.0	23.8	46
Tennessee	★	. . .	. . .	. . .	. . .	36.4	37.5	10
Texas	★	★	★	. . .	. . .	38.9	28.9	28
Utah	W	★	★	. . .	★	37.5	31.8	20
Vermont	★	★	★	W	★	33.3	26.7	34
Virginia	★	★	★	. . .	. . .	16.7	50.0	8
Washington	★	★	W	★	★	33.3	33.3	21
West Virginia	★	. . .	★	★	★	35.3	25.0	30
Wisconsin	★	W	W	★	★	43.5	31.8	7
Wyoming	★	. . .	. . .	★	W	58.3	22.7	14

Sources: Data for elected officials are current as of January 2004 and have been provided by the Center for American Women and Politics, Eagleton Institute of Politics, Rutgers University. Data for appointed officials are current as of summer 2003 (thus not reflecting subsequent gubernatorial changes in California and Utah) and have been provided by the Center on Women in Government and Civil Society, SUNY, Albany.

Key:
★—Denotes that this position is filled through a statewide election.
W—Denotes that this position is filled through a statewide election and is held by a woman.
. . .—Denotes that this position is filled through methods other than a statewide election.
(a)—Top advisors in governors' offices who were appointed by governors.
(b)—Department heads with major policymaking responsibilities (including heads of departments, agencies, offices, boards, commissions and authorities) who were appointed by governors.
(c)—These state rankings are based on representative ratios for each state, which are calculated by dividing the percentage of women policy leaders by the percentage of women in a state's population.

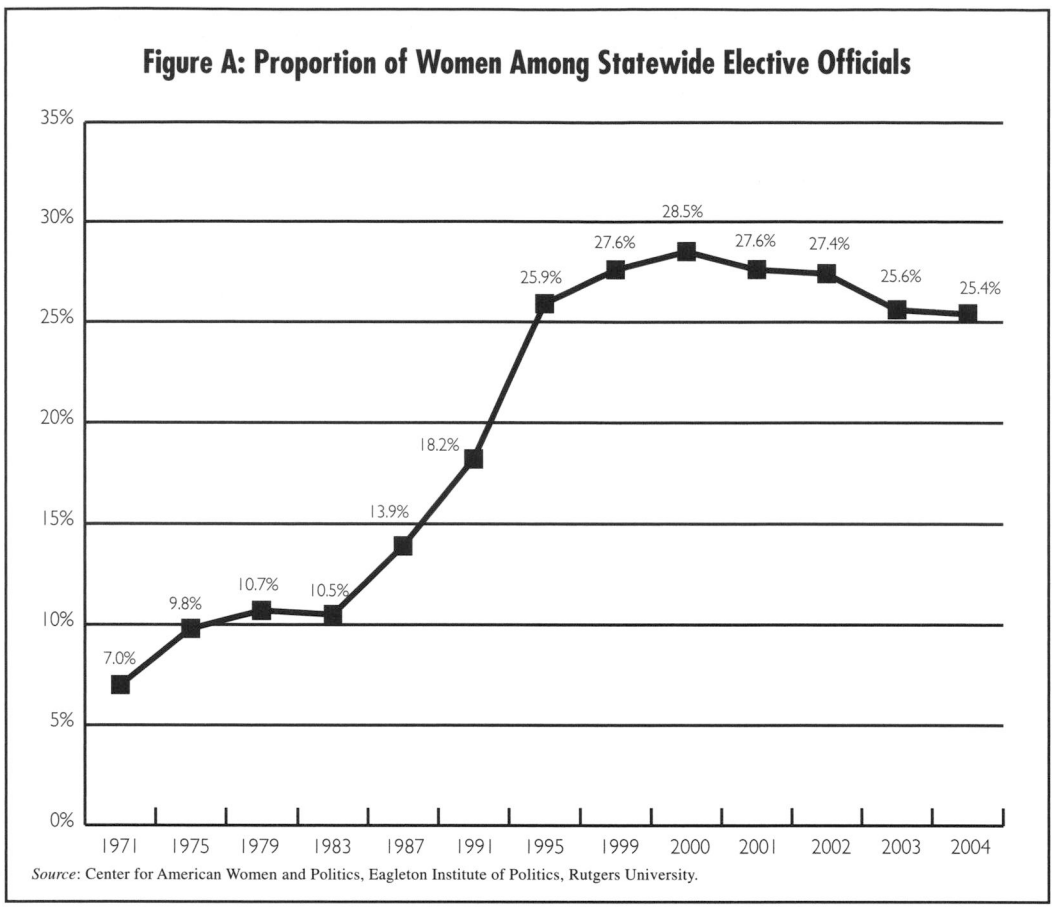

Figure A: Proportion of Women Among Statewide Elective Officials

7.0%
9.8%
10.7%
10.5%
13.9%
18.2%
25.9%
27.6%
28.5%
27.6%
27.4%
25.6%
25.4%

1971   1975   1979   1983   1987   1991   1995   1999   2000   2001   2002   2003   2004

Source: Center for American Women and Politics, Eagleton Institute of Politics, Rutgers University.

missioners. The women serving in statewide elective office include two African Americans (the lieutenant governor of Ohio and the state treasurer of Connecticut) as well as three Latinas (the secretary of state of New Mexico, the attorney general of New Mexico and the superintendent of public instruction for Oregon).

Women are slightly better represented among top appointed officials in state government. According to nationwide data collected by the Center on Women in Government and Civil Society at SUNY-Albany, in late 2003 women constituted 29.3 percent of department heads with major policymaking responsibilities (including heads of departments, agencies, offices, boards, commissions and authorities) who were appointed by governors. Similarly, women are 38.2 percent of the top appointed advisors in governors' offices. These 2003 figures represent a slight decline from 2001, the last time the Center on Women in Government and Civil Society collected these data.[5]

The Judicial Branch

The first woman to win election to a state court of last resort was Florence E. Allen, who was elected to the Ohio Supreme Court in 1922 and re-elected in 1928. Nevertheless, it was not until 1960 that a second woman, Lorna Lockwood of Arizona, was elected to a state supreme court. In 1965, Lockwood's colleagues on the Arizona Supreme Court elected her chief justice, thereby also making her the first woman in history to preside over a state court of last resort.[6]

According to the National Center for State Courts (NCSC), 98, or 29.3 percent, of the 335 justices on state courts of last resort in late 2003 were women. Of the 52 chief justices of these courts, 17, or 32.7 percent, were women. The current chief justice of the New Mexico Supreme Court, Petra Jimenez Maes, is the first Latina in the country to hold this position.

Women comprise a majority of justices on the courts of last resort in four states–New York, Vermont, Washington and Wisconsin. Women constitute at least 40 percent of the justices (but less than a majority) on an additional 14 courts of last resort.

Women are slightly less well represented on intermediate appellate courts. According to NCSC, in 2003 women comprised 222, or 23.1 percent, of the judges on intermediate appellate courts throughout the country.[7] There is no state in which women constitute a majority of intermediate appellate court judges.

Legislators

Even before 1920 when women won the right to vote across the country, a few women had been elected to legislatures in states that had granted the franchise to women. By 1971 the proportion of women serving in state legislatures across the country had grown to 4.5 percent, and by 2004 this proportion has increased almost fivefold to 22.4 percent. As Figure B illustrates, the proportion of women

among legislators grew throughout the 1970s and 1980s. The rate of growth slowed in the 1990s, and similar to the pattern for statewide elected officials, the numbers and proportions of women legislators nationally have leveled off since the late 1990s. In fact, fewer women, 1655, served in state legislatures at the beginning of 2004 than in 1999 when there were 1664 women legislators.

Great variation exists across the states in the proportion of legislators who are women. (see Table C) Washington with 36.7 percent has the largest proportion of women in its legislature, followed by Colorado (34.0 percent), Maryland (33.5 percent), Vermont (31.1 percent), Oregon (30.0 percent) and California (30.0 percent). There seems to be no easy explanation for why these states have risen to the top, and indeed scholars who have statistically examined the variation among the states in the representation of women in their legislatures have found no simple patterns.[8] At the other extreme, South Carolina with only 9.4 percent ranks last

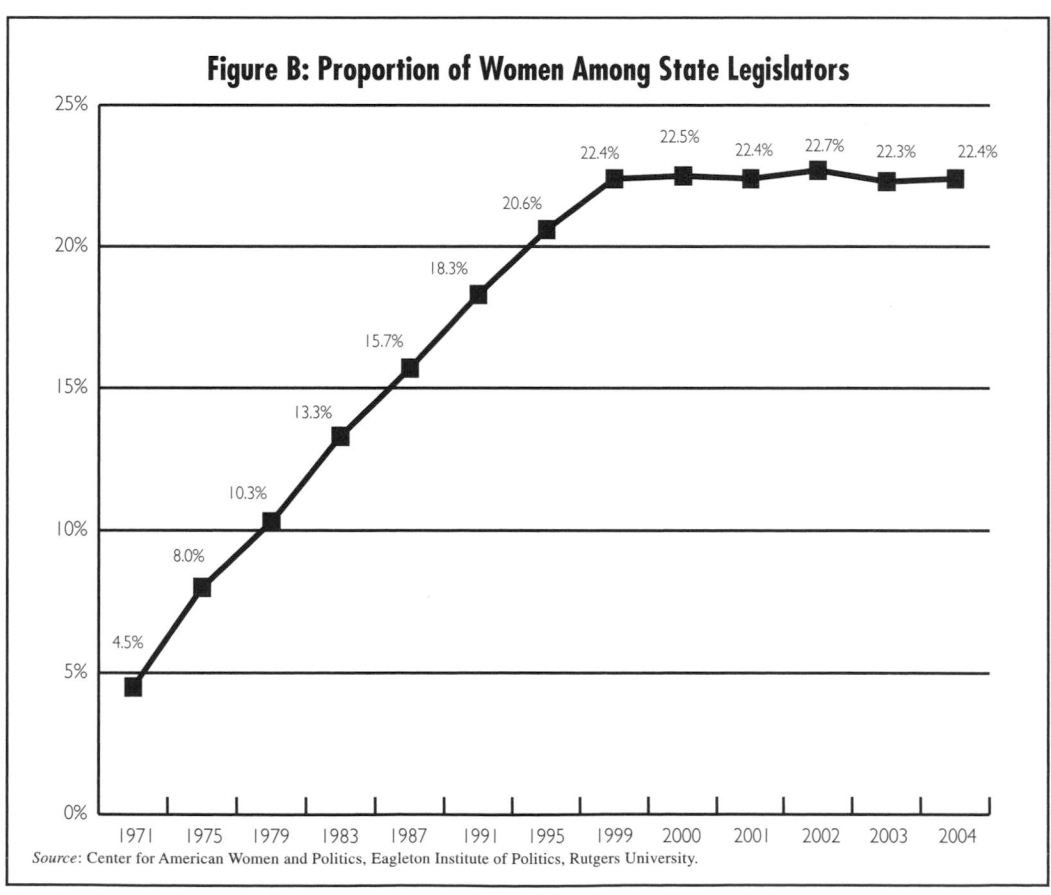

Figure B: Proportion of Women Among State Legislators

Source: Center for American Women and Politics, Eagleton Institute of Politics, Rutgers University.

Table C: Women in State Legislatures

| | Senate | | | House | | | Legislature (both houses) | |
State	Democrats	Republicans	% Women	Democrats	Republicans	% Women	% Women	State rank (a)
Alabama	2	1	8.6%	9	2	10.5	10.0%	49
Alaska	3	1	20.0	3	5	20.0	20.0	32
Arizona	3	5	26.7	8	9	28.3	27.8	12
Arkansas	5	2	20.0	9	6	15.0	16.3	41
California	11	0	27.5	20	5	31.3	30.0	5
Colorado	9	1	28.6	14	10	36.9	34.0	2
Connecticut	6	2	22.2	29	18	31.1	29.4	8
Delaware	4	3	33.3	4	7	26.8	29.0	9
Florida	5	5	25.0	15	15	25.0	25.0	21
Georgia	11	2	23.2	29	9	21.1	21.6	26
Hawaii	7	0	28.0	8	6	27.5	27.6	14
Idaho	1	3	11.4	9	15	34.3	26.7	19
Illinois	8	4	20.3	24	13	31.4	27.7	13
Indiana	7	6	26.0	7	7	14.0	18.0	36
Iowa	1	5	12.0	16	9	25.0	20.7	28
Kansas	3	7	25.0	17	19	28.8	27.9	11
Kentucky	0	4	10.5	9	2	11.0	10.9	48
Louisiana	5	1	15.4	13	5	17.1	16.7	39
Maine (b)	9	4	37.1	26	11	24.5	26.9	18
Maryland	12	3	31.9	37	11	34.0	33.5	3
Massachusetts	10	1	27.5	34	6	25.0	25.5	20
Michigan	5	6	28.9	15	9	21.8	23.6	23
Minnesota	11	11	34.3 (c)	16	16	23.9	27.4	15
Mississippi	4	0	7.7	13	5	14.8	12.6	47
Missouri	4	3	20.6	24	11	21.5	21.3	27
Montana	7	1	16.0	19	10	29.0	24.7	22
Nebraska (d)	—Nonpartisan—		18.4	—Unicameral—			18.4	35
Nevada	4	3	33.3	8	3	26.2	28.6	10
New Hampshire	2	2	16.7	60	52	28.0	27.4	16
New Jersey	4	2	15.0	10	3	16.3	15.8	43
New Mexico	7	5	28.6	11	10	30.0	29.5	7
New York	6	5	17.7	28	8	24.0	21.2	24
North Carolina	5	2	14.0	17	11	23.3	20.6	29
North Dakota	3	2	10.6	6	12	19.1	16.3	40
Ohio	3	1	12.1	12	11	23.2	20.5	30
Oklahoma	5	2	14.6	6	6	11.9	12.8	46
Oregon	6	1	23.3	11	9	33.3	30.0	5
Pennsylvania	5	3	16.0	10	17	13.3	13.8	45
Rhode Island	7	2	23.7	11	3	18.7	20.4	31
South Carolina	2	0	4.3	7	7	11.3	9.4	50
South Dakota	0	4	11.4	4	9	18.6	16.2	42
Tennessee	4	1	15.2	12	6	18.2	17.4	38
Texas	2	2	12.9	11	20	20.7	19.3	33
Utah	3	2	17.2	7	11	24.0	22.1	25
Vermont	8	1	30.0	26	19	30.7(e)	30.6	4
Virginia	7	1	20.0	6	6	12.0	14.3	44
Washington	16	7	46.9	20	11	31.6	36.7	1
West Virginia	1	4	14.7	14	6	20.0	18.7	34
Wisconsin	3	6	27.3	12	15	27.3	27.3	17
Wyoming	3	2	16.7	6	5	18.3	17.8	37

Source: Center for American Women and Politics, Eagleton Institute of Politics, Rutgers University. Figures are as of January 2004.

Key:
    (a)—States where percentages of women are exactly the same (California and Oregon) are ranked the same; states where percentages round out to the same (Iowa and Missouri; Minnesota and New Hampshire), but are not exactly the same, are ranked differently.
    (b)—In addition, one woman in Maine was elected in November 1997 as a non-voting member representing the Penobscot Nation.
    (c)—Includes one member of the Independence Party.
    (d)—Nebraska has a unicameral legislature with nonpartisan elections.
    (e)—Includes one member of the Progressive Party.

among the 50 states in the representation of women among its legislators. Accompanying South Carolina in the bottom five states are Alabama with 10.0 percent women, Kentucky with 10.9 percent, Mississippi with 12.6 percent and Oklahoma with 12.8 percent. All of these are southern or border states, suggesting that the south lags behind the rest of the country in the representation of women within its legislatures. Indeed, this is generally true with no southern state among the top 20 and only Florida, with 25.0 percent women, above the national average.

In early 2004, women held 410, or 20.8 percent, of all state senate seats and 1245, or 23.0 percent, of all state house seats across the country. Although state legislators nationally have become considerably more Republican over the last decade and a half with legislators now almost evenly divided between the two parties, the same is not true for women legislators. From 1988 to 2004, the proportion of Republicans among women actually decreased slightly from 38.7 percent to 34.4 percent for state senators and from 41.4 percent to 40.2 percent for state representatives. In 2004, as in the past, Democrats substantially outnumber Republicans among women state legislators. Among women state senators nationwide, 63.2 percent are Democrats; among women state representatives, 59.6 percent are Democrats.

Almost one-fifth of women state legislators, 18.4 percent, are women of color. Of the 86 senators and 218 representatives serving in legislatures in early 2004, all but 17 are Democrats. African American women hold 57 seats in state senates and 156 seats in state houses across 37 states. Latinas are concentrated in 14 states; they hold 19 senate and 39 house seats. Asian American women count among their numbers seven senators and 16 representatives in seven states while Native American women hold one senate and eight house seats in four states.

Legislative Leaders

Women made significant inroads into leadership positions within state legislatures in the 1990s and early 2000s. The first woman to hold a major leadership position was Minnie Davenport Craig, a Republican and the only woman in her legislature, who was elected speaker of the house in North Dakota in 1933. Two decades later in 1953, Consuelo Northrop Bailey, a Republican who later became Vermont's and the nation's first lieutenant governor, became speaker of the house in her state. While another woman, Marion West Higgins, served briefly as a speaker in New Jersey in the mid-1960s, it was not until two decades later that women began to ascend

to speakerships with any frequency, with Patricia "Tish" Kelly (D-North Dakota), Vera Katz (D-Oregon), Debra Anderson (D-South Dakota), and Jane Hull (R-Arizona) all becoming speakers in the 1980s.

Through the end of 2003, 20 women (six Democrats and 14 Republicans) in 14 states served as speakers. Oregon has had four women speakers, all serving since the mid-1980s. North Dakota has had three women speakers, and Arkansas has had two, both of whom served in the 1990s. Women speakers of the house in 2003 included: Catherine Hanaway (R-Missouri), Moira K. Lyons (D-CT), Karen Minnis (R-Oregon), Lola Spradley (R-Colorado) and Janet Wentz (R-North Dakota).

Fewer women—nine (three Democrats, six Republicans) in seven states—have served as senate presidents[9] through the end of 2003 with the first, Republican Jan Faiks of Arkansas, elected in 1987. Arkansas and Florida have each had two women senate presidents. Women serving as senate presidents in 2003 were: Beverly Daggett (D-Maine), April Brimmer-Kunz (R-Wyoming) and Mary Kramer (R-Iowa).

Women fare somewhat better when all state legislative leadership positions are considered. In 2003, a total of 46, or 13.6 percent, of all top legislative leadership positions across the country were held by women.[10] Women held 17.9 percent of all Democratic leadership positions but only 9.8 percent of Republican leadership positions across all the states. Women held a majority of the leadership positions (senate and house combined) in three states—Washington, Oregon and Colorado. At the other extreme, half of the states, 25, had no women serving in leadership positions in either chamber of the legislature.

There clearly is a relationship between the representation of women in the legislatures of the various states and the presence of women in legislative leadership. Not only do Washington, Colorado and Oregon rank first, second and fifth, respectively among states in the proportion of women among their legislators, but also seven of the states with the largest proportions of women legislative leaders rank among the top ten states in the proportions of women legislators.

The picture is even brighter for women when chairs of standing committees are examined. Nationally women in 2003 chaired 346, or 18.9 percent, of the standing committees in legislatures.[11] Women comprised 20.3 percent of Democratic and 17.7 percent of Republican committee chairs. Women served as committee chairs in 45 state senates and in all but one house (Pennsylvania). California led the way with 42.6 percent of its legislative committees chaired by women. As with leadership positions, there is a relationship between the proportion of women serving in the legislature and the proportion of women committee chairs; of the 10 states with the largest proportion of women committee chairs, seven also are among the top 10 states in terms of the proportion of women serving in their legislatures.

Looking Toward the Future

Although women have made substantial progress over time in increasing their presence in state government, the recent leveling off of women's numbers among statewide elective officials and state legislators is a puzzling development. For advocates who someday would like to see parity between women and men in government, it is a troubling development as well. At a minimum, the leveling off is evidence that increases over time are not inevitable; there is no invisible hand at work to insure that more women will seek and be elected to office with each subsequent election.

The leveling off has implications for women's representation not only among state legislators and nongubernatorial statewide officeholders, but also among governors and members of Congress. Probably the most striking positive development for women in state government in recent years has been the increase in women governors. Indeed, almost one-third of the women who have ever served their states as chief executives currently hold that office, and all but two of the eight became governor during the past two years. Of the eight sitting governors, seven held statewide elective office before running for governor; four were lieutenant governors, two served as attorney generals, and one was her state's insurance commissioner. Four of the current women governors also served in their state legislatures. Similarly, many of the women who run for Congress have gained experience and visibility in state government before seeking federal office. Of the 59 women members of the U.S. House, 25 served in their state houses, 13 in their state senates, and two in statewide elective offices; of the 14 women U.S. senators, seven served in their state legislatures, two in statewide elective offices, and one in an appointed state cabinet post.

Activists who are interested in increasing the number of women serving in office often refer to a political "pipeline" through which potential women candidates for higher level office come forward from amongst the pool of women who have gained experience at lower levels of office. Clearly, the pipeline has worked well in the case of the current women

governors and members of Congress. But what will happen if the pool of candidates in statewide and state legislative office continues to stagnate or even decline? Then, the number of politically experienced women with the visibility and contacts necessary to step forward to run for governor or U.S. House or Senate seat is also likely to stagnate or decline. While several different factors may be responsible for the recent leveling off in the number of women in statewide elective and state legislative office, a lack of effective recruitment certainly is one of the most important. The experience of women in states that have recently implemented term limits for legislative seats provides compelling evidence regarding the importance of recruitment efforts for determining what the future may hold regarding women's representation in state government. Although variation exists across the states, term limits by and large have not led to the election of more women to state legislatures.[12] This has been particularly true for state houses where more women have been term-limited out in recent elections than have been elected to seats that opened up as a result of term limits. Many of the seats vacated by term-limited incumbents, even women incumbents, have gone uncontested by women candidates. Clearly then, the mere existence of more political opportunities in term-limited states has not been sufficient to increase the number of women legislators in the absence of concerted efforts to recruit women to run for seats that have opened up.

Research has found that women who run for office are less likely than their male counterparts to be "self-starters." Women more often than men seek office only after receiving encouragement from others. For example, one recent study of major party candidates in state legislative races found that only 11 percent of women, compared with 37 percent of men, said that it was entirely their own idea to run for the legislature; in contrast, 37 percent of women, compared with 18 percent of men, reported that they had not seriously thought about running until someone else suggested it.[13] Another recent study of people in the professions from which political candidates are most likely to emerge (i.e., law, business, education and politics) found that notably fewer women (43 percent) than men (59 percent) had ever considered running for office.[14]

Findings such as these suggest that the future for women in state government will depend, at least in part, upon the strength of efforts to actively recruit women for both elected and appointed positions. Legislative leaders, political parties and advocacy organizations can help by renewing their commitment and augmenting their efforts to identify and offer support to potential women candidates, especially in winnable races with open seats or vulnerable incumbents. Political action committees can target much needed financial support and technical assistance to women candidates. Incumbent women officials can help by intensifying their efforts to identify and groom women successors for their own positions as well as potential women candidates for other elective and appointive offices. Efforts such as these may well be critical to insuring that the achievements of the past are not lost and that the numbers and proportions of women in state-level office continue upward over the next several years.

Notes

[1] All statistical information in this essay, unless otherwise noted, has been provided by the Center for American Women and Politics (CAWP), Eagleton Institute of Politics, Rutgers University. Additional information is available at www.cawp.rutgers.edu. I would especially like to thank Gilda Morales and Linda Phillips, my colleagues at CAWP, for their assistance with the data for this essay.

[2] Martin Gruberg, Women in American Politics (Oshkosh, WI: Academia Press, 1968), 189.

[3] Gruberg, 190.

[4] Women did serve as superintendents of public instruction in a few states earlier than this.

[5] "Appointed Policy Makers in State Government A Demographic Analysis: Gender, Race and Ethnicity Data," A Report of the Center for Women in Government and Civil Society, Fall 2001. http://www. cwig. alabany.edu/ ApptPolicyMakers2001Report. htm.

[6] Gruberg, 190, 192.

[7] These are the most recent figures available but are not as up-to-date as the figures for courts of last resort. The National Center for State Courts last comprehensively updated these figures for intermediate appellate court judges in May 2003.

[8] See, for example, Barbara Norrander and Clyde Wilcox, "The Geography of Gender Power: Women in State Legislatures," in Sue Thomas and Clyde Wilcox, ed., Women and Elective Office: Past, Present, and Future (New York: Oxford University Press, 1998).

[9] Excluded from consideration here are women who have served as senate presidents by virtue of holding the office of lieutenant governor.

[10] Top legislative leadership positions include: senate presidents and presidents pro tempore, house speakers and speakers pro tempore, and majority and minority leaders of the senate and the house as listed in State Legislative Leadership, Committees & Staff 2003 (Lexington, KY: The Council of State Governments, 2003). The position of senate president has been excluded from these figures in states where the position is filled by the lieutenant governor.

[11] These numbers represent chairs and co-chairs of all senate, house, and joint standing committees as well as chairs of joint statutory committees and joint commissions as listed in State Legislative Leadership, Committees & Staff 2003.

[12] See Susan J. Carroll, "The Impact of Term Limits on Women," Spectrum: The Journal of State Government 74 (Fall 2001): 19–21.

[13] Gary Moncrief, Peverill Squire, and Malcolm Jewell, Who Runs for the Legislature? (New York: Prentice-Hall, 2001), Table 5.5, 102; see also Susan J. Carroll and Wendy S. Strimling, Women's Routes to Elective Office: A Comparison With Men's (New Brunswick, NJ: Center for the American Woman and Politics, 1983).

[14] Richard L. Fox and Jennifer Lawless, "Entering the Arena: Gender and the Initial Decision to Run for Office," American Journal of Political Science 48 (2004): 264–80.

About the Author

Susan J. Carroll is professor of political science and women's and gender studies at Rutgers University and Senior Scholar at the Center for American Women and Politics (CAWP) of the Eagleton Institute of Politics. She has published numerous works on women legislators, women candidates, and various aspects of women's participation in American politics.

Chapter Eight

STATE MANAGEMENT AND ADMINISTRATION

"State human resources is moving from an administrative, 'paper-pushing' role to
a consultative role allowing it to play a strategic part in
the future success of state government."

— Leslie Scott

"Between 1996-2003, as many as 30 states reduced their number of position
classifications, and only six states reported an increase in the number."

— Keon S. Chi

"The cost of workers' compensation, as measured by insurance rates or benefits
paid per worker, undergoes periodic cycles."

— Gregory Krohm

"The state CIO can serve as an important resource in all business process and
capital planning decisions."

— Jack Gallt, Chris Dixon and Mary Gay Whitmer

"In what was once one of the fastest growing areas of state government, legislators now
employ stringent criteria to determine when new professions should be regulated."

— Pam Brinegar

"The development of personal technology and the application of this new power in
a mobile environment is a key technological trend in telecommunications."

— Wayne W. Hall Jr.

"Privatization continues to be a controversial management issue in state government."

— Keon S. Chi, Kelley A. Arnold, Heather M. Perkins

Trends in State Personnel Administration
By Leslie Scott

During the next few years, state government human resource professionals will be focused on building and maintaining the workforce of the future. With budget deficits, an aging workforce, and rising benefits costs, state governments are challenged and will continue to be so. State human resources is moving from an administrative, "paper-pushing" role to a consultative role allowing it to play a strategic part in the future success of state government.

State Personnel Trends

As the baby boomer generation approaches retirement age, approximately 30 percent of state government employees across the country will be eligible for retirement in 2006.[1] Add to this the thousands of employees who have been laid off or accepted early retirement incentives during the recent state fiscal crises, and state government could be facing not only a lack of institutional knowledge, but employees to maintain the services of state government in just a few years.

The Center for Organization Research suggests that government is experiencing the effects of the aging baby boomer population earlier than the private sector. According to the study, 46.3 percent of government workers are age 45 or older in contrast to the private sector where only 31.2 percent are 45 years or older. The study notes that there are a number of factors leading to this significant difference, but some primary factors are that there was much hiring in the public sector during the late 1960s and 1970s in response to the growing number of government programs. Now, those who were hired during this time are eligible for retirement. In addition, downsizing efforts in the early 1980s and 1990s have left fewer younger employees in the state government ranks.[2]

The Right Workforce at the Right Time

Having the right workforce at the right time is critical to an organization, and state government is no different. Human resource professionals in state government have been working hard during recent years to develop workforce plans to ensure the successful recruitment and retention of talented employees.

Workforce plans vary widely from state to state, but they are intent on accomplishing the same goal—making state government an employer of choice not an employer of last resort. Most of the plans involve aggressive recruitment strategies and allowing more flexibility in hiring and implementing innovative pay practices within the confines of public sector employment. Over the next few years, National Association of State Personnel Executives (NASPE) members will work on ways to enhance the image of public service to appeal to potential employees. These efforts will include focus groups and working with university business and government schools, as well as private sector partners specializing in recruitment.

Planning for the Workforce of the Future

Maine

A significant portion of Maine's workforce planning effort is called the Maine Management Service Program (MMS). This program is a multi-phased initiative for 700 managers, excluded from collective bargaining, in Maine state government who are in policymaking positions. The broad purpose of the MMS is to: accelerate leadership development opportunities, develop and focus on leadership competencies, provide MMS members with more latitude in managing their programs, and set up reward and accountability structures particularly for their positions. This will be different from the traditional set up as managers will have greater flexibility and responsibility to directly manage their own careers; job assignments can be tailored to better use current skills or to develop new skills; human resource decisions will be handled by individual agencies, while preserving merit principles.[3]

While the leadership program is a long-term approach, the state has enacted other approaches designed to help in the short term, since about 50 percent of Maine's employees are eligible for retirement.[4] Significant legislation was enacted that eliminates retirement offsets for employees who retire and later return to work for state government. The decision to rehire retired state government employees or to ease restrictions in doing so has not been without controversy. On one hand, some have seen the hiring of retired state employees currently receiving pensions as "double-dipping" and are worried about the message it might send to the general public. Others see it as a cost-effective solution, hiring already experienced employees who don't need benefits, since states have found it difficult to recruit and retain talented new employees. A number of states that are able to rehire retired employees are not able to hire them for exactly the same positions they previously held. Many also have a limit on the number of hours per week they can work or the salary they can earn, and they must wait for a designated amount of time before being able to rehire them—typically 30 to 90 days.

Pennsylvania

Pennsylvania's approach to solving a possible workforce crisis is to focus on the occupations that are most at-risk of being affected by retirements. They do this by evaluating age and retirement by occupation, using an occupation-specific "retirement probability factor," focusing on hard-to-fill or hard-to-train-for positions; and tailoring recruitment and retention efforts to specific occupations.[5]

Georgia

A more recent effort from Georgia is to focus on total rewards. Total rewards not only looks at cash compensation, but also other factors that come into play when an employee considers a compensation package, such as bonuses and variable pay, benefits and work/life factors. Total rewards assigns a numeric value to total compensation plus benefits in order to create a complete competitive picture that can be compared with private sector companies or even public sector organizations.

The Georgia Merit System has identified several ways to use total rewards, including:
- Assessing its relative position in the labor market;
- Looking at strengths and weaknesses;
- Budgeting and strategically planning;
- Examining recruiting and retention practices or other best practices used;
- Providing a communication tool with employees;
- Implementing positive recommendation for change in the structure and/or balance of benefits and work/life opportunities (professional development, training autonomy, etc.) offered to employees; and
- Reducing turnover and its high cost to the organization.[6]

Recently, Georgia led a NASPE effort among the states that are members of compensation associations to add a total rewards element to their yearly surveys. It is anticipated that by using total rewards, states will be better able to compete with the private sector for employees because they will have a tool to fairly compare compensation packages.

Colorado

Another way states are hoping to attract and retain employees is through civil service reform. In Colorado, Gov. Bill Owens appointed a commission on civil service reform that is striving to modernize what has been described as the country's most constitutionally rigid civil service system, with much of its substance and process embedded in the state's constitution.

Colorado's reform efforts, which must be approved by voters, has focused on the following recommendations from the Governor's Commission on Civil Service Reform:
- Improving employee selection by eliminating the "rule of three" and replacing it with a limited number of qualified candidates as provided by law. Currently, a hiring agency can choose only from what was determined through testing as the top three candidates;
- Enable the next governor to use the Senior Executive Service to more effectively establish and implement policy decision;
- Provide more flexibility to meet sudden and occasional business demands—especially with respect to seasonal needs—by allowing the hiring of temporary employees for up to nine months, increasing it from the current six months;
- Limit the disruptive effects of more senior employees "bumping" other employees out of their jobs in times of budget challenges or reorganization;
- Move the constitutional requirement that state employees be Colorado residents into statute so that the General Assembly can allow exceptions where it would better serve citizens;
- Strengthen the ability to discipline problem employees who create an unfair negative impact on public perception and employee morale;
- Modernize state contracting to strengthen employee retraining and job protections while taking advantage of private investment in technology;
- Provide flexibility for higher education institutions to create separate personnel systems for their employees.[7]

Other states that have most recently led civil service reform efforts include Washington, Florida and Georgia.

Washington

Washington's personnel system reform, which will go into effect in 2005, replacing a 43-year-old civil service system, has three main components: collective bargaining, competitive contracting and a new human resource system.

Collective bargaining actually will increase under the reform efforts. Wages, hours, the dollar amount provided for benefits and other terms and conditions are subject to negotiation between state government and unions. The state will also look to contract out services traditionally provided by state government, an action that will no longer be prohibited. However, state employee groups will be allowed to compete for the jobs.

The Personnel System Reform Act of 2002 requires the state to reduce the number of job classifications, respond to changing technologies, economic and social conditions and needs of students; facilitate reorganization and decentralization of services and enhance mobility and career advancement—all aimed at solving problems identified with the present system. The reform also looks to allow flexibility for hard-to-fill positions and increasing salaries for performance, not just longevity. In addition, the recruitment system also will see some changes, from a listing of desirable qualifications rather than minimum qualifications and no limit to the number of qualified applicants who are referred.[8]

Performance measurement also will play a big part in the new system and all managers and supervisors will be required to have performance management training. In addition to longevity, managers may also consider performance, competencies and business needs during times of reduction in force. Currently, longevity is the deciding factor during times of reduction.

Florida and Georgia

Both Florida and Georgia have also passed legislation that effectively eliminates the protection of a traditional civil service program. These were attempts, like Colorado's and Washington's current efforts, to allow managers more flexibility in hiring and firing—particularly for poor performance—and eliminating seniority for all state workers. Florida's "Service First" initiative was implemented in 2001 and Georgia's program was implemented in 1996 for all employees hired on or after July 1, 1996.

Health Care Benefits for Employees

Another area where changes have come is health care benefits. State governments have struggled during recent years to fund the increases in health care premiums for employees, and it is anticipated that they will continue to do so. According to an October 2003 presentation from West Virginia's Public Employees Insurance Agency, states are particularly challenged to continue providing benefits because of rigid budgeting rules and a limited capacity to absorb large cost increases.

For example, Kentucky estimates that by 2022, increases in health care insurance premiums for employees will eat up all projected increases in the commonwealth's general fund revenue. For states that provide retiree benefits, the retiree pool is getting large as the baby boomer population reaches retirement age. Indiana's research shows that for every $1 in premiums paid for retiree health insurance, $3.61 is spent in healthcare expenses.[9]

States have been forced to implement or at least strongly consider implementation of a number of cost-saving measures. Some of the more common methods are raising co-pays and deductibles, mail service prescription incentives and disease management programs. Other options that some states are working on include provider profiling (measuring the quality and outcomes of health care providers with a plan to encourage utilization of the most effective, and ultimately cost-efficient, providers), a database to analyze factors and trends affecting benefits costs, and nurse call programs.[10]

Another trend in the health care arena is controlling the cost of prescription drugs. States are investigating the possibilities of purchasing prescription drugs from Canada for employees and Medicaid recipients, as prescription drug costs are estimated to be significantly lower because of price controls in Canada. Through its research, Iowa estimates an initial savings of $10 million, or 16.4 percent, per year by purchasing prescriptions drugs through Canada. However, this could be a battle as the recently passed Medicare prescription drug bill forbids re-importation of Canadian drugs unless the U.S. Department of Health and Human Services certifies their safety. Federal officials have expressed concern over the safety of prescription drugs from outside the United States.

Other states have focused efforts on banding together to purchase prescription drugs. In November 2000, West Virginia decided to pool its purchasing power and partnered other states for the purchase of prescription drugs. While a number of states were interested in the program, purchasing and statutory issues and simple renegotiation with pharmacy benefit managers among the state limited this partnership to four, including West Virginia. Other states involved in the purchasing coalition were Delaware, Missouri and New Mexico.[11]

West Virginia only had 20,000 covered lives in its prescription program. By partnering with three states, the number of covered lives became 570,000, creating significant purchasing power. With this program, West Virginia saw a net savings of $7 million, with Missouri and New Mexico experiencing savings of $1.4 million to $2 million.[12]

Overall, state human resource management is utilizing what could be a potential crisis—an aging and retiring workforce and budget problems—to assess and plan for its workforce of the future.

Notes

[1] James B. Carroll and David A. Moss, *State Employee Worker Shortage: The Impending Crisis*, (Lexington, KY: National Association of State Personnel Executives and The Council of State Governments, 2002).

[2] Mary B. Young, *The Aging and Retiring Government Workforce: How Serious is the Challenge? What Are Jurisdictions Doing About It?*, (Lexington, MA: The Center for Organizational Research, a division of Linkage, Inc., 2003).

[3] Maine Bureau of Human Resources, *The Maine Management Service: An Introduction*, (Augusta, ME: Bureau of Human Resources, 2003).

[4] Carroll and Moss, op cit.

[5] Young, op cit.

[6] Marjorie H. Young and the Georgia Merit System, *An Implementation Analysis of Total Rewards into the Southeastern and Central States Surveys*, (Atlanta, GA: Georgia Merit System, 2003).

[7] Governor's Commission on Civil Service Reform, *Final Report of the Commission on Civil Service Reform,* (Denver, CO: State of Colorado, 2003).

[8] State of Washington, *Civil Service Reform*, (Tacoma, WA: State of Washington). http://washingtonworks.wa.gov/civil.htm.

[9] National Association of State Personnel Executives, Healthcare Benefits Survey Response, (Lexington, KY: The National Association of State Personnel Executives, 2003).

[10] Ibid.

[11] Tom Susman, Multi-*State Pharmacy Benefit Management Services—RxIS*, (Charleston, WV: West Virginia Public Employees Insurance Agency, 2003).

[12] Ibid.

About the Author

Leslie Scott is association manager of the National Association of State Personnel Executives (NASPE), an association representing the directors and deputy directors of the central human resource agency in each state and territorial government. Prior to joining NASPE, Scott worked with other state government associations, including the National Association of Government Training and Development, the National Association of State Chief Administrators, and the National Association of State Procurement Officials. She holds a bachelors degree in corporate and organizational communication from Western Kentucky University.

Trends in State Civil Service Systems: Personnel Agencies, Reform Efforts, Classifications and Workforce Planning

By Keon S. Chi

Many states have continued to change their human resource management by restructuring personnel agencies, implementing civil service reform plans, reducing the number of position classifications; and planning for future workforce to meet new expectations and demands.

Civil Service Commissions and Personnel Agencies

States' workers are managed by two or more central state personnel agencies and several line agencies. In most states, executive personnel agencies work in collaboration with independent civil service commissions or boards. Such commissions were established by constitutional provisions in 15 states, and by statutory provisions in other states. Although commissioners are normally appointed by governors and subject to senate confirmation for five to 10-year terms, their authorities and functions vary. In Georgia, the State Personnel Board provides policy directions for a state merit system of personnel administration. In Louisiana, the State Civil Service Commission serves as an impartial review board that enacts and adjudicates civil service rules to regulate state personnel activities and hears appeals from state employees. New Jersey's Civil Service Commission appoints a state personnel director to implement its decisions. And the New York State Civil Service Commission adopts and modifies rules governing a wide range of state civil service matters, handles appeals on such matters as examination qualifications and ratings, position classifications, pay grade determination and disciplinary actions.

Central personnel agencies within the executive branch of state government also vary in their legal basis, structure, method of appointing agency directors and reporting procedures. Eleven states established their personnel agency based on constitutional provisions, while most of the other states created such agencies by statutory provisions. Pennsylvania's agency was created by an executive order. However, all but one state (Texas) maintain a central personnel agency. Some states, like California, have two primary personnel agencies. Half of the states maintain a separate, independent personnel agency, while the other half have their personnel unit within a larger umbrella agency. Personnel agency directors are appointed by their governors in 24 states, by personnel boards in five states and by department heads in 15

states. Top personnel executives in the rest of the states are appointed by other executives such as auditor, secretary of administration and finance, and management and budget directors.

Many states have restructured their personnel agencies over the years. In 2003, for example, Iowa's Department of Personnel was merged into the Department of Administrative Services along with General Services, Information Technology and Accounting agencies. A unit called Human Resource Enterprise within the department is now responsible for personnel management. Wisconsin's former Department of Employment Relations was replaced in 2003 by the new Office of State Employment Relations as a result of the governor's effort to streamline state government. Table A shows the many names currently used by central personnel agencies, and these differences in nomenclature appear to reflect organizational variations as well. No two state personnel agency structures are alike. Although a majority of states have kept the same personnel agency names over the years, several states have recently changed their personnel agency name, some by replacing the term personnel with human resources. Until 1990, for example, only three states used the term human resources. By 1995, six states had adopted it; by 2003, 12 states were using the term human resources for their personnel agencies. Perhaps the new label reflects more employee-focused functions of these agencies.

Despite various agency names, the major functions of state personnel administration are very much the same across the states. Such functions include: merit testing, employee qualifications, human resource management information systems, classification, position allocation, compensation, recruitment, selection, performance systems, position audits, promotion, employee assistance and counseling, training, employee health and welfare programs, affirmative action, labor and employee relations, collective bargaining, grievances and appeals, alternative dispute resolution, retirement, incentive and productivity programs, workers compensation, drug testing and budget recommendations to the legislature (see Table 8.2).

Today fewer state personnel executives are appointed by or report to their governors than in the past. Heads of state personnel agencies in 26 states are currently governor appointed, compared to 33 in 1986 (see Table 8.1). Thirty-nine directors reported directly to their governors two decades ago, and that number decreased to 25 in 1996. Meanwhile, the number of personnel executives appointed by umbrella agency heads or personnel boards has increased. The implication here is that governors tend to have less direct control over state personnel administration than in the past, and therefore it has become more complicated for personnel agency directors to remedy weaknesses in civil service systems unless they have support from the upper-level department heads to whom they report. Changing the way state personnel administrative agencies work is also complicated. In a majority of states, personnel administration cannot be changed by executive actions alone. Because statutes are the legal basis of personnel agencies in most states, legislative commitment and support are necessary for agency reform.

In addition, it is important to note that although central personnel agencies perform the largest role in personnel management, other agencies also have significant duties involving state workforce. In Arizona, for example, although the majority of agencies are subject to the jurisdiction of the Arizona Department of Administration Human Resources System, there are 23 agencies that are not included in this system. These 23 agencies have been informally grouped into 11 separate human resources systems. Each of these systems develops its own employment, compensation, attendance and leave and employee relations policies and procedures. In California, the personnel management bureaucracy consists of not only the State Personnel Board and Department of Personnel Administration but also nine other agencies, such as Public Employment Relations Board (union and labor practice), Department of Fair Employment and Housing (discrimination practices), Office of Administrative Law (personnel rules), Department of General Services (contracts for personnel services), Department of Finance (personnel budget), State Compensation Insur-

ance Fund (employee insurance benefits), Public Employees' Retirement System (health benefit plans), State Board of Control (work assignments) and State Controller (payroll and personnel information system).

Finally, the debate over centralization and decentralization in state personnel administration contin-

Table A: State Personnel Agencies

State	Personnel Agency
Alabama	State Personnel Department
Alaska	Division of Personnel
Arizona	Human Resources Division
Arkansas	Office of Personnel Management
California	State Personnel Board; Department of Personnel Administration
Colorado	Department of Personnel
Connecticut	Department of Administrative Services
Delaware	State Personnel Office
Florida	Human Resource Management
Georgia	State Merit System
Hawaii	Department of Human Resource Development
Idaho	Division of Human Resources
Illinois	Bureau of Personnel
Indiana	State Personnel Department
Iowa	Department of Administrative Services
Kansas	Division of Personnel Services
Kentucky	Personnel Cabinet
Louisiana	Department of State Civil Service
Maine	Bureau of Human Resources
Maryland	Office of Personnel Services and Benefits
Massachusetts	Human Resources Division
Michigan	Department of Civil Service
Minnesota	Department of Employee Relations
Mississippi	State Personnel Board
Missouri	Division of Personnel
Montana	State Personnel Division
Nebraska	State Personnel Division
Nevada	Department of Personnel
New Hampshire	Division of Personnel
New Jersey	Department of Personnel
New Mexico	State Personnel Office
New York	Department of Civil Service
North Carolina	Office of State Personnel
North Dakota	Central Personnel Division
Ohio	Division of Human Resources
Oklahoma	Office of Personnel Management
Oregon	Human Resource Services Division
Pennsylvania	Office of Human Resources
Rhode Island	Office of Personnel Administration
South Carolina	Office of Human Resources
South Dakota	Bureau of Personnel
Tennessee	Department of Personnel
Texas	(No central agency)
Utah	Department of Human Resource Management
Vermont	Department of Personnel
Virginia	Department of Human Resource Management
Washington	Department of Personnel
West Virginia	Division of Personnel
Wisconsin	Office of State Employee Relations
Wyoming	Human Resources Division

Source: The Council of State Governments, 2003.

ues. Nearly every state has decentralized at least some of its central personnel functions. But the real debate is not around the question of whether decentralization in general is desirable or not, or whether a specific state should have a more decentralized personnel system. Rather, the debate appears to be around questions such as: How extensive should decentralization be? What elements of the civil service system should be consistent across state agencies? What issues should be up to individual line agencies to determine? What should the role of the central personnel agency be in a decentralized system? In several states, the central agency plays a facilitator's role, consulting with agencies, assisting them in developing agency policies ad programs, providing training and technical assistance and performing a statewide oversight function.

Civil Service Reform

Civil service systems as we know today did not exist in any of the states before the Pendleton Act of 1883 became effective in the federal government. New York was the first to adopt a civil service system at the state level. In the Empire state, the person (Everett P. Wheeler) who was credited with assistance in drafting the civil service act for the federal government also drafted a merit system for New York. An influential legislator (Theodore Roosevelt) moved civil service legislation through the both houses of the state legislature, and a reform-minded governor (Grover Cleveland) signed it into law in 1883. In 1884, Massachusetts followed New York by enacting its civil service law. Other states followed by adopting the merit system in the following decades; however their civil service systems had undergone constant changes.

In the 1970s, for example, more than half the states were involved in civil service reform. Major reasons for reform efforts included: poor or weak personnel administrative practices which had not kept pace with governmental growth; a need to update antiquated statutes governing civil service systems; the emergence of unionism and collective bargaining; the increased demand of government employees for a clear definition of their status as related to pay, benefits and working conditions; the demand by the public to decrease the cost of services in government; and the impetus of civil service reform at the federal level. There was a general agreement among progressive state policymakers that state civil service systems were in need of radical reform to improve the productivity of state government.[1]

During the late 1980s, states continued to initiate civil service reform projects. One survey conducted by the National Association of State Personnel Executives (NASPE) in 1992 showed as many as 35 states were involved in some form of civil service reform. As for the rationale behind their efforts, these states cited the need to change rules, regulations and policies to meet executive leadership needs and to implement quality management initiatives. The NASPE survey identified governors and personnel agency executives as the main forces behind the reform initiatives in most states, but several states indicated other executive agencies and personnel agency customers were driving the reform efforts as well. Comprehensive or "wholesale" civil service reform was undertaken by a few states; while incremental reform focusing on selected areas of civil service systems were implemented by many other states, typically over a period of several years. Classification, compensation and performance evaluation were the main targets for reform in most states, followed by merit testing, employee benefits, selection procedures, incentive and productivity programs, retirement methods and training. Another survey by NASPE conducted in 1996 showed that state personnel agencies were involved in reform activities in the very much same functional areas as in 1992.[2]

Mostly recently, between 1998 and 2003, according to a survey of state personnel executives on state civil service reform conducted by CSG in 2003, comprehensive civil service reform proposals were initiated or implemented in 10 states (Table 8.8). In addition, during the same period, more than half the states implemented or were completing partial or incremental civil service reform projects in key personnel administration areas, including classification, performance evaluation and recruitment. As in the previous decades, states continue to reform their civil service systems to meet changing work environments and new expectations and demands. Recent civil service reform initiatives, as the many previous personnel reform projects, vary from state to state. One can take a snap shot of civil service reform efforts in the states by highlighting a few with reform measures:

- In Colorado, the Governor's Commission on Civil Service Reform in 2003 submitted a comprehensive civil service reform proposal, addressing a wide range of issues, including the rule of three and restructuring personnel boards.

- Delaware's reform measures, which were under consideration by the Merit Employee Relations Board in 2003 and 2004, were designed to simplify and streamline its merit rules addressing issues such as sexual orientation, pay range and the use of the term human resources instead of the term personnel.

- Since 2001, Florida has been implementing a number of civil service reform measures, including movement of career service employees to the Selected Exempt Service, prohibition of bumping, causes of suspension, discipline, recruitment by agency directors, leave payments, and employee performance evaluation and broadbanding.

- Georgia passed a law in 1996 to make all new hires at will employees, hoping that state workers can be more responsive and agency managers can have more flexibility in hiring, promotion and terminations. However, employees hired under the previous merit system continue to have civil service protections. Under the new law, agency directors are now responsible for several functions that the merit system agency had performed, such as screening job applicants.

- Iowa's Department of Personnel was merged into the Department of Administrative Services in 2003. Human resource functions are now performed by a unit within the Department of Administrative Services.

- Although there were no legal mandates or citizen review recommendations to mandate changes, the Michigan Department of Civil Service has undergone changes in virtually all areas of its responsibility in recent years, including classification and compensation and performance evaluation.

- The New York Department of Civil Service recently transformed the state's 120-year old civil service system "from an inflexible relic of declining relevance into a dynamic and progressive practitioner of quality merit system and human resource management." New York was recognized recently as a most innovative state with its civil service reform.

- Washington state's legislature enacted the Personnel System Reform Act of 2002, calling for sweeping changes to the state's civil service system. In addition to a radical change in the classification system, the act expanded the scope of collective bargaining to be negotiated by the governor's office. Under the new reform plan, the Public Employment Relations Commission administers collective bargaining agreements. The

Personnel Appeals Board is abolished, and the role of the Personnel Resource Board has changed.

Why do states need to reform their civil service systems? What are they trying to change? There are no simple answers. One way to answer these questions might be to examine criticisms of the existing systems and highlight reform proposals or recommendations prepared by civil service study commissions. For example, a 1995 study by the Little Hoover Commission in California found that the state's civil service system was "antiquated and duplicative." The study said, "Oversight overkill, turf cold wars and regulations crafted to circumvent over regulation... structural problems create inefficiency and reduce accountability. Statutory restrictions make it hard to find the right person for the job, to discipline and reward, to promote and dismiss. And tensions between labor and management undermine efforts to collaboratively strive for improvement." To rectify weaknesses of the existing system, the commission recommended eliminating of the State Personnel Board and assigning oversight of personnel management and central leadership to the Department of Personnel Administration to avoid overlap and conflict between the personnel agencies; eliminating the review by the Office of Administrative Law of rules, regulations and negotiated agreements on personnel administration; allowing the Department of Personnel Administration to delegate to individual departments more authority over classification, selection, discipline, compensation and layoff procedures; expanding the Career Executive Assignment program to include all managers and supervisors; enacting legislation to implement the negotiated solution as the sole venue for resolving major disputes; and eliminating the presumption of permanent tenure and automatic pay raises, and to link salary adjustments to performance.[3]

In Pennsylvania, a legislative committee found that executive agency managers often had little or no choice in hiring their employees, the civil service system was "duplicative and unnecessarily complex," and employee appeal decisions were excessively slow. The Legislative Budget and Finance Committee's study called for a fundamental reform by establishing an Office of Administration to administer the personnel system more effectively; replacing the State Civil Service Commission with an independent quasi-judicial merit system hearing board; adopting a single merit-based personnel system covering virtually all non-policymaking employees under the governor's personnel control; merging the civil service and non-civil service systems into one merit-based system that removes the distinction between non-civil service and civil service jobs; allowing agency managers greater discretion in hiring and promotion decisions by expanding beyond the rule of three and eliminating residency requirements; transferring the Civil Service Commission's administrative functions to the Bureau of Personnel Administration; and retaining centralized test development and administration for most positions and decentralize test development and administration responsibilities to agencies on a selective basis.[4]

The Governor's Commission on Civil Service Reform in Colorado released its final report in 2003, criticizing the state's existing civil service system as "a rigid employment system that causes waste and inefficiency and hinders the effectiveness of the state workforce that failed to keep pace with changing legal and economic circumstances." It also pointed out that Colorado is one of only two states that restrict state managers to using the rule of three in hiring employees by constitutional provisions. The commission's recommendations include: adding gender to the list of impermissible bases for appointments and promotions under the fundamental merit principle; changing the constitutional provision to allow the personnel director to have rulemaking authority; eliminating the rule of three to allow interview and appointment of any of a limited number of applicants who are qualified for the position; deleting the constitutional provision that specifies the probationary period in favor of a statutory provision for the current 12-month probationary period; eliminating the residency requirement that applicants be residents of the states; and extending temporary appointments from the current six months to nine months out of 12. The reform proposal, however, did not address the position classification issue.[5]

Job Classifications

Of the many personnel administration areas, classification has been the most talked about topic in state civil service reform. Job classification systems have different purposes. In some states, for example, the system is regarded as a rational means for sorting and naming positions, and in other states, it is an important administrative tool. Yet, in other states, it is merely a tool in developing position specifications. A major problem with classification has been its number. In short, states' civil service systems have been criticized for too many position classifications.

California appeared to reflect the typical problem with state classification systems. That state's civil service system consisted of about 3,500 job classifica-

tions. But more than 1,600 of those contained five or fewer employees. A report by the governor's office said: "This excessively detailed partition of state service greatly conflicts the ability of individuals and all state government to serve California. It punishes those employees who quickly master skills by locking their pay to 'time in grade.' It frustrates managers who need to deploy and re-deploy the knowledge, skills and abilities of their employees to maximize performance."[6] It is good to remember that the National Commission on the State and Local Public Service recommended a drastic reduction of the number of job classifications – from several hundreds or thousands to no more than a few dozen. The report also advocated a simple pay structure to allow agency managers to use greater discretion in rewarding productive employees.[7]

The new trend seems to be encouraging. In recent years, states have been moving toward a gradual reduction in the number of job classifications. Between 1986 and 1996, approximately half of the states reduced the number of job classifications, and the other half increased them. Many of the states that reduced the number began doing so in the late 1980s and early 1990s in response to increasing use of technology and new management techniques that changed the education and experience needed to perform state jobs. Between 1996-2003, as many as 30 states reduced their number of position classifications, and only six states reported an increase in the number (Table B). These states changed their classification systems through various title reduction projects without negatively affecting employee salaries. The number of classifications currently ranges from less than 400 in Massachusetts and Oklahoma to more than 4,000 as in New Jersey and Georgia. Overall, 20 states now have fewer than 1,000 job classifications, while seven states have less than 500. Interestingly, between 2000-2002, the number of classifications was reduced in eight states (Florida, Montana, New Mexico, South Dakota, Texas, Utah, Vermont and Virginia). Under Washington state's Personnel System Reform Act of 2002, which is scheduled for implementation in 2005, the number of job classifications will be substantially reduced. Under reform, the act says, "state services will be delivered more effectively, and agencies will have more flexibility to meet changing needs and employees will have enhanced mobility and career advancement opportunity."

In general, the number of classifications appears to be associated with the number of state employees. The more state workers there are, the more job classifications. California, New Jersey and New York are examples, but there are also exceptions.

Table B: Number of Classifications: 1986, 1996 and 2003

State	1986	1996	2003
Alabama	1,340	1,481	1,400
Alaska	1,000	1,000	959
Arizona	1,450	1,575	1,089
Arkansas	2,100	1,854	1,619
California	4,400	4,500	3,500
Colorado	1,600	951	537
Connecticut	2,500	4,060	2,450
Delaware	1,100	1,300	900
Florida	1,839	3,100	(a)
Georgia	1,500	1,500	4,068
Hawaii	1,583	1,719	1,670
Idaho	1,100	1,633	1,200
Illinois	1,600	1,039	957
Indiana	1,525	1,501	1,385
Iowa	1,200	851	750
Kansas	1,200	762	648
Kentucky	1,442	1,700	2,158
Louisiana	2,440	2,875	2,490
Maine	1,497	1,300	1,107
Maryland	3,000	2,389	2,121
Massachusetts	850	1,150	(b)
Michigan	1,766	1,691	1,681
Minnesota	1,794	2,269	2,061
Mississippi	1,700	2,500	2,000
Missouri	1,080	1,307	1,033
Montana	1,500	1,350	1,300
Nebraska	1,300	1,460	1,200
Nevada	1,200	1,300	1,250
New Hampshire	1,470	1,251	1,000
New Jersey	6,500	6,169	4,707
New Mexico	800	1,200	(c)
New York	7,300	5,950	3,777
North Carolina	3,012	3,500	3,000
North Dakota	960	980	940
Ohio	1,737	2,000	2,500
Oklahoma	1,136	1,407	375
Oregon	1,185	815	700
Pennsylvania	2,700	2,782	2,828
Rhode Island	1,500	1,500	3,412
South Carolina	2,400	2,298	500
South Dakota	510	551	450
Tennessee	1,409	1,680	1,766
Texas	1,324	1,148	950
Utah	2,100	2,200	940
Vermont	1,063	1,300	1,300
Virginia	2,100	1,800	300
Washington	2,400	1,750	2,800
West Virginia	950	750	875
Wisconsin	2,011	2,800	1,870
Wyoming	1,350	774	500

Sources: National Association of State Personnel Executives survey, 1986, 1996; The Council of State Government survey, 1996, 2003.

Key:

(a) In Florida, more than 3,300 classes were consolidated into 23 job families, 38 occupational groups, 228 occupations and 144 broadband levels.

(b) Massachusetts has 200-250 job series.

(c) New Mexico has 245 technical occupation groups and five manager categories.

Texas, for example, employs almost as many people as New York but has only one-fourth of the classifications. The number of job classes may be related to such factors as how often the classification system is updated, how involved the personnel department is in the state budgeting process, how often the legislature requests more titles to support a new or expanded program, how difficult it is to get rid of job classifications once they get in the system, and how much opposition there is from employee unions. Two other factors affecting the number of job classes are organizational structure and the need for new occupations, especially information technology.

One recent development in the classification field is the use of broadbanding, introduced to state governments from the private sector. Under broadbanding, a state typically pares away many salary grades and ranges, collapsing them into fewer or broader and more inclusive classes of positions. The most common reason for adopting this practice, usually applied to both classification and compensation, is to complement the move to a flatter organization. Other reasons are to encourage a broadly skilled workforce, support a new culture or climate, support carrier development opportunities, reduce salary administration efforts and costs, and minimize job analysis and evaluation costs. Recently, many states considered reducing the number of job classes through broadbanding or similar methods that allow managers the flexibility to manage personnel. In 1995, for example, California attempted to reduce its largest group of job classes by 75 percent and the governor directed the State Personnel Board to reduce the 1,617 classes with five or fewer employees (California Governor's Office, 1996). Texas tried to delete 422 job classes, create 47 new classes, change the titles of 215 classes, and reallocate 41 classes. In addition, the state was planning to consolidate most agency-specific classes or to rewrite job descriptions so that each class can be used by all agencies as appropriate.[8]

Florida implemented a broadbanding classification and compensation system in July 2002. The previous system, developed during the 1960s, was criticized as being either too narrow or too wide to be meaningful and was blamed for its inability to allow management flexibility and the need for change. The new system was designed to better deal with "the challenges of increased demand for government services with ongoing technological advancements, and the need to continually improve organizational effectiveness to better serve its citizens." Legislation passed by the Florida Legislature in 2001 called for totally restructuring the state's classification system and limited the number of occupational groups to less than 50. It also provided for a maximum of six classification levels for each occupation in the occupational group and set a limit of 300 job classification levels. The specific goals of the broadbanding system in Florida include: significantly reducing the need to reclassify positions due to work assignment and organizational changes by decreasing the number of classification changes required; establishing broad-based classes allowing flexibility in organizational structure and reducing the levels of supervisory classes; emphasizing pay administration and job-performance evaluation by management rather than use of the classification system to award salary increases; and containing provisions to allow managers the flexibility to move employees through the pay ranges and provide for salary increase additives and lump-sum bonuses. Using the federal Standard Occupational Classification system as the structural foundation, the more than 3,300 classes in the Florida state government were consolidated into 23 job families, 38 occupational groups, 228 occupations and 144 broadband levels.[9]

Workforce Planning

The total number of full-time state employees (not including education) has been on the gradual increase in the past three decades, from 2.3 million (full-time equivalent) in 1970 to 2 million in 1980 to 3.1 million in 1990 and 4.1 million in 2000. Today, the full-time worker in a typical state is white, 43 years old and has 10 years of service in the state government. Approximately half of the state employees are males, but in some states, like Missouri, New Jersey and Texas, females outnumber male workers. In most states, more than 40 percent of state full-time workers have served less than five years for their state. The percentage of minorities among state employees varies, ranging from less than 8 percent in Kentucky to 46 percent in Texas. In North Carolina, 29 percent of state workers are African Americans. In 2002, the average annual salary for state workers ranged from $32,000 in Texas to $47,000 in New Jersey and was on average 10-20 percent behind the labor market. Approximately 70 percent of full-time state employees are classified employees across the states.

State personnel executives are likely to face a workforce shortage in state governments. Some human resource management organizations call it a crisis.[10] An annual report prepared by the director of the Bureau of Human Resources in Maine reported, "Our workforce is aging. 'Baby boomers' make up 50 percent of our workforce. One third of our workforce is age 51 or older. Large-scale turnover in the form of retirements is just a few years away. Nearly 30 percent of our workforce will be eligible to retire within five years and over 50 percent of our managers will be eligible to retire in the same period."[11] A joint study by the NASPE and CSG in 2002 estimated that state governments could lose at least 30 percent of their employees in the next few years due to the growing rate of employee retirement, the composition of current workforce with less-trained workers and worsened state budget problems. A severe worker shortage is expected in 10 states in the next 10 years: Iowa, Kansas, Montana, North Dakota, New Jersey, New York, Oklahoma, Pennsylvania, Rhode Island and Washington.[12]

To meet the workforce shortage, several states have initiated innovative approaches; such methods include the implementation of different recruitment methods, filling vacant positions with retired state employees and the reform of classification and compensation systems. For example, Maine's plan calls for: strategically planning for human resource needs of the future and developing effective programs to recruit and retain people to meet those needs; marketing state government as an honorable career and as a great place to work; enhancing marketing of the "total rewards" for working in state government; promoting preventive health measures for employees and their dependents; educating all employees and managers to recognize the value that diversity brings to the workforce; being flexible in the benefits packages; exploring non-traditional labor markets; and accepting all changes collaboratively with agencies employees and employee labor unions.[13]

States need to define their strategic visions for human resource management for the 21st century. Some states, including Minnesota and California, began to develop such strategic plans more than a decade ago. In 1993, the Minnesota Commission on Reform and Efficiency set the state vision for the civil service system, defining a system that is outcome-based, customer-oriented, simple and user friendly while also being strategic, proactive, and change-based. The vision describes an ideal human resource management system that reflects community values and that "encourages quality employers with creative optional workforce development and increased effectiveness of statewide management teams."[14] According to California's vision, "The ideal system would allow managers to hire the best and brightest quickly; train, retain and motivate the workforce; compensate fairly by rewarding merit;

empower workforce to apply their skills in ways that support the mission of their department; empower managers to reward high performance and to discipline or remove under-performance; and train employees for the challenges of competitive government."[15]

To implement successful civil service reform, it is imperative that governors and legislative leaders walk their talk. They must overcome political pressure to rout the status quo from all quarters, including state employee unions. They must tackle the obstacles to change encountered by state personnel executives, including budget problems, reluctance to change on the part of agency managers, and unions concerns and opposition. Without total leadership commitment, neither ongoing civil service reform efforts nor alternatives to traditional state management approaches can be successfully implemented. Without the necessary financial resources, state managers cannot give the needed higher priority to human resource management.

Notes

[1] D.R. Cooke and E. B. Hammond, "Civil Service Reform." *The Book of the States, 1980-81*, (Lexington, KY: The Council of State Governments, 1980), 242-47.

[2] National Association of State Personnel Executives, *State Personnel Office: Roles and Functions,* (Lexington, KY: National Association of State Personnel Executives, 1996).

[3] Little Hoover Commission, *Too Many Agencies, Too Many Rules: Reforming California's Civil Service*, (May 4, 1995).

[4] Legislative Budget and Finance Committee, *Study on Civil Service Reform, (*Pennsylvania General Assembly, April 1998).

[5] Governor's Commission on Civil Service Reform, *Civil Service Reform*, (2003).

[6] California Governor's Office, *Competitive Government: A Plan for Less Bureaucracy, More Results*, (Sacramento, CA: California's Governor's Office, 1996).

[7] National Commission on the State and Local Public Service (Winter Commission), *Hard Truths/Tough Choices: An Agenda for State and Local Reform*, (Albany, NY: Rockefeller Institute of Government, 1993).

[8] Texas Office of the State Auditor, *A Biennial Report of Recommended Changes to the Classification Plan*, (Austin, TX: Office of the State Auditor, September 1996).

[9] State of Florida, *Broadbanding Report. Broadbanding Classification and Compensation System, (*Department of Management Service, December 2001).

[10] P. Stewart and M. Young, *The HR Challenges Raised by the Aging-and-Retiring Government Workforce*, (The Center for Organizational Research, 2003).

[11] http://state.me.us/bhr/annual

[12] J.B. Carroll and D. A. Moss, *State Employee Worker Shortage. The Impending Crisis,* (Lexington, KY: The Council of State Governments and National Association of State Personnel Executives, October 2002).

[13] http://state.me.us/bhr/annual

[14] Commission on Reform and Efficiency, *Human Resources Management in Minnesota State Government*, Summary Report, (St. Paul, MN: Commission on Reform and Efficiency, 1993).

[15] California Governor's Office.

About the Author

Keon S. Chi is editor in chief of *The Book of the States* and *Spectrum: The Journal of State Government*. He is a senior fellow for The Council of State Governments and professor of political science at Georgetown College.

Table 8.1
THE OFFICE OF STATE PERSONNEL EXECUTIVE:
SELECTION, PLACEMENT AND STRUCTURE

State or other jurisdiction	Method of selection	Reports to: Governor	Reports to: Personnel board	Reports to: Other	Directs departmental employees	Legal basis for personnel department	Organizational status Separate agency	Organizational status Part of a larger agency
Alabama	B	...	★	...	★	S	★	...
Alaska	D	...	...	★ (a)	★	C,S	...	★
Arizona	D	...	...	★ (a)	★	C,S	...	★
Arkansas	D	★	...	★ (a)	★	S	★	...
California	B	...	★	...	★	C	★	...
Colorado	D	...	...	★ (a)	...	C	...	★
Connecticut	G	★	...	...	★	S	...	★
Delaware	D	...	...	★	★	S	★	...
Florida	D	...	...	★ (a)	★ (b)	C,S	...	★
Georgia	G	★	★	...	★	C,S,E	★	...
Hawaii	G	★	...	...	...	S	★	...
Idaho	G	★	...	...	★	S	...	★
Illinois	D	...	...	★ (a)	★	S	...	★
Indiana	G	★	...	...	★	S	★	...
Iowa	D	...	...	★ (a)	★	S	...	★
Kansas	(j)	...	...	★ (j)	★	S	...	★
Kentucky	G	★	...	...	★	S	★	...
Louisiana	B	...	★	...	★	C	★	...
Maine	D	...	...	★ (a)	...	S	...	★
Maryland	D	...	...	★ (a)	★	S	...	★
Massachusetts	G (k)	...	...	★ (k)	★	S	★	...
Michigan	(c)	...	...	★ (c)	★	C,S (d)	★	...
Minnesota	G	★	...	...	★	S	★	...
Mississippi	B	...	★	...	★	S	★	...
Missouri	G	...	...	★ (a)	★	C,S	...	★
Montana	D	...	...	★ (a)	★	S	...	★
Nebraska	D	...	...	★ (a)	★	S	...	★
Nevada	G	★	...	...	...	S	★	...
New Hampshire	(e)	...	...	★ (a)	★	S	...	★
New Jersey	G (f)	★	...	...	★	C,S	★	...
New Mexico	B	★	★	...	...	S	★	...
New York	G	★	...	...	★	C,S	★	...
North Carolina	G	★	...	...	★	S	...	★
North Dakota	(g)	...	...	★ (g)	★	S	...	★
Ohio	D	...	...	★ (a)	(n)	S	...	★
Oklahoma	G	★	...	...	★	S	★	...
Oregon	D	...	...	★ (a)	...	S	...	★
Pennsylvania	G, D	...	...	★ (a)	★	E	...	★
Rhode Island	...	...	...	...	...	...	...	★
South Carolina	(h)	...	...	★ (h)	★	S	...	★
South Dakota	G	★	...	...	...	S	...	★
Tennessee	G	★	...	...	★	S	★	...
Texas	(l)	...	...	★ (l)	...	S	...	★
Utah	G	★	...	...	★	S	★	...
Vermont	G	★	...	...	...	S	★	...
Virginia	G	...	...	★ (i)	★	S	★	...
Washington	G	★	...	...	★	S	★	...
West Virginia	G	...	...	★ (a)	...	S	★	...
Wisconsin	G	★	...	...	★	S	★	...
Wyoming	D	...	...	★ (a)	...	S	...	★
Dist. of Columbia	(m)	...	...	★ (m)	★	S	★	...
Guam	D	...	...	★ (a)	...	S	...	★
No. Mariana Islands	G	★	...	...	★	S	★	...

See footnotes at end of table.

THE OFFICE OF STATE PERSONNEL EXECUTIVE:
SELECTION, PLACEMENT AND STRUCTURE — Continued

Source: The Council of State Governments' survey of state personnel offices, October 2003.

Key:

★ — Yes

. . . — No; or state/jurisdiction did not respond to survey.

B — Appointment by personnel board.

D — Appointment by department head.

G — Appointment by governor.

C — Constitution.

S — Statute.

E — Executive Order.

R — Rules.

(a) Reports to department head.

(b) The director of human resource management directs the employees of the Division of Human Resource Management (HRM). HRM administers and manages the policies and programs of the state personnel system, which is comprised of Career Service, Selected Exempt Service and Senior Management Service pay plans.

(c) Civil Service Commission.

(d) The Civil Service Commission and the state personnel director are constitutionally established. The Department of Civil Service was statutorily created.

(e) Governor, Department Head, Nominated by Commissioner of Administrative Services, Appointed by Governor & Council.

(f) Confirmed by the Senate.

(g) Office of Management and Budget Director.

(h) Budget and Control Board Chief of Staff.

(i) Secretary of Administration.

(j) Cabinet secretary.

(k) Nominated by secretary of administration and finance. Reports to the secretary of administration and finance and the governor.

(l) Appointed by state auditor, subject to approval by Legislative Audit Committee. Reports to state auditor.

(m) Appointed by mayor. Reports to deputy mayor.

(n) Directs employees of the Human Resources Division.

Table 8.2
STATE PERSONNEL ADMINISTRATION: FUNCTIONS

State or other jurisdiction	Administers merit testing	Establishes qualifications	Provides human resource information system	Human resource planning	Classification	Position allocation	Compensation	Recruitment	Selection	Performance evaluation	Position audits	Other personnel function audits	Employee promotion	Employee assistance & counseling	Human resource development
Alabama	CPA	CPA	SR	SR	CPA	CPA	CPA	SR	DA	SR	CPA	CPA	SR	DA	SR
Alaska	CPA	CPA	CPA	SR	CPA	CPA	SR	SR	SR	SR	CPA	CPA	SR	SR	SR
Arizona	CPA	SR	SR	CPA	CPA	CPA	CPA	SR	DA	DA	CPA	CPA	DA	SR	SR
Arkansas	CPA	CPA	CPA	SR	CPA	CPA	CPA	DA	DA	DA	CPA	DA	DA	DA	SR
California	CPA	CPA	CPA	CPA	SR	SR	SR	DA	CPA	SR	SR	SR	DA	DA	SR
Colorado	DA	CPA, DA	CPA	CPA	CPA	DA	CPA	DA	DA	DA	CPA	CPA	DA	CPA	CPA
Connecticut	CPA	CPA	O	SR	CPA	O	CPA	SR	CPA	DA	CPA	N.A.	SR	DA	DA
Delaware	N.A.	CPA	CPA	SR	CPA	CPA	CPA	DA	DA	DA	DA	N.A.	DA	SR	SR
Florida	N.A.	DA (d)	CPA	SR	CPA	DA	CPA	DA	DA	DA	DA	N.A.	DA	DA	DA
Georgia	SR	SR	SR	SR	SR	DA	SR	DA	SR	SR	DA	DA	DA	SR	SR
Hawaii	CPA	CPA	CPA	CPA, SR	CPA, O	O	CPA	CPA, O, SR	O, SR	SR	CPA	CPA	O	SR	SR
Idaho	CPA	CPA	SR	SR	CPA	O	SR	SR	SR	DA	CPA	...	SR	SR	SR
Illinois	CPA	CPA	SR	SR	CPA	O	SR	SR	SR	DA	CPA	CPA	DA	SR	SR
Indiana	CPA	CPA	CPA	SR	CPA	SR	CPA	DA	DA	DA	SR	SR	DA	DA	DA
Iowa	CPA	CPA	CPA, O	SR	CPA	CPA	CPA	DA	SR	SR	CPA	N.A.	DA	O	SR
Kansas	N.A.	SR	CPA	SR	SR	SR	SR	SR	DA	DA	SR	SR	DA	SR	DA
Kentucky	CPA	CPA	CPA	CPA	CPA	CPA	CPA	SR	CPA	SR	CPA	CPA	SR	CPA	SR
Louisiana	SR	CPA	CPA	SR	SR	SR	SR	SR	DA	DA	SR	CPA	DA	DA	SR
Maine	SR	SR	CPA	SR	SR	SR	SR	SR	DA	DA	SR	N.A.	SR	DA	SR
Maryland	SR	CPA	CPA	CPA	SR	O	CPA	SR	DA	DA	CPA	CPA	SR	CPA	SR
Massachusetts	CPA	CPA, DA	SR, CPA	SR	SR	DA	CPA	DA	SR, CPA	SR, CPA	CPA	CPA	DA	O	SR
Michigan	CPA	CPA	SR	SR	CPA	CPA	CPA	SR	SR	SR	CPA	SR	DA	CPA	SR
Minnesota	SR	SR	CPA	SR	SR	SR	SR	SR	SR	DA	SR	SR	DA	SR	DA
Mississippi	CPA	CPA	SR	SR	CPA	SR	CPA	SR	DA	DA	SR	SR	DA	DA	DA
Missouri	SR	CPA	SR	CPA, DA	CPA	CPA	SR	SR	SR	DA	CPA	SR	DA	O	CPA, DA
Montana	DA	DA	CPA	DA	CPA	DA	SR	DA	DA	DA	DA	N.A.	DA	CPA	N.A.
Nebraska	N.A.	CPA	SR	CPA	CPA	SR	CPA	CPA	O	O	CPA	CPA	O	O	SR
Nevada	SR	CPA	SR	SR	SR	DA	SR	DA	DA	SR	SR	SR	DA	SR	SR
New Hampshire	CPA	SR	CPA	SR	CPA	N.A.	SR	SR	DA	SR	CPA	CPA	SR	SR	DA
New Jersey	CPA	CPA	CPA	SR	CPA	O	CPA	SR	DA	DA	CPA	CPA	DA	CPA	SR
New Mexico	N.A.	CPA	O	SR	CPA	CPA	CPA	CPA	DA	DA	CPA	O	SR	DA	SR
New York	CPA	SR	SR	DA	CPA	DA	SR	SR	DA	O	CPA	CPA	SR	DA	DA
North Carolina	N.A.	SR	CPA	SR	CPA	SR	SR	DA	DA	SR	DA	CPA	DA	SR	SR
North Dakota	SR	CPA	SR	DA	CPA	N.A.	SR	SR	DA	DA	CPA	SR	DA	N.A.	SR
Ohio	SR	SR	CPA	DA	SR	SR	CPA	SR	DA	DA	CPA	N.A.	DA	O	SR

See footnotes at end of table.

STATE PERSONNEL ADMINISTRATION: FUNCTIONS — Continued

State or other jurisdiction	Administers merit testing	Establishes qualifications	Provides human resource information system	Human resource planning	Classification	Position allocation	Compensation	Recruitment	Selection	Performance evaluation	Position audits	Other personnel function audits	Employee promotion	Employee assistance & counseling	Human resource development
Oklahoma	CPA	CPA	CPA	SR	CPA	SR	CPA	SR	SR	SR	SR	CPA	SR	SR	SR
Oregon	SR	CPA	CPA	SR	CPA	DA	CPA	SR	SR	DA	CPA	SR	DA	SR	SR
Pennsylvania	O	CPA	CPA	SR	SR	SR	SR	SR	DA	SR	SR	SR	DA	SR	SR
Rhode Island	...	...	...	...	...	...	...	...	...	...	...	...	...	...	...
South Carolina	DA	CPA, DA	CPA	CPA, DA	CPA	CPA, O	CPA, DA	CPA, DA	...	DA	CPA, DA	CPA, DA	DA	CPA, DA, O	CPA, DA
South Dakota	N.A.	CPA	CPA	CPA	CPA	CPA	CPA	SR	SR	CPA	CPA	N.A.	SR	N.A.	CPA
Tennessee	CPA	CPA	DA	SR	CPA	CPA	CPA	DA	CPA	CPA	CPA	CPA	CPA	...	SR
Texas	N.A.	DA	DA	DA	CPA	N.A.	CPA	DA	DA	DA	CPA	DA	DA	DA	DA
Utah	DA	SR	CPA	SR	SR	SR	CPA	DA	DA	DA	SR	SR	SR	DA	SR
Vermont	CPA	CPA	CPA	CPA	CPA	CPA	CPA	CPA	O	O	CPA	O	O	O	CPA
Virginia	...	SR	CPA	SR	SR	SR	SR	SR	DA	SR	SR	SR	DA	SR	SR
Washington	...	CPA	CPA	SR	CPA	DA	CPA	SR	SR	DA	SR	CPA	DA	CPA	SR
West Virginia	CPA	CPA	SR	SR	CPA	CPA	CPA	SR	SR	DA	CPA	SR	SR	SR	SR
Wisconsin	SR	SR	CPA	SR	SR	SR	CPA	SR	O	SR	SR	SR	SR	O	CPA
Wyoming	N.A.	CPA	SR	CPA	SR	CPA	SR	CPA	DA	CPA	CPA	N.A.	DA	N.A.	CPA
Dist. of Columbia	CPA	CPA	SR	CPA	CPA	O	CPA	CPA	CPA, SR	CPA	CPA	CPA	CPA, SR	CPA, O	CPA
Guam	CPA	CPA	CPA, SR	CPA	CPA	SR	CPA	CPA	CPA	SR	CPA	CPA	CPA	SR	SR
No. Mariana Islands	CPA	CPA	CPA, SR	CPA	SR	CPA	CPA	CPA	CPA	CPA	CPA	CPA	CPA	O	CPA

See footnotes at end of table.

STATE PERSONNEL ADMINISTRATION: FUNCTIONS — Continued

State or other jurisdiction	Training	Employee health & wellness programs	Affirmative action	Labor & employee relations	Retirement	Employee incentive	Productivity system	Customer surveys	Child care/elder care	Workers compensation	Group health insurance	Deferred compensation	Drug testing	Budget recommendations to legislature	Cafeteria benefits
Alabama	SR	O	DA	SR	O	N.A.	DA	DA	N.A.	O	O	O	DA	DA	O
Alaska	SR	SR	CPA	O	O	SR	...	N.A.	N.A.	SR	O	O	SR	SR	O
Arizona	SR	CPA	SR	SR	SR	SR	CPA	CPA	CPA	O	CPA	O	DA	CPA	N.A.
Arkansas	CPA, SR	CPA, SR	DA	CPA	DA	CPA, DA	CPA, DA	CPA, DA	CPA	O	CPA	CPA	DA	CPA	CPA
California	SR	CPA, SR	CPA, SR	CPA, SR	CPA	CPA	CPA	SR	CPA	CPA, SR	CPA	CPA	CPA, SR	SR	CPA
Colorado	CPA, DA	CPA	N.A.	CPA	CPA, O	CPA, DA	CPA	CPA, DA	CPA, DA	CPA	CPA	CPA	CPA, DA	CPA	N.A.
Connecticut	DA	DA	O	O	CPA	N.A.	N.A.	DA	O	CPA	O	O	O	O	N.A.
Delaware	SR	CPA	SR	SR	CPA	DA	DA	DA	O	CPA	CPA	O	DA	DA	N.A.
Florida	DA	DA	DA	SR	CPA	DA	DA	DA	SR	CPA	O	CPA	DA	DA	N.A.
Georgia	SR	SR	SR	SR	O	SR	SR	SR	O	O	O	CPA	CPA	CPA	CPA
Hawaii	SR	N.A.	DA	SR	O	N.A.	N.A.	N.A.	N.A.	CPA	O	CPA	SR	O	SR
Idaho	SR	SR	SR	SR	O	DA	DA	SR	N.A.	CPA	CPA	O	DA	O	O
Illinois	SR	SR	SR	SR	O	CPA	SR	SR	CPA	SR	CPA	CPA	DA	SR	SR
Indiana	SR	SR	SR	SR	SR	CPA	SR	SR	SR	CPA	CPA	SR	SR	CPA	CPA
Iowa	SR	SR	SR	CPA	SR	CPA	O	CPA	DA	CPA	CPA	CPA	DA	CPA	CPA
Kansas	DA	CPA	SR	SR	N.A.	SR	SR	SR	DA	CPA	CPA	CPA	CPA	CPA	CPA
Kentucky	SR	CPA	SR	SR	SR	SR	SR	SR	SR	CPA	CPA	CPA	N.A.	SR	CPA
Louisiana	SR	DA	SR	SR	O	N.A.	N.A.	DA	DA	O	O	O	DA	O	N.A.
Maine	SR	SR	SR	SR	O	N.A.	CPA	CPA	N.A.	SR	CPA	SR	SR	O	O
Maryland	SR	SR	SR	CPA	O	SR	N.A.	N.A.	N.A.	O	CPA	O	DA	CPA	CPA
Massachusetts	SR	O	SR	SR	O	N.A.	N.A.	DA	N.A.	SR	O	CPA	DA	DA	N.A.
Michigan	SR	CPA	SR	SR	CPA	N.A.	N.A.	SR	N.A.	SR	CPA	CPA	CPA	SR	CPA
Minnesota	SR	DA	SR	SR	O	CPA	DA	SR	SR	SR	CPA	CPA	DA	CPA	N.A.
Mississippi	SR	DA	DA	DA	CPA	DA	CPA	CPA, DA	N.A.	O	CPA	CPA	DA	CPA	N.A.
Missouri	CPA, DA	DA	SR	SR	O	N.A.	N.A.	N.A.	N.A.	O	CPA	O	N.A.	CPA	CPA
Montana	SR	CPA	SR	CPA	O	N.A.	DA	DA	CPA	CPA	CPA	CPA	DA	CPA	CPA
Nebraska	SR	SR	CPA	CPA	O	N.A.	N.A.	DA	O	O	CPA	CPA	SR	SR	N.A.
Nevada	SR	O	SR	SR	O	SR	DA	SR	N.A.	O	O	CPA	DA	O	N.A.
New Hampshire	SR	SR	SR	CPA	DA	CPA	CPA	N.A.	...	CPA	O	CPA	DA	O	...
New Jersey	SR	SR	SR	SR	O	DA	N.A.	SR	O	O	CPA	O	SR	O	N.A.
New Mexico	SR	O	O	O	O	SR	N.A.	N.A.	O	O	CPA	DA	CPA	SR	N.A.
New York	DA	O	SR	DA	O	DA	DA	DA	DA	O	O	CPA	SR	DA	CPA
North Carolina	SR	DA	SR	SR	O	CPA	N.A.	N.A.	N.A.	CPA	O	CPA	DA	SR	N.A.
North Dakota	SR	O	DA	...	O	SR	N.A.	N.A.	N.A.	O	O	O	DA	O	...
Ohio	SR	SR	O	SR	O	DA	DA	SR	N.A.	O	CPA	N.A.	CPA (a)	DA	CPA

See footnotes at end of table.

STATE PERSONNEL ADMINISTRATION: FUNCTIONS — Continued

State or other jurisdiction	Training	Employee health & wellness programs	Affirmative action	Labor & employee relations	Retirement	Employee incentive	Productivity system	Customer surveys	Child care/elder care	Workers compensation	Group health insurance	Deferred compensation	Drug testing	Budget recommendations to legislature	Cafeteria benefits
Oklahoma	SR	SR	SR	N.A.	O	SR	SR	SR	N.A.	O	O	O	N.A.	SR	O
Oregon	SR	DA	SR	CPA	SR	N.A.	SR	SR	N.A.	DA	CPA	CPA	SR	CPA	CPA
Pennsylvania	SR	DA	SR	SR	O	DA	DA	DA	CPA	CPA	CPA	CPA	SR	CPA	N.A.
Rhode Island	CPA, DA	CPA, DA	DA, O	CPA, DA	CPA	DA	DA	CPA, DA	DA	O	...	CPA	DA	O	...
South Carolina	CPA	CPA	CPA	N.A.	O	CPA	N.A.	N.A.	N.A.	CPA	CPA	O	CPA	N.A.	CPA
South Dakota	CPA	CPA	CPA	N.A.	O	CPA	N.A.	N.A.	N.A.	O	O	O	DA	N.A.	CPA
Tennessee	SR	...	SR	SR	O	SR	SR	CPA	CPA	O	O	DA	DA	DA	SR
Texas	DA	DA	DA	DA	O	DA	DA	DA	DA	O	O	O	DA	DA	O
Utah	SR	DA	SR	SR	O	N.A.	DA	SR	N.A.	O	O	O	DA	SR	N.A.
Vermont	SR	CPA	CPA	CPA	CPA	SR	N.A.	SR	O	O	CPA	CPA	N.A.	SR	N.A.
Virginia	SR	SR	...	...	SR	SR	...	SR	...	SR	CPA	SR	DA	CPA	...
Washington	SR	SR	SR	SR	O	N.A.	N.A.	SR	CPA	O	O	O	DA	SR	O
West Virginia	O	O	O	SR	O	SR	DA	O	N.A.	O	O	O	DA	DA	O
Wisconsin	O	O	SR	CPA	O	N.A.	N.A.	N.A.	N.A.	O	O	O	O	SR	O
Wyoming	SR	CPA	DA	CPA	DA	N.A.	N.A.	CPA	N.A.	DA	CPA	DA	DA	CPA	CPA
Dist. of Columbia	CPA	N.A.	O	O	SR	CPA	N.A.	O	N.A.	O	CPA	CPA	O	SR	N.A.
Guam	SR	SR	SR	CPA	SR	CPA	SR	SR	N.A.	N.A.	CPA	N.A.	CPA	SR	CPA
No. Mariana Islands	DA	O	CPA	O	O	CPA	CPA	N.A.	N.A.	O	O	O	CPA	CPA	N.A.

Source: The Council of State Governments' survey of state personnel offices, October 2003.

Key:

CPA — Functions performed in centralized personnel agency.

DA — Functions performed in a decentralized agency.

O — Functions performed by other agency.

SR — Functions are a shared responsibility.

N.A. — Not applicable.

. . . — State did not respond to survey.

(a) Drug tests are not conducted by a state agency but they are coordinated by a centralized personnel agency.

Table 8.3
CLASSIFICATION AND COMPENSATION PLANS

State	Legal basis for classification	Current number of classifications in state	Requirement for periodic comprehensive classification review plan	Date of most recent comprehensive review of classification	Legal basis for compensation plan	Compensation schedules determined by:
Alabama	S	1,308	★	(ii)	J, M, S	P, L (o)
Alaska	C, S, R, CB (q)	959	...	(a)	J, G, V, S	P, L, CB
Arizona	S, R	1,089	...	(e)	J, M	P
Arkansas	S	3,309 (kk)	...	1991	J, M	L
California	C, S, CB	3,500	...	(a)	J, M, G, V, S	P, CB
Colorado	C, S, R	537	★	(f)	J, M, F, S	P
Connecticut	S, CB	2,450	...	(n)	J, S	P, CB
Delaware	S (r)	900	...	1987	S	P, L, GV
Florida	S	(c)	★	2002	S	P, L, GV
Georgia	S, R, EO	4,086	...	1996	S	P, L, GV
Hawaii	S	1,670	...	(s)	J, M, G, F, V , (t)	GV, CB
Idaho	S	1,200	...	1993	S, J, M, F	P, L
Illinois	S, R	957	...	(d)	J, M, G, F, V, S	P, L, GV, CB
Indiana	S	1,385	...	(h)	(m)	P
Iowa	S	750	...	1971	J, M, F, V, S	P, CB
Kansas	S	643	...	(bb)	J, M, G, S	GV, (u)
Kentucky	S	2,158	...	(dd)	J, M, S	GV, P
Louisiana	C	2,490	...	1987	(v)	GV, P
Maine	S	1,107	...	1977 (d)	J, M, F, S	CB
Maryland	S	2,121	...	N.A.	J, S	P, CB
Massachusetts	S, CB	200-250	...	1997 (d) (w)	J, M, G, F, V, S (ee)	P, L, GV, CB (ff)
Michigan	C	(gg)	...	(d)	C	(b)
Minnesota	S	2,061	...	1999	J, F, V, S	L, CB
Mississippi	S	2,000	...	(d)	S	P
Missouri	S, R	1,033	...	(d)	S	GV, CB, (o)
Montana	S	1,300	...	(mm)	J, M, F, V, S	L (cc)
Nebraska	S	1,200	...	1999	J, M, V, CB	P, CB, L
Nevada	S, R	1,250	...	(d)	S	GV, L, (p)
New Hampshire	S, CB	1,000	...	(i)	J, M, CB	P, L, CB
New Jersey	S	(jj)	...	N.A.	S	P, CB , F, (x)
New Mexico	S	(hh)	...	2002	J, M	P
New York	S, R	3,777	...	(d)	J, M, G	P
North Carolina	S	3,000	...	(a)	J, M, F	P, L
North Dakota	S	940	...	(d)	J, M, F, S	P
Ohio	S, CB	2,500	...	1986	S, V	L, CB
Oklahoma	S	375	...	1999	J, M, F, V, S (y)	P
Oregon	S, CB	700	...	1990	M, S, CB	P, L, CB
Pennsylvania	S	2,828	...	(d)(e)	J, M, V	GV, CB
Rhode Island	...	(ll)	...	...	...	...
South Carolina	S, R	500	...	1996 (d)	J, M, G, F, S	P
South Dakota	S	450	...	2001	S	P, L, GV
Tennessee	S	1,766	...	...	J, M	P
Texas	S	950	★	2002	M, G, F	(z)
Utah	S	940	...	2002	J, M, V, S	P, L
Vermont	S	1,300	...	2000	J, V, S	L, CB
Virginia	S	300	★	2001	J, M, G, F	GV, P, L
Washington	S	2,800	...	N.A.	M, G, V, S	(k)
West Virginia	S, R	875	...	1994	S	P, L, GV
Wisconsin	S, R	1,870	...	(g)(h)	S	P, L, CB
Wyoming	R	500	...	(l)	J, M, S	P
District of Columbia	S, R, CB	304	★	(aa)	S	P, CB
Guam	S	1900	★	1991	J, M, F, S	P, L, GV
No. Mariana Islands	S	700	★	(a)	G, F, S	L

See footnotes at end of table.

CLASSIFICATION AND COMPENSATION PLANS — Continued

Source: The Council of State Governments' survey of state personnel offices, October 2003.

Key:

★— Yes

. . .—No; or state did not respond to survey.

C—Constitution.

F—Performance.

G—Geographic.

J—Job Analysis.

L—Legislature.

M—Market.

P—Personnel Department.

S—Statute.

R—Regulation.

V—Longevity/Seniority.

CB—Collective Bargaining.

GV—Governor.

EO—Executive Order.

N.A.—Not available.

(a) Date not known.

(b) In Michigan, the civil service commission, appointed by the governor, must approve collective bargaining agreements for exclusively represented employers. The employee relations board makes recommendations for non-exclusively represented employers.

(c) Florida has a broadband classification system comprised of 23 job families, 38 occupational groups, 232 occupations (classifications) and 146 broadband levels.

(d) Continually or ongoing.

(e) Classes reviewed on a case by case basis as the need arises.

(f) System was completely redesigned as of January 1, 1995. Have been performing consolidation studies on nine occupational groups since. Perform studies of specific classes or class series as needed. Currently examining broadbanding.

(g) Currently undergoing a review of one-tenth of classified employees.

(h) Periodically.

(i) Every 5–10 years.

(j) Periodically, based on need, review specific occupational categories.

(k) State Personnel Board.

(l) Last total review of all positions was in 1987. Since that time, the state reviews by occupational grouping on a rotating basis.

(m) Equitable distribution of funds allocated by the legislature.

(n) The calendar for job classification reviews for the majority of Connecticut's job classifications (i.e., bargaining unit classifications) has been set by agreement.

(o) State Personnel Board.

(p) Personnel commission.

(q) State or federal employment laws have impact when their provisions supercede normal classification or compensation rules.

(r) State merit rules.

(s) Reviews are done in segments, not overall.

(t) Salary schedules are negotiated. They cover pay rates for each pay grade including steps recognizing length of satisfactory service. Market and geographic differentials may be approved for positions in labor market shortages. Variable pay increases for managers recognize performance.

(u) Personnel recommends to governor for approval.

(v) Civil service rules

(w) Applies to non-management positions. Review for management positions will occur in the next year.

(x) Modified Hay System.

(y) Statute provides use of several optional Pay Movement Mechanisms that include pay-for-performance, skill-based pay, market adjustments and equity adjustments. All state employees with two years service or more receive statutorily established lump-sum longevity payments that increase with each two years of service.

(z) State Classification Office.

(aa) Last complete review during the late 1980s. Classification review of clerical occupational series undertaken in September and November 2003.

(bb) Phased review—last phase completed in 1994. Phased approach on hold pending approval of changes in statutes and regulations to decentralize classification.

(cc) After recommendation from central personnel and bargaining.

(dd) None in over 20 years.

(ee) Only a limited number of titles have salary determined by geography or by statute. Only a couple of bargaining units have longevity pay. Both management and non-management schedules have steps whereby an employee advances to the next step based on 12 months of satisfactory performance.

(ff) Legislature and Governor approves annual management salary schedules. Legislature and governor must approve any collective bargaining contracts/increases before they are implemented.

(gg) 606 classifications; 1,681 classifications including levels within the classification series.

(hh) 245 technical occupation groups and five manager categories.

(ii) Twenty percent per year are reviewed.

(jj) New Jersy reports 8, 266 classifications. This includes 4,707 state titles, 3,375 county or municipal titles and 184 common titles.

(kk) Includes classified and unclassified positions.

(ll) Rhode Island reports total classifications of 3,412. Classified service—1,835; Unclassified service—1,491, this classification includes elected officials and support staff, members of boards and commissions appointed by the governor, directors of state departments, and judges; Non-classified—86, this classification includes the state educational system either the Dept. of Elementary and Secondary Education or the Dept. of Higher Education.

(mm) Montana has been transitioning to a broadband classification system since 1999. In 2002 over half of the classifications had been reviewed and moved into the broadband system.

Table 8.4
SELECTED EMPLOYEE LEAVE POLICIES

State or other jurisdiction	Annual leave			Sick leave		Other types of leave reimbursed (c)	Child care offered on state property
	Accrual 1st year (in days/year)	Accrual 5th year (in days/year)	Employees reimbursed for unused leave	Accrual 1st year (in days/year)	Employees reimbursed for unused sick leave		
Alabama	13	16.25	★ (a)	13	(b)	C	. . .
Alaska	24 (y)	27 (y)	★	(y)	(y)	(i)	. . .
Arizona	12	15	(a)	12	(b)	V, C	★
Arkansas	12	15	★	12	(b)	A	. . .
California	16.5	18	★ (a)	12	(b)	. . .	★ (n)
Colorado	12	12	★ (a)	10	(b)	C	★ (n)
Connecticut	15	15	★ (a)	15	★ (b)	. . .	. . .
Delaware	15	15	★	15	★ (b)	C	. . .
Florida	13	15.5	★ (a)	13	★ (b)	C (j)	★
Georgia	15	18	★ (a)	15	(b)	(k)	★
Hawaii (x)	12 (u)	18 (u)	(a)	12 (u)	. . .	C	. . .
Idaho	12	15	★ (a)	12	(b)	C	. . .
Illinois	10	10	★	12	(b)	(aa)	★
Indiana	15 (s)	18 (t)	★ (a)	9	. . .	. . .	★
Iowa	(h)	(h)	★ (a)	18	★ (b)	C	. . .
Kansas	12.03	15.28	(a)	12	(b)	C	. . .
Kentucky	12	15	★ (a)	12	(b)	C	. . .
Louisiana	12	15	★ (a)	12	(b)	C	★ (n)
Maine	12	15	★ (a)	12	(b)	C	. . .
Maryland	10	15	★ (a)	15	(b)	. . .	. . .
Massachusetts	10 (v)	15	★ (a)	15	(b)	P, C (w)	★ (n)
Michigan	14 (d)	17.9 (d)	★	13	(b)	A	. . .
Minnesota	13	16.25	★	13	(b)	V	. . .
Mississippi	18	21	★ (a)	12	. . .	. . .	. . .
Missouri	15	15	. . .	15	(b)	A, C	. . .
Montana	15	15	★	12	★ (b)	. . .	. . .
Nebraska	12	12	★ (a)	12	★ (b)	. . .	★ (n)
Nevada	15	15	★	15	★	C	. . .
New Hampshire	12	15	★	15	★	A (l), (m)	. . .
New Jersey	12	15	(a)	12	★ (b)	C	★ (n)
New Mexico	10	12	★ (a)	12	★ (b)	. . .	. . .
New York	13	13	★ (a)	(q)	(b)	P (o)	★
North Carolina	11.75	16.75	(a)	8	(b)	. . .	. . .
North Dakota	12	15	★	12	(b)	C	. . .
Ohio	14	20	★ (a)	10	★ (b)	C (p)	★
Oklahoma	15	18	★ (a)	15	. . .	C (z)	. . .
Oregon	12	15	★ (a)	12	. . .	P	. . .
Pennsylvania	7 (e)	15	★ (a)	13	★ (b)	C, P	★ (bb)
Rhode Island	. . .	. . .	. . .	. . .	. . .	C	. . .
South Carolina	15	15	★ (a)	15	(b)	C	★ (n)
South Dakota	15	15	★	14	★ (b)	. . .	. . .
Tennessee	12 (f)	18 (f)	★	12	. . .	A, C	★
Texas	12	15	(a)	12	. . .	. . .	★
Utah	13	16.25	. . .	13	. . .	C	. . .
Vermont	12	15	★ (a)	12	(b)	C	. . .
Virginia	4 hours (g)	5 hours (g)	★ (g)	8 (r)	. . .	A, C, V	★ (n)
Washington	12	15	★	12	. . .	C	★
West Virginia	15	15	★ (a)	18	(b)	C	★
Wisconsin	10	10	. . .	16.25	★ (b)	. . .	. . .
Wyoming	12	15	★ (a)	12	★ (b)	. . .	★ (n)
Dist. of Columbia	13	20	★		13	. . .	C . . .
Guam	13	20	★ (a)	13	(b)	. . .	. . .
No. Mariana Islands	13	19	(a)	13	(b)	. . .	. . .

See footnotes at end of table.

SELECTED EMPLOYEE LEAVE POLICIES — Continued

Source: The Council of State Governments' survey of state personnel offices, October 2003.

Key:
★ — Yes
. . . — No
A — Annual leave.
C — Compensatory leave.
P — Personal leave.
V — Vacation leave.

(a) Alabama —Up to 480 hours upon separation. Arizona —Covered employees may accrue up to 240 hours; reimbursement may occur when transferring to another agency, upon leaving state service, or when management approves payment for excesses beyond 240 hours. California —Reimbursement at time of separation. Colorado —Payout for unused leave is up to the maximum accrual rate and at the time of separation. Connecticut—Upon leaving state service. Florida—Civil service can receive payment up to 240 hours of unused annual leave. The 240-hour cap is over an employee's entire career with the state. Selected Exempt Service and Senior Management Service employees may receive payment up to 480 hours of unused annual leave. The lifetime cap provision does not apply. Georgia—Employees forfeit annual leave after accruing 360 hours. On separation from state employment, employees are paid for all accrued leave and all forfeited leave. Employees may also use accrued and forfeited leave as service credit towards retirement. Hawaii—Unused leave is paid upon separation from employment. Idaho—Upon separation. Indiana — Up to 30 days vacation (unused at time of expiration). Iowa—At time employment terminates. Kansas—Employees can convert annual leave in excess of the maximum accumulation allowed to sick leave. Currently a 20 hour maximum — proposal to change is pending. Annual leave balances are paid out at the time of employee separation. Kentucky—If separated by proper resignation or retirement, but shall not exceed the maximum amounts established by regulation. Louisiana—Up to 300 hours annual leave upon separation. Maine—Reimbursement limited to 240 hours upon termination for most employees. Maryland—A maximum of 400 hours may be carried from one calendar year into the next. Employee may be paid for forfeited annual leave at the discretion of their agency. Massachusetts—Departments can request permission from the Human Resources Division to allow a higher accrual rate for newly hired managers which is commensurate with their years of comparable experience. Mississippi—Employees reimbursed for a maximum of 240 hours of unused annual leave upon separation from state employment. Nebraska—Balanced to 35 days on December 31 each year. New Jersey—Employees who do not use their allotted vacation leave during a single year may roll it over to the following calendar year. But employees may not have more than two years worth of unused vacation leave at any time. New Mexico—Employees may be reimbursed up to a maximum of 240 hours at their current hourly rate. New York—Upon separation from state service, employees may receive a lump sum payment for accrued and unused vacation credits up to a maximum of 30 days if they meet eligibility requirements for that payment. North Carolina—Receive pay when separated up to 30 days. Ohio— Up to 40 hours. Personal leave can be cashed out annually at 100 percent of base rate of pay. Unused vacation leave is reimbursed only if such leave was denied during the past 12 months and the employee is at the maximum accrual limit. Oklahoma—Separating employees will be reimbursed for unused annual leave up to 480 hour maximum. Oregon—Up to 250 hours upon separation. Pennsylvania — Unused annual leave may be carried over to maximum of 45 days. Annual leave in excess of 45 days is converted to sick leave after seven pay periods, mot to exceed a 300 sick days balance. Unused leave is paid on separation from service. South Carolina—One additional bonus day of leave is rewarded for each service year above 10 years, to a maximum of 30 days. Forty-five days may be carried forward to the next calendar year. Employees are paid for unused leave only upon termination or retirement. Texas—Hours in excess of maximum allowable carryover limits are credited to employee's sick leave balance. Vermont—Accumulation cap of annual days based upon years of service. Annual leave carries over from year to year as long as it doesn't go over the accumulation cap. When an employee separates from service, up to 60 hours of annual leave accrued is paid. West Virginia—Paid on any type of separation or may be used to purchase additional service credit or insurance coverage when retiring from active employment. Wyoming—Only on termination or retirement. Guam—Reimbursement is made only upon resignation, retirement or separation. Northern Mariana Islands—Classified employees get lump sum unused annual leave when they retire or leave government service and not before. Unclassified employees can elect to get lump sum on their annual leave after completion of an employment contract or carry over if they are offered.

(b) Alabama— May be paid for one-half upon retirement. Arizona —Sick leave in excess of 500 hours is reimbursed on a partial basis at retirement. Arkansas —As of July 1, 1999, sick leave not used is reimbursed upon retirement. California —Service credit given at time of retirement. Colorado—Employees who retire are paid one-fourth of their unused sick leave, up to the maximum accrual rate. Connecticut—At retirement, with limitations. Delaware—Reimbursed for retirement up to a maximum of 45 days. If laid off or upon death, also up to maximum of 45 days. Florida—Employees may receive payment upon separation of employment if they have 10 years of service. Twenty-five percent of sick leave is paid up to 480 hours. Georgia—Employees forfeit sick leave after accruing 720 hours. Forfeited sick leave may be restored to employees in the event of extended illness. Forfeited sick leave counts as service credit towards retirement. Illinois — Only sick leave accrued between January 1, 1984 and December 31, 1997 is subject to reimbursement. Idaho—Partial reimbursement at retirement for health insurance premiums. Iowa—After at least 240 hours of sick leave is accrued, employees may elect to accrue additional vacation in lieu of the normal sick leave accrual at the rate of one hour of vacation for three hours of sick leave. At the time of retirement, some employees can receive compensation for up to $2,000 of unused sick leave. Kansas—Upon retirement, employees who have met length of service and sick leave accumulation requirements are reimbursed for a portion of the unused sick leave. Kentucky—However, upon retirement if unused sick leave amounts to a month, then the months are used for final compensation for retirement. Louisiana—At retirement unused balance is applied toward additional service credit. Maine—Up to 30 days may be credited toward service time for retirement benefit calculations. Maryland—Upon retirement, an employee's sick leave is added on a day for day basis to their service credit for calculation of retirement benefit amount. Massachusetts—Employees who are retiring can cased out 20 percent of their sick leave balance. Michigan—Only employees hired prior to October 1, 1980 are reimbursed for unused sick leave in increments up to 50 percent based upon the number of accumulated hours. Employees hired prior to October 1, 1980 are paid 50 percent of their sick leave upon retirement or death. Minnesota—Eligible employees who meet separation criteria. Missouri—Unused sick leave is creditable toward retirement. Montana—Reimbursed for one-fourth of value. Nebraska—Balanced to 1440 hours on December 31 each year. New Jersey—Sick leave may be carried over from year to year. At the time of retirement, eligible employees can receive supplemental compensation on retirement (SCOR). The maximum amount is $15,000. SCOR is computed at the rate of one-half the employee's daily rate of pay for each day of earned and unused accumulated sick leave at the effective date of retirement. New Mexico—In accordance with the provisions of NMSA 1978, Section 10-7-10, employees who have accumulated 600 hours of unused sick leave are entitled to be paid for unused sick leave in excess of 600 hours at a rate equal to 50 percent of their hourly rate of pay for up to 120 hours of sick leave. Payment for unused sick leave may be madeonly once per fiscal year on either the payday immediately following the first full pay period in January or the first full pay period in July. Immediately prior to retirement from theclassified service, employees who have accumulated 600 hours of unused sick leave are entitled to be paid for unused sick leave in excess of 600 hours at a rate equal to 50 percent of their hourly rate for up to 400 hours of sick leave. New York—Although there is no lump sum payment for unused sick leave at time of separation, a specified number of days of unused sick leave may be applied at retirement toward health insurance premiums and counted as additional retirement service credit. North Carolina—May apply unused leave toward retirement. North Dakota—Upon termination, an employee with 10 years of continuous service is eligible for 10 percent payout of accrued sick leave. Ohio—Reimbursed up to 75 percent of base rate of pay. Pennsylvania — Unused sick leave may be carried over to a maximum of 300 days. Unused sick leave is paid on retirement (but not other separations) on a sliding scale from 30 percent to 50 percent based on years of service. South Carolina—Ninety days of unused sick leave may be credited as service credit upon retirement. South Dakota—One-fourth after seven years of service. Vermont—No limit placed on the total accumulation of earned sick leave, carries over from year to year. West Virginia—Depending on employee's date of hire, may be used to purchase additional service credit or insurance coverage when retiring from active employment. Wisconsin—Under sick leave plan, employees can be reimbursed for hours when they retire by converting to a pool of money to pay for health insurance. Wyoming—Only on termination to a maximum of 480 hours (or one-half of total hours accumulated). Guam—Reimbursement is made, however, for one-half of sick leave accrued by employees who are in the Defined Contribution Retirement Plan. Northern Mariana Islands—Unused sick leave is converted to service time when an employee separates from government service for retirement purposes.

(c) For information on the specific methods of reimbursement, state personnel departments should be consulted.

SELECTED EMPLOYEE LEAVE POLICIES — Continued

(d) Includes 16 hours of personal leave that all employees receive on October 1 of each year.

(e) In Pennsylvania, management gets 10 days.

(f) In Tennessee, annual leave can be carried over according to the following: 1-5 years, 30 days; 5-10 years, 36 days; 10-20 years, 39 days; and 20+ years, 42 days.

(g) Annual leave can be carried over according to the following: 1-5 years, 24 days; 5-10 years, 30 days; 10-20 years, 36 days; and 20+ years, 42 days.

(h) In first year - 10 vacation days, plus two unscheduled holidays. In fifth year - 15 vacation days, plus two unscheduled holidays.

(i) Some collective bargaining agreements provide special leave terms such as educational leave.

(j) Special compensatory time.

(k) Employees may convert up to 24 hours of unused sick leave to personal leave each year.

(l) Floating holidays.

(m) Bonus.

(n) At some facilities.

(o) Pregnancy or childbirth, child care leave, workers' compensation, leave without pay (at discretion of agency).

(p) Overtime eligible employees are paid for compensatory time not used within 180 days.

(q) The amount of sick leave that can be accrued varies by bargaining unit.

(r) In Virginia, there are an additional 4 days for family personal leave.

(s) In Indiana, 12 vacation days, 3 personal days.

(t) In Indiana, 12 vacations days, 3 bonus vacation days, 3 personal days.

(u) Accrued leave and sick leave are 21 days for employees hired on or before July 1, 2001.

(v) Twelve days for managers and confidentials.

(w) Organ donation leave, bereavement leave and blood donation leave.

(x) Applies to seven of the eight bargaining units administered by the Human Resources Department. Excluded are the earnings for firefighters which are based upon 24-hour shifts.

(y) Leave provisions exist in statute, but most employees in the executive branch receive leave in accordance with terms of the applicable collective bargaining agreement. The statute provides personal leave (the usual type in collective bargaining agreements as well). The statutory amount for personal leave is listed in the annual leave section. The amount is about the same as the amount available in the collective bargaining agreement covering the largest group of employees in the classified service.

(z) Employees may use a maximum of 10 days of enforced leave for family illnesses or emergencies per year, however this leave is charged against sick leave balance.

(aa) Personal Business Days—three per year; four per year if no sick time was used in the preceding year.

(bb) Currently offered at four locations.

Table 8.5
STATE EMPLOYEES: PAID HOLIDAYS**

State or other jurisdiction	Major holidays (a)	Martin Luther King's Birthday (b)	Lincoln's Birthday	President's Day (c)	Washington's Birthday (c)	Good Friday	Memorial Day (d)	Columbus Day (e)	Veteran's Day	Day after Thanksgiving	Day before or after Christmas	Day before or after New Year's	Election Day (f)	Other (g)
Alabama	★	★		★ (i)	★			★	★	(k)	(k)			★
Alaska	★	★		★			★		★					★
Arizona	★	★		★			★		★	(k)	Before			
Arkansas	★	★	★	★			★	★	★	★				★
California	★	★	★		★		★	★	★					★
Colorado	★	★		★			★	★	★	★			★	★
Connecticut	★	★	★	★		★	★	★	★	★				★
Delaware	★	★		★		★	★	★	★	★			★	★
Florida	★	★			(l)		★	★	★	(l)	(l)			★
Georgia	★	★					★	★	★	★				
Hawaii	★	★		★		★	★	★	★				★	★
Idaho	★	★		★			★	★	★					
Illinois	★	★	(m)	★			★	★	★	(m)	(m)		★	★
Indiana	★	★ (h)			(m)	★	★	★	★	★				
Iowa	★	★					★		★					
Kansas	★	★		★			★		★	★				★
Kentucky	★	★	★	★		(n)	★	★	★	★	★		(t)	★
Louisiana	★	★		★		★	★	★	★	★			(u)	★
Maine	★	★			★		★	★	★	★				★
Maryland	★	★	★	★			★	★	★	★			★	★
Massachusetts	★	★		★			★	★	★	★				
Michigan	★	★		★			★	★	★	(k)	(k)	★		★
Minnesota	★	★		★			★	★	★	(k)	(k)			
Mississippi	★	★					★	★	★	(k)				
Missouri	★	★	★	★			★ (v)	★	★	★				★
Montana	★	★		★			★	★	★	★			★	★
Nevada	★	★		★	★		★	★	★	★				★
New Hampshire	★	★		★			★	★	★	★				★
New Jersey	★	★			★		★	★	★	(k)				
New Mexico	★	★	(j)	(o)			★	★	★	(o)				★
New York	★	★	(j)	★			★	★	★	★			(w)	★
North Carolina	★	★			★	★	★	★	★	★	(x)		(j)	★
North Dakota	★	★	★	★		★	★	★	★		(p)			
Ohio	★	★		★			★	★	★					

See footnotes at end of table.

STATE EMPLOYEES: PAID HOLIDAYS** — Continued

State or other jurisdiction	Major holidays (a)	Martin Luther King's Birthday (b)	Lincoln's Birthday	President's Day (c)	Washington's Birthday (c)	Good Friday	Memorial Day (d)	Columbus Day (e)	Veteran's Day	Day after Thanksgiving	Day before or after Christmas	Day before or after New Year's	Election Day (f)	Other (g)
Oklahoma	★	★	…	★	…	…	★	…	★	★	(k)	(k)	…	…
Oregon	★	★	…	★	…	…	★	…	★	(k)	(k)	(k)	…	…
Pennsylvania	★	★	…	★	…	…	★	★	★	★	…	…	★	★
Rhode Island	★	★	…	…	…	…	★	★	★	★	★	…	…	★
South Carolina	★	★	…	★	★	…	★	…	★	…	…	…	…	…
South Dakota	★	★	…	★	…	(k)	★	(y)	★	(k)	(k)	(k)	…	★
Tennessee	★	★	…	★	…	★	★	(q)	★	(q)	(k)	…	…	★
Utah	★	★	…	★	…	…	★	★	★	★	★	…	…	★
Vermont	★	★	…	★	★	(r)	★	★	★	★	…	★	…	…
Virginia	★	★	…	★	…	…	★	…	★	★	(k)	(k)	…	★
Washington	★	★	…	★	…	…	★	★	★	★	(s)	(s)	…	★
West Virginia	★	★	★	…	…	…	★	★	★	(k)	(s)	★	★	…
Wisconsin	★	★	…	★	…	…	…	…	★	…	…	…	…	…
Wyoming	★	★	…	★	…	…	★	…	★	…	…	…	…	…
Dist. of Columbia	★	★	…	★	…	…	★	★	★	★	…	…	…	…
Guam	★	★	…	…	…	…	★	…	★	…	…	…	…	…
No. Mariana Islands	★	…	…	…	…	★	…	…	★	…	…	★	…	…

** Holidays in addition to any other authorized paid personal leave granted state employees.

Source: The Council of State Governments' survey of state personnel offices, October 2003.

Note: In some states, the governor may proclaim additional holidays or select from a number of holidays for observance by state employees. In some states, the list of paid holidays is determined by the personnel department at the beginning of each year; as a result, the number of paid holidays may change from year to year. Number of paid holidays may also vary across some employee classifications. If a holiday falls on a weekend, generally employees get the day preceding or following.

Key:
★ — Paid holiday granted.
… — Paid holiday not granted.
(a) New Year's Day, Independence Day, Labor Day, Thanksgiving Day, and Christmas Day.
(b) Third Monday in January.
(c) Generally, third Monday in February; Washington's Birthday or President's Day. In some states the holiday is called President's Day or Washington-Lincoln Day. Most frequently, this day recognizes George Washington and Abraham Lincoln.
(d) Last Monday in May in all states indicated, except Vermont where holiday is observed on May 30. Generally, states follow the federal government's observance (last Monday in May) rather than the traditional Memorial Day (May 30).
(e) Second Monday in October.
(f) General election day only, unless otherwise indicated. In Indiana, primary and general election days.

(g) Additional holidays: Alabama—Mardi Gras Day (or personal leave day) (Tuesday before Ash Wednesday), Confederate Memorial Day (fourth Monday in April), Jefferson Davis' Birthday (First Monday in June).
Alaska—Seward's Day (last Monday in March), Alaska Day (October 18).
Arkansas—Employee's birthday.
California—One personal holiday.
Delaware—Return Day, after 12 noon (Thursday after a general election) in Sussex County only.
Florida—One personal day is granted every July 1. This personal day does not accrue.
Georgia—Confederate Memorial Day (forth Monday in April).
Hawaii—Admission Day (third Friday in August), Prince Kuhio Day (March 26), King Kamehameha Day (June 11).
Illinois—Three personal holidays per year.
Kansas—One discretionary holiday.
Louisiana—Mardi Gras Day (Tuesday before Ash Wednesday), Inauguration Day (every four years, in Baton Rouge only).
Maine—Patriot's Day (third Monday in April).
Massachusetts—Patriot's Day (third Monday in April), Evacuation Day (June 17 - Suffolk County only), Bunker Hill Day (March 17 - Suffolk County only).
Minnesota—One floating holiday.
Mississippi—Confederate Memorial Day (last Monday in April).
Missouri—Harry Truman's Birthday (May 8).

STATE EMPLOYEES: PAID HOLIDAYS** — Continued

Nebraska—Arbor Day (last Friday in April).

Nevada—Nevada Day (last Friday in October).

Rhode Island—Victory Day (second Monday in August).

South Carolina—Confederate Memorial Day (May 10).

Texas—The following are partial staffing state holidays where state offices are scheduled to be open: Confederate Heroes Day (January 19), Texas Independence Day (March 2), San Jacinto Day (April 21), Emancipation Day (June 19) and Lyndon Johnson's Birthday (August 27). The following are optional holidays that a state employee may observe in lieu of any state holiday on which the employee's agency is required to be open: Rosh Hashanah, Yom Kippur, Good Friday and Cesar Chavez Day (March 31).

Utah—Pioneer Day (July 24).

Virginia—Lee-Jackson Day (Friday preceding the third Monday in January).

Washington—One floating holiday.

(h) Celebrated as Robert E. Lee's Birthday.

(i) Celebrated as Thomas Jefferson's Birthday.

(j) Floating holiday; Employee may choose either to work on that day or to take it off. If an employee works on the floating holiday, they may take another day off at any time within one year with supervisory approval.

(k) At the discretion of the governor. In South Carolina, the day after Christmas is an established holiday.

(l) In Georgia, Robert E. Lee's Birthday is observed on the day after Thanksgiving, and Washington's birthday is observed the day after Christmas.

(m) In Indiana, Lincoln's Birthday is observed on the day after Thanksgiving, and Washington's birthday is observed the day before Christmas.

(n) In Kentucky half day.

(o) In New Mexico, President's Day is observed on the day after Thanksgiving.

(p) In North Dakota, offices close at noon on December 24th, but it is not considered a holiday.

(q) In Tennessee, state employees have selected by ballot to observe Columbus Day on the day after Thanksgiving during the past few years.

(r) In Texas, a state employee may observe Good Friday in lieu of any state holiday on which the employee's agency is required to be open.

(s) Half day on Christmas Eve and New Year's Eve if they fall on Monday, Tuesday, Wednesday or Thursday.

(t) Up to four hours.

(u) Every two years.

(v) Also for Jefferson Davis' Birthday.

(w) Employees are allowed up to two hours paid administrative leave to vote.

(x) Three days when Christmas Day falls on Tuesday, Wednesday or Thursday; Two days when Christmas Day falls on Friday or Monday.

(y) Celebrated as Native American's Day.

Table 8.6
ALTERNATIVE WORKING ARRANGEMENTS FOR STATE EMPLOYEES

State or other jurisdiction	Flextime	Share leave	Telecommute	Job sharing	Incentives/credits for not using sick leave
Alabama (p)	★	. . .	. . .	★	. . .
Alaska (c)	★	★	★	★	. . .
Arizona	★	★	★	★	★
Arkansas	★	. . .	★	★	★
California	★	★	★	★	. . .
Colorado	★	★	★	★	★ (d)
Connecticut	★	★	★	. . .	. . .
Delaware	★	. . .	★	. . .	. . .
Florida	★	★ (n)	★	★	. . .
Georgia	★	★	★	★	. . .
Hawaii	★	★	★	. . .	★
Idaho	★	★	★	★	★
Illinois	★	★	★	★	★
Indiana	★	. . .	★	★	. . .
Iowa	★	. . .	★	. . .	★
Kansas (e)	★	★	★	★	. . .
Kentucky	★	★	★	. . .	★ (b)
Louisiana	★	★	★	★	★ (f)
Maine	★	★	. . .	★	. . .
Maryland	★	. . .	★	. . .	. . .
Massachusetts (g)	★	★ (h)	★	★	. . .
Michigan (i)	★	★	★	★	. . .
Minnesota	★	. . .	★	★	. . .
Mississippi	. . .	. . .	. . .	. . .	. . .
Missouri	★	★	★ (limited)	★ (limited)	. . .
Montana	★	★	. . .	★	★ (o)
Nebraska	★	★	★	★	. . .
Nevada	★	★	★	★	★
New Hampshire	★	. . .	. . .	★	★
New Jersey	★	★	★	★	★ (j)
New Mexico	★ (q)	. . .	★ (q)	★ (q)	★
New York	★	★	★	★	★
North Carolina	★	★	★	★	. . .
North Dakota	★	★	★	★	. . .
Ohio	★	. . .	. . .	. . .	★ (r)
Oklahoma	★	★	★	. . .	. . .
Oregon	★	★	★	★	. . .
Pennsylvania	. . .	. . .	★ (s)	★	★ (t)
Rhode Island	★	. . .	★	★	★
South Carolina	★	(k)	★	★	. . .
South Dakota	★	. . .	★	★	. . .
Tennessee	★	★	★	★	. . .
Texas	★	. . .	★	★	. . .
Utah	★	★	★	★	★
Vermont	★	. . .	★ (limited)	★	★
Virginia	★	★	★	★	★
Washington	★	★	★	★	. . .
West Virginia (l)	★	★ (m)	★	★	. . .
Wisconsin	★	. . .	★	★	★
Wyoming	★	★	★	★	. . .
Dist. of Columbia	. . .	. . .	. . .	. . .	. . .
Guam	N.A.	★	. . .	. . .	. . .
No. Mariana Islands	. . .	. . .	. . .	. . .	★ (b)

Source: The Council of State Governments' survey of state personnel offices, October 2003.

Key:

★ — Yes

. . . — No

N.A. — Not applicable.

(a) Information not available.

(b) Unused sick leave converts to service credit upon retirement.

(c) The arrangements checked, most of which are not in general use, may be available in collective bargaining agreements. The terms of these vary and are subject to change when successor agreements are negotiated.

(d) One-fourth unused sick leave is paid out at retirement.

(e) Most of these options at agency discretion.

(f) A small number of agencies offer rewards for not using leave through a Rewards and Recognition program.

(g) Alternative work arrangements are at the discretion of the agency head and supervisor and must be negotiated with the union and proved by the Human Resources Division.

(h) Collective sick leave bank for all employees for personal illness only; no direct allowed to specific employees unless legislation is passed on behalf of a particular employee.

(i) Each department establishes their own work rules governing these options. Only the Department of Corrections provides incentives for not using sick leave.

(j) At the time of retirement, eligible employees can receive supplemental compensation on retirement (SCOR). The maximum amount is $15,000. SCOR is computed at the rate of one-half the employee's daily rate of pay for each day of earned and unused accumulated sick leave at the effective date of retirement.

ALTERNATIVE WORKING ARRANGEMENTS FOR STATE EMPLOYEES — Continued

(k) South Carolina administers a leave pool which allows employees to draw upon unused leave donated by employees to be used in emergency situations.

(l) Alternative working arrangements are at the discretion of each agency/ department director.

(m) Annual leave donation program established by statute and implemented by rule.

(n) Agency optional programs: Sick leave pool—Requires employees to have one year of state service and have a minimum of 64 hours of accrued sick leave. Sick leave transfer plan—Agencies may adopt intra or inter agency sick leave transfer plans to be requested by and donated to employees who have exhausted all of their leave.

(o) Payout at one-fourth of unused leave.

(p) Utilized by certain agencies only.

(q) Agency specific

(r) When 40.1 thru 80 hours of sick leave are used within a 12 month period, it is paid at 70 percent of base rate of pay (versus being paid at 100 percent for hours used less than 40.1 or more than 80).

(s) Telecommuting may be approved on a temporary basis for those employees whose work is critical to the agency and cannot be performed by others.

(t) Incentives/credits for not using sick leave include employee compensation upon retirement for a percentage of unused sick leave balances which exceed 100 days.

Table 8.7
PERFORMANCE EVALUATIONS

State or other jurisdiction	Is employee evaluation in your state mandatory?			
	Mandatory by law	Annual evaluation	Separate evaluation for managers and employees	Agency heads allowed customization in evaluation
Alabama	★	★	. . .	. . .
Alaska	★	★ (a)	. . .	. . .
Arizona	. . .	★	. . .	★
Arkansas	------	------	----N.A.----	------
California	★	★	★	★
Colorado (b)	★	★	. . .	. . .
Connecticut (c)	. . .	. . .	. . .	. . .
Delaware	★	★	. . .	★
Florida	★	★	. . .	★
Georgia	★	★	. . .	. . .
Hawaii	★	★	★	(d)
Idaho	★	★	★	★
Illinois	. . .	★	★	★
Indiana	------	------	----N.A.----	------
Iowa	★	★	. . .	★ (e)
Kansas	★	★	. . .	★
Kentucky	★	★	★	. . .
Louisiana	★	★	★	★
Maine	★	★	. . .	. . .
Maryland	★	★	. . .	★
Massachusetts	★	★	★	. . .
Michigan	★	★	★	★
Minnesota	. . .	. . .	★	★
Mississippi	★	★	. . .	. . .
Missouri (f)	. . .	★	★	★
Montana	. . .	★ (g)	. . .	★
Nebraska	. . .	★	. . .	★
Nevada	★	★	. . .	★
New Hampshire	------	------	----N.A.----	------
New Jersey	★	★	★	★
New Mexico	★	★	. . .	. . .
New York (h)	. . .	★	★	★
North Carolina	★	★	. . .	★
North Dakota	★ (i)	★	. . .	★
Ohio (j)	★	★	★	. . .
Oklahoma	★	★	. . .	. . .
Oregon	★	★	★	★
Pennsylvania	. . .	★	(k)	(l)
Rhode Island	------	------	----N.A.----	------
South Carolina	------	------	----N.A.----	------
South Dakota	. . .	★	. . .	★
Tennessee	------	------	----N.A.----	------
Texas	. . .	. . .	. . .	★
Utah (m)	. . .	★	. . .	★
Vermont	. . .	. . .	. . .	. . .
Virginia				
Washington	★	★	★	N.A.
West Virginia	★	★ (g)	Additional evaluation criteria provided for managers.	★
Wisconsin	★	★	. . .	★
Wyoming	. . .	★	. . .	(n)
Dist. of Columbia	★	★	★	. . .
Guam	★	annual, 18 mos. & 24 mos.		. . . . . .
No. Mariana Islands	. . .	. . .	. . .	

See footnotes at end of table.

PERFORMANCE EVALUATIONS — Continued

Source: The Council of State Governments' survey, November 2003.

Key:

★– Yes

. . .—No

N.A.—Did not respond.

(a) Regulations and various collective bargaining agreements generally refer to the evaluations being done on a merit anniversary date rather than annually, but the interval is still about once a year in general.

(b) Agencies must use the statewide core competencies and number of rating levels. Agencies develop their own forms and descriptive labels for the ratings levels. They develop performance objectives and additional competencies if desired.

(c) Managers are covered by statute, labor units are covered by the separate bargaining agreements.

(d) Generally no, unless customization/changes are needed for special circumstances (e.g. to meet hospital accreditation requirements).

(e) To customize, agencies must first have alternative system reviewed by the Dept. of Management for adherence to the State's Accountable Government Act. So far, only the Highway Patrol Division and the Division of Criminal Investigation of the Dept. of Public Safety have received such approval. Department directors and staff of the Governor are reviewed on different systems also.

(f) The state of Missouri has begun the transition from performance evaluation, which looks back at performance; to performance management, which is a more forward outlook that incorporates planning for individual and organizational success, based on effective communication, shared knowledge of organizational objectives, performance expectations and development opportunities.

(g) By rule.

(h) In accordance with New York state policy, employee performance is evaluated regularly. While each bargaining unit has its own performance evaluation program, each one generally involves the development of a performance plan by an employee with his or her supervisor, a review of employee performance, recognition of positive employee accomplishments, and suggestions for further improving the employee's contribution to the organization. Such reviews are usually conducted annually for each New York state employee.

(i) Administrative rule.

(j) Ohio uses standard evaluation forms that vary by 9 classification groupings (e.g. clerical, trades/technical, professional/paraprofessional).

(k) Managers and supervisors are rated on an additional supervision criteria.

(l) Agencies typically do not customize evaluations; however, attorneys, senior management service, Imagine PA staff, and PA Liquor Control Board Wine and Spirits shop employees have separate evaluation forms.

(m) DHRM sets statewide policy that gives agencies flexibility to adopt a variety of approaches to performance evaluation.

(n) Agency directors are not evaluated.

(o) The mayor has a performance contract with all of this cabinet members, based on shared goals in all the contracts as well as unique performance measures specific to each agency.

(p) Performance evaluation is in the personnel regulation and must be performed in order for deserving employees to get their within grade increases but not mandated by state law.

Table 8.8
CIVIL SERVICE REFORM

Has your state implemented a comprehensive (wholesale) or incremental civil service reform in the past five years?

State or other Jurisdiction	Comprehensive (wholesale) civil service reform	Extent of civil service reform	Incremental civil service reform	Functional areas where reform has taken place
Alabama	...		...	
Alaska	...		... (a)	
Arizona	...		★ (b)	
Arkansas	--N.A.--			
California	...		...	
Colorado	★	Currently underway with target date to general electorate Nov. 2004.	★	B,CL,CO,E,M,P,R,S,T
Connecticut	...		★	S,M
Delaware	★	Simplify and streamline Merit Rules - currently under consideration of Merit Employee Relations Board.		...
Florida	★		...	
Georgia	★	Effective July 1, 1996, all classification, selection and salary administration authority was decentralized to agencies. Final authority for resolution of grievances and adverse actions was also decentralized to agencies on this date. Employees hired before July 1, 1996 who remain on classified positions still have appeal rights to the State Personnel Board.	...	
Hawaii	★		...	
Idaho	...		★	CL,CO,P,T
Illinois	...		★	CL,CO,S,R,M
Indiana	--N.A.--			
Iowa	★	A complete review of our predecessor agency, the Iowa Dept. of Personnel, by our new director was made four years ago (1999) at the behest of the Governor, resulting in the 100-Day Plan and a major reorganization of the department. On July 1, 2003, IDOP was merged into the new Department of Administrative Services. Human resource functions previously assigned to IDOP were retained in the Human Resources unit. Administrative/support functions were transferred to the new combined units in these areas within the new department. Fee-for-service billing established by a customer council was also implemented along with a marketplace (competitive) funding approach for training and development functions.	...	
Kansas			★ (c)	CL,CO,P,S,R,T,E,B
Kentucky	...		★	CL,CO,P,S,R,M,T,E,B
Louisiana			★ (d)	CL,CO,P,S,R,M,T
Maine	...		★ (e)	CL,CO,P,S,R,M,T
Maryland	--N.A.--			
Massachusetts	...		★ (f)	CL,S,R,M
Michigan	★	There have been no legal mandates or citizens review committee recommendations to mandate change, however, the Dept. of Civil Service has undergone changes in virtually all areas of its responsibility within the last five years. The DCS worked collaboratively with all human resource directors and the State Employer to create a Human Resources Transformation Plan that changed our way of doing business in many respects. We have undergone significant organizational structural and business-related changes.	★	CL,CO,P,S,R,M,T,E,B
Minnesota	...		★ (g)	S,R,M
Mississippi	...		★ (h)	P,S,R,M
Missouri	...		...	
Montana	★		★	CL,CO
Nebraska	...		...	
Nevada	...		★ (i)	P,S,R,M
New Hampshire	--N.A.--			
New Jersey	...		★	P
New Mexico	...		★	CL,CO
New York	★	The Dept. of Civil Service has transformed the state's 120 year-old civil service system from an inflexible relic of declining relevance into a dynamic and progressive practitioner of quality merit system and human resources management. The department has achieved a multitude of improvements which have benefited state and local management, government employees and the tax-paying public. These achievements have been accomplished with the unprecedented cooperation of other governmental control agencies, legislative liaisons, employee organizations, and the career staff of the dept. Quality standards: new inter-agency transfer provision, effective testing of provisionals, annual promotion testing, prompt test results, enhanced hiring flexibility, targeted title control, superlative customer service, comprehensive outreach network, advanced information systems	★	CL,CO,S,R,M

See footnotes at end of table.

CIVIL SERVICE REFORM — Continued

Has your state implemented a comprehensive (wholesale) or incremental civil service reform in the past five years?

State or other Jurisdiction	Comprehensive (wholesale) civil service reform	Extent of civil service reform	Incremental civil service reform	Functional areas where reform has taken place
North Carolina	...		★	CL
North Dakota	...		...	
Ohio	...		...	
Oklahoma	★	Classification and Compensation Act of 1999 consolidated approximately 2000 classifications into approximately 370 job families. Central office retains assignment of job family to positions, but the level within the job family is the responsibility of each agency appointing authority. Old 13 step salary schedule was replaced with wide salary bands and agencies given greater flexibility over pay within appropriate salary band. New pay movement mechanisms give agencies more latitude on pay as well. New performance management process adopted tying performance to accountabilities of the job and all agencies required to use OPM official form for performance appraisals.	★ (j)	
Oregon	...		★	CL,CO,P,S,R,M,B
Pennsylvania	...		★ (k)	S,R,M
Rhode Island	--N.A.--			
South Carolina	...		★ (l)	P,R,T,E,B
South Dakota	...		★ (m)	S
Tennessee	--N.A.--			
Texas	...		...	
Utah	...		★ (n)	CL
Vermont	...		...	
Virginia	--N.A.--			
Washington	★	Currently in process with 7/1/05 deadline, CB, CC,CSR, new HRMS	...	
West Virginia	...		...	
Wisconsin	...		★	CL,CO,S,B
Wyoming	...		★ (o)	CL,CO
Dist. of Columbia	...		★ (p)	CO,P,T,B
Guam	...		...	
No. Mariana Islands	...		...	

Source: The Council of State Governments' survey, November 2003.

Key:
★ – Yes
. . . – No
B – Benefit
N.A. – Did not respond
CL – Classification
P – Performance evaluation
CO – Compensation
R – Recruitment
E – Employee relations
S – Selection/hiring
M – Merit testing
T – Training

(a) The state has not implemented a civil service reform, but it has begun a major transition to consolidate the personnel functions spread out among 14 departments into a central agency within the Division of Personnel in the Department of Administration. This transition, which was begun Sept. 16, 2003, is targeted for completion July 1, 2004. The responses to this survey for 2004 were prepared as if the functions were already fully centralized. At the time the survey was completed in October 2003, however, the transition was just underway. Some HR staff and functions were still in the various departments; however, the supervision of all the HR functions had already been transferred to the director of the Division of Personnel.

(b) A Personnel Rules Review Committee was established to help guide incremental reform.

(c) We have decentralized a number of HR functions to agencies (for example recruitment, training, performance reviews) and have proposed regulation changes to further decentralize. Additionally, we are examining every HR function, evaluating effectiveness and efficiency. If not a wholesale reform, it's close.

(d) Workforce planning.

(e) Reform limited to high level civil service managers who are not covered by collective bargaining agreements - the Maine Management Service was created several years ago and civil service policies were reformed for those employees at that time.

(f) Essential Functions Study/Study of current classifications and identifica-tion of essential functions and classification reforms resulting in consolida-tion of number of classifications.

(g) Went to a skills matching selection system using Resumix Software and web-based tools.

(h) We currently are taking a comprehensive review of the performance evaluation system. We are nearly completion of a comprehensive recruit-ment handbook; we discontinued written and proficiency testing, effective October 2003; and as a part of our Total Workforce Initiative Project, we continuously seek improvements to our civil service components, particu-larly those involving the selection component.

(i) Performance evaluation form and rating scale revised; regulations re-vised to make evaluation more flexible and responsive to agency needs.

(j) "Incremental" reform is ongoing. Primary feature of this reform is del-egation of HR processes, i.e., allocation of positions and certification of qualification of applicants for promotion to individual agencies through del-egation agreements.

(k) During the past few years the Pennsylvania State Civil Service Com-mission has pursued several administrative enhancements to include online applications, computerized examinations, the electronic posting of available jobs on a centralized Web site, and allowing non-civil service employees to be appointed from promotion lists as opposed to employment lists.

(l) The areas of classification, compensation and merit testing were part of the 1996 system reforms. While merit testing was completely decentral-ized, all other areas noted above are constantly monitored for needed and potential revision.

(m) Moved from training and experience rating to evaluation of knowl-edge, skills and abilities.

(n) Last year we implemented a title reduction project reducing over 2500 classifications titles to 940.

(o) Implemented broad banding in January 1998 and decentralized com-pensation at the same time.

(p) Created the Management Supervisory Service, which converted 1,000 middle managers to "at-will" status. Implemented new performance man-agement program. Changed pay progression within grade. We have devel-oped the regulations for a new compensation system which requires approval by the legislative branch.

Trends and Issues in Workers' Compensation in the States
By Gregory Krohm

By almost any metric, the performance of state workers' compensation systems varies greatly, with large swings in claims, costs and disputes over just a few years. As a result of this dynamic environment, a handful of states "reform" their workers' compensation statutes almost annually.

Introduction

Unlike most other social insurance programs, workers' compensation systems change often, sometimes quite radically. States are responding to substantial differences in local interest groups, cost pressures, industrial mixes and labor markets. This review will consider recent changes in coverage law, benefit levels, system cost and program delivery.

It is important to understand that workers' compensation systems in some states are seas of tranquility compared to others where major reform proposals are introduced in almost every legislative session. For example, California, Texas and Florida have been particularly active in making statutory changes in all areas of their workers' compensation law over the past 10 years. At the other extreme, states like Nebraska and Wisconsin have had only minor adjustments/updates in statutes over the same period.

Coverage of Law

Since workers' compensation's inception in the United States in 1911, there has been a steady expansion of state laws to cover more workers under more situations. According to the National Academy of Social Insurance (NASI), between 87 to 94 percent of the civilian workforce (depending how you measure the workforce) is covered by workers' compensation. Coverage is triggered by injury or disease associated with an increasingly broad set of circumstances surrounding work. The trend may continue by small increments and extensions in most states.

Often, these changes in coverage are triggered by court cases that define or redefine the concept of employment, such as with professional employer organizations or independent contractors. Look for continued flux in coverage in the following areas:

Professional Employers. In many states, there is a large and growing portion of the workforce supplied via "Professional Employer Organizations" or "Employment Outsourcing." If not treated correctly under workers' compensation law, such organizations confuse and burden the normal systems for regulating coverage and compliance of employers. This issue will continue to smolder as the number and market share of PEOs expands.

Stress and Psychological Injury. Compensability of claims for work-induced stress has been gradually creeping into workers' compensation. Most jurisdictions recognize claims for stress or psychological injury that ensue directly from a clear or traumatic event. The legal battleground for the future will be on compensating psychological conditions that come from general working conditions rather than from a clear-cut event.

Non-objective Injury Complaints. With more effective safety procedures being enforced and the growing importance of office work in the United States, traumatic injury is on the decline. In its place, there is a growing problem with claims of work injury stemming from conditions that are difficult to diagnose and measure. Among the common sources of non-objective injuries are multiple chemical sensitivity and sick building syndrome. Although these constitute less than 1 percent of lost time claims, they are difficult to adjust and resolve.

Interjurisdictional Claims. Claims for benefits outside the normal base of operations of an employer and employee are increasingly common. Coverage for cross-border claims is inconsistent and can lead to unwelcome surprises and extra costs for injured workers and their employers. The problem is worsened by international commerce that brings Mexican and Canadian workers into the United States for temporary operations, such as trucking or contract services.

Repetitive Motion Injury. Look for a continued trend in claims from repetitive motion induced injury to hands, wrists and arms. While often labeled incorrectly as "carpal tunnel," such claims of discomfort or loss of use involve a variety of diagnoses and job situations. Some experts contend the complaints are unfairly attributed to work; others see a need for major safety improvements to protect workers from these "ergonomic" injuries. While the federal Occupational Safety and Health Administration (OSHA) has put to rest any plans for rule making on ergonomic safety and relief for workers with such complaints, it has launched a voluntary compliance program. The ergonomics issue is still smoldering.

Table A: Workers' Compensation Coverage Rates, 2000*

Workers' compensation coverage rates

State or other jurisdiction	Percent of total employment (including self-employed) (1)	Percent of wage and salary employment only (2)	Percent of UI covered wage and salary employment (3)
Alabama	84.4	90.5	95.0
Alaska	87.3	96.2	100.0
Arizona	89.8	95.8	100.0
Arkansas	85.1	91.4	96.0
California	89.1	97.9	100.0
Colorado	89.3	96.4	100.0
Connecticut	90.4	97.1	100.0
Delaware	89.4	94.0	99.0
Florida	87.7	92.9	96.0
Georgia	88.1	93.5	96.7
Hawaii	90.4	98.1	100.0
Idaho	86.1	95.6	100.0
Illinois	91.4	96.4	99.3
Indiana	89.5	95.3	98.6
Iowa	85.8	93.7	99.7
Kansas	87.1	94.0	98.8
Kentucky	86.8	92.9	99.1
Louisiana	89.1	95.3	100.0
Maine	84.9	96.0	100.0
Maryland	90.8	96.4	100.0
Massachusetts	90.7	96.4	99.2
Michigan	88.8	94.4	97.8
Minnesota	88.7	95.7	100.0
Mississippi	83.7	91.0	94.4
Missouri	85.2	91.1	94.9
Montana	80.4	93.1	100.0
Nebraska	82.9	91.5	98.4
Nevada	92.5	96.7	99.0
New Hampshire	87.4	96.0	100.0
New Jersey	91.2	95.7	100.0
New Mexico	81.2	89.0	95.2
New York	90.4	95.8	99.9
North Carolina	87.3	93.7	97.7
North Dakota	80.1	90.3	98.8
Ohio	91.1	96.7	100.0
Oklahoma	86.5	95.4	100.0
Oregon	85.7	95.6	99.0
Pennsylvania	90.2	96.1	100.0
Rhode Island	82.3	86.4	89.3
South Carolina	86.6	92.2	95.8
South Dakota	82.7	93.0	100.0
Tennessee	85.7	92.4	95.6
Texas	73.7	79.8	83.5
Utah	88.7	94.9	100.0
Vermont	86.7	96.5	100.0
Virginia	88.6	93.5	97.9
Washington	88.8	95.9	100.0
West Virginia	86.6	91.8	100.0
Wisconsin	85.8	92.4	97.8
Wyoming	82.6	93.0	100.0
District of Columbia	94.4	96.2	99.2
US Total	**87.5**	**93.9**	**97.6**

*In all columns federal employees are classified in the states where they work.
Source: National Academy of Social Insurance, for details see *Workers' Compensation Coverage: Technical Note on Estimates*, available at www.nasi.org

Benefit Levels

The issue of statutorily required benefits for specific types of injuries has been highly politicized. In most states, benefits have expanded and contracted with the political fortunes of interest groups. There is little logic or objectivity in how some benefits are structured. Benefit payments as a percentage of payroll in each state vary widely, as shown in the following table (Table B). The variation is a result of injury rates, benefits provided in the law, and how benefits are applied in practice.

Indemnification of temporary disability is a quite stable, and relatively uncontroversial, issue. The norm is two-thirds of recent wages (tax free), up to a statutory maximum, after a three to seven day waiting period. Deviations from this norm are minor. The focus of controversy and change is in the indemnification of permanent injury. Payments for permanent total injury and permanent partial injury vary widely from state to state. The controversy stems from two sour-ces. First, when is permanent injury compensable? Second, how should the degree of the permanent injury be measured?

System Cost

System costs have gone through a regular cycle of ups and downs. The growth phase of the cycle fuels reformers that want to cut benefits. The downside invites expansion benefits. However, pricing cycles, in addition to law changes, stem from the so-called "underwriting cycle." Historically insurance pricing has tended to fluctuate up and down in a seven to nine year cycle. The biggest cost drivers in workers' compensation during the foreseeable future are discussed below.

Medical Costs. Since the 1980s, medical costs have risen at much faster rates than all other system costs. Nationwide, the medical cost of treating injured workers now exceeds 45 percent of all benefits paid, according to estimates by the NASI for 2001. After a brief slowdown, the escalation in medical costs is now the number one target for cost containment in workers' compensation. The states are scouring every possible avenue for cost containment. A popular target is cutting provider reimbursement through lowering fee schedules for treatments to injured workers. Other techniques include restricting injured workers to certain providers or managed care programs.

Loss Adjustment Expense. The cost of handling claims went up rapidly in the 1990s as claims payers used more investigation and medical containment procedures. The so-called "Allocated Loss Adjustment Expense" now accounts for 11.8 percent of net premium paid by employers.[1] These high costs for claims handling have begun to decline in the past few years as part of an industry wide drive to reduce administrative expenses.

Injury Rates. Interestingly, injury rates per hundred workers are at record low levels. This has helped to abate the rising medical costs of workers' compensation. There are some early indications that this long running trend of decline in injury rates may have bottomed out. Injury rates may begin to inch up in the next few years.

Catastrophes. The 9/11 attack produced the largest workers' compensation claims occurrence in history. The National Council on Compensation Insurance estimates the workers' compensation loss arising out of that day's incidents to be between $1-3 billion.[2]

Regulators and payers have been concerned with the adequacy of funds for covering other such catastrophe situations. Intense lobbying by the insurance industry resulted in the Terrorism Risk Insurance Act of 2002, which provides a temporary reinsurance backstop for the industry in the event of a foreign act of terrorism.

However, it is doubtful that insurers and other government funds are formally reserving for another 9/11 or its equivalent. Estimates of workers' compensation claims costs from terrorist attacks range up to $100 billion from a single event, such as a "dirty bomb" explosion in a crowded port or a biochemical release.

Program Delivery

The administration of workers' compensation is immensely more variable and state-specific than other major social insurance programs, such as Social Security, Unemployment Insurance, Medicare or Medicaid. The differences across states are widely regarded by multistate insurers and employers as a high cost of business.

State administrative practices have tended to be unstable. There are at least two reasons:

- Political cycles may change the philosophy of government, e.g., hands off market-driven types versus paternalistic government types. Compounding this change of philosophy cycle is the rapidity of administrative turnover in states.

- Technology has opened vast new possibilities for streamlining some regulatory procedures. Unfortunately, these new regulatory systems are expensive to implement in the short run.

Some recent issues that promise to continue as unsettled and volatile administrative issues are discussed below.

Table B: State Worker's Compensation Benefits Per $100 of Covered Wages, By State, 1997-2001

State or other jurisdiction	2001	Change (a)	
		2000-2001	1997-2001
Alabama	$ 1.10	.04	-.12
Alaska	1.82	.18	.21
Arizona	0.54	.19(1)	-.31
Arkansas	0.70	.00	-.03
California	1.58	.09	-.02
Colorado	0.72	-.34	-.74
Connecticut	0.86	-.03	-.34
Delaware	0.94	-.06	-.26
Florida	1.25	-.01	-.29
Georgia	0.83	.04 -	.06
Hawaii	1.58	.09	-.26
Idaho	1.29	.10	-.01
Illinois	0.94	.01	-.03
Indiana	0.59	-.02	.00(2)
Iowa	0.98	.09	.12
Kansas	0.89	-.03	-.13
Kentucky	1.04	.06	-.06
Louisiana	0.95	-.03	-.03
Maine	1.60	-.09	-.56
Maryland	0.93	.02	-.18
Massachusetts	0.53	-.05	-.17
Michigan	0.92	.02	-.07
Minnesota	0.97	.09	-.06
Mississippi	1.03	.00	.00
Missouri	1.39	.00	-.11
Montana	1.90	-.07	-.06
Nebraska	0.98	.08	-.13(3)
Nevada	1.13	.00	-.18
New Hampshire	1.01	.13	-.07(4)
New Jersey	0.71	-.01	-.10
New Mexico	0.86	.04(5)	-.04
New York	0.77	-.01	-.11
North Carolina	0.74	.00	.00
North Dakota	1.05	.02	-.05
Ohio	1.27	.07	-.08
Oklahoma	1.28	-.03	-.58
Oregon	0.88	.08	-.11
Pennsylvania	1.29	-.01	-.32
Rhode Island	0.79	.01	-.19
South Carolina	1.08	-.15	-.07
South Dakota	0.84	.06	-.16
Tennessee	0.88	.04	.14
Texas	0.74	-.02	-.01
Utah	0.69	.05(6)	-.03
Vermont	1.20	-.15	-.07(7)
Virginia	0.58	-.04	-.09
Washington	1.68	.11	.04
West Virginia	3.92	-.03	.01
Wisconsin	1.12	.17	.13
Wyoming	1.55	.14	.11
District of Columbia	0.39	00	-.12
Total non-federal	1.04	.01	-.10
Federal Employees (b)	1.65	.05	.05
Total	1.07	.01	-.11

Source: National Academy of Social Insurance estimates based on Tables 3 and 8.

(a) In states with a note, there was a difference in methods between the two years being compared for at least one component of the estimates. Some of the percent change in benefits, therefore, might be due to the differing methods. The notes are below. For more detail on state by state methodologies, see *Sources and Methods: A Companion to Workers' Compensation: Benefits, Coverage, and Costs, 2001 New Estimates* section of the Academy's website at www.nasi.org.

(b) Includes FECA only.

(1) Deductible data were not available for 2000. Deductibles were estimated using the average percentage of deductibles for all states where the data were available.

(2) Self-insurance data were not available for 1997 or 1998. The average percentage total benefits paid by self-insurers in the state in 1999 and 2000 was used.

(3) No data were available from the state for 1999. Estimates for 1999 are based on data from A.M. Best. Estimates for 1998 use the same methodology

as those for 2000 and 2001. Estimates for 1997 are also the same as 2000 and 2001 with the exception of the self-insurance estimate which is based on the average percentage of total benefits paid by self-insurers in the state in 1998–2001.

(4) The state agency was able to provide private carrier data for 1997 and 1998 only. The agency also provided self-insurance data for 1998. The 1999–2001 estimates are based on A.M. Best data and self-insurance imputations as described in Appendix E.

(5) The state agency was unable to provide state fund benefit data for 2001. The 2001 estimates for state fund benefits are based on the percentage of total benefits paid by the state fund in 2000.

(6) The state agency was only able to provide state fund and medical data for 1999 and 2000. For all other years and insurance carriers estimates are based on data received from A.M. Best and self-insurance imputations as described in Appendix E.

(7) The state agency was only able to provide data for 1997 and 1998. Estimates for 1999–2001 are based on data received from AM. Best and self-insurance imputations as described in Appendix E.

Privacy. No doubt, Americans are highly concerned about the privacy of their personal medical and financial data. This concern fostered a sweeping new set of privacy protections for medical records under a rule by the federal Department of Health and Human Services, first published in December 1999. This rule, done in compliance with the Health Insurance Portability and Accountability Act (HIPAA), was not supposed to include workers' compensation. However, an indirect effect on workers' compensation is that medical providers' pay increased attention to the need for broad, open-ended records requests by workers' compensation claims adjusters. There were sporadic and isolated problems in the months immediately before and after the implementation of the privacy rule on April 14, 2003. Now it seems that normal functions of the workers' compensation claims process are little affected by HIPAA's privacy requirements.

Electronic Data Interchange. In many ways, Electronic Data Interchange (EDI) is linked to the privacy issue. Business and government have been in relentless pursuit of electronic exchange of data, to take the place of paper reporting. The International Association of Industrial Accident Boards and Commissions has invested heavily in developing standards for electronic reports. At present, about 25 states are using EDI in some fashion to receive regulatory reports from payers. This trend will increase as more states adopt and promote EDI. Insurers have complained that the efficiency gains they hoped for from the use of EDI are being dashed by the inconsistent application of EDI across states.

Alternative Dispute Resolution. Workers' compensation is supposed to be a frictionless system, at least compared to the tort-based compensation for injury that it replaced. However, litigation or the involvement of administrative hearings in settling cases or determining benefits is regarded by workers, payers, and administrators as a system burden. Many states with high numbers of disputed claims have resorted to varying types and degrees of alternative dispute resolution. Roughly, one-third of the states have some formal system for intervening in disputes to forestall a full administrative hearing. This trend is likely to continue.

Medicare Set Asides. The Medicare Secondary Payers Act of 1981 makes Medicare a secondary payer for medical bills where coverage exists under a workers' compensation or general health insurance plan. Medicare, via its administrative arm, the Centers for Medicare and Medicaid Services (CMS), has been aggressive in asserting their rights in settlements of claims. CMS has been seeking recovery of their payments with liens against payers and beneficiaries to recover funds Medicare incorrectly paid as the secondary payer. This new detection and enforcement program has created anxiety and complaint among attorneys and claims adjusters.

Agency Budgets. The dramatic deficits confronting most states during the past two years have caused their workers' compensation agencies to adjust to reduced budgets. Hardest hit are travel and training budgets. Programs that are not directly tied to service delivery have been pared back. For example, research departments have been slashed or eliminated. Major reorganizations and staff reductions have been implemented in California, Florida, and Michigan, among other states.

Funding Sources. In response to general purpose revenue shortfalls, several states have elected to fund more of the costs of workers' compensation regulatory agencies through premium taxes and assessments on self insured employers. California and Illinois are the biggest workers' compensation agencies to receive major new funding from "user taxes."

Benchmarking. Many states have a strong interest in comparative data to benchmark the performance of their workers' compensation systems against other jurisdictions. This is sometimes instigated by outside stakeholders and sometimes by internal management of the workers' compensation agency. Good premium and injury rate comparisons exist on a countrywide basis. More progress is being made in detailed benchmarks of system administration.

Conclusion

By almost any metric, the performance of state workers' compensation systems varies greatly. The performance of systems is quite erratic, with large swings in claims, costs and disputes over just a few years. As a result of this dynamic environment, a handful of states "reform" their workers' compensation statutes almost annually. These changes are more the result of interest group fights in the legislature than fact-based public policy analysis. Other states are more incremental and cautious in their system changes, often patterning reforms after other states with successful programs.

The cost of workers' compensation, as measured by insurance rates or benefits paid per worker, undergoes periodic cycles. At present, insurance rates are on an upswing after years of decline. Benefits paid per worker are increasing. Medical cost seems to be the principal cost driver.

States have responded to budgetary pressures in a

variety of ways. Some agencies have gone through virtually no interruption in their staffing or services. Others have seen substantial cutbacks, which have hurt services and system improvements.

Notes

[1] National Council on Compensation Insurance, "2002 Calendar Accident Year Underwriting Results." Data available at: http://www.ncci.com/media/dowloads/cay.xls.

[2] NCCI, Filing Memorandum, Item B-138, 2002. These workers' compensation losses are especially sobering when one considers the fact that New York has relatively modest death benefits, and that the day and hour of the assault reduced the exposure to losses.

References

Eccleston, Stacey, Igor Polevoy, Xiaoping Zhao, and Michael Watson. *The Anatomy of Workers' Compensation Medical Costs and Utilization: Trends and Interstate Comparisons 1996-1999*, Cambridge, MA: Workers Compensation Research Institute, March 2002.

IAIABC Journal. International Association of Industrial Accident Boards and Commissions, published biannually.

Larson's Workers' Compensation (Desk Edition). Matthew-Bender & Co, updated annually.

National Academy of Social Insurance. *Workers' Compensation: Benefits, Coverage, and Costs*." Washington, DC, published annually.

U.S. Department of Labor. *State Workers' Compensation Administrative Profiles*. Washington, DC: U.S. Government Printing Office, October 1996.

U.S. Chamber of Commerce. *Analysis of Workers' Compensation Laws*. Washington, DC, published annually.

Workers' Compensation Policy Review (from John Burton's Workers' Compensation Resources), published quarterly.

About the Author

Gregory Krohm is executive director of the International Association of Industrial Accident Boards and Commissions in Madison, Wis. Prior to this, he served as the administrator for the Wisconsin Division of Workers' Compensation. He teaches courses in private and social insurance at the University of Wisconsin – Madison.

The author is indebted to **Alan Wickman, Melissa Wilson** and **Faith Howe** for insightful comments. This paper expresses the opinion of the author only, and not necessarily those of reviewers or members of the IAIABC.

Trends in State Information and Technology Management

By Jack Gallt, Chris Dixon and Mary Gay Whitmer

The rapid pace of technological change and innovation that transformed government service delivery in the 1990s has been slowed in recent years by the bleak fiscal realities facing most states. Although the demand for online services and 24/7 access to information remains strong, information technology (IT) initiatives must now demonstrate a clear return on investment with an emphasis on system integration and infrastructure consolidation. States are also recognizing the importance of centralized IT oversight, common standards and shared solutions to save money and deliver more effective services to citizens and businesses.

Government operations and the delivery of services have been transformed over the past decade through the application of advanced information and communication technologies. Citizens and businesses routinely interact with state government today via the Internet—paying taxes, renewing licenses and permits, locating information and communicating with their elected representatives. Despite the recent economic downturn, the public demand for more information and greater convenience in dealing with government will continue to increase.

Information technology has made government more accessible, responsive and cost effective, yet it is not enough to simply automate existing practices. The real challenge is to use information technology to implement change across the state enterprise based on a thorough examination of business cases and desired outcomes, making sure limited state resources are spent most effectively. The strategic use of IT can help drive down the administrative expenses of internal functions like human resources, finance and training, and reduce program costs in areas such as health care, human services and criminal justice.

IT Governance

State government IT spending grew steadily during the 1990s, thanks to rising revenues and the need to modernize outdated systems and software. This growth was not always well planned, leading in some cases to overbuilt infrastructures, redundant systems and applications, and large, decentralized IT support organizations.

Most states have addressed these problems by adopting a more disciplined IT governance framework that focuses on improving operational efficiency and business responsiveness. Governance consists of the leadership, organizational structures, direction and processes that ensure information technology sustains and extends the enterprise's mission

and objectives in a planned manner. The most effective structure is one that takes a statewide view of IT, supports horizontal as well as vertical information sharing, moves the state toward conducting business electronically, and leverages limited resources. The position of state chief information officer (CIO) is generally responsible for coordinating state IT investments across the enterprise. State CIOs rely on a variety of means to manage the state's IT resources, including making recommendations for standards, procurement, project management and IT planning activities (see Table A "Statewide Management Responsibilities of the CIO").

A growing number of states have adopting a federated IT model—one that centralizes common infrastructure components and services such as e-mail, data centers and network management, while decentralizing systems and applications unique to individual agencies or departments. This is frequently accompanied by the creation of a statewide IT planning and oversight body designed to establish a common IT vision and improve information sharing and collaboration among agencies. These oversight bodies are typically made up of representatives from state executive branch agencies, the legislative and judicial branches, and the private sector (see Table B "Composition of IT Governing Boards").

Role of the State CIO

While recent state budget crises have not fundamentally changed the role of the state CIO, they have put that role in a new light. First, the deficits have shifted the interests of governors and legislatures away from Web-based services toward an emphasis on back-end cost savings where government conducts internal transactions and shares information across jurisdictions and levels. This has re-oriented the CIO toward systems integration and streamlining with enterprise resource planning (ERP) systems, data center consolidations, e-procurement, and the use of standards to facilitate information sharing across state government via the Internet.

Second, budget deficits have put pressure on the state CIO to bring good news to the table in tough times. State CIOs have been forced to show that they are more than just "techies" and provide the governor and legislature with policy guidance to help find savings through development of statewide IT standards, effective IT project management, and consistent IT procurement to reduce costs and ensure standards compliance. State CIOs are also being called upon to find ways for IT to integrate and automate state business processes, yielding hard savings that can be reallocated to other state priorities.

Finally, budget deficits have forced governors to re-evaluate executive branch structures in search of more efficient arrangements, including how the state manages its information technology assets. State CIOs, who typically report to cabinet heads or the governor directly (see Figure A "State CIO Reporting"), have been successful in making the case that, while they do not provide direct services to citizens, businesses, or other governments, they can provide the infrastructure that allows other agencies to better deliver their services. Thus, the state CIO has become a primary enabler for achieving new efficiencies that cut across all government programs.

Enterprise Architecture

The state CIO is increasingly being asked to help establish and enforce IT policies and standards. Driven by the need to eliminate duplicative spending and encourage interagency data sharing and integration, states are looking to reduce the range of information systems, platforms and applications being used by agencies and departments. Developing an "enterprise architecture" is critical for states in

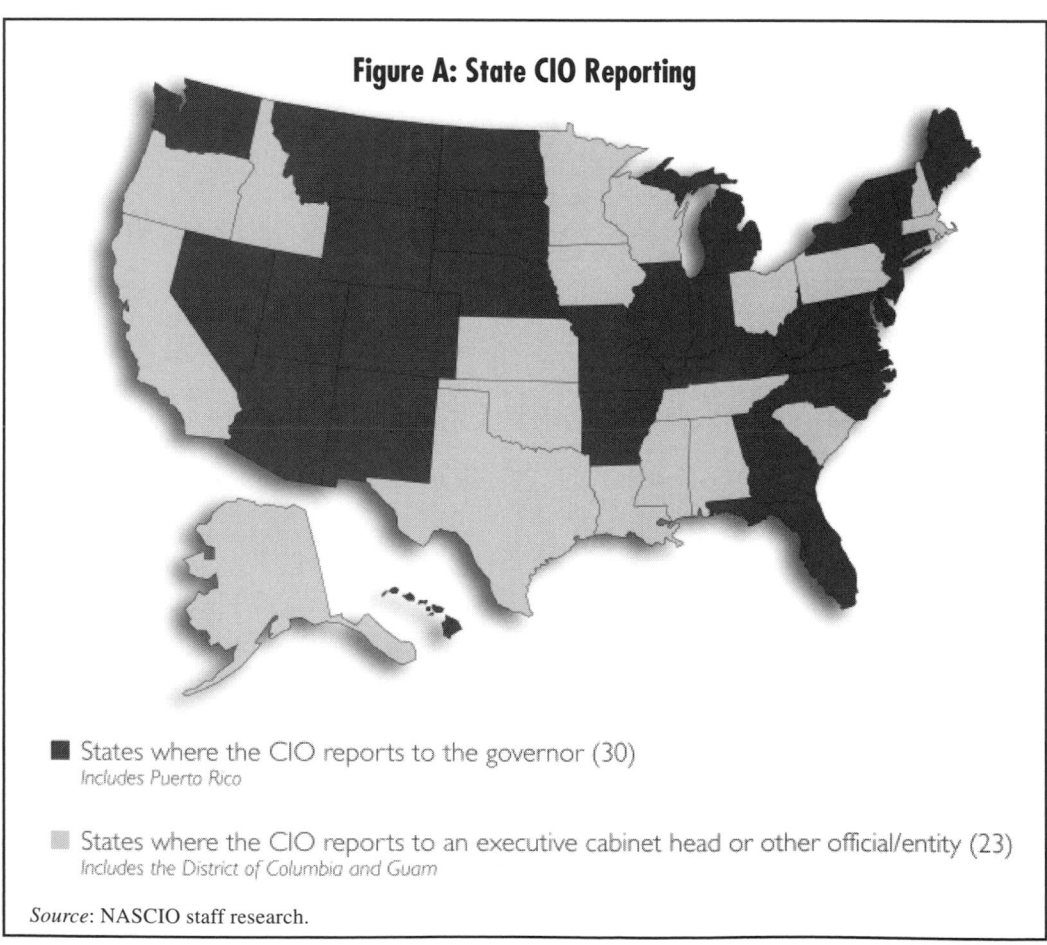

Figure A: State CIO Reporting

■ States where the CIO reports to the governor (30)
Includes Puerto Rico

▪ States where the CIO reports to an executive cabinet head or other official/entity (23)
Includes the District of Columbia and Guam

Source: NASCIO staff research.

meeting the fiscal and programmatic challenges that lie ahead. Enterprise architecture can be described as a methodology for developing an organization's IT support functions and provides the blueprint for the integration of information and services. An adaptive enterprise architecture framework enables information sharing across traditional barriers, enhances government's ability to deliver timely and effective services, and supports agencies in their efforts to improve government functions.

Since 1998, the National Association of State Chief Information Officers' (NASCIO) Enterprise Architecture Program has helped state and local government agencies improve information sharing across government boundaries, as well as position government enterprises for the digital government age. The portfolio of products developed through the program guide enterprises in crafting their own architecture framework and supports the design, implementation and maintenance of their network and system infrastructure.

Business Case Development

As a result of the recent economic downturn, many states have exhausted traditional budget cuts and drawn down their rainy day funds. In light of this difficult economic situation, state CIOs have been working to identify and advocate ways in which technology can streamline government business processes to create new efficiencies and substantial cost savings.

To educate and persuade state government leaders of technology's benefits, state CIOs have worked to develop better business cases for technology-related projects. Keys to developing better state IT business cases include: (1) tailoring them to specific audiences, whether state budget officials, legislators or agency leaders, (2) distilling them into a simple, to-the-point form, (3) and determining ways to calculate the benefits and cost-opportunities associated with new or continued state technology projects, such as through return on investment (ROI) and total cost of ownership (TCO) calculations.

CIOs are also finding that business cases can be used to demonstrate the value of the state IT enterprise in terms of the benefits that state agencies and citizens receive in return for the state's investment in technology.

Procurement

The authority of state CIOs over IT procurement varies from state-to-state (see Table C "Statewide IT Procurement Authority"). However, state CIOs rec-ognize the importance of maximizing the value that states receive from their IT purchases. Through their collective IT procurement experience, the CIOs have identified the following strategies for maximizing the value of IT procurements: (1) garnering volume discounts on the purchase of hardware and software for the state enterprise, (2) streamlining the procurement process to make the purchase of technology more efficient in order to keep pace with the ever-changing technology landscape, and (3) implementing and refining performance-based contracting and benefits funding to maximize vendor performance through incentives and risk sharing.

Security

Chemical, biological, radiological, nuclear and other threats to the critical infrastructure of the states have driven a new emphasis on security. The technological aspects of detecting, preventing or recovering from various types of attacks have brought the state CIO into contact with public health, public safety, law enforcement, and emergency management officials who are seeking to deploy sensors and communications infrastructure as part of a comprehensive counter-terrorism effort. As part of this first response team, state CIOs are instrumental in providing statewide wireless communications (i.e., radio) interoperability as well as other reliable telecommunications infrastructure that can support the necessary information gathering and sharing on a daily basis and during emergencies.

As custodians of state government's critical information assets, state CIOs are charged with securing IT facilities (e.g., data and operations centers), and networks from a variety of physical and electronic-based threats (e.g., viruses, worms, Web site defacements, server hijackings, etc.) that can originate from both inside and outside of the state IT organization. Also, a variety of state and federal privacy mandates have driven states to implement strong access controls on information systems in order to protect citizens' personal information from exposure to unauthorized parties. These new responsibilities have led nearly every state to establish a state chief information security officer (CISO) position, reporting to the CIO, and working closely with the rest of the state's homeland security leadership.

Privacy

State government collects and uses citizens' personal and confidential information for a wide range of reasons, from providing benefits to protecting the public's safety. While the collection of such information is by no means a new phenomenon, the technological advances of the past several years have made government information more accessible than ever before and raised concerns regarding how to protect citizens' privacy.

Prior to the technological revolution, government information was locked away in paper form within agency file cabinets, which provided it a degree of obscurity. In moving that information to a form that is electronically accessible via government databases and Internet-enabled computer systems, states have had to address three fundamental questions: (1) What is the effect of moving confidential data from paper to an electronic medium? (2) How can technology best be used to ensure compliance with existing and evolving privacy policies? (3) What is the impact that technology may have on information made available through open access laws?

The state CIOs play an important role in addressing these questions. To that end, many CIOs are now evaluating and modernizing existing state privacy policies and educating state agencies, legislators and others about the importance of citizens' confidence in state government's ability to protect the privacy of their personal information.

In recent years, Congress has enacted legislation to protect the privacy of certain types of personal information. For example, the Health Insurance Portability and Accountability Act of 1996 (HIPAA) extends privacy protections to individually identifiable health information. The CIOs also are taking steps to educate state agencies about their responsibilities under HIPAA and other federal privacy laws and what they need to do to comply with such laws.

Conclusion

The effective management of information technology assets is an important issue for state government. A decline in state revenues does not have to mean a decline in state IT capability. Technology should be viewed as an integral part of effective program and policy solutions and the state CIO can serve as an important resource in all business process and capital planning decisions.

References

Deloitte Research. *Cutting Fat, Adding Muscle: The Power of Information Technology in Addressing Budget Shortfalls*. New York, NY: Deloitte Research, 2003, http://www.dc.com/Insights/research/public/cutting_fat.asp.

National Association of State Chief Information Officers. *Business Case Basics and Beyond: A Primer on State Government IT Business Cases*. Lexington, KY: National Association of State Chief Information Officers, 2003.

National Association of State Chief Information Officers. *Compendium of Digital Government in the States*. Lexington, KY: National Association of State Chief Information Officers, 2003.

National Association of State Chief Information Officers. *Federal Privacy Law Compendium*. Lexington, KY: National Association of State Chief Information Officers, 2003.

National Association of State Chief Information Officers. *Innovative Funding for Innovative State IT: New Trends and Approaches for State IT Funding*. Lexington, KY: National Association of State Chief Information Officers, 2003.

National Association of State Chief Information Officers. *Transition Handbook*. Lexington, KY: National Association of State Chief Information Officers, 2002, https://www.nascio.org/publications/transition_handbook.pdf.

National Governors Association. *Using Information Technology to Transform State Government*. Washington, D.C.: National Governors Association, 2003, http://www.nga.org/center/divisions/1,1188,C_ISSUE_BRIEF^D_5151,00.html.

About the Authors

Jack Gallt is an issues coordinator for the National Association for State Chief Information Officers (NASCIO) with responsibility for coordinating association activities in the areas of wireless technology, spectrum management, public safety communications and criminal justice information sharing.

Chris Dixon is an issues coordinator for the National Association for State Chief Information Officers (NASCIO) with responsibility for coordinating association activities in the areas of digital government, homeland security, cybersecurity and economic development.

Mary Gay Whitmer is an issues coordinator for the National Association for State Chief Information Officers (NASCIO) with responsibility for coordinating association activities in the areas of privacy, business case development, innovative funding and procurement.

Table A
STATEWIDE MANAGEMENT RESPONSIBILITIES OF THE CIO

State or other jurisdiction	Architecture/ Standards Development	Budgeting	HR/ Hiring	Outsourcing	Personnel Policy	Planning	Policies	Privacy Policies	Procurement	Project Management	System Auditing	Training
Alabama	N.A.	N.A.	N.A.	N.A.	N.A.	N.A.	N.A.	N.A.	N.A.	N.A.	N.A.	N.A.
Alaska	N.A.	N.A.	N.A.	N.A.	N.A.	N.A.	N.A.	N.A.	N.A.	N.A.	N.A.	N.A.
Arizona	RAM	RA	...	RAM	...	RA	RAM	RAM	RAM	RA	RAM	RA
Arkansas	RAM	R	...	RAM	R	RAM	RAM	RAM	RAM	RM	RAM	R
California	RA	R	R	RA	RAM	R	AM	RAM	AM	RA	RAM	RAM
Colorado	N.A.	N.A.	N.A.	N.A.	N.A.	N.A.	N.A.	N.A.	N.A.	N.A.	N.A.	N.A.
Connecticut	RAM	RA	R	RAM	RAM	R	RAM	RAM	RAM	RAM	RAM	RAM
Delaware	RA	RAM	R	RAM	R	RA	RAM	RAM	RM	R	R	R
Florida	RA	R	...	R	...	R	RA	RA	...	...	R	...
Georgia	RAM	RA	R	RAM	R	R	RAM	RAM	RAM	RAM	RAM	RAM
Hawaii	RAM	...	...	R	R	RM	RAM	RM	RM	R	R	R
Idaho	RA	A		R		RAM	RA	RAM	RA	RAM	A	A
Illinois	N.A.	N.A.	N.A.	N.A.	N.A.	N.A.	N.A.	N.A.	N.A.	N.A.	N.A.	N.A.
Indiana	N.A.	N.A.	N.A.	N.A.	N.A.	N.A.	N.A.	N.A.	N.A.	N.A.	N.A.	N.A.
Iowa	RAM	R	...	RAM	R	RA	RA	RAM	RA	RAM	RAM	R
Kansas	RAM	RAM	R	A	AM	R	RAM	RAM	RAM	RA	RAM	R
Kentucky	RAM	RA	...	RAM	R	RA	RAM	RA	RM	RA	RA	R
Louisiana	RA	RA	...	RA	M	RA	RA	RA	RA	RA	RA	...
Maine	RM	R	R	A	R	R	RAM	RAM	RAM	A	R	R
Maryland	RAM	R	RA	RAM	AM	RAM	RAM	RAM	RAM	RAM	RAM	R
Massachusetts	N.A.	N.A.	N.A.	N.A.	N.A.	N.A.	N.A.	N.A.	N.A.	N.A.	N.A.	N.A.
Michigan	RAM	RAM	RAM	RAM	R	RAM	RAM	RAM	RAM	RAM	RAM	RAM
Minnesota	M	AM	RAM	A	RM	RAM	M	M	M	M	A	A
Mississippi	RAM	R	R	RAM	RA	RAM	RAM	R	RAM	RAM	R	RAM
Missouri	RAM	R	...	...	R	RAM	RA	RA	R	...	RAM	...
Montana	RM	R	...	AM	...	AM	AM	AM	RAM	AM	M	RM
Nebraska	N.A.	N.A.	N.A.	N.A.	N.A.	N.A.	N.A.	N.A.	N.A.	N.A.	N.A.	N.A.
Nevada	R	A	RA	RAM	R	RAM	RAM	RA	RA	RAM	A	R
New Hampshire	AM	RA	...	RAM	R	AM	AM	AM	RA	RA	R	R
New Jersey	RAM	RM	...	AM	R	RAM	RA	R	RAM	RAM	RM	RM
New Mexico	RM	RAM	R	RAM	R	RAM	RM	RM	RAM	RM	RAM	...
New York	RAM	R	...	R	R	RAM	RAM	RAM	RAM	M	M	R
North Carolina	R	R	...	R	...	R	A	A	R	AM	A	...
North Dakota	RAM	RM	...	A	R	RA	RAM	RAM	RAM	RA	RA	R
Ohio	RAM	...	...	...	...	RM	RAM	RAM	RAM	RA	RA	...
Oklahoma	N.A.	N.A.	N.A.	N.A.	N.A.	N.A.	N.A.	N.A.	N.A.	N.A.	N.A.	N.A.
Oregon	RAM	R	...	R	...	RAM	RAM	RAM	RAM	RAM	...	R
Pennsylvania	RAM	RAM	RA	RAM	R	RAM	AM	AM	R	RAM	RAM	RAM
Rhode Island	RA	R	R	R	R	RA	RA	RA	RA	R	R	R
South Carolina	R	...	...	...	...	...	R	A	A	M	...	A
South Dakota	RAM	RAM	RAM	RAM	RAM	RAM	RAM	RAM	RAM	RAM	RAM	RAM
Tennessee	RAM	R	...	RA	...	R	R	RAM	R	RAM	RAM	...
Texas	RA	R	...	RAM	R	A	RA	RAM	RA	RAM	R	RA
Utah	RAM	RA	R	RAM	RA	R	RAM	RAM	RA	RAM	RAM	R
Vermont	RAM	...	...	A	...	...	RAM	RAM	RAM	A	A	...
Virginia	A	A	...	RA	A	R	R	AM	R	AM	RAM	A
Washington	A	R	...	...	...	RM	M	M	RAM	RAM	...	...
West Virginia	RA	...	...	RA	R	RAM	RAM	R	RA	RA	RA	RA
Wisconsin	RAM	R	...	R	R	R	RAM	RA	RA	R	M	M
Wyoming	A	RA	...	RA	...	R	R	...	RA	RA	...	R
Dist. Of Columbia	RAM	RAM	R	RAM	R	R	RAM	RAM	RAM	A	RAM	...
Count*	43	38	17	39	31	41	43	42	42	41	39	33

Source: National Association of State Chief Information Officers, December 2003.

Note: This figure represents the number of states responding affirmatively (i.e., R, A, or M) in each category.

Key:

R—Recommend agency practices.

A—Approves agency practices.

M—Manages for agencies.

. . .—Not applicable.

N.A. — Not available.

Table B
COMPOSITION OF IT GOVERNING BOARDS

State or other jurisdiction	Number of representatives from each category								CIO role on board
	Agency	Elected officials	Judicial branch	Legislative branch	Local government	Public education	Private sector	Other	
Alabama	N.A.	N.A.	N.A.	N.A.	N.A.	N.A.	N.A.	N.A.	N.A.
Alaska	N.A.	N.A.	N.A.	N.A.	N.A.	N.A.	N.A.	N.A.	N.A.
Arizona	4	...	1	2	1	1	4	1	Chair or Leader
Arkansas	5	...	...	...	...	1	1	...	Chair or Leader
California	...............Under consideration...............								Member (voting)
Colorado	N.A.	N.A.	N.A.	N.A.	N.A.	N.A.	N.A.	N.A.	N.A.
Connecticut	...	...	...	...	...	...	...	1	Chair or Leader
Delaware	2	1	1	1	...	...	...	4	Chair or Leader
Florida	...	...	...	...	...	...	...	...	Not applicable
Georgia	...	...	1	4	...	...	7	...	Other leadership role
Hawaii	...	...	...	...	...	...	...	...	Not applicable
Idaho	3	...	1	4	1	2	2	2	Chair or Leader
Illinois	N.A.	N.A.	N.A.	N.A.	N.A.	N.A.	N.A.	N.A.	N.A.
Indiana	N.A.	N.A.	N.A.	N.A.	N.A.	N.A.	N.A.	N.A.	N.A.
Iowa	7	...	1	4	...	...	5	2	Member (voting)
Kansas	4	...	2	1	2	1	3	4	Member (voting)
Kentucky	17	5	1	1	...	2	...	...	Chair or Leader
Louisiana	12	8	1	2	...	1	5	1	Other leadership role
Maine	8	1	1	1	...	2	2	5	Other leadership role
Maryland	12	1	1	4	1	3	6	5	Other leadership role
Massachusetts	N.A.	N.A.	N.A.	N.A.	N.A.	N.A.	N.A.	N.A.	N.A.
Michigan	19	...	1	3	...	...	...	1	...
Minnesota	3	...	1	4	...	1	8	1	Chair or Leader
Mississippi	...	...	...	2	...	...	...	5	Advisory capacity only
Missouri	31	...	1	2	...	...	...	...	Member (non-voting)
Montana	9	1	1	3	2	2	1	...	Member (voting)
Nebraska	N.A.	N.A.	N.A.	N.A.	N.A.	N.A.	N.A.	N.A.	N.A.
Nevada	...............Composition at governor's discretion...............								
New Hampshire	8	...	...	1	2	...	2	5	Member (voting)
New Jersey	4	...	...	...	...	...	...	3	Chair or Leader
New Mexico	4	...	2	2	...	2	5	3	Chair or Leader
New York	...	...	...	...	...	...	...	80	Chair or Leader
North Carolina	5	5	1	...	2	2	4	3	Member (non-voting)
North Dakota	3	...	...	...	...	2	1	8	Member (non-voting)
Ohio	...	...	...	...	...	...	...	...	Other leadership role
Oklahoma	N.A.	N.A.	N.A.	N.A.	N.A.	N.A.	N.A.	N.A.	N.A.
Oregon	5	...	...	...	...	...	1	...	Advisory capacity only
Pennsylvania	...	...	...	...	...	...	...	...	Not applicable
Rhode Island	5	1	...	2	2	3	3	2	Chair or Leader
South Carolina	...	...	...	...	...	...	...	...	Not applicable
South Dakota	...	...	...	...	...	...	...	...	Not applicable
Tennessee	2	...	1	7	...	...	2	3	Other leadership role
Texas	7	...	...	...	...	...	...	3	Other leadership role
Utah	...	...	...	...	...	...	...	...	Other leadership role
Vermont	9	1	1	1	...	...	...	...	Chair or Leader
Virginia	...	...	...	...	...	...	...	...	Chair or Leader
Washington	1	...	1	4	...	2	2	5	Member (voting)
West Virginia	13	6	1	1	...	1	...	4	Other leadership role
Wisconsin	13	1	...	...	4	2	...	...	Chair or Leader
Wyoming	3	5	...	...	...	...	...	...	Advisory capacity only
Dist. Of Columbia	...	...	...	...	...	...	...	...	Other leadership role
Count*	28	13	20	22	9	17	20	22	

Source: National Association of State Chief Information Officers, December 2003.

Note: This figure represents the number of states responding affirmatively in each category.

. . . — Not applicable.

N.A. — Not available.

Table C
STATEWIDE IT PROCUREMENT RESPONSIBILITY

State or other jurisdiction	Hardware	Software	Services
Alabama	N.A.	N.A.	N.A.
Alaska	N.A.	N.A.	N.A.
Arizona	CPO	CPO	CPO
Arkansas	Shared	Shared	Shared
California	CPO	CPO	CPO
Colorado	N.A.	N.A.	N.A.
Connecticut	ITO	ITO	ITO
Delaware	Shared	Shared	Shared
Florida	ITO	ITO	ITO
Georgia	ITO	ITO	ITO
Hawaii	Shared	Shared	Shared
Idaho	Shared	Shared	Shared
Illinois	N.A.	N.A.	N.A.
Indiana	N.A.	N.A.	N.A.
Iowa	ITO	ITO	ITO
Kansas	Shared	Shared	Shared
Kentucky	Shared	Shared	Shared
Louisiana	CPO	CPO	CPO
Maine	ITO	ITO	ITO
Maryland	Shared	Shared	Shared
Massachusetts	N.A.	N.A.	N.A.
Michigan	Shared	Shared	Shared
Minnesota	Shared	Shared	ITO
Mississippi	ITO	ITO	ITO
Missouri	CPO	CPO	CPO
Montana	Shared	Shared	Shared
Nebraska	N.A.	N.A.	N.A.
Nevada	ITO	Shared	ITO
New Hampshire	Shared	Shared	Shared
New Jersey	Shared	Shared	Shared
New Mexico	Shared	Shared	Shared
New York	Shared	Shared	Shared
North Carolina	ITO	ITO	ITO
North Dakota	Shared	Shared	ITO
Ohio	ITO	ITO	ITO
Oklahoma	N.A.	N.A.	N.A.
Oregon	Shared	Shared	Shared
Pennsylvania	CPO	CPO	ITO
Rhode Island	CPO	CPO	CPO
South Carolina	Shared	Shared	Shared
South Dakota	Shared	Shared	Shared
Tennessee	No data	CPO	ITO
Texas	ITO	ITO	ITO
Utah	CPO	CPO	CPO
Vermont	Shared	Shared	ITO
Virginia	Shared	Shared	CPO
Washington	Shared	Shared	Shared
West Virginia	Shared	Shared	Shared
Wisconsin	ITO	ITO	ITO
Wyoming	Shared	Shared	Shared
District of Columbia	Shared	Shared	Shared

Source: The National Association of State Chief Information Officers, December 2003.

Key:
ITO—IT Office/Department.
CPO—Central Procurement Office.
Shared—Shared responsibilities between ITO and CPO.
N.A.—Not available.

Trends and Issues in State Professional Licensing
By Pam Brinegar

In what was once one of the fastest growing areas of state government, legislators now employ stringent criteria to determine when new professions should be regulated. Consequently, many emerging professions opt for credentialing in the private sector, although for some of these, a circular relationship is developing between private and public credentialing. Other trends and issues for professional regulators include new technological tools, shifting economic terrain, increased consumer involvement and international trade agreements.

Professional and occupational licensing is a field that often remains out of public view, yet has tremendous economic impact. As Paul Teske puts it, "Regulation is one of the most important activities that governments perform, because it constrains and shapes the important decisions that economic actors make. Whether regulation is prominent, as in the antitrust case against Microsoft, or behind the scenes, like the occupational regulation of lawyers and doctors, its political-economic effects are important and pervasive throughout the economy. Regulation also largely imposes costs on private actors, so its effects do not show up clearly in public budgets, as do the effects of taxation and government spending patterns."[1]

Regulatory Agencies

There are several good primers on how professional and occupational licensing agencies are structured and what basic functions they perform.[2] Three levels of state regulation exist: licensure, certification and registration, ranging from the most to least restrictive respectively.[3] Essentially, working under an enabling statute and regulations, agencies qualify candidates for licensure through checking their educational[4] and other credentials against state requirements, administering an examination and issuing licenses to those who successfully meet all criteria. Their functions include license renewals, continuing education and professional discipline. Currently, in 37 states and the District of Columbia, professions are regulated by central agencies which share varying degrees of administrative tasks with the licensing boards. In the other states, licensing boards are independent agencies. Aside from ensuring resources to carry out their missions (a concern which has plagued almost all state agencies in recent years), issues of currency for state regulators include labor shortages, practitioner quality assurance, examination fraud, identity theft, use of new technological tools, professional mobility and federal initiatives. This article will touch on three of these as well as on the emerging trends surrounding

the proliferation of voluntary credentialing and international trade agreements.

Quality Assurance

One of the most critical issues facing state lawmakers is determining how to ensure that licensed practitioners are competent throughout their practical careers. The initial licensure process in any profession is established to ensure that candidates have met the minimum requirements for entry into professional practice. Practitioners rarely spend their lives performing the tasks on which they were originally evaluated for licensure, and the question becomes how to ensure continuing fitness to practice. Many states require continuing education programs for at least some regulated professions, but that requirement is far from uniform for most professions.[5] Critics of continuing education have expressed concern that it may not be targeted to what the licensee does on a daily basis and that it has failed to stop practitioner incompetence. Often, it is only through the disciplinary process that a practitioner's deficiencies are addressed. As is the case in other countries, some U.S. professions are now considering the use of practitioner self-assessment tools to identify continuing educational needs.

Technology

Use of new technology is the area of fastest growth and the one most pervasively influencing state regulation. This circumstance affects the educational preparation of the professional, their credentialing (or licensing), service delivery, and demonstration of continued competence. Technology affords greater access as candidates can take computerized licensing examinations in even remote locations while consumers can verify licensees and check for disciplinary actions online. Questions about balancing access to information by consumers versus practitioners' rights have led to interesting debates. New concerns about the security of tests and facilities abound, as do issues regarding online provision of services or the supply of drugs from overseas.

Federal Initiatives

The federal government remains reluctant to become involved in state professional licensing, although there are a few recent exceptions. Following the exposure of dubious and sometimes outright fraudulent accounting practices in major U.S. firms, the accounting profession found itself under scrutiny from the government, consumers and concerned practitioners. A federal reform measure designed to restore investor confidence in the markets and in the credibility of financial statements, The Investor Protection, Auditor Reform, and Transparency Act of 2002 (known as the Sarbanes-Oxley Act) established a Public Company Accounting Oversight Board. The board must perform annual inspections of accounting firms that audit 100 or more public companies and at least tri-annual inspections of other public company auditors. Auditors of publicly held companies may not provide other services to those companies.[6] In May 2002, the U.S. General Accounting Office issued a comprehensive report on domestic auditing which is available online.[7]

P.L. 106-50, known as The Veterans Small Business and Entrepreneurship Act, was passed "to create uniform guidelines and standards for the professional certification of members of the Armed Services to aid in their efficient and orderly transition to civilian occupations and professions and to remove potential barriers in the areas of licensure and certification." Discussion has begun on how former military personnel can receive appropriate state-issued credentials for their military training.

In an effort to interest the federal government in standardizing professional requirements, the issue of whether states really have the presumed right to regulate health care practitioners within their borders has been raised and is likely to become an issue in the future if mobility among countries becomes easier than among states.[8] Despite this, Alderson and Montesano's assessment that "in both Canada and the United States, where the power to regulate is derived from a federal constitution, any attempts to legislate a national regulatory regime would entail serious and profound consequences involving the nature of federalism as well as the very nature of the polities themselves"[9] is accurate.

Proliferation of Voluntary Credentialing

Just over 50 years ago, The Council of State Governments (CSG) published an instrumental report on professional regulation that identified "the problem of licensing occupations" as the rate at which new professions were being regulated by the states.[10] The rate continued unabated until the number of regulated professions grew to more than 1,100 (see Tables A and B for selected professions). Of this number, fewer than 60, or less than 6 percent, of these are regulated by all of the states. It is almost unheard of for any two states to agree on the regulatory standards for even a single profession, although interstate professional mobility for some professions is accomplished through endorsement agreements in which jurisdictions agree to accept each other's licensing requirements.

Legislatures intended that licensing and renewal fees would cover the cost of regulating professions, but this was often not the case. The high cost of developing a defensible examination could be difficult to recover, and the expense of disciplining incompetent and unethical practitioners was often greater than anticipated. Also, they increasingly began to realize that in many cases, state oversight had been granted for inappropriate reasons, such as protection of the professionals instead of the public. Schoon and Smith clarify the appropriate focus:

> By stating that the public is the primary stakeholder of licensure activities, we must also state who or what is not a stakeholder. Included in this group are members of the licensed profession, the schools that prepare and train these professionals, the companies that provide resources to the profession, or any other group that has any interest in the practice of the profession other than public protection.[11]

Throughout the country, concerned about rising costs and armed with a recently published framework for evaluating when licensure was appropriate,[12] state houses began to refuse regulation to new petitioners. Early control measures included the use of sunset[13] and sunrise[14] legislation, neither of which was entirely satisfactory, although the process works quite well today.[15]

Largely as a result of the difficulty of achieving state licensure, emerging professions increasingly evaluate and certify practitioners through private sector voluntary credentialing organizations. These organizations usually require that members meet standards of professional practice, codes of ethics and continuing education. They also may have mechanisms for professional discipline and are likely to require recertification of credential holders. Many voluntary groups submit their certification programs to a third-party accreditation organization such as the

National Organization for Competency Assurance or the American National Standards Institute to ensure that their programs are properly structured to ensure protection of consumers.

An interesting twist is that once a group of the voluntarily credentialed becomes large enough, it may choose to seek state licensure. Such groups will have developed sufficient resources to meet initial legislative audit requirements and will have paid for the development of a defensible credentialing examination that can be used as the standard for state regulation, helping to make it cost effective for the state to proceed with licensing of the profession. Often this initiative is tied to a desire to gain government reimbursement for services that licensing can provide.

Trade Agreements

Some professions (notably accountants, architects, engineering, education and attorneys) have worked with the World Trade Organization (WTO) and the Office of the United States Trade Representative to enter into or plan for agreements intended to facilitate mutual recognition of licensees among member countries. The WTO oversees the General Agreement on Trade in Services (GATS) which permits mutual recognition either through a harmonization of local regulations or direct agreement between member countries. Since services, including the professions and occupations, represent the fastest growing sector of the global economy, they have been included in the multilateral trade negotiations since January 2000.

The North American Free Trade Agreement (NAFTA) also provides a structure through which individual professions and their regulatory bodies may reach agreement on the terms for mutual recognition of professional credentials. Under both treaties, agreements reached between countries are not binding on the states in the United States, which receive the agreement terms in the form of recommendations which they individually may or may not incorporate into their statutes or regulations.

Consumer Involvement

Some proponents of voluntary credentialing and of federal standards for professions feel that state licensure is too restrictive to continue as a model for regulating professionals. Indeed, after decades of studying state regulation, licensing policy pioneer Ben Shimberg observed that:

> In theory, licensing may have seemed like a good way of rectifying market failure occasioned by a lack of adequate information upon which consumers could base judgments about the competence

of service providers or, even more serious, by the lack of constraints on the practice of occupation with the potential for danger to the health, safety and welfare of the public.... However, the manner in which licensure has functioned over the past century raises questions about how well it has actually served the public.[16]

Shimberg's charge has been difficult to answer because what serves the public's interest has never been defined. In the past, the public has been very little aware of or involved in professional regulation. Consumers more often tried to seek redress through the courts than through state professional discipline processes. Today, there is a growing collaborative effort between individuals and those who provide professional services to them, including a growing understanding of the role of regulatory agencies. In part because of the enormous amount of information freely available through the Internet, today's consumers are better informed, presented with more choices than ever before, and are making more sophisticated demands. At the same time, there is a trend toward a growing environmental awareness on the part of regulatory agencies and, as more readily shareable information grows, they are becoming much less insular. As regulatory agencies demystify the system and encourage access, the public has become much less peripheral to the regulatory process, and their interests are finally becoming defined.

Notes

[1] P. Teske, "State Legislative Oversight of Regulation," Second Annual Conference on State Politics and Policy: Legislatures and Representation in the U.S. States, University of Wisconsin-Milwaukee, May 25, 2002.

[2] See for example K. Schmitt and B. Shimberg, *Demystifying Occupational and Professional Regulation: Answers to Questions You May Have Been Afraid to Ask*, (Lexington, KY: The Council on Licensure, Enforcement and Regulation, 1996).

[3] Licensure, the most restrictive form of state regulation, specifies that it is illegal to practice a state-licensed profession without meeting state-defined standards, usually consisting of at least specified educational and additional examination requirements. No one without a license may practice the profession as defined in a scope-of-practice act. Certification, also known as title protection, may use requirements similar to those for licensure, but it does not prevent individuals from performing the tasks of the profession as long as they do not use the regulated title. The term certification is widely used in the private sector as well, which is a source of considerable confusion not only for consumers, but for those involved with state and voluntary certification programs as well. Registration, the least restrictive form of state regulation, usually consists of little more than requiring individuals to file their names, addresses and qualifications with a designated state agency.

[4] Modern state professional regulation can be traced in part to an 1889 U.S. Supreme Court *Dent v. West Virginia* decision which held that a state licensing board could determine the educational requirements necessary to hold a license for practicing medicine. Before that decision, the practice of a profession was widely considered an individual property right and candidates could set their own course of preparation, often consisting of an apprenticeship during which they would "read the law" with a licensed attorney or practice medicine under the supervision of a licensed physician. By 1860 professional standards for lawyers (and other professions) had become virtually nonexistent and professional associations began to form for the primary purpose of disbarring the most incompetent practitioners in an effort to salvage the profession's reputation. (A.J. Sestric, *Journal of the Missouri Bar*, July-August 1997). The relationship between these associations, which represented the interests of the professions, and the government agencies, which existed to protect the health and welfare of a state's citizens, has been an uneasy one. The original licensing boards were comprised of members of the professional association since they were the area experts; however, over time, concerns developed regarding whether these board members could fairly represent the interests of both the licensees and the consumers. In response board composition has changed considerably, reducing or eliminating the number of board members who can represent professional associations and adding consumer members.

[5] Continuing education for selected professions: http://www.clearhq.org/fall_news_03_CErequirements.htm.

[6] For a summary of all provisions in the act, see http://www.tscpa.org/welcome/tscpaSum.html.

[7] *The Accounting Profession: Status of Panel on Audit Effectiveness Recommendations to Enhance the Self-Regulatory System*, http://www.gao.gov/new. items/d02411.pdf.

[8] Historically, under Article X of the U.S. Constitution, states have the authority to regulate activities that affect the health, safety and welfare of their citizens including the practice of the healing arts within their borders. However, the states' power to regulate health care may not be absolute because the commerce clause of the Constitution limits states' ability to erect barriers against interstate trade and the practice of health care has been held to be interstate trade for the purposes of antitrust laws. Interestingly, the potential conflict between the states' power to regulate health professionals and the prohibition against restraints on interstate commerce has not been addressed by the courts. States may regulate matters of "legitimate local concern" even though interstate commerce may be affected. U.S. Department of Commerce, Telemedicine Report to Congress, 1997. Report online: http://www.ntia.doc.gov/reports/telemed/legal.htm.

[9] D. Alderson and D. Montesano, *Regulating, De-Regulating and Changing Scopes of Practice in the Health Professions: A Jurisdictional Review*, (A Report Prepared for the Ontario Health Professions Regulatory Advisory Council, April 2003).

[10] *Occupational Licensing Legislation in the States*, (Chicago: The Council of State Governments, 1952). CSG hypothesized that this uncontrolled situation was directly related to basic economic, societal and governmental trends in the United States including growing urban population and large-scale manufacturing. These were accompanied by an increased use of government to regulate portions of the economy for the "benefit of the people as a whole." The authors wrote that "over the span of the last two generations, there has been [such] an extraordinary increase in state legislation requiring governmental examination and licensure…that today there are at least seventy-five different professions, skills, trades or other occupations for which varying combinations of qualifications, examinations and licenses are required in order to practice." Of those 75 professions, only 14, or approximately 19 percent, were regulated by all of the then 48 states.

[11] C.G. Schoon and I.L. Smith, "The Licensure and Certification Mission," *The Licensure and Certification Mission*, (New York: Professional Examination Service, 2000).

[12] B. Shimberg and D. Roederer, *Questions a Legislator Should Ask*. 2d., K. Schmitt, ed., (Lexington, KY, The Council on Licensure, Enforcement and Regulation, 1994).

This influential pamphlet said that regulation should meet a public need, provide the minimum amount of oversight to meet that need, avoid overlap with other regulated services, provide for continued competence and professional discipline, and involve the public in the process. In other words, it educated legislators to understand that the only valid reason to regulate a profession is to protect consumers from any harm they may experience as a result of practice of the profession or occupation.

[13] Sunset is the automatic termination of regulatory boards and agencies unless legislative action is taken to reinstate them. Ultimately, 36 states adopted sunset legislation. The most common outcomes of sunset reviews were not terminations of agencies and boards as predicted, but numerous administrative and structural changes.

[14] Sunrise is a process under which an occupation or profession wishing to receive state certification or licensure must propose the components of the legislation, along with cost and benefit estimates of the proposed regulation. The profession must then convince the legislators that consumers will be unduly harmed if the proposed legislation is not adopted. At least 19 states adopted sunrise legislation.

[15] What is more common at this time is the statutory inclusion of sunset provisions in new laws as well as the periodic examination of agencies through performance audits, also known as legislative or evaluation audits. In some states, the process is carried out through the state auditor's office, while in others, a branch of the legislative research agency conducts the reviews.

Sample reports are available through the National Association of State Auditors, Comptrollers and Treasurers Audit Report Search Site http://www.osc.state.ny.us/nsaa/.

[16] B. Shimberg, "The Role That Licensure Plays in Society," *The Licensure and Certification Mission*, (New York: Professional Examination Service, 2000).

About the Author

Pam Brinegar is the executive director of The Council on Licensure, Enforcement and Regulation (CLEAR), which provides educational programs for professional licensing officials. CLEAR is an affiliate of The Council of State Governments.

Table A
STATE REGULATION OF SELECTED NON-HEALTH OCCUPATIONS AND PROFESSIONS: NOVEMBER 2003

State or other jurisdiction	Accountant, Certified Public	Architect	Auctioneer	Barber	Cosmetologist	Embalmer (a)	Engineer, Professional (b)	Funeral Director	Insurance Agent	Insurance Broker	Landscape Architect	Polygraph Examiner	Real Estate Agent	Real Estate Broker	Surveyor, Land
Alabama	L	L	L	…	L	L	L	L	L	L	L	L	L	L	L
Alaska	L	L	…	L	L	L	L	L	L	L	…	L	L	L	L
Arizona	L	L	L	L	L	L	L	L	L	L	…	L	L	L	L
Arkansas	L	L	L	L	L	L	L	L	L	L	L	L	L	L	L
California	L	L	…	L	L	L	L	L	L	L	…	L	L	L	L
Colorado	L	L	…	L	L	…	L	…	L	L	…	L	L	L	L
Connecticut	L	L	…	L	L	L	L	L	L	L	C	…	L	L	L
Delaware	L	L	L	L	L	L	…	L	L	L	L	…	L	L	L
Florida	L	L	L	L	L	L	L	L	L	L	…	L	L	L	L
Georgia	L	L	L	L	L	L	L	L	L	L	…	L	L	L	L
Hawaii	L	L	…	L	L	L	L	L	L	L	…	L	L	L	L
Idaho	L	L	…	L	L	…	L	L	L	L	L	…	L	L	L
Illinois	L	L	L	L	L	L	L	L	L	L	…	L	L	L	L
Indiana	L	L	L	L	L	L	L	L	L	L	L	…	L	L	L
Iowa	L	L	…	L	L	…	L	L	L	L	L	L	L	L	L
Kansas	L	L	…	L	L	L	L	L	L	L	L	…	L	L	L
Kentucky	L	L	L	L	L	L	L	L	L	L	…	L	L	L	L
Louisiana	L	L	L	L	L	L	L	L	L	L	L	L	L	L	L
Maine	L	L	L	L	L	L	L	L	L	L	L	L	L	L	L
Maryland	L	L	…	L	L	…	L	L	L	L	…	L	L	L	L
Massachusetts	L	L	L	L	L	L	L	L	L	L	L	L	L	L	L
Michigan	L	L	…	L	L	…	L	L	L	L	…	L	L	L	L
Minnesota	L	L	L	L	L	…	L	L	L	L	…	L	L	L	L
Mississippi	L	L	L	L	L	L	L	L	L	L	…	L	L	L	L
Missouri	L	L	L	L	L	L	L	L	L	L	L	L	L	L	L
Montana	L	L	…	L	L	L	L	L	L	L	…	L	L	L	L
Nebraska	L	L	…	L	L	L	L	L	L	L	L	L	L	L	L
Nevada	L	L	L	L	L	L	L	L	L	L	L	L	L	L	L
New Hampshire	L	L	L	L	L	L	L	L	L	L	L	…	L	L	L
New Jersey	L	L	…	L	L	…	L	L	L	L	…	L	L	L	L
New Mexico	L	L	…	L	L	L	L	L	L	L	L	L	L	L	L
New York	L	L	…	L	L	L	L	L	L	L	L	…	L	L	L
North Carolina	L	L	L	L	L	L	L	L	L	L	C	L	L	L	L
North Dakota	L	L	L	L	L	L	L	L	L	L	L	L	L	L	L
Ohio	L	L	L	L	L	L	L	L	L	L	L	…	L	L	L
Oklahoma	L	L	…	L	L	L	L	L	L	L	L	L	L	L	L
Oregon	L	L	…	L	L	L	L	L	L	L	…	L	L	L	L
Pennsylvania	L	L	L	L	L	…	L	L	L	L	L	…	L	L	L
Rhode Island	L	L	L	L	L	L	L	L	L	L	L	…	L	L	L
South Carolina	L	L	L	L	L	L	L	L	L	L	L	L	L	L	L
South Dakota	L	L	…	L	L	L	L	L	L	L	L	L	L	L	L
Tennessee	L	L	L	L	L	L	L	L	L	L	…	L	L	L	L
Texas	L	L	L	L	L	L	L	L	L	L	…	L	L	L	L
Utah	L	L	…	L	L	…	L	L	L	L	L	L	L	L	L
Vermont	L	L	L	L	L	L	L	L	L	L	…	L	L	L	L
Virginia	L	L	L	L	L	L	L	L	L	…	C	L	L	L	L
Washington	L	L	L	L	L	L	L	L	L	L	L	…	L	L	L
West Virginia	L	L	L	L	L	L	L	L	L	L	L	L	L	L	L
Wisconsin	L	L	L	L	L	…	L	L	L	L	L	…	L	L	L
Wyoming	L	L	…	L	L	L	L	L	L	L	L	…	L	L	L
Dist. of Columbia	L	L	L	L	L	…	L	L	L	L	…	…	L	L	L

Sources: Council on Licensure, Enforcement and Regulation, November 2003 and various national associations of state boards.

Key:
C — Certification
L — Licensure
R — Registration

(a) In some states, embalmers are not licensed separately from funeral directors; embalming is part of the funeral director's job.

(b) In addition to licensing professional engineers, some states regulate engineers by specific areas of expertise, such as civil engineers.

Table B
STATE REGULATION OF HEALTH OCCUPATIONS AND PROFESSIONS: NOVEMBER 2003

State or other jurisdiction	Acupuncturist	Chiropractor	Professional	Counselor(a), Alcoholism	Counselor, Drug	Counselor, Pastoral	Counselor, Substance Abuse (b)	Dentist	Dental Assistant (c)	Dental Hygienist	Denturist	Dietitian	Emergency Medical Technician (d)	Hearing Aid Dealer & Fitter
Alabama	…	L	L	…	…	…	…	L	…	L	…	…	L	L
Alaska	L	L	L	…	…	…	…	L	…	L	…	L	L	L
Arizona	L	L	C	C	C	…	C	L	C	L	L	L	L	L
Arkansas	L	L	C	…	…	…	…	L	R	L	…	R	L	L
California	L	L	L	…	…	…	…	L	L	L	…	…	L	L
Colorado	L	L	L	C	C	…	C	L	…	L	…	C	L	L
Connecticut	…	L	L	L	L	…	L	L	C	L	…	C	L	L
Delaware	L	L	L	C	C	…	C	L	…	L	…	…	L	L
Florida	L	L	L	…	…	…	…	L	…	L	…	C	L	L
Georgia	L	L	…	…	…	…	…	L	…	L	…	…	L	L
Hawaii	L	L	L	C	C	…	C	L	…	L	…	C	L	L
Idaho	L	L	L	…	…	…	…	L	…	L	L	…	L	L
Illinois	L	L	L	…	…	…	…	L	…	L	…	L	L	L
Indiana	L	L	L	…	…	…	…	L	L	L	…	C	L	L
Iowa	L	L	C	…	…	…	…	L	…	L	…	L	L	L
Kansas	…	L	L	C	C	C (e)	C	L	…	L	…	…	L	L
Kentucky	L	L	L	L	C	L	L	L	…	L	…	…	L	L
Louisiana	L	L	L	C,L	C,L	L	L	L	…	L	…	…	L	L
Maine	L	L	L	C,L	C,L	…	…	L	…	L	L	…	L	L
Maryland	L	L	C	…	…	…	…	L	L	L	…	…	L	L
Massachusetts	L	L	…	…	…	…	…	L	…	L	…	C	L	L
Michigan	…	L	…	…	…	…	…	L	…	L	…	…	L	L
Minnesota	L	L	…	…	…	…	…	L	L	L	…	…	L	L
Mississippi	L	L	…	…	…	…	…	L	L	L	…	…	L	L
Missouri	L	L	…	…	…	…	…	L	…	L	…	C	L	L
Montana	L	L	L	…	…	…	…	L	…	L	L	…	L	L
Nebraska	L	L	L	…	…	…	C,L	L	L	L	…	C	L	L
Nevada	L	L	C	C	C	C	C	L	L	L	…	…	L	L
New Hampshire	…	L	C	C	C	C	C	L	…	L	…	…	L	L
New Jersey	L	L	L	C	C	…	C	L	…	L	…	…	L	L
New Mexico	L	L	L	L	L	…	L	L	R	L	…	L	L	L
New York	L	L	L	L	L	…	C	L	C	L	…	C	L	L
North Carolina	L	L	L	L	L	…	C	L	L	L	…	…	L	L
North Dakota	…	L	L	…	…	…	…	L	L	L	…	…	L	L
Ohio	L	L	L	…	…	…	L	L	L	L	…	L	L	L

See footnotes at end of table.

Key:
C — Certification
L — Licensure
R — Registration
… — Not regulated

STATE REGULATION OF HEALTH OCCUPATIONS AND PROFESSIONS: NOVEMBER 2003 — Continued

State or other jurisdiction	Acupuncturist	Chiropractor	Professional	Counselor (a), Alcoholism	Counselor, Drug	Counselor, Pastoral	Counselor, Substance Abuse (b)	Dentist	Dental Assistant (c)	Dental Hygienist	Denturist	Dietitian	Emergency Medical Technician (d)	Hearing Aid Dealer & Fitter
Oklahoma	...	L	L	...	...	...	...	L	C	L	...	L	L	L
Oregon	L	L	L	...	...	...	...	L	...	L	L	L	L	L
Pennsylvania	R	L	L(f)	...	...	...	...	L	...	L	...	C	L	L
Rhode Island	L	L	L	...	...	...	C	L	...	L	...	L	L	L
South Carolina	R	L	L	...	...	...	...	L	...	L	...	...	L	L
South Dakota	...	L	L	...	...	...	...	L	L	L	...	L	L	L
Tennessee	L	L	L	L	L	...	...	L	L	L	...	C	L	L
Texas	L	L	L	L	L	...	...	L	...	L	...	L	L	L
Utah	L	L	L	...	...	...	...	L	...	L	...	C	L	L
Vermont	L	L	L	L	L	...	L	L	L	L	...	...	L	L
Virginia	L	L	L	C	C	...	...	L	...	L	...	C	L	L
Washington	L	L	C	C	C	...	...	L	...	L	L	L	L	L
West Virginia	L	L	C	...	...	...	...	L	...	L	...	L	L	L
Wisconsin	...	L	C	...	...	...	L	L	...	L	...	C	L	L
Wyoming	...	L	L	...	...	...	...	L	L	L	...	...	L	L
Dist. of Columbia	L	L	L	...	...	...	R	L	L	L	...	L	L	...

Key:
C — Certification
L — Licensure
R — Registration
. . . — Not regulated

STATE REGULATION OF HEALTH OCCUPATIONS AND PROFESSIONS: NOVEMBER 2003 — Continued

State or other jurisdiction	Homeopath	Massage Therapist	Nurse, Licensed Practical (g)	Nurse Midwife (g)	Nurse, Practitioner (g)	Nurse, Registered (g)	Nurse Home Administrator	Occupational Therapist	Occupational Therapy Assistant	Optician (h)	Optometrist	Osteopath	Pharmacist	Physical Therapist
Alabama	...	L	L	L	L	L	L	L	L	...	L	L	L	L
Alaska	L	...	L	L	L	L	L	L	L	L	L	L	L	L
Arizona	L	L	L	L	L	L	L	L	L	L	L	L	L	L
Arkansas	...	L	L	L	L	L	L	L	L	L	L	L	L	L
California	...	...	...	L	L	L	L	C	C	C	L	L	L	L
Colorado	...	...	L	L	L	L	L	L	L	L	L	L	L	L
Connecticut	L	...	L	L	L	L	L	L	L	...	L	L	L	L
Delaware	...	L	L	L	L	L	L	L	L	L	L	L	L	L
Florida	...	L	L	L	L	L	L	L	L	L	L	L	L	L
Georgia	...	...	L	L	L	L	L	L	L	...	L	L	L	L
Hawaii	...	L	L	L	L	L	L	L	L	L	L	L	L	L
Idaho	...	...	L	L	L	L	L	C	C	...	L	L	L	L
Illinois	...	L	L	L	L	L	L	L	L	L	L	L	L	L
Indiana	...	...	L	L	L	L	(i)	C	C	...	L	L	L	L
Iowa	...	L	L	L	L	L	L	L	L	L	L	L	L	L
Kansas	...	...	L	L	L	L	L	L	L	...	L	L	L	L
Kentucky	...	...	L	L	C	L	L	L	L	...	L	L	L	L
Louisiana	...	L	L	L	C	L	L	L	L	L	L	L	L	L
Maine	...	L	L	L	L	L	L	R	R	R	L	L	L	L
Maryland	...	C	L	L	L	L	L	L	L	L	L	L	L	L
Massachusetts	...	...	L	C	C	L	L	L	L	...	L	L	L	L
Michigan	...	...	L	C	C	L	L	R	R	...	L	L	L	L
Minnesota	...	L	L	C	L	L	L	L	L	R	L	L	L	L
Mississippi	...	...	L	L	L	L	L	L	L	L	L	L	L	L
Missouri	...	C	L	L	L	L	L	L	L	L	L	L	L	L
Montana	...	...	L	L	L	L	L	L	L	...	L	L	L	L
Nebraska	...	L	L	...	L	L	L	L	L	...	L	L	L	L
Nevada	L	...	L	L	L	L	L	L	L	...	L	L	L	L
New Hampshire	...	L	L	L	L	L	L	L	L	...	L	L	L	L
New Jersey	...	C	L	L	L	L	L	L	L	...	L	L	L	L
New Mexico	...	L	L	L	L	L	L	L	L	...	L	L	L	L
New York	...	L	L	L	L	L	L	L	L	...	L	L	L	L
North Carolina	...	L	L	L	L	L	L	L	L	...	L	L	L	L
North Dakota	...	L	L	L	L	L	L	L	L	...	L	L	L	L
Ohio	...	...	L	L	L	L	L	L	L	...	L	L	L	L

See footnotes at end of table.

Key:
C — Certification
L — Licensure
R — Registration
. . . — Not regulated

STATE REGULATION OF HEALTH OCCUPATIONS AND PROFESSIONS: NOVEMBER 2003 — Continued

State or other jurisdiction	Homeopath	Massage Therapist	Nurse, Licensed Practical (g)	Nurse Midwife (g)	Nurse, Practitioner (g)	Nurse, Registered (g)	Nurse Home Administrator	Occupational Therapist	Occupational Therapy Assistant	Optician (h)	Optometrist	Osteopath	Pharmacist	Physical Therapist
Oklahoma	...	...	L	C	C	L	L	L	L	...	L	L	L	L
Oregon	...	L	L	L	C	L	L	L	L	...	L	L	L	L
Pennsylvania	...	...	L	L	L	L	L	L	L	...	L	L	L	L
Rhode Island	...	L	L	L	L	L	L	L	L	L	L	L	L	L
South Carolina	...	...	L	L	L	L	L	L	L	L	L	L	L	L
South Dakota	...	...	L	L	L	L	L	L	L	...	L	L	L	L
Tennessee	...	R	L	L	L	L	L	L	L	...	L	L	L	L
Texas	...	L	L	L	L	L	L	L	L	L	L	L	L	L
Utah	...	...	L	L	L	L	(i)	L	L	...	L	L	L	L
Vermont	...	...	L	L	L	L	L	L	L	L	L	L	L	L
Virginia	...	C	L	L	L	L	L	L	L	L	L	L	L	L
Washington	...	L	L	L	L	L	L	L	L	L	L	L	L	L
West Virginia	...	R	L	L	L	L	L	L	...	L	L	L	L	L
Wisconsin	...	...	L	L	C	L	L	L	L	L	L	L	L	L
Wyoming	...	...	L	L	C	L	L	L	L	...	L	L	L	L
Dist. of Columbia	...	L	L	L	C	L	L	L	L	...	L	L	L	L

See footnotes at end of table.

Key:
C — Certification
L — Licensure
R — Registration
... — Not regulated

STATE REGULATION OF HEALTH OCCUPATIONS AND PROFESSIONS: NOVEMBER 2003—Continued

State or other jurisdiction	Physical Therapist Assistant	Physician	Physician Assistant	Podiatrist	Psychologist	Radiologic Technologist	Radiation Therapist	Respiratory Therapist	Sanitarian	Social Worker (j)	Speech Language Pathologist and Aud	Therapist Marriage and Family	Veterinarian	Veterinary Technician
Alabama	L	L	L	L	L	...	...	...	...	L	...	L	L	L
Alaska	L	L	L	L	L	...	...	L	...	...	...	L	L	L
Arizona	L	L	C	L	L	C	L	L	R	C	...	C	L	L
Arkansas	L	L	C	L	L	L	L	L	R	L	...	L	L	R
California	L	L	L	L	L	C	L	L	...	L	...	L	L	C
Colorado	...	L	C	L	L	...	...	L	...	L	...	L	L	R
Connecticut	R	L	C	L	L	L	...	L	...	L	...	L	L	...
Delaware	L	L	L	L	L	L	L	L	L	L	...	L	L	R
Florida	L	L	L	L	L	L	L	L	L	L	...	L	L	...
Georgia	L	L	L	L	L	L	L	L	...	L	...	L	L	L
Hawaii	...	L	L	L	L	...	...	...	L	L	...	L	L	R
Idaho	L	L	L	L	L	L	L	L	L	L	...	L	L	R
Illinois	L	L	C	L	L	C	L	R	...	L	...	L	L	L
Indiana	L	L	C	L	L	L	L	C	R	L	...	L	L	L
Iowa	L	L	L	L	L	L	...	L	...	L	...	L	L	R
Kansas	L	L	L	L	L	...	L	L	...	L	...	C	L	L
Kentucky	L	L	L	L	L	L	L	L	L	L	...	L	L	L
Louisiana	L	L	L	L	L	L	L	L	L	L	...	L	L	L
Maine	L	L	L	L	L	L	L	L	...	L	...	L	L	R
Maryland	L	L	L	L	L	R	L	L	C	L	...	C,L	L	L
Massachusetts	L	L	L	L	L	L	...	L	L	L	...	L	L	R
Michigan	...	L	L	L	L	R	L	L	R	C	...	L	L	L
Minnesota	...	L	L	L	L	L	...	R	R	L	...	L	L	R
Mississippi	L	L	L	L	L	...	L	L	L	L	...	L	L	L
Missouri	L	L	L	L	L	...	...	L	C	L	...	L	L	L
Montana	L	L	L	L	L	L	...	L	L	L	...	...	L	R
Nebraska	C	L	C	L	L	...	L	L	R	L	...	C	L	L
Nevada	L	L	L	L	L	...	...	L	R	L	...	L	L	R
New Hampshire	L	L	L	L	L	...	...	L	L	L	...	L	L	L
New Jersey	L	L	L	L	L	L	L	L	...	L	...	L	L	L
New Mexico	L	L	L	L	L	C	L	L	L	C,L	...	C	L	L
New York	L	L	L	L	L	L	L	L	...	C,L	...	L	L	R
North Carolina	L	L	L	L	L	...	...	L	...	C,L	...	L	L	L
North Dakota	L	L	L	L	L	L	L	L	...	L	...	L	L	L
Ohio	L	L	L	L	L	L	L	L	...	L	...	L	L	L

See footnotes at end of table.
Key:
C — Certification
L — Licensure
R — Registration
... — Not regulated

STATE REGULATION OF HEALTH OCCUPATIONS AND PROFESSIONS: NOVEMBER 2003—Continued

State or other jurisdiction	Physical Therapist Assistant	Physician	Physician Assistant	Podiatrist	Psychologist	Radiologic Technologist	Radiation Therapist	Respiratory Therapist	Sanitarian	Social Worker (j)	Speech Language Pathologist and Aud	Therapist Marriage and Family	Veterinarian	Veterinary Technician
Oklahoma	L	L	L	L	L	…	…	L	L	L	L	L	L	L
Oregon	R	L	L	L	L	…	L	L	L	C,L	L	L	L	L
Pennsylvania	L	L	C	L	L	…	…	C	…	L(f)	L	L(f)	L	C
Rhode Island	L	L	L	L	L	L	L	L	…	L	L	L(f)	L	…
South Carolina	L	L	L	L	L	C	C	L	R	L	L	L	L	L
South Dakota	L	L	L	L	L	…	…	L	C	L	L	L	L	L
Tennessee	L	L	L	L	L	L	L	L	L	L	L	L	L	L
Texas	L	L	C	L	L	L	L	…	L	L	L	L	L	…
Utah	…	L	C	L	L	L	L	…	…	L	…	L	L	R
Vermont	L	L	…	L	L	L	…	L	…	L	L	L	L	…
Virginia	L	L	…	L	L	L	…	L	…	L	L	L	L	L
Washington	…	L	L	L	L	C	L	L	…	C,L	L	…	L	L
West Virginia	L	L	L	L	L	L	L	L	L	L	L	L	L	L
Wisconsin	L	L	L	L	L	…	L	L	…	C,L	L	L	L	L
Wyoming	L	L	…	L	L	…	L	L	…	L	L	…	L	L
Dist. of Columbia	L	L	L	L	L	…	L	L	…	L	L	L	…	…

Sources: Council on Licensure, Enforcement and Regulation, November 2003 and various national associations of state boards.

Key:
C — Certification
L — Licensure
R — Registration
… — Not regulated

(a) In some states, professional counselors can practice without a license as long as they do not use the title "licensed professional counselor."

(b) In some states, substance abuse counselors use the title "addiction counselor/therapist."

(c) In some states, certification is required for dental assistants to perform expanded functions and take x-rays.

(d) There are eight categories of emergency medical technicians, from basic to paramedic to task-specific certifications. No state regulates all categories, but every state regulates at least one category.

(e) In Kentucky, pastoral counselors must be certified only if their practice is fee-based.

(f) In Pennsylvania, professional counselors, social workers, and marriage and family therapists do not need a license to practice unless they hold themselves out to be licensed.

(g) Some states recognize various categories of advanced practice nurses (e.g. geriatric, school health, and women's health).

(h) In many states, opticians are not licensed separately from optometrists; making and selling eyeglasses is part of the optometrist's job.

(i) In Indiana and Utah, nursing home administrators are not licensed as such, but they are licensed more broadly as health facility administrators.

(j) In some states, social work practice is regulated at one or more of the following levels: basic, intermediate, advanced, and clinical. Certification may be required for practice at the lower levels and licensure required for practice at the higher levels.

Table C
STATE PROFESSIONAL AND OCCUPATIONAL LICENSING CONTACTS

State or other jurisdiction	Centralized agency	Title	Contact	City and State	Phone	E-mail
Alabama	No centralized agency					
Alaska	AK Division of Occupational Licensing	Director	Rick Urion	Juneau, AK 99811-0806	(907) 465-2534	rick_urion@dced.state.ak.us
Arizona	No centralized agency					
Arkansas	No centralized agency					
California	CA Department of Consumer Affairs	Director	Kathleen Hamilton	Sacramento, CA 95814	(916) 445-4465	kathleen_Hamilton@dca.ca.gov
Colorado	CO Dept of Regulatory Agencies, Division of Registrations	Division Director	Rosemary McCool	Denver, CO 80202	(303) 894-7711	rose.mccool@dora.state.co.us
Connecticut	CT Dept. of Public Health, Bureau of Regulatory Services	Bureau Chief	Richard Edmonds	Hartford, CT 06134-0308	(860) 509-8022	richard.edmonds@po.state.ct.us
Delaware	DE Dept of Administrative Svcs., Division of Professional Regulation	Acting Director	Kay Warren	Dover, DE 19904-2467	(302) 744-4500	kwarren@state.de.us
Florida	FL Dept. of Business & Professional Regulation	Secretary	Diane Carr	Tallahassee, FL 32399-1027	(850) 413-0755	call.center@dbpr.state.fl.us
	FL Department of Health	Secretary	John O. Agwunobi	Tallahassee, FL 32399-1701	(850) 245-4321	health@doh.state.fl.us
	FL Department of Health, Division of Medical Quality Assurance	Division Director	Amy Jones	Tallahassee, FL 32399-3251	(850) 245-4224	Amy_Jones@doh.state.fl.us
Georgia	Office of Secretary of State, GA Professional Licensing Boards Division	Division Director	Mollie Fleeman	Macon, GA 31217-3858	(478) 207-1320	mlfleeman@sos.state.ga.us
Hawaii	HI Dept. of Commerce & Consumer Affairs, Professional Licensing Div.	Division Administrator	Noe Noe Tom	Honolulu, HI 96801	(808) 586-2690	pvl@dcca.state.hi.us
Idaho	ID Bureau of Occupational Licenses	Bureau Chief	Rayohn Jacobsen	Boise, ID 83702-5642	(208) 334-3233	rjacobsen@ibol.state.id.us
Illinois	IL Department of Professional Regulation	Director	Fernando E. Grillo	Springfield, IL 62786	(217) 785-0800	xmccraven@ildpr.com
Indiana	IN Health Professions Bureau	Executive Director	Lisa R. Hayes	Indianapolis, IN 46204	(317) 232-2960	lhayes@hpb.state.in.us
Indiana	IN Professional Licensing Agency	Executive Director	Gerald Quigley	Indianapolis, IN 46204	(317) 232-3997	gguigley@pla.state.in.us
Iowa	IA Department of Public Health, Bureau of Professional Licensure	Bureau Chief	Lois Churchill	Des Moines, IA 50319-0075	(515) 281-6385	lchurchi@idph.state.ia.us
	IA Department of Commerce, Professional Licensing Division	Acting Director	Bill Schroeder	Ankeny, IA 50021-3941	(515) 281-7396	bill.schroeder@iowa.gov
Kansas	No centralized agency					
Kentucky	KY Dept. of Administration, Division of Occupations & Professions	Director	Nancy Black	Frankfort, KY 40602-1360	(502) 564-3296	nancyl.black@mail.state.ky.us
Louisiana	No centralized agency					
Maine	ME Office of Licensing & Registration, Dept of Prof. & Fin. Regulation	Director	Anne L. Head	Augusta, ME 04333-0035	(207) 624-8633	anne.l.head@maine.gov
Maryland	MD Dept. of Labor, Licensing & Regulation	Secretary	James D. Fielder, Jr.	Baltimore, MD 21202	(410) 230-6020	jfielder@dllr.state.md.us
	MD Dept. of Labor, Licensing, & Regulation	Deputy Commissioner	Harry Loleas	Baltimore, MD 21202-3658	(410) 230-6226	hloleas@dllr.state.md.us
	MD Dept. of Health & Mental Hygiene	Secretary	Nelson J. Sabatini	Baltimore, MD 21201-2399	(410) 767-6860	nsabatini@dhmh.state.md.us
Massachusetts	MA Division of Professional Licensure	Director	Anne L. Collins	Boston, MA 02114	(617) 727-1183	acollins@state.ma.us
Michigan	MI Bureau of Health Services, Dept. of Consumer & Ind. Svcs.	Director	Melanie Brim	Lansing, MI 48909-8170	(517) 373-8068	bhseinfo@michigan.gov
	MI Bureau of Commercial Services, Dept. of Consumer & Ind. Svc.	Director	Andrew L. Metcalf	Lansing, MI 48909	(517) 241-9223	bcsinfo@michigan.gov
Minnesota	No centralized agency					
Mississippi	No centralized agency					
Missouri	MO Div. of Professional Registration	Division Director	Marilyn Taylor Williams	Jefferson City, MO 65102-1335	(573) 751-1081	mwilliam@mail.state.mo.us

See footnotes at end of table.

STATE PROFESSIONAL AND OCCUPATIONAL LICENSING CONTACTS — Continued

State or other jurisdiction	Centralized agency	Title	Contact	City and State	Phone	E-mail
Montana	MT Business Standards Division	Division Administrator	James F. Brown	Helena, MT 59620-0517	(406) 841-2042	jbrown@state.mt.us
Nebraska	NE Health & Human Services, Regulation & Licensure	Credentialing Div. Admin.	Helen Meeks	Lincoln, NE 68509-4986	(402) 471-0179	Helen.Meeks@hhss.state.ne.us
	NE Dept. of Health & Human Services, Regulation and Licensure	Director	Richard P. Nelson	Lincoln, NE 68509-5007	(402) 471-8566	dick.nelson@hhss.state.ne.us
Nevada	No centralized agency					
New Hampshire	No centralized agency					
New Jersey	Office of the Attorney General, NJ Division of Consumer Affairs	Director	Reni Erdos	Newark, NJ 07101	(973) 504-6200	askconsumeraffairs@lps.state.nj.us
New Mexico	NM Regulation & Licensing Department	Superintendent	Arturo Jaramillo	Santa Fe, NM 87504-5101	(505) 827-1131	arturo.jaramillo@state.nm.us
New York	NY State Education Department, Office of the Professions	Deputy Commissioner	Johanna Duncan-Poitier	Albany, NY 12234-1000	(518) 474-3862	jpoitier@mail.nysed.gov
North Carolina	No centralized agency					
North Dakota	No centralized agency					
Ohio	No centralized agency					
Oklahoma	No centralized agency					
Oregon	Health Licensing Office	Administrator	Susan K. Wilson	Salem, OR 97301-1287	(503) 378-8667	susan.k.wilson.@state.or.us
Pennsylvania	PA Department of State, Bureau of Professional & Occupational Affairs	Commissioner	...	Harrisburg, PA 17105-2649	(717) 783-7192	ra-bpoa@state.pa.us
Rhode Island	RI Department of Health, Division of Health Services Regulation	Associate Director	Donald Williams	Providence, RI 02908	(401) 222-6015	donw@doh.state.ri.us
South Carolina	SC Department of Labor, Licensing & Regulation	Director	Adrienne Youmans	Columbia, SC 29211-1329	(803) 896-4390	youmansa@llr.sc.gov
South Dakota	SD Department of Health	Secretary	Doneen Hollingsworth	Pierre, SD 57501-2536	(605) 773-3361	doh.info@state.sd.us
Tennessee	TN Division of Health Related Boards, Department of Health	Director	Robbie Bell	Nashville, TN 37247-1010	(615) 741-2040	rbell@state.tn.us
	Dept. of Commerce & Insurance, TN Division of Regulatory Boards	Assistant Commissioner	Robert Gowan	Nashville, TN 37243-0572	(615) 741-3449	Robert.Gowan@state.tn.us
Texas	TX Department of Licensing & Regulation	Dir of Lic. & E-Commerce	Don Dudley	Austin, TX 78711	(512) 463-6599	don.dudley@license.state.tx.us
	TX Department of Licensing & Regulation	Executive Director	William Kuntz	Austin, TX 78711	(512) 463-3173	bill@license.state.tx.us
	TX Department of Health, Professional Licensing & Certification	Division Director	Jim Zukowski	Austin, TX 78756-3183	(512) 834-6628	jim.zukowski@tdh.state.tx.us
Utah	UT Department of Commerce, Div. of Occupational and Professional Licensing	Director	J. Craig Jackson	Salt Lake City, UT 84114-6741	(801) 530-6039	cjackson@utah.gov
Vermont	Secretary of State's Office, VT Office of Professional Regulation	Director	Jessica G. Porter	Montpelier, VT 05609-1101	(802) 828-2458	jporter@sec.state.vt.us

See footnotes at end of table.

STATE PROFESSIONAL AND OCCUPATIONAL LICENSING CONTACTS — Continued

State or other jurisdiction	Centralized agency	Title	Contact	City and State	Phone	E-mail
Virginia	VA Dept. of Health Professions	Director	Robert A. Nebiker	Richmond, VA 23230-1712	(804) 662-9919	mebiker@dhp.state.va.us
	VA Dept. of Professional & Occupational Regulation	Director	Louise Fontaine Ware	Richmond, VA 23230	(804) 367-8519	ware@dpor.state.va.us
Washington	WA Department of Health	Secretary	Mary Selecky	Olympia, WA 98504-7890	(360) 236-4030	mary.selecky@doh.wa.gov
	WA Department of Licensing	Director	Fred Stephens	Olympia, WA 98507	(360) 902-3933	fstephens@dol.wa.gov
	WA Department of Health, Health Systems Quality Assurance	Assistant Secretary	Ron Weaver	Olympia, WA 98504-7850	(360) 236-4600	ron.weaver@doh.wa.gov
West Virginia	No centralized agency					
Wisconsin	WI Department of Regulation & Licensing	Secretary	Donsia Strong Hill	Madison, WI 53708-8935	(608) 266-8609	dorl@drl.state.wi.us
	WI Dept of Regulation & Licensing	Deputy Secretary	Mary Woolsey Schlaefer	Madison, WI 53708-8935	(608) 266-8609	mary.schlaefer@drl.state.wi.us
Wyoming	WY Dept. of Administration, Professional Licensing Boards	Occup. Licensing Director	Veronica Skoranski	Cheyenne, WY 82002	(307) 777-7788	vskora@state.wy.us
Dist. Of Columbia	DC Department of Health	Director	James A. Buford	Washington, DC 20002	(202) 442-5888	doh@dc.gov
	DC Department of Consumer and Regulatory Affairs	Director	David A. Clark	Washington, DC 20002	(202) 442-4400	clard@dcra.dc.gov

Source: Council on Licensure Enforcement and Regulation, December 2003.
Note: Since there are literally hundreds of autonomous boards in the states, it is the centralized agencies that are represented in this listing.

State Government Telecommunications: Personal Technology as a New Public Commons
By Wayne W. Hall Jr.

The development of personal technology and the application of this new power in a mobile environment is a key technological trend in telecommunications. For legislators and other public policymakers, this trend commands attention because of what is being created: a vast social commons. In this environment, state government policymakers will be required as never before to pay attention to the information security and integrity of individuals.

State governments as a rule have struggled to keep pace with technical change since the widespread introduction of personal computers beginning in the 1980s. Prior to that development, state technology agencies could take time to experiment, develop or implement technology more or less free from the demands of technology users. AT&T controlled the public telephone network and a handful of technology companies, such as IBM, controlled most computing platforms. The technology behind both was highly centralized and accessible only by specialists, who could manipulate it to create the applications of value to government.

The development of desktop computing signaled a shift toward more decentralized work arrangements. Desktop computers could be linked together and information exchanged in local networks, which created a demand for more and faster connections between computers, not only in the local area network but to the Internet as well. This self-perpetuating cycle continues today. Most policymakers now recognize the importance of broadband communications as an economic and developmental necessity.

The rapid growth of the public Internet also signaled the end of an era of top-down information technology management in state government. In short, it created a network for the rest of us. As one industry observer has noted: "The obscure commands scribbled on Post-It Notes affixed to monitors in offices everywhere were replaced with two simple words: Click here."[1]

The Internet is an organizing force without peer. People previously unknown to each other can communicate, share information and collaborate (or compete) on an enormous scale, which leads to all sorts of interesting outcomes, a fact not lost on social scientists, who are beginning to pay attention to the group dynamics made possible in this unique environment.

A Network for the Rest of Us

Part of what makes the Web unique lies in the technology. The Internet is powered by something called Internet Protocol, or "IP," a suite of rules that enables machines on the Internet to communicate using the same language.

In existing circuit-switched networks, an open voice connection is maintained end-to-end. There is literally a starting and ending point to each call with a continuous connection between handsets. Switches serve as the brains of this network, sorting out all the paths necessary to connect two points. Grossly simplified, it is not so far removed from a wire strung between two tin cans.

But in an IP network, transmissions are chopped into fragments, or packets, each with a home and destination address. Each packet is routed, along separate paths if needed, until reassembled and interpreted at the destination by software as speech, data or video. The result is a "stateless" or "connectionless" network since no connection is maintained between the beginning and end points. This technological shift is a powerful force. Without it, the Internet and the innumerable relationships it creates would be impossible.

In the early development of the telephone network, party lines permitted many individuals to participate on an open circuit, though not everyone could talk at the same time. In a packet switched world those individuals can not only talk at the same time, but be understood using applications created to take advantage of the network such as e-mail and instant messaging. The result is a rising tide of information, the enormity of which creates its own privacy, security and archival issues.[2]

The Network as Public Commons

Many individuals are familiar with Moore's law, which says that the number of transistors per square inch on computer chips will double roughly every

18 months, leading to more and more powerful processors. Fewer know about Metcalf's law, which says the value of a network can be expressed as the square of the number of users. By that measure, the value of the public Internet can hardly be overstated.

No longer are the network brains confined to the large switches at the center of the public telephone network, but rather in the everyday devices used—and owned—by consumers, the notebook computers, handheld digital devices, wireless phones and the like. This trend is unlikely to reverse course anytime soon. In the technologists' idiom, these devices are the network "edge."

Newer technologies may eliminate the "center" altogether. For example, "mesh networks" forgo the idea of an organized infrastructure. There is no hierarchy of machines. Each device in the network is automatically aware of and can communicate with any other device, making the network infinitely flexible, redundant and survivable. Although the U.S. Department of Defense initially provided much of the research funding, the private sector is now beginning to make these concepts into workable applications.

Chip maker Intel announced in December 2003 a chipset that will permit personal computers to run their own wireless networks, which will further decentralize the networking geography. Networking company Sun Microsystems once used the motto, "The network is the computer." This slogan is more and more true everyday. A new and very important network is being created that combines personal technology with mobility with packet networking.

Inventory Management as Policy Issue

Indeed, all the technologies necessary for a continuing networking revolution are falling into place: expanding broadband access to a colossal consumer network called the Web, automatic identification technologies, such as Radio Frequency Identification (RFID), and mobility, enabled by wireless communications devices such as cell phones and wireless digital assistants. But each advance in communications technology brings with it policy considerations.

RFID embeds micro-sized radios in everyday objects to relay information about that particular object to a machine reader. It belongs to a category of technologies called automatic identification technologies, or auto-IDs. It's like a bar code but with significant differences. Auto-ID technologies can be microscopically small and relatively inexpensive to use. Current manufacturing techniques can create some auto-ID tags as small as three microns thick, or about 25 times smaller than the width of a human hair. Embedded in everyday products, this group of technologies can be used to track almost anything. As an inventory management tool, it can virtually eliminate inefficiency. The U.S. Department of Defense will require all of its suppliers to use RFID tags down to individual rolls of toilet paper on pallets by January, 2005.[3] Wal-Mart has also thrown its weight behind these technologies in an effort to manage its massive supply chain. With further advances in sensors, a farmer, for example, might use auto-ID technologies to scan and analyze the temperature, moisture and mineral content of soil from a moving tractor. Decisions about what crops to plant in the coming spring could be made based on the exact soil condition.

Policymakers may be called upon to address concerns with auto-ID technologies since they could also be used to track *people*, not just objects. Indeed, Wal-Mart cancelled an in-store application that would have tracked razor inventory using auto-ID technologies. The official explanation that the company wanted to focus its tracking efforts elsewhere did not stop speculation that privacy concerns played a role. The key question on the minds of some: just what was being tracked?

Unwired

Wireless networking will be the next boom in communications technology. Already a number of new wireless technology standards are providing access to information in new ways. "Wi-Fi," a technology that provides short-range communications at high speeds, is exploding as "hot spots" materialize all over.[4] Many of those hot spots provide Web access to a growing legion of "unwired" consumers, who, in addition to getting information from the Web, may soon begin to place phone calls using that same technology as their point of network entry. Although the security details are being worked out, until recently those hotspots could, in theory if not in practice, provide data entry to state networks as well. This concerns technology managers in state government since it places a portion of the network they are responsible for outside their immediate control.

Other wireless technologies such as Bluetooth hold great promise for managing data over a wide assortment of devices in the home and office environment. The Federal Communications Commission continues to make radio spectrum available to encourage the private sector to create new services that exploit these and other emerging technologies.

Finally, a growing number of consumers have abandoned traditional phone service in favor of wireless phone services. This has obvious business ramifications for telephone companies, which compete with wireless carriers for customers and provide so much of the universal service support to educational, rural and disadvantaged consumers.

Bottom-Up Change

Consumers are adopting new mobility and Internet technologies as fast as they can be developed, in many cases much faster than state government. Whether it is peer-to-peer networking, which confronted the music industry with unchecked swapping of copyrighted work, Wi-Fi network access, instant messaging, or the use of the Internet to place phone calls, the so-called "early adopters" are likely to be everyday users, not large organizations with a dedicated technology mission. State government as an enterprise is very comfortable with a top-down command structure. Unfortunately for it, change is rapidly occurring from the bottom-up and cannot be controlled without banning whole technologies, a shortsighted and unenforceable solution.

All of this matters to our society because the problems of technology are not simply a matter for technologists. The development of computing and ad hoc networking technologies, for instance, raises an intriguing question because sometime in the not too distant future everything *knowable* will also be instantly transportable. In that strange environment, the question must be asked: *what* do we want to know and *who* do we want to know it?[5]

This tension between what we can know and what we should know may not be easy to solve because there is a new dynamic among the governed, what has been called an emerging digital majority. It expects control over any governmental relationship that involves personal information, finances and services consumed.[6] And its interests extend far beyond comparison shopping on the Web or making online dinner reservations. This majority is also interested in what its government is up to.

Something to Say

One candidate in the 2004 Democratic presidential primary race clearly tapped into the organizational power of the Internet to connect with supporters.[7] Using Web-based technology to coordinate backing, the result was a financial and political boon to his candidacy—so much so that he opted out of current campaign finance limits, confident in his ability to raise and spend his own funds. This clever use of the Web as an organizational tool may or may not result in political victory, but it has definitely changed the way political campaigns will be managed in the future.

Another example of Web use is "OneVoice," an organization whose specific purpose is to bypass a political process that it sees as unresponsive to a moderate majority on both sides of the Israeli-Palestinian conflict.[8] OneVoice uses the Web as a tool in its efforts to organize that hypothetical majority, to forge areas of consensus to present to leaders in both governments.

"E-government" in this context is much more than a Web portal or a way to distribute business and hunting licenses, valuable as those services may be. Rather, networking technologies increasingly amplify the voice of ordinary citizens to speak up and communicate in a coordinated fashion their wants and needs.

Notes

[1] Chad Dickerson, "The battle for decentralization," *Infoworld*, (May 2, 2003), http://www.infoworld.com/infoworld/article/03/05/02/18OPconnection_1.html.

[2] Kevin Maney, "Computers try to keep up with information flood," *USA Today*, (November 18, 2003), http://www.usatoday.com/tech/columnist/kevinmaney/2003-11-18-maney_x.htm. Maney takes note of a University of California—Berkeley report which suggests the world created five "exabytes" of information in 2002. Maney puts it in perspective: ". . . an exabyte is 1,000 petabytes, which is 1,000 terabytes, which in turn is 1,000 gigabytes, which finally gets into the range of today's PCs. One gigabyte equals enough books to fill a pickup."

[3] Ann Bednarz, "Defense Department Goes on Offense with RFID," *Network World*, (November 3, 2003), http://www.nwfusion.com/news/2003/1103forresterside.html.

[4] The official designation for Wi-Fi is Institute of Electrical and Electronics Engineers (IEEE) standard 802.11

[5] Deloitte & Touche, "2003 TMT Trends Annual Report: Silver Linings," http://www.deloitte.com/dtt/cda/doc/content/2003%20Annual%20TMT%20Trends%281%29.pdf. Ester Dyson answers the question: "What's Next?"

[6] Paul Taylor, Chief Strategy Officer, Center for Digital Government, has addressed NASTD, Telecommunications and Technology Professionals Serving State Government, on two occasions. He argues persuasively for an emerging digital majority.

[7] Edward Cone, "The Marketing of a President," *Baseline*, (November 17, 2003), http://www.baselinemag.com/article2/0,3959,1386051,00.asp.

About the Author

Wayne W. Hall Jr. has worked with the NASTD—Telecommunications and Technology Professionals Serving State Government—for 15 years. He is currently the technology and research manager for NASTD.

Table A
PRIMARY STATE TELECOMMUNICATION AND TECHNOLOGY CONTACTS

State or other jurisdiction	Department	Company	Title	Contact	Phone number
Alabama	Dept. of Finance	Information Svcs. Div.	Manager of Voice Operations	Julie Robertson	334-242-3052
Alaska	Dept. of Administration	Information Technology Group	Director & Chief Technology Officer	Stan Herrera	907-465-5735
Arizona	Dept. of Administration	Div. of Information Systems	ATS Manager	Sandy Clancy	602-542-1439
Arkansas	...	IT Services	Network Provisioning Manager	Don McDaniel	501-682-5027
California	Dept. of General Svcs.	Telecommunications Div.	Deputy Director	Barry Hemphill	916-657-9482
Colorado	Dept. of Personnel & Administration	Div. of Information Technologies	Network Manager	Paul Nelson	303-866-2872
Connecticut	Dept. of Information Technology	...	Life Member	Robert Dixon	860-622-2435
Delaware	State of Delaware	Dept. of Technology & Information	Business Office Team Leader	Kay Buck	302-739-9649
Florida	State Technology Office	Enterprise Interoperability	Chief, Enterprise Information Solutions Officer	John Ford	850-921-2334
Georgia	Georgia Technology Authority	Telecommunications Div.	Chief Network Officer	Renee Herr	404-656-3992
Hawaii	DAGS	ICSD	Acting Administrator	Melvin Morris	808-586-1920
Idaho	Dept. of Administration	Div. of Information Technology & Communication Svcs.	Administrator	Joe Roche	208-332-1841
Illinois	Central Management Svcs.	Div. of Telecommunications	Chief of Operations	Alice Engle	217-782-4140
	Central Management Svcs.	Div. of Telecommunications	Data Provisioning Manager	Steve Hayden	217-524-5033
Indiana	Dept. of Administration	Div. of Information Technology	Product Services Manager	Tom Gedig	317-233-9794
Iowa	...	Iowa Communications Network	Executive Director	John Gillispie	515-725-4707
Kansas	Dept. of Administration	Div. of Information Systems & Communications	Acting Deputy Director, Telecommunications	David Timpany	785-296-6150
Kentucky	Governor's Office for Technology	Office of Infrastructure Svcs.	Director, Security Services	Mark McChesney	502-564-6687
Louisiana	Office of Information Technology Svcs.	Div. of Administration	Deputy CIO	Allen Doescher	225-342-7105
Maine	Dept. of Administrative & Financial Svcs.	Bureau of Information Svcs.	Director, Network Services	Ellen Lee	207-624-8866
Maryland	Dept. of Budget & Management	OIT Telecommunications	Director, Enabling Technologies & Administrations	Kathleen Lange	410-767-4202
Massachusetts	...	Information Technology Div.	Telecommunications Contract Manager	Bob Spicer	617-626-4644
Michigan	Dept. of Information Technology	Telecommunications Svcs.	Director	Thomas Fogle	517-335-0029
Minnesota	Dept. of Administration	InterTechnologies Group	Project Manager	Jack Ries	651-296-7515
Mississippi	Information Technology Svcs.	Data Svcs.	Data/Video Network Manager	Jimmy Webster	601-359-2690
Missouri	Office of Administration	DIS Technology Svcs.	Telecommunication Services Manager	Nancy Bochat	573-751-5067
Montana	Dept. of Administration	Information Technology Svcs. Div.	Chief, Network Technology Services Bureau	Carl Hotvedt	406-444-1780
Nebraska	...	Div. of Communications	Director	Brenda Decker	402-471-3717
Nevada	Dept. of Information Technology	State of Nevada	Director, Telecommunications	David Richards	775-684-5820
New Hampshire	Dept. of Administrative Svcs.	Information Technology Management	Director	Thomas Towle	603-271-3764
New Jersey	...	Office of Information Technology	Telecommunications Manager	David Blackwell	609-633-0195
New Mexico	GSD/ISD	Office of Communications	IT Manager	Karen Baltzley	505-827-2959
New York	Office for Technology	Div. of Telecommunications	First Deputy Director	Peter Arment	518-402-2324
North Carolina	Information Technology Svcs.	Telecommunications Svcs.	Director	Steve Stoneman	919-981-5261
North Dakota	...	Information Technology Dept.	Director	Mike Ressler	701-328-3190
Ohio	Dept. of Administrative Svcs.	Telecommunications	Network Operations Manager	Roger Smith	614-644-5436
Oklahoma	Office of State Finance	Communications Operations-ISD Enterprise Network Svcs.	Information Systems Network Administrator	Joe Airington	405-521-4170
Oregon	...		Manager	Stephen Macartney	503-373-7211
Pennsylvania	...	Bureau of Commonwealth Telecommunications Svcs.	Assistant Director	Valerie Long	717-772-4236
Rhode Island	Dept. of Administration	Office of Library & Information Svcs.	Acting CIO	Howard Boksenbaum	401-222-4444
South Carolina	Division of the State CIO	S.C. State Budget & Control Board	Deputy CIO	Tom Fletcher	803-896-0404

See footnotes at end of table.

PRIMARY STATE TELECOMMUNICATION AND TECHNOLOGY CONTACTS — Continued

State or other jurisdiction	Department	Company	Title	Contact	Phone number
South Dakota	. . . .	Div. of Telecommunications	Director	Dennis Nincehelser	605-773-4264
Tennessee	Ofice for Information Resources	State of Tennessee	Planning Consultant	Jack McFadden	615-741-5080
Texas	Dept. of Information Resources	Telecommunications	Director	Eddie Esquivel	512-475-2297
Utah	Dept. of Administrative Svcs.	Information Technology Svcs.	Sr. Network Planner	Bill Theel	801-538-3698
Vermont	Dept. of Information & Innovation	State Of Vermont	Telecommunications Manager	Hale Irwin	802-828-3760
Virginia	Virginia Information Technologies Agency	Telecommunications and Network Operations	Director	Robert Davidson	804-371-5545
Washington	Dept. of Information Svcs.	Telecommunications Svcs.	Deputy Director of Operations	Michael McVicker	360-902-3129
West Virginia	Dept. of Administration	IS&C	Information Systems Specialist	Carlos Neccuzi	304-558-5472
Wisconsin	Dept. of Electronic Government	Bureau of Infrastructure & Networks	Bureau Director	Bob Stuessy	608-264-6186
Wyoming	Dept. of A & I	Information Technology Division	Administrator	Earl Atwood	307-777-5600
Puerto Rico	. . . .	Office of Budget & Management	Director	Melba Acosta	787-725-9420

Source: National Association of State Telecommunication Directors, December 2003.

Privatization in State Government: Trends and Issues

By Keon S. Chi, Kelley A. Arnold and Heather M. Perkins

Privatization continues to be a controversial management issue in state governments. In the past five years, 1997-2002, the extent of privatization activities in the states has largely remained the same as in the previous five years or slightly increased. The main reasons for privatization are a lack of personnel or expertise and cost savings. In most cases, privatized services account for less than 5 percent of agency services, while reported costs savings range from none to less than 5 percent. But many state agency directors surveyed seem to have no clear ideas as to how much has been actually saved from privatization. Nevertheless, privatization is likely to continue in the states in the next few years as in the past decade.

Every year, new privatization initiatives are being implemented in the states. To cite just a few recent examples, Florida Gov. Jeb Bush in August 2002 signed a seven-year, $280 million contract with a private firm to provide selected human resource services and save the state approximately $80 million during the contract period. In early 2003, New York Gov. George E. Pataki proposed to privatize certain state assets to lower the Medicaid cost and other government programs. Nevada Gov. Kenny Guinn reported to the Legislature that privatization of the state workers compensation system resulted in a reduction of nearly 800 positions in the state government and relieved the state of a $2 billion liability. He chose the state motor pool and printing operations as candidates for privatization. Virginia Gov. Mark R. Warner said he was planning to continue with public-private partnerships for education and transportation. Maine Gov. John Baldacci proposed privatiz-

ing wholesale and retail liquor operations for greater efficiency.

Rationale for privatization is difficult to generalize. Former Michigan Gov. John Engler seemed to represent the prevailing opinion of state policymakers who initiate privatization when he said:

It's my belief that the private sector is often better at getting the job done than government. First, the competition promotes operating cost effectively, and the greater accountability helps ensure quality products and services. The private sector also excels at using innovative technology to solve problems, while government agencies do not always have the same latitude to innovate or take risks. Finally, the private sector has vast resources in computer technology, high volume proceeding equipment, and specialized personnel, plus the flexibility to assign them wherever they are needed most.[1]

Incumbent Michigan Gov. Jennifer Granholm in 2003 directed the state Department of Management and Budget to review all state contacts for cost overruns and potential cost savings.

On the other hand, opposition to privatization efforts has been persistent over the years. Since the early 1990s, the AFL-CIO has led anti-privatization initiatives by saying, "Privatization/contracting must be stopped, the dismantling of our governments cannot be tolerated." Similarly, Gerald W. McEntee, president of the American Federation of State, County and Municipal Employees (AFSCME), warns:

For public employees and the people we serve, the price of privatization is high—and getting higher. For workers, privatization threatens job security, pay and benefits, working conditions and career opportunities. For the public, it means less quality, less access and less accountability. For local economies, because privatization is often

Figure A: Trends in Privatization Activity in the Past Five Years (1998-2002)

- Increased 25.0%
- Remained the Same 52.6%
- Decreased 11.8%
- No Response 10.5%

Source: Survey of state budget directors and legislative service agency directors, December 2002. *Question*: "Which of the following best describes the amount of privatization activity in the past five years?"

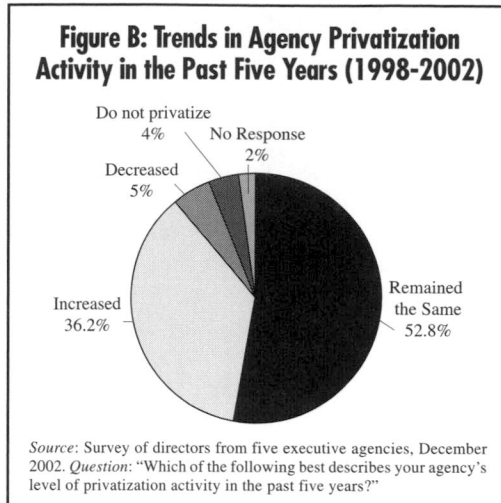

Figure B: Trends in Agency Privatization Activity in the Past Five Years (1998-2002)

Source: Survey of directors from five executive agencies, December 2002. *Question*: "Which of the following best describes your agency's level of privatization activity in the past five years?"

non-union, it means fewer good jobs and a reduced tax base.[2]

The topic of privatization — outsourcing or contracting — seems to have re-emerged recently as a controversial management issue for state policymakers. Governors, agency directors and legislators in many states are asking for either further promotion or curtailment of such public-private partnership cooperation to deal with the faltering economy and dwindling revenues in the past two to three years. There appears to be no consensus as to the effectiveness of privatization in part due to the lack of empirical data as well as the complexity of the issue. This article first discusses the background of privatization in state governments, reports findings of a recent national survey of selected agency directors in the 50 state governments, offers lessons learned from the previous experiences and raises key issues for future privatization activities.

Trends in Privatization

Since the early 1980s, The Council of State Governments (CSG) has monitored and disseminated information on privatization trends in state government. In 1993, CSG published a report, "Privatization in State Government: Options for the Future" in its *State Trends and Forecasts* series. In 1997, CSG's Center for State Trends and Innovations conducted a 50-state survey on privatization in 19 state agencies; the survey findings were reported in a 1998 monograph, "Private Practices: A Review of Privatization in State Government."[3] CSG conducted another national survey of state officials to identify

recent privatization trends between October 2002 and December 2002. The survey was sent to 450 state budget and legislative service agency directors and heads of five executive branch agencies: personnel, education, health and human services, corrections and transportation. The survey yielded an overall response rate of nearly 77 percent.

Budget and Legislative Service Directors

According to the 2002 CSG survey, the level or amount of privatization in the states between 1997 and 2002 has remained the same in most states or slightly increased in some states. Only five of the 38 state budget directors who responded to the survey reported privatization has decreased in their state in the recent past (Figure A). Survey results from heads of the five line agencies in the states showed very much the same trend, confirming that privatization has become a routine management tool in state government in the past decade (Figures B and C). As in the 1997 survey, most state agency directors indicated in the 2002 survey that the extent of privatized services and programs has remained relatively moderate, mostly less than 10 percent. When asked about the amount of privatization that has occurred within the state, 12 budget directors replied that their state has privatized on average at least 6 percent of the their services (Arizona, Connecticut, Indiana, Massachusetts, Minnesota, Missouri, North Carolina, Oklahoma, Virginia, Washington, Wisconsin and Wyoming).

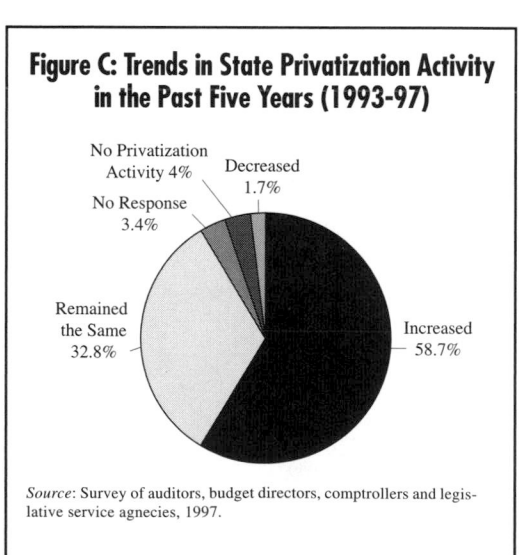

Figure C: Trends in State Privatization Activity in the Past Five Years (1993-97)

Source: Survey of auditors, budget directors, comptrollers and legislative service agencies, 1997.

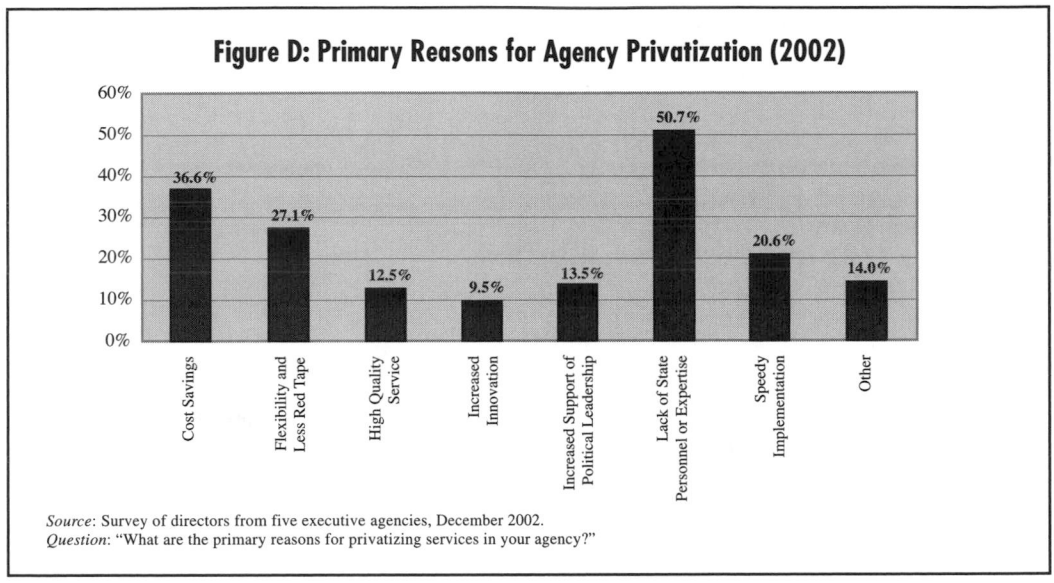

Figure D: Primary Reasons for Agency Privatization (2002)

Source: Survey of directors from five executive agencies, December 2002.
Question: "What are the primary reasons for privatizing services in your agency?"

State budget and legislative service agency directors offered slightly different reasons for and cost savings estimates from privatization when compared with responses from line agency directors. For example, the primary reason for privatization given by a majority of the budget directors was cost savings, while the lack of personnel or expertise was the number one reason for contracting out according to a majority of state agency heads (Figure D). In the 1997 survey, support of political leadership was cited as the second major reason, followed by cost savings, for privatization, but in the 2002 survey, support or pressures from political leadership was not mentioned as a main reason for privatization in most state agencies (Figure E).

Contracting has been the most widely used method by state governments to privatize, followed, to a much less extent, by public-private partnerships (Figure F). For example, Michigan Governor's Education Technology Fund is a public-private partnership

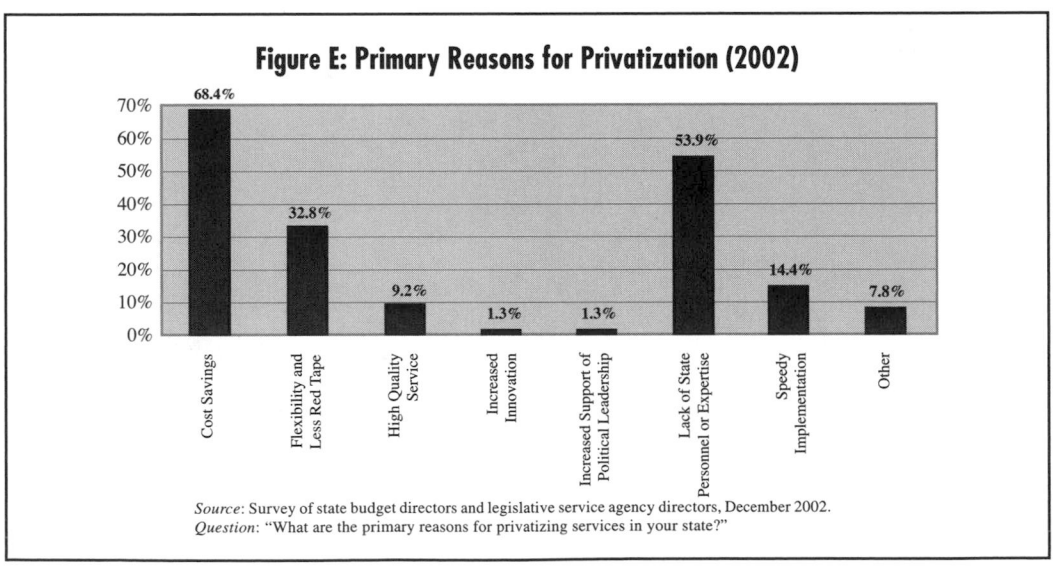

Figure E: Primary Reasons for Privatization (2002)

Source: Survey of state budget directors and legislative service agency directors, December 2002.
Question: "What are the primary reasons for privatizing services in your state?"

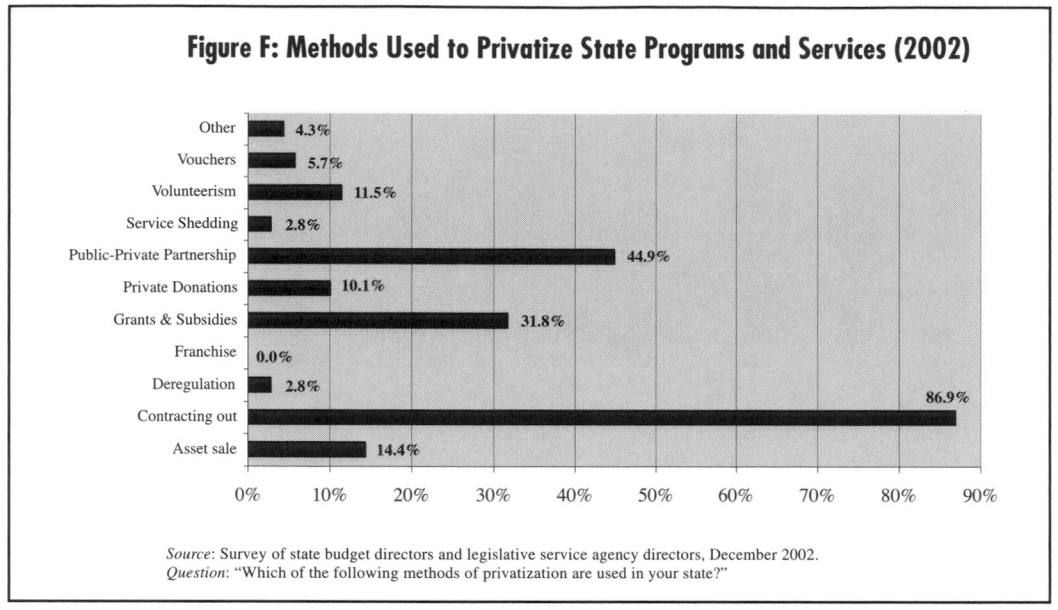

Figure F: Methods Used to Privatize State Programs and Services (2002)

Method	Percentage
Other	4.3%
Vouchers	5.7%
Volunteerism	11.5%
Service Shedding	2.8%
Public-Private Partnership	44.9%
Private Donations	10.1%
Grants & Subsidies	31.8%
Franchise	0.0%
Deregulation	2.8%
Contracting out	86.9%
Asset sale	14.4%

Source: Survey of state budget directors and legislative service agency directors, December 2002.
Question: "Which of the following methods of privatization are used in your state?"

between the state and the Intel Corporation (along with several other businesses) and the purpose is to provide educators with online professional development opportunities through Michigan Virtual University. Several other states also have examples of using one of the three major methods of privatization. The Alaska Office of Management and Budget reported that the state recently implemented the largest privatization in the history of the state involving a telecommunication partnership. A Virginia respondent reported the recently enacted Public-Private Education Infrastructure Act was expected to increase the number of public-private partnerships throughout the Commonwealth. In addition, 15 states have reported passing legislation in past five years relating to privatization (Alaska, Arizona, Connecticut, Illinois, Kentucky, Massachusetts, Nevada, New Jersey, North Carolina, Oklahoma, Oregon, Vermont, Virginia,

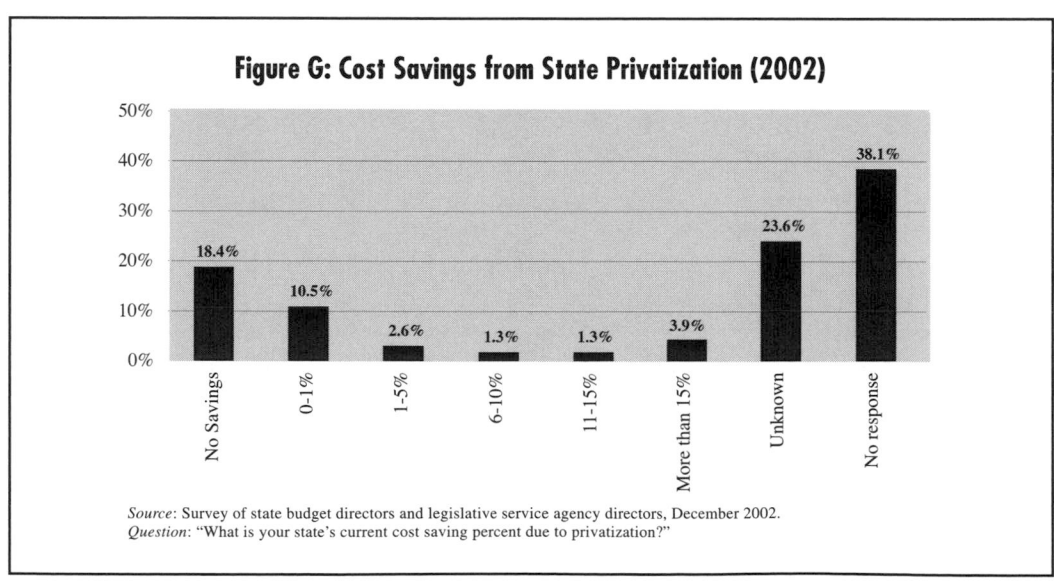

Figure G: Cost Savings from State Privatization (2002)

Category	Percentage
No Savings	18.4%
0-1%	10.5%
1-5%	2.6%
6-10%	1.3%
11-15%	1.3%
More than 15%	3.9%
Unknown	23.6%
No response	38.1%

Source: Survey of state budget directors and legislative service agency directors, December 2002.
Question: "What is your state's current cost saving percent due to privatization?"

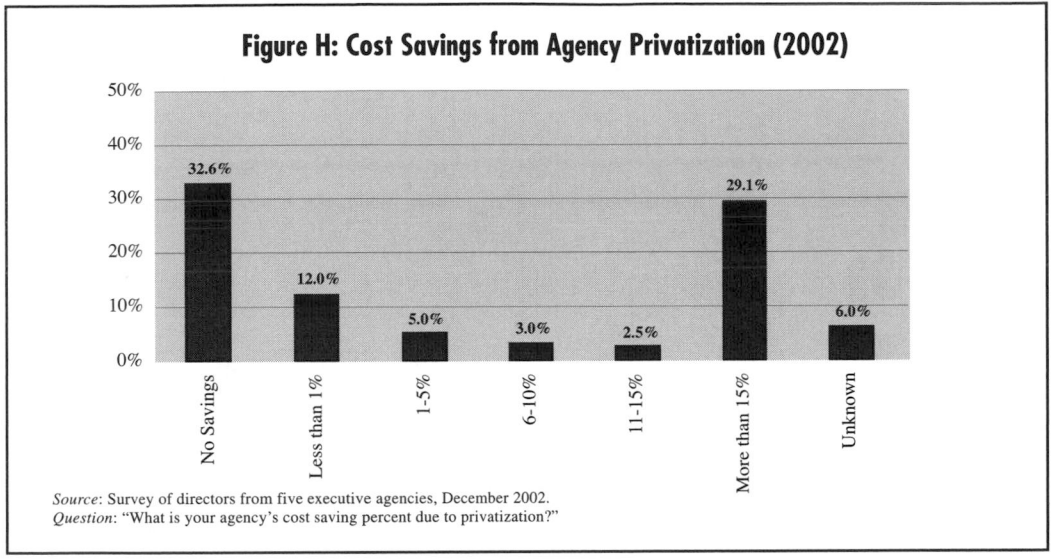

Figure H: Cost Savings from Agency Privatization (2002)

Source: Survey of directors from five executive agencies, December 2002.
Question: "What is your agency's cost saving percent due to privatization?"

Washington and Wisconsin). Washington passed a law in 2002 authorizing state agencies and institutions of higher education to contract out for services that were historically provided by classified civil service employees. It also allows those employees whose positions would be displaced by these contracts to form employee business units and these units will be able to compete for and bid on the contracts along with private companies.

Most budget and legislative service agency directors reported savings from privatization to be 5 percent or less. But many of them could not answer whether privatization saved their state agency money or not, while 18 percent said it has resulted in no savings (Figure G). Budget and legislative service agency directors in Arizona, Connecticut and Virginia reported much higher savings rates—more than 15 percent. It is interesting to note that these officials, based on their information on privatization on a statewide basis, showed differ-

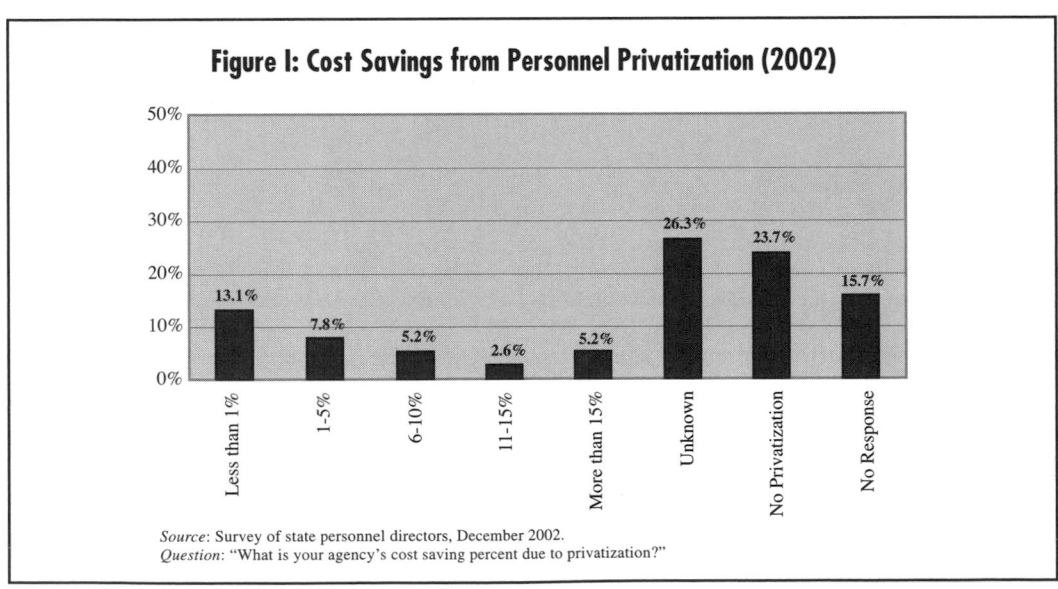

Figure I: Cost Savings from Personnel Privatization (2002)

Source: Survey of state personnel directors, December 2002.
Question: "What is your agency's cost saving percent due to privatization?"

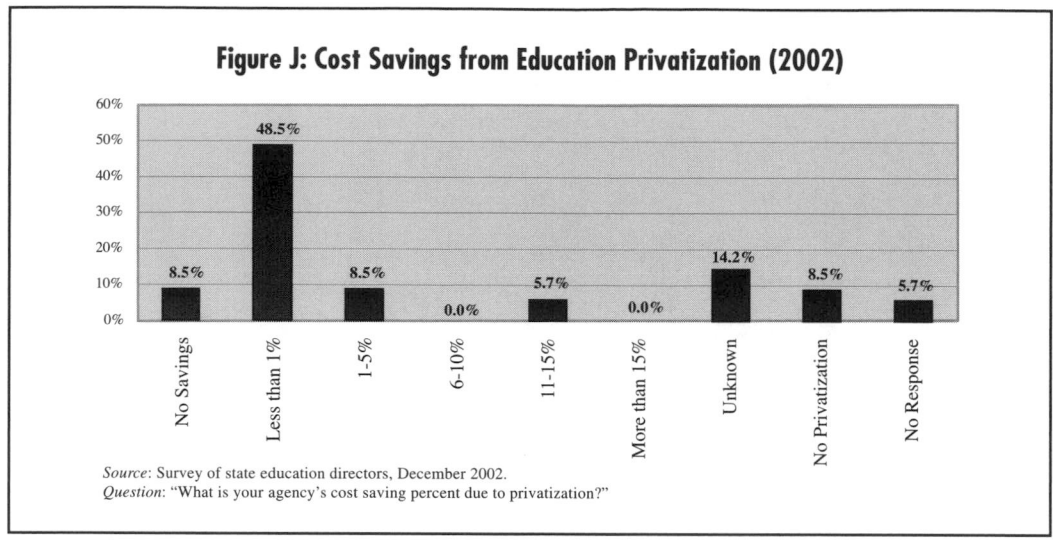

Figure J: Cost Savings from Education Privatization (2002)

Source: Survey of state education directors, December 2002.
Question: "What is your agency's cost saving percent due to privatization?"

ent estimates on cost savings from privatization. For example, 29 percent of agency heads reported cost savings to be more than 15 percent, and 33 percent of the agency heads reported no savings from privatization (Figure H).

Selected State Agencies
Personnel

The level of privatization activities in state personnel agencies between 1997 and 2002 has re-mained the same as in the previous five years. The primary reasons for privatizing services among state personnel departments were a lack of state personnel and expertise, cost savings and high quality private services. The services that were privatized frequently by personnel divisions include workers' compensation claim processing, flexible spending benefits, training consultants and information technology services (Table A). Kansas's personnel agency director reported that they outsource benefits services due "to

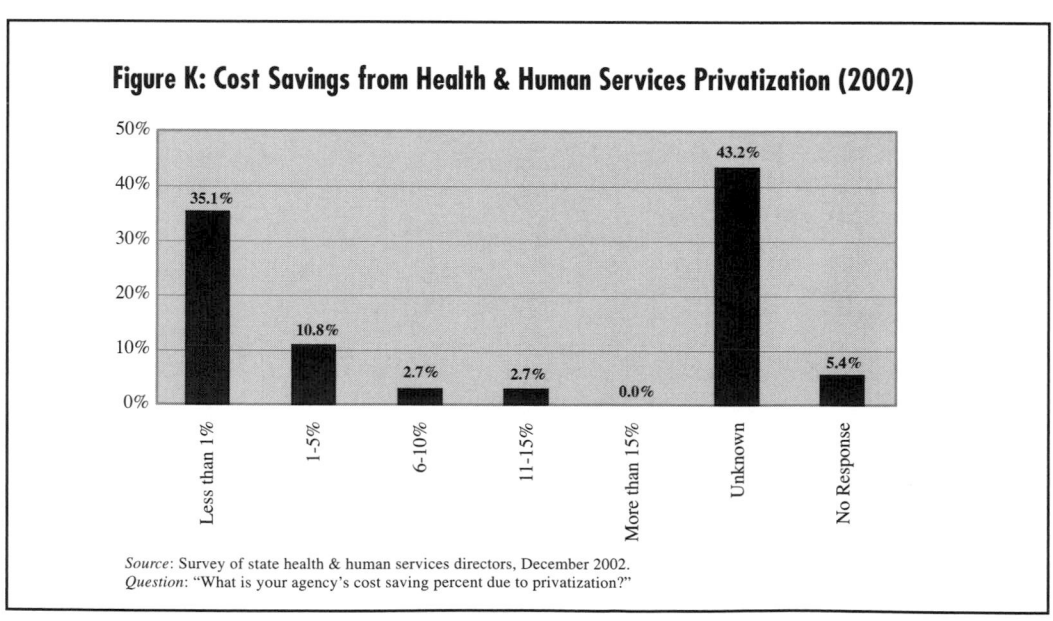

Figure K: Cost Savings from Health & Human Services Privatization (2002)

Source: Survey of state health & human services directors, December 2002.
Question: "What is your agency's cost saving percent due to privatization?"

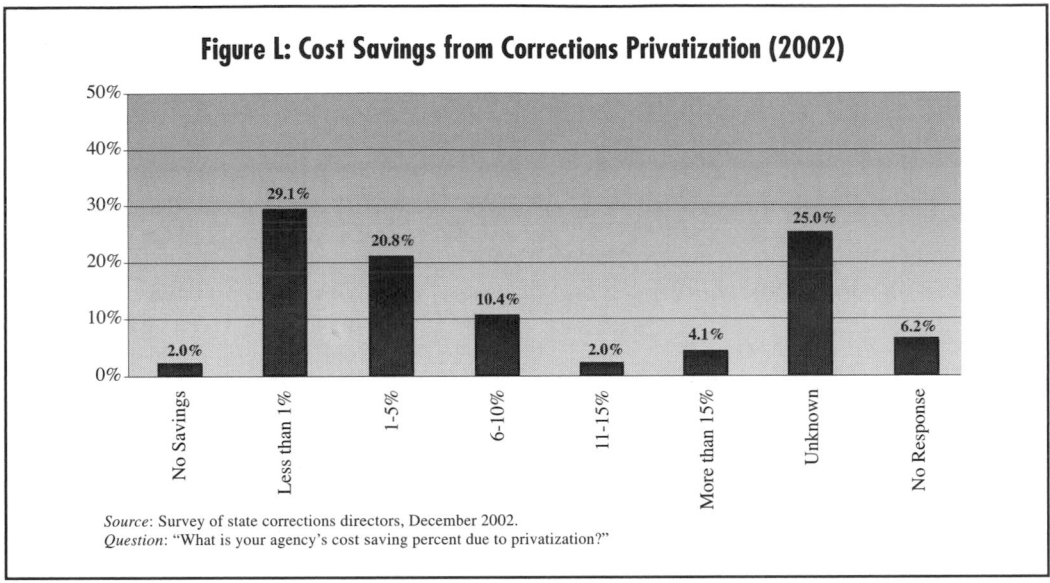

Figure L: Cost Savings from Corrections Privatization (2002)

Source: Survey of state corrections directors, December 2002.
Question: "What is your agency's cost saving percent due to privatization?"

the complexity of these services. There are also more employee self-service options with regards to benefits." Arizona utilized outside consultants to provide training services in order to supplement in house resources. South Dakota's claims administration for health and worker's compensation was contracted to a third party since 1998.

States that have privatized more than 10 percent of their personnel services include Connecticut and Florida. On the other hand, 10 agencies replied that

their state agency did not privatize more than 1 percent of personnel services (Arizona, California, Idaho, Illinois, New Hampshire, South Dakota, Tennessee, Utah, Wisconsin and Wyoming). Contracting was the most widely used method in personnel privatization, but public-private partnerships also were used frequently. Cost savings from personnel contracts were largely unknown or undocumented, according to the survey results, although a small number of the respondents reported some savings,

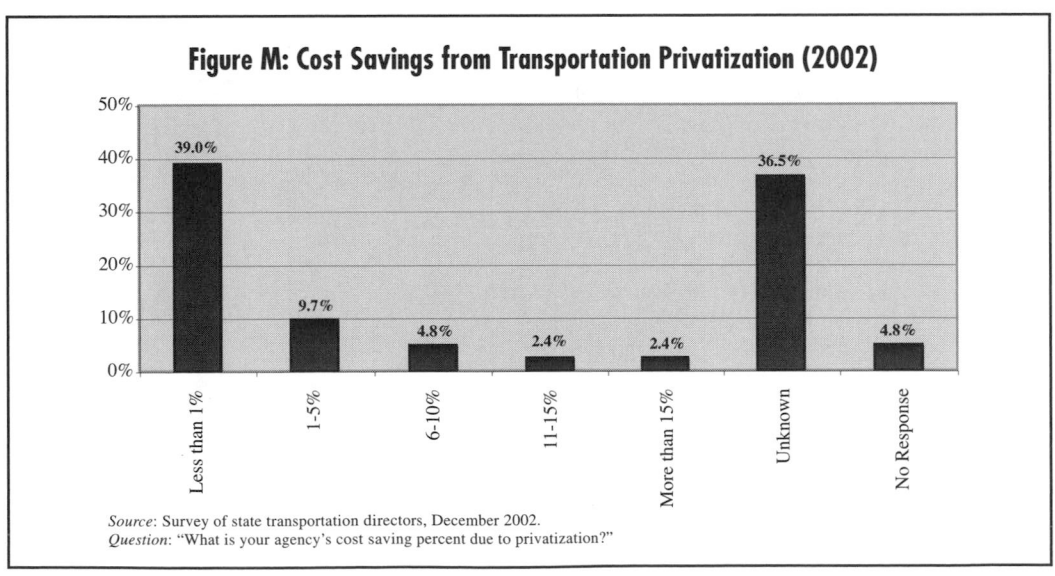

Figure M: Cost Savings from Transportation Privatization (2002)

Source: Survey of state transportation directors, December 2002.
Question: "What is your agency's cost saving percent due to privatization?"

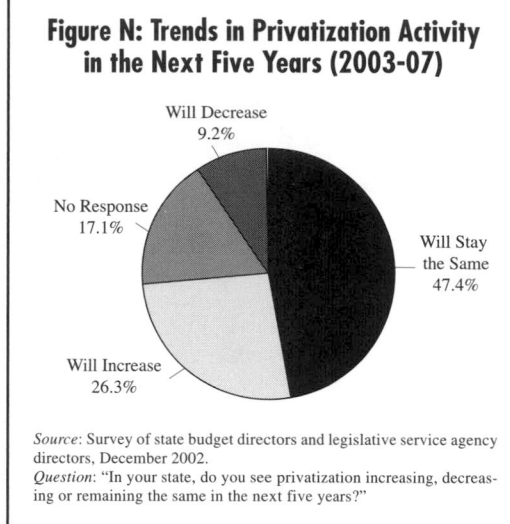

Figure N: Trends in Privatization Activity in the Next Five Years (2003-07)

Will Decrease
9.2%

No Response
17.1%

Will Stay
the Same
47.4%

Will Increase
26.3%

Source: Survey of state budget directors and legislative service agency directors, December 2002.
Question: "In your state, do you see privatization increasing, decreasing or remaining the same in the next five years?"

ranging from less than 1 percent to more than 15 percent (Figure I). Connecticut and Michigan reported a savings of more than 15 percent from personnel privatization.

Education

In the past five years, the extent of privatization in state education agencies, responsible for K-12 education, has stayed the same in most states or increased somewhat in some states. Services privatized by education departments include information technology, statewide assessment testing, special education, and facilities services. Montana signed two contracts within the past five years for statewide student assessment tests with private testing companies. Alabama's head of the education department said that the use of professional services contracts increased to secure expertise not available in the department.

Michigan and Nebraska's education agencies privatized more than 15 percent of their programs and services, while most education agencies have privatized between 1 percent and 5 percent. The Michigan respondent said that contractual services increased in the past five years due to the department's inability to fill staff vacancies. Ohio hired more information technology contractors due to the lack of staff expertise; 25 education directors reported that the primary reason for privatizing education services was a lack of personnel and expertise. The percentage of education services privatized has been less than 15 percent in half the education agencies surveyed. Along with contracting, grants and subsidies and public-private part-

nerships also were used to implement education privatization. Nearly one half the education agency heads surveyed said the savings from privatized services was less than 1 percent. Maryland and Nebraska reported cost savings from privatization to be between 11 percent and 15 percent (Figure J).

Health and Human Services

As in the education agencies, the percentage of human services privatization has also remained the same in the past five years. Only Ohio reported a decrease. Ohio made a decision to shift its management information system staffing from contract staff to state employees in order to save money. The lack of personnel or expertise in the agencies, along with flexibility and less red tape, was the primary reason for privatization; only one out of four cited cost savings as the primary reason for privatized services. Sixteen directors of health and human services agencies reported that more than 10 percent of their services were privatized. Among privatized services in these agencies, case management, child support enforcement services and community-based services, mental health and drug treatment programs, have been the most popular areas.

Oklahoma reported that future cost savings and cost avoidance was projected in a recent outsourcing of a state school for the developmentally disabled. Ten additional states also reported that cost savings was a primary reason for privatizing services offered by the health and human services agencies.

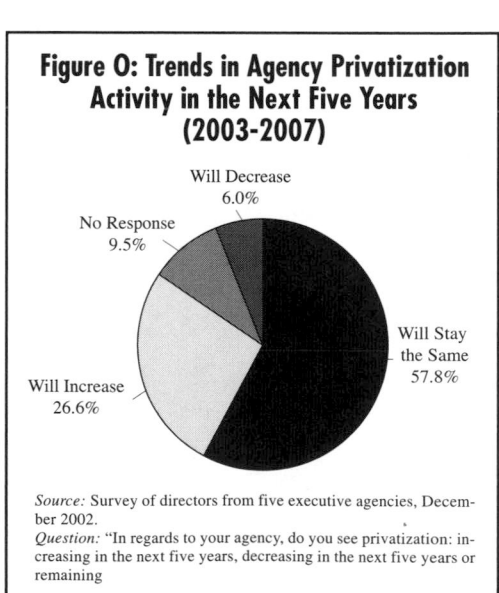

Figure O: Trends in Agency Privatization Activity in the Next Five Years (2003-2007)

Will Decrease
6.0%

No Response
9.5%

Will Stay
the Same
57.8%

Will Increase
26.6%

Source: Survey of directors from five executive agencies, December 2002.
Question: "In regards to your agency, do you see privatization: increasing in the next five years, decreasing in the next five years or remaining

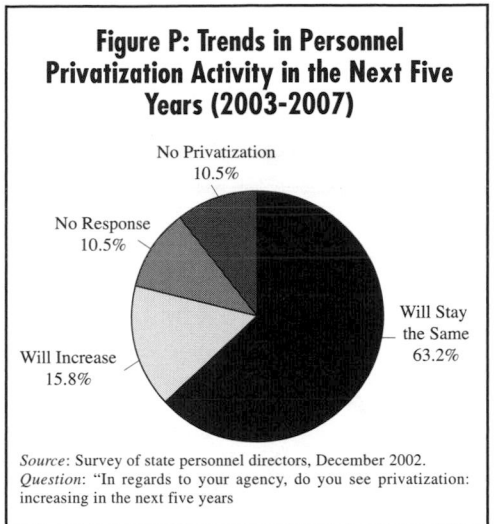

Figure P: Trends in Personnel Privatization Activity in the Next Five Years (2003-2007)

No Privatization
10.5%

No Response
10.5%

Will Increase
15.8%

Will Stay the Same
63.2%

Source: Survey of state personnel directors, December 2002.
Question: "In regards to your agency, do you see privatization: increasing in the next five years

Maryland was downsizing facilities for developmental disabilities and transferring the clients to private sector community programs. The state was also closing many county-run mental health clinics and contracting with private sector organizations to provide the care. Like in the other agencies, contracting has been most widely used. But slightly more than one-third of the respondents reported cost savings from privatization as less than 1 percent. Nearly half the agency directors could not give the amount of cost savings (Figure K).

Corrections

Twenty-one states, or 44 percent of the state corrections agency directors who responded to the survey, reported an increase in privatization between 1997 and 2002. About 40 percent of the survey respondents put percentage of privatized corrections services between 1 percent and 10 percent, while 14 state corrections department directors reported that more than 15 percent of their services were privatized; these states include Alaska, Colorado, Hawaii, Kansas, Louisiana, Massachusetts, New Mexico, Oklahoma, New Mexico, Oklahoma, South Dakota Tennessee and Wyoming. Medical care for inmates was reported as a service privatized by at least 23 states. The Nevada Department of Corrections requested a proposal to privatize pharmacy services. A lack of state beds and prison overcrowding prompted several states to seek arrangements with private prison facilities. Connecticut contracted out with the Virginia Department of Corrections to house 500 inmates due to lack of facilities. Alaska

and Hawaii reported having contracts with out-of-state jails and prisons. According to the Alaska Department of Corrections, "it costs approximately $114 per day in-state and out-of-state it only costs $62."

The main reasons for privatizing correctional services include cost savings, lack of state personnel or expertise and flexibility. Alabama reported that inmate medical services were contracted out because it offered a higher quality of service and the state had a lack of personnel to staff the services. Connecticut placed individuals in privately contracted non-profit halfway houses because it cost less than incarceration. Thirty-one additional states, besides Alabama and Connecticut, also reported that privatization was used mainly as a cost-savings tool. Contracting is the most often used method in privatizing corrections services. Alaska and Indiana reported their cost savings from privatization to be more than 15 percent. But most respondents said cost savings has been less than 5 percent (Figure L).

Transportation

Directors of 24 state departments of transportation, or 59 percent of the transportation survey respondents, reported an increase in privatization over the past five years, while 17 directors said the level of privatization has remained the same in the past five years. Respondents from 20 state transportation departments, or 40 percent of the respondents, reported that more than 15 percent of their services and programs had been privatized. On the other hand, five states (Colorado, Florida, Georgia, Michi-

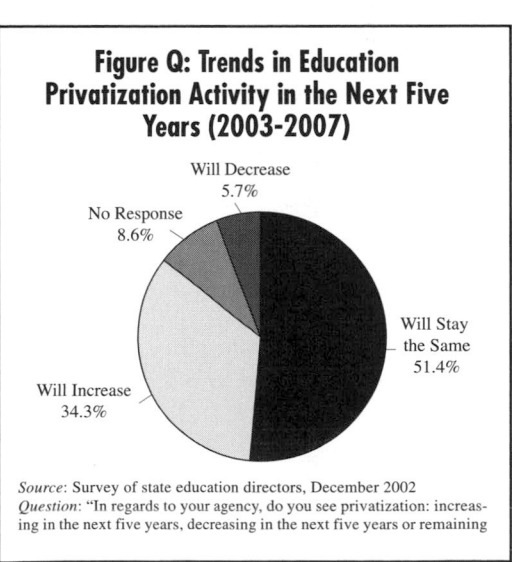

Figure Q: Trends in Education Privatization Activity in the Next Five Years (2003-2007)

Will Decrease
5.7%

No Response
8.6%

Will Increase
34.3%

Will Stay the Same
51.4%

Source: Survey of state education directors, December 2002
Question: "In regards to your agency, do you see privatization: increasing in the next five years, decreasing in the next five years or remaining

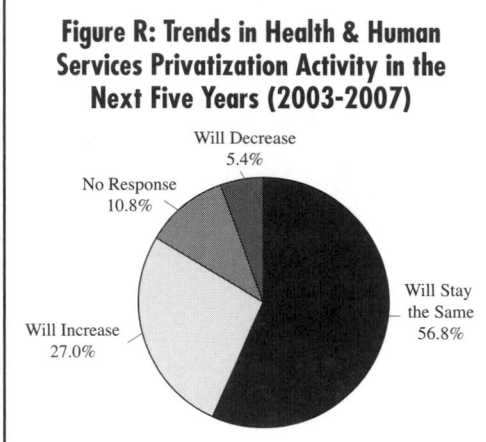

Figure R: Trends in Health & Human Services Privatization Activity in the Next Five Years (2003-2007)

Will Decrease 5.4%

No Response 10.8%

Will Stay the Same 56.8%

Will Increase 27.0%

Source: Survey of state health & human services directors, December 2002.
Questions: "In regards to your agency, do you see privatization: increasing in the next five years, decreasing in the next five years

gan and Montana) reported a drastic decrease in transportation privatization.

Privatized services included highway construction and maintenance, design and engineering, information technology and inspections. Wyoming's transportation agency head stated that it was easier to hire temporary consultants and contractors rather than to put permanent employees on payroll; this practice created less concern for layoffs. California contracted out for special engineering services due to a lack of staff with specialized skills. California's respondent said, "The department contracts out for special engineering services for which it does not have the expertise on staff." In addition, 29 state departments of transportation cited a lack of state personnel and expertise as one of the primary reasons for privatizing services. North Carolina's director said his department must use outside sources due to the difficulty in hiring qualified people. Most privatization projects took the form of contracting, but public-private joint projects were used by at least 10 states. Nearly 39 percent of the transportation agency directors who responded to the survey said their cost savings from privatization was less than 1 percent (Figure M). Connecticut and Kansas's reported cost savings exceeded 10 percent.

The Next Five Years

Privatization as a management approach is likely to continue in state agencies. Nearly half the state officials who responded to the 2002 CSG survey

said privatization in their state or agency was likely to increase, and the other half said the extent of privatization was likely to remain the same in their state (Figures N-T). This forecast seems quite plausible in view of the lingering fiscal crisis in the states, dwindling federal aid to state and local governments, governors' management improvement efforts and the most recent federal privatization initiatives. In November 2002, the Bush administration announced that it would place 850,000 federal jobs—nearly half the federal civilian employees—up for competition from private contractors in the next few years. While its impact on state governments is unknown, it is safe to conclude that privatization will continue to be a public option in most state agencies at least in the next several years.

Issues in Privatization

There are a number of key issues for state policymakers to consider when contemplating privatization either on a statewide or agency-wide basis. Such issues and questions include legal restrictions, lessons learned from previous privatization experiments, productivity, employee displacement, the role of government and accountability due to the blurring line between the public and private sectors

Restrictions

In many states, privatization initiatives have encountered various challenges. To implement privatization initiatives, constitutional provisions had

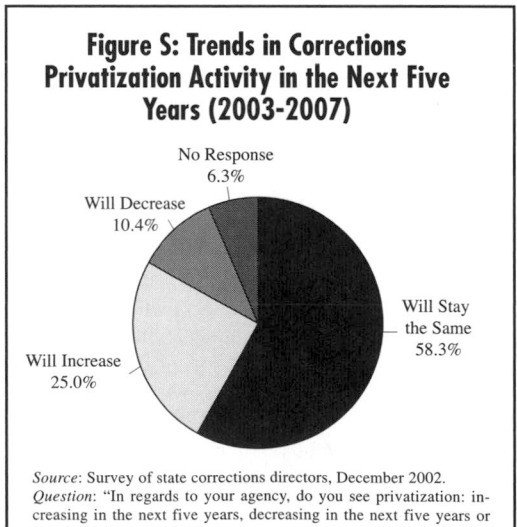

Figure S: Trends in Corrections Privatization Activity in the Next Five Years (2003-2007)

No Response 6.3%

Will Decrease 10.4%

Will Stay the Same 58.3%

Will Increase 25.0%

Source: Survey of state corrections directors, December 2002.
Question: "In regards to your agency, do you see privatization: increasing in the next five years, decreasing in the next five years or remaining the same?"

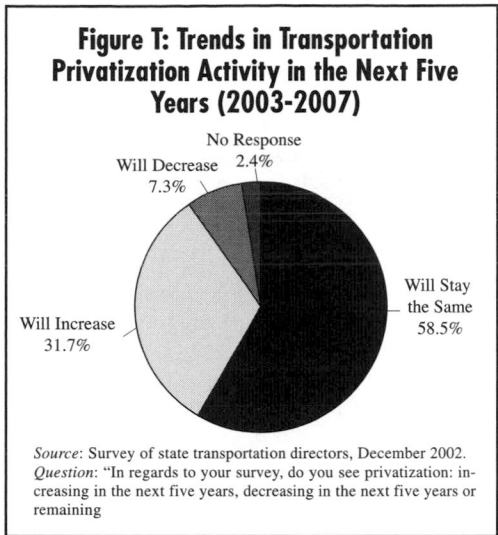

Figure T: Trends in Transportation Privatization Activity in the Next Five Years (2003-2007)

No Response 2.4%
Will Decrease 7.3%
Will Increase 31.7%
Will Stay the Same 58.5%

Source: Survey of state transportation directors, December 2002. *Question*: "In regards to your survey, do you see privatization: increasing in the next five years, decreasing in the next five years or remaining

to be clarified in some states, while, in other states, legal restrictions had to be lifted by legislative measures. In several cases, state civil service systems were blamed as a barrier to privatization.

In addition, in certain cases, federal laws and regulations posed some obstacles to privatization efforts. For example, the major federal barriers that inhibit privatization of state and local enterprises include grant requirements, regulatory requirements and tax policy. According to a Joint Economic Committee staff report released in 1996: "Grant requirements dictate that state and local governments return any undepreciated portions of their federal grants to the federal government. This makes privatization more expensive and encourages continued government control. Regulatory requirements inhibit private investment. For example, tolls are prohibited on most interstate highways. Without tolls, private investors have no way to raise revenues and investment will not occur. Tax policy subsidizes government-owned enterprises but not privately-owned businesses. As a result, competition does not take place on a level playing field, which makes state-owned enterprises appear more efficient than they are and discourages private competitors."[4] In 1996, the National Governors Association adopted a policy asking Congress to remove such federal barriers to allow greater opportunities for privatization, particularly in asset sales, in state and local government.

Lessons

Until recently, as one observer put it, the subject of privatization has been discussed by scholars, poli-

ticians and practitioners in an exaggerated and dogmatic manner.[5] It seems that now is the time to engage in more serious discussions since we now have more information and some empirical data on privatization, albeit still insufficient, than we had in the past. Any meaningful debate on the merits and demerits of privatization should be based on practical lessons policy makers and public administrators have learned over the years; some of the lessons from privatization experiences in state government may be highlighted in four areas.

First, thus far privatization has proven to be neither a cure-all panacea for ineffective government nor a dangerous concept harmful to government operations. As the CSG survey findings would indicate, state policymakers now tend to consider privatization as a cost saving device or as a way to manage their agencies and deliver public services without hiring new staff or experts in certain areas. It appears that privatization has now become a less ideological, less partisan, pragmatic approach for policymakers to consider.

Second, state policymakers should not treat all privatization initiatives equally. For example, contracting out facilities maintenance by a state agency has less serious implications as privatizing management of state prisons or running a mental health facility. Selling off state assets is different from contracting out janitorial services in state agencies. Privatization in state agencies is not the same as it is in city governments either. Privatization has different implications and consequences depending the nature and forms of privatization.

Third, there is no question that government can be more effective than businesses in certain program areas, especially when it comes to customer services.[6] There is no reason to propose privatization when citizens and service clients are satisfied with ongoing government programs and services. Privatization may be considered when policymakers decide that they can deliver more or better services with less taxpayer money by using the private sector.

Fourth, it should be noted, one of the purposes of privatization, according to it supporters, is to dismantle government monopoly in service delivery in favor of private competition. If there is no real competition among able and willing private providers, a privatization initiative is unlikely to realize its stated goals and objectives because such a situation is likely to replace government monopoly with private monopoly. This lesson is particularly pertinent in an era of business restructuring and mergers.

Lastly, it is important to assess practical lessons

learned from state and local experiences for successful privatization projects. Two useful sources of such information are available: one by the U.S. General Accounting Office and another by The Council of State Governments (CSG). Based on its study of selected states and cities, the GAO identified the following six components of a successful privatization initiative: a committed political leader to champion it; a government organizational structure to implement it, legislation to reduce resources to government agencies as an incentive to privatize, reliable cost data, plans for government employee transition to the private sector and monitoring results of privatization.[7] One previous report by CSG also offered specific suggestions for successful implementation of privatization projects. These include: political leadership and support, clear and measurable goals, data collection, monitoring, evaluation, safe guards, team efforts and employee participation in the privatization-planning phase.[8]

Productivity

One key issue is on contracting or outsourcing. Is contracting out a better tool to improve government productivity - effectiveness and efficiency - compared to traditional, in-house productivity techniques? With some exceptions, a majority of state officials who responded to the 1997 and 2002 CSG surveys estimated the savings from their privatization activities to be less than 5 percent. But a more interesting finding from the surveys is that many agency directors could not provide estimates of cost savings from privatization. Nonetheless, state officials have continued to privatize due to the perceived efficiency the private sector might have demonstrated. Some critics and opponents of privatization have focused on the way government is calculating cost savings from privatization.[9] One review of the literature on early privatization activities concluded that privatization may well result in economy but the achievement of productivity is problematic.[10] It is important to follow up with case studies of reliable empirical data.

In addition, there are a number of questions to address the efficiency issue at operational levels when contemplating contracting out government services. For example: Which government office should conduct a cost analysis - a central agency or the agency seeking to privatize? Should an employee group, a potential contractor and private consultant be designated to perform a cost comparison? When should cost analysis be conducted - before or after a contractor is chosen? What should be included in contractor costs - contract price, contract administration and oversight costs, transition costs, conversion costs? What costs should be included in total government costs - direct costs, cost of benefits, indirect costs, avoidable costs? Should there a minimum threshold of cost savings to privatize a service or function? And, what performance period should be used to determine projected cost savings - one year or several years?

Employee Displacement

One of the most difficult issues faced by state policymakers when implementing privatization is its impact on government employees. Not surprisingly, the strongest resistance to privatization usually comes from employee unions and state employees, including those whose jobs may be affected. In fact state employees in several states filed lawsuits against their government to oppose privatization. In some cases, agency directors have addressed such employee concerns by reassigning personnel within government, allowing them to compete with private vendors or consulting with employee organizations. They also have adopted measures to deal with employees affected by privatization by requiring private contractors to give preferential treatment in hiring, offering enhanced severance packages or allowing an early retirement option. Some have expressed concerns about the impact of privatization on minorities in the public services.[11] Little research has been done to determine whether racial minorities and women have been negatively affected by privatization initiatives.

The Role of Government

As many researchers on privatization contend, the privatization movement was initiated in part to reduce the role of government by handing over, or eliminating, some of its functions or services to the private sector. David Osborne, the co-author of *Reinventing Government*, disagreed with this widely held assumption by saying, "Privatization is simply the wrong starting point for a discussion of the role of government. Services can be contracted to the private sector, but governance cannot."[12] Under privatization, policymakers should not delegate its authority or responsibility to oversee private contractor performance. As long as privatized services are financed by taxpayers, policymakers are accountable for private providers' performance, including their mismanagement, and must pay attention to the dangers of corruption, service interruption and unfair labor practices by the private sector. When addressing the role of government under

Table A: Most Popular Privatized Services

Program or service	*States*
Most Popular Privatized Corrections Programs and Services	
Medical/health care services	Ala., Alaska, Ark., Del., Fla., Ind., Kan., Maine, Md., Mass., Minn., Miss., Neb., Nev., N.J., N.M., N.Y., N.C., N.D., Ohio, Pa., S.D., Tenn., Va., W.Va., Wyo.
Food services	Ariz., Fla., Ind., Kan., Md., Mass., Minn., Miss., Neb., N.M., Ohio, Pa., R.I., S.D., Tenn., Va., W.Va.
Substance abuse treatment	Ariz., Del., Fla., Idaho, Mass., N.M., Texas, Utah
Mental health services	Alaska, Idaho, Kan., Md., Ohio, Tenn., W.Va.
Private prisons	Ind., Miss., Mont., Okla., Tenn., Texas, Wyo.
Inmate housing	Alaska, Ariz., Fla., Hawaii, Idaho, Ky., N.M.
Most Popular Privatized Education Programs and Services	
Information technology	Ga., La., Md., Mich., Mo., N.J., N.D., Ohio, Ore., R.I., S.D., Tenn., Texas, Vt., Wis., Wyo.
Professional development/training	Mich., N.H., R.I., S.C., S.D., Tenn., Vt.
Statewide student assessment	Mont., Ore., Tenn., Vt., Wyo.
Product/program development	Iowa, Md., Mich., Vt., Wyo.
Special education	Iowa, Mont., Ore., R.I., Tenn.
Most Popular Privatized Health & Human Services Programs and Services	
Mental health services	Alaska, Ariz., Del., Ga., Idaho, Md., Okla., Pa., Utah, W.Va.
Child welfare services	Alaska, Ga., Mo., N.M., N.D., Okla., Pa., Utah
Substance abuse treatment/ prevention	Alaska, Ark., Del., Fla., N.J., Pa.
Child support administration	Ga., Idaho, Neb., N.M., Ohio, Okla.
Medical services/staff	Fla., Ky., Neb., R.I., W.Va.
Most Popular Privatized Personnel Programs and Services	
Training program staff/development	Calif., Conn., Iowa, La., Mich., N.D., Okla., Tenn., Wash., Wyo.
Information technology	Conn., Fla., Idaho, Ill., Minn., Mont.
Workers' compensation claims processing	Conn., Iowa, S.D.
Health insurance claims processing	Mont., S.D.
General program administration/support	Ill., Iowa
Consultants	Idaho, Iowa
Collective bargaining negotiations	Fla., Iowa
Most Popular Privatized Transportation Services Programs and Services	
General project design/engineering	Colo., Conn., Del., Hawaii, Kan., La., Mich., Miss., Mont., Neb., N.C., Okla., Ore., Pa., Tenn., Texas, Vt., Wis., Wyo.
General construction/maintenance	Conn., Hawaii, Iowa, Kan., Mich., Miss., Mont., Neb., N.J., N.C., Okla., Ore., Pa., Tenn., Wash., Wis.
Information technology	Iowa, Kan., Minn., Mont., Ore., Pa., Tenn., Texas, Wis.
Inspections	Ark., Conn., Del., Kan., Minn., Miss., Okla., R.I.
Grass mowing	Ark., Del., La., Miss., Mont., S.C., Vt.
Rest area operation/maintenance	Ind., La., Minn., Mont., S.C., Wis., Wyo.
Highway construction/maintenance	Ariz., Ark., Conn., Iowa, Ky., La., Texas

Source: Survey of directors from five executive agencies, December 2002.
Question: "Please list the services that have been privatized by your agency."

privatization, state policymakers should also identify core functions and services government must perform by itself for public interest. But there is no consensus on such activities called "inherently governmental activities." In general terms, inherently governmental activities include those that "require either the exercise of discretion in applying government authority or the making of value judgments in making decisions for the government. Government functions normally fall into two categories: the act of government and monetary transactions and entitlements."[13] In the privatization debate, the concept of "governmental"

received little attention from public administration researchers.[14] Whether any inherently governmental activities should be privatized is an important question to consider.

Sector Blurring

The recent privatization trend has further intensified the blurring of the lines between the public and private sectors. In addition to sale of assets, contracting out and traditional public-private partnership projects, for example, many states have recently replicated private management practices, notably strategic planning and benchmarking, quality management, and performance measurement. Some states reformed their civil service system to incorporate private sector practices such as broad banding, performance-based pay and hiring of at-will employees under a radically reformed personnel policy.

How should we react to the further blurring of private and public sectors? Alarmists have argued that privatization might contribute to the "disintegration of government" because they view the public and private sectors as adversaries, competing against each other. One observer said, "sector blurring violates sound constitutional principles and ultimately threatens the ability of elected and appointed officials to maintain an orderly and responsible democratic government."[15] Others have countered the alarmist view by saying that "sector blurring does not mean that public law is any less important or that the Constitution is any less the centerpiece of American government."[16] However, many privatization advocates would agree that the two sectors should be regarded as partners and collaborators. As one observer put it, "They are not opposing alternatives. Business and government are not engaged in a zero-sum game.... The public management skills needed for sustained, successful public-private partnerships require leadership and clarity of executive responsibility."[17] Nonetheless, the question of whether sector blurring should be considered a blessing or a curse needs to be debated continuously by policymakers and researchers from the perspective of future public administration and management.

Notes

[1] John Engler, "Privatization : Heed the Call," *ASI Solutions* (Winter 1996), 2.

[2] www.afscme.org/private.

[3] Keon S. Chi and Cindy Jasper, *Private Practices: A Review of Privatization in State Government*, (Lexington, KY: The Council of State Governments, 1998).

[4] Joint Economic Committee Staff Report, *Federal Barriers to state and Local Privatization*, (U.S. Senate, 1996).

[5] Charles T. Goodsell, "Privatization and the Public Interest" (Remarks presented at the Conference on Contracting for Services, Atlanta, GA, April 24, 1986).

[6] George Frederickson, "When It's Better to Be A Customer of Government," *Governing* (April 1996), 10.

[7] U.S. General Accounting Office, *Privatization: Lessons Learned by State and Local Governments*, (Washington, D.C.: U.S. General Accounting Office, 1997).

[8] Keon S. Chi and Cindy Jasper.

[9] Elliott Sclar, *The Privatization of Public Service*, (Washington, D.C.: Economic Policy Institute, 1998).

[10] Timothy K. Barnekov and Jeffrey A. Raffel, "Public Management of Privatization," *Public Productivity & Management Review* (Winter 1990), 135-52.

[11] Dennis J. Palumbo, "The Political Side of Privatization," *Journal of Management Science & Policy Analysis* (Winter 1989), 25-40.

[12] David Osborne, "Privatization: One Answer, Not the Answer," *Governing* (April 1992), 83.

[13] U.S. General Accounting Office, *Terms Related to Privatization Activities and Processes*, (Washington, D.C.: U.S. General Accounting Office, 1997).

[14] Larkin Dudley, "Questions Unanswered: Comparing Federal and State Arguments Surrounding Inherently Governmental Functions" (Paper presented at the 55th Annual Meeting of the American Society for Public Administration, Kansas City, MO, 1994).

[15] Ronald C. Moe, "Exploring the Limits of Privatization," *Public Administration Review* (November/December 1987), 453-60.

[16] Barry Bozeman, "Exploring the Limits of Public and Private Sectors: Sector Boundaries as Maginot Line," *Public Administration Review* (March/April 1988), 672-5.

[17] Annamarie Hauck Walsh, "Privatization: Implications for Public Management," *IPA Report* (Spring 1996), 1-9.

About the Authors

Keon S. Chi is editor in chief of *The Book of the States* and *Spectrum: The Journal of State Government*. He has served on the editorial board of *Public Administration Review, American Journal of Public Administration, State and Local Government Review* and *Public Integrity*.

Kelley A. Arnold is the publications and customer service coordinator for The Council of State Governments. She holds a master's degree in communications from the University of Kentucky.

Heather M. Perkins, an associate editor of *The Book of the States*, is an editorial associate for The Council of State Governments. She also serves as the associate editor of *Spectrum: The Journal of State Government*.

Table B
METHODS OF PRIVATIZATION USED BY STATE GOVERNMENTS, BY REGION: 2002

State	Asset sale	Contracting out	Deregulation	Grants & subsidies	Private donations	Public-private partnership	Service shedding	Volunteerism	Vouchers
Eastern Region									
Connecticut	...	...	...	★	...	★	...	...	...
Delaware	★	...	...	...	...	...	...	...	...
Maine	...............(a)								
Massachusetts	...	★	...	★	...	...	...	...	...
New Hampshire	...............(a)								
New Jersey	...	★	...	...	...	★	...	...	...
New York	★	★	★	...	...	★	...	...	...
Pennsylvania	...	★	...	...	...	...	...	...	...
Rhode Island	...............(a)								
Vermont	...............(a)								
Midwest Region									
Illinois	...	★	...	...	...	...	...	...	...
Indiana	...	★	...	★	★	...	...	...	★
Iowa	...	★	...	...	...	★	...	...	...
Kansas	...............(a)								
Michigan	★	★	...	★	...	★	...	★	...
Minnesota	...	★	...	...	...	★	...	...	...
Nebraska	...	★	...	...	...	...	...	...	...
North Dakota	...............(a)								
Ohio	...............(a)								
South Dakota	...	★	...	★	...	★	...	...	...
Wisconsin	...	★	...	...	...	★	...	...	★
Southern Region									
Alabama	...............(a)								
Arkansas	...............(a)								
Florida	...............(a)								
Georgia	...	★	...	...	...	★	★	...	...
Kentucky	...	★	...	...	...	...	...	...	...
Louisiana	★	...	...	★	...	...	...	...	...
Maryland	★	★	★	...	...	★	...	...	★
Mississippi	...	★	...	★	...	★	...	★	...
Missouri	...	★	...	★	...	★	...	...	...
North Carolina	...	★	...	★	★	★	...	★	...
Oklahoma	★	★	...	★	★	★	...	★	...
South Carolina	...	★	...	★	★	★	...	...	...
Tennessee	...	★	...	...	...	...	...	...	...
Texas	...............(a)								
Virginia	★	★	...	...	...	...	...	★	...
West Virginia	...	★	...	...	...	...	...	...	...
Western Region									
Alaska	★	★	...	★	...	★	...	...	...
Arizona	...	★	...	★	...	★	...	...	...
California	...............(a)								
Colorado	...	★	...	...	...	...	...	...	...
Hawaii	...............(a)								
Idaho	...	★	...	...	...	★	...	...	...
Montana	...............(a)								
Nevada	...	★	...	★	...	★	...	★	...
New Mexico	...	★	...	...	...	...	...	...	...
Oregon	...	★	...	...	...	★	...	...	...
Utah	...	★	...	...	...	...	...	...	...
Washington	★	★	...	★	★	★	...	★	...
Wyoming	...	★	...	...	...	★	...	...	...

Source: The Council of State Governments' Survey of State Budget Directors, December 2002. Question: "Which of the following methods of privatization are used in your state?"

Key:
★ — Yes
... — No
(a) Did not respond.

Table C
SELECT STATE AGENCY PRIVATIZATION STATISTICS, BY REGION: 2002

State	Department of Corrections	Department of Education	Department of Health & Human Services	Department of Personnel	Department of Transportation
Eastern Region					
Connecticut	A	(a)	(a)	(n)	E
Delaware	(a)	(a)	E	(a)	(b)
Maine	B	(a)	(a)	(a)	E
Massachusetts	E (l)	B	(a)	(q)	(a)
New Hampshire	(g)	B	A	(q)	E
New Jersey	A (m)	B	E	(a)	E
New York	A	(a)	(a)	(a)	(a)
Pennsylvania	C	(a)	E	(n)	E
Rhode Island	B	D	E (v)	(a)	B
Vermont	D	D	A	(a)	(c)
Midwest Region					
Illinois	(a)	A	B	A	(a)
Indiana	C	B	(a)	(a)	B
Iowa	(n)	B	A	(n)	E (d)
Kansas	E (o)	A	E	(n)	C
Michigan	A	E	A	C	E
Minnesota	C	(a)	(q)	(q)	(e)
Nebraska	B	E	B	(a)	B
North Dakota	B	A	E	B	A
Ohio	C	A	(a)	(a)	(a)
South Dakota	E	C	(a)	A	(f)
Wisconsin	(a)	B	(a)	(q)	(a)
Southern Region					
Alabama	B	A	(q)	(q)	(a)
Arkansas	A	(a)	B	(q)	C
Florida	(n)	(a)	A	D (y)	E
Georgia	C	C	D	B	E
Kentucky	B	A	(w)	(q)	E
Louisiana	E	B	(a)	B	E
Maryland	(a)	D	E (x)	(a)	(g)
Mississippi	B	(q)	(a)	(a)	D
Missouri	C	B	B	(a)	(a)
North Carolina	A	(a)	(n)	B	(h)
Oklahoma	E (p)	(a)	C	B	E (i)
South Carolina	(q)	B	(a)	B	B
Tennessee	E (r)	B	(a)	A	C
Texas	D	D	(q)	(q)	E
Virginia	B	(a)	(a)	(a)	(a)
West Virginia	D (s)	A	D	(q)	(a)
Western Region					
Alaska	E (t)	B	A	B	E
Arizona	B	(a)	E	A	E
California	B	(a)	(a)	A	D (j)
Colorado	E	(a)	(a)	(a)	C
Hawaii	E	(a)	(a)	(a)	E
Idaho	B	A	B	A	(a)
Montana	B	B	(a)	(a)	E
Nevada	A	(q)	C	(a)	E
New Mexico	E	(a)	C	(q)	E (k)
Oregon	(a)	C	E	(a)	E
Utah	A	A	E	A	C
Washington	C	(q)	E	B	A
Wyoming	E (u)	B	A	A	B

See footnotes at end of table.

SELECT STATE AGENCY PRIVATIZATION STATISTICS, BY REGION: 2002 — Continued

Source: The Council of State Governments' Survey of State Agency Directors, December 2002. Question: "How many services and programs in your agency are currently privatized?"

Key:

A — Less than 1 percent of services are currently privatized.

B — 1–5 percent of services are currently privatized.

C — 6–10 percent of services are currently privatized.

D — 11–15 percent of services are currently privatized.

E — More than 15 percent of services are currently privatized.

(a) Did not respond.

(b) This is not tracked.

(c) Not able to quantify. Privatization is used to supplement, not replace, state personnel.

(d) All highway construction and significant amount of highway project design is privatized.

(e) On a dollar basis, approximately 55 percent of the department's budget is devoted to hiring outside consulting and contracting firms for design engineering and construction activities.

(f) With regards to supplementing staff, it is less than 1 percent. The DOT contracts out all construction and major maintenance activities and has done so historically.

(g) Unknown.

(h) Construction and maintenance: 6-10 percent; Preconstruction, planning and environment: more than 15 percent.

(i) In this context, DOT is referring to "out-sourcing" or "contracting-out" services.

(j) Approximately 13 percent of our capital outlay support work is budgeted to be done by private contractors. Our annual usage of privatized work has been less budgeted.

(k) New Mexico contracts 75 percent of all road construction, that is different that "privatization."

(l) Based on number of program/services only, not financial figures.

(m) Inmate medical care is the only area which has been privatized.

(n) Data not available.

(o) Approximately 21 percent of the department's operating budget is contracted services procured through a competitive process, although not all contractors are "private."

(p) Private prisons account for approximately 25 percent of our agency budget.

(q) Agency does not engage in privatization.

(r) 17 percent of the budget.

(s) In terms of dollars expended this fiscal year.

(t) All halfway houses, half of medical services and out-of-state prison services are privatized.

(u) About 25 percent of the budget is for contract services.

(v) Percentage represents dollars spent on contracts relative to personnel and operating. The percentage of the department's total budget is less than 1 percent.

(w) Office of Inspector General: less than 1 percent; Dept. for Public Health and Dept. for Mental Health & Mental Retardation: 1-5 percent; Medicaid Benefits program: more than 15 percent. Medicaid Benefits program utilizes a fiscal agent under a contractual arrangement to administer the volume of data produced by this program.

(x) Current budget is 90 percent contracts and grants.

(y) Outsourced—not privatized.

Table D
TRENDS IN PRIVATIZATION, BY REGION

State	Amount of privatization activity in the past five years					Amount of privatization activity in the next five years		
	Dramatically increased	Increased	Stayed the same	Decreased	Dramatically decreased	Increasing	Decreasing	Remaining the same
Eastern Region								
Connecticut	...	★	...	...	...	★	...	...
Delaware	...	...	★	...	...	...	...	★
Maine	....(a)...							
Massachusetts	...	...	★	...	...	...	...	★
New Hampshire	....(a)...							
New Jersey	...	...	...	★	...	...	★	...
New York	...	...	★	...	...	★	...	...
Pennsylvania	...	★	...	...	...	...	...	★
Rhode Island	....(a)...							
Vermont	...	...	★	...	...	...	...	★
Midwest Region								
Illinois	...	★	...	...	...	...	★	...
Indiana	...	...	★	...	...	...	...	★
Iowa	...	...	★	...	...	....................(a)....................		
Kansas	....(a)...							
Michigan	...	...	★	...	...	....................(b)....................		
Minnesota	...	...	★	...	...	★	...	...
Nebraska	...	...	★	...	...	...	...	★
North Dakota	...	★	...	...	...	★	...	...
Ohio	....(a)...							
South Dakota	...	...	★	...	...	...	...	★
Wisconsin	...	★	...	...	...	...	...	★
Southern Region								
Alabama	....(a)...							
Arkansas	...	...	...	★	...	...	★	...
Florida	....(a)...							
Georgia	...	...	...	★	...	★	...	...
Kentucky	...	...	★	...	...	...	...	★
Louisiana	...	...	★	...	...	...	...	★
Maryland	...	...	★	...	...	...	...	★
Mississippi	...	...	★	...	...	...	...	★
Missouri	★	...	...	...	...	★	...	...
North Carolina	...	★	...	...	...	★	...	...
Oklahoma	...	★	...	...	...	....................(c)....................		
South Carolina	...	...	★	...	...	★	...	...
Tennessee	...	...	★	...	...	...	...	...
Texas	....(a)...							
Virginia	...	...	★	...	...	★	...	...
West Virginia	...	...	★	...	...	★	...	...
Western Region								
Alaska	★	...	...	...	...	...	...	★
Arizona	...	★	...	...	...	★	...	...
California	....(a)...							
Colorado	...	...	★	...	...			
Hawaii	....(a)...							
Idaho	...	★	...	...	...	★	...	...
Montana	....(a)...							
Nevada	...	★	...	...	...	★	...	...
New Mexico	...	...	...	★	...	...	★	...
Oregon	...	...	★	...	...	★	...	...
Utah	...	...	...	★	...	....................(b)....................		
Washington	...	...	★	...	...	★	...	...
Wyoming	...	...	★	...	...	...	...	★

Source: The Council of State Government's Survey of State Budget Directors, December 2002. Questions: "Which of the following best describes the amount of privatization activity in the past five years?" "In your state, do you see privatization: increasing in the next five years, decreasing in the next five years or remaining the same?"

Key:
★ — Yes
... — No

(a) Did not respond.
(b) The extent of privatization in the future years is unknown.
(c) Decreasing and remaining the same. The new administration and budget problems will likely impact contract services first.

Chapter Nine

SELECTED STATE POLICIES AND PROGRAMS

"State emergency management agencies are now facing a monumental task of adapting to their new roles in homeland security."

— Amy C. Hughes

"Unlike past federal legislation, it is fair to say that No Child Left Behind affects every child in every school in America."

— Dewayne Matthews

"States look to their higher education institutions to provide high quality education in a range of rapidly changing fields of endeavor."

— John W. Curtis

"Our dilemma is that our agricultural productivity outruns the demand for food and farm prices slowly decline over time hurting farmers and their communities."

— Otto C. Doering III

"The domestic competition to create and retain jobs in the sour economy over the last two years has forced states to get more aggressive than ever in facilitating economic development."

— Jeff Finkle

"The states are doubling their efforts to educate and train people in order to attract and grow industry domestically."

— Mark Arend

"We must look at all forms of energy."

— Robert Middleton

"The federal government should provide funding to the states or other relief to the states for further implementation of federal rules."

— R. Steven Brown

"The 30 states that have established state pharmaceutical assistance programs will need to review the future of these programs in light of Medicare changes."

— Trudi Matthews

"Half the states are reorganizing their state hospitals, including downsizing, reconfiguring, closing and/or consolidating."

— Theodore C. Lutterman, Robert Shaw, Ronald Manderscheid and Noel A. Mazade

"As state officials struggle with budget shortfalls, it is increasingly important to understand the changing nature of state corrections."

— John J. Mountjoy

"As the economy weakened, caseload decline either diminished or reversed. The weaker outcomes demonstrate the substantial challenges of state and local welfare policies."

— Sheila R. Zedlewski

State Emergency Management:
New Realities in a Homeland Security World
By Amy C. Hughes

While 2002 was a year of tremendous change for the emergency management community, year 2003 represents a "settling in" period for the implications of homeland security on the nation's level of preparedness for all hazards. Threats to traditional funding for emergency management and an influx of federal grants funds for everything from haz-mat suits to radio equipment are creating unique challenges for states as they try to maintain a focus on all-hazards preparedness.

Introduction

The Department of Homeland Security is hitting its stride as it continues to formulate its mission as the lead agency for the detection, prevention, response and recovery from disasters, both natural and man-made. In the months since its creation, the state emergency management landscape has changed significantly. State emergency management agencies are now facing a monumental task of adapting to their new roles in homeland security, administering billions of dollars in a long stream of federal funding, serving as administrator for local jurisdictions, and facilitating regional cooperation, while maintaining a hold on the viability of the "all-hazards preparedness" philosophy.

Emergency Management Organizations

State emergency management agencies are responsible for developing emergency operations plans and procedures for all disasters and emergencies (including homeland security); training personnel; and conducting drills and exercises with local governments, state agencies, volunteer organizations and the federal government. Emergency management agencies are also responsible for coordinating and facilitating the provision of resources and supplemental assistance to local governments when events exceed their capabilities. In the aftermath of a disaster or emergency, the emergency management agency coordinates public education, information and warning; conducts damage assessments, resource management and logistics; facilitates mutual aid, sheltering and mass care; manages transportation and evacuation; leads incident management; and oversees the emergency operations center.[1] In times of disaster, the nation's governors depend on the emergency management agency to provide damage estimates, assist the governor's office in crisis communications by providing accurate and realistic information, activate mutual aid agreements to move resources quickly and efficiently, and coordinate with local volunteer organizations to manage donations and supplementary assistance.

The organization of state emergency management agencies varies widely. Currently, in 13 states, the emergency management agency is located within the department of public safety; in 19 states it is located within the military department under the auspices of the adjutant general; and in 11 states, it is located within the governor's office. Regardless of the agencies' organizational structure for daily operations, emergency management ranks high among governors' priorities. In 31 states, the emergency management director is appointed by the governor. The position is appointed by the adjutant general in 11 states and by the secretary of public safety or state police superintendent in eight states.

Homeland Security Structures

The attacks on the World Trade Center and the Pentagon increased public awareness of the potential for domestic terrorism incidents and hastened preparedness efforts by all levels of government. The challenge states face is to integrate homeland security planning and response activities into their existing emergency management and response systems.

All states have designated a homeland security point of contact. This position has become a critical component of a governor's staff and one that has an enormous responsibility to the public for preparing citizens, businesses and governments for the next emergency or large-scale disaster. Ten states have established a unique position of *homeland security director*. In nine states, the emergency management director is the primary point of contact, and in 11 states it is the adjutant general or director of the military department. Increasingly, states are placing the responsibility of homeland security in the hands of the more traditional first responder agencies. In 15 states the public safety secretary serves as homeland security designee. Five states have appointed special advisor positions within the governor's office. These positions operate under the authority of a governor's executive order in 17 states and by statute in 10 others. Eighteen positions or offices operate under the verbal authority of the governor, while seven function by a combination of these authorities (see Table B, "Homeland Security Structures").

To promote interagency cooperation and coordination, 49 states have created a terrorism committee, task force or council. These entities provide direction and focus for statewide planning efforts, funding allocations and overall preparedness activities.

Many states have undergone internal reorganizations to adequately staff and fund homeland security offices and to appropriately realign their resources to accommodate the growing threat of terrorism (see Table C, "Reorganization for Homeland Security"). Nineteen states indicated they had recently completed a reorganization to create an office to address homeland security or to otherwise change the structure of the existing homeland security organization. In 2003, as new governors took office and reassessed the organization of the important roles of state government, several states moved the functions of—and funding streams for—homeland security into agencies with existing responsibilities for public safety.

Several states merged their homeland security and emergency management agencies to provide for greater coordination and to maximize state and federal funds. Doing so allows states to capitalize on the existing capabilities and years of experience and lessons learned from past disasters, which can be readily applied to domestic terrorism events. Emergency management is the central coordination point for all resources and assistance provided during disasters and emergencies, including acts of terrorism. Many states are building upon this experience and leveraging the ability of emergency management to bridge the gaps in communication and mobilize its resources to respond to <u>any</u> type of disaster, however unique, specialized or isolated.

Seven states indicated that reorganization had been proposed or were in the planning stages of reorganization. Twenty-five states reported that reorganization was not in the works. Regardless of the positioning of homeland security in government, states must work to foster and maintain a balance among the detection, prevention, preparedness, response and recovery roles needed to strengthen its resilience to natural and man-made disasters.

Traditional Funding is Losing Out

While new money is in the pipeline for such programs as bioterrorism preparedness and interoperable communications, funding for traditional programs such as the Predisaster Mitigation Program, the National Flood Insurance Program, the Hazard Mitigation Grant Program, and the Emergency Management Performance Grant is losing its foothold. These programs provide long term, critical operational funding for emergency management and the proven, successful programs that minimize the risk to property and life before a disaster occurs.

Earmarking funds for a particular need is a popular legislative strategy, but traditional funding for basic state emergency operations, grants management, technical assistance for locals, training, and public outreach has been lost in a wave of stovepipe funding for equipment, exercises, border and port security, and critical infrastructure protection. These are legitimate needs, but states and locals are struggling to simply maintain adequate staffing levels, pay overtime and administer the funds channeled through their agencies.

Funding for emergency management programs has been stagnant for over a decade, with only modest increases in state operating budgets despite the national focus on homeland security. State budget cuts due to revenue shortfalls have hit emergency management and public safety agencies at a time when more is expected from them. Increased responsibilities for homeland security and the loss of adequate funding for basic operations have taken their toll. In fiscal year 2004, agency budgets ranged from $645,000 to $637 million, including state disaster appropriations. The national average was $37.8 million, a 29 percent reduction from fiscal year 2003. This average represents less than 1 percent of total state government budgets. Despite the deficit, these budgets support an average of 69 full-time employees. Staffing levels in individual agencies range from 1 to 512 full-time employees (see Table A, "State Emergency Management: Agency Structure, Budget and Staffing").

Most new federal funds are being directed specifically toward homeland security activities, while ignoring the needs of basic public safety systems. The nation's emergency management and response system can support homeland security efforts, but must be made more robust and then maintained over the long-term. As their budgets allow, some states are doing their part by appropriating additional funds for homeland security related activities such as planning, training, and exercises; intelligence sharing and analysis; capitol complex security; improvements to local emergency operations centers; critical infrastructure protection; increases in law enforcement personnel; support costs for homeland security staff; and matching funds to assist local jurisdictions in meeting federal grant requirements. However, more can be done. States need the flexibility to direct federal funds to fill the gaps where they cannot – whether it be to develop a specialized response capability to deal with particular threats or to enhance overall emergency preparedness within the state.

New Money, New Problems

Within a very short timeframe the Department of Homeland Security made billions of dollars available to state and local governments for disaster planning, exercises, first responder equipment and additional security for high-population, high-threat areas. When can having too much money be a problem? A report by the nation's mayors[2] indicated that states have been slow to pass through the required grant funds in the timeframe required by the federal government and have not been included in the planning process to distribute the funding. However, along with these grants come stringent deadlines and reporting requirements which do not fit into the traditional governance processes of state and local jurisdictions. States have been unduly criticized for a system they cannot overstep.

States are required to: conduct statewide threat, vulnerability and needs assessments with local jurisdictions; coordinate the distribution and expenditure of the funds with the state homeland security strategic plan and in coordination with the state interagency terrorism taskforce or committees; ensure that sub-grantees adhere to state and federal guidelines and regulations; execute contracts for equipment and services which may take weeks to receive; and maintain accountability throughout the program. The expedited processes and procedures that are necessary for states to meet the 45 to 60 day deadlines result in little time for collaboration and consensus building with local jurisdictions. Local jurisdictions have their own internal purchasing requirements and budgetary restrictions that prevent grant funds from being expended in the time allotted.

Whatever the complaints, this very public debate has highlighted the areas where grant funding can be improved.[3] Future grant funding should include:

- Realistic deadlines for distributing and expending funds;

- Flexibility for states and locals to place resources based on the needs and priorities of each jurisdiction;

- Waivers for states that cannot meet match requirements due to budget constraints;

- Longer-term, stable funding which builds capacity and sustains it;

- A streamlined grant application process.

Several efforts are underway in Congress to consolidate grant programs, simplify the application process, focus funds on the areas where threats and vulnerabilities are greatest, and develop national standards for equipment and training. While this is a step in the right direction, the proposed legislation imposes deadlines and program requirements which may be problematic for state and local jurisdictions.

A New Strategy for Response

The *National Strategy for Homeland Security* calls for the Department of Homeland Security to integrate the current family of federal domestic prevention, preparedness, response, and recovery plans into a single all-hazards plan, and to develop a comprehensive national incident management system to respond to terrorist incidents and natural hazards.[4] The fundamental requirements of this National Response Plan (NRP) are to develop a consistent approach to domestic preparedness as well as to incident management across the life cycle of the incident—from awareness, through prevention and preparedness, and into response and recovery—and to improve the effective use of resources that are available during each step of this cycle.[5]

The NRP:

- Creates a single, all-hazards plan that is flexible enough to accommodate all types of disasters and applies to all of the disciplines involved in the response;

- Emphasizes the unity of effort among all levels of government, private industry, volunteer organizations, and the public;

- Places equal emphasis on awareness, prevention, preparedness, response and recovery;

- Establishes federal authorities to coordinate federal response efforts and outlines involvement of the Department of Homeland Security in incident management.

The plan has wide implications for state and local governments, as they work to integrate the new system into their current response protocols. State and local stakeholder organizations have provided a significant amount of input to ensure that the plan does not create a new system entirely, but rather, takes advantage of the mechanisms states already have in place. The new approach will take time to implement and exercising of the system will be needed.

Mutual Aid Put to the Test

With decreased budgets and increased responsibilities, states are looking to their neighbors for resources and assistance through mutual aid. The Emergency Management Assistance Compact (EMAC) is a national interstate mutual aid agreement that allows states to share resources during times of disaster. EMAC has been in existence since 1992. To date, 48 states, two territories and the District of Columbia are signatories to EMAC. Membership requires that the compact legislation be enacted by the state legislature and signed into law by the governor.

EMAC is a proven national system for mutual aid and has been implemented on a major scale in response to the September 11 terrorist attack on the World Trade Center, Hurricane Lili, the Space Shuttle Columbia disaster, the Rhode Island club fire in 2003, and flooding in West Virginia. Most recently, EMAC was utilized in the response to Hurricane Isabel, which devastated a five state area along the southeastern seaboard. Approximately 120 personnel from no less than 12 states from across the country responded to requests for assistance before and after the storm hit, to conduct damage assessments, serve as backup staff to state and local emergency operations centers, assist stricken victims in obtaining aid, and help with the flow of information to the public and media. This state-to-state mutual aid system leveraged the capability of an entire nation to respond to a regional disaster.

Despite the influx of new money for emergency responders, many local jurisdictions still do not have access to, or enough of, some of the specialized equipment and response teams needed to handle large-scale disasters and unique emergency situations, such as hazardous materials handling and swiftwater rescue. Because resources and funds are limited, states are implementing *intra*-state mutual aid agreements in increasing numbers. An intrastate mutual aid system provides the legal framework and operational mechanism to move resources and people to and from an emergency scene based on pre-established procedures. Twenty-seven states have some form of statewide mutual aid agreement in place or have proposed legislation in the works. Like EMAC, a majority of these agreements are broad enough to apply to all emergency response disciplines. Membership in many of these compacts is voluntary, but states are providing added incentives, such as training, extra funding, cost share relief, and technical assistance to encourage local jurisdictions to join.

Notes

[1] National Emergency Management Association, *If Disaster Strikes Today – Are You Ready to Lead? A Governor's Primer on All-Hazards Emergency Management,* (Lexington, KY: The National Emergency Management Association, 2002).

[2] U.S. Conference of Mayors Homeland Security Monitoring Center, *First Mayors' Report to the Nation: Tracking Federal Homeland Security Funds Sent to the 50 State Governments*, (Washington, D.C.: U.S. Conference of Mayors, 2003).

[3] The Council of State Governments. "States move millions in DHS funds," *State Government News* (May 2003).

[4] The Office of Homeland Security, *National Strategy for Homeland Security*. (Washington, D.C.: The Office of Homeland Security, July 2002). http://www.whitehouse.gov/homeland/book/index.html.

[5] Department of Homeland Security, *National Response Plan*, (Washington, D.C.: Department of Homeland Security, 2004).

About the Author

Amy C. Hughes is a policy analyst for the National Emergency Management Association, an affiliate of The Council of State Governments. She is responsible for national policy research and analysis, publications and promoting information exchange between states on emergency management and homeland security issues.

Table A
STATE EMERGENCY MANAGEMENT: AGENCY STRUCTURE, BUDGET AND STAFFING

State or other jurisdiction	Position appointed	Appointed/ selected by	Reports to	Organizational structure	Agency budget FY 2004 ($ in thousands)	Disaster appropriations ($ in thousands)	Full-time employee positions
Alabama	★	G	G	Governor's Office	4,700	7,600	65
Alaska	★	G	ADJ	Adjutant General/Military Department	2,300	16,500	59
Arizona	★	ADJ	ADJ	Adjutant General/Military Department	1,500	4,000	50
Arkansas	★	G	G	Governor's Office	278,000	9,000	77
California	★	G	G	Governor's Office	637,000	0	512
Colorado	...	CS	ED	Department of Local Affairs	605	6,000	23
Connecticut	★	G	ADJ	Adjutant General/Military Department	3,301	0	30
Delaware	★	SPS	HSD	Safety & Homeland Security Agency	1,400	100	32
Florida	★	G	G	Department of Community Affairs	280,000	0	133
Georgia	★	G	HSD	Homeland Security Agency	3,000	0	100
Hawaii	★	ADJ	ADJ	Department of Defense	1,500	500	40
Idaho	★	ADJ	ADJ	Governor's Office/Military Division	1,220	0	21
Illinois	★	G	G	Governor's Office	30,000	450	267
Indiana	★	G	G	Governor's Office	1,190	200	47
Iowa	★	G	G/ADJ	Department of Public Defense	4,075	1,000	59
Kansas	★	ADJ	ADJ	Adjutant General/Military Department	2,100	1,100	21
Kentucky	★	G	ADJ	Adjutant General/Military Department	4,100	0	79
Louisiana	★	G	G	Adjutant General/Military Department	1,100	0	44
Maine	★	ADJ	ADJ	Adjutant General/Military Department	1,000	0	18
Maryland	★	G	ADJ	Adjutant General/Military Department	8,700	750	45
Massachusetts	★	G	PSS	Public Safety	25,000	0	67
Michigan	...	CS	SPS	State Police	4,100	0	71
Minnesota	★	PSS	PSS	Public Safety	6,000	4,000	62
Mississippi	★	G	G	Governor's Office	94,000	1,730	65
Missouri	★	ADJ	G	Adjutant General/Military Department	6,600	1,000	69
Montana	...	ADJ	ADJ	Adjutant General/Military Department	500	12,000	22
Nebraska	★	ADJ	ADJ	Adjutant General/Military Department	1,200	2,000	32
Nevada	★	G	G	Public Safety	613	7,000	22
New Hampshire	★	G	PSS	Public Safety	3,211	0	40
New Jersey	★	SPS	SPS	State Police	7,100	0	56
New Mexico	★	G	PSS	Public Safety	500	4,250	29
New York	★	G	G	Adjutant General/Military Department	26,851	75,500	120
North Carolina	★	SPS	PSS	Public Safety	3,394	30,000	171
North Dakota	★	ADJ	ADJ	Adjutant General/Military Department	2,500	0	51
Ohio	★	G	PSS	Public Safety	45,000	10,000	96
Oklahoma	★	G	G	Governor's Office	666	7,600	32
Oregon	★	G	SPS	State Police	1,000	0	32
Pennsylvania	★	G	G	Governor's Office	110,000	0	162
Rhode Island	★	ADJ	ADJ	Adjutant General/Military Department	645	0	20
South Carolina	★	ADJ	ADJ	Adjutant General/Military Department	920	1,000	49
South Dakota	★	PSS	PSS	Public Safety	1,500	0	17
Tennessee	★	G	ADJ	Adjutant General/Military Department	2,970	0	101
Texas	★	SPS	SPS	Public Safety	1,300	0	143
Utah	★	PSS	PSS	Public Safety	11,000	0	60
Vermont	★	PSS	PSS	Public Safety	1,850	0	12
Virginia	★	G	PSS	Public Safety	17,000	35,000	101
Washington	★	G	ADJ	Adjutant General/Military Department	88,000	6,600	80
West Virginia	★	G	PSS	Public Safety	1,238	250	37
Wisconsin	★	G	ADJ	Adjutant General/Military Department	14,279	1,395	46
Wyoming	★	G	HSD	Governor's Office	3,500	1,000	23
District of Columbia	★	M	DM	Department of Public Safety	2,000	0	39
Puerto Rico	★	G	G	Governor's Office	3,600	0	0
U.S. Virgin Islands	★	G	ADJ	Adjutant General/Military Department	651	0	20

Source: The National Emergency Management Association, February 2004.
Key:
★- Yes
... - No
G - Governor
GO - Governor's Office
ADJ - Adjutant General
M - Mayor
HSD - Homeland Security Director/Secretary
DM - Deputy Mayor
PSS - Public Safety Secretary/Commissioner/Director
SPS - State Police Superintendent/Commissioner

CS - Civil Service
PS - Public Safety
HS - Homeland Security
SP - State Police

Table B
STATE HOMELAND SECURITY STRUCTURES

State	Homeland Security appropriations	State Homeland Security Advisor		Interagency coordination	
		Designated contact	Operates under authority of	Terrorism committee/ council/taskforce	Operates under authority of
Alabama	★ (a)	Homeland Security Director	SS	★	SS
Alaska	★ (b)	EM Director	EO	★	GA
Arizona	...	EM Director	GA	★	GA
Arkansas	...	EM Director	GA	★	GA
California	★ (c)	Special Advisor	GA/SS	★	EO
Colorado	...	Public Safety Dir./Sec.	SS	★	GA
Connecticut	★ (d)	Public Safety Dir./Sec.	EO	...	GA
Delaware	...	Homeland Security Director	GA	★	EO
Florida	...	Public Safety Dir./Sec.	SS	★	SS
Georgia	★ (e)	Homeland Security Director	EO	★	GA
Hawaii	...	Adjutant General	GA	★	GA
Idaho	...	Adjutant General	SS	★	EO
Illinois	★ (f)	Public Safety Dir./Sec.(t)	GA/EO/SS	★	EO
Indiana	...	Homeland Security Director	SS	★	SS
Iowa	★ (g)	EM Director	GA/SS	★	HSD
Kansas	...	Adjutant General	GA	★	GA
Kentucky	...	Homeland Security Director	SS	★	GA
Louisiana	★ (h)	Adjutant General	EO	★	EO
Maine	...	Adjutant General	GA	★	GA
Maryland	...	Homeland Security Director	EO	★	EO
Massachusetts	...	Public Safety Dir./Sec.	SS	★	AH
Michigan	★ (i)	Adjutant General	EO	★	AH
Minnesota	...	Public Safety Dir./Sec.	EO	★	SS
Mississippi	★ (j)	EM Director	GA	★	EO
Missouri	★ (k)	Homeland Security Director	EO	★	EO
Montana	...	EM Director	EO	★	EO
Nebraska	★ (l)	Lieutenant Governor	GA	★	GA
Nevada	...	Special Advisor	GA	★	SS
New Hampshire	...	Public Safety Dir./Sec.	GA	★	SS
New Jersey	...	Counter-Terrorism Ofc. Dir.	EO/SS	★	SS
New Mexico	...	Public Safety Dir./Sec.	EO	★	EO
New York	★ (m)	Public Safety Dir./Sec.(u)	EO	★	EO
North Carolina	...	Public Safety Dir./Sec.	EO	★	EO
North Dakota	...	EM Director	GA/SS	★	SS
Ohio	...	Public Safety Dir./Sec.(v)	GA	★	GA
Oklahoma	...	Public Safety Dir./Sec.	GA/EO	★	AH
Oregon	...	Adjutant General	GA	★	GA
Pennsylvania	★ (n)	Homeland Security Director	EO	★	EO
Rhode Island	...	Public Safety Dir./Sec.	GA	...	N.A.
South Carolina	...	Public Safety Dir./Sec.(w)	SS	★	SS
South Dakota	...	Homeland Security Coord.	GA	★	HSD
Tennessee	★ (o)	Deputy to the Governor	EO	★	GA
Texas	...	Special Advisor	GA/SS	★	GA/EO/SS
Utah	...	EM Director	SS	★	EO/SS
Vermont	★ (p)	Civil/Military Affairs Sec.	EO	★	EO/SS
Virginia	...	Special Advisor	EO	★	EO
Washington	...	Adjutant General	GA	★	EO
West Virginia	★ (q)	Public Safety Dir./Sec.	GA	★	SS
Wisconsin	...	EM Director	EO	★	EO
Wyoming	★ (r)	Adjutant General	SS	...	N.A.
Dist. of Columbia	...	Dep. Mayor, Public Safety	GA	★	EO
U.S. Virgin Islands	★ (s)	Adjutant General	GA	★	GA/EO

Source: The National Emergency Management Association, February 2004.
Key:
★- Yes
... - No
GA - Gubernatorial authority
EO - Executive order
SS - State statute
HSD - Homeland Security Director
AH - Agency head
(a) $500,000 for planning, training, equipment and coordination activities for terrorism.
(b) $730,000.
(c) $97M for highway patrol augmentation, California Anti-Terrorism Information Center, SSCOT support.
(d) $1M for increased public safety personnel and equipment.
(e) $2M for intelligence staff for Georgia Bureau of Investigations and Geor-

gia Emergency Management Agency.
(f) $1.8M.
(g) $1M for capitol complex security.
(h) $1M for capitol complex security.
(I) $60,000 to assist in meeting federal match requirements.
(j) $1.3M in special funds for improvement to county EOCs.
(k) Approximately $400,000 for Critical Infrastructure Protection and $208,000 for 3 employees and their expenses.
(l) $60,000 to support Lt. Governor and his role as homeland security director.
(m) $85M for personal service and capital projects.
(n) $6M for staff, training, planning, county exercises, GIS support and state-based Urban Search and Rescue Team (USAR) development.
(o) $1.5 M, of which $770,000 is a one time improvement that will not recur for FY 04-05
(p) Approximately $250,000 for 3 staff positions within Vermont State Police.

STATE HOMELAND SECURITY STRUCTURES — Continued

(q) $250,000 to match federal grants.
(r) $104,568 to fund Director of Homeland Security and support costs.
(s) $300,000 for the employment of 4 staff members and office equipment.
(t) Deputy Chief of Public Safety.
(u) Director, Office for Public Security.
(v) Executive Director within Department of Public Safety.
(w) Chief, State Law Enforcement Division.

Table C

STATE GOVERNMENT REORGANIZATION FOR NEW HOMELAND SECURITY RESPONSIBILITIES

State or other jurisdiction	Reorganization planned	Results of reorganization
Alabama	Underway	Will create unique state homeland security agency.
Alaska	Completed	Combined emergency management and homeland security functions.
Arizona	Completed	Combined emergency management and homeland security functions.
Arkansas	Proposed	Emergency management would become bureau under homeland security department; legislation failed during last session.
California	No	N.A.
Colorado	Completed	Homeland security and emergency management functions moved under the Department of Public Safety.
Connecticut	Planned	Considering a merge of emergency management and homeland security functions.
Delaware	Completed	Moved emergency management and homeland security to Department of Public Safety; renamed the Safety & Homeland Security Agency; legislation passed in June 2003.
Florida	No	N.A.
Georgia	Completed	Created Office of Homeland Security and moved emergency management under its jurisdiction.
Hawaii	Planned	Would create homeland security position within Department of Civil Defense.
Idaho	Completed	Formed Bureau of Homeland Security within the governor's office; consolidated the Military Division with the bureaus of Disaster Services and Hazardous Materials.
Illinois	No	N.A.
Indiana	No	N.A.
Iowa	Completed	Combined emergency management and homeland security functions.
Kansas	No	N.A.
Kentucky	Planned	Considering changes to existing homeland security structure as part of a larger reorganization to state government.
Louisiana	Completed	Combined homeland security and emergency management under the Military Department.
Maine	No	N.A.
Maryland	No	N.A.
Massachusetts	Completed	Moved homeland security function from governor's office to Public Safety Office.
Michigan	No	N.A.
Minnesota	Completed	Combined emergency management and homeland security functions.
Mississippi	Completed	Created Office of Homeland Security within emergency management agency.
Missouri	No	N.A.
Montana	No	N.A.
Nebraska	No	N.A.
Nevada	No	N.A.
New Hampshire	Completed	Moved all public health emergency preparedness and bioterrorism response functions to the Department of Safety.
New Jersey	No	N.A.
New Mexico	Proposed	Would create Department of Homeland Security and assume emergency management and other public safety functions; legislation failed during last session.
New York	No	N.A.
North Carolina	No	N.A.
North Dakota	Completed	Placed homeland security and public safety communications under emergency management.
Ohio	No	N.A.
Oklahoma	No	N.A.
Oregon	No	N.A.
Pennsylvania	No	N.A.
Rhode Island	Proposed	Changes are being considered to homeland security structure as part of larger reorganization of state government.
South Carolina	No	N.A.
South Dakota	Completed	Moved homeland security and emergency management functions into the newly created Department of Public Safety.
Tennessee	Completed	Created Office of Homeland Security under governor's office.
Texas	Planned	
Utah	Completed	Combined emergency management and homeland security functions.
Vermont	Completed	Moved homeland security and emergency management functions to the Department of Public Safety.
Virginia	No	N.A.
Washington	No	N.A.
West Virginia	No	N.A.
Wisconsin	No	N.A.
Wyoming	Completed	Moved emergency management from Military Department to new Department of Homeland Security.
District of Columbia	No	N.A.
U.S. Virgin Islands	Completed	Established Office of Homeland Security within emergency management agency.

Source: The National Emergency Management Association, February 2004.
Key:
N.A. - Not applicable.

No Child Left Behind: The Challenge of Implementation
By Dewayne Matthews

Until now, the focus of states on the No Child Left Behind Act (NCLB) has been on compliance. States first struggled to figure out what was required by the legislation, and then concentrated on getting the state plan approved by the U.S. Department of Education. Now that this initial stage has past, states are turning their attention to implementation. They are now trying to understand how to incorporate NCLB into the state's framework of educational governance, and how the legislation can be used to help the state meet its own goals for education performance.

Three years ago, the U.S. Congress, in an unusual show of bipartisanship, passed the landmark No Child Left Behind Act (NCLB). This sweeping legislation, even in these post 9-11 times, is the cornerstone of the administration's domestic policy agenda. As the reauthorization of the Elementary and Secondary Education Act, NCLB affects every facet of federal government programs for K-12 education. However, the impact of the legislation goes far beyond Title I and other federal initiatives. NCLB requires states to make fundamental changes in their approach to education. Under NCLB, states must set performance standards for every school in America, and track student learning across a wide range of student subgroups. It establishes significant consequences for schools, districts and states that fail to meet performance targets. Unlike past federal education legislation, it is fair to say that NCLB affects every child in every school in America. It all adds up to an unprecedented level of federal involvement in education, and a shift of educational decision making from communities and states to the federal government.

It is little wonder that many state policymakers are expressing deep concern about the impact of NCLB on their states, in spite of early and strong support for the principles of NCLB. Most state policymakers and education leaders remain firmly committed to the guiding principle of NCLB – that all children can and should learn. Groups like Achieve, Inc., The Education Trust, and the National Center for Education Accountability have identified schools throughout the United States that consistently reach high levels of student learning even with low income, minority and limited English-proficient students. NCLB asks the question: If these schools can help all children learn, why can't all schools?

While few in the states argue with the goal of NCLB, over the past two decades states have established their own approaches to educational improvement and in some cases NCLB is coming into direct conflict with them. The early excitement about this legislation has now matured into the difficult and complex work of implementation.

The Key Elements of NCLB

While NCLB has elements that affect almost every aspect of the educational system, the sections with the most impact on states are those addressing accountability and teacher quality.

The accountability provisions of NCLB are based on approaches that have been developed in states over the past 20 years. While NCLB requires all states to enact educational standards in grades three through eight and one year in high school, and assess student learning against those standards, almost every state had already established a standards-based accountability system before NCLB was passed, although often not in all the subject areas and grade levels required by the legislation. However, in one key area NCLB broke new ground. NCLB requires states to define a level of performance as "proficient" and hold schools accountable that 95 percent of all students in every identified subgroup reach this level. No large-scale education system has ever attained this level of performance across all groups of students and all schools. Prior to NCLB, almost every state defined their expectations of schools in terms of improvement over time, and schools that showed continuous improvement were deemed in most states to be making satisfactory progress. NCLB says that continuous improvement is not enough – all schools must reach a high standard of performance within a fixed timeframe, or risk sanctions required by the legislation. As a result of the fixed timeframe, schools must meet interim performance targets beginning immediately. These steps are called Adequate Yearly Progress (AYP), which is the heart of the legislation.

Adequate Yearly Progress (AYP): AYP is the difference between where the state wants to be (its standards), and where the state is now (the results of its assessments), divided into annual steps. NCLB requires states to define AYP for all public school students, including charter school students. Although NCLB requires that each state determine AYP, the specific definition is left to states. However, states are required to track performance for these subgroups: low income students, racial and ethnic minorities, limited-English proficient students and students with disabilities. Furthermore, performance must be tracked for schools, districts and the state as a whole. Ninety-five percent of the students in each subgroup in each school are required to participate in the assessment for the school to meet the AYP standard. Schools that fail to meet their state's AYP standard are identified as "needing improvement," even if only one subgroup failed to meet the performance standard.

Each state's definition of AYP is included in an accountability plan, which was submitted by the state education agency to the U.S. Department of Education. All state plans have been approved by the department.

Teacher Quality: For good measure, NCLB requires states to assure that there is a "highly qualified" teacher in every classroom of core academic subjects by the end of the 2005-2006 school year. States must first define what they consider to be a "highly qualified" teacher, although the legislation requires that state definitions assure that teachers be fully licensed or certified by the state and not have had any certification or licensure requirements waived. Then, states must (1) annually increase the percentage of highly qualified teachers until all are highly qualified by 2005-2006, and (2) annually increase the percentage of teachers who are receiving high-quality professional development.

NCLB: The Effects Begin to be Felt

The first major milestone in the implementation of NCLB was the release by states of the list of schools that failed to make AYP in the 2002-2003 school year. The release of these lists was particularly important because, in spite of the best efforts of many state leaders, the press often characterized schools on the list as "failing" rather than the more accurate label of "needs improvement." Given the fact that each state defined its own standards, it was no surprise that the number of schools that were identified varied across states. It was, however, a surprise to some to see the extent of the variation.

The percentage of schools that did not meet AYP varied from a low of 8 percent in Minnesota to a high of 87 percent in Florida. Three states (Kansas, Texas and Connecticut) identified between 10 and 20 percent of their schools as not meeting AYP, while

two states (South Carolina and Idaho) identified between 70 and 80 percent. This wide variation is primarily a result of the difference in standards and proficiency levels across states. It's no wonder that some in states with a large number of schools on the list questioned why they were being "punished" for having high standards.

Another factor that fueled the reaction to the release of the AYP lists was the growing awareness of the differences between the ways AYP was addressed in the state accountability plans approved by the U.S. Department of Education. States were permitted several options in terms of how AYP was calculated. States were allowed to determine the minimum size for each subgroup, and could choose to calculate AYP based on equal annual steps or a "stair-step" approach where increases occur every three years. How states chose to calculate AYP, and how much flexibility they were allowed by the U.S. Department of Education in the approval of their plan, had a lot to do with how many schools made the "needs improvement" list.

States are also being held to the NCLB requirement that 95 percent of students in every subgroup be included in assessments for the school to meet AYP. This means, for example, for a school with 40 students in a subgroup, if only three do not take the test the school will not meet AYP. In many cases, schools have been identified as needing improvement because they did not meet this requirement for one subgroup. Twenty percent of the schools in West Virginia identified as needing improvement were placed on the list because of this requirement. Only three high schools in Hawaii met this requirement.

A further complication in interpreting AYP results is that some states have chosen to maintain their existing state accountability system in parallel with the NCLB system. Florida, Colorado and several other states now have a "federal" list of schools that need improvement, along with a state system that often produces very different results. Some have expressed a concern that having two systems produces confusion among parents, teachers and the media, and sends a mixed message about what schools need to do to improve performance.

The Highly Qualified Teacher Dilemma

Aside from AYP, the provision of NCLB that poses the most difficult implementation challenge is the requirement that all teachers in the state be "highly qualified." Among other steps, states must assure that teachers have been well prepared in the subject they are teaching. While few argue with the intent of the requirement, meeting it is a particular challenge for rural and other hard-to-staff schools.

In rural schools, teachers often must teach a variety of subjects to meet the requirements of state curriculum standards. NCLB requires that teachers demonstrate subject matter expertise in all core subjects they teach. Likewise, some urban schools already find it difficult to recruit and retain teachers. Finding and keeping teachers that meet NCLB requirements is making a difficult situation even more so.

Both the states and the federal government are attempting to address this problem through a variety of approaches. The U.S. Department of Education has funded several initiatives to increase the supply of qualified teachers, particularly through alternative certification routes. States are increasing the availability of professional development to help teachers meet the new requirements. However, this is one area where state budget cuts have directly impacted the capacity of states to meet NCLB requirements. This will be discussed in more detail later.

A New Role for State Education Agencies

While states have focused attention on meeting the direct requirements of NCLB, there are a number of indirect effects that must also be addressed in state implementation. One of the most important is the changing role of state education agencies in monitoring educational performance and helping schools meet AYP requirements. States are coming to terms with two key elements of this change.

The first is that NCLB requires states to track student achievement and report it to the public. This will give states – and the nation – unprecedented information on school performance. It also requires states to create sophisticated student record data systems at their state education agency to accommodate NCLB requirements.

The second is that meeting NCLB performance goals will require states to develop a much stronger capacity to support school improvement efforts at the local and district levels. Schools that are identified as "needing improvement" under NCLB will have to provide technical assistance and professional development to address their shortcomings. Many states are not well equipped to do this. In some states, the number of schools that will make the list of schools needing improvement will be so large as to overwhelm the state education agency's capacity to provide technical support. Even states with well-developed systems of school support, through regional service centers and other approaches, will find it difficult to scale up their capacity to the levels that will be needed. States that now provide only rudimentary levels of support to struggling districts will practically need to start from scratch.

Some states are pinning their hopes for addressing this implementation challenge on the data system itself. A sophisticated system of data on student achievement will allow states to know much more about school performance problems than most do now. With the new data systems, states should have much more detailed information about the nature of performance shortfalls in schools, including the scope of the problem (is it district-wide, or limited to a single subgroup in a specific school?), and the specific subgroups, grade levels and subjects that need to be targeted. The new data systems will also give states the ability to identify schools and districts that are *successful* in these same categories. The National Center for Education Accountability is working with several states to develop the capacity to systematically identify the best practices in successful schools so they can be apply statewide in schools that are not measuring up. NCLB also requires all states to participate in the National Assessment of Educational Progress (NAEP). For the first time, the nation will have comparable data across states on student performance by grade level and subject area. This data may lead to development of a stronger national capacity to understand "what works" in schools.

Is NCLB an Unfunded Mandate?

Behind all the early promise and concern about the implementation of NCLB, states are struggling to understand the cost implications of the legislation. This issue is particularly sensitive because of the unprecedented financial problems of state governments. Some people in the states have already decided that NCLB constitutes an unfunded mandate, which will have a significant short- and long-term impact on state budgets. Others believe NCLB will make the enormous national investment in education more cost-effective.

There are two types of costs states will incur because of NCLB – direct and indirect. Much of the early attention of the states has been focused on the direct costs — things like required state assessments, data collection and reporting. NCLB provides new federal funding for these initiatives, although some are concerned that funding levels will not be sufficient in future years to cover state costs.

More attention is now being paid to the indirect costs of NCLB – paying for the actions states will need to take to meet NCLB student performance requirements. Nobody knows for sure what will be required, but many believe spending on education will need to increase if the performance targets are to be met. For example, spending will increase if states conclude that smaller class sizes are necessary to achieve performance targets. Some are also concerned that NCLB requirements will create a new basis for legal challenges to state education funding systems. However, all this speculation presupposes that there is a direct link between funding levels and school performance. It is not clear at all if the data that will emerge from new state student performance data systems will confirm this link.

The indirect cost tied to NCLB that many states are beginning to focus attention on is that of teacher salaries. NCLB requires that states take steps to assure that there is a highly qualified teacher in every classroom, and makes it much harder for districts to hire teachers that do not fully meet state requirements. The problem of finding, hiring and retaining qualified teachers is particularly acute in two areas – teachers of specific subject areas like math and special education, and teachers for hard-to-staff rural and urban schools. States are attempting to address this issue through improved teacher training programs, stronger teacher recruitment and retention programs, and alternative certification routes. However, states may need to consider such strategies as differential pay or across-the-board salary increases to fully address the problem.

NCLB: What Really Matters?

Until now, the focus of states on NCLB has been on compliance. States first struggled to figure out what was required by the legislation, and then concentrated on getting the state plan approved by the U.S. Department of Education. Now that this initial stage has past, states are turning their attention to implementation. They are now trying to understand how to incorporate NCLB into the state's framework of educational governance, and how the legislation can be used to help the state meet its own goals for education performance. States are beginning to concentrate on three main implementation challenges:

- Creating a data system that provides the level of detail needed, but in a form that can actually be used to improve student performance.

- Creating a system of support for school improvement that can help every school in need of improvement meet AYP expectations.

- Figuring out how to meet the requirement for a highly qualified teacher in every classroom, in a way that is doable, affordable, and that contributes to improved student achievement.

Both state political and educational leadership have been almost unanimous in their support for the premise and the promise of No Child Left Behind. NCLB, if fully realized, represents a chance to make the U.S. education system the very best in the world by creating system in which every child, almost without exception, does well in school. If the nation can meet this promise within 12 years, the implications are staggering to contemplate.

However, simply making the promise will not get it done, and no one knows this better than state leaders. The job of making the promise of NCLB a reality has fallen on the states. For better or worse, NCLB has shifted the national focus of education decision making to rest squarely on student achievement. Everyone involved in making the education system work – from governors and legislators to teachers and principals – need to use the data on student performance to find out where the gaps are, and close them. The stakes are high.

About the Author

Dewayne Matthews is senior advisor to the president at the Education Commission of the States (ECS). Previously, he served as an education policy analyst with the New Mexico Legislature, executive director of the New Mexico Commission on Higher Education, and director of programs and services at the Western Interstate Commission for Higher Education. He holds a Ph.D. in educational leadership and policy studies from Arizona State University.

Table A
NO CHILD LEFT BEHIND BY STATE AND REGION

State or other jurisdiction	NCLB Standards and assessments											NCLB Accountability (AYP)								
	Reading standards	Mathematics standards	Science standards	Annual assessments in reading	Annual assessments in Mathematics	Assessments in science	Assessment in English language proficiency	Inclusion of LEP students	Inclusion of students with disabilities	Inclusion of migrant students	Disaggregation of results	Single accountability system	All schools included	Continuous growth with to 100% proficiency	Annual determination of adequate yearly progress (AYP)	Accountability for all subgroups	Primarily based on academics	Includes graduation rates and additional indicator	Based on separate math and reading objectives	95% of students in all subgroups assessed
Eastern Region																				
Connecticut	●	●	★	★	★	★	★	★	★	★	★	★	★	★	★	★	★	★	★	★
Delaware	●	●	★	★	★	★	★	★	★	★	★	★	★	★	★	★	★	★	★	★
Maine	★	⋮	★	●	●	⋮	★	★	★	★	⋮	★	★	⋮	★	★	★	★	★	⋮
Massachusetts	●	●	●	⋮	⋮	⋮	★	★	★	★	★	★	★	★	★	★	★	★	●	★
New Hampshire	★	★	★	★	●	●	★	★	★	★	★	★	★	★	★	★	★	★	●	★
New Jersey	●	●	★	●	●	●	★	★	★	★	★	★	★	★	★	★	●	●	●	★
New York	●	●	★	●	●	●	★	★	★	★	★	★	●	★	★	★	★	★	★	★
Pennsylvania	●	●	★	●	●	●	★	★	★	★	●	★	★	★	★	★	★	●	★	★
Rhode Island	●	●	★	●	●	⋮	★	★	★	●	●	★	★	●	★	★	★	★	★	★
Vermont	●	●	★	●	●	★	★	★	★	⋮	★	★	★	⋮	★	★	★	★	★	★
Regional totals																				
Appears to be on track	2	2	8	3	3	5	10	10	10	7	8	10	9	8	8	9	8	7	7	8
Appears to be partially on track	7	7	2	6	6	2	0	0	0	2	1	0	1	1	2	0	2	2	3	0
Does not appear to be on track	1	1	0	1	1	2	0	0	0	1	1	0	0	1	0	1	0	1	0	2
Unclear or data unavailable	0	0	0	0	0	0	0	0	0	0	0	0	0	0	0	0	0	0	0	0
Midwestern Region																				
Illinois	★	★	★	★	★	★	★	★	★	★	★	★	★	★	★	★	★	★	★	★
Indiana	★	★	★	★	★	★	★	★	★	★	★	★	★	★	★	★	★	★	★	★
Iowa	★	★	★	★	★	★	★	★	★	★	★	★	★	●	★	★	★	★	★	★
Kansas	●	●	★	●	●	●	★	★	★	★	★	★	★	★	★	★	★	★	★	★
Michigan	●	★	★	●	●	●	★	★	★	★	★	●	●	●	★	●	★	★	●	★
Minnesota	●	●	★	●	●	●	★	★	★	★	★	★	★	●	★	★	★	★	●	★
Nebraska	★	★	★	●	●	★	★	★	★	★	★	★	★	●	★	★	★	★	●	★
North Dakota	★	★	★	★	★	●	★	★	★	★	★	★	★	★	★	★	★	★	★	★
Ohio	★	★	★	★	★	★	★	★	★	★	★	★	★	★	★	★	★	★	★	●
South Dakota	★	★	★	★	★	★	★	★	★	★	★	★	★	●	★	★	★	★	●	●
Wisconsin	●	●	★	●	●	●	⋮	★	★	★	★	⋮	★	⋮	⋮	★	★	⋮	⋮	⋮
Regional totals																				
Appears to be on track	8	7	11	7	6	9	11	11	11	11	11	8	9	6	8	8	8	8	6	7
Appears to be partially on track	3	4	0	4	5	2	0	0	0	0	0	2	2	3	3	2	3	1	3	3
Does not appear to be on track	0	0	0	0	0	0	0	0	0	0	0	1	0	2	0	1	0	2	2	1
Unclear or data unavailable	0	0	0	0	0	0	0	0	0	0	0	0	0	0	0	0	0	0	0	0
Southern Region																				
Alabama	★	★	★	★	★	★	★	★	★	★	★	★	★	⋮	★	★	⋮	★	⋮	⋮
Arkansas	★	★	★	★	★	★	★	★	★	★	★	★	★	★	★	★	★	★	★	★
Florida	★	★	★	★	★	★	★	★	★	★	★	★	★	●	★	★	★	⋮	★	★
Georgia	★	★	★	★	★	★	★	★	★	★	★	★	★	●	★	★	★	★	★	★
Kentucky	●	●	★	●	●	★	★	●	★	⋮	●	★	★	●	●	★	★	●	●	●
Louisiana	★	★	★	●	●	★	⋮	★	★	★	★	★	★	⋮	★	★	★	●	★	★

See footnotes at end of table.

NO CHILD LEFT BEHIND BY STATE AND REGION — Continued

State or other jurisdiction	NCLB Standards and assessments											NCLB Accountability (AYP)								
	Reading standards	Mathematics standards	Science standards	Annual assessments in reading	Annual assessments in Mathematics	Assessments in science	Assessment in English language proficiency	Inclusion of LEP students	Inclusion of students with disabilities	Inclusion of migrant students	Disaggregation of results	Single accountability system	All schools included	Continuous growth to 100 * proficiency	Annual determination of adequate yearly progress (AYP)	Accountability for all subgroups	Primarily based on academics	Includes graduation rates and additional indicator	Based on separate math and reading objectives	95% of students in all subgroups assessed
Maryland	★	★	★	★	★	★	★	★	★	★	★	★	★	★	★	★	★	★	★	★
Mississippi	★	●	★	★	★	●	★	●	★	●	★	★	★	●	★	★	★	★	★	★
Missouri	★	★	★	★	★	★	★	★	★	★	★	★	★	●	★	★	★	★	★	★
North Carolina	★	★	★	★	★	★	★	★	★	★	★	★	★	●	★	★	★	★	★	★
Oklahoma	★	★	★	★	★	★	★	★	★	★	★	★	★	★	★	★	★	★	★	★
South Carolina	★	★	★	★	★	★	★	★	★	★	★	★	★	●	★	★	★	★	★	●
Tennessee	★	★	★	●	●	★	★	●	★	★	★	●	★	●	★	●	★	★	●	●
Texas	★	★	★	●	●	★	★	★	★	★	★	●	★	●	★	●	★	★	★	●
Virginia	★	★	★	★	●	★	★	★	★	★	★	★	★	★	★	★	★	★	★	★
West Virginia	★	★	★	★	●	★		★	★	★	★	★	★	★	★	★	★	★	★	★
Regional totals																				
Appears to be on track	15	14	16	12	12	15	14	14	16	14	16	12	14	9	14	14	14	13	13	11
Appears to be partially on track	1	2	0	4	4	1	0	2	0	1	0	3	1	6	1	2	1	2	2	4
Does not appear to be on track	0	0	0	0	0	0	2	0	0	0	0	1	1	1	1	0	1	1	1	1
Unclear or data unavailable	0	0	0	0	0	0	0	0	0	0	0	0	0	0	0	0	0	0	0	0
Western Region																				
Alaska	●	●		●	●		★	★	★	★	★	★	★	★	★	★	★	★	★	★
Arizona	★	★		★	★		★	★	★	★	★	★	★	★	★	★	★	★	★	
California	★	★		★	★	★	★	★	★	★	★	★	★	★	★	★	★	★	★	★
Colorado	★	★	★	★	★	★	★	★	★	★	★	★	★	●	★	★	★	●	●	●
Hawaii	★	★	★	★	★	★	★	★	★	★	★	★	★	★	★	★	★	●	●	●
Idaho	★	★	★	★	★	★	●	★	★	★	★	★	★	●	★	★	★	●	●	●
Montana	★	★	★	★	★	★	★	★	★	★	★	N.A.			★	★	★			
Nevada	★	★	★	★	★	★	★	★	★	★	★	★	★	★	★	★	★	★	★	★
New Mexico	★	★	★	★	★	★	★	★	★	★	●	★	★	★	★	★	★	●	●	★
Oregon	★	★	★	★	★	★	●	★	★	★	★	★	★	★	★	★	●	●	●	★
Utah	★	★	★	★	★	★	★	★	★	★	★	★	★	★	★	★	●	●	●	●
Washington	★	★	★	★	★	★	★	★	★	★	★	★	★	★	★	★	★	●	★	★
Wyoming	★	★	★	★	★	★	★	★	★	★	★	★	★	★	★	★	★	★	★	★
Regional totals																				
Appears to be on track	12	12	8	8	8	8	11	12	13	13	11	9	8	7	11	12	11	8	8	7
Appears to be partially on track	1	1	1	5	5	1	2	1	0	0	2	2	1	3	1	0	1	3	2	1
Does not appear to be on track	0	0	4	0	0	4	0	0	0	0	0	2	4	3	1	1	1	2	3	5
Unclear or data unavailable	0	0	0	0	0	0	0	0	0	0	0	1	0	0	0	0	0	0	0	0
Dist. of Columbia	★	★	★	●	●		★	★	★	★	★									

See footnotes at end of table.

NO CHILD LEFT BEHIND BY STATE AND REGION — Continued

State or other jurisdiction	NCLB School improvement							NCLB Safe schools			NCLB Supplemental services				NCLB Report card			NCLB Teacher quality		
	Timely identification	Technical Assistance	Public school choice	Rewards and sanctions	School recognition	School restructuring	Corrective action for LEA's	Criteria for unsafe schools	Transfer policy for students in unsafe schools	Transfer policy for victims of violent crime	Criteria for supplemental services	List of approved supplemental services providers	Monitoring of supplemental services providers	Implementation of supplemental services	State report card	Highly qualified teachers definition	Subject matter competence	Test for new elementary teachers	Highly qualified in every classroom	High quality professional development
Eastern Region																				
Connecticut	★	●	★	★	★	★	★	★	★	★	★	★	★	★	★	★	★	★		★
Delaware	●	★	●	★	★	●	★	★	★	★	★	★	●	★	★	●	●	★		●
Maine	●	●	●	●				★	★	★	★	★			●		●	★		●
Massachusetts	●	●	●	●	★	★	★	★	★	★	★	★	★	★	●	★	●	★	●	★
New Hampshire		●						★	★	★	★	★			●		●	★		N.A.
New Jersey	●	●	★	●	●	★	★	★	★	★	★	★	★	★	★	●	●	★		
New York	●	●	●	●	●	★	★	★	★	★	★	★	★	★	★	●	●	●		
Pennsylvania	●	●	●	●	★	★	★	★	★	★	★	★	●	●	●	●	●	●		●
Rhode Island	●	●	●	●	★	N.A.	★	★	★	★	●	★	★	★	●	●	●	●	●	●
Vermont								★	●	●	●	●			★			★	★	●
Regional totals																				
Appears to be on track	4	4	5	7	7	7	8	10	10	10	9	9	7	6	3	3	2	9	0	1
Appears to be partially on track	5	5	5	3	0	0	0	0	0	0	1	0	0	1	7	4	8	1	2	2
Does not appear to be on track	1	1	0	0	3	2	2	0	0	0	0	1	3	3	0	3	0	0	8	6
Unclear or data unavailable	0	0	0	0	0	1	0	0	0	0	0	0	0	0	0	0	0	0	0	1
Midwestern Region																				
Illinois	●	★	●	★	★	★	★	★	★	★	★	★	★	★	★	★	★	★		★
Indiana	★	★	★	★	★	★	★	★	●	★	★	★	★	★	★	★	★	★		★
Iowa	●	★	●	●	●	★	★	★	★	★	★	★	★	★	★	●	★	★		●
Kansas	●	★	●	●	●	★	●	★	★	★	★	★	●	●	★	●	★	★		●
Michigan	●	●	●	●	★	★	★	●	●	●	★	★	★	★	★	●	●	★		●
Minnesota	★	★	★	★	★	★	★	★	★	★	★	★	★	★	★	●	★	★	●	●
Nebraska	●	●	●	●	●	★	●	★	★	★	★	★	●	●	★	●	★	★		●
North Dakota	★	★	★	★	★	★	●	★	★	★	★	★	★	★	●	★	●	★	●	★
Ohio	●	★	●	★	★	★	★	★	★	★	★	★	★	★	●	★	●	●	★	●
South Dakota	●	●	●	●	●	★	★	★	★	★	★	★	★	★	★	●	●	★		●
Wisconsin	★	●	★	★	★	★	★	★	★	★	★	★	★	★	★	★	●	★		●
Regional totals																				
Appears to be on track	4	7	5	5	5	7	4	10	10	10	11	11	9	7	5	6	2	10	1	1
Appears to be partially on track	7	4	6	2	1	0	3	1	1	1	0	0	1	3	6	5	9	0	1	3
Does not appear to be on track	0	0	0	4	5	4	4	0	0	0	0	0	1	1	0	0	0	1	9	7
Unclear or data unavailable	0	0	0	0	0	0	0	0	0	0	0	0	0	0	0	0	0	0	0	0
Southern Region																				
Alabama	●	★	★	★	★	★	★	★	★	★	★	★	★	★	●	★	★	●		
Arkansas	★	★	★	★	★	★	★	★	★	★	★	★	★	★	●	●	N.A.	★		
Florida	★	●	★	★	★	★	●	★	★	★	★	★	★	★	★		★	★	●	
Georgia	★		★	★	★	★		★	★	●	★	★	★	★	★	●	●	★		
Kentucky	★	●	★	★	★	★	★	★	★	★	★	★	★	★	★	●		★		●

See footnotes at end of table.

NO CHILD LEFT BEHIND BY STATE AND REGION—Continued

State or other jurisdiction	NCLB School improvement							NCLB Safe schools			NCLB Supplemental services				NCLB Report card			NCLB Teacher quality		
	Timely identification	Technical Assistance	Public school choice	Rewards and sanctions	School recognition	School restructuring	Corrective action for LEA's	Criteria for unsafe schools	Transfer policy for students in unsafe schools	Transfer policy for victims of violent crime	Criteria for supplemental services	List of approved supplemental services providers	Monitoring of supplemental services providers	Implementation of supplemental services	State report card	Highly qualified teachers definition	Subject matter competence	Test for new elementary teachers	Highly qualified in every classroom	High quality professional development
Louisiana	★	★	★	★	★	★	★	★	★	★	★	★	★	●	●	●	●	★	...	...
Maryland	●	●	●	★	★	★	★	★	★	★	★	★	●	●	●	●	●	★	●	●
Mississippi	★	★	●	★	★	★	★	★	★	★	★	★	★	★	★	●	★	★	...	...
Missouri	★	●	●	★	★	★	★	★	★	★	★	★	★	★	★	★	●	★	...	...
North Carolina	●	★	★	★	★	★	★	★	★	★	★	★	★	★	★	●	●	★	...	...
Oklahoma	●	★	●	★	★	★	★	★	★	★	★	★	●	●	●	●	●	★	...	...
South Carolina	★	●	★	★	★	★	★	★	★	★	★	★	★	★	★	●	●	★	●	●
Tennessee	★	●	●	★	★	★	★	★	★	★	★	★	★	...	...	★	●	★	...	...
Texas	★	★	★	★	★	★	★	★	★	★	★	★	★	★	★	●	★	★	●	...
Virginia	★	★	★	●	●	N.A.	...	★	★	★	★	★	★	★	●	●	★	★	...	...
West Virginia	●	●	★	●	●	N.A.	...	★	★	★	★	★	★	★	●	●	●	★	...	...
Regional totals																				
Appears to be on track	5	8	12	16	16	15	14	15	15	15	16	14	11	10	8	4	5	15	0	11
Appears to be partially on track	11	7	3	0	0	0	0	1	1	1	0	1	1	4	8	9	9	1	3	5
Does not appear to be on track	0	1	1	0	0	0	2	0	0	0	0	1	4	2	0	3	1	0	13	0
Unclear or data unavailable	0	0	0	0	0	1	0	0	0	0	0	0	0	0	0	0	1	0	0	0
Western Region																				
Alaska	★	★	★	★	★	★	★	★	★	★	★	★	★	★	★	★	●	★	...	...
Arizona	●	★	★	●	...	★	...	★	★	★	★	★	★	★	●	●	●	★	...	...
California	★	●	★	★	...	★	★	★	★	★	★	★	★	●	●	●	●	★	...	...
Colorado	★	●	★	...	...	★	★	★	★	★	★	●	★	●	●	●	●	★	●	...
Hawaii	★	●	★	...	...	...	N.A.	★	★	★	★	●	★	●	●	●	●	★	...	...
Idaho	★	★	★	...	...	...	...	★	★	★	●	★	★	●	●	●	●	★	...	...
Montana	★	●	★	...	...	★	...	★	★	★	★	★	★	★	●	●	●	★	●	...
Nevada	★	★	★	★	★	★	★	★	★	★	★	★	★	★	●	●	●	★	...	...
New Mexico	★	●	●	●	★	...	★	●	●	★	●	●	●	●	●	●	●	●	...	...
Oregon	★	●	●	...	...	★	...	★	★	★	★	★	★	★	●	●	★	★	●	...
Utah	★	★	★	●	★	★	★	★	★	★	★	★	●	●	●	★	●	★	...	...
Washington	★	●	★	...	★	★	...	★	★	★	...	★	★	●	●	●	...	★	...	...
Wyoming	★	●	●	...	★	...	...	★	★	★	★	★	★	...	...	...	...	...	...	...
Regional totals																				
Appears to be on track	9	6	10	7	8	7	6	12	10	11	12	10	9	7	3	3	1	10	0	0
Appears to be partially on track	4	7	3	4	0	0	0	1	3	2	0	2	1	5	10	8	8	1	2	2
Does not appear to be on track	0	0	0	2	5	6	6	0	0	0	1	1	3	1	0	2	4	2	11	13
Unclear or data unavailable	0	0	0	0	0	0	1	0	0	0	0	0	0	0	0	0	0	0	0	0
Dist. of Columbia	★		★	●			N.A.	★	★	★	●	★	★	★	...			...		...

Source: Education Commission of the States, No Child Left Behind Database, February 2004.

Key:

★- State appears to be on track.
●- State appears to be partially on track.

... - State does not appear to be on track.
N.A. - Unclear or data not available.
LEP- Limited English Proficient

Table 9.1
MEMBERSHIP AND ATTENDANCE IN PUBLIC ELEMENTARY AND SECONDARY SCHOOLS, BY STATE: 2001–2002 AND 2002–2003

State or other jurisdiction	2001–2002			2002–2003		
	Estimated average daily membership (ADM)	Estimated average daily attendance (ADA)	ADA as a percent of ADM	Estimated average daily membership (ADM)	Estimated average daily attendance (ADA)	ADA as a percent of ADM
United States	. . .	44,591,769	. . .	. . .	44,658,020	. . .
Alabama	730,127	698,350	95.6	726,544	692,593	95.3
Alaska	132,612	114,319	86.2	133,517	114,458	85.7
Arizona	932,380	879,677	94.3	945,255	895,287	94.7
Arkansas	447,594	431,065	96.3	443,207	419,259	94.6
California	. . .	5,879,763	. . .	. . .	6,012,430	. . .
Colorado	. . .	682,007	. . .	. . .	697,277	. . .
Connecticut	540,500	569,540	105.4	575,760	546,970	95.0
Delaware	117,664	109,932	93.4	117,915	109,874	93.2
Florida	2,592,919	2,439,204	94.1	2,557,510	2,405,449	94.1
Georgia	1,470,634	1,370,630	93.2	1,496,012	391,291	93.0
Hawaii	182,561	170,531	93.4	181,648	169,606	93.4
Idaho	. . .	231,080	. . .	. . .	232,000	. . .
Illinois	2,015,140	1,882,208	93.4	2,034,873	1,899,993	93.4
Indiana	956,170	915,834	95.8	959,180	919,507	95.9
Iowa	485,009	462,231	95.3	478,937	456,446	95.3
Kansas	444,470	417,801	94.0	444,653	417,974	94.0
Kentucky	623,768	575,827	92.3	623,933	579,106	92.8
Louisiana	718,883	675,063	93.9	709,312	666,944	94.0
Maine	202,323	190,400	94.1	200,199	188,218	94.0
Maryland	866,431	810,979	93.6	864,205	813,384	94.1
Massachusetts	997,314	931,508	93.4	948,713	900,085	94.9
Michigan	. . .	1,597,231	. . .	. . .	1,608,592	. . .
Minnesota	855,042	800,470	93.6	850,950	799,894	94.0
Mississippi	489,126	464,360	94.9	484,157	459,731	95.0
Missouri	. . .	853,340	. . .	. . .	814,427	. . .
Montana	150,985	138,007	91.4	148,690	136,476	91.8
Nebraska	276,893	262,895	94.9	274,496	260,886	95.0
Nevada	358,425	334,497	93.3	354,264	337,136	95.2
New Hampshire	208,329	197,209	94.7	205,846	194,916	94.6
New Jersey	1,317,561	1,241,276	94.2	1,372,573	1,303,869	95.0
New Mexico	322,031	289,828	90.0	320,986	288,887	90.0
New York	3,028,389	2,728,355	90.1	3,077,762	2,768,015	89.9
North Carolina	1,271,131	1,206,694	94.9	1,288,769	1,223,854	95.0
North Dakota	117,967	111,210	94.3	105,044	97,424	92.7
Ohio	1,796,000	1,649,533	91.8	1,784,993	1,635,044	91.6
Oklahoma	620,036	591,275	95.4	621,543	593,642	95.5
Oregon	519,862	482,313	92.8	522,286	485,066	92.9
Pennsylvania	1,794,000	1,672,000	93.2	1,795,000	1,673,000	93.2
Rhode Island	155,791	144,152	92.5	158,619	147,920	93.3
South Carolina	661,779	634,899	95.9	660,308	637,789	96.6
South Dakota	124,964	117,795	94.3	124,187	117,795	94.3
Tennessee	898,482	847,918	94.4	897,479	851,009	94.8
Texas	. . .	3,863,560	. . .	. . .	3,908,726	. . .
Utah	473,067	447,616	94.6	471,941	446,551	94.6
Vermont	100,919	95,482	94.6	92,777	85,961	92.7
Virginia	1,067,861	1,168,092	109.4	1,179,158	1,074,702	91.1
Washington	1,027,103	962,395	93.7	1,009,468	945,872	93.7
West Virginia	282,182	266,315	94.4	179,686	263,187	146.5
Wisconsin	873,480	840,670	96.2	862,529	828,038	96.0
Wyoming	86,786	82,082	94.6	85,135	80,494	94.5
Dist. of Columbia	67,765	62,343	92.0	64,687	59,594	92.1

Source: Adapted from National Education Association, *Rankings & Estimates: Rankings of the States 2002 and Estimates of School Statistics 2003.* Summary Table D, Estimated ADM and ADA in Public Elementary and Secondary Schools and Number of Public High School Graduates, 2002-2003 (page 87). Reprinted with permission of the National Education Association © 2003. All rights reserved.

Note: Average Daily Membership (ADM) for the school year is an average obtained by dividing the aggregate days of membership by the number of days in which school is in session. Pupils are members of a school from the date they are placed on the current roll until they leave permanently.

Membership is the total number of pupils belonging–the sum of those present and those absent. Average Daily Attendance (ADA) for the school year is the aggregate days pupils were actually present in school divided by the number of days school was actually in session.

Key:
 . . .—Not available.

Table 9.2
ENROLLMENT, AVERAGE DAILY ATTENDANCE AND CLASSROOM TEACHERS
IN PUBLIC ELEMENTARY AND SECONDARY SCHOOLS, BY STATE: 2002-2003

State or other jurisdiction	Total enrollment (a)	Estimated average daily attendance (a)	Classroom teachers (a)	Pupils per teacher based on enrollment	Pupils per teacher based on average daily attendance
United States	47,792,369	44,658,020	3,043,975	15.7	14.6
Alabama	721,633	692,593	46,549	15.5	14.8
Alaska	134,024	114,458	8,052	16.6	14.2
Arizona	940,433	895,287	45,102	20.8	19.8
Arkansas	445,229	419,259	31,771	14.0	13.1
California	6,250,095	6,012,430	314,992	19.8	19.0
Colorado	751,862	697,277	45,196	16.6	15.4
Connecticut	575,760	546,090	42,000	13.7	13.0
Delaware	116,274	109,874	7,661	15.1	14.3
Florida	2,533,628	2,405,449	141,028	17.9	17.0
Georgia	1,496,012	1,391,291	95,875	15.6	14.5
Hawaii	183,829	169,606	11,154	16.4	15.2
Idaho	248,509	232,000	13,848	17.9	16.7
Illinois	2,089,633	1,899,993	134,519	15.5	14.1
Indiana	995,195	919,507	60,542	16.4	15.1
Iowa	482,210	456,446	34,334	14.0	13.2
Kansas	469,634	417,974	32,581	14.4	12.8
Kentucky	629,020	579,106	38,736	16.2	14.9
Louisiana	729,516	666,944	50,255	14.5	13.2
Maine	203,708	188,218	16,161	12.6	11.6
Maryland	866,743	813,384	55,543	15.6	14.6
Massachusetts	987,986	900,085	56,000	17.6	16.0
Michigan	1,730,544	1,608,592	102,033	16.9	15.7
Minnesota	856,863	799,894	56,542	15.1	14.1
Mississippi	491,623	459,731	30,569	16.0	15.0
Missouri	894,029	814,427	67,400	13.2	12.0
Montana	149,574	136,476	10,463	14.2	13.0
Nebraska	283,924	260,886	20,703	13.7	12.6
Nevada	369,498	337,136	19,459	18.9	17.3
New Hampshire	207,628	194,916	14,975	13.8	13.0
New Jersey	1,365,344	1,303,869	103,068	13.2	12.6
New Mexico	320,986	288,887	21,258	15.0	13.5
New York	2,845,000	2,768,015	226,000	12.5	12.2
North Carolina	1,345,889	1,223,854	86,129	15.6	14.2
North Dakota	103,013	97,424	7,745	13.3	12.5
Ohio	1,791,223	1,635,044	122,054	14.6	13.3
Oklahoma	624,176	593,642	40,550	15.3	14.6
Oregon	554,071	485,066	28,967	19.1	16.7
Pennsylvania	1,817,200	1,673,050	118,650	15.3	14.1
Rhode Island	157,996	147,920	13,372	11.8	11.0
South Carolina	671,508	637,789	45,598	14.7	13.9
South Dakota	125,441	117,795	9,018	13.9	13.0
Tennessee	910,364	851,009	58,315	15.6	14.5
Texas	4,223,192	3,908,726	289,680	14.5	13.4
Utah	480,736	446,551	23,144	20.7	19.2
Vermont	99,475	85,961	8,768	11.3	9.8
Virginia	1,176,557	1,074,702	93,069	12.6	11.5
Washington	1,029,131	945,872	52,960	19.4	17.8
West Virginia	281,591	263,187	19,925	14.1	13.2
Wisconsin	881,231	828,038	60,270	14.6	13.7
Wyoming	86,108	80,494	6,622	13.0	12.1
Dist. of Columbia	67,522	59,594	4,769	14.1	12.4

Source: Adapted from National Education Association, *Rankings & Estimates: Rankings of the States 2002 and Estimates of School Statistics 2003.* Summary Tables B, D and F (pages 85, 87, 89). Reprinted with permission of the National Education Association © 2003. All rights reserved.

Key:
(a) Estimated.

Table 9.3
AVERAGE ANNUAL SALARY OF INSTRUCTIONAL STAFF IN PUBLIC ELEMENTARY AND SECONDARY SCHOOLS: 1994–1995 TO 2002–2003

State or other jurisdiction	Average annual salary for: (in unadjusted dollars)							
	1994–95	1995–96	1996–97	1998–99	1999–00	2000–01	2001–02	2002–03
Alabama	$32,597	$32,459	$33,744	$35,820	$36,689	$39,648	$38,744	$39,937
Alaska	48,929	50,516	52,033	46,845	47,262	49,426	50,399	51,142
Arizona	41,325	42,870	44,157	35,025	35,650	47,626	51,089	52,266
Arkansas	29,677	30,607	31,526	32,350	33,386	36,181	36,818	37,117
California	42,538	44,027	45,349	45,400	47,680	52,631	55,787	57,623
Colorado	35,712	36,353	37,445	38,025	38,163	40,604	42,503	42,311
Connecticut	53,020	51,951	52,067	51,584	51,780	54,808	55,780	56,431
Delaware	40,668	42,177	43,085	43,164	44,435	49,080	50,487	53,835
Florida	33,617	34,411	34,983	35,916	36,722	39,460	40,504	40,513
Georgia	34,507	35,786	37,933	39,675	41,023	44,328	46,315	47,897
Hawaii	37,319	37,057	36,986	40,377	40,578	41,401	44,085	45,944
Idaho	31,063	32,285	33,277	34,063	35,162	38,093	39,174	39,715
Illinois	42,448	42,411	44,235	45,569	46,486	49,889	51,310	53,554
Indiana	37,569	38,832	39,998	41,163	41,850	44,595	45,434	46,361
Iowa	32,622	33,529	34,480	34,927	35,678	37,811	39,562	40,289
Kansas	36,709	37,626	38,379	37,405	38,453	36,894	38,134	39,222
Kentucky	34,232	33,115	34,109	35,526	36,380	37,894	39,203	39,203
Louisiana	27,629	28,167	29,013	32,510	33,109	35,267	38,110	38,652
Maine	33,182	33,994	35,015	34,906	35,561	39,659	41,015	42,779
Maryland	42,300	42,958	42,988	42,526	44,048	48,230	50,645	52,248
Massachusetts	48,543	52,663	54,244	45,075	46,250	61,899	61,688	63,278
Michigan	48,507	50,764	52,288	48,207	48,695	50,694	52,676	54,071
Minnesota	38,615	37,680	38,811	39,458	39,802	43,878	43,900	45,959
Mississippi	27,870	28,712	28,648	29,530	31,857	33,244	34,570	35,890
Missouri	32,466	33,870	34,887	34,746	35,656	38,650	40,029	40,823
Montana	30,052	30,908	31,836	31,356	32,121	33,249	34,379	35,754
Nebraska	32,803	34,023	35,045	32,880	33,284	38,359	40,193	40,893
Nevada	36,553	37,879	39,179	38,883	39,390	42,702	42,990	44,042
New Hampshire	39,564	42,188	43,455	37,405	37,734	46,855	47,083	48,188
New Jersey	49,196	50,435	51,949	51,193	52,174	56,691	56,147	57,187
New Mexico	28,866	29,389	30,271	32,398	32,554	34,614	37,073	37,888
New York	48,300	48,754	50,218	49,437	50,173	53,296	56,147	55,000
North Carolina	32,360	31,622	32,571	36,098	39,419	42,638	42,680	43,076
North Dakota	26,515	27,153	27,905	28,976	29,863	31,194	32,630	33,519
Ohio	37,867	39,038	40,087	40,566	41,436	44,319	45,690	47,175
Oklahoma	28,928	30,584	31,000	31,149	31,298	36,314	36,661	36,808
Oregon	40,100	40,980	42,210	42,883	40,919	42,513	46,432	47,796
Pennsylvania	45,422	47,087	48,500	48,457	48,321	50,821	51,920	53,200
Rhode Island	41,464	42,900	44,188	45,650	47,041	53,962	53,013	55,643
South Carolina	31,512	33,155	34,219	34,506	36,081	39,819	41,856	43,313
South Dakota	25,726	27,354	27,767	28,552	29,072	31,142	32,444	33,603
Tennessee	32,452	34,412	35,093	36,500	36,328	38,943	40,072	41,264
Texas	31,444	33,861	35,217	35,041	37,567	40,626	41,625	42,441
Utah	29,672	31,780	33,000	32,950	34,946	37,737	38,457	39,578
Vermont	36,681	37,054	38,167	36,800	37,714	38,393	40,518	43,632
Virginia	34,587	35,535	36,602	37,475	38,123	41,194	42,755	44,211
Washington	37,752	39,594	39,591	38,692	41,013	44,263	45,708	47,291
West Virginia	33,051	33,296	34,360	34,244	35,008	37,181	38,112	39,988
Wisconsin	37,534	39,212	40,389	40,657	41,153	45,221	45,452	46,024
Wyoming	32,300	32,493	32,626	33,500	34,140	35,949	39,161	39,206
Dist. of Columbia	42,088	39,663	40,854	47,150	47,076	50,053	48,352	52,424

Sources: U.S. Department of Education, National Center for Education Statistics, Statistics of State School Systems; National Education Association, *Rankings & Estimates: Rankings of the States 2002 and Estimates of School Statistics 2003*. Summary Table G, Estimated Average Annual Salaries of Total Instructional Staff and of Classroom Teachers, 2001-2002 (Revised) and 2002-2003 (page 90). Reprinted with permission of the National Education Association © 2003. All rights reserved.

Note: Instructional staff includes supervisors, principals, classroom teachers, librarians and other related instructional staff.

Information for the years 1992–93 and 1993–94 can be located in *The Book of the States*, Volume 32, 1998–99.

Information for 1989–90 can be located in *The Book of the States*, Volume 35, 2003.

Trends in Faculty Salaries

By John W. Curtis

Several systematic factors contribute to the variation in faculty salaries. Institutional type is the most significant factor in determining faculty salaries overall; faculty members are also differentiated according to academic rank. Two other important factors are gender and region, and several individual factors are also identified. This article also discusses two policy issues: the widening gap between salaries at private institutions and those in the public sector; and the continuing salary disadvantage faced by women faculty.

Faculty salaries, like much of American higher education itself, are widely differentiated according to several factors. The most significant sources of variation are institutional type (including both the level of degree offered and institutional affiliation) and academic rank. Two other important factors affecting salaries are gender and regional location. Finally, a number of factors affecting the salaries of individual faculty members are specific to each situation, even though commonalities can be observed across the spectrum. These individual factors include the faculty member's discipline, record of publications and scholarship, the presence of collective bargaining and race or ethnicity.

This article provides an overview of the most salient differences in faculty salaries, as identified above, and points to trends which should be of particular interest to policymakers. The source of data presented here is the annual Faculty Compensation Survey conducted by the American Association of University Professors (AAUP). The AAUP survey includes accredited institutions at all levels, both public and private. AAUP has collected and published faculty salary data in its "Annual Report on the Economic Status of the Profession" for nearly six decades. Table B reports average faculty salary at four-year institutions for academic year 2002-03 by state, level and control of institution, and academic rank. (The AAUP collects data from associate degree colleges as well, but the survey response for 2002-03 did not provide sufficient cases for an accurate breakdown by state.)

In comparing faculty salaries between states, the most important factor—and perhaps the most significant source of variation in faculty salaries overall—is institutional type. Institutional type itself can be divided into two components: the level of institution, categorized in the AAUP survey by highest degree; and the control of the institution, generally distinguishing between public and private. Table A shows the variation in national average faculty salary by these two components of institutional type.

Approximately 70 percent of full-time faculty in the United States are employed at public institutions. However, as Table A indicates, faculty salaries at private-independent four-year institutions are 5 to 27 percent higher than those at public institutions. (Private-independent associate degree institutions, by contrast, are few in number and tend to compensate their faculty at lower levels.) Table A distinguishes between two categories of institutions that are often lumped together as "private"—those that are independent and those that are affiliated with a religious denomination. Faculty salaries at institutions in the latter category are generally lower, although the average for church-related doctoral institutions is pushed upward by a relatively small group of large research universities that pay higher salaries. By contrast, in Table B average salaries for private baccalaureate colleges in some states are depressed by combining private-independent and church-related colleges into one category, since the proportion of church-related colleges is much larger in some states and most church-related colleges are in the baccalaureate category.

Tables A and B give an indication for the most current year of the primary issue of interest to state policymakers: the divergence of faculty salaries between public and private sectors. At the national level, and in most states, faculty at public institutions receive lower salaries on average than do faculty at comparable private institutions. But this situation is not static. The AAUP annual report has followed the trend of public/private differentials for many years. As Ronald G. Ehrenberg summarized in the most recent AAUP report,

> Several researchers have used AAUP data to document the decrease in the average salary of faculty members at public academic institutions relative to that of their peers at private institutions that took place between 1978-79 and 2001-

Table A: Average Full-Time Faculty Salary 2002–03, By Institutional Category and Control

	Public	Private-Independent	Church-Related
Doctoral	$70,381	$89,263	$74,865
Master's	58,404	61,265	57,186
Baccalaureate	52,932	60,833	49,108
Associate	50,737	34,641	35,837

Source: American Association of University Professors, Faculty Compensation Survey.

Notes: Includes all full-time primarily instructional faculty, with or without academic rank.

Figures are weighted average (mean) salaries; salaries of faculty members on 12-month contracts have been adjusted to an academic year (9-month) equivalent.

02. Most of the decline occurred before the mid-1990s; the relative salaries of faculty in the public and private sectors remained roughly constant between 1996-97 and 2001-02. ...However, average salaries in public institutions of higher education dropped this past year relative to those in private institutions.[1]

Although average faculty salary alone is not a sufficient indicator of institutional quality, it seems self-evident to observe that, given substantial and widening differences in pay over time, public colleges and universities will have difficulty attracting and keeping the most productive and innovative scholars and teachers. This becomes a public policy issue if we wish to make high-quality higher education accessible to large segments of the public, and not only to those who can pay the cost of and gain admission to private universities and colleges.

For the comparison of average faculty salaries between states, Table B also shows the important distinction between senior faculty members (holding the rank of professor) and generally entry-level faculty (assistant professors). Differences between states in average salary at either rank could indicate a disadvantage in attracting highly-qualified faculty, whether they be established scholars who bring immediate prestige and assume leadership of both scholarly projects and collegiate governance structures, or entry-level faculty who represent the potential for developing research and teaching.

A number of researchers have investigated the continuing salary differences between men and women faculty, differences which cut across institutional type and academic rank. The AAUP has collected institution-level data on average salaries by gender since the mid-1970s. An analysis of those data indicates a remarkably persistent salary disadvantage for women faculty over more than a quarter century. When faculty of the same rank are compared, average salaries for women are 7 to 12 percent lower than those of men. The greatest differences are at the rank of full professor. There are some variations in this comparison by institutional type, as average salaries are more equal in baccalaureate and associate colleges, and are generally more equal at public colleges and universities. However, it is also the case that women faculty are more likely to hold positions that have lower salaries on average: they are more likely than men to be at public community colleges, they are less likely to achieve the rank of professor, and they are less likely to have tenure. (Women are also more likely than men to hold part-time faculty positions, but the AAUP data include salary only for full-time faculty.) As a result, when the weighted average salaries of all women full-time faculty are compared with all full-time men, women receive only about 80 percent of the salary of men. The AAUP data indicate that this has been the case since the late 1970s, with surprisingly little change in the overall figure.

The AAUP data allow only for comparisons of institutional averages. Other investigators have utilized individual-level data to attempt to determine whether gender differences in salary can be attributed to differences in the distribution of women faculty according to other professional characteristics. A recent analysis of 1998 data by the U.S. Department of Education considered some 13 factors that might contribute to the salary difference between men and women faculty.[2] It concluded that, even when all of those factors are controlled in the analysis, men still earn 9.4 percent more than women, on average. Toutkoushian and Conley, in a recent comprehensive review and extension of various analytical models developed during the 1990s, found that progress appeared to have been made in narrowing the "unexplained" salary gap between men and women faculty—that not attributable to differences on observable factors—but that the gap remains at between 4 and 6 percent. As they point out, "[t]hese unexplained wage gaps are not only statistically significant, but are large in a practical sense especially when compounded over a woman's career. These inequities persist across most institution types and fields, and thus we should not lose focus on the fact that more improvement in the situation for women is needed."[3] What many statistical analyses fail to investigate, however, is the reasons that women continue to be overrepresented in the situations that result in lower average salary, as noted above. That, too, is a critical policy issue that remains to be addressed if women are to participate fully in the academic profession.

Faculty salaries also vary by geographic region. The AAUP data, divided into nine regions, indicate that the highest overall average faculty salaries are found in New England,[4] a region dominated by private higher education institutions, and the Pacific,[5] heavily influenced by relatively high salaries in California. An analysis of regional salary trends over time indicates that the regional differences have also been widening. Growth in average salaries over the last 25 years has been most rapid in New England and in the South Atlantic,[6] with salaries in the latter region falling generally into the middle range nationally. Salary growth in the Middle Atlantic region[7] has also generally kept pace, while faculty salaries in the East North Central[8] and, especially, East South Central[9] regions have fallen further behind. The latter two regions are characterized by more public institutions, especially at the doctoral level, reflecting the public/private salary disparities discussed above.

In addition to the broad differences in faculty salaries by categories previously mentioned, salaries for individual faculty members also vary according to a number of specific aspects of the individual situation. In recent years, salary differences between faculty in different disciplines have emerged as a recurring topic for discussion, with the influence of "the market" often cited as the force driving widening disparities even within the same institution. Faculty in fields such as business, engineering, or computer technologies, whose skills have been in demand in the private sector, have frequently been able to secure higher salaries than their colleagues in the humanities and social sciences. Analyses such as the two individual-level studies cited previously have also concluded that faculty members with a more substantial record of publications and scholarship earn higher salaries, even when other factors are taken into account. This likely reflects the continuing premium accorded to research among the several roles of faculty, an emphasis that appears to apply to faculty even in predominantly teaching institutions. Faculty salaries are also affected by the presence of collective bargaining, although a comprehensive recent analysis of the net impact of collective bargaining remains to be done. On the one hand, faculty collective bargaining may lead to higher salary levels for the faculty as a whole, and may lessen inequities within the compensation system; on the other hand, collective bargaining may act to preserve aspects of faculty self-governance and peer review, which can reinforce the differences by discipline and rank discussed above. Finally, the existence of systematic differences in faculty salary by race or ethnicity is a controversial topic, on which there is not conclusive evidence. The U.S. Department of Education analysis referenced above concluded that "...some racial/ethnic differences [in salary] existed in 1998. Compared with White faculty, Asian/Pacific Islander faculty had higher average salaries, were more likely to hold advanced degrees, and had greater representation at public doctoral, research and medical institutions. Black faculty had lower average salaries and were less likely to have advanced degrees or attain tenure or full professorship than White faculty."[10] However, the analysis concluded that when all factors were considered simultaneously, racial or ethnic category did not represent a statistically significant source of differences in faculty salaries.

There are several thousand institutions of higher education in the United States, reflecting the wide variety of institutional traditions, missions, and resources that is a central feature of the American system. Faculty in these institutions fill a number of roles and bring differing professional qualifications to their positions; with more than 400,000 full-time faculty employed in different institutional situations across the country, the variation in faculty salaries is tremendous. This article has provided an overview of the key factors differentiating faculty salaries. It has also identified a critical issue facing state government policymakers: the long-term decline in faculty salaries at public institutions, relative to those at private institutions. States look to their higher education institutions to provide high-quality education in a range of rapidly changing fields of endeavor, as centers of innovation in science and technology, and as sources of solutions to pressing social needs. As enrollments continue to grow, and the need for expanded access to high-quality higher education becomes increasingly apparent, state policymakers must identify sufficient resources to allow their higher education sectors to meet these new demands.

Notes

[1] Ronald G. Ehrenberg, "Unequal Progress: The Annual Report on the Economic Status of the Profession," *Academe* 89, no. 2 (March/April 2003): 26.

[2] U.S. Department of Education, National Center for Education Statistics. *The Condition of Education 2002*, (Washington, D.C.: NCES), 103.

[3] Robert K Toutkoushian and Valerie Martin Conley. "Progress for Women in Academe, but Inequities Persist: Evidence from NSOPF:99." (Paper presented to the annual meeting of the Association for the Study of Higher Education, Portland, Oregon, November 2003), 21.

[4] New England: Connecticut, Maine, Massachusetts, New Hampshire, Vermont and Rhode Island.

[5] Pacific: Alaska, California, Guam, Hawaii, Oregon and

Washington.

⁶ South Atlantic: Delaware, District of Columbia, Florida, Georgia, Maryland, North Carolina, Puerto Rico, South Carolina, Virginia and West Virginia.

⁷ Middle Atlantic: New Jersey, New York and Pennsylvania.

⁸ East North Central: Illinois, Indiana, Michigan, Ohio and Wisconsin.

⁹ East South Central: Alabama, Kentucky, Mississippi and Tennessee.

¹⁰ *The Condition of Education 2002,* 103.

About the Author

John W. Curtis is director of research at the American Association of University Professors in Washington, D.C. He holds a Ph.D. in sociology from Johns Hopkins University, and has worked at colleges and universities in the United States, Germany and Kenya. Opinions expressed in this article are those of the author, and not of the AAUP.

Table B
AVERAGE FULL-TIME FACULTY SALARY IN FOUR-YEAR INSTITUTIONS 2002-03, BY STATE, INSTITUTIONAL CONTROL, INSTITUTION CATEGORY, AND ACADEMIC RANK

State or other jurisdiction	Public Doctoral				Public Master's				Public Baccalaureate			
	Prof.	Assoc.	Asst.	All	Prof.	Assoc.	Asst.	All	Prof.	Assoc.	Asst.	All
United States	$92,405	$64,970	$54,998	$70,381	$74,515	$59,143	$49,091	$58,404	$67,148	$54,755	$45,664	$52,932
Alabama	82,536	60,694	50,761	63,467	64,057	53,284	45,600	50,480	63,257	55,957	50,771	55,411
Alaska	70,957	55,078	48,514	55,974	68,898	55,442	48,481	55,026	. . .	. . .	. . .	. . .
Arizona	87,401	61,716	53,786	68,686	84,631	64,691	51,606	62,593	. . .	. . .	. . .	. . .
Arkansas	80,502	60,769	53,029	62,797	61,780	53,649	42,845	47,791	59,651	52,103	41,989	46,702
California	108,030	69,783	60,294	87,062	83,480	67,685	54,818	69,832	84,866	70,232	61,392	66,955
Colorado	88,824	66,435	56,748	71,590	78,922	60,708	52,878	58,277	61,659	50,338	43,753	47,930
Connecticut	107,574	77,919	62,582	85,646	80,552	62,911	51,386	65,901	. . .	. . .	. . .	. . .
Delaware	101,932	71,122	58,490	76,941	73,793	57,784	47,335	57,275	. . .	. . .	. . .	. . .
Florida	85,027	61,757	53,146	65,206	73,858	59,027	50,171	56,334	71,063	54,500	40,358	54,243
Georgia	100,551	69,213	59,247	75,426	71,007	56,046	46,432	53,780	67,635	56,986	46,105	52,528
Hawaii	87,088	64,193	54,963	70,181	. . .	. . .	. . .	. . .	66,338	54,874	47,955	55,133
Idaho	70,183	56,009	48,389	57,405	62,705	53,390	44,911	49,092	53,485	43,010	36,349	44,753
Illinois	91,457	63,792	54,329	68,159	72,061	58,038	47,460	54,608	. . .	. . .	. . .	. . .
Indiana	89,133	62,451	52,682	67,998	74,941	58,597	49,723	55,895	65,103	52,272	43,869	48,511
Iowa	94,632	66,608	57,725	74,184	76,656	59,885	49,747	58,458	. . .	. . .	. . .	. . .
Kansas	79,620	59,198	50,870	62,208	66,086	53,681	43,882	51,283	. . .	. . .	. . .	. . .
Kentucky	84,523	61,718	51,695	66,931	67,929	55,199	46,812	51,143	. . .	. . .	. . .	. . .
Louisiana	80,393	58,287	51,174	58,450	62,246	52,261	44,901	48,561	. . .	. . .	. . .	. . .
Maine	69,904	58,788	49,074	57,630	71,751	55,693	43,701	55,710	53,873	46,118	38,394	45,056
Maryland	104,471	73,156	64,108	78,505	77,627	62,034	51,130	58,399	89,090	67,860	54,209	70,611
Massachusetts	89,424	71,348	57,223	73,734	72,689	60,090	49,992	61,689	. . .	. . .	. . .	. . .
Michigan	99,536	70,523	58,738	75,893	73,001	59,570	49,776	58,399	. . .	. . .	. . .	. . .
Minnesota	101,323	70,870	61,941	83,798	70,516	60,664	49,958	58,101	68,001	55,084	47,406	55,659
Mississippi	75,980	60,649	49,946	58,289	55,889	50,657	44,363	46,464	53,026	46,783	41,851	43,525
Missouri	87,385	62,445	51,746	61,244	64,316	52,177	43,072	50,352	60,493	48,917	41,143	47,216
Montana	69,094	53,728	46,672	55,369	57,440	46,562	44,619	46,166	58,357	49,619	42,837	49,596
Nebraska	90,695	65,115	56,315	72,586	68,236	57,234	47,189	54,551	59,407	43,044	39,336	46,737
Nevada	94,831	70,485	54,755	71,191	. . .	. . .	. . .	. . .	. . .	. . .	. . .	. . .
New Hampshire	86,882	65,401	53,048	71,031	68,782	55,165	45,768	58,634	. . .	. . .	. . .	. . .
New Jersey	109,893	78,641	61,886	84,930	89,006	70,970	56,060	71,212	87,466	68,781	54,059	69,119
New Mexico	75,480	57,499	49,799	60,155	54,830	44,971	40,225	44,360	. . .	. . .	. . .	. . .
New York	99,073	71,657	59,344	76,968	83,857	65,502	52,045	65,509	81,519	63,456	52,869	62,052
North Carolina	97,860	68,485	58,482	73,267	74,767	59,383	50,596	57,205	66,463	54,276	46,689	53,395
North Dakota	65,359	54,374	47,999	53,325	58,040	47,861	41,478	44,323	43,542	41,864	38,532	39,503
Ohio	87,995	63,085	51,671	66,741	73,873	57,813	47,346	61,467	66,765	54,598	44,490	52,069
Oklahoma	79,869	58,306	49,542	61,025	59,511	50,752	44,381	48,582	54,052	46,338	38,911	43,513
Oregon	77,047	58,725	49,466	58,754	57,874	47,957	40,342	46,627	55,645	46,543	40,788	45,503
Pennsylvania	100,205	70,471	57,534	72,768	86,324	69,488	56,436	68,253	71,705	59,210	49,845	52,386
Rhode Island	86,387	63,645	54,379	74,517	66,043	55,366	48,275	58,002	. . .	. . .	. . .	. . .
South Carolina	85,170	62,403	53,853	66,706	64,163	53,433	43,760	51,990	60,037	51,780	43,974	48,770
South Dakota	68,703	52,813	44,254	51,851	64,450	52,969	46,811	54,251	58,725	50,392	45,870	46,922
Tennessee	81,319	61,070	50,737	63,071	65,547	52,116	44,021	52,367	. . .	. . .	. . .	. . .
Texas	92,732	62,634	55,274	68,171	68,464	56,769	48,823	53,424	75,346	55,325	47,480	55,241
Utah	82,232	58,506	51,459	63,705	61,627	50,041	41,821	48,898	. . .	. . .	. . .	. . .
Vermont	74,845	57,068	48,142	55,754	. . .	. . .	. . .	. . .	51,319	42,920	34,248	43,586
Virginia	97,160	67,209	54,973	72,529	68,081	57,101	45,856	54,594	72,847	56,325	42,423	56,651
Washington	87,990	63,436	58,249	68,770	64,097	52,639	45,791	52,765	. . .	. . .	. . .	. . .
West Virginia	75,096	57,754	46,485	59,257	63,244	50,268	41,136	51,626	57,780	48,856	40,821	46,943
Wisconsin	93,578	69,121	59,890	77,276	67,452	55,275	47,854	56,203	. . .	. . .	. . .	. . .
Wyoming	77,715	58,960	55,273	61,846	. . .	. . .	. . .	. . .	. . .	. . .	. . .	. . .
Dist. of Columbia	. . .	. . .	. . .	. . .	. . .	. . .	. . .	. . .	. . .	. . .	. . .	. . .
Puerto Rico	. . .	. . .	. . .	. . .	. . .	. . .	. . .	. . .	53,542	43,801	36,478	43,018

See footnotes at end of table.

AVERAGE FULL-TIME FACULTY SALARY IN FOUR-YEAR INSTITUTIONS 2002-03, BY STATE, INSTITUTIONAL CONTROL, INSTITUTION CATEGORY, AND ACADEMIC RANK – Continued

State or other jurisdiction	Private											
	Doctoral				Master's				Baccalaureate			
	Prof.	Assoc.	Asst.	All	Prof.	Assoc.	Asst.	All	Prof.	Assoc.	Asst.	All
United States	$114,409	$74,564	$64,509	$85,745	$77,350	$59,634	$48,672	$59,365	$70,391	$53,254	$44,447	$54,513
Alabama	...	...	...	...	72,182	55,289	46,967	57,680	65,081	53,668	43,557	53,938
Alaska	...	...	...	...	...	...	...	...	...	...	...	...
Arizona	...	...	...	...	...	...	...	...	...	...	...	...
Arkansas	...	...	...	...	...	...	...	...	58,895	48,801	42,283	48,777
California	118,055	78,985	67,655	92,479	88,323	65,521	54,353	69,136	87,513	63,847	50,509	69,050
Colorado	85,177	65,704	53,124	67,021	44,547	- -	37,219	42,292	87,825	64,165	49,620	66,485
Connecticut	137,158	79,487	63,819	100,376	85,096	62,537	52,669	65,395	88,395	66,225	51,003	67,151
Delaware	...	...	...	...	56,965	53,085	50,890	52,465	56,981	49,101	41,225	47,863
Florida	95,364	62,661	57,402	68,134	74,787	56,067	47,683	57,547	62,868	53,255	44,058	50,677
Georgia	121,822	79,429	69,037	93,899	71,964	54,291	44,791	51,335	63,020	51,920	41,991	49,713
Hawaii	...	...	...	...	...	...	...	...	...	...	...	...
Idaho	...	...	...	...	...	...	...	43,510	56,923	43,720	40,131	44,514
Illinois	119,792	74,324	64,558	88,795	68,589	56,341	46,443	55,305	64,280	52,198	43,666	51,255
Indiana	112,560	75,267	66,146	89,410	69,657	54,265	43,401	53,016	64,935	50,830	44,997	53,140
Iowa	...	...	...	...	69,930	53,897	44,558	54,973	61,112	49,360	42,144	49,551
Kansas	...	...	...	...	52,385	47,184	45,599	46,380	45,250	38,519	34,733	38,037
Kentucky	...	...	...	...	65,683	56,222	47,014	59,326	56,353	47,911	40,373	47,252
Louisiana	99,130	71,550	60,843	75,189	79,095	57,083	45,815	57,147	57,610	46,268	41,120	48,470
Maine	...	...	...	...	64,820	54,236	44,927	49,790	93,183	63,811	50,564	68,255
Maryland	108,450	75,054	63,182	78,175	76,957	59,549	50,764	59,110	68,710	55,080	45,150	55,745
Massachusetts	126,907	78,925	71,166	95,559	90,822	67,731	55,705	68,571	91,254	64,628	53,114	71,158
Michigan	...	...	...	...	59,665	48,880	42,037	47,903	61,167	49,924	43,433	51,457
Minnesota	79,942	62,521	52,980	62,381	66,927	51,773	42,652	49,364	71,876	54,590	45,956	56,016
Mississippi	...	...	...	...	...	...	...	...	68,415	50,745	46,487	51,963
Missouri	106,994	69,101	59,951	80,088	64,124	52,567	44,190	52,178	56,170	48,106	42,284	46,568
Montana	...	...	...	...	...	...	...	...	46,061	37,242	34,619	41,757
Nebraska	...	...	...	...	78,654	59,013	46,538	55,355	56,127	45,790	40,374	46,742
Nevada	...	...	...	...	...	...	...	...	...	...	...	...
New Hampshire	113,999	81,334	66,471	92,338	73,611	52,913	47,678	59,721	60,587	52,229	42,853	51,365
New Jersey	128,651	74,757	62,367	94,270	77,743	66,370	51,283	62,661	64,867	50,661	41,738	50,763
New Mexico	...	...	...	...	...	...	...	...	55,553	49,584	40,343	49,048
New York	113,614	76,538	64,468	85,161	79,885	62,873	51,396	62,504	82,466	60,806	48,970	62,628
North Carolina	124,869	84,062	72,363	101,709	79,141	61,178	47,998	60,998	60,246	47,240	40,237	47,455
North Dakota	- -	- -	- -	- -	...	...	...	...	46,279	40,149	37,393	39,645
Ohio	101,948	71,933	65,074	81,025	73,496	55,640	46,810	55,696	67,907	53,887	44,378	53,806
Oklahoma	...	...	...	...	72,504	54,660	46,409	54,687	50,902	44,843	37,004	42,441
Oregon	...	...	...	...	78,359	58,060	47,090	61,299	74,913	50,819	46,659	58,080
Pennsylvania	115,433	79,275	72,695	90,820	82,910	63,251	49,839	61,012	73,914	57,472	45,948	56,030
Rhode Island	111,018	71,366	63,980	90,054	72,533	56,040	47,812	53,294	80,920	68,873	57,582	69,773
South Carolina	...	...	...	...	...	...	...	...	66,484	48,824	43,106	51,199
South Dakota	...	...	...	...	...	...	...	...	52,086	45,440	38,188	42,070
Tennessee	112,283	74,219	68,635	84,695	59,582	51,472	44,179	50,102	57,033	45,901	38,725	45,096
Texas	99,046	69,064	60,480	72,531	70,073	55,026	45,534	55,456	57,387	49,179	40,128	46,637
Utah	...	...	...	...	...	...	...	...	- -	- -	- -	- -
Vermont	...	...	...	...	61,235	52,001	41,933	53,424	85,925	60,225	53,354	66,199
Virginia	...	...	...	...	65,396	54,327	45,493	53,852	69,589	52,762	44,205	55,273
Washington	...	...	...	...	71,069	59,409	48,667	58,165	67,973	52,302	46,332	55,421
West Virginia	...	...	...	...	...	...	...	...	52,454	45,697	38,471	43,385
Wisconsin	85,162	64,643	54,515	63,343	55,407	47,502	40,477	44,958	61,641	50,855	43,612	50,064
Wyoming	...	...	...	...	...	...	...	...	...	...	...	...
Dist. of Columbia	100,925	69,911	57,540	76,410	94,568	68,130	53,762	75,045	60,657	48,439	41,703	48,293
Puerto Rico	...	...	...	...	38,647	32,809	28,055	30,356	42,298	33,458	28,922	32,741

Source: American Association of University Professors, Faculty Compensation Survey. More extensive tables and complete definitions are in "The Annual Report on the Economic Status of the Profession 2002-03" *Academe* 89, no. 2 (March/April 2003).

Note: Figures are weighted average (mean) salaries; salaries of faculty members on 12-month contracts have been adjusted to an academic year (9-month) equivalent. Data include primary instructional faculty only.

Key:
. . . – Indicates no response in that category
Prof. – Professor.
Assoc. – Associate professor.
Asst. – Assistant professor.
All – Includes all full-time faculty, with or without academic rank.

Table 9.4
NUMBER OF INSTITUTIONS OF HIGHER EDUCATION AND BRANCHES, BY LEVEL OF CONTROL OF INSTITUTION AND STATE: 2002-2003

State or other jurisdiction	Total	4 years and above			2 years but less than 4 years		
		Public	Private		Public	Private	
			Not-for profit	For profit		Not-for profit	For profit
United States	4,168	631	1,538	297	1,081	127	494
Alabama	75	18	17	6	29	4	1
Alaska	8	3	2	1	2	0	0
Arizona	71	5	12	14	20	3	17
Arkansas	46	11	10	0	22	1	2
California	399	33	148	41	110	17	50
Colorado	77	14	13	18	15	1	16
Connecticut	46	11	18	1	12	1	3
Delaware	10	2	4	0	3	1	0
Florida	161	13	52	35	27	6	28
Georgia	124	21	33	8	53	4	5
Hawaii	20	3	5	3	7	1	1
Idaho	14	4	4	2	3	0	1
Illinois	175	12	85	11	48	5	14
Indiana	99	14	41	5	15	3	21
Iowa	623	3	35	6	16	2	1
Kansas	61	9	21	0	27	2	2
Kentucky	76	8	25	1	26	1	15
Louisiana	88	15	10	3	48	1	11
Maine	32	8	12	0	7	1	4
Maryland	64	14	21	8	16	1	4
Massachusetts	119	15	78	2	16	5	3
Michigan	110	15	58	2	30	1	4
Minnesota	113	11	35	12	41	2	12
Mississippi	41	9	11	0	17	1	3
Missouri	119	13	55	11	19	3	18
Montana	23	6	4	0	12	1	0
Nebraska	38	7	15	0	7	2	7
Nevada	14	3	1	3	3	0	4
New Hampshire	25	5	14	1	4	0	1
New Jersey	57	14	20	2	19	1	1
New Mexico	43	7	7	7	20	1	1
New York	312	47	163	12	35	22	33
North Carolina	126	16	41	4	59	1	5
North Dakota	21	7	4	0	8	1	1
Ohio	179	27	68	2	34	3	45
Oklahoma	53	15	16	3	14	0	5
Oregon	57	9	24	3	17	1	3
Pennsylvania	256	46	97	6	21	14	72
Rhode Island	13	2	10	0	1	0	0
South Carolina	63	12	23	2	21	2	3
South Dakota	26	8	8	4	5	1	0
Tennessee	89	9	45	7	13	3	12
Texas	201	42	50	8	68	4	29
Utah	25	6	3	5	4	1	6
Vermont	27	5	18	1	1	1	1
Virginia	101	15	33	19	24	0	10
Washington	78	11	20	9	34	0	4
West Virginia	37	12	10	0	3	0	12
Wisconsin	68	13	28	6	18	1	2
Wyoming	9	1	0	0	7	0	1
American Samoa	1	0	0	0	1	0	0
District of Columbia	16	2	11	3	0	0	0
Guam	3	1	1	0	1	0	0
No. Marianan Islands	1	1	0	0	0	0	0
Puerto Rico	70	14	35	7	3	3	8
U.S. Virgin Islands	2	2	0	0	0	0	0

Source: U.S. Department of Education, National Center for Education Statistics, Integrated Postsecondary Education Data System (IPEDS), Fall 2002.
Note: Data are not imputed. The item response rate for this table are 100 percent.

Table 9.5
ESTIMATED UNDERGRADUATE TUITION AND FEES AND ROOM AND BOARD RATES IN INSTITUTIONS OF HIGHER EDUCATION, BY CONTROL OF INSTITUTION AND STATE: 2000-2001 AND 2001-2002

State or other jurisdiction	Public 4-year 2000-2001 Total	Public 4-year 2000-2001 Tuition (in-state)	Public 4-year 2001-2002 (a) Total	Public 4-year 2001-2002 (a) Tuition (in-state)	Public 4-year 2001-2002 (a) Room	Public 4-year 2001-2002 (a) Board	Private 4-year 2000-2001 Total	Private 4-year 2000-2001 Tuition	Private 4-year 2001-2002 (a) Total	Private 4-year 2001-2002 (a) Tuition	Private 4-year 2001-2002 (a) Room	Private 4-year 2001-2002 (a) Board	Public 2-year tuition only (in-state) 2000-2001	Public 2-year tuition only (in-state) 2001-2002 (a)
United States	$8,653	$3,501	$9,199	$3,746	$2,811	$2,642	$21,856	$15,470	$22,968	$16,287	$3,571	$3,111	$1,333	$1,379
Alabama	7,349	2,987	7,654	3,245	2,321	2,088	14,136	9,334	15,269	10,229	2,415	2,626	1,672	1,990
Alaska	8,390	2,941	9,258	3,065	3,035	3,157	14,656	9,381	15,675	9,852	4,220	3,382	1,674	1,717
Arizona	7,874	2,346	8,222	2,488	2,719	3,015	15,109	9,322	14,510	9,759	2,616	2,135	924	962
Arkansas	6,797	3,011	7,302	3,387	2,036	1,879	13,377	9,109	14,414	9,952	1,988	2,474	1,158	1,314
California	9,590	2,566	10,320	2,730	3,830	3,760	24,679	12,219	26,203	18,399	4,269	3,535	315	315
Colorado	8,362	2,980	8,808	3,159	2,663	2,987	23,129	15,445	24,351	16,245	3,725	4,380	1,655	1,685
Connecticut	10,521	4,553	11,058	4,772	3,406	2,880	27,737	20,056	29,065	21,075	4,780	3,209	1,868	1,889
Delaware	10,283	4,789	10,889	5,065	3,082	2,742	13,936	8,415	14,698	8,755	3,146	2,798	1,680	1,800
Florida	7,947	2,366	8,361	2,555	3,138	2,667	19,870	13,805	20,978	14,708	3,316	2,954	1,438	1,494
Georgia	7,463	2,699	7,915	2,838	2,730	2,346	19,951	13,770	21,124	1,455	3,763	2,806	1,260	1,293
Hawaii	8,272	2,968	7,987	3,051	2,376	2,560	16,078	8,000	16,627	8,777	3,477	4,373	1,066	1,067
Idaho	6,765	2,628	7,163	2,860	1,993	2,310	17,793	13,664	10,163	5,326	1,862	2,976	1,253	1,410
Illinois	9,532	4,178	10,194	4,567	2,653	2,974	21,784	15,317	22,844	16,194	3,726	2,924	1,532	1,569
Indiana	9,239	3,786	9,783	4,002	2,821	2,960	21,378	16,078	22,545	16,973	2,823	2,749	2,108	2,121
Iowa	7,587	3,157	8,253	3,470	2,512	2,271	19,414	14,630	20,341	15,383	2,289	2,670	2,141	2,362
Kansas	6,654	2,642	6,987	2,700	2,056	2,231	15,670	11,206	16,653	11,987	2,058	2,608	1,378	1,441
Kentucky	6,923	2,898	7,370	3,194	2,131	2,045	14,644	10,176	15,710	10,972	2,261	2,477	1,342	1,561
Louisiana	6,329	2,783	6,689	2,865	1,895	1,929	21,937	15,591	23,050	16,539	3,469	3,042	935	1,009
Maine	9,371	4,267	10,259	4,804	2,716	2,739	22,690	16,450	24,132	17,619	3,214	3,299	2,594	2,642
Maryland	10,834	4,772	11,385	4,973	3,553	2,859	25,670	18,621	27,108	19,652	4,185	3,271	2,301	2,244
Massachusetts	9,207	4,003	9,370	3,999	2,926	2,445	28,666	20,566	29,970	21,526	4,696	3,749	1,894	1,946
Michigan	9,825	4,615	10,565	5,054	2,679	2,832	16,011	11,155	17,046	11,802	2,527	2,717	1,743	1,780
Minnesota	8,127	2,344	9,080	4,494	2,463	2,122	21,332	16,243	22,420	16,986	2,716	2,717	2,507	2,746
Mississippi	7,195	2,969	7,599	3,410	2,252	1,937	13,767	9,659	14,203	10,004	2,047	2,151	1,138	1,362
Missouri	8,203	3,879	8,672	4,111	2,587	1,975	17,886	12,600	18,787	13,218	2,860	2,710	1,472	1,498
Montana	7,615	2,627	8,309	3,467	2,177	2,665	14,454	9,631	15,929	9,926	3,104	2,899	2,004	2,159
Nebraska	7,355	3,101	7,731	3,228	2,105	2,398	16,093	11,619	18,837	14,074	2,386	2,377	1,421	1,498
Nevada	8,247	2,344	8,570	2,437	3,523	2,610	17,835	11,465	19,719	13,510	3,230	2,979	1,369	1,410
New Hampshire	11,720	6,458	12,348	6,728	3,457	2,163	25,184	18,261	26,482	18,186	4,121	3,175	3,933	4,324
New Jersey	12,007	5,609	12,854	6,078	4,034	2,741	23,738	16,680	25,203	17,403	4,113	3,687	2,295	2,236
New Mexico	7,086	2,627	7,587	2,838	2,252	2,497	19,011	14,062	20,508	14,499	3,121	2,888	876	921
New York	10,260	4,063	10,777	4,140	3,637	2,999	25,178	17,433	26,509	18,357	4,697	3,455	2,562	2,584
North Carolina	7,076	2,298	7,667	2,646	2,650	2,371	20,185	14,274	21,024	15,110	2,852	3,062	896	1,014
North Dakota	6,418	2,942	6,843	3,130	1,405	2,308	11,399	8,026	11,840	8,362	1,520	1,959	1,902	2,090
Ohio	9,900	4,502	10,449	4,740	3,043	2,666	20,733	11,840	8,362	15,475	2,820	2,749	2,292	2,373
Oklahoma	6,022	2,259	6,296	2,373	1,744	2,178	15,307	10,587	16,492	11,405	2,343	2,744	1,253	1,214
Oregon	9,394	3,646	10,063	3,862	3,191	3,010	23,123	17,533	24,428	18,308	3,090	3,030	1,637	1,722
Pennsylvania	11,091	5,917	11,861	6,316	2,955	2,590	24,737	17,821	26,002	18,796	3,833	3,373	2,287	2,369
Rhode Island	11,095	4,506	11,610	4,708	3,677	3,225	26,073	18,320	27,192	19,177	4,068	3,946	1,806	1,854

See footnotes at end of table.

ESTIMATED UNDERGRADUATE TUITION AND FEES AND ROOM AND BOARD RATES IN INSTITUTIONS OF HIGHER EDUCATION, BY CONTROL OF INSTITUTION AND STATE: 2000-2001 AND 2001-2002 — Continued

State or other jurisdiction	Public 4-year 2000-2001		Public 4-year 2001-2002 (a)				Private 4-year 2000-2001		Private 4-year 2001-2002 (a)				Public 2-year tuition only (in-state)	
	Total	Tuition (in-state)	Total	Tuition (in-state)	Room	Board	Total	Tuition	Total	Tuition	Room	Board	2000-2001	2001-2002 (a)
South Carolina	9,096	4,701	10,077	5,502	2,485	2,089	17,518	12,713	18,435	13,429	2,511	2,495	1,467	1,787
South Dakota	6,975	3,484	7,469	3,692	1,504	2,273	15,335	11,194	15,935	11,796	1,907	2,232	2,857	2,964
Tennessee	7,614	2,785	8,062	2,975	2,659	2,428	16,890	11,865	18,185	12,728	2,724	2,733	1,441	1,652
Texas	7,614	2,785	8,062	2,975	2,659	2,428	16,890	11,865	18,185	12,728	2,724	2,733	929	981
Utah	6,598	2,226	7,393	2,388	2,002	3,004	8,600	3,754	8,992	4,014	2,445	2,533	1,571	1,679
Vermont	12,847	7,142	13,450	7,470	3,700	2,280	22,454	15,740	23,205	16,407	3,659	3,140	3,004	3,148
Virginia	8,751	3,723	8,988	3,775	2,796	2,417	18,499	13,118	19,541	13,892	2,786	2,863	1,132	1,131
Washington	8,909	3,600	9,986	3,788	2,862	3,337	21,505	15,874	22,612	16,638	3,038	2,936	1,758	1,885
West Virginia	7,290	2,551	7,625	2,645	2,421	2,559	18,285	12,999	18,329	13,136	2,406	2,787	1,661	1,661
Wisconsin	7,396	3,417	7,786	3,691	2,265	1,829	20,317	15,032	21,330	15,907	2,836	2,587	2,262	2,310
Wyoming	7,017	2,575	7,421	2,807	2,012	2,602	(b)	(b)	(b)	(b)	(b)	(b)	1,440	1,490
Dist. of Columbia	(b)	2,070	(b)	2,070	(b)	(b)	26,933	19,186	28,310	20,093	5,090	3,126	(b)	(b)

Source: U.S. Department of Education, National Center for Education Statistics, Integrated Postsecondary Education Data System (IPEDS), "Fall Enrollment" and "Institutional Characteristics" surveys. (This table was prepared November 2002).

Note: Data are for the entire academic year and are average charges. Tuition and fees were weighted by the number of full-time equivalent undergraduates in 2000, but are not adjusted to reflect student residency. Room and board are based on full-time students. Data revised from previously published figures. Detail may not sum to totals due to rounding.

Key:
(a) Preliminary data based on fall 1999 enrollments.
(b) Not applicable.

The How and Why of Agricultural Policy
By Otto C. Doering III

Our agricultural programs were intended to move cash to rural areas during the Great Depression. Today, our programs make large income transfers to farmers. The rationale for this is unarticulated. Our programs could be more closely tied to the basic rationale for government's involvement in agriculture.

How policy affects agriculture is not just the impact of the farm bill. Trade policy, fiscal policy, tax laws, etc. all affect agriculture and other enterprises to varying degrees. What we call agricultural policy may not represent the critical economic drivers that might concern a state or region. The impacts of the 2002 farm bill are likely to be regional in nature, even following the location of specific crops that are addressed by the bill. Our agricultural policies are increasingly held up as too expensive, helping only large farmers, and having unintended negative side effects. Each of these criticisms contains some truth and should be of concern to us. Our dilemma is that our agricultural productivity outruns the demand for food and farm prices slowly decline over time hurting farmers and their communities.

How Did We Get Farm Programs?

The goal of the first farm bill, the 1933 Agricultural Adjustment Act, was to get cash into rural areas during the Great Depression. When the 1933 bill was passed, rural incomes were 40 percent of urban incomes. The rural economy was a barter economy, and cash was being kept under the mattress, if there was any. The challenge for Henry A. Wallace, Franklin Roosevelt's secretary of agriculture, was to get cash to rural areas without paying farmers directly, which would have been politically unacceptable. One device used to accomplish this was the "Ever Normal Granary." Wallace sold this concept in biblical terms of famine and plenty as a program to deal with annual price variation. Simply stated; farmers borrowed money to plant crops, but at harvest crop prices dropped with the new supply. Farmers then had to sell crops at low prices to pay back the banker. The grain merchant who purchased the crop stored it from harvest to spring when prices rose and profited from the farmer's necessity to sell at harvest. Everyone made money except the farmer.

Under the Agricultural Adjustment Act a farmer could take a loan from the government at harvest against a determined value for the crop and pay back the banker. The farmer could sell the crop later when prices rose to pay back the loan to the government, keeping any profit. If the market price stayed below the loan price, the farmer could let the government take the crop given as loan security and not repay the loan. There were two key considerations here. First, the loan rate must be set so that it reflected market conditions—an average between the high and low so that the farmer could sell at the high spring market, pay back the loan, and still have something more than would have been gained from selling at harvest. However, over time Congress raised the loan rate above market averages to transfer more money to farmers for the crops covered by agricultural programs (corn, wheat, cotton, sugar, dairy products, etc.). Thus, farmers turned more of their crops over to the government and government stored and sold more crops at a loss.

The second consideration was supply control. Supporting the income from program crops encouraged more planting, larger crops and lower prices. Starting in 1937, soil conservation programs became the major device for getting cash to rural areas and for limiting crop production while dealing with soil degradation in the Dust Bowl. Farmers were paid to idle cropland for conserving uses and paid cash for conservation improvements they made on the land. Ultimately, signing up for the commodity program required setting aside some proportion of one's land if the secretary determined there was oversupply of one's commodity. In the late 1930s, most federal payments to farmers were conservation payments. Today, the direct income payments dominate because it is politically acceptable to transfer money directly to farmers.

The agricultural programs in the 1930s pumped large amounts of cash into rural areas. The Second World War and the movement of millions off the farm from the '40s through the '60s accelerated the structural change to larger farm units and fewer farmers.

Programs evolved up to the 1996 farm bill adding new devices to get cash into farmer's hands to counter commodity prices that declined over time as production outpaced our population growth and world demand. Commodity loans were no longer the only vehicle to support farmer's income. Direct payments were made to farmers to bring receipts per bushel up to a "target price" set above the loan rate. This gave greater support to farmers without the government having to take in, store and market more grain. So, we adopted a low loan rate requiring less government storage and a higher target price which gave the farmer greater price protection.

Changing the Structure of Farm Programs

The 1996 farm bill changed the structure of farm income support. Congress eliminated all supply control tied to commodity programs—i.e. one no longer could be asked to set aside a percentage of their land if their crop was in surplus. Instead of payments related to target prices, fixed contract payments would be made directly to farmers based on their previous commodity payments irrespective of what mix of crops were now grown or what prices were. Whether prices were high or low, farmers would receive the same annual payment, declining slightly from 1996 to 2002. Farmers liked this in 1996 when prices were high, but found when prices dropped that they did not have the support from the fixed contract payments that they had previously. Ultimately, Congress gave up the attempt to do away with fixed support payments and made additional emergency payments. The concept of the loan had not been given up entirely in 1996 and prices fell so low after 1997 that additional payments were made to farmers for the difference between the extremely low loan price and the even lower market price. The Freedom to Farm program that was supposed to wean farmers away from government support resulted in more government support than before.

When approaching 2002, farmers remembered what happened under the 1996 bill when prices declined. It was only the emergency payments that kept them afloat. Farmers wanted a program that would give them even stronger countercyclical income support.

Insulating Farmers from the Market

The 2002 farm bill insulates farmers from the market more than any previous farm bill—and this from a market oriented administration and Congress. The new bill keeps a loan rate, brings back a target price and continues the direct payments. Table A illustrates the extent to which the 2002 program insu-

lates what the farmer receives from changes in the market price. The example here is for corn, but the result is similar for other program crops like cotton, rice, sugar and wheat. As the table illustrates, when the market price is extremely low the Loan Deficiency Payment (LDP) kicks in and raises the farmers return to the loan rate. The fixed contract payment (left over from the 1996 farm bill) adds another $0.28, and the countercyclical payment (the old target payment from farm bills prior to 1996) adds another $0.34 to bring the farmer's total return to $2.60 per bushel. The numbers in parenthesis for the direct and counter cyclical payments represent what an average farmer in the Corn Belt might actually get given the rules of the program about qualifying yields. In a market that changes from $1.68 to $2.70 the actual variation in prices received by the farmer is $0.45 (from $2.46 to $2.91) not $1.02. If the program were administered to provide the full target price, the price variation would be only $0.38.

Table A: Payments Under Various Corn Market, Target and Loan Prices

Corn Market Price	$1.68		$2.70	
Corn Target Price	2.60		2.60	
Corn Loan Price	1.98		1.98	
Loan Deficiency Payment	.30		No payment	
Counter Cyclical Payment	.34	(.27)	Price too high	
Direct Contract Payment	.28	(.21)	.28	(.21)
Total	$2.60	($2.46)	$2.98	($2.91)

Source: www.agecon.purdue.edu

Is There a Rationale for Farm Programs?

Prior to the 1996 farm bill, Sen. Richard Lugar, then chairman of the Senate Agriculture Committee, asked a series of questions focused on farm programs. What he was really asking for was the rationale for farm programs—i.e., why should we help farmers and not other groups, like dry cleaners put out of business by EPA regulations? His questions were not addressed in the discussion leading up to the bill but there are some good reasons.

1. Improved technology and favorable climate and soils have allowed American farmers to keep ahead of our demand for food. We have continuing surplus production and long term declines in prices for basic commodities that help consumers.

2. Farmers are price takers. International commodity markets set the prices. A farmer cannot in-

fluence the world price by his own actions and can not charge a higher price himself. (American workers are similarly loosing pricing power for their labor as manufacturers move to low labor cost countries.)

3. Farming is a biological process. Once the seed is planted it cannot be shut down. If prices fall after planting the farmer gains little by not fertilizing and harvesting the crop. The farmer cannot close the plant when prices fall, send the workers home and turn out the lights.

4. Farming is dependent on weather. Bad weather can wipe out a crop, and good weather can lead to surplus production where the price falls proportionally more than the increase in the quantity. (Once fed, who buys more food?)

5. Farming is capital and skill intensive. Having farms go in and out of business to adjust for undersupply and oversupply of food would be costly.

6. Finally, food is a strategic good. Few countries want to be too dependent on other countries for their basic food supplies. War or other crises might cut them off.

As a result of these reasons, through our taxes we support farmers and keep the bulk of our cultivated land in production. Because we allow food prices to be determined by a market which is influenced by overproduction, food prices in the U.S. are extremely low. The stability in food prices (at a low level) and the stability added to farm operations by government serves consumers well. This does not mean that our programs are necessarily the best ways to meet national goals for agriculture or that we have the right goals. Our current programs are potentially expensive and ignore the market. They tend to favor some commodities more than others. The farm programs have their own attendant pathologies. Our system leads to consolidation of farms into bigger units. Government payments get capitalized into land values. If a farmer gets a higher return for the crop—a return guaranteed by the government over time—this value gets bid into the value or the rent for that farmland. Finally, high crop subsidies encourage full production even if it degrades the land.

How Does Agriculture Fit Into The Broader Economic Picture?

Less than 2 percent of our people are on the land producing food and the bulk of our food is produced by the larger farms that are an even smaller proportion of the farm population. Our citizens now spend just a little over 10 percent of their dispos-

able income on food. One question is whether agriculture's political muscle outweighs its actual economic importance.

Trade

Commodities have been an important trading good for us since the first European settlements. Much of our economic development in the 18th and 19th centuries was based on exports of commodities and raw materials. At the time of the first Arab oil embargo in the 1970s, the net positive balance of trade from agricultural commodities was seen by agricultural interests as a major factor in earning foreign exchange to allow us to import oil. This is no longer the case. On the one hand, we now import much more oil. On the other hand, even though the value of our agricultural exports has increased by a third from the peak of the early 1980s, our agricultural imports have increased by one and two thirds. A positive agricultural trade balance of $10 to $15 billion today can not make a great contribution to balancing increasing oil imports let alone balancing the increasing trade deficit with China, now estimated at $120 billion. Would we be worse off without agricultural exports? We most certainly would be, but agricultural exports are no longer the driving foreign exchange earning force they were historically for the nation as a whole. The decline in the value of the dollar will give a boost to agricultural exports beyond where they would have been otherwise. However, historically we do not see much of the expected reduction in the growing imports of agricultural products when the value of the dollar decreases.

Where is the Engine of Growth?

The engine of growth in trade for agriculture is in value added agricultural products; meats, processed foods, etc. The engine of growth for commodities is within our domestic economy and is in industrial and process uses of these commodities. This has important implications for states and regions. Industries that add value to agricultural products for export and those industries that increase domestic non-food utilization help state and regional growth.

The Challenge for Agricultural Policy and Economic Growth

The challenge is to maintain those aspects of agricultural programs that we believe meet important goals such as protecting farmers against weather loss and extreme financial fluctuations and also protecting the long-term sustainability of farmland (i.e., meet the most critical rationale for government involvement in agriculture in the most cost effective way). The most important thing for economic growth will be to encourage those aspects of agriculture, value added for food products and other non-food uses that provide this growth at the local level.

References

Gray, Allen, W. May 2002. "2002 Farm Bill: Impacts on Decisions at the Farm." CES paper 342, Purdue University Cooperative Extension Service, W. Lafayette. Discusses the provisions of the 2002 farm bill showing how it affects a typical Corn Belt farm.

Schertz, Lyle and Otto Doering. *The Making of the 1996 Farm Act.* Ames: Iowa State University Press. 1999. De-scribes farm programs, the political process that shapes a farm bill, and lists Senator Lugar's questions.

www.agecon.purdue.edu For background text and fig-ures on trade issues, exports, imports, prices over time, etc. go to "programs and publications," then to "prices and out-look" and click on "2004 outlook, full report."

About the Author

Otto C. Doering III is a professor of Agricultural Eco-nomics at Purdue University. His responsibilities include teaching, research and adult education on issues of agri-culture and natural resources. He has worked in Washing-ton on a number of farm bills, led national environmental studies and served on his state's Commission for Higher Education.

Table B
NUMBER OF FARMS AND FARM ACREAGE BY STATE AND REGION: 2001, 2002, 2003

State	Number of farms			Land in farms (1,000 acres)		
	2003	2002	2001	2003	2002	2001
United States	2,126,860	2,135,360	2,148,630	938,750	940,300	942,070
Eastern Region						
Connecticut	4,200	4,200	4,200	360	360	360
Delaware	2,300	2,400	2,500	530	540	550
Maine	7,200	7,200	7,150	1,370	1,370	1,350
Massachusetts	6,100	6,100	6,100	520	520	520
New Hampshire	3,400	3,400	3,300	450	450	440
New Jersey	9,900	9,900	9,800	820	820	830
New York	37,000	37,000	37,500	7,650	7,660	7,660
Pennsylvania	58,200	58,200	58,500	7,700	7,700	7,710
Rhode Island	850	850	830	60	60	60
Vermont	6,500	6,600	6,600	1,250	1,260	1,270
Regional total	135,650	135,850	136,480	20,710	20,740	20,750
Midwestern Region						
Illinois	73,000	73,000	75,000	27,500	27,500	27,500
Indiana	59,500	60,300	62,100	15,040	15,100	15,100
Iowa	90,000	90600	92,000	31,700	31,800	3,200
Kansas	64,500	64,500	64,500	47,200	47,300	47,300
Michigan	53,300	53,300	53,000	10,090	10,090	10,120
Minnesota	80,000	80,900	81,000	27,700	27,800	27,800
Nebraska	48,500	49,400	50,000	45,900	45,900	4,600
North Dakota	30,300	30,500	30,600	39,400	39,400	39,400
Ohio	77,600	77,800	78,000	14,600	14,610	14,680
South Dakota	31,600	31,800	32,000	43,800	43,800	43,900
Wisconsin	76,500	77,000	77,000	15,600	15,700	15,800
Regional total	684,800	689,100	695,200	318,530	319,000	249,400
Southern Region						
Alabama	45,000	45,000	46,000	8,900	8,900	8,900
Arkansas	47,500	47,500	48,000	14,400	14,500	14,600
Florida	44,000	44,000	44,000	10,200	10,300	10,300
Georgia	49,300	49,300	49,200	10,800	10,800	10,850
Kentucky	87,000	87,000	88,000	13,800	13,800	13,800
Louisiana	27,200	27,500	28,000	7,850	7,900	7,910
Maryland	12,100	12,200	12,300	2,060	2,080	2,100
Mississippi	42,800	42,200	42,000	11,110	11,110	11,130
Missouri	106,000	107,000	108,000	30,200	30,200	30,200
North Carolina	53,500	54,200	55,000	9,100	9,100	9,120
Oklahoma	83,500	83,500	84,000	33,700	33,700	33,800
South Carolina	24,400	24,500	24,500	4,850	4,850	4,880
Tennessee	87,000	87,500	88,000	11,600	11,700	11,800
Texas	229,000	229,000	228,600	130,500	130,500	130,700
Virginia	47,500	47,600	47,900	8,600	8,670	8,680
West Virginia	20,800	20,800	20,800	3,600	3,600	3,600
Regional total	1,006,600	1,008,800	1,014,300	311,270	311,710	312,370
Western Region						
Alaska	610	610	600	900	900	900
Arizona (a)	10,300	10,300	10,400	26,500	26,600	26,700
California	78,500	79,700	81,000	27,100	27,600	27,800
Colorado	31,400	31,400	30,900	31,000	31,100	31,400
Hawaii	5,500	5,500	5,500	1,300	1,300	1,350
Idaho	25,000	25,000	24,500	11,800	11,800	11,800
Montana	28,000	27,900	27,800	60,100	59,800	59,600
Nevada	3,000	3,000	3,050	6,300	6,300	6,300
New Mexico	17,500	17,700	17,800	44,700	44,800	44,800
Oregon	40,000	40,000	40,000	17,200	17,200	17,200
Utah	15,300	15,300	15,500	11,600	11,600	11,600
Washington	35,500	36,000	36,500	15,300	15,350	15,400
Wyoming	9,200	9,200	9,200	34,440	34,500	34,500
Regional total	299,810	301,610	302,750	288,240	288,850	289,350
Regional total without California	268,410	270,210	271,850	257,240	257,750	257,950

Source: U.S. Department of Agriculture, National Agriculture Statistics Service, released February 27, 2004.

Note: A farm is any establishment from which $1,000 or more of agricultural products were sold during the year.

Key:

(a) Includes some accounting for individual farms on reservation land.

Table C
TOTAL NET FARM INCOME, VALUE OF PRODUCTION PER ACRE AND
NET INCOME PER ACRE AND PER OPERATION FOR 2003, BY STATE AND REGION

State or other jurisdiction	Net farm income (in thousands of dollars)	Value of production (a) (dollars per acre)	Net farm income per acre (dollars per acre)	Net farm income per operation (dollars per operation)
United States	$35,323,137	$231	$38	$16,542
Eastern Region				
Connecticut	99,870	1,463	277	23,778
Delaware	81,868	1,442	152	34,112
Maine	46,757	400	34	6,494
Massachusetts	36,810	828	71	6,034
New Hampshire	20,113	422	12	1,553
New Jersey	198,336	1,172	242	20,034
New York	567,612	463	74	15,341
Pennsylvania	610,967	597	79	10,498
Rhode Island	5,796	922	97	6,819
Vermont	105,402	420	84	15,970
Regional total	1,773,531	8,129	1,122	140,633
Midwestern Region				
Illinois	642,008	285	23	8,795
Indiana	107,757	327	7	1,787
Iowa	1,766,835	383	56	19,501
Kansas	375,516	176	8	5,822
Michigan	167,315	384	17	3,139
Minnesota	462,199	311	17	5,713
Nebraska	980,475	211	21	19,848
North Dakota	604,945	95	15	19,834
Ohio	267,950	329	18	3,444
South Dakota	558,670	87	13	17,568
Wisconsin	640,128	401	41	8,313
Regional total	6,573,798	2,989	236	113,764
Southern Region				
Alabama	1,199,561	421	135	26,657
Arkansas	815,668	353	56	17,172
Florida	2,667,272	707	259	60,620
Georgia	1,698,536	479	157	34,453
Kentucky	744,373	280	54	8,556
Louisiana	231,515	251	29	8,419
Maryland	194,827	781	94	15,969
Mississippi	401,418	308	36	9,512
Missouri	450,996	176	15	4,215
North Carolina	1,660,514	890	182	30,637
Oklahoma	758,037	130	22	9,078
South Carolina	177,908	321	37	7,262
Tennessee	339,218	229	29	3,877
Texas	3,686,460	115	28	16,098
Virginia	507,955	307	59	10,671
West Virginia	7,357	136	2	354
Regional total	15,541,615	5,884	1,194	263,550
Western Region				
Alaska	20,113	60	22	32,973
Arizona	1,462,236	126	55	141,965
California	5,197,239	998	188	65,210
Colorado	711,150	162	23	22,648
Hawaii	97,687	378	75	17,761
Idaho	1,255,547	372	106	50,222
Montana	215,619	37	4	7,728
Nevada	92,816	64	15	30,939
New Mexico	677,532	48	15	38,279
Oregon	3,598,776	215	21	8,997
Utah	290,510	108	25	18,988
Washington	969,130	374	63	26,920
Wyoming	99,568	27	3	10,823
Regional total	14,687,923	2,969	615	473,453
Regional total without California	9,490,684	1,971	427	408,243

Source: U.S. Department of Agriculture, Economic Research Service, March 2004.
Key:
(a) Value of agricultural sector production in the value-added accounting model (table).

Job Creation and Retention During the Recession

By Jeff Finkle

The domestic competition to create and retain jobs in the sour economy over the last two years has forced states to get more aggressive than ever in facilitating economic development. However, in pursuing aggressive approaches to recruiting new companies and preserve existing jobs, state and local officials have had to contend with the ramifications of the one of the recession's largest casualties—manufacturing.

Redwood Shores, California-headquartered software company Oracle announced it would relocate 2,000 developer jobs to India. Cigarette manufacturer Philip Morris is in the process of relocating its corporate operations from New York City to an area just outside of Richmond, Virginia, leaving in its wake a dearth of 450 jobs that will reappear in its new hometown. The recession—officially marked as the period between March 2001 and October 2003—has left a great percentage of corporations with an overwhelming need to find more economically friendly environments, either inside or outside the United States. According to an October 2003 *New York Times* article, 15 percent of the 2.81 million jobs that were lost over the last two years found their way to other countries. And according to an Economic Policy Institute analysis of the U.S. Bureau of Labor Statistics' numbers, total payroll employment since the start of the recession has decreased by an average of 1.8 percent nationally.

The country's manufacturing industry is the largest contributor to economic growth, and the biggest employment generator. That being said, according to a report by the National Association of Manufacturers and the Manufacturing Institute, manufacturing production decreased by 7 percent during the 2001 recession, compared to a .5 percent increase in the Gross Domestic Product for that same period. The organizations also conclude that the industry's recovery is proving to be the shallowest in decades. Aside from Nevada—which, with a 3.5 percent increase in jobs, was the only state to see an increase in manufacturing—states across the country were sent reeling from the unexpected devastation brought on by the recession-induced collapse in manufacturing.

Common Thread: Focusing on Growing and Emerging Industries

Having to contend with the dearth in manufacturing that progressed throughout the recession, states have had to refocus their competitive efforts to create and retain jobs. Perhaps the most prominent trend among states' push to create new jobs is the focus on luring new business sectors, specifically, high-end business sectors. The advanced science and high-technology sectors top the list of newly cultivated businesses among most states. Arizona is home to the third largest concentration of semiconductor manufacturers, and while the state has seen a 1.1 percent increase in job growth since the recession began, officials still recognize the overwhelming need to diversify. "So the state has put a considerable amount of resources and a considerable amount of effort into establishing the niche within the bioscience area," says Rick Weddle, president and CEO of the Greater Phoenix Economic Council and chairman-elect of the International Economic Development Council. Those efforts include a 20-year commitment to invest $1.5 billion in university research and development. And the state contributed $100 million for 2002's establishment of the Arizona Genomics Institute & Computational Laboratory at the University of Arizona, Tucson. "The Arizona Genomics Institute works in conjunction with the International Genomics Institute to really map the human genome and to identify opportunities to commercialize compounds and other intellectual property to come out of the process," Weddle explains. "We're attempting to grow a whole new industry cluster instead of trying to target companies specifically." Fruits of the state's labor in this arena are already beginning to appear. In 2002, Arizona convinced the Translational Genomics Research Institute, or TGen, to establish its headquarters in Phoenix. Early projections show that the biomedical research organization could lure as many as 120 new biotech companies to the region over the next decade, thereby creating nearly 13,000 new jobs.

California has the highest concentration of biotechnology companies in the country, but the push to increase that number is very much in force. The California Life Sciences Initiative—put in place in 2002 by former Gov. Gray Davis to define strategies for retaining and luring sciences companies—serves as further evidence that the biotechnology industry is to be an increasingly important source of jobs and revenue as we move through the 21ˢᵗ century. Virginia's Gov. Mark R. Warner followed suit with a similar plan in 2002, establishing the Virginia Biotechnology Initiative and appointing 32-member board to oversee the entity. Pharmaceutical company Eli Lilly took notice and selected Virginia last year for the development of a new $425 million insulin manufacturing facility that will create 700 high-level jobs. Information technology, despite the earth-shattering economic losses resulting from the late 1990s bust of the technology bubble, has continued to be a point of focus for Washington. The state has continued to attract a respectable amount of technology-related companies, primarily due to the presence of an old reliable resident—Microsoft. As of late, the computer technology giant has served as a magnet for a bevy of software and computer game firms.

Taking a broader approach in its economic development endeavors, Connecticut formed the Connecticut Industry Cluster Initiative in 1999, and has since been relying on the tool to carry it through the recession and beyond. The Cluster Initiative focuses on encouraging growth in key industry clusters through workforce training, the implementation of lean techniques, creation of new government policies, and marketing. Two of the state's nine core clusters are bioscience and information technology. "The cluster initiative uses business leaders together with people from academia and government officials to work together and drive policies and programs that will help improve the economy," Rita J. Zangari, deputy commissioner of the Connecticut Department of Economic and Community Development (DECD), explains. "We have a number of established clusters and we have a Governor's Council on Economic Competitiveness that guides the initiative itself. Those groups—both the business leaders and the individual clusters—are working together right now to give us a series of recommendations on competitiveness issues. They're looking at everything from tech transfer initiatives—how Connecticut can get more of its technology out of the research universities and into the commercialization process—to new funding tools, as well as retooling some of our existing funding programs."

Jay Engstrom, administrator of the Idaho Department of Commerce's Economic Development Divi-

sion says the state is not turning its back on any industry sectors, but concedes that biotech and high-tech are specific areas of interest. "Our target is high-paying, high-quality jobs requiring high skills," Engstrom notes. "So, what are those? Biotech and high-tech manufacturing. We do some computer hardware manufacturing here, we do semiconductor, we do a lot of research—Hewlett Packard has a big R&D facility here for the printers. So we have bought pretty heavily into what we're calling science and technology. It's a big area, but why it's so big is because we're trying to focus on building our workforce through higher math, higher sciences; and building the case that we want to train our workforce the best we can for those higher paying, higher quality jobs."

Reeling Them In: Creating Attractive Climate for New Industries

The bioscience and high-technology sectors are high on the list of industries to cultivate in most states. Economic development officials have been pursuing a bevy of means—like Arizona committing to investing in university research and the establishment of research institutions—to distinguish their states from others as a locale with a climate conducive to these sectors. Luring businesses by offering a highly qualified workforce pool is a key tactic. But when the nation's economy took a hit, so too did the country's educational system. A state's ability to provide a highly educated and/or well-trained workforce today and for the short-term has become a vital tool. Among the many teasers that Texas has been peddling to attract new businesses is its highly qualified workforce. With the third largest concentration of scientists and the second largest pool of engineers, it is home to a vast pool of potential employees for the white-collar employment sector. Idaho has found great success with its updated workforce development training fund. "We take a 3 percent offset on our unemployment trust fund and that generates for Idaho about $3 million a year," Engstrom explains. "Then we use those funds as an economic development tool to help existing businesses expand, new businesses move in, or in some instances, if companies can benefit from retraining they're existing workforce when faced with large layoff, we will do that too."

In addition to relying on the qualifications of the local workforce as a draw, states are also attracting new companies with financial incentives. In Texas Gov. Rick Perry signed off on legislation that established the Texas Enterprise Fund, which sets aside

$295 million for aggressive wooing of companies. Some of those funds went to convincing Toyota to choose Texas as the host of its new $800 million manufacturing plant, where the company will employ 2,000 individuals. In Connecticut, economic developers rely on a six-person team of recruiters that actively seeks out domestic and international companies and sells Connecticut's incentives to them. "We have a very attractive urban reinvestment tax credit, where if a company were to locate in an urban area and make a significant capital investment, they get a dollar-for-dollar tax credit on that capital investment that's measured against the economic impact that they create," Connecticut DECD's Zangari explains. "They earn these credits through a certain level of revenue generation that occurs here and we reward them by returning some of that revenue to the company."

Nevada focuses its package of financial incentives on recruiting companies, specifically California companies. Since August, Nevada has taken to actively seeking out businesses in neighboring California for relocation. Big selling points in recruitment range from the ease of relocation within the same time zone, to the state's absence of corporate income tax—or personal income tax, for that matter. Perhaps the largest draw is Nevada's comparably low workers' compensation insurance. "The rates are continuing to skyrocket there, while ours have been decreasing on an average of about 12.3 percent," Nevada Commission on Economic Development director Robert Shriver remarks. "Those are costs that businesses really can't control."

Arkansas, too, has a unique way of selling itself and its financial and geographical attributes. Its failures have turned out to be an effective marketing tool. "We finished a very close second to San Antonio, Texas for the Toyota assembly plant, but competing helped raise the profile of Arkansas," notes Jim Pickens, retiring director of the Arkansas Department of Economic Development. The Toyota campaign sent a very strong message that Arkansas is ready, willing, and able to compete for mega-projects. Once they have the companies' attention, Arkansas officials hammer home benefits of its new comprehensive economic incentive package that refocuses goal-based incentives from headcounts to annual payroll numbers. A high-concentration of Fortune 500 firms and a desirable trafficking location—about halfway between Montreal, Mexico City, and the East and West Coasts—are also big selling points.

The same tools states use to attract companies, works for retaining them, as well. A $50 million incentive package from the Lone Star State's Texas Enterprise Fund helped coax Dallas-based Texas Instruments into building a $3 billion semiconductor manufacturing facility in the city of Richardson, instead of going elsewhere. The TI manufacturing plant is expected to create about 1,000 new jobs when fully operational. Connecticut's business recruitment team used the state's financial incentive resources to secure BAE Systems' commitment to consolidate facilities in California and New Jersey at its site in the city of Cheshire. Connecticut put together an incentive package for the company that entails an approximately $2 million loan featuring rewards tied to the attainment of specified job targets. The expansion is expected to bring in 150 new jobs immediately. Harley-Davidson Financial Services, the loan and insurance arm of Harley-Davidson Motorcycles and an 11-year resident of Nevada, found itself changing its mind about a relocation plan. The state assuaged the company and convinced it to stay by crafting a tax break package that encompassed a 10-year, 50 percent decrease in personal property taxes, and the excising of taxes on an anticipated $10.45 million equipment purchase.

"Economic development is a rough and tumble sport, and it is sometimes played without pads and helmets," Arizona's Jim Pickens remarks, summing up the state of competition for job development and retention across the country. States will have to maintain their efforts, perhaps with the same vigor, to create and retain jobs even as the nation emerges from the recession. The pace will have to be sustained because recovery in manufacturing—the largest contributor to economic growth and the biggest employment generator—is not exactly on the horizon.

About the Author

Jeff Finkle is president and CEO of the International Economic Development Council. Formed through the merger of the Council for Urban Economic Development and the American Economic Development Council in 2001, IEDC represents more that 4,000 members across the U.S. and around the world. Finkle is a nationally recognized expert on economic development and is often called on by the press, the U.S. government, and state and local agencies.

Trends in Job Creation Strategies in the States
By Mark Arend

How can we take a bird's eye view of the economic development landscape and the features on it that are causing state legislators to rethink their workforce development strategies? As industries look farther afield for skilled workers, particularly in high-tech sectors, the states are doubling their efforts to educate and train people in order to attract and grow industry domestically. A state-by-state overview of new job creation initiatives follows the overview.

Is the glass half empty, or is it half full? There is no shortage of data pointing to heavy job losses in the manufacturing sector, nor of reports documenting significant productivity gains in the United States work force and stronger economic indicators. Corporate America's pent-up demand for new capital investment is starting to give way. Where checkbooks were slammed shut in late 2001 and much of 2002, they are open again, and businesses are expanding and investing in new plants and equipment.

But are they investing in new jobs? Are the business climates in the states such that employers will hire from within the states rather than seek labor elsewhere? Is the so-called jobless recovery the end of the story or just the beginning? With voters in most states increasingly willing to replace lawmakers they see as standing in the way of economic prosperity, the importance of economic development—and job creation specifically—has never been more apparent. More than immigration, car taxes, education or any other issue, California's gubernatorial shakeup was about economic development and stopping the exodus of businesses from the state. Perhaps most damaging to the Golden State's business climate is the aversion with which high-tech companies regard California of late. But the entire United States is seeing a loss of jobs in this critical sector.

High-tech Job Losses

The American Electronics Association (AeA) notes in its *Cyberstates 2003* study, that the United States high-tech industry lost 540,000 jobs in 2003, or about 8 percent, of its 6.5 million-jobs level the previous year. Hardest hit was electronics manufacturing, which accounted for more than half the losses. However, "While high-tech employment fell by 8 percent last year, preliminary 2003 data show a significant slowdown in high-tech job losses, with a decline of 4 percent," says William T. Archey, AeA's

president and CEO. "We predict that the 2003 high-tech job losses will total 234,000—down 57 percent from the 540,000 decline in 2002." So is the glass half empty, or is it half full?

Either way, solid economic growth in the United States cannot be counted on into the future if such industrial sectors as electronics manufacturing, software, engineering and communications services are no longer compatible with the states' ability to supply the necessary jobs or business climates. Think of the California problem on a national scale. Before it gets that bad, some new thinking on the part of state lawmakers and the federal government, too, may be in order. If private industry cannot locate the labor it needs in Houston or Hartford, it will not think twice about looking in Hyderabad.

"We are aware of current budget constraints, but now is not the time to cut back on education, particularly in math and science," says Archey. "We need a world class work force to deal with world class challenges. Our second concern," he adds, "is the decline in basic research, particularly in technology, by the federal government. We worry that we have eaten the seed corn of federal research of 20 and 30 years ago and that it is not being replenished."

According to *Cyberstates 2003*:
- California (995,000), Texas (479,000), New York (330,000), Florida (271,000) and Massachusetts (256,000) led the nation in high-tech employment.
- California (-123,000), Texas (-61,000), Massachusetts (-40,000), New Jersey (-29,000) and New York (-28,000) lost the greatest number of high-tech jobs in 2002.
- The District of Columbia (+2,200), Wyoming (+500) and Montana (+100) were the only three states to add tech jobs between 2001 and 2002.
- Colorado led the nation in concentration of high-tech workers in 2002, with 98 high-tech workers per 1,000 private-sector workers, followed by Massachusetts, Virginia, New Mexico and Maryland.

Grading the States

Working from another analysis of state competitiveness, the Corporation for Enterprise Development (CFED) has just released its 17th Annual Development Report Card for the States, which rates—and grades—the states according to 68 measures in three categories: performance, business vitality and development capacity.

Just three states—Massachusetts, Minnesota and Virginia—earned "A"s across the board. Two of these, interestingly, correspond to AeA's list of the states with the highest concentration of high-tech workers. Coincidence? Or do states that proactively cultivate high-tech industries tend to be better at economic development? Earning As and Bs were Colorado, Connecticut, New Jersey, Pennsylvania and Utah. Next in CFED's ranking are the states where Cs and Ds start appearing, which would apply to the vast majority of states, if only eight earned Bs or better. Eleven earned Fs in at least one category.

CFED's report makes the case that despite the myriad and often at-odds economic research and forecasts available, the economy is not a force of nature that cannot be influenced. State economic developers can take several steps to improve the desirability of their states as a location for business, which would in turn stimulate job growth. They include:

- Understanding that investments in education, health, natural resources and research/innovation are effective economic development measures, not other departments' concerns;
- Making business-development resources available to entrepreneurs;
- Helping existing businesses modernize and stay competitive;
- Working to build the assets, not just incomes, of families in the state;
- Understanding and addressing the needs of dislocated workers and businesses in disinvested communities and supporting non-traditional approaches, such as long-term educational support for retraining older workers;
- Being prudent in allocating the state's tax resources so they are not wasted on efforts which do not produce quality jobs.

Let us turn now to what the states are doing specifically to generate jobs in their jurisdictions. Almost universally, education and workforce training were, in fact, where most resources were allocated in 2003. Which states will emerge as major sources of skilled, affordable labor down the road as a result of this investment remains to be seen. In the meantime, here is a look at some recently announced job creation and training measures from around the United States, compiled by *Site Selection* Managing Editor Adam Bruns.

Alabama: In the south, the Mobile Technical Institute opened a new 8,344 sq. ft. facility that will focus on short-term, skill-oriented training specifically targeted to regional employers. The institution offers Administrative Support Specialist and Computer Technical Support diploma programs. In the northern Alabama city of Decatur, plans and fundraising are under way for a $10 million technical high school.

Alaska: Even with a budget $198 million lower than the year before, Gov. Frank Murkowski and the legislature fully funded education at $701.3 million for 2004, a level $32 million higher than 2003.

Arizona: In addition to benefiting from the newly passed Military Reuse Zone benefits at Mesa's Williams Gateway Airport, new corporate arrival Advanced Training Systems International is conducting jet aircraft maintenance training at nearby Chandler-Gilbert Community College located on the Williams Educational Campus. The airport offers three 10,000-ft. runways, a foreign trade zone, and is offering itself for general aviation, air cargo, commercial passenger service, aerospace manufacturing, maintenance and modification.

Arkansas: A new educational grant program has been created, targeting adults looking to improve their workforce skills. Meanwhile, a network of 10 existing workforce training consortia and five more in formation serves the entire state. Leading the charge is Mid-South Community College, in West Memphis, where award-winning training and campus facilities are keeping pace with community and corporate demand.

California: Among the many projects financed in 2003 by bonds from the California Infrastructure and Economic Development Bank are $65 million in bonds issued for the renovation of the California Academy of Sciences in San Francisco and $10.2 million in bonds issued for the expansion of the Claremont University Colleges near Los Angeles.

Colorado: A new law establishes the 13-campus Colorado Community College System as the premier source of basic skills and workforce training in the state. The Community College of Denver and Arapahoe Community College are designing and delivering demonstration programs focused on an accelerated model of the 78-credit hour Associate Degree Nursing (ADN) program funded the through U.S. Department of Labor and HCA private funding. In addition, Tillman Bishop Unified Technical Education Campus (UTEC) in Grand Junction, in conjunction with Delta-Montrose Area Vocational-Technical Center, began accepting applications for a licensed practical nursing program.

Connecticut: In April, Asnuntuck Community College's Manufacturing Technology Center was recognized for five years of success, after growing from an entry-level machine tech program to a 1,000-hour program offering 30 college credits. The center was launched in large part with $1.2 million in support from the Connecticut Department of Economic and Community Development. Besides 300 matriculating students, the center has hosted more than 2,000 members of the existing workforce, including a large number from the 50 companies that make up the state's aerospace components manufacturing cluster.

Delaware: Led by Gov. Ruth Ann Minner, the state has committed more than $1.8 million to help alleviate Delaware's nursing shortage by providing scholarships for future nurses and by expanding the nursing programs at Delaware Technical & Community College campuses statewide. The associated campuses already offer leading programs in HVAC and commercial transportation.

District of Columbia: Among a host of training incentives offered by the D.C. Department of Employment Services is the MetroTech program, which pays approved companies for the full cost of training or certification for IT professionals.

Florida: To foster innovative technology research, Gov. Jeb Bush established the $30 million Centers of Excellence program. The Center of Excellence in Regenerative Health Biotechnology will be established at the University of Florida; the Florida Photonics Center of Excellence at the University of Central Florida; and the Florida Center of Excellence in Biomedical and Marine Biotechnology at Florida Atlantic University. In addition, the Workforce Florida High Skill/High Wages Council is devoting up to $4 million to biotech training.

In Leon County, Tallahassee Community College, an increasingly popular training resource for area employers, has just completed the construction of a 30,000 sq. ft. workforce development center.

Georgia: Over its 36 years, Georgia's renowned QuickStart training program has executed 4,300 projects for 472,000 trainees. Recently passed legislation allows the program to serve existing companies even if they're not creating new jobs, i.e. updating a production system.

Hawaii: Hawaii maintains a network of "one-stop" centers around the state to assist employers and job seekers. The increase in demand for call-center staff has resulted in the development of a public-private call-center training facility located at the Honolulu Community College on Oahu.

Under Act 148 of the 2003 Legislature, the State's Workforce Development Council will further strengthen work force development by pulling together the entire system, including education, federal workforce programs and economic development programs.

Idaho: A measure allowing bonding for facility projects on college campuses across the state was approved, clearing the way for projects estimated to have an economic impact of some $188 million. Backing that measure, even in a year of cutbacks, public K–12 education was funded for $16 million more than in the previous budget year.

Illinois: In August 2003, the city of Chicago, under the aegis of Mayor Richard Daley's Office of Workforce Development, opened a new $650,000 training center at Ford Motor Co.'s Chicago Manufacturing Campus (CMC), the nation's first parts supplier park, on the city's south side. Comau-Pico, specializing in automated assembly instruction, has invested $500,000 in equipment and curriculum development. Upon completion of the two-week, 40-hour curriculum, CMC trainees will receive certification from Comau-Pico in areas such as electrical machine systems, hydraulics, and pneumatics, among others.

Indiana: Energize Indiana is a five-year plan that includes skill assessment of Indiana workers and skills requirement identification for 1,800 different job categories. In addition, the state is tripling the number of job fair events, and introducing company-specific employment fairs for companies in the advanced manufacturing, life sciences, IT and high-tech distribution sectors.

Iowa: The Iowa Values Fund includes $25 million for workforce training. Meanwhile, Iowa Western Community College in Council Bluffs is beefing up its offerings with a new $3.9 million, 34,000 sq. ft. avionics facility at the city airport. The college is out to make its aviation maintenance research and education facilities among the best in the nation. And in north central Iowa, North Iowa Area Community College was pivotal in the formation in fall 2003 of the North Central Iowa Growth Partnership, bringing together the communities of Clear Lake and Mason City.

Kansas: As part of the state budget, $1 million was appropriated to support the National Institute for Aviation Research at Wichita State University.

Kentucky: The 16-district, 62-campus Kentucky

Community and Technical College System serves about 180,000 workers and citizens a year, plus 68,000 students enrolled in credit courses. The system is partnering with regional universities to operate or soon open regional post-secondary education centers in five communities—Elizabethtown, Glasgow, London/Corbin, Hopkinsville and Prestonsburg.

Louisiana: The Incumbent Worker Training Program has been renewed to the tune of $50 million, and modified to provide more "off-the-shelf" options and be more accessible to small business. Workers receiving this training have averaged pay increases of 12.8 percent.

Maine: The scope of the state's technical college system has been expanded to that of a community college system.

Maryland: Anne Arundel Community College was named 2002 Community College of the Year by the National Alliance of Business, in part for its continuing work with Northrop Grumman since 1997. The process drills down further into the state's educational infrastructure, by serving as the catalyst for the school's Teacher Technology Training (T3) project, which trains public school teachers in the effective use of technology in the classroom.

Massachusetts: The Romney "Jobs First" bill proposes a non-degree tuition assistance loan program and grants to encourage training partnerships among community colleges, industry and career centers; and the expansion of the Statewide Technology Transfer Center at the University of Massachusetts to increase the likelihood that technology developed at the school will have commercial application and lead to job creation.

Michigan: The state granted $10 million to Western Michigan University for its new Biosciences Research and Commercialization Center. The funding was authorized with the express purpose of retaining and fostering the talent and expertise cultivated at Pfizer Corp.

Minnesota: The state's workforce development agency has now been merged with its economic development agency, enabling one-stop service to businesses.

Mississippi: Reflecting the rapid pace of corporate expansion in the state, workforce development expenditures in 2003 by the Mississippi Development Authority nearly doubled those of 2002. They included the immediate spending of three-year federal funds in order to establish the framework for job training and placement programs.

Missouri: An audit projects that the state's New Jobs Training Program, launched in 1992, will have helped to create 87,000 new jobs and about $4 billion in increased revenue by 2012. The program, which has received a $72-million investment from the state, allows community colleges to issue bonds to fund training, then pay them off from income taxes withheld from the newly created positions. However, the audit also revealed that about 22 percent of the state's investment has gone to interest on those bonds, and could have been avoided by the establishment of a revolving fund at the program's outset.

Montana: A new workforce training fund has been established by diversion of employee income tax withholding.

Nebraska: The state's 22 career centers, operated by Nebraska Workforce Development, are matched by its 22 detailed annual regional labor market reports. The agency waNInored in 2002 by the U.S. Department of Labor Employment and Training Administration and the National Association of State Workforce Agencies for its internal staff development leadership.

Nevada: Sponsored in part by the state legislature, the Community College of Southern Nevada will see a new 75,000 sq. ft. telecommunications building on its campus by spring 2004. The college sports three campuses and four technical centers under its umbrella.

New Hampshire: In a move to integrate technology and traditional learning, Gov. Craig Benson introduced a pilot program, "Technology Promoting Student Excellence," to bring laptop computers into classrooms in fall 2003.

New Jersey: Gov. James McGreevey's new School Renaissance Zone program is built upon the idea that economic development can be built around revitalized educational facilities. An unrelated law makes technology education a mandatory part of the state's core curriculum. The state's three workforce development departments have been consolidated into one Department of Labor and Workforce Development.

New Mexico: With the infusion of $17 million, the state's workforce training program has been expanded to include service industries as well as manufacturing.

New York: The Ford Motor Co. stamping plant in Buffalo is launching a new training program for its 1,800 workers with the help of a $1.3 million workforce training grant from the state's labor department.

North Carolina: Lawmakers approved $60 million in seed money for growing high-tech industries in North Carolina by authorizing development of a statewide Biomanufacturing Center and Biotechnology Training Center. The biomanufacturing facility will be at North Carolina State University; the biotech center will be at North Carolina Central University.

North Dakota: A total of $5.25 million has been allocated toward centers of excellence at North Dakota universities.

Ohio: Graduate students in higher sciences will be partnered with businesses through the new Third Frontier Graduate Internship program.

Oklahoma: The University of Tulsa's Center for Information Security has partnered with Oklahoma's CareerTech and Community College systems to provide a full curriculum and career path for cyber security and forensics technicians. CareerTech is also reaching out to high school students with pre-engineering programs designed to help meet the corporate demand for engineers. Meanwhile, the High Plains Technology Center in Woodward is expanding its training program for the oil and gas industry to more advanced levels, thanks to a $1.5 million grant.

Oregon: Gov. Ted Kulongoski has approved a grant of $125,000 in Strategic Reserve Funding for North River Boats in Roseburg, Oregon. The grant will enable the company to hire and train new workers. In October 2003, the governor announced a new workforce development strategy at a summit of 450 workforce and economic development professionals from around the state. He is launching several new initiatives to prepare individuals to enter and advance in the workplace and to increase business productivity and competitiveness.

Pennsylvania: The Partnership for Regional Innovation in Manufacturing Education (PRIME), launched in 2000, offers two- and four-year degree programs in engineering and technology tracks, through a partnership between three community colleges and two universities. Much of the programs' interactive learning takes place at the $4 million Computer Integrated Engineering Enterprise-Learning Factory at Robert Morris University near Pittsburgh, but each campus offers its own mix of resources. Around 60 companies offer curriculum feedback and partnership. The program's first students graduated in December 2002. Outreach efforts have included the Manufacturing Pathways Initiative, a summer camp mixing classroom and industrial internships that is coordinated by PRIME, the Pittsburgh Technology Council and Catalyst Connection.

Puerto Rico: In August, a coalition of government, academic and industry leaders announced their intention to raise $14 million to build an Excellence Center for Advanced Technology (ECAT) in Barceloneta for the continuing education of person-nel in the pharmaceutical and biotechnology sectors.

The University of Puerto Rico is in the midst of creating a new microarray analysis center, a bioinformatics center and a clinical proteomics center.

Rhode Island: Plans are under way to fund a new biotech training center at the University of Rhode Island.

South Carolina: More than 5,000 workers from 91 different plants received training from the state's 16-campus Technical College System during the most recent fiscal year. And as a result of new legislation, some $44.6 million is being added to the K–12 education budget.

South Dakota: In July, Gov. Mike Rounds committed $1.3 million to the South Dakota Technology Business Center in Sioux Falls, to be used specifically to attract biotech firms. Construction of the 38,000 sq. ft. facility was to be completed in December 2003; it will house 15–20 companies.

Tennessee: The state is in the midst of renovating its industrial training programs, while also bringing together some aspects of the community and technical college systems.

Texas: Eight different campuses of the University of Texas were granted the authority to issue revenue bonds to finance research facilities.

Utah: The state's leadership in educational attainment is backed by a system of 10 Applied Technology Colleges that provided training to 20,612 individuals from 795 companies during 2001–2002.

Vermont: The Vermont Training Program has been boosted with an additional $400,000 to provide customized workforce training for manufacturers. In addition, incentives for employers to increase workforce training and professional development were doubled.

Virginia: Multiple workforce training programs and councils have been streamlined in order to make better policy and afford companies better service delivery.

Washington: Funding was increased for job skills training, and more of that training will focus on lean manufacturing techniques.

West Virginia: From 700 students in 2001, the state's PROMISE Scholarship Program, dedicated to students who stay in the state to pursue higher education, grew to 3,500 students in 2002. Building on that momentum, recent legislation established centers for economic development and technology advancement at the state's doctoral universities.

Wisconsin: Gov. Jim Doyle plans to introduce legislation to create a $10 million training fund to offer free training to companies that create significant numbers of new, high paying jobs or need to introduce new technologies to retain workers in a competitive world economy.

Wyoming: The state's Quick Start curriculum (based on the award–winning program in Georgia) was expanded to include customer service, manufacturing and warehouse/distribution.

About the Author

Mark Arend is editor of *Site Selection* magazine. Prior to joining the *Site Selection* editorial staff in 1997, he spent 10 years in New York City covering a range of financial service industries. Positions held since 1987 include associate editor of *Wall Street Computer Review* and technology/senior editor of *ABA Banking Journal*. In 1994, as managing editor of *Global Investment Technology,* Arend helped found *Global Investment* Magazine. He is vice president and a co-founder of the Atlanta chapter of the American Society of Business Publication Editors.

Site Selection magazine Managing Editor **Adam Bruns** contributed to this report.

Table A
FINANCIAL ASSISTANCE FOR INDUSTRY

State or other jurisdiction	State-sponsored industrial development authority	Privately sponsored development credit corporation	State authority or agency revenue bond financing	State authority or agency general obligation bond financing	City and/or county revenue bond financing	City and/or County General obligation bond financing	State loans for building construction	State loans for equipment machinery	City and/or county loans for building construction	City and/or county loans for equipment, machinery	State loan guarantees for building construction	State loan guarantees for equipment, machinery	City and/or county loan guarantees for building construction	City and/or county loan guarantees for equipment, machinery	State financing aid for existing plant expansion	State matching funds for city and/or county industrial financing programs	State incentive for establishing industrial plants in areas of high unemployment	City and/or county incentive for establishing industrial plants in areas of high unemployment
Alabama	★	★	★		★	★	★	★	★	★			★	★	★		★	★
Alaska	★		★	★	★	★	★	★			★	★			★	★	★	★
Arizona			★		★	★									★		★	★
Arkansas	★	★	★	★	★	★	★	★	★	★	★	★	★	★	★	★	★	★
California	★	★	★		★	★	★	★	★	★	★	★	★	★	★	★	★	★
Colorado	★		★		★	★									★		★	★
Connecticut	★	★	★	★	★	★	★	★	★	★	★	★			★	★	★	★
Delaware	★	★	★	★	★	★	★	★	★	★	★	★	★	★	★		★	★
Florida			★		★	★			★	★					★		★	★
Georgia	★	★	★		★	★			★	★					★		★	★
Hawaii			★	★	★	★	★	★	★	★	★	★			★		★	★
Idaho			★		★	★											★	★
Illinois	★	★	★		★	★	★	★	★	★	★	★			★	★	★	★
Indiana	★	★	★	★	★	★	★	★	★	★	★	★			★	★	★	★
Iowa			★		★	★	★	★	★	★					★	★	★	★
Kansas	★	★	★	★	★	★	★	★	★	★	★	★	★	★	★	★	★	★
Kentucky	★	★	★	★	★	★	★	★	★	★	★	★			★	★	★	★
Louisiana	★	★	★		★	★	★	★	★	★	★	★		★	★	★	★	★
Maine	★	★	★	★	★	★	★	★	★	★	★	★	★	★	★	★	★	★
Maryland	★	★	★	★	★	★	★	★	★	★	★	★	★	★	★	★	★	★
Massachusetts	★	★	★	★	★	★	★	★	★	★	★	★	★	★	★	★	★	★
Michigan	★	★	★		★	★	★	★	★	★	★	★			★	★	★	★
Minnesota	★	★	★	★	★	★	★	★	★	★	★	★			★	★	★	★
Mississippi	★	★	★	★	★	★	★	★	★	★	★	★			★	★	★	★
Missouri	★	★	★		★	★	★	★	★	★	★	★			★	★	★	★
Montana			★	★	★	★	★	★	★	★	★	★			★		★	★
Nebraska	★		★	★	★	★	★	★	★	★					★		★	★
Nevada	★		★		★	★			★	★					★		★	★
New Hampshire	★	★	★	★	★	★	★	★	★	★	★	★			★	★	★	★
New Jersey	★	★	★		★	★	★	★	★	★	★	★			★		★	★
New Mexico	★	★	★	★	★	★	★	★	★	★	★	★		★	★	★	★	★
New York	★	★	★	★	★	★	★	★	★	★	★	★	★	★	★	★	★	★
North Carolina	★	★	★		★	★	★	★	★	★					★		★	★
North Dakota			★	★	★	★	★	★	★	★	★	★			★	★	★	★
Ohio	★		★	★	★	★	★	★	★	★	★	★			★	★	★	★

See footnotes at end of table.

FINANCIAL ASSISTANCE FOR INDUSTRY — Continued

State or other jurisdiction	State-sponsored industrial development authority	Privately sponsored development credit corporation	State authority or agency revenue bond financing	State authority or agency general obligation bond financing	City and/or county revenue bond financing	City and/or County General obligation bond financing	State loans for building construction	State loans for equipment machinery	City and/or county loans for building construction	City and/or county loans for equipment, machinery	State loan guarantees for building construction	State loan guarantees for equipment, machinery	City and/or county loan guarantees for building construction	City and/or county loan guarantees for equipment, machinery	State financing aid for existing plant expansion	State matching funds for city and/or county industrial financing programs	State incentive for establishing industrial plants in areas of high unemployment	City and/or county incentive for establishing industrial plants in areas of high unemployment
Oklahoma	★	…	★	★	★	★	★	★	★	★	★	★	★	★	★	★	★	★
Oregon	★	★	★	★	★	★	★	★	★	★	★	★	★	★	★	★	★	★
Pennsylvania	★	★	★	★	★	★	★	★	★	★	★	★	★	★	★	★	★	★
Rhode Island	★	★	★	★	★	…	★	★	★	★	★	★	★	★	★	★	★	★
South Carolina	★	…	★	…	★	…	★	★	…	…	…	…	…	…	…	…	…	…
South Dakota	★	…	★	★	★	★	★	★	★	★	…	…	…	★	★	★	★	…
Tennessee	…	…	★	★	★	★	★	★	★	★	★	★	★	★	★	★	★	★
Texas	★	★	★	★	★	★	…	★	★	★	★	★	…	★	★	★	★	…
Utah	★	★	★	…	★	★	★	★	★	★	★	★	★	★	★	★	★	…
Vermont	★	★	★	…	★	★	★	★	★	★	★	★	★	★	★	★	★	★
Virginia	★	★	★	…	★	★	★	★	★	★	…	…	…	★	★	★	★	…
Washington	★	★	★	…	★	★	★	★	★	★	★	★	★	★	★	★	★	★
West Virginia	★	★	★	…	★	…	★	★	★	★	…	…	…	★	★	★	★	…
Wisconsin	★	…	★	…	★	★	…	★	…	★	★	★	…	★	★	★	★	…
Wyoming	★	★	★	★	…	★	★	★	…	★	…	…	…	…	…	…	…	…
Puerto Rico	★	★	★	★	★	★	★	★	★	★	★	★	★	★	★	★	★	★

Source: Site Selection, November 2003.

Note: A significant number of footnotes are published with these charts in the November issue of *Site Selection* magazine. For more information or to obtain a set of the footnotes, contact Editor Mark Arend at mark.arend@conway.com.

Key:
★—Yes
…—No, or state/jurisdiction did not respond to survey.

Table B
TAX INCENTIVES FOR INDUSTRY

State or other jurisdiction	Corporate income tax exemption	Personal Income tax exemption	Excise tax exemption	Tax exemption or moratorium on land, capital improvements	Tax exemption or moratorium on equipment, machinery	Inventory tax exemption on goods in transit (freeport)	Tax exemption on manufacturers' inventories	Sales/use tax exemption on new equipment	Tax exemption on raw materials used in manufacturing	Tax incentive for creation of jobs	Tax incentive for industrial investment	Tax credits for use of specified state products	Tax stabilization agreements for specified industries	Tax exemption to encourage research and development	Accelerated depreciation of industrial equipment
Alabama	★	★	★	★	★	★	★	★	★	★	★			★	★
Alaska		★	★	★				★	★			★			★
Arizona	★	★	★	★	★	★	★	★	★	★	★			★	★
Arkansas	★							★	★	★	★	★		★	
California	★	★	★					★	★	★	★				★
Colorado	★		★	★	★	★	★	★	★	★	★			★	★
Connecticut	★	★	★	★	★	★	★	★	★	★	★		★	★	★
Delaware	★	★	★	★	★	★	★	★	★	★	★			★	★
Florida	★		★		★	★	★	★	★	★	★			★	★
Georgia	★						★	★	★	★	★		★	★	★
Hawaii	★	★	★	★	★	★	★	★	★	★	★			★	★
Idaho	★	★		★	★	★	★	★	★	★	★			★	★
Illinois	★	★		★	★	★	★	★	★	★	★	★		★	★
Indiana	★	★		★	★	★	★	★	★	★	★			★	★
Iowa	★	★		★	★	★	★	★	★	★	★			★	★
Kansas	★	★	★	★	★	★	★	★	★	★	★	★	★	★	★
Kentucky	★	★		★	★	★	★	★	★	★	★			★	★
Louisiana	★	★	★	★	★	★	★	★	★	★	★		★	★	★
Maine	★	★		★	★	★	★	★	★	★	★			★	★
Maryland	★	★	★	★	★	★	★	★	★	★	★		★	★	★
Massachusetts	★	★		★	★	★	★	★	★	★	★		★	★	★
Michigan	★	★	★	★	★	★	★	★	★	★	★		★	★	★
Minnesota	★	★		★	★	★	★	★	★	★	★			★	★
Mississippi	★	★	★	★	★	★	★	★	★	★	★	★	★	★	★
Missouri	★	★		★	★	★	★	★	★	★	★			★	★
Montana	★	★	★	★	★	★	★	★	★	★	★			★	★
Nebraska	★	★		★	★	★	★	★	★	★	★			★	★
Nevada	★				★	★	★	★	★	★	★			★	★
New Hampshire	★	★	★	★	★	★	★	★	★	★	★	★	★	★	★
New Jersey	★	★			★	★	★	★	★	★	★			★	★
New Mexico	★			★	★	★	★	★	★	★	★			★	
New York	★	★	★	★	★	★	★	★	★	★	★			★	★
North Carolina	★	★		★	★	★	★	★	★	★	★			★	
North Dakota	★	★	★	★	★	★	★	★	★	★	★			★	★
Ohio	★	★		★	★	★	★	★	★	★	★			★	★

See footnotes at end of table.

TAX INCENTIVES FOR INDUSTRY — Continued

State or other jurisdiction	Corporate income tax exemption	Personal Income tax exemption	Excise tax exemption	Tax exemption or moratorium on land, capital improvements	Tax exemption or moratorium on equipment, machinery	Inventory tax exemption on goods in transit (freeport)	Tax exemption on manufacturers' inventories	Sales/use tax exemption on new equipment	Tax exemption on raw materials used in manufacturing	Tax incentive for creation of jobs	Tax incentive for industrial investment	Tax credits for use of specified state products	Tax stabilization agreements for specified industries	Tax exemption to encourage research and development	Accelerated depreciation of industrial equipment
Oklahoma	★	★	★	★	★	★	★	★	★	★	★	★	★	★	★
Oregon	…	…	★	★	★	★	★	★	★	…	★	…	…	★	★
Pennsylvania	★	…	★	★	★	★	★	★	★	★	★	★	…	★	★
Rhode Island	…	…	★	★	★	★	★	★	★	★	★	★	★	★	★
South Carolina	★	★	…	★	★	★	★	★	★	★	★	…	…	★	★
South Dakota	★	★	★	★	…	★	★	★	★	★	★	★	…	★	★
Tennessee	★	★	★	★	★	★	…	★	★	★	★	★	…	★	★
Texas	★	★	…	…	★	★	★	★	★	★	★	…	★	★	…
Utah	…	…	…	…	★	★	★	★	★	★	…	★	…	…	★
Vermont	…	…	★	★	★	★	★	★	★	…	★	★	…	…	★
Virginia	★	★	…	★	★	★	★	★	★	★	★	…	★	★	★
Washington	★	★	★	…	…	★	…	★	★	★	★	…	★	★	…
West Virginia	★	★	★	★	★	★	★	★	★	★	★	★	…	★	★
Wisconsin	★	★	…	…	★	★	★	★	★	★	★	…	…	★	★
Wyoming	★	★	★	★	…	★	★	★	★	…	…	…	…	…	…
Puerto Rico	★	★	★	★	★	★	★	★	★	★	★	★	★	★	★

Source: Site Selection, November 2003
Note: A significant number of footnotes are published with these charts in the November issue of Site Selection magazine. For more information or to obtain a set of the footnotes, contact Editor Mark Arend at mark.arend@conway.com.

Key:
★—Yes
…—No; or state/jurisdiction did not respond to survey.

Energy Project Streamlining:
Working More Efficiently, Not Cutting Corners
By Robert Middleton

Since its inception, members of the White House Task Force on Energy Project Streamlining have held over 100 meetings to listen to the concerns of developers, environmentalists, federal and state agencies. The first year's activities and accomplishments were many, mostly falling in the areas of assisting in the resolution of bottlenecks in a number of specific energy projects. In its second year, the task force continues to work on individual energy related projects bottlenecked in the system and has also begun to focus on finding solutions to more systemic issues.

In October 2001, the White House Task Force on Energy Project Streamlining was formed, in response to Executive Order 13212, issued by President George W. Bush in May, 2001. The Executive Order, initiated based on a recommendation in the National Energy Policy, calls for federal agencies to "take appropriate actions, to the extent consistent with applicable law, to expedite projects that will increase the production, transmission, or conservation of energy." These actions must comply with existing laws and regulations and maintain safety, public health and environmental protections. Specifically, the role of the task force is: (1) to monitor and assist the agencies in their efforts to expedite permit review or undertake other actions to accelerate the completion of energy-related projects, increase energy production and conservation, and improve transmission of energy; and (2) to monitor and assist agencies in setting up appropriate mechanisms to coordinate federal, state, tribal, and local permitting in geographic areas where increased permitting activity is expected.

The chairman of the Council on Environmental Quality (CEQ) is the chair of the task force. The task force consists of a cadre of career employees detailed from agencies across the federal government. Task force staff members serve at least three months, but three members have been on the task force since its inception. Agencies that currently have members on the task force are: Department of Interior, Department of Agriculture, Department of Commerce, Department of Energy and the Environmental Protection Agency. However, the agencies involved change as new issues or initiatives are being developed. In the past, other agencies with impacts on the permitting process and energy development had members assigned to the task force, such as the Army Corps of Engineers and the Bureau of Indian Affairs.

It is important to understand that the task force is outcome neutral when it comes to any final permitting decision. All decisions on projects are based on sound science, existing environmental legislation and associated implementing regulations. It is not the intent of the task force to "cut corners" in making decisions. Instead, the task force works with permitting agencies to identify and help remove impediments to timely decisions, many of which come about when a project requires approval from multiple agencies.

Therefore, a large amount of the task force work is facilitating coordination among federal agencies, and state agencies as required. While the task force does not attempt to influence what decision an agency makes, it does help provide federal permittees with some certainty on decision timelines. It is always the intent to work collaboratively with agencies and individual bureaus to develop win-win results. Task force actions may be restricted to a single project, or project component, or may encompass a larger process.

When similar impediments to timely decisions are identified in similar projects, the task force may undertake the development of broader process changes to work toward a more systemic solution. Interagency coordination processes are the major focus of such solutions but, on occasion, the task force may examine processes internal to a single agency. In the future, the task force may also work to develop new legislation to be proposed by the administration.

The task force efforts should result in a variety of benefits for the American public. Its intent is to provide a cost-effective and efficient means of managing valuable domestic energy resources on public lands. In doing this, it will realize a reduced cost of energy to the consumers; a savings of taxpayer dollars by the government; a more upfront collaborative, transparent decision making process for stakeholders; sound decisions based on more complete information; and improved mitigation measures where energy development is permitted to proceed.

The task force must also help structure a system whereby a collaborative process is put in place to allow federal managers to begin planning for the future of public energy development in the United States in an innovative, environmentally sensitive manner. They must look at all forms of energy to include but not limited to: renewables—such as solar, wind, biomass, geothermal and low-impact hydropower—gas, oil, liquefied natural gas, alternate fuels, nuclear and coal.

The task force helps monitor and assist agencies in setting up appropriate mechanisms to coordinate federal, state, tribal and local permitting in geographic areas where increased permitting activity is expected. This has aided in the coordination and integration for decision making; clarity of decision points and decision makers; accountability, such as adhering to statutory or internal deadlines; and doing so by not lowering environmental standards or cutting corners.

When the task force was initiated, efforts were made to identify projects that would benefit from task force involvement. This was done through a series of public meetings. The initial responses to these meetings can be found on the task force Web site (www.etf.energy.gov). Since its inception, task force members have held over 100 meetings to listen to the concerns of developers, environmentalists, federal and state agencies. The first year's activities and accomplishments were many mostly falling in the areas of assisting in the resolution of bottlenecks in a number of specific energy projects. In addition, interagency agreements were drafted to promote better coordination and cooperation among federal agencies and additional support was provided to agencies to streamline their processes. A report summarizing the first year's accomplishments can be found under "Proceedings of the First Year" on the task force Web site. A major lesson from the first year's work was that success in moving projects forward often resulted in others projects getting less attention and falling to the bottom of the pile. This led the task force to recognize the need for more focus on systemic solutions.

In its second year the task force continues to work on individual energy related projects bottlenecked in the system and has also begun to focus on finding solutions to more systemic issues. As mentioned above, the Executive Order directs the task force to assist in setting up appropriate mechanisms to coordinate permitting in geographic areas where increased permitting activity is expected. To further this goal,

the task force has been working with federal agencies and state and local governments involved with energy permitting in the Rocky Mountains. The objective of this work is to build federal and state partnerships to promote a more effective management strategy for energy development and energy policy on federal and state public lands in the Rocky Mountain region. The effort focuses on a three prong approach: developing federal and state partnerships for long-term management of renewables and nonrenewable energy resources on state and federal public lands; allowing more forward looking and strategic planning on a regional basis for the environmentally responsible development, production, and distribution of the nation's valuable energy resources; and developing processes for early collaboration and consultation among the state and federal agencies responsible for managing, authorizing, consulting on, reviewing, or certifying renewable and nonrenewable energy projects on public land. The hope is that through this early and collaborative planning on how to manage these resources, future decisions on where and how to develop them will be made more efficiently and effectively.

Other major task force projects to address more systemic changes are:

- Assisting tribal nations in developing their renewable energy resources and obtaining assistance from federal agencies in funding energy related projects through grants, contracts and direct funding. In addition, the task force is helping to bring tribal nations up to date in managing, evaluating and analyzing energy potential on tribal lands.

- Taking the lead in right-of-way corridor identification and designation. Working with Bureau of Land Management (BLM) and the U.S. Department of Agriculture Forest Service (USFS) in identifying and designating right-of-way corridors in the Western United States. By designating permanent rights-of-way, BLM and USFS will assist in speeding up the permitting process for various energy transportation/transmissions facilities.

- Taking the lead in establishing an interagency Memorandum of Understanding (MOU) for licensing facilities under the Deepwater Ports Act, primarily for the importation of liquefied natural gas (LNG). This MOU coordinates activities of 11 federal agencies in order to meet the 356-day statutory deadline for issuing a licensing decision. This MOU is currently in the process of being signed at the various agencies.

- Taking the lead in developing an interagency agreement for early designation of a lead federal agency for linear right-of-way proposals when the BLM and USFS are involved.
- Taking the lead in the implementation of Section 16 of the Pipeline Safety Improvement Act of 2002 (PSIA). The task force has the responsibility to ensure federal agency participation in the Office of Pipeline Safety-mandated inspection and repairs required by the PSIA. An interagency MOU establishing the policies and procedures for implementation of the PSIA is currently being completed.

The task force continues to work on these broader issues looking for systemic solutions, as well as a large variety of individual projects including: licensing of onshore and offshore liquefied natural gas port facilities, an offshore wind energy farm on the East Coast, backlogs in Applications for Permit to Drill (APD) on federal lands, and renewable and biomass projects.

All concerns and requests for assistance can be forwarded to the following task force contact information:

White House Task Force on
Energy Project Streamlining (WH-1)
1000 Independence Avenue, SW
Washington, D.C. 20585
Phone: 202-586-3464
www.etf.energy.gov

About the Author

Robert Middleton is the director of the White House Task Force on Energy Project Streamlining. Prior to joining the task force, Middleton served since 1993 as chief of staff for the Minerals Management Service.

Table A
STATE INCENTIVES FOR RENEWABLE ENERGY: RULES, REGULATIONS, AND POLICIES, BY STATE AND REGION

State or other jurisdiction	Public benefit funds (a)	Disclosure (b)	Renewable portfolio standards/set asides (c)	Net metering (d)	Interconnection	Extension analysis (e)	Contractor license (f)	Equipment certification (g)	Access laws (h)	Construction and design standards (i)	Green power purchase (j)	Required green power (k)
Eastern Region												
Connecticut	1 S	1 S	1 S	1 S	…	…	1 S	…	…	…	…	…
Delaware	1 S	1 S	1 S	1 S	1 S	…	…	…	…	…	…	…
Maine	1 S	1 S	…	1 S	1 S	…	…	…	1 S	1 S	…	…
Massachusetts	1 S	1 S	1 S	1 S	1 S	…	…	1 S	1 S	…	1 L	…
New Hampshire	1 S	1 S	1 S	1 S	1 S	…	…	…	1 S	…	1 S	…
New Jersey	1 S	1 S	1 S	1 S	1 S	…	…	…	1 S	…	1 S	…
New York	1 S	1 S	…	1 S	1 S	…	…	…	1 S	…	1 S	…
Pennsylvania	1 S	1 S	1 S	1 S	1 S	…	…	…	1 S	…	…	…
Rhode Island	1 S	…	…	1 S	1 S	…	…	…	1 S	…	…	…
Vermont	…	1 S	…	1 S	1 S	…	…	…	1 S	…	…	…
Midwestern Region												
Illinois	1 S	1 S	1 S	1 U	1 U	…	…	…	…	…	1 S, 1 L	…
Indiana	…	…	…	1 S	1 S	…	…	…	1 S	…	…	…
Iowa	…	…	1 S	1 S	1 S	…	…	…	1 S	…	…	1 S
Kansas	…	…	…	…	1 S	…	…	…	1 S	…	…	…
Michigan	…	1 S	…	1 S	1 S	…	1 S	…	1 S	…	…	…
Minnesota	1 S	1 S	2 S	1 S	1 S	…	…	1 S	1 S	1 S	…	1 S
Nebraska	…	…	…	…	…	…	…	…	1 S	…	…	…
North Dakota	1 S	…	…	1 S, 1 U	1 S	…	…	…	1 S	…	…	…
Ohio	1 S	1 S	…	1 S	1 S	…	…	…	1 S	…	1 L	…
South Dakota	…	…	…	1 S	1 S	…	…	…	…	…	…	…
Wisconsin	1 S	…	1 S	1 S	1 S	…	1 L	1 L	1 S, 1 L	1 L	1 L	…
Southern Region												
Alabama	…	…	…	…	…	…	…	…	…	…	…	…
Arkansas	…	…	…	1 S	1 S	…	1 S	1 S	1 S	…	…	…
Florida	1 S	1 S	1 U	2 U	1 S	…	…	…	1 S, 1 L	1 S	…	…
Georgia	…	…	…	1 S	1 S	…	1 S	1 S	1 S, 1 L	…	…	…
Kentucky	…	…	…	1 U	1 S	…	…	…	1 S	…	…	…
Louisiana	…	…	…	1 S	1 S	…	1 S	…	…	…	…	…
Maryland	…	1 S	…	1 S	1 S	…	…	…	1 S	1 S	1 S	…
Mississippi	…	…	…	…	1 S	…	…	…	…	…	…	…
Missouri	…	…	…	1 S	1 S	…	…	…	1 S	…	…	…
North Carolina	…	…	…	…	…	…	…	…	…	1 L	…	…
Oklahoma	…	…	…	1 S	…	…	1 S	1 S	1 S	…	…	…
South Carolina	…	…	…	…	…	…	…	…	…	…	…	…
Tennessee	…	…	…	1 S	1 S	1 S	…	…	1 S	1 S	3 L	…
Texas	1 S, 1 L	1 S	1 S, 1 L	1 S, 2 U	1 S	…	…	…	1 S	…	1 S	…
Virginia	…	1 S	…	1 S	1 S	…	…	…	1 S	…	…	…
West Virginia	…	1 S	…	…	1 S	1 S	…	…	1 S	…	…	…
Western Region												
Alaska	…	…	…	1 U	1 U	…	…	…	1 S	…	…	…
Arizona	…	1 S	1 S	1 U	1 S	1 S	1 S	1 S	1 S	1 S, 3 L	1 L	…
California	1 S	1 S	1 S	1 S	1 S	…	1 S	…	2 S, 5 L	1 S, 4 L	3 L	…
Colorado	…	1 S	1 L	4 U	…	1 S	…	…	1 S, 1 L	4 L	3 L	…

See footnotes at end of table.

STATE INCENTIVES FOR RENEWABLE ENERGY: RULES, REGULATIONS, AND POLICIES, BY STATE AND REGION—Continued

State or other jurisdiction	Public benefit funds (a)	Disclosure (b)	Renewable portfolio standards/ set asides (c)	Net metering (d)	Interconnection	Extension analysis (e)	Contractor license (f)	Equipment certification (g)	Access laws (h)	Construction and design standards (i)	Green power purchase (j)	Required green power (k)
Hawaii	...	...	1 S	1 S	1 S	...	1 S	...	1 S	1 S	...	...
Idaho	...	...	...	3 U	2 U	...	...	...	1 S	...	...	1 S
Montana	1 S	1 S	...	1 S, 1 U	1 S	...	1 S	...	1 S	1 S	...	...
Nevada	...	1 S	1 S	1 S	1 S	...	1 S	...	1 S	1 S	...	1 S
New Mexico	...	1 S	1 S	1 S	1 S	1 S	...	...	1 S	...	...	1 S
Oregon	1 S	1 S	...	1 S, 1 L	1 S	...	...	...	1 S, 2 L	2 L	1 L	...
Utah	...	...	...	1 S	1 S	...	1 S	...	1 S	...	1 L	...
Washington	...	1 S	...	1 S, 1 U	1 S	...	...	...	1 S	1 L	2 L	1 S
Wyoming	...	...	...	1 S	1 S	...	...	...	...	...	...	...
Dist. of Columbia	...	1 S	...	1 S	...	...	...	...	...	...	...	...
American Samoa	...	...	...	...	...	...	...	...	...	...	...	...
Guam	...	...	...	...	...	...	...	...	...	1 S	...	...
No.Mariana Islands	...	...	...	...	...	...	...	...	...	...	...	...
Palua	...	...	...	...	...	...	...	...	...	...	...	...
Puerto Rico	...	...	...	...	...	...	...	...	...	...	...	...
U.S. Virgin Islands	...	...	...	...	...	...	...	...	...	...	...	...

Source: NC Solar Center/ Interstate Renewable Energy Council, Database of State Incentives for Renewable Energy, www. Dsireusa.org - March 2004.

Key:
S - State or Territory
L - Local
U - Utility

(a) Public Benefit Funds (PBF) are typically state-level programs developed through the electric utility restructuring process as a measure to assure continued support for renewable energy resources, energy efficiency initiatives, and low-income support programs. (These funds are also frequently referred to as a system benefits charge, or SBC). Such a fund is most commonly supported through a charge to all customers on electricity consumption, e.g., 0.2 cents/kWh. Examples of how the funds are used include: rebates on renewable energy systems; funding for renewable energy R&D; and development of renewable energy education programs.

(b) "Disclosure" typically refers to the requirement that utilities provide their customers with additional information about the energy they are supplying. This information often includes fuel mix percentages and emissions statistics. Fuel mix information, for example, can be presented as a pie chart on customers' monthly bills. "Certification" is a related issue which refers to the assessment of green power offerings to assure that they are indeed utilizing the type and amount of renewable energy as advertised. One example of green power certification is the Green-e stamp. Both disclosure and certification are designed to help consumers make informed decisions about the energy and supplier they choose. It is worth noting, though, that two states that have not moved ahead with restructure—Florida and Colorado—have enacted disclosure provisions. Indeed, disclosure is often thought of as a good policy to help educate customers about electricity and thereby to prepare markets in advance of retail competition.

(c) Renewables Portfolio Standards (RPS) require that a certain percentage of a utility's overall or new generating capacity or energy sales must be derived from renewable resources, i.e., 1% of electric sales must be from installations. Portfolio Standards most commonly refer to electric sales measured in megawatt-hours (MWh), as opposed to electric capacity measured in megawatts(MW). The term "set asides" is frequently used to refer to programs where a utility is required to include a certain amount of renewables capacity in new

(d) For those consumers who have their own electricity generating units, net metering allows for the flow of electricity both to and from the customer through a single, bi-directional meter. With net metering, during times when the customer's generation exceeds his or her use, electricity from the customer to the utility offsets electricity consumed at another time. In effect, the customer is using the excess generation to offset electricity that would have been purchased at the retail rate. Under most state rules, residential, commercial, and industrial customers are eligible for net

metering, but some states restrict eligibility to particular customer classes.

(e) When an electric customer requests service for a location not currently serviced by the electric grid, they are charged a distance-based fee for the cost of extending power lines to their load. In many cases it is cheaper to have an on-site renewable energy system to meet their electricity needs. Certain states require utilities to provide their customers with information on renewable energy options when a line extension is requested.

(f) Many states have rules regarding the licensing of renewable energy contractors. Contractor licensing requirements can be enacted for solar water heat, active and passive solar space heat, solar industrial process heat, solar thermal electricity, and photovoltaics. These requirements—where they do exist—are designed to ensure that contractors have the necessary experience and knowledge to properly install systems.

(g) Statutes requiring renewable energy equipment to meet certain standards are generally seen as a tool for reducing the chance that consumers will be sold inferior equipment. Beyond being a consumer protecting measure, equipment certification benefits renewables by reducing the number of problem systems and the resulting bad publicity.

(h) These statutes provide for solar or wind easements or access rights. Easements allow for the rights to existing access to a renewable resource on the part of one property owner to be secured from an owner whose property could be developed in such a way as to restrict that resource. This easement is transferred with the property title. Access rights, conversely, automatically provide for the right to continued access to a renewable resource. Solar easements are the most common type of state solar access rule. Furthermore, some states prohibit neighborhood covenants that preclude the use of renewables. At the local level, communities use many different mechanisms to protect solar access, including solar access ordinances, development guidelines requiring proper street orientation, zoning ordinances that contain building height restrictions, and solar permits.

(i) Construction and design policies include state construction policies, green building programs, and energy codes. State construction policies are typically legislative mandates requiring an evaluation of the cost and performance benefits of incorporating renewable energy technologies into state construction projects such as schools and office buildings. Many cities are developing "Green Building" guidelines that require or encourage consideration of renewable energy technologies. Some guidelines are voluntary measures for all building types, while others are requirements for municipal building projects or residential construction. Local energy codes are used to achieve energy efficiency in new construction and reno-

STATE INCENTIVES FOR RENEWABLE ENERGY: RULES, REGULATIONS, AND POLICIES, BY STATE AND REGION—Continued

vations by requiring that certain building projects surpass state requirements for resource conservation. Incorporating renewables is one way to meet code requirements.

(j) Municipalities, state governments, businesses, and other non-residential customers can play a critical role in supporting renewable energy technologies by buying electricity from renewable resources. At the local level, green power purchasing can mean buying green power for municipal facilities, streetlights, water pumping stations and the like. Several states require that a certain percentage of electricity purchased for state government buildings come from renewable resources. A few states allow local governments to aggregate the electricity loads of the entire community to purchase green power and even to join with other communities to form an even larger green power purchasing block. This is often referred to as "Community Choice". Green power purchasing can be achieved via utility green pricing programs, green power marketers (in states with retail competition), special contracts, or community aggregation. DSIRE provides information only on the policies of government agencies and the efforts of community aggregators to purchase green power; it does not track purchases by individual businesses and institutions such as universities.

(k) A handful of states require certain classes of utilities to offer customers the option to purchase power generated from renewable sources. Typically, utilities may provide green power using renewable resources they own or for which they contract; or they may purchase credits from a renewable energy provider certified by the state's Public Utilities Commission.

Table B
STATE FINANCIAL INCENTIVES FOR RENEWABLE ENERGY BY STATE AND REGION

State or other jurisdiction	Personal tax (a)	Corporate tax (b)	Sales tax (c)	Property tax (d)	Rebates (e)	Grants (f)	Loans (g)	Industry recruitment (h)	Leasing/sales (i)	Production incentive (j)
Eastern Region										
Connecticut	...	...	...	1 S	1 P	3 S	1 S	...	...	...
Delaware	...	...	...	...	1 S	...	...	...	...	1 P
Maine	...	...	...	...	1 P	1 S	...	...	...	...
Massachusetts	2 S	3 S	1 S	1 S	2 S, 1 P	2 S	...	...	...	1 P
New Hampshire	...	...	...	1 S	1 P	...	...	...	...	...
New Jersey	...	...	1 S	...	1 S	1 S	...	...	...	1 P
New York	1 S	1 S	...	1 S	4 S, 1 U	2 S	1 S	...	...	1 P
Pennsylvania	...	...	...	...	1 L	2 S, 4 L	4 L	...	...	1 U, 1 P
Rhode Island	1 S	...	1 S	1 S	2 S, 1 P	1 S	...	...	...	1 S, 1 P
Vermont	...	...	1 S	...	1 S, 1 P	...	...	...	...	...
Midwestern Region										
Illinois	...	...	1 S	1 S	4 S, 1 U	2 S, 1 P	...	...	...	1 P
Indiana	...	1 S	...	1 S	...	5 S	...	...	...	1 P
Iowa	...	1 S	2 S	3 S	...	1 S	3 S	...	...	1 P
Kansas	1 S	1 S	...	1 S	...	1 S	...	...	...	1 S, 1 P
Michigan	...	...	...	...	...	4 S	...	3 S	...	1 P
Minnesota	...	...	2 S	1 S	1 S	1 U	2 S	...	...	2 S, 1 P
Nebraska	...	1 S	...	...	...	...	1 S	...	...	1 P
North Dakota	1 S	1 S	1 S	2 S	...	...	...	...	...	1 S, 1 P
Ohio	1 S	2 S	1 S	1 S	...	...	1 S	2 S	...	1 P
South Dakota	...	2 S	...	2 S	...	...	...	...	...	1 S, 1 P
Wisconsin	...	...	...	1 S	1 S, 1 U	2 S	1 S	...	...	1 S, 1 P
Southern Region										
Alabama	1 S	...	...	...	...	1 S	...	...	...	1 U, 1 P
Arkansas	...	...	...	...	...	...	...	1 S	...	1 P
Florida	...	...	1 S	...	2 U	...	...	...	...	1 P
Georgia	1 S	1 S	...	...	...	...	...	...	...	1 U, 1 P
Kentucky	...	...	...	...	...	...	...	...	...	1 U, 1 P
Louisiana	1 S	1 S	...	1 S	...	...	...	...	...	1 P
Maryland	2 S	2 S	2 S	2 S	...	...	2 S	...	...	1 P
Mississippi	...	...	...	...	...	...	1 S	...	...	1 U, 1 P
Missouri	...	1 S	...	...	...	...	1 S	...	...	1 S, 1 P
North Carolina	1 S	1 S	...	1 S	...	...	1 S	1 S	...	1 U, 1P
Oklahoma	1 S	3 S	...	...	...	...	2 S	1 S	...	1 P
South Carolina	...	...	...	...	...	...	...	...	...	1 P
Tennessee	...	...	...	1 S	...	...	1 S	...	...	1 U, 1 P
Texas	...	1 S	...	1 S	1 U	...	1 U	1 S, 1 L	1 U	1 P
Virginia	...	1 S	...	1 S	...	...	...	2 S	...	1 U, 1P
West Virginia	1 S	1 S	...	1 S	...	...	...	...	...	1 P
Western Region										
Alaska	...	...	1 S	...	...	...	1 S	...	...	1 P
Arizona	2 S	...	1 S	...	3 U	...	...	...	...	1 P
California	2 S	2 S	...	1 S	2 S, 6 U	...	1 S, 2 U	...	2 U	1 S
Colorado	1 S	1 S	...	...	1 S, 1 L	...	1 U, 1 L	...	...	2 L, 1 P
Hawaii	1 S	2 S	2 S	...	3 U	...	2 L, 1 U	1 S	...	1 P
Idaho	1 S	1 S	...	...	...	1 P	1 S	...	...	1 P
Montana	3 S	5 S	...	2 S	4 S	1 P, 1 S	1 S	...	...	1 S, 1 P
Nevada	...	...	1 S	2 S	2 U	1 S	...	...	...	1 S, 1 P
New Mexico	...	1 S	...	...	...	...	...	...	...	1 P
Oregon	1 S	1 S	...	1 S	6 U, 2 S	1 P, 1 S	1 S, 4 U	...	...	2 P
Utah	2 S	2 S	1 S	...	...	1 S	1 S	...	...	1 P
Washington	...	...	1 S	...	1 S, 5 U	1 P	2 U	1 S	...	2 U, 2 P
Wyoming	...	1 S	1 S	...	...	1 S	...	...	1 U	1 P
Dist. of Columbia	...	...	...	...	...	...	...	...	...	1 P
American Samoa	...	...	...	...	...	...	...	...	...	...
Guam	...	...	...	...	...	...	...	...	...	...
No. Mariana Islands										
Palau	...	...	...	...	...	...	...	...	...	...
Puerto Rico	1 S	...	2 S	...	...	...	...	...	...	...
U.S. Virgin Islands	...	...	...	...	...	...	...	...	...	...

See footnotes at end of table.

STATE FINANCIAL INCENTIVES FOR RENEWABLE ENERGY BY STATE AND REGION — Continued

*Source:*NC Solar Center/ Interstate Renewable Energy Council, Database of State Incentives for Renewable Energy, www. Dsireusa.org - March 2004.

Key:

S - State or territory

L - Local

U - Utilities or energy service provider

P - Private

. . . - No provision for

(a) Many states offer personal income tax credits or deductions to cover the expense of purchasing and installing renewable energy equipment. Some states offer personal income tax credits up to a certain percentage or predetermined dollar amount for the cost or installation or renewable energy equipment. Allowable credit may be limited to a certain number of years following the purchase or installation or renewable energy equipment. Eligible technologies may include solar and photovoltaic energy systems, geothermal energy, wind energy, biomass, hydroelectric, and alternative fuel technologies.

(b) Corporate tax incentives allow corporations to receive credits or deductions ranging from 10% to 35% against the cost of equipment or installation to promote renewable energy equipment. In some cases, the incentive decreases over time. Some states allow the tax credit only if a corporation has invested a certain dollar amount into a given renewable energy project. In most cases, there is no maximum limit imposed on the amount of the deductible or credit.

(c) Sales tax incentives typically provide an exemption from the state sales tax for the cost of renewable energy equipment.

(d) Property tax incentives typically follow one of three basic structures: exemptions, exclusions, and credits. The majority of the property tax provisions for renewable energy follow a simple model that provides the added value of the renewable device is not included in the valuation of the property for taxation purposes. That is, if a renewable energy heating system costs $1,500 to install versus $1000 for a conventional heating system, then the renewable energy system is assessed at $1000. Property taxes are collected locally, so some states allow the local authorities the option of providing a property tax incentive for renewable energy devices. Six states have such provisions: Connecticut, Iowa, Maryland, New Hampshire, Vermont, and Virginia.

(e) Rebate programs are offered at the state, local, and utility levels to promote the installation of renewable energy equipment. The majority of the programs are available from state agencies and municipally-owned utilities and support solar water heating and/or photovoltaic systems. Eligible sectors usually include residents and businesses, although some programs are available to industry, institutions, and government agencies as well. Rebates typically range from $150 to $4000. In some cases, rebate programs are combined with low or no-interest loans.

(f) States offer a variety of grant programs to encourage the use and development of renewable energy technologies. Most programs offer support for a broad range of renewable energy technologies, while some states focus on promoting one particular type of renewable energy such as wind technology or alternative fuels. Grants are available primarily to the commercial, industrial, utility, education, and government sectors. Some grant programs focus on research and development, while others are designed to help a project achieve commercialization. Programs vary in the amount offered—from $500 to $1,000,000—with some states not setting a limit.

(g) Loan programs offer financing for the purchase of renewable energy equipment. Low-interest or no-interest loans for energy efficiency are a very common strategy for demand-side management by utilities. State governments also offer loans to assist in the purchase of renewable energy equipment. A broad range of renewable energy technologies are eligible. In many states, loans are available to residential, commercial, industrial, transportation, public, and nonprofit sectors. Repayment schedules vary; while most are determined on an individual project basis, some offer a 7-10 year loan term.

(h) This category focuses on special efforts and programs designed to attract renewable energy equipment manufacturers to locate within a state or city. Renewable energy industrial recruitment usually consists of financial incentives like tax credits, grants, or a commitment to purchase a specific amount of the product for use by a government agency. The recruitment incentives are designed to attract industries that will benefit the environment and create jobs. In most cases, the financial incentives are temporary measures that will help support the industries in their early years but include a sunset provision to encourage the industries to become self-sufficient within a number of years.

(i) Utility leasing programs target remote power customers for which line extension would be very costly. The customers can lease the technology, e.g., photovoltaics, from the utility, and in some cases, the customer can opt to purchase the system after a specified number of years. A few utilities sell renewable energy equipment to their customers as part of a buy-down, low-income assistance, lease, or remote power program.A few utilities sell renewable energy equipment to their customers as part of a buy-down, low-income assistance, lease, or remote power program.

(j) Production incentives provide project owners with cash payments based on electricity production on a $/kWh basis, as is the case with the Federal Renewable Energy Production Incentive, or based on the volume of renewable fuels produced on a $/gallon basis, as is the case with a number of state ethanol production incentives. Payments based on performance rather than capital investments can often be a more effective mechanism for ensuring quality projects.

Trends in State Environmental Spending

By R. Steven Brown

The states have expanded their role in environmental protection over the past three decades and now implement most of the federal environmental statutes. With this heightened responsibility has come an increase in state financial commitments to pay for these programs and the states have met this responsibility for years. During the past few years, however, the fiscal crisis in the states, coupled with many new federal environmental rules and a lack of new federal money, has left the states with at least a $1 billion annual gap in the amounts they need to implement current federal law. These shortfalls have been documented in several studies. This situation, if not corrected, may lead to greater risks to the public from exposure to environmental hazards. The federal government should consider providing funding or other relief to the states for further implementation of federal rules.

Delegations to States and Funding Commitments

The federal system of environmental protection in the United States centers on the delegation of many of the federal regulatory programs to the states. The states have increased their role in environmental protection over the past three decades and now implement most of the federal environmental statutes. States now operate 75 percent of the delegable programs – Clean Water Act, Clean Air Act, Resource Conservation and Recovery Act, Safe Drinking Water Act, etc.[1] As recently as 1993, only 40 percent of the programs had been delegated to the states, so the last 10 years have seen a rapid growth in state assumption of these federal programs.

With this heightened responsibility has come an increase in state commitments to pay for these programs and the states have met this responsibility for years. The federal government, primarily through the United States Environmental Protection Agency (EPA), continues to provide grants to states to assist with these programs, but the states themselves provide a substantial portion of the cost of running these programs. The amount varies from program to program and state to state but is 67 percent of the total expenditures overall.[2] The state environmental agencies get the state share of the funding from several sources: state general funds, trust funds and permit fees.

During the past few years, however, the fiscal crisis in the states, coupled with an increase in federal environmental rules and a lack of new federal money, has left the states with at least a $1 billion annual gap in the amounts they need to implement current federal law.

In the 10-year period of increased delegations, state environmental and natural resource agency budgets

had grown from $13.22 billion to $15.1 billion, with most of the budgetary growth from non-federal sources. State funding shortages first began to appear in fiscal 2001.[3] At that time cuts were minor, but they soon began to grow and by fiscal 2003, state environmental and natural resource (including non-EPA programs such as forestry and fish & wildlife) agency budgets had declined from $15.35 billion to $15.1 billion.

Although state general funds are declining for environmental programs, these programs fare no better or worse than other programs in state government. As state agencies lose general funds, they may take a variety of actions to minimize the loss, including cost-cutting measures, transfer of costs to other cost-centers, and program curtailments. At least one state, Illinois, cut nearly the entire 2004 general fund budget contribution to the state agency to zero. When these sorts of reductions occur, water programs are usually affected most because they have the fewest options for other sources of funds, such as permit fees.

Permit fees (charges the state makes to polluters) may provide a substantial portion of the state share, especially with the recent decline in state general fund revenues. However, permit fees are limited with respect to which programs can charge them, how much can be charged, and where the resulting funds can be spent. Fees are charged for some types of permits, but not others. Fees charged to municipal governments (for sewage treatment plant permits for example) are typically lower than those charged for industrial permits. Fees are usually set by the state legislatures. A legislature may also dictate the manner in which the fees can be spent. For example, permit fees may be limited to the cost and review of the permit itself in some states, while other states may

Table A: State Environment/Natural Resource Budgets by Category, 2003

Budget category	Total
Water	
Water resources	$2,186,970,159
Water quality	1,439,087,967
Drinking water	576,505,872
Marine and costal	429,659,056
Subtotal	4,632,193,054
Land management	
Forestry	1,597,786,882
Land management	1,090,775,125
Soil conservation	378,869,448
Mining reclamation	348,707,294
Pesticides control	225,225,047
Geological survey	179,089,909
Subtotal	3,820,453,705
Fish and wildlife	2,835,858,428
Waste management	
Hazardous waste	1,581,965,318
Solid waste	939,234,944
Nuclear waste	49,099,929
Subtotal	1,279,960,353
Total	15,138,765,731

Source: The Environmental Council of the States, 2003

include the costs of an annual inspection as well. The Environmental Council of the States (ECOS) has had more inquiries about permit fees this year than in all previous years combined, and in response we have collected and will publish a State Permit Fees Database this year.[4] During this time of growth in state environmental responsibilities and budgets, the number of new federal environmental rules also grew. From 1996 through 2002, the EPA issued 160 new rules that it deemed had a "state impact." During 2003, another 170 rules with a state impact were completed, in progress, or being proposed.[5]

Funding Gap Studies

Three recent studies[6] have shown there is at least a $1 billion annual funding gap between what the states need to implement the EPA-delegated federal programs and the resources currently on hand. Various national associations of state environmental officials, who polled their members about workload, resources, staffing, and related matters, conducted these three studies. The largest of these was a joint effort of ECOS and the Association of State and Interstate Water Pollution Control Administrators (ASWIPCA). ECOS is the national association of the state environmental agency leaders and ASWIPCA is the national association of state water quality program directors. The study was conducted with the support and participation of the EPA. Following the completion of the study in 2002, the EPA asked the

National Academy of Public Administration (NAPA) to review the results.

What NAPA found was that "between $700 million and $1 billion is a sound national estimate of the gap between the resources that states now have and what they would need to fully implement water programs" of the Clean Water Act. This means states currently have about half what they need to implement the Clean Water Act as enacted by Congress. NAPA went on to say "this national estimate is probably low because it does not include the costs of new and expanding water programs and may also underestimate the costs of state employees." Furthermore, the data for the study was collected before both the September 11, 2001 attacks (and the resultant new security measures) and the cuts in state budgets that began in 2001. ECOS estimates that these two items will result in some additional increase in the shortfall for these programs. Readers should also note that this gap does not include the so-called "infrastructure gap" – the shortage of funds needed to replace aging sewage treatment plants.

What sorts of programs are at risk if the shortfall continues? This will vary from state to state but several areas are likely to be at risk. Watershed planning, including court-ordered studies of Total Maximum Daily Loadings (TMDLs), is endangered because it involves a great deal of monitoring and communication among the industries, farmers, and municipal governments in a watershed. TMDLs are required by the Clean Water Act and are often judicially ordered. Other areas of concern include storm water remedies, combined sewer overflows, and urban sources of water pollution. The Clean Water Act also requires EPA and the states to address these issues.

In 2003 the Association of State Drinking Water Administrators (ASDWA) released a report on the state of the states for the drinking water protection programs delegated to states under the Safe Drinking Water Act. As in other programs, states are required to provide a "match" of non-federal funds to add to the federal funds received through grants used to support local drinking water projects. For drinking water, these funds had been obtained primarily through general fund appropriations, but during the 1990s this source could not meet the demand for the match requirement. Accordingly, many states began to charge permit fees or user fees. Between 1999 and 2001, states increased their combined drinking water contributions from both the general fund and fee programs from $136 million to $151 million. More recently, however, states have begun to see general fund revenues frozen, and have encountered opposi-

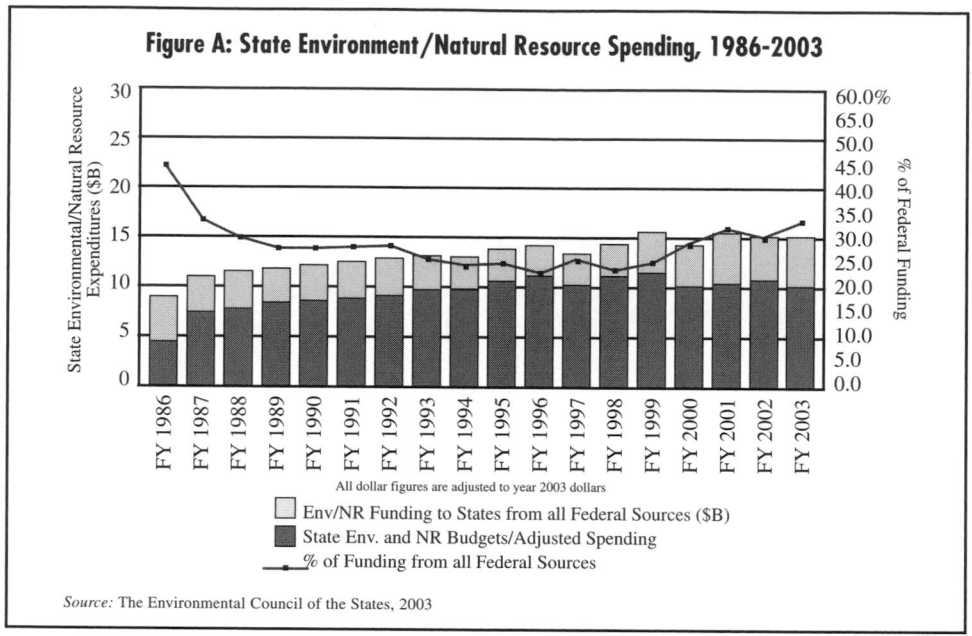

Figure A: State Environment/Natural Resource Spending, 1986-2003

All dollar figures are adjusted to year 2003 dollars

☐ Env/NR Funding to States from all Federal Sources ($B)

■ State Env. and NR Budgets/Adjusted Spending

─■─ % of Funding from all Federal Sources

Source: The Environmental Council of the States, 2003

tion to increases in fee programs. ASDWA found that 33 states were either unsuccessful in increasing fees or did not attempt to do so.

ASDWA found additional funding challenges. First, states are unable to fully spend all funds that are available to them, because of federal matching requirements, federal restrictions on the funding, or even state restrictions. Second, even if these funds could be spent, states are finding a gap between available funding and that which is needed – the gap for drinking water is expected to reach $254 million by 2006.

In 2002, the State and Territorial Air Pollution Program Administrators (STAPPA), the national association of the state air program directors, completed a study of air program financing with the support and cooperation of the EPA. This study found that "under Section 105 of the Clean Air Act [funding] fell short of our needs by nearly $100 million a year." Programs areas at risk include: "hazardous air pollutants; fine particulate matter, especially diesel particulate; compliance; inspections; monitoring; data improvements, including maintaining and improving infrastructures, emission inventories and modeling; haze and visibility monitoring; and outreach to and education of the public and regulated community."

The shortages that states face are caused by a growing number of federal environmental rules passed by Congress and being promulgated by the EPA. Each

year the Office of Management and Budget (OMB) prepares a report to Congress on "unfunded mandates." As part of this report, the OMB includes a section on federal rules that impose a cost of $100 million per year or more on states and local governments (the figure is chosen because it is used in the Unfunded Mandates Act of 1995). In the 2003 report across all of the federal government, seven rules issued over the previous seven years are identified that meet these criteria, and every single one of them is an environmental rule.[7] They include rules on waste combustion, solid waste landfills, drinking water (three of these), and storm water discharges (two of these). There are five other air rules that meet the same criteria as unfunded mandates, but which are exempted by law from the act.

Conclusion

There is no argument made here about whether these programs have benefit to the public – they have already passed this scrutiny, and states accept that they have a benefit. Instead, the argument is over the cost of implementation and who should bear it. The recent state budget problems indicate that states have – after 15 years of continual growth in environmental spending - reached their limit on contributions to federally imposed environmental programs. The federal government should consider providing funding or other relief to states for further implementation of federal rules.

Notes

[1] R. Steven Brown, K. Smaczniak, and M. Jones, "Working for a Living–States Implement Growing Number of National Environmental Laws for EPA," *ECOSTATES* (Fall 2001): 3-6.

[2] R. Steven Brown and Michael J. Kiefer, "Budgets are Bruised, but Still Strong," *ECOSTATES* (Summer 2003): 10-15.

[3] R. Steven Brown, "When the Axe Falls – How State Environmental Agencies Deal with Budget Cuts," *ECOSTATES* (Winter 2002): 16-19.

[4] Daniel Morgan, Michael Kiefer, and R. Steven Brown, *State Permit Fees Database, 2003-2004* (Washington, D.C.: Environmental Council of the States, in press).

[5] Personal communication with Regulatory Management Division of U.S. EPA, December 5, 2003.

[6] *Understanding What States Need to Protect Water Quality,* (Washington, D.C.: National Academy of Public Administration, December 2002); *Public Health Protection Threatened by Inadequate Resources for State Drinking Water Programs,* (Washington, D.C.: Association of State Drinking Water Administrators, April 2003); *Funding Needs of State and Local Air Pollution Control Agencies,* (Washington, D.C.: State and Territorial Air Pollution Program Administrators/Association of Local Air Pollution Control Officials, June 2002).

[7] Office of Management and Budget, *Informing Regulatory Decisions: 2003 Report to Congress on the Costs and Benefits of Federal Regulations and Unfunded Mandates on State, Local and Tribal Entities,* (Washington, D.C.: Office of Management and Budget, 2003), 199.

About the Author

R. Steven Brown is the executive director of the Environmental Council of the States. He helped to form ECOS while at The Council of State Governments, where he led efforts on environment, technology and public safety for 11 years. He is the author of numerous books and articles on the environment and technology.

The Medicare Prescription Drug, Improvement and Modernization Act of 2003: Health Care Changes

By Trudi Matthews

On December 8, 2003, President Bush signed into law the most far-reaching expansion of health care coverage since the Medicare and Medicaid programs were created. The Medicare Prescription Drug, Improvement and Modernization Act of 2003 adds prescription drug coverage for the nation's 40 million seniors and disabled individuals enrolled in Medicare. The law also contains a host of provisions that will have an enormous impact on state health care programs as well as state budgets.

When Medicare was first created in 1965, it did not include coverage for prescription drugs. Most other forms of health insurance did not include coverage for drugs either. Over the years, as drugs became a preferred method for treating illness, employer-sponsored health plans gradually added prescription drug coverage as a standard part of their benefits. With drug costs going up every year, roughly one-third of Medicare beneficiaries lacking any drug coverage, and these individuals paying some of the highest retail prices for drugs, pressure began mounting for Congress to expand Medicare to include coverage for prescription drugs.

Health care analysts watched with bated breath in November 2003 as Congressional leaders in a sudden burst of energy pushed forward a conference agreement on a bill that would add prescription drug coverage to Medicare. Adding to the suspense and irony was that fact that the Republican-controlled House, Senate and administration were leading the charge to enact a bill that would result in the largest expansion of a public health care program since Medicare was created in 1965. And, leading Democrats were opposed to the bill.

Since its enactment by Congress and subsequent approval by the president in December 2003, health care analysts and policymakers have combed through the fine print of the law to pull out the implications for various sectors of health care. Beyond providing a Medicare drug benefit, the law contains a variety of measures including rural health care incentives, health savings accounts and income testing of Medicare Part B premiums. No one doubts that this law will have a far reaching impact on the future of health care in the United States.

States, too, will be affected greatly by the new law. Governors, state legislative leaders and others have argued that Medicare should include prescription drug coverage for dual eligibles, the low-income seniors and disabled individuals enrolled in both Medi-

care and Medicaid. The final law did include transfer of responsibility for dual eligible drugs costs to Medicare, but there are other provisions that make this less of a boon than states had hoped. In addition, states as employers also stand to gain because their health plans routinely covered prescription drug costs for retired state employees because Medicare did not. Many states had also established pharmaceutical assistance programs to assist lower-income elderly with their drug costs. The law addresses these programs as well.

This article will outline some of the features of the new law and its implications related to states. The first section will give an overview of the basic benefits in the law, and then discuss how it will affect states and lastly, the immediate challenges that lie ahead.

Overview of the Medicare Drug Law[1]

The Medicare drug law provides for two basic benefits, one for now and one for later. To give the U.S. Department of Health and Human Services (HHS) time to set up the new prescription drug benefit, Medicare will first establish a prescription drug discount card that becomes available in May 2004. Then in January 2006, the new Medicare Part D will go into effect. In addition to establishing these two basic benefits, the law also contains a host of health care reform measures that will affect states directly and indirectly.

Interim Discount Card

The prescription drug discount card program is aimed at providing interim relief to Medicare beneficiaries by providing them with access to discounted drug prices. The drug cards will be administered through private contractors that will be approved by HHS. The enrollment fee is set at no more than $30. Low-income beneficiaries will receive additional assistance. Medicare will pay low-income individuals' enrollment fee, and drug cards will have a $600 credit that can be applied to their drug costs. People who receive this assistance will have to pay 5 or 10 percent of the cost of each drug depending on their income level. HHS estimates a savings of 15-25 percent off regular retail drug prices for seniors and other Medicare beneficiaries through this program.[2]

New Medicare Part D

Standard Benefit

The new Medicare Part D benefit will have a $35 monthly premium, a $250 deductible, and 75 percent coinsurance for up to $2,250 of drug costs. Above $2,250, beneficiaries would have to pay out-of pocket for additional drug purchases until they reached $3,600 in spending. Beyond $3,600 in spending, the law provides for catastrophic coverage with nominal co-payments per prescription of $2 for generic and $5 or 5 percent of the cost of brand drugs, whichever is greater. The gap between $2,250 and $3,600, often referred to as the "donut hole," was one of the more controversial features of the law. However, it was a feature that enabled it to stay within the $400 billion price tag set aside to pay for the new benefit.

Low-Income Provisions

The standard benefit applies to individuals with higher incomes. For people with incomes below 150 percent of the federal poverty level (or FPL, which is currently $8,980 for a single person, $12,120 for a couple), there will be additional assistance under the law. There is no "donut hole" for Medicare beneficiaries below 150 percent of the federal poverty level. Medicare will cover the full drug costs for institutionalized enrollees without any cost-sharing requirements. The benefit will be structured as follows for different income levels:

- Individuals below 100 percent FPL will have co-payments of $1 for generics, $3 for brand name drugs with no premiums or deductible.

- Individuals under 135 percent FPL will have $2 co-payments for generics, $5 co-payment for brand name drugs with no premiums or deductible; individuals must have assets lower than $6,000 for singles/$9,000 for couples to be eligible for this benefit.

- Individuals under 150 percent FPL will have a $50 deductible, a sliding scale premium, and 15 percent coinsurance up to the catastrophic limit, with $2 and $5 co-payments thereafter; individuals must have assets lower than $10,000 for singles/$12,000 for couples to be eligible for this benefit.

Other Changes

There are a number of major changes to Medicare and health care in general contained in the law that go beyond providing a prescription drug benefit. First, private health plans are given an unprecedented new role in providing benefits under Medicare. Unlike traditional Medicare which is administered directly by the federal government, private health plans will contract with HHS to provide the drug benefit. Additionally, an enhanced Medicare Advantage program will replace the embattled Medicare+Choice program, providing better incentives for managed care organizations to offer comprehensive, integrated health care benefits to Medicare beneficiaries. Thus, as the January 1, 2006, effective date for the new drug benefit approaches, Medicare beneficiaries will face three choices regarding Medicare Part D drug coverage:

- **enroll in a stand-alone prescription drug plan** as a supplement to regular Medicare Parts A and B;

- **enroll in a Medicare Advantage health plan** that covers all health care services including prescription drugs;

- **forgo Part D prescription drug coverage** and access other drug coverage such as that offered by employers to their retirees or remain uninsured.

In addition to the role of private health plans, there are a number of other health care reform measures. The new law expands Health Savings Accounts, eliminating restrictions that had limited their attractiveness to small employers and the uninsured. Individuals with high-deductible insurance plans will be able to set up and contribute as much as $2,600 for a single person or $5,150 for a couple to these accounts. The contributions are tax free as long as the expenses are used for approved health care services, including deductibles and long term care insurance.[3] These new features are expected to assist the growing consumer-directed health insurance and long term care insurance markets. Employers, including state governments, will also receive incentive payments of 28 percent of costs up to $5,000 to maintain drug coverage in retiree health plans. Congressional leaders did not want employers to eliminate retiree drug coverage and hoped through incentive payments to prevent public funds from driving private money out of health care. Finally, Medicare Part B premiums will increase by $10 in 2005 and will be adjusted for inflation thereafter. For the first time, too, individuals who make more than $80,000 annually will have to pay more for Medicare Part B coverage, facing a sliding scale premium based on income.

Implications for States and Territories

The most important change for states is that the new Medicare Part D will assume responsibility for low-income Medicare beneficiary drug costs, relieving states of some of their rising prescription drug costs in Medicaid. Territories will not be eligible to participate in Medicare Part D, but will be eligible for grants to establish a separate benefit. State Medicaid programs provided drug coverage to more than 6 million dual eligibles in 2002 at a per capita cost of $918 in state spending.[4] While the transfer of dual eligibles to Medicare sounds like a fiscal boon to states at first, a number of the law's provisions mean that long-term savings will be more marginal than originally hoped and states may spend more in the short term.

Under the Medicare drug law, states and the Social Security Administration will be responsible for determining who qualifies for low-income assistance. More than 14 million seniors are expected to be eligible for low-income assistance.[5] States will have to hire new staff or retrain others, modify computer systems and make other changes in order to accommodate this requirement.[6] The federal government matching rate for administrative costs in Medicaid is usually 50 percent. Thus, if administrative costs in Medicaid increase significantly, states may see their portion of Medicaid costs rise as well.

In addition, the law requires that Medicaid savings on dual eligibles' drug costs be paid to Medicare. Officially termed as a "state contribution" but more generally known as the clawback provision, this portion of the law levies in essence a federal tax on state Medicaid spending. Based on a complex formula of the number of dual eligibles, their drug costs and other factors, states must pay the federal government 90 percent of what they would have contributed to covering this population under Medicaid. This percentage decreases gradually over the next 10 years to 75 percent in 2015, meaning that states may see more savings as time goes on. Also, falling under the "no good deed goes unpunished" category of the law, states that expanded their Medicaid programs to provide more generous coverage for poor seniors will likely pay significantly more than states that did not, due to the way the clawback formula is calculated.[7]

The Congressional Budget Office (CBO) estimates that state Medicaid spending will decrease by $17.2 billion with nearly 80 percent of these savings coming between 2010 and 2013. However, the CBO estimates found that the added responsibilities for states and contributions to Medicare under the new law mean that states will spend $1.2 billion more between 2004 and 2006.[8] And, a good deal can happen in 10 years with the federal budget.

There are other provisions that may offset some of the added costs to states. There is $200 million set aside for health care costs related to undocumented aliens. The law contains $62.5 million in grant funding for states with pharmaceutical assistance programs. In addition, the law enhances 2004 Disproportionate Share Hospital (DSH) payments by 16 percent.[9] However, there are new audit and reporting requirements under the law aimed at preventing use of DSH accounting devices to increase federal payments to states. These strategies have been popular with states during tough budget times.

The Medicare law also provides the largest enhancement of rural health care since the creation of the program which will help health care access in rural areas in the states. Rural doctors receive a 1.5 percent payment increase, and there are increases for rural health care facilities, bringing them up to par with their urban counterparts over the next decade. Payment increases for rural health care workers, ambulance services, and home health services are also included as well as new incentives to attract health professionals to rural areas.

Immediate Challenges

There are a number of challenges that states face immediately under the law. States will have to provide data to HHS on a monthly basis regarding their enrollment and per capita spending for dual eligibles. HHS will use the data as a basis for calculating state contribution payments and to help with eligibility determinations for the drug discount cards. Moreover, although HHS is responsible for setting eligibility and enrollment for the discount cards, states will need to move quickly to put systems into place to educate seniors about the new discount cards availability and features.

The 30 states that have established state pharmaceutical assistance programs will need to review the future of these programs in light of Medicare changes. States are considering whether to leave them as is, eliminate them, or modify them to fill in the gaps in Medicare Part D.[10] States are prevented from using federal matching funds through Medicaid to fill the gaps in the Medicare drug benefit. Thus, an appropriate role for state-funded pharmaceutical assistance programs may be to provide supplemental drug coverage.

Conclusion

While it is impossible at this point to determine all the changes that states may see under the new Medicare drug law, it is no stretch to say that health care will change fundamentally. The Medicare program had an enormous impact on the American health care system before the new law. Add to this the size and reach of the new law, and the combination ensures that the changes will be of seismic proportions. States will, therefore, face the challenge of both responding to these ground-breaking events as well as shaping their future direction and impact.

Notes

[1] This section is based on an analysis of the law itself available at http://rs9.loc.gov/cgi-bin/query/C?c108:./temp/~c108RRQQi2 as well as several summaries, including Kathryn Kotula and Elaine Ryan, Letter to State Medicaid Directors, American Public Human Services Association/National Association of State Medicaid Directors, November 21, 2003, available at http://www.nasmd.org/Medicare%20Drug%20Bill_Summary.pdf; the American Association of Retired Persons, "What Does the New Medicare Drug Benefit Mean for You?" available at www.aarp.org/bulletin/prescription/articles/a2003-11-26-foryou.html; Health Policy Alternatives, *Prescription Drug Coverage for Medicare Beneficiaries: A Summary of the Medicare Prescription Drug, Improvement, and Modernization Act of 2003*, (Washington, D.C.: Kaiser Commission on Medicaid and the Uninsured, December 2003), available at http://www.kff.org/medicare/6112.cfm; and the Ways and Means Committee, "Summary of the Medicare Conference Agreement", available at http://waysand means. house.gov/media/pdf/healthdocs/confagree ment.pdf.

[2] U.S. Department of Health and Human Services, Press Release, "HHS Announces Immediate Steps To Make Medicare-Approved Drug Discount Card Programs Available Next Spring," available at http://www.hhs.gov/news/press/2003pres/20031210a.html.

[3] U.S. Department of the Treasury, Health Savings Accounts Fact Sheet, http://www.treasury.gov/press/releases/reports/1061hsafactsheet.pdf.

[4] Brian Bruen and John Holahan, *Shifting the Costs of Dual Eligibles: Implications for States and the Federal Government*, (Washington, D.C.: Kaiser Commission on Medicaid and the Uninsured, November 2003), available at http://www.kff.org/medicaid/loader.cfm?url=/commonspot/security/getfile.cfm&PageID=27097.

[5] Congressional Budget Office, Letter to Senator Don Nickles, Chairman of the Committee on Budget, November 20, 2003, available at ftp://ftp.cbo.gov/48xx/doc4814/11-20-MedicareLetter2.pdf.

[6] Kaiser Commission on Medicaid and the Uninsured, "Implications of the New Medicare Prescription Drug Benefit for State Medicaid Budgets," ibid.

[7] Ibid.

[8] Ibid.

[9] Kotula and Ryan.

[10] Raymond Hernandez and Robert Pear, "State Officials Are Cautious on Medicare Drug Benefit," *New York Times*, January 4, 2004.

About the Author

Trudi Matthews is the associate director for health policy for The Council of State Governments. She is responsible for staffing CSG's national Health Capacity Task Force and Emerging Health Trends Subcommittee, as well as writing, researching and planning meetings on a wide variety of health policy issues.

TABLE A
"FULL" DUAL ELIGIBLE ENROLLMENT AND PRESCRIPTION DRUG SPENDING, BY STATE, 2002

State or other jurisdiction	Enrollment		Spending on "full" duals (millions)			State per-capita spending on prescribed drugs (state dollars only)
	Full dual eligibles	Full duals as a share of all dual eligibles	Total	Prescribed drugs	Prescribed drugs as % of total	
United States	6,126,000	85%	$91,056	$13,177	14%	$918
Alabama	121,000	75	1,349	193	14	470
Alaska	9,000	98	144	24	17	1,122
Arizona	57,000	87	765	91	12	562
Arkansas	98,000	81	1,010	151	15	422
California	904,000	97	8,290	1,652	20	888
Colorado	59,000	84	1,014	137	14	1,162
Connecticut	76,000	92	2,252	201	9	1,322
Delaware	9,000	64	236	24	10	1,313
Florida	354,000	87	3,933	937	24	1,153
Georgia	129,000	72	1,622	298	18	947
Hawaii	26,000	96	250	32	13	529
Idaho	10,000	80	163	28	17	799
Illinois	171,000	77	2,976	423	14	1,237
Indiana	103,000	83	1,828	301	16	1,110
Iowa	55,000	82	911	124	14	838
Kansas	39,000	85	792	109	14	1,110
Kentucky	172,000	82	1,961	418	21	730
Louisiana	109,000	77	1,300	252	19	687
Maine	42,000	85	645	106	16	843
Maryland	71,000	78	1,368	182	13	1,282
Massachusetts	193,000	89	3,638	408	11	1,058
Michigan	190,000	88	1,891	358	19	822
Minnesota	92,000	90	2,194	232	11	1,258
Mississippi	133,000	98	1,092	258	24	463
Missouri	138,000	86	1,983	408	21	1,152
Montana	15,000	93	207	33	16	591
Nebraska	35,000	93	533	82	15	949
Nevada	18,000	63	208	33	16	910
New Hampshire	19,000	93	455	52	11	1,371
New Jersey	140,000	82	2,684	381	14	1,359
New Mexico	27,000	69	405	47	12	466
New York	537,000	89	15,217	1,200	8	1,117
North Carolina	225,000	83	2,824	527	19	903
North Dakota	13,000	86	272	28	10	656
Ohio	179,000	82	4,401	496	11	1,142
Oklahoma	77,000	82	869	123	14	471
Oregon	56,000	82	766	156	20	1,134
Pennsylvania	306,000	91	3,339	554	17	822
Rhode Island	27,000	82	715	63	9	1,114
South Carolina	117,000	97	1,199	192	16	503
South Dakota	14,000	78	240	29	12	707
Tennessee	191,000	77	2,058	197	10	375
Texas	363,000	74	4,956	654	13	717
Utah	17,000	89	263	52	20	913
Vermont	22,000	77	248	58	23	977
Virginia	101,000	68	1,450	243	17	1,166
Washington	93,000	87	1,007	239	24	1,275
West Virginia	36,000	72	634	77	12	529
Wisconsin	115,000	93	2,082	274	13	988
Wyoming	6,000	72	128	15	12	956
Dist. of Columbia	17,000	90	287	29	10	504

Source: "*Implications of the New Medicare Prescription Drug Benefit for State Medicaid Budgets,*" (#4162), The Henry J. Kaiser Family Foundation, December 2003. This information was reprinted with permission from the Henry J. Kaiser Family Foundation. The Kaiser Family Foundation, based in Menlo Park, California is a nonprofit, independent national health care philanthropy and is not associated with Kaiser Permanente or Kaiser Industries.

Table 9.6
HEALTH INSURANCE COVERAGE STATUS BY STATE FOR ALL PEOPLE: 2002
(In thousands)

State or other jurisdiction	Total	Covered and not covered by health insurance during the year			
		Covered	Percent	Not covered	Percent
United States	285,933	242,360	84.8%	43,574	15.2%
Alabama	4,440	3,876	87.3	564	12.7
Alaska	635	516	81.3	119	18.7
Arizona	5,442	4,526	83.2	916	16.8
Arkansas	2,692	2,252	83.7	440	16.3
California	35,159	28,761	81.8	6,398	18.2
Colorado	4,477	3,756	83.9	720	16.1
Connecticut	3,382	3,027	89.5	356	10.5
Delaware	798	719	90.1	79	9.9
Florida	16,429	13,586	82.7	2,843	17.3
Georgia	8,426	7,072	83.9	1,354	16.1
Hawaii	1,224	1,101	90.0	123	10.0
Idaho	1,300	1,067	82.1	233	17.9
Illinois	12,504	10,737	85.9	1,767	14.1
Indiana	6,100	5,303	86.9	797	13.1
Iowa	2,903	2,626	90.5	277	9.5
Kansas	2,685	2,404	89.6	280	10.4
Kentucky	4,046	3,498	86.4	548	13.6
Louisiana	4,447	3,627	81.6	820	18.4
Maine	1,269	1,125	88.7	144	11.3
Maryland	5,458	4,728	86.6	730	13.4
Massachusetts	6,470	5,827	90.1	644	9.9
Michigan	9,910	8,752	88.3	1,158	11.7
Minnesota	5,054	4,657	92.1	397	7.9
Mississippi	2,787	2,322	83.3	465	16.7
Missouri	5,585	4,939	88.4	646	11.6
Montana	906	767	84.7	139	15.3
Nebraska	1,704	1,530	89.8	174	10.2
Nevada	2,121	1,703	80.3	418	19.7
New Hampshire	1,266	1,141	90.1	125	9.9
New Jersey	8,604	7,408	86.1	1,197	13.9
New Mexico	1,804	1,452	78.9	388	21.1
New York	19,283	16,241	84.2	3,042	15.8
North Carolina	8,162	6,794	83.2	1,368	16.8
North Dakota	633	564	89.1	69	10.9
Ohio	11,282	9,938	88.1	1,344	11.9
Oklahoma	3,477	2,876	82.7	601	17.3
Oregon	3,510	2,999	85.4	511	14.6
Pennsylvania	12,190	10,809	88.7	1,380	11.3
Rhode Island	1,056	952	90.2	104	9.8
South Carolina	3,997	3,497	87.5	500	12.5
South Dakota	745	659	88.5	85	11.5
Tennessee	5,672	5,058	89.2	614	10.8
Texas	21,529	15,973	74.2	5,556	25.8
Utah	2,310	2,000	86.6	310	13.4
Vermont	619	553	89.3	66	10.7
Virginia	7,118	6,156	86.5	962	13.5
Washington	6,001	5,151	85.8	850	14.2
West Virginia	1,751	1,496	85.4	255	14.6
Wisconsin	5,475	4,938	90.2	538	9.8
Wyoming	488	402	82.3	86	17.7
Dist. of Columbia	572	498	87.0	74	13.0

Source: U.S. Census Bureau, Current Population Survey, *2003 Annual Social and Economic Supplement.*

Table 9.7
NUMBER AND PERCENT OF CHILDREN UNDER 19 YEARS OF AGE, AT OR BELOW
200 PERCENT OF POVERTY, BY STATE: THREE-YEAR AVERAGES FOR 2000, 2001 AND 2002
(In thousands)

State or other jurisdiction	Total children under 19 years, all income levels	At or below 200 percent of poverty		At or below 200 percent of poverty without health insurance	
		Number	Percent	Number	Percent
United States	76,120	28,714	37.7	5,743	7.5
Alabama	1,185	517	43.7	82	6.9
Alaska	199	61	30.7	12	5.8
Arizona	1,547	671	43.4	177	11.4
Arkansas	723	381	52.7	60	8.3
California	10,096	4,226	41.9	968	9.6
Colorado	1,204	385	32.0	106	8.8
Connecticut	872	243	27.9	39	4.5
Delaware	206	57	27.8	8	4.0
Florida	4,036	1,661	41.2	426	10.6
Georgia	2,358	925	39.2	180	7.6
Hawaii	321	113	35.1	14	4.3
Idaho	393	165	42.0	35	8.9
Illinois	3,329	1,152	34.6	228	6.9
Indiana	1,604	558	34.8	109	6.8
Iowa	764	234	30.6	30	3.9
Kansas	706	233	32.9	39	5.5
Kentucky	1,038	423	40.8	68	6.5
Louisiana	1,271	630	49.6	123	9.7
Maine	287	104	36.3	12	4.0
Maryland	1,456	322	22.1	60	4.1
Massachusetts	1,502	458	30.5	40	2.6
Michigan	2,610	841	32.2	106	4.1
Minnesota	1,274	287	22.5	38	3.0
Mississippi	814	405	49.7	57	7.0
Missouri	1,482	452	30.5	43	2.9
Montana	233	101	43.6	20	8.8
Nebraska	458	146	31.9	17	3.7
Nevada	591	229	38.8	66	11.1
New Hampshire	310	68	21.8	9	3.0
New Jersey	2,091	534	25.6	113	5.5
New Mexico	523	266	50.9	58	11.0
New York	4,830	1,893	39.2	277	5.7
North Carolina	2,150	897	41.7	166	7.7
North Dakota	148	55	37.1	8	5.6
Ohio	2,923	966	33.1	157	5.4
Oklahoma	922	434	47.0	98	10.6
Oregon	894	335	37.5	66	7.4
Pennsylvania	2,959	978	33.1	162	5.5
Rhode Island	255	76	29.8	7	2.6
South Carolina	1,062	417	39.3	52	4.9
South Dakota	198	66	33.1	9	4.7
Tennessee	1,464	606	41.4	63	4.3
Texas	6,378	2,998	47.0	1,013	15.9
Utah	776	258	33.3	46	5.9
Vermont	139	44	31.5	3	2.1
Virginia	1,880	552	29.4	104	5.5
Washington	1,611	561	34.8	88	5.5
West Virginia	415	204	49.2	29	6.9
Wisconsin	1,386	414	29.9	36	2.6
Wyoming	129	48	36.9	11	8.2
Dist. of Columbia	118	61	52.1	7	5.9

Source: U.S. Census Bureau, Current Population Survey, 2001, 2002, and 2003 Annual Social and Economic Supplements.

Note: Average of the three years' percentages: not average 'number' divided by average total children. Results may differ slightly based on the method used.

Trends in State Mental Health Agencies

By Theodore C. Lutterman, Robert Shaw, Ronald Manderscheid and Noel A. Mazade

"After a year of study, and after reviewing research and testimony, the Commission finds that recovery from mental illness is now a real possibility. The promise of the New Freedom Initiative— a life in the community for everyone—can be realized. Yet, for too many Americans with mental illnesses, the mental health services and supports they need remain fragmented, disconnected and often inadequate, frustrating the opportunity for recovery."[1] - President Bush's New Freedom Commission on Mental Health. July 2003.

"Across the nation, the demand for mental health services is growing as a result of increased understanding of mental health disorders, the availability of new and effective medications, and the proven efficacy of evidence-based treatment. At the same time, states are facing a crisis as a result of inadequate and diminishing funding, critical workforce shortages and a growing reliance on Medicaid-funded systems."[2] - George Gintoli, Director, South Carolina Department of Mental Health, 2003.

State Mission/Values

The 55 state and territorial state mental health agencies (SMHAs) manage the organization, delivery and financing of mental health services to adults with serious mental illnesses and children and adolescents with serious emotional disturbances. States are developing comprehensive systems and services to help persons with mental illness recover and lead fulfilling lives in the community. SMHAs provide acute and long-term mental health treatment, plus a variety of community-based support services including, but not limited to, supportive employment, housing and education.

During the last century, SMHAs have shifted their resources from providing inpatient care in large state psychiatric hospitals to supporting community-based provider agencies that receive SMHA funds, where the SMHA organizes systems and monitors the quality of the care.

Overview of SMHA Systems

SMHAs have the statutory authority to organize and purchase mental health services in each state. In fiscal year 2001, SMHAs controlled $24 billion in expenditures for systems that serve nearly 5 million citizens. Over two-thirds of these expenditures were community-based services and were mostly dedicated to services for persons with the most severe mental illnesses (e.g., schizophrenia, bi-polar disorder and severe depression).

The SMHA is the central governmental authority in each state responsible for developing comprehensive plans for mental health and it organizes to assure that relevant services are delivered. Other parts of state government play significant roles in the care of people with mental illnesses. These other state agencies include education, the criminal and juvenile justice systems, vocational rehabilitation, housing and employment services. However, it is the SMHAs that serve as the primary vehicle for these services. Since the 1980s, SMHAs have been statutorily required as part of the federal Community Mental Health Services Block Grant, to develop annual comprehensive plans for community-based mental health services. The development of these plans should involve all relevant other state government agencies in forming coordinated plans to serve citizens with mental illnesses in the states.

Location in State Government

Within most states, the SMHA is administratively located within a larger umbrella agency or department. In 2003, 24 SMHAs were located within states' Department of Human Services, eight SMHAs in Departments of Health, and two SMHAs in another state department which often combine health and human services. Fifteen SMHAs were either independent state departments of mental health or departments of mental health and mental retardation (see Figure A).

Among the 15 independent SMHAs, the SMHA director is a member of the governor's cabinet in eight states (Ala., Conn., D.C., Maine, Mo., Ohio, R.I. and Tenn.). In 25 states, the SMHA director reports to a department head, with one level between the SMHAs director and the governor. In 12 states there are two levels between the SMHA and the governor and in three states there are three or more levels between the SMHAs and the governor. In three states (Okla., S.C. and Texas), the SMHA director reports to a mental health board or commission. With regard to governance and oversight, boards or councils are charged with the oversight of the SMHAS in 13 states (Colo., Conn., Iowa, Minn., Mo., Nev., N.M., N.C., Okla., Ore., S.C., Texas and Utah).

Additional Disability Responsibilities within the SMHAs

The SMHAs are often responsible for the provision of other disability-related services. In 23 states, the SMHA is responsible for the provision of substance abuse (both alcohol and other drug abuse) treatment services, and the two agencies are located within the same state umbrella agency in 17 additional states. Ten states have inter-agency agreements between the SMHA and substance abuse agencies to coordinate care (Alaska, D.C., Ill., Mass., N.J., N.Y., Ohio, Texas, Vt. and Wash.).

Twenty years ago, substance abuse services was co-located within the SMHA in 19 states. During the 1980s and early 1990s, many states divided mental health and substance abuse into separate state agencies. In the later 1990s and early 2000s, this trend appears to have reversed and many states. Twenty-four now have organized mental health and substance abuse in the same state agency.

In 14 states, the SMHA is responsible for the provision of mental retardation and developmental disability services (MR/DD). The MR/DD agency is located within the same umbrella agency as the SMHA in 25 states. In 11 states, all three major disability service responsibilities (mental health, substance abuse and MR/DD) are co-located within the SMHA (Ala., Ga., Ky., Maine, Miss., Mo., N.C., R.I., Va., W.Va. and Wis.).

Reorganization of SMHAs

The recent state budget shortages and efforts to streamline government have led to major changes in how SMHAs are organized. Within the last two years, 11 SMHAs have reorganized. Four of these reorganizations involved moving the organizational location of the SMHAs within state government (D.C., Idaho, Ind. and Ore.). Seven of the reorganizations involved shifting additional disability services into or out of the SMHA (Iowa, Md., N.H., Ore., Tenn., Utah and Wyo.). The new disability services moved into the SMHAs were alcohol and other drug services (Ore., Utah and Wis.) and traumatic brain injury (N.H.). In states where disability services were transferred from the SMHA, these services were mental retardation (N.H. and Ore.) and substance abuse (N.H. and Wyo.).

SMHA Responsibilities for Specific Mental Health Special Services and Populations

SMHAs vary widely in the specific services and population groups for which they are responsible. In four states (Conn., Del., N.M. and R.I.), children and adolescent mental health services are located in a separate agency from the adult SMHA. In seven states, the SMHA shares responsibilities for these services with another state agency in the same umbrella department (Colo., Hawaii, Idaho, La., Minn., N.H. and Wyo.).

Adult forensic mental health services are the responsibility of 36 SMHAs, a shared responsibility in 10 SMHAs, and not the responsibility of the SMHA in two states (Iowa and N.D.). Providing services to sexual offenders is the responsibility of nine SMHAs (Alaska, Ariz., Fla., Iowa, Mo., N.M., S.C. and S.D.), a shared responsibility in 18 states, and not the responsibility of the SMHA in 18 others. Providing services for persons with Alzheimer's disease or organic brain syndromes is the primary responsibility of the SMHA in five states (D.C., Ind., N.C., R.I. and Vt.) and is a responsibility the SMHA shares with another state agency in 17 states. In 25 states, the SMHA is not responsible for providing services to persons with Alzheimer's disease. Brain impaired services are a primary responsibility of five SMHAs (Alaska, Calif., Ky., N.C. and R.I.), a shared responsibility in 14 SMHAs, and not a responsibility of the SMHA in 27 states.

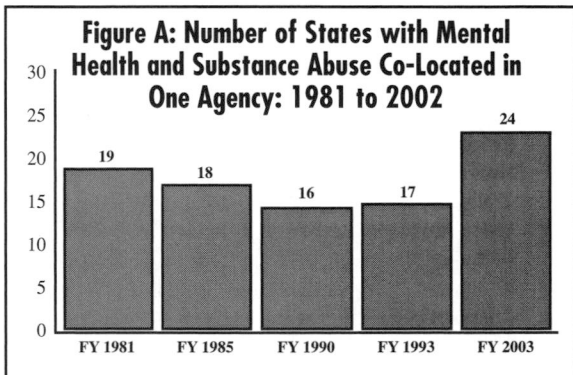

Figure A: Number of States with Mental Health and Substance Abuse Co-Located in One Agency: 1981 to 2002

SMHA Responsibilities
for State Psychiatric Hospitals

In almost every state, the SMHA is responsible for running state-operated psychiatric hospitals and for organizing and funding community-based mental health services. In four states (Colo., Iowa, S.D. and Wis.), the responsibility for the operation of state psychiatric hospitals is not under the authority of the SMHA. In Rhode Island there is no state psychiatric hospital, instead the SMHA operates a general hospital with a psychiatric unit.

State Psychiatric Hospital Closings

States are downsizing and closing state psychiatric hospitals and hospital beds. From 1972 to 1990, according to data from the federal Center for Mental Health Services (CMHS), state and county psychiatric beds decreased over 70 percent (from 361,765 to 98,647). During this time, 14 of 277 state psychiatric hospitals closed. From 1990 to 2000, 44 hospitals were closed as the number of hospital residents decreased to about 54,000 (a further decline of over 40 percent). Since 2000, only two states have closed hospitals (one each in Fla. and Ill.). Four states (Md., Mass., N.C. and S.C.) plan on closing hospitals over the next two years. States continue to close psychiatric hospital beds. In the last five years, 28 states reported closing beds. There are 14 states planning to close almost 1,300 additional beds over the next two years (Ala., Colo., Conn., Del., D.C., Ga., Ind., Mass., Minn., Neb., Pa., Tenn., Texas and Va.). Half of the states were also reorganizing (i.e., downsizing, reconfiguring, consolidating, or privatizing their state hospital systems).

Controlling State Psychiatric Hospital Utilization:

Forty-one SMHAs have community programs that perform a gatekeeping function over admissions to state psychiatric hospitals, including pre-discharge planning (37 states); hospital-community liaison activities (36 states); and preadmission screening (36 states). Gatekeeping services are established by SMHA policy in 27 states, by SMHA regulations in 15 states, and by state statute in 16 states. Virtually all states (46 of 47) report that community programs operate crisis programs to reduce the number of admissions to state psychiatric hospitals. Six states (Ariz., Ill., Ky., Pa., R.I. and Wyo.) have portable benefits that follow a client from a state hospital to the community.

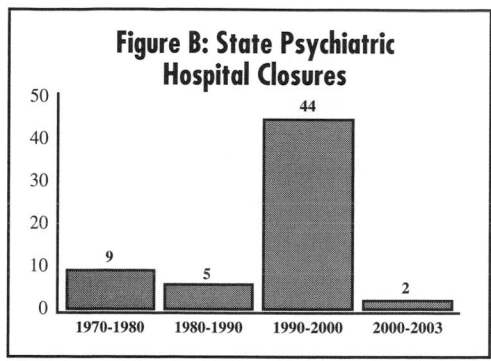

Figure B: State Psychiatric Hospital Closures

Psychiatric Inpatient Bed Shortages:

SMHAs have not been alone in closing psychiatric beds during the last several years. Many states have experienced the closing of private psychiatric hospitals, general hospital psychiatric inpatient beds and Department of Veterans Affairs psychiatric beds (often due to changes in federal reimbursement policies and the impact of managed care restrictions on inpatient services). As a result, some states are now experiencing shortages of acute psychiatric care. Over half (22 of 41) SMHAs are experiencing a shortage in psychiatric beds as a result of the reduction of public and private psychiatric inpatient beds. These bed shortages result in increased waiting lists for state hospital beds in 14 states, increased waits for other psychiatric beds in 12 states, overcrowding in state hospitals in 11 states, and increased resistance to closing additional state hospital beds in seven states.

How SMHAs Organize and Fund Community Mental Health Services:

In FY 2001, the SMHAs expended over $15.4 billion (two-thirds of their mental health budgets) on community-based mental health services and provided community mental health services to approximately 5 million individuals. However, the methods used by states to organize, finance and deliver community mental health services vary widely from state to state.

Three major methods are used by SMHAs to provide community mental health services:

- Contracting with local (usually not-for-profit) community-based mental health providers;

- Funding local governments (city, county or multi-county) mental health authorities, which in turn, operate and contract for community mental health services; and

- Directly providing mental health services in communities using their own state employees.

In many states, combinations of these mechanisms are used. Larger populated states tend to use local governments to organize the delivery of community mental health services, while smaller states often directly operate the community system with their own

Privatization of State Mental Health Agency Operated Services:

In the last two years, Illinois and Oklahoma privatized services at state psychiatric hospitals; South Carolina partially privatized a state psychiatric hospital; and Connecticut has privatized some of its state operated community mental health programs.

Figure C: Methods SMHAs Use to Provide Community Mental Health Services

	SMHA Operates Community Mental Health Services with State Employees	SMHA Directly Contracts with County providers	SMHA Funds City/County/Multi-County Mental Health Authorities
Mechanism is used for at least a portion of the system	14 SMHAs/ Average State Pop= 4,804,316	38 SMHAs/ Average State Pop = 5,496,992	19 SMHAs/ Average State Pop= 8,127,548
Primary mechanism used	6 SMHAs/ Average State Pop= 2,103,947	26 SMHAs/ Average State Pop=4,743,129	14 SMHAs/ Average State Pop= 8,890,517

employees. Of the states directly operating community-based services, two (Conn. and Ga.) reported that they are involved with privatizing the SMHA-operated community mental health providers.

Restructuring of Community Mental Health Services:

Thirty SMHAs are restructuring their community mental health system. Nine states give community programs control over the utilization or budgets of state psychiatric hospitals (Calif., N.H., N.C., N.D., Ohio, Pa., Utah, Vt. and Wis.). Eight states give community mental health programs financial incentives/rewards for reducing state hospital utilization (Calif., Colo., Del., N.H., N.C., Ohio, Pa. and S.C.).

Rural/Frontier Mental Health Services:

Twenty-nine SMHAs report that they have special initiatives to provide mental health services to individuals in rural or frontier areas, such as outreach services, transportation, and telemedicine. Twenty-three SMHAs are using telemedicine to provide services in rural or frontier areas.

Mental Health Prevention/Screening:

Thirty-two states reported that they fund community mental health programs to provide prevention and/or early intervention services. These services were oriented towards children in 31 states, toward adults in nine states, and older adults in six states. Twenty-one SMHAs reported that they fund or operate suicide prevention programs. Seven SMHAs operate or fund hotlines or help lines for suicide prevention.

Eligibility Criteria and SMHA Priority Populations:

Most states have eligibility criteria, such as specific diagnoses (37 states), functional levels (36 states), duration (5 states), and prior history regarding who can receive mental health services from either SMHA operated or funded providers. Twelve states reported that they restrict services to only adults with serious mental illnesses and/or children with serious emotional disturbances. Five states restrict services to adults with serious mental illnesses, but serve children/adolescents with any mental disorder. Twenty-two states have eligibility criteria for serving both adults with serious mental illnesses and adults with other mental illnesses. Only three states reported they have no eligibility criteria.

State Estimates of Population Eligible for Mental Health Services:

Thirty-one states provided information about the estimated population eligible for mental health services in their state. The most common (median) estimate for adults with serious mental illnesses was 5.2 percent of a state's adult population. The median estimate for children and adolescents with serious emotional disturbances was 8.0 percent. States estimated that over 10 million adults and children met the criteria for a serious mental illness or emotional disturbance.

SMHA Estimates of Unmet Need for Mental Health Services:

Twenty-one states report that they have developed estimates of the unmet need for mental health

Figure D: Percent of Population Served

Eligibility Groups for SMHA Services	Average Percent of State Population Served	Number of States Reporting
SMI Adults and SED Children Only	1.4%	7
SMI Adults and any children	0.7	5
Both SMI and Any Mental Illness	2.0	21
No Criteria	1.4	13
No response	1.2	7

services. Twelve states report that they maintain waiting lists for persons in need of mental health services (Ala., Ind., Maine, Mass., Nev., N.Y., Ohio, S.C., Texas, Vt., Va. and W.Va.). Three states report the waiting lists are related to inpatient psychiatric services (Ala., Ind. and S.C.), four states maintain waiting lists for various children's mental health services (Maine, Mass., N.Y. and Vt.), and three states report waiting lists are maintained by local mental health programs or regional boards (Colo., Ohio and S.D.). Twelve states reported maintaining waiting lists for specific services.

Numbers of Persons Served by SMHAs: FY 2002

Forty states reported they served over 4.7 million unduplicated clients across all mental health services during FY 2002 (persons served by SMHA operated or funded programs). On average, these states served approximately 1.5 percent of their state's population, with a range from a maximum of 3.5 percent to 0.1 percent served. States that set eligibility requirements to receive services from the SMHA and limit these services to adults with serious mental illnesses (SMI) and/or children and adolescents with serious emotional disturbances (SED) tend to serve a lower percent of their state's overall population than states that serve broader eligible population groups.

Forty-one states reported that they served 434,838 persons in state psychiatric hospital inpatient settings during FY 2002. Of these, 20,021 (4.6 percent) were children and adolescents and 414,817 (95.4 percent) were adults. Twenty-eight states reported they served a total of 2,951,162 persons in community mental health programs during FY 2002. Of these, 905,419 (30 percent) were children and adolescents, and 2,045,743 (70 percent) were adults.

Provision of Evidence-Based Mental Health Services by SMHAs

In 1999, the landmark *Mental Health: A Report of The Surgeon General*, urged mental health systems to utilize knowledge gained from research to improve service delivery. A number of mental health services have research demonstrated they are effective in addressing mental illnesses. These services have been called "evidence-based practices" (EBPs). Every SMHA was implementing at least one EBP in 2003, and 20 states were offering at least six different EBPs. Many of the EBPs are being offered in parts of a state and fewer EBPs are being implemented statewide. The federal Center for Mental Health Services is developing implementation resource kits for six major EBPs, and has developed a grant program to support states in their implementation efforts. Implementation issues, such as measuring fidelity to service models, methods of financing evidence-based services, and necessary staff training are the focus of major efforts by many SMHAs.

Funding Sources and Expenditures of SMHAs

In FY 2003 and FY 2004, SMHAs Face Major Budget Shortages:

The last few fiscal years (FY 2003 and FY 2004) have become much worse for all state government due to the economic slowdown. Today, almost every state is facing major budget reductions in the current FY 2003, and the National Conference of

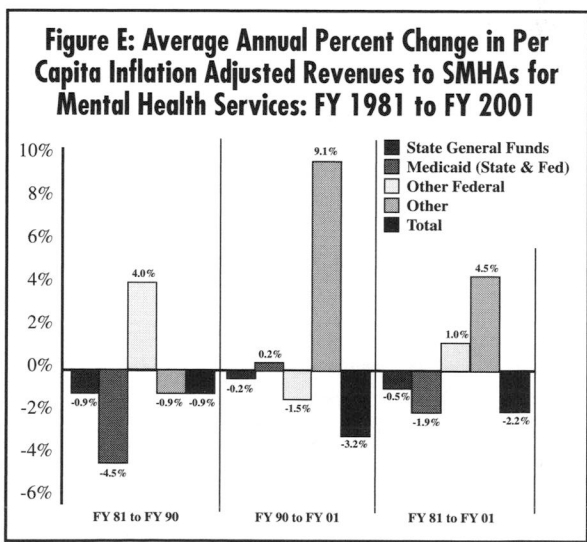

Figure E: Average Annual Percent Change in Per Capita Inflation Adjusted Revenues to SMHAs for Mental Health Services: FY 1981 to FY 2001

Legend: State General Funds; Medicaid (State & Fed); Other Federal; Other; Total

State Legislatures (NCSL) reports that states faced a minimum $68.5 billion budget shortfall for FY 2004.

Medicaid Revenues to SMHA Programs grew Much Faster Than Other Sources in the 1990s:

From FY 1997 to FY 2001 SMHA-controlled revenues for mental health services from Medicaid grew much faster than funds from other sources. Medicaid revenues (state and federal funds) grew from $4.97 billion in FY 1997 to $8.4 billion in FY 2001, an increase of 69 percent. During this same time period, state general and other funds increased from $10.4 billion to $12.4 billion, an increase of 19.4 percent. Total SMHA-controlled revenues increased from $17.3 billion to $23.5 billion, an increase of 36 percent during this time period. However, when adjusted for population growth and inflation, total SMHA-controlled revenues increased only 8 percent over the four years, and declined by 1.7 percent over the last decade.

From FY 1981 to FY 2001 state general (and other state) funds increased by an average of 5 percent per year. However, much of this increase came during the 1980s, when revenues increased by 7.9 percent per year. During the 1990s (FY 1990 to FY 2001), SMHA-controlled revenues from general revenue sources increased only 2.8 percent per year. When revenues are adjusted for the impact of population growth and inflation, state general revenues fell 3.2 percent per year from FY 1990 to FY 2001.

Most of the Growth of SMHA Spending Came from Medicaid:

As a result of the different rates of growth in revenues, in the 1990s, over 61 percent of the growth in SMHA-spending came from Medicaid funds controlled by SMHAs. This is a substantial increase from the 1980s, when Medicaid accounted for only 13 percent of the growth in SMHA spending.

State general revenues accounted for only 29 percent of the increase in SMHA spending for mental health from 1990 to 2001. This is a substantial decline from the 1980s, when state general fund sources accounted for 75 percent of the growth in SMHA mental health spending.

The reliance on Medicaid for funding mental health services has allowed SMHAs to increase services, but at a cost of lost flexibility in the services offered. To use Medicaid, SMHAs have to rely on Medicaid client eligibility rules and approved services, which reduce their flexibility to focus services on targeted high need consumer groups and limits services to Medicaid approved services.

State Tax Dollars Remain the Major Source of Funding of SMHAs:

Despite the growth in Medicaid, SMHAs continue to receive most (67 percent) of their funding from state government sources. In FY 2001, state tax dollars accounted for over $15.7 billion of the funding for SMHAs' mental health services. These funding sources included state general and special funds of over $12.4 billion, and state Medicaid match funds of over $3.2 billion. The federal government was the second largest provider of funds for SMHA services, with FY 2001 dollars totaling almost $6.5 billion of federal funds (28 percent of SMHA total funding).

SMHA-Controlled Mental Health Expenditures Increased by Over $6 Billion from FY 1997 to FY 2001:

In FY 2001, SMHA-controlled expenditures for mental health services totaled over $23.3 billion, an increase of over $6.5 billion (38.3 percent) from FY 1997. This translates into an average annual increase of 8.4 percent per year. Even when controlling for inflation, total SMHA-controlled expenditures for mental health services increased by 18.9 percent over this time period (4.4 percent per year). Over the 20-year period from FY 1981 to FY 2001, SMHA expenditures adjusted for population growth increased by 202 percent. However, when expenditures are adjusted for population growth and inflation, SMHAs experience an 8.2 percent decline over this time period. From FY 1981 to FY 2001, 29 SMHAs had a decrease in expenditures adjusted for inflation and population. In the 4-year period from FY 1997 to FY 2001, 17 SMHAs experienced reductions in inflation-adjusted expenditures for mental health.

Figure F: SMHA-Controlled Revenues for Mental Health: FY 2001

- Local 0.4%
- MH Block 2%
- Other Fed 2%
- Other 5%
- Medicare 2%
- State General Funds 45%
- Fed Medicaid 22%
- State Medicaid 14%
- State Other 8%

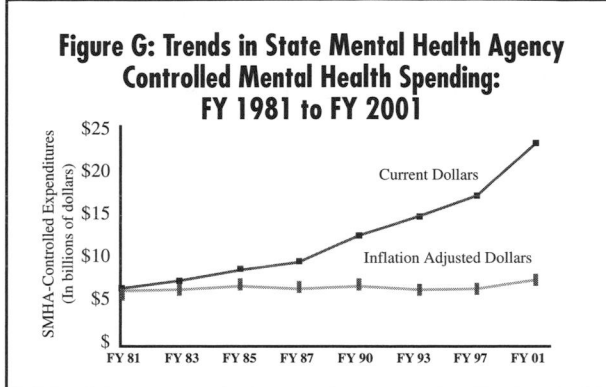

Figure G: Trends in State Mental Health Agency Controlled Mental Health Spending: FY 1981 to FY 2001

State Government Dollars for SMHA-Controlled Mental Health Expenditures Grew Slower than State Government Spending for Other Agencies Between FY 1997 and FY 2001:

Between FY 1997 and FY 2001, the 38.3 percent increase in SMHA-controlled mental health expenditures exceeded the overall growth in state government expenditures for all services (31.3 percent). However, SMHAs have not done as well as other state government agencies in receiving state general fund dollars (up 28 percent between FY 1997 and FY 2001), while on average state government expenditures of state dollars increased 31 percent.

Community-Based Mental Health Services Increased to 66 percent of SMHA Expenditures:

In FY 2001, SMHA-controlled expenditures for community mental health services totaled $15.4 bil-

lion (66 percent of total SMHA expenditures). From FY 1997 to FY 2001, SMHA-controlled expenditures for these community-based mental health services increased by over $5.6 billion, an increase of 57 percent. In FY 1981, SMHA-controlled community mental health expenditures represented only 33 percent of spending. Community mental health services include all non-state hospital inpatient expenditures of SMHAs.

Flat Expenditures at State Psychiatric Hospitals:

SMHAs expended $7.35 billion for state psychiatric hospital inpatient care in FY 2001. This represented a slight increase of $802 million (11.8 percent) from FY 1997. Adjusted for inflation, state psychiatric hospital expenditures decreased by 3.9 percent from FY 1997 to FY 2001, and down by 49.1 percent from FY 1981. State psychiatric hospital inpatient expenditures in FY 2001 represented 32 percent of total SMHA expenditures, down from 49 percent in FY 1993 and 62 percent in FY 1981.

State Hospital Expenditures are Increasingly for Forensic Services:

Expenditures for forensic mental health services in state hospitals increased by 62 percent in FY 1997 to FY 2001, much faster than overall state psychiatric hospital increase of 11.8 percent. Forensic mental health services expenditures have increased to 23.7 percent of total state psychiatric hospital-inpatient expenditures in FY 2001.

Per Capita Expenditures Vary by State and by Region:

In FY 2001, SMHA-controlled mental health expenditures averaged $80.28 for every person in the state's civilian population. There was a substantial variation in levels of per capita expenditures among states that is partially explained by geographic region. Per capita expenditures ranged from a high of $149.61 in Mid-Atlantic states to a low of $47.10 in South Central region states. Adjusted for inflation, 23 states had growth of less than 10 percent and 12 states actually had decreases in mental health expenditures.

Authors' Note

The information in this report was derived from the National Association of State Mental

Figure H: State Mental Health Agency Controlled Expenditures for State Psychiatric Inpatient and Community-Based Services as a Percent of Total Expenditure: FY 1981 to FY 2001

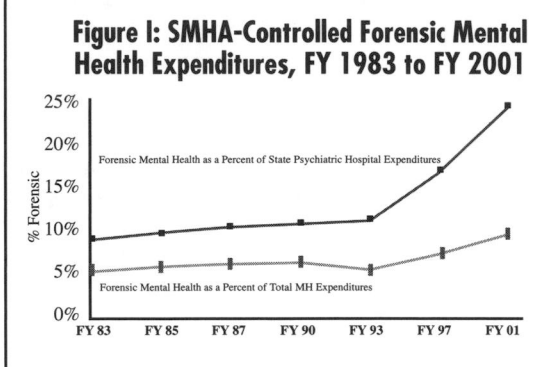

Figure I: SMHA-Controlled Forensic Mental Health Expenditures, FY 1983 to FY 2001

Forensic Mental Health as a Percent of State Psychiatric Hospital Expenditures

Forensic Mental Health as a Percent of Total MH Expenditures

Health Program Directors Research Institute, Inc (NRI) State Mental Health Agency Profiles System and its State Mental Health Agency Revenues and Expenditures Study. Both of these studies have been developed under contract from the Federal Center for Mental Health Services. State specific information on the organization of SMHAs, their services, clients, and expenditures can be found at the NRI's website at www.nri-inc.org.

Notes

[1] New Freedom Commission on Mental Health, *Achieving the Promise: Transforming Mental Health Care in America. Final Report.* DHHS Pub. No. SMH-03-3832. (Rockville, MD:2003).

[2] T. Lutterman, V. Hollen and R. Shaw, *Funding Sources and Expenditures of State Mental Health Agencies: Fiscal Year 2001*, NASMHPD Research Institute, Inc., Alexandria, VA: 2003).

About the Authors

Theodore C. Lutterman is the director of research analysis for the National Association of State Mental Health Program Directors Research Institute, Inc. (NRI).

Robert Shaw is a systems analyst for NRI.

Ronald Manderscheid is the chief, Survey and Analysis Branch, U.S. Center for Mental Health Services.

Noel A. Mazade is executive director of NRI.

Table A
STATE MENTAL HEALTH AGENCY CONTROLLED, BY FUNDING SOURCE: FISCAL YEAR 2001

State or other jurisdiction	State general funds	State Medicaid match	Federal Medicaid	Total Medicaid	Medicare	CMHS Mental Health Block Grant	Other federal	Local government	First- and third-party payments	Other revenues	Other revenues	Fiscal year 2001 per capita
Alabama	$132,715,220	$28,676,452	$67,012,732	$95,689,184	$9,063,348	$5,998,648	$2,149,026	$0	$0	$7,663,669	$253,279,095	$56.73
Alaska (a) (d)	32,773,880	3,818,417	5,739,573	9,557,990	0	755,160	2,910,900	0	2,053,011	3,393,608	51,444,549	81
Arizona (b) (d)	254,978,518	65,882,961	125,316,253	191,199,214	0	6,657,364	31,199,832	0	508,751	32,603,909	517,147,588	97
Arkansas (a)	52,654,112	0	15,435,388	15,435,388	767,921	2,781,208	280,718	0	2,786,080	1,031,971	75,737,398	28
California (b)	1,189,412,583	674,119,479	708,689,708	1,382,809,187	27,655,959	38,949,100	0	0	29,460,978	479,505,186	3,147,792,993	91
Colorado	101,125,569	81,628,434	81,628,434	163,256,868	N.A.	5,193,995	891,932	0	0	12,146,462	282,614,826	64
Connecticut (c)	428,894,351	7,054,454	7,054,454	14,108,908	8,237,952	4,214,516	5,755,016	0	2,134,585	655,983	464,001,312	135
Delaware (c)	61,033,726	5,792,151	6,412,599	12,204,750	1,061,272	457,175	1,977,295	0	544,600	2,687,300	79,966,118	100
Florida (a)	405,204,649	0	93,633,686	93,633,686	3,824,839	24,966,135	58,035,465	0	0	0	585,664,774	36
Georgia	347,218,493	0	2,816,866	2,816,866	11,927,832	9,521,377	7,150,773	0	26	2,011,910	380,647,277	45
Hawaii (b)	205,173,919	0	3,641,593	3,641,593	337,063	1,605,228	3,552,420	0	204,450	78,466	214,593,139	175
Idaho (b)	28,367,800	2,866,800	7,371,700	10,238,500	0	3,603,025	14,987,790	0	0	3,327,200	60,524,315	46
Illinois	593,409,109	0	178,328,635	178,328,635	0	16,248,971	1,874,655	N.A.	0	0	789,861,370	63
Indiana	236,054,637	N.A.	125,151,643	125,151,643	N.A.	8,713,418	6,401,943	N.A.	0	17,845,201	394,166,842	64
Iowa (e)	0	N.A.	N.A.	N.A.	N.A.	N.A.	N.A.	N.A.	0	N.A.	N.A.	
Kansas	58,830,725	11,223,081	77,397,904	88,620,985	0	2,528,707	10,822,749	0	1,041,070	N.A.	161,844,236	60
Kentucky	110,357,300	19,442,390	49,083,383	68,525,774	7,801,936	4,791,260	3,083,422	0	2,358,410	0	196,918,102	48
Louisiana	73,080,264	26,030,402	62,663,535	88,693,937	1,530,872	5,265,451	180,557	0	0	32,175,000	200,926,081	45
Maine	54,563,142	53,191,007	26,117,547	79,308,554	1,287,554	1,448,019	887,092	0	13,370	0	137,507,731	107
Maryland (b)	499,911,577	0	164,900,313	164,900,313	N.A.	10,547,720	2,446,737	0	0	0	677,806,347	126
Massachusetts (d)	671,523,215	0	114,940,834	114,940,834	5,133,720	7,245,465	1,645,707	0	1,269,561	2,839,396	804,597,898	126
Michigan (b) (d)	463,829,552	171,873,163	220,491,109	392,364,272	8,928,618	8,902,776	1,692,190	14,700,746	4,135,780	511,701	895,065,635	90
Minnesota	262,376,066	87,433,556	92,248,833	179,682,389	902,245	5,604,773	24,834,911	29,972,276	8,856,979	5,734,278	517,963,917	104
Mississippi	123,073,199	25,149,340	82,361,190	107,510,530	1,554,022	3,864,148	3,865,959	0	6,924,291	0	246,792,149	86
Missouri (b)	321,220,062	0	123,173,067	123,173,067	9,661,217	6,729,012	3,764,237	0	5,037,873	0	469,585,468	83
Montana	34,278,236	20,107,903	54,053,808	74,161,711		1,470,686	1,811,600	0	0		111,722,233	124
Nebraska	63,085,298	4,548,231	9,594,421	14,142,652	1,375,155	2,011,272	3,966,905	2,518,975	0	5,358,293	92,458,550	54
Nevada (b) (d)	36,256,958	37,743,639	37,743,639	75,487,278	1,663,227	1,940,601	1,411,084	0	2,069,756	1,381,939	120,210,843	57
New Hampshire (d)	43,802,924	41,158,680	41,158,682	82,317,362	4,829,417	1,057,217	3,075,332	0	0	5,402,069	140,484,321	112
New Jersey (b)	600,660,231	50,819,494	50,819,494	101,638,988	16,053,213	15,956,064	3,975,706	1,920,580	22,852,358	0	763,057,140	90
New Mexico (a) (b) (d)	45,820,657		12,965,678	12,965,678	321,307	2,181,353	342,000	0	1,128,776	100,723	62,860,494	34
New York (b) (d)	669,828,808	943,207,649	943,207,649	1,886,415,298	185,650,344	29,600,000	67,469,440	0	171,960,455	133,254,719	3,144,179,064	165
North Carolina (e)	322,752,807	73,588,524	157,096,510	230,685,034	26,745,668	11,431,104	8,778,565	0	15,727,045	0	616,120,223	75
North Dakota	28,804,943	866,233	11,909,715	12,775,948	1,121,998	824,530	3,316,827	0	1,727,293	4,101,900	52,673,439	83
Ohio	439,790,639	58,643,303	181,182,176	239,825,479	10,258,951	20,354,834	16,468,464	0	2,338,841	0	729,037,208	64
Oklahoma	113,372,277	0	5,241,950	5,241,950	5,162,617	3,643,451	1,631,383	0	2,419,590	2,302,142	133,773,410	39
Oregon	71,145,805	92,332,597	138,593,954	230,926,551		3,642,721		0	31,132,563		336,847,640	97
Pennsylvania (a) (b)	1,306,128,617	112,431,437	391,109,274	503,540,711	10,735,000	13,117,716	127,594,925	0	21,207,410	19,350,073	2,001,674,852	163
Rhode Island (b) (c) (d)	12,365,122	30,239,897	35,247,348	65,487,245	0	1,457,929	484,714	9,583,048	1,819,111	1,302,397	92,499,566	87
South Carolina (b) (d)	129,111,870	45,396,969	109,985,194	155,382,163	6,928,900	4,266,646	2,400,611	3,004,164	6,522,067	10,608,442	318,224,863	78

See footnotes at end of table.

STATE MENTAL HEALTH AGENCY CONTROLLED, BY FUNDING SOURCE: FISCAL YEAR 2001 — Continued

State or other jurisdiction	State general funds	State Medicaid match	Federal Medicaid	Total Medicaid	Medicare	CMHS Mental Health Block Grant	Other federal	Local government	First- and third- party payments	Other revenues	Other revenues	Fiscal year 2001 per capita
South Dakota (b)	2,817,434	0	10,713,275	10,713,275	1,995,458	660,906	944,838	0	0	169,631	17,301,542	23
Tennessee	324,559,200	1,440,700	1,613,200	3,053,900	8,170,400	6,255,400	2,336,100	0	50,575,600	252,100	395,202,700	69
Texas (b)	491,187,085	91,149,065	125,366,466	216,515,531	17,127,531	30,924,856	6,436,010	23,768,344	9,657,511	1,357,565	796,974,433	37
Utah (a) (b)	57,825,340	0	8,414,322	8,414,322	1,513,400	2,215,392	2,077,013	0	1,198,612	546,256	73,790,335	33
Vermont (b) (d)	5,402,650	26,850,861	43,619,179	70,470,040	756,381	628,309	1,977,758	0	0	423,197	79,658,335	130
Virginia (b)	312,064,903	57,511,298	61,831,507	119,342,805	15,827,647	7,319,862	1,334,395	0	8,560,957	550,181	465,000,750	65
Washington (b)	52,705,025	219,616,920	228,398,012	448,014,932	8,852,371	8,133,428	655,426	0	6,717,006	486,520	525,564,708	88
West Virginia (b)	37,591,020	373,673	1,121,017	1,494,690	3,196,674	1,827,113	962,986	0	725,301	6,330	45,804,114	25
Wisconsin (e)	255,816,660	31,020,069	68,740,944	99,761,013	5,950,366	6,387,935	279,106	0	9,541,582	11,679,964	389,416,626	72
Wyoming	30,362,057	3,243,624	2,774,768	6,018,392	627,639	553,415	275,350	0	267,983	0	38,104,836	77
Dist. of Columbia	171,891,418	7,769,682	18,730,318	26,500,000	21,525,062	650,581	5,347,545	0	644,231	0	226,558,837	396
Puerto Rico	73,894,064	0	0	0	0	5,228,758	325,000	0	0	0	79,447,822	21
Total	$12,441,103,716	$3,214,242,536	$5,192,843,479	$8,407,086,015	$456,065,096	$370,334,730	$456,070,410	$85,468,133	$389,264,255	$849,705,688	$23,455,098,044	$82
Average (Mean)	239,251,995	63,024,363	101,820,460	161,674,731	9,307,451	7,261,465	8,942,557	1,709,363	7,485,851	16,994,114	459,903,883	
Median	118,222,738	19,442,390	54,053,808	85,469,174	1,995,458	4,791,260	2,336,100	0	1,084,923	1,167,184	253,279,095	77

Source: The National Association of State Mental Health Program Directors Research Institute, Inc. (NRI). March 2004.

Key:

N.A.—Services provided but exact expenditures are unallocable.

(a) Medicaid Revenues for Community Programs are not included in SMHA-Controlled Expenditures.

(b) SMHA-Controlled Expenditures include funds for mental health services in jails or prisons.

(c) Children's Mental Health Expenditures are not included in SMHA-Controlled Expenditures.

(d) SMHA-Controlled Expenditures includes the majority of publicly supported housing provided to Adults with SMI and/or Children with SED.

(e) SMHA did not return data checklist survey.

Table B
STATE MENTAL HEALTH CONTROLLED PER CAPITA EXPENDITURES FOR STATE MENTAL HOSPITAL INPATIENT SERVICES, COMMUNITY SERVICES (STATE HOSPITAL AND OTHER COMMUNITY-BASED),RESEARCH, TRAINING AND ADMINISTRATION: FISCAL YEAR 2001

State or other jurisdiction	State psychiatric hospital inpatient			Community based			Prevention, research, and training			Administration			Total SMHA Expenditures per capita	Total rank
	Amount per capita	Rank	Percent	Amount per capita	Rank	Percent	Amount per capita	Rank	Percent	Amount per capita	Rank	Percent		
Alabama	$23.30	30	41%	$32.07	36	56%	$0.00		0%	$1.60	21	3%	$56.97	39
Alaska (a)(d)	27.10	23	33	49.27	23	61	0.12	22	0	4.87	3	6	81.36	22
Arizona (b)(d)	8.78	50	10	78.59	8	88	0.08	26	0	1.91	16	2	89.36	18
Arkansas (a)	8.67	51	31	18.37	48	65	0.39	11	1	0.82	39	2	28.25	50
California (b)	16.57	42	18	74.11	10	81	0.00		0	0.93	32	1	91.61	15
Colorado	19.01	38	30	44.91	25	70	NA		NA	0.32	46	0	64.24	31
Connecticut (c)	44.72	5	35	72.79	11	56	3.11		2	8.23	2	6	128.85	6
Delaware (c)	59.81	2	65	31.08	37	34	0.00		0	1.81	19	2	92.70	14
Florida (a)	15.43	45	44	19.35	46	55	0.01	31	0	0.62	42	2	35.41	47
Georgia	20.80	35	46	22.14	43	49	0.51	9	1	2.15	13	5	45.59	43
Hawaii (b)	27.73	22	16	125.02	2	71	1.11	4	1	21.35	1	12	175.21	3
Idaho (b)	16.74	41	36	28.45	38	62	0.09	24	0	0.73	40	2	46.01	42
Illinois	24.67	28	39	37.46	32	59	0.16	19	0	1.25	26	2	63.54	32
Indiana	21.17	34	33	42.89	27	66	0.39	12	1	0.25	48	0	64.70	30
Iowa (e)	16.37	43	22	56.82	20	78	0.00		0	NA		NA	73.18	26
Kansas	21.40	33	35	38.00	31	63	0.02	30	0	0.89	35	1	60.31	36
Kentucky	24.88	27	51	22.84	41	47	0.02	29	0	0.90	33	2	48.64	41
Louisiana	26.14	26	58	18.15	49	40	0.00		0	0.90	34	2	45.18	44
Maine	32.26	14	30	69.90	15	65	0.44	10	0	4.71	5	4	107.31	11
Maryland (b)	38.01	8	30	83.01	7	66	0.85	6	1	4.74	4	4	126.62	7
Massachusetts (d)	32.06	16	30	72.01	14	67	1.41	3	1	1.91	17	2	107.38	10
Michigan (b) (d)	29.67	19	33	59.37	17	66	0.08	25	0	0.83	36	1	89.96	17
Minnesota (b)	31.26	17	30	72.68	12	69	0.10	23	0	0.56	43	1	104.60	12
Mississippi (b)	51.72	4	60	33.99	34	39	NA		NA	1.00	28	1	86.71	21
Missouri (b)	30.23	18	50	27.01	39	45	0.00		0	2.73	11	5	59.96	37
Montana	28.85	20	23	90.90	6	73	0.00		0	4.29	6	3	124.04	8
Nebraska	32.15	15	63	17.62	50	35	0.00		0	0.96	30	2	50.73	40
Nevada (b) (d)	20.74	36	36	36.05	33	63	0.00		0	0.53	44	1	57.31	38
New Hampshire (d)	33.11	12	30	76.85	9	69	0.00		0	2.07	15	2	112.03	9
New Jersey (b)	35.15	10	39	53.59	21	59	NA		NA	1.57	22	2	90.31	16
New Mexico (a) (b) (d)	12.02	48	37	20.39	45	63	0.00		0	0.18	49	0	32.60	49
New York (b) (d)	52.42	3	30	116.73	4	66	2.80	2	2	4.01	7	2	175.97	2
North Carolina (e)	34.76	11	46	39.57	30	52	NA		NA	NA		NA	75.57	24
North Dakota	35.43	9	45	42.38	28	54	0.06	28	0	1.03	27	1	78.90	23
Ohio	17.11	40	28	41.46	29	68	0.19	17	0	2.36	12	4	61.12	34
Oklahoma	11.81	49	30	25.38	40	64	0.16	18	0	2.14	14	5	39.49	45
Oregon	23.42	29	24	72.50	13	74	0.00		0	1.47	23	2	97.39	13
Pennsylvania (b)	32.62	13	21	118.26	3	78	0.29	15	0	0.82	38	1	151.98	4
Rhode Island (b) (c) (d)	22.49	31	26	63.22	16	72	0.13	21	0	1.87	18	2	87.71	20
South Carolina (b) (d)	26.88	24	36	43.04	26	58	1.02	5	1	3.05	10	4	73.99	25

See footnotes at end of table.

STATE MENTAL HEALTH CONTROLLED PER CAPITA EXPENDITURES FOR STATE MENTAL HOSPITAL INPATIENT SERVICES, COMMUNITY SERVICES (STATE HOSPITAL AND OTHER COMMUNITY-BASED), RESEARCH, TRAINING AND ADMINISTRATION: FISCAL YEAR 2001—Continued

State or other jurisdiction	State psychiatric hospital inpatient			Community based			Prevention, research, and training			Administration			Total SMHA Expenditures per capita	Total rank
	Amount per capita	Rank	Percent	Amount per capita	Rank	Percent	Amount per capita	Rank	Percent	Amount per capita	Rank	Percent		
South Dakota (b)	40.60	6	67	18.98	47	31	0.24	16	0	0.82	37	1	60.65	35
Tennessee	22.18	32	32	45.91	24	66	0.08	27	0	0.97	29	1	69.13	28
Texas (b)	14.42	47	38	21.77	44	58	0.62	7	2	0.72	41	2	37.53	46
Utah (a)(b)	18.26	39	56	51.72	22	158	0.00		0	0.50	45	2	32.64	48
Vermont (b)(d)	15.68	44	12	111.17	5	85	0.00		0	3.62	8	3	130.46	5
Virginia (b)	38.80	7	60	22.74	42	35	0.56	8	1	3.09	9	5	65.18	29
Washington (b)	28.15	21	32	57.97	18	66	0.38	14	0	1.63	20	2	88.13	19
West Virginia (b)	20.56	37	81	4.01	52	16	0.00		0	0.95	31	4	25.52	51
Wisconsin (e)	15.15	46	21	56.83	19	79	0.15	20	0	0.26	47	0	72.39	27
Wyoming	26.54	25	43	32.89	35	54	0.39	13	1	1.30	25	2	61.12	33
Dist. of Columbia	181.32	1	46	216.52	1	54	0.00	0	0	NA		NA	397.84	1
Puerto Rico	8.10	52	43	9.44	51	50	0.00		0	1.34	24	7	18.88	52
Average (Mean)	25.58	32		53.46	66		0.64		1	1.70		2	81.14	
Median	25.51		35	42.96	63		0.09		0	1.30		2	72.78	

Source: The National Association of State Mental Health Program Directors Research Institute, Inc. (NRI). 2003 SMHA Profiles System.

Note: "Community Services" includes expenditures from state mental hospitals for ambulatory and residential services.

Key:

NA - Services provided but exact expenditures unallocable.

(a) Medicaid Revenues for Community Programs are not included in SMHA-Controlled Expenditures
(b) SMHA-Controlled Expenditures include funds for mental health services in jails or prisons.
(c) Children's Mental Health Expenditures are not included in SMHA-Controlled Expenditures
(d) SMHA-Controlled Expenditures includes the "majority" of publicly supported housing provided to Adults with SMI and/or Children with SED
(e) State mental health agency did not return data checklist.

Table C
ORGANIZATION OF STATE MENTAL HEALTH AGENCIES: FISCAL YEAR 2003

State or other jurisdiction	State mental health location in state government			SMHA responsibility for other disability services		How state mental health agencies organize mental health services			
	Location of state mental health agency	Director is member of governor's cabinet	Children's mental health is law unless in SMHA	Drug abuse	Mental retardation/ developmental disabilities	SMHA directly provides funds, but does not operate	SMHA funds county or city authorities	SMHA directly operates community mental health programs	Primary mechanism used
Alabama	IA	Yes	Yes	Yes	Yes	Yes			SMHA Directly Provides Funds
Alaska	HS	No	Yes	PS	Yes	Yes			SMHA Directly Provides Funds
Arizona	HD	No	Yes	Yes	OA		Yes		SMHA funds county or city mh authorities
Arkansas	HS	No	Yes	OA	PS	Yes			SMHA Directly Provides Funds
California	IA	No	Yes	OA	OA	Yes	Yes		SMHA funds county or city mh authorities
Colorado	HS	No	PU	PS	PS	Yes			SMHA Directly Provides Funds
Connecticut	IA	Yes	OA	Yes	OA	Yes	Yes	Yes	Operates some community & directly funds others
Delaware	HD	No	OA	Yes	PS	Yes		Yes	Operates some community & directly funds others
Florida	O	No	Yes	PS	PS	Yes			SMHA Directly Provides Funds
Georgia	HS	No	Yes	Yes	Yes	Yes			Operates some community & directly funds others
Hawaii	HD	No	PU	PS	PS	Yes		Yes	SMHA directly operates community-based programs
Idaho	HS	No	PU	PS	PS	Yes		Yes	SMHA directly operates community-based programs
Illinois	HS	No	Yes	PS	PS	Yes	Yes		SMHA Directly Provides Funds
Indiana	HS	No	Yes	Yes	PS	Yes			SMHA Directly Provides Funds
Iowa	HS	No	Yes	OA	Yes		Yes		SMHA funds county or city mh authorities
Kansas	HS	No	Yes	PS	PS	Yes			SMHA Directly Provides Funds
Kentucky	HD	No	Yes	Yes	Yes	Yes			SMHA Directly Provides Funds
Louisiana	HD	No	PU	PS	PS		Yes	Yes	SMHA directly operates community-based programs
Maine	IA	Yes	Yes	Yes	Yes	Yes	Yes	Yes	SMHA Directly Provides Funds
Maryland	HD	No	Yes	PS	PS	Yes	Yes		SMHA Directly Provides Funds
Massachusetts	IA	No	Yes	PS	PS	Yes		Yes	SMHA Directly Provides Funds
Michigan	NR		N.R.	Yes	NR				NR
Minnesota	HS	No	PU	PS	PS		Yes		SMHA funds county or city authorities
Mississippi	NR		N.R.	Yes	Yes				NR
Missouri	IA	Yes	Yes	Yes	Yes	Yes			SMHA Directly Provides Funds
Montana	HS	No	Yes	Yes	PS	Yes			SMHA Directly Provides Funds
Nebraska	HS	No	N.R.	Yes	NR	Yes	Yes		SMHA funds county or city authorities
Nevada	IA	No	Yes	PS	Yes			Yes	SMHA directly operates community-based programs
New Hampshire	HS	No	PU	PS	PS	Yes			SMHA Directly Provides Funds
New Jersey	HS	No	Yes	OA	PS	Yes			SMHA Directly Provides Funds
New Mexico	HD	No	OA	Yes	PS	Yes	Yes		SMHA funds county or city mh authorities
New York	IA	No	Yes	No	OA	Yes	Yes	Yes	SMHA funds county or city mh authorities
North Carolina	HS	No	Yes	Yes	Yes	Yes	Yes		SMHA funds county or city mh authorities
North Dakota	HS	No	Yes	Yes	PS	Yes			SMHA Directly Provides Funds
Ohio	IA	Yes	Yes	OA	OA	Yes	Yes		SMHA funds county or city mh authorities
Oklahoma	IA	No	Yes	Yes	OA	Yes	Yes	Yes	SMHA Directly Provides Funds
Oregon	HS	No	Yes	Yes	PS	Yes	Yes	Yes	SMHA Directly Provides Funds
Pennsylvania	HS	No	Yes	OA	PS		Yes		SMHA funds county or city mh authorities
Rhode Island	IA	Yes	OA	Yes	Yes	Yes			SMHA Directly Provides Funds
South Carolina	IA	No	Yes	OA	OA			Yes	SMHA directly operates community-based programs

See footnotes at end of table.

ORGANIZATION OF STATE MENTAL HEALTH AGENCIES: FISCAL YEAR 2003—Continued

State or other jurisdiction	State mental health location in state government			SMHA responsibility for other disability services		How state mental health agencies organize mental health services			
	Location of state mental health agency	Director is member of governor's cabinet	Children's mental health is law unless in SMHA	Drug abuse	Mental retardation/ developmental disabilities	SMHA directly provides funds, but does not operate	SMHA funds county or city authorities	SMHA directly operates community mental health programs	Primary mechanism used
South Dakota	HS	No	Yes	PS	PS	Yes			SMHA Directly Provides Funds
Tennessee	IA	Yes	Yes	OA	OA	Yes			SMHA Directly Provides Funds
Texas	O	No	Yes	OA	PS	Yes			SMHA Directly Provides Funds
Utah	HS	No	Yes	Yes	PS	Yes	Yes		SMHA funds county or city mh authorities
Vermont	HS	No	Yes	PS	Yes	Yes			SMHA Directly Provides Funds
Virginia	IA	No	Yes	Yes	Yes	Yes	Yes		SMHA funds county or city mh authorities
Washington	HS	No	Yes	PS	PS	Yes	Yes		SMHA funds county or city mh authorities
West Virginia	HS	No	Yes	Yes	Yes	Yes			SMHA Directly Provides Funds
Wisconsin	HS	No	Yes	Yes	PS		Yes		SMHA funds county or city mh authorities
Wyoming	HD	No	PU	PS	PS	Yes			SMHA Directly Provides Funds
Dist. of Columbia	IA	Yes	N.R.	OA	OA	Yes		Yes	SMHA directly operates community-based programs

Source: The National Association of State Mental Health Program Directors Research Institute, Inc. (NRI). 2003 SMHA Profiles System.

Key:
IA - Independent agency
HS - Human Services
HD - Health Dept.
O - Other structure
NR - No response
PS - Part of state mental health agency.
PU - Part of umbrella agency.
OA - Other agency

(a) Totals for column: Independent agency - 15; Human services - 24; Health Department - 8; Other structure - 2; No response - 2.
(b) Totals for column: Yes - 8; No - 41
(c) Totals for column: Yes - 36; In same umbrella agency - 7; In other agency - 4; No response - 2.
(d) Totals for column: Part of state mental health agency - 23; Part of umbrella agency - 17; Other agency - 10.
(e) Totals for column: Part of state mental health agency - 14; Part of umbrella agency - 25; Other agency - 9.
(f) Total for column: 38
(g) Total for column: 19
(h) Total for column: 14
(i) Totals for column: Directly funds, but does not operate - 26; Directly operates - 6; Funds city/county authority - 25; Other agency - 9.

Profiles of Prisoners and Prison Programming in the States
By John J. Mountjoy

Crime is down, but prison populations continue to rise. As state officials struggle with budget shortfalls, it is increasingly important to understand the changing nature of state corrections, both from a demographic perspective and a programmatic one. If state officials are to ever solve the "revolving-door-of-corrections," they must provide effective programming and planning whose ultimate goal is the reentry of offenders into society.

Introduction

Crime victimization has fallen steadily since 1994 and property crime rates are at their lowest in more than 20 years. While these numbers are promising to our society, they are not an accurate portrayal of the total state of our criminal justice and corrections systems. With more than 6.7 million citizens under probation, parole, in jail or prison, 3.1 percent of all U.S. citizens (1 in 143) find themselves in the criminal justice system; of these, more than 1.2 million are imprisoned or under supervision by the states. In 2002, state prison populations increased more than 5 percent, with only nine states reporting decreases in population.[1] Between 1995 and 2000, the number of state correctional facilities increased by 3 percent to 1,320.

As states struggle with fiscal crises, programming at all levels of state government has undergone increased scrutiny. Nowhere has this been truer than in state corrections. In 2000, state governments spent more than $35 billion on corrections.[2] Overall, state governments bear the majority burden for corrections, with 62 percent of the total cost across all levels of government, being paid by the states.[3]

In budget balancing efforts, prison programming has often been cut and in extreme circumstances, aging prisons closed. Furthermore, prisoners themselves are changing. More women and juveniles are entering the corrections system and the minority composition of prisons is changing due to an influx of Hispanic and other immigrant populations to the United States. In addition, inmates, like the rest of the population, are living longer which itself presents unique challenges to corrections in terms of programming, needs and costs. Finally, recidivism is the most critical issue facing corrections today with more than half of all released prisoners returning to prison within three years.

Profile of Prisoners

The composition of state prisons is changing. What was once a young-adult to middle-aged white male dominated population has evolved into one much more representative of the population in general and in some instances, over-representative of specific groups most notably black males. In addition, more women and juveniles are being found in state prison populations. For the most part, state prisoners are male, disproportionately black and young.

Gender

While the overall state inmate population continues to grow, it is doing so at a reduced rate—3.2 percent annually, between 1995 and 2002 (Table I). However, the female inmate population increased by 4.9 percent, more than double the male increase of 2.4 percent with women now comprising 6.3 percent of the total state prison population.[4] Since 1995, the total number of female inmates has grown by 42 percent, with approximately one-third of all state female inmates being held in three states—California, Florida and Texas.[5]

At year-end 2002, there were 60 sentenced female inmates per 100,000 women compared to 906 sentenced male inmates per 100,000 men—1 in every 1,666 women and 1 in every 110 men across the country.[6] In addition, the type of crime committed for which the inmate is incarcerated varies widely depending upon gender. For example, males are more likely to be incarcerated for committing a violent crime (50.4 percent vs. 32 percent for female offenders) and female inmates more likely to be incarcerated for committing a drug-related crime (30.4 percent vs. 19.6 percent for male offenders). Further, women are slightly more likely to be incarcerated for property crimes (26.2 percent vs. 18.8 percent for males) and both groups hover around the 10.7 percent mark for public order offenses.[7]

Race/Ethnicity

No area of corrections is changing more rapidly than that of race and ethnicity. At year-end 2001, nearly as many blacks (2,166,000) as whites (2,203,000) had ever served time in prison and His-

Table A: Lifetime Chance of Going to State or Federal Prison for the First Time

	Percent of resident population expected to go to state or federal prison, by year					
	1974	1979	1986	1991	1997	2001
Gender						
Male	3.6%	4.1%	6.0%	9.1%	10.6%	11.3%
Female	0.3	0.4	0.6	1.1	1.5	1.8
Race/Hispanic Origin						
White (a)	1.2	1.4	2.0	2.5	3.1	3.4
Male	2.2	2.5	3.6	4.4	5.4	5.9
Female	0.2	0.2	0.3	0.5	0.7	0.9
Black (a)	7.0	7.2	9.3	16.5	17.7	18.6
Male	13.4	13.4	17.4	29.4	31.0	32.2
Female	1.1	1.4	1.8	3.6	4.9	5.6
Hispanic	2.2	3.3	6.2	9.5	10.5	10.0
Male	4.0	6.0	11.1	16.3	18.0	17.2
Female	0.4	0.4	0.9	1.5	2.2	2.2

Source: U.S. Department of Justice, Bureau of Justice Statistics, *Prevalence of Imprisonment in the U.S. Population*, 1974–2001.

Key:
(a)—Excludes persons of Hispanic origin.

panics numbered about half of either group (997,000).[8] This parity between black and white populations is shocking given that blacks comprise only 12.7 percent of the total U.S. population.[9] Further, nearly 17 percent of all adult black males have served time in prison and based on current trends and incarceration rates, a black male born in 2001 has a 1 in 3 chance of going to prison at some point in his life, while a Hispanic male has a 17.2 percent chance and a white male only around a 6 percent chance; black females, a 1 in 19 chance—six times more likely than their white counterparts. This is quite significant given that in 1974, black males had a lifetime incarceration likelihood of 13.4 percent, Hispanics 4 percent and white males 2.2 percent. The same trend holds true for black females, up from 1.1 percent in 1974 to 5.6 percent in 2001. Hispanic women's likelihood of incarceration rose from 0.4 percent in 1974 to 2.2 percent in 2001, and white females rose to 0.9 percent in 2001, up from 0.2 percent in 1974[10] (Table A). Overall, blacks are more likely to go to prison than other racial and ethnic groups. They comprise the largest group within the active state prison population at 45.4 percent of all state inmates. White prisoners make up 35 percent and Hispanics, 16.9 percent.[11]

The types of offenses committed that resulted in incarceration also vary by race/ethnicity, although in different terms than by gender. For ex-

ample, all three major categories of race/ethnicity committed violent acts, such as murder, rape or assault at much the same rate, around 49 percent of those incarcerated. However, a significant difference exists when looking at drug offenses. Blacks are almost twice as likely to be incarcerated for a drug-related offense as a white inmate—25.4 percent for blacks, 13.5 percent for whites. This figure also holds true for Hispanics with 22.8 percent currently in prison for drug-related offenses. The opposite is true for property offenses, such as burglary, motor vehicle theft and fraud. White inmates incarcerated committed these crimes at a rate of 23.9 percent, as opposed to 16.8 percent for blacks and 15.8 percent for Hispanics.[12] Interestingly, the figures on violent prisoners vs. drug-related offenders seem to fly in the face of some arguments that a majority of state prisoners are non-violent offenders incarcerated due to draconian drug laws. Based on this data, the two groups seem to be evenly split (Table B).

Age

Inmate age is another critical piece of demographic information that is significant in determining corrections costs and programming. While the arrival of new inmates may be slowing, those that are in prison are often younger and are staying longer, due in part to relatively new public policies such as "truth-in-sentencing" laws, mandatory sentencing laws, the abolishment in several states of parole boards and an increase in the severity of crimes committed. While older inmates pose challenges to state correctional systems for specialized health programming, younger inmates pose their own set of difficulties in the development of programming specialized for their educational, health and job training needs. The additional challenge for younger inmates is developing programs that will assist them in making it in a post-release world.

Male prisoners generally fall between the ages of 20 and 39, with the distribution for white males being fairly even in all categories 20 to 54 years of age. Black inmates, on the other hand, tend to have a higher concentration in the 20 to 39 range, while

Table B: Estimated Number of Sentenced Prisoners
Under State Jurisdiction, by Offense, Race and Hispanic Origin, 2001

	All	Male	Female	White	Black	Hispanic
Total	1,208,700	1,132,500	76,200	424,200	548,800	205,300
Violent offenses	596,100	571,700	24,400	208,100	267,700	102,600
Murder (a)	159,200	150,700	8,500	51,500	77,100	27,800
Manslaughter	16,900	15,000	1,900	6,300	6,300	3,500
Rape	30,900	30,600	300	15,100	11,700	2,700
Other sexual assault	87,600	86,600	1,000	50,700	21,300	12,600
Robbery	155,200	150,100	5,200	34,100	91,100	26,200
Assault	118,800	113,200	5,600	38,700	50,300	25,300
Other violent	27,400	25,500	1,900	11,700	10,000	4,700
Property offenses	233,000	213,000	20,000	101,800	92,300	32,500
Burglary	104,700	101,300	3,400	45,700	41,200	14,700
Larceny	45,500	39,600	5,800	17,400	20,300	6,100
Motor vehicle theft	18,000	17,300	700	6,900	6,700	4,200
Fraud	33,700	25,400	8,400	17,100	13,000	3,100
Other property	31,100	29,500	1,600	14,700	11,100	4,500
Drug offenses	246,100	222,900	23,200	57,300	139,500	47,000
Public-order offenses (b)	130,000	121,700	8,300	55,900	47,200	22,300
	3,600	3,200	400	900	1,700	800

Source: U.S. Department of Justice, Bureau of Justice Statistics, *Prisoners in 2002*.
Note: Data are for inmates with a sentence of more than 1 year under the jurisdiction of State correctional authorities. The number of inmates by offense were estimated using the Survey of Inmates in State Correctional Facilities, 1997.

Key:
(a)—Includes nonnegligent manslaughter.
(b)—Includes weapons, drunk driving, court offenses, commercialized vice, morals and decency charges, liquor law violations, and other public-order offenses.
(c)—Includes juvenile offenses and unspecified felonies.

Table C: Number of Sentenced Prisoners Under State or Federal Jurisdiction,
by Offense, Race and Hispanic Origin and Age, 2002

	Male				Female			
	Total (a)	White (b)	Black (b)	Hispanic	Total (a)	White (b)	Black (b)	Hispanic
Total	1,291,326	436,800	586,700	235,000	89,044	35,400	36,000	15,000
18–19	36,400	8,800	17,300	8,400	1,300	700	500	200
20–24	218,300	59,400	105,400	47,400	8,900	3,700	3,100	2,100
25–29	248,400	70,700	123,000	49,300	15,900	5,500	6,500	3,000
30–34	245,700	83,900	111,400	46,200	22,100	8,500	9,200	3,600
35–39	220,600	79,400	102,500	34,200	19,400	7,800	8,300	2,900
40–44	150,200	56,300	64,600	25,300	10,700	4,100	4,700	1,400
45–54	127,300	55,800	48,500	18,800	8,400	3,700	3,000	1,400
55 or older	38,900	21,500	10,800	4,800	1,900	1,200	500	200

Source: U.S. Department of Justice, Bureau of Justice Statistics, *Prisoners in 2002*.

Key:
(a)—Includes American Indians, Alaska Natives, Asians, Native Hawaiians, and other Pacific Islanders.
(b)—Excludes Hispanics.

Hispanics generally fall into the 20 to 34 category. A startling figure is that approximately 10 percent of the total black male population between the ages of 25 to 29 is in prison, compared to 2.4 percent for Hispanics and 1.2 percent for white males. Female prisoners generally fall between the ages of 25 to 44. Both white and black female inmates fall into this category, but Hispanic female inmates are generally a bit younger, fitting into the 20 to 39 age group. All told, black women are twice as likely to end up in prison as Hispanics and more than five times as likely as white females[13] (Table C).

Perhaps the most challenging aspect of age in prisons is that of the older offender, specifically those over the age of 50. In 2000, 8.2 percent of the total state prison population was over 50,[14] up from 6.6 percent in 1996—or 113,000 vs. 63,000.[15] While the most recent number is nearly twice the previous, this gives an indication of the overall growth in state prison populations. As previously noted, it is not a factor of older offenders entering the corrections system; rather it is a factor of offenders being incarcerated longer due to a shift in public policy that is making the criminal justice system and corrections less flexible, with overall annual release rates on the decline—down from 37 percent in 1990 to 33 percent in 2001.[16] Interestingly, states that have "truth-in-sentencing" laws do not historically incarcerate offenders longer than states with no such laws. In 1999, "truth-in-sentencing" states incarcerated inmates for an average of 53 months, while the states with no law held offenders for 52 months.[17]

Prison Programming

Approximately 95 percent of all inmates currently in state prison will one day be released back into the community, with 592,000 prisoners released from state prisons in 2001—up 46 percent from 1990[18] (Table J). In simpler terms, that is 1,600 offenders released back into the community every day. As such, corrections agencies have a responsibility to rehabilitate and prepare inmates for their eventual release back into the community. Currently, states provide a range of mandatory and discretionary programs covering health care, drug and alcohol treatment, education and reentry programming (Table K).

Overall, prison programs work. Inmates that participate in educational, vocational and work-related programs are more successful at avoiding recidivism after release than their counterparts who did not have programming.[19] Considering the alternative (67 percent of released offenders will be rearrested within three years and 47 percent will return to prison, either for a new crime or a technical violation)[20] (Table D), state corrections agencies should be looking at creating more programming.

However, despite a tradition of providing educational and employment training to inmates and the resultant effectiveness in improving outcomes upon release from prison, overall prison programming has declined. In 1991, 42 percent of soon-to-be-released prisoners reported participating in education programs, compared with 37 percent in 1997; vocational programs declined from 31 percent to 27 percent during the same period. A key reason for this decline

Table D: Recidivism of State Prisoners Released in 1983 and 1994, By Offense Type

Most serious offense for which released	Percent of prisoners released in:		Percent rearrested within 3 years, among prisoners released in:		Percent reconvicted within 3 years, among prisoners released in:	
	1993	1994	1983	1994	1983	1994
All released prisoners	100 %	100 %	62.5%	67.5%	46.8%	46.9%
Violent	34.6	22.5	59.6	61.7	41.9	39.9
Property	48.3	33.5	68.1	73.8	53.0	53.4
Drug	9.5	32.6	50.4	66.7	35.3	47.0
Public-order	6.4	9.7	54.6	62.2	41.5	42.0
Other	1.1	1.7	76.8	64.7	62.9	42.1

Source: U.S. Department of Justice, Bureau of Justice Statistics, *Sourcebook of Criminal Justice Statistics* 2001.

has been the rapid growth of prison populations followed by the resultant reshuffling of inmates among institutions to meet the increasing demand for incarceration. As a result, literacy and higher education programs in many states have been cut with a shift to more short-term programs that cost less.[21]

The Urban Institute, in its 2002 report *The Practice and Promise of Prison Programming*, identified nine general characteristics that make prison programming successful.

- Focusing on skills applicable to the job market;
- Matching offenders' needs with program offerings;
- Ensuring that participation is timed to be close to an offenders' release date;
- Providing programming for at least several months;
- Targeting offenders' needs that are changeable and may contribute to crime, such as attitudes and pro-social activities;
- Providing programs that cover each individual's needs and that are well-integrated with other prison programs to avoid potential redundancy or conflict across programs;
- Ensuring that prison programming is followed by treatment and services upon release from prison;
- Relying on effective program design, implementation and monitoring;
- Involving researchers in programs as evaluators.[22]

Health Care

Since 1990, state corrections budgets have increased annually by 7.5 percent and from 1998 to 2001 outpaced overall state budget growth by 3.7 percent.[23] The health care component of state corrections budgets continues to climb and is now just over 10 percent or $3.7 billion, of the total corrections cost.[24] Like the health care costs of private citizens, the cost borne by states on behalf of inmates is enormous and steadily growing. For example, communicable and chronic diseases are rampant in prison with a population that is especially vulnerable to sexually transmitted diseases (STDs). Further, inmates are susceptible to Hepatitis B and C, HIV/AIDS, tuberculosis, and a range of chronic conditions such as hypertension, diabetes and asthma. These often preventable conditions significantly increase the cost of health care, raising it from an average daily cost of $7.15 for a healthy inmate[25] into the tens of thousands of dollars for one treatment for an inmate with a chronic condition, such as hepatitis or HIV/AIDS.

Like many aspects of corrections policy, health care is rife with court mandates which largely determine the minimum levels of programming and services. As a result, many state prisoners have access to better health care than their counterparts on the outside, and in most instances, get that health care for free. For example, 47 states provide MRIs, 44 states provide pacemaker implants, 42 states provide preventive dentistry and 25 states provide organ transplants.[26] To offset these costs, many states have started co-pay programs for inmates, although the recouping of total costs is minimal.

One programmatic factor that is popular throughout a majority of states is the use of private contracts for all or some of their health care services. In 11 states, private providers cover all health care services, in 19 states the corrections agency jointly handles health care services with a private contractor and in eight states health care services are provided by a partnering of the state, private contractors and public health agencies.[27]

Mental illness is also a great cause for concern, with prisons and jails often becoming the dumping ground for those with a range of severe mental problems. Further, the criminal justice and corrections systems have traditionally been without the knowledge and tools to effectively address these issues, one major factor in the enormous scale of the $15 billion annual cost to house inmates with psychiatric problems in Americas jails and prisons.[28]

Prisons are improving their response to this immense need, with 70 percent of all state facilities providing mental health screenings during the intake process, 65 percent of state facilities conducting psychiatric assessments of inmates, 51 percent of state facilities providing 24-hour mental health care, 71 percent providing therapy and counseling to inmates from a trained mental health professional and 66 percent of state facilities help inmates obtain community mental health services once released.[29] (For more policy recommendations regarding the criminal justice system and the mentally ill, visit The Council of State Governments Eastern Regional Conference's *Mental Health Consensus Project*, at http://www.consensusproject.org.)

Elderly inmates pose problems from the stand point of increased costs and specialized health care. In many states, the increase in this population is overwhelming the total corrections health care budget with an inmate over age 60 costing, on average, $70,000 a year to house while a younger inmate costs around $22,000. These costs increase the longer an inmate stays in prison. For example, if a 60-year-old inmate lives to 80 years of age, these costs will rise to $1.4 million annually.[30] Twenty-six states currently have either grouped or geriatric facilities. Eighteen states have specialized hospice or end-of-life care for terminal inmates, while 36 states have medical or compassionate release policies[31] (Table L).

Drug/Alcohol Abuse & Treatment

Drug-related crimes accounted for 12 percent of the 13.9 million arrests made nationally in 2000. Of these, 19 percent were for the manufacture or sale of drugs and 81 percent were for possession.[32] Currently, drug-related offenses account for 21 percent of the total state prison population.[33] As a result, one of the most prevalent groupings of programs in prison is that which addresses drug and alcohol abuse. The need is enormous: 83 percent of all state prisoners reported the past use of drugs and 57 percent reported the use of drugs within the month prior to the commission of the offense for which they are incarcerated. Interestingly, as of 1998 only eight states provided any sort of intake drug-screening; ironic given the destructive nature of abuse both prior to arrival and while in prison[34] (Table E). As of 2000, 39 states provided some sort of drug and alcohol treatment program, ranging from therapeutic communities and special housing to special peer groups, self-help programs and professional counseling.[35]

Education

State prison inmates are generally less educated than their counterparts in the general population (Table F). For example, 39.7 percent of state inmates have not obtained a high school diploma, compared to 18.4 percent of those on the outside. This trend continues when talking about college or other post-secondary education. While 48.4 percent of the general population has completed some form of higher education, only 11.4 percent of inmates have accomplished the same. As expected, educational programs are the single largest set of programs existing in state prisons, with more than 90 percent of institutions offering some form of educational programming and just fewer than 84 percent offering high school/GED courses (Tables G, H). Further, nearly 56 percent currently offer some form of employment or vocational training.[36]

Educational accomplishment by state prisoners varies by gender and race/ethnicity. Minority prisoners are less likely to have received their high school diploma or GED than their white counterparts. Likewise, female offenders are more likely than their male cohorts to have received a secondary education and to have even received some higher education. [37]

Table E: Alchohol - or Drug-Involved State Prisoners Treated for Substance Abuse, By Selected Characteristics, 1997

Characteristic	Estimated number of state prisoners	Treatment for substance abuse		Participation in other substance abuse programs	
		Ever	Since admission	Ever	Since admission
Total	806,758	41.5%	14.6%	49.4%	31.9%
Sex					
Male	754,418	40.5	14.2	49.4	31.9
Female	52,340	55.6	19.6	49.3	31.9
Race/Hispanic origin					
White, non-Hispanic	271,345	51.8	17.0	58.0	36.3
Black, non-Hispanic	367,331	36.6	13.5	46.7	31.6
Hispanic	142,610	33.8	12.5	39.2	23.9
Other	25,472	46.2	16.2	54.2	34.8
Age					
24 or younger	158,705	29.3	10.2	37.9	22.6
25–34	316,744	43.1	15.2	50.2	33.1
35–44	242,579	47.4	16.8	54.4	35.5
45–54	71,936	42.4	14.9	53.9	35.5
55 or older	16,794	36.7	10.1	52.4	31.8

Source: U.S. Department of Justice, Bureau of Justice Statistics, Substance Abuse & Treatment, State and Federal Prisoners, 1997.

Table F: Education By Age, Race/Ethnicity and Gender, 1997

	Percent of state prison inmates		Percent of state prison inmates				Percent of state prison inmates		
	Male	Female	24 or >	25-34	35-44	45 or <	White	Black	Hispanic
Educational Attainment									
8th grade or less	14.3%	13.6%	16.3%	12.1%	12.7%	20.7%	10.9%	11.7%	27.9%
Some high school	25.3	28.2	35.3	27.2	21.7	13.9	16.3	32.4	25.1
GED	28.9	22.3	31.2	29.4	27.8	23.1	35.2	24.8	24.7
High school diploma	20.4	21.6	13.6	21.5	23.5	21.3	22.8	21.0	14.9
Postsecondary	8.8	11.2	3.6	8.3	11.3	14.2	11.4	8.4	5.5
College graduate or <	2.3	3.1	0.1	1.5	3.0	6.9	3.5	1.6	1.9
High school completion									
Completed high school	25.3	30.3	14.1	25.4	30.0	33.4	29.9	25.5	17.2
Earned GED	35.2	27.9	34.4	35.3	35.5	32.0	42.9	30.4	29.7
In prison/jail	26.3	15.9	27.4	26.3	25.0	22.3	30.0	23.2	23.4
Outside prison/jail	8.9	11.9	6.9	9.0	10.5	9.6	12.9	7.2	6.3
Educational programs since admission									
Total	52.0	50.1	57.8	52.4	49.6	46.5	48.8	53.8	52.6
Basic	3.1	3.3	2.5	3.0	3.2	4.3	2.1	3.3	4.8
GED/high school	23.6	21.3	35.5	23.3	19.0	15.4	18.7	26.1	25.0
College	10.0	9.1	6.4	10.1	11.4	11.6	12.4	9.0	7.1
English as 2nd language	1.2	0.5	0.8	1.1	1.4	1.6	0.1	0.1	6.4
Vocational	32.4	29.5	30.5	34.0	32.5	28.7	32.0	33.7	29.1
Other	2.5	3.8	2.3	2.5	2.9	2.8	3.0	2.5	1.8
Number of Prison Inmates	989,419	66,076	208,955	402,693	310,405	133,442	351,742	490,384	179,301

Source: U.S. Department of Justice, Bureau of Justice Statistics, *Education and Correctional Populations, April 2003.*

Table G: Educational Programs Offered in State, Federal and Private Prisons, 2000 and 1995, and Local Jails, 1999

	State prisons		Federal prisons		Private prisons		Jails
Educational programs	2000	1995	2000	1995	2000	1995	1999
With an educational program	91.2%	88.0%	100.0%	100.0%	87.6%	71.8%	60.3%
Basic adult education	80.4	76.0	97.4	92.0	61.6	40.0	24.7
Secondary education	83.6	80.3	98.7	100.0	70.7	51.8	54.8
College courses	26.7	31.4	80.5	68.8	27.3	18.2	3.4
Special education	39.6	33.4	59.7	34.8	21.9	27.3	10.8
Vocational training	55.7	54.5	93.5	73.2	44.2	25.5	6.5
Study release programs	7.7	9.3	6.5	5.4	28.9	32.7	9.3
Without an educational program	8.8	12.0	0.0	0.0	12.4	28.2	39.7
Number of facilities	1,307	1,278	(a)	(a)	242	110	2,819

Source: U.S. Department of Justice, Bureau of Justice Statistics, *Education and Correctional Populations*, April 2003.

Key:
(a)—Changed definitions prevent meaningful comparisons of the numbers of federal facilities, 1995 and 2000.

Table H: Participation in Educational Programs for State and Federal Prison Inmates, 1997 and 1991, for Local Jail Inmates, 1996

Educational programs	Prison inmates				Jails
	State		Federal		
	1997	1991	1997	1991	1996
Total	51.9%	56.6%	56.4%	67.0%	22.9%
Basic	3.1	5.3	1.9	10.4	0.4
GED/high school	23.4	27.3	23.0	27.3	7.8
College courses	9.9	13.9	12.9	18.9	6.1
English as a 2nd language	1.2	(a)	5.7	(a)	(a)
Vocational	32.2	31.2	31.0	29.4	7.0
Other	2.6	2.6	5.6	8.4	3.4
Number of inmates	1,046,136	709,042	87,624	501,159	2,055,942

Source: U.S. Department of Justice, Bureau of Justice Statistics, *Education and Correctional Populations*, April 2003.

Key:
(a)—Not available.

Reentry

The number of inmates exiting prison—600,000 individuals this year alone—and returning to communities they left behind is increasing. The public safety implications are obvious, especially when considering that nearly 1 in 5 of these offenders exits without any post-release supervision. The cost implications of re-entry are also significant: parole revocations are now the fastest growing category of prison admissions.

People with criminal records typically face an overwhelming number of obstacles to successful re-entry, including substance abuse, unemployment and the search for housing. Addressing these problems is difficult under any circumstance, but particularly when service providers tend not to consider people with criminal records as part of their clientele.[38]

Thirty-three percent of the prison population leaves correctional institutions annually. As discussed earlier, because the length of sentences of prisoners has increased, the ratio of the number of persons released to the number incarcerated fell in the 1990s. Given the likely slower growth of the huge prison population in the 2000s, we can expect the re-entry of some 600,000–700,000 inmates into civil society per year in the coming decade.[39] This influx of prisoners back into the community is likely to overwhelm an already over-burdened parole and community supervision system. As a result, while community supervision is viewed as a solution to the growing prob-lem of prison overcrowding, few additional resources are being concentrated on this less expensive and often more effective area of corrections. Effective re-entry programs must address several categories, including education, work training and job placement, familial relationship-building, appropriate housing and living arrangements, direct supervision from probation authorities, medical care (preventative and chronic care) and drug treatment/testing to ensure sobriety.

Conclusion

The effects of recidivism are driving the costs of corrections. While the overall volume of prisoner entry has plateaued, sentences and the length of time served by inmates are growing. Combined with these changes is an overall shift in the composition of the inmate population, with a move towards more women, juveniles and Hispanics. This in turn dictates the various needs of the inmate population and the types of programming that will be successful at ultimately preparing offenders for release. Corrections officials need to be respondent to these changes, providing suitable educational, health and work programs that will benefit not only the inmate, but society in general. The revolving door of corrections is continuing with no end in sight. While state budget shortfalls have forced extensive corrections program cuts, their long-term costs are immeasurable to inmates and communities.

Notes

[1] U.S. Dept. of Justice, Bureau of Justice Statistics, *Prisoners in 2002* NCJ 200248, (Washington, D.C.: U.S. Dept. of Justice, July 2003).

[2] The Council of State Governments, *The Book of the States*, 2003, (Lexington, KY: The Council of State Governments, 2003).

[3] U.S. Dept. of Justice, Bureau of Justice Statistics, *Sourcebook of Criminal Justice Statistics*, 2001, (Washington, D.C.: U.S. Dept. of Justice, 2002).

[4] Ibid.

[5] U.S. Dept. of Justice, Bureau of Justice Statistics, *Prisoners in 2002*.

[6] Ibid.

[7] Ibid.

[8] U.S. Dept. of Justice, Bureau of Justice Statistics, *Prevalence of Imprisonment in the U.S. Population*, 1974–2001 NCJ 197976, (Washington, D.C.: U.S. Dept. of Justice, August 2003).

[9] U.S. Dept. of Commerce, U.S. Census Bureau, *State Population Estimates by Race Alone and Hispanic or Latino Origin*, July 1, 2002, http://www.census.gov.

[10] U.S. Dept. of Justice, Bureau of Justice Statistics, *Prevalence of Imprisonment in the U.S. Population*, 1974–2001.

[11] U.S. Dept. of Justice, Bureau of Justice Statistics, *Prisoners in 2002*.

[12] Ibid.

[13] Ibid.

[14] Ronald Aday, *Aging Prisoners: Crisis in American Corrections*, (Westport, CT: Praeger Publishers, 2003).

[15] Matt Grayson, "Geriatric Jailbirds: Creating Budget Ailments," *State Trends* Summer 1997, no. 3.

[16] U.S. Dept. of Justice, Bureau of Justice Statistics, *Reentry Trends in the U.S.: Releases from State Prison*, http://www.ojp.usdoj.gov/bjs/reentry/releases.htm.

[17] U.S. Dept. of Justice, Bureau of Justice Statistics, *Sourcebook of Criminal Justice Statistics*, 2001, (Washington, D.C.: U.S. Dept. of Justice, 2002).

[18] U.S. Dept. of Justice, Bureau of Justice Statistics, *Prison and Jail Inmates at Midyear 2002* NCJ 198877, (Washington, D.C.: U.S. Dept. of Justice, April 2003).

[19] Sarah Lawrence, Daniel P. Mears, Glenn Dubin, Jeremy Travis, *The Practice and Promise of Prison Programming*, (Washington, D.C.: The Urban Institute, May 2002).

[20] U.S. Dept. of Justice, Bureau of Justice Statistics, *Sourcebook of Criminal Justice Statistics*, 2001.

[21] Sarah Lawrence, *et al.*

[22] Ibid.

[23] National Association of State Budget Officers, *2001 State Expenditure Report*, Summer 2002, http://www.nasbo.org/Publications/2002ExpendReport.pdf.

[24] Chad Kinsella, *TrendsAlert: Corrections Health Care Costs*, (Lexington, KY: The Council of State Governments, December 2003).

[25] U.S. Bureau of Prisons, National Institute of Corrections, *Prison Health Care Survey: An Analysis of factors Influencing Per Capita Costs*, (June 2000).

[26] Ibid.

[27] U.S. Bureau of Prisons, National Institute of Corrections, *Corrections Agency Collaboration with Public Health*, (September 2003).

[28] Treatment Advocacy Center, *Criminalization of Americans with Severe Mental Illnesses*, http://www.psychlaws.org/GeneralResources/Fact3.htm.

[29] U.S. Dept. of Justice, Bureau of Justice Statistics, *Mental Health Treatment in State Prisons, 2000* NCJ 188215, (Washington, D.C.: U.S. Dept. of Justice, July 2001).

[30] Aday.

[31] Ibid.

[32] U.S. Dept. of Justice, Bureau of Justice Statistics, *Sourcebook of Criminal Justice Statistics*, 2001.

[33] U.S. Dept. of Justice, Bureau of Justice Statistics, *Substance Abuse and Treatment, State and Federal Prisoners, 1997*, (Washington, D.C.: U.S. Dept. of Justice), January 1999.

[34] U.S. Bureau of Prisons, National Institute of Corrections, *Prison Health Care Survey: An Analysis of factors Influencing Per Capita Costs*.

[35] American Correctional Association, *Corrections Compendium* 25, no. 6, (June 2000), 13–15.

[36] U.S. Dept. of Justice, Bureau of Justice Statistics, *Education and Correctional Populations* NCJ 195670, (Washington, D.C.: U.S. Dept. of Justice, January 2003).

[37] Ibid.

[38] Reentry Policy Council, Background, The Council of State Governments, Eastern Regional Conference, http://www.reentrypolicy.org/.

[39] Richard Freeman, "Can we close the revolving door?: Recidivism vs. Employment of Ex-Offenders in the U.S.," Urban Institute Reentry Roundtable, New York University Law School, May 19–20, 2003.

About the Author

John J. Mountjoy is associate director for national policy coordination for The Council of State Governments. He has specialized in Public Safety and

Justice policy, managing CSG's national efforts for both the Interstate Compact for Adult Offender Supervision and the Interstate Compact for Juveniles.

He holds both a Masters in Public Administration and a B.A. in Communications from Western Kentucky University.

Table I
CHANGE IN THE NUMBER OF SENTENCED PRISONERS UNDER JURISDICTION OF STATE AND FEDERAL CORRECTIONAL AUTHORITIES, BY REGION AND JURISDICTION, 1995-2001

State or other jurisdiction	Population difference (1995 to 2001)	Percent change	Average annual percent change
United States	259,490	23.9%	3.6%
Federal	52,846	63.2	8.5
State	206,644	20.6	3.2
Northeast	8,609	5.6	0.9
Connecticut	2,857	27.4	4.1
Maine	315	23.8	3.6
Massachusetts (a)(b)	(1,069)	-10.3	-1.8
New Hampshire	377	18.7	2.9
New Jersey	1,076	4.0	0.7
New York	-952	-1.4	-0.2
Pennsylvania	5,647	17.4	2.7
Rhode Island	93	5.1	0.8
Vermont	265	25.3	3.8
Midwest	47,501	24.7	3.7
Illinois	6,690	17.8	2.8
Indiana (a)	4,837	30.1	4.5
Iowa	2,056	34.8	5.1
Kansas	1,523	21.6	3.3
Michigan (a)	7,737	18.8	2.9
Minnesota	1,760	36.3	5.3
Missouri	9,602	50.2	7.0
Nebraska	859	28.6	4.3
North Dakota	473	86.9	11.0
Ohio	618	1.4	0.2
South Dakota	932	49.8	7.0
Wisconsin	10,414	(c)	(c)
South	93,089	20.8	3.2
Alabama	6,008	29.8	4.4
Arkansas	3,556	41.7	6.0
Delaware	1,020	33.8	5.0
Dist. of Columbia (d)	(8,247)	(c)	(c)
Florida	8,532	13.4	2.1
Georgia	11,736	34.3	5.0
Kentucky	3,044	25.2	3.8
Louisiana	10,515	41.7	6.0
Maryland	2,392	11.7	1.9
Mississippi	8,225	67.1	8.9
North Carolina (a)	-282	-1.0	-0.2
Oklahoma	4,629	25.5	3.9
South Carolina	2,591	13.6	2.2
Tennessee	8,465	55.7	7.7
Texas	25,290	19.8	3.1
Virginia	3,934	14.4	2.3
West Virginia	1,681	67.7	9.0
West	57,445	27.7	4.2
Alaska	-122	-6.0	-1.0
Arizona	6,172	30.4	4.5
California (a)	25,550	19.4	3.0
Colorado	6,385	57.7	7.9
Hawaii	1,080	41.7	6.0
Idaho	2,678	80.5	10.3
Montana	1,329	66.5	8.9
Nevada	2,488	32.3	4.8
New Mexico	1,483	37.8	5.5
Oregon	4,898	75.2	9.8
Utah	1,803	52.3	7.3
Washington	3,412	29.4	4.4
Wyoming (a)	289	20.7	3.2

Source: U.S. Department of Justice, Bureau of Justice Statistics, *Sourcebook of Criminal Justice Statistics 2001.*
Key:
(a) Population difference and percent change may be slightly overestimated due to a change in reporting from custody to jurisdiction counts.

(b) Excludes sentenced inmates held in local jails or houses of correction.
(c) Not calculated because of changes in reporting procedures.
(d) Responsibility for sentenced felons was transferred to the Federal Bureau of Prisons as a result of the 1997 Revitalization Act.

Table J
PRISONERS RELEASED FROM STATE OR FEDERAL JURISDICTION,
BY REGION AND JURISDICTION, 1999–2001

State or other jurisdiction	2001	2000	1999	Percent change 1999–2001
United States total	630,207	608,096	576,680	9.3%
Federal	38,370	35,259	31,816	20.6
State	591,837	572,837	544,864	8.6
Northeast	69,373	70,646	65,350	6.2
Connecticut	6,331	5,918	5,283	19.8
Maine	723	677	698	3.6
Massachusetts	2,482	2,889	2,914	-14.8
New Hampshire	1,030	1,044	979	5.2
New Jersey	16,064	15,362	14,734	9.0
New York	28,101	28,828	26,652	5.4
Pennsylvania	10,376	11,759	10,028	3.5
Rhode Island (a)	3,197	3,223	. . .	. . .
Vermont	1,069	946	839	27.4
Midwest	124,030	114,382	106,860	16.1
Illinois	36,313	28,876	25,995	39.7
Indiana	12,207	11,053	10,317	18.3
Iowa	5,357	4,379	4,715	13.6
Kansas	4,270	5,231	4,503	-5.2
Michigan	11,928	10,874	11,243	6.1
Minnesota	4,250	4,244	4,475	-5.0
Missouri	13,892	13,346	12,267	13.2
Nebraska	1,738	1,503	1,558	11.6
North Dakota	715	598	671	6.6
Ohio	24,953	24,793	23	8.9
South Dakota	1,380	1,327	1,311	5.3
Wisconsin	7,027	8,158	6,895	1.9
South	223,185	214,015	202,919	10.0
Alabama	7,905	7,136	8,194	-3.5
Arkansas	6,613	6,308	5,403	22.4
Delaware	2,330	2,260	2,180	6.9
District of Columbia	1,581	3,238	5,471	-71.1
Florida	34,015	33,994	29,889	13.8
Georgia	15,758	14,797	17,173	-8.2
Kentucky	8,234	7,733	6,509	26.5
Louisiana	15,031	14,536	15,241	-1.4
Maryland	10,050	10,004	10,327	-2.7
Mississippi	5,685	4,940	4,136	37.5
North Carolina	8,935	9,687	10,710	-16.6
Oklahoma	8,265	6,628	6,140	34.6
South Carolina	8,627	8,676	7,942	8.6
Tennessee	12,690	13,893	12,361	2.7
Texas	66,228	59,776	52,318	. . .
Virginia	9,816	9,148	7,685	27.7
West Virginia	1,422	1,261	1,240	14.7
West	175,249	173,794	169,735	3.2
Alaska	2,041	2,599	2,504	-18.5
Arizona	9,053	9,100	8,982	0.8
California	129,982	129,621	129,528	0.4
Colorado	6,634	5,881	5,346	24.1
Hawaii	1,581	1,379	1,332	18.7
Idaho	2,539	2,697	1,724	47.3
Montana	1,246	1,031	1,044	19.3
Nevada	4,480	4,374	4,536	-1.2
New Mexico (b)	3,194	3,383	1,997	. . .
Oregon	3,668	3,371	3,185	15.2
Utah	3,151	2,897	2,554	23.4
Washington	6,957	6,764	6,344	9.7
Wyoming	723	697	659	9.7

Source: U.S. Department of Justice, Bureau of Justice Statistics, *Prison and Jail Inmates at Midyear*, 2002.
Key:
. . .—Not calculated due to changes in reporting.
(a) Comparable data were not available for all three years.
(b) Data may not be comparable from year to year due to changing reporting methods.

Table K
NUMBER OF STATE AND FEDERAL CORRECTIONAL FACILITIES PROVIDING
WORK EDUCATION AND COUNSELING PROGRAMS, JUNE 30, 2000

Characteristics		Type of facility			All facilities	
	Total	Federal	State	Private	Confinement	Community
Facilities						
All facilities	1,668	84	1,320	264	1,208	460
With work programs	1,519	77	1,249	193	1,174	345
Prison industries	572	68	482	22	555	17
Facility support services (a)	1,381	77	1,161	143	1,150	231
Farming/agriculture	373	6	346	21	346	27
Public works assignments	953	33	830	90	729	224
Other work programs	287	3	229	55	171	116
Without work programs (b)	149	7	71	71	34	115
With education programs	1,481	77	1,192	212	1,140	341
Basic adult education	1,275	75	1,051	149	1,062	213
Secondary (c)	1,340	76	1,093	171	1,096	244
Special (d)	617	46	518	53	550	67
Vocational training	907	72	728	107	820	87
College	477	62	349	66	410	67
Study release	175	5	100	70	45	130
Without education programs (e)	187	7	128	52	68	119
With counseling programs	1,603	77	1,284	242	1,177	427
Drug dependency, counseling, awareness	1,480	77	1,175	228	1,095	385
Alcohol dependency, counseling, awareness	1,464	77	1,162	225	1,102	362
Psychological, psychiatric counseling	1,038	77	849	112	906	132
Employment	1,076	74	816	186	790	286
Life skills, community adjustment	1,187	75	902	210	895	292
HIV/AIDS	899	69	697	133	734	165
Parenting	763	74	558	131	580	183
Sex offender	338	38	449	51	443	95
Other	400	11	350	39	328	72
Without counseling programs (f)	65	7	158	22	31	33
Inmates participating in work programs (g)	808,118	75,368	682,262	50,488	769,902	38,216

Source: U.S. Department of Justice, Bureau of Justice Statistics, Census of State and Federal Correctional Facilities, 2000.

Key:

(a) Includes office work, administration, food services, laundry, building maintenance, repair, construction and similar programs.

(b) The number without work programs includes 43 facilities that did not report any data for this item.

(c) Includes General Equivalency Diploma (GED).

(d) Includes programs for inmates with learning disabilities.

(e) The number of facilities without education programs includes 42 facilities that did not report any data for this item.

(f) The number of facilities without counseling programs includes 41 facilities that did not report any data for this item.

(g) Inmate participation numbers were not collected for education or counseling programs.

Table L
STATE FACILITIES, SERVICES AND CHALLENGES FOR GERIATRIC INMATES

State	Grouped or in geriatric facilities	Programs or recreational opportunities	Special work assignments	Hospice/ end-of-life programs	Medical or compassionate release	Early release planning
Alabama	★	★	★	★	★	★
Alaska	...	...	...	...	★	★
Arizona	★	★	...	...	★	★
Arkansas	★	...	★	...	★	...
California	...	★	...	★	...	★
Colorado	...	...	...	...	★	★
Connecticut	★	★	...	...	...	...
Delaware	...	...	...	...	...	...
Florida	★	★	★	★	★	★
Georgia	★	★	...	★	★	...
Hawaii	★	★	...	...	★	...
Idaho	...	...	...	...	...	...
Illinois	★	★	...	★	★	...
Indiana	...	★	★	★	★	★
Iowa	...	★	...	...	...	★
Kansas	...	...	...	★	★	★
Kentucky	★	★	★	★	★	★
Louisiana	★	...	★	★	★	★
Maine	...	★	...	...	...	★
Maryland	...	★	...	★	★	★
Massachusetts	...	★	...	...	...	...
Michigan	★	★	...	★	★	★
Minnesota	...	...	★	★	★	★
Mississippi	...	...	...	...	★	★
Missouri	...	★	...	...	★	★
Montana	...	★	...	...	★	...
Nebraska	...	...	...	...	★	★
Nevada	...	...	...	...	...	★
New Hampshire	★	...	★	...	...	...
New Jersey	...	★	...	...	...	...
New Mexico	★	...	...	...	...	...
New York	...	...	...	★	★	★
North Carolina	★	★	★	...	...	★
North Dakota	★	★	...	★	...	★
Ohio	★	★	...	...	★	★
Oklahoma	★	...	...	...	★	...
Oregon	...	★	...	...	★	★
Pennsylvania	★	★	...	...	...	★
Rhode Island	...	...	...	...	★	★
South Carolina	★	★	★	...	★	★
South Dakota	...	...	...	★	★	★
Tennessee	★	...	★	...	★	★
Texas	★	★	★	★	★	★
Utah	...	★	★	★	★	★
Vermont	...	...	...	...	★	★
Virginia	★	...	...	...	★	★
Washington	★	★	...	★	★	★
West Virginia	★	★	★	...	★	★
Wisconsin	★	★	★	...	★	★
Wyoming	★	...	...	...	★	★
Total	26	29	15	18	36	37

Source: Ronald H. Aday, *Aging Prisoners: Crisis in American Corrections.*
Praeger Publishers, Westport, CT, 2003.
Key:
★—Yes.
. . . — No.

Table 9.8
TRENDS IN STATE PRISON POPULATION BY REGION, 2001-2002

State or other jurisdiction	Total population			Percent chamge from -		Incarceration rate June 30, 2002 (a)
	June 30, 2002	December 31, 2001	June 30, 2001	June 30, 2001 to June 30, 2002	December 31, 2001 to June 30, 2002	
United States	1,426,118	1,406,519	1,405,531	1.5%	1.4%	474
Federal	161,681	156,993	152,788	5.8	3.0	49
State	1,264,437	1,249,526	1,252,743	0.9	1.2	425
Eastern Region						
Connecticut (b)	20,243	19,196	18,875	7.2	5.5	397
Delaware (b)	6,957	7,003	7,122	-2.3	-0.7	557
Maine	1,841	1,704	1,693	8.7	8.0	137
Massachusetts (c)	10,620	10,588	10,734	-1.1	0.3	240
New Hampshire	2,476	2,392	2,323	6.6	3.5	197
New Jersey (d)	28,054	28,142	28,108	-0.2	-0.3	326
New York	67,131	67,533	69,158	-2.9	-0.6	346
Pennsylvania	39,275	38,062	37,105	5.8	3.2	318
Rhode Island (b)	3,694	3,241	3,147	17.4	14.0	184
Vermont (b)	1,784	1,741	1,782	0.1	2.5	211
Regional total	182,075	179,602	180,047	1.1	1.3	...
Midwestern Region						
Illinois (d)	43,142	44,348	45,629	-5.5	-2.7	339
Indiana	21,425	20,966	20,576	4.1	2.2	346
Iowa (e)	8,172	7,962	8,101	0.9	2.6	276
Kansas (d)	8,758	8,577	8,543	2.5	2.1	320
Michigan	49,961	48,849	48,371	3.3	2.3	495
Minnesota	6,958	6,606	6,514	6.8	5.3	139
Nebraska	4,031	3,937	3,944	2.2	2.4	227
North Dakota	1,168	1,120	1,080	8.1	4.3	167
Ohio (d)	45,349	45,281	45,684	-0.7	0.2	395
South Dakota	2,900	2,790	2,673	8.5	3.9	378
Wisconsin	21,978	21,533	20,931	5.0	2.1	387
Regional total	213,842	211,969	212,046	0.8	0.8	...
Southern Region						
Alabama	27,495	26,741	27,286	0.8	2.8	593
Arkansas	12,655	12,594	12,332	2.6	0.5	465
Florida (e)	73,553	72,404	72,007	2.1	1.6	451
Georgia (e)	46,417	45,937	45,363	2.3	1.0	552
Kentucky	16,172	15,424	15,400	5.0	4.8	386
Louisiana	36,171	35,810	35,494	1.9	1.0	799
Maryland	24,329	23,752	23,970	1.5	2.4	435
Mississippi	22,001	21,460	20,672	6.4	2.5	728
Missouri	30,034	28,757	28,167	6.6	4.4	531
North Carolina	32,755	31,979	31,142	5.2	2.4	347
Oklahoma (d)	23,435	22,780	23,139	1.3	2.9	672
South Carolina	23,017	22,576	22,267	3.4	2.0	542
Tennessee	24,277	23,671	23,168	4.8	2.6	421
Texas	158,131	162,070	164,465	-3.9	-2.4	685
Virginia	32,739	31,662	30,473	7.4	3.4	452
West Virginia	4,488	4,215	4,130	8.7	6.5	246
Regional total	587,669	581,832	579,475	1.4	1.0	...
Western Region						
Alaska (b)	4,205	4,571	4,197	0.2	-8.0	373
Arizona (e)	29,103	27,710	27,136	7.2	5.0	508
California	160,315	159,444	163,965	-2.2	0.5	450
Colorado (d)	18,320	17,448	17,122	7.0	5.0	414
Hawaii (b)	5,541	5,431	5,412	2.4	2.0	309
Idaho	5,802	6,006	5,688	2.0	-4.4	437
Montana	3,515	3,328	3,250	8.2	5.6	387
Nevada	10,426	10,233	10,291	1.3	1.9	499
New Mexico	5,875	5,668	5,288	11.1	3.7	301
Oregon	11,812	11,410	11,077	6.6	3.5	340
Utah	5,353	5,339	5,440	-1.6	0.3	226
Washington	15,829	15,159	15,242	3.9	4.4	259
Wyoming	1,732	1,684	1,679	3.2	2.9	346
Regional total	277,828	273,431	275,787	0.7	1.6	...
Regional total without California	117,513	113,987	111,822	5.0	3.0	...
Dist. of Columbia	3,023	2,692	5,388	(f)	(f)	55

Source: U.S. Department of Justice, Bureau of Justice Statistics, *Bulletin, Prisoners and Jail Inmates at Midyear 2002* (April 2003).

Key:

. . . — Not available

(a) The number of prisoners with sentences of more than one year per 100,000 residents.

(b) Prisons and jails form one integrated system. Data include total jail and prison population.

(c) The incarceration rate includes an estimated 6,200 inmates sentenced to more than 1 year but held in local jails or houses of corrections.

(d) "Sentenced to more than 1 year" includes some inmates "sentenced to 1 year or less."

(e) Not calculated due to transfer of sentenced felons to the Federal system.

Table 9.9
NUMBER OF SENTENCED PRISONERS ADMITTED AND RELEASED, BY REGION: 1999-2001

State or other jurisdiction	Admissions (a)				Releases (a)			
	2001	2000	1999	Percent change 1999-2001	2001	2000	1999	Percent change 1990-2001
United States	639,569	628,375	617,387	3.6%	630,207	608,096	576,680	9.3%
Federal	45,140	43,732	41,972	7.5	38,370	35,259	31,816	20.6
State	594,429	584,643	575,415	3.3	591,837	572,837	544,864	8.6
Eastern Region								
Connecticut	6,576	6,185	6,306	4.3	6,331	5,918	5,283	19.8
Delaware	2,417	2,709	2,624	-7.9	2,330	2,260	2,180	6.9
Maine	820	751	731	12.2	723	677	689	3.6
Massachusetts	2,215	2,062	2,373	-6.7	2,482	2,889	2,914	-14.8
New Hampshire	1,171	1,051	1,067	9.7	1,030	1,044	979	5.2
New Jersey	14,422	13,653	15,106	-4.5	16,064	15,362	14,734	9.4
New York	25,473	27,601	28,181	-9.6	28,101	28,828	26,652	5.4
Pennsylvania	12,811	11,777	11,082	15.6	10,376	11,759	10,028	3.5
Rhode Island (b)	3,506	3,701	. . .	. . .	3,197	3,223	. . .	. . .
Vermont	972	984	807	20.4	1,069	946	839	27.4
Regional total	70,383	70,474	68,277	3.0	71,703	72,906	64,298	11.5
Midwestern Region								
Illinois	35,289	29,344	27,499	28.3	36,313	28,876	25,995	39.7
Indiana	13,012	11,876	10,564	23.2	12,207	11,053	10,317	18.3
Iowa	4,826	4,656	3,858	25.1	5,357	4,379	4,715	13.6
Kansas	4,502	5,002	4,890	-7.9	4,270	5,231	4,503	-5.2
Michigan	13,105	12,169	12,075	8.5	11,928	10,874	11,243	6.1
Minnesota	4,620	4,406	4,557	1.4	4,250	4,244	4,475	-5.0
Nebraska	1,783	1,688	1,603	11.2	1,738	1,503	1,558	11.6
North Dakota	747	605	715	4.5	715	598	671	6.6
Ohio	24,399	23,780	21,302	14.5	24,953	24,793	22,910	8.9
South Dakota	1,556	1,400	1,395	11.5	1,380	1,327	1,311	5.3
Wisconsin	7,442	8,396	8,868	-16.1	7,027	8,158	6,895	1.9
Regional total	111,281	103,322	97,326	14.3	110,138	101,036	94,593	16.4
Southern Region								
Alabama	7,428	6,296	8,282	-10.3	7,905	7,136	8,194	-3.5
Arkansas	6,977	6,941	6,045	15.4	6,613	6,308	5,403	22.4
Florida	35,064	35,683	32,225	8.8	34,015	33,994	29,889	13.8
Georgia	17,342	17,373	19,871	-12.7	15,758	14,797	17,173	-8.2
Kentucky	7,450	8,116	6,867	8.5	8,234	7,733	6,509	26.5
Louisiana	15,667	15,735	15,981	-2.0	15,031	14,536	15,241	-1.4
Maryland	10,399	10,327	10,987	-5.4	10,050	10,004	10,327	-2.7
Mississippi	6,880	5,796	5,825	18.1	5,685	4,940	4,136	37.5
Missouri	15,183	14,454	13,526	12.3	13,892	13,346	12,267	13.2
North Carolina	9,433	9,848	10,198	-7.5	8,935	9,687	10,710	-16.6
Oklahoma	7,872	7,426	7,635	3.1	8,265	6,628	6,140	34.6
South Carolina	9,218	8,460	8,261	11.6	8,627	8,676	7,942	8.6
Tennessee	14,295	13,675	13,597	5.1	12,690	13,893	12,361	2.7
Texas	61,276	58,197	56,361	. . .	66,228	59,776	52,318	. . .
Virginia	11,310	9,791	8,240	37.3	9,816	9,148	7,685	27.7
West Virginia	1,783	1,577	1,308	36.3	1,422	1,261	1,240	14.7
Regional total	237,577	229,695	225,209	5.4	233,166	221,863	207,535	12.3
Western Region								
Alaska	2,142	2,427	2,405	-10.9	2,041	2,599	2,504	-18.5
Arizona	10,000	9,560	9,021	10.9	9,053	9,100	8,982	0.8
California	126,895	129,640	130,976	-3.1	129,982	129,621	129,528	0.4
Colorado	7,252	7,036	6,702	8.2	6,634	5,881	5,346	24.1
Hawaii	1,700	1,594	1,533	10.9	1,581	1,379	1,332	18.7
Idaho	2,699	3,386	2,307	17.0	2,539	2,697	1,724	47.3
Montana	1,472	1,202	1,277	15.3	1,246	1,031	1,044	19.3
Nevada	4,639	4,929	4,479	3.6	4,480	4,374	4,536	-1.2
New Mexico (c)	2,545	3,161	1,826	. . .	3,194	3,383	1,997	. . .
Oregon	4,473	4,059	4,015	11.4	3,668	3,371	3,185	15.2
Utah	2,864	3,270	3,035	-5.6	3,151	2,897	2,554	23.4
Washington	7,185	7,094	6,795	5.7	6,957	6,764	6,344	9.7
Wyoming	731	638	798	-8.4	723	697	659	9.7
Regional total	174,597	177,996	175,169	-0.3	175,249	173,794	169,735	3.2
Regional total without California	47,702	48,356	44,193	7.9	45,267	44,173	40,207	12.5
Dist. of Columbia	591	3,156	5,733	-89.7	1,581	3,238	5,471	-71.1

Source: U.S. Department of Justice, Bureau of Justice Statistics, *Bulletin, Prisoners and Jail Inmates at Midyear 2002* (April 2003).
Note: Excludes AWOL's and transfers to or from other jurisdictions.
Key:
. . . — Not calculated
(a) Based on inmates under jurisdiction with a sentence of more than one year.

(b) Comparable data were not available for all three years. Data from the most recent comparable year were used to calculate regional and national totals.
(c) Data may not be comparable from year to year due to changing reporting methods.

Table 9.10
STATE PRISON CAPACITIES, BY REGION: 2002

State or other jurisdiction	Rated capacity	Operational capacity	Design capacity	Population as a percent of capacity: (a)	
				Highest capacity	Lowest capacity
Federal	103,897	. . .	. . .	133%	133%
Eastern Region					
Connecticut (b)	. . .	. . .	. . .	. . .	. . .
Delaware	. . .	4,206	3,192	164	216
Maine	1,779	1,779	1,779	104	104
Massachusetts	. . .	. . .	7,721	128	128
New Hampshire	2,419	2,238	2,213	102	112
New Jersey	. . .	. . .	17,122	138	138
New York	61,265	63,531	54,210	105	123
Pennsylvania	34,583	34,583	27,113	113	145
Rhode Island	3,907	3,907	4,061	86	89
Vermont	1,286	1,286	1,226	106	111
Midwestern Region					
Illinois	31,351	31,351	27,256	136	157
Indiana	15,859	21,039	. . .	93	123
Iowa	6,772	6,772	6,772	124	124
Kansas	9,114	. . .	. . .	98	98
Michigan	. . .	51,429	. . .	97	97
Minnesota	7,064	7,064	7,064	97	97
Nebraska	. . .	3,924	3,139	103	129
North Dakota	1,005	952	1,005	109	115
Ohio	36,270	. . .	. . .	120	120
South Dakota	. . .	2,827	. . .	102	102
Wisconsin	. . .	15,559	. . .	117	117
Southern Region					
Alabama	. . .	. . .	12,459	201	201
Arkansas (c)	11,972	12,189	11,299	95	103
Florida	. . .	78,805	58,396	95	129
Georgia	. . .	47,706	. . .	99	99
Kentucky	. . .	12,162	. . .	87	87
Louisiana	19,688	20,010	. . .	98	100
Maryland	. . .	24,263	. . .	99	99
Mississippi (c)	. . .	21,011	. . .	73	73
Missouri	. . .	30,580	. . .	97	97
North Carolina	. . .	28,284	. . .	117	117
Oklahoma (c)	. . .	23,566	. . .	93	93
South Carolina	. . .	22,600	22,955	100	101
Tennessee (c)	19,138	18,691	. . .	96	98
Texas (c)(d)	159,667	154,999	159,667	85	88
Virginia	30,925	. . .	. . .	95	95
West Virginia	. . .	3,593	3,189	101	112
Western Region					
Alaska	3,098	3,206	. . .	93	97
Arizona	26,228	29,406	25,346	100	116
California	. . .	155,087	80,587	103	198
Colorado	. . .	13,925	12,593	116	129
Hawaii	. . .	3,487	2,451	107	152
Idaho	5,871	5,544	4,564	71	92
Montana	. . .	2,460	. . .	78	79
Nevada (c)	10,532	. . .	8,315	96	121
New Mexico (c)	6,245	6,239	5,985	94	98
Oregon	. . .	11,556	11,556	101	101
Utah	. . .	4,196	4,419	97	102
Washington	9,898	12,793	12,793	127	164
Wyoming	1,111	1,051	1,141	98	106

Source: U.S. Department of Justice, Bureau of Justice Statistics, *Prisoners in 2002* (July 2003).

Key:

. . .—Not available.

(a) Population counts are based on the number of inmates held in facilities operated by the jurisdiction. Excludes inmates held in local jails, in other states, or in private facilities.

(b) Connecticut no longer reports capacity due to a law passed in 1995.

(c) Includes capacity of private and contract facilities and inmates housed in them.

(d) Excludes capacity of county facilities and inmates housed in them.

Table 9.11
ADULTS ON PROBATION BY REGION, 2002

State or other jurisdiction	Probation population					Number on probation on 12/31/02 per 100,000 adult residents
	1/1/02	2002		12/31/02	Percent change during 2002	
		Entries	Exits			
United States	3,931,731	2,129,084	2,064,506	3,995,165	1.6	1,854
Federal	31,562	14,349	14,266	31,326	-0.7	15
State	3,900,169	2,114,735	2,050,240	3,963,839	1.6	1,840
Eastern Region						
Connecticut	49,352	23,572	21,940	50,984	3.3	1,947
Delaware	19,995	14,638	14,432	20,201	1.0	3,328
Maine	8,939	6,669	6,162	9,446	5.7	957
Massachusetts	44,119	40,855	40,961	44,013	-0.2	890
New Hampshire (a)(b)	3,665	1,466	1,429	3,702	1.0	387
New Jersey	132,846	43,711	42,374	134,290	1.1	2,062
New York	193,074	41,114	36,146	198,042	2.6	1,358
Pennsylvania (b)	125,928	50,137	45,279	130,786	3.9	1,388
Rhode Island	24,759	6,721	5,566	25,914	4.7	3,168
Vermont	9,266	5,137	4,636	9,767	5.4	2,091
Regional total	611,943	234,020	218,925	627,145	2.4	17,576
Midwestern Region						
Illinois	141,508	61,329	61,293	141,544	0.0	1,506
Indiana	104,116	90,705	88,234	106,587	2.4	2,325
Iowa	22,061	16,603	15,275	23,389	6.0	1,057
Kansas	15,250	23,366	23,399	15,217	-0.2	758
Michigan (a) (b)	170,967	124,702	121,570	173,940	1.7	2,330
Minnesota (b)	120,720	57,236	57,318	120,638	-0.1	3,237
Nebraska	20,847	15,625	17,302	19,170	-8.0	1,493
North Dakota	2,970	2,049	1,820	3,199	7.7	669
Ohio (a) (b)	195,213	133,991	117,924	211,237	8.2	2,469
South Dakota	4,462	3,511	3,014	4,959	11.1	886
Wisconsin (c)	53,820	26,560	24,736	55,644	3.4	1,369
Regional total	851,934	555,677	531,885	875,524	2.6	18,099
Southern Region						
Alabama	40,627	16,767	17,696	39,697	-2.3	1,181
Arkansas	28,119	9,056	9,182	27,993	-0.4	1,384
Florida (a)(b)	292,842	258,077	254,333	294,281	0.5	2,283
Georgia (b)(d)	360,037	193,915	187,067	366,885	. . .	. . .
Kentucky	22,794	13,978	11,916	24,856	9.0	804
Louisiana	35,744	13,268	12,693	36,319	1.6	1,110
Maryland	80,708	42,588	41,314	91,982	1.6	2,010
Mississippi	15,435	8,141	6,943	16,633	7.8	794
Missouri	55,767	23,395	24,578	54,584	-2.1	1,289
North Carolina	110,676	61,122	58,898	112,900	2.0	1,790
Oklahoma (a)(b)	30,269	14,364	15,925	28,708	-5.2	1,105
South Carolina	44,399	13,433	16,224	41,608	-6.3	1,353
Tennessee	40,889	25,643	22,974	42,988	5.1	982
Texas	443,682	193,867	203,056	434,493	-2.1	2,758
Virginia	37,882	30,148	27,671	40,359	6.5	730
West Virginia (b)	6,176	2,983	2,915	6,244	1.1	446
Regional total	1,646,046	920,745	913,385	1,660,530	0.8	20,019
Western Region						
Alaska	4,803	913	767	4,949	3.0	1,095
Arizona (a)	63,073	41,849	38,705	66,217	5.0	16,562
California (a)	350,768	171,400	164,047	358,121	2.1	1,388
Colorado (a) (b)	55,218	33,164	31,190	58,986	6.8	1,748
Hawaii	15,581	6,404	5,213	16,772	7.6	1,780
Idaho (e)	35,670	25,292	29,601	31,361	-12.1	3,263
Montana	6,248	3,598	3,147	6,699	7.2	987
Nevada	12,416	4,750	4,876	12,290	-1.0	762
New Mexico	10,263	9,112	7,749	11,626	13.3	865
Oregon	46,063	17,002	17,304	45,761	-0.7	1,724
Utah	10,292	5,215	4,832	10,675	3.7	671
Washington (a)(b)	165,711	76,358	68,953	173,198	4.5	3,819
Wyoming	4,477	2,447	2,328	4,596	2.7	1,246
Regional total	780,583	397,504	378,712	801,251	2.6	35,910
Regional total without California	429,815	226,104	214,665	443,130	3.0	34,522
District of Columbia	9,663	6,790	7,334	9,389	-2.8	2,032

Source: U.S. Department of Justice, Bureau of Justice Statistics, *Probation and Parole in the United States*, 2002, (August 2003).

Note: Because of incomplete data, the population for some jurisdictions on December 31, 2002, does not equal the population on January 1, 2002, plus entries, minus exits.

Key:
. . .—Not calculated.

(a) All data were estimated.
(b) Data for entries and exits were estimated for nonreporting agencies.
(c) Data for year ending November 30, 2002.
(d) Counts include private agency cases and may overstate the number under supervision.
(e) Counts include estimates for misdemeanors based on annual admissions.

Table 9.12
ADULTS ON PAROLE BY REGION, 2002

State or other jurisdiction	1/1/02	Parole population 2002 Entries	Exits	12/31/02	Percent change during 2002	Number on parole on 12/31/02 per 100,000 adult residents
United States	732,333	468,506	447,991	753,141	2.8	350
Federal	78,113	32,200	27,985	82,972	6.2	39
State	654,220	436,306	420,006	670,169	2.4	311
Eastern Region						
Connecticut	2,126	2,060	1,931	2,255	6.1	86
Delaware	530	262	241	551	4.0	91
Maine	31	1	0	32	3.2	3
Massachusetts (a)	3,718	3,715	3,698	3,718	(f)	(f)
New Hampshire (b)	953	480	470	963	1.0	101
New Jersey	11,931	10,812	10,829	11,914	-0.1	183
New York	56,719	24,416	25,145	55,990	-1.3	384
Pennsylvania (c)	86,238	27,245	15,771	97,712	13.3	1,037
Rhode Island	355	459	392	422	18.9	52
Vermont (b)	900	285	388	797	-11.4	171
Regional total	163,501	69,735	58,865	174,354	6.6	. . .
Midwestern Region						
Illinois (d)	30,148	33,498	28,188	35,458	17.6	377
Indiana	5,339	6,364	5,826	5,877	10.1	128
Iowa	2,614	2,574	2,278	2,910	11.3	131
Kansas (d)	3,991	4,528	4,529	3,990	0.0	199
Michigan	16,501	11,175	10,028	17,648	7.0	236
Minnesota	3,156	3,577	3,330	3,403	7.8	91
Nebraska	530	763	719	574	8.3	45
North Dakota	117	373	341	149	27.4	31
Ohio	17,885	11,828	11,860	17,853	-0.2	209
South Dakota	1,437	1,131	896	1,672	16.4	299
Wisconsin (e)	10,123	6,223	5,923	10,423	3.0	256
Regional total	91,841	82,034	73,918	99,957	8.8	. . .
Southern Region						
Alabama (b)	5,663	2,162	2,516	5,309	-6.3	158
Arkansas	11,357	6,285	5,964	11,678	2.8	577
Florida	5,891	4,369	4,732	5,138	-12.8	40
Georgia	20,809	10,376	9,948	20,912	0.5	331
Kentucky (d)	4,885	3,434	2,316	6,003	22.9	194
Louisiana	23,330	13,573	13,486	23,417	0.4	715
Maryland	13,415	7,478	7,622	13,271	-1.1	325
Mississippi (d)	1,788	912	884	1,816	1.6	87
Missouri	12,864	10,515	9,846	13,533	5.2	320
North Carolina	2,954	3,341	3,490	2,805	-5.0	44
Oklahoma (b)	3,406	1,827	1113	4,120	21.0	159
South Carolina	4,161	857	1,456	3,562	-14.4	116
Tennessee	8,074	3,023	3,164	7,933	-1.7	181
Texas (b)	107,688	30,506	35,126	103,068	-4.3	654
Virginia	4,873	3,006	3,349	4,530	-7.0	82
West Virginia	939	693	633	999	6.4	71
Regional total	232,097	102,357	105,645	228,094	-1.7	. . .
Western Region						
Alaska	522	305	319	508	-2.7	112
Arizona (b)	5,143	6,928	4,130	7,941	(f)	198
California	117,903	149,234	154,335	113,185	-4.0	439
Colorado	5,733	4,738	4,256	6,215	8.4	184
Hawaii	2,608	1,065	1148	2,525	-3.2	268
Idaho	1,657	1,274	968	1,961	18.3	204
Montana (d)	710	681	546	845	19.0	124
Nevada	4,025	2,203	2,257	3,971	-1.3	246
New Mexico	1,562	2,305	1,905	1,962	25.6	146
Oregon	18,290	8,233	7,216	19,307	5.6	727
Utah	3,410	2,245	2,273	3,382	-0.8	213
Washington (b)	155	10	70	95	-38.7	2
Wyoming	557	291	278	570	2.3	154
Regional total	162,275	179,512	179,701	162,467	0.1	. . .
Regional total without California	44,372	30,278	25,366	49,282	11.0	. . .
Dist. of Columbia	5,332	2,272	3,151	4,453	(f)	974

Sources: U.S. Department of Justice, Bureau of Justice Statistics, *Probation and Parole in the United States, 2002* (August 2003).

Note: Because of incomplete data, the population on December 31, 2002, does not equal the population on January 1, 2002, plus entries, minus exits.

Key:

. . . — Number not known.

(a) Data were not reported for 2002. All counts were based on date for 2001.

(b) All data were estimated.

(c) Data for entries and exits were estimated for nonreporting agencies.

(d) Data do not include parolees in one or more of the following categories: absconder, out of state, or inactive.

(e) Data are for the year ending November 30, 2002.

(f) Not calculated.

Table 9.13
CAPITAL PUNISHMENT (as of Fall 2003)

State or other jurisdiction	Capital offenses	Minimum age	Prisoners under sentence of death	Method of execution
Alabama	Intentional murder with 18 aggravating factors.	16	194	Electrocution or lethal injection
Alaska	. . .	. . .	. . .	. . .
Arizona	First degree murder accompanied by at least 1 of 10 aggravating factors. Capital sentencing excludes persons determined to be mentally retarded.	(l)	126	Lethal gas or lethal injection (a)
Arkansas	Capital murder with a finding of at least 1 of 10 aggravating circumstances; treason. Capital sentencing excludes persons determined to be mentally retarded.	14 (m)	40	Lethal injection or electrocution (b)
California	First-degree murder with special circumstances; train-wrecking; treason; perjury causing execution.	18	632	Lethal gas or lethal injection
Colorado	First-degree murder with at least 1 of 15 aggravating factors; treason. Capital sentencing excludes persons determined to be mentally retarded.	18	6	Lethal injection
Connecticut	Capital felony with 8 forms of aggravated homicide. Capital sentencing excludes persons determined to be mentally retarded.	18 (n)	7	Lethal injection
Delaware	First-degree murder with aggravating circumstances. Capital sentencing excludes persons determined to be mentally retarded.	16	21	Hanging or lethal injection (c)
Florida	First-degree murder; felony murder; capital drug-trafficking; capital sexual battery. Capital sentencing excludes persons determined to be mentally retarded.	16	381	Electrocution or lethal injection
Georgia	Murder; kidnapping with bodily injury or ransom when the victim dies; aircraft hijacking; treason. Capital sentencing excludes persons determined to be mentally retarded.	17	116	Lethal injection
Hawaii	. . .	. . .	. . .	. . .
Idaho	First-degree murder with aggravating factors; aggravated kidnapping.	(l)	21	Firing Squad or lethal injection
Illinois	First-degree murder with 1 of 15 aggravating circumstances.	18	18	Lethal injection
Indiana	Murder with 16 aggravating circumstances. Capital sentencing excludes persons determined to be mentally retarded.	18	39	Lethal injection
Iowa	. . .	. . .	. . .	. . .
Kansas	Capital murder with 8 aggravating circumstances. Capital sentencing excludes persons determined to be mentally retarded.	18	7	Lethal injection
Kentucky	Murder with aggravating factors; kidnapping with aggravating factors. Capital sentencing excludes persons determined to be mentally retarded.	16	38	Electrocution or lethal injection (d)
Louisiana	First-degree murder; aggravated rape of victim under age 12; treason.	(l)	92	Lethal injection
Maine	. . .	. . .	. . .	. . .
Maryland	First-degree murder, either premeditated or during the commission of a felony, provided that certain death eligibility requirements are satisfied. Capital sentencing excludes persons determined to be mentally retarded.	18	14	Lethal injection
Massachusetts	. . .	. . .	. . .	. . .
Michigan	. . .	. . .	. . .	. . .
Minnesota	. . .	. . .	. . .	. . .
Mississippi	Capital murder; aircraft piracy.	16 (o)	69	Lethal injection
Missouri	First-degree murder. Capital sentencing excludes persons determined to be mentally retarded.	16	67	Lethal injection or lethal gas
Montana	Capital murder with 1 of 9 aggravating circumstances; capital sexual assault.	(p)	5	Lethal injection assault.
Nebraska	First-degree murder with a finding of at least 1 statutorily-defined aggravating circumstance. Capital sentencing excludes persons determined to be mentally retarded.	18	7	Electrocution
Nevada	First-degree murder with at least 1 of 14 aggravating circumstances.	16	89	Lethal injection

See footnotes at end of table.

CAPITAL PUNISHMENT— Continued

State or other jurisdiction	Capital offenses	Minimum age	Prisoners under sentence of death	Method of execution
New Hampshire	Six categories of capital murder.	17	0	Lethal injection or hanging (e)
New Jersey	Knowing/purposeful murder by one's own conduct; contract murder; solicitation by command or threat in furtherance of a narcotics conspiracy.	18	15	Lethal injection
New Mexico	First-degree murder with at least 1 of 7 statutorily-defined aggravating circumstances. Capital sentencing excludes persons determined to be mentally retarded.	18	2	Lethal injection
New York	First-degree murder with 1 of 12 aggravating factors. Capital sentencing excludes persons determined to be mentally retarded.	18	6	Lethal injection
North Carolina	First-degree murder. Capital sentencing excludes persons determined to be mentally retarded.	17 (f)	207	Lethal injection
North Dakota	. . .	. . .	. . .	. . .
Ohio	Aggravated murder with at least 1 of 9 aggravating circumstances.	18	209	Lethal injection
Oklahoma	First-degree murder in conjunction with a finding of at least 1 of 8 statutorily-defined aggravating circumstances.	16	105	Lethal injection, electrocution or firing squad (g)
Oregon	Aggravated murder.	18	31	Lethal injection
Pennsylvania	First-degree murder with 18 aggravating circumstances.	(l)	241	Lethal injection
Rhode Island	. . .	. . .	. . .	. . .
South Carolina	Murder with 1 of 10 aggravating circumstances. (k)	(l)	74	Electrocution or lethal injection
South Dakota	First-degree murder with 1 of 10 aggravating circumstances; aggravated kidnapping. Capital sentencing excludes persons determined to be mentally retarded.	(q)	4	Lethal injection
Tennessee	First-degree murder with 1 of 15 aggravating circumstances. Capital sentencing excludes persons determined to be mentally retarded.	18	104	Lethal injection or electrocution (h)
Texas	Criminal homicide with 1 of 8 aggravating circumstances.	17	451	Lethal injection
Utah	Aggravated murder. (k)	14 (r)	11	Lethal injection or firing squad
Vermont	. . .	. . .	. . .	. . .
Virginia	First-degree murder with 1 of 13 aggravating circumstances.	14 (j)	27	Electrocution or lethal injection
Washington	Aggravated first-degree murder. Capital sentencing excludes persons determined to be mentally retarded.	18	11	Lethal injection or hanging
West Virginia	. . .	. . .	. . .	. . .
Wisconsin	. . .	. . .	. . .	. . .
Wyoming	First-degree murder.	16	1	Lethal injection or lethal gas (i)
Dist. of Columbia	. . .	. . .	. . .	. . .

Sources: U.S. Department of Justice, Bureau of Statistics, Capital Punishment, 2002 (November 2003). Information on the number of prisoners under death sentence is from the NAACP Legal Defense and Educational Fund Inc., Death Row, U.S.A. Fall 2003.

Note: There were seven prisoners sentenced to death in more than one state. They are included for each state in which they were sentenced to death.

Key:

. . . — No capital punishment statute.

(a) Arizona authorizes lethal injection for persons whose capital sentence was received after 11/15/92; for those sentenced before that date, the condemned may select lethal injection or lethal gas.

(b) Arkansas authorizes lethal injection for those whose capital offense occurred on or after 7/4/83; for those whose offense occurred before that date, the condemned may select lethal injection or electrocution.

(c) Delaware authorizes lethal injection for those whose capital offense occurred after 6/13/86; for those whose offense occurred before that date, the condemned may select lethal injection or hanging.

(d) Kentucky authorizes lethal injection for persons whose capital sentence was received on or after 3/31/98; for those sentenced before that date, the condemned may select lethal injection or electrocution.

(e) New Hampshire authorizes hanging only if lethal injection cannot be given.

(f) The age required is 17 unless the murderer was incarcerated for murder when a subsequent murder occurred; then the age may be 14.

(g) Oklahoma authorizes electrocution if lethal injection is ever held to be unconstitutional, and firing squad if both lethal injection and electrocution are held unconstitutional.

(h) Tennessee authorizes lethal injection for those whose capital offense occurred after 12/31/98; those whose offense occurred before that date may select electrocution.

(i) Wyoming authorizes lethal gas if lethal injection is ever held to be unconstitutional.

(j) The minimum age for transfer to adult court by statute is 14, but the effective age is 16 based on interpretation of U.S. Supreme Court decisions by the state attorney general's office.

(k) Mental retardation is a mitigating factor.

(l) No age specified.

(m) See Arkansas Code Ann. 9-27-318(c)(2)(Supp. 2001).

(n) See Connecticut Gen. Stat. 53a-46a(g)(1).

(o) The minimum age defined by statute is 13, but the effective age is 16 based on interpretation of U.S. Supreme Court decisions by the Mississippi Supreme Court.

(p) Montana law specifies that offenders tried under the capital sexual assault statute be 18 or older. Age may be a mitigating factor for other capital crimes.

(q) Juveniles may be transferred to adult court. Age can be a mitigating factor.

Trends and Issues in Welfare Reform
By Sheila R. Zedlewski

States' welfare challenges are becoming more complex. As the economy weakened, caseload decline either diminished or reversed. Employment rates declined for both welfare recipients and those who recently left welfare. More who left welfare either have returned to it or are disconnected, living without a job, welfare, or someone else who can support them. Fortunately, more who left welfare are staying connected to other government safety net supports. States' welfare offices must combine the message of work and assessment of work barriers with a complex array of services that remediate barriers, track families after they leave welfare, and support working poor families.

Recent Caseload Experience

Temporary Assistance for Needy Families (TANF) caseloads have hovered around 2 million families nationwide since March 2001 following the dramatic 50 percent decline that occurred between fiscal years 1996 and 2000. Caseloads have increased in 28 states since the start of the recession in March 2001 and June 2003 (the most recent data available) and have continued to decline in 22 states (Table C). While net caseload changes have been rather modest in most states, seven states have reported caseload increases of 25 percent or more (Arizona, Nevada, Idaho, Colorado, Mississippi, Indiana and Montana), and four states have reported caseload declines of 25 percent or more (Illinois, New York, Wyoming and Hawaii).

This period marks the first experience with TANF during an economic downturn. Past research that examined caseload change in the Aid to Families with Dependent Children (AFDC) era, would have predicted caseload growth as a result of an economic slowdown (Blank, 2001). However, TANF's work requirements, sanctions and time limits that provide a very different message to families seem to have a deterrent effect on caseload increases. Further, some families that left welfare during the strong economy may have gained enough quarters of coverage to qualify for unemployment insurance, reducing the demand for cash welfare assistance.

Data from the 2002 National Survey of America's Families (NSAF), a nationally-representative survey of over 40,000 nonelderly families, show that caseload dynamics have changed since the economic downturn. Families left welfare at about the same rate during the 2000-2002 period compared with the 1997-1999 period (Loprest, 2003a).[1] However, the share of families that left welfare but returned to it within two years increased during the more recent period, and the rate of new entrants, that is, families

that began to receive welfare benefits for the first time in the past two years, also increased (Zedlewski, 2003). These offsetting dynamics have kept the caseload roughly the same size across the nation in spite of the recession.

Employment

Since the economic downturn, employment rates have declined for both welfare recipients and those who recently left welfare. States' studies of those leaving welfare during the 1996-1999 period, generally showed that 60 percent of leavers were working at any point in time (Acs and Loprest, 2001). Similarly, the 1999 NSAF national data showed that 62 percent of those who left welfare between the 1997-1999 period were working at the time of their interviews (Loprest, 2001). In contrast, the more recent NSAF data show that the employment rate of recent welfare leavers dropped significantly to 56 percent in 2002 (Loprest, 2003a).

The 2002 NSAF data also show, however, a stable employment picture for welfare leavers with jobs. For example, the median wage rate ($8 per hour) was about the same for those who left welfare in the 2000-2002 period as it was for those who left welfare during the 1997-1999 period, and the percent working full time (67 percent) was the same in both time periods. Similarly, the percent reporting that they were working irregular schedules (27 percent) and multiple jobs (12 percent) did not change significantly between the two surveys.

Current employment rates also declined for welfare recipients, from 32.2 percent in 1999 to 27.7 percent in 2002 (Zedlewski, 2003). However, about six in 10 welfare recipients reported in the 2002 NSAF that they had engaged in some work activity (including paid work, job search, education and training) over a 12-month period, about the same level found for 1999 welfare recipients (Zedlewski and Holland, 2003).

The strength of the economy clearly affects the TANF's program goals. States' work first policies were developed during a time when jobs were plentiful in most areas. State welfare offices must recognize that immediate employment is more difficult to achieve in a weaker economy. They will need to work more intensively with local employers to find work opportunities for recipients. They also need to focus on retention services, including ongoing career counseling and job search assistance for those that left but lost their jobs because of a downturn. It may also be a time to focus more resources on education and training so that recipients are engaged in productive activities while waiting for the economy to strengthen and jobs to materialize.

Caseload Composition

Changes in caseload dynamics that included increases in families that entered welfare for the first time in two years, increases in families that left welfare but cycled back within two years, and steady rates of leaving have changed the average time on welfare among the 2002 caseload. A greater share of the caseload was comprised of new entrants (33.8 percent in 2002 compared with 25.9 percent in 1999), and correspondingly families on welfare continuously for at least two years comprised a smaller share of the caseload (37.9 percent in 2002 compared with 47.4 percent in 1999) (Zedlewski, 2003). The NSAF data also show that the average level of disadvantage (including poor mental health, a health condition that prevents work, education less than high school, no work experience in the last three years, having an infant, having a disabled child, and limited English skills) among adults on welfare in 2002 was similar to that found in 1999 (Zedlewski, 2003). However, the 2002 recipients were more disadvantaged in one respect than those on welfare in 1999. A larger share had limited English-speaking ability; more requested their interviews to be conducted in Spanish.

The greater share of new en-

trants among the welfare caseload in 2002 compared with 1999 helps to explain why the average level of disadvantage among the caseload did not change much between these two years. Table A shows the key barriers to employment for three groups: entrants (those who first entered welfare in the past two years), cyclers (those who first received welfare more than two years ago but have received it only intermittently over the past two years), and stayers (those who first received welfare more than two years ago and have been on welfare continuously for the past two years). These data show that entrants tend to be less disadvantaged than welfare cyclers or long-term stayers. A smaller share of the new entrants reported very poor mental health or that health prevents work, and a larger share has completed high school (34.4 percent compared with 44.5 percent of stayers). The recency of their work experience was similar to cyclers and better than long-term welfare stayers (24 percent compared with 38.8 percent). Welfare entrants also were much less likely to request a Spanish language interview (4.5 percent), indicating a greater ability to speak English, compared with welfare stayers (17.9 percent).

Entrants also were less likely to have multiple barriers to employment than welfare stayers (39.2 percent compared with 51.7 percent). Multiple barriers to employment are a significant predictor of vulnerability and unemployment. In sum, since entrants

Table A: Work Barriers of Welfare Recipients by Length of Time on Welfare, 2002 (Percent)

Barriers	Entrants	Cyclers	Stayers	All
Very poor mental health	20.7%	33.3%	26.5%	25.2%
Health prevents work	14.2	18.4	19.8	17.0
Education less than high school	34.4	44.0	44.5	41.8
Last worked three or more years ago	24.0 (b)	24.0 (b)	38.8	29.5
Ha., an infant (a)	23.8 (b)	19.2	14.4 (c)	18.9
Has a child on Supplemental Security Income	8.8	8.0	7.5	8.2
Spanish interview	4.5 (b)	3.8 (b)	17.9 (c)	9.7 (c)
Number of Barriers				
Zero	25.9	19.0	23.1	22.9
One	34.9	33.3	25.2	31.5
Two or more	39.2 (b)	47.6	51.7	45.7

Source: 2002 National Survey of America's Families (Zedlewski, 2003).
Notes: Includes adults receiving TANF and likely to be subject to work requirements (see text). Entrants first entered welfare in the past two years. Cyclers first received welfare more than two years ago but have received it only intermittently over the past two years. Stayers first received welfare more than two years ago and have been on welfare continuously for the past two years.
Key:
(a) An infant child is under the age of one.
(b) Estimate is significantly different from estimate for stayers at the 0.10 level.
(c) Increase from 1999 is significant at the 0.10 level.

made up a larger share of the caseload and they were less disadvantaged, they tended to reduce the average level of disadvantage among the entire caseload.

These data also show that welfare cyclers and long-term stayers are more disadvantaged than those that entered welfare for the first time. States must focus on those recipients with the most significant barriers to employment. Long-term stayers and those that leave but cycle back quickly will be more likely to face time limits in the near term. States' welfare offices must provide services that remove barriers among these recipients. This often requires expensive, comprehensive service interventions. States and localities must improve collaboration among a variety of programs that assist persons with mental illness, substance abuse and skill development. This may require co-location of services, team staffing, automated case management, improved information and referral systems, and common applications across programs (Van Lare, 2003).

States also could focus their job retention services on the more vulnerable welfare leavers – those with limited educations and individual or family health issues. Crisis assistance that helps to stabilize arrangements for transportation and childcare become even more important when jobs are scarce. Employers will lay off those last hired and those with less than perfect attendance records. And the more vulnerable welfare leavers also are less likely to accumulate enough work experience and earnings to qualify for unemployment insurance.

The Well-Being of Welfare Leavers

Another significant change in welfare outcomes during this weaker economic period was an increase in the share of welfare leavers who are "disconnected," that is, not working and not living with a spouse or partner who is working. The 2002 NSAF showed that 13.8 percent of those that left welfare between 2000 and 2002 were disconnected compared with 9.8 percent of those that left between 1997 and 1999 (Loprest, 2003 b). While it is not clear whether the increase in the share that was disconnected is due to higher rates of job loss among those that left welfare for work or an increase in the share that left welfare for reasons other than work (such as sanc-

tions, discouragement or time limits), it is important to recognize that the disconnected are a particularly disadvantaged group.

Table B compares the work barriers of the disconnected with those that left welfare and were still working and with those currently on welfare. The disconnected group had higher rates of health problems, lower education levels, and more limited work experience compared with those that left but were working and those currently on welfare. They also were more likely to have two or more serious barriers to employment compared with working welfare leavers or those on welfare. More than half of the disconnected

Table B: Work Barriers by Welfare Status, 2002 (Percent)

Barriers	Working leavers	On welfare	Disconnected
Very poor mental health	23.8%	25.2%	31.7%
Health prevents work	4.3 (a)	17.0	21.3
Education less than high school	22.3 (a)	41.8 (a)	54.7
Last worked three or more years ago	0.0 (a)	29.5 (a)	44.2
Has an infant	12.4	18.9	13.6
Has a child on Supplemental Security Income	4.8	8.2	10.1
Spanish interview	4.0	9.7 (a)	4.8
Number of barriers			
Zero	55.2 (a)	22.9	15.2
One	32.3	31.5	29.7
Two or more	12.5 (a)	45.7	55.2

Source: 2002 National Survey of America's Families, (from Zedlewski, 2003 and Loprest, 2003c).

Note: Working leavers are defined as those that left welfare since January 2000 and currently have a paid job; those on welfare were on at the time of their interview in 2002; and the disconnected are those that have left welfare since January 2000 and they do not have a job or cash disability income and do not live with a spouse or partner with a job.

Key:
(a) Estimate significantly different from the disconnected at the 0.01 level.

group had two or more barriers to employment compared with about one in 10 leavers with jobs.

Use of Government Safety Net Services

Fortunately, either by choice or through states' outreach efforts, more who left welfare are staying connected to other government safety net supports. Over 35 percent of those that left welfare during 2000-2002 (and stayed off) reported current receipt of food stamps in 2002 compared with 28 percent of those that left in the 1997-1999 period. Further, almost half of adults in the 2002 cohort of welfare leavers had Medicaid benefits compared with four in 10 in the 1999 cohort, and 64.3 percent of children were covered by Medicaid in 2002 compared with 56.9 percent of children in the earlier welfare leaver families. The NSAF data also indicate that families that received government work supports such as child care and health insurance in the first three months after leaving TANF were less likely to return to welfare within two years.

Many states have implemented outreach strategies to inform families that they may still be eligible for food stamps and Medicaid even though they left welfare. In addition, many states have adopted new food stamp options to make it easier for working poor families to retain benefits. Since many of these outreach programs are still underway and new food stamp options were only implemented in 2002, newer data may show further increases in food stamp use by former welfare families. Nonetheless, states need to stay focused on outreach and education so that families understand new program rules. This is particularly critical for immigrant families in the United States for five years whose benefit eligibility was restored by the 2002 Farm Bill.

Summary

The weaker economy has produced weaker welfare outcomes. Caseloads generally are no longer declining; it is more difficult for welfare recipients to find paid employment and more difficult for those that left welfare to retain employment. More single mothers have turned to welfare for the first time as jobs became scarcer. The most vulnerable welfare recipients and leavers, those with mental and physical health issues, limited educations, and little work experience are particularly at risk. In fact, those that left welfare but are not working or living with a working spouse or partner have greater levels of disadvantage than any other group.

These weaker outcomes demonstrate the substantial challenges of state and local welfare policies. The message of work is still vital, but it must be combined with careful attempts to assess work readiness and grant exemptions to those unlikely to find work. Local offices need to find creative ways to increase job availability and provide services that focus on barrier removal. More adults on welfare will face time limits over time and more will find themselves disconnected from cash assistance and employment unless states implement successful policies that move them into paid employment. At the same time, states must continue to focus sufficient TANF dollars on services that support working poor families such as child care. These services can support work and prevent welfare recidivism.

While states face greater welfare program challenges in a weaker economy, they also must prepare

to achieve higher work participation targets when TANF eventually is reauthorized by the U.S. Congress. Although they differ on the details of what can count as work participation and how job placements affect participation targets, both the House bill and the Senate Finance Committee proposal would increase the net work participation requirement relative to current law and fix TANF block grants at current levels. States will have more to do with fixed resources. States need to be thinking creatively about how to maximize resources by encouraging collaborations among local programs that provide employment services. Georgia Good Works! provides one example of a successful supported employment model funded by using TANF dollars and resources from other programs such as Vocational Rehabilitation (Derr, Pavetti, and KewalRamani, 2002).

Notes

[1] The 2002 National Survey of America's Families (NSAF) is a telephone survey with an in-person component for families without telephones. The interviews were conducted between March and September, 2002. This is the third round of the survey; earlier data were collected in 1997 and 1999. The survey was funded by a consortium of private foundations to understand the effects of devolution.

References

Acs, Gregory and Pamela Loprest. 2001. "Final synthesis Report of Findings from ASPE's "Leavers' Grants." Washington, D.C.: U.S. Department of Health and Human Services, Office of the Assistant Secretary for Planning and Evaluation.

Blank, Rebecca. 2001. "What Causes Public Assistance Caseloads to Grow?" *The Journal of Human Resources*, Volume 36, Number 1.

Derr, Michelle, LaDonna Pavetti, and Angelina KewalRamani. 2002. "Georgia GoodWorks!: Transitional Work and Intensive Support for TANF Recipients Nearing the Time Limit." Washington, D.C.: Mathematica Policy Research.

Loprest, Pamela. 2003a. "Fewer Welfare Leavers Employed in Weak Economy," Snapshots3 of America's Families Number 5, Assessing the New Federalism, Washington, D.C.: The Urban Institute.

Loprest, Pamela. 2003b. "Use of Government Benefits Increases among Families Leaving Welfare," Snapshots3 of America's Families Number 6, Assessing the New Federalism, Washington, D.C.: The Urban Institute.

Loprest, Pamela. 2003c. "Disconnected Welfare Leavers Face Serious Risks," Snapshots3 of America's Families Number 7, Assessing the New Federalism, Washington, D.C.: The Urban Institute.

Rahmanou, Hedieh, Elise Richer, and Mark Greenberg, 2003, "Welfare Caseload Remains Relatively Flat in Second Quarter of 2003." Washington, D.C.: Center for Law and Social Policy.

Van Lare, Barry. 2003. "Welfare Reform: The Next Generation," *The Book of the States 2003*, The Council of State Governments.

Zedlewski, Sheila R. 2003. "Work and Barriers to Work among Welfare Recipients in 2002," Snapshots3 of America's Families, Assessing the New Federalism, Washington, D.C.: The Urban Institute.

Zedlewski, Sheila R. and Jennifer Holland. 2003. "Work Activities of Current Welfare Recipients." Snapshots3 of America's Families, No 4. Assessing the New Federalism, Washington, D.C.: The Urban Institute.

About the Author

Sheila R. Zedlewski is the director of the Income and Benefits Policy Center at the Urban Institute. Her recent work has focused on extreme poverty, government program participation and TANF policy. Zedlewski is also one of the team leaders of The Institute's Assessing the New Federalism Project, a multi-year, privately funded study designed to understand the effects of devolution of social welfare policies from the federal to the state governments.

Table C
STATE TANF CASELOAD DATA, CHANGE SINCE RECESSION, MARCH 2001-JUNE 2003

State or other jurisdiction	March 2001	June 2003	Percentage change
United States	2,103,793	2,015,730	-4.0%
Alabama	18,396	19,279	4.8
Alaska	6,181	5,384	-12.9
Arizona	32,909	49,275	49.7
Arkansas	12,022	10,770	-10.4
California	471,668	450,016	-4.6
Colorado	10,696	14,287	33.6
Connecticut	25,101	22,265	-11.3
Delaware	5,887	6,044	2.7
Florida	58,723	58,535	-0.3
Georgia	49,814	55,234	10.9
Hawaii	13,252	9,790	-26.1
Idaho.................................	1,311	1,760	34.2
Illinois	63,626	36,285	-43.0
Indiana	40,421	52,500	29.9
Iowa	19,916	19,952	0.2
Kansas	12,659	15,247	20.4
Kentucky	34,633	31,537	-8.9
Louisiana	25,776	23,343	-9.4
Maine		----------- (a) -----------	
Maryland	28,040	25,568	-8.8
Massachusetts	42,250	48,057	13.7
Michigan	70,192	75,242	7.2
Minnesota	38,316	37,097	-3.2
Mississippi	15,213	20,280	33.3
Missouri	48,670	47,289	-2.8
Montana	4,990	6,323	26.7
Nebraska	10,482	11,965	14.1
Nevada	7,240	10,178	40.6
New Hampshire	5,580	6,290	12.7
New Jersey	47,246	43,006	-9.0
New Mexico	20,986	16,361	-22.0
New York	227,409	146,941	-35.4
North Carolina	43,309	41,108	-5.1
North Dakota	2,909	3,354	15.3
Ohio	87,283	85,570	-2.0
Oklahoma	13,919	14,312	2.8
Oregon	16,031	18,590	16.0
Pennsylvania	87,903	86,038	-2.1
Rhode Island	15,245	13,026	-14.6
South Carolina	16,513	19,220	16.4
South Dakota	2,702	2,766	2.4
Tennessee	59,520	69,751	17.2
Texas	129,602	134,291	3.6
Utah	8,163	9,161	12.2
Vermont..............................	5,586	4,847	-13.2
Virginia	29,410	30,971	5.3
Washington	55,019	54,964	-0.1
West Virginia	13,380	13,750	2.8
Wisconsin	17,207	20,871	21.3
Wyoming	575	401	-30.3
District of Columbia	16,241	16,639	2.5

Source: Rahmanou, Hedieh, Elise Richer, and Mark Greenberg. 2003. "Welfare Caseload Remains Relatively Flat in Second Quarter of 2003," p 7. Washington, D.C., The Center for Law and Social Policy. http://www.clasp.org/DMS/Documents1066331390 .64/caseload_2003_ Q2.pdf

Key:
(a) Data from Maine are unavailable at this time.

Chapter Ten

STATE PAGES

"The strength of state government is not often measured in terms of the state's influence on national programs. Rather the strength of the state is most frequently discussed as state independence, or at least as fiscal and administrative power sufficient to carry out their own function."

— **Morton Grodzins**

Table 10.1
OFFICIAL NAMES OF STATES AND JURISDICTIONS, CAPITALS, ZIP CODES AND CENTRAL SWITCHBOARDS

State or other jurisdiction	Name of state capitol (a)	Capital	Zip code	Area code	Central switchboard
Alabama, State of	State House	Montgomery	36130	334	242-7100
Alaska, State of	State Capitol	Juneau	99801	907	465-4648
Arizona, State of	State Capitol	Phoenix	85007	602	542-4900
Arkansas, State of	State Capitol	Little Rock	72201	501	682-3000
California, State of	State Capitol	Sacramento	95814	916	657-9900
Colorado, State of	State Capitol	Denver	80203	303	866-5000
Connecticut, State of	State Capitol	Hartford	06106	860	240-0100
Delaware, State of	Legislative Hall	Dover	19903	302	739-4114
Florida, State of	The Capitol	Tallahassee	32399	850	488-4441
Georgia, State of	State Capitol	Atlanta	30334	404	656-2000
Hawaii, State of	State Capitol	Honolulu	96813	808	587-0221
Idaho, State of	State Capitol	Boise	83720	208	332-1000
Illinois, State of	State House	Springfield	62706	217	782-2000
Indiana, State of	State House	Indianapolis	46204	317	232-1000
Iowa, State of	State Capitol	Des Moines	50319	515	281-5011
Kansas, State of	Statehouse	Topeka	66612	785	296-0111
Kentucky, Commonwealth of	State Capitol	Frankfort	40601	502	564-3317
Louisiana, State of	State Capitol	Baton Rouge	70804	225	342-4479
Maine, State of	State House Station	Augusta	04333	207	287-6826
Maryland, State of	State House	Annapolis	21401	410	946-5400
Massachusetts, Commonwealth of	State House	Boston	02133	617	722-2000
Michigan, State of	State Capitol	Lansing	48909	517	373-0184
Minnesota, State of	State Capitol	St. Paul	55155	651	296-3962
Mississippi, State of	State Capitol	Jackson	39215	601	359-3770
Missouri, State of	State Capitol	Jefferson City	65101	573	751-2000
Montana, State of	State Capitol	Helena	59620	406	444-3111
Nebraska, State of	State Capitol	Lincoln	68509	402	471-2311
Nevada, State of	State Capitol	Carson City	89701	775	684-5670
New Hampshire, State of	State House	Concord	03301	603	271-1110
New Jersey, State of	State House	Trenton	08625	609	292-6000
New Mexico, State of	State Capitol	Santa Fe	87501	505	986-4600
New York, State of	State Capitol	Albany	12224	518	474-8390
North Carolina, State of	State Capitol	Raleigh	27601	919	733-4111
North Dakota, State of	State Capitol	Bismarck	58505	701	328-2000
Ohio, State of	Statehouse	Columbus	43215	614	466-2000
Oklahoma, State of	State Capitol	Oklahoma City	73105	405	521-2011
Oregon, State of	State Capitol	Salem	97310	503	986-1848
Pennsylvania, Commonwealth of	Main Capitol Building	Harrisburg	17120	717	787-2121
Rhode Island and Providence Plantations, State of	State House	Providence	02903	401	222-2653
South Carolina, State of	State House	Columbia	29211	803	212-6200
South Dakota, State of	State Capitol	Pierre	57501	605	773-3011
Tennessee, State of	State Capitol	Nashville	37243	615	741-2001
Texas, State of	State Capitol	Austin	78701	512	463-4630
Utah, State of	State Capitol	Salt Lake City	84114	801	538-3000
Vermont, State of	State House	Montpelier	05633	802	828-2231
Virginia, Commonwealth of	State Capitol	Richmond	23219	804	698-7410
Washington, State of	Legislative Building	Olympia	98504	360	635-9993
West Virginia, State of	State Capitol	Charleston	25305	304	558-3456
Wisconsin, State of	State Capitol	Madison	53702	608	266-0382
Wyoming, State of	State Capitol	Cheyenne	82002	307	777-7220
District of Columbia	District Building	. . .	20004	202	724-8000
American Samoa, Territory of	Maota Fono	Pago Pago	96799	684	633-4116
Guam, Territory of	Congress Building	Hagatna	96910	671	472-8931
No. Mariana Islands, Commonwealth of	Civic Center Building	Saipan	96950	670	664-0992
Puerto Rico, Commonwealth of	The Capitol	San Juan	00902	787	721-7000
U.S. Virgin Islands, Territory of	Capitol Building	Charlotte Amalie, St. Thomas	00804	340	774-0880

(a) In some instances the name is not official.

Table 10.2
HISTORICAL DATA ON THE STATES

State or other jurisdiction	Source of state lands	Date organized as territory	Date admitted to Union	Chronological order of admission to Union
Alabama	Mississippi Territory, 1798 (a)	March 3, 1817	Dec. 14, 1819	22
Alaska	Purchased from Russia, 1867	Aug. 24, 1912	Jan. 3, 1959	49
Arizona	Ceded by Mexico, 1848 (b)	Feb. 24, 1863	Feb. 14, 1912	48
Arkansas	Louisiana Purchase, 1803	March 2, 1819	June 15, 1836	25
California	Ceded by Mexico, 1848	(c)	Sept. 9, 1850	31
Colorado	Louisiana Purchase, 1803 (d)	Feb. 28, 1861	Aug. 1, 1876	38
Connecticut	Fundamental Orders, Jan. 14, 1638; Royal charter, April 23, 1662	(e)	Jan. 9, 1788 (f)	5
Delaware	Swedish charter, 1638; English charter, 1638	(e)	Dec. 7, 1787 (f)	1
Florida	Ceded by Spain, 1819	March 30, 1822	March 3, 1845	27
Georgia	Charter, 1732, from George II to Trustees for Establishing the Colony of Georgia	(e)	Jan. 2, 1788 (f)	4
Hawaii	Annexed, 1898	June 14, 1900	Aug. 21, 1959	50
Idaho	Treaty with Britain, 1846	March 4, 1863	July 3, 1890	43
Illinois	Northwest Territory, 1787	Feb. 3, 1809	Dec. 3, 1818	21
Indiana	Northwest Territory, 1787	May 7, 1800	Dec. 11, 1816	19
Iowa	Louisiana Purchase, 1803	June 12, 1838	Dec. 28, 1846	29
Kansas	Louisiana Purchase, 1803 (d)	May 30, 1854	Jan. 29, 1861	34
Kentucky	Part of Virginia until admitted as state	(c)	June 1, 1792	15
Louisiana	Louisiana Purchase, 1803 (g)	March 26, 1804	April 30, 1812	18
Maine	Part of Massachusetts until admitted as state	(c)	March 15, 1820	23
Maryland	Charter, 1632, from Charles I to Calvert	(e)	April 28, 1788 (f)	7
Massachusetts	Charter to Massachusetts Bay Company, 1629	(e)	Feb. 6, 1788 (f)	6
Michigan	Northwest Territory, 1787	Jan. 11, 1805	Jan. 26, 1837	26
Minnesota	Northwest Territory, 1787 (h)	March 3, 1849	May 11, 1858	32
Mississippi	Mississippi Territory (i)	April 7, 1798	Dec. 10, 1817	20
Missouri	Louisiana Purchase, 1803	June 4, 1812	Aug. 10, 1821	24
Montana	Louisiana Purchase, 1803 (j)	May 26, 1864	Nov. 8, 1889	41
Nebraska	Louisiana Purchase, 1803	May 30, 1854	March 1, 1867	37
Nevada	Ceded by Mexico, 1848	March 2, 1861	Oct. 31, 1864	36
New Hampshire	Grants from Council for New England, 1622 and 1629; made Royal province, 1679	(e)	June 21, 1788 (f)	9
New Jersey	Dutch settlement, 1618; English charter, 1664	(e)	Dec. 18, 1787 (f)	3
New Mexico	Ceded by Mexico, 1848 (b)	Sept. 9, 1850	Jan. 6, 1912	47
New York	Dutch settlement, 1623; English control, 1664	(e)	July 26, 1788 (f)	11
North Carolina	Charter, 1663, from Charles II	(e)	Nov. 21, 1789 (f)	12
North Dakota	Louisiana Purchase, 1803 (k)	March 2, 1861	Nov. 2, 1889	39
Ohio	Northwest Territory, 1787	May 7, 1800	March 1, 1803	17
Oklahoma	Louisiana Purchase, 1803	May 2, 1890	Nov. 16, 1907	46
Oregon	Settlement and treaty with Britain, 1846	Aug. 14, 1848	Feb. 14, 1859	33
Pennsylvania	Grant from Charles II to William Penn, 1681	(e)	Dec. 12, 1787 (f)	2
Rhode Island	Charter, 1663, from Charles II	(e)	May 29, 1790 (f)	13
South Carolina	Charter, 1663, from Charles II	(e)	May 23, 1788 (f)	8
South Dakota	Louisiana Purchase, 1803	March 2, 1861	Nov. 2, 1889	40
Tennessee	Part of North Carolina until land ceded to U.S. in 1789	June 8, 1790 (l)	June 1, 1796	16
Texas	Republic of Texas, 1845	(c)	Dec. 29, 1845	28
Utah	Ceded by Mexico, 1848	Sept. 9, 1850	Jan. 4, 1896	45
Vermont	From lands of New Hampshire and New York	(c)	March 4, 1791	14
Virginia	Charter, 1609, from James I to London Company	(e)	June 25, 1788 (f)	10
Washington	Oregon Territory, 1848	March 2, 1853	Nov. 11, 1889	42
West Virginia	Part of Virginia until admitted as state	(c)	June 20, 1863	35
Wisconsin	Northwest Territory, 1787	April 20, 1836	May 29, 1848	30
Wyoming	Louisiana Purchase, 1803 (d)(j)	July 25, 1868	July 10, 1890	44
Dist. of Columbia	Maryland (m)	. . .	. . .	. . .
American Samoa		Became a territory, 1900		
Guam	Ceded by Spain, 1898	Aug. 1, 1950	. . .	. . .
No. Mariana Islands	. . .	March 24, 1976	. . .	. . .
Puerto Rico	Ceded by Spain, 1898	. . .	July 25, 1952 (n)	. . .
U.S. Virgin Islands		Purchased from Denmark, March 31, 1917		

See footnotes at end of table.

HISTORICAL DATA ON THE STATES — Continued

Key:

(a) By the Treaty of Paris, 1783, England gave up claim to the 13 original Colonies, and to all land within an area extending along the present Canadian to the Lake of the Woods, down the Mississippi River to the 31st parallel, east to the Chattahoochee, down that river to the mouth of the Flint, border east to the source of the St. Mary's down that river to the ocean. The major part of Alabama was acquired by the Treaty of Paris, and the lower portion from Spain in 1813.

(b) Portion of land obtained by Gadsden Purchase, 1853.

(c) No territorial status before admission to Union.

(d) Portion of land ceded by Mexico, 1848.

(e) One of the original 13 Colonies.

(f) Date of ratification of U.S. Constitution.

(g) West Feliciana District (Baton Rouge) acquired from Spain, 1810; added to Louisiana, 1812.

(h) Portion of land obtained by Louisiana Purchase, 1803.

(i) See footnote (a). The lower portion of Mississippi also was acquired from Spain in 1813.

(j) Portion of land obtained from Oregon Territory, 1848.

(k) The northern portion of the Red River Valley was acquired by treaty with Great Britain in 1818.

(l) Date Southwest Territory (identical boundary as Tennessee's) was created.

(m) Area was originally 100 square miles, taken from Virginia and Maryland. Virginia's portion south of the Potomac was given back to that state in 1846. Site chosen in 1790, city incorporated 1802.

(n) On this date, Puerto Rico became a self-governing commonwealth by compact approved by the U.S. Congress and the voters of Puerto Rico as provided in U.S. Public Law 600 of 1950.

Table 10.3
STATE STATISTICS

State or other jurisdiction	Land area		Population			Density per square mile	No. of Representatives in Congress	Capital	Population	Largest city	Rank in state	Population
	In square miles	Rank in nation	Size	Rank in nation	Percentage change 2002 to 2003							
Alabama	50,744	28	4,500,752	23	0.5	88.7	7	Montgomery	201,425	Birmingham	2	239,416
Alaska	571,951	1	648,818	47	1.1	1.1	1	Juneau	30,711	Anchorage	2	268,983
Arizona	113,635	6	5,580,811	18	2.6	49.1	8	Phoenix	1,371,960	Phoenix	1	1,371,960
Arkansas	52,068	27	2,725,714	32	0.7	52.3	4	Little Rock	184,055	Little Rock	1	184,055
California	155,959	3	35,484,453	1	1.4	227.5	53	Sacramento	435,245	Los Angeles	7	3,798,981
Colorado	103,718	8	4,550,688	22	1.1	43.9	7	Denver	560,415	Denver	1	560,415
Connecticut	4,845	48	3,483,372	29	0.7	719.0	5	Hartford	124,558	Bridgeport	3	140,104
Delaware	1,954	49	817,491	45	1.4	418.4	1	Dover	32,135	Wilmington	2	72,664
Florida	53,927	26	17,019,068	4	2.0	315.6	25	Tallahassee	155,171	Jacksonville	8	762,461
Georgia	57,906	21	8,684,715	9	1.6	150.0	13	Atlanta	424,868	Atlanta	1	424,868
Hawaii	6,423	47	1,257,608	42	1.4	195.8	2	Honolulu	378,155	Honolulu	1	378,155
Idaho	82,747	11	1,366,332	39	1.7	16.5	2	Boise	189,847	Boise	1	189,847
Illinois	55,584	24	12,653,544	5	0.5	227.6	19	Springfield	111,834	Chicago	6	2,886,251
Indiana	35,867	38	6,195,643	14	0.6	172.7	9	Indianapolis	783,612	Indianapolis	1	783,612
Iowa	55,869	23	2,944,062	30	0.3	52.7	5	Des Moines	198,076	Des Moines	1	198,076
Kansas	81,815	13	2,723,507	33	0.4	33.3	4	Topeka	122,103	Wichita	4	355,126
Kentucky	39,728	36	4,117,827	26	0.7	103.7	6	Frankfort	27,660	Louisville-Jefferson (b)	7	693,604
Louisiana	43,562	33	4,496,334	24	0.7	103.2	7	Baton Rouge	225,702	New Orleans	2	473,681
Maine	30,862	39	1,305,728	40	0.8	42.3	2	Augusta	18,560	Portland	9	64,249
Maryland	9,774	42	5,508,909	19	1.1	563.6	8	Annapolis	35,838	Baltimore	7	638,614
Massachusetts	7,840	45	6,433,422	13	0.2	820.6	10	Boston	589,281	Boston	1	589,281
Michigan	56,804	22	10,079,985	8	0.4	177.5	15	Lansing	118,588	Detroit	6	925,051
Minnesota	79,610	14	5,059,375	21	0.7	63.6	8	St. Paul	284,037	Minneapolis	1	375,635
Mississippi	46,907	31	2,881,281	31	0.5	61.4	4	Jackson	180,881	Jackson	1	180,881
Missouri	68,886	18	5,704,484	17	0.6	82.8	9	Jefferson City	39,636	Kansas City	15	443,471
Montana	145,552	4	917,621	44	0.8	6.3	1	Helena	25,780	Billings	6	89,847
Nebraska	76,872	15	1,739,291	38	0.7	22.6	3	Lincoln	232,362	Omaha	1	399,357
Nevada	109,826	7	2,241,154	35	3.4	20.4	3	Carson City	52,457	Las Vegas	2	508,604
New Hampshire	8,968	44	1,287,687	41	1.0	143.6	2	Concord	40,687	Manchester	3	108,398
New Jersey	7,417	46	8,638,396	10	0.7	1,164.7	13	Trenton	85,403	Newark	9	277,000
New Mexico	121,356	5	1,874,614	36	1.2	15.4	3	Santa Fe	62,203	Albuquerque	6	463,874
New York	47,214	30	19,190,115	3	0.3	406.4	29	Albany	95,658	New York City	6	8,084,316
North Carolina	48,711	29	8,407,248	11	1.2	172.6	13	Raleigh	306,944	Charlotte	2	580,597
North Dakota	68,976	17	633,837	48	0.0	9.2	1	Bismarck	55,532	Fargo	2	90,599
Ohio	40,948	35	11,435,798	7	0.2	279.3	18	Columbus	725,228	Columbus	1	725,228
Oklahoma	68,667	19	3,511,532	28	0.6	51.1	5	Oklahoma City	519,034	Oklahoma City	1	519,034
Oregon	95,997	10	3,559,596	27	1.1	37.1	5	Salem	140,977	Portland	1	539,438
Pennsylvania	44,817	32	12,365,455	6	0.3	275.9	19	Harrisburg	48,950	Philadelphia	13	1,492,231
Rhode Island	1,045	50	1,076,164	43	0.7	1,029.8	2	Providence	175,901	Providence	1	175,901
South Carolina	30,110	40	4,147,152	25	1.1	137.7	6	Columbia	117,394	Columbia	1	117,394

See footnotes at end of table.

STATE STATISTICS — Continued

State or other jurisdiction	Land area		Population		Percentage change 2002 to 2003	Density per square mile	No. of Representatives in Congress	Capital	Population	Rank in state	Largest city	Population
	In square miles	Rank in nation	Size	Rank in nation								
South Dakota	75,885	16	764,309	46	0.5	10.1	1	Pierre	13,876	7	Sioux Falls	130,491
Tennessee	41,217	34	5,841,748	16	0.9	141.7	9	Nashville	545,915 (c)	2	Memphis	648,882
Texas	261,797	2	22,118,509	2	1.8	84.5	32	Austin	671,873	4	Houston	2,009,834
Utah	82,144	12	2,351,467	34	1.4	28.6	3	Salt Lake City	181,266	1	Salt Lake City	181,266
Vermont	9,250	43	619,107	49	0.4	66.9	1	Montpelier	8,035	13	Burlington	38,889
Virginia	39,594	37	7,386,330	12	1.4	186.6	11	Richmond	197,456	4	Virginia Beach	433,934
Washington	66,544	20	6,131,445	15	1.1	92.1	9	Olympia	42,514	18	Seattle	570,898
West Virginia	24,078	41	1,810,354	37	0.3	75.2	3	Charleston	53,421	1	Charleston	53,421
Wisconsin	54,310	25	5,472,299	20	0.6	100.8	8	Madison	215,211	2	Milwaukee	590,895
Wyoming	97,100	9	501,242	51	0.5	5.2	1	Cheyenne	53,011	1	Cheyenne	53,011
District of Columbia	63	. . .	563,384	50	-1.0	8,942.6	1 (a)	. . .	. . .	. . .	. . .	. . .
American Samoa (d)	77	. . .	57,291	. . .	22.0	. . .	1 (a)	Pago Pago	4,278	3	Tafuna	8,409
Guam (d)	210	. . .	154,805	. . .	. . .	. . .	1 (a)	Hagatna	1,100	18	Dededo	42,980
No. Mariana Islands (d)	181	. . .	69,221	. . .	. . .	. . .	1 (a)	Saipan	62,392	1	Saipan	62,392
Puerto Rico	3,427	. . .	3,878,523	. . .	0.5	1,131.8	1 (a)	San Juan	421,958	1	San Juan	421,958
U.S. Virgin Islands (d)	134	. . .	108,612	. . .	. . .	. . .	1 (a)	Charlotte Amalie, St. Thomas	11,004	1	Charlotte Amalie, St. Thomas	11,004

Source: U.S. Census Bureau, July 2003.

Key:

. . . — Not applicable

(a) Delegate with privileges to vote in committees and the Committee of the Whole.

(b) Coextensive with Jefferson County.

(c) This city is part of a consolidated city-county government and is coextensive with Davidson County.

(d) Information for territories and cities with a population under 100,000 is from the U.S. Census Bureau, Census 2000.

Alabama

Nickname .... The Heart of Dixie
Motto .... *Aldemus Jura Nostra Defendere*
(We Dare Defend Our Rights)
Flower .... Camellia
Bird .... Yellowhammer
Tree .... Southern (Longleaf) Pine
Song .... *Alabama*
Entered the Union .... December 14, 1819
Capital .... Montgomery

STATISTICS

Land Area (square miles) 50,744
    Rank in Nation 28th
Population 4,500,752
    Rank in Nation 23rd
    Density per square mile 88.7
Capital City .... Montgomery
    Population 201,425
    Rank in State 2nd
Largest City .... Birmingham
    Population 239,416
Number of Representatives in Congress 7
Number of Counties 67
Number of Municipal Governments 451
Number of 2004 Electoral Votes 9
Number of School Districts 128
Number of Special Districts 525

LEGISLATIVE BRANCH

Legislative Body .... Legislature

President of the Senate .... Lt. Gov. Lucy Baxley
President Pro Tem of the Senate .... Lowell Ray Barron
Secretary of the Senate .... Charles McDowell Lee

Speaker of the House .... Seth Hammett
Speaker Pro Tem of the House .... Demetrius C. Newton
Clerk of the House .... William G. Pappas

2004 Regular Session .... Feb. 3-May 17
Number of Senatorial Districts 35
Number of Representative Districts 105

EXECUTIVE BRANCH

Governor .... Bob Riley
Lieutenant Governor .... Lucy Baxley
Secretary of State .... Nancy Worley
Attorney General .... Troy King
Treasurer .... Kay Ivey
Auditor .... Beth Chapman
Comptroller .... Robert Childree

Governor's Present Term 1/03-1/07
Number of Elected Officials in the Executive Branch 7
Number of Members in the Cabinet 28

JUDICIAL BRANCH

Highest Court .... Supreme Court
Supreme Court Chief Justice .... J. Gorman Houston, Jr.
Number of Supreme Court Judges 9
Number of Intermediate Appellate Court Judges 10
Number of U.S. Court Districts 3
U.S. Circuit Court .... 11th Circuit

STATE INTERNET ADDRESSES

Official State Website .... http://www.alabama.gov
Governor's Website .... http://www.governor.state.al.us
State Legislative Website .... http://www.legislature.state.al.us
State Judicial Website .... http://www.judicial.state.al.us

Alaska

Nickname .... The Last Frontier
Motto .... *North to the Future*
Flower .... Forget-Me-Not
Bird .... Willow Ptarmigan
Tree .... Sitka Spruce
Song .... *Alaska's Flag*
Entered the Union .... January 3, 1959
Capital .... Juneau

STATISTICS

Land Area (square miles) 571,951
    Rank in Nation 1st
Population 648,818
    Rank in Nation 47th
    Density per square mile 1.1
Capital City .... Juneau
    Population 31,283
    Rank in State 2nd
Largest City .... Anchorage
    Population 268,983
Number of Representatives in Congress 1
Number of Counties 27
Number of Municipal Governments 149
Number of 2004 Electoral Votes 3
Number of School Districts 53
Number of Special Districts 14

LEGISLATIVE BRANCH

Legislative Body .... Legislature

President of the Senate .... Gene Therriault
Secretary of the Senate .... Kirsten Waid

Speaker of the House .... Pete Kott
Chief Clerk of the House .... Suzanne Lowell

2004 Regular Session .... Jan. 12-May 11
Number of Senatorial Districts 20
Number of Representative Districts 40

EXECUTIVE BRANCH

Governor .... Frank Murkowski
Lieutenant Governor .... Loren Leman
Attorney General .... Gregg Renkes
Treasurer .... Tom Boutin
Auditor .... Pat Davidson
Comptroller .... Betty Martin

Governor's Present Term 12/02-12/06
Number of Elected Officials in the Executive Branch 2
Number of Members in the Cabinet 18

JUDICIAL BRANCH

Highest Court .... Supreme Court
Supreme Court Chief Justice .... Alexander O. Bryner
Number of Supreme Court Judges 5
Number of Intermediate Appellate Court Judges 3
Number of U.S. Court Districts 1
U.S. Circuit Court .... 9th Circuit

STATE INTERNET ADDRESSES

Official State Website .... http://www.state.ak.us
Governor's Website .... http://www.gov.state.ak.us
State Legislative Website .... http://www.legis.state.ak.us
State Judicial Website .... http://www.state.ak.us/courts

Arizona

Nickname .... The Grand Canyon State
Motto .... *Ditat Deus (God Enriches)*
Flower .... Blossom of the Saguaro Cactus
Bird .... Cactus Wren
Tree .... Palo Verde
Songs .... *Arizona March Song and Arizona*
Entered the Union .... February 14, 1912
Capital .... Phoenix

STATISTICS

Land Area (square miles) 113,635
   Rank in Nation 6th
Population 5,580,811
   Rank in Nation 18th
   Density per square mile 49.1
Capital City .... Phoenix
   Population 1,371,960
   Rank in State 1st
Largest City .... Phoenix
Number Representatives in Congress 8
Number of Counties 15
Number of Municipal Governments 87
Number of 2004 Electoral Votes 10
Number of School Districts 410
Number of Special Districts 305

LEGISLATIVE BRANCH

Legislative Body .... Legislature

President of the Senate .... Ken Bennett
President Pro Tem of the Senate .... Timothy Bee
Secretary of the Senate .... Charmion Billington

Speaker of the House .... Jake Flake
Speaker Pro Tem of the House .... Eddie Farnsworth
Chief Clerk of the House .... Norman L. Moore

2004 Regular Session .... Jan. 12-April 30
Number of Senatorial Districts 30
Number of Representative Districts 30

EXECUTIVE BRANCH

Governor .... Janet Napolitano
Secretary of State .... Jan Brewer
Attorney General .... Terry Goddard
Treasurer .... David Petersen
Auditor .... Debra K. Davenport
Comptroller .... D. Clark Partridge

Governor's Present Term 1/03-1/07
Number of Elected Officials in the Executive Branch 11
Number of Members in the Cabinet 38

JUDICIAL BRANCH

Highest Court .... Supreme Court
Supreme Court Chief Justice .... Charles E. Jones
Number of Supreme Court Judges 5
Number of Intermediate Appellate Court Judges 22
Number of U.S. Court Districts 1
U.S. Circuit Court .... 9th Circuit

STATE INTERNET ADDRESSES

Official State Website .... http://www.az.gov
Governor's Website .... http://www.governor.state.az.us
State Legislative Website .... http://www.azleg.state.az.us
State Judicial Website .... http://www.supreme.state.az.us

Arkansas

Nickname .... The Natural State
Motto .... *Regnat Populus (The People Rule)*
Flower .... Apple Blossom
Bird .... Mockingbird
Tree .... Pine
Song ....*Arkansas*
Entered the Union .... June 15, 1836
Capital .... Little Rock

STATISTICS

Land Area (square miles) 52,068
   Rank in Nation 27th
Population 2,725,714
   Rank in Nation 32nd
   Density per square mile 52.3
Capital City .... Little Rock
   Population 184,055
   Rank in State 1st
Largest City .... Little Rock
Number of Representatives in Congress 4
Number of Counties 75
Number of Municipal Governments 499
Number of 2004 Electoral Votes 6
Number of School Districts 310
Number of Special Districts 704

LEGISLATIVE BRANCH

Legislative Body .... General Assembly

President of the Senate .... Lt. Gov. Winthrop Rockefeller
President Pro Tem of the Senate .... Jim Hill
Secretary of the Senate .... Ann Cornwell

Speaker of the House .... Herschel Cleveland
Speaker Pro Tem of the House .... Jimmy Milligan
Chief Clerk of the House .... Jo Renshaw

2004 Regular Session .... Jan. 13-April 13
Number of Senatorial Districts 35
Number of Representative Districts 100

EXECUTIVE BRANCH

Governor .... Mike Huckabee
Lieutenant Governor .... Winthrop Rockefeller
Secretary of State .... Charlie Daniels
Attorney General .... Mike Beebe
Treasurer .... Gus Wingfield
Auditor .... Jim Wood
Comptroller .... Richard Weiss

Governor's Present Term 1/03-1/07
Number of Elected Officials in the Executive Branch 7
Number of Members in the Cabinet 46

JUDICIAL BRANCH

Highest Court .... Supreme Court
Supreme Court Chief Justice .... W. H. Arnold
Number of Supreme Court Judges 7
Number of Intermediate Appellate Court Judges 12
Number of U.S. Court Districts 2
U.S. Circuit Court .... 8th Circuit

STATE INTERNET ADDRESSES

Official State Website .... http://www.state.ar.us
Governor's Website .... http://www.state.ar.us/governor
State Legislative Website .... http://www.arkleg.state.ar.us
State Judicial Website .... http://courts.state.ar.us

California

Nickname .... The Golden State
Motto .... *Eureka* (I Have Found It)
Flower .... Golden Poppy
Bird .... California Valley Quail
Tree .... California Redwood
Song .... *I Love You, California*
Entered the Union .... September 9, 1850
Capital .... Sacramento

STATISTICS

Land Area (square miles) 155,959
   Rank in Nation 3rd
Population 35,484,453
   Rank in Nation 1st
   Density per Square Mile 227.5
Capital City .... Sacramento
   Population 435,245
   Rank in State 7th
Largest City .... Los Angeles
   Population 3,728,981
Number of Representatives in Congress 53
Number of Counties 58
Number of Municipal Governments 475
Number of 2004 Electoral Votes 55
Number of School Districts 985
Number of Special Districts 2,830

LEGISLATIVE BRANCH

Legislative Body .... Legislature

President of the Senate .... Lt. Gov. Cruz Bustamante
President Pro Tem of the Senate .... John L. Burton
Secretary of the Senate .... Gregory Schmidt

Speaker of the Assembly .... Herb J. Wesson Jr.
Speaker Pro Tem of the Assembly .... Christine Kehoe
Chief Clerk of the Assembly .... E. Dotson Wilson

2004 Regular Session .... Dec. 2, 2002-Nov. 30, 2004
Number of Senatorial Districts 40
Number of Representative Districts 80

EXECUTIVE BRANCH

Governor .... Arnold Schwarzenegger
Lieutenant Governor .... Cruz M. Bustamante
Secretary of State .... Kevin Shelley
Attorney General .... Bill Lockyer
Treasurer .... Philip Angelides
Auditor .... Elaine M. Howle
Controller .... Steve Westly

Governor's Present Term 11/03-1/07
Number of Elected Officials in the Executive Branch 8
Number of Members in the Cabinet 13

JUDICIAL BRANCH

Highest Court .... Supreme Court
Supreme Court Chief Justice .... Ronald M. George
Number of Supreme Court Judges 7
Number of Intermediate Appellate Court Judges 105
Number of U.S. Court Districts 4
U.S. Circuit Court .... 9th Circuit

STATE INTERNET ADDRESSES

Official State Website .... http://www.ca.gov
Governor's Website .... http://www.governor.ca.gov
State Legislative Website .... http://www.leginfo.ca.gov
State Judicial Website .... http://www.courtinfo.ca.gov

Colorado

Nickname .... The Centennial State
Motto .... *Nil Sine Numine*
                  (Nothing Without Providence)
Flower .... Columbine
Bird .... Lark Bunting
Tree .... Blue Spruce
Song .... *Where the Columbines Grow*
Entered the Union .... August 1, 1876
Capital .... Denver

STATISTICS

Land Area (square miles) 103,718
   Rank in Nation 8th
Population 4,550,688
   Rank in Nation 22nd
   Density per square mile 43.9
Capital City .... Denver
   Population 560,415
   Rank in State 1st
Largest City .... Denver
Number of Representatives in Congress 7
Number of Counties 63
Number of Municipal Governments 270
Number of 2004 Electoral Votes 9
Number of School Districts 176
Number of Special Districts 1,414

LEGISLATIVE BRANCH

Legislative Body .... General Assembly

President of the Senate .... John Andrews
President Pro Tem of the Senate .... Ken Chlouber
Secretary of the Senate .... Mona Heustis

Speaker of the House .... Lola Spradley
Speaker Pro Tem of the House .... Tambor Williams
Chief Clerk of the House .... Judith Rodrigue

2004 Regular Session .... Jan. 7-May 5
Number of Senatorial Districts 35
Number of Representative Districts 65

EXECUTIVE BRANCH

Governor .... Bill Owens
Lieutenant Governor .... Jane Norton
Secretary of State .... Donetta Davidson
Attorney General .... Ken Salazar
Treasurer .... Mike Coffman
Auditor .... Joanne Hill
Controller .... Arthur Barnhart

Governor's Present Term 1/03-1/07
Number of Elected Officials in the Executive Branch 5
Number of Members in the Cabinet 21

JUDICIAL BRANCH

Highest Court .... Supreme Court
Supreme Court Chief Justice .... Mary Mullarkey
Number of Supreme Court Judges 7
Number of Intermediate Appellate Court Judges 16
Number of U.S. Court Districts 1
U.S. Circuit Court .... 10th Circuit

STATE INTERNET ADDRESSES

Official State Website .... http://www.state.co.us
Governor's Website...http://www.state.co.us/gov_dir/governor_office.html
State Legislative Website .... http://www.leg.state.co.us
State Judicial Website .... http://www.courts.state.co.us

Connecticut

Nickname .... The Constitution State
Motto .... *Qui Transtulit Sustinet*
(He Who Transplanted Still Sustains)
Flower .... Mountain Laurel
Bird .... American Robin
Tree .... White Oak
Song .... *Yankee Doodle*
Entered the Union .... January 9, 1788
Capital .... Hartford

STATISTICS

Land Area (square miles) 4,845
   Rank in Nation 48th
Population 3,483,372
   Rank in Nation 29th
   Density per square mile 719.0
Capital City .... Hartford
   Population 124,558
   Rank in State 3rd
Largest City .... Bridgeport
   Population 140,104
Number of Representatives in Congress 5
Number of Counties 8
Number of Municipal Governments 30
Number of 2004 Electoral Votes 7
Number of School Districts 166
Number of Special Districts 384

LEGISLATIVE BRANCH

Legislative Body .... General Assembly

President of the Senate .... Lt. Gov. M. Jodi Rell
President Pro Tem of the Senate .... Kevin B. Sullivan
Clerk of the Senate .... Thomas P. Sheridan

Speaker of the House .... Moira K. Lyons
Deputy Speakers
  Of the House .... Melody A. Currey, Mary G. Fritz, Wade A. Hyslop Jr.,
Clerk of the House .... Garey E. Coleman

2004 Regular Session .... Feb. 4-May 5
Number of Senatorial Districts 36
Number of Representative Districts 151

EXECUTIVE BRANCH

Governor .... John G. Rowland
Lieutenant Governor .... M. Jodi Rell
Secretary of State .... Susan Bysiewicz
Attorney General .... Richard Blumenthal
Treasurer .... Denise Nappier
Auditor .... Robert Jackle
Comptroller .... Nancy Wyman

Governor's Present Term 1/03-1/07
Number of Elected Officials in the Executive Branch 6
Number of Members in the Cabinet 27

JUDICIAL BRANCH

Highest Court .... Supreme Court
Supreme Court Chief Justice .... William J. Sullivan
Number of Supreme Court Judges 7
Number of Intermediate Appellate Court Judges 9
Number of U.S. Court Districts 1
U.S. Circuit Court .... 2nd Circuit

STATE INTERNET ADDRESSES

Official State Website .... http://www.state.ct.us
Governor's Website .... http://www.state.ct.us/governor
State Legislative Website .... http://www.cga.state.ct.us
State Judicial Website .... http://www.jud.state.ct.us

Delaware

Nickname .... The First State
Motto .... *Liberty and Independence*
Flower .... Peach Blossom
Bird .... Blue Hen Chicken
Tree .... American Holly
Song .... *Our Delaware*
Entered the Union .... December 7, 1787
Capital .... Dover

STATISTICS

Land Area (square miles) 1,954
   Rank in Nation 49th
Population 817,491
   Rank in Nation 45th
   Density per square mile 418.4
Capital City .... Dover
   Population 32,581
   Rank in State 2nd
Largest City .... Wilmington
   Population 73,135
Number of Representatives in Congress 1
Number of Counties 3
Number of Municipal Governments 57
Number of 2004 Electoral Votes 3
Number of School Districts 19
Number of Special Districts 260

LEGISLATIVE BRANCH

Legislative Body .... General Assembly

President of the Senate .... Lt. Gov. John Carney Jr.
President Pro Tem of the Senate .... Thurman G. Adams Jr.
Secretary of the Senate .... Bernard J. Brady

Speaker of the House .... Terry R. Spence
Clerk of the House .... JoAnn M. Hedrick

2004 Regular Session .... Jan. 13-June 30
Number of Senatorial Districts 21
Number of Representative Districts 40

EXECUTIVE BRANCH

Governor .... Ruth Ann Minner
Lieutenant Governor .... John Carney Jr.
Secretary of State .... Harriet Smith Windsor
Attorney General .... M. Jane Brady
Treasurer .... Jack Markell
Auditor .... Thomas Wagner
Comptroller .... Russell T. Larson

Governor's Present Term 1/01-1/05
Number of Elected Officials in the Executive Branch 5
Number of Members in the Cabinet 19

JUDICIAL BRANCH

Highest Court .... Supreme Court
Supreme Court Chief Justice .... E. Norman Veasey
Number of Supreme Court Judges 5
Number of Intermediate Appellate Court Judges 0
Number of U.S. Court Districts 1
U.S. Circuit Court .... 3rd Circuit

STATE INTERNET ADDRESSES

Official State Website .... http://delaware.gov
Governor's Website .... http://www.state.de.us/governor
State Legislative Website .... http://www.legis.state.de.us
State Judicial Website .... http://courts.state.de.us

Florida

Nickname	The Sunshine State
Motto	*In God We Trust*
Flower	Orange Blossom
Bird	Mockingbird
Tree	Sabal Palmetto Palm
Song	*The Swannee River (Old Folks at Home)*
Entered the Union	March 3, 1845
Capital	Tallahassee

STATISTICS

Land Area (square miles)	53,927
Rank in Nation	26th
Population	17,019,068
Rank in Nation	4th
Density per square mile	315.6
Capital City	Tallahassee
Population	155,171
Rank in State	8th
Largest City	Jacksonville
Population	762,461
Number of Representatives in Congress	25
Number of Counties	67
Number of Municipal Governments	404
Number of 2004 Electoral Votes	27
Number of School Districts	67
Number of Special Districts	626

LEGISLATIVE BRANCH

Legislative Body	Legislature
President of the Senate	James E. King Jr.
President Pro Tem of the Senate	Alex Diaz de la Portilla
Secretary of the Senate	Faye W. Blanton
Speaker of the House	Johnnie Byrd
Speaker Pro Tem of the House	Lindsay M. Harrington
Clerk of the House	John B. Phelps
2004 Regular Session	March 2-April 30
Number of Senatorial Districts	40
Number of Representative Districts	120

EXECUTIVE BRANCH

Governor	Jeb Bush
Lieutenant Governor	Toni Jennings
Secretary of State	Glenda Hood
Attorney General	Charlie Crist
Chief Financial Officer	Tom Gallagher
Auditor	William O. Monroe
Governor's Present Term	1/03-1/07
Number of Elected Officials in the Executive Branch	5
Number of Members in the Cabinet	7

JUDICIAL BRANCH

Highest Court	Supreme Court
Supreme Court Chief Justice	Harry Lee Anstead
Number of Supreme Court Judges	7
Number of Intermediate Appellate Court Judges	62
Number of U.S. Court Districts	3
U.S. Circuit Court	11th Circuit

STATE INTERNET ADDRESSES

Official State Website	http://www.myflorida.com
Governor's Website	http://www.state.fl.us/eog
State Legislative Website	http://www.leg.state.fl.us
State Judicial Website	http://www.flcourts.org

Georgia

Nickname	The Empire State of the South
Motto	*Wisdom, Justice and Moderation*
Flower	Cherokee Rose
Bird	Brown Thrasher
Tree	Live Oak
Song	*Georgia on My Mind*
Entered the Union	January 2, 1788
Capital	Atlanta

STATISTICS

Land Area (square miles)	57,906
Rank in Nation	21st
Population	8,684,715
Rank in Nation	9th
Density per square mile	150.0
Capital City	Atlanta
Population	424,868
Rank in State	1st
Largest City	Atlanta
Number of Representatives in Congress	13
Number of Counties	159
Number of Municipal Governments	531
Number of 2004 Electoral Votes	15
Number of School Districts	180
Number of Special Districts	581

LEGISLATIVE BRANCH

Legislative Body	General Assembly
President of the Senate	Lt. Gov. Mark Taylor
President Pro Tem of the Senate	Eric Johnson
Secretary of the Senate	Frank Eldridge Jr.
Speaker of the House	Terry Coleman
Speaker Pro Tem of the House	DuBose Porter
Clerk of the House	Robert E. Rivers Jr.
2004 Regular Session	Jan. 12-To be determined
Number of Senatorial Districts	56
Number of Representative Districts	147

EXECUTIVE BRANCH

Governor	Sonny Perdue
Lieutenant Governor	Mark Taylor
Secretary of State	Cathy Cox
Attorney General	Thurbert E. Baker
Treasurer	W. Daniel Ebersole
Auditor	Russell W. Hinton
Governor's Present Term	1/03-1/07
Number of Elected Officials in the Executive Branch	13
Number of Members in the Cabinet	No formal cabinet system

JUDICIAL BRANCH

Highest Court	Supreme Court
Supreme Court Chief Justice	Norman S. Fletcher
Number of Supreme Court Judges	7
Number of Intermediate Appellate Court Judges	12
Number of U.S. Court Districts	3
U.S. Circuit Court	11th Circuit

STATE INTERNET ADDRESSES

Official State Website	http://www.state.ga.us
Governor's Website	http://gov.state.ga.us/
State Legislative Website	http://www.legis.state.ga.us
State Judicial Website	http://www.georgiacourts.org

Hawaii

Nickname .... The Aloha State
Motto .... *Ua Mau Ke Ea O Ka Aina I Ka Pono*
(The Life of the Land Is Perpetuated in Righteousness)
Flower .... Native Yellow Hibiscus
Bird .... Hawaiian Goose (Nene)
Tree .... *Kukue Tree (Candlenut)*
Song .... *Hawaii Ponoi*
Entered the Union .... August 21, 1959
Capital .... Honolulu

STATISTICS

Land Area (square miles) 6,423
    Rank in Nation 47th
Population 1,257,608
    Rank in Nation 42nd
    Density per square mile 195.8
Capital City .... Honolulu
    Population 378,155
    Rank in State 1st
Largest City .... Honolulu
Number of Representatives in Congress 2
Number of Counties 5
Number of Municipal Governments 1
Number of 2004 Electoral Votes 4
Number of School Districts 1
Number of Special Districts 15

LEGISLATIVE BRANCH

Legislative Body .... Legislature

President of the Senate .... Robert Bunda
Vice President of the Senate .... Donna Mercado Kim
Chief Clerk of the Senate .... Paul T. Kawaguchi

Speaker of the House .... Calvin K.Y. Say
Vice Speaker of the House .... Sylvia Luke
Chief Clerk of the House .... Patricia A. Mau-Shimizu

2004 Regular Session .... Jan. 21-To be determined
Number of Senatorial Districts 25
Number of Representative Districts 51

EXECUTIVE BRANCH

Governor .... Linda Lingle
Lieutenant Governor .... James Aiona
Attorney General .... Mark J. Bennett
Treasurer .... Georgina Kawamura
Auditor .... Marion M. Higa
Comptroller .... Russ K. Saito

Governor's Present Term 12/02-12/06
Number of Elected Officials in the Executive Branch 2
Number of Members in the Cabinet 25

JUDICIAL BRANCH

Highest Court .... Supreme Court
Supreme Court Chief Justice .... Ronald T.Y. Moon
Number of Supreme Court Judges 5
Number of Intermediate Appellate Court Judges 4
Number of U.S. Court Districts 1
U.S. Circuit Court .... 9th Circuit

STATE INTERNET ADDRESSES

Official State Website .... http://www.hawaii.gov
Governor's Website .... http://gov.state.hi.us
State Legislative Website .... http://www.capitol.hawaii.gov
State Judicial Website .... http://www.courts.hi.us

Idaho

Nickname .... The Gem State
Motto .... *Esto Perpetua* (Let It Be Perpetual)
Flower .... Syringa
Bird .... Mountain Bluebird
Tree .... Western White Pine
Song .... *Here We Have Idaho*
Entered the Union .... July 3, 1890
Capital .... Boise

STATISTICS

Land Area (square miles) 82,747
    Rank in Nation 11th
Population 1,366,332
    Rank in Nation 39th
Density per square mile 16.5
Capital City .... Boise
    Population 189,847
    Rank in State 1st
Largest City .... Boise
Number of Representatives in Congress 2
Number of Counties 44
Number of Municipal Governments 200
Number of 2004 Electoral Votes 4
Number of School Districts 115
Number of Special Districts 798

LEGISLATIVE BRANCH

Legislative Body .... Legislature

President of the Senate .... Lt. Gov. Jim Risch
President Pro Tem of the Senate .... Robert L. Geddes
Secretary of the Senate .... Jeannine Wood

Speaker of the House .... Bruce Newcomb
Chief Clerk of the House .... Pamm Juker

2004 Regular Session .... Jan. 12-To be determined
Number of Senatorial Districts 35
Number of Representative Districts 35

EXECUTIVE BRANCH

Governor .... Dirk Kempthorne
Lieutenant Governor .... Jim Risch
Secretary of State .... Ben Ysursa
Attorney General .... Lawrence Wasden
Treasurer .... Ron Crane
Controller .... Keith Johnson

Governor's Present Term 1/03-1/07
Number of Elected Officials in the Executive Branch 7
Number of Members in the Cabinet 22

JUDICIAL BRANCH

Highest Court .... Supreme Court
Supreme Court Chief Justice .... Linda Copple Trout
Number of Supreme Court Judges 5
Number of Intermediate Appellate Court Judges 3
Number of U.S. Court Districts 1
U.S. Circuit Court .... 9th Circuit

STATE INTERNET ADDRESSES

Official State Website .... http://www.state.id.us
Governor's Website http://www2.state.id.us/gov
State Legislative Website http://www2.state.id.us/legislat
State Judicial Website http://www2.state.id.us/judicial

Illinois

Nickname .... The Prairie State
Motto .... *State Sovereignty-National Union*
Flower .... Native Violet
Bird .... Cardinal
Tree .... White Oak
Song .... *Illinois*
Entered the Union .... December 3, 1818
Capital .... Springfield

STATISTICS

Land Area (square miles) 55,584
   Rank in Nation 24th
Population 12,653,544
   Rank in Nation 5th
   Density per square mile 227.6
Capital City .... Springfield
   Population 111,834
   Rank in State 6th
Largest City .... Chicago
   Population 2,886,251
Number of Representatives in Congress 19
Number of Counties 102
Number of Municipal Governments 1,291
Number of 2004 Electoral Votes 21
Number of School Districts 894
Number of Special Districts 3,145

LEGISLATIVE BRANCH

Legislative Body .... General Assembly

President of the Senate .... Emil Jones Jr.
Secretary of the Senate .... Linda Hawker

Speaker of the House .... Michael J. Madigan
House Chief Clerk .... Anthony D. Rossi

2004 Regular Session .... Jan. 14-Dec. 31
Number of Senatorial Districts 59
Number of Representative Districts 118

EXECUTIVE BRANCH

Governor .... Rod Blagojevich
Lieutenant Governor .... Patrick Quinn
Secretary of State .... Jesse White
Attorney General .... Lisa Madigan
Treasurer .... Judy Baar Topinka
Auditor .... William G. Holland
Comptroller .... Daniel Hynes

Governor's Present Term 1/03-1/07
Number of Elected Officials in the Executive Branch 6
Number of Members in the Cabinet 18

JUDICIAL BRANCH

Highest Court .... Supreme Court
Supreme Court Chief Justice .... Mary Ann G. McMorrow
Number of Supreme Court Judges 7
Number of Intermediate Appellate Court Judges 52
Number of U.S. Court Districts 3
U.S. Circuit Court .... 7th Circuit

STATE INTERNET ADDRESSES

Official State Website .... http://www.state.il.us
Governor's Website .... http://www.state.il.us/gov
State Legislative Website .... http://www.legis.state.il.us
State Judicial Website .... http://www.state.il.us/court

Indiana

Nickname .... The Hoosier State
Motto .... *Crossroads of America*
Flower .... Peony
Bird .... Cardinal
Tree .... Tulip Poplar
Song .... *On the Banks of the Wabash, Far Away*
Entered the Union .... December 11, 1816
Capital .... Indianapolis

STATISTICS

Land Area (square miles) 35,867
   Rank in Nation 38th
Population 6,195,643
   Rank in Nation 14th
   Density per square mile 172.7
Capital City .... Indianapolis
   Population 783,612
   Rank in State 1st
Largest City .... Indianapolis
Number of Representatives in Congress 9
Number of Counties 92
Number of Municipal Governments 567
Number of 2004 Electoral Votes 11
Number of School Districts 295
Number of Special Districts 1,125

LEGISLATIVE BRANCH

Legislative Body .... General Assembly

President of the Senate .... Lt. Gov. Katherine Davis
President Pro Tem of the Senate .... Robert D. Garton
Principal Secretary of the Senate .... Mary C. Mendel

Speaker of the House .... B. Patrick Bauer
Speaker Pro Tem of the House .... Chester F. Dobis
Principal Clerk of the House .... Diane Masariu Carter

2004 Regular Session .... Jan. 12-Mar. 14
Number of Senatorial Districts 50
Number of Representative Districts 100

EXECUTIVE BRANCH

Governor .... Joseph E. Kernan
Lieutenant Governor .... Katherine Davis
Secretary of State .... Todd Rokita
Attorney General .... Steve Carter
Treasurer .... Tim Berry
Auditor .... Connie K. Naas

Governor's Present Term 9/03-1/05
Number of Elected Officials in the Executive Branch 7
Number of Members in the Cabinet .... No formal cabinet system

JUDICIAL BRANCH

Highest Court .... Supreme Court
Supreme Court Chief Justice .... Randall T. Shepard
Number of Supreme Court Judges 5
Number of Intermediate Appellate Court Judges 16
Number of U.S. Court Districts 2
U.S. Circuit Court .... 7th Circuit

STATE INTERNET ADDRESSES

Official State Website .... http://www.state.in.us
Governor's Website .... http://www.in.gov/gov
State Legislative Website .... http://www.in.gov/legislative
State Judicial Website .... http://www.in.gov/judiciary

Iowa

Nickname .... The Hawkeye State
Motto .... *Our Liberties We Prize and*
Our Rights We Will Maintain
Flower .... Wild Rose
Bird .... Eastern Goldfinch
Tree .... Oak
Song .... *The Song of Iowa*
Entered the Union .... December 28, 1846
Capital .... Des Moines

STATISTICS

Land Area (square mile) 55,869
   Rank in Nation 23rd
Population 2,944,062
   Rank in Nation 30th
   Density per square mile 52.7
Capital City .... Des Moines
   Population 198,076
   Rank in State 1st
Largest City .... Des Moines
Number of Representatives in Congress 5
Number of Counties 99
Number of Municipal Governments 948
Number of 2004 Electoral Votes 7
Number of School Districts 374
Number of Special Districts 542

LEGISLATIVE BRANCH

Legislative Body .... General Assembly

President of the Senate .... Jeff Lamberti
President Pro Tem of the Senate .... Jeff Angelo
Secretary of the Senate .... Michael E. Marshall

Speaker of the House .... Christopher Rants
Speaker Pro Tem of the House .... Danny Carroll
Chief Clerk of the House .... Margaret A. Thomson

2004 Regular Session .... Jan. 12-To be determined
Number of Senatorial Districts 50
Number of Representative Districts 100

EXECUTIVE BRANCH

Governor .... Thomas Vilsack
Lieutenant Governor .... Sally Pederson
Secretary of State .... Chet Culver
Attorney General .... Thomas Miller
Treasurer .... Michael Fitzgerald
Auditor .... David A. Vaudt
Chief Operating Officer .... Steve Lidner

Governor's Present Term 1/03-1/07
Number of Elected Officials in the Executive Branch 7
Number of Members in the Cabinet .... No formal cabinet system

JUDICIAL BRANCH

Highest Court .... Supreme Court
Supreme Court Chief Justice .... Lewis A. Lavarato
Number of Supreme Court Judges 7
Number of Intermediate Appellate Court Judges 9
Number of U.S. Court Districts 2
U.S. Circuit Court .... 8th Circuit

STATE INTERNET ADDRESSES

Official State Website .... http://www.state.ia.us
Governor's Website .... http://www.governor.state.ia.us/
State Legislative Website .... http://www.legis.state.ia.us
State Judicial Website .... http://www.judicial.state.ia.us

Kansas

Nickname .... The Sunflower State
Motto .... *Ad Astra per Aspera*
(To the Stars through Difficulties)
Flower .... Wild Native Sunflower
Bird .... Western Meadowlark
Tree .... Cottonwood
Song .... *Home on the Range*
Entered the Union .... January 29, 1861
Capital .... Topeka

STATISTICS

Land Area (square miles) 81,815
   Rank in Nation 13th
Population 2,723,507
   Rank in Nation 33rd
   Density per square mile 33.3
Capital City .... Topeka
   Population 122,103
   Rank in State 4th
Largest City .... Wichita
Population 355,126
Number of Representatives in Congress 4
Number of Counties 105
Number of Municipal Governments 627
Number of 2004 Electoral Votes 6
Number of School Districts 304
Number of Special Districts 1,533

LEGISLATIVE BRANCH

Legislative Body .... Legislature

President of the Senate .... Dave Kerr
Secretary of the Senate .... Pat Saville

Speaker of the House .... Doug Mays
Speaker Pro tem of the House .... John D. Ballou
Chief Clerk of the House .... Janet E. Jones

2004 Regular Session .... Jan. 13-April 12
Number of Senatorial Districts 40
Number of Representative Districts 125

EXECUTIVE BRANCH

Governor .... Kathleen Sebelius
Lieutenant Governor .... John Moore
Secretary of State .... Ron Thornburgh
Attorney General .... Phill Kline
Treasurer .... Lynn Jenkins
Auditor .... Barbara J. Hinton
Director, Division of Accounts & Reports .... Dale Brunton

Governor's Present Term 1/03-1/07
Number of Elected Officials in the Executive Branch 6
Number of Members in the Cabinet 14

JUDICIAL BRANCH

Highest Court .... Supreme Court
Supreme Court Chief Justice .... Kay McFarland
Number of Supreme Court Judges 7
Number of Intermediate Appellate Court Judges 10
Number of U.S. Court Districts 1
U.S. Circuit Court .... 10th Circuit

STATE INTERNET ADDRESSES

Official State Website .... http://www.accesskansas.org
Governor's Website .... http://www.ksgovernor.org
State Legislative Website .... http://www.kslegislature.org
State Judicial Website .... http://www.kscourts.org

Kentucky

Nickname	The Bluegrass State
Motto	*United We Stand, Divided We Fall*
Flower	Goldenrod
Bird	Cardinal
Tree	Tulip Poplar
Song	*My Old Kentucky Home*
Entered the Union	June 1, 1792
Capital	Frankfort

STATISTICS

Land Area (square miles)	39,728
Rank in Nation	36th
Population	4,117,827
Rank in Nation	26th
Density per square mile	103.7
Capital City	Frankfort
Population	27,741
Rank in State	7th
Largest City	Louisville-Jefferson Co.
Population	693,604
Number of Representatives in Congress	6
Number of Counties	120
Number of Municipal Governments	424
Number of 2004 Electoral Votes	8
Number of School Districts	176
Number of Special Districts	720

LEGISLATIVE BRANCH

Legislative Body	General Assembly
President of the Senate	David L. Williams
President Pro Tem of the Senate	Richard L. Roeding
Chief Clerk of the Senate	Jay Hartz
Speaker of the House	Jody Richards
Speaker Pro Tem of the House	Larry Clark
Chief Clerk of the House	Lois Pulliam
2004 Regular Session	Jan. 6-April 13
Number of Senatorial Districts	38
Number of Representative Districts	100

EXECUTIVE BRANCH

Governor	Ernest L. Fletcher
Lieutenant Governor	Stephen Pence
Secretary of State	Trey Grayson
Attorney General	Gregory D. Stumbo
Treasurer	Jonathan Miller
Auditor	Crit Luallen
Controller	Ed Ross
Governor's Present Term	12/03-12/07
Number of Elected Officials in the Executive Branch	7
Number of Members in the Cabinet	9

JUDICIAL BRANCH

Highest Court	Supreme Court
Supreme Court Chief Justice	Joseph E. Lambert
Number of Supreme Court Judges	7
Number of Intermediate Appellate Court Judges	14
Number of U.S. Court Districts	2
U.S. Circuit Court	6th Circuit

STATE INTERNET ADDRESSES

Official State Website	http://kentucky.gov
Governor's Website	http://governor.ky.gov/
Legislative Website	http://www.lrc.state.ky.us
Judicial Website	http://www.kycourts.net

Louisiana

Nickname	The Pelican State
Motto	*Union, Justice and Confidence*
Flower	Magnolia
Bird	Eastern Brown Pelican
Tree	Bald Cypress
Songs	*Give Me Louisiana* and *You Are My Sunshine*
Entered the Union	April 30, 1812
Capital	Baton Rouge

STATISTICS

Land Area (square miles)	43,562
Rank in Nation	33rd
Population	4,496,334
Rank in Nation	24th
Density per square mile	103.2
Capital City	Baton Rouge
Population	225,702
Rank in State	2nd
Largest City	New Orleans
Population	473,681
Number of Representatives in Congress	7
Number of Parishes	64
Number of Municipal Governments	302
Number of 2004 Electoral Votes	9
Number of School Districts	78
Number of Special Districts	45

LEGISLATIVE BRANCH

Legislative Body	Legislature
President of the Senate	Donald E. Hines, MD.
President Pro Tem of the Senate	Diana E. Bajoie
Secretary of Senate	Michael S. Baer III
Speaker of the House	Joe R. Salter
Speaker Pro Tem of the House	Sharon Weston Broome
Clerk of the House and Chief of Staff	Alfred W. Speer
2004 Regular Session	March 29-June 21
Number of Senatorial Districts	39
Number of Representative Districts	105

EXECUTIVE BRANCH

Governor	Kathleen B. Blanco
Lieutenant Governor	Mitch Landrieu
Secretary of State	W. Fox McKeithen
Attorney General	Charles C. Foti
Treasurer	John Neely Kennedy
Comptroller	Jerry Luke LeBlanc
Governor's Present Term	1/04-1/08
Number of Elected Officials in the Executive Branch	8
Number of Members in the Cabinet	14

JUDICIAL BRANCH

Highest Court	Supreme Court
Supreme Court Chief Justice	Pascal F. Calogero Jr.
Number of Supreme Court Judges	7
Number of Intermediate Appellate Court Judges	55
Number of U.S. Court Districts	3
U.S. Circuit Court	5th Circuit

STATE INTERNET ADDRESSES

Official State Website	http://www.state.la.us
Governor's Website	http://www.gov.state.la.us
Legislative Website	http://www.legis.state.la.us
Judicial Website	http://www.state.la.us/gov_judicial.htm

Maine

Nickname	The Pine Tree State
Motto	*Dirigo* (I Direct or I Lead)
Flower	White Pine Cone and Tassel
Bird	Chickadee
Tree	White Pine
Song	*State of Maine Song*
Entered the Union	March 15, 1820
Capital	Augusta

STATISTICS

Land Area (square miles)	30,862
Rank in Nation	39th
Population	1,305,728
Rank in Nation	40th
Density per square mile	42.3
Capital City	Augusta
Population	18,560
Rank in State	9th
Largest City	Portland
Population	64,249
Number of Representatives in Congress	2
Number of Counties	16
Number of Municipal Governments	22
Number of 2004 Electoral Votes	4
Number of School Districts	282
Number of Special Districts	222

LEGISLATIVE BRANCH

Legislative Body	Legislature
President of the Senate	Beverly C. Daggett
President Pro Tem of the Senate	Sharon Treat
Secretary of the Senate	Joy J. O'Brien
Speaker of the House	Patrick Colwell
Clerk of the House	Millicent M. MacFarland
2004 Regular Session	Jan. 7-April 23
Number of Senatorial Districts	35
Number of Representative Districts	151

EXECUTIVE BRANCH

Governor	John E. Baldacci
Secretary of State	Dan A. Gwadosky
Attorney General	G. Steven Rowe
Treasurer	Dale McCormick
Auditor	Gail M. Chase
Controller	Edward Karass
Governor's Present Term	1/03-1/07
Number of Elected Officials in the Executive Branch	1
Number of Members in the Cabinet	21

JUDICIAL BRANCH

Highest Court	Supreme Judicial Court
Supreme Court Chief Justice	Leigh Ingalls Saufley
Number of Supreme Court Judges	7
Number of Intermediate Appellate Court Judges	0
Number of U.S. Court Districts	1
U.S. Circuit Court	1st Circuit

STATE INTERNET ADDRESSES

Official State Website	http://www.state.me.us
Governor's Website	http://www.state.me.us/governor
Legislative Website	http://janus.state.me.us/legis
Judicial Website	http://www.courts.state.me.us

Maryland

Nicknames	The Old Line State and Free State
Motto	*Fatti Maschii, Parole Femine* (Manly Deeds, Womanly Words)
Flower	Black-eyed Susan
Bird	Baltimore Oriole
Tree	White Oak
Song	*Maryland, My Maryland*
Entered the Union	April 28, 1788
Capital	Annapolis

STATISTICS

Land Area (square miles)	9,774
Rank in Nation	42nd
Population	5,508,909
Rank in Nation	19th
Density per square mile	563.6
Capital City	Annapolis
Population	35,838
Rank in State	22nd
Largest City	Baltimore
Population	638,614
Number of Representatives in Congress	8
Number of Counties	24
Number of Municipal Governments	157
Number of 2004 Electoral Votes	10
Number of School Districts	24
Number of Special Districts	85

LEGISLATIVE BRANCH

Legislative Body	General Assembly
President of the Senate	Thomas V. Mike Miller Jr.
President Pro Tem of the Senate	Ida G. Ruben
Secretary of the Senate	William B.C. Addison Jr.
Speaker of the House	Michael Erin Busch
Speaker Pro Tem of the House	Adrienne A. Jones
Clerk of the House	Mary Monahan
2004 Regular Session	Jan. 14-April 12
Number of Senatorial Districts	47
Number of Representative Districts	47

EXECUTIVE BRANCH

Governor	Robert Ehrlich Jr.
Lieutenant Governor	Michael Steele
Secretary of State	Karl Aumann
Attorney General	J. Joseph Curran Jr.
Treasurer	Nancy K. Kopp
Auditor	Bruce A. Myers
Comptroller	William Schaefer
Governor's Present Term	1/03-1/07
Number of Elected Officials in the Executive Branch	4
Number of Members in the Cabinet	23

JUDICIAL BRANCH

Highest Court	Court of Appeals
Court of Appeals Chief Judge	Robert M. Bell
Number of Court of Appeals Judges	7
Number of Intermediate Appellate Court Judges	13
Number of U.S. Court Districts	1
U.S. Circuit Court	4th Circuit

STATE INTERNET ADDRESSES

Official State Website	http://www.maryland.gov
Governor's Website	http://www.gov.state.md.us
Legislative Website	http://www.mlis.state.md.us
Judicial Website	http://www.courts.state.md.us/

Massachusetts

Nickname .... The Bay State
Motto .... *Ense Petit Placidam Sub Libertate Quietem*
(By the Sword We Seek Peace,
but Peace Only under Liberty)
Flower .... Mayflower
Bird .... Chickadee
Tree .... American Elm
Song .... *All Hail to Massachusetts*
Entered the Union .... February 6, 1788
Capital .... Boston

STATISTICS

Land Area (square miles) 7,840
    Rank in Nation 45th
Population 6,433,422
    Rank in Nation 13th
    Density per square mile 820.6
Capital City .... Boston
    Population 589,281
    Rank in State 1st
Largest City .... Boston
Number of Representatives in Congress 10
Number of Counties 14
Number of Municipal Governments 45
Number of 2004 Electoral Votes 12
Number of School Districts 349
Number of Special Districts 403

LEGISLATIVE BRANCH

Legislative Body .... General Court

President of the Senate .... Robert E. Travaglini
President Pro Tem of the Senate .... Stanley C. Rosenberg
Clerk of the Senate .... William F. Welch

Speaker of the House .... Thomas M. Finneran
Clerk of the House .... Steven T. James
2004 Regular Session .... Jan. 7-July 31
Number of Senatorial Districts 40
Number of Representative Districts 160

EXECUTIVE BRANCH

Governor .... Mitt Romney
Lieutenant Governor .... Kerry Healey
Secretary of the Commonwealth .... William F. Galvin
Attorney General .... Thomas Reilly
Treasurer & Receiver General .... Timothy Cahill
Auditor .... Joseph DeNucci
Comptroller .... Martin J. Benison

Governor's Present Term 1/03-1/07
Number of Elected Officials in the Executive Branch 6
Number of Members in the Cabinet 10

JUDICIAL BRANCH

Highest Court .... Supreme Judicial Court
Supreme Judicial Court Chief Justice .... Margaret H. Marshall
Number of Supreme Judicial Court Judges 7
Number of Intermediate Appellate Court Judges 25
Number of U.S. Court Districts 1
U.S. Circuit Court .... 1st Circuit

STATE INTERNET ADDRESSES

Official State Website .... http://www.mass.gov
Governor's Website .... http://www.state.ma.us/gov
Legislative Website .... http://www.state.ma.us/legis
Judicial Website .... http://www.state.ma.us/courts

Michigan

Nickname .... The Wolverine State
Motto .... *Si Quaeris Peninsulam Amoenam Circumspice*
(If You Seek a Pleasant Peninsula, Look About You)
Flower .... Apple Blossom
Bird .... Robin
Tree .... White Pine
Song .... *Michigan, My Michigan*
Entered the Union .... January 26, 1837
Capital .... Lansing

STATISTICS

Land Area (square miles) 56,804
    Rank in Nation 22nd
Population 10,079,985
    Rank in Nation 8th
    Density per square mile 177.5
Capital City .... Lansing
    Population 118,588
    Rank in State 6th
Largest City .... Detroit
    Population 925,051
Number of Representatives in Congress 15
Number of Counties 83
Number of Municipal Governments 533
Number of 2004 Electoral Votes 17
Number of School Districts 734
Number of Special Districts 366

LEGISLATIVE BRANCH

Legislative Body .... Legislature

President of the Senate .... Lt. Gov. John Cherry
President Pro Tem of the Senate .... Patricia Birkholz
Secretary of the Senate .... Carol Morey Viventi

Speaker of the House .... Rick Johnson
Speaker Pro Tem of the House .... Larry Julian
Clerk of the House .... Gary L. Randall

2004 Regular Session .... Jan. 14-Dec. 31
Number of Senatorial Districts 38
Number of Representative Districts 110

EXECUTIVE BRANCH

Governor .... Jennifer Ganholm
Lieutenant Governor .... John Cherry
Secretary of State .... Terri Land
Attorney General .... Mike Cox
Treasurer .... Jay B. Rising
Auditor .... Thomas McTavish
Director, Office of Financial Management .... Michael J. Moody

Governor's Present Term 1/03-1/07
Number of Elected Officials in the Executive Branch 36
Number of Members in the Cabinet 24

JUDICIAL BRANCH

Highest Court .... Supreme Court
Supreme Court Chief Justice .... Maura D. Corrigan
Number of Supreme Court Judges 7
Number of Intermediate Appellate Court Judges 28
Number of U.S. Court Districts 2
U.S. Circuit Court .... 6th Circuit

STATE INTERNET ADDRESSES

Official State Website .... http://www.michigan.gov
Governor's Website .... http://www.michigan.gov/gov
Legislative Website .... http://www.michiganlegislature.org
Judicial Website .... http://www.courts.michigan.gov

Minnesota

Nickname	The North Star State
Motto	*L'Etoile du Nord* (The North Star)
Flower	Pink and White Lady-Slipper
Bird	Common Loon
Tree	Red Pine
Song	*Hail! Minnesota*
Entered the Union	May 11, 1858
Capital	St. Paul

STATISTICS

Land Area (square miles)	79,610
Rank in Nation	14th
Population	5,059,375
Rank in Nation	21st
Density per square mile	63.6
Capital City	St. Paul
Population	284,037
Rank in State	2nd
Largest City	Minneapolis
Population	375,635
Number of Representatives in Congress	8
Number of Counties	87
Number of Municipal Governments	854
Number of 2004 Electoral Votes	10
Number of School Districts	415
Number of Special Districts	403

LEGISLATIVE BRANCH

Legislative Body	Legislature
President of the Senate	James Metzen
Secretary of the Senate	Patrick E. Flahaven
Speaker of the House	Steven A. Sviggum
Speaker Pro Tem of the House	Ron Abrams, Lynda Boudreau, Mark Olson
Chief Clerk of the House	Edward A. Burdick
2004 Regular Session	Feb. 2-May 12
Number of Senatorial Districts	67
Number of Representative Districts	67

EXECUTIVE BRANCH

Governor	Tim Pawlenty
Lieutenant Governor	Carol Molnau
Secretary of State	Mary Kiffmeyer
Attorney General	Mike Hatch
Commissioner of Finance	Dan McElroy
Auditor	Patricia Anderson Awanda
Governor's Present Term	1/03-1/07
Number of Elected Officials in the Executive Branch	5
Number of Members in the Cabinet	25

JUDICIAL BRANCH

Highest Court	Supreme Court
Supreme Court Chief Justice	Kathleen A. Blatz
Number of Supreme Court Judges	7
Number of Intermediate Appellate Court Judges	16
Number of U.S. Court Districts	1
U.S. Circuit Court	8th Circuit

STATE INTERNET ADDRESSES

Official State Website	http://www.state.mn.us
Governor's Website	http://www.governor.state.mn.us
Legislative Website	http://www.leg.state.mn.us
Judicial Website	http://www.courts.state.mn.us/home/

Mississippi

Nickname	The Magnolia State
Motto	*Virtute et Armis* (By Valor and Arms)
Flower	Magnolia
Bird	Mockingbird
Tree	Magnolia
Song	*Go, Mississippi*
Entered the Union	December 10, 1817
Capital	Jackson

STATISTICS

Land Area (square miles)	46,907
Rank in Nation	31st
Population	2,881,281
Rank in Nation	31st
Density per square mile	61.4
Capital City	Jackson
Population	180,881
Rank in State	1st
Largest City	Jackson
Number of Representatives in Congress	4
Number of Counties	82
Number of Municipal Governments	296
Number of 2004 Electoral Votes	6
Number of School Districts	152
Number of Special Districts	458

LEGISLATIVE BRANCH

Legislative Body	Legislature
President of the Senate	Lt. Gov. Amy Tuck
President Pro Tem of the Senate	Travis Little
Secretary of the Senate	John O. Gilbert
Speaker of the House	William J. McCoy
Speaker Pro Tem of the House	J.P. Compretta
Clerk of the House	F. Edwin Perry
2004 Regular Session	Jan. 6-May 9
Number of Senatorial Districts	52
Number of Representative Districts	122

EXECUTIVE BRANCH

Governor	Haley Barbour
Lieutenant Governor	Amy Tuck
Secretary of State	Eric Clark
Attorney General	Jim Hood
Treasurer	Tate Reeves
Auditor	Phil Bryant
Comptroller	Margaret Hill
Governor's Present Term	1/04-1/08
Number of Elected Officials in the Executive Branch	8
Number of Members in the Cabinet	No formal cabinet system

JUDICIAL BRANCH

Highest Court	Supreme Court
Supreme Court Chief Justice	Edwin Lloyd Pittman
Number of Supreme Court Judges	9
Number of Intermediate Appellate Court Judges	10
Number of U.S. Court Districts	2
U.S. Circuit Court	5th Circuit

STATE INTERNET ADDRESSES

Official State Website	http://www.ms.gov
Governor's Website	http://www.governor.state.ms.us
Legislative Website	http://www.ls.state.ms.us
Judicial Website	http://www.mssc.state.ms.us

Missouri

Nickname	The Show Me State
Motto	*Salus Populi Suprema Lex Esto*
	(The Welfare of the People Shall Be the Supreme Law)
Flower	White Hawthorn Blossom
Bird	Bluebird
Tree	Flowering Dogwood
Song	*Missouri Waltz*
Entered the Union	August 10, 1821
Capital	Jefferson City

STATISTICS

Land Area (square miles)	68,886
Rank in Nation	18th
Population	5,704,484
Rank in Nation	17th
Density per square mile	82.8
Capital City	Jefferson City
Population	39,636
Rank in State	15th
Largest City	Kansas City
Population	443,471
Number of Representatives in Congress	9
Number of Counties	115
Number of Municipal Governments	946
Number of 2004 Electoral Votes	11
Number of School Districts	524
Number of Special Districts	1,514

LEGISLATIVE BRANCH

Legislative Body	Legislative Assembly
President of the Senate	Lt. Gov. Joe Maxwell
President Pro Tem of the Senate	Peter Kinder
Secretary of the Senate	Terry L. Spieler
Speaker of the House	Catherine Hanaway
Speaker Pro Tem of the House	Rod Jetton
Clerk of the House	Stephen S. Davis
2004 Regular Session	Jan. 7-May 30
Number of Senatorial Districts	34
Number of Representative Districts	163

EXECUTIVE BRANCH

Governor	Bob Holden
Lieutenant Governor	Joe Maxwell
Secretary of State	Matt Blunt
Attorney General	Jeremiah W. Nixon
Treasurer	Nancy Farmer
Auditor	Claire McCaskill
Director, Division of Accounting	James Carder
Governor's Present Term	1/01-1/05
Number of Elected Officials in the Executive Branch	6
Number of Members in the Cabinet	17

JUDICIAL BRANCH

Highest Court	Supreme Court
Supreme Court Chief Justice	Ronnie L. White
Number of Supreme Court Judges	7
Number of Intermediate Appellate Court Judges	32
Number of U.S. Court Districts	2
U.S. Circuit Court	8th Circuit

STATE INTERNET ADDRESSES

Official State Website	http://www.state.mo.us
Governor's Website	http://www.gov.state.mo.us
Legislative Website	http://www.moga.state.mo.us
Judicial Website	http://www.osca.state.mo.us

Montana

Nickname	The Treasure State
Motto	*Oro y Plata* (Gold and Silver)
Flower	Bitterroot
Bird	Western Meadowlark
Tree	Ponderosa Pine
Song	*Montana*
Entered the Union	November 8, 1889
Capital	Helena

STATISTICS

Land Area (square miles)	145,552
Rank in Nation	4th
Population	917,621
Rank in Nation	44th
Density per square mile	6.3
Capital City	Helena
Population	25,780
Rank in State	6th
Largest City	Billings
Population	89,847
Number of Representatives in Congress	1
Number of Counties	56
Number of Municipal Governments	129
Number of 2004 Electoral Votes	3
Number of School Districts	453
Number of Special Districts	592

LEGISLATIVE BRANCH

Legislative Body	Legislature
President of the Senate	Bob Keenan
President Pro Tem of the Senate	Walter McNutt
Secretary of the Senate	Rosana Skelton
Speaker of the House	Doug Mood
Speaker Pro Tem of the House	Jeff Laszloffy
Chief Clerk of the House	Marilyn Miller
2004 Regular Session	No regular session in 2004
Number of Senatorial Districts	50
Number of Representative Districts	100

EXECUTIVE BRANCH

Governor	Judy Martz
Lieutenant Governor	Karl Ohs
Secretary of State	Bob Brown
Attorney General	Mike McGrath
Treasurer	Scott Darkenwald
Auditor	John Morrison
Administrator, State Accounting	Cathy Muri
Governor's Present Term	1/01-1/05
Number of Elected Officials in the Executive Branch	6
Number of Members in the Cabinet	17

JUDICIAL BRANCH

Highest Court	Supreme Court
Supreme Court Chief Justice	Karla M. Gray
Number of Supreme Court Judges	7
Number of Intermediate Appellate Court Judges	0
Number of U.S. Court Districts	1
U.S. Circuit Court	9th Circuit

STATE INTERNET ADDRESSES

Official State Website	http://www.state.mt.us
Governor's Website	http://www.discoveringmontana.com/gov2
Legislative Website	http://leg.state.mt.us
Judicial Website	http://www.lawlibrary.state.mt.us

Nebraska

Nickname .... The Cornhusker State
Motto .... *Equality Before the Law*
Flower .... Goldenrod
Bird .... Western Meadowlark
Tree .... Western Cottonwood
Song .... *Beautiful Nebraska*
Entered the Union .... March 1, 1867
Capital .... Lincoln

STATISTICS

Land Area (square miles) 76,872
   Rank in Nation 15th
Population 1,739,291
   Rank in Nation 38th
   Density per square mile 22.6
Capital City .... Lincoln
   Population 232,362
   Rank in State 2nd
Largest City .... Omaha
   Population 399,357
Number of Representatives in Congress 3
Number of Counties 93
Number of Municipal Governments 531
Number of 2004 Electoral Votes 5
Number of School Districts 576
Number of Special Districts 1,146

LEGISLATIVE BRANCH

Legislative Body .... Unicameral Legislature

President of the Legislature .... Lt. Gov. David Heineman
Speaker of the Legislature .... Curt Bromm
Chairperson of Executive Board,
   Legislative Council .... Pat Engel
Vice Chairperson of Executive Board,
   Legislative Council .... Jim Cudaback
Clerk of the Legislature .... Patrick J. O'Donnell

2004 Regular Session .... Jan.8-To be determined
Number of Legislative Districts 49

EXECUTIVE BRANCH

Governor .... Mike Johanns
Lieutenant Governor .... David Heineman
Secretary of State .... John Gale
Attorney General .... Jon Bruning
Treasurer .... Ron Ross
Auditor .... Kate Witek
State Accounting Administrator .... Paul Carlson

Governor's Present Term 1/03-1/07
Number of Elected Officials in the Executive Branch ... 6
Number of Members in the Cabinet 29

JUDICIAL BRANCH

Highest Court .... Supreme Court
Supreme Court Chief Justice .... John V. Hendry
Number of Supreme Court Judges 7
Number of Intermediate Appellate Court Judges ... 6
Number of U.S. Court Districts 1
U.S. Circuit Court .... 8th Circuit

STATE INTERNET ADDRESSES

Official State Website .... http://www.state.ne.us
Governor's Website .... http://gov.nol.org
Legislative Website .... http://www.unicam.state.ne.us
Judicial Website .... http://court.nol.org

Nevada

Nickname .... The Silver State
Motto .... *All for Our Country*
Flower .... Sagebrush
Bird .... Mountain Bluebird
Tre e .... Bristlecone Pine and Single-leaf Pinon
Song .... *Home Means Nevada*
Entered the Union .... October 31, 1864
Capital .... Carson City

STATISTICS

Land Area (square miles) 109,826
   Rank in Nation 7th
Population 2,241,154
   Rank in Nation 35th
   Density per square mile 20.4
Capital City .... Carson City
   Population 52,457
   Rank in State 6th
Largest City .... Las Vegas
   Population 508,604
Number of Representatives in Congress 3
Number of Counties 17
Number of Municipal Governments 19
Number of 2004 Electoral Votes 5
Number of School Districts 17
Number of Special Districts 158

LEGISLATIVE BRANCH

Legislative Body .... Legislature

President of the Senate .... Lt. Gov. Lorraine Hunt
President Pro Tem of the Senate .... Mark Amodei
Secretary of the Senate .... Claire Clift

Speaker of the Assembly .... Richard Perkins
Speaker Pro Tem of the Assembly .... Wendell Williams
Chief Clerk of the Assembly .... Nancy Tribble

2004 Regular Session .... No regular session in 2004
Number of Senatorial Districts 12
Number of Representative Districts 42

EXECUTIVE BRANCH

Governor .... Kenny Guinn
Lieutenant Governor .... Lorraine Hunt
Secretary of State .... Dean Heller
Attorney General .... Brian Sandoval
Treasurer .... Brian Krolicki
Auditor .... Paul V. Townsend
Controller .... Kathy Augustine

Governor's Present Term 1/03-1/07
Number of Elected Officials in the Executive Branch ... 6
Number of Members in the Cabinet .... No formal cabinet system

JUDICIAL BRANCH

Highest Court .... Supreme Court
Supreme Court Chief Justice .... Deborah Agosti
Number of Supreme Court Judges 7
Number of Intermediate Appellate Court Judges ... 0
Number of U.S. Court Districts 1
U.S. Circuit Court .... 9th Circuit

STATE INTERNET ADDRESSES

Official State Website .... http://www.nv.gov
Governor's Website .... http://www.gov.state.nv.us
Legislative Website .... http://www.leg.state.nv.us
Judicial Website .... http://silver.state.nv.us/elec_judicial.htm

New Hampshire

Nickname .... The Granite State
Motto .... *Live Free or Die*
Flower .... Purple Lilac
Bird .... Purple Finch
Tree .... White Birch
Song .... *Old New Hampshire*
Entered the Union .... June 21, 1788
Capital .... Concord

STATISTICS

Land Area (square miles) 8,968
    Rank in Nation 44th
Population 1,287,687
    Rank in Nation 41st
    Density per square mile 143.6
Capital City .... Concord
    Population 40,687
    Rank in State 3rd
Largest City .... Manchester
    Population 108,398
Number of Representatives in Congress 2
Number of Counties 10
Number of Municipal Governments 13
Number of 2004 Electoral Votes 4
Number of School Districts 178
Number of Special Districts 148

LEGISLATIVE BRANCH

Legislative Body .... General Court

President of the Senate .... Thomas R. Eaton
President Pro Tem of the Senate .... Carl R. Johnson
Clerk of the Senate .... Steven J. Winter

Speaker of the House .... Gene Chandler
Speaker Pro Tem of the House .... Sheila T. Francoeur
Clerk of the House .... Karen O. Wadsworth

2004 Regular Session .... Jan. 7-June 30
Number of Senatorial Districts 24
Number of Representative Districts 88

EXECUTIVE BRANCH

Governor .... Craig Benson
Secretary of State .... William M. Gardner
Attorney General .... Peter Heed
Treasurer .... Michael A. Ablowich
Auditor .... Thomas E. Martin
Comptroller .... Thomas Martin

Governor's Present Term 1/03-1/05
Number of Elected Officials in the Executive Branch 1
Number of Members in the Cabinet .... No formal cabinet system

JUDICIAL BRANCH

Highest Court .... Supreme Court
Supreme Court Chief Justice .... John T. Broderick, Jr.
Number of Supreme Court Judges 5
Number of Intermediate Appellate Court Judges 0
Number of U.S. Court Districts 1
U.S. Circuit Court .... 1st Circuit

STATE INTERNET ADDRESSES

Official State Website .... http://www.state.nh.us
Governor's Website .... http://www.nh.gov/governor/
Legislative Website .... http://www.gencourt.state.nh.us
Judicial Website .... http://www.courts.state.nh.us/

New Jersey

Nickname .... The Garden State
Motto .... *Liberty and Prosperity*
Flower .... Violet
Bird .... Eastern Goldfinch
Tree .... Red Oak
Song .... I'm From New Jersey
Entered the Union .... December 18, 1787
Capital .... Trenton

STATISTICS

Land Area (square miles) 7,417
    Rank in Nation 46th
Population 8,638,396
    Rank in Nation 10th
    Density per square mile 1,164.7
Capital City .... Trenton
    Population 85,650
    Rank in State 9th
Largest City .... Newark
    Population 277,000
Number of Representatives in Congress 13
Number of Counties 21
Number of Municipal Governments 324
Number of 2004 Electoral Votes 15
Number of School Districts 604
Number of Special Districts 276

LEGISLATIVE BRANCH

Legislative Body .... Legislature

President of the Senate .... Richard J. Codey
President Pro Tem of the Senate .... Shirley K. Turner
Secretary of the Senate .... Ellen M. Davenport

Speaker of the Assembly .... Albio Sires
Speaker Pro Tem of the Assembly .... Donald Tucker
Clerk of the General Assembly .... Christine Riebe

2004 Regular Session .... Jan. 13-Dec. 31
Number of Senatorial Districts 40
Number of Representative Districts 40

EXECUTIVE BRANCH

Governor .... James McGreevey
Secretary of State .... Regena Thomas
Attorney General .... Peter C. Harvey
Treasurer .... John E. McCormac
Auditor .... Richard L. Fair
Controller .... Charlene Holzbaur

Governor's Present Term 1/02-1/06
Number of Elected Officials in the Executive Branch 1
Number of Members in the Cabinet 19

JUDICIAL BRANCH

Highest Court .... Supreme Court
Supreme Court Chief Justice .... Deborah T. Poritz
Number of Supreme Court Judges 7
Number of Intermediate Appellate Court Judges 32
Number of U.S. Court Districts 1
U.S. Circuit Court .... 3rd Circuit

STATE INTERNET ADDRESSES

Official State Website .... http://www.state.nj.us
Governor's Website .... http://www.state.nj.us/governor
Legislative Website .... http://www.njleg.state.nj.us
Judicial Website .... http://www.judiciary.state.nj.us

New Mexico

Nickname .... The Land of Enchantment
Motto .... *Crescit Eundo* (It Grows As It Goes)
Flower .... Yucca (Our Lord's Candles)
Bird .... Chaparral Bird
Tree .... Pinon
Songs .... *Asi es Nuevo Mexico and*
O, Fair New Mexico
Entered the Union .... January 6, 1912
Capital .... Santa Fe

STATISTICS

Land Area (square miles) 121,356
    Rank in Nation 5th
Population 1,874,614
    Rank in Nation 36th
    Density per square mile 15.4
Capital City .... Santa Fe
    Population 62,203
    Rank in State 3rd
Largest City .... Albuquerque
    Population 463,874
Number of Representatives in Congress 3
Number of Counties 33
Number of Municipal Governments 101
Number of 2004 Electoral Votes 5
Number of School Districts 89
Number of Special Districts 628

LEGISLATIVE BRANCH

Legislative Body .... Legislature

President of the Senate .... Lt. Gov. Diane Denish
President Pro Tem of the Senate .... Richard Romero
Chief Clerk of the Senate .... Margaret Larragoite

Speaker of the House .... Ben Lujan
Chief Clerk of the House .... Stephen R. Arias

2004 Regular Session .... Jan. 20-Feb. 19
Number of Senatorial Districts 42
Number of Representative Districts 70

EXECUTIVE BRANCH

Governor .... Bill Richardson
Lieutenant Governor .... Diane Denish
Secretary of State .... Rebecca Vigil-Giron
Attorney General .... Patricia Madrid
Treasurer .... Robert E. Vigil
Auditor .... Domingo P. Martinez
Controller .... Anthony Armijo

Governor's Present Term 1/03-1/07
Number of Elected Officials in the Executive Branch 12
Number of Members in the Cabinet 17

JUDICIAL BRANCH

Highest Court .... Supreme Court
Supreme Court Chief Justice .... Petra Jimenez Maes
Number of Supreme Court Judges 5
Number of Intermediate Appellate Court Judges 10
Number of U.S. Court Districts 1
U.S. Circuit Court .... 10th Circuit

STATE INTERNET ADDRESSES

Official State Website .... http://www.state.nm.us
Governor's Website .... http://www.governor.state.nm.us
Legislative Website .... http://legis.state.nm.us
Judicial Website .... http://www.nmcourts.com

New York

Nickname .... The Empire State
Motto .... *Excelsior* (Ever Upward)
Flower .... Rose
Bird .... Bluebird
Tree .... Sugar Maple
Song .... *I Love New York*
Entered the Union .... July 26, 1788
Capital .... Albany

STATISTICS

Land Area (square miles) 47,214
    Rank in Nation 30th
Population 19,190,115
    Rank in Nation 3rd
    Density per square mile 406.4
Capital City .... Albany
    Population 95,658
    Rank in State 6th
Largest City .... New York City
    Population 8,084,316
Number of Representatives in Congress 29
Number of Counties 62
Number of Municipal Governments 616
Number of 2004 Electoral Votes 31
Number of School Districts 703
Number of Special Districts 1,135

LEGISLATIVE BRANCH

Legislative Body .... Legislature

President of the Senate .... Lt. Gov. Mary Donohue
President Pro Tem and Majority Leader of the Senate ... Joseph L. Bruno
Secretary of the Senate .... Steven M. Boggess

Speaker of the Assembly .... Sheldon Silver
Speaker Pro Tem of the Assembly .... Ivan C. Lafayette
Acting Clerk of the Assembly .... June Egeland

2004 Regular Session .... Jan. 7-Dec. 31
Number of Senatorial Districts 62
Number of Representative Districts 150

EXECUTIVE BRANCH

Governor .... George Pataki
Lieutenant Governor .... Mary Donohue
Secretary of State .... Randy Daniels
Attorney General .... Eliot Spitzer
Treasurer .... Aida Brewer
Controller .... Alan G. Hevesi

Governor's Present Term 1/03-1/07
Number of Elected Officials in the Executive Branch 4
Number of Members in the Cabinet 75

JUDICIAL BRANCH

Highest Court .... Court of Appeals
Court of Appeals Chief Justice .... Judith S. Kaye
Number of Court of Appeals Judges 7
Number of Intermediate Appellate Court Judges 70
Number of U.S. Court Districts 4
U.S. Circuit Court .... 2nd Circuit

STATE INTERNET ADDRESSES

Official State Website .... http://www.state.ny.us
Governor's Website .... http://www.state.ny.us/governor
Senate Website .... http://www.senate.state.ny.us
Assembly Website .... http://assembly.state.ny.us
Judicial Website .... http://www.courts.state.ny.us

North Carolina

Nickname .... The Tar Heel State and Old North State
Motto .... *Esse Quam Videri*
(To Be Rather Than to Seem)
Flower .... Dogwood
Bird .... Cardinal
Tree .... Long Leaf Pine
Song .... *The Old North State*
Entered the United States .... November 21, 1789
Capital .... Raleigh

STATISTICS

Land Area (square miles) 48,711
    Rank in Nation 29th
Population 8,407,248
    Rank in Nation 11th
    Density per square mile 172.6
Capital City .... Raleigh
    Population 306,944
    Rank in State 2nd
Largest City .... Charlotte
    Population 580,597
Number of Representatives in Congress 13
Number of Counties 100
Number of Municipal Governments 541
Number of 2004 Electoral Votes 15
Number of School Districts 120
Number of Special Districts 319

LEGISLATIVE BRANCH

Legislative Body .... General Assembly

President of the Senate .... Lt. Gov. Beverly Perdue
President Pro Tem of the Senate .... Marc Basnight
Principal Clerk of the Senate .... Janet Pruitt

Democratic Speaker of the House .... James B. Black
Republican Speaker of the House .... Richard T. Morgan
Principal Clerk of the House .... Denise Weeks

2004 Regular Session .... May 10-To be determined
Number of Senatorial Districts 50
Number of Representative Districts 120

EXECUTIVE BRANCH

Governor .... Michael Easley
Lieutenant Governor .... Beverly Perdue
Secretary of State .... Elaine Marshall
Attorney General .... Roy A. Cooper III
Treasurer .... Richard H. Moore
Auditor .... Ralph Campbell Jr.
Controller .... Robert Powell

Governor's Present Term 1/01-1/05
Number of Elected Officials in the Executive Branch 10
Number of Members in the Cabinet 10

JUDICIAL BRANCH

Highest Court .... Supreme Court
Supreme Court Chief Justice .... I.B. Lake Jr.
Number of Supreme Court Judges 7
Number of Intermediate Appellate Court Judges 12
Number of U.S. Court Districts 3
U.S. Circuit Court .... 4th Circuit

STATE INTERNET ADDRESSES

Official State Website .... http://www.ncgov.com
Governor's Website .... http://www.governor.state.nc.us
Legislative Website .... http://www.ncleg.net
Judicial Website .... http://www.nccourts.org

North Dakota

Nickname .... Peace Garden State
Motto .... *Liberty and Union, Now and Forever,*
One and Inseparable
Flower .... Wild Prairie Rose
Bird .... Western Meadowlark
Tree .... American Elm
Song .... *North Dakota Hymn*
Entered the Union .... November 2, 1889
Capital .... Bismarck

STATISTICS

Land Area (square miles) 68,976
    Rank in Nation 17th
Population 633,837
    Rank in Nation 48th
    Density per square mile 9.2
Capital City .... Bismarck
    Population 55,532
    Rank in State 2nd
Largest City .... Fargo
    Population 90,599
Number of Representatives in Congress 1
Number of Counties 53
Number of Municipal Governments 360
Number of 2004 Electoral Votes 3
Number of School Districts 230
Number of Special Districts 764

LEGISLATIVE BRANCH

Legislative Body .... Legislative Assembly

President of the Senate .... Lt. Gov. Jack Dalrymple
President Pro Tem of the Senate .... Herb Urlacher
Secretary of the Senate .... William R. Horton

Speaker of the House .... Janet Wentz
Clerk of the House .... Brad Faye

2004 Regular Session .... No regular session in 2004
Number of Senatorial Districts 47
Number of Representative Districts 47

EXECUTIVE BRANCH

Governor .... John Hoeven
Lieutenant Governor .... Jack Dalrymple
Secretary of State .... Alvin Jaeger
Attorney General .... Wayne Stenehjem
Treasurer .... Kathi Gilmore
Auditor .... Robert R. Peterson
Comptroller .... Sheila Peterson

Governor's Present Term 12/00-12/04
Number of Elected Officials in the Executive Branch 10
Number of Members in the Cabinet 18

JUDICIAL BRANCH

Highest Court .... Supreme Court
Supreme Court Chief Justice .... Gerald W. VandeWalle
Number of Supreme Court Judges 5
Number of Intermediate Appellate Court Judges 0
Number of U.S. Court Districts 1
U.S. Circuit Court .... 8th Circuit

STATE INTERNET ADDRESSES

Official State Website .... http://discovernd.com
Governor's Website .... http://www.governor.state.nd.us
Legislative Website .... http://www.state.nd.us/lr
Judicial Website .... http://www.court.state.nd.us

Ohio

Nickname .... The Buckeye State
Motto .... *With God, All Things Are Possible*
Flower .... Scarlet Carnation
Bird .... Cardinal
Tree .... Buckeye
Song .... *Beautiful Ohio*
Entered the Union .... March 1, 1803
Capital .... Columbus

STATISTICS

Land Area (square miles) 40,948
    Rank in Nation 35th
Population 11,435,798
    Rank in Nation 7th
    Density per square mile 279.3
Capital City .... Columbus
Population 725,228
    Rank in State 1st
Largest City .... Columbus
Number of Representatives in Congress 18
Number of Counties 88
Number of Municipal Governments 942
Number of 2004 Electoral Votes 20
Number of School Districts 662
Number of Special Districts 631

LEGISLATIVE BRANCH

Legislative Body .... General Assembly

President of the Senate .... Doug White
President Pro Tem of the Senate .... Randall Gardner
Clerk of the Senate .... Matthew T. Schuler

Speaker of the House .... Larry Householder
Speaker Pro Tem of the House .... Gary W. Cates
Legislative Clerk of the House .... Laura P. Clemens

2004 Regular Session .... Jan. 6-Dec. 31
Number of Senatorial Districts 33
Number of Representative Districts 99

EXECUTIVE BRANCH

Governor .... Bob Taft
Lieutenant Governor .... Jennette Bradley
Secretary of State .... J. Kenneth Blackwell
Attorney General .... Jim Petro
Treasurer .... Joseph T. Deters
Auditor .... Betty D. Montgomery
Director, Office of Management & Budget .... Thomas W. Johnson

Governor's Present Term 1/03-1/07
Number of Elected Officials in the Executive Branch 6
Number of Members in the Cabinet 24

JUDICIAL BRANCH

Highest Court .... Supreme Court
Supreme Court Chief Justice .... Thomas J. Moyer
Number of Supreme Court Judges 7
Number of Intermediate Appellate Court Judges 68
Number of U.S. Court Districts 2
U.S. Circuit Court .... 6th Circuit

STATE INTERNET ADDRESSES

Official State Website .... http://www.state.oh.us
Governor's Website .... http://governor.ohio.gov/
Legislative Website .... http://www.ohio.gov/ohio/GovState.stm#ohleg
Judicial Website .... http://www.sconet.state.oh.us

Oklahoma

Nickname .... The Sooner State
Motto .... *Labor Omnia Vincit* (Labor Conquers All Things)
Flower .... Mistletoe
Bird .... Scissor-tailed Flycatcher
Tree .... Redbud
Song .... *Oklahoma*
Entered the Union .... November 16, 1907
Capital .... Oklahoma City

STATISTICS

Land Area (square miles) 68,667
    Rank in Nation 19th
Population 3,511,532
    Rank in Nation 28th
    Density per square mile 51.1
Capital City .... Oklahoma City
Population 519,034
    Rank in State 1st
Largest City .... Oklahoma City
Number of Representatives in Congress 5
Number of Counties 77
Number of Municipal Governments 590
Number of 2004 Electoral Votes 7
Number of School Districts 544
Number of Special Districts 560

LEGISLATIVE BRANCH

Legislative Body .... Legislature

President of the Senate .... Lt. Gov. Mary Fallin
President Pro Tem of the Senate .... Cal Hobson
Secretary of the Senate .... Michael Clingman

Speaker of the House .... Larry E. Adair
Speaker Pro Tem of the House .... Danny Hillard
Chief Clerk/Administrator of the House .... Larry Warden

2004 Regular Session .... Feb. 2-May 28
Number of Senatorial Districts 50
Number of Representative Districts 101

EXECUTIVE BRANCH

Governor .... Brad Henry
Lieutenant Governor .... Mary Fallin
Secretary of State .... Susan Savage
Attorney General .... W. A. Drew Edmondson
Treasurer .... Robert Butkin
Auditor .... Jeff McMahan
Comptroller .... Brenda Bolander

Governor's Present Term 1/03-1/07
Number of Elected Officials in the Executive Branch 11
Number of Members in the Cabinet 10-15

JUDICIAL BRANCH

Highest Court .... Supreme Court
Supreme Court Chief Justice .... Joseph M. Watt
Number of Supreme Court Judges 9
Number of Intermediate Appellate Court Judges 12
Number of U.S. Court Districts 3
U.S. Circuit Court .... 10th Circuit

STATE INTERNET ADDRESSES

Official State Website .... http://www.state.ok.us
Governor's Website .... http://www.governor.state.ok.us/
Legislative Website .... http://www.lsb.state.ok.us
Judicial Website .... http://www.oscn.net

Oregon

Nickname	The Beaver State
Motto	*She Flies with Her Own Wings*
Flower	Oregon Grape
Bird	Western Meadowlark
Tree	Douglas Fir
Song	*Oregon, My Oregon*
Entered the Union	February 14, 1859
Capital	Salem

STATISTICS

Land Area (square miles)	95,997
Rank in Nation	10th
Population	3,559,596
Rank in Nation	27th
Density per square mile	37.1
Capital City	Salem
Population	140,977
Rank in State	3rd
Largest City	Portland
Population	539,438
Number of Representatives in Congress	5
Number of Counties	36
Number of Municipal Governments	240
Number of 2004 Electoral Votes	7
Number of School Districts	197
Number of Special Districts	927

LEGISLATIVE BRANCH

Legislative Body	Legislative Assembly
President of the Senate	Peter Courtney
President Pro Tem of the Senate	Lenn Hannon
Secretary of the Senate	Judy Hall
Speaker of the House	Karen Minnis
Chief Clerk of the House	Ramona Kenady
2004 Regular Session	No regular session in 2004
Number of Senatorial Districts	30
Number of Representative Districts	60

EXECUTIVE BRANCH

Governor	Ted Kulongoski
Secretary of State	Bill Bradbury
Attorney General	Hardy Myers
Treasurer	Randall Edwards
Auditor	Catherine Pollino
Controller	John Radford
Governor's Present Term	1/03-1/07
Number of Elected Officials in the Executive Branch	6
Number of Members in the Cabinet	No formal cabinet system

JUDICIAL BRANCH

Highest Court	Supreme Court
Supreme Court Chief Justice	Wallace P. Carson Jr.
Number of Supreme Court Judges	7
Number of Intermediate Appellate Court Judges	10
Number of U.S. Court Districts	1
U.S. Circuit Court	9th Circuit

STATE INTERNET ADDRESSES

Official State Website	http://www.oregon.gov
Governor's Website	http://www.governor.state.or.us
Legislative Website	http://www.leg.state.or.us
Judicial Website	http://www.ojd.state.or.us

Pennsylvania

Nickname	The Keystone State
Motto	*Virtue, Liberty and Independence*
Animal	White-tailed Deer
Flower	Mountain Laurel
Tree	Hemlock
Song	Pennsylvania
Entered the Union	December 12, 1787
Capital	Harrisburg

STATISTICS

Land Area (square miles)	44,817
Rank in Nation	32nd
Population	12,365,455
Rank in Nation	6th
Density per square mile	275.9
Capital City	Harrisburg
Population	48,540
Rank in State	13th
Largest City	Philadelphia
Population	1,492,231
Number of Representatives in Congress	19
Number of Counties	67
Number of Municipal Governments	1,018
Number of 2004 Electoral Votes	21
Number of School Districts	501
Number of Special Districts	1,885

LEGISLATIVE BRANCH

Legislative Body	General Assembly
President of the Senate	Lt. Gov. Catherine Baker Knoll
President Pro Tem of the Senate	Robert C. Jubelirer
Secretary-Parliamentarian of the Senate	Mark R. Corrigan
Speaker of the House	John M. Perzel
Chief Clerk of the House	Ted Mazia
2004 Regular Session	Jan. 6-Dec. 10
Number of Senatorial Districts	50
Number of Representative Districts	203

EXECUTIVE BRANCH

Governor	Ed Rendell
Lieutenant Governor	Catherine Baker Knoll
Secretary of State	Pedro A. Cortes
Attorney General	Gerald J. Pappert
Treasurer	Barbara Hafer
Auditor	Robert P. Casey, Jr.
Comptroller	Harvey Eckert
Governor's Present Term	1/03-1/07
Number of Elected Officials in the Executive Branch	6
Number of Members in the Cabinet	19

JUDICIAL BRANCH

Highest Court	Supreme Court
Supreme Court Chief Justice	Ralph J. Cappy
Number of Supreme Court Judges	7
Number of Intermediate Appellate Court Judges	24
Number of U.S. Court Districts	3
U.S. Circuit Court	3rd Circuit

STATE INTERNET ADDRESSES

Official State Website	http://www.state.pa.us
Governor's Website	http://www.governor.state.pa.us/
Legislative Website	http://www.legis.state.pa.us
Judicial Website	http://www.courts.state.pa.us

Rhode Island

Nicknames .... Little Rhody and Ocean State
Motto .... *Hope*
Flower .... Violet
Bird .... Rhode Island Red
Tree .... Red Maple
Song .... *Rhode Island*
Entered the Union .... May 29, 1790
Capital .... Providence

STATISTICS

Land Area (square mile) 1,045
   Rank in Nation 50th
Population 1,076,164
   Rank in Nation 43rd
   Density per square mile 1,029.8
Capital City .... Providence
Population 175,901
   Rank in State 1st
Largest City .... Providence
Number of Representatives in Congress 2
Number of Counties 5
Number of Municipal Governments 8
Number of 2004 Electoral Votes 4
Number of School Districts 36
Number of Special Districts 75

LEGISLATIVE BRANCH

Legislative Body .... General Assembly

President of the Senate .... Lt. Gov. Charles Fogarty
President Pro Tem of the Senate .... John C. Revens Jr.
Clerk of the Senate .... Raymond T. Hoyas Jr.

Speaker of the House .... William J. Murphy
Speaker Pro Tem of the House .... Peter F. Kilmartin
Clerk of the House .... Louis D'Antuono

2004 Regular Session .... Jan. 6-To be determined
Number of Senatorial Districts 38
Number of Representative Districts 75

EXECUTIVE BRANCH

Governor .... Don Carcieri
Lieutenant Governor .... Charles J. Fogarty
Secretary of State .... Matthew Brown
Attorney General .... Patrick Lynch
Treasurer .... Paul J. Tavares
Auditor .... Ernest A. Almonte
Controller .... Lawrence Franklin

Governor's Present Term 1/03-1/07
Number of Elected Officials in the Executive Branch 5
Number of Members in the Cabinet .... Not available

JUDICIAL BRANCH

Highest Court .... Supreme Court
Supreme Court Chief Justice .... Frank J. Williams
Number of Supreme Court Judges 5
Number of Intermediate Appellate Court Judges 0
Number of U.S. Court Districts 1
U.S. Circuit Court .... 1st Circuit

STATE INTERNET ADDRESSES

Official State Website .... http://www.state.ri.us
Governor's Website .... http://www.governor.state.ri.us
Legislative Website .... http://www.rilin.state.ri.us
Judicial Website .... http://www.courts.state.ri.us

South Carolina

Nickname .... The Palmetto State
Motto .... *Animis Opibusque Parati*
   (Prepared in Mind and Resources) and
   Dum Spiro Spero (While I breathe, I Hope)
Flower .... Yellow Jessamine
Bird .... Carolina Wren
Tree .... Palmetto
Songs .... *Carolina* and *South Carolina on My Mind*
Entered the Union .... May 23, 1788
Capital .... Columbia

STATISTICS

Land Area (square miles) 30,110
   Rank in Nation 40th
Population 4,147,152
   Rank in Nation 25th
   Density per square mile 137.7
Capital City .... Columbia

Population 117,394
   Rank in State 1st
Largest City .... Columbia
Number of Representatives in Congress 6
Number of Counties 46
Number of Municipal Governments 269
Number of 2004 Electoral Votes 8
Number of School Districts 90
Number of Special Districts 301

LEGISLATIVE BRANCH

Legislative Body .... General Assembly

President of the Senate .... Lt. Gov. Andre Bauer
President Pro Tem of the Senate .... Glenn F. McConnell
Clerk and Director of Senate Research .... Jeffrey S. Gossett

Speaker of the House .... David H. Wilkins
Speaker Pro Tem of the House .... W. Douglas Smith
Clerk of the House .... Sandra K. McKinney

2004 Regular Session .... Jan. 13-June 3
Number of Senatorial Districts 46
Number of Representative Districts 124

EXECUTIVE BRANCH

Governor .... Mark Sanford
Lieutenant Governor .... R. Andre Bauer
Secretary of State .... Mark Hammond
Attorney General .... Henry McMaster
Treasurer .... Grady L. Patterson Jr.
Auditor .... Thomas L. Wagner, Jr.
Comptroller .... Richard Eckstrom

Governor's Present Term 1/03-1/07
Number of Elected Officials in the Executive Branch 9
Number of Members in the Cabinet 15

JUDICIAL BRANCH

Highest Court .... Supreme Court
Supreme Court Chief Justice .... Jean Hoefer Toal
Number of Supreme Court Judges 5
Number of Intermediate Appellate Court Judges 91
Number of U.S. Court Districts 1
U.S. Circuit Court .... 4th Circuit

STATE INTERNET ADDRESSES

Official State Website .... http://www.myscgov.com
Governor's Website http://www.scgovernor.com/
Legislative Website .... http://www.scstatehouse.net
Judicial Website .... http://www.judicial.state.sc.us

South Dakota

Nicknames	The Mt. Rushmore State
Motto	*Under God the People Rule*
Flower	American Pasque
Bird	Chinese ring-necked pheasant
Tree	Black Hills Spruce
Song	*Hail, South Dakota*
Entered the Union	November 2, 1889
Capital	Pierre

STATISTICS

Land Area (square miles)	75,885
Rank in Nation	16th
Population	764,309
Rank in Nation	46th
Density per square mile	10.1
Capital City	Pierre
Population	13,876
Rank in State	7th
Largest City	Sioux Falls
Population	130,491
Number of Representatives in Congress	1
Number of Counties	66
Number of Municipal Governments	308
Number of 2004 Electoral Votes	3
Number of School Districts	176
Number of Special Districts	376

LEGISLATIVE BRANCH

Legislative Body	Legislature
President of the Senate	Lt. Gov. Dennis Daugaard
President Pro Tem of the Senate	Arnold Brown
Secretary of the Senate	Patricia Adam
Speaker of the House	Matthew Michels
Speaker Pro Tem of the House	Christopher Madsen
Chief Clerk of the House	Karen Gerdes
2004 Regular Session	Jan. 13-To be determined
Number of Senatorial Districts	35
Number of Representative Districts	35

EXECUTIVE BRANCH

Governor	Mike Rounds
Lieutenant Governor	Dennis Daugaard
Secretary of State	Chris Nelson
Attorney General	Larry Long
Treasurer	Vernon L. Larson
Auditor	Rich Sattgast
Governor's Present Term	1/03-1/07
Number of Elected Officials in the Executive Branch	10
Number of Members in the Cabinet	20

JUDICIAL BRANCH

Highest Court	Supreme Court
Supreme Court Chief Justice	David E. Gilbertson
Number of Supreme Court Judges	5
Number of Intermediate Appellate Court Judges	0
Number of U.S. Court Districts	1
U.S. Circuit Court	8th Circuit

STATE INTERNET ADDRESSES

Official State Website	http://www.state.sd.us
Governor's Website	http://www.state.sd.us/governor
Legislative Website	http://legis.state.sd.us
Judicial Website	http://www.sdjudicial.com

Tennessee

Nickname	The Volunteer State
Motto	*Agriculture and Commerce*
Flower	Iris
Bird	Mockingbird
Tree	Tulip Poplar
Songs	*When It's Iris Time in Tennessee;* The Tennessee Waltz; My Homeland, Tennessee *My Tennessee;* and *Rocky Top*
Entered the Union	June 1, 1796
Capital	Nashville

STATISTICS

Land Area (square miles)	41,217
Rank in Nation	34th
Population	5,841,748
Rank in Nation	16th
Density per square mile	141.7
Capital City	Nashville
Population	545,915
Rank in State	2nd
Largest City	Memphis
Population	648,882
Number of Representatives in Congress	9
Number of Counties	95
Number of Municipal Governments	349
Number of 2004 Electoral Votes	11
Number of School Districts	138
Number of Special Districts	475

LEGISLATIVE BRANCH

Legislative Body	General Assembly
Speaker of the Senate	Lt. Gov. John S. Wilder
Speaker Pro Tem of the Senate	Jo Ann Graves
Chief Clerk of the Senate	Russell Humphrey
Speaker of the House	James O. Naifeh
Speaker Pro Tem of the House	Lois M. DeBerry
Chief Clerk of the House	Burney T. Durham
2004 Regular Session	Jan. 13-To be determined
Number of Senatorial Districts	33
Number of Representative Districts	99

EXECUTIVE BRANCH

Governor	Phil Bredesen
Lieutenant Governor	John S. Wilder
Secretary of State	Riley Darnell
Attorney General	Paul G. Summers
Treasurer	Dale Sims
Auditor	Art Hayes
Comptroller of the Treasury	John Morgan
Governor's Present Term	1/03-1/07
Number of Elected Officials in the Executive Branch	1
Number of Members in the Cabinet	28

JUDICIAL BRANCH

Highest Court	Supreme Court
Supreme Court Chief Justice	Frank F. Drowota III
Number of Supreme Court Judges	5
Number of Intermediate Appellate Court Judges	24
Number of U.S. Court Districts	3
U.S. Circuit Court	6th Circuit

STATE INTERNET ADDRESSES

Official State Website	http://www.state.tn.us
Governor's Website	http://www.state.tn.us/governor
Legislative Website	http://www.legislature.state.tn.us
Judicial Website	http://www.tsc.state.tn.us

Texas

Nickname .... The Lone Star State
Motto .... *Friendship*
Flower .... Bluebonnet (Buffalo Clover, Wolf Flower)
Bird .... Mockingbird
Tree .... Pecan
Song .... *Texas, Our Texas*
Entered the Union .... December 29, 1845
Capital .... Austin

STATISTICS

Land Area (square miles) 261,797
  Rank in Nation 2nd
Population 22,118,509
  Rank in Nation 2nd
  Density per square mile 84.5
Capital City .... Austin
  Population 671,873
  Rank in State 4th
Largest City .... Houston
  Population 2,009,834
Number of Representatives in Congress 32
Number of Counties 254
Number of Municipal Governments 1,196
Number of 2004 Electoral Votes 34
Number of School Districts 1,040
Number of Special Districts 2,245

LEGISLATIVE BRANCH

Legislative Body .... Legislature

President of the Senate .... Lt. Gov. David Dewhurst
President Pro Tem of the Senate .... Eddie Lucio Jr.
Secretary of the Senate .... Patsy Spaw

Speaker of the House .... Tom Craddick
Speaker Pro Tem of the House .... Sylvester Turner
Chief Clerk of the House .... Robert Haney

2004 Regular Session .... No regular session in 2004
Number of Senatorial Districts 31
Number of Representative Districts 150

EXECUTIVE BRANCH

Governor .... Rick Perry
Lieutenant Governor .... David Dewhurst
Secretary of State .... Geoffrey S. Connor
Attorney General .... Greg Abbott
Comptroller of Public Accounts .... Carole Keeton Strayhorn
Auditor .... Lawrence F. Alwin

Governor's Present Term 1/03-1/07
Number of Elected Officials in the Executive Branch 9
Number of Members in the Cabinet .... No formal cabinet system

JUDICIAL BRANCH

Highest Court .... Supreme Court
Supreme Court Chief Justice .... Thomas R. Phillips
Number of Supreme Court Judges 18
Number of Intermediate Appellate Court Judges 80
Number of U.S. Court Districts 4
U.S. Circuit Court .... 5th Circuit

STATE INTERNET ADDRESSES

Official State Website .... http://www.state.tx.us
Governor's Website .... http://www.governor.state.tx.us
Legislative Website .... http://www.capitol.state.tx.us
Judicial Website .... http://www.courts.state.tx.us

Utah

Nickname .... The Beehive State
Motto .... *Industry*
Flower .... Sego Lily
Bird .... California Seagull
Tree .... Blue Spruce
Song .... *Utah, We Love Thee*
Entered the Union .... January 4, 1896
Capital .... Salt Lake City

STATISTICS

Land Area (square miles) 82,144
  Rank in Nation 12th
Population 2,351,467
  Rank in Nation 34th
  Density per square mile 28.6
Capital City .... Salt Lake City
  Population 181,266
  Rank in State 1st
Largest City .... Salt Lake City
Number of Representatives in Congress 3
Number of Counties 29
Number of Municipal Governments 236
Number of 2004 Electoral Votes 5
Number of School Districts 40
Number of Special Districts 300

LEGISLATIVE BRANCH

Legislative Body .... Legislature

President of the Senate .... L. Alma Mansell
Secretary of the Senate .... Annette B. Moore

Speaker of the House .... Martin R. Stephens
Chief Clerk of the House .... Carole E. Peterson

2004 Regular Session .... Jan. 19-March 3
Number of Senatorial Districts 29
Number of Representative Districts 75

EXECUTIVE BRANCH

Governor .... Olene S. Walker
Lieutenant Governor .... Gayle F. McKeachnie
Attorney General .... Mark L. Shurtleff
Treasurer .... Edward T. Alter
Auditor .... Auston G. Johnson
Comptroller .... Mark E. Austin

Governor's Present Term 11/03-1/05
Number of Elected Officials in the Executive Branch 5
Number of Members in the Cabinet 19

JUDICIAL BRANCH

Highest Court .... Supreme Court
Supreme Court Chief Justice .... Christine M. Durham
Number of Supreme Court Judges 5
Number of Intermediate Appellate Court Judges 7
Number of U.S. Court Districts 1
U.S. Circuit Court .... 10th Circuit

STATE INTERNET ADDRESSES

Official State Website .... http://www.utah.gov
Governor's Website .... http://www.utah.gov/governor/
Legislative Website .... http://www.le.state.ut.us
Judicial Website .... http://utcourts.gov

Vermont

Nickname	The Green Mountain State
Motto	*Freedom and Unity*
Flower	Red Clover
Bird	Hermit Thrush
Tree	Sugar Maple
Song	*Hail, Vermont!*
Entered the Union	March 4, 1791
Capital	Montpelier

STATISTICS

Land Area (square miles)	9,250
Rank in Nation	43rd
Population	619,107
Rank in Nation	49th
Density per square mile	66.9
Capital City	Montpelier
Population	8,035
Rank in State	13th
Largest City	Burlington
Population	38,889
Number of Representatives in Congress	1
Number of Counties	14
Number of Municipal Governments	47
Number of 2004 Electoral Votes	3
Number of School Districts	288
Number of Special Districts	152

LEGISLATIVE BRANCH

Legislative Body	General Assembly
President of the Senate	Lt. Gov. Brian Dubie
President Pro Tem of the Senate	Peter Welch
Secretary of the Senate	David A. Gibson
Speaker of the House	Walter E. Freed
Clerk of the House	Donald G. Milne
2004 Regular Session	Jan. 6-To be determined
Number of Senatorial Districts	13
Number of Representative Districts	106

EXECUTIVE BRANCH

Governor	James Douglas
Lieutenant Governor	Brian Dubie
Secretary of State	Deborah Markowitz
Attorney General	William H. Sorrell
Treasurer	Jeb Spaulding
Auditor	Elizabeth Ready
Comptroller	Robert Hofmann
Governor's Present Term	1/03-1/05
Number of Elected Officials in the Executive Branch	6
Number of Members in the Cabinet	7

JUDICIAL BRANCH

Highest Court	Supreme Court
Supreme Court Chief Justice	Jeffrey L. Amestoy
Number of Supreme Court Judges	5
Total Number of Appellant Court Judges	0
Number of U.S. Court Districts	1
U.S. Circuit Court	2nd Circuit

STATE INTERNET ADDRESSES

Official State Website	http://vermont.gov
Governor's Website	http://www.vermont.gov/governor/
Legislative Website	http://www.leg.state.vt.us
Judicial Website	http://www.vermontjudiciary.org

Virginia

Nickname	The Old Dominion
Motto	*Sic Semper Tyrannis* (Thus Always to Tyrants)
Flower	Dogwood
Bird	Cardinal
Tree	Dogwood
Song	*Carry Me Back to Old Virginia*
Entered the Union	June 25, 1788
Capital	Richmond

STATISTICS

Land Area (square miles)	39,594
Rank in Nation	37th
Population	7,386,330
Rank in Nation	12th
Density per square miles	186.6
Capital City	Richmond
Population	197,456
Rank in State	4th
Largest City	Virginia Beach
Population	433,934
Number of Representatives in Congress	11
Number of Counties	135
Number of Municipal Governments	229
Number of 2004 Electoral Votes	13
Number of School Districts	135
Number of Special Districts	196

LEGISLATIVE BRANCH

Legislative Body	General Assembly
President of the Senate	Lt. Gov. Tim Kaine
President Pro Tem of the Senate	John H. Chichester
Clerk of the Senate	Susan Clarke Schaar
Speaker of the House	William J. Howell
Clerk of the House	Bruce F. Jamerson
2004 Regular Session	Jan.14-Mar.13
Number of Senatorial Districts	40
Number of Representative Districts	100

EXECUTIVE BRANCH

Governor	Mark Warner
Lieutenant Governor	Tim Kaine
Secretary of the Commonwealth	Anita A. Rimler
Attorney General	Jerry W. Kilgore
Treasurer	Jody M. Wagner
Auditor	Walter J. Kucharski
Comptroller	David Von Moll
Governor's Present Term	1/02-1/06
Number of Elected Officials in the Executive Branch	3
Number of Members in the Cabinet	12

JUDICIAL BRANCH

Highest Court	Supreme Court
Supreme Court Chief Justice	Leroy R. Hassell Sr.
Number of Supreme Court Judges	7
Total Number of Appellant Court Judges	11
Number of U.S. Court Districts	2
U.S. Circuit Court	4th Circuit

STATE INTERNET ADDRESSES

Official State Website	http://www.virginia.gov
Governor's Website	http://www.governor.state.va.us
Legislative Website	http://legis.state.va.us
Judicial Website	http://www.courts.state.va.us

Washington

Nickname .... The Evergreen State
Motto .... *Alki* (Chinook Indian word meaning By and By)
Flower .... Coast Rhododendron
Bird .... Willow Goldfinch
Tree .... Western Hemlock
Song .... *Washington, My Home*
Entered the Union .... November 11, 1889
Capital .... Olympia

STATISTICS

Land Area (square miles) 66,544
   Rank in Nation 20th
Population 6,131,445
   Rank in Nation 15th
   Density per square mile 92.1
Capital City .... Olympia
   Population 42,530
   Rank in State 18th
Largest City .... Seattle
   Population 570,426
Number of Representatives in Congress 9
Number of Counties 39
Number of Municipal Governments 279
Number of 2004 Electoral Votes 11
Number of School Districts 296
Number of Special Districts 1,173

LEGISLATIVE BRANCH

Legislative Body .... Legislature

President of the Senate .... Lt. Gov. Brad Owen
President Pro Tem of the Senate .... Shirley Winsley
Secretary of the Senate .... Milton H. Doumit Jr.

Speaker of the House .... Frank Chopp
Speaker Pro Tem of the House .... John Lovick
Chief Clerk of the House .... Rich Nafziger

2004 Regular Session .... Jan. 12-March 11
Number of Senatorial Districts 49
Number of Representative Districts 49

EXECUTIVE BRANCH

Governor .... Gary Locke
Lieutenant Governor .... Brad Owen
Secretary of State .... Sam Reed
Attorney General .... Christine O. Gregoire
Treasurer .... Michael J. Murphy
Auditor .... Brian Sonntag
Director of Office of Financial Management .... Marty Brown

Governor's Present Term 1/01-1/05
Number of Elected Officials in the Executive Branch 9
Number of Members in the Cabinet 28

JUDICIAL BRANCH

Highest Court .... Supreme Court
Supreme Court Chief Justice .... Gerry L. Alexander
Number of Supreme Court Judges 9
Total Number of Appellant Court Judges 22
Number of U.S. Court Districts 2
U.S. Circuit Court .... 9th Circuit

STATE INTERNET ADDRESSES

Official State Website .... http://access.wa.gov
Governor's Website .... http://www.governor.wa.gov
Legislative Website .... http://www.leg.wa.gov
Judicial Website .... http://www.courts.wa.gov

West Virginia

Nickname .... The Mountain State
Motto .... *Montani Semper Liberi*
(Mountaineers Are Always Free)
Flower .... Rhododendron
Bird .... Cardinal
Tree .... Sugar Maple
Songs .... *West Virginia, My Home Sweet Home;*
The West Virginia Hills;
and *This is My West Virginia*
Entered the Union .... June 20, 1863
Capital .... Charleston

STATISTICS

Land Area (square miles) 24,078
   Rank in Nation 41st
Population 1,810,354
   Rank in Nation 37th
   Density per square mile 75.2
Capital City .... Charleston
   Population 53,421
   Rank in State 1st
Largest City .... Charleston
Number of Representatives in Congress 3
Number of Counties 55
Number of Municipal Governments 234
Number of 2004 Electoral Votes 5
Number of School Districts 55
Number of Special Districts 342

LEGISLATIVE BRANCH

Legislative Body .... Legislature

President of the Senate .... Earl Ray Tomblin
President Pro Tem of the Senate .... William R. Sharpe Jr.
Clerk of the Senate .... Darrell E. Holmes

Speaker of the House of Delegates .... Robert S. Kiss
Speaker Pro Tem of the House of Delegates .... John Pino
Clerk of the House of Delegates .... Gregory M. Gray

2004 Regular Session .... Jan. 14-March 13
Number of Senatorial Districts 16
Number of Representative Districts 58

EXECUTIVE BRANCH

Governor .... Bob Wise
Secretary of State .... Joe Manchin
Attorney General .... Darrell V. McGraw Jr.
Treasurer .... John D. Perdue
Auditor .... Glen B. Gainer III

Governor's Present Term 1/01-1/05
Number of Elected Officials in the Executive Branch 6
Number of Members in the Cabinet 10

JUDICIAL BRANCH

Highest Court .... Supreme Court of Appeals
Supreme Court of Appeals Chief Justice .... Larry Starcher
Number of Supreme Court of Appeals Judges 5
Total Number of Appellant Court Judges 0
Number of U.S. Court Districts 2
U.S. Circuit Court .... 4th Circuit

STATE INTERNET ADDRESSES

Official State Website .... http://www.wv.gov/
Governor's Website .... http://www.state.wv.us/governor
Legislative Website .... http://www.legis.state.wv.us/legishp.html
Judicial Website .... http://www.state.wv.us/wvsca

Wisconsin

Nickname* .... The Badger State
Motto .... *Forward*
Flower .... Wood Violet
Bird .... Robin
Tree .... Sugar Maple
Song .... *On, Wisconsin!*
Entered the Union .... May 29, 1848
Capitol .... Madison

STATISTICS

Land Area (square miles) 54,310
    Rank in Nation 25th
Population 5,472,299
    Rank in Nation 20th
    Density per square mile 100.8
Capital City .... Madison
    Population 215,211
    Rank in State 2nd
Largest City .... Milwaukee
    Population 590,895
Number of Representatives in Congress 8
Number of Counties 72
Number of Municipal Governments 585
Number of 2004 Electoral Votes 10
Number of School Districts 431
Number of Special Districts 684

LEGISLATIVE BRANCH

Legislative Body .... Legislature

President of the Senate .... Alan J. Lasee
President Pro Tem of the Senate .... Robert T. Welch
Chief Clerk of the Senate .... Robert J. Marchant

Speaker of the Assembly .... John Gard
Speaker Pro Tem of the Assembly .... Stephen J. Freese
Chief Clerk of the Assembly .... Patrick Fuller

2004 Regular Session .... Jan. 13-To be determined
Number of Senatorial Districts 33
Number of Representative Districts 99

EXECUTIVE BRANCH

Governor .... James Doyle
Lieutenant Governor .... Barbara Lawton
Secretary of State .... Douglas LaFollette
Attorney General .... Peg Lautenschlager
Treasurer .... Jack C. Voight
Auditor .... Janice L. Mueller
Controller .... William J Rafferty

Governor's Present Term 1/03-1/07
Number of Elected Officials in the Executive Branch 6
Number of Members in the Cabinet 16

JUDICIAL BRANCH

Highest Court .... Supreme Court
Supreme Court Chief Justice .... Shirley S. Abrahamson
Number of Supreme Court Judges 7
Total Number of Appellant Court Judges 16
Number of U.S. Court Districts 2
U.S. Circuit Court .... 7th Circuit

STATE INTERNET ADDRESSES

Official State Website .... http://www.wisconsin.gov
Governor's Website .... http://www.wisgov.state.wi.us
Legislative Website .... http://www.legis.state.wi.us
Judicial Website .... http://www.courts.state.wi.us

* unofficial

Wyoming

Nicknames .... The Equality State and The Cowboy State
Motto .... *Equal Rights*
Flower .... Indian Paintbrush
Bird .... Western Meadowlark
Tree .... Cottonwood
Song .... *Wyoming*
Entered the Union .... July 10, 1890
Capital .... Cheyenne

STATISTICS

Land Area (square miles) 97,100
    Rank in Nation 9th
Population 501,242
    Rank in Nation 51st
    Density per square mile 5.2
Capital City .... Cheyenne
    Population 53,658
    Rank in State 1st
Largest City .... Cheyenne
Number of Representatives in Congress 1
Number of Counties 23
Number of Municipal Governments 98
Number of 2004 Electoral Votes 3
Number of School Districts 48
Number of Special Districts 546

LEGISLATIVE BRANCH

Legislative Body .... Legislature

President of the Senate .... April Brimmer Kurtz
Vice President of the Senate .... John Schiffer
Chief Clerk of the Senate .... Diane Harvey

Speaker of the House .... Fred Parady
Speaker Pro Tem of the House .... Rodney Anderson
Chief Clerk of the House .... Jerry Fox

2004 Regular Session .... Feb. 9-Mar.9
Number of Senatorial Districts 30
Number of Representative Districts 58

EXECUTIVE BRANCH

Governor .... Dave Freudenthal
Secretary of State .... Joe Meyer
Attorney General .... Pat Crank
Treasurer .... Cynthia M. Lummis
Auditor .... Max Maxfield

Governor's Present Term 1/03-1/07
Number of Elected Officials in the Executive Branch 5
Number of Members in the Cabinet 20

JUDICIAL BRANCH

Highest Court .... Supreme Court
Supreme Court Chief Justice .... William U. Hill
Number of Supreme Court Judges 5
Total Number of Appellant Court Judges 0
Number of U.S. Court Districts 1
U.S. Circuit Court .... 10th Circuit

STATE INTERNET ADDRESSES

Official State Website .... http://www.state.wy.us
Governor's Website http://www.state.wy.us/governor/governor_home.asp
Legislative Website .... http://legisweb.state.wy.us
Judicial Website .... http://www.courts.state.wy.us

District of Columbia

Motto .... *Justitia Omnibus* (Justice to All)
Flower .... American Beauty Rose
Bird .... Wood Thrush
Tree .... Scarlet Oak
Became U.S. Capital .... December 1, 1800

STATISTICS

Land Area (square miles) 63
Population 563,384
    Density per square mile 9378.0
Delegate to Congress* 1
Number of Municipal Governments 1
Number of 2004 Electoral Votes 3
Number of School Districts 2
Number of Special Districts 1

*Committee voting privileges only.

LEGISLATIVE BRANCH

Legislative Body .... Council of the District of Columbia

Chair .... Linda W. Cropp
Chair Pro Tem .... Jack Evans
Secretary to the Council .... Phyllis Jones
2004 Regular Session .... Jan. 2-Dec.31

EXECUTIVE BRANCH

Mayor .... Anthony Williams
Secretary of the District of Columbia .... Beverly D. Rivers
Corporation Counsel .... Robert Rigsby
Chief Financial Officer .... N. Anthony Calhoun
Auditor .... Deborah Nichols

Mayor's Present Term 1/01-1/05
Number of Elected Officials in the Executive Branch 10
Number of Members in the Cabinet 10

JUDICIAL BRANCH

Highest Court .... D.C. Court of Appeals
Court of Appeals Chief Justice .... Annice M. Wagner
Number of Court of Appeals Judges 9
Number of U.S. Court Districts 1

INTERNET ADDRESSES

Official Website .... http://www.washingtondc.gov
Mayor's Website .... http://dc.gov/mayor/index.shtm
Legislative Website .... http://www.dccouncil.washington.dc.us
Judicial Website .... http://www.dcbar.org

American Samoa

Motto .... *Samoa-Maumua le Atua* (Samoa, God Is First)
Flower .... Paogo (Ula-fala)
Plant .... Ava
Song .... *Amerika Samoa*
Became a Territory of the United States 1900
Capital .... Pago Pago

STATISTICS

Land Area (square miles) 77
Population 57,291
    Density per square mile 744.0
Capital City .... Pago Pago
    Population 4,100
    Rank in Territory 3rd
Largest City .... Tafuna
Population 8,409
Delegate to Congress 1
Number of School Districts 1

LEGISLATIVE BRANCH

Legislative Body .... Legislature

President of the Senate .... Lutu Tenari S. Fuimaono
President Pro Tem of the Senate .... Faiivae A. Galeai
Secretary of the Senate .... Leo'o V. Ma'o

Speaker of the House .... Matagi Mailo Ray McMoore
Vice Speaker .... Savali Talavou Ale
Chief Clerk of the House .... Fialupe Lutu

2004 Regular Session .... Jan.12, 2004-To be determined
Number of Senatorial Districts 12
Number of Representative Districts 17

EXECUTIVE BRANCH

Governor .... Togiola T.A. Tulafono
Lieutenant Governor .... Aitofele Sunia
Attorney General .... Fiti Sunia
Treasurer .... Francis Leasiolagi
Auditor .... Francis Sefo

Governor's Present Term 4/03-1/05
Number of Members in the Cabinet 16

JUDICIAL BRANCH

Highest Court .... High Court
High Court Chief Justice .... Michael Kruse
Number of High Court Judges 6

INTERNET ADDRESSES

Official Website .... http://www.asg-gov.com/
Governor's Website .... http://www.government.as/gov.htm
Legislative Website .... http://www.government.as/legislative.htm
Judicial Website .... http://www.government.as/highcourt.htm

Guam

Nickname .... Hub of the Pacific
Flower .... Puti Tai Nobio (Bougainvillea)
Bird .... Toto (Fruit Dove)
Tree .... Ifit (Intsiabijuga)
Song .... *Stand Ye Guamanians*
Stone .... Latte
Animal .... Iguana
Ceded to the United States
    by Spain .... December 10, 1898
Became a Territory .... August 1, 1950
Request to become a
    Commonwealth Plebiscite .... November 1987
Capital .... Hagatna

STATISTICS

Land Area (square miles) 210
Population 154,805
    Density per square mile 737.1
Capital .... Hagatna
    Population 1,122
    Rank in Territory 18th
Largest City .... Dededo
Population 42,980
Delegate to Congress 1
Number of School Districts 1

LEGISLATIVE BRANCH

Legislative Body .... Legislature

Speaker .... Vincente Pangelinan
Vice Speaker .... Frank Aguon Jr.
Clerk of the Legislature .... Robert Rabago, Bill Murphy
Legislative Secretary of the Senate .... Tina Rose Muna Barnes

2004 Regular Session .... Jan. 12,2004- To be determined
Number of Senatorial Districts 15

EXECUTIVE BRANCH

Governor .... Felix Perez
Lieutenant Governor .... Kaleo Moylan
Attorney General .... Douglas Moylan
Treasurer .... Y'Asela A. Pereira
Comptroller .... Arleen Pierce

Governor's Present Term 1/03-1/07
Number of Elected Officials in the Executive Branch 10
Number of Members in the Cabinet 55

JUDICIAL BRANCH

Highest Court .... Supreme Court
Supreme Court Chief Justice .... F. Philip Cabullido
Number of Supreme Court Judges 3

INTERNET ADDRESSES

Official Website .... http://ns.gov.gu
Governor's Website .... http://ns.gov.gu/government.html
Legislative Website .... http://www.guam.net/gov/senate
Judicial Website .... http://www.justice.gov.gu

Northern Mariana Islands

Flower .... Plumeria
Bird Marianas Fruit Dove
Tree Flame Tree
Song .... *Gi TaloGi Halom Tasi*
Administered by the United States
    a trusteeship for the United Nations .... July 18, 1947
Voters approved a proposed constitution .... June 1975
U.S. president signed covenant agreeing to
    commonwealth status for
    the islands .... March 24, 1976
Became a self-governing
    Commonwealth .... January 9, 1978
Capital .... Saipan

STATISTICS

Land Area (square miles) 181
Population 69,221
    Density per square mile 382.4
Capital City .... Saipan
    Population 62,392
Largest City .... Saipan
Delegate to Congress 1
Number of School Districts 1

LEGISLATIVE BRANCH

Legislative Body .... Legislature

President of the Senate .... Paul A. Manglona
Vice President of the Senate .... Thomas P. Villagomez
Clerk of the Senate .... Nicolasa B. Borja

Speaker of the House .... Heinz S. Hofschneider
Vice Speaker of the House .... Manuel Agulto Tenorio
Clerk of the House .... Evelyn C. Fleming

2004 Regular Session .... Not Available
Number of Senatorial Districts 9
Number of Representative Districts 18

EXECUTIVE BRANCH

Governor .... Juan N. Babauta
Lieutenant Governor .... Diego Benavente
Attorney General .... Pamela Brown
Treasurer .... Antoinette S. Calvo
Auditor .... Michael S. Sablan
Comptroller .... Bernadita Palacios

Governor's Present Term 1/02-1/06
Number of Elected Officials in the Executive Branch 10
Number of Members in the Cabinet 16

JUDICIAL BRANCH

Highest Court .... Commonwealth Supreme Court
Commonwealth Supreme Court Chief Justice .... Miguel S. Demapan
Number of Commonwealth Supreme Court Judges 3

INTERNET ADDRESSES

Official Website .... http://www.saipan.com/gov
Governor's Website .... http://www.mariana-islands.gov.mp
Legislative Website .... http://www.saipan.com/gov/branches/senate
Judicial Website http://cnmilaw.org/htmlpage/hpg34.htm

Puerto Rico

Nickname .... Island of Enchantment
Motto .... *Joannes Est Nomen Ejus*
(John is Thy Name)
Flower .... Maga
Bird Reinita
Tree Ceiba
Song .... *La Borinquena*
Became a Territory of the
United States .... December 10, 1898
Became a self-governing Commonwealth .... July 25, 1952
Capital .... San Juan

STATISTICS

Land Area (square miles) 3,427
Population 3,878,532
Density per square mile 1,111.3
Capital City .... San Juan
Population 442,447
Largest City .... San Juan
Delegate to Congress* 1
Number of School Districts 1

*Committee voting privileges only.

LEGISLATIVE BRANCH

Legislative Body .... Legislative Assembly
President of the Senate .... Antonio J. Fas Alzamora
Vice President
of the Senate .... Velda Gonzalez de Modestti
Secretary of the Senate .... Jose Ariel Nazario-Alvarez

Speaker of the House .... Carlos Vizcarrondo Irizarry
Speaker Pro Tem .... Ferdinand Perez-Roman
Clerk of the House .... Nester Duprey-Salgado

2004 Regular Session Jan.12-June 30

EXECUTIVE BRANCH

Governor .... Sila M. Calderón
Secretary of State .... Ferdinand Mercado
Attorney General .... Anabelle Rodriquez
Treasurer .... Juan Flores Galarza
Controller .... Manuel Diaz-Saldana

Governor's Present Term 1/01-1/05
Number of Elected Officials in the Executive Branch 10
Number of Members in the Cabinet 140

JUDICIAL BRANCH

Highest Court .... Supreme Court
Supreme Court Chief Justice .... Jose A. Andreu Garcia
Number of Supreme Court Judges 7

INTERNET ADDRESSES

Official State Website .... http://www.puertorico.pr
Governor's Website .... http://www.fortaleza.gobierno.pr
Senate Website .... http://www.camaradepuertorico.org
House Website .... http://www.camaradepuertorico.org
Judicial Website .... http://www.tribunalpr.org

U.S. Virgin Islands

Nickname .... The American Paradise
Motto .... United in Pride and Hope
Flower .... The Yellow Cedar
Bird Yellow Breast or Banana Quit
Song .... *Virgin Islands March*
Purchased from Denmark .... March 31, 1917
Capital .... Charlotte Amalie, St. Thomas

STATISTICS

Land Area (square miles)* 134
Population 108,612
Density per square mile 810.5
Capital City .... Charlotte Amalie, St. Thomas
Population 12,500
Largest City .... Charlotte Amalie, St. Thomas
Delegate to Congress** 1
Number of School Districts 1

*The U.S. Virgin Islands is comprised of three large islands (St. Croix, St. John, and St. Thomas) and 50 smaller islands and cays.
**Committee voting privileges only.

LEGISLATIVE BRANCH

Legislative Body .... Legislature

President .... David Jones
Vice President .... Lorraine L. Berry
Legislative Secretary of the Senate .... Shawn-Michael Malone
2004 Regular Session .... Jan. 12-ending date to be determined

EXECUTIVE BRANCH

Governor .... Charles W. Turnbull
Lieutenant Governor .... Vargrave Richards
Attorney General .... Iver A. Stirdiron
Treasurer .... Bernice A. Turnbull
Auditor .... Steven G. Van Beverhoudt

Governor's Present Term 1/03-1/07
Number of Elected Officials in the Executive Branch 10
Number of Members in the Cabinet 21

JUDICIAL BRANCH

Highest Court .... Territorial Court
Territorial Court Chief Justice .... Raymond L. Finch
Number of Territorial Court Judges 3
U.S. Circuit Court 3rd

INTERNET ADDRESSES

Official Website .... http://www.usvi.org
Governor's Website .... http://www.usvi.org
Legislative Website .... http://www.senate.gov.vi
Judicial Website .... http://www.vid.uscourts.gov

Index